FUNDAMENTALS OF
FINANCIAL ACCOUNTING

FRED PHILLIPS
University of Saskatchewan

ROBERT LIBBY
Cornell University

PATRICIA A. LIBBY
Ithaca College

BRANDY MACKINTOSH
University of Saskatchewan

Mc
Graw
Hill
Education

Fundamentals of Financial Accounting
Fifth Canadian Edition

The Internet addresses listed in the text were accurate at the time of publication. The inclusion of a website does not indicate an endorsement by the authors or McGraw−Hill Ryerson, and McGraw−Hill Ryerson does not guarantee the accuracy of information presented at these sites.

ISBN−13: 978−1−25−926986−8
ISBN−10: 1−25−926986−8

1 2 3 4 5 6 7 8 9 0 TCP 22 21 20 19 18

Printed and bound in Canada

Care has been taken to trace ownership of copyright material contained in this text; however, the publisher will welcome any information that enables it to rectify any reference or credit for subsequent editions.

Portfolio Director, Business & Economics, International: *Nicole Meehan*
Portfolio Manager: *Keara Emmett*
Director, Portfolio Marketing: *Joy Armitage Taylor*
Content Development Manager: *Denise Foote*
Content Developer: *Tammy Mavroudi*
Senior Portfolio Associate: *Stephanie Giles*
Supervising Editors: *Janie Deneau & Jeanette McCurdy*
Photo/Permissions Researcher: *Indu Arora*
Copy Editor: *Judy Sturrup*
Plant Production Coordinator: *Michelle Saddler*
Manufacturing Production Coordinator: *Emily Hickey*
Cover and Interior Design: *Katherine Strain*
Composition: *MPS Limited*
Cover Photo: © *Marianne de Jong / Adobe Stock*
Printer: *Transcontinental Printing Group*

Dedication

Barb, Harrison, and Daniel, my Mom, and (memory of) my Dad

FRED PHILLIPS

Herman and Doris Hargenrater,
Laura Libby, Oscar and Selma Libby

PATRICIA AND ROBERT LIBBY

Mom and Dad—Thank you for teaching me the importance
of doing things right the first time around and for inspiring
me to work hard and always do my best. And
to Pat, Payton, and Avery—thank you for your support
and for teaching me something new every day.

BRANDY MACKINTOSH

Meet the Authors

Fred Phillips

Fred Phillips is a professor and the George C. Baxter Scholar at the University of Saskatchewan, where he teaches introductory financial accounting. He also has taught introductory accounting at the University of Texas at Austin and the University of Manitoba. Fred has an undergraduate accounting degree, a CPA, CA (Canada), and a PhD from the University of Texas at Austin. He previously worked as an audit manager at KPMG.

Fred's main career interest is accounting education. He has been recognized with more than 26 awards, as chosen by his students and peers. In 2006, Fred was awarded the title Master Teacher at the University of Saskatchewan. In 2011, he was admitted to the 3M National Teaching Fellowship, the highest honour for undergraduate teaching in Canada. In 2012, Fred received the L. S. Rosen Outstanding Educator Award, the American Accounting Association's Innovation in Auditing and Assurance Education Award, and the American Accounting Association's Award for Outstanding Research in Accounting Education. Most recently, he received the Edwards MPAcc Teaching Effectiveness Award and, for the third time in his career, the University of Saskatchewan Student Union's Teaching Excellence Award. His peer−reviewed publications include education−focused research and instructional cases in *Issues in Accounting Education*, as well as professional judgment studies in *Journal of Accounting Research* and *Organizational Behavior and Human Decision Processes*, among others. Fred is a current member of the Teaching, Curriculum, & Learning and Two−Year College sections of the American Accounting Association. In his spare time, he likes to play tennis, drink iced cappuccinos, and relax with his family.

Robert Libby

Robert Libby is the David A. Thomas Professor of Accounting and Accounting Area Coordinator at Cornell University, where he teaches the introductory financial accounting course. He previously taught at the University of Illinois, Pennsylvania State University, the University of Texas at Austin, the University of Chicago, and the University of Michigan. He received his BS from Pennsylvania State University, and his MAS and PhD from the University of Illinois; he also successfully completed the CPA exam (Illinois).

Bob was selected as the AAA Outstanding Educator in 2000, and received the AAA Outstanding Service Award in 2006 and the AAA Notable Contributions to the Literature Award in 1985 and 1996. He has received the Core Faculty Teaching

Award multiple times at Cornell. Bob is a widely published author and researcher specializing in behavioural accounting. He has published numerous articles in *The Accounting Review*; *Journal of Accounting Research*; *Accounting, Organizations, and Society*; and other accounting journals. He has held a variety of offices, including vice president, in the American Accounting Association, and he is a member of the American Institute of CPAs and the editorial boards of *The Accounting Review* and *Accounting, Organizations, and Society*.

Patricia A. Libby

Patricia Libby is associate professor of accounting at Ithaca College, where she teaches the undergraduate financial accounting course. She previously taught graduate and undergraduate financial accounting at Eastern Michigan University and the University of Texas. Before entering academe, she was an auditor with Price Waterhouse (now PricewaterhouseCoopers) and a financial administrator at the University of Chicago. She is also faculty advisor to Beta Alpha Psi and the Ithaca College Accounting Association. She received her BS from Pennsylvania State University, her MBA from DePaul University, and her PhD from the University of Michigan; she also successfully completed the CPA exam (Illinois).

Pat conducts research on using cases in the introductory course and other parts of the accounting curriculum. She has published articles in *The Accounting Review*, *Issues in Accounting Education*, and *The Michigan CPA*.

Brandy Mackintosh

Brandy Mackintosh is an assistant professor at the Edwards School of Business at the University of Saskatchewan, where she teaches introductory, intermediate, and advanced financial accounting. She has also taught external auditing and advanced financial reporting at the graduate level. Brandy has an undergraduate accounting degree, and is a CPA, CA (Canada). Prior to joining the University of Saskatchewan, she worked as an audit manager at Deloitte.

Brandy was selected as the Edwards School of Business Most Effective Professor in 2015 and again in 2016. She also received the Edwards School of Business Most Approachable Professor Award in 2014 and 2016. Brandy has received the University of Saskatchewan Student Union's Teaching Excellence Award multiple times, most recently in 2015. Her scholarly interests relate to accounting education and case writing. She has published cases in *Issues in Accounting Education*, and most recently won the 2016 Canadian Academic Accounting Association case—writing competition.

BRIEF CONTENTS

CONTENTS

CHAPTER 4

Adjustments, Financial Statements, and Financial
Results   166

Pizza Palace Inc.   166

CHAPTER 5

Fraud, Internal Control, and Cash   232

Koss Corporation   232

CHAPTER 6

Merchandising Operations and the Multi-Step Income
Statement   282

Walmart   282

Your Personal Coach . . .

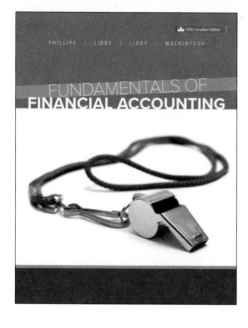

Phillips, Libby, Libby, and Mackintosh's *Fundamentals of Financial Accounting*, fifth Canadian edition, arms students with a secret weapon for success in financial accounting—the best personal coach on the market. The cover of this text features the quintessential representation of a coach—a whistle. Simple, maybe, but this whistle captures the essence of this text brand as your coach. The following are highlights of Phillips's innovative student—centred approach:

WRITING THAT STUDENTS CAN READ. What does it mean to say that a book is "readable"? In the case of *Fundamentals of Financial Accounting*, fifth Canadian edition, it simply means that it's the most enjoyable accounting textbook your students have ever read. Through a mix of conversational wording, humour, and everyday examples, *Fundamentals of Financial Accounting* achieves a style that maintains rigour without sacrificing student engagement. Open this textbook to any page and read for yourself; *Fundamentals of Financial Accounting* offers **the most engaging read** of any financial text.

STUDENT-FRIENDLY COVERAGE OF DIFFICULT TOPICS. Written with students in mind, *Fundamentals of Financial Accounting* handles difficult concepts in a way that reflects the balance of preparer and user concepts, and keeps students from being overwhelmed.

- The **accounting process** is covered in three chapters (2, 3, and 4).
- The purpose of a **statement of cash flows** is introduced at the beginning of the text, but the mechanics of preparing one are studied at the end.
- **Ratios** are introduced throughout the chapters and then pulled together at the end (13).
- **Individual concepts** are introduced throughout the text as needed to explain specific accounting practices and then pulled together at the end.
- **Award—Winning Continuing Case:** Key accounting judgments that affect business decisions in the workplace are learned by students through an award—winning continuing case in the assignment material for Chapters 5 through 12.

...in Financial Accounting

CURRENT. Phillips reflects current accounting standards in Canada. Covering both International Financial Reporting Standards (IFRS) and Accounting Standards for Private Enterprise (ASPE), Phillips discusses key differences between IFRS and ASPE in a boxed feature at the end of each chapter.

BALANCED. Phillips delivers a balanced approach. Throughout, understanding the preparation of financial statements is balanced with the importance of using the financial statements to guide decision making.

EXTENSIVE END-OF-CHAPTER EXERCISES AND PROBLEMS. Students build confidence and success with a wealth of end-of-chapter discussion questions, exercises, coached and comprehensive problems, skills development cases, and continuing cases.

Stay Focused . . .

The best way to learn to prepare and use financial statements is to study accounting in real business contexts.

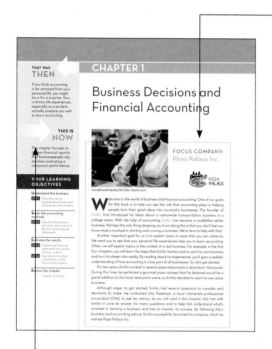

FOCUS COMPANY APPROACH. The Focus Company approach integrates each chapter's material with a real—world company, its decisions, and its financial statements.

Not all students learn financial accounting with ease. With so many distractions these days, it is difficult to keep both majors and non—majors focused on the big picture. The authors of *Fundamentals of Financial Accounting* fifth Canadian edition understand the challenges instructors face and the need for a financial accounting text that is relevant, easy to read, and current.*Fundamentals of Financial Accounting* responds by using carefully chosen focus companies that students not only recognize but are familiar with because they have visited or used those companies' products.

Students often feel that they lack the real—world experience needed to understand accounting, a subject they believe has little impact on their daily lives. *Fundamentals of Financial Accounting*'s chapter openers provide real—world situations and examples that illustrate how accounting principles are part of day—to—day activities that students might not have thought about from an accounting perspective, from companies like the local pizza restaurant to the world's most familiar businesses, such as Hudson's Bay Company, Walmart, Cedar Fair, Molson Coors Brewing Company, Under Armour, and General Mills. Through crisp, clear, and engaging writing, the financial decisions these companies make and the financial statements they use come alive for students and they are able to see the big picture of how accounting relates to the real world—their world.

THAT WAS THEN/THIS IS NOW. To provide connectivity in students' minds, each chapter opens by briefly putting into perspective the information learned in the previous chapter and what will be learned in the present chapter.

KEY TERMS. All key terms are defined within the text in which the terms are first introduced, reinforcing student under—standing and recapping important text points.

. . . on the Real World

SPOTLIGHT FEATURES. Each chapter includes Spotlight features focusing on financial reporting, IFRS and ASPE, ethics, the world, business decisions, internal controls, and Canada. These features are designed to further engage students and provide instructors with material for in–class discussion.

SPOTLIGHT ON Financial Reporting

The Ultimate Irony: Teacher Late with Report

K12 Inc. claims to be the leader in computer-based instruction for grades K th
get its own computerized accounting systems working in time to meet an impo
deadline. K12 admitted that it was struggling with "the integration of diverse a
that it would be about a month late releasing its annual report.
The company explained that it had recently acquired several other companie
ent computerized accounting systems. To ensure all of the transactions were

Spotlight on Financial Reporting These features con–nect chapter topics with real–world disclosures provided in the financial statements of our focus companies and other contrasting companies.

Spotlight on IFRS and ASPE Specific discussions on International Financial Reporting Standards (IFRS) and how they differ from Accounting Standards for Private Enterprises (ASPE) are grouped together in the Spotlight on IFRS and ASPE box at the end of each chapter.

SPOTLIGHT ON IFRS and ASPE

As International Financial Reporting Standards (IFRS) are adopted around t
transaction analysis process in this chapter becomes even more important.
the U.S., which explains accounting rules in detail, ASPE and IFRS are less de
judgment when analyzing transactions. This difference in emphasis exists b
are used across many different countries, where business practices and leg
placing slightly more emphasis on general principles than on detailed rules, II
easily and broadly applied around the world.

SPOTLIGHT ON Ethics

35 Days Hath September?

It seems some managers—specifically those at Computer Associates (CA)–h
period assumption. CA was charged with financial statement fraud for imp
five days of sales in September–a month that has only thirty days. To mak
had met their September sales targets, CA included the first five days of s
September income statement. This accounting fraud led managers to be p
earned and tricked investors into thinking CA was a successful company.

Spotlight on Ethics The text ensures that students start off with a solid grounding in ethics. Shining the spotlight on ethical issues in each chapter prompts the student to think about tough ethical decisions and to practise mak–ing these decisions in the end–of–chapter cases.

Spotlight on the World Students are kept apprised of the ongoing changes in the accounting profession around the world through these features.

SPOTLIGHT ON The World

Direct versus Indirect Method Presentation

ASPE and IFRS currently allow companies to use either the direct or indirec
Accounting Standards Board (FASB) and the International Accounting Stand
spoken in the past about removing this choice and allowing only the direct me
method is more detailed and shows the operating cash receipts and cash pay
with the objective of a cash flow statement. However, the indirect method sh
accrual income to cash flows from operations, which is an advantage over t

SPOTLIGHT ON Business Decisions

Lehman Brothers' Operating Cash Flows and the Financial Crisis

Lehman Brothers, Holdings, Inc. was one of the largest and most profitable
panies in the world. But cash flow and working capital management problem
bankruptcy only a month before the stock market crash of 2008. The following
net income and net operating cash flows reveals the company's problems:

15.0

Spotlight on Business Decisions Found throughout the text, these features help students to develop strong decision–making skills by illustrating the relevance of accounting in real–world decision making and the lessons learned from global economic crises.

Spotlight on Controls These features highlight appli–cations of internal control principles in the workplace.

SPOTLIGHT ON Controls

Sources of Inventory Shrinkage

Independent verification of inventory quantities is important. A recent study :
$34 billion of inventory goes missing from U.S. retailers each year.[1] Althoug
cause of shrinkage (accounting for 36 percent of lost units), an even larger po
from employee theft. To avoid hiring dishonest employees, companies scre
employment and criminal background checks. To deter and detect employee
tags, surveillance cameras, and complex computer programs that monitor ca

SPOTLIGHT ON Canada

Mentorship Program Offers Vision to Aboriginal Youth

The Martin/CPA Canada Accounting Mentorship Program (AMP) was an e
Prime Minister Paul Martin and CPA Lloyd Posno. AMP's purpose is to pai
youth who seek university degrees and develop their interest in pursuing busir
in accounting.
   The AMP high-school students who aspire to complete post-secondary
with accountants from seven of the profession's top firms. These students parti

Spotlight on Canada These boxes feature information on accounting and business practices specific to Canadian Aboriginal communities.

Dedicated and Coached...

A PROVEN TEACHING AND LEARNING METHODOLOGY. Faculty agree the accounting cycle is the most critical concept to learn and master for students studying financial accounting. The approach to this topic in Phillips/Libby/Libby/Mackintosh is based on the belief that students struggle with the accounting cycle when transaction analysis is covered in one chapter. If students are exposed to the accounting equation, journal entries, and T-accounts for both balance sheet and income statement accounts in a single chapter, many are left behind and are unable to grasp material in the next chapter, which typically covers adjustments and financial statement preparation.

The accompanying graphic shows how, unlike other textbooks, the Phillips/Libby/Libby/Mackintosh approach spreads transaction analysis coverage over two chapters so that students have the time to master the material. In Chapter 2 of Fundamentals of Financial Accounting, students are exposed to the accounting equation and transaction analysis for transactions that affect only balance sheet accounts. This provides students with the opportunity to learn the basic structure and tools used in accounting in a simpler setting. In Chapter 3, students are exposed to more complex transactions that affect both balance sheet and income statement accounts. As a result of this progressive approach to transaction analysis, students learn more, as documented in peer-reviewed research.[1] We have also seen that our approach prepares students to learn adjustments, financial statement preparation, and more advanced topics.

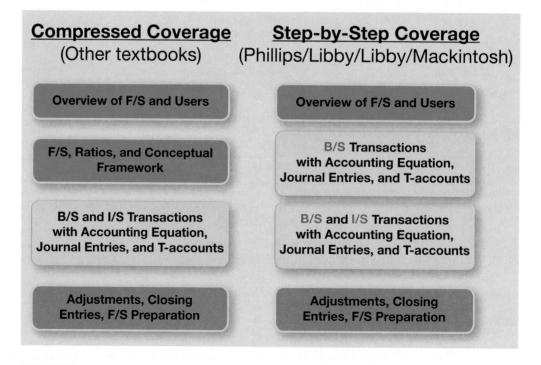

Compressed Coverage (Other textbooks)	**Step-by-Step Coverage** (Phillips/Libby/Libby/Mackintosh)
Overview of F/S and Users	Overview of F/S and Users
F/S, Ratios, and Conceptual Framework	B/S Transactions with Accounting Equation, Journal Entries, and T-accounts
B/S and I/S Transactions with Accounting Equation, Journal Entries, and T-accounts	B/S and I/S Transactions with Accounting Equation, Journal Entries, and T-accounts
Adjustments, Closing Entries, F/S Preparation	Adjustments, Closing Entries, F/S Preparation

[1] F. Phillips and L. Heiser, "A Field Experiment Examining the Effects of Accounting Equation Emphasis and Transaction Scope on Students Learning to Journalize," Issues in Accounting Education 26, pp. 681–699 (2011).

. . . for Student Motivation and Success

COACH'S TIP. Virtually every student has been inspired by a great coach at some time or another. Throughout the chapters, Coach's Tips provide students with advice and guidance on learning the material. Coach's Tips appear again in the problem material to offer encouragement as students work to reinforce what they've learned.

COACH'S TIP

Any account name containing *receivable* is an asset and any containing *payable* is a liability.

COACHED PROBLEMS. Every chapter includes three problem sets: Coached Problems, Group A Problems, and Group B Problems. The Coached Problems go beyond the traditional check figures to advise students on the process of solving a problem in addition to its outcome.

HOW'S IT GOING? Research shows that students learn best when they are actively engaged in the learning process. *Fundamentals of Financial Accounting* provides plenty of this active learning feature to engage the student, provide interactivity, and promote efficient learning. These quizzes ask students to pause at strategic points throughout each chapter to ensure they understand key points before moving ahead. Answers are strategically placed at the end of the chapter summary so that students don't acciden-tally read them before answering the questions.

HOW'S IT GOING?

Self-Study Practice 1.1

In the space provided, indicate (a) the type of account (A = asset, L = liability, SE = shareholders' equity, R = revenue, E = expense), and (b) whether it is reported on the income statement (I/S), statement of retained earn-ings (SRE), balance sheet (B/S), or statement of cash flows (SCF).

SOLUTION TO SELF-STUDY PRACTICE

Solution to SP1.1

	Type	Statement
1.	A	B/S
2.	E	I/S

THE USER FRAMEWORK. The USER Framework provides a "road map" to each chapter, showing how accounting functions work at all levels of the firm. Students learn to

Understand the business decisions that managers make,

Study the accounting methods used,

Evaluate the reported results from the viewpoint of financial statement users, and

Review how the accounting methods affect the managers' decisions.

ANALYZE, RECORD, SUMMARIZE. A systematic accounting process is used to capture and report the financial effects of a company's activities. This process includes three basic steps:

Step 1: Analyze Transactions

Transaction analysis involves determining whether a transaction exists and, if it does, analyzing its impact on the accounting equation.

Steps 2 and 3: Record and Summarize

One way to record and summarize the financial effects of transactions would be to enter your understanding of their effects into a spreadsheet. By summing each spreadsheet column, you could compute new balances at the end of each month and report them on a balance sheet.

These helpful steps appear throughout various chapters to support learning.

Review and Practice Materials . . .

REVIEW OF THE CHAPTER

To effectively evaluate and guide student success with the appropriate feedback, you need homework and test materials that are easy to use and tied to the chapter discussions.

Each chapter of *Fundamentals of Financial Accounting* is followed by an extensive variety of end–of–chapter material that applies and integrates topics presented in the chapter. We have retained many of the popular items from prior editions and added new types of end–of–chapter materials, including a Homework Helper, multi–perspective discussion questions, comprehensive problems, and continuing cases.

DEMONSTRATION CASE. Each chapter provides demonstration cases of activities in real–life situations. These exercises have students analyzing, preparing, and summarizing actual information.

CHAPTER SUMMARY. Each chapter concludes with an end–of–chapter summary, organized by chapter learning objectives, that revisits the learning objectives from the beginning of the chapter.

KEY TERMS. The Key Terms list includes all key terms used in the chapter. In addition to the definitions avail–able in the text of each chapter, full definitions of all key terms are found in the Glossary near the end of the text.

HOMEWORK HELPER. The Homework Helper imme–diately precedes each chapter's homework materials, highlighting subtleties discussed in the chapter and pro–viding practice advice so that students can avoid common pitfalls when completing homework.

PRACTICE MATERIAL

QUESTIONS. Each chapter includes ten to twenty multi–perspective discussion questions that ask students to explain and discuss terms and concepts presented in the chapter. Selected questions, denoted with an icon, are designed to help students begin developing critical think–ing skills. These questions are ideal for sparking debate at the beginning of class or when transitioning between or reviewing topics.

MINI-EXERCISES. Each of these assignments illustrates and applies a single learning objective from the chapter.

. . . Build Confidence and Success

EXERCISES. These additional assignments illustrate and apply single and multiple learning objectives from the chapter.

EXERCISES

E1-1 **Reporting Amounts on the Four Basic Financial Statements**   LO1-2
Using the following table and the equations underlying each of the four basic financial statements, show (a) that the balance sheet is in balance, (b) that net income is properly calculated, (c) what caused changes in the retained earnings account, and (d) what caused changes in the cash account.

COACHED PROBLEMS

CP1-1 **Preparing an Income Statement, Statement of Retained Earnings, and Balance Sheet**
Assume that you are the president of Nuclear Company. At the end of the first year of operations (December 31, 2017), the following financial data for the company are available: LO1-2

| Cash | $12,000 |
| Accounts Receivable | 59,500 |

PROBLEMS (COACHED, GROUP A, AND GROUP B). Each chapter includes three problem sets to help students develop decision–making skills. Coached problems include question–specific tips to assist students who need a little help getting started. Groups A and B are similar problems, but without the coaching. Excel templates are tied to selected end–of–chapter assignments designated with the excel icon.

LEVEL UP QUESTIONS. In each chapter, particularly challenging questions, designated by the Level Up icon, require students to combine multiple concepts to advance to the next level of accounting knowledge.

LO1-2   M1-15 **Relationships Among Financial Statements**
Items from the income statement, statement of retained earnings, and balance sheet of Electronic Arts Inc. are listed below in alphabetical order. Solve for the missing amounts, and explain whether the company was profitable.
TIP: Use Exhibit 1.6 to identify relations among the items, then solve for amounts.

	Electronic Arts Inc.
Contributed Capital	$2,430
Dividends	0

COMPREHENSIVE PROBLEMS

LO2-3, 3-3, 4-1,   C4-1 **From Recording Transactions (Including Adjusting Journal Entries) to Preparing Finan**
4-2, 4-3, 4-4,   **Statements and Closing Journal Entries**
4-5, 4-6
Consider the following, using what you learned in Chapters 2, 3, and 4.
Brothers Harry and Herman Hausyerday began operations of their machine shop (
H Tool Co.) on January 1, 2010. The annual reporting period ends December 31. The
balance on January 1, 2017, appears below (the amounts are rounded to thousands of do

COMPREHENSIVE PROBLEMS. Selected chapters include problems that cover topics from earlier chapters to refresh, reinforce, and build an integrative understanding of the course material. These are a great resource for helping students stay up to date throughout the course.

SKILLS DEVELOPMENT CASES. Each chapter offers cases designed to help students develop analytical, critical thinking, and technological skills. These cases are ideal for individual assignments, class discussions, and group projects. Encourage your students to find financial infor–mation in an actual annual report. The first case of every chapter presents an opportunity to connect your students with real–world financial reporting.

SKILLS DEVELOPMENT CASES

LO1-2, 1-2, 1-3   S1-1 **Finding Financial Information**
Refer to the summarized financial statements of The Home Depot in Appendix A at back of this book.

Required:
1. What is the amount of net income for the year ended January 29, 2017?

CONTINUING CASE

CC1-1 **Financial Statements for a Business Plan**
Nicole Mackisey is thinking of forming her own spa business, Nicole's Getaway Spa   LO1-2, 1-3
(NGS). Nicole expects that she and two family members will each contribute $10,000 to the
business and receive 1,000 shares each.
Nicole forecasts the following amounts for the first year of operations, ending
December 31, 2017: cash on hand and in the bank, $2,150; amounts due from customers
from spa treatments, $1,780; building and equipment, $70,000; amounts owed to beauty

CONTINUING CASE. In Chapter 1, students are introduced to Nicole's Getaway Spa (NGS). In each chapter, the Continuing Case feature extends this case and requires students to apply topics from the current chapter. Chapters 5 through 12 present a continuing case involving the Wiki Art Gallery (WAG) (see Appendix D). This case depicts a setting in which accounting infor–mation is used to determine a company's selling price. By examining accounting decisions in an easy–to–use multiple–choice format, students learn that not all num–bers are what they appear at first glance.

What's New in the Fifth Edition?

In response to feedback and guidance from numerous financial accounting faculty, the authors have made many important changes to the fifth Canadian edition of *Fundamentals of Financial Accounting*, including the following:

- Integrated new focus companies, including Molson Coors Brewing Company and Koss Corporation, a headphone manufacturer
- Reorganized topics within Chapters 5 through 7 to improve cohesiveness and introduce additional depth
- An introduction to the topic of fraud (as in the fourth edition) in Chapter 5 that now also discusses and illustrates the related topic of internal controls, including cash controls and electronic documentation of cash disbursements
- A discussion in Chapter 6 that illustrates merchandising operations, including inventory sales (as in the fourth edition); however, this topic is now preceded by merchandise inventory purchases, consistent with the natural sequence of business events
- A focus in Chapter 7 on inventory costing and valuation (as in the fourth edition) that now includes a discussion of inventory turnover and gross profit analyses in assessing the likelihood of inventory write−downs
- New end−of−chapter material in each chapter to support new topics and learning objectives, with more than fifty **revised** and updated end−of−chapter assignments, exercises, problems, and cases
- A **new** Spotlight on Canada box that discusses accounting and business practices specific to Canadian Aboriginal communities
- Additional Help Me Solve It animations that walk students through an end−of−chapter question hand−picked by the author to provide students with insight into understanding and completing the question

Fundamentals of Financial Accounting fifth Canadian edition has also kept certain features that reviewers noted were very useful and necessary. These include

- Comparisons of the key differences between Accounting Standards for Private Enterprises (ASPE) and International Financial Reporting Standards (IFRS) in a boxed feature at the end of each chapter
- Comprehensive problems (spanning multiple chapters)
- Two critical thinking cases with questions throughout most chapters, in easy to use multiple−choice format.
- Check figures for some Exercises and Group A and Group B Problems, just to name a few

DETAILED CHANGES BY CHAPTER

CHAPTER 1

- **New** description of financial statement users, with new illustration (Exhibit 1.2)
- Updated dates for sample financial statements
- Expanded discussion of conceptual framework, with new illustration (Exhibit 1.10)
- Revisions to end of chapter material: updated numerical data for real−world companies, revised annual report case to reflect updated financial statements

CHAPTER 2

- **New** illustration of accounting cycle
- Expanded learning objectives to include trial balance preparation
- Revised illustration of T−accounts to include normal balance (Exhibit 2.7)
- Updated dates for sample financial statements
- Update analysis of current ratios in Spotlight on Financial Reporting
- Revisions to end of chapter material: updated numerical data for real−world companies, revised annual report case to reflect updated financial statements

CHAPTER 3

- Updated dates for sample financial statements
- Changed terminology from "unearned revenue" to "deferred revenue" to align better with new Revenue Recognition standards
- **New** IFRS/ASPE comparison box in relation to new Revenue Recognition standards
- **New** illustrations to compare timing of revenue recog−nition and cash receipt (Exhibit 3.5)
- **New** illustrations to compare timing of expense recog−nition and cash payment (Exhibit 3.6)
- **New** transactions to illustrate contemporary technol−ogy, such as online Facebook advertising and automated monthly disbursements
- **New** format for accounting equation effects to illustrate link between income statement and balance sheet
- Updated demonstration case
- Revisions to end of chapter material: updated numer−ical data for real−world companies, revised exercises to include transaction analysis and determination of income effects, revised annual report case to reflect updated financial statements

CHAPTER 4

- Updated dates for sample financial statements
- **New** illustration to tie adjustments to accounting cycle (Exhibit 4.2)
- **New** illustration of adjustment effects on balance sheet and income statement (Exhibit 4.5)
- Continued use of new accounting equation format illustrating link between income statement and balance sheet
- Updated demonstration case
- Revisions to end of chapter material: updated numerical data for real−world companies, revised exercises to encourage reflection on income effects of adjustments, revised annual report case to reflect updated financial statements

CHAPTER 5

- Substantial changes from the fourth edition: removed the discussion of press releases, the illustration of European financial statements, the introduction of the basic business model, and repeated coverage of external users. Inserted an explanation of internal control and cash reporting along with supporting examples.
- **New** focus company (Koss Corporation) to illustrate how internal control deficiencies allowed the VP Finance to steal $31.5 million to pay for extravagant credit card purchases
- **New** categorization of fraud types
- Expand discussion of internal control to include new COSO cube
- **New** illustration of electronic documents used to process cash disbursements
- **New** discussion of petty cash transactions and p−cards in Spotlight on Controls
- **New** discussion and illustration of reporting restricted cash
- Revisions to end of chapter material: updated numerical data for real−world companies, revised exercises to encourage reflection on income effects of adjustments, revised annual report case to reflect updated financial statements

CHAPTER 6

- Substantial changes from the fourth edition: removed internal control topics (now in Chapter 5), and relocated journal entries for inventory purchases (previously in Chapter 7) to accompany inventory sales in this chapter (Chapter 6)
- Updated focus company illustrations with Walmart and new Planet Fitness material contrast financial statements of service company with merchandiser (Exhibit 6.2)

- **New** illustration of cost−of−goods−sold equations to distinguish periodic and perpetual inventory systems
- Expanded discussion of shrinkage to include book−to−physical adjustment
- **New** exhibit comparing journal entries for inventory purchase and sale transactions (Exhibit 6.8) in a perpetual system (periodic system entries are included in the chapter supplement)
- **New** supplement created to discuss the concept of bundled sales, which stems from the new Revenue Recognition standards
- Expanded discussion to include using the net method for sales discounts and estimating significant returns of sales
- Updated demonstration case
- Revisions to end of chapter material: updated numerical data for real−world companies, revised exercises to encourage reflection on income effects of adjustments, revised annual report case to reflect updated financial statements

CHAPTER 7

- Inventory purchases and the corresponding journal entries have been removed and are now in Chapter 6 to accompany inventory sales.
- **New** Spotlight on Financial Reporting discussing the LCM write−down at Lululemon for its see−through yoga pants fiasco
- Updated inventory turnover analysis in Exhibit 7.7, involving Harley−Davidson, McDonalds, and HBC
- **New** Spotlight on Financial Reporting to tie inventory turnover and gross profit to LCM
- Updated demonstration case
- Revisions to end of chapter material: updated numerical data for real−world companies, revised exercises to encourage reflection on income effects of adjustments, revised annual report case to reflect updated financial statements

CHAPTER 8

- Updated focus company illustrations with VF Corporation—the maker of North Face jackets, JanSport backpacks, Wrangler jeans, and Vans shoes
- Updated Spotlight on Financial Reporting showing days to collect for Kellogg Company
- Updated receivables turnover analysis in Exhibit 8.7, involving VF Corporation, Kellogg's, and Skechers
- **New** Spotlight on Business Decisions showing how Target monitors its additional revenues over its costs of having customers pay for items on credit
- Updated demonstration case featuring Rocky Mountain Chocolate Factory

- Revisions to end of chapter material: updated numerical data for real—world companies, revised exercises to encourage reflection on income effects of adjustments, revised annual report case to reflect updated financial statements

CHAPTER 9

- Updated focus company illustrations with Cedar Fair
- Eliminated discussion of cash—only tangible asset purchase
- Revised depreciation formula presentations to highlight depreciation rates
- **New** illustration to explain calculation and journalizing of gain/loss on disposal
- Revised amortization presentation to show Accumulated Amortization rather than directly reducing asset
- Updated fixed asset turnover analysis in Exhibit 9.5, involving Cedar Fair, Six Flags, and Yahoo!
- **New** illustration in Homework Helper to show common causes of changes in account balances
- Revisions to end of chapter material: updated numerical data for real—world companies, revised exercises to encourage reflection on income effects of adjustments, revised annual report case to reflect updated financial statements

CHAPTER 10

- Updated focus company illustrations with General Mills
- **New** Spotlight on Business Decisions to discuss accounting for crowdfunding liabilities arising from Kickstarter and Prosper arrangements
- Replaced quick ratio with debt—to—assets ratio
- Revisions to end of chapter material: updated numerical data for real—world companies, revised exercises to encourage reflection on income effects of adjustments, revised annual report case to reflect updated financial statements

CHAPTER 11

- **New** focus company, Molson Coors Brewing Company
- Revised list of reasons for stock repurchases, supported by new Spotlight on Business Decisions involving Safeway's treasury stock purchase to boost EPS
- Expanded illustration of dividend journal entries to include closing entry
- **New** section to illustrate simple statement of shareholders' equity
- **New** Spotlight on the World to discuss the U.S. government's JOBS Act and crowdfunding equity
- **New** ratio analyses in Exhibit 11.7, involving Molson Coors Brewing Company and Anheuser—Busch Inbev

- Inserted cash dividends into demonstration case A
- Revisions to end of chapter material: updated numerical data for real—world companies, revised exercises to encourage reflection on income effects of adjustments, revised annual report case to reflect updated financial statements

CHAPTER 12

- Updated focus company illustrations and financial information for Under Armour Inc.
- Final section of chapter illustrates user analyses that are possible with direct method but not indirect method presentation
- Deleted spreadsheet approach, previously in chapter supplement
- Revised demonstration cases to be more consistent with approaches illustrated in chapter
- Revisions to end of chapter material: updated numerical data for real—world companies, revised exercises to encourage reflection on income effects of adjustments, revised annual report case to reflect updated financial statements

CHAPTER 13

- Updated information regarding the focus company (Home Depot), including all narrative interpreting and comparing financial results
- Revised Exhibit 13.5 and related discussion to reflect changes made to all other chapters
- **New** Spotlight on Business Decisions to discuss impact of supply chain financing on current ratio
- Revisions to end of chapter material: updated numerical data for real—world companies, revised exercises to encourage reflection on income effects of adjustments, revised annual report case to reflect updated financial statements

APPENDIXES A & B: HOME DEPOT SUMMARIZED FINANCIAL STATEMENTS AND EXCERPTS FROM THE FISCAL 2016 ANNUAL REPORT OF LOWE'S COMPANIES INC.

- Summarized financial statements of The Home Depot and updated excerpts from the fiscal 2016 Lowe's Annual Reports

APPENDIX C: PRESENT AND FUTURE VALUE CONCEPTS

- Reviewed and updated all end—of—chapter material

APPENDIX D: WIKI ART GALLERY, INC.

- The award winning critical thinking case, WIKI Art Gallery, Inc., is now included as an appendix instead of online in Connect. This is to allow for easier access and referencing for students when they are completing the multiple choice questions relating to this case through-out most chapters.

APPENDIX E: INVESTMENTS IN OTHER CORPORATIONS

- Updated focus company—Rogers Communications
- Revised discussion of mergers and acquisitions

SUPERIOR LEARNING SOLUTIONS AND SUPPORT

The McGraw–Hill Education team is ready to help you assess and integrate any of our products, technology, and services into your course for optimal teaching and learning performance. Whether it's helping your students improve their grades or putting your entire course online, the McGraw–Hill Education team is here to help you do it. Contact your Learning Solutions Consultant today to learn how to maximize all of McGraw–Hill Education's resources!

For more information, please visit us online: **http://www.mheducation.ca/he/solutions**

Advice on Working in Teams

Accounting information is always created and shared with others, making teamwork an important skill to develop. Our research finds that whether you select your own teammates or your instructor assigns them to you, taking certain steps can improve the chances of your team being successful.[2]

1. **Know what you want.** Talk with your teammates about the quality of work your team aspires to produce and the amount of commitment to reach that goal. Define the general rules by which the team will work. How will the team determine who does what? How often will you meet, and for how long? How will you keep in touch between meetings? Spending a few minutes at the start to put these "rules" in writing can save you much frustration and disappointment later.

2. **Plan how to get there.** Team projects can feel overwhelming at first, and you may be tempted to quickly split up the work so that everyone can get started on it. Do not do this. Take the time to identify (a) the specific steps needed to complete the project, (b) the skills required at each step, and (c) the strengths of each team member. Two benefits of being in a team are that you do not have to be an expert in everything and you do not have to do it all yourself. So assign work to team members based on their strengths and workloads, ensuring that everyone gets to do their fair share. Our research shows that teams earn better grades when everyone participates in a meaningful way.

3. **Work as a team.** Teams are more than just groups of people. To be a team, you must be committed to the same goal and be willing to "step up" when you can. Teams can accomplish much when working as single unit, but not without the individual effort made by team members. Our research shows that the highest project grades are earned when team members work together, bringing their skills and abilities to bear on each task.

4. **Build the team.** Teams rarely are perfect when they first start. It takes time to build the trust that is needed when relying on others. Help team members along by scheduling times to review one another's work and to give constructive feedback on how it can be improved. As a team, assess the whole team's performance and the openness of its communication. Do this often, and small difficulties will be less likely to turn into big problems.

[2]S. Hilton and F. Phillips, "Instructor–Assigned and Student–Selected Groups: A View from Inside," *Issues in Accounting Education* 25, pp 15–33 (2010).

Advice on Using Your Text

What does it take to do well in your Financial Accounting course? Our research finds that the way you read and use your textbook can have a major impact on your course performance.[3] The following graphic summarizes our primary findings, which suggests four things you can do to improve your chances of earning a good grade.

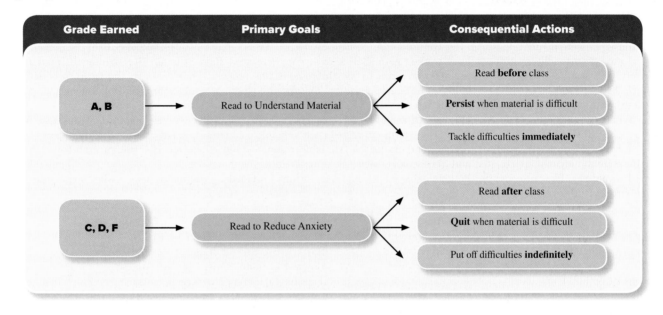

1. **Read the chapters to learn rather than just to get through them.** Learning doesn't miraculously occur just because your eyes have skimmed all the assigned lines of the textbook. You have to think and focus while reading to embed the material in your understanding and memory. Use the text's learning objectives to focus on what's really important in the chapters.

2. **Don't be discouraged if you initially find some material challenging to learn.** At one time or another, both the best and weakest students describe themselves as both "confused" and "having a good grasp of the material," "anxious" and "confident," and "overwhelmed" and "uncomfortable." The simple fact is that learning new material can be challenging and initially confusing for anyone. Success does not depend as much on whether you become confused as it does on what you do when you become confused.

3. **Clear up confusion as it arises.** A key difference between the most successful students and the least successful students is how they respond to difficulty and confusion. When successful students are confused or unsure, they immediately try to enhance their understanding through re–reading, self–testing, and seeking outside help if necessary. In contrast, unsuccessful students try to reduce anxiety by delaying further reading or by resorting to memorizing without understanding. Aim to clear up confusion when it arises because accounting, in particular, is a subject for which your understanding of later material depends on a thorough grasp of earlier material.

4. **Think of reading as the initial stage of studying.** Abandon the idea that "studying" only occurs during the final hours before an exam. By initially reading with the same intensity that occurs when later reviewing for an exam, you can create extra time for practising exercises and problems. This combination of concentrated reading and extensive practice is likely to contribute to better learning and superior exam scores.

---

[3]B.J. Phillips and F. Phillips, "Sink or Skim: Textbook Reading Behaviors of Introductory Accounting Students," *Issues in Accounting Education* 22, pp 21–44 (2007).

Acknowledgements

I am extremely grateful to have had this opportunity to work on yet another edition of this textbook. The entire process continues to be an incredible journey that you can truly appreciate only when you have been directly involved. The process has been rewarding and enjoyable thanks to the contributions made by everyone.

The committed team at McGraw−Hill Education was outstanding. They are truly a talented group of individuals who, with all of their efforts, have made this project come together. A huge thank you goes out to Keara Emmett, the portfolio manager, for her talent, commitment, and support throughout this process. Thank you to the content developers, Tammy Mavroudi and Lindsay MacDonald, for all of their guidance during this project. Tammy's wealth of information, patience, and insights were invaluable to me. Her constant communication with me was essential to the success of this project.

I am exceptionally grateful to have worked with such a great copy editor as Judy Sturrup. Her significant input and careful attention to details and deadlines were vital to me throughout this process. Thank you to the entire production staff: Jeanette McCurdy, Emily Hickey, and Michelle Saddler. Thanks also to our technical checker, Rob Ducharme; your attention to detail has been greatly appreciated.

I am extremely appreciative for the dedication and professionalism that was shown by everyone involved, as this made my job more manageable, including all the reviewers who provided such valuable comments and suggestions for improvements.

I am also genuinely grateful to Fred Phillips for his valuable resources and expertise. His guidance and wealth of knowledge are greatly appreciated and his commitment to be of assistance was unwavering.

I would also like to recognize the invaluable advice and suggestions provided by the many people who participated in the manuscript development reviews. For this assistance, I thank the following colleagues:

Reviewers for the Fifth Canadian Edition
Alym Amlani, *Kwantlen Polytechnic University*
Lorraine Cipparrone, *Sheridan College*
Pat Corkum, *Acadia University*
Megan Costiuk, *University of Regina*
Jaime Morales, *Trent University*
Barrie Tober, *Niagara College*

Reviewers for previous editions
Ron Baker, *University of Regina*
Hilary Becker, *Carleton University*
Paul Berry, *Mount Allison University*
Catherine Byers, *Seneca College of Applied Arts*
Andrea Chance, *George Brown College, University of Guelph*
Ann Clarke−Okah, *Carleton University*
Robert Collier, *University of Ottawa*
Patricia Corkum, *Acadia University*
Sandra Daga, *University of Toronto at Scarborough*
Angela Davis, *University of Winnipeg*
Han Donker, *University of Northern British Columbia*
Cynthia Duncan, *Seneca College*
Gerry Dupont, *Carleton University*
Ian Feltmate, *Acadia University*
Deirdre Fitzpatrick, *George Brown College*
George Gekas, *Ryerson University*
Elizabeth Grasby, *Western University*
Else Grech, *Ryerson University*
Colin Haime, *Vancouver Island University*
Rosalie Harms, *University of Winnipeg*
Mahlon Harvey, *University of Winnipeg*
Gordon Holyer, *Vancouver Island University*
Melissa Jean, *Western University*

Glen Kobussen, *University of Saskatchewan*
Walter Krystia, *Ryerson University*
Rafik Kurji, *Mount Royal University*
Howard Leaman, *University of Guelph−Humber*
Jennifer Li, *Brock University*
Ken Macaulay, *St. Francis Xavier University*
Amy MacFarlane, *University of Prince Edward Island*
Marie Madil−Payne, *George Brown College*
Chima Mbagwu, *Wilfrid Laurier University*
Kelsie McKay, *Georgian College*
Muriel McKenna, *Seneca College of Applied Arts & Technology*
Carol Meissner, *Georgian College*
Jaime Morales, *Trent University*
Robert C. Nichols, *Capilano University*
Vanessa Oltmann, *Vancouver Island University*
Michel Paquet, *SAIT Polytechnic*
Jay Perry, *Niagara College*
Jane Raycraft, *Capilano University*
Giuseppina Salvaggio, *Dawson College*
Ramesh Saxena, *Humber College*
John Siambanopoulos, *Western University*
Glenys Sylvestre, *University of Regina*
Tanya Tang, *University of British Columbia*
Rod Tilley, *Mount Saint Vincent University*
Barrie Tober, *Niagara College*
Gilles Valade, *Thompson Rivers University*
Helen Vallee, *Kwantlen Polytechnic University*
Peggy Wallace, *Trent University*
Shu−Lin Wong, *Memorial University of Newfoundland*
Richard Wright, *Fanshawe College*
Eliza Zuliani, *University of Toronto*

I want to thank my husband, our two daughters, and the other members of my family. Words alone cannot express the gratitude I feel for their encouragement, support, and patience throughout this process. Thank you for being just as excited about this edition as I am!

Brandy Mackintosh Edwards School of Business University of Saskatchewan

The Complete Course Solution

We listened to educators from around the world, learned about their challenges, and created a whole new way to deliver a course.

Connect2 is a collaborative teaching and learning platform that includes an instructionally designed complete course framework of learning materials that is flexible and open for instructors to easily personalize, add their own content, or integrate with other tools and platforms.

- Save time and resources building and managing a course.
- Gain confidence knowing that each course framework is pedagogically sound.
- Help students master course content.
- Make smarter decisions by using real-time data to guide course design, content changes, and remediation.

MANAGE — Dynamic Curriculum Builder

Quickly and easily launch a complete course framework developed by instructional design experts. Each Connect2 course is a flexible foundation for instructors to build upon by adding their own content or drawing upon the wide repository of additional resources.

- Easily customize Connect2 by personalizing the course scope and sequence.
- Get access to a wide range of McGraw-Hill Education content within one powerful teaching and learning platform.
- Receive expert support and guidance on how best to utilize content to achieve a variety of teaching goals.

MASTER — Student Experience

Improve student performance with instructional alignment and leverage Connect2's carefully curated learning resources. Deliver required reading through Connect2's award-winning adaptive learning system.

- Teach at a higher level in class by helping students retain core concepts.
- Tailor in-class instruction based on student progress and engagement.
- Help focus students on the content they don't know so they can prioritize their study time.

MEASURE — Advanced Analytics

Collect, analyze and act upon class and individual student performance data. Make real-time course updates and teaching decisions backed by data.

- Visually explore class and student performance data.
- Easily identify key relationships between assignments and student performance.
- Maximize in-class time by using data to focus on areas where students need the most help.

Course Map

The flexible and customizable course map provides instructors full control over the pre-designed courses within Connect2. Instructors can easily add, delete, or rearrange content to adjust the course scope and sequence to their personal preferences.

Implementation Guide

Each Connect2 course includes a detailed implementation guide that provides guidance on what the course can do and how best to utilize course content based on individual teaching approaches.

Instructor Resources

A comprehensive collection of instructor resources are available within Connect2. Instructor Support and Seminar Materials provide additional exercises and activities to use for in-class discussion and teamwork.

Business Decisions and Financial Accounting

wavebreakmedia/Shutter-stock.com

FOCUS COMPANY:
Pizza Palace Inc.

PIZZA
PALACE

Welcome to the world of business and financial accounting. One of our goals for this book is to help you see the role that accounting plays in helping people turn their good ideas into successful businesses. The founder of FedEx first introduced his ideas about a nationwide transportation business in a college essay. With the help of accounting, FedEx has become a multibillion-dollar business. Perhaps the only thing stopping you from doing this is that you don't feel you know what is involved in starting and running a business. We're here to help with that.

Another important goal for us is to explain topics in ways that you can relate to. We want you to see that your personal life experiences help you to learn accounting. Often, we will explain topics in the context of a real business. For example, in the first four chapters, you will learn the steps that Emilio Santos took to start his own business and turn his dream into reality. By reading about his experiences, you'll gain a realistic understanding of how accounting is a key part of all businesses. So, let's get started.

For ten years, Emilio worked in several pizza restaurants in downtown Vancouver. During this time, he perfected a gourmet pizza concept that he believed would be a great addition to the local restaurant scene, so Emilio decided to start his own pizza business.

Although eager to get started, Emilio had several questions to consider and decisions to make. He contacted Ally Paddison, a local chartered professional accountant (CPA), to ask her advice. As you will read in this chapter, Ally met with Emilio in June to answer his many questions and to help him understand what's involved in starting a business and how to monitor its success. By following Ally's business and accounting advice, Emilio successfully launched his company, which he named Pizza Palace Inc.

ORGANIZATION OF THE CHAPTER

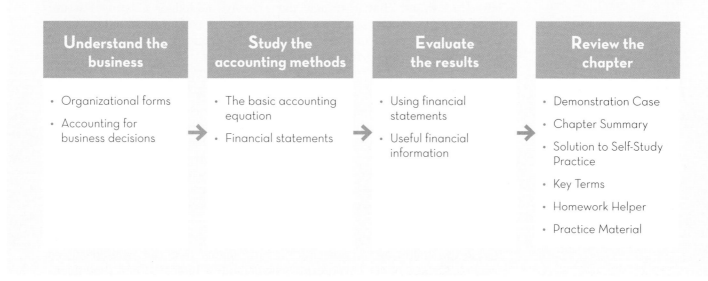

Understand the business	Study the accounting methods	Evaluate the results	Review the chapter
• Organizational forms • Accounting for business decisions	• The basic accounting equation • Financial statements	• Using financial statements • Useful financial information	• Demonstration Case • Chapter Summary • Solution to Self-Study Practice • Key Terms • Homework Helper • Practice Material

Understand the Business

ORGANIZATIONAL FORMS

"Emilio, we should start by talking about how you want to organize your business."

©The McGraw-Hill Companies Inc./Brian Moeskau, photographer

 "Well, I'm opening a gourmet pizza restaurant. What else do I need to know?"

©The McGraw-Hill Companies Inc./Brian Moeskau, photographer

Ally outlined three primary ways in which businesses can be organized: sole proprietorship, partnership, and corporation.

LEARNING OBJECTIVE 1-1

Describe various organizational forms and business decision makers.

Sole Proprietorship

This is a form of business owned (and usually operated) by one individual. It is the easiest form of business to start because it doesn't require any special legal procedures. The owner just gets a business licence and they're good to go. A sole proprietorship is considered a part of the owner's life, with all profits (or losses) becoming part of the taxable income of the owner, and the owner is personally liable for all debts of the business.

Partnership

A partnership is similar to a sole proprietorship, except that prof— its, taxes, and legal liability are the responsibility of two or more owners instead of just one. It is slightly more expensive to form than a sole proprietorship because a lawyer typically is needed to draw up a partnership agreement, which describes how profits are shared between partners and how that would change if new partners are added or existing partners leave. The key advantage of a partnership over a sole proprietorship is that, because it has more owners, a partnership typically has more resources available to it, which can fuel the business's growth.

Corporation

Unlike sole proprietorships and partnerships, a corporation is a separate entity from both a legal and accounting perspective. This means that the corporation, not its owners, is legally responsible for its own taxes and debts. Thus, owners cannot lose more than their investment in the corporation, which is a major advantage to the owners. Two disadvantages of incorporation are that the legal fees for creating a corporation can be high and income tax returns must be filed for both the corporation and its owners.

Corporations can raise large amounts of money for growth because they divide ownership of the corporation into shares that can be sold to new owners. A share of the corporation's ownership is indicated in a legal document called a *share certificate*. The owners of a company's shares (shareholders) can buy and sell shares privately or publicly on a stock exchange if the company has legally registered to do so. Most corporations start out as private companies and will apply to become public companies ("go public") if they need a lot of financing, which they obtain from selling new share certificates to investors. Some big-name corporations, like London Drugs and Kal Tire, haven't gone public because they get enough financing from private sources, but many that you are familiar with, such as Rogers Communications Inc. and Boston Pizza International Inc., are public companies.

Other

The only other form of business ownership in Canada is one that offers limited liability, and is called a limited liability partnership (LLP). In this business form, the partners have limited liability, depending upon their contribution to the partnership. Sometimes partners make only financial contributions to a partnership and are not involved in actively running the business. We focus on corporations in this book.

> "I'm interested in limiting my legal liability and getting some financing by selling ownership shares to investors and putting in some of my own personal money, so I will create a private corporation called Pizza Palace Inc. What's next?"

ACCOUNTING FOR BUSINESS DECISIONS

Most companies exist to earn profits for their shareholders. They earn profits by selling goods or services to customers for more than they cost to produce. Pizza Palace will be successful if it is able to sell pizzas for more than it costs the company to make them. To know just how successful his company is, Emilio will need to establish and maintain a good system of financial record-keeping—an accounting system. **Accounting** is an information system designed by an organization to capture (analyze, record, and summarize) the activities affecting its financial condition

Accounting: A system of analyzing, recording, and summarizing the results of a business's activities and then reporting the results to decision makers.

and performance, and then report the results to decision makers, both inside and outside the organization. It's such a key part of business that business people typically talk about their companies using accounting terms, which is why accounting terminology is often called the "language of business."

Every organization needs accountants to assist in reporting financial information for decision making and to help its owners understand the financial effects of those business decisions. Emilio can get this help in one of two ways. He can hire an accountant to work as an employee of his business (a private accountant) or he can contract with someone like Ally, who provides advice to a variety of businesses (a public accountant). Because Emilio's business is small, he doesn't yet need a full-time accountant. Instead, he agrees that Pizza Palace will pay fees to Ally for basic services. She'll help him to set up an accounting system and advise him on key business decisions.

> "How will an accounting system help me run my business?"

The main goal of an accounting system is to capture information about the operating, investing, and financing activities of a company so that it can be reported to decision makers, both inside and outside the business. Exhibit 1.1 illustrates this role and shows that this information can be presented in two kinds of reports.

Managerial accounting reports include detailed financial plans and continually updated reports about the operating performance of the company. These reports are made available only to the company's employees (internal users) so that they can make business decisions related to production, marketing, human resources, and finance. For example, managerial accounting reports are needed when determining whether to build, buy, or rent a building; whether to continue or discontinue making particular products; how much to pay employees; and how much to borrow. As

EXHIBIT 1.1	The Accounting System Reports Information for Decision Makers

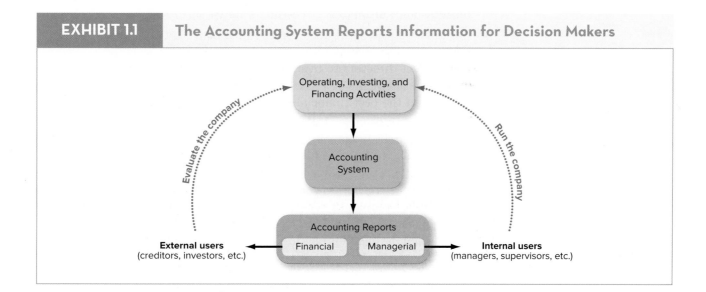

manager of Pizza Palace, Emilio will regularly need managerial accounting reports to monitor the quantity of supplies on hand, evaluate the various costs associated with making and selling his gourmet pizza, and assess the productivity of his employees.

 "Others outside your business will need financial information about your restaurant. For example, where will the money come from to start your business?"

"My wife and I will contribute $30,000 from personal savings. But I'll still need to ask the bank for a $20,000 loan to buy equipment. What will the bank want to know?"

Financial statements: Accounting reports that summarize the financial results of business and financing activities.

Ally described financial accounting reports, called **financial statements**, which are prepared periodically to provide information to people not employed by the business. These external financial statement users aren't given access to detailed internal records of the company, so they rely extensively on the financial statements. The four main groups of external users are (1) creditors, (2) investors, (3) directors, and (4) government.

- Creditors include suppliers, banks, and anyone to whom money is owed. *Suppliers* want to be sure they will be paid for the goods and services they deliver, so they will evaluate a company's financial statements and check its credit history before allowing it to buy on credit. Banks use financial statements to evaluate the risk that they will not be repaid the money they've loaned to a company. Because banks take a risk when they loan money to a company, they want periodic financial reports to evaluate how well the company is doing so they can intervene if it looks like the company will have trouble repaying its loan.

- Investors include existing and potential shareholders. *Shareholders* look to accounting information to assess the financial strength of a business and, ultimately, to estimate its value.

- Directors is the short title for the members of a company's *board of directors*. The shareholders of public companies or large private companies elect directors to oversee the company's managers. Directors use financial statements to ensure the company's managers make decisions that are in the best financial interests of its shareholders.

- Government agencies look closely at companies' financial statements. For example, Canadian securities regulations are managed through laws and agencies established by Canada's thirteen provincial and territorial governments. Each province and territory has a securities commission or equivalent authority that keeps a close watch on the information that public companies report in financial statements. Also, the provincial, territorial, and federal governments use financial statement information to ensure taxes are computed correctly.

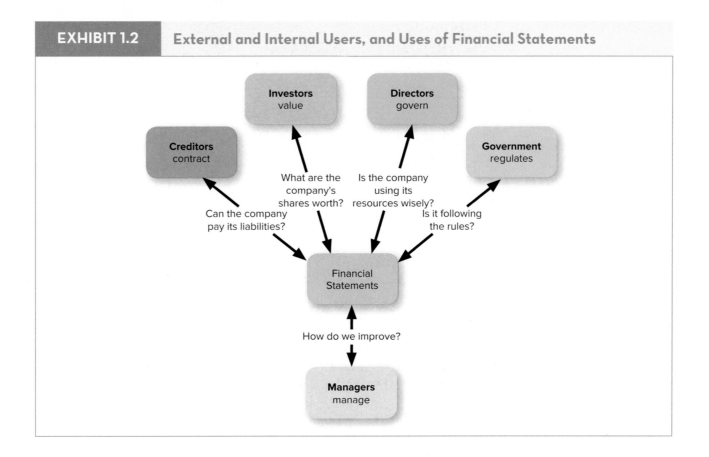

Exhibit 1.2 shows that, along with managers inside the company, these external user groups are key users of financial statement information. In the case of Pizza Palace, the bank will be the main external user. Emilio will be expected to prepare financial statements to obtain the loan and then regularly provide updated financial reports until the loan is repaid. If the company's shares are ever sold to other investors, these shareholders will rely on financial statements to estimate the value of their shares and determine whether to buy, sell, or hold Pizza Palace shares.

While Emilio understood everything Ally had told him up to this point, he had another major concern.

"I want to sound intelligent when I talk to my banker, but I don't know much about accounting."

 "This is a common concern for new business owners, so let's start with the most basic thing you need to know about accounting."

THE BASIC ACCOUNTING EQUATION

LEARNING OBJECTIVE 1-2

Describe the purpose, structure, and content of the four basic financial statements.

One of the central concepts of financial reports is that what a company owns must equal what the company owes to its creditors and shareholders. In accounting, there are special names for what a company owns (assets) and the claims on these items by creditors (liabilities) and shareholders (equity), as shown below.

Resources Owned . . .	=	Resources Owed . . .	
by the **company**		to **creditors**	to **shareholders**
Assets	**=**	**Liabilities**	**+ Shareholders' Equity**

Basic accounting equation: $A + L = SE$, where A = assets, L = liabilities, and SE = shareholders' equity.

Separate entity assumption: The financial reports of a business are assumed to include the results of only that business's activities.

The relationship between assets (A), liabilities (L), and shareholders' equity (SE) is known as the **basic accounting equation**. The business itself, not the shareholders who own the business, is viewed as owning the assets and owing the liabilities. This is called the **separate entity assumption**, which requires that a business's financial reports include only the activities of the business and not those of its shareholders.

The elements of the basic accounting equation are fundamental to reading and understanding financial statements, so let's look at each in detail.

Assets

An asset is an economic resource presently controlled by the company; it has measurable value and is expected to benefit the company by producing cash inflows or reducing cash outflows in the future. For Pizza Palace, assets include things like cash, supplies, and cookware, and equipment such as tables, chairs, and pizza ovens. Some companies may have assets that don't appear on their financial statements, such as good, hardworking employees. These employees do not appear on the financial statements because they don't have measurable value.

Liabilities

Liabilities are measurable amounts that the company owes to creditors. If Pizza Palace borrows from a bank, it would owe a liability called a *Note Payable*. This particular name is used because banks require borrowers to sign a legal document called a *note*, which describes details about the company's promise to repay the bank. Pizza Palace is likely to also owe suppliers for ingredients and other supplies delivered to Pizza Palace. When a company buys goods from another company, it usually does so on credit by promising to pay for the goods at a later date. The amount owed is called an *Account Payable* because purchases made using credit are said to be "on account." Pizza Palace could also owe wages to employees (*Salaries and Wages Payable*) and taxes to governments (*Taxes Payable*). From a legal perspective, creditors have priority over shareholders. Thus, if a company goes out of business, liabilities must be paid before any amounts are paid to shareholders.

Shareholders' Equity

Shareholders' equity represents the owners' claims on the business. As illustrated below, these claims arise for two reasons:

1. The owners have a claim on amounts they contributed directly to the company in exchange for its shares (Contributed Capital).

2. The owners have a claim on amounts the company has earned through profitable business operations (Retained Earnings).

Retained Earnings is particularly important because a business can survive only if it is profitable. It will be profitable if the total amount earned from selling goods and services is greater than the costs incurred to generate those sales. Theoretically, these prof—its belong to the company's owners, so they increase shareholders' equity. Through these profits, owners can get more money back from the company than they paid in (a return on their invest—ment). Given the importance of a company's profits, accounting systems separately track the two components of profit: revenues and expenses.

Revenues   Revenues are earned by selling goods or services to custom—ers. For Pizza Palace, revenues are measured at the amount the company charges its customers for pizza.

Expenses   Expenses are all costs of doing business that are necessary to earn revenues. For Pizza Palace, these include advertising, utilities, rent, wages, insurance, repairs, and supplies used in making pizza. Expenses are said to be incurred to generate revenues. The word *incurred* means that the activities giving rise to a cost (e.g., running an ad, using electricity) have occurred in the period in which the related revenues have been generated.

Net Income   Although *profit* is used in casual conversation, the preferred term in accounting is *net income*. Net income is calculated as revenues minus expenses. For Pizza Palace to be profitable, its rev—enues must be greater than its expenses. (If revenues are less than expenses, the company would have a net loss, but for now we'll optimistically assume that Pizza Palace is going to earn a profit.) By generating net income, a company increases its shareholders' equity, as

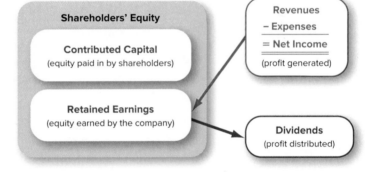

illustrated below. This net income can be left in the company to accumu—late (with the prior year's net income that has been retained) or it can be paid out to the company's shareholders for their own personal use (called *dividends*).

Dividends   A company's net income (profit) is accumulated in Retained Earnings until a decision is made to distribute it to shareholders in what is called a *dividend*. The simplest type of dividend, and the most common for a small business like Pizza Palace, is a dividend paid in cash. Dividends are not an expense incurred to generate earnings. Rather, dividends are an optional distribution of earnings to shareholders, approved by the company's board of directors. Dividends are reported as a reduction in Retained Earnings. If Emilio wanted, he could choose to leave all the prof—its in Pizza Palace by never declaring a dividend.

"Okay, I think I get it. But can you tell me how all those items relate to each other and where they are reported in the financial statements?"

FINANCIAL STATEMENTS

Assets, liabilities, shareholders' equity, revenues, expenses, and dividends appear in different reports that collectively are called *financial statements*. The term *financial statements* refers to four accounting reports, typically prepared in the following order:

1. **Income Statement**
2. **Statement of Retained Earnings**
3. **Balance Sheet**
4. **Statement of Cash Flows**

Financial statements can be prepared at any time during the year, although they are most commonly prepared monthly, every three months (quarterly reports), and at the end of the year (annual reports). Companies are allowed to choose their fiscal year–end date. The fiscal year can be a twelve–month period ending on a day other than December 31, or the fiscal year can be what is called a calendar year–end, which is a twelve–month period ending on December 31. Toy maker Mattel, Inc. uses a calendar year–end because this is the start of its slow business period. The Saskatchewan Roughriders Football Club Inc. has chosen a fiscal year–end of March 31, which is during the off–season of the football schedule and is a slower time of year for the organization.

The Income Statement

Income statement: Reports the amount of revenues less expenses for a period of time. Also called the *statement of operations*.

The first financial statement prepared is the **income statement** (also called the *statement of operations*). Ally gives Emilio Exhibit 1.3 to show what Pizza Palace's income statement might look like for the month ended September 30, assuming he is able to open his restaurant on September 1. The heading of the income statement identifies who, what, and when: the

---

EXHIBIT 1.3 Income Statement

PIZZA PALACE

		Explanation
PIZZA PALACE INC. **Income Statement (Projected)** **For the Month Ended September 30, 2017**		Who: Name of the business What: Title of the statement When: Accounting period
Revenues		
Sales Revenue	$ 11,000	Revenue earned from the sale and delivery of pizza to customers
Total Revenues	11,000	**Total amount earned during September**
Expenses		
Supplies Expense	4,000	Cost of pizza ingredients used up in September
Salaries and Wages Expense	2,000	Cost of salaries and employee wages for work done in September
Rent Expense	1,500	Cost of rent for the month of September
Utilities Expense	600	Cost of utilities used in September
Insurance Expense	300	Cost of insurance coverage for September
Advertising Expense	100	Cost of advertising done in September
Income Tax Expense	500	Cost of taxes on September's income
Total Expenses	9,000	**Total expenses incurred in September to generate revenues**
Net Income	$ 2,000	**Difference between total revenues and total expenses**

---

name of the business, the title of the report, and the time period covered by the financial statement. Larger businesses with thousands or millions of dollars in revenues and expenses add a fourth line under the date to indicate if the numbers reported are rounded to the nearest thousand or million.

For international companies, this fourth line also reports the currency used in the report. An international company based in Canada will trans—late any foreign currency into Canadian dollars—basically assuming all its business was done in Canadian dollars. This is the **unit of measure assumption**. There is also the option for these companies to report in a currency other than Canadian dollars. Many well—known Canadian pub—licly traded companies, such as Lululemon Athetica, report in U.S. dollars. We also see it in the reporting currency used in other countries: Nestlé (Swiss franc), Lego (Danish krone), and Adidas (euro). Companies with complex activities report a statement of comprehensive income that shows net income as well as gains and losses relating to pensions, certain invest—ments, and foreign currency translations.

The body of an income statement has three major captions—revenues, expenses, and net income—corresponding to the equation for the income statement (Revenues − Expenses = Net Income). Individual types of revenues and expenses would be reported under the revenue and expense headings. These **accounts**, as they are called, are typical for most businesses, whether small or big. Notice that each major caption has an underlined subtotal, and the "bottom line" amount for net income has a double underline to highlight it. Finally, a dollar sign appears at the top and bottom of the column of numbers.

When listing the accounts on the income statement, revenues are on top, usually with the largest, most relevant revenue listed first. Then expenses are subtracted, again from largest to smallest, except that Income Tax Expense is the last expense listed. Net Income is the difference between total revenues and total expenses. This format, which groups revenues separately from expenses and reports a single measure of income, is called a **single—step income statement**. Other income statement formats are possible, as will be explained in Chapter 6.

"So, does the $2,000 of Net Income mean I'll have that much more cash?"

"No. Net Income is a measure of how much better off your business is, not how much cash you made."

Ally's point is one of the key ideas of the income statement. It's quite common for a business to provide goods or services to customers in one month but not collect cash from them until a later month. Similarly, expenses for the current month's activities may actually be paid in a different month. You'll have a chance to learn about this in more detail later, but it's worth trying to understand from the beginning that revenues don't necessarily equal cash coming in during the month, and expenses don't always equal cash going out during the month.

Emilio seemed disappointed to see only $2,000 of projected net income for the first month. Ally reassured him that it's typical for new businesses like Pizza Palace to initially struggle to generate a profit because they have lots of expenses related to advertising and employee training but relatively small revenues because they haven't yet built a loyal customer base. Pizza Palace's net income will likely increase in the future after the business becomes well known. When the company sells more pizza, revenues will increase without a major increase in expenses, except for the cost of ingredients and supplies that will be used in making the additional pizzas.

 "I guess that's not so bad. It does make me want to watch my expenses and try to boost my pizza sales quickly. What about the amount Pizza Palace owes to the bank? Should we talk about the balance sheet?"

"Before we look at that, I want to show you the next statement that connects the income statement to the balance sheet, so you'll understand the relationships between the reports."

The Statement of Retained Earnings

Statement of retained earnings: Reports the way that net income and the distribution of dividends affected the financial position of the company during the period.

Pizza Palace will report a **statement of retained earnings**, as shown in Exhibit 1.4. A more comprehensive statement of shareholders' equity that explains changes in all shareholders' equity accounts is provided by large corporations. But for Pizza Palace, most changes in shareholders' equity relate to generating and distributing earnings, so a statement of retained earnings is just as good as a full-blown statement of shareholders' equity.

The heading in Exhibit 1.4 identifies the name of the company, the title of the report, and the accounting period. The statement starts with the Retained Earnings balance at the beginning of the period. Remember that retained earnings are the profits that have accumulated in the company

EXHIBIT 1.4	Statement of Retained Earnings	PIZZA PALACE

PIZZA PALACE INC. Statement of Retained Earnings (Projected) For the Month Ended September 30, 2017		Explanation
		Who: Name of the business
		What: Title of the statement
		When: Accounting period
Retained Earnings, September 1, 2017	$ 0	Last period's ending Retained Earnings balance
Add: Net Income	2,000	Reported on the income statement (Exhibit 1.3)
Subtract: Dividends	(1,000)	Distributions to shareholders in the current period
Retained Earnings, September 30, 2017	$1,000	This period's ending Retained Earnings balance

over time. Because this is a new business, there aren't any accumulated profits yet, so the beginning balance is $0. Next, the statement adds Net Income, and subtracts any Dividends for the current period, to arrive at Retained Earnings at the end of the period.[1] Again, a dollar sign is used at the top and bottom of the column of numbers and a double underline appears at the bottom.

The Balance Sheet

The next financial report is the **balance sheet**. It is also known as the statement of financial position. The balance sheet's purpose is to report the amount of a business's assets, liabilities, and shareholders' equity at a specific point in time.

Exhibit 1.5 presents Pizza Palace's projected balance sheet. Think of the balance sheet as a picture or screen capture of Pizza Palace's resources and claims to resources at the end of a particular day (in this case, September 30, 2017).

Notice again that the heading specifically identifies the name of the company and title of the statement. Unlike the other financial reports, the balance sheet is presented for a point in time (at September 30, 2017, in this case). The assets are listed in order of how soon they are to be used or turned into cash. Likewise, liabilities are listed in order of how soon each is to be paid or settled.

Balance sheet: Reports the amount of assets, liabilities, and shareholders' equity of a business at a point in time.

EXHIBIT 1.5	Balance Sheet		PIZZA PALACE

PIZZA PALACE INC. **Balance Sheet (Projected)** **At September 30, 2017**		Explanation Who: Name of the business What: Title of the statement When: Point in time
Assets		Resources controlled by the company
Cash	$14,000	Amount of cash on hand and in the business's bank account
Accounts Receivable	1,000	Pizza Palace's right to collect from customers for prior credit sales
Supplies	3,000	Amount of food and paper supplies on hand
Equipment	40,000	Cost of ovens, tables, etc.
Total Assets	$58,000	Total amount of the company's resources
Liabilities and Shareholders' Equity		Claims on the company's resources
Liabilities		Creditors' claims on the company's resources
Accounts Payable	$ 7,000	Amount owed to suppliers for prior credit purchases (on account)
Note Payable	20,000	Amount of loan owed to the bank (for promissory note)
Total Liabilities	27,000	**Total claims on the resources by creditors**
Shareholders' Equity		Shareholders' claims on the company's resources
Contributed Capital	30,000	Amount shareholders contributed for company shares
Retained Earnings	1,000	Total earnings retained in the business (Exhibit 1.4)
Total Shareholders' Equity	31,000	Total claims on the company's resources by shareholders
Total Liabilities and Shareholders' Equity	$58,000	**Total claims on the company's resources**

The balance sheet first lists the assets of the business, which for Pizza Palace total $58,000. The second section lists the business's liabilities and shareholders' equity balances, also totalling $58,000. The balance sheet "balances" because the resources equal the claims to the resources. The basic accounting equation (also called the *balance sheet equation*) reflects the business's financial position at September 30, 2017:

Assets	=	Liabilities	+	Shareholders' Equity
58,000	=	$27,000	+	$31,000

COACH'S TIP

Any account name containing *receivable* is an asset and any containing *payable* is a liability.

Cash is the first asset reported on the balance sheet. The $14,000 would represent the total amount of cash on hand and in Pizza Palace's bank account. The $1,000 reported as Accounts Receivable represent Pizza Palace's right to collect from customers for sales made on credit. Pizza Palace intends to allow local colleges and universities to buy pizza for fundraising events on account by running a tab for which Pizza Palace sends a bill after the deliveries are made. The $3,000 reported for Supplies indicates the cost of pizza supplies on hand at the balance sheet date. The same is true for the $40,000 of Equipment. According to the cost principle of accounting, assets are initially reported on the balance sheet based on their original cost to the company.

Under liabilities, Ally includes $7,000 of Accounts Payable as the amount that Pizza Palace owes suppliers for food and paper supplies purchased on account. The Note Payable is the written promise to repay the loan from the bank. As with all liabilities, these are financial obligations of the business arising from past business activities.

Finally, within shareholders' equity, Contributed Capital reflects the dollar amount of the company's shares given when Emilio and his wife contribute $30,000 to the company. Retained Earnings reports the earnings as of September 30, 2017, that are expected to be retained in the company. It matches the ending amount of Retained Earnings on the statement of retained earnings (Exhibit 1.4).

"Besides monitoring my revenues and expenses, it looks like I need to make sure I have enough assets to pay my liabilities."

"Sharp observation! Your creditors are most interested in your ability to pay cash to them in the future. However, not all assets can be easily turned into cash and not all revenues and expenses are received or paid in cash. So there is one more important financial statement."

The Statement of Cash Flows

Statement of cash flows: Reports the operating, investing, and financing activities that caused increases and decreases in cash during the period.

Pizza Palace's projected income statement (back in Exhibit 1.3) shows a positive net income of $2,000. However, net income is not necessarily equal to cash, because revenues are reported when earned and expenses when incurred, regardless of when cash is received or paid. The fourth financial report of interest to external users, then, is the **statement of cash flows**. It includes only those activities that result in cash changing

EXHIBIT 1.6   Statement of Cash Flows

PIZZA PALACE

PIZZA PALACE INC. Statement of Cash Flows (Projected) For the Month Ended September 30, 2017		Explanation Who: Name of the entity What: Title of the statement When: Accounting period
Cash Flows from Operating Activities		Activities directly related to earning income
Cash Received from Customers	$10,000	Amount of cash received from customers
Cash Paid to Employees and Suppliers	(5,000)	Amount of cash paid to employees and suppliers of goods/services
Cash Provided by Operating Activities	5,000	Cash inflows minus outflows ($10,000 − $5,000)
Cash Flows from Investing Activities		Activities related to the sale/purchase of productive assets
Cash Used to Buy Equipment	(40,000)	Amount of cash spent on equipment
Cash Used in Investing Activities	(40,000)	
Cash Flows from Financing Activities		Activities involving investors and banks
Capital Contributed by Shareholders	30,000	Amount of cash received from owners
Cash Dividends Paid to Shareholders	(1,000)	Amount of cash paid to owners
Cash Borrowed from the Bank	20,000	Amount of cash received from the bank
Cash Provided by Financing Activities	49,000	Cash inflows minus outflows ($30,000 − $1,000 + $20,000)
Change in Cash	14,000	Sum of three categories of cash flows ($5,000 − $40,000 + $49,000)
Beginning Cash, September 1, 2017	0	Cash balance at the beginning of the accounting period
Ending Cash, September 30, 2017	$ 14,000	Cash balance reported on the balance sheet (Exhibit 1.5)

hands. Exhibit 1.6 shows Pizza Palace's projected statement of cash flows for the month ended September 30, 2017.

The statement of cash flows is divided into three types of activities:

1. **Operating:** These activities are directly related to running the business to earn profit. They include buying supplies, making pizza, serving food to customers, cleaning the store, buying advertising, renting a building, repairing ovens, obtaining insurance coverage, and so on.

2. **Investing:** These activities involve buying and selling productive resources with long lives (such as buildings, land, equipment, and tools), purchasing investments, and lending to others. As Exhibit 1.6 shows, Pizza Palace expects to spend $40,000 cash to purchase equipment.

3. **Financing:** Borrowing from banks, repaying bank loans, receiving cash from shareholders for company shares, and paying dividends to shareholders are all considered financing activities.

Pizza Palace's statement of cash flows is typical of a start–up business or a business in expansion. The negative number for investing cash flows occurs because the company needs to buy a significant amount of equipment. The bank will be interested in watching how the cash flows reported on this statement change in the future in order to assess Pizza Palace's ability to make cash payments on the loan.

Notes to the Financial Statements

The four basic financial statements are not complete without notes to help financial statement users understand how the amounts were derived and

COACH'S TIP

Parentheses are used on the statement of cash flows to indicate negative cash flows; if the number is left positive, this represents a cash inflow.

what other information may affect their decisions. We'll talk about these notes in more detail in later chapters.

Relationships Among the Financial Statements

Exhibit 1.7 shows how the four basic financial statements connect to one another. The arrows show that

1 Net Income, from the income statement, is a component in determining ending Retained Earnings on the statement of retained earnings;

2 Retained Earnings from the statement of retained earnings is then reported on the balance sheet; and

3 Cash on the balance sheet is equal to the Ending Cash reported on the statement of cash flows.

EXHIBIT 1.7   Relationships Among the Financial Statements

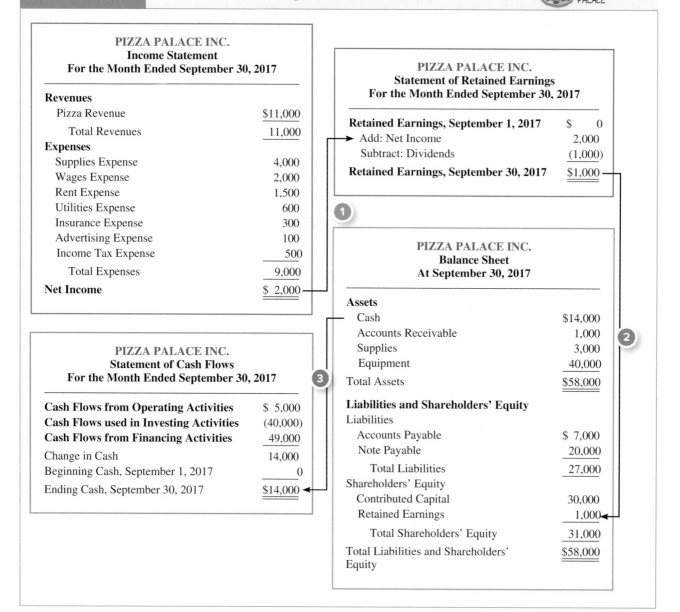

PIZZA PALACE INC.
Income Statement
For the Month Ended September 30, 2017

Revenues	
Pizza Revenue	$11,000
Total Revenues	11,000
Expenses	
Supplies Expense	4,000
Wages Expense	2,000
Rent Expense	1,500
Utilities Expense	600
Insurance Expense	300
Advertising Expense	100
Income Tax Expense	500
Total Expenses	9,000
Net Income	$ 2,000

PIZZA PALACE INC.
Statement of Retained Earnings
For the Month Ended September 30, 2017

Retained Earnings, September 1, 2017	$ 0
Add: Net Income	2,000
Subtract: Dividends	(1,000)
Retained Earnings, September 30, 2017	$1,000

PIZZA PALACE INC.
Balance Sheet
At September 30, 2017

Assets	
Cash	$14,000
Accounts Receivable	1,000
Supplies	3,000
Equipment	40,000
Total Assets	$58,000
Liabilities and Shareholders' Equity	
Liabilities	
Accounts Payable	$ 7,000
Note Payable	20,000
Total Liabilities	27,000
Shareholders' Equity	
Contributed Capital	30,000
Retained Earnings	1,000
Total Shareholders' Equity	31,000
Total Liabilities and Shareholders' Equity	$58,000

PIZZA PALACE INC.
Statement of Cash Flows
For the Month Ended September 30, 2017

Cash Flows from Operating Activities	$ 5,000
Cash Flows used in Investing Activities	(40,000)
Cash Flows from Financing Activities	49,000
Change in Cash	14,000
Beginning Cash, September 1, 2017	0
Ending Cash, September 30, 2017	$14,000

Financial Statement	Purpose: To report . . .	Structure	Examples of Content
Income Statement	The financial performance of the business during the current accounting period.	Revenues − Expenses = Net Income	Sales revenue, wages expense, supplies expense, rent expense
Statement of Retained Earnings	The accumulation of earnings retained in the business during the current accounting period with that of prior periods.	Beginning Retained Earnings + Net Income (this period) − Dividends (this period) = Ending Retained Earnings	Net income is from the income statement. Dividends are amounts distributed this period.
Balance Sheet	The financial position of a business at a point in time.	Assets = Liabilities + Shareholders' Equity	Cash, receivables, supplies, equipment, accounts payable, notes payable, contributed capital, retained earnings
Statement of Cash Flows	Activities that caused increases and decreases in cash during the current accounting period.	+/− Operating Cash Flows +/− Investing Cash Flows +/− Financing Cash Flows = Change in Cash + Beginning Cash = Ending Cash	Cash collected from customers, cash paid to suppliers, cash paid for equipment, cash borrowed from banks, cash received from selling shares

A summary of the four basic financial statements is presented in Exhibit 1.8.

You have seen lots of new and important material in this section. Before moving on, take a moment to complete the self-study practice. This is the best way to make sure you've paid enough attention when reading about how business activities are reported in financial statements.

🔦 HOW'S IT GOING?

Self-Study Practice 1.1

In the space provided, indicate (a) the type of account (A = asset, L = liability, SE = shareholders' equity, R = revenue, E = expense), and (b) whether it is reported on the income statement (I/S), statement of retained earnings (SRE), balance sheet (B/S), or statement of cash flows (SCF).

Account Title	Type	Statement
1. Land	_____	_____
2. Wages Expense	_____	_____
3. Accounts Receivable	_____	_____
4. Rent Revenue	_____	_____
5. Contributed Capital	_____	_____
6. Note Payable	_____	_____

After you have finished, check your answers with the solution, which follows the chapter summary.

"So, you've just seen how your financial statements should look in one month and how they relate. Are you feeling okay with all this?"

"It actually makes me anxious to get started. What will my external users look for?"

Evaluate the Results

USING FINANCIAL STATEMENTS

The financial statements are a key source of information when external users, like creditors and investors, make decisions concerning a company. As you will see throughout this course, the amounts reported in the financial statements can be used to calculate percentages and ratios that reveal important insights into a company's performance. For now, however, let's consider how creditors and investors might gain valuable information simply by reading the dollar amounts reported in each financial statement.

- Creditors are mainly interested in assessing the following:

  1. **Is the company generating enough cash to make payments on its loan?** Answers to this question will come from the statement of cash flows. In particular, creditors are interested in seeing whether operating activities are producing positive cash flows. Pizza Palace's expected net inflow of $5,000 cash from operating activities is very good for a new business. Find it in Exhibit 1.6.

  2. **Does the company have enough assets to cover its liabilities?** Answers to this question will come from comparing assets and liabilities reported on the balance sheet. Pizza Palace is expected to own slightly more than twice what it owes to creditors at September 30 (total assets of $58,000 versus total liabilities of $27,000). With $14,000 in Cash, Pizza Palace would be able to immediately pay all of its Accounts Payable and part of its Note Payable, if needed.

- Investors expect a return on their contributions to a company. The return may be immediate (through dividends) or long-term (through selling share certificates at a price higher than their original cost). Dividends and higher share prices are more likely if a company is profitable. As a result, investors look closely at the income statement (and statement of retained earnings) for information about the company's ability to generate profits (and distribute dividends).

"I've heard a lot about fraud and 'cooking the books.' How do users know that the information they're getting is useful and can be trusted?"

USEFUL FINANCIAL INFORMATION

Ally indicated that useful financial information results when businesses apply generally accepted accounting principles in an ethical business environment.

LEARNING OBJECTIVE 1-4

Describe factors that contribute to useful financial information.

Generally Accepted Accounting Principles

As it turns out, the system of financial statement reporting in use today has a long history—all the way back to a publication in 1494 by an Italian monk and mathematician, Luca Pacioli. Today, the Chartered Professional Accountants of Canada (CPA Canada) has the primary responsibility for setting the underlying rules of accounting in Canada. As a group, these rules are called **Generally Accepted Accounting Principles (GAAP)**. (The abbreviated form is pronounced like the name of the clothing store.)

The Accounting Standards Board (AcSB) is an independent body supported by CPA Canada to develop and establish the standards and guidelines that govern financial accounting and reporting in Canada, using guidance from the International Accounting Standards Board (IASB). After much deliberation, the AcSB determined that one of two different sets of accounting rules would be appropriate for use in Canada. Publicly accountable profit–oriented enterprises, such as Lululemon and Shoppers Drug Mart, must follow the principles and rules set out in the **International Financial Reporting Standards (IFRS)**. In contrast, private enterprises whose shares are not traded on a public stock exchange can choose to follow either IFRS or Canadian Accounting Standards for Private Enterprises (ASPE). Each of these sets of standards is discussed below.

What does **publicly accountable profit–oriented enterprise** mean? According to the *CPA Canada Handbook*, a publicly accountable enterprise is an entity, other than a not–for–profit organization, that

- has issued, or is in the process of issuing, debt or equity instruments that are, or will be, outstanding and traded in a public market (a domestic or foreign stock exchange, or an over–the–counter market), or
- holds assets in a fiduciary capacity for a broad group of outsiders as one of its primary businesses.

A debt or equity instrument is a document that has a monetary value or represents a legally enforceable agreement between two or more parties regarding a right to payment of money. A fiduciary is an individual, corporation, or association that is holding assets for another party, often with the legal authority and duty to make decisions regarding financial matters on behalf of the other party. Banks, credit unions, and insurance companies are all examples of fiduciaries.

So, what does this mean for companies that do not meet these criteria? A **private enterprise** is a profit–oriented entity that is not a publicly accountable enterprise and therefore is not required to use IFRS. A private enterprise may still choose to use IFRS if, for example, it is expecting to become publicly accountable in the near future. IFRS deals with many complex accounting issues and disclosures that may not be applicable to private enterprises. Given this, and the fact that many private enterprises have a limited number of users of their financial statements, it usually does not make financial sense for these types of companies to incur the additional time and costs of reporting their financial statements under IFRS.

Generally accepted accounting principles (GAAP): Rules of accounting approved by the Canadian Institute of Chartered Accountants for use in Canada.

International financial reporting standards (IFRS): Rules of accounting created by the International Accounting Standards Board (IASB) for international use.

Publicly accountable profit-oriented enterprise: Has shares or debt trading in a public market or holds assets in a fiduciary capacity for someone else and is required to use IFRS.

Private enterprise: Does not have publicly traded shares in an open market, nor does it hold assets in a fiduciary capacity for some-one else. Has the option to use IFRS or ASPE.

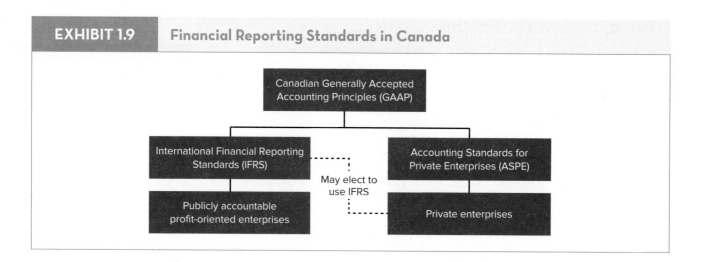

EXHIBIT 1.9   Financial Reporting Standards in Canada

Accounting standards for private enterprises (ASPE): Rules of accounting that address issues that are more relevant in a private enterprise environment and therefore can be used by private enterprises only.

An alternative for private enterprises is to use the Canadian **Accounting Standards for Private Enterprises (ASPE).** These standards address accounting issues that are more typical in a private enterprise environment that may not require the complexities and detailed disclosures that a publicly accountable enterprise would need.

Exhibit 1.9 illustrates the financial reporting options available to Canadian companies. Both IFRS and ASPE are considered to be GAAP. The focus of the material in this textbook is on private enterprises; however, at the end of each chapter, we'll use a feature called Spotlight on IFRS and ASPE to alert you to the important differences between ASPE and IFRS.

The main goal of ASPE and IFRS is to ensure companies produce financial information that is useful to existing and potential investors, lenders, and other creditors in making decisions about providing resources to the companies. As shown in Exhibit 1.10, for financial information to be judged useful, it must possess two fundamental characteristics: *relevance and faithful representation.*

Information is relevant if it makes a difference in decision making, and it is a faithful representation if it fully depicts the economic substance

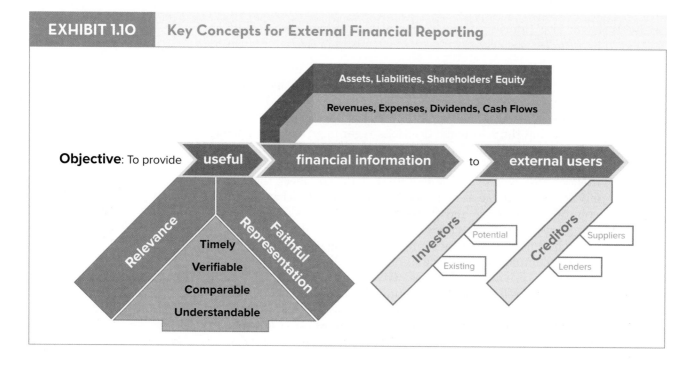

EXHIBIT 1.10   Key Concepts for External Financial Reporting

of business activities. The usefulness of financial information is enhanced when it is (i) timely, (ii) verifiable, (iii) comparable, and (iv) understandable. Information is *timely* if it is available in time to influence decision makers. The Toronto Stock Exchange requires public companies to issue their annual financial statements within ninety days of year-end. Information is *verifiable* if others, such as external auditors, reach similar values using similar methods. It is *comparable* if the same accounting principles are used over time and across companies. It is *understandable* if reasonably informed users can comprehend and interpret it.

To achieve these objectives, the AcSB and IASB have developed a framework that outlines the financial elements to be measured (shown in green in Exhibit 1.10) and the main external users for whom the financial information is intended (shown in beige in Exhibit 1.10).

"Who is responsible for ensuring that businesses follow GAAP?"

"Overall, users expect information that is truthful, and this assumes that the company is following strong ethical business and accounting practices."

Canadian auditing standards (CAS): Provide auditors with up-to-date tools and required procedures in order to carry out high-quality financial statement audits in today's complex business environment.

Ally told Emilio that a company's managers have primary responsibility for following GAAP. To provide additional assurance, some private companies and all public companies hire independent auditors to scrutinize their financial records. Auditors must follow **Canadian Auditing Standards (CAS)** while planning and performing financial statement audits. Canadian Auditing Standards provide auditors with the required tools, procedures, and guidance they need to carry out high–quality audits. These auditors must then report whether, beyond reasonable doubt, the financial statements represent what they claim to represent and whether they comply with GAAP. In a sense, GAAP are to auditors and accountants what Canada's Criminal Code is to lawyers and the public.

SPOTLIGHT ON Canada

First Nations Financial Transparency Act

On March 27, 2013, the First Nations Financial Transparency Act (FNFTA) received Royal Assent in Parliament. Royal Assent is the final stage of the legislative process, the formal process by which a bill passed by both chambers of Parliament becomes law. The First Nations Financial Transparency Act requires that 581 First Nations, defined as an Indian band under the Indian Act, make their audited consolidated financial statements and a Schedule of Remuneration and Expenses of the chief and council available to their members as well as publish it on a website. These financial documents include

- audited consolidated financial statements,
- a Schedule of Remuneration and Expenses,
- the auditor's written report respecting the consolidated financial statements, and
- the auditor's report or the review engagement report, as the case may be, respecting the Schedule of Remuneration and Expenses.

As well, as of 2014–2015, and in compliance with the legislation, the Minister of Indigenous and Northern Affairs was required to publish, on the departmental website, the audited consolidated financial statement and the Schedule of Remuneration and Expenses of chief and council of each First Nation, when received.

If a First Nation did not follow the requirements, then funding from the government was withheld. The purpose of the FNFTA was to improve the financial transparency and accountability of First Nations by requiring the public disclosure of First Nations' financial information.

Since that time, a change in government has occurred in Canada, and on December 18, 2015, the new Minister of Indigenous and Northern Affairs issued a statement indicating that the department

- has stopped all discretionary compliance measures related to the First Nations Financial Transparency Act,
- is reinstating funding withheld from First Nations under these measures, and
- is suspending any court actions against First Nations that have not complied with the Act.

At the time of publication of this book, the Government of Canada is engaging with First Nations leaders and members, as well as First Nations organizations and institutions, in order to seek input on how to best support mutual transparency and accountability between First Nations and the Government of Canada. Through this engagement, participants will be asked to

- suggest new approaches to mutual transparency and accountability, and
- comment on options that could support mutual transparency and accountability.

The Government of Canada is open to considering all options. Feedback from this engagement will lay the groundwork for a new way forward.

Source: First Nations Financial Transparency Act, from: https://www.aadnc-aandc.gc.ca/eng/1322056355024/1322060287419

Ethical Conduct

Ethics refers to the standards of conduct for judging right from wrong, honest from dishonest, and fair from unfair. Intentional financial misreporting is both unethical and illegal. As you will see throughout this course, some accounting and business issues have clear answers that are either right or wrong. However, many situations require accountants, auditors, and managers to weigh the pros and cons of alternatives before making final decisions. To help ensure these decisions are made in a professional and ethical manner, CPA Canada requires that all its members adhere to a Code of Professional Conduct. Despite this code of conduct, some individuals have been involved in accounting scandals and fraud. These fraud cases (and their consequences) will be discussed in greater detail in Chapter 5.

Ethical conduct is just as important for small private businesses as it is for large public companies. Ally's advice to Emilio and to all managers is to strive to create an ethical environment and establish a strong system of checks and controls inside the company. Do not tolerate blatant acts of fraud, such as employees making up false expenses for reimbursement, punching in a time card belonging to a co-worker who will be late for work, or copying someone's ideas and claiming them as his or her own. Also, be aware that not all ethical dilemmas are clear-cut. Some situations will make it necessary to weigh one moral principle (e.g., honesty) against another (e.g., loyalty). Advise employees that, when faced with an ethical dilemma, they should follow a three-step process:

1. **Identify who will be affected by the situation**—both those who will appear to benefit (often the manager or employee) and those who will be harmed (other employees, the company's reputation, owners, creditors, and the public in general).

2. **Identify the alternative courses of action.**

3. **Choose the alternative that is the most ethical**—and that stakeholders would be proud to have reported in the news.

Often, there is no one right answer to ethical dilemmas and hard choices will need to be made. In the end, however, following strong ethical practices is a key factor in business success and in ensuring good financial reporting.

SPOTLIGHT ON Ethics

Accounting Scandals

Accounting scandals are driven by greed and the fear of personal or business failure. Initially, some people may appear to benefit from fraudulent reporting. In the long run, however, fraud harms most individuals and organizations. When it is uncovered, the corporation's stock price drops dramatically. In one case involving MicroStrategy, the stock price dropped 65 percent in a single day of trading, from $243 to $86 per share.

Creditors are also harmed by fraud. As a result of a fraud at Pigeon King International, creditors lost $23 million due to the bankruptcy that resulted from the fraudulent acts. Innocent employees are also harmed by fraud. At Enron, 5,600 employees lost their jobs and many lost all of their retirement savings. The auditing firm Arthur Andersen, which once employed 28,000 people, went out of business after becoming entangled in the WorldCom and Enron frauds.

Epilogue for Pizza Palace

Emilio got going quickly and, in August, created a corporation called Pizza Palace Inc. The next three chapters will take you step by step through the financing, investing, and operating decisions that occurred at Pizza Palace during its first month of business. We will look at the way accountants collect data about business activities and process this data to construct the financial statements. The key to success in this course is to practise the skills that are presented in this textbook. It is very difficult to learn accounting without doing the assignments and keeping up with the reading.

Supplement 1A

CAREERS THAT DEPEND ON ACCOUNTING KNOWLEDGE

Accounting knowledge can make the difference in your ability to land a dream job, whether you hope to work in production and operations management, human resources, finance, or marketing. Exhibit 1S.1 shows non-accounting jobs that could be available to you at the world's leading companies and explains how accounting knowledge can be vital to these positions.

EXHIBIT 1S.1	Accounting Knowledge Can Benefit All Majors

Production and Operations Management

Production Manager, Nintendo: Figure out how to make $250 3DS for $100.71.

Outsourcing Specialist, Apple: Coordinate more than 20 suppliers of parts for the next iPad, at the same total cost as legacy iPads.

Human Resources

Compensation Analyst, Google: Develop affordable, attractive global pay programs.

Labor Relations Manager, National Basketball Players' Association: Assist in salary renegotiations involving the $58 million salary cap and 57% revenue sharing guarantee.

Accounting

Finance

Investment Analyst, Goldman Sachs: Assess value of investing $50 million in Facebook.

Financial Analyst, Target Corporation: Help credit card segment reduce the number of days awaiting collections from customers.

Marketing

Brand Manager, H.J. Heinz Company: Set prices to achieve 5% annual sales growth.

Customer Business Developer, Procter & Gamble: Collaborate with accounting to enhance customer profits and cash flows.

©Rubberball/Getty Images

Sources: http://techland.time.com/2011/03/29/the-incredibly-cheap-100-nintendo-3ds, http://blogs.forbes.com/johnray/2011/03/11/isuppli-teardown-of-the-ipad-2-investor-edition/, http://isuppli.com/Teardowns/News/Pages/iPad-2-Carries-Bill-of-Materials-of-$326-60-IHS-iSuppli-Teardown-Analysis-Shows.aspx, http://www.nytimes.com/2011/05/25/sports/basketball/players-accuse-nba-of-failing-to-bargain-in-good-faith.html?_r=1&ref=nationallaborrelationsboard.

As mentioned earlier, the focus of this textbook is on the Accounting Standards for Private Enterprises (ASPE), and the Spotlight on IFRS and ASPE segment of every chapter will alert you to the significant differences between ASPE and IFRS (International Financial Reporting Standards).

Topic	ASPE	IFRS
Four basic financial reports that comprise the financial statements	Under ASPE, the four basic financial reports are labelled as follows: **1. Income Statement** The income statement presents net income resulting from revenue, expense, gain, and loss transactions for the period. ASPE does not use other comprehensive income.	Under IFRS, these reports can also be referred to in the following ways: **1. Statement of Comprehensive Income** The statement of comprehensive income includes all revenues and gains, and expenses and losses reported in net income, as well as other comprehensive income. Other comprehensive income consists of other gains or losses that are not required by primary sources of GAAP to be included in net income. An example would be unrealized gains and losses on revaluation of property, plant, and equipment under the revaluation model discussed in greater detail in Chapter 9.
	2. Statement of Retained Earnings The statement of retained earnings reconciles the opening retained earnings balance at the beginning of an accounting period with the ending retained earnings balance at the end of the accounting period. This would include items affecting retained earnings such as net income and dividends.	**2. Statement of Changes in Equity** The statement of changes in equity reports the changes in each individual shareholder's equity account, as well as the overall change in total shareholders' equity during the year. This will include comprehensive income. This statement is usually presented in a columnar format with a column for each shareholder's equity account and total shareholders' equity.
	3. Balance Sheet **4. Statement of Cash Flows**	**3. Statement of Financial Position** **4. Statement of Cash Flows**

Review the Chapter

This section provides a chance to solidify your understanding of key points. It's worth your time to work through the following demonstration case, scan the chapter summary, test your understanding of key terms, and then practise, practise, practise.

DEMONSTRATION CASE

The introductory case presented here reviews the items reported on the income statement, statement of retained earnings, and balance sheet. To do so, we'll use the financial statements of a fictional company, Over Armour, Inc. that develops, markets, and distributes athletic apparel and gear. Following is a list of items and amounts (in thousands of Canadian dollars) in Over Armour's financial statements for the quarter ended September 30, 2017.

Accounts Payable	$129,724	Other Expenses	$ 1,736
Accounts Receivable	151,086	Other Liabilities	10,425
Cash	40,152	Property and Equipment	70,645
Contributed Capital	176,330	Retained Earnings, September 30, 2014	143,445
Dividends	0	Retained Earnings, July 1, 2014	117,782
General and Administrative Expenses	71,788	Sales Revenues	231,946
Income Tax Expense	19,080	Total Assets	474,886
Inventories	163,612	Total Expenses	206,283
Net Income	25,663	Total Liabilities	155,111
Notes Payable	14,962	Total Liabilities and Shareholders' Equity	474,886
Operating Expenses	113,679	Total Revenues	231,946
Other Assets	49,391	Total Shareholders' Equity	319,775

Required:

1. Prepare an income statement, a statement of retained earnings, and a balance sheet for the quarter, following the formats in Exhibits 1.2, 1.3, and 1.4.

2. Describe the content of these three statements.

3. Name the other statement that Over Armour would include in its financial statements.

4. Did financing for Over Armour's assets come primarily from liabilities or from shareholders' equity?

5. Explain why Over Armour would subject its statements to an independent audit.

Suggested Solution

1. The first step to reach a solution is to distinguish accounts as belonging to the income statement (revenues and expenses), the statement of retained earnings (retained earnings and dividends), or the balance sheet (assets, liabilities, and shareholders' equity). Organize the accounts in the proper format and follow the flow from one to another (as shown by the arrows in the following statements).

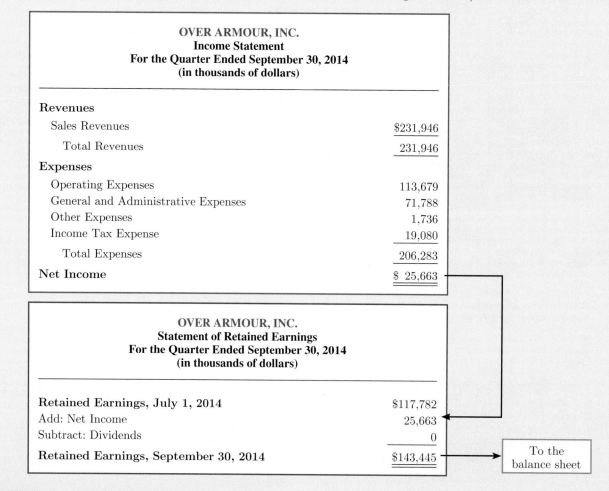

OVER ARMOUR, INC.
Income Statement
For the Quarter Ended September 30, 2014
(in thousands of dollars)

Revenues	
Sales Revenues	$231,946
Total Revenues	231,946
Expenses	
Operating Expenses	113,679
General and Administrative Expenses	71,788
Other Expenses	1,736
Income Tax Expense	19,080
Total Expenses	206,283
Net Income	$ 25,663

OVER ARMOUR, INC.
Statement of Retained Earnings
For the Quarter Ended September 30, 2014
(in thousands of dollars)

Retained Earnings, July 1, 2014	$117,782
Add: Net Income	25,663
Subtract: Dividends	0
Retained Earnings, September 30, 2014	$143,445

To the balance sheet

```
                OVER ARMOUR, INC.                          ┌─────────────┐
                   Balance Sheet                           │  From the   │
                At September 30, 2014                       │  statement  │
                (in thousands of dollars)                   │ of retained │
                                                            │  earnings   │
                                                            └─────────────┘

Assets
   Cash                                          $  40,152
   Accounts Receivable                              151,086
   Inventories                                      163,612
   Property and Equipment                            70,645
   Other Assets                                      49,391
Total Assets                                      $474,886

Liabilities
   Accounts Payable                               $129,724
   Notes Payable                                    14,962
   Other Liabilities                                10,425
      Total Liabilities                             155,111

Shareholders' Equity
   Contributed Capital                              176,330
   Retained Earnings                                143,445  ◄──────┘
      Total Shareholders' Equity                    319,775
Total Liabilities and Shareholders' Equity        $474,886
```

2. The income statement reports the most common measure of financial performance for a business: net income (revenues minus expenses during the accounting period). The statement of retained earnings links the net income number from the income statement to the end—of—period retained earnings balance on the balance sheet. The balance sheet reports the amount of assets, liabilities, and shareholders' equity of a business at a point in time.

3. Over Armour would also present a statement of cash flows.

4. The balance sheet indicates that financing for Over Armour's assets is provided primar— ily from shareholders' equity ($319,775,000) rather than liabilities ($155,111,000).

5. Like all public companies, Over Armour will subject its financial statements to an audit because the Canadian Securities Administrators require an independent audit. Also, an audit will give users greater confidence in the accuracy of financial statement infor— mation because the people who audit the statements are required to meet professional standards of ethics and competence.

CHAPTER SUMMARY

Describe various organizational forms and business decision makers.   LO1-1

- Sole proprietorships are owned by one individual, are relatively inexpensive to form, and are not treated legally as separate from their owners. Thus, all profits or losses become part of the taxable income of the owner, who is also responsible personally for all debts of the business.

- Partnerships are businesses legally similar to sole proprietorships, but with two or more owners.

- Corporations are separate legal entities (thus, corporations pay taxes) that issue shares to investors (shareholders) and are more costly to establish. Shareholders cannot be held liable for more than their investment in the corporation. Private corporations issue shares to a few individuals while public corporations issue shares in the stock market.

- Business decision makers include creditors (banks, suppliers), investors (shareholders), customers, governments, and other external users.

Describe the purpose, structure, and content of the four basic financial statements.

- The *income statement* reports the net amount that a business earned (net income) over a period of time by subtracting the costs of running the business (expenses) from the total amount earned (revenues).
- The *statement of retained earnings* explains changes in the retained earnings account over a period of time by considering increases (from net income) and decreases (from dividends to shareholders).
- The *balance sheet* reports what the business owns (reported as assets) at a particular point in time and how much of the financing for these assets came from creditors (reported as liabilities) and shareholders (reported as shareholders' equity).
- The *statement of cash flows* explains changes in the cash account over a period of time by reporting inflows and outflows of cash from the business's operating, investing, and financing activities.

LO1-3 **Explain how financial statements are used by decision makers.**

- Creditors are mainly interested in assessing whether the company (1) is generating enough cash to make payments on its loan, and (2) has enough assets to cover its liabilities. Answers to these questions are indicated by the statement of cash flows and the balance sheet.
- Investors look closely at the income statement for information about a company's ability to generate profits, and at the statement of retained earnings for information about a company's dividend distributions.

LO1-4 **Describe factors that contribute to useful financial information.**

- Companies generate useful financial information by applying generally accepted accounting principles in an ethical business environment. Companies can use either IFRS or ASPE, depending on the type of enterprise involved.
- To be useful, information must be relevant and a faithful representation of reality. Information is more useful when it is comparable, verifiable, timely, and understandable.

SOLUTION TO SELF-STUDY PRACTICE

Solution to SP1.1

	Type	Statement
1.	A	B/S
2.	E	I/S
3.	A	B/S
4.	R	I/S
5.	SE	B/S
6.	L	B/S

KEY TERMS

Accounting

Accounting Standards for Private Enterprises (ASPE)

Accounts

Balance Sheet

Basic Accounting Equation

Canadian Auditing Standards (CAS)

Financial Statements

Generally Accepted Accounting Principles (GAAP)

Income Statement

International Financial Reporting Standards (IFRS)

Private Enterprise

Publicly Accountable Profit— Oriented Enterprise

Separate Entity Assumption

Statement of Cash Flows

Statement of Retained Earnings

Unit of Measure Assumption

Complete definitions are also provided in the glossary at the end of this text.

HOMEWORK HELPER

Alternative terms
- The balance sheet also can be called the *statement of financial position*.
- The income statement also can be called the *statement of operations*.
- Net income can also be called *net earnings*.

Helpful reminders
- The balance in each account is reported once and only once in one of the following: the balance sheet, income statement, or statement of retained earnings.

Frequent mistakes
- Dividends are not expenses. Dividends relate to distributing (not generating) earnings. Consequently, a company's dividends are reported on its statement of retained earnings (not its income statement).

PRACTICE MATERIAL

QUESTIONS (⑤ Symbol indicates questions that require analysis from more than one perspective.)

1. Define *accounting*.
2. Valeri is opening a hair salon but she does not know what business form she should select. What can you tell her about the advantages and disadvantages of operating as a sole proprietorship versus a corporation? ⑤
3. Briefly explain the difference between financial accounting and managerial accounting.
4. The accounting process generates financial reports for both internal and external users. Describe some of the specific groups of internal and external users.
5. Explain what the *separate entity assumption* means when it says that a business is treated as separate from its owners for accounting purposes.
6. List the three main types of business activities on the statement of cash flows and give an example of each.
7. What information should be included in the heading of each of the four primary financial statements?
8. What are the purposes of (*a*) the balance sheet, (*b*) the income statement, (*c*) the state—ment of retained earnings, and (*d*) the statement of cash flows?
9. Explain why the income statement, statement of retained earnings, and statement of cash flows would be dated "For the Year Ended December 31, 2017," whereas the balance sheet would be dated "At December 31, 2017."
10. Briefly explain the difference between *net income* and *net loss*.
11. Describe the basic accounting equation that provides the structure for the balance sheet. Define the three major components reported on the balance sheet.
12. Describe the equation that provides the structure for the income statement. Explain the three major items reported on the income statement.
13. Describe the equation that provides the structure for the statement of retained earnings. Explain the four major items reported on the statement of retained earnings.
14. Describe the equation that provides the structure for the statement of cash flows. Explain the three major types of activities reported on the statement.
15. Briefly describe the organization that is responsible for developing accounting measure—ment rules (generally accepted accounting principles) in Canada.
16. What is the main goal for accounting rules in Canada and around the world? What characteristics must financial information possess to reach that goal?

17. Briefly define what an ethical dilemma is and describe the steps to consider when evaluating ethical dilemmas.

18. In what ways might accounting frauds be similar to cases of academic dishonesty?

MINI-EXERCISES

LO1-1 **M1-1 Identifying Definitions with Abbreviations**

Abbreviation	Full Designation
1. CPA	Chartered Professional Accountant
2. GAAP	_____
3. IASB	_____
4. CSA	_____
5. IFRS	_____
6. ASPE	_____

LO1-1, 1-2, 1-4 **M1-2 Matching Definitions with Terms or Abbreviations**

Match each definition with its related term or abbreviation by entering the appropriate letter in the space provided.

Term or Abbreviation	Definition
_____ 1. Investing activities	A. A system that collects and processes financial information about an organization and reports that information to decision makers
_____ 2. Private company	B. Measurement of information about a business in the monetary unit (dollars or other national currency)
_____ 3. Corporation	C. An unincorporated business owned by two or more persons
_____ 4. Accounting	D. A company that sells its shares privately and is not required to release its financial statements to the public
_____ 5. Partnership	E. An incorporated business that issues shares as evidence of ownership
_____ 6. AcSB	F. Buying and selling productive resources with long lives
_____ 7. Financing activities	G. Transactions with lenders (borrowing and repaying cash) and shareholders (selling company shares and paying dividends)
_____ 8. Unit of measure	H. Activities directly related to running the business to earn profit
_____ 9. GAAP	I. Accounting Standards Board
_____ 10. Public company	J. A company that has its shares bought and sold by investors on established stock exchanges
_____ 11. Operating activities	K. Generally accepted accounting principles

Match each definition with its related term by entering the appropriate letter in the space provided.

Term	Definition
____ 1. Relevance	A. The financial reports of a business are assumed to include the results of only that business's activities
____ 2. Faithful representation	
____ 3. Comparability	B. The resources owned by a business
____ 4. Separate entity	C. Financial information that can be compared across businesses because similar accounting methods have been applied
____ 5. Assets	
____ 6. Liabilities	D. The total amounts invested and reinvested in the business by its owners
____ 7. Shareholders' equity	
____ 8. Revenues	E. The costs of business necessary to earn revenues
____ 9. Expenses	E. A feature of financial information that allows it to influence a decision
____ 10. Unit of measure	
	G. Earned by selling goods or services to customers
	H. The amounts owed by the business
	I. Financial information that depicts the economic substance of business activities
	J. The assumption that states that results of business activities should be reported in an appropriate monetary unit

M1-4 Matching Financial Statement Items to Balance Sheet and Income Statement Categories   LO1-2

According to its annual report, "Procter & Gamble markets a broad range of laundry, cleaning, paper, beauty care, health care, food and beverage products in more than 180 countries around the world, with leading brands including Tide, Crest, Crisco, Vicks, and Max Factor." The following are items taken from its recent balance sheet and income statement. For each item, indicate (*a*) the type of account (A = asset, L = liability, SE = shareholders' equity, R = revenue, E = expense), and (*b*) whether it is reported on the income statement (I/S) or balance sheet (B/S).

____ 1. Accounts Payable		____ 5. Selling and Administrative Expenses
____ 2. Accounts Receivable		____ 6. Sales Revenue
____ 3. Cash		____ 7. Notes Payable
____ 4. Income Tax Expense		____ 8. Retained Earnings

M1-5 Matching Financial Statement Items to Balance Sheet and Income Statement Categories   LO1-2

For each item, indicate (a) the type of account (A = asset, L = liability, SE = shareholders' equity, R = revenue, E = expense), and (b) whether it is reported on the income statement (I/S) or balance sheet (B/S).

____ 1. Accounts Receivable		____ 5. Cash
____ 2. Sales Revenue		____ 6. Advertising Expense
____ 3. Equipment		____ 7. Accounts Payable
____ 4. Supplies Expense		____ 8. Retained Earnings

M1-6 Matching Financial Statement Items to Balance Sheet and Income Statement Categories

Tootsie Roll Industries manufactures and sells more than 64 million Tootsie Rolls and 20 million Tootsie Roll Pops each day. The following items were listed on Tootsie Roll's recent income statement and balance sheet. For each item, indicate (a) the type of account (A = asset, L = liability, SE = shareholders' equity, R = revenue, E = expense), and (b) whether it is reported on the income statement (I/S) or balance sheet (B/S).

_____ 1. Accounts Receivable

_____ 2. Selling and Administrative Expenses

_____ 3. Cash

_____ 4. Equipment

_____ 5. Advertising Expense

_____ 6. Sales Revenue

_____ 7. Notes Payable

_____ 8. Retained Earnings

_____ 9. Accounts Payable

M1-7 Matching Financial Statement Items to Balance Sheet and Income Statement Categories

General Mills is a manufacturer of food products, such as Lucky Charms cereal, Pillsbury crescent rolls, and Green Giant vegetables. The following items were presented in the company's financial statements. For each item, indicate (a) the type of account (A = asset, L = liability, SE = shareholders' equity, R = revenue, E = expense), and (b) whether it is reported on the income statement (I/S) or balance sheet (B/S).

_____ 1. Accounts Payable

_____ 2. Contributed Capital

_____ 3. Equipment

_____ 4. Accounts Receivable

_____ 5. Notes Payable

_____ 6. Cash

_____ 7. Retained Earnings

_____ 8. Selling and Administrative Expenses

_____ 9. Sales Revenue

_____ 10. Supplies

M1-8 Matching Financial Statement Items to the Basic Financial Statements

Prior to being acquired in November 2007 by Luxottica Group—an Italian eyewear company—Oakley, Inc. reported the following items in its financial statements. For each item, indicate whether it is reported on the income statement (I/S), statement of retained earnings (SRE), balance sheet (B/S), and/or statement of cashflows (SCF).

_____ 1. Dividends

_____ 2. Total Shareholders' Equity

_____ 3. Sales Revenue

_____ 4. Total Assets

_____ 5. Cash Flows from Operating Activities

_____ 6. Total Liabilities

_____ 7. Net Income

_____ 8. Cash Flows from Financing Activities

M1-9 Matching Financial Statement Items to the Basic Financial Statements

Match each element with its financial statement by entering the appropriate letters in the space provided.

Element	Financial Statement
_____ 1. Cash Flows from Financing Activities	A. Balance Sheet
_____ 2. Expenses	B. Income Statement
_____ 3. Cash Flows from Investing Activities	C. Statement of Retained Earnings
_____ 4. Assets	D. Statement of Cash Flows
_____ 5. Dividends	
_____ 6. Revenues	
_____ 7. Cash Flows from Operating Activities	
_____ 8. Liabilities	

M1-10 Reporting Amounts on the Statement of Cash Flows

LO1-2

Learning which items belong in each category of the statement of cash flows is an important first step in understanding their meaning. Use a letter to mark each item in the following list as a cash flow from Operating, Investing, or Financing activities. *Put parentheses around the letter if it is a cash* outflow *and use no parentheses if it's an* inflow.

_____ 1. Cash paid for dividends   _____ 4. Cash paid to employees

_____ 2. Cash collected from customers   _____ 5. Cash paid to purchase equipment

_____ 3. Cash received when signing a note _____ 6. Cash received from issuing shares

M1-11 Reporting Amounts on the Statement of Cash Flows

LO1-2

Learning which items belong in each category of the statement of cash flows is an important first step in understanding their meaning. Use a letter to mark each item in the following list as a cash flow from Operating, Investing, or Financing activities. *Put parentheses around the letter if it is a cash* outflow *and use no parentheses if it's an* inflow.

_____ 1. Cash paid to purchase equipment _____ 4. Cash paid for dividends

_____ 2. Cash collected from clients   _____ 5. Cash paid to suppliers

_____ 3. Cash received from selling   _____ 6. Cash received from issuing shares
       equipment

M1-12 Preparing a Statement of Retained Earnings

LO1-2

Stone Culture Corporation was organized on January 1, 2016. For its first two years of operations, it reported the following:

Net Income for 2016	$36,000	Dividends for 2017	$ 20,000
Net Income for 2017	45,000	Total assets at the end of 2016	125,000
Dividends for 2016	15,000	Total assets at the end of 2017	242,000

On the basis of the data given, prepare a statement of retained earnings for 2016 (its first year of operations) and 2017.

M1-13 Relationships Among Financial Statements

LO1-2

Items from the income statement, statement of retained earnings, and balance sheet are listed below in alphabetical order. For the companies shown in each column, solve for the missing amounts.

     TIP: Use Exhibit 1.6 to identify relations among the items, then solve for the amounts.

	Apple Inc.	Alphabet Inc.	Intel Corp.
Contributed Capital	$11	$18	$17
Dividends	0	0	4
Net Income	(a)	(d)	(g)
Retained Earnings, Beginning of Year	23	20	26
Retained Earnings, End of Year	(b)	(e)	(h)
Total Assets	(c)	(f)	(i)
Total Expenses	51	20	33
Total Liabilities	27	12	13
Total Revenues	65	29	44

M1-14 Relationships Among Financial Statements

Items from the income statement, statement of retained earnings, and balance sheet are listed below in alphabetical order. For the companies shown in each column, solve for the missing amounts.

TIP: Use Exhibit 1.6 to identify relations among the items, then solve for the amounts.

	Amazin' Corp.	Best Tech, Inc.	Colossal Corp.
Contributed Capital	$5	$15	$100
Dividends	10	5	50
Net Income	(a)	(d)	(g)
Retained Earnings, Beginning of Year	30	0	200
Retained Earnings, End of Year	(b)	(e)	(h)
Total Assets	(c)	(f)	(i)
Total Expenses	75	30	200
Total Liabilities	30	30	350
Total Revenues	100	50	300

LO1-2 **M1-15 Relationships Among Financial Statements**

LEVEL UP

Items from the income statement, statement of retained earnings, and balance sheet of Electronic Arts Inc. are listed below in alphabetical order. Solve for the missing amounts, and explain whether the company was profitable.

TIP: Use Exhibit 1.6 to identify relations among the items, then solve for amounts.

	Electronic Arts Inc.
Contributed Capital	$2,430
Dividends	0
Net Income	(a)
Retained Earnings, Beginning of Year	370
Retained Earnings, End of Year	(b)
Total Assets	4,900
Total Expenses	(c)
Total Liabilities	2,400
Total Revenues	3,600

LO1-2, 1-3 **M1-16 Preparing an Income Statement, Statement of Retained Earnings, and Balance Sheet**

Assume the following information was reported in the December 31, 2017, financial statements of WestJet (listed alphabetically, amounts in millions).

Accounts Payable	$1,731	Other Assets	$ 2,581
Accounts Receivable	845	Other Liabilities	3,107
Aircraft Fuel Expense	2,536	Other Operating Expenses	2,145
Cash	2,213	Other Revenue	336
Contributed Capital	2,153	Property and Equipment	10,874
Dividends	14	Repairs and Maintenance Expense	616
Income Tax Expense	413	Retained Earnings (as of December 31, 2017)	4,788
Interest Expense	69	Salaries Expense	3,213
Landing Fees Expense	560	Supplies on Hand	259
Notes Payable	4,993	Ticket Revenues	9,861

1. Prepare an income statement for the year that ended December 31, 2017.
2. Prepare a statement of retained earnings for the year ended December 31, 2017.
   TIP: Assume the balance in retained earnings was $4,157,000,000 at January 1, 2017.
3. Prepare a balance sheet at December 31, 2017.
4. Using the balance sheet, indicate whether the total assets of WestJet at the end of the year were financed primarily by liabilities or shareholders' equity.

EXERCISES

LO1-2

E1-1 Reporting Amounts on the Four Basic Financial Statements

Using the following table and the equations underlying each of the four basic financial statements, show (a) that the balance sheet is in balance, (b) that net income is properly calculated, (c) what caused changes in the retained earnings account, and (d) what caused changes in the cash account.

Assets	$18,200	Beginning Retained Earnings	$3,500
Liabilities	13,750	Ending Retained Earnings	4,300
Shareholders' Equity	4,450	Cash Flows from Operating Activities	1,600
Revenue	10,500	Cash Flows from Investing Activities	(1,000)
Expenses	9,200	Cash Flows from Financing Activities	(900)
Net Income	1,300	Beginning Cash	1,000
Dividends	500	Ending Cash	700

LO1-2

E1-2 Reporting Amounts on the Four Basic Financial Statements

Using the following table and the equations underlying each of the four basic financial state—ments, show (a) that the balance sheet is in balance, (b) that net income is properly calculated, (c) what caused changes in the retained earnings account, and (d) what caused changes in the cash account.

Assets	$79,500	Beginning Retained Earnings	$20,500
Liabilities	18,500	Ending Retained Earnings	28,750
Shareholders' Equity	61,000	Cash Flows from Operating Activities	15,700
Revenue	32,100	Cash Flows from Investing Activities	(7,200)
Expenses	18,950	Cash Flows from Financing Activities	(5,300)
Net Income	13,150	Beginning Cash	3,200
Dividends	4,900	Ending Cash	6,400

LO1-2, 1-3

E1-3 Preparing a Balance Sheet

Designer Footwear Inc. is a designer shoe warehouse that sells luxurious and fashionable shoes at prices that people can actually afford. Its balance sheet, at November 1, 2017, contained the following (listed alphabetically, amounts in thousands).

Accounts Payable	$136,405	Other Liabilities	$ 79,148
Accounts Receivable	11,888	Property, Plant, and Equipment	233,631
Cash	45,570	Retained Earnings	179,538
Contributed Capital	291,248	Total Assets	785,383
Notes Payable	99,044	Total Liabilities and Shareholders' Equity	?
Other Assets	494,294		

Required:

1. Prepare the balance sheet as of November 1, solving for the missing amount.
2. As of November 1, did most of the financing for assets come from creditors or shareholders?

E1-4 Completing a Balance Sheet and Inferring Net Income

Ken Young and Kim Sherwood organized Reader Direct as a corporation; each contributed $49,000 cash to start the business and received 4,000 shares. The store completed its first year of operations on December 31, 2017. On that date, the following financial items for the year were determined: cash on hand and in the bank, $47,500; amounts due from customers from sales of books, $26,900; property and equipment, $48,000; amounts owed to publishers for books purchased, $8,000; one–year note payable to a local bank for $2,850. No dividends were declared or paid to the shareholders during the year.

Required:

1. Complete the balance sheet at December 31, 2017:

Assets		Liabilities and Shareholders' Equity	
Cash	$ _____	**Liabilities**	
Accounts Receivable	_____	Accounts Payable	$ _____
Property and Equipment	_____	Note Payable	_____
		Total Liabilities	_____
		Shareholders' Equity	
		Contributed Capital	_____
		Retained Earnings	13,550
		Total Shareholders' Equity	_____
Total Assets	$ _____	Total Liabilities and Shareholders' Equity	$ _____

2. Using the retained earnings equation and an opening balance of $0, work backward to compute the amount of net income for the year ended December 31, 2017.

3. As of December 31, 2017, did most of the financing for assets come from creditors or shareholders?

4. Assuming that Reader Direct generates net income of $3,000 and pays dividends of $2,000 in 2018, what would be the company's ending Retained Earnings balance at December 31, 2018?

E1-5 Labelling and Classifying Business Transactions

The following items relate to business transactions involving Collectibles Canada.

a. Coins and currency
b. Amounts that Collectibles Canada owes to suppliers of coins and currency
c. Amounts that Collectibles Canada can collect from customers
d. Amounts owed to bank for loan to buy building
e. Property on which buildings will be built
f. Amounts distributed from profits to shareholders
g. Amounts earned by Collectibles Canada by selling coin–collecting supplies
h. Unused paper in Collectibles Canada head office
i. Cost of paper used up during month
j. Amounts contributed to Collectibles Canada by shareholders

Required:

1. Identify an appropriate label (account name) for each item as it would be reported in the company's financial statements.

2. Classify each item as an asset (A), liability (L), shareholders' equity (SE), revenue (R), or expense (E).

E1-6 Preparing an Income Statement and Inferring Missing Values

LO1-2, 1-3

Cineplex Entertainment operates movie theatres and food concession counters throughout Canada. Assume its income statement for the quarter ended September 30, 2017, reported the following (listed alphabetically, amounts in thousands of dollars):

Admissions Revenues	$455,700	Net Income	?
Concessions Expenses	25,500	Other Expenses	$233,800
Concessions Revenues	188,900	Other Revenues	31,200
Film Rental Expenses	247,000	Rent Expense	90,000
Selling and Administrative Expenses	65,700	Total Expenses	?

Required:

1. Solve for the missing amounts and prepare an income statement for the quarter ended September 30, 2017.

   TIP: First put the items in the order they would appear on the income statement and then solve for the missing values.

2. What are Cineplex's main source of revenue and two biggest expenses?

E1-7 Preparing an Income Statement

LO1-2

Home Realty, Incorporated, has been operating for three years and is owned by three investors. J. Doe owns 60 percent of the 9,000 total outstanding shares and is the managing executive in charge. On December 31, 2017, the following financial items for the entire year were determined: sales revenue, $166,000; selling expenses, $97,000; interest expense, $6,300; promotion and advertising expenses, $9,025; and income tax expense, $18,500. Also during the year, the company declared and paid the owners dividends amounting to $12,000. Prepare the company's income statement.

Check Figures:
Total Expenses = $130,825

E1-8 Inferring Values Using the Income Statement and Balance Sheet Equations

LO1-2

Review the chapter explanations of the income statement and the balance sheet equations. Apply these equations in each of the following independent cases to compute the two missing amounts for each case. Assume that it is the end of the first full year of operations for the company.

TIP: First identify the numerical relationships among the columns using the balance sheet and income statement equations. Then compute the missing amounts.

Independent Cases	Total Revenues	Total Expenses	Net Income (Loss)	Total Assets	Total Liabilities	Shareholders' Equity
A	$100,000	$82,000	$	$150,000	$70,000	$
B		80,000	12,000	112,000		60,000
C	80,000	86,000		104,000	26,000	
D	50,000		13,000		22,000	77,000
E		81,000	(6,000)		73,000	28,000

E1-9 Preparing an Income Statement and Balance Sheet

LO1-2, 1-3

Five individuals organized Moncton Clay Corporation on January 1. At the end of January 31, the following monthly financial data are available:

Total Revenues	$131,000
Operating Expenses	90,500
Cash	30,800
Accounts Receivable	25,300
Supplies	40,700
Accounts Payable	25,700
Contributed Capital	30,600

No dividends were declared or paid during January.

Required:

1. Complete the following income statement and balance sheet for the month of January.

MONCTON CLAY CORPORATION
Income Statement
For the Month Ended January 31

Total Revenues	$_____
Operating Expenses	_____
Net Income	$_____

MONCTON CLAY CORPORATION
Balance Sheet
At January 31

Assets

Cash	$_____
Accounts Receivable	_____
Supplies	_____
Total Assets	$_____

Liabilities

Accounts Payable	$_____
Total Liabilities	_____

Shareholders' Equity

Contributed Capital	_____
Retained Earnings	_____
Total Shareholders' Equity	_____
Total Liabilities and Shareholders' Equity	$_____

---

2. Discuss whether Moncton Clay Corporation will be able to pay its liabilities. Consider the relationship between total assets and total liabilities.

LO1-2, 1-3 **E1-10 Analyzing and Interpreting an Income Statement**

Three individuals organized Pest B—Gone Professionals on January 1 to provide insect extermination services. The company paid dividends of $10,000 during the year. At the end of the first year of operations, the following income statement was prepared:

PEST B-GONE PROFESSIONALS
Income Statement
For the Year Ended December 31

Revenues		
Service Revenue	$192,000	
Sales Revenue	24,000	
Total Revenues		$216,000
Expenses		
Supplies Expense	$ 76,000	
Salaries and Wages Expense	33,000	
Advertising Expense	22,000	
Other Expenses	46,000	
Total Expenses		177,000
Net Income		$ 39,000

Required:

1. What was the amount of average monthly revenue?
2. What was the average amount of monthly salaries and wages expense?
3. Explain why advertising is reported as an expense.
4. Explain why the dividends are not reported as an expense.
5. Can you determine how much cash the company had on December 31? Answer yes or no, and explain your reasoning.

E1-11 Matching Cash Flow Statement Items to Business Activity Categories

LO1-2

Tech Data Corporation is a leading distributor of computer peripherals and network solutions, and was ranked by *Fortune* as the second–most admired company in its industry category. The following items were taken from one of its cash flow statements. Mark each item in the following list with a letter to indicate whether it is a cash flow from Operating, Investing, or Financing activities. *Put parentheses around the letter if it is a cash* outflow *and use no parentheses if it's an* inflow.

___ 1. Cash paid to suppliers and employees
___ 2. Cash received from customers
___ 3. Cash received from borrowing long–term debt
___ 4. Cash received from issuing shares
___ 5. Cash paid to purchase equipment

E1-12 Matching Cash Flow Statement Items to Business Activity Categories

LO1-2

The Coca–Cola Company is one of the world's leading manufacturers, marketers, and distrib–utors of non–alcoholic beverage concentrates and syrups, producing more than 300 beverage brands. Mark each item in the following list with a letter to indicate whether it is a cash flow from Operating, Investing, or Financing activities. *Put parentheses around the letter if it is a cash* outflow *and use no parentheses if it's an* inflow.

___ 1. Purchases of equipment
___ 2. Cash received from customers
___ 3. Cash received from issuing shares
___ 4. Cash paid to suppliers and employees
___ 5. Cash paid on notes payable
___ 6. Cash received from selling equipment

COACHED PROBLEMS

CP1-1 Preparing an Income Statement, Statement of Retained Earnings, and Balance Sheet

Assume that you are the president of Nuclear Company. At the end of the first year of oper–ations (December 31, 2017), the following financial data for the company are available:

LO1-2

Cash	$12,000
Accounts Receivable	59,500
Supplies on Hand	8,000
Equipment	36,000
Accounts Payable	30,297
Notes Payable	1,470
Sales Revenue	88,000
Operating Expenses	57,200
Other Expenses	8,850
Contributed Capital	61,983
Dividends	200

Required:

1. Prepare an income statement for the year that ended December 31, 2017.

   TIP: Begin by classifying each account as asset, liability, shareholders' equity, revenue, or expense. Each account is reported on only one financial statement.

   TIP: Net Income = $21,950

2. Prepare a statement of retained earnings for the year ended December 31, 2017.

   TIP: Because this is the first year of operations, the beginning balance in Retained Earnings will be zero.

3. Prepare a balance sheet at December 31, 2017.

   TIP: The balance sheet includes the ending balance from the statement of retained earnings.

   TIP: Total Assets = $115,500

LO1-3 **CP1-2 Interpreting the Financial Statements**

Refer to CP1–1.

Required:

1. Evaluate whether the company was profitable.
2. Evaluate whether the company could have paid a greater amount in dividends.
3. Evaluate whether the company is financed mainly by creditors or shareholders.
4. Determine the amount of cash increase or decrease that would be shown in the statement of cash flows.

LO1-2 **CP1-3 Reporting Amounts on the Four Basic Financial Statements**

Assume that Fitness and Fun, Inc. reported the following information for the nine–month period ended September 30, 2017. Items are listed alphabetically and are in thousands of dollars.

Accounts Payable	$ 102,665	Other Liabilities	$ 86,234
Accounts Receivable	5,318	Retained Earnings (January 1, 2017)	199,890
Cash (January 1, 2017)	5,354	Gym Revenues	575,667
Cash (September 30, 2017)	7,119	Gym Operating Expenses	350,835
Contributed Capital	381,728	Advertising and Marketing Expenses	23,608
Supplies on Hand	14,739	Selling and Administrative Expenses	83,207
Notes Payable	647,120	Interest and Other Expenses	20,316
Accrued Liabilities	119,482	Income Tax Expense	38,895
Property and Equipment	1,451,641		
Other Assets	117,108		

Other cash flow information:	
Cash received from issuing common shares	$ 9,061
Cash paid to purchase equipment	354,255
Cash paid to suppliers and employees	472,265
Repayments of borrowings	13,043
Cash received from customers	574,824
Cash received from borrowings	95,558
Cash received from sale of long-term assets	161,885
Dividends paid to shareholders	0

Required:

Prepare the four basic financial statements for the nine months ended September 30, 2017.

   TIP: Prepare the four statements in the following order:

a. Income statement

   TIP: Net Income = $58,806,000

b. Statement of retained earnings

   TIP: Closing Retained Earnings = $258,696,000

c. Balance sheet

   TIP: Total Assets = $1,595,925,000

d. Statement of cash flows

   TIP: Cash Provided by Operating Activities = $102,559,000

   TIP: Cash Used in Investing Activities = $192,370,000

   TIP: Cash Provided by Financing Activities = $91,576,000

CP1-4 Interpreting the Financial Statements

Refer to CP1–3.

Required:

1. Did Fitness and Fun Inc. rely more on creditors or shareholders for its financing at September 30, 2017? What is your information source?
2. Was the shareholders' equity at September 30, 2017, comprised more of contributions made by shareholders directly to the company or amounts earned and retained through profitable business operations? What is your information source?

GROUP A PROBLEMS

PA1-1 Preparing an Income Statement, Statement of Retained Earnings, and Balance Sheet

You are the president of High Power Corporation. At the end of the first year of operations (December 31, 2017), the following financial data for the company are available:

Cash	$13,300
Accounts Receivable	9,550
Supplies	5,000
Equipment	86,000
Accounts Payable	32,087
Notes Payable	1,160
Sales Revenue	91,000
Operating Expenses	58,700
Other Expenses	8,850
Contributed Capital	59,103
Dividends	1,950

Check Figures:
Net Income = $23,450
Total Liabilities = $33,247

Required:

1. Prepare an income statement for the year ended December 31, 2017.
2. Prepare a statement of retained earnings for the year ended December 31, 2017.
3. Prepare a balance sheet at December 31, 2017.

PA1-2 Interpreting the Financial Statements

Refer to PA1–1.

Required:

1. Evaluate whether the company was profitable.
2. Evaluate whether the company could have paid a greater amount for dividends.
3. Evaluate whether the company is financed mainly by creditors or shareholders.
4. Determine the amount of cash increase or decrease that would be shown in the state—ment of cash flows.

PA1-3 Preparing an Income Statement, Statement of Retained Earnings, and Balance Sheet

Assume that you are the owner/operator of College Park Veterinary Clinic. At the end of the second year of operations (June 30, 2017), the following financial data for the company are available:

Check Figures:
Retained Earnings, June 30, 2017 = $600
Total Assets = $411,600

Cash	$ 5,000
Accounts Receivable	125,600
Supplies	25,000
Property and Equipment	242,500
Other Assets	13,500
Accounts Payable	87,000
Notes Payable	150,000
Other Liabilities	37,000
Sales Revenue	250,000
Operating Expenses	185,700
Selling and Administrative Expenses	53,400
Advertising and Marketing Expenses	27,800
Interest Expense	5,000
Retained Earnings, July 1, 2016	50,000
Contributed Capital	137,000
Dividends	27,500

Required:

1. Prepare an income statement for the year ended June 30, 2017.
2. Prepare a statement of retained earnings for the year ended June 30, 2017.
3. Prepare a balance sheet at June 30, 2017.

LO1-3 **PA1-4 Interpreting the Financial Statements**

Refer to PA1–3.

Required:

1. Evaluate whether the company was profitable.
2. Evaluate whether the company could have paid a greater amount in dividends.
3. Evaluate whether the company is financed mainly by creditors or shareholders.
4. Is it possible to determine the amount of cash increase or decrease that would be shown in the statement of cash flows from the information presented? If not, why not?

LO1-2 **PA1-5 Reporting Amounts on the Four Basic Financial Statements**

Assume that the following information for the year ended December 31, 2017, was reported by Bloomin' Brands, the company that owns and operates Outback Steakhouse and Carrabba's Italian Grill restaurants. Amounts are in millions of dollars.

Cash (balance on January 1, 2017)	84	Other Revenues	21
Cash (balance on December 31, 2017)	94	Property, Fixtures, and Equipment	1,549
Food and Supplies Expenses	1,415	Restaurant Sales Revenue	3,920
Accounts Payable	166	Wages and Taxes Payable	120
Selling and Administrative Expenses	235	Utilities and Other Expenses	1,104
Food and Supply Inventories	87	Wages Expense	1,087
Notes Payable	235	Retained Earnings, January 1, 2017	1,074
Other Assets	529	Contributed Capital	86
Other Liabilities	517		

Other cash flow information:	
Cash paid to purchase equipment	$ 384
Cash paid to suppliers and employees	2,578
Cash received from customers	2,946
Cash received from bank borrowings	375
Repayments of bank borrowings	294
Cash received from sale of fixtures and equipment	32
Other cash outflows used for financing activities	62
Other cash outflows used for investing activities	2
Common shares issued to owners in exchange for cash	16
Dividends declared and paid in cash	39

Required:

Prepare the four basic financial statements for 2017.

GROUP B PROBLEMS

PB1-1 **Preparing an Income Statement and Balance Sheet**

LO1-2

Assume that you are the president of Aerospace Explorations. At the end of the first year of operations (December 31, 2017), the following financial data for the company are available:

Cash	$13,900
Accounts Receivable	9,500
Supplies	9,000
Equipment	86,000
Accounts Payable	30,277
Notes Payable	1,220
Sales Revenue	94,000
Operating Expenses	60,000
Other Expenses	8,850
Contributed Capital	62,853
Dividends	1,100

Required:

1. Prepare an income statement for the year ended December 31, 2017.
2. Prepare a statement of retained earnings for the year ended December 31, 2017.
3. Prepare a balance sheet at December 31, 2017.

PB1-2 **Interpreting the Financial Statements**

LO1-3

Refer to PB1−1.

Required:

1. Evaluate whether the company was profitable.
2. Evaluate whether the company could have paid a greater amount in dividends.
3. Evaluate whether the company is financed mainly by creditors or shareholders.
4. Determine the amount of cash increase or decrease that would be shown in the statement of cash flows.

PB1-3 **Preparing an Income Statement and Balance Sheet**

Assume that you are the president of Rock Point
Adventures Inc. At the end of the second year of operations (June 30, 2017), the following financial data for the company are available:

LO1-2

Bank Overdraft	$ 2,058
Accounts Receivable	124,579
Supplies	14,356
Property and Equipment	136,897
Other Assets	3,857
Accounts Payable	58,973
Notes Payable	74,985
Other Liabilities	3,765
Sales Revenue	143,098
Rental Revenue	34,986
Concessions Revenue	25,873
Operating Expenses	74,390
Rent Expense	25,198
Concessions Expenses	21,985
Other Expenses	4,278
Contributed Capital	58,346
Retained Earnings, July 1, 2016	53,456
Dividends	50,000

Required:

1. Prepare an income statement for the year ended June 30, 2017.
2. Prepare a statement of retained earnings for the year ended June 30, 2017.
3. Prepare a balance sheet at June 30, 2017.

LO1-2 **PB1-4 Interpreting the Financial Statements**

Refer to PB1–3.

Required:

1. Evaluate whether the company was profitable.
2. Evaluate whether the company could have paid a greater amount for dividends.
3. Evaluate whether the company is financed mainly by creditors or shareholders.
4. Is it possible to determine the amount of cash increase or decrease that would be shown in the statement of cash flows from the information presented? If not, why not.

LO1-2 **PB1-5 Reporting Amounts on the Four Basic Financial Statements**

Check Figure:
Net Income =
$81,282
Cash Provided
by Operating
Activities =
$152,655

Assume that the Cheesecake Factory reported the following information for the fiscal year ended August 31, 2017. Amounts are in thousands of dollars.

Accounts Payable	$ 45,570	Other Assets	$ 186,453
Accounts Receivable	11,639	Other Liabilities	126,012
Wages Payable	117,226	Other Revenues	8,171
Cash (balance on September 1, 2016)	31,052	Retained Earnings (beginning)	440,510
Cash (balance on August 31, 2017)	44,790	Prepaid Rent	43,870
Food and Supplies Expense	333,528	Property and Equipment	732,204
Selling and Administrative Expenses	72,751	Restaurant Sales Revenue	1,315,325
Food and Supply Inventories	20,775	Utilities and Other Expenses	414,978
Notes Payable	39,381	Wages Expense	420,957
Contributed Capital	239,744	Dividends	49,994

Other cash flow information:	
Additional investments by shareholders	$ 33,555
Cash paid to purchase equipment	243,211
Cash paid to suppliers and employees	1,123,353
Repayments of borrowings	170,242
Cash received from customers	1,276,008
Cash received from borrowings	175,000
Cash received from sale of long-term assets	115,975
Dividends declared and paid in cash	49,994

Required:

Prepare the four basic financial statements for the fiscal year ended August 31, 2017.

SKILLS DEVELOPMENT CASES

LO1-2, 1-2, 1-3 **S1-1 Finding Financial Information**

Refer to the summarized financial statements of The Home Depot in Appendix A at the back of this book.

Required:

1. What is the amount of net income for the year ended January 29, 2017?
2. What amount of sales revenue was earned for the year ended January 29, 2017?

3. How much inventory does the company have on January 29, 2017?

4. How much does The Home Depot have in cash on January 29, 2017?

5. The Home Depot's shares are traded on the New York Stock Exchange under the symbol HD. What kind of company does this make The Home Depot?

S1-2 Comparing Financial Information

LO1-1, 1-2, 1-3

Refer to the financial statements of Lowe's Companies, Inc. in Appendix B and the summarized financial statements of The Home Depot in Appendix A at the back of this book.

Required:

1. Was Lowe's Companies, Inc.'s net income for the year ended February 3, 2017, greater (or less) than The Home Depot's?

2. Was Lowe's sales revenue for the year ended February 3, 2017, greater (or less) than The Home Depot's?

3. Did Lowe's have more (or less) inventories than The Home Depot at the end of the 2016 fiscal year?

4. Did Lowe's have more (or less) cash than The Home Depot at the end of the 2016 fiscal year?

5. Is Lowe's the same type of business organization as The Home Depot?

6. On an overall basis, was Lowe's or The Home Depot more successful in the 2016 fiscal year?

S1-3 Internet-Based Team Research: Examining an Annual Report

LO1-1, 1-2, 1-3

As a team, select an industry to analyze. Reuters provides lists of industries at www.reuters .com/finance/personal-finance. Another source is csimarket.com. Each group member should access the annual report for one publicly traded company in the industry, with each member selecting a different company. In addition to the company's own website, a great source is the Canadian Securities Administrators' System for Electronic Document Analysis and Retrieval (SEDAR) service. This free source is available by going to the Search Database section of www.sedar.com, clicking on Search for Public Company Documents, and then filling in the required information.

Required:

1. On an individual basis, each team member should write a short report that lists the following information:

   a. What type of business organization is it?

   b. What types of products or services does it sell?

   c. On what day of the year does its fiscal year end?

   d. For how many years does it present complete balance sheets? Income statements? Cash flow statements?

   e. Are its financial statements audited by independent CPAs? If so, by whom?

   f. Did its total assets increase or decrease over the last year?

   g. Did its net income increase or decrease over the last year?

2. Then, as a team, write a short report comparing and contrasting your companies using these attributes. Discuss any patterns across the companies that you as a team observe. Provide potential explanations for any differences discovered.

S1-4 Ethical Decision Making: A Real-Life Example

LO1-2, 1-3, 1-4

In June 2005, John Rigas, the 80-year-old founder and former chief executive officer (CEO) of Adelphia Communications was sentenced to fifteen years in jail for defrauding investors and lenders of over a billion dollars. His son, the former chief financial officer (CFO), was sentenced to twenty years in jail.

To understand the charges, you need to first understand a bit about Adelphia's history. Adelphia started as a one-town cable company in 1952 but, at the time the fraud accusations were made public, had grown into the sixth-largest cable television provider in the United

States. Because the company started as a family—owned business, Adelphia's operations were always a central part of the personal lives of the Rigas family members. However, the extent to which their personal lives were mixed in with the business activities was never clear to shareholders—until they were reported in an article in the August 12, 2002, issue of *Fortune*.

Answer the questions using information from the table below that summarizes how the Rigas family allegedly spent over $1.2 billion of Adelphia's money—money that ultimately belonged to Adelphia's shareholders.

Required:

1. What is the accounting concept that the Rigas family is accused of violating?
2. Based on the information provided in the following table, can you determine which of the family's dealings are clearly inappropriate and which are clearly appropriate?
3. As a shareholder, how might you attempt to ensure that this kind of behaviour does not occur or, at least, does not occur without your knowing about it?
4. Aside from Adelphia's shareholders, who else might be harmed by these actions committed by the Rigas family?

Family Assets—Sort Of		
Some of the notable ways the Rigas family used Adelphia shareholder dollars.		
On the Receiving End	Who's Behind the Entity	How Much?
Dobaire Designs	Adelphia paid this company, owned by Doris Rigas (John's wife), for design services.	$ 371,000
Wending Creek Farms	Adelphia paid John Rigas's farm for lawn care and snowplowing.	$ 2,000,000
SongCatcher Films	Adelphia financed the production of a movie by Ellen Rigas (John's daughter).	$ 3,000,000
Eleni Interiors	The company made payments to a furniture store run by Doris Rigas and owned by John.	$ 12,000,000
The Golf Club at Wending Creek Farms	Adelphia began developing a ritzy golf club.	$ 13,000,000
Wending Creek 3656	The company bought timber rights that would eventually revert to a Rigas family partnership.	$ 26,000,000
Praxis Capital Ventures	Adelphia funded a venture capital firm run by Ellen Rigas's husband.	$ 65,000,000
Niagara Frontier Hockey LP	Adelphia underwrote the Rigas's purchase of the Buffalo Sabres hockey team.	$ 150,000,000
Highland 2000	Adelphia guaranteed loans to a Rigas family partnership, which used the funds to buy shares.	$1,000,000,000
Total		$1,271,371,000

LO1-4

S1-5 Ethical Decision Making: A Mini-Case

You are one of three partners who own and operate Mary's Maid Service. The company has been operating for seven years. One of the other partners has always prepared the company's annual financial statements. Recently, you proposed that the statements be audited each year because it would benefit the partners and prevent possible disagreements about the division of profits. The partner who prepares the statements proposed that his uncle, who has a lot of financial experience, can do the job at little cost. Your other partner remained silent.

Required:

1. What position would you take on the proposal? Justify your response in writing.
2. What would you strongly recommend? Give the basis for your recommendation.

LO1-2, 1-3, 1-4

S1-6 Critical Thinking: Developing a Balance Sheet and Income Statement

On September 30, Ashley and Jason started arguing about who is better off. Jason said he was better off because he owned a PlayStation console that he bought last year for $250. He figures that, if needed, he could sell it to a friend for $180. Ashley argued that she was better off because she had $1,000 cash in her bank account and a piece of art that she bought two years ago for $800 but could now probably sell for $1,400.

Jason countered that Ashley still owed $250 on a loan and that Jason's dad promised to buy him a Porsche if he does really well in his accounting class. Jason said he had $6,000 cash in his bank account right now because he just received a $4,800 student loan. Ashley knows that Jason also owes a tuition instalment of $800 for this term.

Ashley and Jason met again in early November. They each asked how the other was doing. Ashley claimed that she'd become much more successful than Jason. She had a part–time job, where she earned $1,500 per month. Jason laughed at Ashley because he had won $1,950 on a lottery ticket he bought in October, and that was merely for the "work" of standing in line for a minute. It was just what he needed, because his apartment costs $800 each month. Ashley, on the other hand, pays $470 for her share of the rent. Both Ashley and Jason have other normal living costs that total $950 each month.

1. Prepare a financial report that compares what Ashley and Jason each own and owe on September 30. Make a list of any decisions you had to make when preparing your report.

2. In a written report, identify and justify which of the two characters is better off. If you were a creditor, to whom would you rather lend money?

3. Prepare a report that compares what Ashley and Jason each earned during October. List any decisions you had to make when preparing your report.

4. In a written report, identify and justify which of the two characters is more successful. If you were a creditor considering a three–year loan to one of these characters, to whom would you rather lend money?

S1-7 Preparing an Income Statement and Balance Sheet

LO1-2

eXcel

Electronic Arts is the world's leading developer and publisher of interactive entertain–ment software for personal computers and advanced entertainment systems made by Sony, Nintendo, and Microsoft.

Assume that the company is revising its methods for displaying its financial statements, and the controller in the accounting department has asked you to create electronic worksheets that the department can use as its standard format for financial statement reporting. The controller has provided you with an alphabetical list of statement categories and account names (below), with corresponding balances (in millions) as of September 30. She has asked you to use a spreadsheet program to create two worksheets that organize the accounts into a properly formatted balance sheet and income statement, and that use formulas to compute the amounts represented by question marks below.

Accounts Payable	$ 171	Liabilities		Revenue	
Accounts Receivable	328	Net Income	?	Sales Revenue	$675
Assets		Notes Payable	$ 12	Selling Expense	223
Cash	2,412	Other Assets	283	Shareholders' Equity	
Contributed Capital	986	Other Expenses	1	Total Assets	?
Cost of Goods Sold Expense	284	Other Liabilities	587	Total Expenses	?
Expenses		Promotion Expense	107	Total Liabilities	?
Income Tax Expense	9	Property and Equipment	364	Total Liabilities and Shareholders' Equity	?
Inventories	367	Retained Earnings	1,998	Total Shareholders' Equity	?

Not knowing where to start, you emailed your friend Owen for advice on using a spreadsheet. Owen's detailed reply follows.

Required:

Follow Owen's advice to create a balance sheet and income statement, with each statement saved on a separate worksheet in a file called *me*EA.xls where the *me* part of the file name uniquely identifies you.

From: Owentheaccountant@yahoo.com
To: Helpme@hotmail.com
Cc:
Subject: Excel Help

Hey, pal. Long time, no chat. Here's the scoop on creating those worksheets, with a screenshot too. If you need more help, let me know and I'll submit an application for your position there. ☺

1. Start up Excel to open a new spreadsheet file. You'll need only two worksheets for this assignment, so delete the third worksheet by right-clicking on the *Sheet3* tab at the bottom of the worksheet and selecting Delete. While you're at it, rename *Sheet1* and *Sheet2* to *Balance Sheet* and *Income Statement* by double-clicking on the worksheet tabs and typing in the new names.

2. Plan the layout for your reports. Use the first column as a blank margin, the second column for account names and their headings, and the third column for the numbers corresponding to each account name or total. If you want to apply the same format to all worksheets, begin by right-clicking on the tab at the bottom of a worksheet and choosing Select All Sheets. Next, resize the first column by clicking on the A at the top of that column, then from the Home tab, in the Cells group, click on Format then Column Width . . . , and enter a width of 2. Using this same procedure, resize columns B and C to 50 and 15, respectively.

3. Starting with cell B1, enter the company's name. Enter the report name and date in cells B2 and B3. To merge cells so these headings span more than one column, select the cells to be merged and then click on Format in the Cells group, select Format Cells . . . and click the Merge Cells box in the Text Control section of the Alignment tab. Continue with the body of the report in cell B5, entering any necessary amounts in column C.

4. To use formulas to compute subtotals and totals, the equals sign = is entered first into the cell and is followed immediately by the formula. So, to add a series of amounts, say C7 through C11, use a formula like = SUM(C7:C11), as shown in the screenshot below.

5. After you enter all the data and calculate totals, be sure to save the file. To do this, just click on the Office button in the top left and choose Save As . . . .

6. If you need to print the worksheets, it might be best to highlight what you want printed, then click on the Office button, choose Print. . . , and choose Selection in the Print What box.

7. Go to it, you accounting guru!

CONTINUING CASE

CC1-1 Financial Statements for a Business Plan

Nicole Mackisey is thinking of forming her own spa business, Nicole's Getaway Spa (NGS). Nicole expects that she and two family members will each contribute $10,000 to the business and receive 1,000 shares each.

Nicole forecasts the following amounts for the first year of operations, ending December 31, 2017: cash on hand and in the bank, $2,150; amounts due from customers from spa treatments, $1,780; building and equipment, $70,000; amounts owed to beauty supply outlets for spa equipment, $4,660; notes payable to a local bank, $38,870.

Cash dividends of $2,000 will be paid to the shareholders during the year. Nicole also forecasts that first–year sales revenues will be $40,000, wages will be $24,000, the cost of supplies used up will be $7,000, selling and administrative expenses will be $5,000, and income taxes will be $1,600.

Required:

1. Based on Nicole's estimates, prepare a (forecasted) income statement for Nicole's Getaway Spa for the year ended December 31, 2017.
2. Prepare a (forecasted) statement of retained earnings for Nicole's Getaway Spa for the year ended December 31, 2017.
3. Prepare a (forecasted) balance sheet for Nicole's Getaway Spa at December 31, 2017.
4. As of December 31, 2017, would most of the financing for assets come from creditors or shareholders?

Endnote

1. For companies that have a net loss (expenses exceed revenues), the statement of retained earnings would subtract the net loss rather than add net income. Also, if retained earnings is negative it is referred to as a deficit and the statement would be called *Statement of Deficit*.

THAT WAS
THEN

In the previous chapter, you were introduced to the four main financial statements: the balance sheet, income statement, statement of retained earnings, and statement of cash flows.

THIS IS
NOW

This chapter focuses on just the balance sheet and the accounting system used to produce it.

YOUR LEARNING OBJECTIVES

Understand the business

LO2-1 Identify financial effects of common business activities that impact the balance sheet.

Study the accounting methods

LO2-2 Apply transaction analysis to accounting transactions.

LO2-3 Use journal entries and T-accounts to show how transactions affect the balance sheet.

LO2-4 Prepare a trial balance and a classified balance sheet.

Evaluate the results

LO2-5 Interpret the balance sheet using the current ratio and an understanding of related concepts.

Review the chapter

Chapter Summary

CHAPTER 2

The Balance Sheet

pxhidalgo/Getty Images

FOCUS COMPANY:
Pizza Palace Inc.

PIZZA PALACE

You read in Chapter 1 about Emilio Santos's plans for starting a pizza company in Vancouver. Emilio's local CPA, Ally, advised him that all businesses, big and small, need systems for gathering and organizing financial information. Like most public accounting firms, Ally offers professional services that can help smaller companies like Pizza Palace track the financial results of their activities. With Ally's help, Emilio will implement an accounting system to do this for Pizza Palace. This system will provide the financial information that he needs to manage the company and to report its results to others interested in his business.

The focus in this chapter is on the activities that occurred during August when Emilio was establishing Pizza Palace, long before it could open its doors to customers. You will learn how these activities are captured in an accounting system, leading to the assets, liabilities, and shareholders' equity that are reported in a balance sheet.

Later, in Chapter 3, you will learn about the operating activities that occur after a business opens its doors to customers and begins generating the revenues and expenses that are reported in an income statement. Your introduction to the accounting system will conclude in Chapter 4, where you will learn about the steps needed to adjust the accounting records before finalizing and evaluating a company's financial results.

ORGANIZATION OF THE CHAPTER

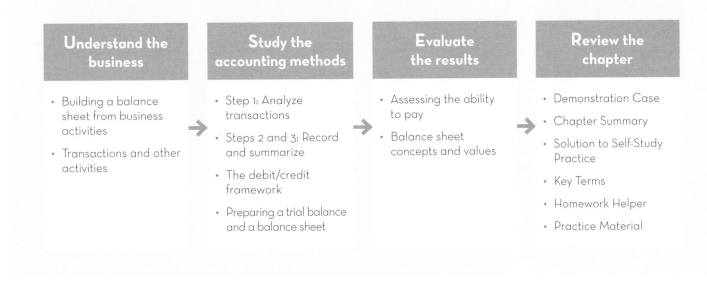

Understand the business	Study the accounting methods	Evaluate the results	Review the chapter
• Building a balance sheet from business activities • Transactions and other activities	• Step 1: Analyze transactions • Steps 2 and 3: Record and summarize • The debit/credit framework • Preparing a trial balance and a balance sheet	• Assessing the ability to pay • Balance sheet concepts and values	• Demonstration Case • Chapter Summary • Solution to Self-Study Practice • Key Terms • Homework Helper • Practice Material

Understand the Business

BUILDING A BALANCE SHEET

After meeting with Ally, Emilio understood that before he could open his restaurant, he would have to establish the business. This would involve acquiring **assets** that Pizza Palace would use for many months or years to come. The assets would be owned by Pizza Palace, but creditors would have a claim to those assets equal to the amount of the company's **liabilities**. As owners of Pizza Palace, Emilio and his wife also would have a claim on the company's assets (**shareholders' equity**), but their claim would be secondary to creditors' claims. Emilio remembered that the balance sheet was structured like the basic accounting equation $(A = L + SE)$, but it was only by accounting for Pizza Palace's activities that he truly learned how a balance sheet was built.

A key activity for any start-up company, such as Pizza Palace, is to obtain financing. Two sources of financing are available to businesses: equity and debt. *Equity* refers to financing a business through owners' contributions and reinvestments of profit. *Debt* refers to financing the business through loans. A business is obligated to repay debt financing, but it is not obligated to repay its equity financing.

Like most small business owners, Emilio and his wife used their personal savings to make an initial cash contribution to the company. They decided to contribute $50,000, which is more than they had originally planned, but by relying more on equity financing, the company wouldn't require quite as much debt financing. In exchange for their investment in the company, Emilio and his wife will receive a document called a *share certificate*. This certificate indicates the number of shares they have acquired in the company and serves as evidence of their ownership.

Emilio had determined that Pizza Palace would need additional money to become established, so on behalf of the company, he applied for a loan from a bank. Soon after the loan was approved, Pizza Palace received $20,000 cash in exchange for its promise to repay the loan in two years. The terms for repaying the loan were described in detail in a legal document

LEARNING OBJECTIVE 2-1

Identify financial effects of common business activities that impact the balance sheet.

Assets: Resources presently owned by a business that generate future economic benefits.

Liabilities: Amounts presently owed by a business.

Shareholders' equity: The amount invested and reinvested in a company by its shareholders. Also called *owners' equity* or *stockholders' equity*.

called a *promissory note*. The initial financing activities of Pizza Palace are pictured in Exhibit 2.1.

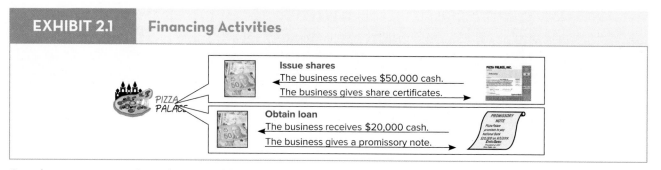

Canadian money image: CarpathianPrince/Shutterstock.com; Bank note image used with the permission of the Bank of Canada; Share certification: ©David A. Tietz/Editorial Image, LLC

After obtaining initial financing, a company will start investing in assets that will be used later when the business opens. In the case of Pizza Palace, Emilio first spent $42,000 cash by writing company cheques to buy and install restaurant booths, cash registers, and other equipment. The company also needed to buy operating assets, such as cookware and related items like pizza pans, pizza cutters, serving plates, cutlery, drink glasses, napkin holders, and cheese and spice shakers.

These items could be purchased with cash, but that would be inconvenient and inefficient. Instead, businesses typically buy goods or services from others on credit, by promising to pay within thirty days of the purchase. Pizza Palace bought $630 worth of these items on credit, as indicated by the supplier's bill (or *invoice*). These examples are pictured in Exhibit 2.2.

| EXHIBIT 2.2 | Investing Activities |

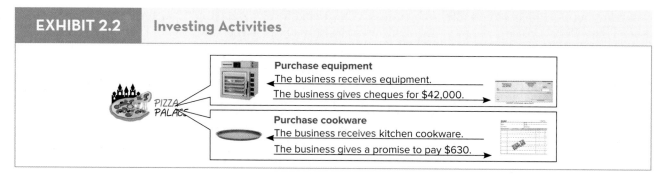

Pizza oven: courtesy of Toastmaster; Cheque: ©David A. Tietz/Editorial Image, LLC; Pizza pan: ©Jamie Duplass/Alamy; Invoice: ©Studio 101/Alamy

By carefully reading Exhibits 2.1 and 2.2, you will see three features that will be important for understanding how accounting works:

1. The company always documents its activities. Share certificates, promissory notes, cheques, invoices, and other documents indicate the nature of the underlying business activity.

2. The company always receives something and gives something. This is a basic feature of all business activities. A business enters into an exchange either to earn a profit immediately or to obtain resources that will allow it to earn a profit later. This is the fundamental idea of business: to create value through exchange. Any exchange that affects the company's assets, liabilities, or shareholders' equity must be captured in and reported by the accounting system. Because the accounting system captures both what is received and what is given, it is often referred to as a *double-entry* system.

3. Each exchange is analyzed to determine a dollar amount that represents the value of items given and received. This value is called the cost and is used to measure the financial effects of the exchange, as required by the **cost principle**.

Cost principle: Assets and liabilities should initially be recorded at their original cost to the company.

As illustrated in Exhibit 2.3, these three features are key inputs into the process used when accounting for business activities. After each activity is documented, accountants assign names to the items exchanged and then analyze their financial effects on the accounting equation. The ultimate goal is to capture these financial effects so that they can be reported in the financial statements for use by decision makers inside and outside the company. Take a moment right now to read Exhibit 2.3.

EXHIBIT 2.3	Accounting for Business Activities

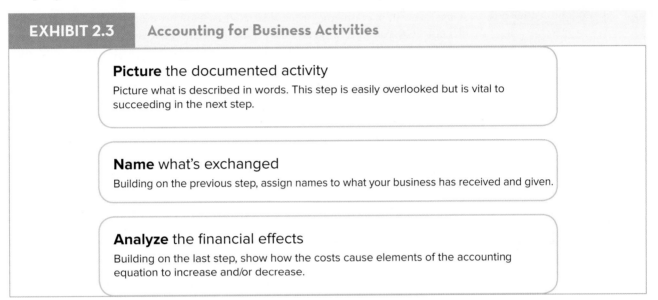

Picture the documented activity
Picture what is described in words. This step is easily overlooked but is vital to succeeding in the next step.

Name what's exchanged
Building on the previous step, assign names to what your business has received and given.

Analyze the financial effects
Building on the last step, show how the costs cause elements of the accounting equation to increase and/or decrease.

TRANSACTIONS AND OTHER ACTIVITIES

Business activities that affect the basic accounting equation $(A = L + SE)$ are called **transactions**. Transactions are of special importance because they are the only activities that enter the financial accounting system. Transactions include two types of activities:

Transactions: An exchange or event that has a direct economic effect on the assets, liabilities, or shareholders' equity of a business.

1. **External exchanges.** These are exchanges that occur between the company and someone else that involve assets, liabilities, and/or shareholders' equity. When Starbucks sells you a Frappucino®, it is exchanging an icy taste of heaven for your cash, so Starbucks would record this in its accounting system.

2. **Internal events.** These are exchanges that occur within the company itself. For example, when Red Bull combines sugar, water, taurine, and caffeine, something magical happens: these ingredients turn into Red Bull Energy Drink. This internal event is a transaction because it has a direct financial effect whereby some assets (supplies of sugar, etc.) are used up to create a different asset (an inventory of Red Bull drinks).

Some important activities that occur will not be captured by the accounting system because they are not transactions. For example, during the first month of business, Emilio signed a contract on behalf of Pizza Palace to rent restaurant space in a building the following month. This activity was not a transaction because no assets or services were exchanged at that time. The landlord exchanged a promise to rent the building for Pizza Palace's promise to pay rent, but an exchange that only includes promises is not an accounting transaction.

For this same reason, Pizza Palace's accounting system did not cap—ture other activities such as placing orders with suppliers or promising to hire employees. Documents were created to indicate that these activities occurred, but they were appropriately excluded from the accounting records because these were not transactions. Later, when these promises result in actually receiving or giving an asset or service, they will become transac—tions to be captured by the accounting system.

Study the Accounting Methods

A systematic accounting process is used to capture and report the financial effects of a company's activities. This process, represented by the circular graphic, is called the accounting cycle because it repeats itself over and over.

For now, we will focus on the first three steps:

Analyze → Record → Summarize

STEP 1: ANALYZE TRANSACTIONS

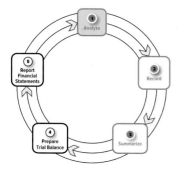

The process in Exhibit 2.3 is commonly referred to as *transaction analy—sis*, which involves determining whether a transaction exists and, if it does, analyzing its impact on the accounting equation. Two simple ideas are used when analyzing transactions:

1. Duality of effects. It's a fancy name, but the idea is simple. Every transaction has at least two effects on the basic accounting equation. To remember this, just think of expressions like "give and receive" or "push and pull" or, if you're a closet scientist, Newton's Third Law of Motion.

2. A = L + SE. You know this already, right? Well, just remember that the dollar amount for assets must always equal the total of liabilities plus shareholders' equity for every accounting transaction. If it doesn't, then you are missing something and you should go back to the first idea (duality of effects).

As part of transaction analysis, a name is given to each item exchanged. Accountants refer to these names as *account titles*. To ensure account titles are used consistently, every company establishes a **chart of accounts**—a list that designates a name and reference number that the company will use when accounting for each item that it exchanges. A partial chart of accounts for Pizza Palace is shown in Exhibit 2.4. (The chart of accounts shown in Chapter 2 includes only balance sheet accounts. Chapter 3 will expand this to include additional assets and liabilities as well as revenue and expense accounts.) A more comprehensive chart of accounts to use when completing homework assignments is presented in the Homework Helper.

Chart of accounts: A summary of all account names (and corresponding account numbers) used to record financial results in the accounting system.

The chart of accounts is tailored to each company's business, so although some account titles are common across all companies (Cash, Accounts Payable), others may be used only by a particular company (such as Cookware). Depending on the company, you may see a liability for a bank loan called a *Note Payable* or a *Loan Payable*.[1]

The best way to learn how to account for business activities is to work through examples. Skim the names and descriptions that are in Exhibit 2.4 one more time, and then let's look more closely at Pizza Palace's business activities.

EXHIBIT 2.4   Pizza Palace's (Partial) Chart of Accounts   PIZZA PALACE

Account Number	Account Name	Description
101	Cash	Dollar amount of coins, paper money, funds in bank
113	Cookware	Cost of cutlery, pizza pans, dishes, etc.
135	Equipment	Cost of pizza ovens, restaurant booths, dishwashers, etc.
201	Accounts Payable	Owed to suppliers for goods or services bought on credit
222	Note Payable	Owed to lenders, as per terms of promissory note
301	Contributed Capital	Shares issued for contributions made to the company
310	Retained Earnings	Accumulated earnings (not yet distributed as dividends)

(a) **Issue Shares to Owners.** Emilio Santos incorporates Pizza Palace Inc. on August 1. The company issues shares to Emilio and his wife as evidence of their contribution of $50,000 cash, which is deposited in the company's bank account.

COACH'S TIP

Analyze transactions from the standpoint of the business, not of its owners.

Picture — Receives ← → Gives

Name
- Pizza Palace has received $50,000 in cash.
- Pizza Palace gave $50,000 of shares (contributed capital).

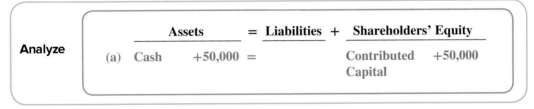

Analyze

	Assets	=	Liabilities	+	Shareholders' Equity
(a) Cash	+50,000	=			Contributed Capital +50,000

Canadian money: CarpathianPrince/Shutterstock.com; Bank note image used with the permission of the Bank of Canada; Share certificate: ©David A. Tietz/Editorial Image, LLC

Notice that in the accounting equation table above, we included reference (a) so that we can refer back to the original transaction description if needed. You, too, should use transaction letters (or numbers or dates) as references in your homework problems. The goal of transaction analysis is to identify the specific accounts affected, the dollar amount of the change in the accounts, and the direction of this change ($+$ or $-$) on the accounting equation category. In example (a), an asset (Cash) increases by $50,000, which equals the increase in the shareholders' equity account (Contributed Capital).

(b) **Invest in Equipment.** **Pizza Palace pays $42,000 cash to buy restaurant booths and other equipment.**

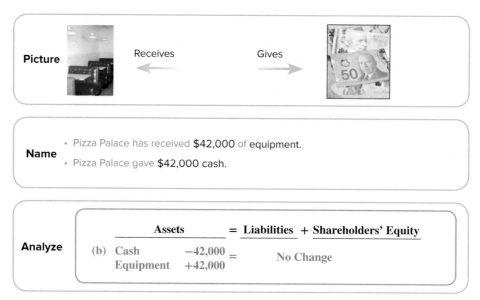

| | Picture | Receives | ← | Gives | → | |

| **Name** | • Pizza Palace has received $42,000 of equipment.
• Pizza Palace gave $42,000 cash. |

		Assets		= Liabilities	+ Shareholders' Equity
Analyze	(b)	Cash	−42,000	=	No Change
		Equipment	+42,000		

Restaurant booths: ©Creatrixcordis/iStock; Canadian money: CarpathianPrince/ Shutterstock.com; Bank note image used with the permission of the Bank of Canada

Notice that even though transaction (b) did not affect liabilities or shareholders' equity, the accounting equation remained in balance because the decrease in one asset (Cash) was offset by the increase in another asset (Equipment). The accounting equation must always balance (be equal) for each transaction.

(c) **Obtain Loan from Bank.** **Pizza Palace borrows $20,000 from a bank, depositing those funds in its bank account and signing a formal agreement to repay the loan in two years.**

| | Picture | Receives | ← | Gives | → | PROMISSORY NOTE |

| **Name** | • Pizza Palace has received $20,000 cash.
• Pizza Palace gave a note payable to the bank for $20,000. |

		Assets	=	Liabilities	+ Shareholders' Equity
Analyze	(c)	Cash +20,000	=	Note +20,000	
				Payable	

Canadian money: CarpathianPrince/Shutterstock.com; Bank note image used with the permission of the Bank of Canada

COACH'S TIP

Notes payable are like accounts payable except that they (1) earn interest, (2) can be outstanding for long periods (more than one year), and (3) are documented using formal documents called *notes*.

(d) **Invest in Equipment.** Pizza Palace purchases and receives $18,000 in pizza ovens and other restaurant equipment, paying $16,000 in cash and giving an informal promise to pay $2,000 at the end of the month.

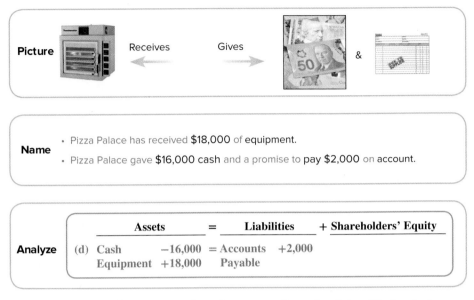
If you ever run into a transaction that you have no idea how to analyze, try to break it down. Rather than trying to solve it all at once, begin by looking just for what is received. Another strategy is to look for any cash exchanged, because by getting a handle on that part of the transaction, the other parts often become easier to see. Always be sure to summarize the effects in terms of the accounting equation, because it must balance if you've detected all the accounts affected by the transaction.

(e) **Order Cookware.** Pizza Palace orders $630 of pans, dishes, and other cookware. None have been received yet.

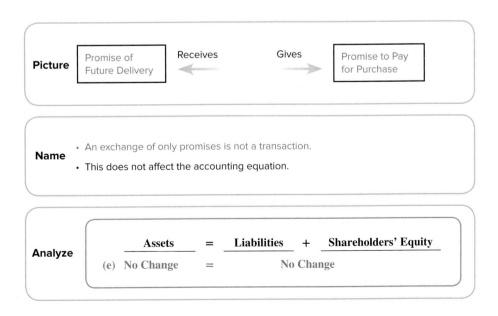

Not all documented business activities are considered accounting trans—actions. As shown in (e), Pizza Palace and the supplier have documented the order, but it involves an exchange that consists only of promises, so it is not an accounting transaction.

(f) **Pay Supplier.** Pizza Palace pays $2,000 to the equipment supplier in (d).

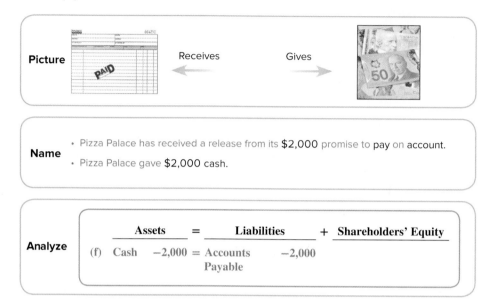

	Picture	Receives ←	Gives →

Name
- Pizza Palace has received a release from its $2,000 promise to pay on account.
- Pizza Palace gave $2,000 cash.

Analyze

		Assets	=	Liabilities	+	Shareholders' Equity
(f)	Cash	−2,000	=	Accounts Payable	−2,000	

Invoice: ©Studio 101/Alamy; Canadian money: CarpathianPrince/Shutterstock.com; Bank note image used with the permission of the Bank of Canada

In (f), Pizza Palace fulfills its liability to a supplier. Thus, the Accounts Payable decrease because, in exchange for its payment to the supplier, Pizza Palace receives a release from its original promise to pay the supplier $2,000.

(g) **Receive Cookware.** Pizza Palace receives $630 of the cookware ordered in (e) and promises to pay for it next month.

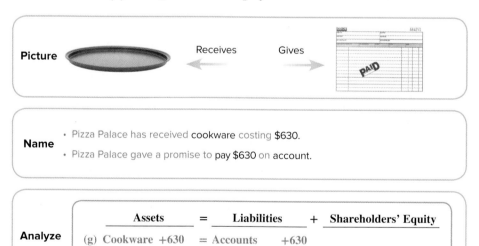

	Picture	Receives ←	Gives →

Name
- Pizza Palace has received cookware costing $630.
- Pizza Palace gave a promise to pay $630 on account.

Analyze

		Assets	=	Liabilities	+	Shareholders' Equity
(g)	Cookware	+630	=	Accounts Payable	+630	

Pizza pan: ©Jamie Duplass/Alamy; Invoice: ©Studio 101/Alamy

As we said before, the best way to learn accounting is to do examples, so try the following practice question.

HOW'S IT GOING?

Self-Study Practice 2.1

Complete the following transaction analysis steps by filling in the empty blanks and boxes.

NIKE, Inc. purchased equipment costing $500,000, paying $200,000 cash and signing a formal promissory note to pay the balance several years from now.

Picture

Receives

Gives

PROMISSORY NOTE

NIKE INC. promises to pay National Equipment $300,000 on 1/1/2019.

&

Name

Nike has received_____.

Nike gave_____.

Analyze

Assets	=	Liabilities	+	Shareholder's Equity

After you have finished, check your answer with the solution, which follows the chapter summary.

STEPS 2 AND 3: RECORD AND SUMMARIZE

In the previous section, you learned how to analyze transactions, which ended with an understanding of the financial effects of each transaction on a company's asset, liability, and shareholders' equity accounts. In an academic setting, we have encouraged you to write down these accounting equation effects. In the workplace, an accountant would not actually cap– ture the effects in this way. Instead, after determining the financial effects of a transaction, an accountant would capture the effects through two additional steps: recording and summarizing.

One way to record and summarize the financial effects of transactions would be to enter your understanding of their effects into a spreadsheet like the one shown in Exhibit 2.5. By summing each spreadsheet column, you could compute new balances at the end of each month and report them on a balance sheet.

A spreadsheet makes it easy to see the individual impact of each trans– action and how transactions combine with beginning balances to yield ending balances, but it is impractical for most large organizations to use. Instead, most companies record and summarize the financial effects of transactions with computerized accounting systems, which can handle a large num– ber of transactions. These systems follow the accounting cycle, which is repeated day after day, month after month, and year after year.

EXHIBIT 2.5   Using a Spreadsheet to Record and Summarize Transactions

			Assets		=	Liabilities		+	Shareholders' Equity
		Cash	Cookware	Equipment		Accounts Payable	Notes Payable		Contributed Capital
3	Beginning	0	0	0	=	0	0		0
4	(a)	+50,000			=				+50,000
5	(b)	-42,000		+42,000	=				
6	(c)	+20,000			=		+20,000		
7	(d)	-16,000		+18,000	=	+2,000			
8	(e)		no change		=		no change		
9	(f)	-2,000			=	-2,000			
10	(g)		+630		=	+630			
11	Ending	10,000	630	60,000	=	630	20,000	+	50,000

Exhibit 2.5.xlsx - Microsoft Excel

As shown in Exhibit 2.6, the three–step analyze–record–summarize process is applied to daily transactions, as well as adjustments at the end of each month, before a trial balance and the financial statements are prepared. The same three steps also are part of the closing process that occurs

EXHIBIT 2.6   Elements of the Accounting Cycle

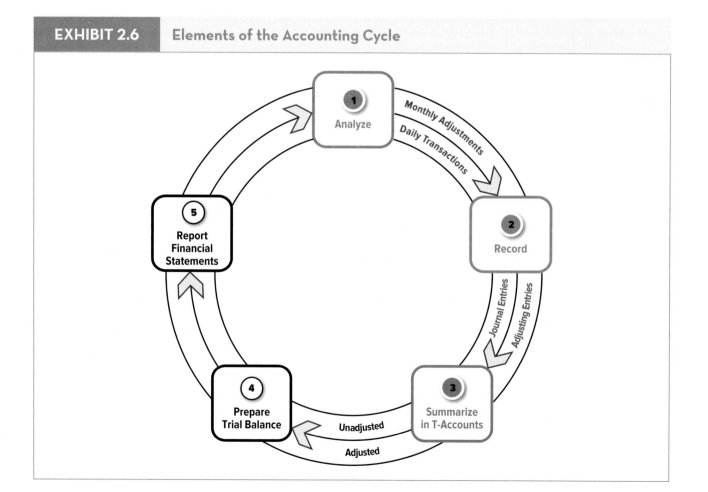

at the end of each year. Our focus in Chapter 2 is on applying the three–step process during the period to activities that affect only balance sheet accounts. After you have become comfortable with this process, you will learn (in Chapter 3) to apply this process to operating activities that affect both balance sheet and income statement accounts. In Chapter 4, you will learn how the process is applied at the end of the accounting period, when the accounting records are adjusted and closed.

The three–step process of analyzing, recording, and summarizing is a lot like what you do as a student when attending class, taking notes, and preparing for exams. Day after day, you analyze what is said in class and you record important points in a notebook, which is kind of like an academic diary or journal. Later, when preparing for exams, you transform your notes into summary sheets, which you then use to study for exams. The same ideas are used in the accounting cycle. Transactions are analyzed, and their financial effects are entered into **journals** each day they occur. Later, these journal entries are summarized in **ledger** accounts that keep track of the financial effects on each account. To make this process as efficient as possible, journals and ledger accounts share the same underlying framework discussed in the following section.

> **Journals:** Used to record the effects of each day's transactions, organized by date.
>
> **Ledger:** Used to summarize the effects of journal entries on each account; organized by account.

THE DEBIT/CREDIT FRAMEWORK

The framework used for journals and ledger accounts was created more than 500 years ago, yet it continues to exist in accounting systems today. Although computers now perform many routine accounting tasks involving journals and ledger accounts, using most computerized systems still requires an understanding of how these accounting records work.

LEARNING OBJECTIVE 2-3

Use journal entries and T-accounts to show how transactions affect the balance sheet.

To understand this framework, think of the accounting equation (A = L + SE) as an old–fashioned weight scale that tips at the equals sign. Assets—like Cash and Equipment—are put on the left side of the scale, and liabilities and shareholders' equity accounts are put on the right. Likewise, each individual account has two sides, with one side used for increases and the other for decreases, similar to what is shown in Exhibit 2.7.

EXHIBIT 2.7	The Debit/Credit Framework

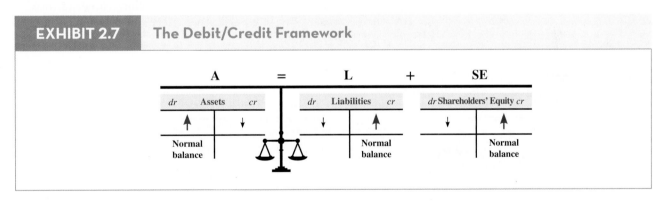

Take special note of two important rules illustrated in Exhibit 2.7:

1. **Accounts increase on the same side as they appear in A = L + SE.** Accounts on the left side of the accounting equation increase on the left side of the account and accounts on the right side of the equation increase on the right:
   - Assets increase on the left side of the account.
   - Liabilities increase on the right side of the account.
   - Shareholders' equity accounts increase on the right side of the account.
   - Decreases are the opposite, as shown in Exhibit 2.7.

Debit: The left side of an account, or the act of entering an amount into the left side of an account.

Credit: The right side of an account, or the act of entering an amount into the right side of an account.

2. Left is debit (*dr*), right is credit (*cr*). The terms (and abbreviations) **debit** (*dr*) and **credit** (*cr*) come from Latin words that had meaning back in the day, but today they just mean *left* and *right*. When combined with how increases and decreases are entered into accounts, the following rules emerge:

- Use debits for increases in assets (and for decreases in liabilities and shareholders' equity accounts).
- Use credits for increases in liabilities and shareholders' equity accounts (and for decreases in assets).

Accountants didn't dream up this debit/credit framework just to confuse you. The purpose of this double–entry system is to introduce another check on the accuracy of accounting numbers. In addition to requiring that A = L + SE, the double–entry system also requires that debits = credits. In other words, the dollar value of all debits has to equal the dollar value of all credits. If either of these relationships is not equal, then you know for sure that you've made an error that will need to be corrected.

Step 1: Analyzing Transactions

The debit/credit framework does not change this first step of the accounting process. Continue to use the approach shown in Exhibit 2.3 to determine the financial effects of transactions, which you will learn to enter into the accounting system in step 2.

Step 2: Recording Journal Entries

Journal entries: Indicate the effects of each day's transactions in a debits-equal-credits format.

The financial effects of transactions are entered into a journal using a debits–equal–credits format, as shown in Exhibit 2.8. When looking at these **journal entries**, as they are called, notice the following:

- A date is included for each transaction.
- Debits appear first (on top). Credits are written below the debits and are indented to the right (both the words and the amounts). The order of the debited accounts or credited accounts doesn't matter, as long as for each journal entry debits are on top and credits are on the bottom and indented.
- Total dollar value of debits equals total dollar value of credits for each transaction (e.g., see the entry on August 5 where $18,000 = $16,000 + $2,000).

EXHIBIT 2.8	Formal Journal Page

General Journal					Page G1
Date	Account Titles and Explanation	Ref.	Debit	Credit	
2017					
Aug. 1	Cash		50,000		
(a)	Contributed Capital			50,000	
	(Financing from shareholders.)				
Aug. 2	Equipment		42,000		
(b)	Cash			42,000	
	(Bought equipment using cash.)				
Aug. 5	**Equipment**		18,000		
(d)	Cash			16,000	
	Accounts Payable			2,000	
	(Bought equipment using cash and credit.)				

- Dollar signs are not used because the journal is understood to be a record of financial effects.
- The reference column (Ref.) will be used later (in step 3) to indicate when the journal entry has been summarized in the ledger accounts.
- A brief explanation of the transaction is written below the debits and credits.
- The line after the explanation is left blank before writing the next journal entry.

When writing journal entries in this course, we'll make a few minor changes to the formal entries, which should make it easier for you to learn the most important aspects of recording journal entries. The way we would show the journal entry for August 5 is

d	dr **Equipment** (+A)	18,000	
	cr **Cash** (−A)...		16,000
	cr **Accounts Payable** (+L)..		2,000

Note the main differences between our simplified format and a formal journal entry:
- When a date is not given, use some form of reference for each trans-action, such as (d), to identify the event.
- Omit the reference column and transaction explanation to simplify the entry.
- Indicate whether you are debiting (dr) or crediting (cr) each account. This will help to reinforce the debit/credit framework shown in Exhibit 2.7. Plus, it will make it easier to interpret journal entries when indents are not clear (sometimes an issue in handwritten homework).
- Include the appropriate account type (A, L, or SE) along with the direction of the effect (+ or −) next to each account title to clarify the effects of the transaction on each account. Again, this will rein-force the debit/credit framework and help you to determine whether the accounting equation has remained in balance.

Step 3: Summarizing in Ledger Accounts

By themselves, journal entries show the effects of each individual transac-tion but they do not provide account balances. That's why ledger accounts are needed. After journal entries have been recorded (in step 2), their dollar amounts are transferred (a **posting**) to each ledger account affected by the transaction so that account balances can be computed. In most com-puterized accounting systems, this happens automatically. In homework assignments, you'll have to do it yourself, so Exhibit 2.9 shows you how this is done using the journal entry for August 5. If account numbers are provided, keep track of the posting of journal entries to general ledger accounts by writing the account number in the Ref. column of the journal and the journal page number in the Ref. column of the ledger.

As we did earlier for journal entries, we will use a simplified format for ledger accounts to make it easier to focus on their main features. The sim-plified version of a ledger account is called a **T−account**. Each T−account represents the debit and credit columns of a ledger account. Exhibit 2.10 shows the T−accounts for Pizza Palace's Equipment, Cash, and Accounts

Posting: The process of transferring details of journal entries into the correspond-ing ledger accounts.

T-Account: A simplified version of a ledger account used for summarizing the effects of journal entries.

EXHIBIT 2.9   Posting from the Journal to the Ledger

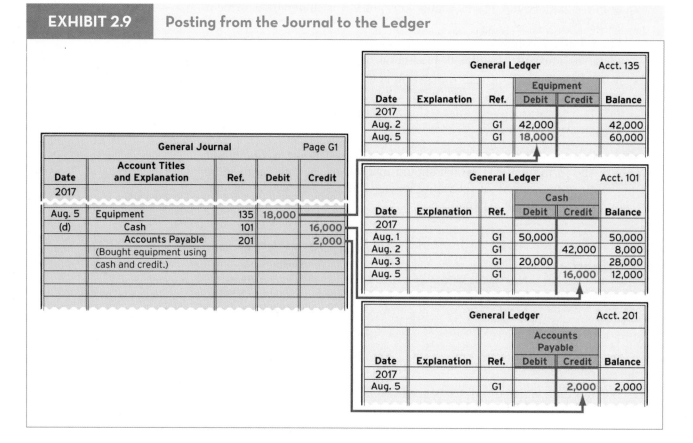

Payable based on transactions (a) through (d). It also shows how an indi—vidual journal entry's effects would be summarized in these T—accounts. The debit to Equipment in the journal entry is copied into the debit (left) side of its T—account. The credits to Cash and Accounts Payable are copied into the credit (right) side of those T—accounts. (If you've forgotten why the transaction is recorded this way, take a quick look back at Exhibit 2.7 or at the graphic below.)

EXHIBIT 2.10   Posting from a Simplified Journal Entry to T-Accounts

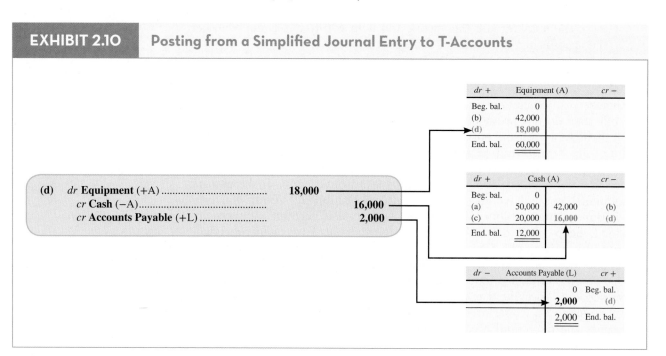

In Exhibit 2.10, notice the following:

- Every account starts with a begin‐ning balance, usually on the side where increases are summarized. For balance sheet accounts, the ending balance from the prior period is the beginning balance for the current period. Because Pizza Pal‐ace is in its first month of business, the beginning balance in each account is zero in this example.

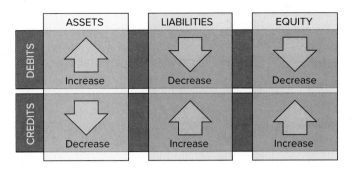

- Dollar signs are not needed in journal entries and T–accounts.

- Each amount is accompanied by a reference to the related journal entry, which makes it easy to trace back to the original transaction should errors occur.

- To find ending account balances, express the T–accounts as equations:

	Equipment	Cash	Accounts Payable
Beginning balance	0	0	0
Add: "+" side	42,000	+50,000	+2,000
	18,000	+20,000	
Subtract: "−" side		−42,000	
		−16,000	
Ending balance	60,000	12,000	2,000

COACH'S TIP

Assets normally end with a debit balance (because debits to assets normally exceed credits) and liabilities and shareholders' equity accounts normally end with credit balances (credits exceed debits).

Knowing how to use T–accounts in this way will help you answer homework questions that involve solving for missing values in accounts.

- The ending balance is double underlined to distinguish it from transactions and symbolize the final result of a computation. The ending balance is shown on the side that has the greater total dollar amount.

SPOTLIGHT ON Financial Reporting

The Ultimate Irony: Teacher Late with Report

K12 Inc. claims to be the leader in computer-based instruction for grades K through 12, yet it couldn't get its own computerized accounting systems working in time to meet an important financial reporting deadline. K12 admitted that it was struggling with "the integration of diverse accounting systems," and that it would be about a month late releasing its annual report.

The company explained that it had recently acquired several other companies that were using differ-ent computerized accounting systems. To ensure all of the transactions were accounted for properly, K12 needed extra time to conduct a thorough review of its systems. Investors weren't comforted by this explanation and reacted by selling their shares of K12, causing a drop in the company's stock price. Meeting deadlines is as important in the business world as it is in academics.

Source: K12 Inc., "K12 Inc. Releases Selected Preliminary FY 2011 Financial Data and Announces Delay in Filing Annual Report," press release, 2011, www.sec.gov.

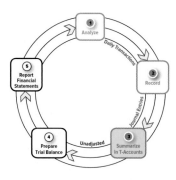

Pizza Palace Inc.'s Accounting Records

In this section, we will work with you to account for the transactions that were presented earlier in this chapter for Pizza Palace. Because we showed the *analyze* step in detail earlier, we do not show it in detail here. Instead, we pick up where step 1 left off—with the effects of each transaction on the accounting equation. By reviewing steps 2 and 3 of the accounting cycle in detail, you will be able to practise using the new concepts of debits, credits, journal entries, and T–accounts. Study the following examples carefully. The biggest mistake people make when first learning accounting is that they think they understand how it all works without actually going through enough examples. To understand accounting, you have to practise, practise, practise, as if you're learning to play a new sport or a musical instrument.

(a) **Issue Shares to Owners.** Emilio Santos incorporates Pizza Palace Inc. on August 1. The company issues shares to Emilio and his wife as evidence of their contribution of $50,000 cash, which is deposited in the company's bank account.

1 Analyze

	Assets	=	Liabilities	+	Shareholders' Equity	
(a) Cash	+50,000	=			Contributed Capital	+50,000

2 Record

(a)	*dr* Cash (+A)	50,000	
	cr Contributed Capital (+SE).............................		50,000

3 Summarize

dr +	Cash (A)	*cr* −		*dr* −	Contributed Capital (SE)	*cr* +
Beg. bal.	0				0	Beg. bal.
(a)	50,000				50,000	(a)

(b) **Invest in Equipment.** Pizza Palace pays $42,000 cash to buy restaurant booths and other equipment.

1 Analyze

	Assets		=	Liabilities	+	Shareholders' Equity
(b) Cash		−42,000	=			
Equipment		+42,000				

2 Record

(b)	*dr* Equipment (+A)	42,000	
	cr Cash (−A)		42,000

3 Summarize

dr +	Cash (A)	*cr* −		*dr* +	Equipment (A)	*cr* −
Beg. bal.	0			Beg. bal.	0	
(a)	50,000	42,000	(b)	(b)	42,000	

(c) **Obtain Loan from Bank.** Pizza Palace borrows $20,000 from a bank, depositing those funds in its bank account and signing a formal agreement to repay the loan in two years.

1 Analyze

Assets		=	Liabilities		+	Shareholders' Equity
(c) Cash	+20,000	=	Note Payable	+20,000		

2 Record

(c)	dr **Cash** (+A)	20,000	
	cr **Note Payable** (+L)		20,000

3 Summarize

dr +	Cash (A)		cr −		dr −	Note Payable (L)		cr +
Beg. bal.	0						0	Beg. bal.
(a)	50,000	42,000	(b)				20,000	(c)
(c)	20,000							

(d) **Invest in Equipment.** Pizza Palace purchases $18,000 in pizza ovens and other restaurant equipment, paying $16,000 in cash and giving an informal promise to pay $2,000 at the end of the month.

1 Analyze

Assets		=	Liabilities		+	Shareholders' Equity
(d) Cash	−16,000	=	Accounts Payable	+2,000		
Equipment	+18,000					

2 Record

(d)	dr **Equipment** (+A)	18,000	
	cr **Cash** (−A)		16,000
	cr **Accounts Payable** (+L)		2,000

3 Summarize

dr +	Cash (A)		cr −		dr +	Equipment (A)	cr −		dr −	Accounts Payable (L)	cr +
Beg. bal.	0				Beg. bal.	0					0 Beg. bal.
(a)	50,000	42,000	(b)		(b)	42,000					2,000 (d)
(c)	20,000	16,000	(d)		(d)	18,000					

(e) **Order Cookware.** Pizza Palace orders $630 of pans, dishes, and other cookware. None have been received yet. Because this event involves the exchange of only promises, it is not considered a transaction. No journal entry is needed.

(f) Pay Supplier. Pizza Palace pays $2,000 to the equipment supplier in (d).

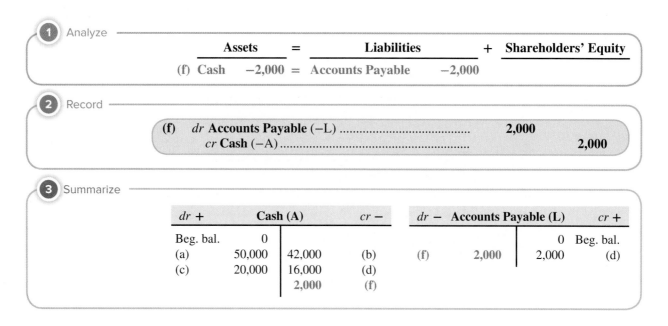

(g) Receive Cookware. Pizza Palace receives $630 of the cookware ordered in (e) and promises to pay for it next month.

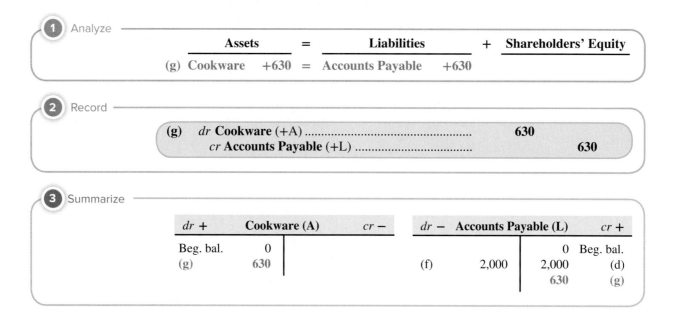

Prepare a trial balance and a classified balance sheet.

Trial balance: An internal report that lists all accounts and their balances to check on the equality of total recorded debits and total recorded credits.

Exhibit 2.11 summarizes the journal entries and T−accounts affected by events (a) through (g) for Pizza Palace. It also reports the ending bal−ances for each account.

PREPARING A TRIAL BALANCE AND BALANCE SHEET

The next step in the accounting cycle is to prepare an internal accounting report called a **trial balance**. It checks that the accounting records are in balance by determining whether debits = credits. If total debits don't equal total credits, the balance sheet will not balance. The trial balance lists the

EXHIBIT 2.11   Journal Entries and T-Accounts for Pizza Palace

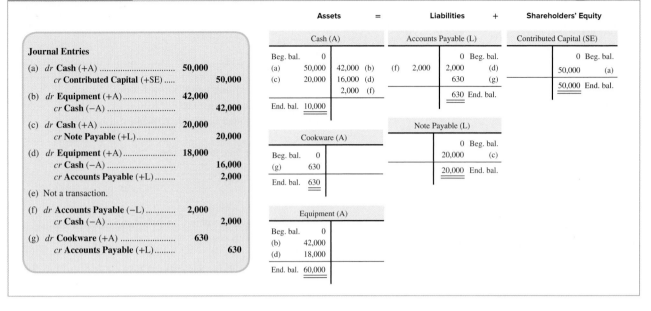

ending balance in every T–account and then computes total debits and total credits, as shown in Exhibit 2.12. Because the column totals are equal, Pizza Palace's balance sheet can be prepared.

Exhibit 2.13 shows Pizza Palace's balance sheet based on the transactions in this chapter. The balance sheet is prepared by taking the ending balances for each account in the trial balance and grouping them as assets, liabilities, and shareholders' equity in balance sheet format. We've used a balance sheet format in Exhibit 2.13 called the **classified balance sheet**. A classified bal–ance sheet contains subcategories for assets and liabilities labelled *current*. **Current assets** are assets the business will use up or turn into cash within

Classified balance sheet: A balance sheet that classifies current assets and current liabilities separately from long-term assets and long-term liabilities.

EXHIBIT 2.12   Trial Balance for Pizza Palace

PIZZA PALACE INC.
Trial Balance
At August 31, 2017

	Debit	Credit
Cash	10,000	
Cookware	630	
Equipment	60,000	
Accounts Payable		630
Note Payable		20,000
Contributed Capital		50,000
Totals	70,630	70,630

Trial balance provides a check on debits = credits equality

Ending balances in T-accounts in Exhibit 2.11

EXHIBIT 2.13 Classified Balance Sheet

PIZZA PALACE INC. Balance Sheet At August 31, 2017		Explanation of Classification
		Who: Name of business What: Title of the statement When: Point in time
Assets		
Current Assets		Current assets are expected to be used up or turned into cash within 12 months.
Cash	$10,000	Cash in the company's bank account to be used up.
Cookware	630	Pizza pans and dishes will likely be used up or replaced before August 31, 2018.
Total Current Assets	10,630	
Equipment	60,000	Ovens and restaurant booths will be used for many years.
Total Assets	$70,630	
Liabilities and Shareholders' Equity		
Current Liabilities		Current liabilities will be paid or fulfilled within 12 months.
Accounts Payable	$ 630	Amounts owed to suppliers are usually paid within one or two months.
Total Current Liabilities	630	
Note Payable	20,000	The promissory note is not to be repaid until September 1, 2019.
Total Liabilities	20,630	
Shareholders' Equity		
Contributed Capital	50,000	Shareholders' equity accounts are not classified as current or noncurrent.
Retained Earnings	0	
Total Shareholders' Equity	50,000	
Total Liabilities and Shareholders' Equity	$70,630	

Current assets: Expected to be used up or converted into cash within 12 months of the balance sheet date.

Current liabilities: (1) Debts and obligations that are expected to be paid, settled, or fulfilled within twelve months of the balance sheet date. (2) Short-term obligations that will be paid with current assets within the current operating cycle or one year, whichever is longer.

Non-current: Assets and liabilities that do not meet the definition of current. Also described as long-term.

12 months of the balance sheet date. **Current liabilities** are debts and other obligations that will be paid or fulfilled within 12 months of the balance sheet date.

In our example, Accounts Payable is the only current liability. The other liability—Note Payable—is expected to be paid in two years, so it is considered **non—current**. Most companies list assets in order of liquidity (how soon they will be used up or turned into cash) and liabilities in order of maturity (how soon they will be paid in cash or fulfilled by providing a service). Refer to the Spotlight on IFRS and ASPE, which discusses the presentation differences between ASPE and IFRS.

Like Pizza Palace's Equipment and Note Payable accounts, its share—holders' equity accounts are understood to be long—term in nature, although they are not labelled as such. Exhibit 2.13 includes the Retained Earnings account in shareholders' equity despite its zero balance because we don't want you to forget about this account. It will become a key link to the income statement, when this is introduced in Chapter 3.

Evaluate the Results

Interpret the balance sheet using the current ratio and an understanding of related concepts.

ASSESSING THE ABILITY TO PAY

The classified balance sheet format makes it easy to see whether current assets are sufficient to pay current liabilities. In Pizza Palace's case, $10,630 of current assets is greater than the $630 of current liabilities, making it obvious that the company's current assets are sufficient to cover its current liabilities.

The only problem with looking at total dollar amounts is the difficulty in comparing them across companies. It is far easier to express the relationship as a ratio, by dividing current assets by current liabilities. This calculation is known as the *current ratio*. It is used to evaluate liquidity, which is the ability to pay liabilities as they come due in the short run. Generally speaking, a high current ratio suggests good liquidity. Pizza Palace's current ratio ($10,630 ÷ $630 = 16.9) is unusually high. Current ratios typically vary from 1.0 to 2.0. Recently, Yum! Brands, Inc.'s current ratio was 0.55, as shown below.

ACCOUNTING DECISION TOOLS

Name of Measure	Formula	What It Tells You
Current ratio	$\dfrac{\text{Current Assets}}{\text{Current Liabilities}}$	• Whether current assets are sufficient to pay current liabilities • A higher ratio means better ability to pay

SPOTLIGHT ON Financial Reporting

Balance Sheet and Current Ratio Example

Yum! Brands, Inc. is the world's largest restaurant company, well known for its brands such as KFC, Taco Bell, and Pizza Hut. Yum! Brands is significantly larger than Pizza Palace, but the structure of its balance sheet and its account titles are quite similar. Its current ratio is typical of many large companies.

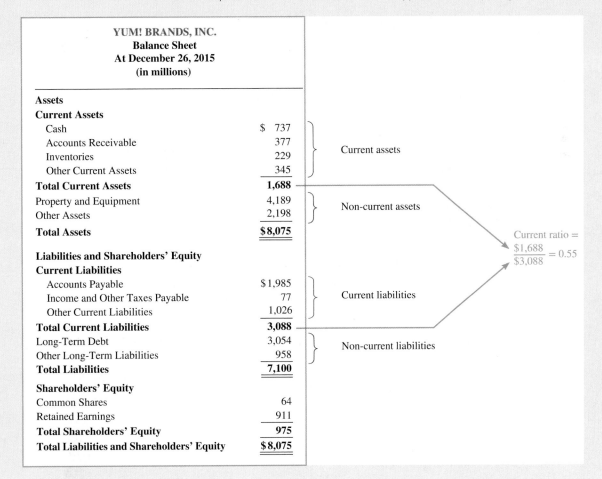

YUM! BRANDS, INC.
Balance Sheet
At December 26, 2015
(in millions)

Assets		
Current Assets		
Cash	$ 737	Current assets
Accounts Receivable	377	
Inventories	229	
Other Current Assets	345	
Total Current Assets	**1,688**	
Property and Equipment	4,189	Non-current assets
Other Assets	2,198	
Total Assets	**$8,075**	
Liabilities and Shareholders' Equity		
Current Liabilities		
Accounts Payable	$1,985	Current liabilities
Income and Other Taxes Payable	77	
Other Current Liabilities	1,026	
Total Current Liabilities	**3,088**	
Long-Term Debt	3,054	Non-current liabilities
Other Long-Term Liabilities	958	
Total Liabilities	**7,100**	
Shareholders' Equity		
Common Shares	64	
Retained Earnings	911	
Total Shareholders' Equity	**975**	
Total Liabilities and Shareholders' Equity	**$8,075**	

$$\text{Current ratio} = \frac{\$1,688}{\$3,088} = 0.55$$

BALANCE SHEET CONCEPTS AND VALUES

The purpose of a balance sheet is to report what a company owns and owes, but not necessarily what the company is worth. Some people mistakenly believe that the balance sheet reports a company's current value. To them, this is not a crazy idea because the balance sheet lists a company's assets and liabilities, so the net difference between the two must be the company's worth. In fact, *net worth* is a term that many accountants and analysts use when referring to shareholders' equity. So why is it wrong to think that the balance sheet reports a company's current value?

The answer comes from knowing that accounting is based on recording and reporting transactions, as you have seen over and over in this chapter. This focus on transactions does two things to the balance sheet: (1) it affects what is (and is not) recorded, and (2) it affects the amounts assigned to recorded items.

1. **What is (and is not) recorded?**
   Measurable exchanges, such as a purchase of ovens, are recorded. Pizza Palace's gourmet pizza recipes, on the other hand, were not acquired in an exchange, so they are not listed on the balance sheet.

2. **What amounts are assigned to recorded items?**
   Following the cost principle, assets and liabilities are first recorded at the amounts that were measurable at the time that transactions occurred. Later, if an asset's value increases (known as its fair market value), the increase is generally not recorded under ASPE. However, if an asset's value falls, it is generally reported at that lower value. Thus, the amount reported on the balance sheet may not be the asset's current value.

In order to determine the value of a company, fair market values must be considered. As was just mentioned, some of these adjustments to fair

---

SPOTLIGHT ON Financial Reporting

Current Ratios Before and After a Financial Crisis

During 2008, companies experienced a crisis unlike anything since the Great Depression of the 1930s. Financial institutions, such as Lehman Brothers, had collapsed or were on the verge of collapse. Consequently, banks became ultra-conservative and stopped lending to one another, which severely limited the amount of cash available to lend to businesses. The best way for a company to survive this credit crisis was to have a strong balance sheet, which meant having lots of cash and other current assets relative to the amount of liabilities owed.

The graph at the right shows the current ratios of three large pizza companies before and after the financial crisis. Notice how both Papa John's and Domino's Pizza significantly increased their ratios of current assets to current liabilities soon after the financial crisis began in the fall of 2008. California Pizza Kitchen did not follow this same path. After four years of declining financial results, California Pizza was sold to a private company in 2011.

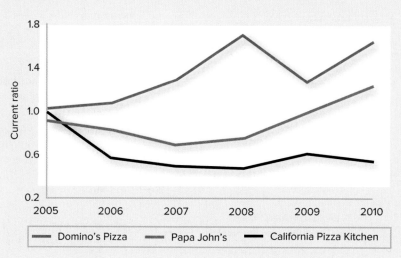

---

market value are not recorded under ASPE, and therefore the balance sheet data alone is not enough to value a company. It is a good starting point, however, because the balance sheet itself details the current snapshot of the assets and liabilities of the company, but doesn't take into account any future economic factors or the possibility of future profitability.

Summary of the Accounting Cycle

To show that the accounting process explained in this chapter can apply to any business, Exhibit 2.14 illustrates it for a fictitious construction company.

EXHIBIT 2.14	Summary of the Accounting Cycle

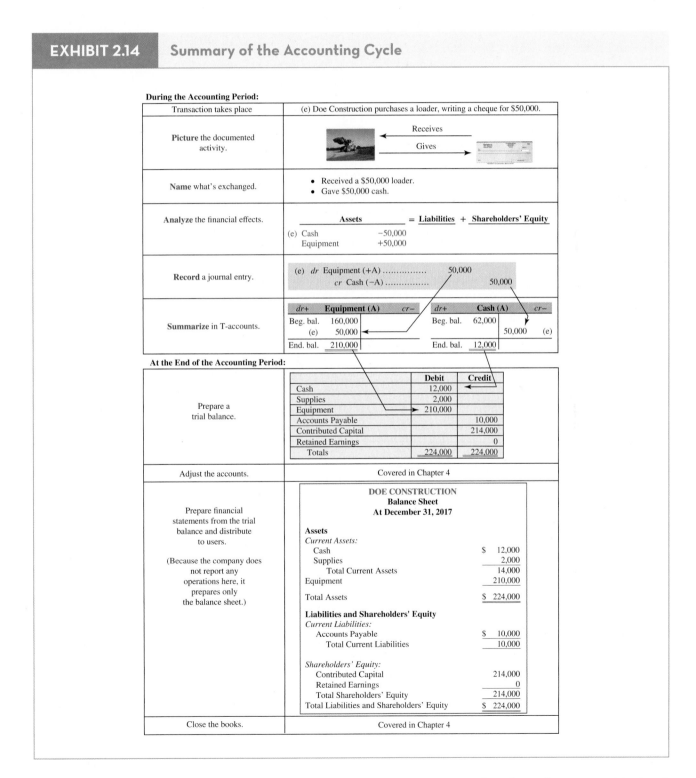

During the Accounting Period:

Transaction takes place	(e) Doe Construction purchases a loader, writing a cheque for $50,000.
Picture the documented activity.	Receives / Gives
Name what's exchanged.	• Received a $50,000 loader. • Gave $50,000 cash.
Analyze the financial effects.	Assets = Liabilities + Shareholders' Equity (e) Cash −50,000 Equipment +50,000
Record a journal entry.	(e) *dr* Equipment (+A) .... 50,000 *cr* Cash (−A) 50,000
Summarize in T-accounts.	*dr+* Equipment (A) *cr−* *dr+* Cash (A) *cr−* Beg. bal. 160,000 Beg. bal. 62,000 (e) 50,000 50,000 (e) End. bal. 210,000 End. bal. 12,000

At the End of the Accounting Period:

		Debit	Credit
Prepare a trial balance.	Cash	12,000	
	Supplies	2,000	
	Equipment	210,000	
	Accounts Payable		10,000
	Contributed Capital		214,000
	Retained Earnings		0
	Totals	224,000	224,000

Adjust the accounts.	Covered in Chapter 4

Prepare financial statements from the trial balance and distribute to users. (Because the company does not report any operations here, it prepares only the balance sheet.)	**DOE CONSTRUCTION** **Balance Sheet** **At December 31, 2017** **Assets** *Current Assets:* Cash $ 12,000 Supplies 2,000 Total Current Assets 14,000 Equipment 210,000 Total Assets $ 224,000 **Liabilities and Shareholders' Equity** *Current Liabilities:* Accounts Payable $ 10,000 Total Current Liabilities 10,000 *Shareholders' Equity:* Contributed Capital 214,000 Retained Earnings 0 Total Shareholders' Equity 214,000 Total Liabilities and Shareholders' Equity $ 224,000

Close the books.	Covered in Chapter 4

As International Financial Reporting Standards (IFRS) are adopted around the world, the three-step transaction analysis process in this chapter becomes even more important. In contrast to GAAP in the U.S., which explains accounting rules in detail, ASPE and IFRS are less detailed and require more judgment when analyzing transactions. This difference in emphasis exists because IFRS standards are used across many different countries, where business practices and legal environments vary. By placing slightly more emphasis on general principles than on detailed rules, IFRS standards are more easily and broadly applied around the world.

Differences Between ASPE and IFRS

As discussed earlier in this chapter, a private entity will distinguish between current and non-current assets and liabilities on the entity's balance sheet. Under IFRS, a public company has a choice as to how the company's balance sheet is presented. A public company can present its assets and liabilities, with current followed by non-current on the balance sheet, except when the presentation based on liquidity would provide more reliable and relevant information. In the latter case, the company would then present all assets and liabilities in the order of liquidity.

Also discussed in this chapter was the cost principle, where assets and liabilities should be originally recorded at the initial cost to the company. If the asset's value increases, ASPE does not allow companies to record this increase. Under IFRS, a public company has the option of recording an asset at cost using the cost model, or it can choose to use the revaluation model.

The revaluation model under IFRS allows a company to report property, plant, and equipment assets at their fair value at the date of the revaluation, as long as the fair value can be measured reliably. Fair value of an asset is considered to be the price that could be received upon selling that asset. So, in other words, the company can record the asset's increases and decreases in value from one revaluation date to the next. See the Spotlight on IFRS and ASPE in Chapter 9 for more details.

Supplement 2A

ACCOUNTING CAREERS

Every business, government, and not—for—profit organization needs financial advice from an accountant. As shown in Exhibit 2S.1, accountants provide advice either as an employee in a single organization (private accounting) or in a CPA firm (public accounting). Because accounting is in great demand, it continues to be a popular career choice for college graduates.

Accountants may pursue a variety of certifications, including the CPA (Chartered Professional Accountant), CFE (Certified Fraud Examiner), CIA (Certified Internal Auditor), CFP (Certified Financial Planner), CFF (Certified in Financial Forensics), and CFA (Chartered Financial Analyst), among others. For additional information on accounting careers, certifications, salaries, and opportunities, visit www.cpacanada.ca, www.acfe.com, and www.chapters.theiia.org.

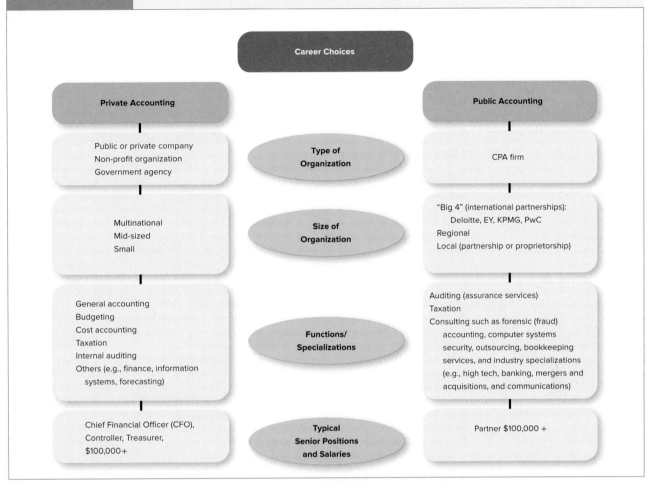

Collaborative Relationships Help Many

CPA Canada and AFOA Canada (formerly Aboriginal Financial Officers Association of Canada) have come together to explore ways that the two organizations can bring value to their members.

AFOA Canada is a membership-driven organization and was founded as a not-for-profit association in 1999. The organization supports Aboriginal professionals to manage and govern their communities and organizations with a focus on enhancing finance, management, and leadership practices and skills. It is the only organization in Canada that focuses on the capacity development and day-to-day needs of those Aboriginal professionals who are working in all of these areas.

CPA Canada will be providing Aboriginal professionals with an efficient pathway to the new CPA Canada Advanced Certificate in Accounting and Finance (ACAF). ACAF is an online education program created for students looking for junior and intermediate careers in accounting and finance. CPA Canada will also work to integrate some course material from its ACAF program into the Certified Aboriginal Financial Manager (CAFM) curriculum. This will provide CAFM students with an accelerated route to obtain the ACAF.

CPA Canada will also be looking for opportunities to increase exposure of its members and students to Indigenous culture and history through professional development and education programs. The CAFM designation includes a module on Aboriginal history and culture that could be used to educate CPAs and students who work with Aboriginal communities.

Source: https://www.cpacanada.ca/en/connecting-and-news/news/media-centre/2016/february/mou-afoa

Review the Chapter

This section provides a chance to solidify your understanding of key points. It's worth your time to work through the following demonstration case, scan the chapter summary, test your understanding of key terms, and then practise, practise, practise.

DEMONSTRATION CASE

eXcel

On April 1, 2017, three university students started Goodbye Grass Corporation (GGC). A summary of GGC's transactions completed through April 30, 2017, follows:

a. Issued shares to the three investors in exchange for cash contributions totalling $9,000.
b. Acquired rakes and other hand tools (equipment) for $600, paying the hardware store $200 cash and agreeing informally to pay the balance in three months.
c. Ordered lawn mowers and edgers costing $4,000 from XYZ Lawn Supply, Inc.
d. Purchased four hectares of land for the future site of a storage garage. Paid cash, $5,000.
e. Received the mowers and edgers that had been ordered and signed a promissory note to pay XYZ Lawn Supply in full in sixty days.
f. Sold for $1,250 one hectare of land to the city for a park and accepted a note from the city indicating payment would be received by GGC in six months.
g. One of the owners borrowed $3,000 from a local bank for personal use.

Required:

1. Analyze each event to determine its effects on the accounting equation.
2. Prepare journal entries to record transactions listed above (omit explanations).
3. Set up T—accounts for Cash, Note Receivable (from the city), Equipment (hand tools and mowing equipment), Land, Accounts Payable (to hardware store), Note Payable (to equipment supply company), and Contributed Capital. Indicate the beginning balances of $0 in each T—account, and then summarize the effects of each journal entry in the appropriate T—accounts. Determine the ending balance in each account.
4. Use the amounts in the T—accounts developed in requirement 3 to prepare a trial balance in order to ensure that the total dollar value of debits equals the total dollar value of cred—its for the ending balances of these T—accounts.

5. Use the trial balance developed in requirement 4 to prepare a classified balance sheet for Goodbye Grass Corporation at April 30, 2017. Show the balances for all assets, liabilities, and shareholders' equity accounts.

6. As of April 30, 2017, has financing for GGC's assets come primarily from liabilities or shareholders' equity?

7. Use the necessary information from the classified balance sheet developed in requirement 5 to calculate the current ratio for GGC as of April 30, 2017. Evaluate GGC's liquidity and explain how this could potentially impact GGC's suppliers and creditors.

Suggested Solution

1. Analyze the transactions:

	Assets				=	Liabilities		+ Stockholders' Equity
	Cash	Note Receivable	Equipment	Land	=	Accounts Payable	Notes Payable	Contributed Capital
(a)	+9,000				=			+9,000
(b)	−200		+600		=	+400		
(c)		No change*			=			No change
(d)	−5,000			+5,000	=			No change
(e)			+4,000		=		+4,000	
(f)	+1,250			−1,250	=			No change
(g)		No change**			=			No change

*Event (c) is not considered a transaction because it involves only the exchange of promises. **Event (g) is not considered a transaction of the company because the separate entity assumption (from Chapter 1) states that transactions of the owners are separate from transactions of the business.

2. Record the journal entries:

(a)	dr Cash (+A)	9,000	
	cr Contributed Capital (+SE)		9,000
(b)	dr Equipment (+A)	600	
	cr Cash (−A)		200
	cr Accounts Payable (+L)		400
(c)	This is not an accounting transaction, so a journal entry is not needed.		
(d)	dr Land (+A)	5,000	
	cr Cash		5,000
(e)	dr Equipment (+A)	4,000	
	cr Note Payable (+L)		4,000
(f)	dr Note Receivable (+A)	1,250	
	cr Land (−L)		1,250
(g)	This is not a transaction of the business, so a journal entry is not needed.		

3. Summarize journal entries in T−accounts:

Assets = **Liabilities** + **Shareholders' Equity**

Cash (A)

Beg. bal.	0		
(a)	9,000	200	(b)
		5,000	(d)
End. bal.	3,800		

Equipment (A)

Beg. bal.	0		
(b)	600		
(e)	4,000		
End. bal.	4,600		

Accounts Payable (L)

		0	Beg. bal.
		400	(b)
		400	End. bal.

Contributed Capital (SE)

		0	Beg. bal.
		9,000	(a)
		9,000	End. bal.

Note Receivable (A)

Beg. bal.	0		
(f)	1,250		
End. bal.	1,250		

Land (A)

Beg. bal.	0		
(d)	5,000	1,250	(f)
End. bal.	3,750		

Note Payable (L)

		0	Beg. bal.
		4,000	(e)
		4,000	End. bal.

4. Prepare a trial balance from the ending balances in the T–accounts:

GOODBYE GRASS CORPORATION
Trial Balance
At April 30, 2017

	Debit	Credit
Cash	3,800	
Note Receivable	1,250	
Equipment	4,600	
Land	3,750	
Accounts Payable		400
Note Payable		4,000
Contributed Capital		9,000
Totals	13,400	13,400

5. Prepare a classified balance sheet from the trial balance:

GOODBYE GRASS CORPORATION
Balance Sheet
At April 30, 2017

Assets		Liabilities	
Current Assets		Current Liabilities	
Cash	$ 3,800	Accounts Payable	$ 400
Note Receivable	1,250	Note Payable	4,000
Total Current Assets	5,050	Total Current Liabilities	4,400
Equipment	4,600		
Land	3,750	**Stockholders' Equity**	
		Contributed Capital	9,000
		Retained Earnings	0
		Total Stockholders' Equity	9,000
Total Assets	$13,400	Total Liabilities and Stockholders' Equity	$13,400

6. The primary source of financing for GGC's assets (totalling $13,400) has come from shareholders' equity ($9,000) rather than from liabilities ($4,400).

7. $\text{Current Ratio} = \dfrac{\text{Current Assets}}{\text{Current Liabilities}}$

$= \dfrac{5,050}{4,400}$

$= 1.15$

GGC's current ratio is 1.15 and greater than 1, which indicates that the company's assets are greater than its liabilities. This suggests good liquidity and would convey to existing and potential suppliers and creditors that GGC is able to pay its liabil–ities as they become due. This, in turn, represents lower risk involved for suppliers and creditors with respect to lending money to GGC. This is attractive for any new suppliers or creditors that GGC would like to do business with in the future.

CHAPTER SUMMARY

LO2-1 **Identify financial effects of common business activities that impact the balance sheet.**

- Financing activities involve debt transactions with lenders (e.g., Notes Payable) and equity transactions with investors (e.g., Contributed Capital).

- Investing activities involve buying and selling long–term assets (e.g., Buildings, Equipment).
- Operating activities involve day–to–day transactions with suppliers, employees, and customers, and typically affect current assets and current liabilities.

Apply transaction analysis to accounting transactions. LO2-2

- Transactions include external exchanges and internal events.
- Transaction analysis is based on the duality of effects and the basic accounting equation. *Duality of effects* means that every transaction affects at least two accounts.
- Transaction analysis follows a systematic approach: picturing the documented business activity; naming the assets, liabilities, or shareholders' equity that are exchanged; and analyzing the financial effects on the basic accounting equation.

Use journal entries and T-accounts to show how transactions affect the balance sheet. LO2-3

- *Debit* means left and *credit* means right.
- Debits increase assets and decrease liabilities and shareholders' equity.
- Credits decrease assets and increase liabilities and shareholders' equity.
- Journal entries express, in debits–equal–credits form, the effects of a transaction on various asset, liability, and shareholders' equity accounts. Journal entries are used to record financial information in the accounting system, which is later summarized by accounts in the ledger (T–accounts).
- T–accounts are a simplified version of the ledger, which summarizes transaction effects for each account. T–accounts show increases on the left (debit) side for assets, which are on the left side of the accounting equation. T–accounts show increases on the right (credit) side for liabilities and shareholders' equity, which are on the right side of the accounting equation.

Prepare a trial balance and a classified balance sheet. LO2-4

- A *trial balance* checks on the equality of debit and credit balances.
- A *classified balance sheet* separately classifies assets as current if they will be used up or turned into cash within one year. Liabilities are classified as current if they will be paid, settled, or fulfilled within one year.

Interpret the balance sheet using the current ratio and an understanding of related concepts. LO2-5

- The current ratio divides current assets by current liabilities to determine the extent to which current assets are likely to be sufficient for paying current liabilities.
- Because accounting is transaction based, the balance sheet does not necessarily represent the current value of a business.
- The amounts recorded for assets and liabilities may not represent current values because under the cost principle they generally are recorded at cost, using the exchange amounts established at the time of the initial transaction.

ACCOUNTING DECISION TOOLS

Name of Measure	Formula	What It Tells You
Current ratio	$\dfrac{\text{Current Assets}}{\text{Current Liabilities}}$	• Whether current assets are sufficient to pay current liabilities • A higher ratio means better ability to pay

Solution to SP2.1

Nike has received equipment costing $500,000.
Nike gave $200,000 cash and a $300,000 note.

Assets		=	Liabilities		+	Shareholders' Equity
Cash	−200,000	=	Note	+300,000		
Equipment	+500,000		Payable			

KEY TERMS

Assets	Debit	Posting
Chart of Accounts	Journal Entries	Shareholders' Equity
Classified Balance Sheet	Journals	T−account
Cost Principle	Ledger	Transactions
Credit	Liabilities	Trial Balance
Current Assets	Non−current	

Complete definitions are also provided in the glossary at the end of this text.

HOMEWORK HELPER

Account Name	Description
Assets	
Cash	Includes cash in the bank and in the cash register
Short−term Investments	Investments in government securities and certificates of deposit
Accounts Receivable	The right to collect from customers for prior sales on credit
Interest Receivable	The right to collect interest from others
Inventories	Goods on hand that are being held for resale
Supplies	Items on hand that will be used to make goods or provide services
Prepaid Insurance	Amount paid to obtain insurance covering future periods
Prepaid Rent	Amount paid for rent relating to future periods
Notes Receivable	Amounts loaned to others under a formal agreement (Note)
Land	Cost of land to be used by the business
Buildings	Cost of buildings the business will use for operations
Equipment	Cost of equipment used to produce goods or provide services
Software	Cost of purchased computer programs and code
Intangible Assets	Trademarks, brand names, goodwill, and other assets that lack a physical presence
Liabilities	
Accounts Payable	Amounts owed to suppliers for goods or services bought on credit
Wages Payable	Amounts owed to employees for salaries, wages, and bonuses
Accrued Liabilities	Amounts owed to others for advertising, utilities, interest, etc.
Deferred Revenues	Amounts (customer deposits) received in advance of providing goods or services to customers

Notes Payable	Amounts borrowed from lenders; involves signing a promissory note
Interest Payable	Amount due on loans as the cost of borrowing
Bonds Payable	Amounts borrowed from lenders; involves issuance of bonds
Other Liabilities	A variety of liabilities with smaller balances
Shareholders' Equity	
Contributed Capital	Amount of cash (or other property) contributed in exchange for the company's shares
Retained Earnings	Amount of accumulated earnings not distributed as dividends

Alternative terms

- Shareholders' equity also can be called *stockholders' equity*.
- The balance sheet also can be called the *statement of financial position*.

Helpful reminders

- It's easier to account for a transaction if you can accurately determine how it might affect Cash before determining its impact on other account(s).
- The word *pay* and the expression *purchase with cash* both imply a reduction in Cash.

Frequent mistakes

- When accounting for transactions, avoid thinking of yourself as the customer, investor, or creditor. Instead, put yourself in the position of the company you're accounting for.
- *Shareholders'* is plural; *shareholder's* is singular.

PRACTICE MATERIAL

QUESTIONS (⊖ Symbol indicates questions that require analysis from more than one perspective.)

1. Define the following:
   a. Asset
   b. Current Asset
   c. Liability
   d. Current Liability
   e. Contributed Capital
   f. Retained Earnings

2. Define a transaction and give an example of each of the two types of events that are considered to be transactions.

3. For accounting purposes, what is an account? Explain why accounts are used in an accounting system.

4. What is the basic accounting equation?

5. Explain what *debit* and *credit* mean.

6. Briefly explain what is meant by *transaction analysis*. What are the two principles underlying transaction analysis?

7. What two different accounting equalities must be maintained in transaction analysis?

8. What is a journal entry? What is the typical format of a journal entry?

9. What is a T—account? What is its purpose?

10. Explain the cost principle.

11. To obtain financing for her hair salon, Valeri asked you to prepare a balance sheet for her business. When she sees it, she is disappointed that the assets

exclude a value for her list of loyal customers. What can you tell her to explain why this "asset" has been excluded? Knowing this, what should she tell her banker when they meet next week? $

12. Is transaction analysis as important under IFRS as it is under ASPE? Why or why not?

MINI-EXERCISES

LO2-3 **M2-1 Identifying Increase and Decrease Effects on Balance Sheet Accounts**

Complete the following table by entering either *increases* or *decreases* in each column.

	Debit	Credit
Assets	_____	_____
Liabilities	_____	_____
Shareholders' Equity	_____	_____

LO2-3 **M2-2 Identifying Debit and Credit Effects on Balance Sheet Accounts**

Complete the following table by entering either the word *debit* or *credit* in each column.

	Debit	Credit
Assets	_____	_____
Liabilities	_____	_____
Shareholders' Equity	_____	_____

LO2-3, 2-3, 2-5 **M2-3 Matching Terms with Definitions**

Match each term with its related definition by entering the appropriate letter in the space provided. There should be only one definition per term (i.e., there are more definitions than terms).

Term	Definition
____ 1. Journal entry	A. An exchange or event that has a direct and measurable financial effect
____ 2. A = L + SE; Debits = Credits	B. Four periodic financial statements
____ 3. Transaction	C. The two equalities in accounting that aid in providing accuracy
____ 4. Liabilities	D. The results of transaction analysis in debits−equal−credits format
____ 5. Assets	E. The account that is debited when money is borrowed from a bank
____ 6. Income statement, balance sheet, statement of retained earnings, and statement of cash flows	F. A resource owned by a business, with measurable value and expected future benefits
	G. Cumulative earnings of a company that are not distributed to the owners
	H. Every transaction has at least two effects
	I. Amounts presently owed by a business
	J. Assigning dollar amounts to transactions

LO2-1, 2-4 **M2-4 Classifying Accounts on a Balance Sheet**

The following are a few of the accounts of Aim Delivery Corporation:

_____ 1. Wages Payable   _____ 8. Income Taxes Payable

_____ 2. Accounts Payable   _____ 9. Equipment

_____ 3. Accounts Receivable   _____ 10. Notes Payable (due in six months)

_____ 4. Buildings   _____ 11. Retained Earnings

_____ 5. Cash   _____ 12. Supplies

_____ 6. Contributed Capital   _____ 13. Utilities Payable

_____ 7. Land

In the space provided, classify each as it would be reported on a balance sheet. Use the following codes:

CA = Current Asset   CL = Current Liability   SE = Shareholders' Equity

NCA = Non−current Asset   NCL = Non−current Liability

M2-5 Identifying Accounts on a Classified Balance Sheet and Their Normal Debit or Credit Balances

LO2-1, 2-3, 2-4

According to a recent report of Hasbro, Inc., the company is "a worldwide leader in children's and family games and toys." Hasbro produces products under several brands including Tonka, Milton Bradley, Playskool, and Parker Brothers. The following are several of the accounts from a recent balance sheet:

_____ 1. Accounts Receivable   _____ 6. Property, Plant, and Equipment

_____ 2. Short−Term Bank Loan   _____ 7. Retained Earnings

_____ 3. Contributed Capital   _____ 8. Accounts Payable

_____ 4. Long−Term Debt   _____ 9. Cash

_____ 5. Income Taxes Payable

Required:

1. Indicate how each account normally should be categorized on a classified balance sheet. Use the following codes:

CA = Current Asset   CL = Current Liability   SE = Shareholders' Equity

NCA = Non−current Asset   NCL = Non−current Liability

2. Indicate whether the account normally has a debit or credit balance.

M2-6 Identifying Accounts on a Classified Balance Sheet and Their Normal Debit or Credit Balances

LO2-1, 2-3, 2-4

Netflix, Inc. is the world's leading Internet subscription service for movies and TV shows, with more than 20 million members. The following are several of the accounts included in a recent balance sheet:

_____ 1. Accrued Liabilities   _____ 5. Long−Term Debt

_____ 2. Prepaid Rent   _____ 6. Property and Equipment

_____ 3. Cash   _____ 7. Retained Earnings

_____ 4. Contributed Capital   _____ 8. Accounts Payable

Required:

1. Indicate how each account normally should be categorized on a classified balance sheet. Use the following codes:

CA = Current Asset   CL = Current Liability   SE = Shareholders' Equity

NCA = Non−current Asset   NCL = Non−current Liability

2. Indicate whether the account normally has a debit or credit balance.

M2-7 Identifying Events as Accounting Transactions

Do the following events result in a recordable transaction for The Toro Company? Answer Yes or No for each. If you answered No, explain why.

_____ 1. Toro purchased robotic manufacturing equipment that it paid for by signing a Note Payable.

_____ 2. Toro's president purchased shares in another company for his own portfolio.

_____ 3. The company lent $550 to an employee.

_____ 4. Toro ordered supplies from Office Max to be delivered next week.

_____ 5. Six investors in Toro sold their shares to another investor.

_____ 6. The company borrowed $2,500,000 from a local bank.

M2-8 Identifying Events as Accounting Transactions

With forty locations in eight provinces, Discount Books is the country's favourite new—and—used bookstore chain. Do the following events result in a recordable transaction for Discount Books? Answer Yes or No for each.

_____ 1. Discount Books bought an old laundromat in Toronto.

_____ 2. The privately held company issued shares to new investors.

_____ 3. The company signed an agreement to rent store space in Columbia Plaza near Vancouver.

_____ 4. The company paid for renovations to prepare its Calgary store for operations.

_____ 5. The vice—president of the company spoke at a literacy luncheon in Saskatchewan, which contributed to building the company's reputation as a responsible company.

M2-9 Determining Financial Statement Effects of Several Transactions

For each of the following transactions of Spotlighter Inc. for the month of January, indicate the accounts, amounts, and direction of the effects on the accounting equation. The first transaction (*a*) has been completed for you.

a. Borrowed $3,940 from a local bank on a note due in six months

b. Received $4,630 cash from investors and issued shares to them

c. Purchased $920 in equipment, paying $190 cash and promising the rest on a note due in one year

d. Paid $372 cash for supplies

e. Bought $700 of supplies on account

	Assets	=	Liabilities	+	Shareholders' Equity
(a)	Cash +3,940		Notes Payable +3,940		

M2-10 Preparing Journal Entries

For each of the transactions in M2–9 [including (*a*)], write the journal entry using the format shown in this chapter (omit explanations).

M2-11 Posting to T-Accounts

For each of the transactions in M2–9 [including (*a*)], post the effects to the appropriate T—accounts and determine ending account balances.

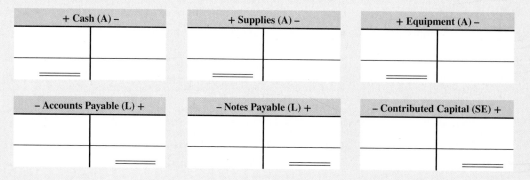

M2-12 Reporting a Classified Balance Sheet

Given the transactions in M2—9 [including (a)], prepare a classified balance sheet for Spotlighter Inc. as of January 31.

M2-13 Identifying Transactions and Preparing Journal Entries

J.K. Builders was incorporated on July 1. Prepare journal entries for the following events from the first month of business. If the event is not a transaction, write No Transaction.

a. Received $70,000 cash invested by owners and issued shares.

b. Bought an unused field from a local farmer by paying $60,000 cash. As a construction site for smaller projects, it is estimated to be worth $65,000 to J.K. Builders.

c. A lumber supplier delivered lumber supplies to J.K. Builders for future use. The lumber supplies would have normally sold for $10,000, but the supplier gave J.K. Builders a 10 percent discount. J.K. Builders has not yet received a bill from the supplier.

d. Borrowed $25,000 from the bank with a plan to use the funds to build a small workshop in August. The loan must be repaid in two years.

e. One of the owners sold $10,000 worth of his shares to another shareholder for $11,000.

M2-14 Determining Financial Statement Effects of Transactions

Analyze the accounting equation effects of the transactions in M2—13 using the format shown in the chapter, and compute total assets, total liabilities, and total shareholders' equity.

M2-15 Identifying Transactions and Preparing Journal Entries

Joel Henry founded JHenryBooks.com at the beginning of August, selling new and used books online. He is passionate about books, but does not have a lot of accounting experience. Help Joel by preparing journal entries for the following events. If the event is not a transaction, write No Transaction.

a. The company purchased equipment for $4,000 cash. The equipment is expected to be used for ten or more years.

b. Joel's business bought $7,000 worth of books from a publisher. The company will pay the publisher within 45 to 60 days.

c. Joel's friend Sam lent $4,000 to the business. Sam had Joel write a note promising that JHenryBooks.com would repay the $4,000 in four months. Because they are good friends, Sam is not going to charge Joel interest.

d. The company paid $1,500 cash for books purchased on account earlier in the month.

e. JHenryBooks.com repaid the $4,000 loan established in (c).

M2-16 Determining Financial Statement Effects of Transactions

Analyze the accounting equation effects of the transactions in M2—15 using the format shown in the chapter, and compute total assets, total liabilities, and total shareholders' equity.

M2-17 Identifying Transactions and Preparing Journal Entries

Sweet Shop Co. is a chain of candy stores that has been in operation for the past ten years. Prepare journal entries for the following events, which occurred at the end of the most recent year. If the event is not a transaction, write No Transaction.

a. Ordered and received $12,000 worth of cotton candy machines from Candy Makers Inc., which Sweet Shop Co. will pay for in forty—five days.

b. Sent a cheque for $6,000 to Candy Makers Inc. for the cotton candy machines from (a).

c. Received $400 from customers who bought candy on account in previous months.

d. To help raise funds for store upgrades estimated to cost $20,000, Sweet Shop Co. issued 1,000 shares for $15 each to existing shareholders.

e. Sweet Shop Co. bought ice cream trucks for $60,000 total, paying $10,000 cash and signing a long–term note for $50,000.

LO2-2, 2-4   **M2-18 Determining Financial Statement Effects of Transactions**

Analyze the accounting equation effects of the transactions in M2−17 using the format shown in the chapter, and compute total assets, total liabilities, and total shareholders' equity.

LO2-3   **M2-19 Identifying Transactions and Preparing Journal Entries**

Katy Williams is the manager of Blue Light Arcade. The company provides entertainment for parties and special events. Prepare journal entries for the following events relating to the year ended December 31. If the event is not a transaction, write No Transaction.

a. Blue Light Arcade received $50 cash on account for a birthday party held two months ago.

b. Agreed to hire a new employee at a monthly salary of $3,000. The employee starts work next month.

c. Paid $2,000 for a table–top hockey game purchased last month on account.

d. Repaid a $5,000 bank loan that had been outstanding for six months. (Ignore interest.)

e. The company purchased an air hockey table for $2,200, paying $1,000 cash and signing a short–term note for $1,200.

LO2-2, 2-4   **M2-20 Determining Financial Statement Effects of Transactions**

Analyze the accounting equation effects of the transactions in M2−19 using the format shown in the chapter, and compute total assets, total liabilities, and total shareholders' equity.

LO2-4   **M2-21 Ordering Current Assets and Current Liabilities Within a Classified Balance Sheet**

Charlie's Crispy Chicken (CCC) operates a fast–food restaurant. When accounting for its first year of business, CCC created several accounts. Using the following descriptions, prepare a classified balance sheet at September 30, 2017. Are CCC's current assets sufficient to be converted into cash to cover its current liabilities? How can you tell?

Account Name	Balance	Description
Accounts Payable	$ 2,000	Payment is due in 30 days
Bank Loan Payable	10,000	Payment is due in 2021
Cash	1,800	Includes cash in register and in bank account
Contributed Capital	20,000	Shares issued in exchange for owners' contributions
Food Ingredients	400	Includes frozen chicken, french fries, beverages, etc.
Kitchen Equipment	13,000	Includes deep fryers, microwaves, dishwasher, etc.
Kitchen Supplies	1,400	Includes serving trays, condiment dispensers, etc.
Land	8,900	Held for future site of new restaurant
Note Payable	15,000	Payment is due in 2023
Restaurant Booths	25,000	Likely to be used through 2027
Retained Earnings	3,000	Total earnings through September 30, 2017
Utilities Payable	300	Payment is due in 30 to 45 days
Wages Payable	200	Payment is due in 7 days

M2-22 Preparing a Classified Balance Sheet

The following accounts are taken from the financial statements of Knight Entertainments Resorts, Inc. at its September 30, 2017, year—end. (Amounts are in thousands.)

General Expenses	$ 48,735
Salaries Payable	22,082
Interest Expense	32,066
Accounts Payable	58,462
Other Current Liabilities	115,663
Food and Beverage Revenue	12,065
Cash	88,761
Accounts Receivable	56,777
Other Current Assets	283,692
Property and Equipment	1,647,050
Long—Term Note Payable	1,835,192
Contributed Capital	32
Retained Earnings	44,849

Required:

1. Prepare a classified balance sheet at September 30, 2017.

   TIP: This exercise requires you to remember material from Chapter 1. (Some of the above accounts are not reported on the balance sheet.)

2. Using the balance sheet, indicate whether the total assets of Knight Entertainments Resorts, Inc. at the end of the year were financed primarily by liabilities or by shareholders' equity.

3. Were the current assets sufficient to cover the current liabilities at September 30, 2017? Show the ratio and calculations that indicate this.

M2-23 Calculating and Interpreting the Current Ratio

LO2-5

The balance sheet of Robust Ribs Restaurant reports current assets of $30,000 and current liabilities of $15,000. Calculate and interpret the current ratio. Does it appear likely that Robust Ribs will be able to pay its current liabilities as they come due in the next year?

M2-24 Evaluating the Impact of Transactions on the Current Ratio

LO2-5

Refer to M2—23. Evaluate whether the current ratio of Robust Ribs Restaurant will increase or decrease as a result of the following transactions.

a. Paid $2,000 cash for a new oven

b. Borrowed $5,000 cash from a bank, issuing a note that must be repaid in three years

c. Received a $2,000 cash contribution from the company's main shareholder

d. Purchased $500 of napkins, paper cups, and other disposable supplies on account

M2-25 Analyzing the Impact of Transactions on the Current Ratio

LO2-5

BSO, Inc. has current assets of $1,000,000 and current liabilities of $500,000, resulting in a current ratio of 2.0. For each of the following transactions, determine whether the current ratio will increase, decrease, or remain the same. Consider each item, (a) to (d), independently of the others.

a. Purchased $20,000 of supplies on credit

b. Paid Accounts Payable in the amount of $50,000

c. Recorded $100,000 of cash contributed by a shareholder for common stock

d. Borrowed $250,000 from a local bank, to be repaid in 90 days

EXERCISES

LO2-1, 2-2, 2-3 **E2-1 Matching Terms with Definitions**

Match each term with its related definition by entering the appropriate letter in the space provided. There should be only one definition per term (but there are more definitions than terms).

Term	Definition
____ 1. Separate Entity Assumption	A. Economic resources to be used or turned into cash within one year
____ 2. Balance Sheet	B. Reports assets, liabilities, and shareholders' equity
____ 3. Current Assets	C. Decrease assets; increase liabilities and shareholders' equity
____ 4. Notes Payable	D. Increase assets; decrease liabilities and shareholders' equity
____ 5. Duality of Effects	E. Accounts for a business separate from its owners
____ 6. Retained Earnings	F. The two equalities in accounting that aid in providing accuracy
____ 7. Debit	G. A standardized format used to accumulate data about each item reported on financial statements
	H. The principle that assets should be recorded at their original cost to the company
	I. The account credited when money is borrowed from a bank using a promissory note
	J. Cumulative earnings of a company that are not distributed to the owners
	K. Every transaction has at least two effects

LO2-1, 2-2 **E2-2 Identifying Account Titles**

The following are independent situations.

a. A company orders and receives ten personal computers for office use, for which it signs a note promising to pay $25,000 within three months.

b. A company purchases for $21,000 cash a new delivery truck that has a list ("sticker") price of $24,000.

c. A women's clothing retailer orders thirty new display stands for $300 each for future delivery.

d. A new company is formed and issues 100 shares for $12 per share to investors.

e. A company purchases a piece of land for $50,000 cash. An appraiser for the buyer valued the land at $52,500.

f. The owner of a local company buys a $10,000 car for personal use. (When answering the questions below, consider this from the company's point of view.)

g. A company borrows $1,000 from a local bank and signs a six-month note for the loan.

h. A company pays $1,500 owed on its note payable. (Ignore interest.)

Required:

1. Indicate titles of the appropriate accounts, if any, affected in each of the above events. Consider what the company gives and receives.

2. At what amount would you record the delivery truck in (b)? The piece of land in (e)? What measurement principle are you applying?

3. What reasoning did you apply in (c)? For (f), what accounting concept did you apply?

E2-3 Classifying Accounts and Their Usual Balances

LO2-1, 2-3, 2-4

Digital Design Diversions, Inc. (DDDI) designs, develops, and distributes video games for computers and advanced game systems such as Playnation, Y–Box, and Yeee. DDDI has been operating for only one full year.

Required:

For each of the following accounts from DDDI's recent balance sheet, complete the following table. Indicate whether the account is classified as a current asset (CA), non–current asset (NCA), current liability (CL), non–current liability (NCL), or shareholders' equity (SE), and whether the account usually has a debit (dr) or credit (cr) balance.

Account	Balance Sheet Classification	Debit or Credit Balance
1. Land		
2. Retained Earnings		
3. Notes Payable (due in three years)		
4. Accounts Receivable		
5. Supplies		
6. Contributed Capital		
7. Equipment		
8. Accounts Payable		
9. Cash		
10. Taxes Payable		

E2-4 Determining Financial Statement Effects of Several Transactions

LO2-1, 2-2

The following events occurred at Favanta Company:

a. Received $10,000 cash from owners and issued shares to them

b. Borrowed $7,000 cash from a bank and signed a note due later this year

c. Purchased land for $12,000; paid $1,000 in cash and signed a note for $11,000

d. Bought and received $800 of equipment on account

e. Purchased $3,000 of equipment, paying $1,000 in cash and charged the rest on account

Required:

For each of the events (a) through (e), perform transaction analysis and indicate the account, amount, and direction of the effect (+ for increase and − for decrease) on the accounting equation. Check that the accounting equation remains in balance after each transaction. Use the following headings:

Event	Assets	=	Liabilities	+	Shareholders' Equity

E2-5 Determining Financial Statement Effects of Several Transactions

LO2-1, 2-3, 2-5

NIKE, Inc., with its Canadian headquarters in Thornhill, Ontario, is one of the world's leading manufacturers of athletic shoes and sports apparel. The following activities occurred during a recent year. The amounts are in millions of dollars.

a. Purchased $216 in equipment; paid by signing a $5 long–term note and fulfilling the rest with cash.

    b. Issued $21 in additional shares for cash contributions made by shareholders.

    c. Several Nike investors sold their own shares to other investors on the stock exchange for $110 per share.

Required:

1. For each of these events, perform transaction analysis and indicate the account, amount (in millions), and direction of the effect on the accounting equation. Check that the accounting equation remains in balance after each transaction. Use the following headings:

Event	Assets	=	Liabilities	+	Shareholders' Equity

2. Explain your response to transaction (*c*).

3. Did these transactions change the extent to which Nike relied on creditors versus shareholders for financing? Explain.

LO2-3

E2-6 Recording Investing and Financing Activities

Refer to E2–4.

Required:

For each of the events in E2–4, prepare journal entries, checking that debits equal credits.

LO2-3, 2-5

E2-7 Recording Investing and Financing Activities

Refer to E2–5.

Required:

1. For each of the events in E2–5, prepare journal entries, checking that debits equal credits.

2. Explain your response to event (*c*).

LO2-2, 2-3

E2-8 Analyzing the Effects of Transactions in T-Accounts

Harrigan Service Company, Inc. was incorporated by Ian Harrigan and five other managers. The following activities occurred during the year:

Check Figure:

Ending Cash
balance =
$57,000 Debit

    a. Received $60,000 cash from the managers; each was issued 1,000 shares

    b. Purchased equipment for use in the business at a cost of $12,000; one–fourth was paid in cash and the company signed a note for the balance (due in six months)

    c. Signed an agreement with a cleaning service to pay it $120 per week to clean the corporate offices, beginning next week

    d. Ian Harrigan borrowed $10,000 for personal use from a local bank, signing a one–year note

Required:

1. Create T–accounts for the following accounts: Cash, Equipment, Note Payable, and Contributed Capital. Beginning balances are zero. For each of the above transactions, record its effects in the appropriate T–accounts. Include referencing and totals for each T–account.

2. Using the balances in the T–accounts, fill in the following amounts for the accounting equation:

    Assets $ _____ = Liabilities $ _____ + Shareholders' Equity $ _____

3. Explain your response to events (*c*) and (*d*).

LO2-1, 2-2, 2-4

E2-9 Inferring Investing and Financing Transactions, and Preparing a Balance Sheet

During its first week of operations, January 1 to 7, 2017, Cosy Comfort Furniture Company completed six transactions with the dollar effects indicated in the following schedule:

	Assets			=	Liabilities	+	Shareholders' Equity
	Cash	Equipment	Land		Notes Payable		Contributed Capital
Beginning	$ 0	$ 0	$ 0	=	$ 0		$ 0
(a)	+12,000			=			+12,000
(b)	+50,000			=			+50,000
(c)	−4,000		+12,000	=	+8,000		
(d)	+4,000			=	+4,000		
(e)	−7,000	+7,000		=			
(f)			+3,000	=	+3,000		
Ending	$	$	$	=	$		$

Required:

1. Write a brief explanation of transactions (a) through (f). Explain any assumptions that you made.
2. Compute the ending balance in each account and prepare a classified balance sheet for Cosy Comfort Furniture Company on January 7, 2017.
3. As of January 7, 2017, has most of the financing for Cosy Comfort's investments in assets come from liabilities or shareholders' equity?

Check Figure:
Ending Notes
Payable balance =
$65,000 Credit

E2-10 Inferring Investing and Financing Transactions and Preparing a Balance Sheet

LO2-1, 2-2, 2-4

During its first month of operations, March 2017, Falla Fashions, Inc. completed four trans—actions with the dollar effects indicated in the following schedule:

DOLLAR EFFECT OF EACH OF THE FOUR TRANSACTIONS

Accounts	(a)	(b)	(c)	(d)	Ending Balance
Cash	$50,000	$(4,000)	$(5,000)	$(4,000)	
Computer Equipment				4,000	
Delivery Truck		25,000			
Short—Term Bank Loan				5,000	
Long—Term Notes Payable		21,000			
Contributed Capital	50,000				

Required:

1. Write a brief explanation of transactions (a) through (d). Explain any assumptions that you made.
2. Compute the ending balance in each account and prepare a classified balance sheet for Falla Fashions, Inc. at the end of March 2017.
3. As of March 31, 2017, has most of the financing for Falla's investment in assets come from liabilities or shareholders' equity?

E2-11 Analyzing Accounting Equation Effects, Recording Journal Entries, and Summarizing Financial Statement Impact

LO2-2, 2-3, 2-4

Rawlco Communications operates fifteen radio stations throughout the West. The following events are representative of those occurring during September.

a. Placed an order for office supplies costing $2,000; Supplier intends to deliver later in the month

b. Purchased equipment that cost $30,000; paid $10,000 cash and signed a promissory note to pay $20,000 in one month *c*. Negotiated and signed a one–year bank loan, and as a result, deposited $5,000 cash in the company's chequing account

d. Hired a new finance manager on the last day of the month

e. Received an investment of $10,000 cash from the company's owners, in exchange for issuing shares

f. Supplies ordered in (*a*) were received, along with a bill for $2,000

Required:

1. Indicate the specific account, amount, and direction of effects for each transaction on the radio station's accounting equation. If an event is not considered a transaction, explain why.
2. Prepare journal entries to record each transaction.
3. Rawlco began the month with $220,000 in total assets. What total assets would be reported on the balance sheet after events (*a*) through (*f*)?

LO2-1, 2-3, 2-5

E2-12 Recording Journal Entries and Preparing a Classified Balance Sheet

Assume Downer.com was organized on May 1, to compete with Despair, Inc.®—a company that sells demotivational posters and office products. The following events occurred during the first month of Downer.com's operations.

a. Received $60,000 cash from the investors who organized Downer.com Corporation

b. Borrowed $20,000 cash and signed a note due in two years

c. Ordered computer equipment costing $16,000

d. Purchased $9,000 in equipment, paying $2,000 in cash and signing a six–month note for the balance

e. Received the equipment ordered in (*c*), paid for half of it, and put the rest on account

Required:

1. Summarize the financial effects of transactions (*a*) through (*e*) in a table or spreadsheet similar to Exhibit 2.5.
2. Prepare journal entries for each transaction. Be sure to use referencing and categorize each account as an asset (A), liability (L), or shareholders' equity (SE). If a transaction does not require a journal entry, explain the reason.
3. Prepare a classified balance sheet at May 31. Include Retained Earnings with a balance of zero.

LO2-2, 2-3, 2-4

E2-13 Analyzing the Effects of Transactions Using T-Accounts; Preparing and Interpreting a Balance Sheet

Lee Delivery Company Inc. (LDC) was incorporated in 2017. The following transactions occurred during the year:

Check Figure:

Ending Equipment balance = $22,000

a. Received $40,000 cash from organizers in exchange for shares in the new company

b. Purchased land for $12,000, signing a two–year note (Ignore interest)

c. Bought two used delivery trucks at the start of the year at a cost of $10,000 each; paid $2,000 cash and signed a note due in three years for the rest (Ignore interest.)

d. Paid $2,000 cash to a truck repair shop for a new motor, which increased the cost of one of the trucks

e. Shareholder Jonah Lee paid $122,000 cash for a house for his personal use

Required:

1. Analyze each item for its effects on the accounting equation of LDC, for the year ended December 31, 2017.

   TIP: Transaction (a) is presented below as an example.

		Assets	=	Liabilities	+	Shareholders' Equity	
(a)	Cash	+40,000	=			Contributed Capital	+40,000

TIP: The new motor in transaction (d) is treated as an increase to the cost of the truck.

2. Record the effects of each item using a journal entry.

    TIP: Use the simplified journal entry format shown in the demonstration case for this chapter.

3. Summarize the effects of the journal entries by account, using the T–account format shown in the chapter.

4. Prepare a classified balance sheet for LDC at the end of 2017.

5. Using the balance sheet, indicate whether LDC's assets at the end of the year were financed primarily by liabilities or shareholders' equity.

E2-14 Explaining the Effects of Transactions on Balance Sheet Accounts Using T-Accounts

LO2-1, 2-2, 2-3

Heavey and Lovas Furniture Repair Service, a company with two shareholders, began opera–tions on June
1. The following T–accounts indicate the activities for the month of June.

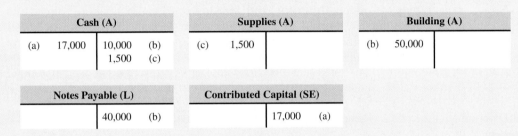

Required:

Explain transactions (a) through (c) that resulted in the entries in the T–accounts; that is, for each account, what transactions made it increase and/or decrease?

E2-15 Calculating and Evaluating the Current Ratio

LO2-1, 2-5

Delamy Design Ltd. is a clothing designer, marketer, and distributor. The company reported the following in recent balance sheets (amounts in thousands):

	September 30, 2017	December 31, 2016
Assets		
Current Assets:		
Cash	$73,324	$ 92,962
Accounts Receivable	81,336	58,270
Inventories	25,816	20,440
Other Current Assets	5,512	5,002
Total Current Assets	185,988	176,674
Property, Equipment, and Other	54,128	25,820
Long–Term Assets		
Total Assets	$ 240,116	$202,494
Liabilities and Shareholders' Equity		
Current Liabilities:		
Accounts Payable	$ 19,207	$ 18,694
Other Current Liabilities	12,880	10,633
Income Taxes Payable	3,512	—
Total Current Liabilities	35,599	29,327
Long–Term Liabilities	1,709	312
Shareholders' Equity	202,808	172,855
Total Liabilities and Shareholders' Equity	$240,116	$202,494

Required:

1. Calculate the current ratio at September 30, 2017, and December 31, 2016.

2. Did the company's current ratio increase or decrease? What does this imply about the company's ability to pay its current liabilities as they come due?

3. What would Delamy's current ratio have been if, on September 30, 2017, the company was to have paid down $10,000 of its Accounts Payable? Does paying down Accounts Payable in this case increase or decrease the current ratio?

4. Are the company's total assets financed primarily by liabilities or shareholders' equity at September 30, 2017?

LO2-2, 2-3, 2-4, 2-5 **E2-16 Analyzing and Recording Transactions, and Preparing and Evaluating a Balance Sheet**

Business Sim Corp. (BSC) issued 1,000 shares to Kelly in exchange for $12,000. BSC borrowed $30,000 from the bank, promising to repay it in two years. BSC paid $35,000 for computer equipment with cheque number 101 and signed a note for $5,000 due in six months. BSC received $900 of supplies purchased on account. BSC's loan contains a clause ("covenant") that requires BSC to maintain a ratio of current assets to current liabilities of at least 1.3.

Required:

1. Identify the transactions and analyze their accounting equation effects, using the format shown in the chapter.

2. Prepare journal entries for the transactions described above, and post them to T-accounts.

3. Assuming BSC entered into no other activities during its first year ended September 30, 2017, prepare the company's classified balance sheet. Include a balance of zero in Retained Earnings.

4. Determine and explain whether BSC is complying with or violating its loan covenant.

COACHED PROBLEMS

LO2-2, 2-5 **CP2-1 Determining Financial Statement Effects of Various Transactions**

The four friends who organized Healthcare Services (HS) on January 1, 2017, each invested $10,000 in the company and were issued 8,000 common shares. To date, they are the only shareholders. During the first month (January 2017), the company had the following five events:

a. Collected a total of $40,000 from the organizers and issued the shares

b. Purchased a building for $65,000, equipment for $16,000, and three hectares of land for $12,000; paid $13,000 in cash and signed a note for the balance, which is due to be paid in 15 years

c. One shareholder reported to the company that 500 shares of his HS shares had been sold and transferred to another shareholder for $5,000 cash

d. Purchased supplies for $3,000 cash

e. Sold one hectare of land for $4,000 cash to another company

Required:

1. Was Healthcare Services organized as a partnership or corporation? Explain the basis for your answer.

2. During the first month, the records of the company were inadequate. You were asked to prepare a summary of the preceding transactions. To develop a quick assessment of their economic effects on Healthcare Services, you have decided to complete the spreadsheet that follows and to use plus (+) for increases and minus (−) for decreases for each account.

TIP: Transaction (a) is presented below as an example.

TIP: In transaction (b), five different accounts are affected.

	Assets					=	Liabilities	+	Shareholders' Equity	
	Cash	Supplies	Land	Building	Equipment	=	Notes Payable		Contributed Capital	Retained Earnings
(a)	+40,000								+40,000	

3. Did you include the transaction between the two shareholders—event (c)—in the spreadsheet? Why?

> TIP: Think about whether this event caused HS to receive or give up anything.

4. Based only on the completed spreadsheet, provide the following amounts (show computations):

a. Total assets at the end of the month

b. Total liabilities at the end of the month

c. Total shareholders' equity at the end of the month

d. Cash balance at the end of the month

e. Total current assets at the end of the month

5. As of January 31, 2017, has the financing for HS's investment in assets primarily come from liabilities or from shareholders' equity?

CP2-2 Recording Transactions (in a Journal and T-Accounts); Preparing and Interpreting the Balance Sheet LO2-2, 2-3, 2-4, 2-5

Athletic Professional Training Company (APTC) was incorporated as a private company on June 1, 2017. The company's accounts included the following at July 1, 2017:

Accounts Payable	$4,000	Land	$100,000
Building	200,000	Notes Payable	17,000
Cash	16,000	Retained Earnings	0
Contributed Capital	318,000	Supplies	5,000
Equipment	18,000		

During the month of July, the company did the following:

a. Issued 2,000 shares for $200,000 cash

c. Borrowed $30,000 cash from a local bank, payable June 30, 2017

c. Bought a building for $141,000; paid $41,000 in cash and signed a three-year note for the balance

d. Paid cash for equipment that cost $100,000

e. Purchased supplies for $10,000 on account

Required:

1. Analyze transactions (a) through (e) to determine their effects on the accounting equation. Using a spreadsheet format with a column for each account, enter the July 1, 2017, amounts in the first line under the account headings, and calculate ending balances.

> TIP: You won't need new accounts to record the transactions described above, so have a quick look at the ones listed before you begin.

> TIP: In transaction (c), three different accounts are affected.

2. Record the transaction effects determined in requirement 1 using journal entries.

3. Summarize the journal entry effects from requirement 2 using T–accounts.

> TIP: Create a T–account for each account listed above. Enter the July 1, 2017, balances as the month's beginning balances.

4. Prepare a classified balance sheet at July 31, 2017.

> TIP: Total Assets equals $679,000.

5. As of July 31, 2017, has the financing for APTC's investment in assets come primar–ily from liabilities or shareholders' equity?

CP2-3 Recording Transactions (in a Journal and T-Accounts); Preparing and Interpreting the Balance Sheet LO2-2, 2-3, 2-4, 2-5

Plaudere Plastics Company (PPC) has been operating for three years. Note the December 31, 2017, account balances:

Cash	$ 35,000	Land	$ 30,000
Accounts Receivable	5,000	Supplies	5,000
Inventory	40,000	Accounts Payable	37,000
Notes Receivable (due 2020)	2,000	Notes Payable (due 2020)	80,000
Equipment	80,000	Contributed Capital	150,000
Factory Building	120,000	Retained Earnings	50,000

During the year 2017, the company had the following summarized activities:

a. Purchased equipment that cost $21,000; paid $5,000 cash and signed a two–year note for the balance

b. Issued an additional 2,000 shares for $20,000 cash

c. Borrowed $30,000 cash from a local bank, payable on June 30, 2019

d. Purchased supplies for $4,000 cash

e. Built an addition to the factory for $41,000; paid $12,000 in cash and signed a three–year note for the balance

f. Hired a new president to start January 1, 2018; the contract was for $95,000 for each full year worked

Required:

1. Analyze transactions (a) through (f) to determine their effects on the accounting equation.

   TIP: You won't need new accounts to record the transactions described above, so have a quick look at the ones listed in the beginning of this question before you begin.

   TIP: In transaction (e), three different accounts are affected.

   TIP: In transaction (f), consider whether PPC owes anything to its new president for the year ended December 31, 2017.

2. Record the transaction effects determined in requirement 1 using journal entries.
3. Summarize the journal entry effects from requirement 2 using T–accounts.

   TIP: Create a T–account for each account listed above. Enter the December 31, 2016, balances as the 2017 beginning balances.

4. Explain your response to event (f).
5. Prepare a classified balance sheet at December 31, 2017.

   TIP: Total Assets equals $412,000.

6. As of December 31, 2017, has the financing for PPC's investment in assets primarily come from liabilities or shareholders' equity?

GROUP A PROBLEMS

LO2-2, 2-5

PA2-1 Determining Financial Statement Effects of Various Transactions

Model trains for sale to toy stores are produced by Whistle Stop Incorporated, a small man–ufacturing company. Whistle Stop also has a small service department that repairs customers' model trains for a fee. The company has been in business for five years. At the end of the most recent year, 2016, the accounting records reflected total assets of $500,000 and total liabilities of $200,000. During the current year, 2017, the following summarized events occurred:

a. Issued additional shares for $100,000 cash

b. Borrowed $120,000 cash from the bank and signed a ten–year note

c. Built an addition on the factory for $200,000 and paid cash to the contractor

d. Purchased equipment for the new addition for $30,000, paying $3,000 in cash and signing a note due in six months for the balance

e. Returned a $3,000 piece of equipment, from (*d*), because it proved to be defective; received a reduction of the note payable

f. Purchased a delivery truck (equipment) for $10,000; paid $5,000 cash and signed a nine−month note for the remainder

g. A shareholder sold $5,000 worth of his shares in Whistle Stop Incorporated to his neighbour

Required:

1. Complete the spreadsheet that follows, using plus (+) for increases and minus (−) for decreases for each account. The first transaction is used as an example.

	Assets			=	Liabilities	+	Shareholders' Equity	
	Cash	Equipment	Building	=	Notes Payable		Contributed Capital	Retained Earnings
(a)	+100,000						+100,000	

2. Did you include event (*g*) in the spreadsheet? Why or why not?

3. Based on beginning balances plus the completed spreadsheet, provide the following amounts (show computations):

   a. Total assets at the end of the year

   b. Total liabilities at the end of the year

   c. Total shareholders' equity at the end of the year

4. As of December 31, 2017, has the financing for Whistle Stop's investment in assets primarily come from liabilities or shareholders' equity?

PA2-2 Determining Financial Statement Effects of Various Transactions   LO2-2, 2-5

eXcel

Lex Systems Inc. is a computer software company that makes online public access cataloguing systems for library, business, or home use. It also has a small service department that provides initial data inputting for a fee. The company has been in business for ten years. At the end of the most recent year, 2016, the accounting records reflected total assets of $100,000 and total liabilities of $25,000. During the current year, 2017, the following summarized events occurred:

a. Repaid $5,000 cash on a bank note borrowed in a previous year

b. Bought a computer from a shareholder for $2,000; signed a one−year note for the liability

c. Disposed of a printer that was obsolete (net book value of zero) by turning it in to a salvage centre; no proceeds from the disposal

d. Purchased office equipment for $1,000; paid cash

e. Paid a $500 cash dividend to the shareholders

f. Made a $10,000 down payment on a $50,000 building; signed a four−year note for the remainder

g. A shareholder sold $5,000 worth of his shares in Lex Systems Inc. to the company at cost

Required:

1. Complete the spreadsheet that follows, using plus (+) for increases and minus (−) for decreases for each account. The first transaction is given as an example.

	Assets			=	Liabilities	+	Shareholders' Equity	
	Cash	Equipment	Building	=	Notes Payable		Contributed Capital	Retained Earnings
(a)	−5,000				−5,000			

2. Did you include event (c) in the spreadsheet? Why or why not?
3. Based on beginning balances plus the completed spreadsheet, provide the following amounts (show computations):

   a. Total assets at the end of the year

   b. Total liabilities at the end of the year

   c. Total shareholders' equity at the end of the year

4. As of December 31, 2017, has the financing for Lex Systems Inc.'s investment in assets primarily come from liabilities or from shareholders' equity?

LO2-2, 2-3, 2-4, 2-5 **PA2-3 Recording Transactions (in a Journal and T-Accounts); Preparing and Interpreting the Balance Sheet**

Deliberate Speed Corporation (DSC) was incorporated as a private company on June 1, 2017. The company's accounts included the following at June 30, 2017:

Accounts Payable	$10,000	Land	$200,000
Building	100,000	Notes Payable, due 2019	2,000
Cash	26,000	Retained Earnings	259,000
Contributed Capital	180,000	Supplies	7,000
Equipment	118,000		

Check Figure:

Ending Contributed Capital balance = $580,000

During the month of July, the company had the following activities:

a. Issued 4,000 shares for $400,000 cash

b. Borrowed $90,000 cash from a local bank, payable June 30, 2020

c. Bought a factory building for $182,000; paid $82,000 in cash and signed a three–year note for the balance

d. Paid cash for equipment that cost $200,000

e. Purchased supplies for $30,000 on account

Required:

1. Analyze transactions (a) through (e) to determine their effects on the accounting equation.
2. Record the transaction effects determined in requirement 1 using a journal entry format.
3. Summarize the journal entry effects from requirement 2 using T–accounts.
4. Prepare a classified balance sheet at July 31, 2017.
5. As of July 31, 2017, has the financing for DSC's investment in assets primarily come from liabilities or from shareholders' equity?

LO2-2, 2-3, 2-4, 2-5 **PA2-4 Recording Transactions (in a Journal and T-Accounts); Preparing and Interpreting the Balance Sheet**

Fruity Farms was incorporated as a private company on January 1, 2017. The company's accounts included the following at January 31, 2017:

Accounts Payable	$20,000	Land	$100,000
Building	50,000	Notes Payable, due 2019	22,000
Bank Overdraft	9,000	Retained Earnings	74,000
Contributed Capital	75,000	Supplies	3,000
Equipment	47,000		

Check Figure:

Ending Retained Earnings balance = $59,000

During the month of February, the company had the following activities:

a. Paid a dividend to shareholders of $15,000

b. Repaid $10,000 cash to a local bank

c. Issued 500 shares for $50,000 cash

d. Purchased equipment for $30,000, paying $3,000 in cash and signing a note due in six months for the balance

e. Purchased supplies for $3,000 on account

Required:

1. Analyze transactions (*a*) through (*e*) to determine their effects on the accounting equation.
2. Record the transaction effects determined in requirement 1 using a journal entry format.
3. Summarize the journal entry effects from requirement 2 using T−accounts.
4. Prepare a classified balance sheet at February 28, 2017.
5. As of February 28, 2017, has the financing for Fruity Farm's investment in assets primarily come from liabilities or from shareholders' equity?

PA2-5 Recording Transactions (in a Journal and T-Accounts); Preparing and Interpreting the Balance Sheet   LO2-2, 2-3, 2-4, 2-5

Alezandray's Interiors, Inc., is a leading international manufacturer and retailer of home fur−nishings. The following is from Alezandray's balance sheet as of September 30, 2017. (Dollars are in millions.)

Cash	$ 80	Accounts Payable	$ 29
Accounts Receivable	12	Wages and Other Expenses Payable	111
Inventories	188	Long−Term Debt	203
Other Current Assets	26	Other Long−Term Liabilities	44
Property, Plant, and Equipment	355	Contributed Capital	356
Other Assets	99	Retained Earnings	20

Assume that the following events occurred in the quarter ended December 31 (dollars are in millions):

a. Paid $2,000,000 cash for an additional "other asset"

b. Issued additional shares for $2,000,000 in cash

c. Purchased property, plant, and equipment; paid $2,000,000 in cash and signed a note to pay the remaining $9,000,000 in two years

d. Sold, at cost, other assets for $1,000,000 cash

e. Conducted negotiations to purchase a sawmill, which is expected to cost $36,000,000

Required:

1. Analyze transactions (*a*) through (*e*) to determine their effects on the accounting equation. Use the format shown in the demonstration case.
2. Record the transaction effects determined in requirement 1 using journal entries.
3. Summarize the journal entry effects from requirement 2 using T−accounts. Use the September 2017 ending balances as the beginning balances for the October to December 2017 quarter.
4. Explain your response to event (*e*).
5. Prepare a classified balance sheet at December 31, 2017.
6. As of December 31, 2017, has the financing for Alezandray's investment in assets primarily come from liabilities or from shareholders' equity?

GROUP B PROBLEMS

PB2-1 Determining Financial Statement Effects of Various Transactions   LO2-2, 2-5

Swish Watch Corporation manufactures, sells, and services expensive watches. The company has been in business for three years. At the end of the most recent year, 2016, the accounting records reported total assets of $2,255,000 and total liabilities of $1,780,000. During the current year, 2017, the following summarized events occurred:

a. Issued additional shares for $109,000 cash

b. Borrowed $186,000 cash from the bank and signed a ten-year note

c. A shareholder sold $5,000 of his shares in Swish Watch Corporation to another investor

d. Built an addition onto the factory for $200,000 and paid cash to the construction company

e. Purchased equipment for the new addition for $44,000, paying $12,000 in cash and signing a six-month note for the balance

f. Returned a $4,000 piece of equipment, from (e), because it proved to be defective; received a cash refund

Required:

1. Complete the spreadsheet that follows, using plus (+) for increases and minus (−) for decreases for each account. The first transaction is given as an example.

	Assets			=	Liabilities	+	Shareholders' Equity	
	Cash	Equipment	Building	=	Notes Payable		Contributed Capital	Retained Earnings
(a)	+109,000						+109,000	

2. Did you include event (c) in the spreadsheet? Why?

3. Based on beginning balances plus the completed spreadsheet, provide the following amounts (show computations):

   a. Total assets at the end of the year.

   b. Total liabilities at the end of the year.

   c. Total shareholders' equity at the end of the year.

4. As of December 31, 2017, has the financing for Swish Watch Corporation's investment in assets primarily come from liabilities or from shareholders' equity?

LO2-2, 2-5 **PB2-2 Determining Financial Statement Effects of Various Transactions**

Blockhead and Sons is a motor vehicle repair centre specializing in engine repair. At the end of the most recent year, 2016, the accounting records reported total assets of $746,000 and total liabilities of $534,000. During the current year, 2017, the following summarized events occurred:

a. Repaid $50,000 cash on a bank note borrowed in a previous year

b. Bought a tow truck (equipment) from a supplier for $25,000; signed a one-year note for the liability

c. Disposed of a computer that was obsolete (net book value of zero) by turning it in to a salvage centre; no proceeds from the disposal

d. Purchased shop equipment for $100,000; paid cash

e. Paid a $50,000 cash dividend to the shareholders

f. Made a $100,000 down payment on a $500,000 building; signed a forty-year note for the remainder

g. Borrowed $100,000 cash from the bank and signed a ten-year note

Required:

1. Complete the spreadsheet that follows, using plus (+) for increases and minus (−) for decreases for each account. The first transaction is given as an example.

	Assets			=	Liabilities	+	Shareholders' Equity	
	Cash	Equipment	Building	=	Notes Payable		Contributed Capital	Retained Earnings
(a)	−50,000				−50,000			

2. Did you include event (c) in the spreadsheet? Why?

3. Based on beginning balances plus the completed spreadsheet, provide the following amounts (show computations):

   a. Total assets at the end of the year

   b. Total liabilities at the end of the year

   c. Total shareholders' equity at the end of the year

4. As of December 31, 2017, has the financing for Blockhead and Sons's investment in assets primarily come from liabilities or from shareholders' equity?

PB2-3 Recording Transactions (in a Journal and T-Accounts); Preparing and Interpreting the Balance Sheet

LO2-2, 2-3, 2-4, 2-5

Bearings & Brakes Corporation (B&B) was incorporated as a private company on June 1, 2017. The company's accounts included the following at June 30, 2017:

Accounts Payable	$50,000	Land	$444,000
Factory Building	500,000	Notes Payable, due 2019	5,000
Cash	90,000	Retained Earnings	966,000
Contributed Capital	170,000	Supplies	9,000
Equipment	148,000		

During the month of July, the company had the following activities:

a. Issued 6,000 shares for $600,000 cash

b. Borrowed $60,000 cash from a local bank, payable June 30, 2020

c. Bought a factory building for $166,000; paid $66,000 in cash and signed a three−year note for the balance

d. Paid cash for equipment that cost $90,000

e. Purchased supplies for $90,000 on account

Check Figure:
Ending Notes Payable balance = $165,000
Total Assets = $2,041,000

Required:

1. Analyze transactions (a) through (e) to determine their effects on the accounting equation. Use the format shown in the demonstration case.

2. Record the transaction effects determined in requirement 1 using a journal entry format.

3. Summarize the journal entry effects from requirement 2 using T−accounts.

4. Prepare a classified balance sheet at July 31, 2017.

5. As of July 31, 2017, has the financing for B&B's investment in assets primarily come from liabilities or from shareholders' equity?

PB2-4 Recording Transactions (in a Journal and T-Accounts); Preparing and Interpreting the Balance Sheet

LO2-2, 2-3, 2-4, 2-5

Lakeshore Cottages was incorporated as a private company on January 1, 2017. The compa−ny's accounts included the following at January 31, 2017:

Accounts Payable	$156,000	Land	$144,000
Building	500,000	Notes Payable, due 2019	583,000
Cash	24,000	Retained Earnings	66,000
Contributed Capital	170,000	Supplies	99,000
Equipment	208,000		

During the month of February, the company had the following activities:

a. Borrowed $150,000 cash from a local bank, payable June 30, 2020

b. Repaid $250,000 cash to a local bank

c. Issued 1,500 shares for $150,000 cash

d. Purchased equipment for $30,000, paying $3,000 in cash and signing a note due in six months for the balance

e. Purchased supplies for $30,000 on account

Required:

1. Analyze transactions (a) through (e) to determine their effects on the accounting equation. Use the format shown in the demonstration case.
2. Record the transaction effects determined in requirement 1 using a journal entry format.
3. Summarize the journal entry effects from requirement 2 using T−accounts.
4. Prepare a classified balance sheet at February 28, 2017.
5. As of February 28, 2017, has the financing for Lakeshore Cottages' investment in assets primarily come from liabilities or from shareholders' equity?

LO2-2, 2-3, 2-4, 2-5 **PB2-5 Recording Transactions (in a Journal and T-Accounts); Preparing and Interpreting the Balance Sheet**

Starbucks is a coffee company—a *big* coffee company. During a ten−year period, the number of Starbucks locations grew from 165 to over 8,800 stores in fifty countries. Assume the following is from Starbucks' annual report for the year ended September 30, 2017, and dollars are reported in thousands.

Cash	$ 269,800	Accounts Payable	$ 324,900
Accounts Receivable	329,500	Short−Term Bank Loans	1,864,800
Inventories	692,800	Long−Term Debt	549,600
Other Current Assets	455,900	Other Long−Term Liabilities	442,400
Property, Plant, and Equipment	2,956,400	Contributed Capital	40,100
Other Long−Term Assets	968,200	Retained Earnings	2,450,800

Check Figure:
Total Current Liabilities = $2,189,700

Assume that the following events occurred in the following quarter, which ended December 31, 2017. Dollars are in thousands.

a. Paid $10,000 cash for additional other long−term assets

b. Issued additional shares for $5,100 in cash

c. Purchased property, plant, and equipment; paid $11,200 in cash and signed additional long−term loans for $9,500

d. Sold, at cost, other long−term assets for $6,000 cash

e. Conducted negotiations to purchase a coffee farm, which is expected to cost $8,400

Required:

1. Analyze transactions (a) through (e) to determine their effects on the accounting equation. Use the format shown in the demonstration case.
2. Record the transaction effects determined in requirement 1 using journal entries.
3. Summarize the journal entry effects from requirement 2 using T−accounts. Use the September 2017 ending balances (reported above) as the beginning balances for the October–December 2017 quarter.

4. Explain your response to event (*e*).
5. Prepare a classified balance sheet at December 31, 2017.
6. As of December 31, 2017, has the financing for the investment in assets made by Starbucks primarily come from liabilities or from shareholders' equity?

SKILLS DEVELOPMENT CASES

S2-1 Finding and Analyzing Financial Information
LO2-1, 2-4, 2-5

Refer to the summarized financial statements of The Home Depot in Appendix A at the back of this book.

Required:

1. What is the company's fiscal year—end? Where did you find the exact date?
2. Use the company's balance sheet to determine the amounts in the accounting equation (A = L + SE).
3. What is the amount of the company's current liabilities on January 29, 2017? Are current assets sufficient to cover current liabilities?
4. Has financing for the company's investment in assets primarily come from liabilities or from shareholders' equity?

S2-2 Finding and Analyzing Financial Information
LO2-1, 2-4, 2-5

Refer to the summarized financial statements of The Home Depot in Appendix A and Lowe's Companies, Inc. in Appendix B at the back of this book.

Required:

1. Use each company's balance sheet to determine the amounts in the accounting equation (A = L + SE). Is The Home Depot or Lowe's Companies, Inc. larger in terms of total assets?
2. Does The Home Depot have more or less current liabilities than Lowe's Companies, Inc. at the end of the 2016 fiscal year? Which company has a larger current ratio?
3. On the balance sheet, Lowe's Companies, Inc. reports inventories of $10,458,000,000. Does this amount represent the expected selling price? Why or why not?
4. Has financing for Lowe's Companies, Inc.'s investment in assets primarily come from liabilities or from shareholders' equity at February 3, 2017? Thinking back to Chapter 1, what does this imply about the risk assumed by Lowe's Companies, Inc.'s investors, relative to those investing in The Home Depot?

S2-3 Team Research, Financial Analysis, Technology, and Communication: Examining the Balance Sheet
LO2-1, 2-4, 2-5

In teams, select an industry to analyze. From the Internet, each team member should access the annual report for one publicly traded company in the industry, with each member selecting a different company. (See S1—3 in Chapter 1 for a description of possible resources for these tasks.)

Required:

1. On an individual basis, each team member should write a short report that lists the follow—ing information:
   a. The date of the balance sheet
   b. The major non—current asset accounts and any significant changes in them
   c. The major non—current liability accounts and any significant changes in them
   d. Any significant changes in total shareholders' equity
   e. Whether financing for the investment in assets primarily comes from liabilities or from shareholders' equity
2. Then, as a team, write a short report comparing and contrasting your companies using the above dimensions. Discuss any similarities across the companies that you observe as a team, and provide potential explanations for any differences discovered.

S2-4 Ethical Reasoning, Critical Thinking, and Communication: A Real-Life Fraud

In the world of financial fraud, the "Ponzi scheme" is famous. Here is the story behind how the scam got its name.

Charles Ponzi started the Security Exchange Company on December 26, 1919. He thought he had discovered a way to purchase American stamps in a foreign country at significantly lower amounts than they were worth in the United States. He claimed his idea was so successful that anyone who gave money to his company would be repaid their original loan plus 50 percent interest within ninety days. Friends and family quickly offered their money to Ponzi and they were handsomely rewarded, being repaid their original loan and the 50 percent interest within just forty–five days.

Thanks to an article in the *New York Times*, word spread quickly about Ponzi's business, attracting thousands of people seeking a similar payback. He might have had a successful business had his idea actually worked. The problem, however, was that it didn't. The 50 percent interest paid to early investors did not come from the profits of a successful underlying business idea (which didn't even exist) but, instead, was obtained fraudulently from funds contributed by later lenders. Eventually, the Ponzi scheme collapsed on August 10, 1920, after an auditor examined Ponzi's accounting records.

Required:

1. Assume that on December 27, 1919, Ponzi's first three lenders provided his company with $5,000 each. Use the basic accounting equation to show the effects of these transactions on December 27, 1919.

2. If the first two lenders are repaid their original loan amounts plus the 50 percent interest promised to them, how much cash is left in Ponzi's business to repay the third lender? Given what you discovered, how was it possible for Ponzi's company to remain in "business" for over eight months?

3. Who was harmed by Ponzi's scheme?

Epilogue: After taking in nearly $15 million from 40,000 people, Ponzi's company failed with just $1.5 million in total assets. Ponzi spent four years in prison but, after also being found guilty at a subsequent trial, jumped bail—and then became involved in fraudulently selling swampland in Florida.

In December 2008, Bernard Madoff was arrested for using a modern–day Ponzi scheme to defraud investors of $65,000,000,000. On June 29, 2009, he was sentenced to 150 years in prison.

S2-5 Ethical Reasoning, Critical Thinking, and Communication: A Mini-Case

You work as an accountant for a small land development company that desperately needs additional financing to continue in business. The president of your company is meeting with the manager of a local bank at the end of the month to try to obtain this financing. The president has approached you with two ideas to improve the company's reported financial position.

First, he claims that, because a big part of the company's value comes from its knowledgeable and dedicated employees, you should report their "intellectual abilities" as an asset on the balance sheet.

Second, he claims that, although the local economy is doing poorly and almost no one is buying land or new houses, he is optimistic that eventually things will turn around. For this reason, he asks you to continue reporting the company's land on the balance sheet at its cost, rather than the much lower amount that real estate appraisers say it's really worth.

Required:

1. Thinking back to Chapter 1, why do you think the president is so concerned with the amount of assets reported on the balance sheet?

2. What accounting concept introduced in Chapter 2 relates to the president's first suggestion to report "intellectual abilities" as an asset?

3. What accounting concept introduced in Chapter 2 relates to the president's second suggestion to continue reporting land at its cost?

4. Who might be hurt by the president's suggestions if you were to do as he asks? What should you do?

S2-6 Financial Analysis and Critical Thinking: Evaluating the Reliability of a Balance Sheet LO2-1, 2-4, 2-5

Betsey Jordan asked a local bank for a $50,000 loan to expand her small company. The bank asked Betsey to submit a financial statement of the business to supplement the loan application. Betsey prepared the following balance sheet.

Balance Sheet
At June 30, 2017

Assets	
Cash	$ 9,000
Inventory	30,000
Equipment	46,000
Personal Residence (monthly payments, $2,800)	300,000
Remaining Assets	20,000
Total Assets	$405,000
Liabilities	
Short−Term Debt to Suppliers	62,000
Long−Term Debt on Equipment	38,00
Total Debt	100,000
Shareholders' Equity	305,000
Total Liabilities and Shareholders' Equity	$405,000

Required:

The balance sheet has several flaws. However, there is at least one major deficiency. Identify it and explain its significance.

S2-7 Using Technology to Analyze Transactions and Prepare a Balance Sheet LO2-2

Assume you recently obtained a part−time accounting position at the corporate head−quarters of Elizabeth Arden, Inc. in Miami Lakes, Florida. Elizabeth Arden is a leading manufacturer and marketer of prestige beauty products, prominently led by the Red Door line of fragrances. Assume that the following table summarizes accounts and their balances reported by Elizabeth Arden, Inc. in a September 30 balance sheet. Amounts are in thousands.

Cash	$ 14,300	Short−Term Notes Payable	$125,000
Accounts Receivable	285,400	Accounts Payable	111,800
Inventories	199,700	Other Current Liabilities	75,700
Other Current Assets	31,600	Long−Term Debt	323,600
Property and Equipment	35,800	Other Long−Term Liabilities	10,100
Other Non−current Assets	224,100	Contributed Capital	101,800
		Retained Earnings	42,900

Assume the company entered into the following transactions during October (amounts in thousands):

a. Purchased an additional manufacturing facility at a cost of $15,000 by issuing a promis−sory note that becomes payable in three years.

b. Used $7,000 cash to repay one of the short−term loans.

c. Issued additional shares for $20,000 cash contributed by shareholders.

d. Used cash to buy land for $8,000.

Required:

The controller at Elizabeth Arden has asked you to create a spreadsheet in which to display the following:

1. The account balances at September 30
2. The effects of the four October transactions
3. Totals that combine the September 30 balances with the October transactions.

You feel like you might be ready to tackle this assignment, but just to be sure, you email your friend Owen for advice. Here's his reply.

From: Owentheaccountant@yahoo.com
To: Helpme@hotmail.com
Cc:
Subject: Excel Help

1. My thinking is that you'll really impress your boss if you set up the spreadsheet to look like a bunch of T-accounts, one beside another. Use two columns for each balance sheet account (with the account name spanning the two columns) to make it look just like a T-account. You do remember how to use the cell merge command to make a header span two columns, right? If not, check the last e-mail I sent you (S1-7, Chapter 1). Here's a screenshot of how your worksheet might look just before you enter the October transactions.

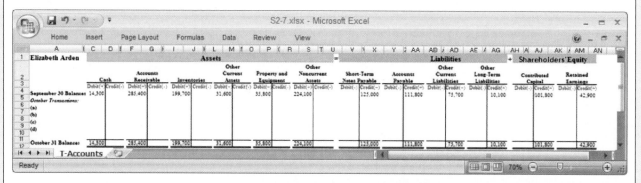

2. For spreadsheet skills in addition to cell merging, you might try creating a balance sheet with cells that are linked to the corresponding cells in the T-accounts. To do this, open a worksheet in the same file as the T-accounts. Then click on a cell in the balance sheet worksheet where you want to import a number from the T-accounts, then type =, then click on the tab for the T-account worksheet, click on the cell with the total to be transferred, and then press Enter. This links the cells so that any changes to the T-accounts automatically update the balance sheet. Also, Excel will let you hide row and column gridlines if you want. Just search Excel's help index for "hide gridlines."

3. I guess the only thing that's left is to remind you that to compute the ending balances in each T-account, you have to add the increases to the beginning balance and subtract the decreases. So, to compute the totals for a particular account, your formula might look like =(SUM(C4:C9)-SUM(D5:D9)).

4. Oh yeah, when you're all done, don't forget to save the file using a name that uniquely identifies you.

CONTINUING CASE

LO2-1, 2-2,
2-3, 2-4, 2-5

CC2-1 Accounting for the Establishment of a Business

Nicole has decided that she is going to start her business, Nicole's Getaway Spa (NGS). A lot has to be done when starting a new business. Here are some transactions that have occurred prior to April 30, 2017.

a. Received $80,000 cash when issuing 8,000 new shares
b. Purchased some land by paying $2,000 cash and signing a note payable for $7,000 due in 2017
c. Hired a new esthetician for a salary of $1,000 a month, starting next month
d. Bought $1,000 in soaps and aromatherapy supplies for the spa on credit
e. NGS purchased a company car for $18,000 cash (list price of $21,000) to assist in running errands for the business

f. Nicole sold 100 of her own personal shares to Raea Gooding for $300

g. Paid $350 of the amount owed in (*d*)

Required:

1. For each of the events, prepare journal entries if a transaction exists, checking that debits equal credits. If a transaction does not exist, explain why there is no transaction.
2. Assuming that the beginning balances in each of the accounts are zero, complete T−accounts to summarize the transactions (*a*) through (*g*).
3. Prepare a classified balance sheet at April 30, 2017, using the information given in the transactions.
4. Calculate the current ratio at April 30, 2017. What does this ratio indicate about the ability of NGS to pay its current liabilities?

Endnote

1. The account names you see in the financial statements of most large businesses are actually aggregations (or combinations) of several specific accounts. For example, Papa John's International keeps separate accounts for land, buildings, and equipment but combines them into one title on its balance sheet called *Property and Equipment*.

THAT WAS

THEN

In the previous chapter, you learned how to analyze, record, and summarize the effects of transactions on balance sheet accounts.

THIS IS

NOW

This chapter focuses on analyzing, recording, and summarizing the effects of operating transactions on balance sheet and income statement accounts.

YOUR LEARNING OBJECTIVES

Understand the business

LO3-1 Describe common operating transactions and select appropriate income statement account titles.

Study the accounting methods

LO3-2 Explain and apply the revenue and expense recognition principles.

LO3-3 Analyze, record, and summarize the effects of operating transactions, using the accounting equation, journal entries, and T-accounts.

LO3-4 Prepare an unadjusted trial balance.

Evaluate the results

LO3-5 Evaluate net profit margin, but beware of income statement limitations.

Review the chapter

Chapter Summary

CHAPTER 3

The Income Statement

Andersen Ross/Blend Images LLC

FOCUS COMPANY:
Pizza Palace Inc.

You read about Emilio Santos and his new gourmet pizza business, Pizza Palace, in Chapter 2. Using money he and his wife had contributed, plus a loan from the bank, he purchased the ovens, restaurant booths, and other equipment he needed to run the business. The next step in his business plan is to draw customers into the restaurant and provide them with the product and service that will keep them coming back. These day-to-day operating activities will determine whether the company makes a profit.

The first goal of this chapter is to help you understand common operating activities and see how an income statement indicates whether a business generated a profit (or loss). Then we'll show how the transaction analysis approach from Chapter 2 can be used to analyze and record transactions affecting the income statement. Finally, at the end of the chapter, we will highlight some uses and limitations of the income statement.

ORGANIZATION OF THE CHAPTER

Understand the business	Study the accounting methods	Evaluate the results	Review the chapter
• Operating activities • Income statement accounts	• Cash basis accounting • Accrual basis accounting • The expanded accounting equation • Unadjusted trial balance • Review of revenues and expenses	• Net profit margin • Income statement limitations	• Demonstration Cases • Chapter Summary • Solutions to Self-Study Practice • Key Terms • Homework Helper • Practice Material

Understand the Business

OPERATING ACTIVITIES

Operating activities are the day—to—day functions involved in running a business. Unlike the investing and financing activities discussed in Chapter 2, which occur infrequently and typically produce long—lasting effects, operating activities occur regularly and often have a shorter dura—tion of effect. Operating activities include buying goods and services from suppliers and employees, and selling goods and services to customers and then collecting cash from them. The period that begins with buying goods and ser—vices and continues through to collecting cash from customers is known as the *operating cycle*. Exhibit 3.1 illustrates the operating cycle for Pizza Palace.

LEARNING OBJECTIVE 3-1

Describe common operating transactions and select appropriate income statement account titles.

EXHIBIT 3.1	Typical Operating Cycle Activities

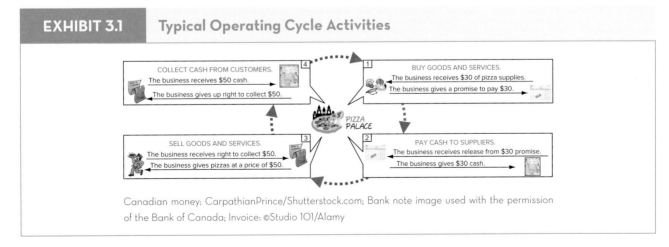

Canadian money: CarpathianPrince/Shutterstock.com; Bank note image used with the permission of the Bank of Canada; Invoice: ©Studio 101/Alamy

Although most businesses have the same steps in their operating cycles, the length of time for each step varies from company to company. For example, Pizza Palace usually collects cash from restaurant customers within minutes of making a sale, whereas the breakfast cereal company Kellogg Canada Inc. might wait several weeks to collect on sales it makes to grocery stores.

To be successful, Emilio must closely monitor Pizza Palace's operating activities. Operating activities are the primary source of revenues and expenses, and thus can determine whether a company earns a profit (or incurs a loss). Although Emilio may intuitively sense how his business is doing, a more reliable management approach is to evaluate the revenues and expenses reported on the income statement. Emilio takes a quick look at the projected income statement Ally prepared (Exhibit 3.2) based on the operating activities that were expected for Pizza Palace (in Chapter 1). This projected income statement will provide a benchmark against which he can evaluate actual results.

| EXHIBIT 3.2 | Projected Income Statement | PIZZA PALACE |

PIZZA PALACE INC. Income Statement For the Month Ended September 30, 2017		Explanation Who: Name of the business What: Title of the statement When: Accounting period
Revenues		
Pizza Revenue	$11,000	Revenue reported from the sale of pizza to customers in September
Total Revenues	11,000	**Total amount earned during September**
Expenses		
Supplies Expense	4,000	Cost of pizza ingredients used up in September
Wages Expense	2,000	Cost of employee wages for work done in September
Rent Expense	1,500	Cost of rent for the month of September
Utilities Expense	600	Cost of utilities used in September
Insurance Expense	300	Cost of insurance coverage for September
Advertising Expense	100	Cost of advertising done in September
Income Tax Expense	500	Cost of taxes on September's income
Total Expenses	9,000	**Total expenses incurred in September to generate revenues**
Net Income	$2,000	**Difference between total revenues and total expenses**

INCOME STATEMENT ACCOUNTS

The income statement summarizes the financial impact of operating activities undertaken by the company during the accounting period. It includes three main sections: revenues, expenses, and net income.

Revenues

Revenues: Amounts earned by selling goods or services to customers.

Revenues are the amounts a business charges its customers when it provides goods or services. If Pizza Palace sells 1,100 pizzas in September and charges $10 per pizza, Pizza Revenue would total $11,000. Revenue is reported when the company transfers control of a good or service to a customer, regardless of when the company is paid by the customer. The amount of revenue earned during the period is the first thing reported in the body of the income statement.

Expenses

Expenses: Costs of business necessary to earn revenues.

Expenses are costs of operating the business, incurred to generate revenues in the period covered by the income statement. Expenses are reported when the company uses something, like space in a building, supplies for providing services, or the efforts of employees. Basically, whenever a business uses up its resources to generate revenues during the period, it reports an expense, whether or not payment for the resources has occurred. Expenses are reported in the body of the income statement after revenues. Some of Pizza Palace's typical expenses are listed in the income statement shown in Exhibit 3.2.

Net Income

Net income is calculated by subtracting expenses from revenues; it is a total, not an account like Pizza Revenue or Wages Expense. Because it is a total, net income summarizes the overall impact of revenues and expenses in a single number. It is called a *net loss* if expenses are greater than revenues and a *net income* if revenues are greater than expenses. Net income indicates the amount by which shareholders' equity increases as a result of a company's profitable operations. For this reason, net income (or loss) is a closely watched measure of a company's success.

Exhibit 3.2 shows how revenues, expenses, and net income would be reported in Pizza Palace's income statement. Each account title describes the specific type of revenue or expense arising from the business's particular operations. This is true for all companies. Pizza Palace reports "Pizza Revenues," but Rogers Plus reports "Cable Service Revenue." Google reports "Traffic Acquisition Expenses," and Air Canada reports "Airport and Navigation Fees." You'll become more comfortable with various account titles as this course progresses, but to keep things simple, right now we'll stick to common types of revenues and expenses.

The income statement in Exhibit 3.2 is for the month ended September 30, 2017. As it turns out, September 30, 2017, is a Saturday. There is nothing particularly special about this date—it's just the last day of the month. By dividing the company's long life into shorter chunks of time, Emilio applies the **time period assumption**. It allows him to measure and evaluate Pizza Palace's financial performance on a timely basis. If net income is low in the current month, Emilio will find out about it quickly and be able to take steps to become more profitable in the following month.

Notice that the income statement only reports the financial effects of business activities that occurred during the current period. They relate only to the current period and do not have a lingering financial impact beyond the end of the current period. This is a key distinction between the income statement and the balance sheet. The revenues and expenses on an income statement only report the financial impact of activities in the current period, whereas items on a balance sheet will continue to have a financial impact beyond the end of the current period. Balance sheet accounts are considered permanent, whereas income statement accounts are considered temporary. Another way people describe this difference is that the balance sheet takes stock of what exists at a point in time, whereas the income statement depicts the flow of what happened over a period of time.

Net income: The excess of revenues over expenses.

COACH'S TIP

A more complete list of revenue and expense account titles appears in the Homework Helper section.

Time period assumption: The long life of a company is divided into shorter periods, such as months, quarters, and years.

HOW'S IT GOING?

Self-Study Practice 3.1

For each item listed below, indicate whether the company should report it on the income statement this period (yes/no). If yes, indicate an appropriate account title for the item described.

Description	Yes/No	Account Title
1. The Royal Bank of Canada charges customers a monthly service fee.	_____	_____
2. Canadian Tire buys a new building to use as a retail store.	_____	_____
3. Dell pays to deliver computers to customers.	_____	_____
4. Tim Hortons buys supplies to be used next month.	_____	_____
5. Shoppers Drug Mart pays this week's wages to employees.	_____	_____

After you have finished, check your answers with the solution, which follows the chapter summary.

35 Days Hath September?

It seems some managers—specifically those at Computer Associates (CA)—haven't learned the **time period assumption**. CA was charged with financial statement fraud for improperly recording thirty-five days of sales in September—a month that has only thirty days. To make it look like managers had met their September sales targets, CA included the first five days of sales from October in its September income statement. This accounting fraud led managers to be paid bonuses they hadn't earned and tricked investors into thinking CA was a successful company.

When the truth was revealed later, CA's shareholders quickly abandoned the company, causing its share price to fall 43 percent in a single day. CA ultimately paid shareholders $225 million to make up for its bad accounting and agreed to ensure that all inappropriate management bonuses were paid back to the company. In addition, several marketing and accounting personnel were sent to jail.

Proper revenue reporting is obviously a very serious matter.

Study the Accounting Methods

CASH BASIS ACCOUNTING

What's a good way to determine whether you're doing well financially? Many people simply look at the balance in their bank accounts to gauge their financial performance. If the overall balance increased this month, they take that as a sign that they've done a good job of managing their finances. If it has gone down, that's a clue they need to tame their spending next month. The bank balance tends to give a decent measure of financial performance because cash flows (in and out) occur closely in time to the activities that caused those cash flows. Reporting income on this basis, called **cash basis accounting**, is fine for managing personal finances, but not for running a business.

Cash basis accounting:
Reports revenues when cash is received and expenses when cash is paid; this is not allowed under GAAP.

Cash basis accounting doesn't measure financial performance very well when transactions are conducted using credit rather than cash. Credit often introduces a significant delay between the time an activity occurs and the time it impacts a bank account balance. If you are paid for work once a month, for example, the results of your hard work don't show up until the end of the month. Similarly, if you go crazy with your credit card at the mall, these transactions won't affect your bank balance until you pay the bill the following month.

Because most companies use credit for their transactions, cash basis accounting is not likely to correspond to the business activities that actually occur during a given period. Imagine if Pizza Palace paid its employees to cater a party in one month but didn't receive its customer's payment for these services until the following month. Under cash basis accounting, Pizza Palace would report expenses in Month 1 but wouldn't report revenues until it received the payment from its customer in Month 2. This leads to a rather distorted view of the company's financial performance, as shown in Exhibit 3.3.

Under cash basis accounting, the company would report a net loss in Month 1 and a huge net income in Month 2, when the truth is that the business activities generated revenue of $15,000, expenses of $10,000, and net income of $5,000, all of which relate to the activities that occurred in Month 1 when the party was catered. A better method of accounting is needed—one that reports the revenues and related expenses during the same period.

EXHIBIT 3.3 **Cash Basis Accounting Can Distort Reported Profits**

Alamy Stock Photo

	MONTH 1 (No cash is received, but **cash is paid**.)		MONTH 2 (**Cash is received**, but no cash is paid.)	
Revenues	$	0	Revenues	$15,000
Expenses		10,000	Expenses	0
Net Income (Loss)		$(10,000)	Net Income	$15,000

ACCRUAL BASIS ACCOUNTING

An alternative method of accounting would be to report revenues and expenses when services are provided, regardless of when cash is received or paid. This approach, called **accrual basis accounting**, produces a better measure of the profits arising from the company's activities. As shown in Exhibit 3.4, accrual accounting would require that Pizza Palace report all its revenues, expenses, and net income in the period in which the catering service occurs (Month 1). In the following month, Pizza Palace doesn't cater any parties, so it does not report revenues and expenses.

According to ASPE and IFRS, accrual basis accounting is the only acceptable method for external reporting of income. The cash basis can be used internally by some small companies, but ASPE and IFRS do not allow it for external reporting. The "rule of accrual" is that the financial effects of business activities are measured and reported when the activities actually occur, not when the cash related to them is received or paid. That is, revenues are recognized when the company provides goods or services to customers and expenses when they are incurred. The two basic accounting principles that determine when revenues and expenses are recognized under accrual basis accounting are called the *revenue recognition* and *expense recognition* principles.

LEARNING OBJECTIVE 3-2

Explain and apply the revenue and expense recognition principles.

Accrual basis accounting: Reports revenues when they are earned and expenses when they are incurred, regardless of the timing of cash receipts or payments; required under GAAP.

EXHIBIT 3.4 **Accrual Basis Accounting Relates Profit to Underlying Activities**

Alamy Stock Photo

	MONTH 1 (No cash is received, but **service is provided**.)		MONTH 2 (Cash is received, but **no service is provided**.)	
Revenues		$15,000	Revenues	$ 0
Expenses		10,000	Expenses	0
Net Income (Loss)		$ 5,000	Net Income	$ 0

Revenue Recognition Principle

According to the **revenue recognition principle**, revenues should be recognized when they are earned. The word *recognized* means revenues are measured and recorded in the accounting system. The word *earned*

Revenue recognition principle: The requirement under accrual basis accounting to record revenues when they are earned, not necessarily when cash is received for them.

means the company has fulfilled its obligation to the customer by doing what it promised to do. For example, when Pizza Palace delivers a pizza to a customer, one would agree that the promise to the customer has been fulfilled. As a result, the customer is able to direct the use of and obtain the benefits from the good or service.

All companies expect to receive cash in exchange for providing goods and services, but the timing of cash receipts does not dictate when revenues are recognized. Instead, the key factor in determining when to recognize revenue is whether the company has provided goods or services to custom— ers during the accounting period. Three possible cases exist, as shown on the timeline in Exhibit 3.5.

EXHIBIT 3.5	Timing of Reporting Revenue versus Cash Receipts

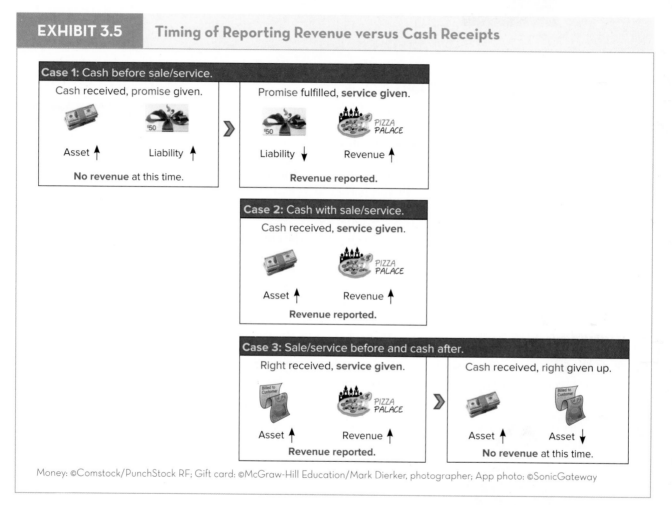

Money: ©Comstock/PunchStock RF; Gift card: ©McGraw-Hill Education/Mark Dierker, photographer; App photo: ©SonicGateway

Case 1: Cash before sale/service. Airlines, magazine publishers, insurance companies, and retail stores routinely receive cash before delivering goods and services. For example, Pizza Palace receives cash for gift cards that customers can redeem later when purchasing from its restaurant. Pizza Palace will record the cash received when it issues the gift card, but since it hasn't yet delivered goods or services to these customers, no revenue is recorded. Instead, Pizza Palace has an obligation to accept the gift card as payment in the future.

Deferred revenue:
A liability representing a company's obligation to provide goods or services to customers in the future.

This obligation is a liability called **Deferred Revenue**, and it is recorded on the balance sheet equal to the amount of cash received for the gift card. Revenue will be reported later; in other words, it is deferred until the goods or services are provided in exchange for the gift card.

Case 2: Cash with sale/service. Cash sales are common for companies selling to consumers. For example, Pizza Palace collects cash within moments of delivering pizza to a customer. In this case, cash and revenue are reported at the same time.

Case 3: Sale/service before and cash after. This situation typically arises when a company sells to a customer on account. Selling on account means that the company provides goods or services to a customer—not for cash, but for the right to collect cash in the future. This right is an asset account called *Accounts Receivable*. Thus, if Pizza Palace delivers pizza sold on account to a university organization, Pizza Palace records Pizza Revenue on the income statement and Accounts Receivable on the balance sheet. Later, when payment is received, Pizza Palace will increase its Cash account and decrease its Accounts Receivable account. No additional revenue is reported when the payment is received because the revenue was already recorded when the pizza was delivered.

SPOTLIGHT ON Financial Reporting

Revenue Recognition Policy

Every company is required (under ASPE and IFRS) to report its revenue recognition policy in its notes to the financial statements. Pizza Palace adheres to the same revenue recognition policy as Papa John's, which explains its policy as follows:

> **Papa John's International, Inc.**
>
> Restaurant sales are recognized as revenues when the products are delivered to or carried out by customers.

It's worthwhile to make sure that you understand what sparks the recording of revenues, because in the next section you'll see that this also triggers the recording of expenses. To ensure that you have a handle on this, spend a minute on the following Self–Study Practice.

HOW'S IT GOING?

Self-Study Practice 3.2

The following transactions are typical operating activities for Nova Scotia Seas, a scuba diving and instruction company. Indicate the amount of revenue, if any, that should be recognized in June for each activity.

Operating Activity	Amount of Expense Incurred in June
1. In June, Nova Scotia Seas provided $32,000 in diving instruction to customers for cash.	
2. In June, new customers paid $8,200 cash for diving trips to be provided by Nova Scotia Seas; $5,200 in trips were made in June and the rest will be provided in July.	
3. In June, customers paid $3,900 cash for instruction they received in May.	

After you have finished, check your answers with the solution, which follows the chapter summary.

Expense Recognition Principle ("Matching")

The business activities that generate revenues also create expenses. Under accrual basis accounting, expenses are recognized in the same period as the revenues to which they relate, not necessarily the period in which cash is paid for them. For example, for Pizza Palace to deliver pizza in September, it must rent space in a building and have its employees work that month. Under accrual basis accounting, Pizza Palace would report rent expense and wages expense in September, even if the rent was paid in August and the wages were paid in October.

This is what accountants call the **expense recognition principle (matching)**: record expenses in the same period as the revenues with which they can reasonably be associated. If an expense cannot be directly associated with revenues, it is recorded in the period that the underlying business activity occurs. For example, because it's not clear how or when advertising affects revenue, advertising expense is simply reported in the period that ads are run. Notice that it is the timing of the underlying business activities, not the cash payments, that dictates when expenses are recognized. Three possible cases are shown in Exhibit 3.6.

EXHIBIT 3.6   Timing of Reporting Expenses versus Cash Payments

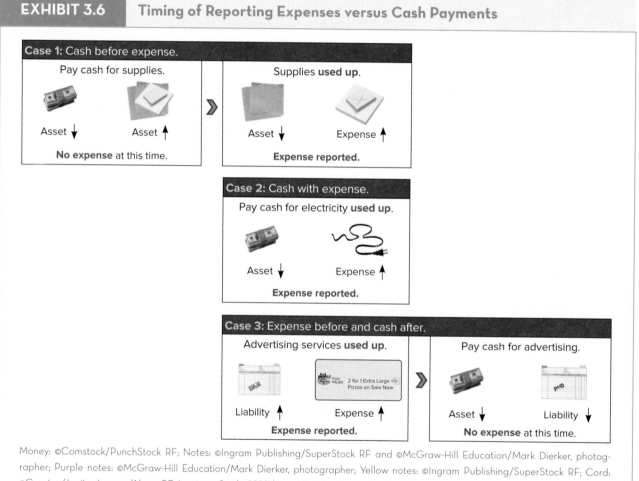

Money: ©Comstock/PunchStock RF; Notes: ©Ingram Publishing/SuperStock RF and ©McGraw-Hill Education/Mark Dierker, photographer; Purple notes: ©McGraw-Hill Education/Mark Dierker, photographer; Yellow notes: ©Ingram Publishing/SuperStock RF; Cord: ©Creatas/Jupiter Images/Alamy RF; Invoice: ©Studio 101/Alamy RF; Advertisement: ©SonicGateway

Case 1: Cash before expense. It is common for businesses to pay for something that provides benefits only in future periods. For example, Pizza Palace might buy paper napkins now, but not use them until next month. Under the expense recognition principle, the expense from using these supplies (Supplies Expense) is reported next month, when the supplies are used to earn revenue, not in the month when the supplies were purchased. This month, the supplies represent an asset (Supplies). Similar situations arise when a company prepays rent or insurance in one month and uses up these assets in a later month.

Case 2: Cash with expense. Pizza Palace has arranged to make automatic monthly payments at the end of each month to its utility company for electricity. Because the electricity is used up in the current month, it is an expense of the current month.

Case 3: Expense before and cash after. Most businesses acquire goods or services on credit, so it is common for them to incur the expense of using up the benefits of goods or services in the current month and pay for them in a later month. For example, Pizza Palace places ads online but does not pay for this service until the following month. Because the ads run in the current month, they are an expense that will be reported on this month's income statement. Because the cost has not yet been paid at the end of the month, the balance sheet reports a corresponding liability called Accounts Payable. Similar situations arise when employees work in the current period but are not paid their wages until the following period. This period's wages are reported as Salaries and Wages Expense on the income statement, and any unpaid wages are reported as Salaries and Wages Payable on the balance sheet.

It's time for you to practise determining which costs should be reported as expenses on an income statement that's been prepared using accrual basis accounting. As you work through the next Self–Study Practice, feel free to glance at Exhibit 3.6 for help.

HOW'S IT GOING?

Self-Study Practice 3.3

The following transactions are typical operating activities for Nova Scotia Seas, a scuba diving and instruction company. Indicate the amount of expense, if any, that should be recognized in June for each activity.

Operating Activity	Amount of Expense Incurred in June
1. In June, Nova Scotia Seas paid $6,000 cash for insurance for July to December.	
2. In June, Nova Scotia Seas paid $4,000 in wages to employees for work performed in June.	
3. In June, Nova Scotia Seas used $2,400 of electricity, to be paid in July.	

After you have finished, check your answers with the solution, which follows the chapter summary.

THE EXPANDED ACCOUNTING EQUATION

When we introduced the basic accounting equation in Chapter 2, we didn't mention how to account for the income statement effects of operating activities. You already had enough to learn about the effects of investing and financing activities on assets, liabilities, and contributed capital. The time has now come for you to learn how to analyze, record, and summarize the effects of activities affecting the income statement. To do this, you first need to know how the debit/credit framework works with revenues and expenses.

Let's start with the basic accounting equation from Chapter 2: assets equal liabilities plus shareholders' equity, or A = L + SE. For now, we're going to focus on the shareholders' equity category. As you already know from Chapters 1 and 2, shareholders' equity represents shareholders' claims on the company, which come from either (1) Contributed Capital, given to the company by shareholders in exchange for shares, or (2) Retained Earnings, generated by the company itself through profitable operations. Retained Earnings is the part that expands to include revenues and expenses, as shown in Exhibit 3.7.

EXHIBIT 3.7   The Expanded Debit/Credit Framework

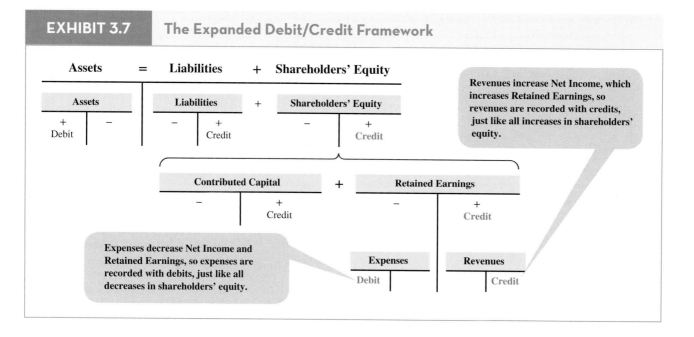

Assets   =   Liabilities   +   Shareholders' Equity

Revenues increase Net Income, which increases Retained Earnings, so revenues are recorded with credits, just like all increases in shareholders' equity.

Expenses decrease Net Income and Retained Earnings, so expenses are recorded with debits, just like all decreases in shareholders' equity.

Take a moment to look at how Exhibit 3.7 encourages you to think of revenues and expenses as subcategories within Retained Earnings. They are shown this way because revenues and expenses eventually flow into Retained Earnings, but they aren't initially recorded there. Instead, each revenue and expense is accumulated in a separate account, making it easier to identify the amount to report for each item on the income statement. At the end of each accounting year, these separate revenue and expense accounts are transferred to (or "closed") into Retained Earnings through a process that we'll demonstrate in Chapter 4. For now, just focus on learning how revenues and expenses are recorded to indicate increases and decreases in the company's earnings, with corresponding effects recorded in the company's asset and/or liability accounts.

Because revenue and expense accounts are subcategories of Retained Earnings, they are affected by debits and credits in the same way as all shareholders' equity accounts. You already know that increases in shareholders' equity are recorded on the right side. You also know that revenues increase net income, which increases the shareholders' equity account Retained Earnings. So putting these ideas together should lead to the conclusion that revenues are recorded on the right (credit).

Here's the logic again: increases in shareholders' equity are on the right—revenues increase shareholders' equity, and revenues are recorded on the right (credit). Decreases in shareholders' equity are recorded on the left side, so to show that expenses decrease net income and retained earnings, expenses are recorded on the left (debit). Exhibit 3.7 summarizes these effects.

Transaction Analysis, Recording, and Summarizing

To learn how to use your new knowledge of the revenue and expense recognition principles, the expanded accounting equation, and the debit/credit framework, you'll need lots of practice. Let's continue analyzing, recording, and summarizing as we did in Chapter 2, except now we'll focus on Pizza Palace's operating activities in September.

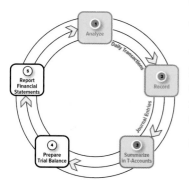

(a) **Provide Services for Cash.** In September, Pizza Palace delivered pizza to customers for $15,000 cash. These activities qualify as accounting transactions because Pizza Palace received cash and delivered pizza, which generates revenues. The increase in Cash (an asset) must be recorded (with a debit) along with the revenue (which, as a subcategory of shareholders' equity), is recorded with a credit.

To indicate that the pizza deliveries increase revenue, which ultimately increases shareholders' equity, we use the notation (+R, +SE) in the journal entry. The increase in Cash is summarized in the Cash T−account, which carried a debit balance of $10,000 forward from the end of August (Chapter 2). The revenues earned are recorded in a new account called *Pizza Revenue*, which has a beginning balance of zero because the company began operating only this month.

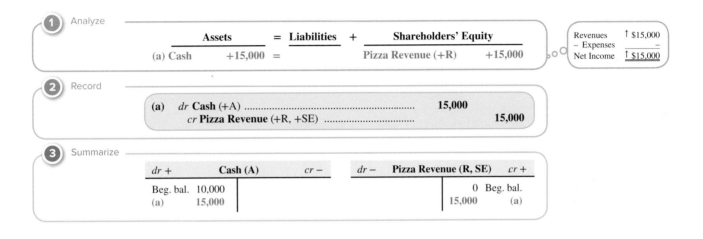

(b) Receive Cash for Future Services. Pizza Palace issued three $100 gift cards at the beginning of September. Pizza Palace receives cash but gives only gift cards, which creates an obligation to accept the gift cards as payment for pizzas in the future. This obligation is recorded as a liability called *Deferred Revenue*.

> **COACH'S TIP**
>
> The word *deferred* in the Deferred Revenue account means the company hasn't done everything it was paid to do. The revenue is therefore deferred until the good or service has been provided. The company has a liability to do the work or return the cash.

1 Analyze

	Assets	=	Liabilitie		+	Shareholders' Equity
(b)	Cash +300	=	Deferred Revenue	+300		

2 Record

(b)	dr **Cash** (+A)	300	
	cr **Deferred Revenue** (+L)		300

3 Summarize

dr +	Cash (A)	cr −		dr −	Deferred Revenue (L)	cr +
Beg. bal.	10,000				0	Beg. bal.
(a)	15,000				300	(b)
(b)	300					

(c) **Provide Services on Credit.** Pizza Palace delivers $500 of pizza to a university organization, billing this customer on account. Once again, this is another instance where revenues are recorded based on whether the work has been done, not whether cash has been received. Because the pizza has been delivered, Pizza Palace has earned revenue and now has the right to collect $500 from the university organization. The right to collect money is an asset called *Accounts Receivable*. Use a debit to increase this asset, and a credit to increase revenue.

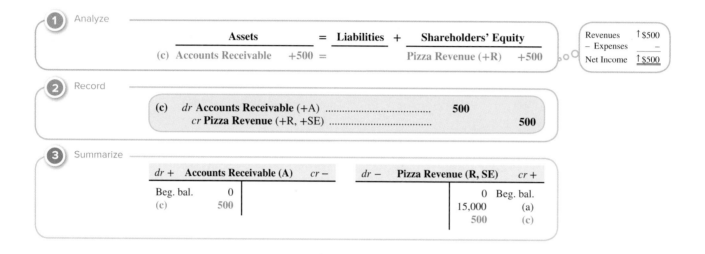

1 Analyze

	Assets	=	Liabilities	+	Shareholders' Equity
(c) Accounts Receivable	+500 =				Pizza Revenue (+R) +500

Revenues	↑$500
– Expenses	–
Net Income	↑$500

2 Record

(c) dr **Accounts Receivable** (+A) 500
        cr **Pizza Revenue** (+R, +SE) 500

3 Summarize

dr +	Accounts Receivable (A)	cr −
Beg. bal.	0	
(c)	500	

dr −	Pizza Revenue (R, SE)	cr +
	0	Beg. bal.
	15,000	(a)
	500	(c)

(d) **Receive Payment on Account** Pizza Palace received a $300 cheque from the university organization, as partial payment of its account balance. This transaction does not involve additional pizza deliveries, so no additional revenue is generated. Instead, the receipt of cash reduces the amount that Pizza Palace can collect from this customer in the future, so it causes a decrease in Accounts Receivable.

1 Analyze

	Assets	=	Liabilities	+	Shareholders' Equity
(d) Cash	+300				
Accounts Receivable	−300				

2 Record

(d) dr **Cash** (+A) 300
        cr **Accounts Receivable** (−A) 300

3 Summarize

dr +	Cash (A)	cr −
Beg. bal.	10,000	
(a)	15,000	
(b)	300	
(d)	300	

dr +	Accounts Receivable (A)		cr −
Beg. bal.	0		
(c)	500	300	(d)

Self-Study Practice 3.4

Analyze, record, and summarize the following June transaction: **Nova Scotia Seas provided $3,000 of diving instruction in June to customers who will pay cash in July.**

1 Analyze

Assets = Liabilities + Shareholders' Equity

2 Record

dr [   ] ([ ]) .... [   ]
cr [   ] ([   ]) ... [   ]

3 Summarize

dr ( ) cr   dr ( ) cr

After you have finished, check your answers with the solution, which follows the chapter summary.

(e) Pay Cash to Employees. Pizza Palace wrote cheques to employees totalling **$8,700** for wages related to hours worked in September. The expense recognition principle requires that all expenses that relate to revenues reported in the current period be recorded in the current period. Because this transaction involves using the efforts of employees to make and deliver pizza, it represents an expense. We show (+E, −SE) because as expenses increase, net income decreases, which causes shareholders' equity to decrease.

COACH'S TIP

To review why expenses are recorded using a debit, see Exhibit 3.7.

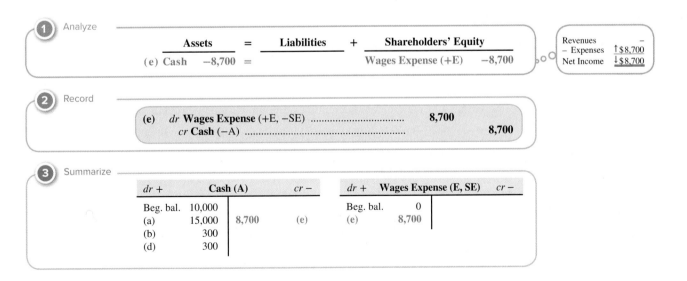

1 Analyze

	Assets	=	Liabilities	+	Shareholders' Equity	
(e) Cash	−8,700	=			Wages Expense (+E) −8,700	

Revenues	−
− Expenses	↑$8,700
Net Income	↓$8,700

2 Record

(e) dr **Wages Expense** (+E, −SE) 8,700
      cr **Cash** (−A) 8,700

3 Summarize

dr +	Cash (A)	cr −		dr +	Wages Expense (E, SE)	cr −
Beg. bal.	10,000			Beg. bal.	0	
(a)	15,000	8,700 (e)		(e)	8,700	
(b)	300					
(d)	300					

(f) Pay Cash in Advance. On September 1, Pizza Palace paid **$7,200** in advance for September, October, and November rent. This transaction involves paying for the right to use the rented building for three months following the payment. This payment provides an eco–nomic resource to Pizza Palace (building space for three months), so it will initially be reported as an asset called *Prepaid Rent*. Each month, when the rented space has been used, Pizza Palace will reduce Prepaid Rent and show the amount used up as Rent Expense. The adjustment needed to report that September's share of the total rent expense $(1/3 \times \$7,200 = \$2,400)$ will be covered in Chapter 4. For now, we will record just the $7,200 rent prepayment.

1 Analyze

	Assets		=	Liabilities	+	Shareholders' Equity
(f) Cash		−7,200				
Prepaid Rent		+7,200				

2 Record

(f) *dr* **Prepaid Rent (+A)** 7,200
        cr **Cash (−A)** 7,200

3 Summarize

dr +	Cash (A)		*cr* −
Beg. bal.	10,000		
(a)	15,000	8,700	(e)
(b)	300	7,200	(f)
(d)	300		

dr +	Prepaid Rent (A)		*cr* −
Beg. bal.	0		
(f)	7,200		

Prepayments for insurance and other time–based services would be analyzed and recorded in a similar manner.

(g) **Pay Cash in Advance.** On September 2, Pizza Palace wrote a cheque for $1,600 for pizza sauce, dough, cheese, and paper products. This transaction provides another example of a prepayment that is initially recorded as an asset. The supplies are an asset because they

1 Analyze

	Assets		=	Liabilities	+	Shareholders' Equity
(g) Cash		−1,600				
Supplies		+1,600				

2 Record

(g) *dr* **Supplies (+A)** 1,600
        cr **Cash (−A)** 1,600

3 Summarize

dr +	Cash (A)		*cr* −
Beg. bal.	10,000		
(a)	15,000	8,700	(e)
(b)	300	7,200	(f)
(d)	300	1,600	(g)

dr +	Supplies (A)		*cr* −
Beg. bal.	0		
(g)	1,600		

can be used to make and sell pizza in the future. Later, when that happens and the supplies have been used up, Pizza Palace will reduce the Supplies account balance and report the amount used up as Supplies Expense. The adjustment to be made at the end of September will be covered in Chapter 4.

(h) **Incur Cost to Be Paid Later. Pizza Palace placed Facebook sidebar ads in September** and received a bill for $400 to be paid in October. This cost was incurred for September advertising services, so according to the expense recognition principle, it should be recorded as an expense in September. Rather than pay cash for this expense, Pizza Palace gave a promise to pay, which increases the liability called *Accounts Payable*.

> **COACH'S TIP**
>
> The beginning balance in Accounts Payable is carried forward from the previous month's activities discussed in Chapter 2

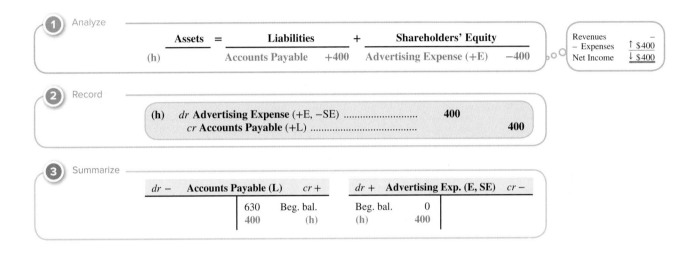

1 Analyze

	Assets	=	Liabilities	+	Shareholders' Equity	
(h)			Accounts Payable +400		Advertising Expense (+E)	−400

Revenues	−
− Expenses	↑ $400
Net Income	↓ $400

2 Record

(h) *dr* **Advertising Expense (+E, −SE)** 400
     cr **Accounts Payable (+L)** 400

3 Summarize

dr −	Accounts Payable (L)	*cr* +
	630	Beg. bal.
	400	(h)

dr +	Advertising Exp. (E, SE)	*cr* −
Beg. bal.	0	
(h)	400	

(i) **Pay Cash for Expenses. Pizza Palace was notified by its bank that an automatic monthly payment of $600 was transmitted to its utility company for electricity use in September.** Just like transaction (e), the cash payment and expense occurred during the same period.

1 Analyze

	Assets	=	Liabilities	+	Shareholders' Equity	
(i)	Cash −600	=			Utilities Expense (+E)	−600

Revenues	−
− Expenses	↑ $600
Net Income	↓ $600

2 Record

(i) *dr* **Utilities Expense (+E, −SE)** 600
     cr **Cash (−A)** 600

3 Summarize

dr +	Cash (A)		*cr* −
Beg. bal.	10,000		
(a)	15,000	8,700	(e)
(b)	300	7,200	(f)
(d)	300	1,600	(g)
		600	(i)

dr +	Utilities Expense (E, SE)	*cr* −
Beg. bal.	0	
(i)	600	

Self-Study Practice 3.5

For a little break and some practice, let's return one last time to Nova Scotia Seas. Analyze, record, and summarize the effects of the following transaction for June: **Nova Scotia Seas paid $4,000 in wages to employees who worked in June**.

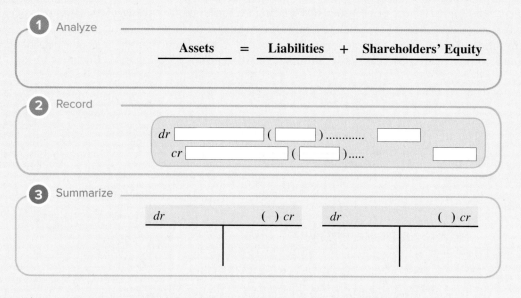

After you have finished, check your answers with the solution, which follows the chapter summary.

Calculating Account Balances.   After entering ("posting") the effects of each journal entry into the T−accounts, we can now calculate the ending balances. In Exhibit 3.8, we have included all the T−accounts for Pizza Palace (from this chapter as well as Chapter 2). You've heard it before, but we'll just remind you that the ending balance in each account is the amount by which the total of the increase (+) side exceeds the total of the decrease (−) side.

UNADJUSTED TRIAL BALANCE

LEARNING OBJECTIVE 3-4

Prepare an unadjusted trial balance.

After summarizing journal entries in the various accounts and then cal−culating ending balances for each account, you should check that the total recorded debits equal the total recorded credits by preparing an unadjusted trial balance.

The unadjusted trial balance shown in Exhibit 3.9 is similar to the one shown In Chapter 2. The only difference is that we now have income statement accounts (revenues, expenses) to list after the balance sheet accounts. As before, use the debit column for accounts showing an ending debit balance and the credit column for accounts showing an ending credit balance. Lastly, add the two columns and see if the total dollar amount of debits equals the total dollar amount of credits.

If your trial balance indicates that total debits don't equal total credits, you should be concerned because this means you've made an error some−where in preparing or posting the journal entries to the T−accounts. Don't panic or start randomly changing numbers. The first thing to do when you find yourself in a hole is stop digging. Calmly look at the difference

EXHIBIT 3.8 T-Accounts for Pizza Palace

PIZZA PALACE

| Assets | = | Liabilities | + | Shareholders' Equity |

Cash (A) — dr + / cr −

Beg. bal.	10,000		
(a)	15,000	8,700	(e)
(b)	300	7,200	(f)
(d)	300	1,600	(g)
		600	(i)
End. bal.	7,500		

Accounts Receivable (A) — dr + / cr −

Beg. bal.	0		
(c)	500	300	(d)
End. bal.	200		

Supplies (A) — dr + / cr −

Beg. bal.	0	
(g)	1,600	
End. bal.	1,600	

Prepaid Rent (A) — dr + / cr −

Beg. bal.	0	
(f)	7,200	
End. bal.	7,200	

Cookware (A) — dr + / cr −

Beg. bal.	630	

Equipment (A) — dr + / cr −

Beg. bal.	60,000	

Accounts Payable (L) — dr − / cr +

		630	Beg. bal.
		400	(h)
		1,030	End. bal.

Deferred Revenue (L) — dr − / cr +

		0	Beg. bal.
		300	(b)
		300	End. bal.

Note Payable (L) — dr − / cr +

		20,000	Beg. bal.

Contributed Capital (SE) — dr − / cr +

		50,000	Beg. bal.

Retained Earnings (SE) — dr − / cr +

		0	Beg. bal.

Pizza Revenue (R, SE) — dr − / cr +

		0	Beg. bal.
		15,000	(a)
		500	(c)
		15,500	End. bal.

Wages Expense (E, SE) — dr + / cr −

Beg. bal.	0	
(e)	8,700	
End. bal.	8,700	

Utilities Expense (E, SE) — dr + / cr −

Beg. bal.	0	
(i)	600	
End. bal.	600	

Advertising Exp. (E, SE) — dr + / cr −

Beg. bal.	0	
(h)	400	
End. bal.	400	

> Beginning balances in this exhibit (September 1) are the ending balances in Exhibit 2.12 (August 31).

between total debits and credits, and consult the Homework Helper section for tips on how to find the error causing that difference.

Be aware that even if total debits equal total credits, it's still possible that you've made an error. For example, if you accidentally debit an asset rather than an expense, or credit Accounts Payable instead of Deferred Revenue, total debits would still equal total credits. So if the trial balance doesn't balance, you know you've made an error for sure. If the trial bal‑ance does balance, it's still possible that you've made a mistake.

If you haven't already scanned the trial balance in Exhibit 3.9, take a moment to do it now. Notice that the title says unadjusted trial balance. It is called this because several adjustments will have to be made at the end of the accounting period to update the accounts. For example, some of the benefits of Prepaid Rent were used up in September, but this hasn't been recorded yet. If you're really sharp, you'll also have noticed that income taxes haven't been calculated and recorded yet.

Although it's possible to prepare preliminary financial statements using the numbers on the unadjusted trial balance, most companies don't. They wait until after the final adjustments are made. These adjustments will

EXHIBIT 3.9   Sample Unadjusted Trial Balance

PIZZA PALACE INC.
Unadjusted Trial Balance
At September 30, 2017

Account Name	Debits	Credits
Cash	$ 7,500	
Accounts Receivable	200	
Supplies	1,600	
Prepaid Rent	7,200	
Cookware	630	
Equipment	60,000	
Accounts Payable		$ 1,030
Deferred Revenue		300
Note Payable		20,000
Contributed Capital		50,000
Retained Earnings		0
Pizza Revenue		15,500
Wages Expense	8,700	
Utilities Expense	600	
Advertising Expense	400	
Totals	$86,830	$86,830

Balance sheet accounts

Income statement accounts

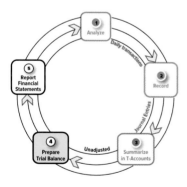

ensure the revenues and expenses are up to date and complete so that the (adjusted) net income number will provide a good indication about whether the company was profitable during the period. Don't worry about how to make the end-of-period adjustments yet. We'll spend most of Chapter 4 on that. For now, just realize that the accounts still have to be adjusted before we can prepare financial statements that follow generally accepted accounting principles.

REVIEW OF REVENUES AND EXPENSES

Up to this point in the chapter, you've analyzed some transactions—nine, actually—that involve operating activities. While this is a good introduction, it doesn't quite prepare you for the variety of operating activities that most companies engage in. What you really need is a general summary of everything you've learned about revenues, expenses, and journal entries, and then lots of practice applying it to a broad range of activities. Let's start with revenues.

Remember that revenues are recorded when the business fulfills its promise to provide goods or services to customers, which is not necessarily the same time that cash is received. Because of this, we look at three cases where cash is received: (1) before the revenue is earned by delivering goods or services, (2) in the same period the revenue is earned, and (3) after the revenue is earned. The journal entries for these situations are shown in the following panels.

COACH'S TIP

A trial balance is prepared by simply listing and summing the T-account balances.

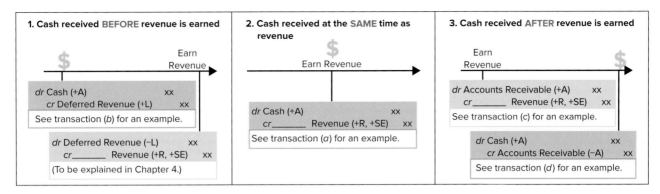

These three panels correspond to the revenue transactions for Pizza Palace analyzed earlier in this chapter, but they can be applied to any business. We use a generic label "_____ Revenue" with the expectation that you will fill in the blank with whatever type of revenue you are recording. That is, when accounting for revenue from delivering pizza, you should use an account name like Pizza Revenue. A more complete list of account names is provided in the Homework Helper section.

Let's look at a similar summary for expenses now. Under accrual accounting, expenses are recorded when incurred (by using up the economic benefits of acquired items). Expenses are not necessarily incurred at the same time that cash is paid. Because of this, we look at three cases where cash is paid: (1) before the expense is incurred, (2) in the same period the expense is incurred, and (3) after the expense is incurred. The corresponding journal entries are summarized in the following panels.

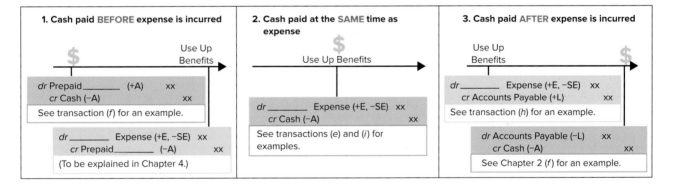

Again, we use generic labels like "Prepaid _____" and "_____ Expense" with the expectation that you will fill in the blank with whatever type of item you are recording (e.g., Prepaid Rent, Rent Expense, Prepaid Insurance, Insurance Expense).

Evaluate the Results

NET PROFIT MARGIN

The income statement provides the main measure of a company's operating performance for one particular period. The key thing to look for is whether net income is positive (revenues exceed expenses). Beyond that, it's useful to consider whether revenues are growing faster than expenses. If so, the company's net income will be increasing.

Currently, Pizza Palace's accounting records report revenues of $15,500 and expenses of $8,700, $600, and $400, suggesting a net income of $5,800.

Net Profit Margin: Indicates how much profit is earned from each dollar of revenue.

This net income of $5,800 is about 37.4 percent of the $15,500 of revenues ($5,800 ÷ $15,500 = 0.3741). This **net profit margin**, as it is called, implies that Pizza Palace earned 37.4 cents of net income from each dollar of pizza revenue. But Ally cautions Emilio that these measures are preliminary and will change when the accounting records are adjusted at the end of September. The adjustment process is the main topic of Chapter 4.

ACCOUNTING DECISION TOOLS

Name of Measure	Formula	What It Tells You
Net profit margin	$\dfrac{\text{Net Income}}{\text{Total Revenue}}$	• The amount of profit from each dollar of revenue • A higher ratio means better performance

As Emilio realized, a good accountant like Ally monitors how well other companies are doing. She was able to advise Emilio that pizza companies usually have low net profit margins because their ingredients are relatively expensive. For example, as shown below, Papa John's net profit margin has been around 5 percent, except during the financial crisis when it was 3 percent.

SPOTLIGHT ON Financial Reporting

Net Profit Margin Before and After the Financial Crisis

The following graph indicates the net profit margins of three dominant pizza companies: Papa John's, Domino's Pizza, and California Pizza Kitchen. The graph shows a significant decline in net profit margin leading into the financial crisis of 2008, with a good recovery in 2009 for two of the companies. Unfortunately, California Pizza Kitchen was unable to reverse its declining profit margin and was sold to a private company in 2011.

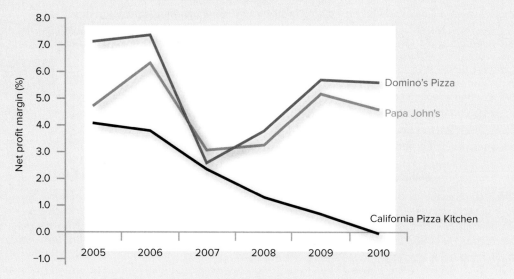

INCOME STATEMENT LIMITATIONS

Although an income statement is useful for assessing a company's performance, it does have some limitations that lead to common misconceptions. One of the most common is that some people think net income equals the amount of cash generated by the business during the period. While this is the way many of us think about our own income, it's not the way companies recognize revenues and expenses on the income statement when using accrual basis accounting.

A second, related misconception is that a company's net income represents the change in the company's value during the period. While a company's net income is one source of value to the company, many other determinants of its value are not included in the income statement. A good example is the increase in the value of Pizza Palace's name as it grows its reputation for making great pizza.

A third common misconception is that the measurement of income involves only counting. Proper counting is essential to income measurement, but estimation also plays a role. For example, Pizza Palace's equipment will not last forever. Instead, it will be "used up" over time to generate the company's revenue. It should therefore be expensed over the period in which it is used. Doing so requires an estimate of the period over which each category of equipment will be used. We will discuss this particular example in Chapter 4; many other examples of the role of estimates in income measurement will arise in later chapters.

SPOTLIGHT ON Ethics

Why All the Scandals?

You may have heard about accounting scandals, such as those at Enron and WorldCom (now owned by Verizon Communications), in which managers have been accused of "cooking the books." Why did they do it? The simple answer is greed. Companies whose earnings have fallen often experience a decline in their share prices, which usually leads to pay reductions or even job losses for senior executives. When a company is actually performing poorly, greed may lead some managers to falsify revenues and hide expenses to make it look like the company is still doing well.

While this sometimes fools people for a short time, it rarely works in the long run and often leads to very bad consequences. Several cases involving faulty revenue and expense accounting follow. As you look at these cases, imagine what it must have been like to be Bernie Ebbers—the person who received a twenty-five-year prison sentence at age sixty-five. It is probably just as bad as being Barry Minkow, who was sentenced to twenty-five years in jail when he was twenty-one.

The CEO	The Fraud	Conviction/Plea	The Outcome
Bernie Ebbers, 65 WorldCom	Recorded operating expenses as if they were assets; resulted in the largest fraud in U.S. history	Convicted July 2005	Sentenced to 25 years
Garth Drabinsky, 61 Livent Inc.	Moved operating expenses from one period to another; recorded operating expenses as if they were assets	Convicted August 2009	Sentenced to 7 years
Sanjay Kumar, 44 Computer Associates	Recorded sales in the wrong accounting period	Pleaded guilty April 2006	Sentenced to 12 years
Martin Grass, 49 Rite Aid Corporation	Recorded rebates from drug companies before they were earned	Pleaded guilty June 2003	Sentenced to 8 years
Barry Minkow, 21 ZZZZ Best	Made up customers and sales to show profits when, in reality, the company was a sham	Convicted December 1988	Sentenced to 25 years

Due to the nature of the material in Chapter 3, there are many similarities between ASPE and IFRS. Both require the same basis of accounting for external reporting of financial statements, and both have revenue and expense recognition principles. The revenue recognition principle under IFRS has recently changed and is a more comprehensive framework for revenue recognition than that found under ASPE. This framework is outlined below. The expense recognition principle is the same under both sets of standards.

Topic	ASPE	IFRS
Basis of Accounting	Accrual basis of accounting is the only acceptable method for external reporting of financial statements.	Accrual basis of accounting is the only acceptable method for external reporting of financial statements.
Revenue Recognition Principle	Revenues should be recognized when they are earned.	Revenues should be recognized when the transfer of promised goods or services to customers has occurred, in an amount that reflects the consideration to which the company expects to be entitled in exchange for those goods and services. Revenue is to be recognized by the company when control over the goods or services is transferred to the customer. This is applied through a five-step model: 1. Identify the contract. 2. Identify separate performance obligations. 3. Determine the transaction price. 4. Allocate transaction price to the performance obligations. 5. Recognize revenue when each performance obligation is satisfied.
Expense Recognition Principle	Expenses are recognized in the same period as the revenues to which they relate.	Expenses are recognized in the same period as the revenues to which they relate.

Review the Chapter

This section provides a chance to solidify your understanding of key points. It's worth your time to work through the following demonstration cases, scan the chapter summary, test your understanding of key terms, and then practise, practise, practise.

DEMONSTRATION CASE A

1. From the following list of balance sheet and income statement account balances for Castle Cruises Corporation, prepare an income statement for the year ended November 30, 2017. (Amounts are reported in millions of Canadian dollars.)
2. Explain what the results suggest about the cruise ship company's operating performance. For the same period last year, net income was $1,990,000,000 (in Canadian dollars) and net profit margin was 15.3 percent.

Transportation Expenses	$ 2,232	Wages Expense	$1,470	Selling Expenses	$ 1,629
Passenger Ticket Revenue	11,210	Fuel Expenses	1,774	Prepaid Expenses	267
Onboard Revenue	3,436	Accounts Payable	512	Ship Expenses	4,308
Food Expenses	856	Income Tax Expense	47	Deferred Revenue	2,519

Suggested Solution

1. Income Statement

CASTLE CRUISES CORPORATION
Income Statement
For the Year Ended November 30, 2017
(in millions)

Revenues	
Passenger Ticket Revenue	$11,210
Onboard Revenue	3,436
Total Revenues	14,646
Expenses	
Ship Expenses	4,308
Transportation Expenses	2,232
Selling Expenses	1,629
Fuel Expenses	1,774
Wages Expense	1,470
Food Expenses	856
Income Tax Expense	47
Total Expenses	12,316
Net Income	$ 2,330

2. The net income of $2,330,000,000 indicates that Castle Cruises Corporation was profit− able, meaning that the revenues it earned were greater than the expenses it incurred. Its net profit margin was 15.9 percent of total revenues ($2,330,000,000 ÷ $14,646,000,000 = 0.159). This is a positive sign. It is an improvement over the net income of $1,990,000,000 and net profit margin of 15.3 percent reported in the prior year.

DEMONSTRATION CASE B

This case is a continuation of the Goodbye Grass Corporation case introduced in Chapter 2. The company was established, and property and equipment were purchased. The balance sheet at April 30, 2017, based on only the investing and financing activities (from Chapter 2) is as follows:

GOODBYE GRASS CORPORATION
Balance Sheet
At April 30, 2017

Assets		Liabilities	
Current Assets		Current Liabilities	
Cash	$ 3,800	Accounts Payable	$ 400
Note Receivable	1,250	Note Payable	4,000
Total Current Assets	5,050	Total Current Liabilities	4,400
Equipment	4,600	**Shareholders' Equity**	
Land	3,750	Contributed Capital	9,000
		Retained Earnings	0
		Total Shareholders' Equity	9,000
		Total Liabilities and	
Total Assets	$13,400	Shareholders' Equity	$ 13,400

The following activities also occurred during April 2017:

a. The company purchased and used gasoline for mowers and edgers, paying $90 in cash at a local gas station.

b. In early April, received $1,600 cash from the city in advance for lawn maintenance service for April through July ($400 each month). The entire amount is to be recorded as Deferred Revenue.

c. In early April, purchased $300 of insurance covering six months, April through September. The entire payment is to be recorded as Prepaid Insurance.

d. Mowed lawns for residential customers who are billed every two weeks. A total of $5,200 of service was billed and is to be recorded in April.

e. Residential customers paid $3,500 on their accounts.

f. Paid wages every two weeks. Total cash paid in April was $3,900.

g. Received a bill for $320 from the local gas station for additional gasoline purchased on account and used in April.

h. Paid $100 on Accounts Payable.

Required:

1. Analyze activities (a) through (h) with the goal of indicating their effects on the basic accounting equation (Assets = Liabilities + Shareholders' Equity), using the format shown in the chapter.

2. Prepare journal entries to record the transactions identified among activities (a) through (h).

   TIP: Treat insurance (in c) in the same manner as Pizza Palace's rent in transaction (f).

3. Summarize the effects of each transaction in the appropriate T–accounts. Before enter–ing these effects, set up T–accounts for Cash, Accounts Receivable, Note Receivable, Prepaid Insurance, Equipment, Land, Accounts Payable, Deferred Revenue, Note Payable, Contributed Capital, Retained Earnings, Mowing Revenue, Wages Expense, and Fuel Expense. The beginning balance in each T–account should be the amount shown on the balance sheet above or $0 if the account does not appear on the balance sheet. After posting the journal entries to the T–accounts, compute ending balances for each of the T–accounts.

4. Use the amounts in the T–accounts to prepare an unadjusted trial balance for Goodbye Grass Corporation at April 30, 2017.

5. Alongside the trial balance, indicate which accounts would be reported on the balance sheet and which would be reported on the income statement.

   After completing the above requirements, check your answers with the following solution.

Suggested Solution

1. Transaction analysis

		Assets	=	Liabilities		+	Shareholders' Equity	
(a)	Cash	−90	=				Fuel Expense (+E)	−90
(b)	Cash	+1,600	=	Deferred Revenue	+1,600			
(c)	Cash	−300	=		No change			
	Prepaid Insurance	+300						
(d)	Accounts Receivable	+5,200	=				Mowing Revenue (+R)	+5,200
(e)	Cash	+3,500	=		No change			
	Accounts Receivable	−3,500						
(f)	Cash	−3,900	=				Wages Expense (+E)	−3,900
(g)	No change		=	Accounts Payable	+320		Fuel Expense (+E)	−320
(h)	Cash	−100	=	Accounts Payable	−100			

2. Journal entries

a.	dr Fuel Expense (+E, −SE)............................	90	
	cr Cash (−A)..		90
b.	dr Cash (+A)...	1,600	
	cr Deferred Revenue (+L).........................		1,600
c.	dr Prepaid Insurance (+A)...........................	300	
	cr Cash (−A)..		300
d.	dr Accounts Receivable (+A).......................	5,200	
	cr Mowing Revenue (+R, +SE)...................		5,200
e.	dr Cash (+A)...	3,500	
	cr Accounts Receivable (−A)......................		3,500
f.	dr Wages Expense (+E, −SE).......................	3,900	
	cr Cash (−A)..		3,900
g.	dr Fuel Expense (+E, −SE)..........................	320	
	cr Accounts Payable (+L)...........................		320
h.	dr Accounts Payable (−L)............................	100	
	cr Cash (−A)..		100

3. T−accounts

Assets	=	Liabilities	+	Shareholders' Equity

Cash (A) — dr + / cr −

dr +	Cash (A)		cr −
Beg. bal.	3,800		
(b)	1,600	90	(a)
(e)	3,500	300	(c)
		3,900	(f)
		100	(h)
End. bal.	4,510		

dr +	Accounts Receivable (A)		cr −
Beg. bal.	0		
(d)	5,200	3,500	(e)
End. bal.	1,700		

dr +	Note Receivable (A)		cr −
Beg. bal.	1,250		
End. bal.	1,250		

dr +	Prepaid Insurance (A)		cr −
Beg. bal.	0		
(c)	300		
End. Bal.	300		

dr +	Equipment (A)		cr −
Beg. bal.	4,600		
End. bal.	4,600		

dr +	Land (A)		cr −
Beg. bal.	3,750		
End. bal.	3,750		

dr −	Accounts Payable (L)		cr +
		400	Beg. bal.
(h)	100	320	(g)
		620	End. bal.

dr −	Deferred Revenue (L)		cr +
		0	Beg. bal.
		1,600	(b)
		1,600	End. bal.

dr −	Note Payable (L)		cr +
		4,000	Beg. bal.
		4,000	End. bal.

dr −	Contributed Capital (SE)		cr +
		9,000	Beg. bal.
		9,000	End. bal.

dr −	Retained Earnings (SE)		cr +
		0	Beg. bal.
		0	End. bal.

dr +	Wages Expense (E)		cr −
Beg. bal.	0		
(f)	3,900		
End. bal.	3,900		

dr −	Mowing Revenue (R)		cr +
		0	Beg. bal.
		5,200	(d)
		5,200	End. bal.

dr +	Fuel Expense (E)		cr −
Beg. bal.	0		
(a)	90		
(g)	320		
End. bal.	410		

4. Unadjusted trial balance

GOODBYE GRASS CORPORATION
Unadjusted Trial Balance
At April 30, 2017

Account Name	Debits	Credits	
Cash	$ 4,510		⎫
Accounts Receivable	1,700		
Note Receivable	1,250		
Prepaid Insurance	300		
Equipment	4,600		Balance
Land	3,750		sheet
Accounts Payable		$ 620	
Deferred Revenue		1,600	
Note Payable		4,000	
Contributed Capital		9,000	
Retained Earnings		0	⎭
Service Revenue		5,002	⎫
Salaries and Wages Expense	3,900		Income
Fuel Expense	410		statement
Totals	$20,420	$20,420	⎭

CHAPTER SUMMARY

LO3-1 **Describe common operating transactions and select appropriate income statement account titles.**

- The income statement reports the results of transactions that affect net income, which include
  Revenues—amounts charged to customers for sales of goods or services provided
  Expenses—costs of business activities undertaken to earn revenues
- See Exhibit 3.2 for basic income statement format.

LO3-2 **Explain and apply the revenue and expense recognition principles.**

- There are two key concepts underlying accrual basis accounting and the income statement.
  Revenue recognition principle—recognize revenues when they are earned by providing goods or services
  Expense recognition principle ("matching")—recognize expenses when they are incurred in generating revenue, regardless of when cash is paid

LO3-3 **Analyze, record, and summarize the effects of operating transactions, using the accounting equation, journal entries, and T-accounts.**

- The expanded transaction analysis model includes revenues and expenses as subcategories of Retained Earnings. Increases, decreases, and normal account balances (dr or cr) are shown below.

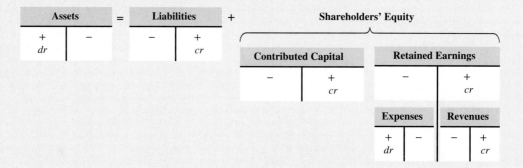

Prepare an unadjusted trial balance.

- The unadjusted trial balance is a list of all accounts and their unadjusted balances and is used to check on the equality of recorded debits and credits.

Evaluate net profit margin, but beware of income statement limitations.

- *Net profit margin* expresses net income as a percentage of total revenues.
- The income statement indicates whether the company is profitable, but it might not explain whether cash increased or decreased.
- The income statement does not directly measure the change in value of a company during the period.
- Estimation plays a key role when measuring income.

ACCOUNTING DECISION TOOLS

Name of Measure	Formula	What It Tells You
Net profit margin	$\dfrac{\text{Net Income}}{\text{Total Revenue}}$	• The amount of profit from each dollar of revenue • A higher ratio means better performance

SOLUTION TO SELF-STUDY PRACTICE

Solution to SP3.1

	Yes/No	Account Title
1.	Yes	Service Fee Revenue
2.	No	(A building is an asset not an expense.)
3.	Yes	Delivery Expense
4.	No	(Supplies are assets until used up.)
5.	Yes	Salaries and Wages Expense

Solution to SP3.2

1. $32,000
2. $5,200 in June (The remaining $3,000 will be recognized as revenue in July; until then, it is reported as a liability called *Deferred Revenue*.)
3. No revenue in June for this activity; revenue was earned and recognized in May (along with Accounts Receivable). The cash received in June reduces Accounts Receivable.

Solution to SP3.3

1. No expense in June for the $6,000 payment; the $6,000 will be reported as an asset called *Prepaid Insurance* until used up in July to December.
2. $4,000
3. $2,400: This cost relates to business activities in June, so the $2,400 is reported as an expense in June (a corresponding liability is reported on the balance sheet).

Solution to SP3.4

1.

Assets		=	Liabilities	+	Shareholders' Equity	
Accts. Receivable	+3,000 =				Diving Revenue (A)	+3,000

2. *dr* Accounts Receivable (+A).................3,000

    cr Diving Revenue (+R, +SE).......................3,000

3.

dr +	Accts. Rec. (A)	cr −		dr −	Diving Revenue (R, SE)	cr +
(June)	3,000				3,000	(June)

Solution to SP3.5

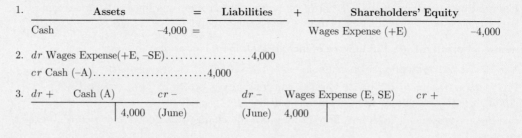

1.

Assets		=	Liabilities	+	Shareholders' Equity	
Cash	−4,000	=			Wages Expense (+E)	−4,000

2. dr Wages Expense(+E, −SE)................4,000
   cr Cash (−A)........................4,000

3.

$dr +$	Cash (A)	$cr -$		$dr -$	Wages Expense (E, SE)	$cr +$
	4,000 (June)			(June) 4,000		

KEY TERMS

Accrual Basis Accounting	Expense Recognition Principle (Matching)	Revenue Recognition Principle
Cash Basis Accounting		Revenues
Deferred Revenue	Net Income	Time Period Assumption
Expenses	Net Profit Margin	

Complete definitions are also provided in the glossary at the end of this text.

HOMEWORK HELPER

Account Name	Description
Revenues	
Sales Revenue	Arises from delivering products in the ordinary course of business
Service Revenue	Arises from providing services in the ordinary course of business
Rental Revenue	Amounts earned by renting out company property
Interest Revenue	Amounts earned on savings and loans to others
Dividend Revenue	Dividends earned from investing in other companies
Expenses	
Cost of Goods Sold	Cost of products sold in the ordinary course of business
Repairs & Maintenance Expense	Cost of routine maintenance and upkeep of buildings/equipment
Advertising Expense	Cost of advertising services obtained during the period
Depreciation Expense	Cost of plant and equipment used up during the period
Insurance Expense	Cost of insurance coverage for the current period
Salaries and Wages Expense	Cost of employees' salaries and wages for the period
Rent Expense	Cost of rent for the period
Supplies Expense	Cost of supplies used up during the period
Delivery Expense	Cost of freight to deliver goods to customers
Utilities Expense	Cost of power, light, heat, Internet, and telephone for the period
Amortization Expense	Cost of intangible assets used up or expired during the period
Interest Expense	Interest charged on outstanding debts owed during the period
Income Tax Expense	Taxes charged on net income reported for the period

Alternative terms

- *Net income* also can be called *net earnings* or *net profit*.
- *Prepaid Rent* and *Prepaid Insurance* can be called *Prepaid Expenses*, which is reported as a current asset on the balance sheet.
- The income statement may also be called *statement of comprehensive income, statement of earnings*, or *statement of operations*.

Helpful reminders

- To properly understand why Prepaid Expenses is an asset and Deferred Revenue is a liability, emphasize the first word (prepaid and deferred).
- If the trial balance doesn't balance, look at the difference between total debits and total credits. If the difference is
  - the same as one of your T–account balances, you probably forgot to include the account in your trial balance.

- twice the amount of an account balance, you may have included it in the wrong column of the trial balance.
- twice the amount of a transaction, you may have posted a debit as a credit or a credit as a debit in your T−accounts.
- evenly divisible by 9, you may have reversed the order of two digits in a number (a transposition error) or left a zero off the end of a number.
- evenly divisible by 3, you may have hit the key above or below the one you intended to hit (like a 9 instead of a 6) on your numeric keypad.

Frequent mistakes

- *Accrual* is *not* spelled *accural*.

PRACTICE MATERIAL

QUESTIONS (⊜ Symbol indicates questions that require analysis from more than one perspective.)

1. Show the income statement equation and define each element.

2. When accounting was developed in the fourteenth and fifteenth centuries, some businesses had very short lives. For instance, a business might have been created for a ship to sail from Europe to North America and return with furs and other goods. After the goods were delivered and profits were distributed among those who financed the shipment, the business ceased to exist. In more recent centuries, businesses began to experience longer lives. Identify the accounting concept that is needed when accounting for businesses with long lives. Explain what this concept means and why it is necessary for modern−day accounting. ⊜

3. Define *accrual basis accounting* and contrast it with *cash basis accounting*.

4. Why is it appropriate to use cash basis accounting in your personal life but not in the business world? ⊜

5. What does it mean to *recognize* an accounting transaction?

6. When is revenue typically recognized under accrual basis accounting?

7. Explain the expense recognition (or "matching") principle.

8. Explain why shareholders' equity is increased by revenues and decreased by expenses.

9. Explain why revenues are recorded as credits and expenses as debits.

10. Complete the following table by entering either *debit* or *credit* in each cell:

Item	Increase	Decrease
Revenues		
Expenses		

11. Complete the following table by entering either *increase* or *decrease* in each cell:

Item	Debit	Credit
Revenues		
Expenses		

12. What basic characteristic distinguishes items reported on the income statement from items reported on the balance sheet?

13. Which of the four basic accounting reports indicates that it is appropriate to consider revenues and expenses as subcategories of retained earnings? Explain.

14. What is the difference between Accounts Receivable and Revenue?

15. What is the difference between Accounts Payable for advertising and Advertising Expense?

16. For each of the following situations, indicate whether it represents an accounting error and explain why it is or is not an error. Also state whether a trial balance would indicate that an error exists for each situation. ⊜

    a. Cash received from a customer was debited to Accounts Receivable and credited to Cash.

    b. Revenue was recognized when a customer purchased a gift card for future use.

c. An expense was recorded as an asset.

d. The debit side of a journal entry was recorded in the accounts, but the credit side was not.

e. A company shareholder purchased a new car, but this event was not recorded by the company.

17. What are three limitations of the income statement that often lead to misconceptions?

MINI-EXERCISES

LO3-2 **M3-1 Reporting Cash Basis versus Accrual Basis Income**

Bachman Music Company had the following transactions in March:

a. Sold music lessons to customers for $10,000; received $6,000 in cash and the rest on account

b. Paid $600 in wages for the month

c. Received a $200 bill for utilities that will be paid in April

d. Received $1,000 from customers as deposits on music lessons to be given in April

Complete the following statements for March:

Cash Basis Income Statement		Accrual Basis Income Statement	
Revenues		Revenues	
Cash Sales	$_____	Sales to Customers	$_____
Customer Deposits	_____		
Expenses		Expenses	
Wages Paid	_____	Wages Expense	_____
		Utilities Expense	_____
Cash Income	$_____	Net Income	$_____

LO3-2 **M3-2 Identifying Accrual Basis Revenues**

The following transactions are July activities of Bill's Extreme Bowling, Inc., which operates several bowling centres. If revenue is to be recognized in July, indicate the amount. If revenue is not to be recognized in July, explain why.

Activity	Amount or Explanation
a. Bill collected $12,000 from customers for services related to games played in July.	
b. Bill invoiced a customer for $250 for a party held at the centre on the last day of July. The bill is to be paid in August.	
c. The men's and women's bowling leagues gave Bill advance payments totalling $1,500 for the fall season that starts in September.	
d. Bill received $1,000 from credit sales made to customers last month (in June).	

LO3-3 **M3-3 Identifying Accrual Basis Expenses**

Again, the following transactions are July activities of Bill's Extreme Bowling, Inc. If an expense is to be recognized in July, indicate the amount. If an expense is not to be recognized in July, explain why.

Activity	Amount or Explanation
e. Bill paid $1,500 to plumbers for repairing a broken pipe in the restrooms.	
f. Bill paid $2,000 for the June electricity bill and received the July bill for $2,500, which will be paid in August.	
g. Bill paid $5,475 to employees for work in July.	

M3-4 Recording Accrual Basis Revenues

LO3-3

For each of the transactions in M3—2, write the journal entry using the format shown in the chapter.

M3-5 Recording Accrual Basis Expenses

LO3-3

For each of the transactions in M3—3, write the journal entry using the format shown in the chapter.

M3-6 Determining the Accounting Equation Effects of Operating Activities Involving Revenues and Expenses

LO3-2, 3-3

For each of the following July transactions of Bill's Extreme Bowling, Inc. complete the spreadsheet, indicating the amount and effect (+ for increase and – for decrease) of each transaction under the accrual basis. Write NE if there is no effect. Include revenues as a subcategory of shareholders' equity, as shown for transaction (a), which is provided as an example.

Transaction	Assets	Liabilities	Shareholders' Equity
a. Bill collected $12,000 from customers for games played in July.	+12,000	NE	Games Fee Revenue (+R) + 12,000
b. Bill invoiced a customer for $250 for a party held at the centre on the last day of July. The bill is to be paid in August.			
c. Bill received $1,000 from credit sales made to customers last month (in June).			
d. The men's and women's bowling leagues gave Bill advance payments totalling $1,500 for the fall season that starts in September.			
e. Bill paid $1,500 to plumbers for repairing a broken pipe in the restrooms.			
f. Bill paid $2,000 for the June electricity bill and received the July bill for $2,500, which will be paid in August.			
g. Bill paid $5,475 to employees for work in July.			

M3-7 Preparing an Income Statement

LO3-1

Given the transactions in M3—6 [including transaction (a)], prepare an income statement for Bill's Extreme Bowling, Inc., for the month ended July 31. (This income statement would be considered preliminary because it uses unadjusted balances.)

M3-8 Identifying Accrual Basis Revenues

LO3-2

The following transactions are February activities of Swing Hard Incorporated, which offers indoor golfing lessons in Western Canada. If revenue is to be recognized in February, indicate the amount. If revenue is not to be recognized in February, explain why.

Activity	Amount or Explanation
a. Swing Hard collected $15,000 from customers for lesson services given in February.	
b. Swing Hard sold a gift card for golf lessons for $150 cash in February.	
c. Swing Hard received $4,000 from services provided on account to customers in January.	
d. Swing Hard collected $2,250 in advance payments for services to start in June.	
e. Swing Hard billed a customer $125 for services provided between February 25 and February 28. The bill is to be paid in March.	

LO3-2   **M3-9 Identifying Accrual Basis Expenses**

The following transactions are February activities of Swing Hard Incorporated, which offers indoor golfing lessons in Western Canada. If an expense is to be recognized in February, indicate the amount. If an expense is not to be recognized in February, explain why.

Activity	Amount or Explanation
f. Swing Hard paid $4,750 to its golf instructors for the month of February.	
g. Swing Hard paid $1,750 for electricity used in the month of January.	
h. Swing Hard received an electricity bill for $800 for the month of February, to be paid in March.	

LO3-3   **M3-10 Recording Accrual Basis Revenues**

For each of the transactions in M3–8, write the journal entry using the format shown in the chapter.

LO3-3   **M3-11 Recording Accrual Basis Expenses**

For each of the transactions in M3–9, write the journal entry using the format shown in the chapter.

LO3-3   **M3-12 Preparing Accrual Basis Journal Entries for Business Activities**

Quick Cleaners Inc. (QCI) has been in business for several years. It specializes in cleaning houses but has some small–business clients, as well. Prepare journal entries for the following transactions, which occurred during a recent month:

a. QCI incurred $600 of heating and electrical costs this month and will pay them next month.

b. QCI issued $25,000 of QCI shares for cash.

c. QCI paid wages for the current month, totalling $2,000.

d. QCI performed cleaning services on account worth $2,800.

e. Some of Quick Cleaners's equipment was repaired at a total cost of $150. The company paid the full amount immediately.

LO3-3   **M3-13 Preparing Accrual Basis Journal Entries for Business Activities**

Junk2Trade is an online company that specializes in matching buyers and sellers of used items. Buyers and sellers can purchase a membership with Junk2Trade, which provides them advance notice of potentially attractive offers. Prepare journal entries for the following trans–actions, which occurred during a recent month, and determine Junk2Trade's preliminary net income.

a. Junk2Trade provided online advertising services for another company for $200 on account.

b. On the last day of the month, Junk2Trade paid $50 cash to run an advertisement promot–ing the company's services. The advertisement ran that day in the local newspaper.

c. Junk2Trade received $200 cash in membership fees for the month from new members.

d. Junk2Trade received an electricity bill for $85, for usage this month. The bill will be paid next month.

e. Junk2Trade billed a customer $180 for helping to sell some junk. The company expects to receive the customer's payment by the end of next month.

LO3-3   **M3-14 Preparing Accrual Basis Journal Entries for Business Activities**

An international children's charity collects donations, which are used to buy clothing and toys for children in need. The charity records donations of cash and other items as Donations Revenue when received. Prepare journal entries for the following transactions, which occurred during a recent month, and determine the charity's preliminary net income.

a. The charity received $4,000 in cash and cheques from a door–to–door campaign.

b. The charity paid $2,000 cash for employee wages this month.

c. The charity paid $1,000 cash on a short–term loan from the bank (ignore interest).

d. The charity bought $3,000 worth of new toy supplies from a large toy manufacturer, paying $1,000 cash and signing a short–term note for $2,000.

e. A manufacturer generously donated an additional $2,500 of toy supplies.

M3-15 Preparing Accrual Basis Journal Entries for Business Activities

LO3-3

An auto body repair shop has been in business for twenty–three years. Prepare journal entries for the following transactions, which occurred during a recent month, and determine the auto body shop's preliminary net income.

a. Shop signed a long–term note and received a $150,000 loan from a local bank.

b. Shop billed a customer $2,000 for repair services just completed. Payment is expected in forty–five days.

c. Shop wrote a cheque for $600 of rent for the current month.

d. Shop received $450 cash from a customer for work done the same day.

e. The company incurred $400 in advertising costs for the current month and is planning to pay these costs next month.

M3-16 Determining the Accounting Equation Effects of Operating Activities Involving Revenues and Expenses

LO3-2, 3-3

The following transactions are February activities of Swing Right Incorporated, which offers golfing lessons in Western Canada. For each of the following transactions, complete the spreadsheet, indicating the amount and effect (+ for increase and – for decrease) of each transaction under the accrual basis. Write NE if there is no effect. Include revenues as a sub–category of shareholders' equity, as shown for transaction (*a*), which is provided as an example.

Transaction	Assets	Liabilities	Shareholders' Equity
a. Swing Right collected $15,000 from customers for lessons given in February.	+15,000	NE	Lesson Revenue (+R) + 125,000
b. Swing Right sold a gift card for golf lessons for $150 cash in February.			
c. Swing Right received $4,000 from credit sales made to customers in January.			
d. Swing Right collected $2,250 in advance payments for golf lessons to start in June.			
e. Swing Right billed a customer $125 for golf lessons given from February 25 through February 28. The bill is to be paid in March.			
f. Swing Right paid $4,750 for wages to its golf instructors for the month of February.			
g. Swing Right paid $1,750 for electricity used in the month of January.			
h. Swing Right received an electricity bill for $800 for the month of February, to be paid in March.			

M3-17 Preparing an Income Statement

LO3-2

Given the transactions in M3–16 [including transaction (*a*)], prepare an income statement for Swing Right Incorporated for the month ended February 28. (This income statement would be considered preliminary because it uses unadjusted balances.)

M3-18 Preparing Financial Statements from a Trial Balance

LO3-1, 3-4

The following accounts are taken from Buck Up! Inc., a company that specializes in horse–breaking services and rodeo lessons, at December 31, 2017.

BUCK UP! INC.
Unadjusted Trial Balance
At December 31, 2017

Account Name	Debits	Credits
Cash	$ 59,750	
Accounts Receivable	3,300	
Prepaid Insurance	1,200	
Equipment	64,600	
Land	23,000	
Accounts Payable		$ 29,230
Deferred Revenue		1,500
Long−Term Notes Payable		74,000
Contributed Capital		5,000
Retained Earnings		14,500
Dividends	3,500	
Horse−Breaking Revenue		25,200
Rodeo Lesson Revenue		10,500
Wages Expense	3,900	
Maintenance Expense	410	
Other Expenses	270	
Totals	$159,930	$159,930

Required:

Using the unadjusted trial balance provided, create a classified balance sheet, statement of retained earnings, and income statement for Buck Up! Inc. for the year ended December 31, 2017. (These financial statements would be considered preliminary because they use unadjusted balances.)

> TIP: Create the income statement first, followed by the statement of retained earnings, and finally the classified balance sheet. Follow the formats presented in Exhibits 1.2, 1.3, and 2.13.

LO3-1, 3-4　**M3-19　Preparing an Income Statement**

Assume that the following accounts are taken from the December 31, 2017, financial state−ments of Rogers Communications Inc. (Amounts are in millions.)

Subscription Revenue	$24,904
Other Revenues	12,779
Salaries Expense	9,653
Cash	1,516
Accounts Receivable	7,296
Interest Expense	2,299
Accounts Payable	1,470
Advertising Revenue	8,799
Long-Term Debt	37,004
Other Expenses	381
Deferred Revenue	1,178
Equipment	18,048
Income Tax Expense	2,336
Operating Expense	27,426

Required:

Prepare an income statement for the year ended December 31, 2017.

   TIP: Some of the above accounts are not reported on the income statement.

M3-20 Calculating and Interpreting Net Profit Margin

Expedia and Priceline compete as online travel agencies. Historically, Expedia has focused more on flights whereas Priceline has focused on hotel bookings. The following amounts were reported by the two companies in 2012. Calculate each company's net profit margin expressed as a percent (to one decimal place). Which company has generated a greater return of profit from each revenue dollar?

(in millions)	Net Income	Total Assets	Total Liabilities	Total Revenues
Expedia	$ 280	$7,090	$4,800	$4,030
Priceline	1,420	6,570	2,670	5,260

M3-21 Calculating and Interpreting Net Profit Margin

Kijojo Auctions runs an online auction company. Its end—of—year financial statements indi—cate the following results. Calculate the company's net profit margin expressed as a percent (to one decimal place) and indicate whether it represents an improvement or deterioration relative to the 15.0 percent net profit margin earned in the previous year.

Total assets = $100,000   Expenses = $80,000

Total liabilities = $60,000   Retained earnings (beginning of year) = $15,000.

Contributed Capital = $10,000   Dividends = $5,000

EXERCISES

E3-1 Matching Definitions with Terms

Match each definition with its related term by entering the appropriate letter in the space provided.

Term	Definition
_____ 1. Expenses	A. Record expenses when incurred in earning revenue.
_____ 2. Revenues	B. A liability account used to record the obligation to provide future services or return cash that has been received before revenues have been earned.
_____ 3. Revenue recognition principle	
_____ 4. Cash basis accounting	
_____ 5. Deferred Revenue	C. Costs that result when a company sacrifices resources to generate revenues.
_____ 6. Accrual basis accounting	D. Record revenues when earned, not necessarily when cash is received.
_____ 7. Prepaid Expenses	
_____ 8. Expense recognition principle	E. Record revenues when received and expenses when paid.
	F. A type of asset account used to record the benefits obtained when cash is paid before expenses are incurred.
	G. Record revenues when earned and expenses when incurred.
	H. The amount businesses charge to customers for providing goods or services.

E3- Identifying Accrual Basis Revenues

According to the revenue principle, revenues should be recognized when they are earned, which happens when the company performs acts promised to the customer. For most businesses, this condition is met at the point of delivery of goods or services. Assume that the following transactions occurred in September 2017:

a. A customer pays $10 cash for ten song files from Apple's iTunes store. Answer from Apple's standpoint.

Check Figure [Part (b)]:

Revenue earned = $2,000

b. The Home Depot provides a carpet installation for $2,000 cash. A comparable installation by other companies costs $3,000.

c. Shaw Communications is scheduled to install digital cable at 1,000 homes during the month of September. The installation charge is $100 per home. The terms require payment within thirty days of installation. Answer from Shaw's standpoint.

d. Shaw completes the installations described in (c). Answer from Shaw's standpoint.

e. Shaw receives payment from customers for the installations described in (c). Answer from Shaw's standpoint.

f. A customer purchases a ticket from WestJet in September for $500 cash to travel in December. Answer from WestJet's standpoint.

Required:

For each of the transactions, if revenue is to be recognized in September, indicate the amount. If revenue is not to be recognized in September, explain why.

LO3-1, LO3-2   **E3-3 Identifying Accrual Basis Revenues**

According to the revenue principle, revenues should be recognized when they are earned, which happens when the company performs acts promised to the customer. For most businesses, this condition is met at the point of delivery of goods or services. The following transactions occurred in September 2017:

a. Gilligan Enterprises Inc. issues $26,000,000 in new common shares.

b. Western University receives $20,000,000 cash for 80,000 five−game season football tickets. None of the games have been played.

c. Western University plays the first football game referred to in (b).

d. Harld Construction Company signs a contract with a customer for the construction of a new $500,000 warehouse to be started in October. At the signing, Harld receives a cheque for $50,000 as a deposit to be applied against amounts earned during the first phase of construction. Answer from Harld's standpoint.

e. A popular snowboarding magazine company today receives a total of $1,800 from subscrib−ers. The subscriptions begin in the next fiscal year, which is after September 30. Answer from the magazine company's standpoint.

f. Fido sells a $100 cell phone plan for service in September to a customer who charges the sale on his credit card. Answer from the standpoint of Fido.

Required:

For each of the transactions, if revenue is to be recognized in September, indicate the amount. If revenue is not to be recognized in September, explain why.

LO3-1, LO3-2   **E3-4 Identifying Accrual Basis Expenses**

Under accrual basis accounting, expenses are recognized when incurred, which means the activity giving rise to the expense has occurred. Assume the following transactions occurred in January 2017:

a. Gateway pays its computer service technicians $90,000 in salary for work done in January 2017. Answer from Gateway's standpoint.

b. At the beginning of January, Turnboldt Construction Company pays $4,500 in rent for February to April 2017.

c. Assume that McGraw−Hill Education—publisher of this textbook and *BusinessWeek*—use $1,000 worth of electricity and natural gas in January for which it has not yet been billed.

d. Pooler Company receives and pays in January a $1,500 invoice from a consulting firm for services received in January.

e. The campus bookstore receives consulting services at a cost of $5,000. The terms indicate that payment is due within thirty days of the consultation.

f. Schergevitch Incorporated has its delivery van repaired in January for $280 and charges the amount on account.

Required:

For each of the transactions, if an expense is to be recognized in January, indicate the amount. If an expense is not to be recognized in January, indicate why.

E3-5 Identifying Accrual Basis Expenses

LO3-1, LO3-2

Under accrual basis accounting, expenses are recognized when incurred. Assume that the following transactions occurred in January 2017:

a. American Express pays its salespeople $3,500 in commissions related to December financial advisory services sales. Answer from American Express's standpoint.

b. On January 31, American Express determines that it will pay its salespeople $4,200 in commissions related to January sales. The payment will be made in early February. Answer from American Express's standpoint.

c. The City of Ottawa hires Waste Management, Inc. to provide trash collection services beginning in January. The city pays $7.2 million for the entire year. Answer from the City's standpoint.

d. The University of Saskatchewan pays $10,000 in advance for refundable airline tickets to fly the basketball team to a tournament in Toronto. The first game will be played in March. Answer from the university's standpoint.

e. A Business College employee works eight hours, at $15 per hour, on January 31; payday is not until February 3. Answer from the college's point of view.

f. Wang Company paid $3,600 for a fire insurance policy on January 1. The policy covers twelve months beginning on January 1. Answer from Wang's point of view.

g. Ziegler Company, a farm equipment company, receives a phone bill for $230 of calls made in January. The bill has not been paid to date.

Check Figure [Part (c)]:
Expenses incurred = $600,000

Required:

For each of the transactions, if an expense is to be recognized in January, indicate the amount. If an expense is not to be recognized in January, indicate why.

E3-6 Determining Accounting Equation Effects and Net Income

LO3-2, LO3-3

The following transactions occurred during a recent year:

a. Paid wages of $1,000 for the current period

b. Borrowed $5,000 cash from local bank

c. Purchased $2,000 of equipment on credit

d. Earned $400 of sales revenue, collected cash

e. Received $800 of utilities services on credit

f. Earned $1,700 of service revenue on credit

g. Paid $300 cash on account to a supplier

h. Incurred $70 of delivery expenses, paid cash

i. Earned $400 of service revenue, collected half in cash, balance on credit

j. Collected $100 cash from customers on account

k. Incurred $300 of advertising costs, paid half in cash, balance on credit

Required:

For each of the transactions, complete the table below, indicating the account, amount, and direction of the effect (+ for increase and − for decrease) of each transaction under the accrual basis. Write NE if there is no effect. Include revenues and expenses as subcategories of share—holders' equity, as shown for transaction (a), which is provided as an example. Also determine the company's preliminary net income.

Transaction	Assets		=	Liabilities	+	Shareholders' Equity	
(a)	Cash	−1,000		NE		Wages Expense (+E)	−1,000

E3-7 Determining Accounting Equation Effects and Net Income

Wolverine World Wide, Inc. manufactures military, work, sport, and casual footwear and leather accessories under a variety of brand names, such as Cat Footwear, Hush Puppies, Wolverine, and Harley–Davidson Footwear. Assume that the following transactions occurred during a recent year. (Dollars are in thousands.)

a. Made cash sales of $49,000

b. Purchased $3,000 of additional supplies on account

c. Borrowed $58,000 on long–term notes

d. Purchased $18,600 in additional equipment, paying in cash

e. Incurred $27,000 in selling expenses, paying two–thirds in cash and owing the rest on account

f. Paid $4,700 in rent for this period

Required:

For each of the transactions, complete the table below, indicating the account, amount, and direction of the effect (+ for increase and – for decrease) and amount of each transaction under the accrual basis. Write NE if there is no effect. Include revenues and expenses as subcategories of shareholders' equity, as shown for transaction (a), which is provided as an example. Also determine the company's preliminary net income.

Transaction	Assets		Liabilities	Shareholders' Equity	
(a)	Cash	+49,000	NE	Sales Revenue (+R)	+49,000

E3-8 Recording Journal Entries and Determining Net Income

Sysco is a global leader in marketing and distributing food products to restaurants, health–care and educational facilities, lodging establishments, and other customers who prepare meals away from home. The following transactions are typical of those that occurred in a recent year, but the amounts are simplified. (Dollars are in thousands.)

a. Borrowed $80,000 from a bank, signing a short–term note payable

b. Provided $100,000 in service to customers, with $95,000 on account and the rest received in cash

c. Purchased plant and equipment for $130,000 in cash

d. Paid employee wages of $1,000

e. Received $410 on account from a customer

f. Paid $4,000 cash for travel costs during the year

g. Paid $8,200 cash on accounts payable

h. Incurred $20,000 in utility expenses during the year, of which $15,000 was paid in cash and the rest owed on account

Required:

For each of the transactions, prepare accrual basis journal entries. Determine whether the accounting equation remains in balance and debits equal credits after each entry. Also, calculate the company's preliminary net income.

E3-9 Recording Journal Entries and Determining Net Income

Silver Star Mountain Resort is a ski resort northeast of Vernon in British Columbia. Besides maintaining well–groomed ski runs, the company sells lift tickets, ski lessons, and ski equip–ment. It operates several restaurants and rents townhouses to vacationing skiers. The following hypothetical December 2017 transactions are typical of those that occur at the resort.

a. Borrowed $500,000 from the bank on December 1, signing a note payable due in six months

b. Purchased a new snowplow for $20,000 cash on December 31

c. Purchased ski supplies for $10,000 on account

d. Incurred $22,000 in routine maintenance expenses for the chairlifts; paid cash

e. Received $72,000 for season passes (beginning in the new year) *f*. Sold daily lift passes this month for a total of $76,000 cash

g. Received a $320 deposit on a townhouse to be rented for five days in January 2018

h. Paid half the charges incurred on account in (*c*)

i. Paid $18,000 in wages to employees for the month of December

Required:

Prepare accrual basis journal entries for each transaction. Be sure to categorize each account as an asset (A), liability (L), shareholders' equity (SE), revenue (R), or expense (E), and check that debits equal credits for each journal entry. Also, calculate the company's preliminary net income.

E3-10 Recording Journal Entries and Determining Net Income and Net Profit Margin

LO3-2, 3-3

Rowland & Sons Air Transport Service Ltd. has been in operation for three years. The fol-lowing transactions occurred in February 2017:

Feb. 1	Paid $200 for rent of hangar space in February
Feb. 4	Received customer payment of $800 to ship several items to Victoria next month
Feb. 7	Flew cargo from Winnipeg to Regina; the customer paid in full ($900 cash)
Feb. 10	Paid pilot $1,200 in wages for flying in February
Feb. 14	Paid $100 for an advertisement run in the local paper on February 14
Feb. 18	Flew cargo for two customers from Edmonton to Lake Louise for $1,700; one customer paid $500 cash and the other asked to be billed $1,200
Feb. 25	Purchased on account $1,350 in spare parts for the planes

Required:

Prepare journal entries for each transaction. Be sure to categorize each account as an asset (A), liability (L), shareholders' equity (SE), revenue (R), or expense (E). Also, calculate the compa-ny's preliminary net income and net profit margin expressed as a percent (to one decimal place).

E3-11 Recording and Posting Accrual Basis Journal Entries

LO3-2, 3-3

Ricky's Piano Rebuilding Company has been operating for one year (2016). At the start of 2017, its income statement accounts had zero balances and its balance sheet account balances were as follows:

Cash	$ 6,000	Accounts Payable	$ 8,000
Accounts Receivable	25,000	Deferred Revenue (deposits)	3,200
Supplies	1,200	Notes Payable	40,000
Equipment	8,000	Contributed Capital	8,000
Land	6,000	Retained Earnings	9,000
Building	22,000		

Required:

1. Create T-accounts for the balance sheet accounts and for these additional accounts: Piano Rebuilding Revenue, Rent Revenue, Wages Expense, and Utilities Expense. Enter the beginning balances.

2. Prepare journal entries for the following January 2017 transactions, using the letter of each transaction as a reference:

   a. Received a $500 deposit from a customer who wanted her piano rebuilt in February

   b. Rented a part of the building to a bicycle repair shop; $300 rent received for January

   c. Delivered five rebuilt pianos to customers who paid $14,500 in cash

   d. Delivered two rebuilt pianos to customers for $7,000 charged on account

   e. Received $6,000 from customers as payment on their accounts

   f. Received a utility bill for $350 for January services to be paid in February

g. Ordered $800 in supplies

h. Paid $1,700 to suppliers on account in January

i. Paid $10,000 in wages to employees in January for work done this month

j. Received and paid cash for the supplies in (g)

3. Post the journal entries to the T–accounts. Show the unadjusted ending balances in the T–accounts.

LO3-4   **E3-12 Preparing an Unadjusted Trial Balance**

Refer to E3–11.

Required:

Use the balances in the completed T–accounts in E3–11 to prepare an unadjusted trial balance at the end of January 2017.

LO3-2, 3-3   **E3-13 Analyzing Transactions from the Perspectives of Different Companies**

LEVEL UP

Over–the–Top Technologies (OTT) operates a computer repair and Web consulting business. News Now (NN) publishes a local newspaper. The two companies entered into the following transactions.

a. NN billed OTT for $500 of advertising services provided this month on account.

b. OTT repaired some of NN's equipment this month, for $135 on account.

c. NN collected $500 cash from OTT for the advertising services provided in (*a*).

d. NN paid $60 cash to OTT for OTT advertising NN's online newspaper this month on OTT's Website.

e. OTT and NN signed a promissory note, documenting OTT's $1,000 cash loan to NN this month with repayment to occur in six months.

Required:

Show the journal entries that OTT and NN would record for items (*a*) through (*e*). Use a two–part table, with the left side showing OTT's journal entries and the right side showing NN's journal entries.

LO3-2, 3-3, 3-4   **E3-14 Inferring Operating Transactions and Preparing an Unadjusted Trial Balance**

Virtual Golf Corporation operates indoor golf simulators that allow individual customers and golf club members to experience courses like Pebble Beach and Augusta without leaving their own neighbourhoods. Its stores are located in rented space in malls and shopping centres. During its first month of business ended April 30, 2017, Virtual Golf Corporation completed seven transactions with the dollar effects indicated in the following schedule:

| Accounts | Assets | | | | = | Liabilities | + | Shareholders' Equity | |
	Cash	Accounts Receivable	Supplies	Equipment	Accounts Payable	Deferred Revenue	Contributed Capital	Retained Earnings
Beginning balance	$ 0	$ 0	$ 0	$ 0	$ 0	$ 0	$ 0	$ 0
a	+100,000						+100,000	
b	−30,000			+30,000				
c	−200		+1,000		+800			
d	+9,000	+1,000						Sales Revenue +10,000
e	−1,000							Wages Expense −1,000
f					+1,200			Utilities Expense −1,200
g	+2,000					+2,000		
Ending balance	$ 79,800	$ 1,000	$ 1,000	$ 30,000	$ 2,000	$ 2,000	$ 100,000	

Required:

1. Write a brief explanation of transactions (a) through (g). Include any assumptions that you made.

2. Using the ending balance in each account, prepare an unadjusted trial balance for Virtual Golf Corporation on April 30, 2017.

E3-15 Inferring Transactions and Computing Effects Using T-Accounts

LO3-1, 3-2, 3-3

Assume a recent annual report of Dow Jones & Company, the world leader in business and financial news and information (and publisher of the *Wall Street Journal*), included the following accounts. Dollars are in millions.

dr + Accounts Receivable (A) cr –			dr + Prepaid Expenses (A) cr –			dr – Unearned Revenue (L) cr +		
1/1	313		1/1	25			240	1/1
	2,573	x		43	y	z	328	
12/31	295		12/31	26			253	12/31

Required:

1. For each T–account, describe the typical transactions that cause it to increase and decrease.

2. Express each T–account in equation format (Beginning + Increase Side – Decrease Side = Ending) and then solve for the missing amounts (in millions). For example, the Accounts Receivable T–account can be expressed as $313 + 2{,}573 - x = 295$. By rearranging the equation, you can solve for $313 + 2{,}573 - 295 = x$.

E3-16 Determining Accounting Equation Effects of Several Transactions

LO3-1, 3-2, 3-3

In January, Tongo Inc. had the following transactions. Indicate the accounts, amounts, and direction of the effects on the accounting equation under the accrual basis. The solution for transaction (a) is provided.

a. Received $9,500 cash for consulting services rendered in January

b. Issued shares to investors for $10,000 cash

c. Purchased $12,000 of equipment, paying 25 percent in cash and owing the rest on a note due in two years

d. Received $7,500 cash for consulting services to be performed in February

e. Bought $1,000 of supplies on account

f. Received utility bill for January for $1,250, due February 15

g. Consulted for customers in January for fees totalling $15,900, due in February

h. Received $12,000 cash for consulting services rendered in December

i. Paid $500 toward supplies purchased in (e)

	Assets		=	Liabilities	+	Shareholders' Equity	
(a)	Cash	+9,500	=			Service Revenue (+R)	+9,500

E3-17 Preparing Journal Entries

LO3-3

For each of the transactions in E3–16 [including transaction (a)], write the journal entry using the format shown in this chapter.

E3-18 Posting to T-Accounts

LO3-3

For each of the transactions in E3–16 [including transaction (a)], post the effects to the appropriate T–accounts and determine ending account balances. Beginning account balances have been given. Transaction (a) has been posted as an example in the first T–account.

dr +	Cash (A)	cr –
1/1	10,000	
(a)	9,500	

dr –	Accounts Payable (L)	cr +
		5,000 1/1

dr –	Contributed Capital (SE)	cr +
		12,000 1/1

dr +	Accounts Receivable (A)	cr –
1/1	12,500	

dr –	Unearned Revenue (L)	cr +
		2,500 1/1

dr –	Retained Earnings (SE)	cr +
		8,800 1/1

dr +	Supplies (A)	cr –
1/1	800	

dr –	Note Payable (L)	cr +
		0 1/1

dr –	Service Revenues (R)	cr +
		0 1/1
		9,500 (a)

dr +	Equipment (A)	cr –
1/1	5,000	

dr +	Utilities Expense (E)	cr –
1/1	0	

LO3-4 **E3-19 Creating an Unadjusted Trial Balance**

Based on the transactions posted to T–accounts in E3–18, create an unadjusted trial balance for Tongo Inc. for the month ended January 31. Distinguish the balance sheet and income statement accounts as shown in Exhibit 3.9.

LO3-2, 3-3 **E3-20 Inferring Transactions and Creating Financial Statements**

An analysis of transactions made during July 2017 by NepCo, an Internet service provider, during its first month of operations is shown below. Increases and decreases affecting revenues and expenses are explained.

		Assets			=	Liabilities	+		Stockholders' Equity	
	Cash	Accounts Receivable	Supplies	Equipment		Accounts Payable		Contributed Capital	Retained Earnings	
(a)	+11,000							+11,000		
(b)						+710			−710	Utilities expense
(c)		+5,000							+5,000	Service revenue
(d)	−6,000			+10,000		+4,000				
(e)	+1,000								+1,000	Service revenue
(f)			+550			+550				
(g)	−3,000					−3,000				
(h)	−2,000								−2,000	Wage expense
(i)	−750								−750	Rent expense
(j)	+1,500	−1,500								
	1,750	3,500	550	10,000		2,260		11,000	2,540	

Required:

1. Describe the business activities that led to the accounting equation effects for each trans–action shown above.
2. Prepare an income statement and a statement of retained earnings for July, and a classified balance sheet as of July 31, 2017. (These financial statements would be considered prelim–inary because they use unadjusted balances.)

E3-21 Determining the Effects of Various Transactions

E&Z Reader was founded in January 2017 to provide text reading and recording services. Selected transactions for E&Z Reader's first month of business are as follows:

a. Issued shares to investors for $50,000 cash

b. Billed customers $10,500 for services performed in January

c. Purchased car for $24,500 for use in the business; paid in cash

d. Purchased $2,400 of supplies on account

e. Received $7,500 cash from customers billed in transaction (b)

f. Used $1,500 in utilities, which will be paid in February

g. Paid employees $3,500 cash for work done in January

h. Paid $1,200 cash toward supplies purchased in transaction (d)

Required:

For each transaction, complete the following:

1. Give the name of the account being debited or credited.
2. Give the basic account type (A, L, SE, R, E).
3. Indicate whether the account is increased (+) or decreased (−) due to the transaction.
4. Indicate whether the account normally holds a debit or credit balance.

Transaction (a) has been given as an example.

Debit Side of Journal Entry			
Account Name	Account Type	Direction of Change	Normal Balance
(a) Cash	A	+	Debit

Credit Side of Journal Entry			
Account Name	Account Type	Direction of Change	Normal Balance
Contributed Capital	SE	+	Credit

COACHED PROBLEMS

CP3-1 Recording Non-quantitative Journal Entries

The following list includes a series of accounts for B−Ball Corporation, which has been operating for three years. These accounts are listed alphabetically and numbered for identi−fication. Following the accounts is a series of transactions. For each transaction, indicate the account(s) that should be debited and credited by entering the appropriate account number(s) to the right of each transaction. If no journal entry is needed, write NE after the transaction. Transaction (a) is used as an example.

TIP: In transaction (h), remember what the matching principle says.

TIP: Think of transaction (j) as two transactions that (1) incur expenses and liability and (2) pay part of the liability.

Account No.	Account Title	Account No.	Account Title
1	Accounts Payable	8	Note Payable
2	Accounts Receivable	9	Prepaid Insurance
3	Cash	10	Rent Expense
4	Contributed Capital	11	Service Revenue
5	Equipment	12	Supplies Expense
6	Income Tax Expense	13	Supplies
7	Income Tax Payable		

Transactions	Debit	Credit
a. Purchased equipment for use in the business; paid one—third cash and signed a note payable for the balance	5	3, 8
b. Received cash for issuing shares to new investors	——	——
c. Paid cash for rent this period	——	——
d. Collected cash for services performed this period	——	——
e. Collected cash on accounts receivable for services performed last period	——	——
f. Performed services this period on credit	——	——
g. Paid cash on accounts payable for expenses incurred last period	——	——
h. Purchased supplies to be used later; paid cash	——	——
i. Paid three—fourths of the income tax expense for the year; the balance to be paid next year	——	——
j. On the last day of the current period, paid cash for an insurance policy covering the next two years	——	——

LO3-2, 3-3   **CP3-2 Recording Journal Entries**

Ryan Olson organized a new company, MeToo, Inc. The company provides networking man—agement services on social networking sites. You have been hired to record the transactions occurring in the first two weeks of operations, beginning May 1, 2017.

a. May 1: Issued 1,000 shares to investors for $30 per share

b. May 1: Borrowed $50,000 from the bank to provide additional funding to begin operations; note is due in two years

c. May 1: Paid $2,400 for a one—year fire insurance policy
    TIP: For convenience, simply record the full amount of the payment as an asset (Prepaid Insurance). At the end of the month, this account will be adjusted to its proper balance. We will study this adjustment process in Chapter 4, so just leave it as Prepaid Insurance for now.

d. May 3: Purchased furniture and fixtures for the store for $15,000 on account; amount is due within thirty days

e. May 5: Placed advertisements in local newspapers for a total of $250 cash

f. May 9: Sold services for $400 cash

g. May 14: Made full payment for the furniture and fixtures purchased on account on May 3

Required:

For each of the transactions, prepare journal entries. Be sure to categorize each account as an asset (A), liability (L), shareholders' equity (SE), revenue (R), or expense (E).

LO3-1, 3-2, 3-3, 3-4   **CP3-3 Analyzing the Effects of Transactions Using T-Accounts and Preparing an Unadjusted Trial Balance**

eXcel

Barbara Jones opened Barb's Book Business on February 1, 2017. The company specializes in editing accounting textbooks. You have been hired as manager. Your duties include maintain—ing the company's financial records. The following transactions occurred in February 2017, the first month of operations:

a. Received shareholders' cash contributions totalling $16,000 to form the corporation; issued shares

b. Paid $2,400 cash for three months' rent for office space
    TIP: For convenience, simply record the full amount of the payment as an asset (Prepaid Rent). At the end of the month, this account will be adjusted to its proper balance. We will study this adjustment process in Chapter 4, so just leave it as Prepaid Rent for now.

c. Purchased supplies for $300 cash

d. Signed a promissory note, payable in two years; deposited $10,000 in the company's bank account *e*. Used the money from (*d*) to purchase equipment for $2,500 and furniture and fixtures for $7,500

f. Placed an advertisement in the local paper for $425 cash

g. Made sales totalling $1,800; $1,525 was in cash and the rest on account

h. Incurred and paid employee wages of $420

i. Collected accounts receivable of $50 from customers

j. Repaired one of the computers for $120 cash

   TIP: Most repairs involve costs that do *not* provide additional future economic benefits.

Required:

1. Set up appropriate T–accounts for Cash, Accounts Receivable, Supplies, Prepaid Rent, Equipment, Furniture and Fixtures, Notes Payable, Contributed Capital, Service Revenue, Advertising Expense, Wages Expense, and Repair Expense. All accounts begin with zero balances.

   TIP: When preparing the T–accounts, you might find it useful to group them by type: assets, liabilities, shareholders' equity, revenues, and expenses.

2. Record in the T–accounts the effects of each transaction for Barb's Book Business in February, referencing each transaction in the accounts with the transaction letter. Show the unadjusted ending balances in the T–accounts.

3. Prepare an unadjusted trial balance at the end of February.

   TIP: Total Debits equals $27,800.

4. Refer to the revenues and expenses shown on the unadjusted trial balance. Based on this information, write a short memo to Barbara offering your opinion on the results of operations during the first month of business.

CP3-4 Analyzing, Journalizing, and Interpreting Business Activities

LO3-3, 3-5

LEVEL UP

Longlake Tennis Club (LTC) operates an indoor tennis facility. The company charges a $150 annual membership fee plus a member rental rate of $20 per court per hour. LTC's fiscal year end is August 31. LTC's revenue recognition policy is described in its financial statement notes as follows:

Revenue Recognition

LTC earns revenue from two sources. Annual membership fees are earned by providing twelve months of services to members, so the fees are reported as membership revenue as they are earned over that twelve–month period. Court rental fees are earned by renting courts each day, so they are reported as service revenue, as courts are used by members.

   On August 31, ten new members joined and paid the annual membership fee in cash. The memberships do not begin until September 1. For the week ended September 11, LTC provided 190 court hours of rental services for members and collected its fees in cash. On September 13, LTC purchased and received tennis balls and other supplies. The regular retail price was $220, but LTC negotiated a lower amount ($200) that is to be paid in October.

   On September 15, LTC paid $1,500 to employees for the hours they worked from September 1 to 15. For the two weeks ended September 25, LTC provided 360 court hours for members and collected its fees in cash. On September 26, LTC's courts were used for a member's birthday party. LTC expects the member to pay the special event–booking fee of $210 on Saturday, October 2.

   On September 27, LTC wrote a $300 cheque to an advertising company to prepare advertising flyers that will be inserted in local newspapers on October 1. On September 29, LTC received $210 on account for the member's birthday party that was held on September 26. On September 30, LTC submitted its electricity and natural gas meter readings online. According to the utilities suppliers' websites, the total charges for the month will be $300. This amount will be paid on October 17 through a pre–authorized online payment.

Required:

1. Indicate the accounting equation effects of the August and September events, using a table similar to the one shown for Demonstration Case B. Reference each transaction by date.

2. Prepare journal entries to record the August and September events described above. Reference each transaction by date.

3. Using your answer to requirement 1 or 2, calculate LTC's preliminary net income for September. Is LTC profitable, based on its preliminary net income?

4. Identify at least two adjustments that LTC will be required to make before it can prepare a final income statement for September.

> TIP: Scan the accounts used to answer requirements 1 and 2, looking for amounts that are no longer accurate at September 30.

GROUP A PROBLEMS

LO3-1, 3-2, 3-3

Check Figure [Part (g)]:
Debit 15 and Credit 5

PA3-1 Recording Non-quantitative Journal Entries

The following is a series of accounts for Dewan & Allard Incorporated, which has been operating for two years. The accounts are listed alphabetically and numbered for identification. Following the accounts is a series of transactions. For each transaction, indicate the account(s) that should be debited and credited by entering the appropriate account number(s) to the right of each transaction. If no journal entry is needed, write NE after the transaction. Transaction (*a*) is given as an example.

Account No.	Account Title	Account No.	Account Title
1	Accounts Payable	9	Land
2	Accounts Receivable	10	Note Payable
3	Advertising Expense	11	Prepaid Insurance
4	Buildings	12	Service Revenue
5	Cash	13	Supplies Expense
6	Contributed Capital	14	Supplies
7	Income Tax Expense	15	Wages Expense
8	Income Tax Payable		

Transactions	Debit	Credit
a. Issued shares to new investors for cash	5	6
b. Performed services for customers this period on credit	——	——
c. Purchased on credit but did not use supplies this period	——	——
d. Prepaid a fire insurance policy this period to cover the next twelve months	——	——
e. Purchased a building this period by making a 20 percent cash down payment and signing a note payable for the balance	——	——
f. Collected cash for services that had been provided and recorded in the prior year	——	——
g. Paid cash for wages that had been incurred this period	——	——
h. Paid cash for supplies that had been purchased on accounts payable in the prior period	——	——
i. Paid cash for advertising expense incurred in the current period	——	——
j. Incurred advertising expenses this period to be paid next period	——	——
k. Collected cash for services rendered this period	——	——
l. Recorded income taxes for this period to be paid at the beginning of the next period	——	——
m. Shares sold by shareholder this period for an amount above the original issuance price	——	——

LO3-2, 3-3

PA3-2 Preparing Accrual Basis Journal Entries for Business Activities

Diana Mark is the president of TempEmp, Inc., a company that provides temporary employees for not-for-profit companies. TempEmp has been operating for five years; its revenues have increased each year. You have been hired to help Diana in analyzing the following transactions for the first two weeks of April 2017:

April 2	Purchased office supplies for $500 on account
April 5	Billed the local United Way office $1,950 for temporary services provided
April 8	Paid $250 for supplies purchased and recorded on account last period
April 8	Placed an advertisement in the local paper for $400 cash
April 9	Purchased new equipment for the office costing $2,300 cash
April 10	Paid employee wages of $1,200, which were incurred in April
April 11	Received $1,000 on account from the local United Way office, billed on April 5
April 12	Purchased land as the site of a future office for $10,000; paid $2,000 down and signed a note payable for the balance
April 13	Issued 2,000 additional shares for $40 per share in anticipation of building a new office
April 14	Billed Family & Children's Services $2,000 for services rendered this month
April 15	Received the April telephone bill for $245 to be paid next month

Required:

For each of the transactions, prepare journal entries. Be sure to categorize each account as an asset (A), liability (L), shareholders' equity (SE), revenue (R), or expense (E).

PA3-3 Preparing Accrual Basis Journal Entries for Business Activities

LO3-2, 3-3

The following transactions are February 2017 activities of InGolfHelp, which offers indoor golfing lessons. You have been hired to analyze the following transactions for a week in February 2017:

February 15	InGolfHelp collected $15,000 from customers for lessons given in February.
February 15	InGolfHelp sold a gift card for golf lessons for $150 cash in February.
February 18	InGolfHelp received $4,000 from credit sales made to customers in January.
February 18	InGolfHelp collected $2,250 in advance payments for golf lessons to start in June.
February 19	InGolfHelp billed a customer $125 for golf lessons given between February 15 and February 18. The bill is to be paid in March.
February 20	InGolfHelp paid $4,750 to its golf instructors for the month of February.
February 21	InGolfHelp paid $1,750 for electricity used in the month of January.
February 22	InGolfHelp received an electricity bill for $800 for the month of February, to be paid in March.

Required:

For each of the transactions, prepare journal entries. Be sure to categorize each account as an asset (A), liability (L), shareholders' equity (SE), revenue (R), or expense (E).

PA3-4 Analyzing the Effects of Transactions Using T-Accounts, Preparing an Unadjusted Trial Balance, and Determining Net Income and Net Profit Margin

LO3-1, 3-2, 3-3, 3-4, 3-5

Sunny Valley Stables Inc. was established on April 1, 2017. The company provides stables, care for animals, and grounds for riding and showing horses. You have been hired as the new assistant financial controller. The following transactions for April 2017 are provided for your review.

Check Figure:
Ending cash balance
$134,560 dr

a. Received contributions from five investors of $200,000 in cash ($40,000 each)

b. Built a barn for $142,000; paid half the amount in cash on April 1 and signed a three–year note payable for the balance

c. Provided $15,260 in animal care services for customers, all on credit

d. Rented stables to customers who cared for their own animals; received cash of $13,200

e. Received from a customer $1,500 to board her horse in May, June, and July (record as Deferred Revenue) *f.* Purchased hay and feed supplies on account for $3,210

g. Paid $840 in cash for water utilities incurred in the month

h. Paid $1,700 on accounts payable for previous purchases

i. Received $1,000 from customers on accounts receivable

j. Paid $4,000 in wages to employees who worked during the month

k. At the end of the month, prepaid a two−year insurance policy for $3,600

l. Received an electric utility bill for $1,200 for usage in April; bill will be paid next month

Required:

1. Set up appropriate T−accounts. All accounts begin with zero balances.
2. Record in the T−accounts the effects of each transaction for Sunny Valley Stables in April, referencing each transaction in the accounts with the transaction letter. Show the unad−justed ending balances in the T−accounts.
3. Prepare an unadjusted trial balance as of April 30, 2017.
4. Refer to the revenues and expenses shown on the unadjusted trial balance. Based on this information, calculate preliminary net income and determine whether the net profit margin is better or worse than the 30.0 percent earned by a close competitor.

LO3-2, 3-3, 3-4

PA3-5 Analyzing the Effects of Transactions Using T-Accounts and Preparing an Unadjusted Trial Balance

You have been hired as the new assistant financial controller for Autobody Corp., an auto body repair shop. Prepare journal entries for the following transactions, which occurred during August 2017.

a. At the end of the month, prepaid a two−year insurance policy for $5,000

b. Received contributions from three investors of $90,000 in cash ($30,000 each)

c. Purchased a building for $250,000; paid a deposit of $25,000 in cash on August 15 and signed a nine−year note payable for the balance

d. Paid $8,000 in wages to employees who worked during the month

e. Rented an unused service bay to an oil change franchise; received cash of $26,000

f. Provided $30,000 in repair services for customers, all on credit

g. Received from a customer $5,000 to store some vehicles on the property for the winter (record as Deferred Revenue)

h. Paid $750 in cash for water utilities used during the month

i. Received an electric utility bill for $1,800 for usage in August; bill will be paid next month

j. Purchased cleaning supplies on account for $6,000

k. Paid $3,500 on accounts payable for previous purchases

l. Received $3,000 from customers on accounts receivable

Required:

1. Set up appropriate T−accounts. All accounts begin with zero balances.
2. Record in the T−accounts the effects of each transaction for Autobody Corp. in April, ref−erencing each transaction in the accounts with the transaction letter. Show the unadjusted ending balances in the T−accounts.
3. Prepare an unadjusted trial balance as of August 31, 2017.
4. Refer to the revenues and expenses shown on the unadjusted trial balance. Based on this information, write a short memo to the five owners offering your opinion on the results of operations during the first month of business.

GROUP B PROBLEMS

LO3-1, 3-2, 3-3

PB3-1 Recording Non-quantitative Journal Entries

Abercrombie & Fitch Co. is a specialty retailer of casual apparel. The company's brand was established in 1892. It was first publicly traded in 1996 and was spun off from The Limited in

1998. Assume that the following is a series of accounts for Abercrombie. The accounts are listed alphabetically and numbered for identification. Following the accounts is a series of hypo—thetical transactions. For each transaction, indicate the account(s) that should be debited and credited by entering the appropriate account number(s) to the right of each transaction. If no journal entry is needed, write NE after the transaction. Transaction (*a*) is given as an example.

Check Figure [Part (*i*)]: Debit 3 and Credit 6

Account No.	Account Title	Account No.	Account Title
1	Accounts Payable	7	Prepaid Rent
2	Accounts Receivable	8	Rent Expense
3	Cash	9	Supplies Expense
4	Contributed Capital	10	Supplies
5	Equipment	11	Deferred Revenue
6	Interest Revenue	12	Wages Expense

Transactions	Debit	Credit
a. Incurred wages expense; paid cash	12	3
b. Collected cash on account	___	___
c. Used up supplies (washroom paper towels, etc.) this period	___	___
d. Sold gift certificates to customers; none redeemed this period	___	___
e. Purchased equipment, paying part in cash and charging the balance on account	___	___
f. Paid cash to suppliers on account	___	___
g. Issued additional shares for cash	___	___
h. Paid rent to landlords for next month's use of mall space	___	___
i. Earned and received cash for interest on investments	___	___

PB3-2 Preparing Accrual Basis Journal Entries for Business Activities

LO3-2, 3-3

Robin Harrington established Timely Delivery on January 1, 2017. The following transactions occurred during the company's most recent quarter.

a. Issued shares for $80,000

b. Provided delivery service to customers, receiving $72,000 in accounts receivable and $16,000 in cash

c. Purchased equipment costing $82,000 and signed a long—term note for the full amount

d. Incurred repair costs of $3,000 on account

e. Collected $65,000 from customers on account

f. Borrowed $90,000 by signing a long—term note

g. Prepaid $74,400 cash to rent equipment and aircraft next quarter

h. Paid employees $38,000 for work done during the quarter

i. Purchased (with cash) and used immediately $49,000 in fuel for delivery equipment

j. Paid $2,000 on accounts payable

k. Ordered, but haven't yet received, $700 in supplies

Required:

For each of the transactions, prepare journal entries. Be sure to categorize each account as an asset (A), liability (L), shareholders' equity (SE), revenue (R), or expense (E).

PB3-3 Preparing Accrual Basis Journal Entries for Business Activities

LO3-2, 3-3

SmartAutoTrader is an online company that specializes in matching buyers and sellers of used items. Buyers and sellers can purchase a membership with SmartAutoTrader, which provides them with advance notice of potentially attractive offers. The following transactions occurred during the company's most recent quarter:

a. SmartAutoTrader provided online advertising services for another company for $200 on account.

b. On the last day of the month, SmartAutoTrader paid $50 cash to run an advertisement promoting the company's services. The advertisement ran that day in the local newspaper.

c. The company received $200 cash in membership fees for the month from new members.

d. SmartAutoTrader received an electricity bill for $85, for usage this month. The bill will be paid next month.

e. The company billed a customer $180 for expediting the sale of some items. SmartAutoTrader expects to receive the customer's payment by the end of next month.

f. SmartAutoTrader received $4,000 in cash and cheques from membership sales.

g. SmartAutoTrader paid $2,000 cash for employee wages this month.

h. The company paid $1,000 cash on a loan from the bank (ignore interest).

i. The company bought $3,000 worth of supplies from a large manufacturer, paying $1,000 cash and signing a short−term note for $2,000.

j. SmartAutoTrader signed a long−term note and received a $150,000 loan from a local bank.

k. The company billed a customer $2,000 for services provided. Payment is expected in forty−five days.

l. The company wrote a cheque for $600 for rent.

m. SmartAutoTrader received $450 cash from a customer for work done the same day.

n. The company incurred $400 in advertising costs for the current month and is planning to pay these costs next month.

Required:

For each of the transactions, prepare journal entries. Be sure to categorize each account as an asset (A), liability (L), shareholders' equity (SE), revenue (R), or expense (E).

LO3-1, 3-2, 3-3, 3-4, 3-5

PB3-4 Analyzing the Effects of Transactions Using T-Accounts and Preparing an Unadjusted Trial Balance

Since June 1, 2017, FunnyFlatables has been renting out fun items like moon walks and inflatable slides for parties and corporate events. The company has obtained the use of an abandoned ice rink located in a local shopping mall, where its rental products are displayed and available for casual hourly rental by mall patrons. The following transactions occurred during the first month of operations.

a. Received $50,000 cash in exchange for company shares

b. Purchased inflatable rides and inflation equipment, paying $20,000 cash

c. Received $5,000 cash from casual hourly rentals at the mall

d. Rented rides and equipment to customers for $10,000; received cash of $2,000 and the rest is due from customers

e. Received $2,500 from a large corporate customer as a deposit on a party booking for July 1

f. Began to prepare for the July 1 party by purchasing various party supplies on account for $600

g. Paid $6,000 in cash for renting the mall space this month

h. Prepaid next month's mall space rental charge of $6,000

i. Received $1,000 from customers on accounts receivable

j. Paid $4,000 in wages to employees for work done during the month

k. Paid $1,000 to run a television advertisement this month

Required:

1. Set up appropriate T−accounts. All accounts begin with zero balances.
2. Record in the T−accounts the effects of each transaction for FunnyFlatables in June, referencing each transaction in the accounts with the transaction letter. Show the unadjusted ending balances in the T−accounts.
3. Prepare an unadjusted trial balance for the end of June 2017.
4. Refer to the revenues and expenses shown on the unadjusted trial balance to calculate preliminary net income and determine whether the net profit margin is better or worse than the 30.0 percent earned by a close competitor.

PB3-5 Analyzing the Effects of Transactions Using T-Accounts and Preparing an Unadjusted Trial Balance

LO3-1, 3-2, 3-3, 3-4

Assume you are the owner of The University Shopper, which specializes in items of special interest to university students. You opened your doors for business on September 1, 2017. The following transactions occurred during the first month of operations.

a. Contributed $5,000 cash to the company in exchange for shares

b. Paid $1,000 to run a television advertisement this month

c. Received $5,000 cash from photocopier rentals

d. Received $2,500 from a university student council as a deposit for a large order of items to be delivered for Christmas

e. Purchased sales equipment, paying $10,000 cash

f. Paid $5,000 in cash for renting the space on campus this month

g. Paid yourself $5,000 in wages for work done during the month

h. Sold goods totalling $10,000 for the month; received cash of $5,000 and the rest is due from customers (friends)

i. Began to prepare for the large Christmas order by purchasing inventory on account for $6,000

j. Prepaid next month's rental charge of $5,000

k. Received $1,000 from customers on accounts receivable

Required:

1. Set up appropriate T−accounts. All accounts begin with zero balances.

2. Record in the T−accounts the effects of each transaction for The University Shopper in September, referencing each transaction in the accounts with the transaction letter. Show the unadjusted ending balances in the T−accounts.

3. Prepare an unadjusted trial balance for the end of September 2017.

4. Refer to the revenues and expenses shown on the unadjusted trial balance and write a short memo to your parents, who loaned you the money to start the company, offering your opinion on the results of operations during the first month of business.

Check Figure:
Ending Accounts Receivable balance = $4,000 dr

COMPREHENSIVE PROBLEM

C3-1 Analyzing, Recording, and Posting, and Preparing and Evaluating Financial Statements

LO2-2, 2-3, 2-4, 3-2, 3-3, 3-4, 3-5

Using the material learned from the first three chapters, answer the following question.

Vanishing Games Corporation (VGC) operates a massive multi−player online game, charging players a monthly subscription of $15. At the start of 2017, VGC's income statement accounts had zero balances and its balance sheet account balances were as follows:

Cash	$1,500,000	Accounts Payable	$ 108,000
Accounts Receivable	150,000	Deferred Revenue	73,500
Supplies	14,700	Notes Payable (due 2019)	60,000
Equipment	874,500	Contributed Capital	2,500,000
Land	1,200,000	Retained Earnings	1,419,700
Building	422,000		

In addition to the above accounts, VGC's chart of accounts includes the following: Subscription Revenue, Licensing Revenue, Wages Expense, Advertising Expense, and Utilities Expense.

Required:

1. Analyze the effect of the January 2017 transactions listed below on the accounting equa− tion, using the format shown in this chapter's Demonstration Case B.

a. Received $50,000 cash from customers for subscriptions that had already been earned in 2016

b. Received $25,000 cash from Electronic Arts, Inc. for licensing revenue earned in the month of January 2017

c. Purchased ten new computer servers for $33,500; paid $10,000 cash and signed a three−year note for the remainder owed

d. Paid $10,000 for an Internet advertisement run on Yahoo! in January 2017

e. Sold 15,000 monthly subscriptions at $15 each for services provided during the month of January 2017; half was collected in cash and half was sold on account

f. Received an electric and gas utility bill for $5,350 for January 2017 services; bill will be paid in February

g. Paid $378,000 in wages to employees for work done in January 2017

h. Purchased $3,000 of supplies on account

i. Paid $3,000 cash to the supplier in (h)

2. Prepare journal entries for the January 2017 transactions listed in requirement 1, using the letter of each transaction as a reference.

3. Create T−accounts, enter the beginning balances shown above, post the journal entries to the T−accounts, and show the unadjusted ending balances in the T−accounts.

4. Prepare an unadjusted trial balance as of January 31, 2017.

5. Prepare an income statement for the month ended January 31, 2017, using unad−justed balances from requirement 4.

6. Prepare a statement of retained earnings for the month ended January 31, 2017, using the beginning balance given above and the net income from requirement 5. Assume VGC has no dividends.

7. Prepare a classified balance sheet at January 31, 2017, using your response to requirement 6.

8. Why does the income statement total not equal the change in cash?

SKILLS DEVELOPMENT CASES

LO3-1   **S3-1 Finding Financial Information**

Refer to the summarized financial statements of The Home Depot in Appendix A at the end of this text.

Required:

1. Did The Home Depot's sales revenues increase or decrease in the year ended January 29, 2017, as compared to the previous year? By how much? Calculate this change as a per−centage of the previous year's sales revenues by dividing the amount of the change by the previous year's sales revenues and multiplying by 100.

2. The Home Depot's largest expense for its 2016 fiscal year was Cost of Sales. Did The Home Depot's Cost of Sales increase or decrease in the year ended January 29, 2017, as compared to the previous year? By how much?

LO3-1   **S3-2 Comparing Financial Information**

Refer to the summarized financial statements of The Home Depot in Appendix A and those of Lowe's Companies, Inc. in Appendix B at the back of this book.

Required:

1. Did Lowe's Companies, Inc.'s sales revenues increase or decrease in the year ended February 3, 2017, as compared to the previous year? By how much? Calculate this change as a per−centage of the previous year's sales revenues. Is the trend in Lowe's Companies, Inc.'s sales revenues more or less favourable than The Home Depot's?

2. State the amount of the largest expense on the income statement of Lowe's Companies, Inc. for the year ended February 3, 2017, and describe the transaction represented by the expense. Did this expense increase or decrease, and by what percentage, as compared to the previous year?

LO3-1, 3-5   **S3-3 Internet-Based Team Research: Examining the Income Statement**

In teams, select an industry to analyze. Via the Internet, each team member should access the annual report for one publicly traded company in the industry, with each member selecting a different company. (See S1−3 in Chapter 1 for a description of possible resources for these tasks.)

Required:

1. On an individual basis, each team member should write a short report that lists the following information:

   a. The major revenue and expense accounts on the most recent income statement

   b. Description of how the company has followed the conditions of the revenue principle

   c. The percentage of revenues that go to covering expenses and that are in excess of expenses (i.e., the percentage that remains as net income)

2. Then, as a team, write a short report comparing and contrasting your companies using these attributes. Discuss any patterns across the companies that you as a team observe. Provide potential explanations for any differences discovered.

S3-4 Ethical Decision Making: A Real-Life Example

LO3-1, 3-2, 3-3, 3-5

Read the following excerpt from a complaint filed by the Securities and Exchange Commission against WorldCom (posted online at http://www.sec.gov/litigation/complaints/comp17829.htm).

> WorldCom officers and employees fraudulently made and caused the making of false and fictitious entries in WorldCom's general ledger which effectively "transferred" a significant portion of its line cost expenses to a variety of capital asset accounts, thereby effectively recharacterizing, without any supporting documentation, and in a manner inconsistent with GAAP, the operating expenses it had incurred for access to third party networks as "assets."

1. When a company incurs a cost, its accountants have to decide whether to record the cost as an asset or expense. When costs are recorded as an asset, they are said to be *capitalized*. This builds on ideas first presented in Chapter 2, where you learned that it was appropriate to record costs as assets, provided that they possess certain characteristics. What are those characteristics?

2. The author of the article argues that, even with clear rules like those referenced in question 1 above, accounting still allows managers to use "tricks" like capitalizing expenses. What do you suppose the author means by the expression *capitalizing expenses?*

3. Suppose that, in the current year, a company inappropriately records a cost as an asset when it should be recorded as an expense. What is the effect of this accounting decision on the current year's net income? What is the effect of this accounting decision on the following year's net income?

4. Do you think it is always easy and straightforward to determine whether costs should be capitalized or expensed? Do you think it is always easy and straightforward to determine whether a manager is acting ethically or unethically? Give examples to illustrate your views.

S3-5 Ethical Decision Making: A Mini-Case

LO3-1, 3-2, 3-5

Mike Lynch is the manager of an insurance company's Toronto office. As the regional manager, his pay package includes a base salary, commissions, and a bonus when the region sells new policies in excess of its quota. Mike has been under enormous pressure lately, stemming largely from two factors. First, he is experiencing mounting personal debt due to some unfortunate circumstances. Second, compounding his worries, the region's sales of new insurance policies have dipped below the normal quota for the first time in years.

You have been working for Mike for two years, and like everyone else in the office, you consider yourself lucky to work for such a supportive boss. You also feel great sympathy for his personal problems. In your position as accountant for the regional office, you are only too aware of the drop in new policy sales and the impact this will have on the manager's bonus. While you are working on the year–end financial statements, Mike stops by your office.

Mike asks you to change the manner in which you have accounted for a new property insurance policy for a large local business. A cheque for the premium, substantial in amount, came in the mail on December 31, the last day of the reporting year. The premium covers a period beginning on January 5. You deposited the cheque and correctly debited Cash and credited Deferred Revenue. Mike says, "Hey, we have the money this year, so why not count the revenue this year? I never did understand why you accountants are so picky about these things, anyway. I'd like you to change the way you've recorded the transaction. I want you to credit a revenue account. And anyway, I've done favours for you in the past, and I am asking for such a small thing in return." With that, he leaves your office.

Required:

How should you handle this situation? What are the ethical implications of Mike's request? Who are the parties who would be helped or harmed if you went along with the request? If you fail to comply with his request, how will you explain your position to him? Justify your answers in writing.

LO3-1, 3-2, 3-4   **S3-6 Critical Thinking: Analyzing Changes in Accounts, and Preparing a Trial Balance**

Hordichuk Painting Service Company was organized on January 20, 2017, by three individuals, each receiving 5,000 shares from the new company. The following is a schedule of the cumulative account balances immediately after each of the first nine transactions, ending on January 31, 2017.

Accounts	Cumulative Balances								
	a	b	c	d	e	f	g	h	i
Cash	$75,000	$70,000	$85,000	$71,000	$61,000	$61,000	$46,000	$44,000	$60,000
Accounts Receivable			12,000	12,000	12,000	26,000	26,000	26,000	10,000
Supplies					5,000	5,000	4,000	4,000	4,000
Equipment		20,000	20,000	20,000	20,000	20,000	20,000	20,000	20,000
Land				18,000	18,000	18,000	18,000	18,000	18,000
Accounts Payable					3,000	3,000	3,000	1,000	1,000
Notes Payable		15,000	15,000	19,000	19,000	19,000	19,000	19,000	19,000
Contributed Capital	75,000	75,000	75,000	75,000	75,000	75,000	75,000	75,000	75,000
Paint Revenue			27,000	27,000	27,000	41,000	41,000	41,000	41,000
Supplies Expense							1,000	1,000	1,000
Wages Expense					8,000	8,000	23,000	23,000	23,000

Required:

1. Analyze the changes in this schedule for each transaction, then explain the transaction. Transactions (a) and (b) are examples:

   a. Cash increased $75,000, and Contributed Capital (shareholders' equity) increased $75,000. Therefore, transaction (a) was an issuance of the capital shares of the corporation for $75,000 cash.

   b. Cash decreased $5,000, Equipment (an asset) increased $20,000, and Notes Payable (a liability) increased $15,000. Therefore, transaction (b) was a purchase of equipment for $20,000. Payment was made as follows: cash, $5,000; notes payable, $15,000.

2. Based only on the preceding schedule, prepare an unadjusted trial balance.

LO3-2, 3-3, 3-4   **S3-7 Analyzing Transactions and Preparing an Unadjusted Trial Balance**

e**X**cel

Assume you recently started up a new company called Slusher Gusher that rents out machines for making frozen drinks like smoothies, frozen juices, tea slush, and iced cappuccinos. For $100, your business will deliver a machine, provide supplies (straws, paper cups), set up the machine, and pick up the machine the next morning. Drink mixes and other supplies are sold by other businesses in your city. This is a one-person operation, and you are responsible for everything from purchasing to marketing to operations to accounting.

You've decided that you'll just write notes about what happens during the month and do the accounting at the end of the month. You figure this will be more efficient. Plus, by waiting until the end of the month to do the accounting, you'll be less likely to make a mistake, because by that time you'll better understand the accounting cycle. Your notes said the following about your first month of operations:

Oct. 2	Incorporated Slusher Gusher (Slusher Gusher Inc.) and contributed $10,000 for shares in the company.
Oct. 12	Paid cash to buy three frozen drink machines on eBay at a total cost of $1,500. What a deal!
Oct. 13	Paid cash to buy $70 of supplies. Walmart was packed.
Oct. 16	Received $500 cash for this past week's rentals. I'm rich!
Oct. 17	Determined that $45 of supplies had been used up. Hmm, looks like I'll need some more.
Oct. 20	Bought $100 of supplies on account. I can't believe the party store gave me credit like that.
Oct. 23	Feeling tired after a busy week (six rentals this time). Received $400 cash and expect to receive $200 more sometime this week.
Oct. 25	Received $100 cash from one of the customers who hadn't paid up yet. Called the other customer to remind him I'm waiting.
Oct. 26	Ran an advertisement in the local paper today. Paid $25 cash.
Oct. 27	Received $150 cash for a two–machine All Saints' Day party to be held on November 1. It's a good thing I got this money because no other bookings are in sight for the rest of the month.

Required:

Create a spreadsheet in which to record the effects of the October transactions and calculate end–of–month totals. Using the spreadsheet, prepare a trial balance that checks whether debits = credits. Because you want to be sure that you do this right, you email your friend Owen for advice. Here's his reply:

From: Owentheaccountant@yahoo.com
To: Helpme@hotmail.com
Cc:
Subject: Excel Help

Wow, you're a CEO already? I always thought you were a mover and a shaker! So you want my advice on how to set up your spreadsheet? My advice is read the last e-mail I sent. The main thing that's new here is you'll need to include some columns for revenue and expenses under the shareholders' equity heading. Here's a screenshot of how your worksheet might look just before you enter the October transactions. Notice that because shareholders' equity is decreased by expenses, the debit side is used to record expenses.

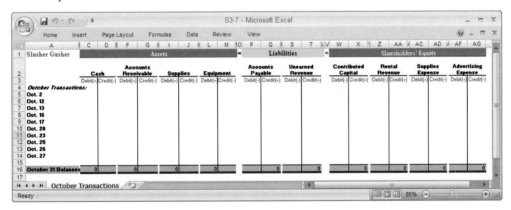

To prepare the trial balance, create three columns. In the first, enter the account names (one per row). In the second column, link in each debit balance by entering = in a cell and then clicking on the debit total from the T-account. Repeat this with all the accounts. Then do the same with the credit balances. At the bottom of the trial balance, use the SUM function to compute total debits and credits. Don't forget to save the file using a name that uniquely identifies you (as my true hero).

CONTINUING CASE

CC3-1 Accounting for Business Operations

Starting in May 2017, Nicole decided that she has everything she needs to open her doors to customers. To keep up with competition, Nicole has added items such as gift certificates and has started to advertise her company more and put things into place to keep her business going in the long term. Here is a sample of some transactions that occurred in the month of May at Nicole's Getaway Spa.

May 1	Paid $3,000 cash for an insurance policy that covers the period from June 1 until May 31 next year
May 4	Ordered five new massage tables from Spa Supplies Unlimited for $250 each for future delivery
May 7	Provided $860 of spa services to customers on account
May 10	Purchased spa supplies for $800 on account to use at Nicole's Getaway Spa
May 13	Received a bill for $45 for running an advertisement in the newspaper in May; bill was paid in cash
May 16	Paid one–quarter of the amount owed from May 10
May 19	Sold $1,900 of gift certificates to customers for cash
May 20	Obtained financing from the bank by signing a $5,000 note payable
May 22	Received two of the massage tables ordered on May 4 and paid cash for the two tables
May 25	Paid $500 cash for utility bills for services received and billed in May

Required:

For each of the transactions, prepare journal entries using the date of the transaction as the reference.

CHAPTER 4

In the previous chapter, you learned how to analyze, record, and summarize the effects of operating transactions on balance sheet and income statement accounts.

THIS IS
NOW

This chapter concludes the accounting cycle by focusing on adjustments, financial statement preparation, and the closing process.

Adjustments, Financial Statements, and Financial Results

Iakov Filimonov/ Shutterstock.com

FOCUS COMPANY:
Pizza Palace Inc.

In Chapter 3, you saw that Pizza Palace sold a lot of pizza during its first month of operations—more than owner–manager Emilio Santos had expected. Emilio was very curious to know how the business performed, so he computed net income based on the company's unadjusted balances. When he saw that $15,500 of revenues had led to net income of $5,800 (a net profit margin of 37.4 percent), Emilio was very excited.

Emilio's CPA, Ally, cautioned him that, because he had been using unadjusted amounts in his computations, his results were not meaningful. She emphasized that under accrual accounting, adjustments need to be made at the end of an accounting period to (1) update amounts already recorded in the accounting records and (2) include events that had occurred but had not yet been recorded. These adjustments ensure that the recognition of revenues and expenses occurs in the proper period, and that assets and liabilities are reported at appropriate amounts.

In the first section of this chapter, we'll help you to understand why adjustments are a necessary part of accrual basis accounting. In the second part of the chapter, we'll show you how to determine what adjustments are needed, and how they are recorded and summarized in the accounting system. This second section concludes with the final steps involved in the accounting cycle. In the third part of this chapter, you will learn the importance of adjustments for external financial statement users, and as always, the final section provides lots of opportunities for you to review and work with the material presented in this chapter.

ORGANIZATION OF THE CHAPTER

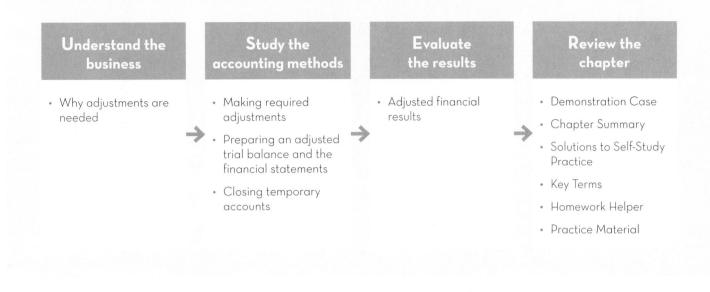

Understand the business	Study the accounting methods	Evaluate the results	Review the chapter
• Why adjustments are needed	• Making required adjustments • Preparing an adjusted trial balance and the financial statements • Closing temporary accounts	• Adjusted financial results	• Demonstration Case • Chapter Summary • Solutions to Self-Study Practice • Key Terms • Homework Helper • Practice Material

Understand the Business

WHY ADJUSTMENTS ARE NEEDED

Accounting systems are designed to record most recurring daily transactions, particularly any involving cash. As cash is received or paid, it is recorded in the accounting system. This focus on cash works well, especially when cash receipts and payments occur in the same period as the activities that lead to revenues and expenses.

As you learned in Chapter 3, however, cash is not always received in the period in which the company earns the related revenue; likewise, cash is not always paid in the period in which the company incurs the related expense. In these situations, **adjustments** are made to the accounting records at the end of the period to ensure that assets and liabilities are reported at appropriate amounts. These adjustments also ensure that the related revenues and expenses are reported in the proper period, as required by the revenue and expense recognition principles.

Adjustments involve both income statement and balance sheet accounts. They are needed to ensure that

- revenues are recorded when the company has fulfilled an obligation (the revenue recognition principle),
- expenses are recorded in the same period as the revenues to which they relate (the expense recognition or "matching" principle),
- assets are reported at amounts representing the economic benefits that remain at the end of the current period, and
- liabilities are reported at amounts owed at the end of the current period that will require a future sacrifice of resources.

Companies wait until the end of the accounting period to adjust their accounts because adjusting the records daily would be costly and time−consuming. In practice, almost every financial statement account could require adjustment. Rather than trying to memorize examples, you should instead focus on learning the general nature of adjustments and the process for determining them. In general, adjustments can be grouped into two categories: (1) deferrals and (2) accruals.

1. Deferral Adjustments

The word *defer* means to postpone until later. In accounting, we say an expense or revenue has been deferred if we have postponed reporting it on the income statement until a later period. As you saw in Chapter 3, when Pizza Palace pays its rent in advance, the expense is initially deferred as an asset on the balance sheet (in an account called *Prepaid Rent*). The adjustment part comes later, at the end of the month, when one month of the prepaid rent benefits have been used up. The deferral adjustment involves reducing Prepaid Rent and increasing Rent Expense on the income statement.

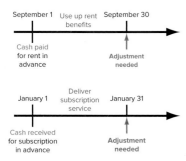

Deferral adjustments also can involve revenues. For example, when *Chatelaine* receives cash for subscriptions before it has delivered maga—zines to subscribers, this revenue is initially deferred as a liability on the balance sheet (in an account called *Deferred Subscriptions Revenue*). The liability indicates the company's obligation to deliver magazines in the future. Later, when the company delivers the magazines, thereby meeting its obligation and earning the revenue, a deferral adjustment is made to reduce Deferred Subscriptions Revenue on the balance sheet and increase Subscriptions Revenue on the income statement.

There are two key ideas that you should note here:

1. **Deferral adjustments are used to decrease balance sheet accounts and increase corresponding income statement accounts.** Previously deferred amounts exist on the balance sheet because the company paid cash before incurring the expense or received cash before earning revenue. When revenues are earned (as defined by the revenue recognition principle) or expenses incurred (as defined by the expense recognition principle), the previously deferred amounts are adjusted and amounts are transferred to the income statement using a deferral adjustment.

2. **Each deferral adjustment involves one asset and one expense account, or one liability and one revenue account.** The left side of Exhibit 4.1 shows a partial list of accounts that commonly require deferral adjustments.

EXHIBIT 4.1   Examples of Accounts Affected by Adjustments

Deferral Adjustments				Accrual Adjustments			
	Balance Sheet	**Income Statement**			**Balance Sheet**	**Income Statement**	
Assets	Supplies	Supplies Expense	**Expenses**	**Assets**	Interest Receivable	Interest Revenue	**Revenues**
	Prepaid Rent	Rent Expense			Rent Receivable	Rent Revenue	
	Prepaid Insurance	Insurance Expense					
Liabilities	Deferred Ticket Revenue	Ticket Sales Revenue	**Revenues**	**Liabilities**	Income Tax Payable	Income Tax Expense	**Expenses**
	Deferred Subscriptions Revenue	Subscriptions Revenue			Wages Payable	Wages Expense	
					Interest Payable	Interest Expense	

2. Accrual Adjustments

Accrual adjustments are needed when a company has earned revenue or incurred an expense in the current period but has not yet recorded it because the related cash will not be received or paid until a later period. For example, Pizza Palace will eventually pay taxes on the income it earns this period, so an accrual adjustment will be needed at the end of the month to record increases in its Income Tax Expense and Income Tax Payable accounts. This adjustment matches Income Tax Expense to the period in which the company earned the income that caused the income taxes.

Likewise, if interest revenue is earned on investments this month but not received in cash until a later month, an accrual adjustment is needed at the end of the current month to record increases in the company's Interest Revenue and Interest Receivable accounts.

There are two key ideas that you should note here:

1. **Accrual adjustments are used to record revenue or expenses when they occur prior to receiving or paying cash, and to adjust corresponding balance sheet accounts.**

2. **Each accrual adjustment involves one asset and one revenue account, or one liability and one expense account.** Notice that this differs from deferral adjustments, which pair assets with expenses and liabilities with revenues. The right side of Exhibit 4.1 shows a partial list of accounts that require accrual adjustments.

HOW'S IT GOING?

Self-Study Practice 4.1

For each of the following, indicate whether a deferral (D) or accrual (A) adjustment is required on October 31, and what two accounts will be affected by it.

	Type of Adjustment	Accounts Affected	
		Balance Sheet	Income Statement
1. In October, Air Canada provided flight services to customers who had paid for their tickets in August.			
2. Hertz Car Rental earned vehicle rent from customers in October, but is not expecting payment until November.			
3. In October, Fortune magazine incurred interest on a bank loan that must be paid at the end of the year.			
4. In October, Apple Inc. used up one month of insurance coverage that it had prepaid in July.			

After you have finished, check your answers with the solution, which follows the chapter summary.

HOW'S IT GOING?

Self-Study Practice 4.2

For each situation in the left column, choose two applicable reasons for an adjustment from the right column.

_____ 1. Brand Affinity Technologies received a $500 bill for this month's celebrity advertising services. It will pay the bill next month.

_____ 2. Concerts, for which Live Nation Entertainment sold $10,000 of tickets last month, were performed this month.

_____ 3. Chiquita Brands International used up $5,000 of the benefits of its banana harvesting and transportation equipment.

_____ 4. International Flavors and Fragrances completed a project to develop a new scent for Hilton Hotels, for which it will be paid $1,000 next month.

A. Revenue can be recorded because the company has fulfilled an obligation.

B. Expense has been incurred.

C. Liability has been incurred.

D. Liability has been fulfilled.

E. Asset has been acquired.

F. Asset has been used up.

After you have finished, check your answers with the solution, which follows the chapter summary.

MAKING REQUIRED ADJUSTMENTS

LEARNING OBJECTIVE 4-2

Prepare adjustments needed at the end of the period.

Adjusting journal entries (AJEs): Record the effects of each period's adjustments in a debits-equal-credits format.

The process of making adjustments is similar to the process used to account for daily transactions, which you learned about in Chapters 2 and 3. As Exhibit 4.2 shows, the main difference is that adjustments are made at the end of each accounting period immediately prior to preparing financial statements. Adjustments are not made on a daily basis because it's more efficient to do them all at once at the end of each period.

After determining the necessary adjustments (in step 1), they are recorded using **adjusting journal entries (AJEs)** (in step 2) and then summarized in the accounts (in step 3). An adjusted trial balance is prepared to ensure total debits still equal total credits after the adjusting journal entries have been posted to the accounts. If the trial balance is in balance, the financial statements can be prepared.

EXHIBIT 4.2	Month-End Adjustments as Part of the Accounting Cycle

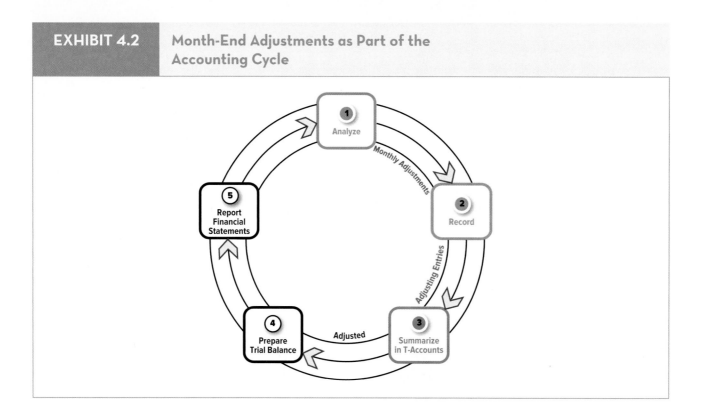

Adjustment Analysis, Recording, and Summarizing

The first step, Analyze, involves determining the necessary adjustments to make to the accounting records. To complete this step, you need to know the balance currently reported in each account, then determine what should be reported as the balance, and finally figure out the adjustment that will take you from the current (unadjusted) balance to the desired (adjusted) balance. This thinking process is illustrated by Exhibit 4.3.

The unadjusted trial balance is a key starting point for the adjustment process because it presents the unadjusted balances for every account, which will help you identify accounts that require adjustment. Exhibit 4.4 shows Pizza Palace's unadjusted trial balance at the end of September. This trial balance is identical to what you saw in Exhibit 3.9, except we've included

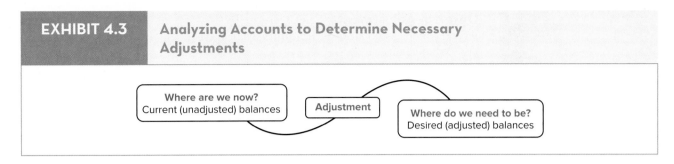

balances for all accounts in Pizza Palace's chart of accounts, including those that currently have zero balances. Alongside the unadjusted trial balance, we've identified accounts requiring adjustment at the end of September.

In the remainder of this section, we show how to analyze, record, and summarize the required adjustments. Read these pages carefully; they con—tain the topics that people typically find the most challenging in this chapter.

EXHIBIT 4.4   Unadjusted Trial Balance

PIZZA PALACE INC.
Unadjusted Trial Balance
At September 30, 2017

Explanation of Adjustments Needed

Account Name	Debit	Credit	
Cash	$ 7,500		
Accounts Receivable	200		Increase for right to collect cash from Emilio's friend for pizza delivery [see (e)].
Supplies	1,600		Decrease for supplies used up during September [see (a)].
Prepaid Rent	7,200		Decrease for prepaid September rent benefits now used up [see (b)].
Cookware	630		
Equipment	60,000		Adjust for equipment benefits used up in September [see (c)].
Accumulated Depreciation		$ 0	
Accounts Payable		1,030	
Deferred Revenue		300	Decrease for gift card obligations met in September [see (d)].
Wages Payable		0	Increase for September wages incurred but not yet paid [see (f)].
Income Tax Payable		0	Increase for tax owed on income generated in September [see (h)].
Interest Payable		0	Increase for interest owed on unpaid note in September [see (g)].
Dividends Payable		0	Increase for cash dividends declared in September [see (i)].
Note Payable		20,000	
Contributed Capital		50,000	
Retained Earnings		0	
Dividends Declared	0		
Pizza Revenue		15,500	Increase for revenues earned by delivering pizza to Emilio's friend [see (e)].
Wages Expense	8,700		Increase for employees' September wages not yet recorded [see (f)].
Rent Expense	0		Increase for expense incurred for September rent [see (b)].
Supplies Expense	0		Increase for supplies used up in September [see (a)].
Depreciation Expense	0		Increase for expense incurred by using equipment in September [see (c)].
Utilities Expense	600		
Advertising Expense	400		
Interest Expense	0		Increase for September interest incurred on unpaid note [see (g)].
Income Tax Expense	0		Increase for taxes on income generated in September [see (h)].
Totals	**$86,830**	**$86,830**	

©Bernd Euler/VISUM/The
Image Works

Deferral Adjustments Let's begin by looking at deferral adjustments, which are used to update amounts that have been previously deferred on the balance sheet.

(a) Supplies Used During the Period. **Of the $1,600 in supplies received in early September, $400 remains on hand at September 30.**

The supplies were initially recorded as an asset on September 2 (in Chapter 3), but some of them have now been used up as of September 30. The expense recognition principle requires an adjustment be made to report the cost of supplies used up this month as an expense (to match against revenues). To determine the cost of supplies used up, you have to do a little calculating. If you had $1,600 of supplies available for use and only $400 of supplies are left at the end of the month, then the $1,200 difference must be the cost of supplies used this month. In accounting terms, you should reduce the asset (Supplies) by $1,200 and show this amount as an expense (Supplies Expense).

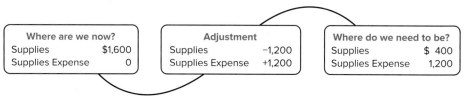

Where are we now?		Adjustment		Where do we need to be?	
Supplies	$1,600	Supplies	−1,200	Supplies	$ 400
Supplies Expense	0	Supplies Expense	+1,200	Supplies Expense	1,200

The effects of this adjustment on the accounting equation are shown below, along with the required adjusting journal entry (AJE) and the accounts affected by it.

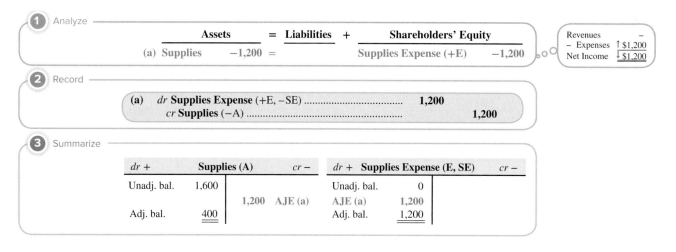

① Analyze

	Assets	= Liabilities +	Shareholders' Equity	
(a) Supplies	−1,200 =		Supplies Expense (+E)	−1,200

Revenues   −
− Expenses   ↑ $1,200
Net Income   ↓ $1,200

② Record

(a)	*dr* **Supplies Expense** (+E, −SE)	1,200	
	cr **Supplies** (−A)		1,200

③ Summarize

dr +	**Supplies (A)**	*cr* −		*dr* +	**Supplies Expense (E, SE)**	*cr* −
Unadj. bal.	1,600			Unadj. bal.	0	
		1,200 AJE (a)		AJE (a)	1,200	
Adj. bal.	400			Adj. bal.	1,200	

COACH'S TIP

In step 1 above, the notation "Supplies Expense (+E) −1,200" implies that the increase in an expense causes a decrease in shareholders' equity (through its negative impact on net income and retained earnings). To review this point see Exhibit 3.7.

The financial statement effects of this adjustment are pictured in Exhibit 4.5.

(b) Rent Benefits Expired During the Period. **Three months of rent were prepaid on September 1 for $7,200, but one month has now expired, leaving only two months prepaid at September 30.**

To picture how costs relate to various time periods, it's useful to draw a timeline like the one shown in Exhibit 4.6.

The timeline in Exhibit 4.6 shows that the September prepayment of $7,200 represented three equal months of $2,400. The benefits of the first month (pictured in red) have now expired, so they should be reported as an expense on the September income statement. Only two of the three months (2/3) remain prepaid on September 30. Thus, the $7,200 that was prepaid on September 1 needs to be adjusted on September 30 to $4,800 (2/3 × $7,200), which is the cost of the two remaining months of Prepaid Rent.

EXHIBIT 4.5 — Adjusting for Assets Used Up

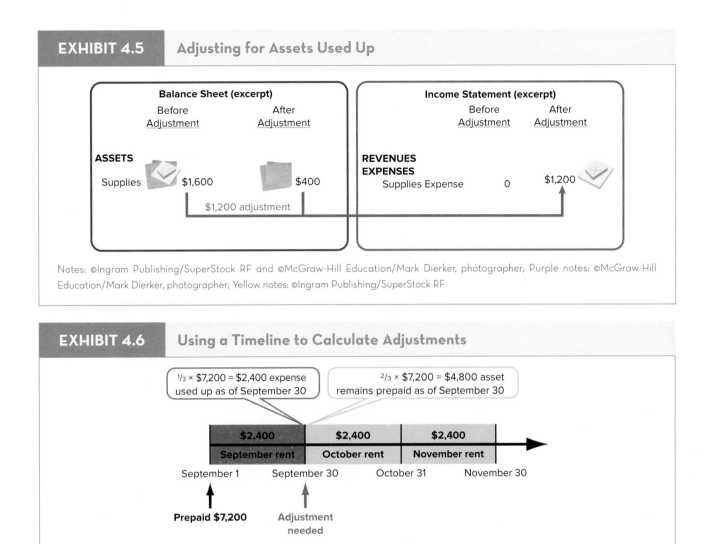

Balance Sheet (excerpt)

	Before Adjustment	After Adjustment
ASSETS		
Supplies	$1,600	$400

$1,200 adjustment

Income Statement (excerpt)

	Before Adjustment	After Adjustment
REVENUES		
EXPENSES		
Supplies Expense	0	$1,200

Notes: ©Ingram Publishing/SuperStock RF and ©McGraw-Hill Education/Mark Dierker, photographer; Purple notes: ©McGraw-Hill Education/Mark Dierker, photographer; Yellow notes: ©Ingram Publishing/SuperStock RF

EXHIBIT 4.6 — Using a Timeline to Calculate Adjustments

⅓ × $7,200 = $2,400 expense used up as of September 30

⅔ × $7,200 = $4,800 asset remains prepaid as of September 30

$2,400	$2,400	$2,400
September rent	October rent	November rent

September 1   September 30   October 31   November 30

Prepaid $7,200   Adjustment needed

The preceding analysis has determined that an adjustment is needed to reduce Prepaid Rent by $2,400, from $7,200 to $4,800. Likewise, the adjustment needs to increase Rent Expense by $2,400. These effects are accounted for as follows:

1 Analyze

	Assets	=	Liabilities	+	Shareholders' Equity	
(b) Prepaid Rent	−2,400	=			Rent Expense (+E)	−2,400

Revenues   −
− Expenses   ↑ 2,400
Net Income   ↓ 2,400

2 Record

(b)	dr Rent Expense (+E, −SE)	2,400	
	cr Prepaid Rent (−A)		2,400

2 Summarize

dr +	Prepaid Rent (A)	cr −		dr +	Rent Expense (E, SE)	cr −
Unadj. bal.	7,200			Unadj. bal.	0	
		2,400 AJE (b)		AJE (b)	2,400	
Adj. bal.	4,800			Adj. bal.	2,400	

Similar adjustments are made for other prepayments such as Prepaid Insurance. If the company pays the cost of services in advance of receiving them, the company initially defers that cost as an asset on the balance

Self-Study Practice 4.3

On September 30, Apple Inc. paid $24,000 for insurance for October, November, and December. On October 31, unadjusted balances for Prepaid Insurance and Insurance Expense were $24,000 and $0, respectively. Based on this information, (1) analyze the accounting equation effects of the adjustment required on October 31, (2) record the adjusting journal entry, and (3) summarize the effects of the adjusting journal entry in the T-accounts shown below.

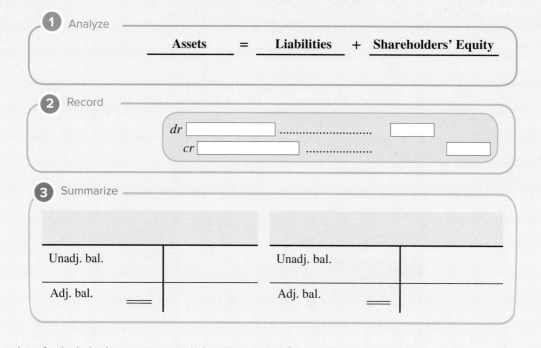

1 Analyze

| Assets | = | Liabilities | + | Shareholders' Equity |

2 Record

dr [   ] .... [   ]
cr [   ] .... [   ]

3 Summarize

| Unadj. bal. | | Unadj. bal. | |
| Adj. bal. | | Adj. bal. | |

After you have finished, check your answers with the solution, which follows the chapter summary.

Carrying value (net book value, book value): The amount an asset or liability is reported at ("carried at") in the financial statements. For assets, it's the acquisition cost less accumulated depreciation. It is also known as *net book value* or *book value*.

Depreciation: (1) The process of allocating the cost of buildings, vehicles, and equipment to the accounting periods in which they are used; also referred to as *amortization*. (2) The allocation of the cost of long-lived tangible assets over their productive lives using a systematic and rational method. Also called *amortization*.

sheet. At the end of each accounting period in which the services are used up, a deferral adjustment is made to decrease the asset and increase the related expense on the income statement. Practise doing this one more time in the following Self–Study Practice.

Notice that for events in (a), (b), and the Self–Study Practice, the deferral adjustments have two effects: (1) they reduce the **carrying value** of assets on the balance sheet, and (2) they transfer the amount of the reductions to related expense accounts on the income statement. This happens whether we're adjusting supplies, prepaid rent, or even long–term assets like buildings, vehicles, and equipment. When accounting for the use of long–term assets like buildings, vehicles, and equipment, there is one slight difference in how the carrying value is reduced, as we'll explain next.

(c) **Depreciation Is Recorded for Use of Equipment. The restaurant equipment, which was estimated to last five years, has now been used for one month, representing an estimated expense of $1,000.**

The **expense recognition "matching" principle** indicates that when equipment is used to generate revenues in the current period, part of its cost should be transferred to an expense account in that period. This process is referred to as **depreciation**, so an income statement account named *Depreciation Expense* reports the cost of equipment use in the current period. It is important to note that this process can also be referred to as *amortization*. The terms *depreciation* and *amortization* can be used interchangeably. On the balance sheet, we reduce the amount reported for equipment but we don't take the amount of depreciation directly out of the equipment account. Rather, a **contra—account** is created to keep track of all the depreciation recorded against the equipment. This contra—account, named *Accumulated Depreciation*, is like a negative asset account that is subtracted from the Equipment account in the assets section of the balance sheet, as shown in Exhibit 4.7.

Contra-account: An account that is an offset to, or reduction of, another account.

EXHIBIT 4.7	Reporting Accumulated Depreciation on the Balance Sheet

PIZZA PALACE INC.
Balance Sheet (excerpt)
At September 30, 2017

<u>Assets</u>

Equipment	$60,000	← Original cost of equipment
Less: Accumulated Depreciation	(1,000)	← Running total of depreciation recorded
Equipment, Net of Accumulated Depreciation	59,000	← Carrying value (or book value)

COACH'S TIP

Recording depreciation for the use of long-lived assets is a lot like recording the use of supplies. The only difference is that a contra-account is used so that a record of the original costs is maintained for long-lived assets throughout their long lives.

In our analyses below, we use a small x to indicate a contra—account, so the notation for a contra—account for an asset is "xA." An increase in a contra—asset account $(+xA)$ decreases total assets on the balance sheet $(-A)$.

1 Analyze

Assets	= Liabilities +	Shareholders' Equity	
(c) Accumulated Depreciation (+xA) $\quad$ −1,000 =		Depreciation Expense (+E) $\quad$ −1,000	

Revenues	−
− Expenses	↑ $1,000
Net Income	↓ $1,000

2 Record

(c)	*dr* Depreciation Expense (+E, −SE)	1,000	
	cr Accumulated Depreciation (+xA, −A)		1,000

3 Summarize

dr +	Equipment (A)	*cr* −
Unadj. bal.	60,000	
Adj. bal.	60,000	

dr −	Accumulated Depreciation (xA)	*cr* +
Unadj. bal.		0 $\quad$ Unadj. bal.
	1,000	AJE (c)
Adj. bal.	1,000	Adj. bal.

dr +	Depreciation Expense (E, SE)	*cr* −
Unadj. bal.	0	
AJE (c)	1,000	
Adj. bal.	1,000	

There are four aspects of this example that you should note:

1. **Accumulated Depreciation is a balance sheet account and Depreciation Expense is an income statement account.** As a balance sheet account, Accumulated Depreciation will increase over time as it accumulates the depreciation of each period until the asset is no longer used. As an income statement account, Depreciation Expense will include only the depreciation of the current accounting year.

2. **By recording depreciation in Accumulated Depreciation, separate from the Equipment account, you can report both the original cost of equipment and a running total of the amount that has been depreciated.** This gives financial statement users a rough idea of how much of the asset's original cost (representing its original usefulness) has been used up as of the balance sheet date. In our example, approximately 1/60 ($1,000/$60,000) of the equipment's total usefulness has been used up as of September 30.

3. **The normal balance in a contra-account is always the opposite of the account it offsets.** Accumulated Depreciation is recorded with a credit because the account that it offsets, Equipment, is recorded with a debit.

4. **The amount of depreciation depends on the method used for determining it.** There are different depreciation methods that can be used to calculate how much depreciation is expensed each period. These methods (and their formulas) will be discussed in greater detail in Chapter 9. At this point, it's important to know, that the process of depreciation is allocating the cost of the asset over a period of time that the asset is being used to generate revenue.

Just as deferral adjustments are used to record expenses incurred when assets are used up, they also are used to record the revenues earned when a company meets its obligation to provide goods or services to customers. For example, when Air Canada, the Globe and Mail, and Rogers Communications Inc. receive cash in advance of providing flights, newspapers, and cellphone service, they initially increase (debit) Cash and increase (credit) a liability account called *Deferred Revenue*. Later, when they meet their obligations, a deferral adjustment is recorded, reducing the liability (with a debit) and reporting the revenue earned from these services (with a credit). Let's see how this idea applies to Pizza Palace.

COACH'S TIP

The word *deferred* in the Deferred Revenue account title means that the company hasn't done what it was paid to do and the revenue is deferred until the obligation is performed. In other words, the company has an obligation (liability) to do the work or return the cash.

(d) Gift Cards Redeemed for Service. **Pizza Palace redeemed $160 of gift cards that customers used to pay for pizza.**

The unadjusted trial balance reports $300 of Deferred Revenue, which represents Pizza Palace's obligation to honour gift cards previously issued to customers. By accepting $160 of gift cards in exchange for pizza this month, Pizza Palace has fulfilled a portion of its obligation and has earned additional revenue. Thus, a deferral adjustment is needed to reduce Deferred Revenue and increase Pizza Revenue.

1 Analyze

	Assets	=	Liabilities		+	Shareholders' Equity		
(d)			Deferred Revenue	−160		Pizza Revenue (+R)	+160	

Revenues	↑ 160
− Expenses	−
Net Income	↑ 160

2 Record

(d)	dr Deferred Revenue (−L)	160	
	cr Pizza Revenue (+R, +SE)...........................		160

3 Summarize

dr −	Deferred Revenue (L)		cr +		dr −	Pizza Revenue (R, SE)		cr +
		300	Unadj. bal.				15,500	Unadj. bal.
AJE (d)	160						160	AJE (d)
		140	Adj. bal.				15,660	Adj. bal.

Accrual Adjustments Let's now look at common examples of accrual adjustments, which are adjustments that make the accounting records complete by including transactions that have occurred but have not been recorded.

(e) Revenues Earned but Not Yet Recorded. **Pizza Palace provided $40 of pizza to Emilio's close friend on the last day of September, with payment to be received in October.**

Companies that regularly provide services on credit will design their accounting systems to record transactions like this on a daily basis. However, for a business like Pizza Palace that does not typically extend credit to its customers, these kinds of events may require an accrual adjustment at month–end. Because these revenues and the right to collect them (Accounts Receivable) are earned in September, the **revenue recognition principle** indicates they should be recorded in September. Thus, an accrual adjustment is needed on September 30 to increase Accounts Receivable on the balance sheet and increase Pizza Revenue on the income statement.

Revenue recognition principle: The requirement under accrual basis accounting to record revenues when they are earned, not necessarily when cash is received for them.

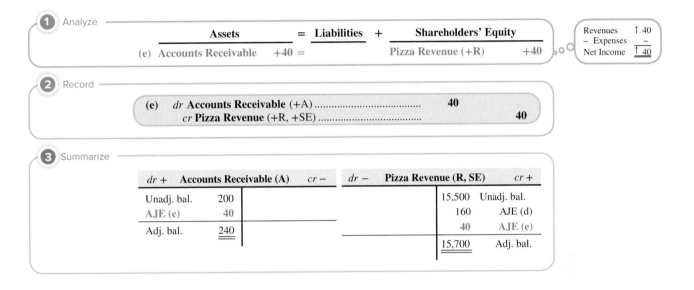

Other situations require accrual adjustments for revenue earned but not yet recorded. For example, interest on investments is earned daily but typically is received in cash on a yearly basis, so each month an accrual adjustment is made to increase Interest Receivable and Interest Revenue for amounts earned but not yet recorded. Also, if a company provides professional accounting, advertising, or legal services over two or more accounting periods, it typically will not receive cash or bill its customer until the services have been provided in full. Consequently, an adjustment is needed to record the portion of the total revenue that has been earned as of the end of the month.

(f) Wage Expense Incurred but Not Yet Recorded. **Pizza Palace owes $300 of wages to employees for work done on the last day of September.**

Back in Chapter 3, Pizza Palace paid employees $8,700 for work done through September 29 ($300 per day). As of September 30, one additional day of work has been completed at a cost of $300. Although this amount will not be paid until October, the expense relates to work done (and revenues generated) in September, so the expense recognition principle

September 2017						
S	M	T	W	T	F	S
					1	2
3	4	5	6	7	8	9
10	11	12	13	14	15	16	Paid
17	18	19	20	21	22	23
24	25	26	27	28	29	30
Owed						

requires an adjustment be made to accrue the $300 of additional wages incurred and owed by Pizza Palace, as follows.

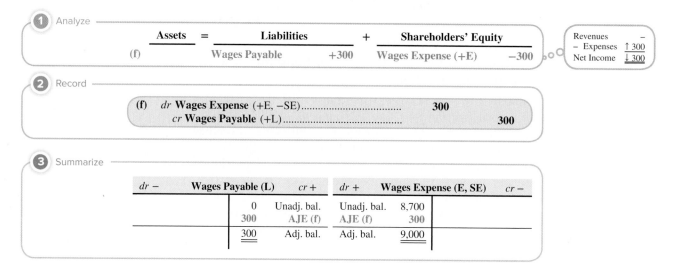

When the $300 of wages is paid in cash the following month, Pizza Palace will decrease Wages Payable (with a debit) and decrease Cash (with a credit).

Accrual adjustments also may be required for other expenses, like property taxes and interest, if incurred and owed during the current period (but not yet recorded). The adjusting journal entry required for each of these items would be similar to the one shown in (g), with an expense recorded (with a debit) and a liability increased (with a credit). For purposes of our Pizza Palace example, we'll assume that the only remaining expenses to record are the accruals for interest (in g) and income taxes (in h), both of which are incurred this month but won't be paid until a later period.

(g) **Interest Expense Incurred but Not Yet Recorded.** **Pizza Palace has not paid or recorded the $100 interest that it owes for this month on its note payable to the bank.**

Pizza Palace incurs interest each month on its unpaid note payable to the bank. An adjustment is needed to record the Interest Expense relating to September and, because this interest has not yet been paid, the adjustment also must record a liability called *Interest Payable*.

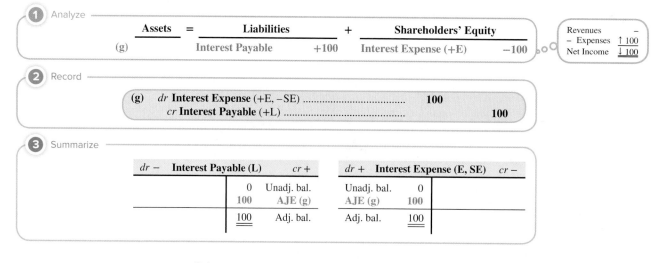

(h) **Income Taxes Incurred but Not Yet Recorded.** **Pizza Palace pays income tax at an average rate equal to 40 percent of the company's income before taxes.**

Just like you, a corporation is responsible for income tax when it generates more revenue than expenses in the current period. Income tax is calculated by multiplying (1) the company's adjusted income (before income taxes) by (2) the company's tax rate. To calculate adjusted income (before income tax), the following table starts with the unadjusted revenue and expense numbers from the unadjusted trial balance (Exhibit 4.4) and then includes the effects of adjustments to revenues and expenses. Multiply the adjusted income before income tax ($1,000) by the tax rate (40 percent) to get the amount of income tax ($400).

	Revenues	Expenses	
Unadjusted totals	$15,500	$ 9,700	◄ Calculated from Exhibit 4.4 ($9,700 = $8,700 + $600 + $400)
Adjustments: (a)		+ 1,200	
(b)		+ 2,400	
(c)		+ 1,000	
(d)	+ 160		
(e)	+ 40		
(f)		+ 300	
(g)		+ 100	
Adjusted totals	$15,700 −	$14,700	= $1,000 ◄ Adjusted income before income tax expense

The unadjusted trial balance shows that no income tax has been recorded (both Income Tax Payable and Income Tax Expense are $0). Because income was reported in September, the expense recognition principle requires that we record the $400 tax expense in September. The tax hasn't been paid yet, so a liability is recorded.

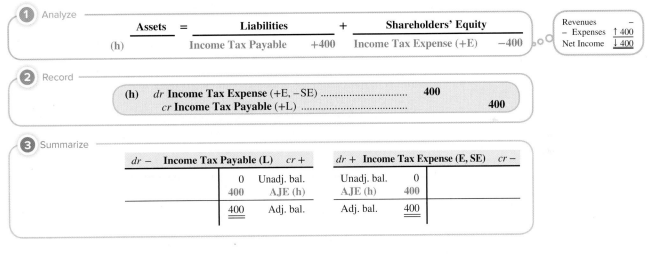

1 Analyze

Assets	=	Liabilities	+	Shareholders' Equity	
(h)		Income Tax Payable +400		Income Tax Expense (+E) −400	

Revenues −
− Expenses ↑ 400
Net Income ↓ 400

2 Record

(h) dr Income Tax Expense (+E, −SE) 400
    cr Income Tax Payable (+L) 400

3 Summarize

dr −	Income Tax Payable (L)	cr +		dr +	Income Tax Expense (E, SE)	cr −
	0	Unadj. bal.		Unadj. bal.	0	
	400	AJE (h)		AJE (h)	400	
	400	Adj. bal.		Adj. bal.	400	

Additional Comments

There are three final points to learn before finishing this section. First, notice that none of the adjusting journal entries affected the Cash account. Adjusting journal entries never involve cash. Second, adjusting entries always include one balance sheet and one income statement account.

The third point relates to dividends, which a corporation uses to distribute profits to shareholders as a return on their investment in the corporation. The decision to pay a dividend is made by the company's board of directors *after* profits have been generated, so dividends are not expenses of the business. Instead, they are a reduction of the retained earnings. Consequently, dividends are not reported on the income statement, but instead are subtracted on the Statement of Retained Earnings (as shown in Chapter 1). Dividends are recorded in their own special account called *Dividends Declared*. Because dividends reduce shareholders' equity, they are recorded with a debit, just

HOW'S IT GOING?

Self-Study Practice 4.4

Assume that, prior to accruing marketing expenses of $5 million, Pixar's adjusted income before income taxes was $245 million. Assuming the company's average tax rate was 40 percent, (1) analyze the effect of the required income tax adjustment on the accounting equation, and (2) prepare the adjusting journal entry, assuming that no amounts have been recorded yet for income taxes.

1 Analyze

Assets	=	Liabilities	+	Shareholders' Equity

2 Record

dr _____ .... [   ]
cr _____ .... [   ]

After you have finished, check your answers with the solution, which follows the chapter summary.

like all reductions in shareholders' equity. Now that we know Pizza Palace has generated a profit for the month, we'll assume that the company pays a dividend to shareholders. (Technically speaking, a dividend can occur any time during the year, so it is typically recorded as a transaction when declared, rather than at the end of the period as an adjusting journal entry. But we'll show it here for convenience.)

(i) Dividend Declared. Pizza Palace declares a $500 cash dividend to be paid at a later date.

The dividend is recorded as a reduction in shareholders' equity in a special account called *Dividends Declared*. Because it reduces shareholders' equity, it is recorded as a debit. The corresponding increase in dividends payable is recorded as a credit.

1 Analyze

	Assets	=	Liabilities		+	Shareholders' Equity	
(i)		=	Dividends Payable	+500		Dividends Declared (+D)	−500

2 Record

(i)	dr Dividends Declared (+D, −SE)	500	
	cr Dividends Payable (+L)		500

3 Summarize

dr −	Dividends Payable (L)	cr +		dr +	Dividends Declared (D, SE)	cr −
	0	Unadj. bal.		Unadj. bal.	0	
	500	(i)		(i)	500	
	500	Adj. bal.		Adj. bal.	500	

It is important to note that companies have key financial requirements or restrictions that the board of directors must consider when declaring a cash dividend. These will be further discussed in Chapter 11.

Exhibit 4.8 summarizes the work we've done to this point. Starting with the unadjusted trial balance prepared at the end of Chapter 3 (see the left side of Exhibit 4.8), we determined the adjusting journal entries that needed to be recorded at the end of this month (see the right side of Exhibit 4.8). Next, we posted adjusting journal entries (a) through (i) to the T−accounts, as summarized in Exhibit 4.9. Next, we need to check that the accounting records are still in balance by using the adjusted T−account balances to pre−pare an adjusted trial balance. Assuming the trial balance shows that debits equal credits, we will finally be able to prepare the financial statements.

| EXHIBIT 4.8 | Summary of Unadjusted Balances and Adjusting Journal Entries | |

PIZZA PALACE INC.
Unadjusted Trial Balance
At September 30, 2017

Account Name	Debit	Credit
Cash	$ 7,500	
Accounts Receivable	200	
Supplies	1,600	
Prepaid Rent	7,200	
Cookware	630	
Equipment	60,000	
Accumulated Depreciation		$ 0
Accounts Payable		1,030
Deferred Revenue		300
Wages Payable		0
Income Tax Payable		0
Interest Payable		0
Dividends Payable		0
Note Payable		20,000
Contributed Capital		50,000
Retained Earnings		0
Dividends Declared	0	
Pizza Revenue		15,500
Wages Expense	8,700	
Rent Expense	0	
Supplies Expense	0	
Depreciation Expense	0	
Utilities Expense	600	
Advertising Expense	400	
Interest Expense	0	
Income Tax Expense	0	
Totals	**$86,830**	**$86,830**

PIZZA PALACE INC.
General Journal

(a) *dr* Supplies Expense (+E, −SE) 1,200
         cr Supplies (−A) 1,200

(b) *dr* Rent Expense (+E, −SE) 2,400
         cr Prepaid Rent (−A) 2,400

(c) *dr* Depreciation Expense (+E,−SE) 1,000
         cr Accumulated Depreciation (+xA, −A) .. 1,000

(d) *dr* Deferred Revenue (−L) 160
         cr Pizza Revenue (+R, +SE) 160

(e) *dr* Accounts Receivable (+A) 40
         cr Pizza Revenue (+R, +SE) 40

(f) *dr* Wages Expense (+E, −SE) 300
         cr Wages Payable (+L) 300

(g) *dr* Interest Expense (+E, −SE) 100
         cr Interest Payable (+L) 100

(h) *dr* Income Tax Expense (+E, −SE) 400
         cr Income Tax Payable (+L) 400

(i) *dr* Dividends Declared (+D, −SE) 500
         cr Dividends Payable (+L) 500

Next step: Post these adjusting journal entries as shown in Exhibit 4.9.

PREPARING AN ADJUSTED TRIAL BALANCE AND THE FINANCIAL STATEMENTS

Adjusted Trial Balance

An **adjusted trial balance** is prepared to check that the accounting records are still in balance after having posted all adjusting entries to the

Prepare an adjusted trial balance.

EXHIBIT 4.9   Pizza Palace's Adjusted Accounts

PIZZA PALACE

dr +	Cash (A)	cr −
Unadj. bal.	7,500	
Adj. bal.	**7,500**	

dr +	Accounts Receivable (A)	cr −
Unadj. bal.	200	
AJE (e)	40	
Adj. bal.	**240**	

dr +	Supplies (A)	cr −
Unadj. bal.	1,600	
		1,200 AJE (a)
Adj. bal.	**400**	

dr +	Prepaid Rent (A)	cr −
Unadj. bal.	7,200	
		2,400 AJE (b)
Adj. bal.	**4,800**	

dr +	Cookware (A)	cr −
Adj. bal.	**630**	

dr +	Equipment (A)	cr −
Adj. bal.	**60,000**	

dr −	Accumulated Depreciation (xA)	cr +
		0 Unadj. bal.
		1,000 AJE (c)
		1,000 Adj. bal.

Next step: Summarize these adjusted balances in an adjusted trial balance as shown in Exhibit 4.10.

dr −	Accounts Payable (L)	cr +
		1,030 Adj. bal.

dr −	Deferred Revenue (L)	cr +
		300 Unadj. bal.
AJE (d)	160	
		140 Adj. bal.

dr −	Wages Payable (L)	cr +
		0 Unadj. bal.
		300 AJE (f)
		300 Adj. bal.

dr −	Income Tax Payable (L)	cr +
		0 Unadj. bal.
		400 AJE (h)
		400 Adj. bal.

dr −	Interest Payable (L)	cr +
		0 Unadj. bal.
		100 AJE (g)
		100 Adj. bal.

dr −	Dividends Payable (L)	cr +
		0 Unadj. bal.
		500 AJE (i)
		500 Adj. bal.

dr −	Note Payable (L)	cr +
		20,000 Adj. bal.

dr −	Contributed Capital (SE)	cr +
		50,000 Adj. bal.

dr −	Retained Earnings (SE)	cr +
		0 Adj. bal.

dr +	Dividends Declared (D, SE)	cr −
Unadj. bal.	0	
(i)	500	
Adj. bal.	**500**	

dr −	Pizza Revenue (R, SE)	cr +
		15,500 Unadj. bal.
		160 AJE (d)
		40 AJE (e)
		15,700 Adj. bal.

dr +	Wages Expense (E, SE)	cr −
Unadj. bal.	8,700	
AJE (f)	300	
Adj. bal.	**9,000**	

dr +	Rent Expense (E, SE)	cr −
Unadj. bal.	0	
AJE (b)	2,400	
Adj. bal.	**2,400**	

dr +	Supplies Expense (E, SE)	cr −
Unadj. bal.	0	
AJE (a)	1,200	
Adj. bal.	**1,200**	

dr +	Depreciation Expense (E, SE)	cr −
Unadj. bal.	0	
AJE (c)	1,000	
Adj. bal.	**1,000**	

dr +	Utilities Expense (E, SE)	cr −
Adj. bal.	**600**	

dr +	Advertising Expense (E, SE)	cr −
Adj. bal.	**400**	

dr +	Interest Expense (E, SE)	cr −
Unadj. bal.	0	
AJE (g)	100	
Adj. bal.	**100**	

dr +	Income Tax Expense (E, SE)	cr −
Unadj. bal.	0	
AJE (h)	400	
Adj. bal.	**400**	

Adjusted trial balance: A list of all accounts and their adjusted balances to check on the equality of recorded debits and credits.

T−accounts. To prepare an adjusted trial balance, just copy the adjusted T−account balances (Exhibit 4.9) into the debit or credit columns of the adjusted trial balance (left side of Exhibit 4.10).

List the accounts in the order they will appear in the balance sheet, statement of retained earnings, and income statement. As you can see in Exhibit 4.10, the trial balance proves that Pizza Palace's accounting records are in balance (total debits = $89,170 = total credits), so the financial statements can be prepared. The balance for each account in the trial balance is reported only once on either the income statement, statement of retained earnings, or balance sheet.

PIZZA PALACE INC. Adjusted Trial Balance At September 30, 2017		
Account Name	**Debits**	**Credits**
Cash	$ 7,500	
Accounts Receivable	240	
Supplies	400	
Prepaid Rent	4,800	
Cookware	630	
Equipment	60,000	
Accumulated Depreciation		$ 1,000
Accounts Payable		1,030
Deferred Revenue		140
Wages Payable		300
Income Tax Payable		400
Interest Payable		100
Dividends Payable		500
Note Payable		20,000
Contributed Capital		50,000
Retained Earnings		0
Dividends Declared	500	
Pizza Revenue		15,700
Wages Expense	9,000	
Rent Expense	2,400	
Supplies Expense	1,200	
Depreciation Expense	1,000	
Utilities Expense	600	
Advertising Expense	400	
Interest Expense	100	
Income Tax Expense	400	
Totals	$89,170	$89,170

PIZZA PALACE INC. Income Statement For the Month Ended September 30, 2017	
Revenues	
Pizza Revenue	$15,700
Total Revenues	15,700
Expenses	
Wages Expense	9,000
Rent Expense	2,400
Supplies Expense	1,200
Depreciation Expense	1,000
Utilities Expense	600
Advertising Expense	400
Interest Expense	100
Income Tax Expense	400
Total Expenses	15,100
Net Income	$ 600

PIZZA PALACE INC. Statement of Retained Earnings For the Month Ended September 30, 2017	
Retained Earnings, September 1	$ 0
Add: Net Income	600
Subtract: Dividends Declared	(500)
Retained Earnings, September 30	$ 100

To the Balance Sheet.

Typically, the income statement is prepared first because the net income number from it flows into the statement of retained earnings, and then the retained earnings number from the statement of retained earnings flows into the balance sheet. As you will see in later chapters of this book, the statement of cash flows and notes to the financial statements are prepared last because they include information obtained from the income statement, statement of retained earnings, and balance sheet (plus other sources).

Income Statement and Statement of Retained Earnings

Prepare the income statement by creating the usual heading (who, what, when) and listing the names and amounts for each revenue and expense account from the adjusted trial balance, as shown in Exhibit 4.10. Notice that each major category of items on the income statement is subtotalled prior to computing net income for the period.

Account balances from the adjusted trial balance are also used in the statement of retained earnings, as shown in Exhibit 4.10. Notice

LEARNING OBJECTIVE 4-4

Prepare financial statements.

COACH'S TIP

Dividends Declared is reported only on the statement of retained earnings.

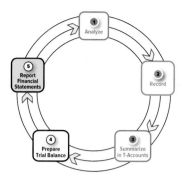

that the amount coming from the adjusted trial balance is the beginning—of—year balance for Retained Earnings. This account balance doesn't yet include revenues, expenses, and dividends for the current period because they've been recorded in their own separate accounts. Eventually we will transfer ("close") those accounts into Retained Earnings, but that's done only at the end of the year. For now, the Retained Earnings account on the adjusted trial balance provides the opening amount on the statement of retained earnings. The amount for Net Income on the next line of the statement of retained earnings comes from the income statement, and the Dividends Declared number comes from the adjusted trial balance.

Balance Sheet

Like the other statements, the balance sheet is prepared from the adjusted trial balance, as shown in Exhibit 4.11. When preparing the balance sheet,

---

EXHIBIT 4.11 **Preparing the Balance Sheet** PIZZA PALACE

PIZZA PALACE INC.
Adjusted Trial Balance
At September 30, 2017

Account Name	Debits	Credits
Cash	$ 7,500	
Accounts Receivable	240	
Supplies	400	
Prepaid Rent	4,800	
Cookware	630	
Equipment	60,000	
Accumulated Depreciation		$ 1,000
Accounts Payable		1,030
Deferred Revenue		140
Wages Payable		300
Income Tax Payable		400
Interest Payable		100
Dividends Payable		500
Note Payable		20,000
Contributed Capital		50,000
Retained Earnings		0
Dividends Declared	500	
Pizza Revenue		15,700
Wages Expense	9,000	
Rent Expense	2,400	
Supplies Expense	1,200	
Depreciation Expense	1,000	
Utilities Expense	600	
Advertising Expense	400	
Interest Expense	100	
Income Tax Expense	400	
Totals	$89,170	$89,170

PIZZA PALACE INC.
Balance Sheet
At September 30, 2017

Assets

Current Assets		
Cash		$ 7,500
Accounts Receivable		240
Supplies		400
Prepaid Rent		4,800
Cookware		630
Total Current Assets		13,070
Equipment	$60,000	
Accumulated Depreciation	(1,000)	59,000
Total Assets		$72,570

Liabilities and Shareholders' Equity

Liabilities

Current Liabilities		
Accounts Payable		$ 1,030
Deferred Revenue		140
Wages Payable		300
Income Tax Payable		400
Interest Payable		100
Dividends Payable		500
Total Current Liabilities		2,470
Note Payable		20,000
Total Liabilities		22,470
Shareholders' Equity		
Contributed Capital		50,000
Retained Earnings		100
Total Shareholders' Equity		50,100
Total Liabilities and Shareholders' Equity		$72,570

From the Statement of Retained Earnings.

watch out for three things. First, remember to classify assets and liabilities as current if they will be turned into cash or used up within twelve months. Liabilities should be classified as current if they will be fulfilled (paid) within twelve months. Second, note that Accumulated Depreciation is reported in the assets section (and are subtracted from the accounts to which they are contra–accounts). Third, get the Retained Earnings balance from the state–ment of retained earnings, not from the adjusted trial balance. (The adjusted trial balance still reports only the period's opening Retained Earnings balance.)

Statement of Cash Flows and Notes

We don't want you to forget that the statement of cash flows (SCF) and notes to the financial statements must also be prepared as part of the financial statements. But for now, we'll leave coverage of the SCF for Chapter 12 and we'll slide information about financial statement notes into each of the remaining chapters.

CLOSING TEMPORARY ACCOUNTS

LEARNING OBJECTIVE 4-5

Explain the closing process.

The last step of the accounting cycle is referred to as the *closing process.* As shown in the first column of Exhibit 4.12, this step is performed only at the end of the year, after the financial statements have been prepared. The closing process cleans up the accounting records to get them ready to begin tracking the results in the following year. It's kind of like zeroing the trip odometer on your car or hitting the reset button on your Xbox.

EXHIBIT 4.12	Year-End Closing Concludes the Accounting Cycle

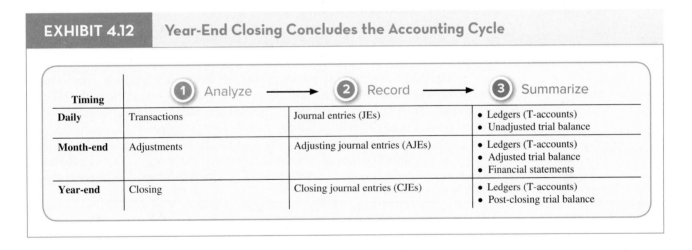

Timing	① Analyze	② Record	③ Summarize
Daily	Transactions	Journal entries (JEs)	• Ledgers (T-accounts) • Unadjusted trial balance
Month-end	Adjustments	Adjusting journal entries (AJEs)	• Ledgers (T-accounts) • Adjusted trial balance • Financial statements
Year-end	Closing	Closing journal entries (CJEs)	• Ledgers (T-accounts) • Post-closing trial balance

Closing Income Statement and Dividend Accounts

In Chapter 3, you learned to think of revenue and expense accounts as subcategories of Retained Earnings, which are used to track earnings–re–lated transactions of the current year. Earlier in this chapter, you saw that the Dividends Declared account is similarly used to track dividends declared during the current year. At the end of each year, after all the year's transactions and adjustments are recorded, all revenue, expense, and dividends declared accounts are closed by moving their balances to their permanent home in Retained Earnings. The Retained Earnings account, like all other balance sheet accounts, is a **permanent account** because its ending balance from one year becomes its beginning balance for the following year. In contrast, revenues, expenses, and dividends declared are considered **temporary accounts** because they are used to track only the current year's results and then are closed before the next year's activities are recorded.

Permanent account: An account that tracks financial results from year to year by carrying its ending balances into the next year.

Temporary accounts: Accounts that track financial results for a limited period of time by having their bal–ances zeroed out at the end of each accounting year.

The closing process serves two purposes:

1. **Transfer net income (or loss) and dividends to Retained Earnings.** After the closing journal entries are prepared and posted, the balance in the Retained Earnings account will agree with the statement of retained earnings and the balance sheet.

2. **Establish zero balances in all income statement and dividend accounts.** After the closing journal entries are prepared and posted, the balances in the temporary accounts are reset to zero to start accumulating next year's results.

Closing journal entries follow the usual debits—equal—credits format used for the transaction journal entries (in Chapters 2 and 3) and adjusting journal entries (shown earlier in this chapter). Because they're the last thing done during the year, they're posted immediately to the accounts. (Some computerized systems record and post closing journal entries automatically.) Two closing journal entries are needed:

1. Debit each revenue account for the amount of its credit balance, credit each expense account for the amount of its debit balance, and record the difference in Retained Earnings. If you've done it correctly, the amount credited to Retained Earnings should equal Net Income on the Income Statement. (If the company has a net loss, Retained Earnings will be debited.)

2. Credit the Dividends Declared account for the amount of its debit balance and debit Retained Earnings for the same amount.

Exhibit 4.13 shows the closing process for Pizza Palace (assuming, for the sake of illustration, that it closes its books on the last day of September).

Post-Closing Trial Balance

After the closing journal entries are posted, all temporary accounts should have zero balances. This would include all revenue, expense, and dividends declared accounts. These accounts will be ready for summarizing transactions recorded next year. Therefore only balance sheet accounts (permanent accounts) will have an ending balance that will carry forward to be next year's opening balance. The ending balance in Retained Earnings is now up to date (it matches the year—end amount on the statement of retained earnings and balance sheet) and is carried forward as the beginning balance for the next year.

As the last step of the accounting cycle, you should prepare a **post—closing trial balance** (shown in Exhibit 4.14). In this context, *post* means *after*, so a post—closing trial balance is an *after—closing* trial balance that is prepared as a final check that total debits still equal total credits and that all temporary accounts have been closed.

Now that we've completed the accounting cycle, it seems appropriate to summarize it one more time. Exhibit 4.12 showed one way to organize the various steps of the accounting cycle. Exhibit 4.15 presents the same ideas in a slightly different format. The steps in the coral, blue, and gold boxes are done daily, monthly, and yearly, respectively.

Post-closing trial balance: An internal report prepared as the last step in the accounting cycle to check that debits equal credits and all temporary accounts have been closed.

Evaluate the Results

ADJUSTED FINANCIAL RESULTS

Explain how adjustments affect financial results.

Throughout this chapter, you have learned various adjustments that must be made to the accounting records when finalizing and preparing the financial statements. These adjustments help to ensure that all revenues and expenses

① Analyze

The analysis step for closing the temporary accounts requires only that you identify, from the adjusted trial balance, the temporary accounts with debit balances (to be credited below) and credit balances (to be debited below).

② Record

CJE 1. Close revenue and expense accounts:

dr Pizza Revenue (−R) 15,700
    cr Wages Expense (−E) 9,000
    cr Rent Expense (−E) 2,400
    cr Supplies Expense (−E) 1,200
    cr Depreciation Expense (−E) 1,000
    cr Utilities Expense (−E) 600
    cr Advertising Expense (−E) 400
    cr Interest Expense (−E) 100
    cr Income Tax Expense (−E) 400
    cr Retained Earnings (+SE) 600

CJE 2. Close the dividends declared account:

dr Retained Earnings (−SE) 500
    cr Dividends Declared (−D) 500

③ Summarize

EXHIBIT 4.14　Pizza Palace's Post-Closing Trial Balance

COACH'S TIP

Total debits on the post-closing trial balance don't equal the total assets on the balance sheet because Accumulated Depreciation (a credit balance on the trial balance) is subtracted from assets on the balance sheet.

PIZZA PALACE INC.
Post-Closing Trial Balance
At September 30, 2017

Account Name	Debits	Credits
Cash	$ 7,500	
Accounts Receivable	240	
Supplies	400	
Prepaid Rent	4,800	
Cookware	630	
Equipment	60,000	
Accumulated Depreciation		$ 1,000
Accounts Payable		1,030
Deferred Revenue		140
Wages Payable		300
Income Tax Payable		400
Interest Payable		100
Dividends Payable		500
Note Payable		20,000
Contributed Capital		50,000
Retained Earnings		100
Dividends Declared	0	
Pizza Revenue		0
Wages Expense	0	
Rent Expense	0	
Supplies Expense	0	
Depreciation Expense	0	
Utilities Expense	0	
Advertising Expense	0	
Interest Expense	0	
Income Tax Expense	0	
Totals	$73,570	$73,570

EXHIBIT 4.15　The Accounting Process

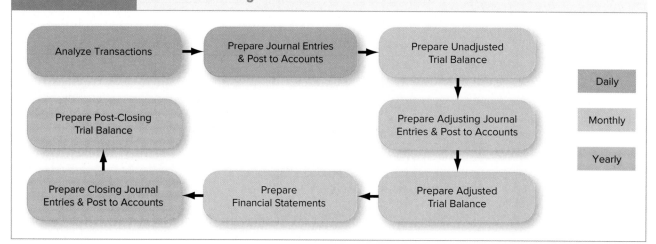

are reported in the period in which they are earned and incurred. As a result of these adjustments, the financial statements present the best picture of whether the company's business activities were profitable that period, and what economic resources the company owns and owes at the end of that period. Without these adjustments, the financial statements present an incomplete and misleading picture of the company's financial performance.

Pizza Palace provides a good example of the extent to which unadjusted balances may change during the adjustment process. Chapter 3 ended with Emilio believing that Pizza Palace had earned a sizeable profit (net income of $5,800 from revenue of $15,500, resulting in a net profit margin of 37.4 percent). After making the required adjustments in this chapter, the company's adjusted results indicated a much different picture (net income of $600 from revenue of $15,700, yielding a net profit margin of 3.8 percent).

Consequently, Emilio learned that he had much to improve upon in the upcoming months. His new goal is to increase the company's revenue by expanding his customer base, while at the same time trying to control expenses. He is well aware that even large companies go out of business if they fail to maintain revenues and control their expenses.

SPOTLIGHT ON Financial Reporting

Financial Crisis: Anatomy of a Business Failure

Until its bankruptcy in late 2008 and liquidation in early 2009, Circuit City was one of the largest electronics stores in the United States. However, Circuit City's inability to maintain sales and control expenses ultimately led to its demise. Notice how quickly the company's stock price fell as it reported deteriorating financial results.

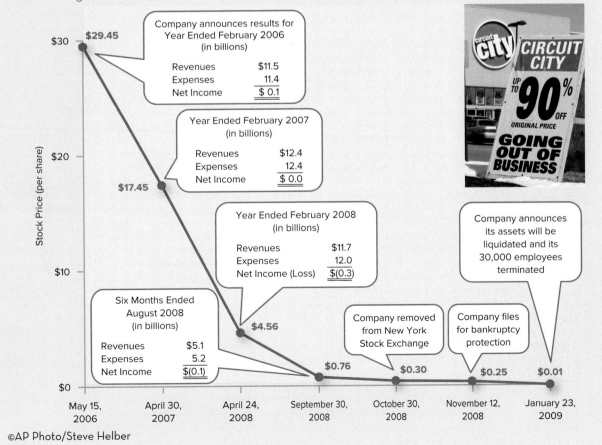

©AP Photo/Steve Helber

Given the nature of the material in this chapter, there are no significant differences between ASPE and IFRS.

Review the Chapter

This section provides a chance to solidify your understanding of key points. It's worth your time to work through the following demonstration case, scan the chapter summary, test your understanding of key terms, and then practise, practise, practise.

DEMONSTRATION CASE

We take our final look at the accounting activities of Goodbye Grass Corporation by illustrating the activities at the end of the accounting cycle: the adjustment process, financial statement preparation, and the closing process. No adjustments have been made to the accounts yet. Your starting point will be the following unadjusted trial balance dated April 30, 2017:

GOODBYE GRASS CORPORATION
Unadjusted Trial Balance
At April 30, 2017

Account Name	Debits	Credits
Cash	$ 4,510	
Accounts Receivable	1,700	
Note Receivable	1,250	
Interest Receivable	0	
Prepaid Insurance	300	
Equipment	4,600	
Accumulated Depreciation		$ 0
Land	3,750	
Accounts Payable		620
Deferred Revenue		1,600
Wages Payable		0
Interest Payable		0
Income Tax Payable		0
Dividends Payable		0
Note Payable		4,000
Contributed Capital		9,000
Retained Earnings		0
Dividends Declared		0
Mowing Revenue		5,200
Interest Revenue		0
Wages Expense	3,900	
Fuel Expense	410	
Insurance Expense	0	
Depreciation Expense	0	
Interest Expense	0	
Income Tax Expense	0	
Totals	$20,420	$20,420

By reviewing the unadjusted trial balance, you identify three deferral accounts (Prepaid Insurance, Equipment, and Deferred Revenue) that may need to be adjusted in addition to accruals that may be necessary relating to wages, income taxes, and interest on the Note Receivable and Note Payable. The following information is determined at the end of the accounting cycle:

Deferral Adjustments

a. One–fourth of the $1,600 cash received from the city at the beginning of April for future mowing service was earned in April. The $1,600 in Deferred Revenue represents four months of service (April through July).

b. Insurance purchased at the beginning of April for $300 provides coverage for six months (April through September). The insurance coverage for April has now been used.

   TIP: Account for the expiry of prepaid insurance just like the expiry of prepaid rent.

c. Mowers, edgers, rakes, and hand tools (equipment) have been used in April to generate revenues. The company estimates $300 in depreciation each year.

Accrual Adjustments

d. Wages have been paid through April 28. Employees worked the last two days of April and will be paid in May. Wages amount to $200 per day.

e. Interest incurred and payable on the short–term note payable is $45 for the month of April.

f. Interest earned and receivable on the short–term note receivable is $10 for the month of April.

g. The estimated income tax rate for Goodbye Grass Corporation is 35 percent.

h. Dividends were declared on April 30 for $200.

Required:

1. Analyze items (a) through (h) and identify the effects of required adjustments on the basic accounting equation (Assets = Liabilities + Shareholders' Equity), using the format shown in the chapter.

2. Record the adjusting journal entries required at the end of April.

3. Summarize the effects of each adjusting journal entry in T–accounts for each account affected. Obtain beginning balances from the unadjusted trial balance, then post the adjusting journal entries from requirement 2, and calculate adjusted April 30 balances.

4. Prepare an adjusted trial balance to ensure debit and credit balances are equal, remem–bering to include all accounts in the trial balance (and not just the ones affected by the adjusting journal entries).

5. Prepare an income statement, a statement of retained earnings, and a classified balance sheet from the amounts in the adjusted trial balance.

6. Prepare the closing journal entries that would be required if Goodbye Grass Corporation's fiscal year ended April 30, 2017.

7. Prepare the post–closing trial balance as a final check that all debits still equal credits and that all temporary accounts have been closed.

After completing requirements 1 to 7, check your answers with the following solution.

Suggested Solution

1. Adjustment analysis:

   a. The unadjusted balances are $1,600 for Deferred Revenue and $5,200 for Mowing Revenue. One–fourth of the $1,600 was earned in April ($400 = ¼ × $1,600), bringing total mowing revenues for the month to $5,600 ($5,200 + $400). Three–fourths of the $1,600 remain unearned at the end of April ($1,200 = ¾ × $1,600). To reach these desired balances, we need an adjust–ment that decreases Deferred Revenue by $400 and increases Mowing Revenue by $400.

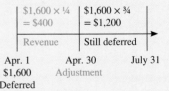

Assets	=	Liabilities	+	Shareholders' Equity
		Deferred Revenue −400		Mowing Revenue (+R) +400

   b. The unadjusted balances are $300 for Prepaid Insurance and $0 for Insurance Expense. One–sixth of the $300 expired in April, resulting in an insurance expense for the month of $50 (⅙ × $300). Five of the six months of insurance coverage remain unused at the

$300 × ⅙ = $50	$300 × ⅚ = $250
Expense	Still prepaid

Apr. 1   Apr. 30   Oct. 31
$300   Adjustment
Prepaid

end of April ($250 = ⅚ × $300). To reach these desired balances, we need an adjustment that decreases Prepaid Insurance by $50 and increases Insurance Expense by $50.

Assets	=	Liabilities	+	Shareholders' Equity
Prepaid Insurance −50				Insurance Expense (+E) −50

c. The unadjusted balances are $0 for Accumulated Depreciation and $0 for Depreciation Expense. Yearly depreciation of $300 equals $25 for just one month ($300 × $\frac{1}{12}$). To go from the unadjusted balances of $0 to the desired adjusted balances of $25, we increase the expense and contra–account balances by $25.

Assets	= Liabilities +	Shareholders' Equity
Accumulated Depreciation (+xA) −25		Depreciation Expense (+E) −25

d. The unadjusted balances are $0 for Wages Payable and $3,900 for Wages Expense. Because the final two days of work done in April are unpaid, we need to record a liability for $400 (2 × $200). Total wages expense for the month should include the $3,900 paid for work from April 1 to 28 plus the $400 not yet paid for work on April 29 and 30. To reach these desired balances, we need an adjustment increasing Wages Payable by $400 and increasing Wages Expense by $400.

Assets =	Liabilities	+	Shareholders' Equity
	Wages Payable +400		Wages Expense (+E) −400

e. The unadjusted balances are $0 for Interest Payable and $0 for Interest Expense. Interest of $45 was incurred in April, so the adjustment needs to increase both accounts by $45.

Assets =	Liabilities	+	Shareholders' Equity
	Interest Payable +45		Interest Expense (+E) −45

f. The unadjusted balances are $0 for Interest Receivable and $0 for Interest Revenue. Interest of $10 was earned in April, so the adjustment needs to increase both accounts by $10.

Assets	= Liabilities +	Shareholders' Equity
Interest Receivable +10		Interest Revenue (+R) +10

g. The unadjusted balances are $0 for Income Tax Payable and $0 for Income Tax Expense. The amount of calculated income taxes will increase both of these accounts. Income taxes are calculated as 35 percent of adjusted income before tax for the month, as follows:

	Revenues	Expenses	
Unadjusted totals	$5,200	$4,310	← Calculated from unadjusted trial balance
Adjustments: (a)	+400		($4,310 = $3,900 + $410)
(b)		+ 50	
(c)		+ 25	
(d)		+ 400	
(e)		+ 45	
(f)	+ 10		
Adjusted totals	$5,610	$4,830	= $780 Adjusted income before income tax
			× 35% Tax rate
			$273 **Income tax**

Assets =	Liabilities	+	Shareholders' Equity
	Income Tax Payable +273		Income Tax Expense (+E) −273

h. The unadjusted balances are $0 for Dividends Payable and $0 for Dividends Declared. Dividends of $200 were declared in April, so the adjustment needs to increase both accounts by $200.

Assets =	Liabilities	+	Shareholders' Equity
	Dividends Payable +200		Dividends Declared (+D) −200

2. Adjusting journal entries

   a.   *dr* Deferred Revenue (−L)   400
           cr Mowing Revenue (+R, +SE)   400

   b.   *dr* Insurance Expense (+E, −SE)   50
           cr Prepaid Insurance (−A)   50

   c.   *dr* Depreciation Expense (+E, −SE)   25
           cr Accumulated Depreciation (+xA, −A)   25

   d.   *dr* Wages Expense (+E, −SE)   400
           cr Wages Payable (+L)   400

   e.   *dr* Interest Expense (+E, −SE)   45
           cr Interest Payable (+L)   45

   f.   *dr* Interest Receivable (+A)   10
           cr Interest Revenue (+R, +SE)   10

   g.   *dr* Income Tax Expense (+E, −SE)   273
           cr Income Tax Payable (+L)   273

   h.   *dr* Dividends Declared (+D, −SE)   200
           cr Dividends Payable (+L)   200

3. T−accounts affected by adjusting journal entries (*See Chapter 3 for balances of T−accounts not affected by adjusting journal entries.*)

dr +	Interest Receivable (A)	*cr −*
Beg. bal.	0	
(f)	10	
End. bal.	10	

dr −	Interest Payable (L)	*cr +*
		0 Beg. bal.
		45 (e)
		45 End. bal.

dr +	Insurance Expense (E, SE)	*cr −*
Beg. bal.	0	
(b)	50	
End. bal.	50	

dr +	Prepaid Insurance (A)	*cr −*
Beg. bal.	300	
	50	(b)
End. bal.	250	

dr −	Income Tax Payable (L)	*cr +*
		0 Beg. bal.
		273 (g)
		273 End. bal.

dr +	Depreciation Expense (E, SE)	*cr −*
Beg. bal.	0	
(c)	25	
End. bal.	25	

dr −	Accumulated Depreciation (xA)	*cr +*
		0 Beg. bal.
		25 (c)
		25 End. bal.

dr −	Mowing Revenue (R, SE)	*cr +*
		5,200 Beg. bal.
		400 (a)
		5,600 End. bal.

dr +	Interest Expense (E, SE)	*cr −*
Beg. bal.	0	
(e)	45	
End. bal.	45	

dr −	Deferred Revenue (L)	*cr +*
		1,600 Beg. bal.
(a)	400	
		1,200 End. bal.

dr −	Interest Revenue (R, SE)	*cr +*
		0 Beg. bal.
		10 (f)
		10 End. bal.

dr +	Income Tax Expense (E, SE)	*cr −*
Beg. bal.	0	
(g)	273	
End. bal.	273	

dr −	Wages Payable (L)		cr +
		0	Beg. bal.
		400	(d)
		400	End. bal.

dr +	Wages Expense (E, SE)		cr −
Beg. bal.	3,900		
(d)	400		
End. bal.	4,300		

dr −	Dividends Payable (L)		cr +
		0	Beg. bal.
		200	(h)
		200	End. bal.

dr +	Dividends Declared (D, SE)		cr −
Beg. bal.	0		
(h)	200		
End. bal.	200		

4. Adjusted trial balance

GOODBYE GRASS CORPORATION
Adjusted Trial Balance
At April 30, 2017

Account Name	Debits	Credits	
Cash	$ 4,510		
Accounts Receivable	1,700		
Note Receivable	1,250		
Interest Receivable	10		
Prepaid Insurance	250		
Equipment	4,600		
Accumulated Depreciation		$ 25	
Land	3,750		To Balance Sheet
Accounts Payable		620	
Deferred Revenue		1,200	
Wages Payable		400	
Interest Payable		45	
Income Tax Payable		273	
Dividends Payable		200	
Note Payable		4,000	
Contributed Capital		9,000	
Retained Earnings		0	To Statement of Retained Earnings
Dividends Declared	200		
Mowing Revenue		5,600	
Interest Revenue		10	
Wages Expense	4,300		
Fuel Expense	410		To Income Statement
Insurance Expense	50		
Depreciation Expense	25		
Interest Expense	45		
Income Tax Expense	273		
Totals	$21,373	$21,373	

5. Income statement, statement of retained earnings, and balance sheet

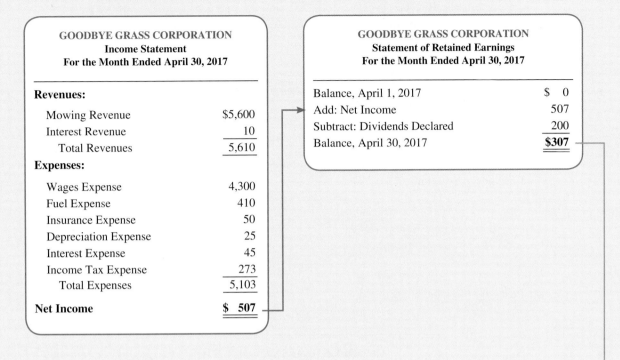

GOODBYE GRASS CORPORATION		
Income Statement		
For the Month Ended April 30, 2017		
Revenues:		
Mowing Revenue	$5,600	
Interest Revenue	10	
Total Revenues	5,610	
Expenses:		
Wages Expense	4,300	
Fuel Expense	410	
Insurance Expense	50	
Depreciation Expense	25	
Interest Expense	45	
Income Tax Expense	273	
Total Expenses	5,103	
Net Income	$ 507	

GOODBYE GRASS CORPORATION	
Statement of Retained Earnings	
For the Month Ended April 30, 2017	
Balance, April 1, 2017	$ 0
Add: Net Income	507
Subtract: Dividends Declared	200
Balance, April 30, 2017	$307

GOODBYE GRASS CORPORATION			
Balance Sheet			
At April 30, 2017			
Assets		**Liabilities and Shareholders' Equity**	
Current Assets:		Liabilities	
Cash	$ 4,510	Current Liabilities:	
Accounts Receivable	1,700	Accounts Payable	$ 620
Note Receivable	1,250	Deferred Revenue	1,200
Interest Receivable	10	Wages Payable	400
Prepaid Insurance	250	Interest Payable	45
Total Current Assets	7,720	Income Tax Payable	273
Equipment	$ 4,600	Dividends Payable	200
Less: Accumulated Depreciation	(25)	Note Payable	4,000
Equipment, Net	4,575	Total Current Liabilities	6,738
Land	3,750	Shareholders' Equity	
Total Assets	$16,045	Contributed Capital	9,000
		Retained Earnings	307
		Total Shareholders' Equity	9,307
		Total Liabilities and Shareholders' Equity	$16,045

6. Closing journal entry

If Goodbye Grass Corporation had adopted an April 30 year–end, the company would require a journal entry to close its revenue and expense accounts into Retained Earnings. It would also need a second journal entry to close the Dividends Declared account into Retained Earnings. The closing journal entry needed to close revenues and expenses into Retained Earnings is as follows:

dr Mowing Revenue (−R)	5,600	
dr Interest Revenue (−R)	10	
cr Wages Expense (−E)		4,300
cr Fuel Expense (−E)		410
cr Insurance Expense (−E)		50
cr Depreciation Expense (−E)		25
cr Interest Expense (−E)		45
cr Income Tax Expense (−E)		273
cr Retained Earnings (+SE)		507

The second closing journal entry needed to close Dividends Declared into Retained Earnings is as follows:

dr Retained Earnings (+SE)	200	
cr Dividends Declared (−D)		200

7. Post−closing trial balance

GOODBYE GRASS CORPORATION
Post-Closing Trial Balance
At April 30, 2017

Account Name	Debits	Credits
Cash	$ 4,510	
Accounts Receivable	1,700	
Note Receivable	1,250	
Interest Receivable	10	
Prepaid Insurance	250	
Equipment	4,600	
Accumulated Depreciation		$ 25
Land	3,750	
Accounts Payable		620
Deferred Revenue		1,200
Wages Payable		400
Interest Payable		45
Income Tax Payable		273
Dividends Payable		200
Note Payable		4,000
Contributed Capital		9,000
Retained Earnings		307
Dividends Declared	0	
Mowing Revenue		0
Interest Revenue		0
Wages Expense	0	
Fuel Expense	0	
Insurance Expense	0	
Depreciation Expense	0	
Interest Expense	0	
Income Tax Expense	0	
Totals	$16,070	$16,070

CHAPTER SUMMARY

Explain why adjustments are needed. LO4-1

Adjustments are needed to ensure that

- revenues are recorded when earned (the revenue recognition principle),
- expenses are recorded when incurred to generate revenues (the expense recognition principle),
- assets are reported at amounts representing the economic benefits that remain at the end of the current period, and
- liabilities are reported at amounts owed at the end of the current period that will require a future sacrifice of resources.

Prepare adjustments needed at the end of the period. LO4-2

- The process for preparing adjustments includes
    1. analyzing the unadjusted balances in balance sheet and income statement accounts, and calculating the amount of the adjustment needed, using a timeline where appropriate;
    2. preparing an adjusting journal entry to make the adjustment; and
    3. summarizing the adjusting journal entry in the applicable ledger (T–accounts).
- Each adjusting journal entry affects one balance sheet and one income statement account.

Prepare an adjusted trial balance. LO4-3

An adjusted trial balance is a list of all accounts with their adjusted debit or credit balances indicated in the appropriate column to provide a check on the equality of the debits and credits.

Prepare financial statements. LO4-4

Adjusted account balances are used in preparing the following financial statements:

- Income Statement: Revenues − Expenses = Net Income
- Statement of Retained Earnings: Beginning Retained Earnings + Net Income − Dividends Declared = Ending Retained Earnings
- Balance Sheet: Assets = Liabilities + Shareholders' Equity
- The statement of cash flows and notes to the financial statements are important components of adjusted financial statements, but they will be studied in later chapters.

Explain the closing process. LO4-5

- Closing journal entries are required to (1) transfer net income (or loss) and dividends declared into retained earnings and (2) prepare all temporary accounts (revenues, expenses, dividends declared) for the following year by establishing zero balances in these accounts.
- Two closing journal entries are needed:
    1. Debit each revenue account, credit each expense account, and record the difference (equal to net income) in Retained Earnings.
    2. Credit the Dividends Declared account for the amount of its balance and debit Retained Earnings for the same amount.

Explain how adjustments affect financial results. LO4-6

Adjustments help ensure that all revenues and expenses are reported in the period in which they are earned and incurred as a result of a company's activities. Without these adjustments, the financial statements present an incomplete and potentially misleading picture of the company's financial performance.

SOLUTION TO SELF-STUDY PRACTICE

Solution to SP4.1

Type / Balance Sheet & Income Statement Accounts

1. D / Deferred Revenue & Flight Service Revenue
2. A / Rent Receivable & Rent Revenue
3. A / Interest Payable & Interest Expense
4. D / Prepaid Insurance & Insurance Expense

Solution to SP4.2

1. B, C   3. B, F
2. A, D   4. A, E

Solution to SP4.3

1.

Assets		=	Liabilities	+	Shareholders' Equity	
Prepaid Insurance	−8,000	=			Insurance Expense (+E)	−8,000

2.
```
dr Insurance Expense (+E, −SE) ...................................  8,000
     cr Prepaid Insurance (−A) ...................................           8,000
```

3.

dr +	Prepaid Insurance (A)	cr −		dr +	Insurance Expense (E, SE)	cr −
Unadj. bal.	24,000			Unadj. bal.	0	
		8,000	AJE	AJE	8,000	
Adj. bal.	<u>16,000</u>			Adj. bal.	<u>8,000</u>	

Solution to SP4.4

1. Adjusted income before taxes = $245 \cdot \$5 = \$240$ (million).
   Income tax = $\$240 \cdot 40\% = \$96$ (million).

Assets	=	Liabilities	+	Shareholders' Equity	
	=	Income Tax Payable +96		Insurance Expense (+E)	−400

2.
```
dr Income Tax Expense (+E, −SE) ...................................  96
     cr Income Tax Payable (+L) ...................................        96
```

KEY TERMS

Adjusted Trial Balance

Adjusting Journal Entries (AJEs)

Adjustments

Carrying Value (Net Book Value, Book Value)

Contra−Account

Depreciation

Revenue Recognition Principle

Permanent Account

Post−Closing Trial Balance

Temporary Accounts

Complete definitions are also provided in the glossary at the end of this text.

HOMEWORK HELPER

Alternative terms

- *Accrued Liabilities* is a generic account name that can include liabilities recorded using accrual adjustments for salaries, utilities, income taxes, and many other items.
- *Amortization* is used in ASPE whereas *depreciation* is used in IFRS. These terms can be and are used interchangeably with depreciation being used most often.

- When determining each adjustment, draw timelines to picture where you are now, where you need to be, and the adjustment to get yourself there.
- Cash is never part of an accrual or deferral adjustment.
- The income statement is the temporary home for revenue and expense accounts, and their permanent home is Retained Earnings in the shareholders' equity section of the balance sheet.

Frequent mistakes

- Accumulated Depreciation and Depreciation Expense are not the same accounts. Accumulated Depreciation is a permanent balance sheet account that accumulates each period of depreciation. Depreciation Expense is a temporary income statement account that reports only the current period's depreciation.
- Dividends are not expenses, but rather are distributions to shareholders of the company's prior profits that have accumulated in Retained Earnings.
- The amount in Retained Earnings on an adjusted trial balance is not reported on the balance sheet; it is the beginning balance on the statement of retained earnings. The ending balance from the statement of retained earnings is reported on the balance sheet.

PRACTICE MATERIAL

QUESTIONS (⊖ Symbol indicates questions that require analysis from more than one perspective.)

1. Briefly explain the purposes of adjustments.
2. Explain the relationships between adjustments and the following Chapter 3 concepts: (*a*) the time period assumption, (*b*) the revenue recognition principle, and (*c*) the expense recognition principle.
3. List the two types of adjusting journal entries and give an example of an adjustment affecting revenues and expenses for each type.
4. Explain the effect of adjusting journal entries on cash.
5. What is a contra–asset? Give an example of one.
6. Explain the differences between depreciation expense and accumulated depreciation.
7. What is an adjusted trial balance? What is its purpose?
8. On December 31, a company makes a $9,000 payment for renting a warehouse in January, February, and March of the following year. Show the accounting equation effects of the transaction on December 31, as well as the adjustments required on January 31, February 28, and March 31.
9. Using the information in question 8, determine the amounts and accounts that will be reported on the January 31 balance sheet and the income statement for the month ended January 31.
10. Using the information in question 8, prepare the journal entry and adjusting journal entries to be made on December 31, January 31, February 28, and March 31.
11. What is the equation for each of the following statements: (*a*) income statement, (*b*) balance sheet, and (*c*) statement of retained earnings?
12. Explain how the financial statements in question 11 relate to each other.
13. What is the purpose of closing journal entries?
14. How do permanent accounts differ from temporary accounts?
15. Why are the income statement accounts closed but the balance sheet accounts are not?
16. Is Dividends Declared considered an asset, liability, or shareholders' equity account? Is it a permanent or temporary account? Does it normally have a debit or credit balance?
17. What is a post–closing trial balance? Is it a useful part of the accounting cycle? Explain.
18. The owner of a local business complains that the adjustments process consumes a lot of time and delays reporting month–end financial results. How would you convince her of the importance of this process? ⊖

MINI-EXERCISES

M4-1 Understanding Concepts Related to Adjustments

Match each situation below to two applicable reasons that an adjustment must be made.

_____ 1. WestJet Airlines provided flights this month for customers who paid cash last month for tickets.

_____ 2. Shoppers Drug Mart received a telephone bill for services this month, which must be paid next month.

_____ 3. The Jim Pattison Group completed work on an advertising campaign that will be collected next month.

_____ 4. The Lyton Foundation used up some of the benefits of its 3,250 m² building (when teaching students about forensic science, aerospace, and video production).

A. Revenue has been earned

B. Expense has been incurred

C. Liability has been incurred

D. Liability has been fulfilled

E. Asset has been acquired

F. Asset has been used up

M4-2 Matching Transactions with Type of Adjustment

Match each transaction with the type of adjustment that will be required, by entering the appropriate letter in the space provided.

Transaction	Type of Adjustment
_____ 1. Supplies for office use of $500 were purchased during the year, of which $100 remained on hand (unused) at year–end.	A. Accrual adjustment
	B. Deferral adjustment
_____ 2. Interest of $250 on a note receivable was earned at year–end, although collection of the interest is not due until the following year.	
_____ 3. At year–end, wages payable of $3,600 had not been recorded or paid.	
_____ 4. At year–end, one–half of a $2,000 advertising project had been completed for a client, but nothing had been billed or collected.	
_____ 5. A gift card was redeemed for $600 of services.	

Using the information provided, prepare the adjusting journal entries required.

M4-3 Determining Accounting Equation Effects of Adjustments

For each of the following transactions for the SkyBlue Corporation, give the accounting equation effects of the adjustments required on December 31, 2017, for the month:

a. Collected $2,400 rent for the period December 1, 2017, to February 28, 2018, which was credited to Deferred Revenue on December 1, 2017.

b. Paid $1,200 for a two–year insurance premium on December 1, 2017, and debited Prepaid Insurance for that amount.

c. Used a machine purchased on December 1, 2017, for $48,000. The company estimates *annual* depreciation of $4,800.

Using the information, prepare the adjusting journal entries required on December 31, 2017.

M4-4 Determining Accounting Equation Effects of Adjustments

For each of the following transactions for the SkyBlue Corporation, give the accounting equation effects of the adjustments required at the end of the month on December 31, 2017:

a. Received a $600 utility bill for electricity usage in December to be paid in January 2018.

b. Owed wages to ten employees who worked three days at $100 each per day at the end of December. The company will pay employees at the end of the first week of January 2018.

c. On December 1, 2017, loaned money to an employee who agreed to repay the loan in one year along with $1,200 for one full year of interest. No interest has been recorded yet.

Using the information, prepare the adjusting journal entries required on December 31, 2017.

M4-5 Preparing Journal Entries for Deferral Transactions and Adjustments

LO4-2

For each of the following separate situations, prepare journal entries to record the initial transaction on September 30 and the adjustment required on October 31.

a. Hockey Helpers paid $4,000 cash on September 30 to rent an arena for the months of October and November.

b. Super Stage Shows received $16,000 on September 30 for season tickets that admit patrons to a theatre event that will be held twice (on October 31 and November 30).

c. Risky Ventures paid $3,000 on September 30 for insurance coverage for the months of October, November, and December.

M4-6 Preparing Journal Entries for Deferral Transactions and Adjustments

LO4-2

For each of the following separate situations, prepare journal entries to record the initial transaction on December 31 and the adjustment required on January 31.

a. On December 31, 2016, Magnificent Magazines received $12,000 for subscriptions to maga—zines that will be published and distributed in January through December 2017.

b. Walker Window Washing paid $1,200 cash for supplies on December 31, 2016. As of January 31, 2017, $200 of these supplies had been used up.

c. Indoor Raceway received $3,000 on December 31, 2016, from race participants for three races. One race was held January 31, 2017; the other two will be in March 2017.

M4-7 Preparing Journal Entries for Deferral and Accrual Adjustments

LO4-2

Service Pro Corp (SPC) determined that its unadjusted net income was $10,000 for the year ended September 30, 2017. For the following transactions and events, show the adjusting entries that SPC would make on September 30, 2017.

a. At September 30, Prepaid Insurance shows a balance of zero, but Insurance Expense shows a debit balance of $2,340, representing the cost of a three—year fire insurance policy that was purchased on September 1, 2017.

b. On August 31, 2017, Cash was debited and Service Revenue was credited for $1,500. The $1,500 related to fees for a three—month period starting September 1, 2017.

c. The company's income tax rate is 20 percent. An income tax instalment of $2,000 was paid for this year on September 1, at which time it was recorded in Prepaid Expenses.

M4-8 Reporting Adjusted Account Balances

LO4-3, 4-4

Indicate whether each of the following accounts would be reported on the balance sheet (BS) or income statement (IS) of Home Repair Company. Further, if the account is reported on the balance sheet, indicate whether it would be classified with current assets (CA), non—current assets (NCA), current liabilities (CL), non—current liabilities (NCL), or stockholders' equity (SE). If the account is reported on the income statement, indicate whether it would be classi—fied as revenue (R) or expense (E). Finally, for each account, indicate whether the company's accounting records would normally show a debit (dr) or credit (cr) balance.

Account	Financial Statement?	Classification?	Normal dr or cr Balance?
Interest Expense			
Prepaid Rent			
Amortization Expense			
Deferred Revenue			
Retained Earnings			
Accumulated Depreciation			

M4-9 Preparing an Adjusted Trial Balance

Macro Company had the following adjusted accounts and balances at year—end (June 30, 2017):

Accounts Payable	$ 300	Depreciation Expense	$ 110	Prepaid Expenses	$ 40
Accounts Receivable	550	Income Tax Expense	110	Salaries Expense	660
Accrued Liabilities	150	Income Tax Payable	30	Sales Revenue	3,600
Accumulated		Interest Expense	180	Supplies	710
Depreciation	250	Interest Revenue	50	Rent Expense	400
Administrative Expense	820	Land	200	Retained Earnings	120
Buildings and Equipment	1,400	Long-Term Debt	1,300	Deferred Revenue	100
Cash	1,020				
Contributed Capital	300				

Required:

Prepare an adjusted trial balance for Macro Company at June 30, 2017.

LO4-4 **M4-10 Reporting an Income Statement**

The SkyBlue Corporation has the following adjusted trial balance at December 31, 2017.

	Debit	Credit
Cash	$ 1,230	
Accounts Receivable	2,000	
Prepaid Insurance	2,300	
Notes Receivable	3,000	
Equipment	12,000	
Accumulated Depreciation		$ 2,600
Accounts Payable		1,600
Accrued Liabilities Payable		3,820
Wages Payable		1,000
Income Taxes Payable		2,900
Deferred Rent Revenue		600
Contributed Capital		2,400
Retained Earnings		1,000
Dividends Declared	300	
Sales Revenue		42,030
Rent Revenue		300
Wages Expense	21,600	
Depreciation Expense	1,300	
Utilities Expense	1,220	
Insurance Expense	1,400	
Rent Expense	9,000	
Income Tax Expense	2,900	
Total	$58,250	$58,250

Prepare an income statement for the SkyBlue Corporation for the year ended December 31, 2017. How much net income did the company generate during 2017?

LO4-4 **M4-11 Reporting a Statement of Retained Earnings**

Refer to M4—9. Prepare a statement of retained earnings for 2017.

LO4-4 **M4-12 Reporting a Balance Sheet**

Refer to M4—9. Prepare a classified balance sheet at December 31, 2017. Are the SkyBlue Corporation's assets financed primarily by debt or equity?

M4-13 Recording Closing Journal Entries LO4-5

Refer to the adjusted trial balance in M4–9. Prepare closing journal entries on December 31, 2017.

M4-14 Preparing and Posting Adjusting Journal Entries LO4-2

At December 31, the unadjusted trial balance of H&R Tacks reports Supplies of $9,000 and Supplies Expense of $0. On December 31, supplies costing $7,700 are on hand. Prepare the adjusting journal entry on December 31. In separate T–accounts for each account, enter the unadjusted balances, post the adjusting journal entry, and report the adjusted balance.

M4-15 Preparing and Posting Adjusting Journal Entries LO4-2

At December 31, the unadjusted trial balance of H&R Tacks reports Equipment of $30,000 and zero balances in Accumulated Depreciation and Depreciation Expense. Depreciation for the period is estimated to be $6,000. Prepare the adjusting journal entry on December 31. In separate T–accounts for each account, enter the unadjusted balances, post the adjusting journal entry, and report the adjusted balance.

M4-16 Preparing and Posting Adjusting Journal Entries LO4-2

At December 31, the unadjusted trial balance of H&R Tacks reports Prepaid Insurance of $7,200 and Insurance Expense of $0. The insurance was purchased on July 1 and provides coverage for twenty–four months. Prepare the adjusting journal entry on December 31. In separate T–accounts for each account, enter the unadjusted balances, post the adjusting journal entry, and report the adjusted balance.

M4-17 Preparing and Posting Adjusting Journal Entries LO4-2

At December 31, the unadjusted trial balance of H&R Tacks reports Deferred Revenue of $5,000 and Service Revenues of $33,800. One half of the deferred revenue has been earned as of December 31. Prepare the adjusting journal entry on December 31. In separate T–accounts for each account, enter the unadjusted balances, post the adjusting journal entry, and report the adjusted balance.

M4-18 Preparing and Posting Adjusting Journal Entries LO4-2

At December 31, the unadjusted trial balance of H&R Tacks reports Wages Payable of $0 and Wages Expense of $20,000. Employees have been paid for work done up to December 27, but the $1,200 they have earned for December 28 to 31 has not yet been paid or recorded. Prepare the adjusting journal entry on December 31. In separate T–accounts for each account, enter the unadjusted balances, post the adjusting journal entry, and report the adjusted balance.

M4-19 Preparing and Posting Adjusting Journal Entries LO4-2

At December 31, the unadjusted trial balance of H&R Tacks reports Interest Payable of $0 and Interest Expense of $0. Interest incurred and owed in December totals $500. Prepare the adjusting journal entry on December 31. In separate T–accounts for each account, enter the unadjusted balances, post the adjusting journal entry, and report the adjusted balance.

M4-20 Preparing and Posting Journal Entries for Dividends LO4-2

At December 31, the unadjusted trial balance of H&R Tacks reports Dividends Declared of $0 and Dividends Payable of $0. A $200 dividend was declared on December 27, with payment in cash to occur three weeks later. Prepare the required journal entry. In separate T–accounts for each account, enter the unadjusted balances, post the journal entry, and report the adjusted balance.

M4-21 Preparing an Adjusted Trial Balance LO4-3

The adjusted trial balance for PI Detectives reported the following account balances: Accounts Receivable, $500; Supplies, $9,000; Prepaid Insurance, $7,200; Equipment,

LEVEL
UP

$28,000; Accumulated Depreciation, $4,000; Accounts Payable, $200; Deferred Revenue, $5,000; Notes Payable, $3,000; Contributed Capital, $22,000; Retained Earnings, $5,700; Dividends, $3,000; Service Revenue, $33,800; Wages Expense, $20,000; and Depreciation Expense, $1,000. Prepare an adjusted trial balance as of December 31, and solve for its missing Cash balance.

LO4-2, 4-4, 4-5   **M4-22 Progression of Prepaid Expenses over Several Periods**

LEVEL UP

Midcounty Manufacturing purchased a three−year insurance policy for $30,000 on January 2, 2016. Prepare any journal entries, adjusting journal entries, and closing journal entries required on January 2, 2016, December 31, 2016, and December 31, 2017. Summarize these entries in T−accounts for Prepaid Insurance, Insurance Expense, Cash, and Retained Earnings. Assume the January 2, 2016, balances in these accounts were $0, $0, $90,000, and $80,000, respectively. Given only the entries for insurance, indicate what amounts would be reported for each of these accounts on the balance sheets and income statements prepared on December 31, 2016, and December 31, 2017.

EXERCISES

LO4-3   **E4-1 Preparing an Adjusted Trial Balance from Adjusted Account Balances**

Glidden Consulting provides marketing research for clients in the retail industry. The com−pany had the following adjusted balances at December 31, 2017 (listed alphabetically):

Accounts Payable		Accumulated Depreciation		Consulting Fees Earned		General and Administrative Expense	
	86,830	18,100			2,564,200	320,050	

Accounts Receivable		Building and Equipment		Contributed Capital		Income Taxes Payable	
225,400		323,040			233,370		2,030

Accrued Liabilities		Cash		Dividends Declared		Interest Expense	
	25,650	173,000		5,000		17,200	

Land		Other Revenue		Supplies		Utilities Expense	
60,000			20,800	12,200		25,230	

Notes Payable		Prepaid Expenses		Training Expenses		Wages and Benefits Expense	
	160,000	10,200		18,600		1,590,000	

Other Assets		Rent Expense		Travel Expense	
145,000		152,080		23,990	

Other Operating Expenses		Retained Earnings		Deferred Consulting Fees	
188,000			?		32,500

Required:

1. Prepare an adjusted trial balance listing the accounts in proper order at December 31, 2017. Solve for the ? in Retained Earnings.
2. Does the Retained Earnings balance determined in requirement 1 represent the balance at December 31, 2017, or December 31, 2016? Explain.

LO4-1   **E4-2 Identifying Adjustments by Scanning a Trial Balance**

Coach, Inc. is a maker of handbags and other women's and men's accessories. Assume the following were reported in Coach's adjusted trial balance and were used to prepare its June 30, 2017, year−end financial statements.

COACH, INC.
Adjusted Trial Balance
At June 30, 2017

(in millions)	Debit	Credit
Cash	$ 698	
Accounts Receivable	107	
Inventories	345	
Prepaid Expenses	234	
Property and Equipment	755	
Accumulated Depreciation		$ 291
Other Assets	426	
Accounts Payable		134
Wages Payable		304
Income Taxes Payable		12
Other Current Liabilities		308
Contributed Capital		24
Retained Earnings		709
Sales Revenue		3,181
Cost of Sales	774	
Selling and Administrative Expenses	1,260	
Interest Revenue		48
Income Tax Expense	412	
	$5,011	$5,011

Required:

1. Based on the information in the trial balance, list two pairs of balance sheet and income statement accounts that likely required *deferral adjustments* as of June 30 (no computations are necessary).

2. Based on the information in the trial balance, list two pairs of balance sheet and income statement accounts that likely required *accrual adjustments* as of June 30 (no computations are necessary).

E4-3 Recording Initial Transactions and Subsequent Adjustments

LO4-1, 4-2

During the month of September, the Bridge City Go—Kart Company had the following business activities:

a. On September 1, paid rent on the track facility for six months at a total cost of $12,000

b. On September 1, received $60,000 for season tickets for 12—month admission to the racetrack

c. On September 1, booked the racetrack for a private organization that will use the track one day per month for $2,000 each time, to be paid in the following month. The organization uses the track on September 30

d. On September 1, hired a new manager at a monthly salary of $3,000, to be paid the first Monday following the end of the month

Required:

First prepare the journal entry, if any, required to record each of the initial business activities on September 1. Then prepare the adjusting journal entries, if any, required on September 30.

E4-4 Recording Adjusting Journal Entries

LO4-2

Mobol, a wireless phone carrier, completed its first year of operations on December 31, 2017. All of the 2017 entries have been recorded, except for the following:

a. At year—end, employees earned wages of $6,000, which will be paid on the next payroll date, January 13, 2018.

b. At year—end, the company had earned interest revenue of $3,000. It will be collected March 1, 2018.

Required:

1. What is the annual reporting period for this company?
2. Identify whether each required adjustment is a deferral or an accrual.
3. Show the accounting equation effects of each required adjustment, using the format shown in the demonstration case.
4. Why are these adjustments needed?

LO4-1, 4-2
Check Figure
[Part (a)]:
Wages Payable is
credited $6,000.

E4-5 Recording Adjusting Journal Entries

Refer to E4—4.

Required:

Record the required adjusting journal entry for transactions (a) and (b).

LO4-1, 4-2

E4-6 Determining Adjustments and Accounting Equation Effects

Fesel Company is making adjusting journal entries for the year ended December 31, 2017. In developing information for the adjusting journal entries, you learned the following:

a. A two—year insurance premium of $7,200 was paid on January 1, 2017, for coverage beginning on that date. As of December 31, 2017, the unadjusted balances were $7,200 for Prepaid Insurance and $0 for Insurance Expense.

b. At December 31, 2017, you obtained the following data relating to shipping supplies:

Unadjusted balance in Shipping Supplies on December 31, 2017	$15,000
Unadjusted balance in Shipping Supplies Expense on December 31, 2017	72,000
Shipping supplies on hand, counted on December 31, 2017	10,000

Required:

Check Figure
[Req. 2]:
Shipping Supplies
Expense =
$77,000

1. Of the $7,200 paid for insurance, what amount should be reported on the 2017 income statement as Insurance Expense? What amount should be reported on the December 31, 2017, balance sheet as Prepaid Insurance?
2. What amount should be reported on the 2017 income statement as Shipping Supplies Expense? What amount should be reported on the December 31, 2017, balance sheet as Shipping Supplies?
3. Using the format shown in the demonstration case, indicate the accounting equation effects of the adjustment required for transaction (a) dealing with insurance and transaction (b) dealing with shipping supplies.

LO4-2

E4-7 Recording Adjusting Journal Entries

Refer to E4—6.

Required:

Prepare adjusting journal entries at December 31, 2017, for transaction (a) dealing with insurance, and transaction (b) dealing with shipping supplies.

LO4-1, 4-2, 4-6

E4-8 Recording Typical Adjusting Journal Entries

Nickleby's Ski Store is completing the accounting process for its first year ended December 31, 2017. The transactions during 2017 have been journalized and posted. The following data are available to determine adjusting journal entries:

a. The unadjusted balance in Office Supplies was $850 at December 31, 2017. The unadjusted balance in Supplies Expense was $0 at December 31, 2017. A year—end count showed $100 of supplies on hand.

b. Wages earned by employees during December 2017, unpaid and unrecorded at December 31, 2017, amounted to $3,700. The last paycheques were issued December 28; the next payments will be made on January 6, 2018. The unadjusted balance in Wages Expense was $40,000 at December 31, 2017.

c. A portion of the store's basement is now being rented for $1,100 per month to K. Frey. On November 1, 2017, the store collected six months' rent in advance from Frey in the amount of $6,600. It was credited in full to Deferred Rent Revenue when collected. The unadjusted balance in Rent Revenue was $0 at December 31, 2017.

d. The store purchased delivery equipment at the beginning of the year. The estimated depreciation for 2017 is $3,000, although none has been recorded yet.

e. On December 31, 2017, the unadjusted balance in Prepaid Insurance was $4,800. This was the amount paid in the middle of the year for a two−year insurance policy, with coverage beginning on July 1, 2017. The unadjusted balance in Insurance Expense was $800, which was the cost of insurance from January 1 to June 30, 2017.

f. Nickleby's store did some ski repair work for Frey. At the end of December 31, 2017, Frey had not paid for work completed, amounting to $750. This amount has not yet been recorded as Repair Shop Revenue. Collection is expected during January 2018.

Required:

Earlier in 2017, Nickleby's store had already provided, recorded, and collected cash for $5,000 of repair services for other customers.

1. For each of the items listed above, indicate the account names and adjusted balances that should be reported on Nickleby's year−end balance sheet and income statement.

2. For each situation, prepare the adjusting journal entry that should be recorded for Nickleby's at December 31, 2017.

E4-9 Determining Accounting Equation Effects of Typical Adjusting Journal Entries   LO4-2, 4-6

Refer to E4−8.

Required:

For each of the transactions in E4−8, indicate the amount and direction of effects of the adjusting journal entry on the elements of the accounting equation. Using the following format, indicate + for increase, − for decrease, and NE for no effect. Include account names using the format shown for the following sample.

Transaction	Assets	Liabilities	Shareholders' Equity
(a)	Office Supplies −750		Supplies Expense (+E) −750
Etc.			

E4-10 Reporting Depreciation   LO4-4

The adjusted trial balance for Rowdy Profits Corporation reports that its equipment cost $250,000. For the current year, the company has recorded $30,000 of depreciation, which brings the total depreciation to date to $150,000.

Balance Sheet   Income Statement
Assets   Revenues
Liabilities   Expenses
Shareholders' Equity

Required:

Using the headings shown above, indicate the location and amounts that would be used to report the three items on the company's balance sheet and income statement.

E4-11 Recording Transactions Including Adjusting and Closing Journal Entries   LO4-2, 4-5

The following accounts are used by Mouse Potato, Inc., a computer game maker.

Codes	Account	Codes	Account
A	Accounts Receivable	K	Note Payable
B	Accumulated Depreciation	L	Office Equipment
C	Cash	M	Office Supplies
D	Contributed Capital	N	Retained Earnings
E	Depreciation Expense	O	Service Revenue
F	Dividends Declared	P	Supplies Expense
G	Dividends Payable	Q	Deferred Service Revenue
H	Interest Expense	R	Wage Expense
I	Interest Payable	S	Wages Payable
J	Interest Revenue	T	None of the above

Required:

For each of the following independent situations, give the journal entry by entering the appropriate code(s) and amount(s). The first one has been provided as an example.

Check Figure
[Part (f)]:
Debit "P" for $250;
credit "M" for $250

	Independent Situations	Debit		Credit	
		Code	Amount	Code	Amount
a.	Accrued wages, unrecorded and unpaid at year-end are $400.	R	400	S	400
b.	Service revenue collected in advance is $600.				
c.	Dividends declared and paid during year are $900.				
d.	Depreciation expense for year is $1,000.				
e.	Service revenue earned but not yet collected at year-end is $1,000.				
f.	Balance in Office Supplies account is $400; supplies on hand at year-end is $150.				
g.	At year-end, interest on note payable not yet recorded or paid is $220.				
h.	Adjusted balance at year-end in Service Revenue account is $75,000. Give the journal entry to close this one account at year-end.				
i.	Adjusted balance at year-end in Interest Expense account is $420. Give the journal entry to close this one account at year-end.				

LO4-1, 4-2   **E4-12 Inferring Transactions from Accrual and Deferral Accounts**

Deere & Company was founded in 1837 and today is the world's leading producer of agricultural equipment. Assume the following information is taken from its annual report for the year ended October 31, 2013 (in millions of dollars):

Income Tax Payable				Wages Payable				Interest Payable		
	135	Beg. bal.			1,060	Beg. bal.			140	Beg. bal.
712	?	(a)	(b)	?	19,575		1,127	?	(c)	
	79	End. bal.			1,175	End. bal.			150	End. bal.

Required:

1. For each accrued liability account, describe the typical transactions that cause it to increase and decrease.
2. Express each T−account in equation format and then solve for the missing amounts for (a), (b), and (c) (in millions). For example, the Interest Payable T−account can be expressed as follows: Beg. bal. (140) + increases (?) − decreases (1,127) = End. bal. (150). By rearranging the equation, you can solve for? = 150 + 1,127 − 140.

LO4-2, 4-6   **E4-13 Analyzing the Effects of Adjusting Journal Entries on the Income Statement and Balance Sheet**

On December 31, 2017, J. Alan and Company prepared an income statement and balance sheet but failed to take into account four adjusting journal entries. The income statement, prepared on this incorrect basis, reported income before income tax of $30,000. The balance sheet (before the effect of income taxes) reflected total assets of $90,000, total liabilities of $40,00, and shareholders' equity of $50,000. The data for the four adjusting journal entries follow:

a. Depreciation of $8,000 for the year on equipment was not recorded.

b. Wages amounting to $17,000 for the last three days of December 2017 were not paid and not recorded (the next payroll will be on January 10, 2018).

c. Rent revenue of $4,800 was collected on December 1, 2017, for office space for the three–month period December 1, 2017, to February 28, 2018. The $4,800 was credited in full to Deferred Rent Revenue when collected.

d. Income taxes were not recorded. The income tax rate for the company is 30 percent.

Required:

Complete the following table to show the effects of the four adjusting journal entries (indicate deductions with parentheses):

Items	Net Income	Total Assets	Total Liabilities	Stockholders' Equity
Amounts reported	$30,000	$90,000	$40,000	$50,000
Effect of Depreciation	_____	_____	_____	_____
Effect of wages	_____	_____	_____	_____
Effect of rent revenue	_____	_____	_____	_____
Adjusted balances	6,600	82,000	55,400	26,600
Effect of income tax	_____	_____	_____	_____
Correct amounts	_____	_____	_____	_____

E4-14 Reporting an Adjusted Income Statement

On December 31, 2017, Dyer Inc. completed its first year of operations. Because this is the end of the annual accounting period, the company bookkeeper prepared the following preliminary income statement:

Income Statement, 2017		
Rental Revenue		$114,000
Expenses:		
Salaries and Wages Expense	$28,500	
Maintenance Expense	12,000	
Rent Expense	9,000	
Utilities Expense	4,000	
Gas and Oil Expense	3,000	
Other Expenses	1,000	
Total Expenses		57,500
Income		$ 56,500

You are an independent CPA hired by the company to audit the firm's accounting systems and financial statements. In your audit, you developed additional data as follows:

a. Wages for the last three days of December amounting to $310 were not recorded or paid.

b. The $400 telephone bill for December 2017 has not been recorded or paid.

c. Depreciation on rental autos, amounting to $23,000 for 2017, was not recorded.

d. Interest of $500 was not recorded on the note payable by Dyer Inc.

e. The Rental Revenue account includes $4,000 of revenue to be earned in January 2018.

f. Maintenance supplies costing $600 were used during 2017, but this has not yet been recorded.

g. The income tax expense for 2017 is $7,000, but it won't actually be paid until 2018.

Required:

1. What adjusting journal entry for each item (a) through (g) should be recorded at December 31, 2017? If none is required, explain why.
2. Prepare, in proper form, an adjusted income statement for 2017.
3. Did the adjustments have a significant overall effect on the company's net income?

Check Figure
[Req. 2]:
Net income from the adjusted income statement = $20,690

E4-15 Recording Adjusting Entries and Preparing an Adjusted Trial Balance

Ninja Sockeye Star prepared the following unadjusted trial balance at the end of its second year of operations, ending December 31, 2017.

Account Titles	Debit	Credit
Cash	$12,000	
Accounts Receivable	6,000	
Prepaid Rent	2,400	
Machinery	21,000	
Accumulated Depreciation		$ 1,000
Accounts Payable		1,000
Utilities Payable		0
Income Tax Payable		0
Contributed Capital		29,800
Retained Earnings		2,100
Sales Revenue		45,000
Wages Expense	25,000	
Utilities Expense	12,500	
Rent Expense	0	
Depreciation Expense	0	
Income Tax Expense	0	
Totals	$78,900	$78,900

Other data not yet recorded at December 31, 2017 includes the following:

a. Rent expired during 2017, $1,200
b. Depreciation expense for 2017, $1,000
c. Utilities payable, $9,000
d. Income tax expense, $800

Required:

1. Using the format shown in the demonstration case, indicate the accounting equation effects of each required adjustment.
2. Prepare the adjusting journal entries required at December 31, 2017.
3. Summarize the adjusting journal entries in T−accounts. After entering the beginning bal−ances and computing the adjusted ending balances, prepare an adjusted trial balance as of December 31, 2017.

LO4-2, 4-3   **E4-16 Recording Four Adjusting Journal Entries and Preparing an Adjusted Trial Balance**

Mint Cleaning Inc. prepared the following unadjusted trial balance at the end of its second year of operations, ending December 31, 2017. To simplify this exercise, the amounts given in the unadjusted trial balance are in thousands of dollars.

Account Titles	Debit	Credit
Cash	$ 38	
Accounts Receivable	9	
Prepaid Insurance	6	
Machinery	80	
Accumulated Depreciation		$ 0
Accounts Payable		9
Contributed Capital		76
Retained Earnings		4
Sales Revenue		80
Administrative Expenses	26	
Wages Expense	10	
Totals	$169	$169

Other data not yet recorded at December 31, 2017, is as follows:

a. Insurance expired during 2017, $5
b. Depreciation expense for 2017, $4
c. Wages payable, $7
d. Income tax expense, $9

Required:

1. Prepare the adjusting journal entries for 2017.
2. Using T–accounts, determine the adjusted balances in each account and prepare an adjusted trial balance as of December 31, 2017.

E4-17 Reporting an Income Statement, Statement of Retained Earnings, and Balance Sheet

LO4-4

Refer to E4–16.

Required:

Check Figure:
Total assets = $124

Using the adjusted balances in E4–16, prepare an income statement, statement of retained earnings, and balance sheet for 2017.

E4-18 Recording Closing Entries

LO4-5

Refer to E4–16.

Required:

Using the adjusted balances in E4–16, give the closing journal entry for 2017. What is the purpose of "closing the books" at the end of the accounting period?

E4-19 Analyzing, Recording, and Summarizing Business Activities and Adjustments

LO4-1, 4-2, 4-6

The following relates to a magazine company called My Style Mag (MSM). You will use your understanding of the relationships among (1) business activities, (2) accounting equation effects, (3) journal entries, and (4) T–accounts to complete a four–part table similar to the following. Prepare a separate table for each item (a) through (f).

(1)	(Description of the business activity.)				

(2)	**Assets**	**=**	**Liabilities**	**+**	**Shareholders' Equity**

(3)	Account Names	Debit	Credit

(4)		

Required:

For each item (a) through (f) listed below, use the information provided to prepare and com–plete a four–part table similar to that shown above.

a. | (1) | On January 22, 2017, MSM received $24,000 cash from customers for one-year subscriptions to the magazine for February 2017 to January 2018. |

b.

(3)	Account Names	Debit	Credit
Jan. 31	Utilities Expense (+E, – SE)	3,000	
	Accounts Payable (+L)		3,000

c.

(2)	Assets	=	Liabilities	+	Shareholders' Equity
Feb. 28			Deferred Subscription Revenue −2,000		Subscription Revenue (+R) +2,000

d. | (1) | On March 31, 2017, MSM recorded an adjusting entry for the month's depreciation of $10,000. |

e.

(4)	Cash		Prepaid Rent
	5,000 Apr. 1	Apr. 1 5,000	

f.

(4)	Accounts Receivable		Advertising Revenue
	Apr. 30 10,000		10,000 Apr. 30

COACHED PROBLEMS

LO4-3, 4-5   **CP4-1 Preparing an Adjusted Trial Balance, Closing Journal Entry, and Post-Closing Trial Balance**

The following is a list of accounts and amounts reported for Empire Inc., for the fiscal year ended December 31, 2017. The accounts have normal debit or credit balances and the dollars are rounded to the nearest thousand.

Accounts Payable	$ 15,291	Long-Term Debt	$ 531
Accounts Receivable	60,914	Other Assets	27,294
Accrued Liabilities	12,098	Other Revenue	1,288
Accumulated Depreciation	7,315	Product Cost Expense	171,208
Cash	79,613	Property and Equipment	34,031
Contributed Capital	91,768	Retained Earnings	80,226
Income Tax Expense	11,787	Sales Revenue	332,110
Inventories	27,086	Selling, General, and Administrative Expenses	128,694

Required:

1. Prepare an adjusted trial balance at December 31, 2017. Is the Retained Earnings balance of $80,226 the amount that would be reported on the balance sheet as of December 31, 2017?

   TIP: Empire Inc. did not declare a dividend during 2017, but it did earn net income.

   TIP: Total Debits equals $540,627.

2. Prepare the closing entry required at December 31, 2017.

3. Prepare a post–closing trial balance at December 31, 2017.

   TIP: Total Debits equals $228,938.

CP4-2 Analyzing and Recording Adjusting Journal Entries

LO4-1, 4-2

The annual accounting year of Jordan Company ends on December 31. It is now December 31, 2017, and all of the 2017 entries have been made except for the following:

a. The company owes interest of $700 on a bank loan. The interest will be paid on September 30, 2018, when the loan is repaid. No interest has been recorded.

b. On September 1, 2017, Jordan collected six months' rent of $4,800 on storage space. At that date, Jordan debited Cash and credited Deferred Revenue for $4,800.

c. The company earned service revenue of $3,300 on a special job that was completed December 29, 2017. Collection will be made during January 2018. No entry has been recorded.

d. On November 1, 2017, Jordan paid a one-year premium for property insurance of $4,200 for coverage starting on that date. Cash was credited and Prepaid Insurance was debited for this amount.

e. At December 31, 2017, wages earned by employees but not yet paid totalled $1,100. The employees will be paid on the next payroll date, January 15, 2018.

f. Depreciation of $1,000 must be recognized on a service truck purchased this year.

g. The income, after all adjustments other than income taxes, was $30,000. The company's income tax rate is 30 percent. Compute and record income tax expense.

Required:

1. Determine the accounting equation effects of each required adjustment.

    TIP: In transaction (*b*), Jordan Company has met its obligation for four of the six months, thereby earning 4/6 of the rent collected.

    TIP: In transaction (*d*), two months of insurance coverage has now expired.

2. Give the adjusting journal entry required for each transaction at December 31, 2017.

CP4-3 Determining Accounting Equation Effects of Adjusting Journal Entries

LO4-2, 4-6

Refer to CP4-2.

Required:

Indicate the effects (account, amount, and direction) of each adjusting journal entry. Use + for increase, − for decrease, and NE for no effect. Provide an appropriate account name for any revenue and expense effects.

    TIP: The first transaction is done for you as an example.

Transaction	Assets	Liabilities	Shareholders' Equity
a	NE	Interest Payable +700	Interest Expense (+E) −700
b			
etc.			

CP4-4 Identifying and Preparing Adjusting Journal Entries

LO4-1, 4-2, 4-3, 4-6

Golf Academy Limited provides private golf lessons. Its unadjusted trial balance at December 31, 2017, follows, along with information about selected accounts.

Account Names	Debit	Credit	Further Information
Cash	$31,900		As reported on December 31 bank statement.
Supplies	600		Based on count, only $200 of supplies still exist.
Deferred Revenue		$ 3,500	Of this amount, $3,000 was received for December lessons and $500 for January lessons.
Wages Payable		0	Employees were paid $1,000 for ten days of work through December 28 but have not yet been paid for work on December 29 and 30.
Income Tax Payable		0	The company has paid last year's income taxes but not this year's taxes.
Interest Payable		0	The company has not paid the $100 of interest owed on its note payable for the current period.
Note Payable		12,000	This one-year note was taken out this year on December 1.
Contributed Capital		1,000	This amount was contributed to the company in prior years.
Retained Earnings		3,000	This is the balance reported at the end of last year.
Lesson Revenue		51,500	Most customers pay cash for lessons each time they are provided, but some customers paid in advance.
Wages Expense	36,100		An employee worked through December 30, but did not work on December 31.
Supplies Expense	2,400		This is the cost of supplies used through November 30.
Interest Expense	0		The company has not paid the $100 of interest owed on its note payable for the current period.
Income Tax Expense	0		The company has an average tax rate of 30 percent.
Totals	**$71,000**	**$71,000**	

Required:

1. Calculate the (preliminary) unadjusted net income for the year ended December 31, 2017.

   TIP: Net Income equals $13,000.

2. Name the five pairs of balance sheet and income statement accounts that require adjustment.

3. Calculate the desired balances for each account listed in the unadjusted trial balance.

   TIP: Total Debits equals $75,890.

4. Prepare the adjusting journal entries that are required at December 31, 2017.

5. Calculate the adjusted net income that the company should report for the year ended December 31, 2017. By how much did the adjustments in requirement 4 cause net income to increase or decrease?

   TIP: Net Income equals $10,710.

GROUP A PROBLEMS

LO4-3, 4-5

PA4-1 Preparing a Trial Balance, Closing Journal Entry, and Post-Closing Trial Balance

ElecBooks Corporation provides an online bookstore for electronic books. The following is a simplified list of accounts and amounts reported in its accounting records. The accounts have normal debit or credit balances. Amounts in the list of accounts are rounded to the nearest thousand dollars. Assume the year ended on September 30, 2017.

Accounts Payable	$ 221	Other Current Assets	$ 71
Accounts Receivable	191	Other Long-Lived Assets	461
Accrued Liabilities	354	Other Operating Expenses	197
Accumulated Depreciation	300	Prepaid Expenses	94
Cash	307	Property and Equipment	2,142
Contributed Capital	151	Retained Earnings	1,445
Depreciation Expense	340	Selling Expenses	2,605
General and Administrative Expenses	357	Service Revenues	6,369
Income Tax Expense	302	Short-Term Bank Loan	476
Interest Revenue	92	Store Operating Expenses	2,166
Long-Term Debt	196	Supplies	546
		Deferred Revenue	175

Required:

1. Prepare an adjusted trial balance at September 30, 2017. Is the Retained Earnings balance of $1,445,000 the amount that would be reported on the balance sheet as of September 30, 2017?
2. Prepare the closing entry required at September 30, 2017.
3. Prepare a post-closing trial balance at September 30, 2017.

**Check Figure
[Req. 3]:**
Total debits and
total credits =
$3,812,000

PA4-2 Analyzing and Recording Adjusting Journal Entries

LO4-1, 4-2

Brokeback Towing Company is at the end of its accounting year, December 31, 2017. The following data that must be considered were developed from the company's records and related documents:

a. On July 1, 2017, a three-year insurance premium on equipment in the amount of $600 was paid and debited in full to Prepaid Insurance on that date. Coverage began on July 1.

b. At the end of 2017, the unadjusted balance in the Office Supplies account was $1,000. A physical count of supplies on December 31, 2017, indicated supplies costing $300 were still on hand.

c. On December 31, 2017, YY's Garage completed repairs on one of Brokeback's trucks at a cost of $800. The amount is not yet recorded. It will be paid during January 2018.

d. In December, the 2017 property tax bill for $1,600 was received from the city. The taxes, which have not been recorded, will be paid on February 15, 2018.

e. On December 31, 2017, the company completed the work on a contract for an out-of-province company for $7,900 payable by the customer within 30 days. No cash has been collected and no journal entry has been made for this transaction.

f. On July 1, 2017, the company purchased a new hauling van. Depreciation for July to December 2017, estimated to total $2,750, has not been recorded.

g. As of December 31, the company owes interest of $500 on a bank loan taken out on October 1, 2017. The interest will be paid on September 30, 2018, when the loan is repaid. No interest has been recorded yet.

h. The income before any of the adjustments or income taxes was $30,000. The company's federal income tax rate is 30 percent. Compute adjusted income based on all of the preceding information, and then determine and record income tax expense.

Required:

1. Give the adjusting journal entry required for each transaction at December 31, 2017.
2. Without the adjustments made in requirement 1, by what amount would Brokeback's net income have been understated or overstated?

PA4-3 Determining Accounting Equation Effects of Adjusting Journal Entries

LO4-2, 4-6

Refer to PA4-2.

Required:

Indicate the accounting equation effects (amount and direction) of each adjusting journal entry. Use + for increase, − for decrease, and NE for no effect. Provide an appropriate account name for any revenue and expense effects.

Transaction	Assets	Liabilities	Shareholders' Equity
(a)			
(b)			
Etc.			

PA4-4 Identifying and Preparing Adjusting Journal Entries

LO4-1, 4-2, 4-3, 4-6

Val's Hair Emporium is a hair salon. Its unadjusted trial balance as of December 31, 2017, follows, along with information about selected accounts.

Account Names	Debit	Credit	Further Information
Cash	$ 3,800		As reported on December 31 bank statement.
Supplies	4,300		Based on count, only $3,200 of supplies still exist.
Prepaid Rent	6,000		This amount was paid November 1 for rent through the end of January.
Accounts Payable		$ 1,500	This represents the total amount of bills received for supplies and utilities through December 15. Val estimates that the company has received $450 of utility services through December 31 for which it has not yet been billed.
Wages Payable		0	Stylists have not yet been paid $150 for their work on December 31.
Income Tax Payable		0	The company has paid last year's income taxes but not this year's taxes.
Contributed Capital		2,000	This amount was contributed to the company in prior years.
Retained Earnings		900	This is the balance reported at the end of last year.
Hair Styling Revenue		75,800	Customers pay cash when they receive services.
Wages Expense	29,100		This is the cost of stylist wages through December 30.
Utilities Expense	12,200		This is the cost of utilities through December 15.
Rent Expense	20,000		This year's rent was $2,000 per month.
Supplies Expense	4,800		This is the cost of supplies used through November 30.
Income Tax Expense	0		The company has an average tax rate of 30 percent.
Totals	**$80,200**	**$80,200**	

Required:

1. Calculate the (preliminary) unadjusted net income for the year ended December 31, 2017.
2. Name the five pairs of balance sheet and income statement accounts that require adjustment.
3. Calculate the desired balances for each account listed in the unadjusted trial balance.
4. Prepare the adjusting journal entries that are required at December 31, 2017.
5. Calculate the adjusted net income that the company should report for the year ended December 31, 2017. By how much did the adjustments in requirement (4) cause net income to increase or decrease?

GROUP B PROBLEMS

LO4-3, 4-5   **PB4-1 Preparing a Trial Balance, Closing Journal Entry, and Post-Closing Trial Balance**

Regis Corporation operates hair salons under various brand names including Supercuts, Mia & Maxx, and Style America. Assume the following is a simplified list of accounts and amounts (in millions) reported in the company's accounts for the year ended June 30, 2017.

Accounts Payable	$ 70	Income Tax Expense	$ 54
Accounts Receivable	38	Interest Expense	36
Accrued Liabilities	208	Inventories	212
Accumulated Depreciation	586	Long-Term Liabilities	982
Cash	128	Other Current Assets	67
Contributed Capital	247	Other Long-Lived Assets	1,309
Cost of Operations	1,690	Property, Plant, and Equipment	1,068
Depreciation Expense	131	Retained Earnings	644
General and Administrative Expenses	337	Rent Expense	406
		Salon Revenue	2,739

Required:

1. Prepare an adjusted trial balance at June 30, 2017. Is the Retained Earnings balance of $644,000,000 the amount that would be reported on the balance sheet as of June 30, 2017?

2. Prepare the closing entry required at June 30, 2017.

3. Prepare a post-closing trial balance at June 30, 2017.

PB4-2 Analyzing and Recording Adjusting Journal Entries

LO4-1, 4-2

Cactus Company's annual accounting year ends on June 30. It is June 30, 2017, and all of the 2017 entries except the following adjusting journal entries have been made:

Check Figure
[Part h]:
Income Tax
Expense = $9,000

a. The company earned service revenue of $2,000 on a special job that was completed June 29, 2017. Collection will be made during July 2017; no entry has been recorded.

b. On March 31, 2017, Cactus paid a six-month premium for property insurance in the amount of $3,200 for coverage starting on that date. Cash was credited and Prepaid Insurance was debited for this amount.

c. At June 30, 2017, wages of $900 were earned by employees but not yet paid. The employees will be paid on the next payroll date, which is July 13, 2017.

d. On June 1, 2017, Cactus collected two months' maintenance revenue of $450. At that date, Cactus debited Cash and credited Deferred Maintenance Revenue for $450. One half of it has now been earned but not yet recorded.

e. Depreciation of $1,500 must be recognized on a service truck purchased on July 1, 2016.

f. Cash of $4,200 was collected on May 1, 2017, for services to be rendered evenly over the next year, beginning on May 1. Deferred Service Revenue was credited when the cash was received. Some of it has now been earned but not yet recorded.

g. The company owes interest of $600 on a bank loan taken out on February 1, 2017. The interest will be paid when the loan is repaid on January 31, 2018.

h. The income before any of the adjustments or income taxes was $31,675. The company's federal income tax rate is 30 percent. Compute adjusted income based on all of the preceding information, and then determine and record income tax expense.

Required:

1. Determine the accounting equation effects of each required adjustment.

2. Give the adjusting journal entry required for each transaction at June 30, 2017.

PB4-3 Determining Accounting Equation Effects of Adjusting Journal Entries

LO4-2, 4-6

Refer to PB4-2.

Required:

Indicate the accounting equation effects (amount and direction) of each adjusting journal entry. Use + for increase, − for decrease, and NE for no effect. Provide an appropriate account name for any revenue and expense effects.

Transaction	Assets	Liabilities	Shareholders' Equity
(a)			
(b)			
(c)			
Etc.			

PB4-4 Identifying and Preparing Adjusting Journal Entries

LO4-1, 4-2, 4-3, 4-6

Learn to Play, Inc. is a one-person company that provides private piano lessons. Its unadjusted trial balance at December 31, 2017, follows, along with information about selected accounts.

Account Names	Debit	Credit	Further Information
Cash	$ 23,800		As reported on December 31 bank statement.
Supplies	300		Based on count, only $200 of supplies still exist.
Deferred Revenue		$ 1,500	Of this amount, $500 was received for December lessons and $1,000 for January lessons.
Wages Payable		0	Employees were paid $500 for ten days of work through December 28. They have not yet been paid for work on December 29 and 30.
Income Tax Payable		0	The company has paid last year's income tax but not this year's tax.
Interest Payable		0	The company has not paid the $100 of interest owed on its note payable for the current period.
Note Payable		12,000	This one-year note was taken out this year on December 1.
Contributed Capital		1,000	This amount was contributed to the company in prior years.
Retained Earnings		3,000	This is the balance reported at the end of last year.
Lesson Revenue		25,500	Most customers pay cash for lessons each time they are provided, but some customers pay in advance.
Wages Expense	18,100		Employees worked through December 30, but did not work on December 31.
Supplies Expense	800		This is the cost of supplies used through November 30.
Interest Expense	0		The company has not paid the $100 of interest owed on its note payable for the current period.
Income Tax Expense	0		The company has an average tax rate of 30 percent.
Totals	**$43,000**	**$43,000**	

Required:

1. Calculate the (preliminary) unadjusted net income for the year ended December 31, 2017.
2. Name the five pairs of balance sheet and income statement accounts that require adjustment.
3. Calculate the desired balances for each account listed in the unadjusted trial balance.
4. Prepare the adjusting journal entries that are required at December 31, 2017.
5. Calculate the adjusted net income that the company should report for the year ended December 31, 2017. By how much did the adjustments in requirement 4 cause net income to increase or decrease?

COMPREHENSIVE PROBLEMS

LO2-3, 3-3, 4-1, 4-2, 4-3, 4-4, 4-5, 4-6 — **C4-1 From Recording Transactions (Including Adjusting Journal Entries) to Preparing Financial Statements and Closing Journal Entries**

Consider the following, using what you learned in Chapters 2, 3, and 4.

Brothers Harry and Herman Hausyerday began operations of their machine shop (H & H Tool Co.) on January 1, 2010. The annual reporting period ends December 31. The trial balance on January 1, 2017, appears below (the amounts are rounded to thousands of dollars to simplify).

Account Titles	Debit	Credit
Cash	$ 3	
Accounts Receivable	5	
Supplies	12	
Land	0	
Equipment	60	
Accumulated Depreciation (on Equipment)		$ 6
Other Assets	4	
Accounts Payable		5
Notes Payable		0
Wages Payable		0
Interest Payable		0
Income Tax Payable		0
Contributed Capital		65
Retained Earnings		8
Dividends Declared	0	
Service Revenue	0	
Depreciation Expense	0	
Income Tax Expense	0	
Interest Expense	0	
Supplies and Operating Expenses	0	
Totals	$84	$84

Transactions during 2017 (in thousands of dollars) are as follows:

a. Borrowed $12 cash on a short–term note payable
b. Purchased land for future building site, paid cash, $9
c. Earned revenues for 2017, $160, including $40 on credit and $120 collected in cash
d. Issued additional shares for $3
e. Recognized operating expenses for 2017, $85, including $15 on credit and $70 paid in cash
f. Collected accounts receivable, $24
g. Purchased other assets, $10 cash
h. Paid accounts payable, $13
i. Purchased supplies on account for future use, $18
j. Signed a $25 service contract to start February 1, 2018
k. Declared and paid a cash dividend, $17

Data for adjusting journal entries are as follows:

l. Supplies counted on December 31, 2017, $10
m. Depreciation for the year on the equipment, $6
n. Accrued interest on notes payable, $1
o. Wages earned since the December 24 payroll not yet paid, $12
p. Income tax for the year, $8; will be paid in 2018

Required:

1. Set up T–accounts for the accounts on the trial balance and enter beginning balances.
2. Record journal entries for transactions (a) through (k), and post them to the T–accounts.
3. Prepare an unadjusted trial balance.
4. Record and post the adjusting journal entries (l) through (p).
5. Prepare an adjusted trial balance.
6. Prepare an income statement, statement of retained earnings, and balance sheet.
7. Prepare and post the closing journal entries.

8. Prepare a post–closing trial balance.

9. How much net income did H & H Tool Co. generate during 2017? Is the company financed primarily by liabilities or shareholders' equity?

LO2-3, 3-3, 4-1, 4-2, 4-3, 4-4, 4-5, 4-6

C4-2 From Recording Transactions (Including Adjusting Journal Entries) to Preparing Financial Statements and Closing Journal Entries

Consider the following, using what you learned in Chapters 2, 3, and 4.

Drs. Elaine Newton and Alicia Donland began operation of their physical therapy clinic, called Northward Physical Therapy, on January 1, 2016. The annual reporting period ends December 31. A trial balance was created with amounts rounded to the nearest thousand dollars. The trial balance on January 1, 2017, was as follows:

Account Titles	Debit	Credit
Cash	$7	
Accounts Receivable	3	
Supplies	3	
Equipment	6	
Accumulated Depreciation (equipment)		$1
Other Assets	6	
Accounts Payable		5
Notes Payable		0
Wages Payable		0
Interest Payable		0
Income Tax Payable		0
Deferred Revenue		0
Contributed Capital		15
Retained Earnings		4
Dividends Declared	0	
Service Revenue		0
Depreciation Expense	0	
Income Tax Expense	0	
Interest Expense	0	
Operating Expenses	0	
Totals	$25	$25

Transactions during 2017 were as follows:

a. Borrowed $22,000 cash on July 1, 2017, signing a six–month note payable

b. Purchased equipment for $25,000 cash on July 1, 2017

c. Issued additional shares for $5,000

d. Earned revenues for 2017 of $55,000, including $8,000 on credit and $47,000 received in cash

e. Recognized operating expenses for 2017 of $30,000, including $5,000 on credit and $25,000 in cash

f. Purchased other assets, $3,000 cash

g. Collected accounts receivable, $9,000

h. Paid accounts payable, $10,000

i. Purchased supplies on account for future use, $7,000

j. Received a $3,000 deposit from a hospital for a contract to start January 5, 2018

k. Declared and paid a cash dividend, $4,000

Data for adjusting journal entries were as follows:

l. Supplies of $3,000 were counted on December 31, 2017

m. Depreciation for 2017, $4,000

n. Accrued interest on notes payable of $1,000

o. Wages incurred since the December 27 payroll not yet paid, $3,000

p. Income tax expense for 2017 was $4,000, and will be paid in 2018

**Check Figure
[Req. 6]:**
Net income =
$6,000 Retained
Earnings Dec. 31/17
= $6,000

Required:

1. Set up T−accounts for the accounts on the trial balance and enter beginning balances.
2. Record journal entries for transactions (*a*) through (*k*), and post them to the T−accounts.
3. Prepare an unadjusted trial balance.
4. Record and post the adjusting journal entries (*l*) through (*p*).
5. Prepare an adjusted trial balance.
6. Prepare an income statement, statement of retained earnings, and balance sheet.
7. Prepare and post the closing journal entries.
8. Prepare a post−closing trial balance.
9. How much net income did the physical therapy clinic generate during 2017? Is the business financed primarily by liabilities or shareholders' equity?

C4-3 From Recording Transactions (Including Adjusting Journal Entries) to Preparing Financial Statements and Closing Journal Entries

LO2-3, 3-3, 4-1,
4-2, 4-3, 4-4,
4-5, 4-6

Consider the following, using what you learned in Chapters 2, 3, and 4.

Alison and Chuck Renny began operations of their furniture repair shop (Lazy Sofa Furniture, Inc.) on January 1, 2016. The annual reporting period ends December 31. A trial balance was created with amounts rounded to the nearest thousand dollars. The trial balance on January 1, 2017, was as follows:

Account Titles	Debit	Credit
Cash	$ 5	
Accounts Receivable	4	
Supplies	2	
Small Tools	6	
Equipment	0	
Accumulated Depreciation		$ 0
Other Assets	9	
Accounts Payable		7
Notes Payable		0
Wages Payable		0
Interest Payable		0
Income Tax Payable		0
Deferred Revenue		0
Contributed Capital		15
Retained Earnings		4
Dividends Declared	0	
Service Revenue		0
Depreciation Expense	0	
Income Tax Expense	0	
Interest Expense	0	
Operating Expenses	0	
Totals	$26	$26

Transactions during 2017 are as follows:

a. Borrowed $21,000 cash on July 1, 2017, signing a six−month note payable
b. Purchased equipment for $18,000 cash on July 1, 2017
c. Issued additional shares for $5,000
d. Earned revenues for 2017 in the amount of $65,000, including $9,000 on credit and $56,000 received in cash
e. Recognized operating expenses for 2017, $35,000, including $7,000 on credit and $28,000 in cash

f. Purchased additional small tools, $3,000 cash

g. Collected accounts receivable, $8,000

h. Paid accounts payable, $11,000

i. Purchased on account supplies for future use, $10,000

j. Received a $3,000 deposit on work to start January 15, 2018

k. Declared and paid a cash dividend, $10,000

These are the data for adjusting journal entries:

l. Supplies of $4,000 were counted on December 31, 2017

m. Depreciation for 2017, $2,000

n. Accrued interest on notes payable of $1,000

o. Wages earned since the December 24 payroll not yet paid, $3,000

p. Income tax for 2017 was $4,000, and will be paid in 2018

**Check Figure
[Req. 6]:**
Total liabilities
and shareholders'
equity for Dec.
31/17 = $71,000

Required:

1. Set up T−accounts for the accounts on the trial balance and enter beginning balances.

2. Record journal entries for transactions (*a*) through (*k*), and post them to the T−accounts.

3. Prepare an unadjusted trial balance.

4. Record and post the adjusting journal entries (*l*) through (*p*).

5. Prepare an adjusted trial balance.

6. Prepare an income statement, statement of retained earnings, and balance sheet.

7. Prepare and post the closing journal entries.

8. Prepare a post−closing trial balance.

9. How much net income did Lazy Sofa Furniture, Inc. generate during 2017? Is the company financed primarily by liabilities or shareholders' equity?

LO2-3, 3-3, 4-2,
4-3, 4-4

C4-4 From Recording Transactions to Preparing Accrual and Deferral Adjustments and Reporting Results on the Balance Sheet and Income Statements

Consider the following, using what you learned in Chapters 2, 3, and 4.

Run Heavy Corporation (RHC) is a corporation that manages a local rock band. RHC was formed with an investment of $10,000 cash, paid in by the leader of the band on January 3. On January 4, RHC purchased music equipment by paying $2,000 cash and signing an $8,000 promissory note payable in three years.

On January 5, RHC booked the band for six concert events, at a price of $2,500 each. Of the six events, four were completed between January 10 and 20. On January 22, cash was collected for three of the four events. The other two bookings were for February concerts, but on January 24, RHC collected half of the $2,500 fee for one of them.

On January 27, RHC paid $3,140 cash for the band's travel−related costs. On January 28, RHC paid its band members a total of $2,400 cash for salaries and wages for the first three events. As of January 31, the band members hadn't yet been paid wages for the fourth event completed in January, but they would be paid in February at the same rate as for the first three events.

As of January 31, RHC has not yet recorded the $100 of monthly depreciation on the equipment. Also, RHC has not yet paid or recorded the $60 interest owed on the promissory note at January 31. RHC is subject to a 15 percent tax rate on the company's income before tax.

Required:

1. Prepare journal entries to record the transactions and adjustments needed on each of the dates indicated above.

2. Post the journal entries from requirement 1 to T−accounts, calculate ending balances, and prepare an adjusted trial balance.

3. Prepare a classified balance sheet and income statement as of and for the month ended January 31.

LO4-2, 4-4

C4-5 From Recording Transactions to Preparing Accrual and Deferral Adjustments and Reporting Results on the Balance Sheet and Income Statements

Consider the following, using what you learned in Chapters 2, 3, and 4.

House of Tutors, Inc. (HTI) is a company that runs a tutoring service for high school and university students. The company reported the following amounts in its post—closing trial balance, prepared at August 31 at the end of its first fiscal year.

Accounts Payable	$ 60	Equipment	$ 12,000
Accounts Receivable	220	Interest Payable	40
Accumulated Depreciation	1,200	Note Payable (long-term)	8,000
Cash	700	Retained Earnings	820
Common Shares	2,900	Supplies	100

The company encountered the following events during September:

a. HTI provided 100 hours of regular hourly tutoring at the rate of $20 per hour, all of which was collected in cash.

b. HTI paid tutors at the hourly rate of $10 per hour. On September 28, HTI paid for 90 hours of tutor time and promised to pay the remaining hours worked.

c. HTI hosted an all—night review session on September 29 for people cramming for midterm exams, at a special price of $10 per attendee. Rather than collect cash at the time of the review session, HTI will send bills in October to the 75 people who attended the review session.

d. At the beginning of the night—long review session, HTI paid $200 cash to its tutors for wages. No additional salaries and wages will be paid for the review session.

e. HTI collected $200 cash on account from students who received tutoring during the summer.

f. HTI also collected $250 cash from a high school for a tutoring session to be held in October.

g. HTI determined that depreciation for September should be $100.

h. Although HTI adjusted its accounts on August 31, it has not yet paid the $40 monthly interest owed on the promissory note, for either August or September. The note is due in three years.

i. HTI has only $40 of supplies left at September 30.

j. HTI's income taxes are approximately 30 percent of income before tax.

Required:

1. Prepare HTI's journal entries and adjusting journal entries.

2. Prepare HTI's income statement and statement of retained earnings for the month ended September 30.

3. Prepare HTI's classified balance sheet at September 30.

C4-6 Recording/Posting Transactions and Adjustments, and Preparing Trial Balances and Financial Statements—Requires Calculating Depreciation and Interest

LO2-3, 3-3, 4-2, 4-4

Consider the following, using what you learned in Chapters 2, 3, and 4.

Fast Deliveries, Inc. (FDI) was organized in December last year, and had limited activity last year. The resulting balance sheet at the beginning of the current year is provided below.

FAST DELIVERIES, INC.
Balance Sheet at January 1

Assets:		Liabilities:	
Cash	$10,900	Accounts Payable	$ 500
Accounts Receivable	800	Shareholders' Equity:	
Supplies	400	Contributed Capital	11,000
		Retained Earnings	600
		Total Liabilities and Shareholders'	
Total Assets	$12,100	Equity	$12,100

Two employees have been hired, at a monthly salary of $2,200 each. The following trans—actions occurred during January of the current year. For your reference, the chapter to which each event relates is indicated in the first column.

Ch.	January	
2	1	$5,700 is paid for twelve months' insurance starting January 1. (Record as an asset.)
2	2	$4,200 is paid for three months of rent beginning January 1. (Record as an asset.)
2	3	FDI borrows $30,000 cash from First State Bank at 6% annual interest; this note is payable in two years.
2	4	A delivery van is purchased using cash. Including tax, the total cost was $24,000.
2	5	Shareholders contribute $6,000 of additional cash to FDI for its common stock.
2	6	Additional supplies costing $1,000 are purchased on account and received.
2	7	$600 of accounts receivable arising from last year's December sales are collected.
2	8	$400 of accounts payable from December of last year are paid.
3	9	Performed services for customers on account. Mailed invoices totaling $10,400.
3	10	$7,600 of services are performed for customers who paid immediately in cash.
3	16	$2,200 of salaries are paid for the first half of the month.
3	20	FDI receives $3,500 cash from a customer for an advance order for services to be provided later in February.
3	25	$4,500 is collected from customers on account (see January 9 transaction).

Ch. 4 Additional information for adjusting entries:

January

31a.   A $1,200 bill arrives for January utility services. Payment is due February 15.

31b.   Supplies on hand on January 31 are counted and determined to have cost $250.

31c.   As of January 31, FDI had completed 60% of the deliveries for the customer who paid in advance on January 20.

31d.   Accrue one month of interest on the bank loan. Yearly interest is determined by multiplying the amount borrowed by the annual interest rate (expressed as 0.06).
For convenience, calculate January interest as one-twelfth of the annual interest.

31e.   Assume the van will be used for four years, after which it will have no value. Thus, each year, one-fourth of the van's benefits will be used up, which implies annual depreciation equal to one-fourth of the van's total cost. Record depreciation for the month of January, equal to one-twelfth of the annual depreciation expense.

31f.   Salaries earned by employees for the period from January 16–31 are $1,100 per employee and will be paid on February 3.

31g.   Adjust the prepaid asset accounts (for rent and insurance) as needed.

Required:

1. Record journal entries for the transactions that occurred from January 1–31.

2. If you are completing this problem manually, set up T−accounts using the beginning balances shown in the January 1 balance sheet, post the transactions from requirement 1, and prepare an adjusted trial balance at January 31. If you are completing this problem in Connect using the general ledger tool, this requirement will be completed for you.

3. Using the given information, record all adjusting journal entries needed at January 31.

4. If you are completing this problem manually, post the adjusting journal entries from require−ment 3 into T−accounts and prepare an adjusted trial balance. If you are completing this problem in Connect using the general ledger tool, this requirement will be completed for you.

5. Prepare an income statement and statement of retained earnings for the month ended January 31, and prepare a classified balance sheet at January 31.

SKILLS DEVELOPMENT CASES

LO4-1, 4-6   **S4-1 Finding Financial Information**

Refer to the summarized financial statements of The Home Depot in Appendix A at the end of this book.

Required:

1. How much does The Home Depot have recorded as other current assets on the balance sheet as of January 29, 2017? Give a couple of examples of items that could make up this other current assets amount.

2. How much did The Home Depot owe for accounts payable at January 29, 2017? Was this an increase or decrease from the previous year?

S4-2 Comparing Financial Information

LO4-1, 4-6

Refer to the summarized financial statements of The Home Depot in Appendix A and Lowe's Companies, Inc. in Appendix B at the back of this book.

Required:

1. How much did Lowe's Companies, Inc. owe for salaries and wages at February 3, 2017? Was this an increase or decrease from the previous year? What factors could cause these two numbers to be different?

2. Refer to the Revenues note in the Summary of Significant Accounting Policies that follows Lowe's Companies, Inc.'s statements of cash flows. How does the company account for customer payments received in advance of providing services? What adjusting journal entry must Lowe's Companies, Inc. make when it provides these services?

S4-3 Internet-Based Team Research: Examining Deferrals and Accruals

LO4-1, 4-4

As a team, select an industry to analyze. Using the Internet, each team member should access the annual report for one publicly traded company in the industry, with each member selecting a different company. (See question S1–3 in Chapter 1 for a description of possible resources for these tasks.)

Required:

1. On an individual basis, each team member should write a short report listing the following:
   a. The company's total assets and total liabilities at the end of each year
   b. The company's prepaid expenses and accrued liabilities at the end of each year
   c. The percentage of prepaid expenses to total assets and the percentage of accrued liabilities to total liabilities
   d. A description of and explanation for the types of accrued liabilities reported in the notes to the financial statements
2. Discuss any patterns that you as a team observe. Then, as a team, write a short report comparing and contrasting your companies according to the preceding attributes. Provide potential explanations for any differences discovered.

S4-4 Ethical Decision Making: A Real-Life Example

LO4-1, 4-2, 4-6

On December 12, 2002, the U.S. Securities and Exchange Commission (SEC) filed a lawsuit against four executives of Safety–Kleen Corp., a leading provider of industrial waste collection and disposal services. The primary issue was that the executives had directed others in the company to record improper adjustments in 1999 and 2000, which had the effect of overstating net income during those periods. The following table was included in the SEC's court documents to demonstrate the (combined) effect of proper and improper adjustments on net income. (All amounts are in millions.)

	Year (Quarter)				
	1999(Q1)	1999(Q2)	1999(Q3)	1999(Q4)	2000(Q1)
Net income before adjustments	$ 90.9	$ 76.7	$ 47.9	$ 57.3	$ 47.0
Effect of adjustments	36.6	30.9	75.5	53.1	69.8
Net income after adjustments	**$127.5**	**$107.6**	**$123.4**	**$110.4**	**$116.8**

The following excerpts from the SEC's complaint describe two of the allegedly improper adjustments:

Improper Capitalization of Operating Expenses

26. As part of the fraudulent accounting scheme, [three top executives] improperly recorded several adjusting entries to capitalize certain operating expenses. These adjustments caused the company to materially overstate both its assets and its earnings. For example, at the end of the third quarter of fiscal 1999, they improperly capitalized approximately $4.6 million of payroll expenses relating to certain marketing and start-up activities.

Improper Treatment of Accruals

33. During the fourth quarter of fiscal 1999, Humphreys [the CFO] created additional fictitious income by directing [other accounting executives] to eliminate a $7.6 million accrual that had been established to provide for management bonuses that had been earned in fiscal 1999, but were to be paid the following quarter. Humphreys' action suggested that no bonuses were going to be paid for that year. In fact, the bonuses for 1999 were paid as scheduled.

Required:

1. Discuss whether large adjustments, such as those included by Safety—Kleen in 1999 and 2000, necessarily indicate improper accounting procedures.

2. What does the SEC's document mean in paragraph 26 when it says three top executives "improperly recorded several adjusting entries to *capitalize* certain operating expenses"? Drawing on concepts presented in Chapters 2 and 3, explain why it is improper to record payroll expenses for marketing personnel as assets.

3. Assume the $7.6 million in bonuses referred to in paragraph 33 were recorded in the third quarter of 1999. What journal entry would have been used to record this accrual? Assume this accrual was eliminated in the fourth quarter of 1999. What adjusting journal entry would have been recorded to eliminate (remove) the previous accrual? What journal entry would have been used to record the $7.6 million in bonuses paid in the first quarter of 2000 (assuming the accrual had been removed in the fourth quarter of 1999)? What accounting concept is violated by recording an expense for management bonuses when they are paid rather than when they are earned by managers?

Epilogue: In April 2005, a federal judge found the company's former CEO and CFO liable for $200 million for their role in the fraud.

LO4-1, 4-4, 4-6 **S4-5 Ethical Decision Making: A Mini-Case**

Assume you work as an assistant accountant in the head office of a DVD movie kiosk business, similar to Coinstar Inc. With the increasing popularity of online movie rental operations, your company has struggled to meet its earnings targets for the year.

It is important for the company to meet its earnings targets this year because the company is renegotiating a bank loan next month, and the terms of that loan are likely to depend on the company's reported financial success. Also, the company plans to issue more shares to the public in the upcoming year, to obtain funds for establishing its own presence in the online movie rental business.

The chief financial officer (CFO) has approached you with a solution to the earnings dilemma. She proposes that the depreciation period for the inventory of reusable DVDs be extended from three months to fifteen months. She explains that by lengthening the depreciation period, a smaller amount of depreciation expense will be recorded in the current year, resulting in a higher net income. She claims that generally accepted accounting principles require estimates like this, so it wouldn't involve doing anything wrong.

Required:

Discuss the CFO's proposed solution. In your discussion, consider the following questions. Will the change in depreciation affect net income in the current year in the way that the CFO described? How will it affect net income in the following year? Is the CFO correct when she claims that the change in estimated depreciation is allowed by GAAP? Who relies on the video company's financial statements when making decisions? Why might their decisions be affected by the CFO's proposed solution? Is it possible that their decisions would not be affected? What should you do?

S4-6 Critical Thinking: Adjusting an Income Statement and Balance Sheet for Deferrals and Accruals

LO4-1, 4-2, 4-4, 4-6

Pirate Pete Moving Corporation has been in operation since January 1, 2017. It is now December 31, 2017, the end of the annual accounting period. The company has not done well financially during its first year, although revenue has been fairly good. Three shareholders manage the company, but they have not given much attention to record keeping. In view of a serious cash shortage, they have applied to your bank for a $20,000 loan. As a loan officer, you requested a complete set of financial statements. The following 2017 annual financial statements were prepared by the company's office staff.

PIRATE PETE MOVING CORPORATION Income Statement for the year ended December 31, 2017	
Transportation Revenue	$85,000
Expenses:	
Salaries Expense	17,000
Supplies Expense	12,000
Other Expenses	18,000
Total Expenses	47,000
Net Income	$38,000

PIRATE PETE MOVING CORPORATION Balance Sheet At December 31, 2017	
Assets	
Cash	$ 2,000
Accounts Receivable	3,000
Supplies	6,000
Equipment	40,000
Prepaid Insurance	4,000
Remaining Assets	27,000
Total Assets	$82,000
Liabilities	
Accounts Payable	$ 9,000
Shareholders' Equity	
Contributed Capital	35,000
Retained Earnings	38,000
Total Liabilities and Shareholders' Equity	$82,000

After briefly reviewing the statements and looking into the situation, you requested that the statements be redone (with some expert help) to incorporate depreciation, accruals, supply counts, income taxes, and so on. As a result of a review of the records and supporting documents, the following additional information was developed:

a. The Supplies amount of $6,000 shown on the balance sheet has not been adjusted for supplies used during 2017. A count of the supplies on hand on December 31, 2017, showed $1,800.

b. The insurance premium paid in 2017 was for years 2017 and 2018. The total insurance premium was debited in full to Prepaid Insurance when paid in 2017 and no adjustment has been made.

c. The equipment cost $40,000 when it was purchased January 1, 2017. It had an estimated annual depreciation of $8,000. No depreciation has been recorded for 2017.

d. Unpaid (and unrecorded) salaries at December 31, 2017, amounted to $2,200.

e. At December 31, 2017, transportation revenue collected in advance amounted to $7,000. This amount was credited in full to Transportation Revenue when the cash was collected earlier during 2017.

f. Income taxes for the year are calculated as 25 percent of income before tax.

Required:

1. Prepare the adjusting journal entries required on December 31, 2017, based on the preceding additional information. You may need to create new accounts not yet included in the income statement or balance sheet.

2. Redo the preceding statements after taking into account the adjusting journal entries. One way to organize your response is as follows:

		Changes			
Items	Amounts Reported	Plus	Minus	Corrected Amounts	
(List here each item from the two statements)					

3. Recording the adjusting journal entries had the following effects:

   a. *Increase* or *decrease* (select one) net income by $_____

   b. *Increase* or *decrease* (select one) total assets by $_____

4. Write a letter to the company explaining the results of the adjustments and your preliminary analysis.

LO4-3, 4-4, 4-6

S4-7 Aggregating Accounts on an Adjusted Trial Balance to Prepare an Income Statement, Statement of Retained Earnings, and Balance Sheet

Assume you recently were hired for a job in Evansville, Indiana, at the head office of Escalade, Inc.—the company that makes Goalrilla™ and Goaliath® basketball systems, and is the exclusive supplier of Ping Pong® and Stiga® equipment for table tennis. Your first assignment is to review the company's lengthy adjusted trial balance to determine the accounts that can be combined ("aggregated") into single line items that will be reported on the financial statements. By querying the accounting system, you were able to obtain the following alphabetical list of accounts and their adjusted balances (in thousands) for the year ended December 31.

Accounts Payable	$ 2,792	Inventory of Finished Goods	$ 10,263	Prepaid Insurance	$ 108
Accounts Receivable	34,141	Inventory of Goods being Made	4,536	Prepaid Rent	434
Accrued Interest Payable	42	Inventory of Supplies and Materials	5,750	Rent Expense	7,350
Accrued Wages Payable	5,856	Long-Term Bank Loan	14,000	Retained Earnings	27,571
Accrued Warranties Payable	1,324	Long-Term Contract Payable	1,837	Salaries Expense	3,582
Accumulated Depreciation	26,198	Long-Term Note Payable	2,700	Sales Commissions Expense	3,349
Cash	3,370	Manufacturing Equipment	12,962	Sales of Basketball Systems	98,998
Contributed Capital	7,165	Notes Payable (current)	11,390	Sales of Other Products	28,710
Cost of Goods Sold	111,164	Notes Receivable	400	Sales of Ping Pong Tables	27,747
Depreciation Expense	862	Office Building	2,301	Shipping Expenses	1,448
Factory Buildings	7,070	Office Equipment	2,363	Transport Equipment	7,560
Income Tax Expense	5,804	Office Supplies Expense	69	Deferred Revenue	8,144
Income Tax Payable	1,189	Other Accrued Liabilities	1,638	Utilities Expense	2,111
Insurance Expense	2,368	Other Long-Term Assets	28,310	Wages Expense	3,024
Interest Expense	950	Packaging Expenses	1,010	Warranties Expense	1,226
Interest Receivable	415			Warehouse Buildings	3,001

Required:

With the above account names and balances, prepare an adjusted trial balance using a spreadsheet. Also prepare an income statement, a statement of retained earnings, and a balance sheet that import their numbers from the adjusted trial balance or from the other statements where appropriate. If similar accounts can be aggregated into a single line item for each financial statement, use a formula to compute the aggregated amount. To be sure that you understand how to import numbers from other parts of a spreadsheet, you email your friend Owen for advice. His reply is as follows.

Hey, pal. You're bouncing from job to job like one of those ping-pong balls that your company sells. OK, to import a number from another spreadsheet, you first click on the cell where you want the number to appear. For example, if you want to enter the Cash balance in the balance sheet, click on the cell in the balance sheet where the cash number is supposed to appear. Enter the equals sign (=) and then click on the tab that takes you to the worksheet containing the adjusted trial balance. In that worksheet, click on the cell that contains the amount you want to import into the balance sheet and then press Enter. This will create a link from the adjusted trial balance cell to the balance sheet cell. At the end of this message, I've pasted a screen shot showing the formula I would enter on the balance sheet to import the total of three related inventory accounts from the adjusted trial balance. Don't forget to save the file using a name that indicates who you are.

S4-7.xls - Microsoft Excel

Home | Insert | Page Layout | Formulas | Data | Review | View

C7   =SUM('Trial Balance'!C8:C10)

	A	B	C
1		Escalade, Inc.	
2		Balance Sheet	
3		As of December 31 (in thousands)	
4		ASSETS	
5		Cash	$ 3,370
6		Receivables	34,956
7		Inventories	20,549
8		Prepaids	542
9		Total Current Assets	59,417
10		Property, plant, and equipment	35,257
11		less accumulated depreciation	(26,198)
12		Other long-term assets	28,310
13		Total Assets	$ 96,786
14		LIABILITIES	
15		Accounts payable	$ 2,792
16		Notes payable	11,390
17		Income tax payable	1,189
18		Deferred Revenue	8,144
19		Other liabilities	8,860
20		Total Current Liabilities	32,375
21		Long-term debt	18,537
22		Total Liabilities	50,912
23		SHAREHOLDERS' EQUITY	
24		Contributed capital	7,165
25		Retained earnings	38,709
26		Total Shareholders' Equity	45,874
27		Total Liabilities and Shareholders' Equity	$ 96,786
28			

Trial Balance / Income Statement / Statement of

Ready   100%

CONTINUING CASE

CC4-1 Adjusting the Accounting Records

Assume it is now December 31, 2017, and Nicole has just completed her first year of operations at Nicole's Getaway Spa. Looking through her trial balance, she notices that there are some items that have either not been recorded or are no longer up to date.

a. Nicole's Getaway Spa is renting its space at a cost of $600 per month. On September 1, 2017, Nicole paid eight months rent in advance using cash. This prepayment was recorded in the account Prepaid Rent back in September.

b. The building purchased at the beginning of the year for $47,000 cash has estimated depre‐ciation of $2,000 for 2017, but none has been recorded yet.

c. Wages to the support staff at Nicole's Getaway Spa have been paid up to December 26, 2017. The support staff worked both December 27 and 28 and will be paid on January 5, 2018. Wages amount to $1,000 per day.

d. The insurance policy, purchased on June 1 for $3,000 cash, provides coverage for twelve months. The insurance coverage since June has now been used up.

e. The unadjusted amount in the Spa Supplies account was $2,000 at December 31, 2017, for supplies purchased on account. A year‐end count showed $700 of supplies remain on hand.

f. On the last day of December, a customer obtained spa services by using a $90 gift certif‐icate that was purchased earlier in the month. Use of the gift certificate to pay for these services had not yet been recorded.

Required:

1. For each of the items listed above, identify whether an accrual adjustment, a deferral adjustment, or no adjustment is required.

2. For each of the deferral adjustments, prepare the initial journal entry that would have been recorded.

3. Prepare the adjusting journal entries that should be recorded for Nicole's Getaway Spa at December 31, 2017, assuming that the items have not been adjusted prior to December 31, 2017.

THAT WAS
THEN

In the previous chapters, you learned about the accounting system that produces the basic financial statements.

THIS IS
NOW

This chapter explains how internal control works behind the scenes to improve operations and prevent fraud, particularly when it comes to one key asset: cash.

YOUR LEARNING OBJECTIVES

Understand the business

LO5-1 Define fraud and internal control.

LO5-2 Explain common principles and limitations of internal control.

Study the accounting methods

LO5-3 Apply internal control principles to cash receipts and payments.

LO5-4 Perform the key control of reconciling cash to bank statements.

Evaluate the results

LO5-5 Explain the reporting of cash.

Review the chapter

Chapter Summary

Supplemental material

LO5-S1 Describe the operations of petty cash systems.

CHAPTER 5

Fraud, Internal Control, and Cash

©Csondy/Getty Images RF

FOCUS COMPANY:
Koss Corporation

Chapters 1, 2, 3, and 4, explained the key roles that accounting systems and financial statements play when establishing and operating a small business like Pizza Palace. This chapter introduces another key part of an accounting system: internal controls, which are the behind-the-scenes practices that help businesses achieve their objectives.

When operating effectively, internal controls can improve operations, enhance the reporting of financial and non-financial information, and enable compliance with laws and regulations. But when internal controls fail, the results can be disastrous. Just ask the people at Koss Corporation—known for making headphones and earbuds. The company's former vice-president of finance recently admitted she exploited weaknesses in the company's internal controls and stole $31.5 million to pay for extravagant purchases she made with personal credit cards.

This chapter will help you understand why frauds occur and how internal controls can help prevent them. The chapter will also help you learn an internal control practice to use in your personal life every month to protect your own cash. Had it been used properly at Koss, the company could have avoided much of its losses.[1]

Logo courtesy of Koss.

ORGANIZATION OF THE CHAPTER

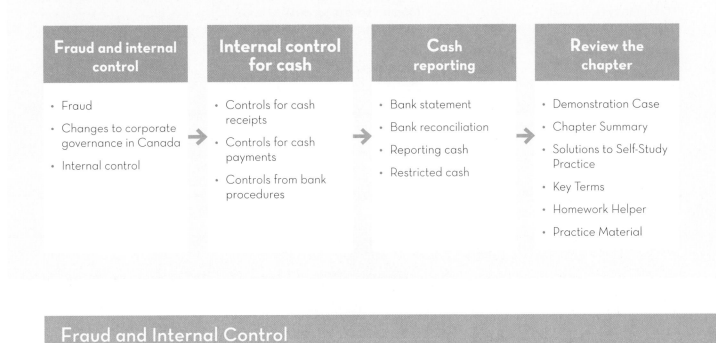

Fraud and internal control	Internal control for cash	Cash reporting	Review the chapter
• Fraud • Changes to corporate governance in Canada • Internal control	• Controls for cash receipts • Controls for cash payments • Controls from bank procedures	• Bank statement • Bank reconciliation • Reporting cash • Restricted cash	• Demonstration Case • Chapter Summary • Solutions to Self-Study Practice • Key Terms • Homework Helper • Practice Material

Fraud and Internal Control

FRAUD

A **fraud** is generally defined as an attempt to deceive others for personal gain. In 2014, Canada's Anti—Fraud Centre recorded 42,200 reported complaints of fraud nationally, with losses totalling nearly $75 million.[2] Employee fraud is often grouped into three categories:

1. *Corruption.* Corruption involves misusing a position of trust for inappropriate personal gain. Current and former members of the Canadian Senate claimed travel and living—allowance expenses from the Senate for which they were not eligible. Nine of these cases were referred for police investigation and some senators were criminally charged.

2. *Asset misappropriation.* Asset misappropriation is, quite simply, theft (embezzlement). Cash is usually the target, but other assets can be misappropriated. A vice—president of product development at Tiffany & Co. admitted to stealing and reselling $1.3 million of jewellery that belonged to her employer. The company discovered the pieces missing when counting its inventory.

3. *Financial statement fraud.* This type of fraud involves misreporting amounts in the financial statements, usually to portray more favourable financial results than actually exist. The most famous cases occurred at Enron (now bankrupt) and WorldCom (now part of Verizon). WorldCom violated GAAP by recording $11 billion of expenses as assets; the result was larger total assets on the balance sheet and more net income on the income statement.

As Exhibit 5.1 shows, financial statement fraud occurs infrequently but causes the greatest losses. In contrast, asset misappropriation is more frequent but tends to involve smaller amounts.

Why would an employee commit fraud? Research has found that three factors exist when fraud occurs. These factors work together, as suggested by the *fraud triangle* shown in Exhibit 5.2 and described below.

EXHIBIT 5.1 | Users and Uses of Accounting Information

Frequency (% of cases)

| Asset Misappropriation | 68% |

| Corruption | 26% |

← Financial Statement Fraud (6%)

Median Loss ($ per case)

| Financial Statement Fraud | $1,000,000 |

| Corruption | $250,000 |

← Asset Misappropriation ($120,000)

Source: Association of Certified Fraud Examiners 2012 *Report to the Nations on Occupational Fraud and Abuse.*

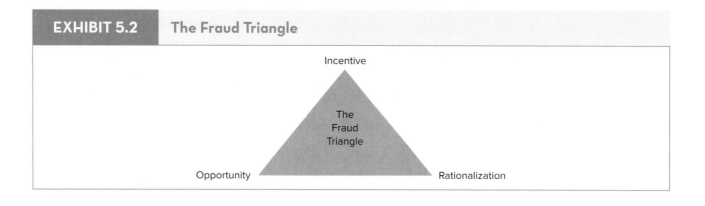

EXHIBIT 5.2 | The Fraud Triangle

Incentive

The Fraud Triangle

Opportunity

Rationalization

Loan covenants: Terms of a loan agreement that, if broken, entitle the lender to renegotiate loan terms or to force repayment.

1. ***Incentive.*** The employee has a reason for committing fraud. Sometimes the reason is personal financial pressure. For example, the VP at Koss stole because her $145,000 salary was not enough to pay the monthly credit card bills that reached as high as $1 million. In other cases, the incentive is to make the business appear successful so as to attract investors, bring in new business partners, or meet loan requirements. Many lending agreements include **loan covenants**, which require the company to achieve financial targets, such as maintaining specific levels of assets or shareholders' equity. If loan covenants are not met, the lender can require the company to pay a higher interest rate, repay its loan balance on demand, or put up extra collateral to secure the loan. To avoid this, dishonest managers may misreport the company's financial status.

2. ***Opportunity.*** The employee has a means of committing fraud. Opportunities to commit fraud usually stem from weak internal controls. That was certainly the case at Koss, where the VP transferred $16 million out of the company without approval or review by the chief financial officer. She also took advantage of deficiencies in the company's petty cash authorizations to pay for $390,000 of her personal purchases. Finally, she covered up these thefts with journal entries that were not properly authorized.

3. ***Rationalization.*** The employee perceives the misdeed as unavoidable or justified. In the Koss case, the defense attorney argued the VP suffered from addiction and mental illness, which led to uncontrollable compulsive behaviour. In many other cases, fraudsters rationalize their actions through a feeling of personal entitlement, which outweighs moral principles such as honesty and concern for others. These employees often feel they are underpaid, so fraud is their way to get even and be paid what they think they deserve.

Livent: The Final Act

The Live Entertainment Corporation of Canada, Inc. also known as Livent, was a theatre production company in Toronto. It was founded in 1990 by Garth Drabinsky and Myron Gottlieb, former Cineplex Odeon Corp. execu-tives, and went public in 1993.

Livent appeared to be a very successful company, winning three Tony Awards, including Best Musical. It opened a refurbished theatre on Broadway in New York City at a cost of $22.5 million (U.S.) and had plans to build a second theatre in Toronto for $30 million.

All was not as it seemed, however. In April 1998, former Hollywood agent and Disney executive Michael Ovitz made a deal to invest $20 million (U.S.) in Livent for control of the company. It was then that the Livent facade started to crumble. Ovitz's management team reported "massive, systematic accounting irregularities that permeated the company." By November, Livent had filed for bankruptcy and civil lawsuits were filed against Drabinsky and Gottlieb, alleging that they overstated earnings and assets, and hid losses to make Livent's financial situation appear better than it was. It is claimed that investors lost approximately $500 million.

After an eleven-month trial, on March 25, 2009, Drabinsky and Gottlieb were convicted of two counts of fraud and one count of uttering forged documents. Drabinsky was sentenced to serve seven years in jail and Gottlieb received a sentence of six years.

Several features of the Livent scandal make it similar to other major financial frauds. These sim-ilarities are consistent with the fraud triangle referred to earlier in this chapter. The incentive in this situation was that Livent had a constant and growing need for additional capital. The opportunity was created from the weaknesses in the control system, which allowed the accountants to develop computer software for senior management to track the real numbers and the manipulated numbers at the same time. The management team was very aggressive and growth-oriented, and felt that their actions were justified, as evidenced by the matter-of-fact manner in which they organized and carried out the fraud.

Fraud affects all sizes and types of companies, but its impact on public companies is a major concern. When investors lose, the economy suffers. To reduce fraud among public companies, the Canadian regulators have introduced significant laws.

CHANGES TO CORPORATE GOVERNANCE IN CANADA

The Canadian financial reporting environment has significantly changed over the past decade, due to the occurrence of several high−profile accounting frauds and scandals that occurred in the late 1990s and early 2000s. Confidence in the stock markets was shaken by frauds involv−ing Enron and WorldCom. Investors, of course, had serious reservations about the reliability of reported financial information and the credibility of external auditors.

In response to these high−profile frauds, the U.S. Congress reacted to the crisis in 2002 by creating the **Sarbanes−Oxley Act (SOX)**. The Act requires top managers of public companies to sign a report certifying their responsibilities for the financial statements, maintain an audited system of internal controls to ensure accuracy in the accounting reports, and main− tain an independent committee to oversee top management and ensure that

Sarbanes-oxley act (SOX): Created by the U.S. Congress after the fall of Enron due to accounting fraud. Includes regulations on many topics, including internal control systems and certification of executives.

they cooperate with auditors. As a result of the Act, corporate executives face severe consequences—twenty years in prison and $5 million in fines—if they are found guilty of committing accounting fraud.

Following closely what the United States did in response to these scandals, the Government of Ontario passed Bill 198, also known as the Budget Measures Act or C–SOX (pronounced see–sox). Bill 198 replicates many of the SOX requirements that resulted in the Canadian Securities Administrators (CSA) introducing a series of new rules that accommodated the unique nature of the Canadian financial market. Similar to the U.S. Act, these rules also require CEO/CFO certification, the adoption of a system of internal controls to ensure the accuracy of the company's financial reporting, and in addition, an expanded role for the audit committee.

Major Canadian public companies are required to have fully independent and financially literate audit committees. There are, however, some differences between C–SOX and SOX. One major difference is the auditor involvement around the internal controls assessment made by management. SOX requires auditors to assess and report on the effectiveness of the internal controls that management has reported on. There is no requirement under C–SOX for the same auditor involvement around the management's report on internal controls.

Also in this time of change, the Canadian Public Accountability Board was established. One of its main objectives is to conduct inspections of audit firms that audit reporting issuers of the provincial and territorial securities commissions. This, in turn, monitors the independence that auditors must have from their clients. The Canadian Securities Administrators also introduced a series of rules that accommodated the uniqueness of the Canadian financial market. All Canadian publicly accountable enterprises must comply with these rules and regulations. Some of the key requirements are summarized in Exhibit 5.3 and are explained below.

EXHIBIT 5.3	Significant Changes Made to the Canadian Financial Reporting Environment

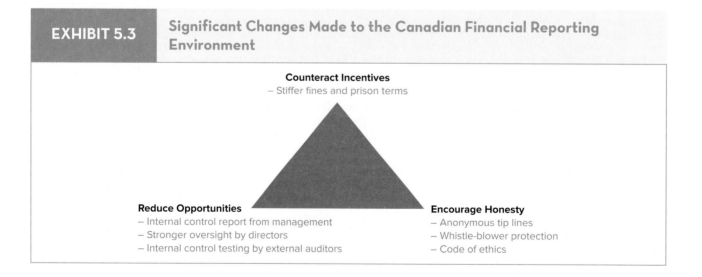

Counteract Incentives
– Stiffer fines and prison terms

Reduce Opportunities
– Internal control report from management
– Stronger oversight by directors
– Internal control testing by external auditors

Encourage Honesty
– Anonymous tip lines
– Whistle-blower protection
– Code of ethics

1. *Counteract incentives.* Those who willfully misrepresent financial results face stiff penalties, including fines of up to $5 million plus repayment of any fraud proceeds. Also, maximum jail sentences have been increased to twenty years, which can quickly add up, because federal sentencing guidelines allow judges to declare consecutive jail terms for each violation. The VP at Koss was charged with six counts of fraud, so she was facing a maximum prison term of 120 years.

2. *Reduce opportunities.* This is the part of the fraud triangle most affected by the new Act. To reduce fraud opportunities and improve companies' internal control over financial reporting, all public companies are required to do the following:

- *Establish an audit committee of independent directors.* This committee strives to ensure the company's accounting, internal control, and audit functions are effective.

- *Evaluate and report on the effectiveness of internal control over financial reporting.* This evaluation must be completed by management and, for large public companies listed on a U.S. stock exchange, by external auditors, as well. An external audit of control effectiveness can be expensive, so it is optional for small public companies. Sadly, Koss executives felt the company's resources "would be better spent on strategic planning" than auditing, so they did not ask external auditors to test and report on their company's internal controls. Had they done so, the massive fraud might have been detected earlier. You will learn more about internal control in the following section.

3. *Encourage honesty.* Admittedly, it's difficult for any law to achieve this, but some parts of the act help honest employees confront those inclined to rationalize and conceal fraud. For example, public companies must have tip lines that allow employees to secretly submit concerns about questionable accounting or auditing practices. The Securities and Exchange Commission in the United States recently paid $14 million to one of these whistleblowers for a tip that led to a fraud discovery. The Ontario Securities Commission has adopted a Whistleblower Program that grants legal protection to whistleblowers to prevent retaliation by those charged with fraud. If you tattle on your boss for submitting a fraudulent expense claim, you can't be fired for it. Finally, companies are required to adopt a code of ethics for their senior financial officers. Google begins its code with "Don't be evil," and then explains what this means in plain English.

HOW'S IT GOING?

Self-Study Practice 5.1

Identify whether each of the following increases (+) or decreases (−) the risk of fraud, arising from incentives (I), opportunities (O), or rationalizing/concealing (R).

Account Title	+/−	I/O/R
1. Enron was notorious for its "rank and yank" practice that involved ranking the financial performance of each business unit and then firing managers in the lowest 20 percent.		
2. Nintendo of America conducts pre-employment screening before hiring anyone.		
3. The H. J. Heinz Company board of directors is one of the strongest boards in North America, according to Institutional Shareholder Services.		

After you have finished, check your answers with the solution placed after the chapter summary.

INTERNAL CONTROL

Objectives

Internal control:
Processes by which a company provides reasonable assurance regarding the reliability of the company's financial reporting, the effectiveness and efficiency of its operations, and its compliance with applicable laws and regulations.

Internal control consists of the actions taken by people at every level of an organization to achieve its objectives:

- *Operations.* Operational objectives focus on completing work efficiently and effectively and protecting assets by reducing the risk of fraud.
- *Reporting.* Reporting objectives include producing reliable and timely accounting information for use by people both inside and outside of the organization.
- *Compliance.* Compliance objectives focus on adhering to laws and regulations.

In your personal life, these actions include basic steps such as locking your door (operations), checking the accuracy of your banking records (reporting), and staying within the speed limit when driving (compliance).

Components

Most organizations use the following control components as a framework when analyzing their internal control systems.

1. *Control environment.* The control environment refers to the attitude that people in the organization hold regarding internal control. It is influenced by the policies that a company's board of directors and senior managers set, their demonstrated commitment to integrity and ethical values, the character of the people they hire, and how they evaluate others. A strong control environment helps employees understand the value of internal controls to their organization's success.
2. *Risk assessment.* Managers should continuously assess the potential for fraud and other risks that could prevent the company from achieving its objectives.
3. *Control activities.* Control activities include various work responsibilities and duties completed by employees to reduce risks to an acceptable level. We discuss these activities in detail in the next section of this chapter.
4. *Information and communication.* An effective internal control system generates and communicates information about activities affecting the organization to support sound decision making.
5. *Monitoring activities.* The internal control system is evaluated often to determine whether it is working as intended. Deficiencies should be communicated to those responsible for taking corrective action, including senior management and/or the board of directors.

As shown in Exhibit 5.4, the control objectives and components apply to all levels of an organization. Although a chief financial officer and a cashier are assigned different responsibilities, their work combines to achieve the same control objectives through the components of control shown below.

Principles of Control Activities

Explain common principles and limitations of internal control.

The control objectives and components outlined in the previous sections are supported by fundamental principles of control. We focus this section on how five key principles, shown in Exhibit 5.5, are used in control activities you are likely to see early in your career. We want you to understand these control

EXHIBIT 5.4

Relationship of Control Objectives and Components to Organizational Levels

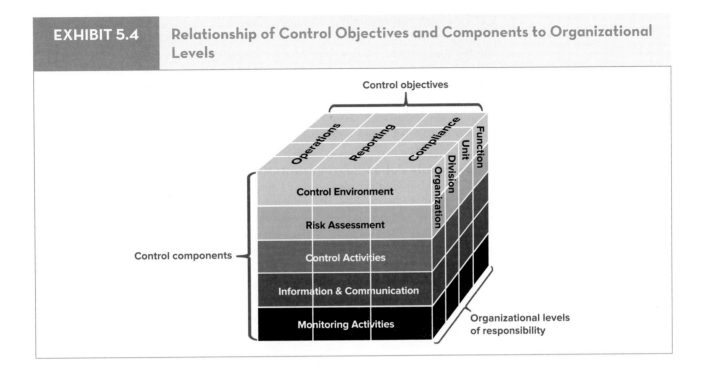

examples so that when you encounter them or other controls on the job, you will appreciate them and ensure others respect them. The principles apply to all areas of business, including human resource management, finance, market—ing, and general business operations, but our focus here is on accounting.

EXHIBIT 5.5   Five Common Principles of Internal Control

Principle	Explanation	Example
① Establish responsibility	Assign each task to only one employee.	Give a separate cash register drawer to each cashier at the beginning of a shift.
② Segregate duties	Do not make one employee responsible for all parts of a process.	Inventory buyers do not also approve payments to suppliers.
③ Restrict access	Do not provide access to assets or information unless it is needed to fulfill assigned responsibilities.	Secure valuable assets such as cash and restrict access to computer systems (via passwords, firewalls).
④ Document procedures	Prepare documents to show activities that have occurred.	Pay suppliers using prenumbered checks and digitally documented electronic fund transfers.
⑤ Independently verify	Check others' work.	Compare the cash balance in the company's accounting records to the cash balance reported by the bank and account for any differences.

1 **Establish responsibility.** Whenever possible, assign each task to only one employee. Doing so will allow you to determine who caused any errors or thefts that occur. That's why retail companies assign a separate cash register drawer to each employee at the beginning of a shift. If two cashiers were to use the same drawer, it would be impossible to know which cashier caused the drawer to be short on cash. With only one person responsible for adding and removing money from the drawer, there's no doubt about who is responsible for a cash shortage.

2 **Segregate duties.** Segregation of duties involves assigning responsibilities so that one employee can't make a mistake or commit a dishonest act without someone else discovering it. That's why inventory buyers do not approve payments to suppliers. Without this control, buyers could create their own fictitious supply company and approve unwarranted payments to the supply company. Segregation of duties is most effective when a company assigns responsibilities for related activities to two or more people and assigns responsibilities for record keeping to people who do not have access to the assets for which they are accounting. One employee should not initiate, approve, record, and have access to the items involved in the same transaction. A lack of segregation of duties at Koss created the opportunity for fraud because the VP had access to both the company's cash and record keeping that allowed her to conceal her theft through fraudulent journal entries.

3 **Restrict access.** Some controls involve rather obvious steps such as physically locking up valuable assets and electronically securing access to other assets and information. Companies restrict access to cheque–signing equipment, require a passcode to open cash registers, and protect computer systems with firewalls. If employees do not need assets or information to fulfill their assigned responsibilities, they are denied access.

4 **Document procedures.** Digital and paper documents are such common features of business that you may not realize they represent an internal control. By documenting each business activity, a company creates a record of whether goods were shipped, customers were billed, cash was received, and so on. Without these documents, a company wouldn't know what transactions have been or need to be entered into the accounting system. To enhance this control, most companies assign sequential numbers to their documents and check that they are used in numerical sequence. This check occurs frequently, sometimes daily, to ensure that every transaction is recorded and that each document number corresponds to one and only one accounting entry.

5 **Independently verify.** A business can perform independent verification in various ways. The most obvious is to hire someone (an auditor) to check that the work done by others within the company is appropriate and supported by documentation. Independent verification also can be made part of a person's job. For example, before a cheque is issued to pay the bill for a truckload of merchandise, a clerk first verifies that the bill relates to goods actually received and is calculated correctly. A third form of independent verification involves comparing the company's accounting information to information kept by an independent third party. For example, the company may compare internal cash records to a statement of account issued by the bank. The next section of this chapter demonstrates this procedure, called a bank reconciliation.

Control Limitations

Internal controls can never completely prevent and detect errors and fraud for two reasons. First, an organization will implement internal controls only to the extent that their benefits exceed their costs. Companies could nearly eliminate shoplifting by body searching every customer who leaves the store, but such an irritating policy would soon drive customers away. The cost of the lost sales would far exceed the benefits of reduced shoplifting. For smaller companies, the cost of hiring additional employees to fully segregate duties exceeds the benefits. In these cases, other controls, such as independent verification by top management, must compensate for the lack of segregation of duties.

A second limitation is that internal controls can fail as a result of human error or fraud. People do make simple mistakes when performing control procedures, especially if they are tired, careless, or confused. Criminally minded employees have been known to override (disarm) internal controls or collude (work together) to get around them. The fraud at Koss involved collusion between the VP and her assistant.

SPOTLIGHT ON Controls

Is That a Control, Too?

The five principles covered in this section do not represent all possible forms of internal control. Many other policies and procedures exist, some of which contribute in subtle ways to internal control. For example, most businesses establish a **mandatory vacation** policy for employees who handle cash because it is difficult for them to cover prior thefts while they are away from the business.

Another simple control is an **anonymous hotline** that allows anyone to tip off independent auditors about suspected fraud. The Association of Certified Fraud Examiners claims that more than 40 percent of workplace fraud cases are identified in this way. A final example of a control that can limit losses from theft is **bonding** employees, which involves obtaining an insurance policy that partially reimburses the organization for losses caused by employee fraud.

Internal Control for Cash

Internal control for cash is important for two main reasons. First, the risk of cash-handling errors is significant because the volume of cash transactions is enormous. Second, because cash is valuable, portable, and "owned" by the person who possesses it, it poses a high risk of theft. To reduce these risks, internal controls are vital.

LEARNING OBJECTIVE 5-3

Apply internal control principles to cash receipts and payments.

CONTROLS FOR CASH RECEIPTS

Businesses can receive cash in two different ways. They can receive it in person at the time of a sale or from a remote source as payment on an account. Most businesses receive cash either physically, in the form of dollars, coins, and cheques payable to the business, or through electronic transactions involving credit cards, debit cards, and electronic funds transfers. Regardless of the way or form in which a business receives cash, the primary internal control goal for cash receipts is to ensure that the business receives the appropriate amount of cash and safely deposits it in the bank.

Cash Received In Person

To properly segregate duties involving cash receipts, specific responsibilities are assigned to employees, as shown in Exhibit 5.6. Cashiers collect cash and issue a receipt at the point of sale. Supervisors take custody of the cash at the end of each cashier's shift and deposit it in the bank. Accounting staff then ensure the receipts from cash sales are properly recorded in the accounting system. Segregating these duties ensures that those who handle the cash (cashiers and supervisors) do not have access to those who record it (the accounting staff). If this segregation of duties did not exist, employees could steal the cash and cover up the theft by changing the accounting records.

| EXHIBIT 5.6 | Internal Controls for Processing Cash Received in Person |

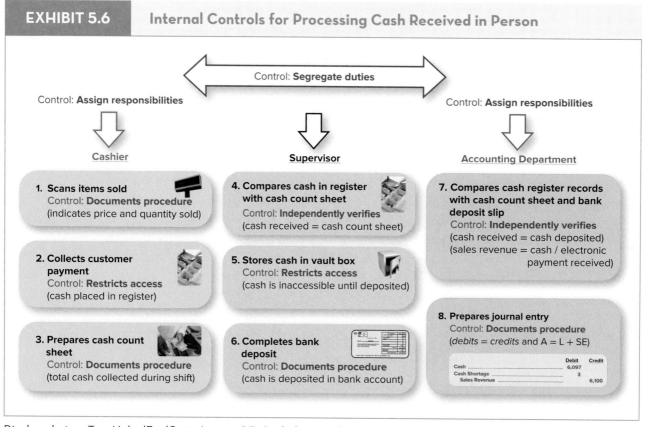

Display photo: ©Tom Hahn/E+/Getty Images RF; Cash drawer photo: ©Tetra Images/Getty Images RF; Safe photo: ©PhotoDisc/Getty Images RF; Cash count photo: ©PhotoLink/Getty Images RF

Exhibit 5.6 shows, in boxes 1–3, that the cashier uses the cash register and its accompanying point–of–sale accounting system to perform three important functions: (1) document the amount charged for each item sold, (2) restrict access to cash, and (3) document the total cash sales. In documenting each item sold (both on screen and on a paper or emailed receipt), the cash register reduces errors by allowing customers to dispute any overcharges. By restricting access, the cash register reduces the risk of cash being lost or stolen. By documenting the total cash sales, the cash register provides an independent record of the amount of cash the cashier should have collected and passed on for deposit at the bank. The cashier uses this information when completing a cash count sheet at the end of each shift. The cash count sheet documents the amount of cash the cashier received and determines any cash shortage or overage that occurred during the shift.

Exhibit 5.6 also shows, in boxes 4–6, that the supervisor performs important controls such as independently verifying each cashier's count sheet, a copy of which is sent to the accounting department. The supervisor is also responsible for placing the cash in a locked vault until it is taken to the bank for deposit. At that time, a deposit slip listing the amounts included in the deposit is prepared and presented to the bank for a teller to verify. After verifying and receiving the funds, the bank teller stamps the deposit slip, which is then forwarded to the company's accounting department.

The accounting department performs two key tasks, shown in boxes 7 and 8 of Exhibit 5.6. It compares the record of cash sales maintained by the cash register with the count sheet prepared by the cashier and the stamped bank deposit slip returned by the bank. This comparison provides indepen–dent verification that the amount of cash rung up at the time of sale was deposited into the bank account.

Based on this information, a journal entry is prepared to record Sales Revenue at the amount rung up at the cash register and Cash at the amount deposited in the bank. Any difference between the two amounts is recorded in a Cash Shortage (or Overage) account, which is reported on the income statement as a miscellaneous expense (or revenue). For example, if cashiers rang up sales totalling $6,100 but had only $6,097 to deposit, the following financial statement effects would be recorded with the journal entry that follows.

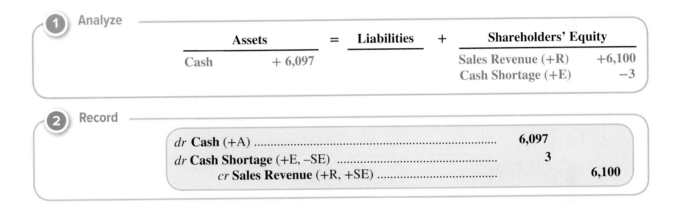

1 Analyze

	Assets	=	Liabilities	+	Shareholders' Equity	
Cash	+ 6,097				Sales Revenue (+R)	+6,100
					Cash Shortage (+E)	−3

2 Record

dr Cash (+A)	6,097	
dr Cash Shortage (+E, –SE)	3	
cr Sales Revenue (+R, +SE)		6,100

Cash Received from a Remote Source

Cash Received by Mail Businesses receive cheques in the mail when customers pay on account. Because this cash is not received in the form of currency and coins, a cashier is not needed to enter these amounts into a cash register. Instead, the clerk who opens the mail performs this function. In fact, to visualize the following description, you need only glance back at Exhibit 5.6 and replace boxes 1–5 with the following duties performed by a mail clerk.

Like a point–of–sale cash register, the mail clerk records all amounts received on a cash receipt list, which here also include the customers' names and the purpose of each payment. The customer typically explains the purpose of the payment using a remittance advice, which the customer includes with the payment. Ideally, someone supervises the clerk who opens the mail to ensure that he or she takes no cash that may have been remit–ted by a customer. As evidence of this supervision, both the mail clerk and the supervisor sign the completed cash receipts list. To ensure that no one diverts the cheques for personal use, the clerk stamps each cheque For

Deposit Only, which instructs the bank to deposit the cheque in the company's account rather than exchange it for cash.

After these steps have been completed, the cash received is separated from the record of cash received. Cheques and money orders are given to the person who prepares the bank deposit, whereas the cash receipts list and remittance advices are sent to the accounting department. As in step 7 of Exhibit 5.6, the accounting department then compares the total on the cash receipts list with the stamped deposit slip received from the bank. This comparison serves to independently verify that all cash received by mail was deposited in the bank. The accounting department then uses the cash receipts list to record the journal entries that debit Cash and credit Accounts Receivable from each customer.

Cash Received Electronically Businesses also receive payments from customers via electronic funds transfer (EFT). An EFT occurs when a customer electronically transfers funds from his or her bank account to the company's bank account. Most businesses encourage customers to use EFTs because they speed up collections. A company may not receive mailed payments for five to seven days, but it receives EFTs almost immediately. And because these payments are deposited directly into the company's bank account, EFTs eliminate the need for some internal controls. To process an EFT, the accounting department merely records journal entries to debit Cash and credit Accounts Receivable from each customer.

HOW'S IT GOING?

Self-Study Practice 5.2

The five internal control principles are represented in the following diagram. (One principle appears twice.) Identify the principle associated with each numbered box.

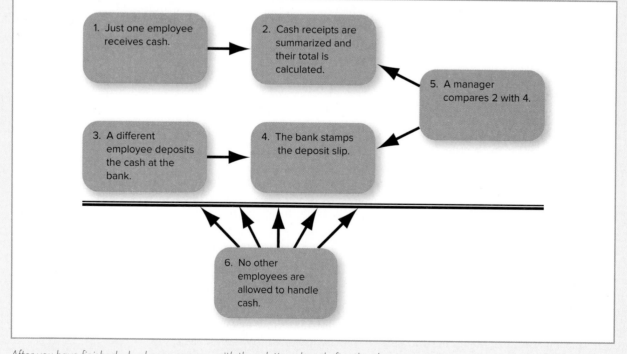

After you have finished, check your answers with the solution placed after the chapter summary.

CONTROLS FOR CASH PAYMENTS

Most cash payments involve (1) writing a cheque or completing an electronic funds transfer (EFT) to a supplier or (2) paying employees via EFT. In the rare case where a company pays for purchases with dollar bills and coins, it uses (3) a petty cash system. The primary goal of internal controls for all cash payments is to ensure that the business pays only for properly authorized transactions.

Cash Paid by Cheque for Purchases on Account

Businesses usually purchase goods and services on account and pay for them later by cheque or EFT. Most companies rely on a voucher system to control these transactions. A **voucher system** is a process for approving and documenting all purchases and payments made on account. A voucher is simply a collection of documents prepared at each step in the system. Exhibit 5.7 lists typical steps involved in obtaining goods or services from a supplier, documents prepared at each step, and examples of the related cash controls and applicable control principles.

Voucher system: A process for approving and documenting all purchases and payments on account. (267)

EXHIBIT 5.7	Steps, Documentation, and Controls in a Voucher System

Steps	Documentation	Sample Control(s)		Control Principle
1. Request that goods or services be ordered.	Purchase requisition	Ensure that the request is made by someone who is approved to order goods or services of the type and amount requested.	**1**	Establish responsibility.
2. Order goods or services.	Purchase order	Place the order only with approved suppliers at approved prices.	**3**	Restrict access.
3. Receive goods or services.	Receiving report	Record goods received.	**4**	Document procedures.
		Notify the accounting department so that the purchase and liability can be recorded.	**2**	Segregate duties.
4. Obtain bill for goods or services.	Supplier invoice	Ensure that the supplier charges only for items received at approved prices.	**5**	Independently verify.
5. Write cheque to pay the bill.	Company cheque	Use prenumbered cheque and account for its sequence. Missing cheques may signal theft.	**4**	Document procedures.
		Make payments only when a purchase is supported by complete voucher documentation.	**5**	Independently verify.
		Mark the voucher "paid" after each cheque is written to avoid duplicating the payment.	**4**	Document procedures.
		Notify the accounting department of the payment so that it can be recorded.	**2**	Segregate duties.

Below we illustrate how Exhibit 5.7 is applied in practice by Wonderful Merchandise and Things (WMT).

1. As Exhibit 5.7 indicates, the purchasing system begins with an authorized employee completing a manual or electronic purchase requisition form. In the purchase requisition example shown, Kelly Watson has requested office supplies. These items are requested regularly, so they are selected from a drop-down list of items that Kelly is authorized to request. The purchase requisition is sequentially numbered so that

Purchase Requisition

Online Data Entry
Wonderful Merchandise & Things (WMT) — Purchase Requisition

| Date Requested: | 8/13/2017 | Requisition Number: | 201408211 |

Item Number	Description	Quantity	Unit Cost	Total Cost
12-307-10	Multipurpose 8.5 x 11 paper	10	$ 2.33	23.30
11-998-12	Boxes of blue gel pens	2	$ 5.60	11.20
			Total:	$ 34.50

Requested by: Select Name: Kelly Watson; Signature: K Watson; Phone: 314-555-1212
Approved by: Select Name: Jordan Sparks; Signature: J W Sparks; Date: 8/14/2017

Purchase Order

Online Data Entry
Wonderful Merchandise & Things (WMT) — Purchase Order

| Date Ordered: | 8/16/2017 | Order Number: | PO-2015-08-998 |

Supplier: Supplier ID #: 2267 Name: Super Supply Co.
Street address: 223 Western Avenue
City, Province, Postal Code: Edmonton AB T5T 0B8

Deliver to: Building: Administration Bldg
Street Address: 89 Simpsons Road
City, Province: Camrose AB T4V 0Z5

Item Number	Description	Quantity	Unit Cost	Total Cost
12-307-10	Multipurpose 8.5 x 11 paper	10	$ 2.33	23.30
11-998-12	Boxes of blue gel pens	2	$ 5.60	11.20
			Total:	$ 34.50

Approved by: Select Name: Pat Rock; Signature: P Rock; Date: 8/16/2017

Receiving Report

Wonderful Merchandise & Things (WMT) — Receiving Report

Received from: Super Supply Co., 223 Western Avenue, Edmonton, AB

Check Carrier: X FEDEX SVC; CANADA POST (USPS); TRUCK; SHIPPER'S TRUCK; AIR EXPRESS; OTHER — August 23, 2017

Our Order Number: PO-2015-08-998; Date Shipped: August 22, 2017; Shipped to Attention of: ; Location: Central Supply; Phone:

QTY	Description	Number of Cartons	Weight Each	Weight Total	Condition	Rec'd by Intls
10	Packages of paper	1	20	20	Good	RT
2	Boxes of pens	1	1	1	Good	RT

Shipment: Complete or Partial — COMPLETE; Total Number of Cartons: 3; Total Weight: 22; Number & Condition of Items: Good 12 Missing 0 Damaged 0

Received by: RT; Date: August 23, 2017; Checked by: FB; Date: 08-23-2017

Invoice

INVOICE #9705 — Super! Supply Co.

31 August 2017 — PAYMENT DUE BY: September 30, 2017

Bill to: Wonderful Merchandise & Things, 89 Simpsons Road, Camrose, AB, T4V 0Z5

Submit payment to: SUPER SUPPLY CO., 223 Western Avenue, Edmonton, AB, T5T 0B8

QUANTITY	DETAILS	UNIT PRICE	LINE TOTAL
10	Paper	2.33	23.30
2	Boxes of pens	5.60	11.20
	Discount		
	Net Total		$34.50
	Tax		

Terms: n/30 — CDN$ TOTAL — $34.50

---

missing requisitions can be easily identified. The purchase requisition must be approved by a supervisor before an order is placed with a supplier. No journal entry is made at this stage because the company has not entered into an exchange, so a transaction has not yet occurred.

2. After the purchase requisition is approved, the company's purchasing agent completes a pre–numbered purchase order. Unlike the purchase requisition, the purchase order identifies the company that will supply the goods. In the example shown here, this company is chosen from a drop–down list of approved suppliers. In this case, the supplier is Super Supply Co. The purchase order also indicates the specific location to which the goods are to be delivered, as well as the approved cost for the items. The purchase order is then sent to the company supplying the goods. A copy of the purchase order is also transmitted to the company's own account–ing department to forewarn them of the pending purchase. However, at this point, the company has only promised to pay for the items on order, but has not received them, so a journal entry is not recorded yet.

3. When the goods are received, a receiving report is prepared. As shown in this example, the receiving report indicates the date, quantity, and condition of items received. A copy of the receiving report is sent to WMT's accounting department to notify them that the goods have been received and are in good order, so that the purchase can be recorded (in step 4).

4. The next piece of documentation in the voucher system will be an invoice sent to WMT from Super Supply Co. The employees at WMT's accounting department will verify that infor–mation on the invoice matches information on both the receiving report and purchase order (often called a three–way match). Specifically, they will check that the quantity of items billed on the invoice matches the quantity WMT received, as indicated on its receiving report, and that the cost per item on the invoice matches the approved cost indicated previously on the purchase order. Assuming the supplier invoice is accurate, the accounting department will prepare a journal entry to record the pur–chase of office supplies on account. Then, the supplier invoice will be included with the other documents in a voucher that will be submitted for payment. An example of the voucher package of documents is shown here, with the supplier invoice on top.

5. The final step in the voucher system, shown in Exhibit 5.7, is for WMT to process a cheque or electronic funds transfer to pay for the items purchased and received. When the cheque or funds transfer is prepared, WMT's accounting department reduces both the Cash account and the Accounts Payable to the supplier (created in step 4). The voucher also is marked Paid so that it cannot be accidentally or intentionally resubmitted for duplicate payment.

Notice in Exhibit 5.7 how employee responsibilities are limited to specific tasks that occur only after obtaining and documenting proper authorization in the prior step. The purchasing, receiving, and bill payment duties are segregated to ensure that the company obtains and pays only for the goods or services that have been properly authorized and received.

Cash Paid to Employees via Electronic Funds Transfer

Most companies pay salaries and wages to employees through EFTs, which are known by employees as direct deposits. The company initiates the EFT when it instructs its bank to transfer the pay due each employee directly from the company's bank account to each employee's bank account. This system is convenient and efficient for the employer, because it eliminates the tasks of physically writing and distributing the cheques, and for the employee, who has access to the funds without having to deposit a cheque. One risk, however, is that the bank might accidentally overpay or underpay an employee by transferring the wrong amount of money out of the company's bank account.

To reduce this risk, many companies use an imprest system for paying employees. An **imprest system** restricts the total amount paid to others by limiting the amount of money available to be transferred. Using an imprest payroll system, the company instructs the bank to transfer the total net pay of all employees for the pay period out of the company's general bank account and into a special payroll account established for that purpose. Then the bank transfers the individual amounts from the payroll account to the employees' chequing accounts. If the transfers occur without error, the special payroll account equals zero after all employees have been paid. If the account is overdrawn or a balance remains, the company knows that an error has occurred.

Imprest system: A process that controls the amount paid to others by limiting the total amount of money available for making payments to others.

Cash Paid to Reimburse Employees (Petty Cash)

To avoid the time and cost of writing cheques for business expenses that are small in amount, most organizations use a petty cash fund. A petty cash fund is a system used to reimburse employees for expenditures they have made on behalf of the organization.

Like the imprest payroll account described above, a petty cash fund acts as a control by establishing a limited amount of cash to use for specific types of expenses. The main difference between the two is that, rather than transferring funds from a general bank account to another special account at the bank, the company removes cash from its general bank account to hold at its premises in a locked cash box. The company's petty cash custo—dian is responsible for operating the petty cash fund. Because this employee

---

SPOTLIGHT ON Controls

Pcards: Efficient Control of Small-Dollar Transactions

When using a petty cash system, administrative costs of processing small-dollar purchases can exceed the cost of the items themselves. To avoid these costs and implement tighter controls over small-dollar purchases, many organizations, such as the Saskatoon Public School Division, have turned to purchasing cards, or Pcards.

Pcards work like a credit card by allowing employees to purchase business-related items using a plastic card issued by a financial institution. The financial institution keeps track of the purchases and sends a monthly bill to the company for all purchases the company's employees make. With all small transactions combined into one monthly bill, the company avoids having to reimburse each employee for each individual transaction. The company can also tighten controls before the purchases occur by setting limits on the amounts and types of allowable purchases.

has access to cash, he or she should be supervised, and the petty cash fund should be subject to surprise audits. At Koss, the fund was operated by the VP's assistant with review only by the VP, who colluded with her assistant to process $390,000 of personal purchases. The fund was not audited. Step–by–step procedures for properly establishing and operating a petty cash fund are explained in Supplement 5A.

CONTROLS FROM BANK PROCEDURES

Banks provide important services to individuals and businesses. They accept deposits, process payments to others, and provide statements that account for these and other transactions. Their services help businesses to control cash in several ways:

1. **Restricting access.** Because banks provide a secure place to deposit cash, businesses need to keep only a limited amount of cash on hand, which reduces the risk that it will be stolen or misplaced.

2. **Documenting procedures.** By processing payments made by cheque or EFT, banks facilitate and document business transactions.

3. **Independently verifying.** Company accountants can use the statement of account prepared by the bank to double–check the accuracy of the cash records. By comparing these two sets of records and investigating any differences, they can verify that the company's records are accurate or identify necessary adjustments.

Cash Reporting

The balance in a company's cash records usually differs from the balance in the bank's records for a variety of valid reasons described in this part of the chapter. To determine the appropriate amount to report on the balance sheet and statement of cash flows, an internal accounting report is prepared to compare the company's cash records with the bank's.

The process of comparing two sets of records is called called *reconciling*, so the report is called a **bank reconciliation**. A bank reconciliation is a key internal control because it provides independent verification of all cash transactions that the bank has processed for the company. This procedure is done monthly, ideally by a company employee whose duties are segregated from recording and handling cash. This segregation of duties did not exist at Koss, which allowed the VP's embezzlement to remain undetected through six years. You should prepare a monthly bank reconciliation in your own life. To prepare a bank reconciliation, you must first understand the items on a bank statement.

Bank reconciliation:
Process of using both the bank statement and the case accounts of a business to determine the appropriate amount of cash in a bank account, after taking into consideration delays or errors in processing cash transactions.

BANK STATEMENT

LEARNING OBJECTIVE **5-4**

Perform the key control of reconciling cash to bank statements.

For each account a business opens, the bank generates a statement that it makes available online. The format varies from bank to bank, but the statement that's shown in Exhibit 5.8 is typical. This statement, prepared by Anysavings Bank for one of the accounts opened by Wonderful Merchandise and Things (WMT), provides an overall summary of the account (labelled ① in Exhibit 5.8). The summary is followed by a list of specific transactions posted to the account (labelled ② through ④) and a running balance in the account (labelled ⑤). In the following section, we explain the transactions that caused changes in the account's balance.

EXHIBIT 5.8   Sample Bank Statement

CHEQUING ACCOUNT STATEMENT

ANYSAVINGS BANK   123 Young Street
Toronto, ON M4B 2C4

ACCOUNT NUMBER:	877-95861
STATEMENT DATE:	June 30, 2017

Wonderful Merchandise and Things (WMT)
1000 Blank Road
Toronto, ON M4B 1B2

Please examine statement and cheques promptly. If no error is reported within ten days, the account will be considered correct. Please report change of address. For questions or problems call Anysavings Bank's Hotline 1-800-555-5100

Your opening balance	$ 7,762.40	
① Total deposits into your account	3,620.00	
Total withdrawals from your account	(744.00)	
Your closing balance on June 30, 2017	**$ 10,638.40**	

Details of your account activity

Date	Description ②	Withdrawals ($) ③	Deposits ($) ④	Balance ($) ⑤
June 1				7,762.40
June 6	Cheque # 100	500.00		7,262.40
June 6	Deposit		3,000.00	10,262.40
June 19	Cheque # 101	55.00		10,207.40
June 23	Cheque # 102	100.00		10,107.40
June 23	Deposit		500.00	10,607.40
June 24	Interest earned		20.00	10,627.40
June 25	NSF Cheque	18.00		10,609.40
June 26	EFT Deposit		100.00	10,709.40
June 30	Cheque # 104	65.00		10,644.40
June 30	Service charges	6.00		10,638.40
Closing Balance				**10,638.40**

Cheques Cleared

After a cheque is written, the payee (to whom the cheque is written) usually presents the cheque to a financial institution for deposit or cash. That financial institution contacts the cheque writer's bank, which in turn withdraws the amount of the cheque from the cheque writer's account and reports it as a deduction on the bank statement. The cheque is then said to have **cleared the bank.**

Cheques are listed on the bank statement in the order in which they clear the bank. Look closely at the Description column in Exhibit 5.8 and you will see that four cheques cleared the bank in June. Because WMT's cheques are used in their prenumbered order, the bank statement provides a hint that cheque 103 did not clear the bank this month. (This fact will be important later when we prepare the bank reconciliation.)

Deposits Made

Deposits are listed on the bank statement in the order in which the bank processes them. If you make a deposit after the bank closes (using an ATM or a night deposit chute), it will not appear on the bank statement until the bank processes it the following business day. Knowing this detail will help you to prepare the bank reconciliation.

Other Transactions

The balance in a bank account can change for a variety of reasons other than cheques and deposits. For example, the account balance increases when the account earns interest and when funds are transferred into the account electronically. The account balance decreases when the bank charges a service fee or transfers funds out of the account electronically.

To understand how these items are reported on a bank statement, it is important to realize that the bank statement is presented from the bank's point of view. The amounts in a company's bank account are liabilities to the bank because they will eventually be used by or returned to

COACH'S TIP

Bank statements often refer to cheques as debits and deposits as credits. This apparent reversal of debit and credit rules occurs because the bank reports from its perspective, not yours. To the bank, your account is a liability that decreases when you take money out (debit the liability) and increases when you deposit money (credit the liability).

the account holder. As with all liabilities, increases are reported as credits on the bank statement. Amounts that are removed from a bank account reduce the bank's liability, so they are reported as debits on the bank statement. Banks typically explain the reasons for these increases (credits) and decreases (debits) with symbols or in a short memo, appropriately called a credit memo or debit memo.

BANK RECONCILIATION

A bank reconciliation involves comparing the company's records to the bank's statement of account to determine whether they agree. The company's records can differ from the bank's records for two basic reasons: (1) the company has recorded some items that the bank doesn't know about at the time it prepares the statement of account or (2) the bank has recorded some items that the company doesn't know about until the bank statement is examined. Exhibit 5.9 lists specific causes of these differences, which we discuss below.

EXHIBIT 5.9	Reconciling Differences

Your Bank May Not Know About	You May Not Know About
1. Errors made by the bank	3. Interest the bank has put into your account
2. Time lags	4. Electronic funds transfers (EFTs)
a. Deposits that you made recently	5. Service charges taken out of your account
b. Cheques that you wrote recently	6. Cheques you deposited but that bounced
	7. Errors made by you

1. **Bank errors.** Bank errors happen in real life, just as they do in Monopoly. If you discover a bank error, you should ask the bank to correct its records, but you should not change yours.

2. **Time lags.** Time lags are common. A time lag occurs, for example, when you make a deposit outside the bank's normal business hours. *You* know you made the deposit, but your bank does not know until it processes the deposit the next day. Time lags involving deposits are called deposits in transit. Another common time lag is an outstanding cheque. This lag occurs when you write a cheque to a company, but your bank doesn't find out about it until that company deposits the cheque in its own bank, which then notifies your bank. As you will see later, although deposits in transit and outstanding cheques may be a significant part of a bank reconciliation, they do not require any further action on your part because you have already recorded them.

3. **Interest deposited.** You may know that your bank pays interest, but you probably do not know exactly how much interest you'll get because it varies depending on the average balance in your account. When you read your bank statement, you'll learn how much interest you need to add to your records.

4. **Electronic funds transfer (EFT).** It doesn't happen every day, but occasionally funds may be transferred into or out of your account without your knowing about it. If you discover these electronic transfers on your bank statement, you will need to adjust your records.

5. **Service charges.** These are the amounts the bank charges for processing your transactions. Rather than send you a bill and wait for you to pay it, the bank just takes the amount directly out of your account. You will need to reduce the Cash balance in your accounting records for these charges.

6. **NSF cheques.** Customers' cheques that you deposited in the bank but were later rejected ("bounced") because of insufficient funds in your customers' own bank accounts are referred to as **NSF (not sufficient funds) cheques.** Because the bank increased your account when the cheque was deposited, the bank decreases your account when it discovers the deposit was not valid. You will need to reduce your Cash balance by the amount of these bounced cheques (and any additional bank charges), and you will have to try to collect these amounts from the cheque writer.

7. **Your errors.** You may have made mistakes or forgotten to record some amounts in your records. If so, you will need to adjust your records for these items.

Bank Reconciliation Illustrated

The ending cash balance shown on the bank statement does not usually agree with the ending cash balance shown by the related Cash account on the books of the company. For example, the Cash account of WMT at the end of June might contain the information shown in the following T–account.

dr +	**Cash (A)**		cr −
June 1 balance	7,762.40		
June 6 deposit	3,000.00	500.00	Cheque 100 written June 4
June 23 deposit	500.00	55.00	Cheque 101 written June 17
June 30 deposit	1,800.00	100.00	Cheque 102 written June 20
		145.00	Cheque 103 written June 24
		56.00	Cheque 104 written June 30
		815.00	Cheque 105 written June 30
Ending balance	11,391.40		

Notice that WMT's ending cash balance of $11,391.40 differs from the $10,638.40 ending cash balance shown on the bank statement in Exhibit 5.8. To determine the appropriate cash balance, these balances need to be reconciled.

Exhibit 5.10 shows the bank reconciliation prepared by WMT for the month of June. The completed reconciliation finds that the up–to–date cash balance is $11,478.40, an amount that differs from both the banks statement and WMT's accounting records. This balance is the amount that WMT will report as Cash on its balance sheet after adjusting its records with the journal entries that we present later.

To prepare the bank reconciliation in Exhibit 5.10, WMT compared the entries in its Cash account to the bank statement (Exhibit 5.8) with the following goals:

1. **Identify the deposits in transit.** A comparison of WMT's recorded deposits with those listed on the bank statement revealed that WMT made a deposit of $1,800 on June 30 that was not listed on the bank statement. More than likely, the bank will process this deposit the next business day (July 1). WMT doesn't have to change its records for this item because it already was recorded in WMT's books on June 30. It is simply a timing difference, so WMT entered the amount on the bank reconciliation as an addition to update the bank's records.

2. **Identify the outstanding cheques.** A comparison of the cheques listed on the bank statement with the company's record of written cheques showed cheques numbered 103 and 105 were still outstanding at the end of June (that is, they had not cleared the bank). They were entered on the reconciliation (in Exhibit 5.10) as a deduction from the bank account because the bank will eventually reduce the account balance when these

EXHIBIT 5.10   Sample Bank Reconciliation

WMT BANK RECONCILIATION
At June 30

UPDATES TO BANK STATEMENT			UPDATES TO COMPANY'S BOOKS		
Ending cash balance per bank statement		$10,638.40	Ending cash balance per books		$11,391.40
Additions			Additions		
(1) Deposit in transit		1,800.00	(3a) Interest received from the bank		20.00
		12,438.40	(3b) EFT received from customer		100.00
					11,511.40
Deductions			Deductions		
(2) Outstanding cheques:			(3c) NSF cheque of R. Smith		18.00
# 103	145.00		(3d) Bank service charges		6.00
# 105	815.00	960.00	(4) Error in recording cheque 104		9.00
Up-to-date ending cash balance		$11,478.40	Up-to-date ending cash balance		$11,478.40

cheques clear the bank. (WMT had already deducted cheques 103 and 105, so WMT does not change its cash records.)

3. **Record other transactions on the bank statement and correct your errors.**

- **Interest received** from the bank, $20—entered on the bank reconciliation in Exhibit 5.9 as an addition to the company's books because it's included in the bank balance but not yet in the company's books.

- **Electronic funds transfer** received from customer, $100—entered on the bank reconciliation as an addition to the book balance because it's included in the bank balance but not yet in the company's books.

- **NSF cheque** rejected, $18—entered on the bank reconciliation as a deduction from the company's books because it was deducted from the bank statement balance but has not yet been deducted from the company's cash records.

- **Service charges,** $6—entered on the bank reconciliation as a deduction from the company's books because it has been deducted from the bank balance but not yet removed from the Cash account in the company's books.

- **Your company errors,** $9—after accounting for the items listed above, WMT found that the reconciliation was out of balance by $9. Upon checking the journal entries made during the month, WMT found that cheque 104 was recorded in the company's accounts as $56 when, in fact, the cheque had been filled out for $65 (in payment of Accounts Payable). As Exhibit 5.8 shows, the bank correctly processed the cheque (on June 30) as $65. To correct its own error, WMT must deduct $9 ($65 − $56) from the company's–books side of the bank reconciliation and record a corresponding journal entry (below).

Now that we know the up–to–date cash balance is $11,478.40, we need to prepare and record journal entries that will bring the Cash account to that balance. Remember that the entries on the Bank Statement side of the bank reconciliation do not need to be adjusted by WMT because they will work out automatically when the bank processes them next month. Only the items on the company's books side of the bank reconciliation need to be recorded in the company's records, using the following journal entries:

Interest Received:

(a) dr Cash (+A)... 20

      cr Interest Revenue (+R, +SE)... 20

      To record interest received from the bank.

EFT Received from Customer:

(b) dr Cash (+A)... 100

      cr Accounts Receivable (−A)... 100

      To record electronic funds transfer received from customer.

Customer's Cheque Rejected as NSF:

(c) dr Accounts Receivable (+A).. 18

      cr Cash (−A)... 18

      To record amount rejected by bank and still owed by customer.

Service Charges:

(d) dr Office Expenses (+E, −SE)...................................... 6

      cr Cash (−A)... 6

      To record service charge deducted by bank.

Company Error (Understated Payment to Supplier):

(e) dr Accounts Payable (−L).. 9

      cr Cash (−A)... 9

      To correct error made in recording a cheque paid to a creditor.

After the reconciling entries are posted, the Cash balance matches the bank reconciliation ($11,478.40).

Cash (A)

Before reconciliation	11,391.40		
(a)	20.00	18.00	(c)
(b)	100.00	6.00	(d)
		9.00	(e)
Up-to-date balance	11,478.40		

HOW'S IT GOING?

Self-Study Practice 5.1

Indicate which of the following items, which were discovered when preparing a bank reconciliation for HBC, will need to be recorded in the Cash account on the company's books.

1. Outstanding cheques
2. Deposits in transit
3. Bank service charges
4. NSF cheques that were deposited

After you have finished, check your answers with the solution placed after the chapter summary.

Granny Does Time

Grandmothers seem so trustworthy. But in one well-known case, a granny stole nearly half a million dollars from the small company where she worked as a bookkeeper. How did she do it? It was easy, because the owner knew little accounting, so he gave her responsibility for all of the company's accounting work but never independently verified her work.

Granny realized this lack of internal control gave her unlimited opportunity, so she wrote cheques to herself and recorded them as inventory purchases. Then, when she did the bank reconciliation, she destroyed the cheques to cover her tracks. Granny kept this fraud going for eight years, but then confessed after becoming overwhelmed with guilt. The next chapter will tell you why no one ever became suspicious about the recorded inventory purchases that didn't actually occur.

REPORTING CASH

LEARNING OBJECTIVE 5-5

Explain the reporting of cash.

Cash: Money or any instrument that banks will accept for deposit and immediate credit to a company's account, such as a cheque, money order, or a bank draft.

Cash equivalents: Short-term, highly liquid investments purchased within three months of maturity.

Cash, as reported on the balance sheet, includes **cash** deposited with banks, petty cash on hand, and cash equivalents. **Cash equivalents** are short–term, highly liquid investments purchased within three months of maturity. They are considered equivalent to cash because they are both readily convertible to known amounts of cash and so near to maturity that there is little risk their value will change. In your personal life, cash equivalents could include term deposits you've purchased within three months of maturity. For companies, cash equivalents include money market funds, government bonds, and other highly liquid investments. Exhibit 5.11 shows how Whole Foods Markets, Inc. reported $351 million in cash and cash equivalents on its balance sheet at September 25, 2016.

EXHIBIT 5.11	Example of Cash Reporting

WHOLE FOODS MARKET, INC.
Balance Sheet (excerpts)
At September 25, 2017

(in millions)

Assets

Current assets	
Cash and Cash Equivalents	$ 351
Short-term Investments	379
Restricted Cash	122
Accounts Receivable	242
Inventory	517
Prepaids and Other Assets	364
Total Current Assets	1,975

RESTRICTED CASH

Restricted cash: Not available for general use but rather restricted for a specific purpose.

Companies are sometimes legally or contractually required to set aside cash for a specific purpose and are not allowed to use it for day–to–day operations. This **restricted cash** must be reported separately on the balance sheet, as shown in Exhibit 5.11. The notes to the financial statements of Whole Foods Market, Inc. explained that a portion of the $122 million of restricted cash was set aside as a rent guarantee for landlords and the rest was put up as collateral for insurance claims with the Workers' Compensation Board. By reporting this restricted cash separately from the $351 million in cash and cash equivalents, Whole Foods more clearly conveys to financial statement users the actual amount of cash available to pay liabilities. The restricted cash in Exhibit 5.11 was classified as a current asset because it was expected to be used up within a year. Restricted cash that is not expected to be used up within a year would be classified as a non–current asset.

SPOTLIGHT ON IFRS and ASPE

Given the nature of the material in this chapter, there are no significant differences between ASPE and IFRS

Supplement 5A

PETTY CASH SYSTEMS

A petty cash system involves three steps: (1) putting money into petty cash to establish a fund, (2) paying money out to reimburse others, and (3) putting money back into petty cash to replenish the fund.

LEARNING OBJECTIVE **5-S1**

Describe the operations of petty cash systems.

1. **Put money into the fund.** The company establishes the fund by writ‑ ing a cheque to the petty cash custodian. The amount of the cheque equals the total estimated payments to be made from the fund over a fairly short period, such as a month or quarter. The custodian cashes the cheque and places the funds in the locked cash box. At this time, the petty cash still belongs to the company, so it represents an asset that must be recorded in the accounting system. Establishing a $100 petty cash fund involves the following accounting equation effects and journal entry.

1 Analyze

	Assets	= Liabilities +	Shareholders' Equity
Cash	– 100		
Petty Cash	+100		

2 Record

	Debit	Credit
Petty Cash	100	
Cash		100

2. **Pay money out of the fund.** The custodian determines when to make payments out of the cash box following policies established by the company's managers. Usually, these policies limit the size and nature of payments to items such as postage, taxi fares, and low–cost sup‑ plies. Petty cash policies require that payments be documented using a petty cash receipt signed by both the custodian and the payee.

No. 22	Petty Cash Receipt	
Paid: $21.00	Date:	7/9/17
To: Yellow Checker Cab (receipt attached)		
For: Taxi Fare to Airport	Account: Travel Expense	
Payment Approved by:	Payment Received by:	
Chris Cattani	John Glovonal	
Custodian		

The custodian attaches any related documents, such as a bill of sale or an invoice, to the petty cash receipt and places it in the cash box.

Documents such as these act as controls to ensure that petty cash payments are made only for approved purchases. Because these receipts involve such small amounts, payments out of petty cash are not recorded in the accounting system until the fund is replenished. To ensure that the fund is operating appropriately, however, most companies require that an internal auditor or man– ager conduct surprise audits of the fund. At any point, the sum of the petty cash receipts and the funds in the cash box should equal the fund's total when it was established.

3. **Replenish the fund.** When the amount of cash in the cash box runs low, the petty cash custodian asks that the fund be replenished. To support this request, the petty cash custodian presents a summary of payments and all supporting petty cash receipts to the accounting department. After reviewing these items, the accounting department marks the receipts Paid and issues a cheque to the custodian for the total amount spent. The amount of the cheque is recorded as a reduction in Cash (with a credit), and the various items that were paid are recorded in their corresponding accounts (with debits). For example, the following accounting equation effects and journal entry would be recorded if the custodian requested a cheque for $67 to replenish the fund after payments were made for supplies ($40), travel ($21), and a dozen Tim Hortons donuts awarded to the employee of the month ($6).

COACH'S TIP

If the total of cash and receipts in the cash box is less (or more) than the fund total, the fund is referred to as being short (or over). Shortages (overages) are recorded in an account called Cash Short (Over) and reported on the income statement as miscellaneous expense (or revenue).

1 Analyze

Assets		= Liabilities +	Stockholders' Equity	
Cash	−67		Travel Expense (+E)	−21
Supplies	+40		Office Expense (+E)	−6

2 Record

	Debit	Credit
Supplies	40	
Travel Expense	21	
Office Expense	6	
Cash		67

Because petty cash transactions are recorded only when the fund is replen– ished, some companies have a policy of replenishing all petty cash funds at the end of each accounting period so that the expenses are recorded in the appropriate period. Other companies do not observe this policy on the grounds that unrecorded petty cash transactions are "immaterial" (too small to affect the decisions of financial statement users).

Review the Chapter

This section provides a chance to solidify your understanding of key points. It's worth your time to work through the following demonstration case, scan the chapter summary, test your understanding of key terms, and then practise, practise, practise.

DEMONSTRATION CASE

Bardash Corporation has just received a statement for its chequing account for the month ended September 30. The bank's statement of account showed the following:

Bank balance, September 1	$1,150
Deposits during September	650
Checks cleared during September	900
Bank service charge	25
Interest earned	5
EFT received from Bardash customer	20
NSF check written by Bardash customer	(15)
Bank balance, September 30	885

The bank had not yet reported a deposit of $50 made on September 29 and a Bardash cheque for $200 had not cleared its account. Bardash's September 30 Cash balance was $759. The company's accountant discovered that one of Bardash's cheques for $19, paid on account to a supplier, had been recorded as $10.

Required:

1. Complete the September bank reconciliation. What adjustments, if any, does Bardash need to make?
2. Why is it important for individuals and businesses to prepare a bank reconciliation each month?

After completing the requirements, check your answers with the following solution.

Suggested Solution

1. Bardash's bank reconciliation

Updates to Bank Statement		Updates to Company's Books	
September 30 cash balance	$ 885	September 30 cash balance	$759
Additions		Additions	
Deposit in transit	50	(a) Interest earned	5
Deductions		(b) EFT from customer	20
Outstanding check	(200)	Deductions	
Up-to-date cash balance	$ 735	(c) Bank service charge	(25)
		(d) NSF check	(15)
		(e) Recording error	(9)
		Up-to-date cash balance	$735

Bardash needs to record the following reconciling entries:

		Debit	Credit
(a)	Cash..	5	
	Interest Revenue.......................................		5
(b)	Cash..	20	
	Accounts Receivable..................................		20
(c)	Office Expenses...	25	
	Cash...		25
(d)	Accounts Receivable..................................	15	
	Cash...		15
(e)	Accounts Payable......................................	9	
	Cash...		9

2. Bank statements, whether personal or business, should be reconciled each month to help ensure that a correct balance is reflected in the depositor's books. Failure to reconcile a bank statement increases the chance that an error will not be discovered and may result in NSF cheques being written. Businesses reconcile their bank statements for an additional reason: the up–to–date balance that is calculated during reconciliation is included in Cash reported on the balance sheet.

CHAPTER SUMMARY

LO5-1 **Define fraud and internal control.**

- Fraud is an attempt to deceive others for personal gain. Employee fraud includes collusion, asset misappropriation, and financial statement fraud.
- Internal control consists of the actions taken by people at every level of an organization to achieve its objectives relating to operations, reporting, and compliance. The components of internal control include the control environment, risk assessment, control activities, information and communication, and monitoring activities.

LO5-2 **Explain common principles and limitations of internal control.**

- Most employees working within a company will encounter five basic principles: (1) establish responsibility for each task; (2) segregate duties so that one employee cannot initiate, record, approve, and handle a single transaction; (3) restrict access to only those employees who have been assigned responsibility; (4) document procedures performed; and (5) independently verify work done by others inside and outside the business.
- Internal controls may be limited by cost, human error, and fraud.

LO5-3 **Apply internal control principles to cash receipts and payments.**

- When applied to cash receipts, internal control principles require that (1) cashiers be held individually responsible for the cash they receive; (2) different individuals be assigned to receive, maintain custody of, and record cash; (3) cash be stored in a locked safe until it has been securely deposited in a bank; (4) cash register receipts, cash count sheets, daily cash summary reports, and bank deposit slips be prepared to document the cash received and deposited; and (5) cash register receipts be matched to cash counts and deposit slips to independently verify that all cash was received and deposited.
- When applied to cash payments, internal control principles require that (1) only certain individuals or departments initiate purchase requests; (2) different individuals be assigned to order, receive, and pay for purchases; (3) access to cheques and valuable property be restricted; (4) purchase requisitions, purchase orders, receiving reports, and pre–numbered cheques be used to document the work done; and (5) each step in the payment process occurs only after the preceding step has been independently verified using the documents listed in (4).

LO5-4 **Perform the key control of reconciling cash to bank statements.**

- The bank reconciliation requires determining two categories of items: (1) those that have been recorded in the company's books but not in the bank's statement of account and (2) those that have been reported in the bank's statement of account but not in the company's books. The second category of items provides the data needed to adjust the Cash account to the balance that will be reported on the balance sheet.

LO5-5 **Explain the reporting of cash.**

- Cash is combined with cash equivalents in current assets. Cash equivalents are highly liquid investments purchased within three months of maturity.
- Restricted cash is reported separately, as a current asset if expected to be used up within one year or, if not, as a non–current asset.

SOLUTIONS TO SELF-STUDY PRACTICE

Solution to SP5.1

1. +I (greater pressure to report stronger financial results)
2. −R (less likely to hire employees that will rationalize/ conceal fraud)
3. −O (strong oversight by directors)

Solution to SP5.2

1. Establish responsibility
2. Document procedures
3. Segregate duties
4. Document procedures
5. Independently verify
6. Restrict access

Solution to SP5.3

Only 3 and 4 need to be recorded.

3. Bank service charges are deducted from the company's bank account, so Cash must be reduced and Office Expense must be recorded.
4. All cheques are recorded on the books as increases in the Cash account when they are deposited. When the bank later rejects an NSF cheque, Cash must be decreased and the related Accounts Receivable increased.

KEY TERMS

Bank Reconciliation	Imprest System	Restricted Cash
Cash	Internal Control	Sarbanes−Oxley Act (SOX)
Cash Equivalents	Loan Covenants	Segregation of Duties
Fraud	NSF (Not Sufficient Funds) Cheques	Voucher System

Complete definitions are also provided in the glossary at the end of this text.

HOMEWORK HELPER

Alternative terms

- Under IFRS, the balance sheet is called the *statement of financial position*, and the income statement is called the *statement of comprehensive income*.
- The up−to−date ending cash balance is also called the *true cash balance* or *correct cash balance*.

Helpful reminders

- When preparing a bank reconciliation, your goals are to determine which transactions the bank has not yet processed and which transactions your company has not yet processed. You will record transactions correctly processed by the bank but not yet processed by your company.
- If you are having trouble reconciling cash balances, you may be overlooking an outstand−ing cheque or deposit. Try counting the number of cheques or deposits processed by the bank and by your company to ensure you have identified them all.

Frequent mistakes

- Do not change your cash records for reconciling items related to updating the bank statement.

PRACTICE MATERIAL

QUESTIONS (⑤ Symbol indicates questions that require analysis from more than one perspective.)

1. What are three categories of employee fraud? Which is most common? Which is associated with the largest losses?

2. What are the three points of the fraud triangle? Is fraud more or less likely to occur if one of these elements is missing?

3. Why would managers misrepresent the financial results of their companies? What are the incentives for doing this?

4. What aspect(s) of the changes made to corporate governance in Canada might counteract the incentive to commit fraud?

5. What aspect(s) of the changes made to corporate governance in Canada might reduce the opportunities for fraud?

6. What aspect(s) of the changes made to corporate governance in Canada might allow honest employees to prevail?

7. What three types of objectives are the focus of internal control?

8. What are the five components of an internal control system?

9. What are five common internal control principles?

10. Why is it a good idea to assign each task to only one employee?

11. Why should responsibilities for certain duties, like cash handling and cash recording, be separated? What types of responsibilities should be separated?

12. What are some of the methods for restricting access?

13. In what ways does documentation act as a control?

14. In what ways can independent verification occur?

15. In what way does a mandatory vacation policy act as a control?

16. What are two limitations of internal control?

17. What is the primary internal control goal for cash receipts?

18. What internal control functions are performed by a cash register and point–of–sale system? How are these functions performed when cash is received by mail? ⑤

19. How is cash received in person independently verified?

20. What is the primary internal control goal for cash payments?

21. What are the purposes of a bank reconciliation? What balances are reconciled?

22. Define cash and cash equivalents and indicate the types of items that should be reported as cash and cash equivalents.

23. Define restricted cash and indicate how it should be reported on the balance sheet.

24. (Supplement 5A) What are the arguments for and against replenishing all petty cash funds at the end of each accounting period? ⑤

MINI-EXERCISES

M5-1 Matching Circumstances to the Fraud Triangle

Match each of the following circumstances to the corresponding element of the fraud triangle by entering the appropriate letter in the space provided.

_____ 1. Employee has significant personal debt.

_____ 2. One employee receives and deposits customer cheques.

_____ 3. CFO feels she is underpaid relative to other financial officers.

_____ 4. Manager approval is not required for expense reports.

A. Incentive
B. Opportunity
C. Rationalize

M5-2 Identifying Internal Controls over Financial Reporting

LO5-2, 5-3

Fox Erasing has a system of internal control with the following procedures. Match the proce—dure to the corresponding internal control principle.

Procedure	Internal Control Principle
_____ 1. The treasurer signs cheques.	A. Establish responsibility
_____ 2. The treasurer is not allowed to make bank deposits.	B. Segregate duties
_____ 3. The company's cheques are prenumbered.	C. Restrict access
_____ 4. Unused cheques are stored in the vault.	D. Document procedures
_____ 5. A bank reconciliation is prepared each month.	E. Independently verify

M5-3 Identifying Internal Control Principles Applied by a Merchandiser

LO5-2, 5-3

Identify the internal control principle represented by each point in the following diagram.

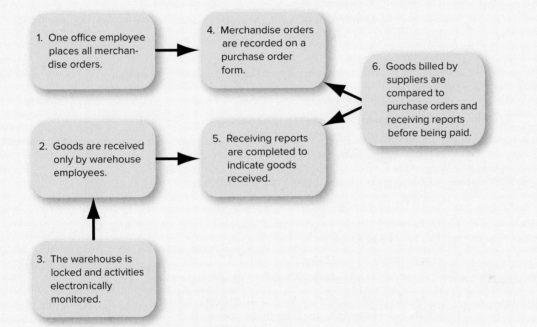

1. One office employee places all merchandise orders.

4. Merchandise orders are recorded on a purchase order form.

6. Goods billed by suppliers are compared to purchase orders and receiving reports before being paid.

2. Goods are received only by warehouse employees.

5. Receiving reports are completed to indicate goods received.

3. The warehouse is locked and activities electronically monitored.

M5-4 Matching Cash Receipt Processes to Internal Control Principles

LO5-3

Match each of the cash receipt activities to the internal control principle to which it best relates. Enter the appropriate letter in the space provided.

_____ 1. A list of cheques received in the mail is prepared.	A. Establish responsibility
_____ 2. Total cash receipts are compared to the amount on the bank deposit slip.	B. Segregate duties
_____ 3. A password is required to open the cash register.	C. Restrict access
_____ 4. Price changes at the checkout require a manager's approval.	D. Document procedures
_____ 5. Cashiers are required to count the cash in their register at the beginning and end of each shift.	E. Independently verify

M5-5 Identifying Internal Control Weaknesses in Descriptions of the Cash Receipts Process

Each situation below describes an internal control weakness in the cash receipts process. Identify which of the five internal control principles is violated, explain the weakness, and then suggest a change that would improve internal control.

a. Cashiers prepare a cash count summary, attach tapes from the cash register showing total receipts, and then prepare a bank deposit slip, which they take to the bank for deposit. After the deposit is made, all documents are forwarded to the accounting department for review and recording.

b. The receptionist opens the mail each morning, sorts it into piles, and then gives cheques received from customers to the mail clerk for delivery to the accounting department, where a cash receipts list is prepared.

c. The accounting department receives cash register totals each day and promptly files them by cash register number. The accounting department also receives cash count sheets from cashiers each day and files them by employee number. The accounting department receives stamped bank deposit slips the morning after the bank deposit is made, prepares the journal entry, and files the deposit slips by date.

d. To avoid boredom, the employee who works the cash register at the movie theatre trades off with either the employee who collects the tickets or an employee who works at the concessions stand.

e. To enhance efficiency, cashiers are assigned the responsibility of authorizing price changes at the cash register.

M5-6 Matching Cash Payment Processes to Internal Control Principles

Match each of the following cash payment activities to the internal control principle to which it best relates. Enter the appropriate letter in the space provided.

_____ 1. The business manager has the only key to the cheque–signing equipment.

_____ 2. The purchasing manager orders all goods and services for the business.

_____ 3. A bank reconciliation is prepared monthly.

_____ 4. Pre–numbered cheques are used for all payments.

_____ 5. The company asks suppliers to deliver their merchan– dise to the warehouse but mail their invoices to the accounting department.

A. Establish responsibility

B. Segregate duties

C. Restrict access

D. Document procedures

E. Independently verify

M5-7 Identifying Internal Control Weaknesses in Descriptions of Cash Payment Processes

Each situation below describes an internal control weakness in the cash payments process. Identify which of the five internal control principles is violated, explain the weakness, and then suggest a change that would improve internal control.

a. The warehouse clerk is responsible for ordering inventory when levels become low and advising the accounting department to issue a payment to the supplier when ordered goods are received.

b. For each purchase, the accountant compares the purchase order (prepared by the pur– chasing manager) to the receiving report (prepared by warehouse employees), and then attaches these documents to the corresponding supplier invoice and files them by supplier name. The accountant then prepares a cheque, which the owner signs and sends to the mail clerk for mailing.

c. The cheque–signing machine is stored with a supply of blank cheques in the lunchroom closet.

d. Purchase orders can be approved by the purchasing manager, accountant, or warehouse supervisor, depending on who is the least busy.

M5-8 Organizing Items on the Bank Reconciliation

LO5-4

Indicate whether the following items would be added (+) or subtracted (−) from the company's books or the bank statement side of a bank reconciliation.

Reconciling Item	Bank Statement	Company's Books
a. Outstanding cheques of $12,000		
b. Bank service charge of $15		
c. Deposit in transit of $2,300		
d. Interest earned of $5		

M5-9 Preparing Journal Entries after a Bank Reconciliation

LO5-4

Using the information in M5−8, prepare any journal entries needed to adjust the company's books.

M5-10 Identifying Outstanding Cheques

LO5-4

Use the following bank statement and T−account to identify outstanding cheques that should be included in the May 31 bank reconciliation.

BANK STATEMENT				
Date	**Cheques**	**Deposits**	**Other**	**Balance**
May 1				$200
4	#2 $ 10	$ 50		240
12	#4 100		NSF Cheque $50	90
28	#5 20			70
30	#6 15	200		255
May 31	#8 55		Service charge 5	195

Cash (A)			
May 1	200		
May 3	50	10	May 3 #2
		70	May 4 #3
		100	May 8 #4
		20	May 11 #5
		15	May 21 #6
May 29	200	25	May 29 #7
May 30	150	55	May 30 #8
May 31	305		

M5-11 Identifying Outstanding Deposits

LO5-4

Use the information in M5−10 to identify outstanding deposits that should be included in the May 31 bank reconciliation.

M5-12 Preparing a Bank Reconciliation

LO5-4

Use the information in M5−10 to prepare the May 31 bank reconciliation.

M5-13 Accounting for Unrecorded Items on Bank Reconciliation

LO5-4

Use your answer to M5−12 to prepare any journal entries needed as a result of the May 31 bank reconciliation.

M5-14 Reporting Cash and Cash Equivalents

LO5-5

Indicate (Yes or No) whether each of the following is properly included in Cash and Cash Equivalents.

_____ 1. $10,000 of government Treasury bills purchased ten days prior to their maturity

_____ 2. $50,000 of government Treasury bills purchased to satisfy a legal requirement to set aside funds for a landfill cleanup

_____ 3. $10,000 of cash owed by customers on sales made within twenty days of year—end

_____ 4. $1,000 of cash in the petty cash custodian's locked cash box

LO5-S1 **M5-15 (Supplement 5A) Accounting for Petty Cash Transactions**

The petty cash custodian reported the following transactions during the month. Prepare the journal entry to record the replenishment of the fund.

A $10 cash payment is made to Starbucks to purchase coffee for a business client, a $40 cash payment is made for supplies purchased from Office Depot, and a $30 cash payment is made to UPS to deliver goods to a customer.

LO5-S1 **M5-16 (Supplement 5A) Accounting for Petty Cash Transactions**

On September 30, Hector's petty cash fund of $100 is replenished. At the time, the cash box contained $18 cash and receipts for taxi fares ($40), delivery charges ($12), and office supplies ($30). Prepare the journal entry to record the replenishment of the fund.

EXERCISES

LO5-1, 5-2 **E5-1 Identifying the Internal Control Principle and Financial Reporting Control Objective**

At most movie theatres, one employee sells tickets and another employee collects them. One night, when you're at the movies, your friend comments that this is a waste of the theatre's money.

Required:

1. Identify the name of the control principle to which this situation relates.
2. Explain to your friend what could happen if the same person did both jobs.

LO5-1, 5-2 **E5-2 Identifying Financial Reporting Control Objectives**

Your student club recently volunteered to go door to door collecting cash donations on behalf of a local charity. The charity's accountant went berserk when you said you wrote receipts only for donors who asked for one.

Required:

Identify the control principle that you violated, and explain why the accountant reacted so strongly. What controls might be appropriate to use in the future?

LO5-3 **E5-3 Identifying Internal Control Principles in Cash Receipt Processes**

Locker Rentals Corp. (LRC) operates locker rental services at several locations throughout the city, including the airport, bus depot, shopping malls, and athletics facilities. Unlike some of the old mechanical lockers that charge a fixed amount per use, LRC's lockers operate electron—ically and are able to charge based on hours of use. The locker system transmits a daily message to LRC's office indicating the number of hours that lockers have been used. The office manager uses this to determine when cash should be picked up at each location. LRC's cash receipts system is described below.

a. Two employees (cash collection clerks) are responsible for collecting cash from the lock—ers. Based on instructions from the office manager, one clerk collects cash from specific locations on the west side of the city and the other collects from specific locations on the east side.

b. When each cash collection clerk returns the cash, a supervisor counts the cash and pre—pares a cash count sheet.

c. The supervisor summarizes the cash count sheets in a pre—numbered daily cash summary and files the pre—numbered cash count sheets by date.

d. The supervisor places the cash in a locked cashbox until it is taken to the bank for deposit.

e. The supervisor, not the cash collection clerks, takes the cash to the bank for deposit.

f. The supervisor prepares a duplicate deposit slip, which the bank stamps after the deposit is made, to indicate the date and amount of the deposit.

g. The supervisor sends the stamped bank deposit slip and daily cash summary to the accountant, who compares them before preparing a journal entry debiting Cash and crediting Locker Rental Revenue.

Required:

1. For each statement (*a*) through (*g*), identify the internal control principle being applied.
2. After several months, LRC's supervisor is arrested for stealing nearly $10,000 from the company. Identify the internal control weakness that allowed this theft to occur.

E5-4 Identifying Internal Control Principles in Cash Payment Processes

LO5-3

Home Repair Corp. (HRC) operates a building maintenance and repair business. The business has three office employees—a sales manager, a materials/crew manager, and an accountant. HRC's cash payments system is described below.

a. After a contract is signed with a customer, the sales manager prepares a pre–numbered purchase requisition form that indicates the materials needed for the work at the repair site.

b. Based on the purchase requisition form, the materials/crew manager prepares and sends a pre–numbered purchase order to suppliers of materials, advising them of the specific materials needed and the repair site to which they should be delivered.

c. The materials/crew manager is the only employee authorized to order goods.

d. Upon receiving a supplier's invoice, the accountant compares it to terms indicated on the purchase order, noting in particular the prices charged and quantity ordered.

e. If these documents are in agreement, the accountant prepares a pre–numbered cheque, stamps the invoice Paid, and prepares a journal entry to record the payment. The journal entry explanation references the sequential number on the purchase order.

f. HRC's owner prepares monthly bank reconciliation and reviews cheques returned with the bank statement to ensure they have been issued to valid suppliers.

Check Figures:
[Part (*b*)]:
Segregate duties/
Document
procedures

Required:

1. For each statement (*a*) through (*f*), identify the internal control principle being applied.
2. Using the above description, prepare a list of steps and documentation similar to Exhibit 5.7. Which document in Exhibit 5.7 is excluded from the above description?
3. After several months, HRC's materials/crew manager is arrested for having $20,000 of materials delivered to his home but charged to the company. Identify the internal control weakness that allowed this theft to occur.

E5-5 Preparing a Bank Reconciliation and Journal Entries, and Reporting Cash

LO5-3

Hills Company's June 30 bank statement and the June ledger account for cash are summarized here:

Check Figures:
Up-to-date cash
balance = $6,370

	Withdrawals	Deposits	Balance
Balance, June 1			$ 7,200
Deposits during June		$18,000	25,200
Cheques cleared during June	$19,100		6,100
Bank service charges	30		6,070
Balance, June 30			6,070

+	Cash (A)		−	
June 1	Balance	6,800		
June	Deposits	19,000	19,400	Cheques written	June
June 30	Balance	6,400		

Required:

1. Prepare a bank reconciliation. A comparison of the cheques written with the cheques that have cleared the bank shows outstanding cheques of $700. Some of the cheques that cleared in June were written prior to June. No deposits in transit were noted in May, but a deposit is in transit at the end of June.

2. Give any journal entries that should be made as a result of the bank reconciliation.

3. What is the balance in the Cash account after the reconciliation entries?

4. In addition to the balance in its bank account, Hills Company also has $300 cash on hand. This amount is recorded in a separate T−account called Cash on Hand. What is the total amount of cash that should be reported on the balance sheet at June 30?

LO5-4   **E5-6 Preparing a Bank Reconciliation and Journal Entries, and Reporting Cash**

The September 30 bank statement for Cadieux Company and the September ledger account for cash are summarized here:

	Withdrawals		Deposits	Balance
Balance, September 1				$2,000
September 7–NSF Cheque	$ 100			1,900
September 11			$3,000	4,900
September 12	#101	800		4,100
September 17	#102	1,700		2,400
September 26	#103	2,300		100
September 29–EFT deposit			150	250
September 30–Service Charge		20		230

BANK (handwritten, left margin)

ADD (handwritten)   SUBTRACT (handwritten)

		+	Cash (A)	−		
Sept 1	Balance	2,000				
Sept 10		3,000	800	Sept 10	#101	
Sept 30		2,500	1,700	Sept 15	#102	
			2,300	Sept 22	#103	
			50	Sept 28	#104	
Sept 30	Balance	2,650				

BOOKS (handwritten, left margin)

No outstanding cheques and no deposits in transit were noted in August. However, there are deposits in transit and cheques outstanding at the end of September. The NSF cheque and electronic funds transfer (EFT) involved transactions with Cadieux Company's customers.

Required:

1. Prepare a bank reconciliation.
2. Give any journal entries that should be made as the result of the bank reconciliation.
3. What should the balance in the Cash account be after recording the journal entries in requirement 2?
4. If the company also has $400 of cash on hand (recorded in a separate account), what total amount of cash should the company report on the September 30 balance sheet?

LO5-5   **E5-7 Reporting Cash, Cash Equivalents, and Restricted Cash**

Assume Expedia, Inc. reported total cash of approximately $1,400 million at September 30, 2017. Of this amount, $20 million was set aside to "fulfill the requirement of an aviation authority of a certain foreign country to protect against the potential non−delivery of travel services in that country" in the short term. Another $410 million was invested in money mar−ket funds and time deposits with original maturities of less than ninety days. The remaining $970 million was held in bank accounts. Expedia also reported $420 million in short−term investments (maturing in 90–360 days), $43 million of deferred revenue, $695 million of accounts receivable, $180 million of prepaid insurance, and $3,660 of goodwill. Show the current assets section of Expedia's balance sheet.

> **TIP:** Some items are not current assets.

E5-8 Preparing a Balance Sheet

LO5-5

Gatti Corporation reported the following balances at June 30.

Accounts Payable	$110	Depreciation Expense	$ 15	Restricted Cash (short–term)	$ 20
Accounts Receivable	70	Dividends	5	Retained Earnings	40
Accumulated Depreciation—Equipment	40	Equipment	300	Salaries and Wages Expense	400
Cash	10	Notes Payable (long–term)	60	Service Revenue	480
Cash Equivalents	15	Notes Payable (short–term)	30	Deferred Revenue	40
Contributed Capital	100	Petty Cash	5	Utilities Expense	60

Required:

1. What amount should be reported as Cash and Cash Equivalents?
2. Prepare a classified balance sheet. Do not show the components that add up to your answer in requirement 1 but rather show only the line Cash and Cash Equivalents.

E5-9 (Supplement 5A) Recording Petty Cash Transactions

LO5S-1

Sunshine Health established a $100 petty cash fund on January 1. From January 2 through 10, payments were made from the fund, as listed below. On January 12, the fund had only $10 remaining; a cheque was written to replenish the fund.

- January 2—Paid cash for deliveries to customers—$23
- January 7—Paid cash for taxi fare incurred by office manager—$50
- January 10—Paid cash for pens and other office supplies—$17

Required:

1. Prepare the journal entry, if any, required on January 1.
2. Prepare the journal entries, if any, required on January 2 through 10.
3. Prepare the journal entries, if any, required on January 12.

E5-10 (Supplement 5A) Recording Petty Cash Transactions

LO5S-1

Mountain Air Company established a $200 petty cash fund on January 1. From January 2 through 15, payments were made from the fund, as listed below. On January 17, the fund was replenished with a cheque for $158.

- January 3—Paid cash for deliveries to customers—$43
- January 8—Paid cash to restaurant for catering office lunch—$83
- January 15—Paid cash for supplies—$32

Required:

1. Prepare the journal entry, if any, required on January 1.
2. Prepare the journal entries, if any, required on January 2 through 15.
3. Prepare the journal entries, if any, required on January 17.

COACHED PROBLEMS

CP5-1 Evaluating Internal Control Strengths and Weaknesses in Cash Receipts and Disbursements

LO5-3

The following procedures are used by Richardson Light Works.

a. When customers pay cash for lighting products, the cash is placed in a cash register and a receipt is issued to the customer.

b. At the end of each day, the cash is counted by the cashier and a cash count sheet is prepared.

c. The manager checks the accuracy of the cash count sheet before taking the cash to the bank for deposit.

d. The journal entry to record cash sales is prepared using the cash count sheets.

e. Cheques are written to suppliers immediately after supplier invoices are received.

f. Receiving reports are prepared to indicate the quantity and condition of goods received from suppliers, based on inspections made by warehouse personnel.

Required:

1. Indicate whether each procedure represents a strength or weakness. Explain your reasons.

2. For each weakness, describe a change in procedures that would address the weakness.

LO5-4, 5-5   **CP5-2 Identifying Outstanding Cheques and Deposits in Transit, and Preparing a Bank Reconciliation and Journal Entries**

The April 30 bank statement for KMaxx Company and the April ledger account for cash are summarized here:

Date	Cheques		Deposits	Other		Balance
Balance, April 1						$6,000
April 5	#101	$ 700				5,300
April 9			$2,500			7,800
April 12	#102	200				7,600
April 19	#103	500				7,100
April 22	#104	1,000				6,100
April 27				EFT Payment	$200	5,900
April 29				NSF cheque	100	5,800
April 30				Service charge	25	5,775

		+	Cash (A)	−		
April 1	Balance	6,000				
April 8		2,500	700	April 2	#101	
April 28		500	200	April 10	#102	
			500	April 15	#103	
			1,100	April 20	#104	
			300	April 29	#105	
April 30	Balance	6,200				

No outstanding cheques and no deposits in transit were noted in March. However, there are deposits in transit and cheques outstanding at the end of April. The electronic funds transfer (EFT) involved an automatic monthly payment to one of KMaxx's creditors. Cheque #104 was written for $1,100. The NSF cheque had been received from a customer.

Required:

1. Prepare a bank reconciliation for April.

     TIP: Put a check mark beside each item that appears on both the bank statement and what's already been recorded in the accounting records (shown in the T−account). Items left unchecked will be used in the bank reconciliation.

2. Give any journal entries that should be made as a result of the bank reconciliation.

     TIP: Remember to make entries only for items that affect the company's books, not the bank.

3. What should the balance in the Cash account be after recording the journal entries in requirement 2?
4. If the company also has $1,000 of cash on hand (recorded in a separate account), what total amount should the company report as Cash and Cash Equivalents on the April 30 balance sheet?

CP5-3 Identifying Outstanding Cheques and Deposits in Transit and Preparing a Bank Reconciliation and Journal Entries

LO5-4, 5-5

The August bank statement and cash T–account for Martha Company follow:

Date	Withdrawals	Deposits	Balance
Aug. 1			$17,470
2–Cheque	$300		17,170
3		$12,000	29,170
4–Cheque	400		28,770
5–Cheque	250		28,520
9–Cheque	890		27,630
10–Cheque	310		27,320
15		4,000	31,320
21–Cheque	400		30,920
24–Cheque	21,000		9,920
25		7,000	16,920
30–Cheque	800		16,120
30–Interest earned		20	16,140
31–Service charge	10		16,130

+		Cash (A)	–	
Aug. 1	Balance	17,470	Cheques written	
Deposits				
Aug. 2		12,000	300	Aug. 1
12		4,000	400	2
24		7,000	250	3
31		5,000	310	4
			890	5
			290	15
			550	17
			800	18
			400	19
			21,000	23
Aug. 31	Balance	20,280		

No deposits were in transit and no cheques were outstanding at the end of July.

Required:

1. Identify and list the deposits in transit at the end of August.
   TIP: Put a check mark beside each item that appears on both the bank statement and what's already been recorded in the accounting records (shown in the T–account).
2. Identify and list the outstanding cheques at the end of August.
3. Prepare a bank reconciliation for August.
   TIP: Any items in the accounting records without check marks should appear on the bank statement side of the bank reconciliation. Any items in the bank statement without check marks should appear on the company's books side of the bank reconciliation.
   TIP: Up–to–date cash balance equals $20,290.

4. Give any journal entries that the company should make as a result of the bank reconciliation. Why are they necessary?

5. After the reconciliation journal entries are posted, what balance will be reflected in the Cash account in the ledger?

6. If the company also has $100 on hand, which is recorded in a different account called Cash on Hand, what total amount of Cash and Cash Equivalents should be reported on the August 31 balance sheet?

LO5-5, 5S-1 **CP5-4 (Supplement 5A) Reporting Petty Cash Transactions**

Superior Cabinets maintains a petty cash fund for minor business expenditures. The petty cash custodian, Mo Smith, describes the events that occurred during the last two months:

1. I established the fund by cashing a Superior Cabinets' cheque for $300, made payable to me.

2. Liz Clay provided a receipt for $50 for various supplies. I paid $50 cash to her.

3. James Flyer provided a $70 taxi receipt, so I paid $70 cash to him.

4. Ricky Ricota claimed to do photocopying for Superior Cabinets at The UPS Store for $97 but had misplaced the receipt. I took him at his word and paid $97 cash to him.

5. On the last day of the month, I prepared a summary of expenditures and requested the fund be replenished. I received and cashed a Superior Cabinets cheque for $217, placing the cash into the locked cash box.

6. James Flyer provided receipts for taxi costs ($75), so I paid $75 cash to him.

7. Woo Riun provided a $147 receipt from a local delivery company for an expedited delivery to a customer. I paid her $147 cash.

8. Ricky Ricota claimed to have purchased $35 of envelopes, but again he had misplaced the receipt. He showed me a big stack of envelopes, so I paid him $35 cash.

9. After requesting that the fund be replenished, I received and cashed a Superior Cabinets check for $257, placing the cash into the locked cash box.

10. After suggesting that the petty cash fund be increased, I received and cashed a Superior Cabinets cheque for $100, which I placed in the locked cash box.

Required:

1. Prepare journal entries where required.

   TIP: Remember that petty cash journal entries are recorded only when the fund is established and reimbursed, not when each payment is made.

2. If Superior Cabinets has $1,000 cash in the bank, $500 of government Treasury bills purchased last month with a six-week maturity, and $750 of cash set aside for legal reasons, how much will the company report on the balance sheet as Cash and Cash Equivalents?

   TIP: Don't forget to include the amount in the Petty Cash fund.

GROUP A PROBLEMS

LO5-3 **PA5-1 Evaluating Internal Control Strengths and Weaknesses in Cash Receipts and Disbursements**

e**X**cel

The following procedures are used by Tico Taco Shop.

a. Customers pay cash for all food orders. Cash is placed in a cash register and a receipt is issued when requested by the customer.

b. At the end of each day, the cashier counts the cash, prepares a cash count sheet, and has the manager review and sign the cash count sheet.

c. At three times during the day, excess cash is removed from the cash register and placed in a vault until it is taken for night deposit at the local bank.

d. Orders for drink cups, straws, condiments, and other supplies are written on pre−numbered purchase order forms and are approved by the manager before being sent to an authorized supplier.

e. When supplies are received, they are stacked just inside the back door to the kitchen, which is left unlocked because part−time employees frequently arrive and leave at various times during the day.

Required:

1. Indicate whether each procedure represents a strength or weakness. Explain your reasons.

2. For each weakness, describe a change in procedures that would address the weakness.

PA5-2 Preparing a Bank Reconciliation and Journal Entries, and Reporting Cash

LO5-4, 5-5

Check Figures:
Up-to-date cash
balance = $17,180

The bookkeeper at Martin Company has asked you to prepare a bank reconciliation as of May 31. The bank statement for May 1 and the May T−account for cash showed the transactions listed below.

Martin Company's bank reconciliation at the end of April showed a cash balance of $18,800. No deposits were in transit at the end of April, but a deposit was in transit at the end of May.

		Withdrawals	Deposits	Balance
Balance, May 1				$18,800
May 2			$ 8,000	26,800
May 5	#301	$11,000		15,800
May 7	#302	6,000		9,800
May 8			10,000	19,800
May 14	#303	500		19,300
May 17–Interest Earned			120	19,420
May 22–NSF cheque		280		19,140
May 27	#304	4,600		14,540
May 31–Service charges		60		14,480
Balance, May 31				14,480

+		Cash (A)	−		
May 1	Balance	18,800	11,000	May 2	#301
May 1		8,000	6,000	May 4	#302
May 7		10,000	500	May 11	#303
May 29		4,000	4,600	May 29	#304
			1,300	May 29	#305
May 31	Balance	17,400			

Required:

1. Prepare a bank reconciliation for May.

2. Prepare any journal entries required as a result of the bank reconciliation. Why are they necessary?

3. After the reconciliation journal entries are posted, what balance will be reflected in the Cash account in the ledger?

4. If the company also has $50 on hand, which is recorded in a different account called Cash on Hand, what total amount of Cash and Cash Equivalents should be reported on the balance sheet at the end of May?

PA5-3 Identifying Outstanding Cheques and Deposits in Transit and Preparing a Bank Reconciliation and Journal Entries

eXcel

The December bank statement and cash T—account for Stewart Company follow:

Date	Withdrawals	Deposits	Balance
Dec. 1			$48,000
2–Cheque	$ 500		47,500
4–Cheque	7,000		40,500
6–Cheque	120		40,380
11–Cheque	550	$28,000	67,830
13–Cheque	1,900		65,930
17–Cheque	12,000		53,930
23–Cheque	80	36,000	89,870
26–Cheque	900		88,970
28–Cheque	2,200		86,770
30–Cheque	17,000	19,000	88,770
30–NSF*	300		88,470
31–Cheque	1,650		86,820
31–Interest earned		50	86,870
31–Service charge	150		86,720

*NSF cheque from J. Left, a customer

	+	Cash (A)	–	
Dec. 1	Balance	48,000	Cheques written during December:	
Deposits				
Dec. 11		28,000	500	60
23		36,000	7,000	900
30		19,000	120	150
31		13,000	550	17,000
			1,900	3,500
			12,000	1,650
			2,200	
Dec. 31	Balance	96,470		

There were no deposits in transit or outstanding cheques at November 30.

Required:

1. Identify and list the deposits in transit at the end of December.
2. Identify and list the outstanding cheques at the end of December.
3. Prepare a bank reconciliation for December.
4. Give any journal entries that the company should make as a result of the bank reconciliation. Why are they necessary?
5. After the reconciliation journal entries are posted, what balance will be reflected in the Cash account in the ledger?
6. If the company also has $300 on hand, which is recorded in a different account called *Cash on Hand*, what total amount of Cash and Cash Equivalents should be reported on the December 31 balance sheet?

PA5-4 (Supplement 5A) Reporting Petty Cash Transactions

Harristown Hockey Club (HHC) maintains a petty cash fund for minor club expenditures. The petty cash custodian, Wayne Crosby, describes the events that occurred during the last two months:

a. I established the fund by cashing a cheque from HHC for $250, made payable to me.

b. Tom Canuck provided a $70 receipt for repairs to the club's computer, so I paid $70 cash to him.

c. Kim Harra provided a receipt for $50 for various supplies she planned to use to decorate the arena later this year. I paid $50 cash to her.

d. Trainer Jim bought some equipment that the club intends to use for the next few years. He gave me the receipt and I paid him $80.

e. On the last day of the month, I prepared a summary of expenditures and requested the fund be replenished. I received and cashed a cheque from HHC for $200, placing the cash in a locked cash box.

f. Wendy Wignes provided receipts for supplies purchased for the club's office for use next month. I paid $125 cash to her.

g. Destiny Hook provided a phone bill showing she had paid $30 for telephone calls made to contact referees for the annual tournament. I paid her $30 cash.

h. Gutty McTavish submitted a receipt for $35 for a haircut he received. I did not pay him.

i. On the last day of the month, I received and cashed a cheque from HHC for $155, placing the cash in the locked cash box.

Required:

1. Prepare journal entries where required.
2. If HHC has $1,000 cash, $500 of government Treasury bills purchased four months ago, and $750 of cash set aside for its workers' compensation insurance, how much will the company report on the balance sheet as Cash and Cash Equivalents?

GROUP B PROBLEMS

PB5-1 Evaluating Internal Control Strengths and Weaknesses in Cash Receipts and Disbursements

LO5-3

The following procedures are used by Principal Wholesale Incorporated:

a. All sales are made on account, with each sale being indicated on a sequentially numbered sales invoice.

b. Customer payments are received in the mail by the office receptionist, who sends the cheques to a cashier for deposit and the remittance advices to the accounting department for recording against the customer's account balance.

c. The office receptionist is assigned the job of handling all customer complaints.

d. When a customer has a legitimate complaint about goods sold to the customer on account, the receptionist will phone the accounting department to request that the customer's account be credited for the sales allowance.

e. The company's inventory is stored in a locked warehouse that is monitored by surveillance cameras.

f. Payments to the company's suppliers are made only after the supplier's invoice is received and compared to the receiving report.

Required:

1. Indicate whether each procedure represents a strength or weakness. Explain your reasons.
2. For each weakness, describe a change in procedures that would address the weakness.

PB5-2 Preparing a Bank Reconciliation and Journal Entries, and Reporting Cash

The bookkeeper at Tony Company has asked you to prepare a bank reconciliation as of February 28. The February 28 bank statement and the February T–account for cash showed the following (summarized):

		Withdrawals		Deposits	Balance
Balance, February 1					$49,400
February 2	#101	$15,000			34,400
February 4				$7,000	41,400
February 5–NSF Cheque		320			41,080
February 9	#102	11,000			30,080
February 12	#103	7,500			22,580
February 14				9,500	32,080
February 19	#104	9,000			23,080
February 23				14,150	37,230
February 26	#105	6,700			30,530
February 27–Interest earned				150	30,680
February 28–Service charges		40			30,640

		+	Cash (A)	–		
Feb 1	Balance	49,400				
Feb 2		7,000	15,000	Feb 1	#101	
Feb 13		9,500	11,000	Feb 7	#102	
Feb 21		14,150	7,500	Feb 11	#103	
Feb 28		7,800	9,000	Feb 17	#104	
			6,700	Feb 25	#105	
			1,200	Feb 29	#106	
Feb 28	Balance	37,450				

Tony Company's bank reconciliation at the end of January showed no outstanding cheques. No deposits were in transit at the end of January, but a deposit was in transit at the end of February.

Required:

1. Prepare a bank reconciliation for February.
2. Prepare any journal entries required as a result of the bank reconciliation. Why are they necessary?
3. After the reconciliation journal entries are posted, what balance will be reflected in the Cash account in the ledger?
4. If the company also has $50 on hand, which is recorded in a different account called *Cash on Hand*, what total amount of Cash and Cash Equivalents should be reported on the balance sheet at the end of February?

PB5-3 Identifying Outstanding Cheques and Deposits in Transit and Preparing a Bank Reconciliation and Journal Entries

Check Figures:
Total deposits in transit at Sept. 30: $21,000

The September bank statement and cash T–account for Terrick Company follow:

Date	Withdrawals	Deposits	Balance
Sept. 1			$ 75,900
2–Cheque	$620		75,280
4–Cheque	2,000		73,280
6–Cheque	1,500		71,780
11–Cheque	300	$14,000	85,480
13–Cheque	650		84,830
17–Cheque	10,000		74,830
23–Cheque	90	27,000	101,740
26–Cheque	700		101,040
28–Cheque	8,000		93,040
29–Cheque	730	17,000	109,310
29–NSF cheque*	500		108,810
30–Cheque	400		108,410
30–Interest earned		60	108,470
30–Service charges	40		108,430

*NSF cheque from B. Frank, a customer

	+		Cash (A)		–
Sept. 1	Balance	75,900	Cheques written during September:		
Deposits			620		8,000
Sept. 11		14,000	2,000		730
23		27,000	1,500		400
29		17,000	300		500
30		21,000	650		6,000
			10,000		90
			700		
Sept. 30	Balance	123,410			

There were no deposits in transit or outstanding cheques at August 31.

Required:

1. Identify and list the deposits in transit at the end of September.
2. Identify and list the outstanding cheques at the end of September.
3. Prepare a bank reconciliation for September.
4. Give any journal entries that the company should make as a result of the bank reconcilia–tion. Why are they necessary?
5. After the reconciliation journal entries are posted, what balance will be reflected in the Cash account in the ledger?
6. If the company also has $200 on hand, which is recorded in a different account called *Cash on Hand*, what total amount of Cash and Cash Equivalents should be reported on the September 30 balance sheet?

PB5-4 (Supplement 5A) Reporting Petty Cash Transactions

Service World maintains a petty cash fund. The fund custodian encountered the following events.

a. The fund was established when a cheque for $300 was cashed and deposited in a locked cash box. An employee submitted a receipt for a customer delivery costing $20 and was reimbursed in full from petty cash.

b. An employee submitted a receipt for a customer delivery costing $20 and was reimbursed in full from petty cash.

Fraud, Internal Control, and Cash   CHAPTER 5   275

c. Another employee submitted a receipt for $60 for locksmith repairs to the office door and was reimbursed in full from petty cash.

d. An employee submitted a receipt for newspaper advertising that cost the company $50. She was given $50 from the petty cash box.

e. The petty cash custodian received and cashed a cheque that fully replenished the petty cash fund.

f. An employee submitted a receipt for $35 for supplies and was reimbursed in full from petty cash.

g. An employee submitted a receipt for $65 for filling up his personal vehicle. He was not reimbursed because it would violate company policy.

h. At the end of the month, a cheque was given to the petty cash custodian that would not only replenish the petty cash fund but also increase the total fund to $400.

Required:

1. Prepare any required journal entries.
2. If Service World has $1,000 cash, $500 of government Treasury bills purchased last month with a six–week maturity, and $750 of cash set aside for legal reasons, how much will the company report on the balance sheet as Cash and Cash Equivalents?

COMPREHENSIVE PROBLEM

LO2-2, 2-4, 2-5, 3-3, 3-5, 4-2, 4-3, 4-4, 5-4, 5-5

LEVEL UP

C5-1 Recording Transactions and Adjustments, Reconciling Items, and Preparing Financial Statements

On January 1, Pulse Recording Studio (PRS) had the following account balances.

Accounts Receivable	$ 7,000	Equipment	$ 30,000
Accounts Payable	8,500	Notes Payable (long-term)	12,000
Accumulated Depreciation—Equipment	6,000	Prepaid Rent	3,000
Cash	3,800	Retained Earnings	5,300
Cash Equivalents	1,500	Supplies	500
Contributed Capital	10,000	Deferred Revenue	4,000

The following transactions occurred during January.

a. Received $2,500 cash on January 1 from customers on account for recording services completed in December.

b. Wrote cheques on January 2 totaling $4,000 for amounts owed on account at the end of December.

c. Purchased and received supplies on account on January 3, at a total cost of $200.

d. Completed $4,000 of recording sessions on January 4 that customers had paid for in advance in December.

e. Received $5,000 cash on January 5 from customers for recording sessions started and completed in January.

f. Wrote a cheque on January 6 for $4,000 for an amount owed on account.

g. Converted $1,000 of cash equivalents into cash on January 7.

h. On January 15, completed EFTs for $1,500 for employees' salaries and wages for the first half of January.

i. Received $3,000 cash on January 31 from customers for recording sessions to start in February.

Required:

1. Prepare journal entries for the January transactions.
2. Enter the January 1 balances into T–accounts, post the journal entries from requirement 1; calculate January 31 balances.

3. Use the January 31 balance in Cash from requirement 2 and the following information to prepare a bank reconciliation. PRS's bank reported a January 31 balance of $6,300.

10.	The bank deducted $500 for an NSF cheque from a customer deposited on January 5.
11.	The cheque written January 6 has not cleared the bank, but the January 2 payment has cleared.
12.	The cash received and deposited on January 31 was not processed by the bank until February 1.
13.	The bank added $5 cash to the account for interest earned in January.
14.	The bank deducted $5 for service charges.

4. Prepare journal entries for items (10) through (14) from the bank reconciliation, if applicable, and post them to the T–accounts. If a journal entry is not required for one or more of the reconciling items, indicate "no journal entry required."

5. Prepare adjusting journal entries on January 31, using the following information.

15.	Depreciation for the month is $200.
16.	Salaries and wages totalling $1,500 have not yet been recorded for January 16–31.
17.	Prepaid Rent will be fully used up by March 31.
18.	Supplies on hand at January 31 were $500.
19.	Received $600 invoice for January electricity charged on account to be paid in February but is not yet recorded.
20.	Interest on the promissory note of $60 for January has not yet been recorded or paid.
21.	Income tax of $1,000 on January income has not yet been recorded or paid.

6. Post the adjusting journal entries from requirement 5 to the T–accounts and prepare an adjusted trial balance.

7. Prepare an income statement for January and a classified balance sheet at January 31. Report PRS's cash and cash equivalents as a single line on the balance sheet.

8. Calculate the current ratio at January 31 and indicate whether PRS has met its loan covenant that requires a minimum current ratio of 1.2.

9. Calculate the net profit margin and indicate whether PRS has achieved its objective of 10 percent.

SKILLS DEVELOPMENT CASES

S5-1 Finding Financial Information

LO5-2, 5-5

Refer to the summarized financial statements of The Home Depot in Appendix A at the back of this book.

Required:

How much does the company report for Cash and Cash Equivalents, at January 29, 2017?

S5-2 Comparing Financial Information

LO5-2, 5-5

Refer to the summarized financial statements of The Home Depot in Appendix A and Lowe's Companies Inc. in Appendix B at the back of this book.

Required:

1. Does Lowe's report more or less Cash and Cash Equivalents than The Home Depot at the beginning of February 2017?
2. According to the company's management and independent registered public accounting firm, were the internal controls over financial reporting at Lowe's and its subsidiaries effective at that time?

S5-3 Internet-Based Team Research: Examining an Annual Report

LO5-2, 5-5

As a team, select an industry to analyze. Using the Internet, each team member should access the annual report for one publicly traded company in the industry, with each member selecting a different company (see S1–3 in Chapter 1 for a description of possible resources for these tasks).

Required:

1. On an individual basis, each team member should write a short report that incorporates the following:

    a. Read management's report on internal control effectiveness. Did any material weaknesses or deficiencies exist during the year? Did the external auditors agree with management's assessment?

    b. How much did the company report in total Cash and Cash Equivalents? Does the company present sufficient information to determine the proportion of Cash versus Cash Equivalents? Does the company report Restricted Cash?

2. Then, as a team, write a short report comparing and contrasting your companies using these attributes. Discuss any patterns across the companies that you observe as a team. Provide potential explanations for any differences discovered.

LO5-1, 5-2 **S5-4 Ethical Decision Making: A Real-Life Example**

When some people think about inventory theft, they imagine a shoplifter running out of a Famous Footwear store with goods stuffed inside a jacket or bag. But that's not what the managers thought at the Famous Footwear store on Chicago's Madison Street. No, they suspected their own employees were the main cause of their unusually high inventory theft. One scam involved dishonest cashiers who would let their friends take a pair of Skechers without paying for them. To make it look like the shoes had been bought, cashiers would ring up a sale, but instead of charging $50 for shoes, they would charge only $2 for a bottle of shoe polish. That's when the company's managers decided to put its register–monitoring system to work. In just two years, the company cut its Madison Street inventory losses in half. Here's how a newspaper described the store's improvements:

> **Retailers Crack Down on Employee Theft**
> *SouthCoast Today,* Chicago
> **By Calmetta Coleman,** *Wall Street Journal* **Staff Writer**
>
> . . . Famous Footwear installed a chainwide register-monitoring system to sniff out suspicious transactions, such as unusually large numbers of refunds or voids, or repeated sales of cheap goods.
>
> . . . [B]efore an employee can issue a cash refund, a second worker must be present to see the customer and inspect the merchandise.
>
> . . . [T]he chain has set up a toll-free hotline for employees to use to report suspicions about co-workers.

Required:

1. To which of the three types of employee fraud does this article relate?
2. Explain how the register–monitoring system would allow Famous Footwear to cut down on employee theft.
3. What is the name of the control principle that is addressed by Famous Footwear's new cash refund procedure?
4. Think of and describe at least four different parties that are harmed by the type of inventory theft described in this case.

LO5-1, 5-5 **S5-5 Ethical Decision Making: A Mini-Case**

You are an assistant in the accounting department of Hasher Electronics, a small electronics retailer. Hasher has a loan that requires the company to maintain a minimum cash balance of $125,000, as reported on its year–end balance sheet. Although Hasher has struggled in recent years, as of yesterday it looked as though Hasher would be able to meet this requirement. The cash balance in Hasher's general ledger was $130,000 and the company's credit manager was expecting to receive a $30,000 electronic funds transfer that day on account from your biggest customer. Your department supervisor had been worried about meeting the loan requirement, so she had delayed making payments to Hasher's suppliers for several days. But in anticipation of receiving the EFT, she decided yesterday to issue cheques to suppliers totalling $15,000.

It is now the last day of the fiscal year and your supervisor approaches you with a problem. Your big customer had backed out at the last minute, indicating it had "some financial issues to sort out" before it can transfer money to Hasher. The supervisor says the only way Hasher can meet its loan requirement is to put the $15,000 back into the Cash account and pretend as if the supplier cheques were not issued until after year—end. You questioned whether this would be ethical. Her reply was, "Well, we don't really have a choice. Either we do this, or we violate the terms of the loan agreement and possibly be forced to repay the loan imme—diately. That could put us out of business. Think of all the people who would lose their jobs! Just make a journal entry today to increase Cash and Accounts Payable. Then tomorrow we can reduce Cash and Accounts Payable—probably before many of our suppliers even get the cheques we have written to them."

Required:

1. Who might suffer in the short term if you go along with your supervisor's request? What might happen in the future if you go along with her request this time? If you do not go along, who might suffer in the short term and what could be the long—term consequences?

2. You want to be loyal to your supervisor but honest to others who rely on your work. As an accounting assistant, which of these concerns should be most important? Why?

3. What alternative courses of action can you take? Which of these is "best" given the circumstances?

S5-6 Critical Thinking: Analyzing Internal Control Weaknesses

LO5-1, 5-2

Snake Creek Company has a trusted employee who, as the owner said, "handles all of the bookkeeping and paperwork for the company." This employee is responsible for counting, verifying, and recording cash receipts and payments, making the weekly bank deposit, preparing cheques for major expenditures (signed by the owner), making small expenditures from the cash register for daily expenses, and collecting accounts receivable. The owner asked the local bank for a $20,000 loan. The bank asked that an audit be performed covering the year just ended. The independent auditor (a local CPA), in a private conference with the owner, presented some evidence of the following activities of the trusted employee during the past year:

a. Cash sales sometimes were not entered in the cash register and the trusted employee pocketed approximately $50 per month.

b. Cash taken from the cash register (and pocketed by the trusted employee) was replaced with expense memos with fictitious signatures (approximately $12 per day).

c. $300 collected on an account receivable from a valued out—of—town customer was pocketed by the trusted employee and was covered by making a $300 entry as a debit to Inventory and a credit to Accounts Receivable.

d. $800 collected on an account receivable from a local customer was pocketed by the trusted employee and was covered by making an $800 entry as a debit to Supplies and a credit to Accounts Receivable.

Required:

1. What was the approximate amount stolen during the past year?

   TIP: Assume employees work 5 days a week, 52 weeks a year.

2. What would be your recommendations to the owner?

CONTINUING CASES

CC5-1 Accounting for Cash Receipts, Purchases, and Cash Payments and Reconciling Items

LO5-3, 5-4, 5-5

Nicole's Getaway Spa (NGS) continues to grow and develop. Nicole is now evaluating a computerized accounting system and needs your help in understanding how source documents inform accounting processes. She also needs some help reconciling NGS's bank account.

Required:

1. For each source document shown below, prepare the appropriate journal entry or indicate that no journal entry is required.

   a. Purchase order dated October 13 for massage chairs costing $765 and oil supplies costing $240

Item Number	Description	Quantity	Unit Cost	Total Cost
2-37-10A	Massage chairs with face cradle	3	$ 255.00	$ 765.00
11-98-28K	Bottles of massage oil	40	$ 6.00	$ 240.00
			Total:	$ 1,005.00

Online Data Entry — Nicole's Getaway Spa — Purchase Order

Date Ordered: 10/13/2017 Order Number: PO-333887

Supplier: Supplier ID #: 45 Name: Unlimited Spa Supplies
Street address: 10 - 199 East Road
City, Province, Postal Code: Anytown Canada

Deliver to: Building: Top Shopping Center
Street Address: 100 Main Street
City, Province: Anytown Canada

Approved by: Select Name: Nicole Mackisey Signature: N Mackisey Date: 10/13/2017

   b. Remittance advice from customer for $93, received October 17

REMITTANCE ADVICE

To: Nicole's Getaway Spa
100 Main Street
Anytown, Canada

Customer Account: Capital Gym Club
Invoice Number/Date: 1317700 / September 25
Amount Due: $93.00
Payment Date: October 17
Amount Enclosed: $93.00

Enter the amount you are paying above

   c. Receiving report indicating October 22 receipt of October 13 order. Also received supplier invoice totalling $1,005

Online Data Entry — Nicole's Getaway Spa — Receiving Report

Unlimited Spa Supplies
10 - 199 East Road
Anytown, Canada

CHEQUE CARRIER
X SHIPPER'S TRUCK
UPS/FEDEX

OUR ORDER NUMBER	DATE SHIPPED	SHIPPED TO ATTENTION OF	DATE RECEIVED
PO-333887	10/22 2017	Nicole Mackisey	Thursday, October 22, 2

QTY	DESCRIPTION	WEIGHT EACH	WEIGHT TOTAL	CONDITION OF GOODS	REC'D BY INTLS
3	Equipment - massage chairs	60	180	Good	RS
2	Supplies - bottles of massage oil	20	40	Good	RS
			220		

   d. NGS cheque for payment in full of October 13 order

Nicole's Getaway Spa
100 Main Street
Anytown, Canada

National Bank
200 - 1ˢᵗ Avenue
Anytown, Canada

101

DATE: October 30, 2017

PAY TO THE ORDER OF: One thousand and five dollars and 0/100 $ 1,005.00

Unlimited Spa Supplies
10 – 199 East Road
Anytown, Canada

Per: Nicole Mackisey
Per: K Rowland
Authorized Signatories

⑈0000010⑈ ⑊ ⑈000067894⑈ 12345678⑈   ⑈0000012345⑈

2. Nicole has asked you to prepare a bank reconciliation for NGS. According to her records, NGS's cash balance is $6,000 at December 31, but the bank reports a balance of $5,500.

   a. The bank deducted $250 for an NSF cheque from a customer that was deposited on December 22.

   b. NGS has written cheques totalling $3,500 that have not yet cleared the bank.

   c. The bank added $10 cash to the account for interest earned in December.

   d. NGS made a $3,480 deposit on December 31, which will be recorded by the bank in January.

   e. The bank deducted $10 for service charges.

   f. NGS wrote a cheque to a supplier on account for $300 but mistakenly recorded it as $30.

3. Prepare journal entries for items (a) through (f) from the bank reconciliation, if applicable. If a journal entry is not required for one or more of the reconciling items, indicate "no journal entry required."

4. If NGS also has $120 of petty cash and $1,000 invested in government Treasury bills pur-chased in August, what is the amount of Cash and Cash Equivalents on NGS's December 31 balance sheet?

CC5-2 Wiki Art Gallery (WAG)

LO5-2, 5-7

Refer to the Wiki Art Gallery (WAG) instructional case in Appendix D or access in Connect, and read the case in sufficient depth to answer the following question.

1. Which of the following statements uses the fraud triangle appropriately when identifying the risks of financial misreporting at WAG?

   a. Because Rob prepares WAG's financial statements, the incentive for misstating the financial results is heightened.

   b. Because WAG's financial statements are not audited, the opportunity for misstating the financial results is heightened.

   c. The risk of financial reporting fraud is heightened because Stephen has shown a ten-dency to rationalize and conceal misdeeds.

   d. The pending sale of WAG increases the opportunity for misstating the financial results.

Endnotes

1. Information regarding the Koss fraud has been obtained from the following sources: Koss Corporation 2011 Form 10–K, 2009 Form 10–K, and 2009 Schedule 14A; http://www.milwaukeemag.com /article/3162011–thediva; *Puskala v. Koss* class action complaint (http://securities.stanford .edu/1044/KOSS00_01/2010115_f01c_1000041.pdf); *SEC v. Koss* civil action complaint (http://www.sec.gov/litigation/complaints/2011/comp22138.pdf); and *SEC v. Sachdeva /Mulvaney* civil action complaint (http://www.sec.gov/litigation/complaints/2010 /comp21640.pdf).

2. *CPA Magazine*, April 2017, page 48.

THAT WAS

THEN

Earlier chapters have focused on companies whose operating activities relate to providing services to customers, rather than selling goods.

THIS IS

NOW

This chapter focuses on companies that sell merchandise to customers, and the way they control and report their operating results.

CHAPTER 6

Merchandising Operations and the Multi-step Income Statement

Martin Good/Shutterstock.com

FOCUS COMPANY:
Walmart

Seventeen years after the company was founded, Walmart rang up yearly sales of $1 billion. Fourteen years later, it sold that much in a week. Thanks to the millions of Canadians who shop at Walmart, its sales now average over $1 billion a day. And that's not all. Walmart has been able to earn sizable profits, even during difficult economic times.

One secret to its success is the state-of-the-art accounting system that controls Walmart's merchandise sales and cash collections. In this chapter, you will learn about this kind of system and the other aspects of merchandising companies that make them unique and interesting. You'll also learn how to analyze a merchandiser's financial statements to figure out the amount of mark-up that it includes in the prices you pay. You might be surprised by how much you're contributing to Walmart's profits.

Walmart logo courtesy of Wal-Mart Stores, Inc.: www.walmart.com

ORGANIZATION OF THE CHAPTER

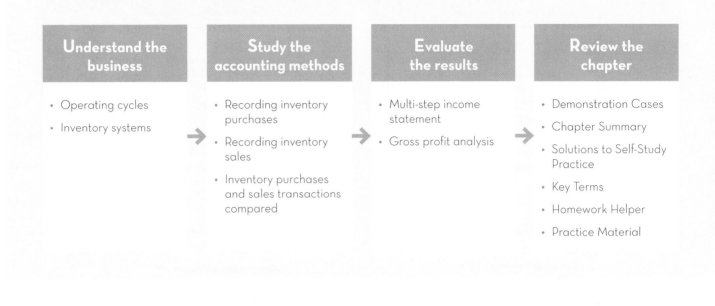

Understand the business	Study the accounting methods	Evaluate the results	Review the chapter
• Operating cycles • Inventory systems	• Recording inventory purchases • Recording inventory sales • Inventory purchases and sales transactions compared	• Multi-step income statement • Gross profit analysis	• Demonstration Cases • Chapter Summary • Solutions to Self-Study Practice • Key Terms • Homework Helper • Practice Material

Understand the Business

OPERATING CYCLES

For any company to be successful, it must complete its operating cycle efficiently. The operating cycle is a series of activities that a company undertakes to generate revenues and, ultimately, cash. Exhibit 6.1 contrasts the operating cycles of service and merchandising companies.

Service companies such as Planet Fitness follow a simple operat—ing cycle: sell services to customers, collect cash from them, and use that money to pay for operating expenses. **Merchandising companies** differ in that their cycle begins with buying products. These products, which are called **inventory**, are sold to customers, which leads to collecting cash that can be used to pay for operating expenses and buy more inventory. Merchandising companies such as Walmart and Costco are called retailers when they sell directly to individual consumers and wholesalers when they sell their inventory to retail businesses for resale to consumers.

This chapter applies equally to both retail and wholesale merchan—disers. This chapter does not include **manufacturing companies** such as Mattel and Goodyear because they make, rather than buy, the products they sell, which introduces complexities that are beyond this introductory course. Accounting for manufacturing companies is explained in managerial and cost accounting courses.

LEARNING OBJECTIVE 6-1

Distinguish between service and merchandising operations.

Service companies: Sell services rather than physical goods.

Merchandising companies: Sell goods that have been obtained from a supplier.

Inventory: Assets acquired for resale to customers.

Manufacturing companies: Sell goods that they have made themselves.

EXHIBIT 6.1	Operating Cycles for Service and Manufacturing Companies

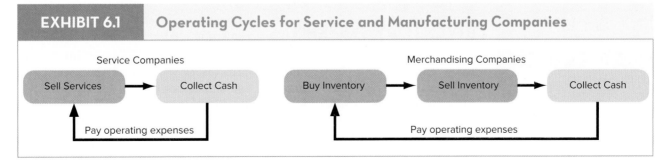

Service Company Example	Merchandising Company Example

PLANET FITNESS, INC.
Balance Sheet (excerpt)
At December 31, 2015
(in thousands)

Assets

Current Assets

Cash and Cash Equivalents	$31,430
Accounts Receivable	19,079
Supplies	4,557
Prepaid Assets	5,152
etc.	

WAL-MART STORES, INC.
Balance Sheet (excerpt)
At January 31, 2016
(in millions)

Assets

Current Assets

Cash and Cash Equivalents	$ 8,705
Accounts Receivable	5,624
Inventory	44,469
Prepaid Assets	1,441
etc.	

Income Statement (excerpt)
(in thousands)

Service Revenue	$330,537
Depreciation Expense	32,158
etc.	

Income Statement (excerpt)
(in millions)

Sales Revenue, net	$478,614
Cost of Goods Sold	360,984
Gross Profit	117,630
Depreciation Expense	3,672
etc.	

The operating cycle differences in Exhibit 6.1 lead to important differences in how service and merchandising companies report their financial results. Exhibit 6.2 shows three key differences in the balance sheet and income statement of a service company (Planet Fitness) and a merchandising company (Walmart). The balance sheet excerpts show that (1) merchandisers report Inventory as a current asset, but service companies do not. Service companies often report Supplies, but they differ from inventory because *supplies are goods acquired for internal use. Inventory consists of goods acquired for resale to customers.* The income statement excerpts show that (2) service companies earn revenue from services whereas merchandisers earn revenue from sales. Finally, (3) merchandisers report an expense called Cost of Goods Sold, which represents the total cost of all goods sold to customers during the period. Service companies do not incur this expense because they do not sell goods.

Of course, some companies operate as both service and merchandising companies. Magicuts, for example, buys shampoo for both internal use (Supplies) and resale to customers (Inventory). The financial statements of such companies separately report all the items shown in Exhibit 6.2.

INVENTORY SYSTEMS

LEARNING OBJECTIVE 6-2

Explain the differences between periodic and perpetual inventory systems.

Three accounts are particularly important to a merchandiser: Inventory, Sales Revenue, and Cost of Goods Sold. Inventory reports the merchandiser's total cost of acquiring goods that it has not yet sold, whereas Sales Revenue and Cost of Goods Sold indicate the total selling price and cost of all goods that the merchandiser did sell to customers during the period. By subtracting Cost of Goods Sold from Sales Revenue, a merchandiser determines its *gross profit*, which represents the profit earned before

EXHIBIT 6.3 | Relationship Between Inventory and Cost of Goods Sold

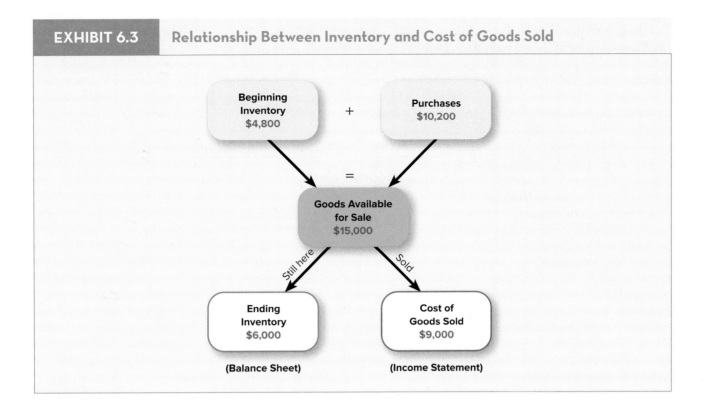

taking into account other expenses such as salaries, wages, depreciation, and so on.

Before we discuss the systems for tracking changes in Inventory, Sales Revenue, and Cost of Goods Sold, you should understand a key relationship between Inventory and Cost of Goods Sold. A merchandiser starts each accounting period with a stock of inventory that we will call beginning inventory (BI). During the accounting period, the cost of new purchases (P) is added to the cost of beginning inventory. As in Exhibit 6.3, the sum of these two amounts (BI + P) represents the cost of **goods available for sale**.

Goods available for sale either will be sold during the period (reported as Cost of Goods Sold (CGS) on the income statement) or will remain on hand (reported as ending inventory (EI) on the balance sheet). Ending inventory for one accounting period becomes beginning inventory for the next period. A **cost of goods sold equation** can express the relationship among these items in two ways, as given below using the numbers from Exhibit 6.3:

Goods available for sale: The sum of beginning inventory and purchases for the period.

Cost of goods sold equation: Expresses the relationship between inventory on hand, purchased, and sold; BI + P − EI = CGS or BI + P − CGS = EI

BI + P − EI = CGS	or	**BI + P − CGS = EI**
$4,800 + 10,200 − 6,000 = $9,000		$4,800 + 10,200 − 9,000 = $6,000

Companies track these costs using either a periodic or perpetual inventory system. As explained below, the equation above on the left is used for a periodic inventory system and the equation above on the right depicts a perpetual inventory system.

If one of the values in the cost of goods sold equation is unknown, you can use either version of the cost of goods sold equation or the inventory T−account to solve for the missing value. See for yourself in the following Self−Study Practice.

HOW'S IT GOING?

Self-Study Practice 6.1

Use the Cost of Goods Sold equation to solve for the missing information for Cases 1 and 2. Then enter the information for either Case 1 or Case 2 into the T-account on the right.

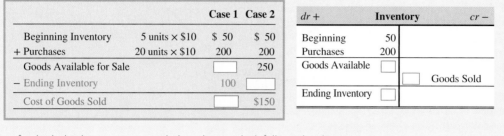

		Case 1	Case 2
Beginning Inventory	5 units × $10	$ 50	$ 50
+ Purchases	20 units × $10	200	200
Goods Available for Sale		☐	250
− Ending Inventory		100	☐
Cost of Goods Sold		☐	$150

dr +	Inventory		cr −
Beginning	50		
Purchases	200		
Goods Available	☐		
		☐	Goods Sold
Ending Inventory	☐		

After you have finished, check your answers with the solution, which follows the chapter summary.

Periodic Inventory System

Periodic inventory system: A system in which ending inventory and cost of goods sold are determined only at the end of the accounting period based on a physical inventory count.

A **periodic inventory system** updates the inventory records for merchandise purchases, sales, and returns only at the end of the accounting period. Although simple to maintain, a major drawback of a periodic system is that accurate records of the inventory on hand and the inventory that has been sold are unavailable during the accounting period. To determine these amounts, employees must physically count the inventory, which they do at the end of the period, when the store is "closed for inventory." Based on the inventory count, the cost of ending inventory (EI) is determined and subtracted to calculate the cost of goods sold (BI + P − EI = CGS). These amounts are then used to adjust the balances for Inventory and Cost of Goods Sold.

Perpetual Inventory System

Perpetual inventory system: A system in which a detailed inventory record is maintained by recording each purchase and sale of inventory during the accounting period.

A **perpetual inventory system** updates inventory records every time an item is bought, sold, or returned. You may not realize it, but the barcode readers at Walmart's checkouts serve two purposes: (1) they calculate and record the sales revenue for each product you're buying and (2) they remove the product and its cost from Walmart's inventory records. Similar scanners are used back in the "employees only" part of the store, where products are unloaded from the trucks or returned to suppliers. As a result of this continuous, or "perpetual," updating, the balances in Walmart's Inventory and Cost of Goods Sold accounts are always up to date.

Inventory Control

Shrinkage: The cost of inventory lost to theft, fraud, and error.

A perpetual inventory system provides the best inventory control because its continuous tracking of transactions allows companies to instantly determine the quantity of products on the shelves and to evaluate the amount of time they have spent there. Using this information, companies can better manage their inventory and save a great deal of money in financing and storage charges. Another benefit of a perpetual inventory system is that it allows managers to estimate **shrinkage**, the term for loss of inventory from theft, fraud, and error. You might wonder how companies can estimate how much of their inventory is missing because isn't it, by definition, *missing?* They use the information in the perpetual inventory system and the following version of the cost of goods sold equation:

$$BI + P − CGS = EI$$

To illustrate, assume Walmart reports the following for one of its lines of cell phones.

Equation	Quantity		Cost per Unit		Total Cost
	Information in the company's perpetual records				
Beginning Inventory	3	×	$100	=	$300
+ Purchases	3	×	$100	=	300
− Goods Sold	(2)	×	$100	=	(200)
= Ending Inventory	4	×	$100	=	$400

vs.

Physical inventory count

Because a perpetual inventory system records all goods purchased and sold, the ending inventory in the company's perpetual records indicates how many units should be on hand. In our example, four units should be on hand at a unit cost of $100, for a total cost of $400. By physically counting the inventory that is actually on hand, the company can determine whether items have been physically removed without being recorded as an approved transaction.

Calculate shrinkage by subtracting the cost of inventory counted from that recorded in the perpetual inventory system. In our example, just three units were on hand, so the shrinkage was one unit, with a cost of $100. This shrinkage will be accounted for by recording a *book–to–physical* adjustment that reduces the Inventory account by one unit ($100) and increases Cost of Goods Sold by $100. In a perpetual inventory system, Inventory and Cost of Goods Sold are not complete until this book–to–physical adjustment is made.

You can't do this kind of analysis with a periodic inventory system because it doesn't provide an up–to–date record of the inventory that should be on hand when you count it. Notice, however, that even if you're using a perpetual inventory system, you still need to count the inventory occasionally (at least yearly) to ensure the accounting records are accurate and any shrinkage is detected. If you don't do this physical count, you could end up like the company in the Spotlight on Controls in Chapter 5. The grandmother was able to falsely record payments to herself as if they were inventory purchases because no one checked to see whether the recorded inventory actually existed.

SPOTLIGHT ON Controls

Sources of Inventory Shrinkage

Independent verification of inventory quantities is important. A recent study suggests that more than $34 billion of inventory goes missing from U.S. retailers each year.[1] Although shoplifting is a major cause of shrinkage (accounting for 36 percent of lost units), an even larger portion (44 percent) results from employee theft. To avoid hiring dishonest employees, companies screen job applicants using employment and criminal background checks. To deter and detect employee theft, they use security tags, surveillance cameras, and complex computer programs that monitor cash registers.

Study the Accounting Methods

RECORDING INVENTORY PURCHASES

LEARNING OBJECTIVE 6-3

In this section, we demonstrate the accounting for inventory purchases, as well as transportation, purchase returns and allowances, and purchase discounts. For purposes of this demonstration, we record all inventory–related

Analyze purchase transactions under a perpetual inventory system.

transactions in the Inventory account. This approach is generally associated with a perpetual inventory system because it maintains an up-to-date balance in the Inventory account at all times. An alternative approach, which maintains separate accounts for purchases, transportation, and so on, is generally used in a periodic inventory system and is demonstrated in Supplement 6B at the end of this chapter.

Inventory Purchases

Most large retailers use perpetual inventory systems that not only monitor inventory quantities, but also automatically issue purchase orders to replenish inventory on hand. The purchase order instructs the supplier to send specified quantities of particular products on certain dates. At the time the purchase order is transmitted, Walmart and the supplier have exchanged only promises, so no journal entry is recorded. A transaction arises when Walmart receives the inventory and is invoiced for it. For example, if Walmart receives $10,500 of bikes purchased on account, the transaction would affect the accounting equation and would be recorded as follows.

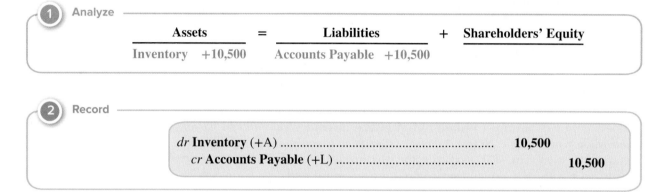

1 Analyze

Assets	=	Liabilities	+	Shareholders' Equity
Inventory +10,500		Accounts Payable +10,500		

2 Record

dr Inventory (+A) 10,500
    cr Accounts Payable (+L) 10,500

The $10,500 owed to the supplier remains in Accounts Payable until it is paid, at which time Accounts Payable is decreased (with a debit) and Cash is decreased (with a credit). The Inventory account remains at $10,500, unless the inventory is sold or any of the following transactions occur.

Transportation Cost

The inventory that Walmart purchases does not magically appear in its stores. It must be shipped from the supplier to Walmart. Depending on the terms of sale, the transportation cost may be paid by either Walmart or the supplier. If the terms of sale are **FOB shipping point**, ownership of the goods transfers to Walmart at the shipping point, so Walmart would pay the transportation cost. This transportation cost (also called freight-in) is recorded as an addition to Walmart's Inventory account because it is a cost Walmart incurs to obtain the inventory. If the terms are **FOB destination**, ownership transfers at the destination, so the supplier incurs the transportation cost.

Assume that Walmart pays $400 cash to a trucker who delivers the $10,500 of bikes to one of its stores. Walmart would account for this transportation cost as follows:

FOB (free on board) shipping point: A term of sale indicating that goods are owned by the customer the moment they leave the seller's premises.

FOB (free on board) destination: A term of sale indicating that goods are owned by the seller until they are delivered to the customer.

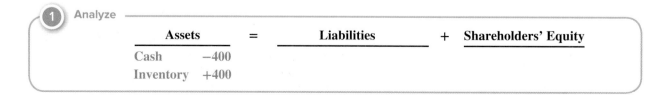

1 Analyze

Assets	=	Liabilities	+	Shareholders' Equity
Cash −400				
Inventory +400				

> *dr* **Inventory** (+A) **400**
>   *cr* **Cash** (−A) **400**

In general, a purchaser should include in the Inventory account any costs needed to get the inventory into a condition and location ready for sale. Costs that are incurred after the inventory has been made ready for sale, such as freight—out to deliver goods to customers, should be treated as selling expenses.

Purchase Returns and Allowances

When goods purchased from a supplier arrive in damaged condition or fail to meet specifications, the buyer can (1) return them for a full refund or (2) keep them and ask for a cost reduction, called an *allowance*. Either way, these **purchase returns and allowances** are accounted for by reducing the cost of the inventory and either recording a cash refund or reducing the liability owed to the supplier.

Purchase returns and allowances: A reduction in the cost of inventory purchases associated with unsatisfactory goods.

Assume, for example, that Walmart returned some of the bikes to the supplier and received a $500 reduction in the balance owed. This purchase return would be analyzed and recorded as follows:

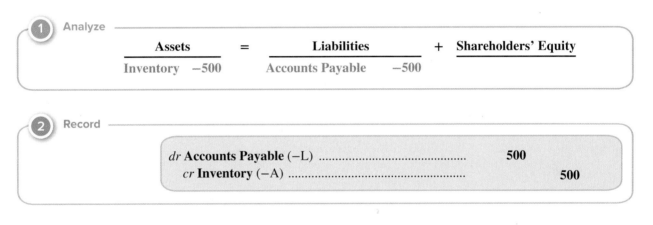

① Analyze

Assets	=	**Liabilities**	+	**Shareholders' Equity**
Inventory −500		Accounts Payable −500		

② Record

> *dr* **Accounts Payable** (−L) **500**
>   *cr* **Inventory** (−A) **500**

Purchase Discounts

When inventory is bought on credit, terms such as "2/10, n/30" may be specified. The "2/10" part means that if the purchaser pays by the 10th day of taking ownership of the goods, a 2 percent **purchase discount** can be deducted from the amount owed. The "n/30" part means that if pay—ment is not made within the 10—day discount period, the full amount will be due 30 days after ownership transferred. See Exhibit 6.4 for an illustra—tion of a 2/10, n/30 purchase on November 1.

Purchase discount: A cash discount received for prompt payment of a purchase on account.

When offered a purchase discount at the time of purchase, the purchaser accounts for it in two stages. Initially, the purchase is accounted for at full cost. Later, if payment is made within the discount period, the purchaser reduces the Inventory account by the amount of the discount because it effectively reduces the cost of the inventory. The purchase discount is calculated using the net amount owing to the supplier, after considering purchase returns and allowances.

Assume, for example, that Walmart's purchase of bikes for $10,500 occurred with terms 2/10, n/30. The initial purchase would be accounted for as shown earlier, by recording a $10,500 increase in Inventory (with a

EXHIBIT 6.4   Interpreting Credit Terms

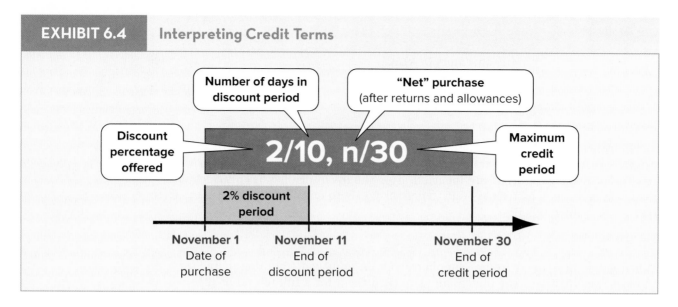

debit) and a $10,500 increase in Accounts Payable (with a credit). In our example, Walmart returned inventory costing $500 and received a $500 reduction in its Accounts Payable. Consequently, Walmart owed the sup−plier $10,000 for the purchase. Multiplying this balance by the 2 percent discount, we find that Walmart's purchase discount is $200 (2% × $10,000 = $200). This discount means that Walmart has to make a payment of only $9,800 ($10,000 − $200 = $9,800) to fully satisfy its $10,000 of Accounts Payable. The $200 discount also reduces the cost of inventory as follows:

COACH'S TIP

The discount would not be applied to the freight-in unless the trucking company offered a discount.

① Analyze

	Assets		=	Liabilities		+	Shareholders' Equity
Cash	+9,800		=	Accounts Payable	−10,000		
Inventory	−200						

② Record

dr **Accounts Payable (−L)** 10,000
    cr **Cash (−A)** 9,800
    cr **Inventory (−A)** 200

Summary of Inventory Purchase Transactions

You have now seen how several types of inventory transactions affect the Inventory account on the balance sheet. Exhibit 6.5 summarizes, in table and T−account forms, how these transactions affect inventory, assuming

EXHIBIT 6.5   Effects of Inventory Transactions Related to Purchases

Beginning Inventory		$ 4,800
+ Purchases	$10,500	
+ Freight-in	400	
− Purchase Returns and Allowances	(500)	
− Purchase Discounts	(200)	
Net Purchases		10,200
Cost of Goods Available for Sale		$15,000

Inventory

Beginning	4,800		
Purchases	10,500	500	Purchase Returns
Freight-in	400	200	Purchase Discounts
Goods Available	15,000		

Self-Study Practice 6.2

On October 1, Best Buy received a shipment of televisions bought for $10,000, on terms 2/10, n/30. Best Buy paid the amount owed on October 8. What accounting equation effects and journal entries would Best Buy record on October 1 and 8?

October 1—Purchase

1 Analyze

Assets	=	Liabilities	+	Shareholders' Equity

2 Record

	Debit	Credit
[ ]	[ ]	
[ ]		[ ]

October 8—Payment

1 Analyze

Assets	=	Liabilities	+	Shareholders' Equity

2 Record

	Debit	Credit
[ ]	[ ]	
[ ]		[ ]
[ ]		[ ]

beginning inventory was $4,800. Take a moment to flip back to Exhibit 6.3 so that you can see that these are the values that will either become assigned to Cost of Goods Sold (when the goods are sold) or remain in Inventory.

Recording Inventory Sales

As required by the revenue recognition principle, merchandisers record revenue when they fulfill their performance obligations by transferring control of the goods to customers. For a retail merchandiser like Walmart, this transfer occurs when a customer buys and takes possession of the goods at checkout. For a wholesale merchandiser, the transfer of control occurs at

LEARNING OBJECTIVE 6-4

Analyze sales transactions under a perpetual inventory system.

a time stated in the written sales agreement. Just like the purchase agreement you saw earlier in this chapter, the sales agreement will specify one of two possible times for transfer of control:

1. **FOB shipping point:** the sale is recorded when the goods leave the seller's shipping department.
2. **FOB destination:** the sale is recorded when the goods reach their destination (the customer).

Unless otherwise indicated, the examples in this book assume that transfer of control occurs when goods are shipped (FOB shipping point), which usually means the buyer pays for all transportation costs.[2]

Every merchandise sale has two components, each of which requires an entry in a perpetual inventory system:

1. **Selling price.** Walmart's *sales price* is recorded as an increase in Sales Revenue and a corresponding increase in either Cash (for a cash sale) or Accounts Receivable (for a credit sale).
2. **Cost.** The *cost* that Walmart incurred to initially buy the merchandise is removed from Inventory and reported as an expense called *Cost of Goods Sold* (CGS).

For example, assume Walmart sells two Schwinn mountain bikes at a price of $200 per bike, for a total of $400 cash. The bikes had previously been recorded in Walmart's Inventory at a total cost of $350. This transaction is illustrated, analyzed, and recorded in Exhibit 6.6.

Notice in Exhibit 6.6 that the first part of Walmart's journal entry involving Cash and Sales Revenue is recorded at the total selling price ($400). The second part involving Cost of Goods Sold and Inventory uses Walmart's total cost ($350). The $50 difference between selling price and cost ($400 − $350) is called the *gross profit*. Gross profit is not directly recorded in an account by itself, but instead is a subtotal produced by subtracting Cost of Goods Sold from Sales Revenue on the income statement.

To simplify, we use only one Sales Revenue account and one Cost of Goods Sold account for our examples. In the workplace, however, merchandising companies use different Sales and Cost of Goods Sold accounts for different product lines. This allows managers at Walmart

---

EXHIBIT 6.6 | **Sale of Merchandise in a Perpetual System**

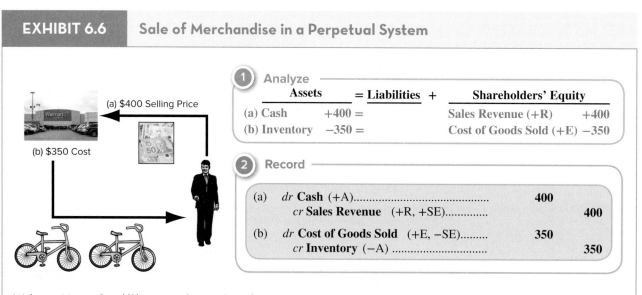

(a) $400 Selling Price

(b) $350 Cost

1 Analyze

Assets		= Liabilities +	Shareholders' Equity	
(a) Cash	+400 =		Sales Revenue (+R)	+400
(b) Inventory	−350 =		Cost of Goods Sold (+E)	−350

2 Record

(a)	*dr* Cash (+A)...	400	
	cr Sales Revenue (+R, +SE)...............		400
(b)	*dr* Cost of Goods Sold (+E, −SE).........	350	
	cr Inventory (−A)		350

Walmart: Martin Good/Shutterstock.com; Canadian Money: CarpathianPrince/Shutterstock.com; Bank note image used with the permission of the Bank of Canada

to separately evaluate sales of different products. When reporting to external financial statement users, Walmart combines these individual accounts into a single number for Sales and a single number for Cost of Goods Sold, which avoids cluttering its income statement with numerous accounts and also prevents its competitors from discovering details about its sales of specific products.

Sales Returns and Allowances

When goods sold to a customer arrive in damaged condition or are otherwise unsatisfactory, the customer can (1) return them for a full refund or (2) keep them and ask for a reduction in the selling price, called an *allowance*. These **sales returns and allowances** require Walmart to revise the previously recorded sale and, in the case of returns, to revise the previously recorded inventory reduction and cost of goods sold. To illustrate this, suppose that after Walmart sold the two Schwinn mountain bikes, the customer returned one to Walmart. Assuming that the bike is still like new, Walmart would refund the $200 selling price to the customer and take the bike back into inventory at its cost of $175.

To account for this transaction, Walmart would make two entries to basically reverse the entries recorded when the bike was sold. We say "basically" because there is one catch: Walmart does not directly reduce its Sales Revenue account. Instead, Walmart tracks sales returns and allowances in a contra-revenue account that is deducted from total sales revenue.

Just as a contra-asset account such as Accumulated Depreciation reduces the total in an asset account such as Equipment, a contra-revenue account such as Sales Returns and Allowances reduces the total in a revenue account such as Sales Revenues. Using a contra-revenue account instead of directly reducing the Sales account allows Walmart to track the value of goods returned, providing clues about whether customers are happy with the quality and price of Walmart's products.[3]

Sales returns are recorded as follows:

> **Sales returns and allowances:** Refunds and price reductions given to customers after goods have been sold and found unsatisfactory.

> **COACH'S TIP**
>
> To indicate that an increase in a contra-revenue account reduces revenues, which reduces shareholders' equity, use (+xR, −SE).

1 Analyze

Assets		=	Liabilities	+	Shareholders' Equity	
Cash	−200	=			Sales Returns & Allowances (+xR)	−200
Inventory	+175	=			Cost of Goods Sold (−E)	+175

2 Record

dr **Sales Returns & Allowances (+xR), −SE**............................	200	
cr **Cash (−A)**		200
dr **Inventory (+A)**...	175	
cr **Cost of Goods Sold (−E), +SE**		175

A sales return that results in issuing store credit rather than a cash refund is accounted for the same way, except that the reduction in Cash is replaced with an increase in the liability Deferred Revenue (for the store gift card that is issued). A sales *allowance* (i.e., a reduction in sales without the return of goods) is accounted for as shown above, except the increase in Inventory and decrease in Cost of Goods Sold are not recorded.

When it is expected that sales returns after the end of the current month are to be significant, they must be estimated and recorded in the current month, as an offset to revenue in the period of the initial sale.

Sales On Account and Sales Discounts

Just as you saw earlier in this chapter for purchase discounts, a merchan—diser can specify terms such as "2/10, n/30" to encourage customers to pay promptly for sales on account. The "2/10" means that if the customer pays by the tenth day after the sale date, a 2 percent **sales discount** will be deducted from the selling price. The "n/30" part implies that if payment is not made within the ten—day discount period, the full amount will be due thirty days after the date of sale.

Sales discount: A sales price reduction given to customers for prompt payment of their account balance.

A company accounts for sales discounts either when the goods are first sold (the *net method*) or later when the payment is received (the *gross method*). The net method is convenient when customers routinely take advantage of sales discounts whereas the gross method may be appropriate when a company's customers do not regularly take the sales discounts. The examples in this book illustrate the gross method.[4]

When a sales discount is offered to and later taken by the customer, the seller accounts for two transactions: (1) the initial sale and (2) the sales discount taken by the customer. Suppose that Walmart sells printer paper on account to a local business for $1,000 with payment terms of 2/10, n/30. The paper had cost Walmart $700. Walmart accounts for this initial sale as follows:

① Analyze

Assets	=	Liabilities	+	Shareholders' Equity
Accounts Receivable +1,000				Sales Revenue (+R) +1,000
Inventory −700				Cost of Goods Sold (+E) −700

② Record

dr Accounts Receivable (+A)	1,000	
cr Sales Rrevenue (+R, +SE)		1,000
dr Cost of Goods Sold (+E, −SE)	700	
cr Inventory (−A)		700

To take advantage of the 2 percent discount, the customer must pay Walmart within ten days. If the customer does so, it will deduct the $20 discount (2% × $1,000) from the total owed ($1,000), and then pay $980 to Walmart. Walmart accounts for the $20 sales discount using a contra—revenue account, as follows:

① Analyze

Assets	=	Liabilities	+	Shareholders' Equity
Cash +980				Sales Discounts (+xR) −20
Accounts Receivable −1,000				

② Record

dr Cash (+A)	980	
dr Sales Discounts (+xR, −SE)	20	
cr Accounts Receivable (−A)		1,000

Sales Revenue	$1,400	**Selling price** of 2 bikes ($400) + paper ($1,000)
Less: Sales Returns and Allowances	(200)	**Selling price** of returned bike ($200)
Sales Discounts	(20)	**Selling price** of paper ($1,000) × 2% (discount)
Net Sales	1,180	$1,400 − $200 − $20 = $1,180
Cost of Goods Sold	875	**Cost** of 2 bikes ($350) − returned bike ($175) + paper ($700)
Gross Profit	$ 305	$1,180 − $875 = $305

If the customer doesn't pay by the end of the discount period, Walmart would not allow the customer to take a discount for early payment. Instead, the customer would have to pay the full $1,000, which Walmart would record as an increase in Cash (debit) and a decrease in Accounts Receivable (credit). What if a customer doesn't pay at all? We discuss that important issue in detail in Chapter 8.

Before leaving the topic of sales discounts, we should clear up a common misconception. Sales discounts differ from the discount that you get as a consumer buying clearance items at a reduced selling price. Reductions in the selling price of merchandise that occur before a sale is made—what Walmart calls "rolling back" prices—are not captured in the accounting system because they are not transactions. To be considered a transaction, a sales discount must occur after the initial sale has been made. These types of sales discounts are given in business–to–business (B2B) transactions for prompt payment on account. We're sorry to say that, as a consumer, you're not likely to be offered this kind of discount.

COACH'S TIP

Sales discounts are calculated after taking into account any sales returns and allowances. Customers that pay a portion of what they owe are entitled to a discount on that portion if they pay within the discount period.

Summary of Sales-Related Transactions

The sales returns and allowances and sales discounts introduced in this section were recorded using contra–revenue accounts. Exhibit 6.7 summarizes how they are reported on the income statement. See the Homework Helper for further information.

By using contra–revenue accounts, accountants and managers are able to monitor and control how sales returns, allowances, and discounts affect the company's business operations. For example, frequent customer returns of defective products would cause an increase in the Sales Returns and

SPOTLIGHT ON Financial Reporting

Revenue Recognition for More Complex Customer Contracts

The IASB issued a new revenue recognition accounting standard effective for 2017 financial statements. The standard requires companies that follow IFRS to recognize revenue at the amount they are entitled to receive when goods and services are transferred to customers. The standard also explains how to handle more complex contracts with customers. For example, when Microsoft sells a contract containing multiple service elements (e.g., a computer system license, installation service, software updates, and ongoing technical support), the contract price is allocated among the service elements and is reported as revenue when each of those performance obligations is satisfied. More detail can be found in Supplement 6A at the end of this chapter. Accounting for complex sales transactions, such as these, will be covered more extensively in your intermediate accounting course.

Transaction:	Purchase (buyer perspective)			Sale (seller perspective)		
Goods ordered	No transaction; no journal entry.			No transaction; no journal entry.		
		Debit	**Credit**		**Debit**	**Credit**
Goods delivered	Inventory	Cost		Accounts Receivable	SP	
	Accounts Payable		Cost	Sales Revenue		SP
				Cost of Goods Sold	Cost	
				Inventory		Cost
		Debit	**Credit**		**Debit**	**Credit**
Goods returned	Accounts Payable	Cost		Sales Returns/Allowances	SP	
(on account)	Inventory		Cost	Accounts Receivable		SP
				Inventory	Cost	
				Cost of Goods Sold		Cost
		Debit	**Credit**		**Debit**	**Credit**
Allowance granted	Accounts Payable	Cost		Sales Returns/Allowances	SP	
(on account)	Inventory		Cost	Accounts Receivable		SP
		Debit	**Credit**		**Debit**	**Credit**
Payment within	Accounts Payable	Cost		Cash	Paid	
discount period	Cash		Paid	Sales Discounts	SP%	
	Inventory		Cost%	Accounts Receivable		SP

SP = Selling price, SP% = Selling price × % Discount, Cost% = Cost × % Discount, Paid = Net cash paid (after discount)

Allowances account. In response to an increase in this account, Walmart's managers might discontinue selling the product or find a new supplier for it.

Accountants rarely report sales returns, allowances, and discounts in an income statement prepared for external users, because that could reveal crucial information to competitors. Instead, when preparing an income statement for external reporting purposes, accountants begin with Net Sales, as shown later in Exhibit 6.9.

INVENTORY PURCHASES AND SALES TRANSACTIONS COMPARED

Exhibit 6.8 summarizes and compares the journal entries for inventory purchases and sales transactions made on account for a perpetual inven—tory system. Notice that purchase transactions affect only balance sheet accounts, whereas sales transactions affect accounts on both the balance sheet and income statement. Also notice that purchase transactions are recorded at the merchandiser's cost, whereas sales transactions involve the selling price (SP) *and* cost of the merchandiser's inventory.

Evaluate the Results

MULTI-STEP INCOME STATEMENT

LEARNING OBJECTIVE 6-5

Prepare and analyze a merchandiser's multi-step income statement.

To survive, a merchandiser must sell goods for more than their cost. That's the only way companies like Walmart can generate enough money to cover operating expenses. To show how much profit is earned from product sales, without being clouded by other operating costs, merchandise companies often present their income statement using a multi—step format.

WAL-MART STORES, INC.
Income Statements
For the Years Ended January 31
(amounts in millions)

	2016	2015	2014
Net Sales	$478,614	$482,229	$473,076
Cost of Goods Sold	360,984	365,086	358,069
Gross Profit	117,630	117,143	115,007
Selling, General, and Administrative Expenses	97,041	93,418	91,353
Income from Operations	20,589	23,725	23,654
Other Income	1.049	1,074	1,002
Income Before Income Tax	21,638	24,799	24,656
Income Tax Expense	6,558	7,985	8,105
Net Income	$ 15,080	$ 16,814	$ 16,551

A **multi–step income statement** is similar to what you saw in the first few chapters, with expenses being subtracted from revenues to arrive at net income. The difference is that a multi–step format separates the revenues and expenses that relate to core operations from all the other (peripheral) items that affect net income. For merchandisers, a key mea–sure is the amount of profit earned over the cost of goods sold, so their multi–step income statements separate Cost of Goods Sold from other expenses. As shown in Exhibits 6.7 and 6.9, this extra step produces a subtotal called **gross profit**, which is the profit the company earned from selling goods, over and above the cost of the goods (also known as *gross margin*). If you buy something for $70 and sell it for $100, you'll have a gross profit of $30.

Notice in Exhibit 6.9 that after the gross profit line, the multi–step income statement presents other items in a format similar to what you saw for a service company in Chapter 3 (Exhibit 3.2). The category called *Selling, General, and Administrative Expenses* includes a variety of operating expenses including wages, utilities, advertising, rent, and the costs of delivering merchandise to customers. These expenses are subtracted from gross profit to yield Income from Operations, which is a measure of the company's income from regular operating activities, before considering the effects of interest, income taxes, and any non–recurring items.

Multi-step income statement: Presents import-ant subtotals, such as gross profit, to help distinguish core operating results from other, less significant items that affect net income.

Gross profit (or gross margin): Net sales minus cost of goods sold. It is a subtotal, not an account.

GROSS PROFIT ANALYSIS

Exhibit 6.9 presents Walmart's income statement in comparative format by showing results for more than one year. This format reveals that Walmart's gross profit increased throughout the three years. The difficulty in interpreting the increasing dollars of gross profit is that Walmart also increased its net sales over these three years, so we don't know whether the increase in gross profit dollars arises solely because Walmart increased its sales volume or whether it also is generating more profit per sale. To determine the amount of gross profit included in each dollar of sales, ana–lysts typically evaluate the gross profit percentage.

ACCOUNTING DECISION TOOLS

Name of Measure	Formula	What It Tells You
Gross profit percentage	$\dfrac{\text{Net Sales} - \text{CGS}}{\text{Net Sales}} \times 100$	• The percentage of profit earned on each dollar of sales, after considering the cost of products sold • A higher ratio means that greater profit is available to cover operating and other expenses

Gross profit percentage: A ratio indicating the percentage of profit earned on each dollar of sales, after considering the cost of products sold.

The **gross profit percentage** measures the percentage of profit earned on each dollar of sales. A higher gross profit percentage means that the company is selling products for a greater markup over its cost. This ratio can be used (1) to analyze changes in the company's operations over time, (2) to compare one company to another, and (3) to determine whether a company is earning enough on each sale to cover its operating expenses.

The graphic here shows that Walmart's gross profit percentage was constant at 24.3 percent across the years ended January 31, 2014, and 2015, and then increased slightly from 24.3 percent to 24.6 percent across the years ended January 31, 2015, and 2016. However, net sales decreased in the year ended January 31, 2016. Thus, the increase in total dollars of gross profit reported in that year could only be caused by an increase in gross profit per sale, not an increase in sales volume.

You might wonder whether it's even worth talking about a mere 0.3 per‑cent change in the gross profit percentage, but a small change in this ratio can lead to a big change in net income. In Walmart's case, because the company has such a huge sales volume (nearly $500 billion), even just one‑tenth of a percentage point increase in gross profit translates into almost half a billion dollars of addition profit ($500 billion × 0.001 = $0.5 billion). Yes, that's *billion*.

Comparing Gross Profit Percentages

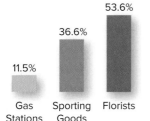

Gross Profit Percentage by Industry

Source: eStatement Studies, 2013-14.

Be aware that gross profit percentages can vary greatly between industries (as shown in the margin) and between companies in the same industry. Walmart's gross profit percentage of 24.6 percent is characteristic of its slogan of "Saving people money so they can live better." Walmart's strat‑egy is to earn a relatively small amount of profit on each dollar of sales, but to compensate by generating a huge volume of sales. In contrast, high‑end department stores carry brand‑name fashions with high‑end prices, resulting in fewer sales but more profit on each sale. In 2016, Hudson's Bay Company reported a 59.5 percent gross profit percentage.

As the following spotlight indicates, gross profit percentages can reveal problems in a merchandiser's operations.

EXHIBIT 6.10   Walmart's Gross Profit Percentage

WALMART'S GROSS PROFIT PERCENTAGE

		2016	2015	2014
$\dfrac{\text{Gross Profit}}{\text{Net Sales}}$	=	$\dfrac{\$117{,}630}{\$478{,}614}$	$\dfrac{\$117{,}143}{\$482{,}229}$	$\dfrac{\$115{,}007}{\$473{,}076}$
	=	0.246	0.243	0.243
		× 100	× 100	× 100
	=	24.6%	24.3%	24.3%

"Shoppers Are Buying More. They're Also Stealing More."

That's how a *Wall Street Journal* story described the 2013 third-quarter results at JC Penney (JCP) Co.[5] What attracted thieves to JCP? For one, customers were given cash refunds rather than store credit, even when they didn't have a sales receipt, so that gave them an *incentive* to steal. Second, they had an *opportunity* to steal because JCP had removed antitheft sensor tags from its products to avoid interfering with radio frequency identification (RFID) tags, which had just been introduced to better track inventory.

Oops. How much did this blunder cost the company? In a conference call with analysts, the CEO indicated that it accounted for a decline of "100 basis points" of gross profit, which is Wall Street lingo for one full percentage point. Given JCP's third-quarter sales of $2.8 billion, one percentage point translates into a loss of $28 million ($2.8 billion × 0.01 = $28 million).

SPOTLIGHT ON IFRS and ASPE

The majority of the differences between ASPE and IFRS for cash and merchandise sales are in the accounting for the inventory costs themselves and the valuation of this inventory. These differences will be outlined in Chapter 7.

Supplement 6A

SALES OF BUNDLED PRODUCTS/SERVICES

LEARNING OBJECTIVE **6-S1**

Record sales of bundled products/services.

A common practice for many businesses is to sell a product and service as a *bundle*, with a single price for the package. For example, ADT sells home security equipment with monitoring services, Rogers sells cable TV equipment with TV programming, Bell sells cell phones with cellular service, Johnson & Johnson sells hospital equipment with training and repair services, and so on. In each case, the total price covers more than one performance obligation. To ensure proper reporting of revenue earned by fulfilling each performance obligation, these companies follow a five–step revenue model as shown below.

Consider a simple example where Sirius XM sells a vehicle equipment kit and twelve–month radio access subscription for a combined price of $200. Separately, the equipment and subscription sell for $100 and $150, respectively. The customer pays the $200 price on October 30, receives the equipment on October 31, and the subscription begins November 1. Sirius XM held the equipment in its Inventory at its $35 cost. The five–step revenue model is used below to determine how much and when revenue from selling the bundle is reported. Exhibit 6A.1 summarizes these steps.

Step 1. Identify the contract. A contract is agreed to online, establishing responsibilities relating to shipping, radio signal access, payment, pricing, and more.

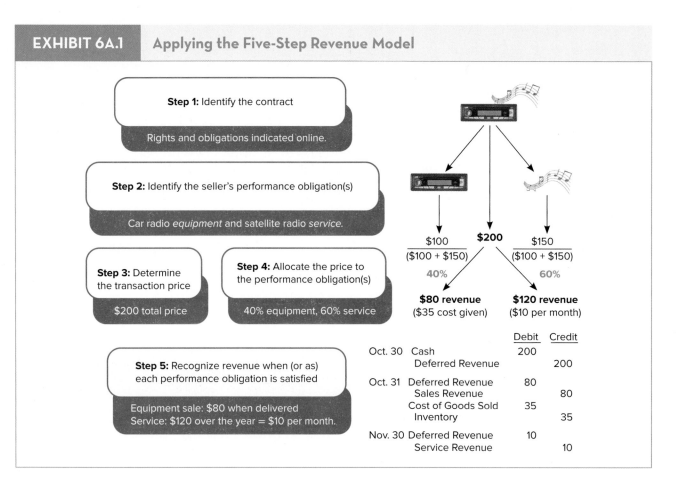

Step 2. Identify the seller's performance obligations. Sirius XM promises to provide radio equipment and one year of radio service, so it has two per–formance obligations.

Step 3. Determine the transaction price. The total price for the transaction is $200, as stated.

Step 4. Allocate the transaction price to the performance obligation(s). This allocation is made based on the standalone selling prices of the equipment and service. When sold separately, the price of the equipment is $100 and the twelve–month service is $150, equaling a total of $250. Relative to this total, the $100 equipment price is 40 percent (calculated as $100 divided by $250) and the $150 radio service is 60 percent (calculated as $150 divided by $250). Thus, the $200 total price for the bundle is allocated 40 percent to equipment and 60 percent to the radio service. In dollars, revenue for delivering the equipment is $80 (40 percent of $200) and revenue from providing the radio service is $120 (60 percent of $200).

Step 5. Recognize revenue when (or as) each performance obligation is satisfied. When the $200 cash is received October 30, Sirius XM has not satisfied its performance obligations, so it records the $200 as a liability (Deferred Revenue). On October 31, when Sirius XM delivers the radio kit, it fulfills the performance obligation to provide equipment, so at that point it reduces its liability and records revenue of $80. If Sirius XM uses a per–petual inventory system, it also records cost of goods sold of $35, reducing Inventory by the same amount. No revenue for the radio service is recorded on October 31 because that performance obligation is fulfilled over time as

PERIODIC RECORDS	PERPETUAL RECORDS

A. Record purchases:

April 14:

	Debit	Credit
Purchases (170 units at $60)	10,200	
Accounts Payable		10,200

A. Record purchases:

April 14:

	Debit	Credit
Inventory (170 units at $60)	10,200	
Accounts Payable		10,200

B. Record sales (but not cost of goods sold):

November 30:

Accounts Receivable	12,000	
Sales Revenue (150 units at $80)		12,000

No cost of goods sold entry

B. Record sales and cost of goods sold:

November 30:

Accounts Receivable	12,000	
Sales Revenue (150 units at $80)		12,000

Cost of Goods Sold	9,000	
Inventory (150 units at $60)		9,000

C. Record end-of-period adjustments:

  a. Count the number of units on hand.
  b. Compute the dollar valuation of the ending inventory.
  c. Compute and record the cost of goods sold.

Beginning Inventory (last period's ending) (80 units at $60)	$ 4,800
Add: Net Purchases	10,200
Cost of Goods Available for Sale	15,000
Deduct: Ending Inventory (physical count—100 units at $60)	6,000
Cost of Goods Sold	$ 9,000

December 31:

Transfer beginning inventory and net purchases to cost of goods sold (act as if all goods were sold):

Cost of Goods Sold	15,000	
Inventory (beginning)		4,800
Purchases		10,200

Adjust the cost of goods sold by subtracting the amount of ending inventory still on hand (recognize that not all goods were sold):

Inventory (ending)	6,000	
Cost of Goods Sold		6,000

C. Record end-of-period adjustments:

At the end of the accounting period, the balance in the Cost of Goods Sold account is reported on the income statement. Computing the cost of goods sold is not necessary because the **Cost of Goods Sold** account is up to date. Also, the **Inventory** account shows the ending inventory amount reported on the balance sheet. A physical inventory count is still necessary to assess the accuracy of the perpetual records and identify theft and other forms of shrinkage. Any shrinkage would be recorded by reducing the **Inventory** account and increasing an expense account **(Cost of Goods Sold)**. This illustration assumes that no shrinkage has been detected.

No entries

PERIODIC	PERPETUAL

Assets		=	Liabilities	+	Stockholders' Equity	
Purchases	+10,200		Accounts Payable +10,200			
Accts. Rec.	+12,000				Sales Revenue (+R)	+12,000
Inventory	−4,800				Cost of Goods Sold (+E)	−15,000
Purchases	−10,200					
Inventory	+6,000				Cost of Goods Sold (−E)	+6,000
Totals	**+13,200**	**=**	**+10,200**			**+3,000**

Assets		=	Liabilities	+	Stockholders' Equity	
Inventory	+10,200		Accounts Payable +10,200			
Accts. Rec.	+12,000				Sales Revenue (+R)	+12,000
Inventory	−9,000				Cost of Goods Sold (+E)	−9,000
Totals	**+13,200**	**=**	**+10,200**			**+3,000**

each month of service is provided. Consequently, $120 remains as a liability in Deferred Revenue. On November 30, Sirius XM will adjust its accounts to show it has fulfilled 1/12 of promised radio services, resulting in $10 of revenue. A similar adjustment to decrease Deferred Revenue and report $10 of Service Revenue is made each month as the promised services are provided.

Supplement 6B

RECORDING INVENTORY TRANSACTIONS IN A PERIODIC SYSTEM

LEARNING OBJECTIVE 6-S2

Record inventory transactions in a periodic system.

As you have learned, businesses using a periodic inventory system update inventory records only at the end of the accounting period. Unlike a perpetual inventory system, a periodic system does not track the cost of goods sold during the accounting period.

This supplement illustrates typical journal entries made when using a periodic inventory system. The table that follows contrasts those entries with the entries that would be recorded using a perpetual inventory system. A summary of the effects of the journal entries on the accounting equation follows them. Note that the total effects and the resulting financial statements are identical. Only the timing and the nature of the entries differ.

Assume for the purposes of this illustration that an electronics retailer stocks and sells just one item and that only the following events occurred:

Jan. 1	Beginning inventory: 80 units at a unit cost of $60
Apr. 14	Purchased 170 additional units on account at a unit cost of $60
Nov. 30	Sold 150 units on account at a unit sales price of $80
Dec. 31	Discounted 100 units at a unit cost of $60

Review the Chapter

This section provides a chance to solidify your understanding of key points. It's worth your time to work through the following demonstration cases, scan the chapter summary, test your understanding of key terms, and then practise, practise, practise.

DEMONSTRATION CASE

Assume Oakley, Inc.—the maker of sunglasses, goggles, and other products—made merchandise costing $137,200 and sold it on credit to Sunglass Hut for $405,000 with terms 2/10, n/30. Some of the merchandise differed from what Sunglass Hut had ordered, so Oakley agreed to give an allowance of $5,000. Sunglass Hut satisfied the remaining balance (of $400,000) by paying within the discount period.

Required:

1. Assuming that Oakley uses a perpetual inventory system, analyze the accounting equation effects and record the journal entries that Oakley would use for the following transactions:
   a. Sale from Oakley to Sunglass Hut
   b. Allowance granted by Oakley
   c. Payment made by Sunglass Hut to Oakley
2. Compute Oakley's net sales, assuming that sales returns and allowances and sales discounts are treated as contra-revenues.

3. Compute Oakley's gross profit and gross profit percentage on the sale. Compare this ratio to the 66.5 percent gross profit percentage earned by the Luxottica Group—the Italian company that makes Killer Loop® and Ray–Ban® sunglasses, which are sold through its Sunglass Hut stores. What does it imply about the two companies?

COACH'S TIP

Transaction (b) depicts an allowance but no return of goods. Had goods been returned, Oakley also would increase its Inventory and decrease its Cost of Goods Sold.

Suggested Solution

1. a. Sale from Oakley to Sunglass Hut

1 Analyze

Assets	= Liabilities +	Shareholders' Equity	
Accounts Receivable +405,000		Sales Revenue (+R)	+405,000
Inventory −137,200		Cost of Goods Sold (+E)	−137,200

2 Record

dr Accounts Receivable (+A)	405,000	
cr Sales Rrevenue (+R, +SE)		405,000
dr Cost of Goods Sold (+E, −SE)	137,200	
cr Inventory (−A)		137,200

b. Allowance granted by Oakley

1 Analyze

Assets	= Liabilities +	Shareholders' Equity
Accounts Receivable +5,000		Sales Returns and allowances (+xR) −5,000

2 Record

dr Sales Returns and allowances (+xR, −SE)	5,000	
cr Accounts Receivable (−A)		5,000

c. Payment made by Sunglass Hut to Oakley

1 Analyze

Assets	= Liabilities +	Shareholders' Equity
Cash +392,000		Sales Discounts (+xR) −800,000
Accounts Receivable −400,000		

2 Record

dr Cash (+A)	392,000	
dr Sales Discounts (+xR, −SE)	800,000	
cr Accounts Receivable (−A)		400,000

2. Sales returns and allowances and sales discounts should be subtracted from sales revenue to compute net sales:

Sales Revenue	$405,000
Less: Sales Returns and Allowances	5,000
Sales Discounts	8,000*
Net Sales	
*$8,000 = 2% × ($405,000 − $5,000)	392,000

3. Gross profit and gross profit percentage are calculated as follows:

	In Dollars	% of Net Sales
Net Sales (calculated in 2 above)	$392,000	100.0%
Less: Cost of Goods Sold	137,200	35.0
Gross Profit	$254,800	65.0%

The 65 percent gross profit percentage indicates that Oakley generates 65 cents of gross profit on each dollar of sales. This is 1.5 cents less gross profit on each dollar of sales than Luxottica ($1.5 = 66.5 - 65.0$). This difference implies that Luxottica is including a higher markup in its selling prices than Oakley is.

CHAPTER SUMMARY

LO6-1   Distinguish between service and merchandising operations.

- Service companies sell services rather than physical goods; consequently, their income statements show costs of services rather than cost of goods sold.
- Merchandising companies sell goods that have been obtained from a supplier. Retail merchandising companies sell directly to consumers, whereas wholesale merchandising companies sell to retail companies.

LO6-2   Explain the differences between periodic and perpetual inventory systems.

- Periodic inventory records are updated only when inventory is counted, usually at the end of each accounting period.
- Perpetual inventory systems promote efficient and effective operations because they provide an up–to–date record of inventory that should be on hand at any given time. They protect against undetected theft because this up–to–date record can be compared to a count of the physical quantity that actually is on hand.

LO6-3   Analyze purchase transactions under a perpetual inventory system.

- The Inventory account should include costs incurred to get inventory into a condition and location ready for sale.
- The cost of inventory includes its purchase price and transportation (freight–in) minus cost reductions for purchase returns and allowances, purchase discounts, and goods sold. Costs to deliver inventory to customers (freight–out) are a selling expense and are not included in inventory.

LO6-4   Analyze sales transactions under a perpetual inventory system.

- In a perpetual inventory system, two entries are made every time inventory is sold: one entry records the sale (and corresponding debit to Cash or Accounts Receivable) and the other entry records the Cost of Goods Sold (and corre–sponding credit to Inventory).
- Sales discounts and sales returns and allowances are reported as contra–revenues, reducing net sales.

LO6-5   Prepare and analyze a merchandiser's multi-step income statement.

- One of the key items in a merchandiser's multi–step income statement is gross profit, which is a subtotal calculated by subtracting cost of goods sold from net sales. The gross profit percentage is calculated and interpreted as follows.

ACCOUNTING DECISION TOOLS

Name of Measure	Formula	What It Tells You
Gross profit percentage	$\dfrac{\text{Net Sales} - \text{CGS}}{\text{Net Sales}} \times 100$	• The percentage of profit earned on each dollar of sales, after considering the cost of products sold • A higher ratio means that greater profit is available to cover operating and other expenses

SOLUTIONS TO SELF-STUDY PRACTICE

Solution to SP6.1

Case 1: Goods available = $250, CGS = $150
Case 2: Ending inventory = $100

Inventory			
Beginning Inventory	50		
Purchases	200		
Goods Available	250		
		150	Goods Sold
Ending Inventory	100		

Solution to SP6.2

	Assets	=	Liabilities	+	Shareholders' Equity
Oct 1	Inventory + 10,000	=	Accounts Payable + 10,000		

> *dr* Inventory (+A) 10,000
>   *cr* Accounts Payable (+L) 10,000

	Assets		=	Liabilities	+	Shareholders' Equity
Oct 8	Cash	−9,800	=	Accounts Payable − 10,000		
	Inventory	−200				

> *dr* Accounts Payable (−L) 10,000
>   *cr* Cash (−A) 9,800
>   *cr* Inventory (−A) 200

KEY TERMS

Cost of Goods Sold (CGS) Equation
FOB (Free On Board) Destination
FOB (Free On Board) Shipping Point
Goods Available for Sale
Gross Profit (or Gross Margin)
Gross Profit Percentage

Inventory
Manufacturing Companies
Merchandising Companies
Multi−step Income Statement
Periodic Inventory System
Perpetual Inventory System
Purchase Discount

Purchase Returns and Allowances
Sales Discount
Sales Returns and Allowances
Service Companies
Shrinkage

Complete definitions are also provided in the glossary at the end of this text.

HOMEWORK HELPER

Multi-step Income Statement Format (heading omitted)

Sales Revenue	$ 100,000
Less: Sales Returns and Allowances	(2,500)
Sales Discounts	(1,500)
Net Sales	96,000
Cost of Goods Sold	55,000
Gross Profit	41,000
Selliing, General, and Administrative Expenses	21,000
Income from Operations	20,000
Other Revenue (Expenses)	5,000
Income before Income Tax Expense	25,000
Income Tax Expense	10,000
Net Income	$ 15,000

Reported Externally

Reported Internally

Alternative terms

- *Gross profit* is also called *gross margin* or *margin*.

Helpful reminders

- Purchase and sales discounts are calculated after taking into account any returns and allowances. A partial payment within the discount period (such as one–half the total amount owed) usually qualifies for a partial discount (one–half of the discount on the total).
- Sales Returns have two components: (1) an adjustment to the selling price (record a contra–revenue and a decrease in Cash or Accounts Receivable) and (2) return of goods previously recorded as sold (record an increase in Inventory and a decrease in Cost of Goods Sold). Sales Allowances involve only the first component, because no goods are returned to the seller.

Frequent mistakes

- Discounts (or "markdowns") in the selling price of merchandise occur prior to making a sale, so they are not recorded. Sales Discounts, given to customers after making a sale, are recorded in a contra–revenue account, to offset the Sales Revenue recorded on the initial sales transaction.
- Gross profit percentage is calculated as a percentage of Net Sales, not Cost of Goods Sold.

PRACTICE MATERIAL

QUESTIONS (Ⓢ Symbol indicates questions that require analysis from more than one perspective.)

1. What is the distinction between service and merchandising companies? What is the distinction between merchandising and manufacturing com–panies? What is the distinction between retail and wholesale merchandising companies?

2. If a Saskatchewan–based company ships goods on September 30 to a customer in Toronto with sales terms FOB destination, does the Saskatchewan–based company include the inventory or the sale in its September financial statements?

3. Define *goods available for sale*. How does it differ from cost of goods sold?

4. Define *beginning inventory* and *ending inventory*.

5. Describe how transportation costs to obtain inventory (freight—in) are accounted for by a merchandising company using a perpetual inventory system. Explain the reasoning behind this accounting treatment.

6. What is the main distinction between perpetual and periodic inventory systems? Which type of system provides better internal control over inventory? Explain why.

7. Why is a physical count of inventory necessary in a periodic inventory system? Why is it still necessary in a perpetual inventory system?

8. What is the difference between FOB shipping point and FOB destination? How do these terms relate to the revenue principle?

9. Describe in words the journal entries that are made in a perpetual inventory system when inventory is sold on credit.

10. What is the distinction between *sales returns* and *sales allowances?*

11. What is a sales discount? Use 1/10, n/30 in your explanation.

12. In response to the weak economy, your company's sales force is urging you, the sales manager, to change sales terms from 1/10, n/30 to 2/10, n/45. Explain what these terms mean and how this switch could increase or decrease your company's profits.

13. Explain the difference between Sales Revenue and Net Sales.

14. Why are contra—revenue accounts used rather than directly deducting from the Sales Revenue account?

15. What is gross profit? How is the gross profit percentage computed? Illustrate its calculation and interpretation assuming Net Sales is $100,000 and Cost of Goods Sold is $60,000.

MINI-EXERCISES

M6-1 Distinguishing Among Operating Cycles

LO6-1

Identify the type of business as service (S), retail merchandiser (RM), wholesale merchandiser (WM), or manufacturer (M) for each of the following.

____ 1. The company reports no inventory on its balance sheet.

____ 2. The company is a true "middleman," buying from a manufacturer and selling to other companies.

____ 3. The company's inventory includes raw materials that will be processed into ready—to—use goods.

____ 4. The company sells goods to consumers.

M6-2 Calculating Shrinkage in a Perpetual Inventory System

LO6-2

Corey's Campus Store has $4,000 of inventory on hand at the beginning of the month. During the month, the company buys $41,000 of merchandise and sells merchandise that cost $30,000. At the end of the month, $13,000 of inventory is on hand. How much shrinkage occurred during the month?

M6-3 Items Included in Inventory

LO6-3

Explain whether the following items should be included in the inventory of The Knot, a company that arranges and supplies wedding services for couples and other wedding consultants.

a. Goods are being held by The Knot on consignment from Emerald Bridal.

b. Goods in transit to Winston Wedding Consultants, sold by The Knot, FOB shipping point.

c. Goods in transit to The Knot, purchased by The Knot, FOB shipping point.

LO6-3 **M6-4** **Items Included in Inventory**

Dillard's, Inc. operates department stores located primarily in the Southwest, Southeast, and Midwest United States. In its 2013 third–quarter report, the company reported Cost of Goods Sold of $1.0 billion, ending inventory for the third quarter of $1.8 billion, and ending inventory for the previous quarter of $1.5 billion. Determine the amount of merchandise purchases for the third quarter.

LO6-3 **M6-5** **Evaluating Inventory Cost Components**

Assume Anderson's General Store bought, on credit, a truckload of merchandise from American Wholesaling costing $23,000. If the company was charged $650 in transportation cost by National Trucking, immediately returned goods to American Wholesaling costing $1,200, and then took advantage of American Wholesaling's 2/10, n/30 purchase discount, how much did this inventory cost Anderson's?

LO6-3 **M6-6** **Preparing Journal Entries for Purchases, Purchase Discounts, and Purchase Returns Using a Perpetual System**

Using the information in M6–5, prepare journal entries to record the inventory transactions, assuming Anderson's uses a perpetual inventory system.

LO6-3, 6-5 **M6-7** **Recording Journal Entries for Purchases and Sales Using a Perpetual Inventory System**

Inventory at the beginning of the year cost $13,400. During the year, the company purchased (on account) inventory costing $84,000. Inventory that had cost $80,000 was sold on account for $95,000. At the end of the year, inventory was counted and its cost was determined to be $17,400. (1) Show the cost of goods sold equation using these numbers. (2) What was the dollar amount of Gross Profit? (3) Prepare journal entries to record these transactions, assuming a perpetual inventory system is used.

LO6-4 **M6-8** **Reporting Net Sales and Gross Profit with Sales Discounts**

Merchandise costing $2,000 is sold for $3,000 on terms 2/10, n/30. If the buyer pays within the discount period, what amount will be reported on the income statement as net sales and as gross profit?

LO6-4 **M6-9** **Recording Journal Entries for Sales and Sales Discounts**

Using the information in M6–8, prepare the journal entries needed at the time of sale and collection, assuming the company uses a perpetual inventory system.

LO6-4 **M6-10** **Choosing between FOB Shipping Point and FOB Destination**

In its 2011 annual report, American Eagle Outfitters states that its "e–commerce operation records revenue upon the estimated customer receipt date of the mer–chandise." Is this FOB shipping point or FOB destination? If American Eagle was to change to the other terms of shipment, would it report its Sales Revenues earlier or later?

LO6-4 **M6-11** **Journal Entries to Record Sales Discounts**

Inventory that cost $500 is sold for $700, with terms of 2/10, n/30. Give the journal entries to record (a) the sale of merchandise and (b) collection of the accounts receivable assuming that it occurs during the discount period.

LO6-2, 6-5 **M6-12** **Calculating Shrinkage and Gross Profit in a Perpetual Inventory System**

LEVEL UP

Nord Store's perpetual accounting system indicated ending inventory of $20,000, cost of goods sold of $100,000, and net sales of $150,000. A year–end inventory count determined that goods costing $15,000 were actually on hand. Calculate (a) the cost of shrinkage, (b) an adjusted cost of goods sold (assuming shrinkage is charged to cost of goods sold), (c) gross profit percentage before shrinkage, and (d) gross profit percentage after shrinkage.

M6-13 Preparing a Multi-step Income Statement

LO6-5

Sellall Department Stores reported the following amounts in its adjusted trial balance prepared as of December 31: Administrative Expenses, $2,400; Cost of Goods Sold, $22,728; Income Tax Expense, $3,000; Interest Expense, $1,600; Interest Revenue, $200; General Expenses, $2,600; Sales Revenue, $42,000; Sales Discounts, $2,200; Sales Returns and Allowances, $1,920; and Delivery (freight–out) Expense, $300. Prepare a multi–step income statement for distribution to external financial statement users, using a format similar to Exhibit 6.11.

M6-14 Computing and Interpreting the Gross Profit Percentage

LO6-5

Using the information in M6–13, calculate the gross profit percentage (rounded to one decimal place). How has Sellall performed, relative to the gross profit percentages reported for Walmart in the chapter?

M6-15 Computing and Interpreting the Gross Profit Percentage

LO6-5

Ziehart Pharmaceuticals reported Net Sales of $178,000 and Cost of Goods Sold of $58,000. Candy Electronics Corp. reported Net Sales of $36,000 and Cost of Goods Sold of $26,200. Calculate the gross profit percentage for both companies (rounded to one decimal place). Which company has a greater proportion of its sales available to cover expenses other than cost of goods sold?

M6-16 Interpreting Changes in Gross Profit Percentage

LO6-5

Luxottica Group, the Italian company that sells Ray Ban and Oakley sunglasses, reported net sales of €7.1 billion in 2012 and €6.2 billion in 2011. Gross profit increased from €4.1 billion in 2011 to €4.7 billion in 2012. Was the increase in gross profit caused by (a) an increase in gross profit per sale, (b) an increase in sales volume, or (c) a combination of (a) and (b)?

M6-17 Determining the Cause of Increasing Gross Profit

LO6-5

Fortune Brands Home & Security, Inc. sells Master Lock padlocks. It reported an increase in net sales from $3.3 billion in 2011 to $3.6 billion in 2012, and an increase in gross profit from $1.0 billion in 2011 to $1.2 billion in 2012. Based on these numbers, determine whether the change in gross profit was caused by an increase in gross profit per sale, an increase in sales volume, or a combination of the two.

M6-18 Understanding Relationships Among Gross Profit and Inventory

LO6-2, 6-5

If net sales are $300,000, cost of goods available for sale is $280,000, and gross profit percentage is 35 percent, what is the amount of ending inventory?

EXERCISES

E6-1 Relating Financial Statement Reporting to Type of Company

LO6-1

For each of the following, indicate whether the item would be reported on the balance sheet (B/S), reported on the income statement (I/S), or not shown in the financial statements (Not) and whether it relates to a service company (SC) or merchandising company (MC).

	Financial Statement	Type of Company
Inventory		
Sales Revenue		
Cost of Goods Available for Sale		
Service Revenue		

E6-2 Inferring Merchandise Purchases

LO6-2

The Gap, Inc. is a specialty retailer that operates stores selling clothes under the trade names Gap, Banana Republic, and Old Navy. Assume that you are employed as a stock analyst and your boss has just completed a review of the annual report of The Gap, Inc. for the third quarter of 2013. She provided you with her notes, but they are missing some information that you need. Her notes show that the inventory for The Gap was $2.4 billion at the end of the quarter and $1.8 billion at the beginning of the quarter. Net Sales for the quarter were $4.0 billion. Gross Profit was $1.6 billion and Net Income was $330 million.

Required:

Determine the Cost of Goods Sold and purchases for the third quarter.

LO6-2   **E6-3 Identifying Shrinkage and Other Missing Inventory Information**

Calculate the missing information for each of the following independent cases:

Cases	Beginning Inventory	Purchases	Cost of Goods Sold	Ending Inventory (perpetual system)	Ending Inventory (as counted)	Shrinkage
A	$100	$700	$300	?	$420	$?
B	200	800	?	150	150	?
C	150	500	200	450	?	10
D	260	?	650	210	200	?

LO6-2   **E6-4 Inferring Shrinkage Using a Perpetual Inventory System**

Hudson's Bay Company (HBC) is Canada's largest diversified general merchandise retailer, with over 600 retail locations and nearly 60,000 associates located in every province in Canada. HBC's two banners are The Bay and Home Outfitters. In 2017, assume that HBC reported Cost of Goods sold of $11,571 million, Ending Inventory for the current year of $3,259 million, and Ending Inventory for the previous year (2016) of $3,641 million.

Required:

If you knew that the cost of inventory purchases was $11,289 million, could you estimate the cost of shrinkage during the year? If so, prepare the estimate and, if not, explain why not.

LO6-2, 6-5   **E6-5 Inferring Missing Amounts Based on Income Statement Relationships**

Check Figure [Case E]: Cost of Goods Sold = $500

Supply the missing dollar amounts for Lewis Retailers's income statement for each of the following independent cases:

Cases	Sales Revenue	Beginning Inventory	Purchases	Cost of Goods Available for Sale	Cost of Goods Sold	Cost of Ending Inventory	Gross Profit
A	$ 650	$ 100	$700	$?	$300	$?	$?
B	900	200	800	?	?	150	?
C	?	150	?	?	200	300	400
D	800	?	600	?	650	250	?
E	1,000	50	900	?	?	?	500

LO6-2, 6-5   **E6-6 Inferring Missing Amounts Based on Income Statement Relationships**

Supply the missing dollar amounts for Clark Retailers's income statement for each of the following independent cases:

Cases	Sales Revenue	Beginning Inventory	>Purchases	Total Available	Ending Inventory	Cost of Goods Sold	Gross Profit	Selling and General Expenses	Income from Operations
A	$800	$100	$700	$?	$500	$?	$?	$200	$?
B	900	200	700	?	?	?	?	150	0
C	?	150	?	?	250	200	400	100	?
D	800	?	600	?	250	?	?	250	100

E6-7 Reporting Purchases and Purchase Discounts Using a Perpetual Inventory System

LO6-3

During the months of January and February, Axen Corporation purchased goods from three suppliers. The sequence of events was as follows:

Jan.	6	Purchased goods for $1,200 from Green with terms 2/10, n/30
	6	Purchased goods from Munoz for $900 with terms 2/10, n/30
	14	Paid Green in full
Feb.	2	Paid Munoz in full
	28	Purchased goods for $350 from Reynolds with terms 2/10, n/45

Required:

Assume that Axen uses a perpetual inventory system, the company had no inventory on hand at the beginning of January, and no sales were made during January and February. Calculate the cost of inventory as of February 28.

E6-8 Recording Journal Entries for Purchases and Purchase Discounts Using a Perpetual Inventory System

LO6-3

Using the information in E6-7, prepare journal entries to record the transactions, assuming Axen uses a perpetual inventory system.

E6-9 Reporting Purchases, Purchase Discounts, and Purchase Returns Using a Perpetual Inventory System

LO6-3

During the month of June, Ace Incorporated purchased goods from two suppliers. The sequence of events was as follows:

Check Figure:
Cost of Inventory = $3,058

June	3	Purchased goods for $3,200 from Diamond Inc. with terms 2/10, n/30
	5	Returned goods costing $1,100 to Diamond Inc. for full credit
	6	Purchased goods from Club Corp. for $1,000 with terms 2/10, n/30
	11	Paid the balance owed to Diamond Inc.
	22	Paid Club Corp. in full

Required:

Assume that Ace uses a perpetual inventory system and that the company had no inventory on hand at the beginning of the month. Calculate the cost of inventory as of June 30.

E6-10 Recording Journal Entries for Purchases, Purchase Discounts, and Purchase Returns Using a Perpetual Inventory System

LO6-3

Using the information in E6-9, prepare journal entries to record the transactions, assuming Ace uses a perpetual inventory system.

E6-11 Items Included in Inventory

LO6-3, 6-4

PC Mall, Inc. is a direct marketer of computer hardware, software, peripherals, and electronics. In a recent annual report, the company reported that its revenue is "recognized upon receipt of the product by the customer."

Required:

1. Indicate whether PC Mall's sales terms are FOB shipping point or FOB destination.
2. Assume PC Mall sold inventory on account to eCOST.com on December 28 that was to be delivered January 3. The inventory cost PC Mall $25,000 and the selling price was $30,000. What amounts, if any, related to this transaction would be reported on PC Mall's balance sheet and income statement in December? In January?
3. Assume PC Mall purchased electronics on December 29 that were shipped that day and received on January 2. For these goods to be included in PC Mall's inventory on December 31, would the terms have been FOB destination or FOB shipping point?

LO6-4

E6-12 Reporting Net Sales with Credit Sales and Sales Discounts

Check Figure:
Net Sales = $228

During the months of January and February, Solitare Corporation sold goods to three customers. The sequence of events was as follows:

Jan. 6   Sold goods for $100 to Wizard Inc. with terms 2/10, n/30; goods cost Solitare $70
     6   Sold goods to SpyderCorp. for $80 with terms 2/10, n/30; goods cost Solitare $60
    14   Collected cash due from Wizard Inc.
Feb. 2   Collected cash due from SpyderCorp
    28   Sold goods for $50 to Bridges with terms 2/10, n/45; goods cost Solitare $30

Required:

Assuming that Sales Discounts are reported as contra–revenue, compute Net Sales for the two months ended February 28.

LO6-4

E6-13 Recording Journal Entries for Net Sales with Credit Sales and Sales Discounts

Using the information in E6–12, prepare journal entries to record the transactions, assuming Solitare uses a perpetual inventory system.

LO6-4

E6-14 Reporting Net Sales with Credit Sales and Sales Discounts

The following transactions were selected from the records of Evergreen Company:

July 12   Sold merchandise to Wally Butler, who paid for the $1,000 purchase with cash. The goods cost Evergreen Company $600.
    15   Sold merchandise to Claudio's Chair Company at a selling price of $5,000 on terms 3/10, n/30. The goods cost Evergreen Company $3,500.
    20   Sold merchandise to Otto's Ottomans at a selling price of $3,000 on terms 3/10, n/30. The goods cost Evergreen Company $1,900.
    23   Collected payment from Claudio's Chair Company from the July 15 sale.
Aug. 25   Collected payment from Otto's Ottomans from the July 20 sale.

Required:

Assuming that Sales Discounts are reported as contra–revenue, compute Net Sales for the two months ended August 31.

LO6-4

E6-15 Recording Journal Entries for Net Sales with Credit Sales and Sales Discounts

Using the information in E6–14, prepare journal entries to record the transactions, assuming Evergreen Company uses a perpetual inventory system.

LO6-4

E6-16 Reporting Net Sales with Credit Sales, Sales Discounts, and Sales Returns

The following transactions were selected from among those completed by Bear's Retail Store:

Nov. 20 Sold two items of merchandise to Cheryl Jahn, who paid the $400 sales price in cash. The goods cost Bear's $300.

     25 Sold 20 items of merchandise to Vasko Athletics at a selling price of $4,000 (total); terms 3/10, n/30. The goods cost Bear's $2,500.

     28 Sold 10 identical items of merchandise to Nancy's Gym at a selling price of $6,000 (total); terms 3/10, n/30. The goods cost Bear's $4,000.

     29 Nancy's Gym returned one of the items purchased on the 28th. The item was in perfect condition, and credit was given to the customer.

Dec. 6 Nancy's Gym paid the account balance in full.

     30 Vasko Athletics paid in full for the invoice of November 25.

Required:

Assuming that Sales Returns and Sales Discounts are reported as contra−revenues, compute Net Sales for the two months ended December 31.

E6-17 Recording Journal Entries for Net Sales with Credit Sales, Sales Discounts, and Sales Returns

LO6-4

Using the information in E6−16, prepare journal entries to record the transactions, assuming Bear's Retail Store uses a perpetual inventory system.

E6-18 Determining the Effects of Credit Sales, Sales Discounts, and Sales Returns and Allowances on Income Statement Categories

LO6-4, 6-5

Rockland Shoe Company records Sales Returns and Allowances and Sales Discounts as contra−revenues. Complete the following table, indicating the amount and direction of effect (+ for increase, − for decrease, and NE for no effect) of each transaction on each item reported in Rockland's income statement prepared for internal use. Be sure to total the effects.

July 12 Rockland sold merchandise to Kristina Zee at its factory store. Kristina paid for the $300 purchase in cash. The goods cost Rockland $160.

     15 Sold merchandise to Shoe Express at a selling price of $5,000, with terms 3/10, n/30. Rockland's cost was $3,000.

     20 Collected cash due from Shoe Express.

     21 Sold merchandise to Fleet Foot Co. at a selling price of $2,000, with terms 2/10, n/30. Rockland's cost was $1,200.

     23 Fleet Foot Co. returned $1,000 of shoes and promised to pay for the remaining goods in August. The returned shoes were in perfect condition and had cost Rockland $600.

Transaction Date:	July 12	July 15	July 20	July 21	July 23	Totals
Sales Revenues						
Sales Returns and Allowances						
Sales Discounts						
Net Sales						
Cost of Goods Sold						
Gross Profit						

E6-19 Analyzing and Recording Sales and Gross Profit With and Without Sales Discounts

LO6-4, 6-5

Cycle Wholesaling sells merchandise on credit terms of 2/10, n/30. A sale for $800 (cost of goods sold of $500) was made to Sarah's Cycles on February 1. Assume Cycle Wholesaling uses a perpetual inventory system.

Required:

1. Give the journal entry Cycle Wholesaling would make to record the sale to Sarah's Cycles.

2. Give the journal entry to record the collection of the account, assuming it was collected in full on February 9.

3. Give the journal entry, assuming, instead, that the account was collected in full on March 2.

4. Calculate the gross profit percentage for the sale to Sarah's Cycles, assuming the account was collected in full on February 9.

LO6-5

Check Figure
[Case A]:
Gross Profit = $2,100

E6-20 Inferring Missing Amounts Based on Income Statement Relationships

Supply the missing dollar amounts for the income statement of Williamson Company for each of the following independent cases:

	Case A	Case B	Case C
Sales Revenues	$8,000	$6,000	$?
Sales Returns and Allowances	150	?	275
Net Sales	?	?	5,920
Cost of Goods Sold	5,750	4,050	5,400
Gross Profit	?	1,450	?

LO6-5

E6-21 Analyzing Gross Profit Percentage on the Basis of a Multi-step Income Statement

The following summarized data were provided by the records of Mystery Incorporated for the year ended December 31:

Administrative Expense	$ 19,000
Cost of Goods Sold	165,000
Income Tax Expense	17,600
Sales Returns and Allowances	7,000
Selling Expense	40,200
Sales of merchandise for cash	240,000
Sales of merchandise on credit	42,000

Required:

1. Based on these data, prepare a multi–step income statement for internal reporting purposes (showing all appropriate subtotals and totals).

2. What was the amount of gross profit? What was the gross profit percentage (calculated using the formula shown in this chapter)? Explain what these two amounts mean.

3. Did the gross profit percentage in the current year improve, or decline, relative to the 38.0 percent gross profit percentage in the prior year?

LO6-5

E6-22 Analyzing Gross Profit Percentage on the Basis of an Income Statement

Grizzly World Wide Inc. prides itself as being the world's leading marketer of Canadian branded non–athletic footwear. The following data (in millions) were taken from its annual report for the fiscal year ended January 31:

Sales of Merchandise	$1,220
Income Tax Expense	45
Cash Dividends Paid	21
Selling and Administrative Expense	345
Cost of Products Sold	735
Interest Expense	3
Other Revenues	3

Required:

1. Based on these data, prepare a multi–step income statement.

2. How much was the gross profit? What was the gross profit percentage? (Round to the nearest tenth of a percentage point.) Explain what these two amounts mean.

3. Evaluate the results in light of the company's 39.2 percent gross profit percent–age in the prior year.

E6-23 (Supplement A) Allocating Transaction Price to Performance Obligations

LO6-S1

A company that usually sells satellite TV equipment for $50 and two years of satellite TV service for $450 has a special, time–limited offer in which it sells the equipment for $300 and gives the two years of satellite service for free. If the com–pany sells one of these packages on July 1, how much revenue should the company recognize on July 1 when it delivers the equipment and receives the full price in cash?

E6-24 (Supplement A) Allocating Transaction Price to Performance Obligations

LO6-S1

A company separately sells home security equipment and twelve months of system monitoring service for $120 and $240, respectively. The company sells an equip–ment/monitoring bundle on January 1 for a total price of $270. How much, and what type of revenue, should the company recognize on the income statement prepared for the period January 1–31?

E6-25 (Supplement B) Recording Purchases and Sales Using Perpetual and Periodic Inventory Systems

LO6-S2

Kangaroo Jim Company reported beginning inventory of 100 units at a per unit cost of $25. It had the following purchase and sales transactions during the year:

Jan 14	Sold 25 units at unit sales price of $45 on account.
Apr. 9	Purchased 15 additional units at a per unit cost of $25 on account.
Sept. 2	Sold 50 units at a sales price of $50 on account.
Dec. 31	Counted inventory and determined 40 units were still on hand.

Required:

Record each transaction, assuming that Kangaroo Jim Company uses (a) a perpet–ual inventory system and (b) a periodic inventory system.

COACHED PROBLEMS

CP6-1 Purchase Transactions Between Wholesale and Retail Merchandisers, Using Perpetual Inventory Systems

LO6-3

The transactions listed below are typical of those involving Amalgamated Textiles and American Fashions. Amalgamated is a wholesale merchandiser, and American Fashions is a retail merchandiser. Assume all sales of merchandise from Amalgamated to American Fashions are made with terms 2/10, n/30, and that the two companies use perpetual inventory systems. Assume that the following trans–actions between the two companies occurred in the order listed during the year ended December 31.

a. Amalgamated sold merchandise to American Fashions at a total price of $230,000. The merchandise cost Amalgamated $175,000.

b. Two days later, American Fashions complained to Amalgamated that some of the merchandise differed from what American Fashions had ordered. Amalgamated agreed to give an allowance of $5,000 to American Fashions.

c. Just three days later, American Fashions paid Amalgamated, which settled all amounts owed.

Required:

1. Indicate the effect (direction and amount) of each transaction on the Inventory balance of American Fashions.
2. Prepare the journal entries that American Fashions would record and show any computations.

   TIP: The selling price charged by the seller is the purchaser's cost.

LO6-4, 6-5 **CP6-2 Reporting Sales Transactions Between Wholesale and Retail Merchandisers Using Perpetual Inventory Systems**

Use the information in CP6–1 to complete the following requirements.

Required:

1. For each of the events (a) through (c), indicate the amount and direction of the effect (+ for increase, − for decrease, and NE for no effect) on Amalgamated Textiles in terms of the following items.

Sales Revenues	Sales Returns and Allowances	Sales Discounts	Net Sales	Cost of Goods Sold	Gross Profit

2. Which of the above items are likely to be reported on Amalgamated's external financial statements, and which items will be combined "behind the scenes"?
3. Prepare the journal entries that Amalgamated Textiles would record, and show any computations.

   TIP: When using a perpetual inventory system, the seller always makes two journal entries when goods are sold.

LO6-4, 6-5 **CP6-3 Recording Cash Sales, Credit Sales, Sales Discounts, and Sales Returns and Allowances, and Analyzing Gross Profit Percentage**

Campus Co–Op, which is operated by students, uses a perpetual inventory system. The following transactions (summarized) have been selected for analysis:

a.	Sold merchandise for cash (cost of merchandise, $152,070)	$275,000
b.	Received merchandise returned by customers as unsatisfactory (but in perfect condition), for cash refund (original cost of merchandise, $800)	1,600
c.	Sold merchandise (costing $9,000) to a customer, on account with terms 2/10, n/30	20,000
d.	Collected half of the balance owed by the customer in (c) within the discount period	9,800
e.	Granted an allowance to the customer in (c)	1,800

Required:

1. Compute Sales Revenue, Net Sales, and Gross Profit for Campus Co–Op.
2. Compute the gross profit percentage (using the formula shown in this chapter).
3. Prepare journal entries to record transactions (a) through (e).
4. Campus Co–Op is considering a contract to sell merchandise to a campus organization for $15,000. This merchandise will cost Campus Co–Op $12,000. Would this contract increase (or decrease) Campus Co–Op's gross profit and gross profit percentage? How should Campus Co–Op decide whether to accept the contract?

   TIP: The impact on gross profit (a dollar amount) may differ from the impact on gross profit percentage.

LO6-5 **CP6-4 Preparing a Multi-step Income Statement with Sales Discounts and Sales Returns and Allowances, and Computing the Gross Profit Percentage**

Psymon Company, Inc. sells construction equipment. The annual fiscal period ends on December 31. The following adjusted trial balance was created from the general ledger accounts on December 31:

Account Titles	Debits	Credits
Cash	$ 42,000	
Accounts Receivable	18,000	
Inventory	65,000	
Property and Equipment	50,000	
Accumulated Depreciation		$ 21,000
Liabilities		30,000
Contributed Capital		90,000
Retained Earnings, January 1		11,600
Sales Revenue		182,000
Sales Returns and Allowances	7,000	
Sales Discounts	8,000	
Cost of Goods Sold	98,000	
Selling Expense	17,000	
Administrative Expense	18,000	
General Expenses	2,000	
Income Tax Expense	9,600	
Totals	$334,600	$334,600

Required:

1. Prepare a multi–step income statement that would be used for internal report–ing purposes. Treat Sales Discounts and Sales Returns and Allowances as contra–revenue accounts.

   TIP: Some of the accounts listed will appear on the balance sheet rather than the income statement.

2. Prepare a multi–step income statement that would be used for external report–ing purposes, beginning with the amount for Net Sales.

3. Compute and interpret the gross profit percentage (using the formula shown in this chapter and rounding to one decimal place).

CP6-5 (Supplement A) Record Journal Entry After Allocating Transaction Price to Performance Obligations

LO6-S1

Great Canadian Oilchange (GCO) sells a package that combines oil change service with a parts package for $30. A customer who supplies the parts (oil and filter) is charged $20 for the service only, and a customer who buys only the oil and filter is charged $20 for these parts. The parts cost GCO $14.

Required:

1. Determine the dollar amount of revenue earned from the oil change service versus the revenue earned from the sale of parts for each combined oil change package.

   TIP: To calculate the percentage of the combined package that relates to the service, divide the standalone selling price of the service by the combined standalone selling prices of both the service and parts.

2. Show the journal entry GCO would record if GCO provides a combined oil change service and parts package on October 7. Assume GCO distinguishes Service Revenue from Sales Revenue arising from the sale of parts, it uses a perpetual inventory system for recording the cost of goods sold, and it collects cash the day the oil change is performed.

CP6-6 (Supplement B) Recording Inventory Transactions Using Periodic and Perpetual Inventory Systems

LO6-S2

Frigid Supplies reported beginning inventory of 200 units, for a total cost of $2,000. The company had the following transactions during the month:

Jan. 3 Sold 20 units on account at a selling price of $15 per unit
6 Bought 30 units on account at a cost of $10 per unit
16 Sold 30 units on account at a selling price of $15 per unit
19 Sold 20 units on account at a selling price of $20 per unit
26 Bought 10 units on account at a cost of $10 per unit
31 Counted inventory and determined that 160 units were on hand

Required:

1. Prepare the journal entries that would be recorded using a periodic inventory system.

2. Prepare the journal entries that would be recorded using a perpetual inventory system, including any book–to–physical adjustment that might be needed.

   TIP: Adjust for shrinkage by decreasing Inventory and increasing Cost of Goods Sold.

3. What is the dollar amount of shrinkage that you were able to determine in (a) requirement 1, and (b) requirement 2? Enter CD (cannot determine) if you were unable to determine the dollar amount of shrinkage.

GROUP A PROBLEMS

LO6-3   **PA6-1 Reporting Purchase Transactions Between Wholesale and Retail Merchandisers Using Perpetual Inventory Systems**

The transactions listed below are typical of those involving New Books Inc. and Readers' Corner. New Books is a wholesale merchandiser and Readers' Corner is a retail merchandiser. Assume all sales of merchandise from New Books to Readers' Corner are made with terms 2/10, n/30, and that the two companies use perpetual inventory systems. Assume the following transactions between the two companies occurred in the order listed during the year ended August 31.

a. New Books sold merchandise to Readers' Corner at a selling price of $550,000. The merchandise cost New Books $415,000.

b. Two days later, Readers' Corner complained to New Books that some of the merchandise differed from what Readers' Corner had ordered. New Books agreed to give an allowance of $10,000 to Readers' Corner.

c. Just three days later, Readers' Corner paid New Books, which settled all amounts owed.

Required:

1. Indicate the effect (direction and amount) of each transaction on the Inventory balance of Readers' Corner.

2. Prepare the journal entries that Readers' Corner would record and show any computations.

LO6-4, 6-5   **PA6-2 Reporting Sales Transactions Between Wholesale and Retail Merchandisers Using Perpetual Inventory Systems**

Use the information in PA6–1 to complete the following requirements.

Required:

1. For each of the events (a) through (c), indicate the amount and direction of the effect (+ for increase, − for decrease, and NE for no effect) on New Books in terms of the following items.

Sales Revenues	Sales Returns and Allowances	Sales Discounts	Net Sales	Cost of Goods Sold	Gross Profit

2. Which of the above items are likely to be reported on New Books' external financial statements, and which items will be combined behind the scenes?

3. Prepare the journal entries that New Books would record, and show any computations.

PA6-3 Recording Sales with Discounts and Returns, and Analyzing Gross Profit Percentage

LO6-4, 6-5

Hair Care Inc. is a wholesaler of hair supplies. Hair Care uses a perpetual inventory system. The following transactions (summarized) have been selected for analysis:

Check Figure:
Net Sales = $60,340

a.	Sold merchandise for cash (cost of merchandise $28,797)	$51,200
b.	Received merchandise returned by customers as unsatisfactory (but in perfect condition), for cash refund (original cost of merchandise $360)	600
c.	Sold merchandise (costing $4,750) to a customer, on account with terms 2/10, n/30	10,000
d.	Collected half of the balance owed by the customer in (c) within the discount period	4,900
e.	Granted an allowance to the customer in (c)	160

Required:

1. Compute Sales Revenue, Net Sales, and Gross Profit for Hair World.
2. Compute the gross profit percentage (using the formula shown in this chapter and rounding to one decimal place).
3. Prepare journal entries to record transactions (a) through (e).
4. Hair Care is considering a contract to sell merchandise to a hair salon chain for $15,000. This merchandise will cost Hair Care $10,000. Would this contract increase (or decrease) Hair Care's gross profit and gross profit percentage? How should Hair Care decide whether to accept the contract?

PA6-4 Preparing a Multi-step Income Statement with Sales Discounts and Sales Returns and Allowances, and Computing the Gross Profit Percentage

LO6-5

Big Billy Corporation is a local grocery store organized seven years ago as a corporation. The store is in an excellent location, and sales have increased each year. The bookkeeper prepared the following statement (assume that all amounts are correct, but note the incorrect terminology and format):

BIG BILLY CORPORATION Profit and Loss December 31		
	Debit	**Credit**
Sales		$420,000
Cost of Goods Sold	$279,000	
Sales Returns and Allowances	10,000	
Sales Discounts	6,000	
Selling Expense	58,000	
Administrative Expense	16,000	
General Expenses	1,000	
Income Tax Expense	15,000	
Net Income	35,000	
Totals	$420,000	$420,000

Required:

1. Prepare a multi–step income statement that would be used for internal reporting purposes. Treat Sales Returns and Allowances as well as Sales Discounts as contra–revenue accounts.

2. Prepare a multi–step income statement that would be used for external report–ing purposes, beginning with the amount for Net Sales.

3. Compute and interpret the gross profit percentage (using the formula shown in this chapter and rounding to one decimal place).

LO6-S1   **PA6-5 (Supplement A) Record Journal Entry After Allocating Transaction Price to Performance Obligations**

Hospital Equipment Company (HEC) acquired several MRI machines for its inven–tory at a cost of $2,300 per machine. HEC usually sells these machines to hospitals at a price of $5,800. HEC also separately sells twelve months of training and repair services for MRI machines for $1,450. HEC is paid $5,800 cash on January 1 for the sale of an MRI machine delivered on January 1. HEC sold the machine at its regular price, but included one free year of training and repair service.

Required:

1. For the machine sold at its regular price, but with one free year of training and repair service, determine the dollar amount of revenue earned from the equip–ment sale versus the revenue earned from the training and repair services.

2. What journal entry would HEC record for the transaction on January 1? (Assume HEC uses a perpetual inventory system for recording the cost of goods sold.)

LO6-S2   **PA6-6 (Supplement B) Recording Inventory Transactions Using Periodic and Perpetual Inventory Systems**

Home Hardware reported beginning inventory of twenty shovels, for a total cost of $100. The company had the following transactions during the month:

Jan. 2   Sold 4 shovels on account at a selling price of $10 per unit
16   Sold 10 shovels on account at a selling price of $10 per unit
18   Bought 5 shovels on account at a cost of $5 per unit
19   Sold 10 shovels on account at a selling price of $10 per unit
24   Bought 10 shovels on account at a cost of $5 per unit
31   Counted inventory and determined that 10 units were on hand

Required:

1. Prepare the journal entries that would be recorded using a periodic inventory system.

2. Prepare the journal entries that would be recorded using a perpetual inventory system, including any book–to–physical adjustment that might be needed.

3. What is the dollar amount of shrinkage that you were able to determine in (a) requirement 1, and (b) requirement 2? Enter CD (cannot determine) if you were unable to determine the dollar amount of shrinkage.

GROUP B PROBLEMS

LO6-3   **PB6-1 Reporting Purchase Transactions Between Wholesale and Retail Merchandisers Using Perpetual Inventory Systems**

The transactions listed below are typical of those involving Southern Sporting Goods and Sports R Us. Southern Sporting Goods is a wholesale merchandiser and Sports R Us is a retail merchandiser. Assume all sales of merchandise from Southern Sporting Goods to Sports R Us are made with terms 2/10, n/30 and that the two companies use perpetual inventory systems. Assume the following transac–tions between the two companies occurred in the order listed during the year ended December 31.

a. Southern Sporting Goods sold merchandise to Sports R Us at a selling price of $125,000. The merchandise cost Southern Sporting Goods $94,000.

b. Two days later, Sports R Us complained to Southern Sporting Goods that some of the merchandise differed from what Sports R Us had ordered. Southern Sporting Goods agreed to give Sport R Us an allowance of $3,000.

c. Just three days later, Sports R Us paid Southern Sporting Goods, which settled all amounts owed.

Required:

1. Indicate the effect (direction and amount) of each transaction on the Inventory balance of Sports R Us.

2. Prepare the journal entries that Sports R Us would record, and show any computations.

PB6-2 Reporting Sales Transactions Between Wholesale and Retail Merchandisers Using Perpetual Inventory Systems   LO6-4, 6-5

Use the information in PB6–1 to complete the following requirements

Required:

1. For each of the events (a) through (c), indicate the amount and direction of the effect (+ for increase, − for decrease, and NE for no effect) on Southern Sporting Goods in terms of the following items.

Sales Revenues	Sales Returns and Allowances	Sales Discounts	Net Sales	Cost of Goods Sold	Gross Profit

2. Which of the above items are likely to be reported on Southern Sporting Goods' external financial statements, and which items will be combined behind the scenes?

3. Prepare the journal entries that Southern Sporting Goods would record, and show any computations.

PB6-3 Recording Sales and Purchases with Discounts and Returns, and Analyzing Gross Profit Percentage   LO6-4, 6-5

Lonny's Building Supplies (LBS) is a locally owned and operated hardware store. LBS uses a perpetual inventory system. The following transactions (summarized) have been selected for analysis:

a.	Sold merchandise for cash (cost of merchandise, $224,350)	$500,000
b.	Received merchandise returned by customers as unsatisfactory (but in perfect condition), for cash refund (original cost of merchandise, $1,900)	3,000
c.	Sold merchandise (costing $3,000) to a customer, on account, with terms 2/10, n/30	5,000
d.	Collected half of the balance owed by the customer in (c) within the discount period	2,450
e.	Granted an allowance to the customer in (c)	950

Required:

1. Compute Sales Revenue, Net Sales, and Gross Profit for LBS.

2. Compute the gross profit percentage (using the formula shown in this chapter rounding to one decimal place).

3. Prepare journal entries to record transactions (a) through (e).

4. LBS is considering a contract to sell building supplies to a local home builder for $20,000. These materials will cost LBS $16,000. Would this contract increase (or decrease) LBS's gross profit and gross profit percentage? How should LBS decide whether to accept the contract?

PB6-4 Preparing a Multi-step Income Statement with Sales Discounts and Sales Returns and Allowances, and Computing the Gross Profit Percentage   LO6-5

Jacquie's Greenhouse Corporation is a local greenhouse organized ten years ago as a corporation. The greenhouse is in an excellent location, and sales have increased each year. The bookkeeper prepared the following statement (assume that all amounts are correct, but note the incorrect terminology and format):

JACQUIE'S GREENHOUSE CORPORATION		
Profit and Loss		
December 31		
	Debit	Credit
Sales		$504,000
Cost of Goods Sold	$311,000	
Sales Returns and Allowances	11,000	
Sales Discounts	8,000	
Selling Expense	61,000	
Administrative Expense	13,000	
General Expenses	3,000	
Income Tax Expense	18,000	
Net Income	79,000	
Totals	$504,000	$504,000

Required:

Check Figure:
Net Sales = $485,000

1. Prepare a multi–step income statement that would be used for internal report–ing purposes. Treat Sales Returns and Allowances as well as Sales Discounts as contra–revenue accounts.

2. Prepare a multi–step income statement that would be used for external report–ing purposes, beginning with the amount for Net Sales.

3. Compute and interpret the gross profit percentage (using the formula shown in this chapter).

LO6-S1   **PB6-5 (Supplement A) Record Journal Entry After Allocating Transactions Price to Performance Obligations**

Sky Communications (SKY) usually sells a cell phone for $320 plus twelve months of cellular service for $480. SKY has a special, time–limited offer in which it gives the phone for free and sells the twelve months of cellular service for $420. Each phone costs SKY $120, which it accounts for in its perpetual inventory system. On July 1, SKY sells one of the special packages, delivers the phone, collects the $420 cash, and starts the cellular service.

Required:

1. For the special offer, how much of the $420 relates to the sale of the cell phone versus the sale of the cellular service?

2. What journal entries should SKY record on July 1 and July 31? (Assume SKY uses a perpetual inventory system for recording the cost of goods sold.)

LO6-S2   **PB6-6 (Supplement B) Recording Inventory Transactions Using Periodic and Perpetual Inventory Systems**

Sigfusson Supplies reported beginning inventory of 100 units for a total cost of $2,000. The company had the following transactions during the month:

Jan. 6	Sold 20 units on account at a selling price of $30 per unit
9	Bought 10 units on account at a cost of $20 per unit
11	Sold 10 units on account at a selling price of $35 per unit
19	Sold 20 units on account at a selling price of $40 per unit
27	Bought 10 units on account at a cost of $20 per unit
31	Counted inventory and determined that 60 units were on hand

Required:

1. Prepare the journal entries that would be recorded using a periodic inventory system.

2. Prepare the journal entries that would be recorded using a perpetual inventory system, including any book–to–physical adjustment that might be needed.

3. What is the dollar amount of shrinkage that you were able to determine in (a) requirement 1, and (b) requirement 2? Enter CD (cannot determine) if you were unable to determine the dollar amount of shrinkage.

COMPREHENSIVE PROBLEM

C6-1 **Accounting for Inventory Orders, Purchases, Sales, Returns, and Discounts**   LO5-4, 6-3, 6-4, 6-5

Consider the following, based on what you learned in Chapters 5 and 6:

a. On October 1, the Business Students' Society (BSS) placed an order for 100 golf shirts at a unit cost of $20, under terms 2/10, n/30.
b. The order was received on October 10, but twenty golf shirts had been damaged in shipment.
c. On October 11, the damaged golf shirts were returned.
d. On October 12, BSS complained that the remaining golf shirts were slightly defective, so the supplier granted a $100 allowance.
e. BSS paid for the golf shirts on October 13.
f. During the first week of October, BSS received student and faculty orders for eighty golf shirts, at a unit price of $37.50, on terms 2/10, n/30.
g. On October 18, the golf shirts were delivered to these customers. Unfortunately, customers were unhappy with the golf shirts, so BSS permitted them to be returned or gave an allowance of $12.50 per shirt.
h. On October 21, one half of the golf shirts were returned by customers to BSS.
i. On October 22, the remaining forty customers were granted the allowance on account.

Required:

1. Prepare journal entries for the transactions described above, using the date of each transaction as its reference. Assume BSS uses perpetual inventory accounts. If you complete this problem in Connect, these journal entries will be summarized for you in T–accounts and a trial balance.
2. Report the financial effects of the above transactions in a multi–step income statement, prepared for internal use, for the month ended October 31. Assume operating expenses, other than cost of goods sold, are $100 and income tax expense is $45.
3. Determine the percentage of net sales that is available to cover operating expenses other than cost of goods sold. By what name is this percentage commonly known?
4. As of October 31, the cheque dated October 13 had not cleared the bank. How should BSS report this on its October 31 bank reconciliation? Give the journal entry that's needed, if any, as a result of including this item in the bank reconciliation.

SKILLS DEVELOPMENT CASES

S6-1 **Finding Financial Information**   LO6-2, 6-5

Refer to the summarized financial statements of The Home Depot in Appendix A at the end of this book.

Required:

1. What amount of Net Sales does the company report during the year ended January 29, 2017?
2. What is the company's Cost of Goods Sold for this same year–end? Compute the company's gross profit percentage for the year ended January 29, 2017, and explain what this means.
3. Assume that The Home Depot experienced no shrinkage in the most current year. Using the balance sheet and income statement, estimate the amount of purchases in the year ended January 29, 2017.

S6-2 Comparing Financial Information

Refer to the summarized financial statements of The Home Depot in Appendix A and Lowe's Companies, Inc. in Appendix B.

Required:

1. Does Lowe's Companies, Inc. report higher or lower Net Sales than The Home Depot during the year ending February 3, 2017?
2. Assuming that Cost of Sales is the same thing as Cost of Goods Sold, compute Lowe's Companies, Inc.'s gross profit percentage for the most recent year. Is it greater or less than The Home Depot's? Based on this, where are consumers likely to find lower markups?
3. Assume that Lowe's Companies, Inc. experienced no shrinkage in the most recent year. Using the balance sheet and income statement, estimate the amount of purchases in the 2016 fiscal year. How much greater (or less) were Lowe's Companies, Inc.'s purchases than The Home Depot's in that year?

S6-3 Internet-Based Team Research: Examining an Annual Report

As a team, select an industry to analyze. Using the Internet, each team member should access the annual report for one publicly traded company in the industry, with each member selecting a different company. (See S1–3 in Chapter 1 for a description of possible resources for these tasks.)

Required:

1. On an individual basis, each team member should write a short report that incorporates the following:
   a. Describe the company's business in sufficient detail to be able to classify it as a service, merchandising, or manufacturing company. What products or services does the company provide?
   b. Calculate the gross profit percentage at the end of the current and prior years, and explain any change between the two years.
2. Then, as a team, write a short report comparing and contrasting your companies using these attributes. Discuss any patterns across the companies that you as a team observe. Provide potential explanations for any differences discovered.

S6-4 Ethical Decision Making: A Real-Life Example

When some people think about inventory theft, they imagine a shoplifter running out of a store with goods stuffed inside a jacket or bag. But that's not what the managers thought at the Famous Footwear store on Chicago's Madison Street. No, they suspected their own employees were the main cause of their unusually high shrinkage. One scam involved dishonest cashiers who would let their friends take a pair of Skechers without paying for them. To make it look like the shoes had been bought, cashiers would ring up a sale, but instead of charging $50 for shoes, they would charge only $2 for a bottle of shoe polish. That's when the company's man-agers decided to put its accounting system to work. In just two years, the company cut its Madison Street inventory losses in half. Here's how a newspaper described the store's improvements:

Retailers Crack Down on Employee Theft
SouthCoast Today, September 10, 2000, Chicago
By Calmetta Coleman, *The Wall Street Journal* Staff Writer

. . . Famous Footwear installed a chainwide register-monitoring system to sniff out suspicious tran-actions, such as unusually large numbers of refunds or voids, or repeated sales of cheap goods.

. . . [B]efore an employee can issue a cash refund, a second worker must be present to see the customer and inspect the merchandise.

. . . [T]he chain has set up a toll-free hotline for employees to use to report suspicions about co-workers.

These improvements in inventory control came as welcome news for investors and creditors of Brown Shoe Company, the company that owns Famous Footwear. Despite these improvements at the Chicago store, Brown Shoe has been forced to shut down operations in other cities.

Required:

1. Explain how the register—monitoring system would allow Famous Footwear to cut down on employee theft.
2. What is the name of the control principle that is addressed by Famous Footwear's new cash refund procedure?
3. If Famous Footwear used a periodic inventory system, rather than a perpetual inventory system, how would the company detect shrinkage?
4. Think of and describe at least four different parties who are harmed by the type of inventory theft described in this case.

S6-5 Ethical Decision Making: A Mini-Case

LO6-5

Assume you work as an accountant in the merchandising division of a large public company that makes and sells athletic clothing. To encourage the merchandising division to earn as much profit on each individual sale as possible, the division manager's pay is based, in part, on the division's gross profit percentage. To encourage control over the division's operating expenses, the manager's pay also is based on the division's net income.

You are currently preparing the division's financial statements. The division had a good year, with sales of $100,000, cost of goods sold of $50,000, sales returns and allowances of $6,000, sales discounts of $4,000, and other selling expenses of $30,000. (Assume the division does not report income taxes.) The division manager stresses that *"it would be in your personal interest"* to classify sales returns and allowances as well as sales discounts as selling expenses rather than as contra—revenues on the division's income statement. He justifies this "friendly advice" by saying that he's not asking you to fake the numbers—he just believes that those items are more accurately reported as expenses. Plus, he claims, being a division of a larger company, you don't have to follow GAAP.

Required:

1. Prepare an income statement for the division using the classifications shown in this chapter. Using this income statement, calculate the division's gross profit percentage.
2. Prepare an income statement for the division using the classifications advised by the manager. Using this income statement, calculate the division's gross profit percentage.
3. What reason (other than reporting "more accurately") do you think is motivat—ing the manager's advice to you?
4. Do you agree with the manager's statement that he's "not asking you to fake the numbers"?
5. Do you agree with the manager's statement about not having to follow GAAP?
6. How should you respond to the division manager's "friendly advice"?

S6-6 Critical Thinking: Analyzing Internal Control Weaknesses

LO6-2

Snake Creek Company has a trusted employee who, as the owner said, "handles all of the bookkeeping and paperwork for the company." This employee is respon—sible for counting, verifying, and recording cash receipts and payments, making the weekly bank deposit, preparing cheques for major expenditures (signed by the owner), making small expenditures from the cash register for daily expenses, and collecting accounts receivable. The owner asked the local bank for a $20,000 loan. The bank asked that an audit be performed covering the year just ended. The independent auditor (a local CPA), in a private conference with the owner, presented some evidence of the following activities of the trusted employee during the past year:

a. Cash sales sometimes were not entered in the cash register, and the trusted employee pocketed approximately $50 per month.

b. Cash taken from the cash register (and pocketed by the trusted employee) was replaced with expense memos with fictitious signatures (approximately $12 per day).

c. The amount of $300 was collected on an account receivable from a valued out−of−town customer, pocketed by the trusted employee who covered it by making a $300 entry as a debit to Sales Returns and a credit to Accounts Receivable.

d. An amount of $800 was collected on an account receivable from a local customer and pocketed by the trusted employee who covered it by making an $800 entry as a debit to Sales Discounts and a credit to Accounts Receivable.

Required:

1. What was the approximate amount stolen during the past year?

    TIP: Assume employees work five days a week, fifty−two weeks a year.

2. What would be your recommendations to the owner?

LO6-5

S6-7 Preparing Multi-step Income Statements and Calculating Gross Profit Percentage

Assume that you have been hired by Big Sky Corporation as a summer intern. The company is in the process of preparing its annual financial statements, and you are asked to prepare an income statement for internal reporting purposes and an income statement for external reporting purposes. Your boss has also requested that you determine the company's gross profit percentage based on the statements that you are to prepare. The following adjusted trial balance was created from the general ledger accounts on May 31, 2017.

Account Titles	Debits	Credits
Cash	$ 57,000	
Accounts Receivable	67,000	
Inventory	103,000	
Property and Equipment	252,000	
Accumulated Amortization		$103,000
Liabilities		75,000
Contributed Capital		120,000
Retained Earnings, June 1, 2016		145,900
Sales Revenue		369,000
Sales Returns and Allowances	9,500	
Sales Discounts	14,000	
Cost of Goods Sold	248,000	
Selling Expense	19,000	
Administrative Expense	23,000	
General Expenses	5,000	
Income Tax Expense	15,400	
Totals	$812,900	$812,900

Your boss wants you to create the spreadsheet in a way that automatically recal−culates net sales and any other related amounts whenever changes are made to the contra−revenue accounts. To do this, you know that you'll have to use formulas throughout the worksheets and even import or link cells from one worksheet to another. Once again, your friend Owen is willing to help.

Required:

Enter the trial balance information into a spreadsheet and complete the following:

1. Prepare a multi−step income statement that would be used for internal report−ing purposes. Classify sales returns and allowances and sales discounts as contra−revenue accounts.

Sounds like you are going to get some great experience this summer. Okay, to import a number from another spreadsheet, you first click on the cell where you want the number to appear. For example, if you want to enter the Net Sales balance in the external income statement, click on the cell in the external income statement where the Net Sales number is supposed to appear. Enter the equals sign (=) and then click on the tab that takes you to the worksheet containing the internal income statement. In that worksheet, click on the cell that contains the amount you want to import into the external income statement and then press Enter. This will create a link from the internal income statement cell to the external income statement cell. Here's a screen shot showing the formula that will appear after you import the number.

			Big Sky Corporation				
			Income Statement				
			For the Year Ended May 31, 2014				
Net sales						345,500	
Cost of goods sold						248,000	
Gross profit							

G5   *fx* ='Internal Income Statement'!G8

Internal Income Statement   External Income Statement

Don't forget to save the file using a name that indicates who you are.

2. Prepare a multi–step income statement that would be used for external reporting purposes, beginning with the amount for Net Sales.

3. Compute the gross profit percentage.

CONTINUING CASES

CC6-1 Accounting for Merchandising Operations

LO6-4, 6-5

Nicole's Getaway Spa (NGS) has been so successful that Nicole has decided to expand her spa by selling merchandise. She sells things such as nail polish, at–home spa kits, cosmetics, and Palacetherapy items. Nicole uses a perpetual inventory system and is starting to realize all of the work that is created when inventory is involved in a business. The following transactions were selected from among those completed by NGS in August.

Aug. 2   NGS sold 10 items of merchandise to Salon World on account at a selling price of $1,000 (total); terms 2/10, n/30. The goods cost NGS $650.

3   NGS sold 5 identical items of merchandise to Cosmetics 4 You on account at a selling price of $825 (total); terms 2/10, n/30. The goods cost NGS $400.

6   Cosmetics 4 You returned one of the items purchased on August 3. The item could still be sold by NGS in the future, and credit was given to the customer.

10   Collected payment from Salon World, fully paying off the account balance.

20   Sold two at–home spa kits to Meghan Witzel for $300 cash. The goods cost NGS $96.

22   Cosmetics 4 You paid its remaining account balance in full.

Required:

1. Prepare journal entries for each transaction.
2. Calculate the amount of Net Sales and Cost of Goods Sold for the transactions listed above. What is Nicole's Getaway Spa's gross profit percentage (round to one decimal place)? Explain to Nicole what this gross profit percentage means.

LO6-4, 6-5   **CC6-2 Wiki Art Gallery (WAG)**

Refer to the Wiki Art Gallery (WAG) instructional case in Appendix D and read the case in sufficient depth to answer the following questions.

1. Is the revenue recognition policy used by Wiki Art Gallery (WAG) for artwork sales in accordance with the revenue recognition principle? Why or why not? Select the correct answer.

   a. Yes, the artwork sales policy is in accordance with the revenue recognition principle because WAG reports sales using FOB shipping point.

   b. Yes, the artwork sales policy is in accordance with the revenue recognition principle because WAG reports sales using FOB destination.

   c. No, the artwork sales policy is not in accordance with the revenue recognition principle because WAG reports revenue as it is earned each month.

   d. No, the artwork sales policy is not in accordance with the revenue recognition principle because WAG reports revenue before it fulfills its obligation to transfer ownership of the artwork to the customer.

2. WAG presents a single–step income statement. Reorganize it into a multi–step format to calculate the gross profit from artwork sales in 2011 and 2010 and the gross profit percentage from artwork sales in 2011 and 2010. Which of the following is consistent with the amounts reported by WAG?

   a. Gross profit from artwork sales was $58,225 in 2011 and $10,400 in 2010, and the gross profit percentage was 72.2 percent in 2011 and 34.2 percent in 2010.

   b. Gross profit from artwork sales was $58,225 in 2011 and $10,400 in 2010, and the gross profit percentage was 41.6 percent in 2011 and 14.9 percent in 2010.

   c. Gross profit from artwork sales was $63,061 in 2011 and $2,417 in 2010, and the gross profit percentage was 45.0 percent in 2011 and 3.45 percent in 2010.

   d. Gross profit from artwork sales was $22,375 in 2011 and $20,000 in 2010, and the gross profit percentage was 27.8 percent in 2011 and 65.8 percent in 2010.

3. Recalculate WAG's gross profit and gross percentage for 2011 after removing the effects of the sale to TEAC (The Eccentric Art Collector). Which of the following is consistent with these revised amounts?

   a. The revised gross profit would be $30,600, resulting in a gross profit percent–age of 38.0 percent.

   b. The revised gross profit would be $8,225, resulting in a gross profit percent–age of 26.9 percent.

   c. The revised gross profit would be $10,600, resulting in a gross profit percent–age of 34.6 percent.

   d. The revised gross profit would be $10,225, resulting in a gross profit percent–age of 33.4 percent.

THAT WAS

THEN

In the previous chapter, we focused on selling goods that were purchased at the same cost per unit.

THIS IS

NOW

This chapter demonstrates how to account for goods purchased at different unit costs.

YOUR LEARNING OBJECTIVES

Understand the business

LO7-1 Describe the issues in managing different types of inventory.

Study the accounting methods

LO7-2 Explain how to report inventory and cost of goods sold.

LO7-3 Compute costs using three inventory costing methods.

LO7-4 Report inventory at the lower of cost and net realizable value.

Evaluate the results

LO7-5 Evaluate inventory management by computing and interpreting the inventory turnover ratio.

Review the chapter

Chapter Summary

Supplemental material

LO7-S1 Compute inventory costs using LIFO.

LO7-S2 Compute inventory costs in perpetual systems.

LO7-S3 Determine the effects of inventory errors.

CHAPTER 7

Inventory and Cost of Goods Sold

Iakov Filimonov/ Shutterstock.com

FOCUS COMPANY:

Hudson's Bay Company

www.hbc.com

Whether you are shopping for gasoline, groceries, or a new electronic gadget, prices always seem to be changing. The political situation in oil-producing nations can cause a stunning increase in prices at the pump. A late freeze in Florida can hike the price of orange juice. Increasing competition can dramatically lower the cost of that new hand-held device.

Like you, companies face similar price changes when they purchase or produce goods. For some products, unit costs increase over time, and for others, technological innovation causes unit costs to decrease. Either way, inventory is likely to include some items that were acquired at a lower unit cost and others that were acquired at a higher unit cost.

Suppose Canada's largest department store, the Hudson's Bay Company (HBC), buys three batches of its multi-stripe beach towels at a cost of $5 per towel for the first batch, $6 per towel for the second batch, and $7 per towel for the third. When HBC sells a beach towel, what cost should it use to compute the Cost of Goods Sold? And what happens at the end of the season when the value of its beach towels falls below cost?

As you will learn in this chapter, accounting rules allow different methods to be used when accounting for inventory, each of which leads to reporting different dollar amounts for Cost of Goods Sold (and the items remaining in inventory). This flexibility allows managers to choose the method that best fits their business environment. But it also means that you must know which method managers are using and how it works. That's what we'll look at in this chapter.

HBC Corporate Collection. Logo used with permission.

ORGANIZATION OF THE CHAPTER

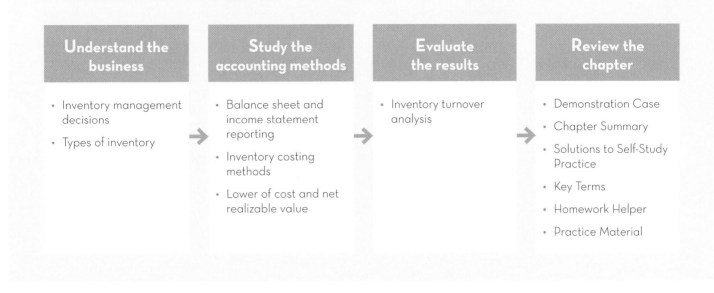

Understand the business	Study the accounting methods	Evaluate the results	Review the chapter
• Inventory management decisions • Types of inventory	• Balance sheet and income statement reporting • Inventory costing methods • Lower of cost and net realizable value	• Inventory turnover analysis	• Demonstration Case • Chapter Summary • Solutions to Self-Study Practice • Key Terms • Homework Helper • Practice Material

Understand the Business

INVENTORY MANAGEMENT DECISIONS

You may not make or sell inventory, but you buy it all the time. The things that concern you as a consumer also concern managers who make inventory decisions. The primary goals of inventory managers are to

LEARNING OBJECTIVE 7-1

Describe the issues in managing different types of inventory.

1. maintain a sufficient quantity of inventory to meet customers' needs,
2. ensure inventory quality meets customers' expectations and company standards, and
3. minimize the cost of acquiring and carrying inventory (including costs related to purchasing, production, storage, spoilage, theft, obsolescence, and financing).

These factors are tricky to manage because as one of them changes (e.g., quality), so, too, do the others (e.g., cost). Ultimately, inventory manage—ment often comes down to purchasing goods that can be sold soon after they are acquired.

TYPES OF INVENTORY

The generic term *inventory* means goods that are held for sale in the normal course of business or are used to produce other goods for sale. Merchandis—ers hold merchandise inventory, which consists of products acquired in a finished condition, ready for sale without further processing. Manufacturers often hold three types of inventory, with each representing a different stage in the manufacturing process. They start with raw materials inventory, such as plastic, steel, or fabrics. When these raw materials enter the pro—duction process, they become part of work in process inventory, which includes goods that are in the process of being manufactured. When com—pleted, work in process inventory becomes finished goods inventory, which is ready for sale just like merchandise inventory. For the purposes of this chapter, we'll focus on merchandise inventory, but be aware that the concepts we cover apply equally to manufacturer's inventory.

Two other accounting terms may be used to describe inventory. Consignment inventory refers to goods a company is holding on behalf of the goods' owner. Typically, this arises when a company is willing to sell the goods for the owner (for a fee) but does not want to take ownership of the goods in the event the goods are difficult to sell. Consignment inventory is reported on the balance sheet of the owner, not the company holding the inventory. Goods in transit are inventory items being transported. This type of inventory is reported on the balance sheet of the owner, not the company transporting it. As you may remember from Chapter 6, ownership of inventory is determined by the terms of the inventory sales agreement. If a sale is made FOB destination, the goods belong to the seller until they reach their destination (the customer). If a sale is made FOB shipping point, inventory belongs to the customer at the point of shipping (from the seller's premises).

Study the Accounting Methods

BALANCE SHEET AND INCOME STATEMENT REPORTING

LEARNING OBJECTIVE 7-2

Explain how to report inventory and cost of goods sold.

Because inventory will be used or converted into cash within one year, it is reported on the balance sheet as a current asset. Goods placed in inventory are initially recorded at cost, which is the amount paid to acquire the asset and prepare it for sale. See Exhibit 7.1 for the way HBC reports inventory.

EXHIBIT 7.1	Reporting Inventory on the Balance Sheet (Partial)

HUDSON'S BAY COMPANY
Balance Sheets (Partial)

(in millions)	January 30, 2016	January 30, 2015
Assets		
Current Assets		
Cash and Cash Equivalents	$ 507	$ 168
Accounts Receivable	512	212
Inventory	3,415	2,319
Prepaid Expenses and Other	194	100

When a company sells goods, it removes their cost from the Inventory account and reports the cost on the income statement as the expense Cost of Goods Sold. See Exhibit 7.2 for how HBC reports the Cost of Goods Sold (CGS) on its partial income statement. Notice that it directly follows Net Sales. The difference between these two line items is a subtotal called *Gross Profit*.

EXHIBIT 7.2 **Reporting Cost of Goods Sold on the Income Statement (Partial)**

HUDSON'S BAY COMPANY
Income Statements (Partial)
For the Years Ended

(in millions)	January 30, 2016	January 30, 2015	February 1, 2014
Net Sales	$11,162	$8,169	$5,223
Cost of Goods Sold	6,638	4,901	3,217
Gross Profit	$ 4,524	$3,268	$2,006

Cost of Goods Sold Equation

Chapter 6 explained that the balance sheet account Inventory is related to the income statement account Cost of Goods Sold through the cost of goods sold equation. The cost of goods sold equation can take one of two forms, depending on whether the inventory costs are updated periodically at year−end (or month−end) when inventory is counted, or perpetually each time inventory is bought or sold

Beginning Inventory + Purchases − Ending Inventory = Cost of Goods Sold	**Periodic Updating**

Beginning Inventory + Purchases − Cost of Goods Sold = Ending Inventory	**Perpetual Updating**

Exhibit 7.3 illustrates how to use these equations with a simple case where a company has beginning inventory of five units that each cost $10, then purchases twenty units with a cost of $10 each, sells fifteen units, and is left with ten units in ending inventory. Exhibit 7.3 shows that, in a peri−odic inventory system, you must calculate the cost of Ending Inventory and then use the cost of goods sold equation to "force out" the Cost of Goods Sold (left table).

In a perpetual inventory system, the Cost of Goods Sold is updated with each inventory transaction, which "forces out" the cost of Ending Inventory (right table). With a perpetual inventory system, you can "prove" the cost of Ending Inventory by calculating it directly using the number of units on hand. Be sure you understand all of the calculations in Exhibit 7.3 before moving on, because we use this as a basis for more calculations later in this chapter.

EXHIBIT 7.3 **Relationship Between Inventory and Cost of Goods Sold**

PERIODIC INVENTORY

Description	# of Units		Unit Cost	Total Cost
Beginning	5	×	$10	$ 50
+ Purchases	20	×	$10	200
Available	25	×	$10	250
− Ending	(10)	×	$10	(100)
= Cost of Goods Sold				$150

PERPETUAL INVENTORY

Description	# of Units		Unit Cost	Total Cost
Beginning	5	×	$10	$ 50
+ Purchases	20	×	$10	200
Available	25	×	$10	250
− Goods Sold	(15)	×	$10	(150)
= Ending Inventory				$100

INVENTORY COSTING METHODS

LEARNING OBJECTIVE 7-3
Compute costs using three inventory costing methods.

In the example presented in the previous section, the cost of all units of the item was the same—$10. If inventory costs normally remained constant, we'd be done right now. But the cost of goods does not always stay the same, just as you notice every time you fill up your car with gas. In recent years, the costs of many items have risen moderately. In other cases, such as electronic products, costs have dropped dramatically.

When the costs of inventory change over time, it is not obvious how to determine the cost of goods sold (and the cost of ending inventory). To see why, think about the following simple example:

May 3	Purchased 1 unit for **$70**
May 5	Purchased 1 more unit for **$75**
May 6	Purchased 1 more unit for **$95**
May 8	Sold 2 units for $125 each

The sale on May 8 of two units, at a selling price of $125 each, would gener‐ ate sales revenue of $250($125 × 2), but what amount would be considered the cost of goods sold? The answer depends on which goods are reported as sold.

Three generally accepted inventory costing methods are available under ASPE and IFRS for determining the cost of goods sold and the cost of goods remaining in ending inventory, regardless of whether a company uses a perpetual or periodic inventory system. The method chosen does not have to correspond to the physical flow of goods, so any one of these three acceptable methods can be used in Canada.

Specific identification:
The inventory costing method that identifies the cost of the specific item that was sold.

The **specific identification** method individually identifies and records the cost of each item sold as Cost of Goods Sold. This method requires accountants to keep detailed records of the purchase cost of each item. This can be accomplished with unique identifiers such as bar coding and, in the case of a car, its vehicle identification number (VIN). In the example just given, if the items sold were identified as the ones received on May 3 and May 6, which cost $70 and $95, the total cost of those items ($70 + $95 = $165) would be reported as Cost of Goods Sold. The cost of the remaining item ($75) would be reported as Inventory on the balance sheet at the end of the period. Companies tend to use the specific identification method when accounting for individually expensive and unique items. Bridal shops and art galleries are two examples of companies that would most likely use the specific identification method due to the uniqueness of their inventories.

The units within each HBC product line are identical, so the company does not use the specific identification method. Like most companies, HBC uses one of the two other cost flow methods to account for inventory items. These two other inventory costing methods are *not based on the physical flow* of goods on and off the shelves. Instead, these methods are based on *assumptions* that account‐ ants make about the flow of inventory costs. These two cost flow assumptions are applied to our simple three–unit example in Exhibit 7.4 as follows:

First-in, first-out (FIFO):
Assumes that the costs of the first goods purchased (first in) are the costs of the first goods sold (first out).

1. **First–in, first–out (FIFO)** assumes that the inventory costs flow out in the order the goods are received. As in Exhibit 7.4, the earliest items received, the $70 and $75 units received on May 3 and 5, become the $145 Cost of Goods Sold on the income statement, and the remaining $95 unit received on May 6 becomes Ending Inventory on the balance sheet.

Weighted average cost:
An inventory costing assump‐ tion that uses the weighted average unit cost of the goods available for sale for both cost of goods sold and ending inventory.

2. **Weighted average cost** uses the weighted average of the costs of goods available for sale for both the cost of each item sold and those remaining in inventory. As in Exhibit 7.4, the average of the costs [($70 + $75 + $95) ÷ 3 = $80] is assigned to the two items sold, resulting in $160 as Cost of Goods Sold on the income statement. The same $80 average cost is assigned to the one item in Ending Inventory reported on the balance sheet.

EXHIBIT 7.4   Cost Flow Assumptions and Financial Statement Effects

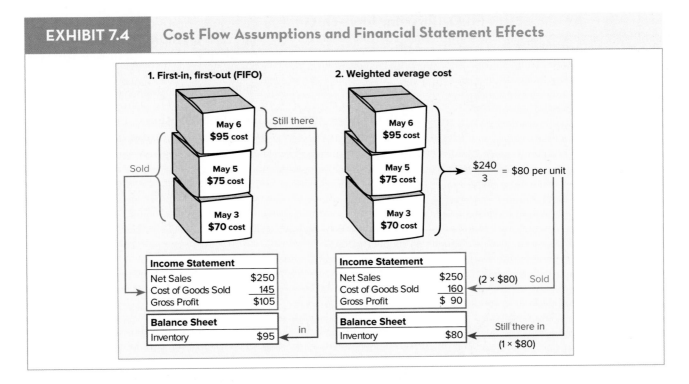

As Exhibit 7.4 illustrates, the choice of cost flow assumption can have a major effect on Gross Profit on the income statement and Inventory on the balance sheet.

Notice that although they're called *inventory* costing methods, their names actually describe how to calculate the cost of goods sold. That is, the first–out part of FIFO refers to the goods that are sold (i.e., first out) not the goods that are still in ending inventory. Here's a summary of whether the oldest, newest, or average unit costs are used to calculate amounts on the balance sheet or income statement.

	FIFO	Weighted Average
Cost of Goods Sold (Income Statement)	Oldest cost	Average cost
Inventory (Balance Sheet)	Newest cost	Average cost

Inventory Cost Flow Computations

Now that you've seen how these cost flow assumptions work, and that they actually make a difference in a company's balance sheet and income state–ment, you're ready for a more realistic example. So, let's assume that dur–ing the first week of October, HBC entered into the following transactions for its multi–striped beach towel. All sales were made at a selling price of $15 per unit. These sales occurred after HBC made two batches of towel purchases, which were added to inventory purchased the previous month.

Date	Description	# of Units	Cost per Unit	Total Cost
Oct. 1	Beginning Inventory	10	$ 7	$ 70
Oct. 3	Purchase	30	8	240
Oct. 5	Purchase	10	10	100
	Goods Available for Sale	50		$410
Oct. 6	Sales	(35)	To calculate	To calculate
	Ending Inventory	15	To calculate	To calculate

FIFO (First-In, First-Out) The first–in, first–out (FIFO) method assumes that the oldest goods (the first into inventory) are the first ones sold (the first out of inventory). So to calculate the cost of the thirty–five units sold, use the costs of the first–in (oldest) goods (10 units at $7 plus 25 of the 30 units at $8 equals a total of $270). The costs of the newer goods are included in the cost of the ending inventory (ten units at $10 plus five units remaining from the thirty units at $8 equals a total of $140). These calculations are summarized in the table below.

FIFO		
Beginning Inventory	10 units × $7	$ 70
+ Purchases	30 units × $8	240
	10 units × $10	100
Goods Available for Sale		410
− Ending Inventory (10 × $10) + (5 × $8)		140
Cost of Goods Sold (10 × $7) + (25 × $8)		$270

Notice in the table that the Cost of Goods Sold can be calculated directly (10 × $7 plus 25 × $8 equals a total of $270) or it can be backed into by subtracting the cost of ending inventory from the cost of goods available for sale ($410 − $140 = $270). This latter approach is helpful if the number of units sold is not known, which can occur when a company uses a periodic inventory system.[1]

Weighted Average Cost The weighted average cost method is found in two steps. The first step is to calculate the total cost of the goods available for sale. You multiply the number of units at each cost by the cost per unit and then add to get the total cost:

Beginning Inventory	10 units × $7	$ 70
+ Purchases	30 units × $8	240
	10 units × $10	100
Goods Available for Sale	**50 units**	**$410**

Then you calculate the weighted average cost per unit using the following formula:

$$\frac{\text{Weighted}}{\text{Average Cost}} = \frac{\text{Cost of Goods Available for Sale}}{\text{Number of Units Available for Sale}} = \frac{\$410}{50 \text{ Units}} = \frac{\$8.20}{\text{per unit}}$$

Cost of goods sold and ending inventory are both calculated using the same weighted average cost per unit, as in the following table.

Weighted Average		
Beginning Inventory	10 units × $7	$ 70
+ Purchases	30 units × $8	240
	10 units × $10	100
Goods Available for Sale	**50 units**	410
− Ending Inventory (15 × $8.20)		123
Cost of Goods Sold (35 × $8.20)		$287

COACH'S TIP

Notice that the name of the method (first-in, first-out) describes how to calculate the cost of goods sold. The cost of ending inventory using FIFO is based on costs last-in.

COACH'S TIP

To calculate weighted average cost, be sure to **weight** the costs by the number of units at each unit cost. Don't simply average the unit costs [($7 + $8 + $10) ÷ 3 = $8.33]. That is a simple average—not a weighted average.

Financial Statement Effects Exhibit 7.5 summarizes the financial statement effects of the FIFO and weighted average cost methods. Remember that these methods differ only in the way they split the cost of goods available for sale between ending inventory and cost of goods sold. If a cost goes into Inventory, it doesn't go into Cost of Goods Sold. Thus, the method that assigns the highest cost to ending inventory will assign the lowest cost to cost of goods sold (and vice versa). As you can see in Exhibit 7.5, the effect on Cost of Goods Sold affects many other items on the income statement, including Gross Profit, Income from Operations, Income Before Income Tax Expense, Income Tax Expense, and Net Income.

EXHIBIT 7.5	Financial Statement Effects of Inventory Costing Methods

Effects on the Income Statement	FIFO	Weighted Average (WA)
Sales	$525	$525
Cost of Goods Sold	270	287
Gross Profit	**255**	**238**
Operating Expenses	125	125
Income from Operations	**130**	**113**
Other Revenue (Expenses)	20	20
Income Before Income Tax Expense	**150**	**133**
Income Tax Expense (assume 30%)	45	40
Net Income	**$105**	**$ 93**
Effects on the Balance Sheet		
Inventory	$140	$123

Depending on whether costs are rising or falling, different methods have different effects on the financial statements. When costs are rising, as they are in our example, FIFO produces a higher inventory value (making the balance sheet *appear* to be stronger) and a lower cost of goods sold (resulting in a higher gross profit, which makes the company *look* more profitable). When costs are falling, these effects are reversed: FIFO produces a lower ending inventory value and a higher cost of goods sold—a double whammy. These are not "real" economic effects, however, because the inventory cost flow assumption does not affect the number of units sold or held in ending inventory. The following graphic summarizes the relative amounts reported:

*To learn about LIFO, see the Spotlight on the World feature below.

Tax Implications and Cash Flow Effects Given the financial statement effects, you might wonder why a company would ever use a method that produces a lower inventory amount and a higher cost of goods sold. The answer is suggested in Exhibit 7.5, in the line called *Income Tax Expense*. When faced with increasing costs per unit, as in our example, a company that uses FIFO will have a higher income tax expense. This income tax effect is a real cost in the sense that the company will actually have to pay more income taxes in the current year, thereby reducing the company's cash.

Consistency in Reporting   A common question is whether managers are free to choose one inventory costing method one period, and then switch to another inventory costing method the next period, depending on whether unit costs are rising or declining during the period. Because this switching would make it difficult to compare financial results across periods, accounting rules discourage it. A change in method is allowed only if it improves the accuracy of the company's financial results. A company can, however, use different methods for inventories that differ in nature or use, provided that the methods are used consistently over time.

HOW'S IT GOING?

Self-Study Practice 7.1

Ultima Euromoda, Inc. purchased one designer suit at a cost of $200 and then purchased three more for $400 each. Three of the suits were then sold at a price of $1,000 each. Compute the Sales Revenue, Cost of Goods Sold, Gross Profit, and the cost of Ending Inventory using (a) FIFO and (b) weighted average. Which inventory costing method will minimize Ultima's income taxes?

After you have finished, check your answers with the solution, which follows the chapter summary.

SPOTLIGHT ON The World

Last-In, First-Out (LIFO)

The last-in, first-out (LIFO) inventory costing method, which is not permitted under ASPE or IFRS, assumes that the newest goods (the last into inventory) are the first ones sold (the first out of inventory). The cost of Ending Inventory using LIFO is based on costs first-in. (Think of this as "first-in, still there" or FIST.)
    LIFO is not permitted for several reasons:

1. In most situations, LIFO does not fairly represent the actual flow of costs.
2. The cost of Ending Inventory that is reported on the balance sheet is not a fair representation of the most recent costs of inventory on hand.
3. The use of LIFO can result in large distortions of reported income when older inventory costs, which are typically lower, are expensed to cost of goods sold.

    LIFO is permitted under U.S. GAAP, since the United States is one country that has not yet adopted IFRS. Public companies in Canada that are listed on a U.S. stock exchange and also on a Canadian exchange are allowed to prepare their financial statements using U.S. GAAP and are permitted to use the LIFO inventory costing method. We have therefore added Supplement 7A, where we examine LIFO more closely, using the same examples that we used in this early part of the chapter.

LOWER OF COST AND NET REALIZABLE VALUE

Report inventory at the lower of cost and net realizable value.

The inventory costing methods that have been discussed so far in this chapter have followed the historical cost principle. This principle requires companies to record inventory at its historical purchase price, or cost.

The price that this inventory could be sold for (the value of inventory), can fall below its recorded cost for two reasons: (1) it's easily replaced by identical goods at a lower cost, or (2) it's become outdated or damaged. The first case is common for high—tech electronics. As companies become more efficient at making cutting—edge products, the products become cheaper to make. The second case commonly occurs with fad items or seasonal goods, such as winter parkas, which tend to drop in value at the end of the season.

In either instance, when the value of inventory falls below its recorded cost, GAAP requires that inventory be written down to its lower net realizable value. This rule is known as reporting inventory at the **lower of cost and net realizable value (LC&NRV)**. It results in inventory that is reported conservatively, at an amount that does not exceed its actual value. Also, by recording the write—down in the period in which a loss in value occurs, companies better match their revenues and expenses of that period.

Let's look at how the inventory write—down is determined and recorded. Assume that HBC's ending inventory includes two items whose estimated values have recently changed: winter parkas and beach towels.[2]

The estimated values of these items can be used as the net realizable value and compared to the original recorded cost per unit. You then take the lower of those two amounts (the lower of cost and net realizable value) and multiply it by the number of units on hand. The result is the amount at which the inventory should be reported after all adjustments have been made:

Lower of cost and net realizable value (LC&NRV): A valuation rule that requires Inventory to be written down when its net realizable value or current replacement cost falls below its original historical cost. Can also be referred to as *lower of cost and market value*

Item	Cost per Item	Net Realizable Value per Item	LC&NRV per Item	Quantity	Total Lower of Cost and Net Realizable Value	Total Recorded Cost	Write—Down
Winter Parkas	$165	$150	$150	1,000	1,000 × $150 = $150,000	$165,000	$15,000
Beach Towels	20	25	20	400	400 × $ 20 = 8,000	8,000	0

Because the net realizable value of the 1,000 winter parkas ($150 × 1,000) is lower than the recorded cost ($165 × 1,000), the recorded amount for ending inventory should be written down by $15 per unit ($165 − $150). Thus, the total write—down should be $15,000 ($15 × 1,000). The effect of this write—down on the accounting equation and the journal entry to record it would be as follows:

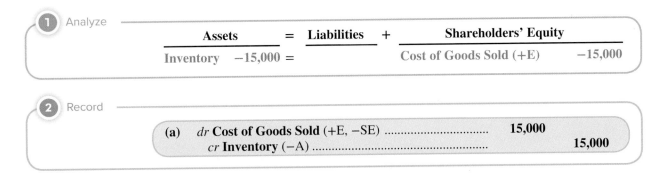

1 Analyze

Assets	=	Liabilities	+	Shareholders' Equity
Inventory −15,000 =				Cost of Goods Sold (+E) −15,000

2 Record

(a)	dr Cost of Goods Sold (+E, −SE)	15,000	
	cr Inventory (−A)		15,000

The beach towels do not need to be written down because their net realizable value ($25) is greater than their original cost ($20). The beach towels remain on the books at their cost of $20 per unit ($8,000 in total). Their value should not be increased based on the higher replacement cost because GAAP requires that they be reported at the lower of cost and net realizable value.

Most companies report their inventory write—down expense as Cost of Goods Sold, even though the written—down goods may not have been sold. This reporting is appropriate because writing down goods that haven't yet

COACH'S TIP

Companies generally report their accounting policy for inventory in the first note to the financial statements.

sold is a necessary cost of carrying the goods that did sell. By recording the write–down in the period in which a loss in value occurs, companies better match their revenues and expenses of that period.

Because investors and analysts view a LC&NRV write–down as a sign of inventory management problems, some executives have gone out of their way to avoid them, as the following Spotlight on Ethics explains. The failure to follow inventory LC&NRV rules is one of the most common types of financial statement misstatements. To learn more about how this mis–statement and other inventory errors can affect the financial statements, see Supplement 7C at the end of this chapter.

Evaluate the Results

INVENTORY TURNOVER ANALYSIS

LEARNING OBJECTIVE 7-5

Evaluate inventory management by computing and interpreting the inventory turnover ratio.

How can you tell whether an increase in a company's inventory balance is good news or bad news? If the increase occurs because management is building up stock in anticipation of higher sales, it could be good news. But if it results from an accumulation of old inventory items that nobody wants, it is probably bad news. Those who work inside the company can easily determine whether the change is good or bad news by talking with the sales managers. But if you are looking at the company's financial statements from the outside, how can you tell?

The method most analysts use to evaluate such changes is called *inventory turnover analysis*. Exhibit 7.6 illustrates the idea behind inventory turnover analysis. As a company buys goods, its inventory balance goes up; as it sells goods, its inventory balance goes down. This process of buying and selling, which is called **inventory turnover**, is repeated over and over during each accounting period for each line of products.

Inventory turnover: The process of buying and selling inventory.

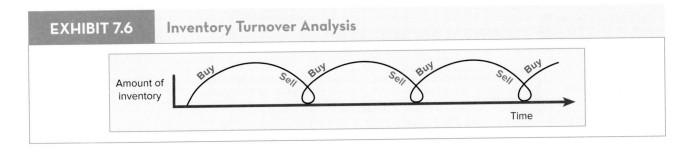

| EXHIBIT 7.6 | Inventory Turnover Analysis |

Analysts can assess how many times, on average, inventory has been bought and sold during the period by calculating the inventory turnover ratio. A higher ratio indicates that inventory moves more quickly from purchase to sale, reducing storage and obsolescence costs. Because less money is tied up in inventory, the excess can be invested to earn interest or reduce borrowing, which reduces interest expense. More efficient purchasing and production techniques, as well as high product demand, will boost this ratio. A sudden decline in the inventory turnover ratio may signal an unexpected drop in demand for the company's products or sloppy inventory management.

Rather than evaluate the number of times inventory turns over during the year, some analysts prefer to think in terms of the length of time (in days) required to sell inventory. Converting the inventory turnover ratio to the number of days needed to sell the inventory is easy. You simply divide 365 days by the year's inventory turnover ratio to get the **days to sell**. This measure provides the same basic information, but it is a little easier to interpret than the inventory turnover ratio. In terms of Exhibit 7.6, the *inventory turnover ratio* indicates the number of loops in a given period; *days to sell* indicates the average number of days between loops.

Days to sell: A measure of the average number of days from the time inventory is bought to the time it is sold.

ACCOUNTING DECISION TOOLS

Name of Measure	Formula	What It Tells You
Inventory turnover ratio	$\dfrac{\text{Cost of Goods Sold}}{\text{Average Inventory}}$	• The number of times inventory turns over during the period • A higher ratio means faster turnover
Days to sell	$\dfrac{365}{\text{Inventory Turnover Ratio}}$	• Average number of days from purchase to sale • A higher number means a longer time to sell

Comparison to Benchmarks

Inventory turnover ratios and the number of days to sell can be helpful in comparing different companies' inventory management practices. But use them cautiously, because these measures can vary significantly between industries. For merchandisers, inventory turnover refers to buying and selling goods, whereas for manufacturers, it refers to producing inventory and delivering it to customers. These differences are reflected in Exhibit 7.7, which shows that McDonald's has a turnover ratio of 52.9, which means that it takes about seven days to sell its entire food inventory (including the stuff in its freezers). The motorcycles at Harley–Davidson hog more time, as indicated by the company's inventory turnover ratio of 6.5, which equates to about 56 days to produce and sell. HBC's inventory turned over only 2.3 times during the year, which is just once every 159 days.

EXHIBIT 7.7	Summary of Inventory Turnover Ratio Analyses

Company	Relevant Information (in millions)				Fiscal 2015 Inventory Turnover Calculation	Fiscal 2015 Days to Sell Calculation
		Fiscal 2015		Fiscal 2014		
Harley–Davidson Motorcycles	CGS	$3,356		$3,543	$\dfrac{\$3,356}{(\$586 + \$449)/2} = 6.5$ times	$\dfrac{365\,\text{days}}{6.5\,\text{times}} = 56.2$ days
	Inventory	$586		$449		
McDonald's	CGS	$5,552		$6,129	$\dfrac{\$5,552}{(\$100 + \$110)/2} = 52.9$ times	$\dfrac{365\,\text{days}}{52.9\,\text{times}} = 6.9$ days
	Inventory	$100		$110		
Hudson's Bay Company	CGS	$6,638		$4,901	$\dfrac{\$6,638}{(\$3,415 + \$2,319)/2} = 2.3$ times	$\dfrac{365\,\text{days}}{2.3\,\text{times}} = 158.7$ days
	Inventory	$3,415		$2,319		

Inventory turnover also can vary significantly between companies within the same industry, particularly if they take different approaches to pricing their inventory. In Chapter 6, we saw that Walmart follows a low–cost pricing policy, which means it sets its sales prices only slightly above cost. This policy led Walmart to earn about 24.6 cents of gross profit on each dollar of sales, whereas Reitmans earned 60.3 cents of gross profit. But when you consider the inventory turnover measures, you can see the full implications of this pricing policy. Walmart turns over its inventory about 8.1 times a year (45 days), whereas Reitmans turns over its inventory 3.4 times a year (106 days). Often, the company with a lower gross profit percentage has a faster inventory turnover.

With inventory turnover ratios varying between industries and companies, it's most useful to compare a company's turnover with its own results from prior periods. For practice at computing and comparing to prior periods, try the following Self–Study Practice.

HOW'S IT GOING?

Self-Study Practice 7.2

HBC's balance sheet and income statement information for prior years are presented in Exhibits 7.1 and 7.2. The inventory balance at the end of fiscal 2014 was $2,349 million.

(a) Calculate HBC's inventory turnover and days to sell for the year ended January 30, 2015 (fiscal 2014).

(b) Did HBC's inventory turnover improve or decline in fiscal 2015 as shown in Exhibit 7.7 compared to fiscal 2014 [calculated in (a)]?

After you have finished, check your answers with the solution, which follows the chapter summary.

Applying Inventory Turnover and Gross Profit to LCM Judgments

Inventory turnover analysis is also useful to accountants when evaluating whether a write-down is needed to report inventory at LC&NRV (lower of cost and net realizable value). Decreasing turnover (and increasing days to sell) suggests that inventory is not selling well and that future price cuts may be needed to sell the inventory.

If these price cuts are large or the inventory currently generates a relatively low gross profit percentage (as discussed in Chapter 6), the price cuts can result in a market value below cost, warranting an LC&NRV write-down. Consequently, *accountants watch for worsening inventory turnover and low gross profit percentages as signals that a write-down may be needed to report inventory at LC&NRV.*

Like ASPE, IFRS requires that inventory be reported at the lower of cost and net realizable value (LC&NRV). However, inventory LC&NRV rules under IFRS differ from ASPE in an important way. With IFRS, if a decline in the net realizable value reverses, perhaps because of an economic recovery, the value of inventory is written back up to its original cost and the recovery is credited to Cost of Goods Sold. With ASPE, reversals of inventory write-downs are not allowed.

Topic	ASPE	IFRS
Inventory valuation	• Inventory is required to be reported at the lower of cost and net realizable value.	• Inventory is required to be reported at the lower of cost and net realizable value.
	• If a write-down of inventory is needed because of the LC&NRV rule, this write-down cannot be reversed, even if a decline in the net realizable value reverses.	• If a write-down of inventory is necessary because of the LC&NRV rule, this write-down can be reversed and the value of inventory can be written back up, but only to its original cost.

Supplement 7A

RECORDING INVENTORY TRANSACTIONS USING LAST-IN, FIRST-OUT (LIFO)

LEARNING OBJECTIVE 7-S1

Compute inventory costs using LIFO.

Inventory Costing Methods

As discussed earlier in this chapter, ASPE and IFRS do not permit companies to use the **last—in, first—out (LIFO)** inventory costing method. However, if a Canadian public company is listed on a U.S. stock exchange, it is permitted to use U.S. GAAP and therefore can apply the LIFO inventory costing method. For this reason, we felt it was appropriate to include in this supplement the examples from the chapter material—but using

Last-in, first-out (LIFO): Assumes that the most recently purchased units (last in) are sold first (first out).

LIFO as the inventory costing method. First, our simple example where the following transactions took place:

May 3	Purchased 1 unit for **$70**
May 5	Purchased 1 more unit for **$75**
May 6	Purchased 1 more unit for **$95**
May 8	Sold 2 units for $125 each

The sale on May 8 of two units, at a selling price of $125 each, would generate sales revenue of $250 ($125 × 2), and the amount of Cost of Goods Sold would depend on which goods are assumed to have been sold. LIFO assumes that the inventory costs flow out in the opposite order to which the goods are received. In other words, the costs of the last goods purchased (last in) are the costs of the first goods sold (first out). As in our example, the latest items received, the $95 and $75 units received on May 6 and 5, become the $170 Cost of Goods Sold on the income statement, and the remaining $70 unit received on May 3 becomes Ending Inventory on the balance sheet. This is shown in Exhibit 7A.1.

EXHIBIT 7A.1	Cost Flow Assumption and Financial Statement Effects Using LIFO

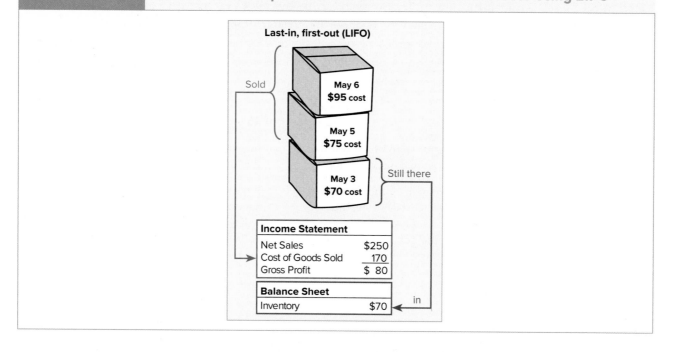

The following summary shows whether the oldest, newest, or average unit costs are used to calculate the amounts on the balance sheet or income statement.

	FIFO	LIFO	Weighted Average
Cost of Goods Sold (Income Statement)	Oldest cost	Newest cost	Average cost
Inventory (Balance Sheet)	Newest cost	Oldest cost	Average cost

Inventory Cost Flow Computations

Now that you've seen how the LIFO cost flow assumption works, let's go back to our more realistic example of HBC. Let's assume that during the first week of October, HBC entered into the following transactions for its multi–striped beach towel. All sales were made at a selling price of $15 per unit. These sales occurred after HBC made two batches of towel purchases, which were added to inventory purchased the previous month.

Date	Description	# of Units	Cost per Unit	Total Cost
Oct. 1	Beginning Inventory	10	$ 7	$ 70
Oct. 3	Purchase	30	8	240
Oct. 5	Purchase	10	10	100
	Goods Available for Sale	50		$410
Oct. 6	Sales	(35)	To calculate	To calculate
	Ending Inventory	15	To calculate	To calculate

The last–in, first–out (LIFO) method assumes that the newest goods (the last into inventory) are the first ones sold (the first out of inventory). So, to calculate the cost of the thirty–five units sold, use the costs of the last–in (newest) goods (ten units at $10 plus twenty–five of the thirty units at $8 equals a total of $300). The costs of the older goods are included in the cost of the ending inventory (ten units at $7 plus five units remaining from the thirty units at $8 equals a total of $110). These calculations are summarized in the table below.

LIFO		
Beginning Inventory	10 units × $7	$ 70
+ Purchases	30 units × $8	240
	10 units × $10	100
Goods Available for Sale		410
− Ending Inventory $(10 \times \$7) + (5 \times \$8)$		110
Cost of Goods Sold $(10 \times \$10) + (25 \times \$8)$		$300

The name of the method (last–in, first–out) describes how to calculate the costs of goods sold. The cost of ending inventory using LIFO is based on costs first–in. (Think of this as "first–in, still there" or FIST.)

As in the table, Cost of Goods Sold can be calculated directly (10 × $10 plus 25 × $8 = a total of $300) or it can be backed into by subtract–ing the cost of ending inventory from the cost of goods available for sale ($410 − $110 = $300). We actually recommend that you do both, as a way to double–check your calculations.

Supplement 7B

FIFO, LIFO, AND WEIGHTED AVERAGE IN A PERPETUAL INVENTORY SYSTEM

There were several good reasons for showing in the previous sections of this chapter how cost flow assumptions are applied in a periodic inventory system, even though most modern companies use perpetual inventory systems.

First, only the LIFO and weighted average calculations differ between periodic and perpetual inventory systems. As we show in the following example, FIFO calculations don't differ between periodic and perpetual systems. FIFO is one of the generally acceptable methods for companies to use in Canada, so even if they calculate costs under a perpetual system, it is identical to calculating costs under a periodic system.

Second, most LIFO companies actually use FIFO during the period and then adjust to LIFO at the end of the period. By waiting until the end of the period to calculate this LIFO adjustment, it's *as if* all pur—chases during the period were recorded before the Cost of Goods Sold was calculated and recorded. In other words, it's as if these companies use a periodic inventory system to determine their LIFO inventory numbers, even though they actually track the number of units bought and sold on a perpetual basis.

Third, companies typically adjust their records at year—end to match a physical count of the inventory on hand, so as a practical mat—ter, these companies are on a periodic costing system for all intents and purposes.

Fourth, the periodic inventory system is easier to visualize, so it's easier for you to learn.

Despite this, it can be useful to know how to apply cost flow assump—tions in a perpetual inventory system. In this supplement, we show how to calculate the Cost of Goods Sold and cost of Ending Inventory on a perpetual basis using the same basic cost flow information used in the body of the chapter. The only difference in the following table is that we have assumed the sales occurred on October 4, prior to the final inventory purchase.

Date	Description	# of Units	Cost per Unit	Total Cost
Oct. 1	Beginning Inventory	10	$ 7	$ 70
Oct. 3	Purchase	30	$ 8	240
Oct. 4	Sales	(35)	To Calculate	To Calculate
Oct. 5	Purchase	10	$10	100
	Ending Inventory	15	To calculate	To calculate

FIFO (First-In, First-Out)

The first—in, first—out (FIFO) method assumes that the oldest goods (the first into inventory) are the first ones sold (the first out of inventory). So to calculate the cost of the thirty—five units sold, use the costs of the first—in (oldest) goods (ten units at $7 plus twenty—five of the thirty units at $8 equals a total of $270). The costs of the newer goods are included in the cost of the ending inventory (five units remaining from the thirty units at $8 plus ten units at $10 equals a total of $140). These calculations are summarized in the left—hand side of the following table (the right—hand side summarizes periodic calculations, which were explained in the body of the chapter).

As you can see, FIFO yields identical amounts under perpetual and periodic. The only difference is that perpetual allows you to "force out" the cost of Ending Inventory so that it can be compared to the cost of goods actually on hand (to determine shrinkage). Periodic requires you to use the cost of goods in Ending Inventory to force out the Cost of Goods Sold (so you cannot determine shrinkage).

FIFO–Perpetual

Beginning Inventory	10 units × $7	$ 70
+ Purchases	30 units × $8	240
	10 units × $10	100
Goods Available for Sale		410
− Cost of Goods Sold $(10 \times \$7) + (25 \times \$8)$		270
Ending Inventory $(10 \times \$10) + (5 \times \$8)$		$140

FIFO–Periodic

Beginning Inventory	10 units × $7	$ 70
+ Purchases	30 units × $8	240
	10 units × $10	100
Goods Available for Sale		410
− Ending Inventory $(10 \times \$10) + (5 \times \$8)$		140
Cost of Goods Sold $(10 \times \$7) + (25 \times \$8)$		$270

LIFO (Last-In, First-Out)

The last–in, first–out (LIFO) method assumes that the newest goods (the last into inventory) as of the date of the sale are the first ones sold (the first out of inventory). So to calculate the cost of the thirty–five units sold, use the costs of the last–in (newest) goods as of the date of the sale (thirty units at $8 plus five of the ten units at $7 equals a total of $275). The costs of the older goods (five units remaining from the ten units at $7 equals $35) plus any later purchases (ten units at $10 equals $100) are included in the cost of the ending inventory ($35 + $100 = $135). These calculations appear in the following table on the left.

LIFO–Perpetual

Beginning Inventory	10 units × $7	$ 70
+ Purchases	30 units × $8	240
Goods Available for Sale		310
− Cost of Goods Sold $(30 \times \$8) + (5 \times \$7)$		275
Goods Available for Sale	5 units × $7	35
+ Purchases	10 units × $10	100
Ending Inventory $(5 \times \$7) + (10 \times \$10)$		$135

LIFO–Periodic

Beginning Inventory	10 units × $7	$ 70
+ Purchases	30 units × $8	240
	10 units × $10	100
Goods Available for Sale		410
− Ending Inventory $(10 \times \$7) + (5 \times \$8)$		110
Cost of Goods Sold $(10 \times \$10) + (25 \times \$8)$		$300

Notice that LIFO–Perpetual calculates Cost of Goods Sold using the cost of goods last–in at the time of the sale, whereas LIFO–Periodic uses the cost of goods last–in at the end of the period.

Weighted Average Cost

In a perpetual inventory system, the weighted average cost must be calculated each time a sale is recorded. Use the same two steps shown in the body of the chapter: (1) calculate the total cost of the goods available for sale, and (2) divide by the number of units available for sale. For example, in the following table on the left, the weighted average cost at the time of sale is calculated by dividing $310 by the forty units available for sale ($310 ÷ 40 = $7.75 per unit). This cost is then multiplied by the number of units sold to calculate Cost of Goods Sold (35 × $7.75 = $271.25). The remaining five units are also valued at the same weighted average cost (5 × $7.75 = $38.75). Additional inventory purchases ($100) are added to these inventory costs to calculate the cost of ending inventory ($38.75 + $100 = $138.75).[4]

Weighted Average–Perpetual		
Beginning Inventory	10 units × $7	$ 70.00
+ Purchases	30 units × $8	240.00
Goods Available for Sale	40 units	310.00
− Cost of Goods Sold (35 × $7.75)		271.25
Goods Available for Sale	5 units	38.75
+ Purchases	10 units × $10	100.00
Ending Inventory	15 units	$138.75

Weighted Average–Periodic		
Beginning Inventory	10 units × $7	$ 70
+ Purchases	30 units × $8	240
	10 units × $10	100
Goods Available for Sale	50 units	410
− Ending Inventory (15 × $8.20)		123
Cost of Goods Sold (35 × $8.20)		$287

Financial Statement Effects

Exhibit 7B.1 summarizes the financial statement effects of using a perpetual inventory system with FIFO, LIFO, or weighted average cost methods. These methods differ only in the way they split the cost of goods available for sale between Ending Inventory and Cost of Goods Sold. If a cost goes into Cost of Goods Sold, it must be taken out of Inventory. Thus, the method that assigns the highest cost to Cost of Goods Sold assigns the lowest cost to Ending Inventory (and vice versa).

EXHIBIT 7B.1 **Financial Statement Effects of Inventory Costing Methods (Perpetual)**

Effects on the Income Statement	FIFO	LIFO	Weighted Average
Sales	$525	$525	$525.00
Cost of Goods Sold	270	275	271.25
Gross Profit	255	250	253.75

Effects on the Balance Sheet	FIFO	LIFO	Weighted Average
Inventory	$140	$135	$138.75

Supplement 7C

THE EFFECTS OF ERRORS IN ENDING INVENTORY

As mentioned earlier in the chapter, the failure to correctly apply the LC&NRV rule to Ending Inventory is considered an error. Other errors can occur when inappropriate quantities or unit costs are used in calculating inventory cost. Regardless of the reason, errors in inventory can significantly affect both the balance sheet and the income statement. As the Cost of Goods Sold equation indicates, a direct relationship exists between Ending Inventory and Cost of Goods Sold because items not in the ending inventory are assumed to have been sold. Thus, any errors in ending inventory will affect the balance sheet (current assets) and the income statement (Cost of Goods Sold, Gross Profit, and Net Income). The effects of inventory errors are felt in more than one year because the ending inventory for one year becomes the beginning inventory for the next year.

To determine the effects of inventory errors on the financial statements in both the current year and the following year, use the Cost of Goods Sold equation. For example, let's assume that ending inventory was overstated in Year 1 by $10,000 due to an error that was not discovered until Year 2. This would have the following effects in Year 1:

YEAR 1	
Beginning Inventory	Accurate
+ Purchases	Accurate
− Ending Inventory	Understated $10,000
= Cost of Goods Sold	Understated $10,000

Because Cost of Goods Sold was understated, Gross Profit and Income before Income Tax Expense would be overstated by $10,000 in Year 1, as shown in Exhibit 7C.1. (Net Income would be overstated, as well, although the effects would be offset somewhat by overstated Income Tax Expense.)

EXHIBIT 7C.1   Two-Year Income Effects of Inventory Error

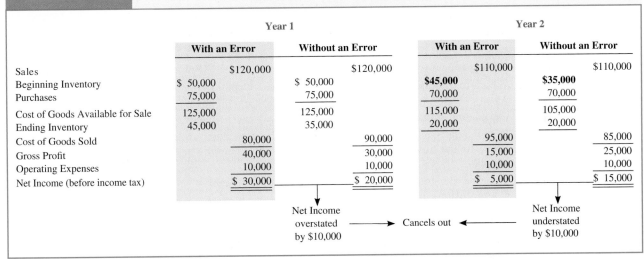

	Year 1		Year 2	
	With an Error	**Without an Error**	**With an Error**	**Without an Error**
Sales	$120,000	$120,000	$110,000	$110,000
Beginning Inventory	$ 50,000	$ 50,000	**$45,000**	**$35,000**
Purchases	75,000	75,000	70,000	70,000
Cost of Goods Available for Sale	125,000	125,000	115,000	105,000
Ending Inventory	45,000	35,000	20,000	20,000
Cost of Goods Sold	80,000	90,000	95,000	85,000
Gross Profit	40,000	30,000	15,000	25,000
Operating Expenses	10,000	10,000	10,000	10,000
Net Income (before income tax)	$ 30,000	$ 20,000	$ 5,000	$ 15,000

Net Income overstated by $10,000 ⟶ Cancels out ⟵ Net Income understated by $10,000

The Year 1 ending inventory becomes the Year 2 beginning inventory, so even if Year 2 ending inventory is calculated correctly, the error in Year 1 creates an error in Year 2, as shown in the following table:

YEAR 2	
Beginning Inventory	Understated $10,000
+ Purchases	Accurate
− Ending Inventory	Accurate
= Cost of Goods Sold	Understated $10,000

Because Cost of Goods Sold is overstated in Year 2, that year's Gross Profit and Income Before Income Tax Expense would be understated by the same amount in Year 2. (Net Income would be understated, as well, although the effects would be offset somewhat by understated Income Tax Expense.)

Ignoring income taxes, the effects of these errors on Net Income in each of the two years is shown in Exhibit 7C.1. Notice that the Cost of Goods Sold is understated in the first year and overstated in the second year. Over the two years, these errors offset one another. Inventory errors will "self−correct" like this only if ending inventory is accurately calculated at the end of the following year and adjusted to that correct balance. (The fact that these errors are self−correcting does not make them acceptable. They are errors.)

Review the Chapter

This section provides a chance to solidify your understanding of key points. It's worth your time to work through the following demonstration case, scan the chapter summary, test your understanding of key terms, and then practise, practise, practise.

DEMONSTRATION CASE

Bondel Electronics sells one type of consumer electronics product. Assume that the following sum-marized transactions were completed during the month ended January 31, 2017, in the order given.

	Units	Unit Cost
Beginning inventory (January 1)	11	$200
New inventory purchases (January 3)	5	209
New inventory purchases (January 4)	9	220
Sale (January 5 at a price of $420 per item)	(12)	
	13	

Required:

1. Using the formats shown in the chapter, compute the Cost of Goods Available for Sale, Ending Inventory, and Cost of Goods Sold under (*a*) FIFO and (*b*) weighted average.
2. Which method would minimize income taxes? Explain your answer.
3. Assuming that operating expenses were $500 and the income tax rate is 25 percent, prepare the income statement for the month using the method selected in requirement 2.
4. If the replacement cost fell to $205 in February, compute the adjustment that would be made to the Inventory account assuming the company uses (*a*) FIFO and (*b*) weighted average.
5. Describe the impact of an adjustment in requirement 4 on the inventory turnover ratio. Computations are not required.

Suggested Solution

1.

(a) FIFO

Beginning Inventory	11 units × $200	$2,200
+ Purchases	5 units × $209	1,045
	9 units × $220	1,980
Goods Available for Sale		5,225
− **Ending Inventory** (9 × $220) + (4 × $209)		**2,816**
Cost of Goods Sold (11 × $200) + (1 × $209)		**$2,409**

(b) Weighted Average

Beginning Inventory	11 units × $200	$2,200
+ Purchases	5 units × $209	1,045
	9 units × $220	1,980
Goods Available for Sale		5,225
− **Ending Inventory** (13 × $209)		**2,717**
Cost of Goods Sold (12 × $209)		**$2,508**

$$\text{Weighted Average Cost} = \frac{\text{Cost of Goods Available for Sale}}{\text{Number of Units Available for Sale}} = \frac{\$5,225}{25 \text{ Units}} = \frac{\$209}{\text{per unit}}$$

2. Weighted average would minimize income taxes. Because costs are rising, weighted average produces higher Cost of Goods Sold, lower Income Before Income Tax Expense, and lower Income Tax Expense.

3.

BONDEL ELECTRONICS
Income Statement
For the Month Ended January 31, 2017

Sales (12 × $420)	$5,040
Cost of Goods Sold	2,508
Gross Profit	2,532
Operating Expenses	500
Income Before Income Tax Expense	2,032
Income Tax Expense (25%)	508
Net Income	$1,524

4. The total net realizable value of the thirteen units in ending inventory, with a per−unit replacement cost of $205, is $2,665 (13 × $205 = $2,665). The LC&NRV analysis follows:

	Cost	Net Realizable Value	LC&NRV	Adjustment Needed
(a) FIFO	$2,816	$2,665	$2,665	$(151) = $2,816 − $2,665
(b) Weighted Average	$2,717	$2,665	$2,665	(52) = $2,717 − $2,665

5. *The ending balance in the inventory account under either method needs to be reported at $2,665, as this is the lower amount in both cases.* An adjustment for LC&NRV decreases the Inventory balance and increases the Cost of Goods Sold. Both of these changes (individually or together) increase the inventory turnover ratio.

CHAPTER SUMMARY

Describe the issues in managing different types of inventory. LO7-1

- Make or buy a sufficient *quantity* of *quality* products, at the lowest possible *cost*, so that they can be sold as quickly as possible to earn the desired amount of gross profit.

- *Merchandise inventory* is bought by merchandisers in a ready−to−sell format. When *raw materials* enter a manufacturer's production process, they become *work in process* inventory, which is further transformed into *finished goods* that are ultimately sold to customers.

Explain how to report inventory and cost of goods sold. LO7-2

- The costs of goods purchased are added to Inventory (on the balance sheet).

- The costs of goods sold are removed from Inventory and reported as an expense called Cost of Goods Sold (on the income statement).

- The costs remaining in Inventory at the end of a period become the cost of Inventory at the beginning of the next period.

- The relationships among beginning inventory (BI), purchases (P), ending inventory (EI), and cost of goods sold (CGS) are BI + P − EI = CGS or BI + P − CGS = EI.

Compute costs using three inventory costing methods. LO7-3

- Four methods can be used to allocate the cost of inventory, but in Canada, only three of these methods are generally accepted, whether a company uses ASPE or IFRS. LIFO is the one method that is not acceptable in Canada. Any of the remaining three methods— specific identification, FIFO, and weighted average—can be used to allocate the cost of inventory available for sale between goods that are sold and goods that remain on hand at the end of the accounting period.

- Specific identification assigns costs to Ending Inventory and Cost of Goods Sold by tracking and identifying each specific item of inventory.
- Under FIFO, the costs first in are assigned to Cost of Goods Sold, and the costs last in (most recent) are assigned to the inventory that is still on hand in Ending Inventory.
- Under weighted average cost, the weighted average cost per unit of inventory is assigned equally to goods sold and those still on hand in Ending Inventory.

LO7-4 **Report inventory at the lower of cost and net realizable value.**

- The lower of cost and net realizable value (LC&NRV) rule ensures inventory assets are not reported at more than they are worth.

LO7-5 **Evaluate inventory management by computing and interpreting the inventory turnover ratio.**

- The inventory turnover ratio measures the efficiency of inventory management. It reflects how many times average inventory was acquired and sold during the period. The inventory turnover ratio is calculated by dividing Cost of Goods Sold by Average Inventory.

ACCOUNTING DECISION TOOLS

Name of Measure	Formula	What It Tells You
Inventory turnover ratio	$\dfrac{\text{Cost of Goods Sold}}{\text{Average Inventory}}$	• The number of times inventory turns over during the period • A higher ratio means faster turnover
Days to sell	$\dfrac{365}{\text{Inventory Turnover Ratio}}$	• Average number of days from purchase to sale • A higher number means a longer time to sell

SOLUTION TO SELF-STUDY PRACTICE

Solution to SP7.1

	(a) FIFO	(b) Weighted Average
Sales Revenue (3 × $1,000)	$3,000	$3,000
Cost of Goods Sold*	1,000	1,050
Gross Profit	2,000	1,950
Ending Inventory	$ 400	$ 350

*(a) $1,000 = (1 × $200) + (2 × $400); (b) $1,050 = 3 × [(1 × $200) + (3 × $400)]/4; Weighted average minimizes Ultima's gross profit and, therefore, minimizes its income taxes.

Solution to SP7.2

(a) $\dfrac{\$4,901}{(\$2,319 + \$2,349)/2} = 2.09\,\text{times}$

$\dfrac{365\,\text{days}}{2.09\,\text{times}} = 174.6\,\text{days}$

(b) HBC's inventory turnover increased in fiscal 2015 which resulted in 15.96 fewer days to sell as compared to the year before.

KEY TERMS

Days to Sell

First–In, First–Out (FIFO)

Inventory Turnover

Last–In, First–Out (LIFO)

Lower of Cost and Net Realizable
Value (LC&NRV)

Specific Identification

Weighted Average Cost

Complete definitions are also included in the glossary at the end of this text.

HOMEWORK HELPER

Alternative terms

- Cost of Goods Sold is also called *Cost of Sales*.
- Days to Sell is also called *Days in Inventory* and *Days' Sales in Inventory*.

Helpful reminders

- The "first–out" part of FIFO and LIFO describes the costs going out of inventory into Cost of Goods Sold. To calculate ending inventory cost using LIFO, think FIST (first–in, still there). For FIFO inventory, think LIST (last–in, still there).

Frequent mistakes

- When calculating weighted average cost, do not simply average the costs per unit. Instead, divide the total cost of goods available for sale by the number of goods available for sale.
- Use Cost of Goods Sold when calculating inventory turnover, do not use Sales Revenue. Also, use the average inventory, not the Ending Inventory balance.

PRACTICE MATERIAL

QUESTIONS (⑤ Symbol indicates questions that require analysis from more than one perspective.)

1. What are three goals of inventory management?

2. Describe the specific types of inventory reported by merchandisers and manufacturers.

3. The chapter discussed three inventory costing methods that are acceptable in Canada. List the three methods and briefly explain each.

4. Which inventory cost flow method is most similar to the flow of products involving (a) a gumball machine, (b) bricks off a stack, and (c) gasoline out of a tank?

5. "Where possible, the inventory costing method should mimic actual product flows." Do you agree? Explain.

6. Contrast the effects of LIFO versus FIFO on ending inventory when (a) costs are rising and (b) costs are falling.

7. Contrast the income statement effect of LIFO versus FIFO (on Cost of Goods Sold and Gross Profit) when (a) costs are rising and (b) costs are falling.

8. Several managers in your company are experiencing personal financial problems and have asked that your company switch from weighted average to FIFO so that they can receive bigger bonuses, which are tied to the company's net income. How would you respond to this request if you were the company's chief financial officer? Would such a switch help the managers? Who could it hurt? ⑤

9. Explain briefly the application of the LC&NRV rule to ending inventory. Describe its effect on the balance sheet and income statement when the net realizable value is lower than cost.

10. As a sales representative for a publicly traded pharmaceutical company, you become aware of new evidence that one of your company's main drugs has significant

life–threatening side effects that were not previously reported. Your company has a large inventory of this drug. What income statement accounts other than Net Sales will be affected by the news? A friend asks you whether he should invest in your company. What should you say? ⑤

11. You work for a made–to–order clothing company whose reputation is based on its fast turnaround from order to delivery. The owner of your company is considering out–sourcing much of the clothing production because she thinks this will improve inventory turnover and customer satisfaction. In what way is she correct? In what way might she be wrong? ⑤

12. (Supplement 7B) Distinguish perpetual inventory systems from periodic inventory sys–tems by describing when and how Cost of Goods Sold is calculated when using LIFO.

13. (Supplement 7C) Explain why an error in Ending Inventory in one period affects the following period.

MINI-EXERCISES

LO7-1   **M7-1 Matching Inventory Items to Type of Business**

Match the type of inventory with the type of business by placing checkmarks in the applicable columns:

	Type of Business	
Type of Inventory	Merchandising	Manufacturing
Merchandise		
Finished goods		
Work in process		
Raw materials		

LO7-1   **M7-2 Reporting Goods in Transit**

Abercrombie & Fitch Co. reported the following in its financial statement notes.

> Ending inventory balances were $427.0 million, $679.9 million, and $464.6 million at February 2, 2013; January 28, 2012; and January 29, 2011, respectively. These balances included inventory in transit balances of $34.8 million, $103.1 million, and $55.0 million at February 2, 2013; January 28, 2012; and January 29, 2011, respectively. Inventory in transit is considered to be all merchandise owned by Abercrombie & Fitch that has not yet been received at an Abercrombie & Fitch distribution center.

Was the inventory in transit sold to Abercrombie & Fitch Co. as FOB shipping point or FOB destination?

LO7-2   **M7-3 Reporting Inventory-Related Accounts in the Financial Statements**

For each of the following, indicate whether it would be reported on the balance sheet (B/S), reported on the income statement (I/S), or not shown in the company's financial statements (Not).

a. Sales Revenue

b. Inventory (held on consignment)

c. Cost of Goods Sold

d. Inventory (out on consignment)

M7-4 Matching Financial Statement Effects to Inventory Costing Methods

Complete the following table by indicating which inventory costing method (FIFO or LIFO) would lead to the effects noted in the rows, for each of the circumstances described in the columns.

	1. Declining Costs	2. Rising Costs
a. Lowest net income		
b. Lowest ending inventory		

M7-5 Matching Inventory Costing Method Choices to Company Circumstances

Indicate whether a company interested in minimizing its income taxes should choose the FIFO or LIFO inventory costing method under each of the following circumstances.

a. Declining costs _____

b. Rising costs _____

M7-6 Calculating Cost of Goods Available for Sale, Ending Inventory, Sales, Cost of Goods Sold, and Gross Profit under Periodic FIFO and Weighted Average Cost

Given the following information, calculate cost of goods available for sale and ending inventory, then sales, cost of goods sold, and gross profit under (a) FIFO and (b) weighted average. Assume that a periodic inventory system is used.

		Units	Unit Cost	Unit Selling Price
July 1	Beginning Inventory	100	$10	
July 13	Purchase	500	13	
July 25	Sold	(200)		$15
July 31	Ending Inventory	400		

M7-7 Calculating Cost of Goods Available for Sale, Cost of Goods Sold, and Ending Inventory under FIFO and Weighted Average Cost (Periodic Inventory)

Aircard Corporation tracks the number of units purchased and sold throughout each accounting period, but applies its inventory costing method at the end of each period as if it uses a periodic inventory system. Given the following information, calculate the cost of goods available for sale, ending inventory, and cost of goods sold, if Aircard uses (a) FIFO or (b) weighted average cost.

		Units	Unit Cost
July 1	Beginning Inventory	2,000	$20
July 5	Sold	1,000	
July 13	Purchased	6,000	22
July 17	Sold	3,000	
July 25	Purchased	8,000	25
July 27	Sold	5,000	

M7-8 Calculating Cost of Goods Available for Sale, Cost of Goods Sold, and Ending Inventory under Periodic FIFO and Weighted Average Cost

In its first month of operations, Literacy for the Illiterate opened a new bookstore and bought merchandise in the following order: (1) 300 units at $7 on January 1, (2) 450 units at $8 on January 8, and (3) 750 units at $9 on January 29. Assuming 900 units are on hand at the end of the month, calculate the cost of goods available for sale, ending inventory, and cost of goods sold under the (a) FIFO and (b) weighted average cost flow assumptions. Assume a periodic inventory system is used.

LO7-4 **M7-9 Reporting Inventory under Lower of Cost and Net Realizable Value (LC&NRV)**

The Jewel Fool had the following inventory items on hand at the end of the year:

	Quantity	Cost per Item	Replacement Cost per Item
Necklaces	50	$75	$70
Bracelets	25	60	50

Determine the lower of cost and net realizable value per unit, and the total amount that should be reported on the balance sheet for each item of inventory.

LO7-4 **M7-10 Preparing the Journal Entry to Record Lower of Cost and Net Realizable Value Adjustments**

During its second and third quarters of fiscal 2014, BlackBerry Limited wrote down its BB10 smartphone inventory by approximately $1,700,000,000 because its cost exceeded its market value. Show the effects of this adjustment on the accounting equation and show the journal entry that the company would have made to record it.

LO7-5 **M7-11 Determining the Effects of Inventory Management Changes on the Inventory Turnover Ratio**

Indicate the most likely effect of the following changes in inventory management on the inventory turnover ratio (+ for increase, − for decrease, and NE for no effect).

_____ a. Inventory delivered by suppliers daily (small amounts) instead of weekly (larger amounts).

_____ b. Shorten production process from ten days to eight days.

_____ c. Extend payments for inventory purchases from fifteen days to thirty days.

LO7-6 **M7-12 Interpreting LC&NRV Financial Statement Note Disclosure**

Zumiez Inc. is a leading action sports retailer, focusing on skateboarding, snowboarding, surfing, and BMX, selling some of its merchandise under the Blue Tomato brand. The company's financial statement notes reported that "Merchandise inventories may include items that have been written down to our best estimate of their net realizable value. Our decisions to write−down our merchandise inventories are based on their current rate of sale, the age of the inventory, the profitability of the inventory and other factors." What ratios and financial measure(s) discussed in this chapter are the company likely using to monitor the

a. "...current rate of sale"?

b. "...age of the inventory"?

c. "...profitability of the inventory"?

LO7-5 **M7-13 Calculating the Inventory Turnover Ratio and Days to Sell**

Complete the following table. Round the inventory turnover ratio to one decimal place before computing days to sell. Round days to sell to one decimal place.

Case	BI	Purchases	CGS	EI	Inventory Turnover Ratio	Days to Sell
a.	$100	$700	$ 600	?	?	?
b.	200	?	1,200	?	6.0	?
c.	?	?	1,000	150	?	36.5

LO7-S2 **M7-14 (Supplement 7B) Calculating Cost of Goods Sold and Ending Inventory under FIFO and LIFO (Perpetual Inventory)**

Refer to M7−7. Calculate the cost of ending inventory and cost of goods sold assuming a perpetual inventory system is used in combination with (a) FIFO and (b) LIFO.

M7-15 (Supplement 7B) Calculating Cost of Goods Sold and Ending Inventory under Perpetual FIFO, LIFO, and Weighted Average Cost

LO7-S2

Repeat M7−8, except assume Literacy for the Illiterate uses a perpetual inventory system and it sold 600 units between January 9 and January 28.

M7-16 (Supplement 7C) Determining the Financial Statement Effects of Inventory Errors

LO7-S3

Assume the 2017 ending inventory of Shea's Shrimp Shack was understated by $10,000. Explain how this error would affect the amounts reported for cost of goods sold and gross profit for 2017 and 2018.

M7-17 (Supplement 7C) Determining the Financial Statement Effects of Inventory Errors

LO7-S3

Repeat M7−14, but assume the 2017 ending inventory was *overstated* by $100,000.

EXERCISES

E7-1 Reporting Goods in Transit and Consignment Inventory

LO7-1

Second Chance Clothing (SCC) obtains goods on consignment and through purchase, and sells them to others. The following events occurred close to SCC's October 31 year−end.

a. On November 2, SCC received goods on consignment from Apparel Corp.

b. On October 31, SCC received goods on consignment from Apparel Corp.

c. Goods in transit to SCC were shipped by Shoe, Inc. on October 31, FOB shipping point.

d. Goods in transit to SCC were shipped by Shoe, Inc. on October 31, FOB destination.

Required:

Indicate (Yes or No) whether SCC should include each item in its inventory balance at October 31.

E7-2 Determining the Correct Inventory Balance

LO7-1, 7-2, 7-4

Seemore Lens Company (SLC) sells contact lenses FOB destination. For the year that ended December 31, the company reported Inventory of $70,000 and Cost of Goods Sold of $420,000.

a. Included in Inventory (and Accounts Payable) are $10,000 of lenses held on consignment.

b. Included in the Inventory balance are $5,000 of office supplies held in SLC's warehouse.

c. Excluded from the Inventory balance are $8,000 of lenses in the warehouse that are ready to send to customers on January 1. On December 31, SLC reported these lenses as sold at a price of $15,000.

d. Included in the Inventory balance are $3,000 of lenses that were damaged in December and will be scrapped in January, with no recoverable value.

Required:

Create a table showing the balances presently reported for Inventory and Cost of Goods Sold, and then displaying the adjustment(s) needed to correctly account for each of items (a) through (d), and finally determining the appropriate Inventory and Cost of Goods Sold balances.

E7-3 Recording Journal Entries to Correct Inventory Misreporting

LO7-1, 7-2, 7-4

Refer to the information in E7−2.

Required:

For each item, (a) through (d), prepare the journal entry to correct the balances presently reported. If a journal entry is not required, indicate so.

E7-4 Calculating Cost of Ending Inventory and Cost of Goods Sold under Periodic FIFO and Weighted Average Cost

Spotter Corporation reported the following for June in its periodic inventory records.

Date	Description	Units	Unit Cost	Total Cost
June 1	Beginning	12	$8	$96
11	Purchase	38	9	342
24	Purchase	20	11	220
30	Ending	24		

Required:

1. Calculate the cost of ending inventory and the cost of goods sold under the (*a*) FIFO and (*b*) weighted average cost methods.
2. Which of the two methods will lead to reporting the highest net income?

E7-5 Calculating Cost of Ending Inventory and Cost of Goods Sold under Periodic FIFO and Weighted Average Cost

Oahu Kiki tracks the number of units purchased and sold throughout each accounting period but applies its inventory costing method at the end of each month as if it uses a periodic inventory system. Assume Oahu Kiki's records show the following for the month of January. Sales totalled 240 units.

	Date	Units	Unit Cost	Total Cost
Beginning Inventory	January 1	120	$8	$960
Purchase	January 15	380	9	3,420
Purchase	January 24	200	11	2,200

Required:

1. Calculate the number and cost of goods available for sale.
2. Calculate the number of units in ending inventory.
3. Calculate the cost of ending inventory and cost of goods sold using the (*a*) FIFO and (*b*) weighted average cost methods.

E7-6 Analyzing and Interpreting the Financial Statement Effects of Periodic FIFO and Weighted Average Cost

Orion Iron Corp. tracks the number of units purchased and sold throughout each year but applies its inventory costing method at the end of the year as if it uses a periodic inventory system. Assume its accounting records provided the following information at the end of the annual accounting period, December 31.

Transactions	Units	Unit Cost
a. Inventory, Beginning	3,000	$12
For the year:		
b. Purchase, April 11	9,000	10
c. Purchase, June 1	8,000	13
d. Sale, May 1 (sold for $40 per unit)	3,000	
e. Sale, July 3 (sold for $40 per unit)	6,000	
f. Operating expenses (excluding income tax expense), $195,000		

Required:

1. Calculate the number and cost of goods available for sale.

2. Calculate the number of units in ending inventory.

3. Compute the cost of ending inventory and cost of goods sold under (a) FIFO and (b) weighted average cost.

4. Prepare an income statement that shows amounts for the FIFO method in one column and for the weighted average method in another column. Include the following line items in the income statement: Sales, Cost of Goods Sold, Gross Profit, Operating Expenses, and Income from Operations.

5. Compare the Income from Operations and the Ending Inventory amounts that would be reported under the two methods. Explain the similarities and differences.

6. Which inventory costing method may be preferred by Orion Iron Corp. for income tax purposes? Explain.

Check Figure
[Req. 3]:
Cost of Goods
Sold – FIFO =
$96,000

E7-7 Analyzing and Interpreting the Financial Statement Effects of FIFO and Weighted Average Cost

LO7-3

Scoresby Inc. tracks the number of units purchased and sold throughout each year but applies its inventory costing method at the end of the year as if it uses a periodic inventory system. Assume its accounting records provided the following information at the end of the annual accounting period, December 31.

Transactions	Units	Unit Cost
a. Inventory, Beginning	3,000	$ 8
For the year:		
b. Purchase, March 5	9,500	9
c. Purchase, September 19	5,000	11
d. Sale, April 15 (sold for $29 per unit)	4,000	
e. Sale, October 31 (sold for $31 per unit)	8,000	
f. Operating expenses (excluding income tax expense), $250,000		

Required:

1. Calculate the number and cost of goods available for sale.

2. Calculate the number of units in ending inventory.

3. Compute the cost of ending inventory and cost of goods sold under (a) FIFO and (b) weighted average cost.

4. Prepare an income statement that shows December 31 amounts for the FIFO method in one column and the weighted average method in another column. Include the following line items in the income statement: Sales, Cost of Goods Sold, Gross Profit, Operating Expenses, and Income from Operations.

5. Compare the Income from Operations and the Ending Inventory amounts that would be reported under the two methods. Explain the similarities and differences.

6. Which inventory costing method may be preferred by Scoresby for income tax purposes? Explain.

E7-8 Evaluating the Effects of Inventory Methods on Income from Operations, Income Taxes, and Net Income (Periodic)

LO7-3

Courtney Company uses a periodic inventory system. The following data was available: beginning merchandise inventory, 1,000 units at $35; purchases, 4,000 units at $38; operating expenses (excluding income taxes), $91,500; ending inventory per physical count at December 31, 900 units; sales price per unit, $75; and average income tax rate, 30 percent.

Required:

1. Complete the body of the following income statement and the cost of goods sold calculation under both the FIFO and weighted average costing methods.

Income Statement	Units	FIFO	Weighted Average
Sales Revenue	_____	$ _____	$ _____
Cost of Goods Sold*	_____	_____	_____
Gross Profit		_____	_____
Operating Expenses		_____	_____
Income from Operations		_____	_____
Income Tax Expense		_____	_____
Net Income		_____	_____

2. Between FIFO and weighted average, which method is preferable in terms of (a) maximizing income from operations or (b) minimizing income taxes? Explain.
3. What would be your answer to requirement 2 if costs were falling? Explain.

*Cost of Goods Sold equation:			
Beginning Inventory	_____	$ _____	$ _____
Purchases	_____	_____	_____
Goods Available for Sale	_____	_____	_____
Ending Inventory	_____	_____	_____
Cost of Goods Sold	_____	_____	_____

LO7-4   **E7-9 Reporting Inventory at Lower of Cost and Net Realizable Value**

Peterson Furniture Designs is preparing its annual financial statements dated December 31. Ending inventory information about the five major items stocked for regular sale follows:

Item	Ending Inventory				
	Quantity on Hand	Unit Cost When Acquired (FIFO)	Net Realizable Value at Year-End	LC&NRV per Item	Total LC&NRV
Alligator Armoires	50	$15	$12		
Bear Bureaus	75	40	40		
Cougar Beds	10	50	52		
Dingo Cribs	30	30	30		
Elephant Dressers	400	10	6		

Required:

1. Complete the final two columns of the table and then compute the amount that should be reported for the ending inventory using the LC&NRV rule applied to each item.
2. Prepare the journal entry that Peterson Furniture Designs would record on December 31.
3. If the net realizable value was recovered to an amount greater than original cost by June 30 of the following year, would the journal entry in requirement 2 be reversed under ASPE? Under IFRS?

LO7-4   **E7-10 Reporting Inventory at Lower of Cost and Net Realizable Value**

Sublime Sandals Company is preparing its annual financial statements dated December 31. Ending inventory information about the four major items stocked for regular sale are as follows:

Product Line	Quantity on Hand	Unit Cost When Acquired (FIFO)	Net Realizable Value at Year-End
Air Flow	20	$12	$14
Blister Buster	75	40	38
Coolonite	35	55	50
Dudesly	10	30	35

Required:

1. Compute the amount that should be reported for the ending inventory, using the LC&NRV rule applied to each item.
2. How will the write-down of inventory to the lower of cost and net realizable value affect the company's expenses reported for the year ended December 31?
3. How would the methods used by Sublime Sandals Company to account for its inventory be affected by a switch from ASPE to IFRS?

Check Figure:
Ending Inventory =
$5,140

E7-11 Failing to Report Inventory at the Lower of Cost and Net Realizable Value

LO7-4

David H. Brooks, a university graduate with an accounting degree and the former CEO of DHB Industries, Inc. was charged in October 2007 with accounting and securities fraud for failing to report the company's inventory at the lower of cost and net realizable value.

From 2001 to 2005, DHB purchased large quantities of a material called Zylon and used it in making bulletproof vests that were sold to the U.S. military and local law enforcement agencies. During this same period, DHB learned that Zylon deteriorated rapidly when exposed to light, heat, and body perspiration. DHB knew that one of its competitors, Second Chance, a manufacturer of body armour, had stopped using Zylon in its vests and, eventually, discontinued its business because customer demand for its Zylon-based vests had evaporated.

DHB did not write down its own inventory of Zylon and Zylon-based vests because it had a large contract to supply the U.S. military with bulletproof vests. In its financial statements for the year ended December 31, 2004, DHB reported inventory of $86 million, sales of $90 million, and net income of $8.3 million, but no inventory write-down. Yet, only eight months later, DHB admitted it should have written down its inventory by $18 million.

Required:

1. Show the impact of the inventory write-down on the accounting equation, and also show the journal entry that should have been recorded on December 31, 2004.
2. Calculate (*a*) the Inventory balance that should have been reported on December 31, 2004, and (*b*) the amount of Net Income that should have been reported for the year ended December 31, 2004. (Assume the inventory write-down does not affect income tax.)
3. DHB's share price reached an all-time high ($20 to $22 per share) in November and December 2004, but then the company's CEO, CFO, and other executives began selling their shares in the company. Within a few weeks, they had cashed in over $200 million of shares. In August 2005, after DHB announced its inventory would have to be written down, the share price fell to less than $5 per share. If you were a lawyer representing DHB's investors, what evidence would you present to assert that a fraud had occurred? If you were a lawyer defending DHB, what counter-arguments would you make?

E7-12 Analyzing and Interpreting the Inventory Turnover Ratio

LO7-5

Polaris Industries Inc. is the biggest snowmobile manufacturer in the world. Assume that it reported the following amounts in its financial statements (in millions):

	2017	2016	2015	2014
Net Sales Revenue	$1,948	$1,780	$1,657	$1,870
Cost of Goods Sold	1,502	1,387	1,297	1,452
Average Inventory	220	224	216	188

Required:

1. Calculate to one decimal place the inventory turnover ratio and average days to sell inventory for 2017, 2016, and 2015.
2. Comment on any trends, and compare the effectiveness of inventory managers at Polaris to inventory managers at a competitor, where inventory turns over 4.5 times per year (81.1 days to sell). Both companies use the same inventory costing method (FIFO).

E7-13 (Supplement 7A) Calculating Cost of Ending Inventory and Cost of Goods Sold under Periodic LIFO

Refer to the information in E7–4.

Required:

1. Calculate the cost of ending inventory and the cost of goods sold under the LIFO cost method.
2. Compare the results of this method to those in E7–4. Where does this method fall in relation to the other two methods with respect to which method will lead to reporting the highest net income?

E7-14 (Supplement 7B) Calculating Cost of Ending Inventory and Cost of Goods Sold under Perpetual FIFO

Refer to the information in E7–5. Assume Oahu Kiki applies its inventory costing method perpetually at the time of each sale. The company sold 240 units between January 16 and 23.

Required:

Calculate the cost of ending inventory and the cost of goods sold using the FIFO method.

E7-15 (Supplement 7B) Calculating Cost of Ending Inventory and Cost of Goods Sold under Perpetual FIFO

Refer to the information in E7–6. Assume Orion Iron applies its inventory costing method perpetually at the time of each sale.

Required:

Calculate the cost of ending inventory and the cost of goods sold using the FIFO method.

E7-16 (Supplement 7C) Analyzing and Interpreting the Impact of an Inventory Error

G. Douglas Corporation prepared the following two income statements:

	First Quarter		Second Quarter	
Sales Revenue		$15,000		$18,000
Cost of Goods Sold				
Beginning Inventory	$ 3,000		$ 4,000	
Purchases	7,000		12,000	
Goods Available for Sale	10,000		16,000	
Ending Inventory	4,000		9,000	
Cost of Goods Sold		6,000		7,000
Gross Profit		9,000		11,000
Operating Expenses		5,000		6,000
Income from Operations		$ 4,000		$ 5,000

During the third quarter, the company's internal auditors discovered that the ending inventory for the first quarter should have been $4,400. The ending inventory for the second quarter was correct.

Check Figure [Req. 3]:
First quarter Income from Operations = $4,400

Required:

1. What effect would the error have on total Income from Operations for the two quarters combined? Explain.
2. What effect would the error have on Income from Operations for each of the two quarters? Explain.
3. Prepare corrected income statements for each quarter. Ignore income taxes.

COACHED PROBLEMS

CP7-1 Analyzing the Effects of Three Alternative Inventory Costing Methods

LO7-3

Scrappers Supplies tracks the number of units purchased and sold throughout each accounting period but applies its inventory costing method at the end of each period, as if it uses a peri—odic inventory system. Assume its accounting records provided the following information at the end of the annual accounting period, December 31.

Transactions	Units	Unit Cost
Beginning inventory, January 1	200	$ 30
Transactions during the year:		
a. Purchase on account, March 2	300	32
b. Cash sale, April 1 ($46 each)	(350)	
c. Purchase on account, June 30	250	36
d. Cash sale, August 1 ($46 each)	(50)	

TIP: Although the purchases and sales are listed in chronological order, Scrappers determines the cost of goods sold *after* all of the purchases have occurred.

Required:

1. Compute the cost of goods available for sale, cost of ending inventory, and cost of goods sold at December 31, under each of the following inventory costing methods:

   a. Weighted average cost

   b. First—in, first—out

   c. Specific identification, assuming that the April 1 sale was selected one—fifth from the beginning inventory and four—fifths from the purchase of March 2. Assume that the sale of August 1, was selected from the purchase of June 30.

   TIP: Cost of goods available for sale is the same for all methods.

2. Of the three methods, which will result in the highest gross profit? Which will result in the lowest income taxes?

CP7-2 Evaluating the Income Statement and Income Tax Effects of Lower of Cost and Net Realizable Value

LO7-4

L. Smart Company prepared its annual financial statements dated December 31. The company used the FIFO inventory costing method, but it failed to apply the LC&NRV to the ending inventory. The preliminary income statement follows:

Sales Revenue		$280,000
Cost of Goods Sold		
Beginning Inventory	$ 30,000	
Purchases	182,000	
Goods Available for Sale	212,000	
Ending Inventory (FIFO cost)	44,000	
Cost of Goods Sold		168,000
Gross Profit		112,000
Operating Expenses		61,000
Income from Operations		51,000
Income Tax Expense (30%)		15,300
Net Income		$ 35,700

TIP: Inventory write—downs do not affect the cost of goods available for sale. Instead, the effect of the write—down is to reduce ending inventory, which increases Cost of Goods Sold and then affects other amounts reported lower in the income statement.

Assume that you have been asked to restate the financial statements to incorporate the LC&NRV. You have developed the following data relating to the ending inventory:

Item	Quantity	Purchase Cost Per Unit	Purchase Cost Total	Current Replacement Cost per Unit (Net Realizable Value)
A	3,000	$3	$ 9,000	$4
B	1,500	4	6,000	2
C	7,000	2	14,000	4
D	3,000	5	15,000	2
			$44,000	

Required:

1. Restate the income statement to reflect the LC&NRV rule of the ending inventory. Apply the lower of cost and net realizable value on an item—by—item basis and show computations.

   TIP: Net Income equals $27,300.

2. Compare and explain the lower of cost and net realizable value effect on each amount that was changed in requirement 1.

   TIP: Net Income decreases by $8,400.

3. What is the conceptual basis for applying the lower of cost and net realizable value to merchandise inventory?

LO7-5 **CP7-3 Calculating and Interpreting the Inventory Turnover Ratio and Days to Sell**

Best Buy is a leading national retailer of brand—name consumer electronics, personal com—puters, and entertainment software. Assume the company reported the following amounts in its financial statements (in millions).

	2017	2016
Net Sales Revenue	$50,272	$49,694
Cost of Goods Sold	37,611	37,534
Beginning Inventory	5,486	4,753
Ending Inventory	5,896	5,486

Required:

1. Determine the inventory turnover ratio and average days to sell inventory for 2017 and 2016. Round your answers to one decimal place.

   TIP: Remember to use costs in both the numerator (CGS) and denominator (average inventory).

2. Comment on any changes in these measures, and compare the effectiveness of inventory managers at Best Buy with GameStop, where inventory turns over 6.0 times per year (61 days to sell).

LO7-S1, 7-S2 **CP7-4 (Supplement 7A and 7B) Analyzing the Effects of the LIFO Inventory Method in a Perpetual Inventory System**

Using the information in CP7—1.

Required:

1. Calculate the Cost of Goods Sold and Ending Inventory for Scrappers Supplies, assuming it applies the LIFO cost method.

2. Now calculate the Cost of Goods Sold and Ending Inventory, assuming it applies the LIFO cost method perpetually at the time of each sale. Compare these amounts to the periodic LIFO calculations you did in requirement 1. Does the use of a perpetual inventory system result in a higher or lower Cost of Goods Sold when costs are rising?

   TIP: In CP7—1, the sale of 350 units on April 1 is assumed, under LIFO, to consist of the 300 units purchased March 2 and fifty units from beginning inventory.

CP7-5 (Supplement 7C) Analyzing and Interpreting the Effects of Inventory Errors

Partial income statements for Murphy & Murphy (M & M) reported the following summarized amounts:

	Quarter 1	Quarter 2	Quarter 3	Quarter 4
Net Sales	$50,000	$49,000	$71,000	$58,000
Cost of Goods Sold	32,500	35,000	43,000	37,000
Gross Profit	17,500	14,000	28,000	21,000

After these amounts were reported, M & M's accountant determined that the inventory at the end of Quarter 2 was understated by $3,000. The inventory balance at the end of the other three quarters was accurately stated.

Required:

1. Restate the partial income statements to reflect the correct amounts, after fixing the inventory error.
2. Compute the gross profit percentage for all four years both (*a*) before the correction and (*b*) after the correction. Does the pattern of gross profit percentages lend confidence to your corrected amounts? Explain. Round your answer to the nearest percentage.

    TIP: Gross profit percentage is calculated as (Gross Profit/Net Sales) × 100.

GROUP A PROBLEMS

PA7-1 Analyzing the Effects of Three Alternative Inventory Methods in a Periodic Inventory System

Gladstone Limited tracks the number of units purchased and sold throughout each accounting period but applies its inventory costing method at the end of each period, as if it uses a periodic inventory system. Assume its accounting records provided the following information at the end of the annual accounting period, December 31.

Transactions	Units	Unit Cost
Beginning inventory, January 1	1,800	$5.00
Transactions during the year:		
a. Purchase, January 30	2,500	6.20
b. Sale, March 14 ($10 each)	(1,450)	
c. Purchase, May 1	1,200	8.00
d. Sale, August 31 ($10 each)	(1,900)	

Required:

1. Compute the amount of goods available for sale, ending inventory, and cost of goods sold under each of the following inventory costing methods at December 31:

    a. Weighted average cost
    b. First—in, first—out
    c. Specific identification, assuming that two—fifths of the March 14 sale was selected from the beginning inventory and three—fifths was from the purchase of January 30; assume that the sale of August 31 was selected from the remainder of the beginning inventory, and that the balance was from the purchase of May 1

2. Of the three methods, which will result in the highest gross profit? Which will result in the lowest income taxes?

**Check Figure
[Req. 1(*a*)]:**
Ending inventory using weighted average cost = $13,330

eXcel

PA7-2 Evaluating the Income Statement and Income Tax Effects of Lower of Cost and Net Realizable Value

Springer Anderson Gymnastics prepared its annual financial statements dated December 31. The company used the FIFO inventory costing method, but it failed to apply the LC&NRV to the ending inventory. The preliminary income statement is as follows:

Sales Revenue		$140,000
Cost of Goods Sold		
Beginning Inventory	$ 15,000	
Purchases	91,000	
Goods Available for Sale	106,000	
Ending Inventory (FIFO cost)	22,000	
Cost of Goods Sold		84,000
Gross Profit		56,000
Operating Expenses		31,000
Income from Operations		25,000
Income Tax Expense (30%)		7,500
Net Income		$ 17,500

Assume that you have been asked to restate the financial statements to incorporate the LC&NRV. You have developed the following data relating to the ending inventory:

Item	Quantity	Purchase Cost Per Unit	Purchase Cost Total	Current Replacement Cost per Unit (Net Realizable Value)
A	1,500	$3	$ 4,500	$4
B	750	4	3,000	2
C	3,500	2	7,000	1
D	1,500	5	7,500	3
			$22,000	

Required:

1. Restate the income statement to reflect the LC&NRV rule of the ending inventory. Apply the lower of cost and net realizable value on an item–by–item basis and show computations.
2. Compare and explain the lower of cost and net realizable value effect on each amount that was changed in requirement 1.
3. What is the conceptual basis for applying the lower of cost and net realizable value to merchandise inventories?

PA7-3 Calculating and Interpreting the Inventory Turnover Ratio and Days to Sell

Harman International Industries is a world–leading producer of loudspeakers and other elec–tronics products, which are sold under brand names like JBL, Infinity, and Harman/Kardon. Assume the company reported the following amounts in its financial statements (in millions):

	2017	2016
Net Sales Revenue	$3,364	$2,855
Cost of Goods Sold	2,479	2,210
Beginning Inventory	334	391
Ending Inventory	353	334

Required:

1. Determine the inventory turnover ratio and average days to sell inventory for 2017 and 2016. Round to one decimal place.

2. Comment on any changes in these measures, and compare the effectiveness of inventory managers at Harman to inventory managers at Pioneer Corporation, where inventory turns over 5.2 times per year (70 days to sell). Both companies use the same inventory costing method (FIFO).

PA7-4 (Supplements 7A and 7B) Analyzing the Effects of the LIFO Inventory Method in a Perpetual Inventory System

Use the information in PA7-1.

Required:

1. Calculate the Cost of Goods Sold and Ending Inventory for Gladstone Company assuming it applies the LIFO cost method.
2. Now calculate the Cost of Goods Sold and Ending Inventory assuming it applies the LIFO cost method perpetually at the time of each sale. Compare these amounts to the periodic LIFO calculations you did in requirement 1. Does the use of a perpetual inventory system result in a higher or lower Cost of Goods Sold when costs are rising?

PA7-5 (Supplement 7C) Analyzing and Interpreting the Effects of Inventory Errors

LO7-S3

Partial income statements for Sherwood Company summarized for a four–year period show the following:

	2014	2015	2016	2017
Net Sales	$2,000,000	$2,400,000	$2,500,000	$3,000,000
Cost of Goods Sold	1,400,000	1,660,000	1,770,000	2,100,000
Gross Profit	$ 600,000	$ 740,000	$ 730,000	$ 900,000

An audit revealed that in determining these amounts, the ending inventory for 2015 was overstated by $20,000. The inventory balance on December 31, 2016, was accurately stated. The company uses a periodic inventory system.

Required:

1. Restate the partial income statements to reflect the correct amounts, after fixing the inventory error.
2. Compute the gross profit percentage for each year (*a*) before the correction and (*b*) after the correction, rounding to the nearest percentage. Do the results lend confidence to your corrected amounts? Explain.

**Check Figure
[Req. 1]:**
2015 Gross Profit =
$720,000

GROUP B PROBLEMS

PB7-1 Analyzing the Effects of Three Alternative Inventory Methods in a Periodic Inventory System

LO7-3

Mojohava Industries tracks the number of units purchased and sold throughout each accounting period but applies its inventory costing method at the end of each period, as if it uses a periodic inventory system. Assume its accounting records provided the following information at the end of the accounting period, January 31. The inventory's selling price is $9 per unit.

Transactions	Unit Cost	Units	Total Cost
Inventory, January 1	$2.50	250	$625
Sale, January 10		(200)	
Purchase, January 12	3.00	300	900
Sale, January 17		(150)	
Purchase, January 26	4.00	80	320

Inventory and Cost of Goods Sold   CHAPTER 7   367

Required:

1. Compute the amount of goods available for sale, ending inventory, and cost of goods sold at January 31, under each of the following inventory costing methods:

   a. Weighted average cost

   b. First–in, first–out

   c. Specific identification, assuming that the January 10 sale was from the beginning inventory and the January 17 sale was from the January 12 purchase

2. Of the three methods, which will result in the highest gross profit? Which will result in the lowest income taxes?

LO7-4 **PB7-2 Evaluating the Income Statement and Income Tax Effects of Lower of Cost and Net Realizable Value**

Mondeara Clothing prepared its annual financial statements dated December 31. The company used the FIFO inventory costing method, but it failed to apply LC&NRV to the ending inventory. The preliminary income statement is as follows:

Net Sales		$420,000
Cost of Goods Sold		
Beginning Inventory	$ 45,000	
Purchases	273,000	
Goods Available for Sale	318,000	
Ending Inventory (FIFO cost)	66,000	
Cost of Goods Sold		252,000
Gross Profit		168,000
Operating Expenses		93,000
Income from Operations		75,000
Income Tax Expense (30%)		22,500
Net Income		$ 52,500

Assume that you have been asked to restate the financial statements to incorporate LC&NRV. You have developed the following data relating to the ending inventory:

Item	Quantity	Acquisition Cost Per Unit	Acquisition Cost Total	Current Replacement Cost per Unit (Net Realizable Value)
A	3,000	$4.50	$13,500	$6.00
B	1,500	6.00	9,000	3.00
C	7,000	3.00	21,000	6.00
D	3,000	7.50	22,500	4.50
			$66,000	

Required:

Check Figure
[Req. 1]:
Net Income =
$43,050

1. Restate the income statement to reflect LC&NRV valuation of the ending inventory. Apply LC&NRV on an item–by–item basis and show your computations.

2. Compare and explain the LC&NRV effect on each amount that was changed in requirement 1.

3. What is the conceptual basis for applying LC&NRV to merchandise inventory?

LO7-5 **PB7-3 Calculating and Interpreting the Inventory Turnover Ratio and Days to Sell**

Assume Amazon.com reported the following amounts in its financial statements (in millions):

	2017	2016
Net Sales	$34,204	$24,509
Cost of Goods Sold	26,561	18,978
Beginning Inventory	2,171	1,399
Ending Inventory	3,202	2,171

Required:

1. Determine the inventory turnover ratio and average days to sell inventory for 2017 and 2016. Round to one decimal place.
2. Comment on any changes in these measures and compare the inventory turnover at Amazon.com to inventory turnover at Barnes & Noble, Inc., where inventory turned over 3.2 times during 2017 (114.1 days to sell). Based on your own experience, what's the key difference between Amazon.com and Barnes & Noble that leads one company's results to be the picture of efficiency and the other to seem like a library?

PB7-4 (Supplement 7A and 7B) Analyzing the Effects of the LIFO Inventory Method in a Perpetual Inventory System

LO7-S1, 7-S2

Use the information in PB7—1.

Required:

1. Calculate the Cost of Goods Sold and Ending Inventory for Mojohava Industries assuming it applies the LIFO cost method.
2. Now calculate the Cost of Goods Sold and Ending Inventory assuming it applies the LIFO cost method perpetually at the time of each sale. Compare these amounts to the periodic LIFO calculations you did in requirement 1. Does the use of a perpetual inventory system result in a higher or lower Cost of Goods Sold when costs are rising?

PB7-5 (Supplement 7C) Analyzing and Interpreting the Effects of Inventory Errors

LO7-S3

Spears & Cantrell announced inventory had been overstated by $30 million at the end of its second quarter. The error wasn't discovered and corrected in the company's periodic inventory system until after the end of the third quarter. The following table shows the amounts (in millions) that were originally reported by the company.

	Q1	Q2	Q3
Net Sales	$3,000	$3,600	$3,750
Cost of Goods Sold	2,100	2,490	2,655
Gross Profit	900	1,110	1,095

Required:

1. Restate the income statements to reflect the correct amounts, after fixing the inventory error.
2. Compute the gross profit percentage for each quarter (*a*) before the correction and (*b*) after the correction, rounding to the nearest percentage. Do the results lend confidence to your corrected amounts? Explain.

Check Figure [Req. 1]:
Second quarter Gross Profit = $1,080

COMPREHENSIVE PROBLEM

C7-1 Computing and Evaluating Financial Statement Effects of Alternative Inventory Costing Methods (Chapters 2 and 7)

LO2-5, 7-3

You have been given responsibility for overseeing a bank's small business loans division. The bank includes loan covenants requiring a minimum current ratio of 1.8 in all small business loans. When you ask which inventory costing method the covenant assumes, the previous loans manager gives you a blank look. To explain to him that a company's inventory costing method is important, you present the following balance sheet information:

Current assets other than inventory	$ 10
Inventory	(a)
Other (non-current) assets	107
Total assets	$ (b)
Current liabilities	$ 36
Other (non-current) liabilities	44
Shareholders' equity	(d)
Total liabilities and shareholders' equity	$ (c)

You ask the former loans manager to find amounts for (a), (b), (c), and (d), assuming the company began the year with five units of inventory at a unit cost of $11, then purchased eight units at a cost of $12 each, and finally purchased six units at a cost of $16 each. A year–end inventory count determined that four units are on hand.

Required:

1. Determine the amount for (a) using FIFO, and then calculate (b) through (d).
2. Determine the amount for (a) using Weighted Average, and then calculate (b) through (d).
3. Determine the current ratios using (i) FIFO and (ii) Weighted Average, and explain why these ratios differ.
4. Determine whether the company would be in violation of or compliance with its loan covenant if the company were to use (i) FIFO and (ii) Weighted Average.

LO4-2, 6-3, 6-4, 7-3, 7-5

C7-2 Recording Inventory Transactions, Making Accrual and Deferral Adjustments, and Preparing and Evaluating Financial Statements (Chapters 4, 6, and 7)

LEVEL UP

Custom College Coasters specializes in logo–imprinted drink coasters. The company reported the following balances in its unadjusted trial balance at December 1.

Cash	$10,005	Accounts Payable	$ 1,500	Cost of Goods Sold	$8,900
Accounts Receivable	2,000	Wages Payable	300	Rent Expense	1,100
Inventory	500	Taxes Payable	0	Wages Expense	2,000
Prepaid Rent	600	Contributed Capital	6,500	Depreciation Expense	110
Equipment	810	Retained Earnings	3,030	Income Tax Expense	0
Accumulated Depreciation	110	Sales Revenue	15,985	Selling Expenses	1,400

The company buys coasters from one supplier. All amounts in Accounts Payable on December 1 are owed to that supplier. The inventory on December 1 consisted of 1,000 coasters, all of which were purchased in a batch on July 10 at a unit cost of $0.50. Custom College Coasters uses the FIFO cost flow method.

During December, the company entered into the following transactions. Some of these transactions are explained in greater detail below.

Dec. 1   Purchased 500 coasters on account from the regular supplier at a unit cost of $0.52, with terms of 2/10, n/30

Dec. 2   Purchased 1,000 coasters on account from the regular supplier at a unit cost of $0.55, with terms of 2/10, n/30

Dec. 15   Paid the supplier $1,600 cash on account

Dec. 17   Sold 2,000 coasters on account at a unit price of $0.90

Dec. 23   Paid employees $500, $300 of which related to work done in November and $200 for wages up to December 22

Dec. 24   Collected $1,000 from customers on account

Dec. 31   Loaded 1,000 coasters on a cargo ship to be delivered to a customer in Hawaii; sale was made FOB destination with terms of 2/10, n/30

Other relevant information includes the following:

a. Custom College Coasters has not yet recorded $200 of selling expenses incurred in December on account.

b. The company estimates that the equipment depreciates at a rate of $10 per month. One month of depreciation needs to be recorded.

c. Wages for the period from December 23 to 31 are $100 and will be paid on January 15.

d. The $600 of Prepaid Rent relates to a six–month period ending on May 31 of the next year.

e. No shrinkage or damage was discovered when the inventory was counted on December 31.

f. The company did not declare dividends and there were no transactions involving contrib–uted capital.

g. The company has a 30 percent tax rate and has made no tax payments this year.

Required:

1. Analyze the accounting equation effects of each transaction and any adjustments required at month–end.

2. Prepare journal entries to record each transaction and any adjustments required at month–end.

3. Summarize the journal entries in T–accounts. Be sure to include the balances on December 1 as beginning account balances. Calculate ending balances and prepare a trial balance.

4. Prepare the year–end income statement, statement of shareholders' equity, and classified balance sheet, using the formats presented in Exhibit 6.9 and Exhibit 4.11.

5. Calculate to one decimal place the inventory turnover ratio and days to sell in 2014, assuming that inventory was $500 on January 1 of this year. Evaluate these measures in comparison to an inventory turnover ratio of 12.0 during the previous year.

SKILLS DEVELOPMENT CASES

S7-1 Finding Financial Information

LO7-2, 7-4, 7-5

Refer to the summarized financial statements of The Home Depot in Appendix A near the end of this text.

1. How much inventory does the company hold on January 29, 2017? Does this represent an increase or decrease in comparison to the prior year?

2. Compute to one decimal place the company's inventory turnover ratio and days to sell for the most recent year.

S7-2 Comparing Financial Information

LO7-2, 7-4, 7-5

Refer to the summarized financial statements of The Home Depot in Appendix A and Lowe's Companies, Inc. in Appendix B at the back of this book.

1. Does Lowe's Companies, Inc. hold more or less inventory than The Home Depot at the end of their 2016 fiscal year on February 3, 2017?

2. Does Lowe's Companies, Inc. follow the lower of cost and net realizable value rule? What method does Lowe's Companies, Inc. use to determine the cost of its inventory? Describe where you found this information.

3. Compute to one decimal place Lowe's Companies, Inc.'s inventory turnover ratio and days to sell for the 2016 fiscal year and compare these to The Home Depot's. What does this analysis suggest to you?

S7-3 Internet-Based Team Research: Examining an Annual Report

LO7-1, 7-2, 7-3, 7-4, 7-5

As a team, select an industry to analyze. Using the internet, each team member should access the annual report for one publicly traded company in the industry, with each member select–ing a different company. (See S1–3 in Chapter 1 for a description of possible resources for these tasks.)

Required:

1. On an individual basis, each team member should write a short report that incorporates the following:

   a. Describe the types of inventory held by the company. Does the company indicate its inventory management goals anywhere in its annual report?

   b. Describe the inventory costing method that is used. Why do you think the company chose this method rather than the other acceptable methods? Do you think its inventory costs are rising or falling?

   c. Calculate the inventory turnover ratio for the current and prior year, and explain any change between the two years. (To obtain the beginning inventory number for the prior year, you will need the prior year's annual report.)

   d. Search the annual report for information about the how the company applies the LC&NRV rule to inventory. Did the company report the amount of inventory written down during the year?

2. Then, as a team, write a short report comparing and contrasting your companies using these attributes. Discuss any patterns across the companies that you as a team observe. Provide potential explanations for any differences discovered.

LO7-2, 7-4 **S7-4 Ethical Decision Making: A Real-Life Example**

Assume you are on a jury hearing a trial involving a large national drugstore chain. Your immediate task is to identify suspicious events in the following evidence that suggest financial fraud may have occurred.

In just seven years, the company grew from 15 to 310 stores, reporting sales of more than $3 billion. Some retail experts believed the company was going to be the next Walmart. The apparent secret of the company's success was its ability to attract customers to its stores by selling items below cost. Then the company would make it easy for customers to buy other items, particularly pharmaceuticals, which earned a high gross profit.

After the inventory was counted and its cost was calculated, the company applied the LC&NRV test. On a store–by–store basis, top management compared the unit cost and net realizable value of inventory items and then prepared journal entries to write down the inventory. Some of the journal entries were large in amount and involved debiting an account called Cookies and crediting the inventory account.

Management reported that the Cookies account was used to accumulate the required write–downs for all the company's stores. Just before the financial statements were finalized, the Cookies account was emptied by allocating part of it back to each of the stores. In one instance, $9,999,999.99 was allocated from Cookies to a store account called Accrued Inventory.

This strategy appeared to be working, so the company's top executives built up massive pharmaceutical inventories at its stores, causing total inventory to increase from $11 million to $36 million to $153 million in three years. The company hadn't installed a perpetual inventory system, so inventory had to be physically counted at each store to determine the cost of goods sold. To help its auditors verify the accuracy of these inventory counts, top management agreed to close selected stores on the day inventory was counted. All they asked was that they be given advance notice of which stores' inventory counts the auditors were planning to attend, so that the temporary closures could be conveyed to employees and customers at those stores.

The external auditors selected four stores to test each year and informed the company several weeks in advance. To further assist the auditors with counting the inventory, top management reduced the inventory levels at the selected stores by shipping some of their goods to other stores that the auditors weren't attending.

Required:

Prepare a list that summarizes the pieces of evidence that indicate that fraud might have occurred and, for each item on the list, explain why it contributes to your suspicion.

Epilogue: This case is based on a fraud involving Phar Mor, as described by David Cottrell and Steven Glover in the July 1997 issue of *CPA Journal*. Phar Mor's management was collectively fined over $1 million and two top managers received prison sentences ranging from thirty–three months to five years. The company's auditors paid over $300 million in civil judgments for failing to uncover the fraud.

S7-5 Ethical Decision Making: A Mini-Case

David Eltner is the CEO of Aquatic Gear Enterprises, a seven–year–old manufacturer of boats. After many long months of debate with the company's board of directors, David obtained the board's approval to expand into water ski sales. David firmly believed that Aquatic Gear could generate significant profits in this market, despite recent increases in the cost of skis.

A board meeting will be held later this month at which David will present the financial results for the first quarter of ski sales. As Aquatic Gear's corporate controller, you reported to David that the results weren't great. Although sales were better than expected at $165,000 (3,000 units at $55 per unit), the cost of goods sold was $147,500. This left a gross profit of $17,500.

David knew this amount wouldn't please the board. Desperate to save the ski division, David asks you to "take another look at the cost calculations to see if there's any way to reduce the cost of goods sold. I know you accountants have different methods for figuring things out, so maybe you can do your magic now when I need it most." You dig out your summary of inventory purchases for the quarter to recheck your calculations, using the LIFO method that has always been used for the company's inventory of boats.

	Date	Units	Unit Cost	Total Cost
Beginning inventory of water skis	January 1	0	—	—
Purchase	January 15	1,500	$30	$ 45,000
Purchase	February 18	2,000	45	90,000
Purchase	March 29	2,500	50	125,000

Required:

1. Calculate Cost of Goods Sold using the LIFO method. Does this confirm the statement you made to David about the Gross Profit earned on water ski sales in the first quarter?
2. Without doing any calculations, do you think it is likely that any alternative inventory costing method will produce a lower Cost of Goods Sold? Explain.
3. Calculate Cost of Goods Sold using the FIFO method. Would use of this method solve David's current dilemma?
4. Is it acceptable within GAAP to report the water skis using one inventory costing method and the boats using a different method?
5. Do you see any problems with using the FIFO numbers for purposes of David's meeting with the board?

S7-6 Calculating and Recording the Effects of Lower of Cost and Net Realizable Value on Ending Inventory

Assume you recently obtained a job with Perfume Passion, the largest specialty retailer of discounted fragrances in Canada. Your job is to estimate the amount of write–down required to value inventory at the lower of cost and net realizable value. The cost of inventory is calculated using the weighted average cost method and, at $368 million, it represents the company's biggest and most important asset. Assume the corporate controller asked you to prepare a spreadsheet that can be used to determine the amount of the LC&NRV write–down for the current year. The controller provides the following hypothetical numbers for you to use in the spreadsheet.

Product Line	Weighted Average Unit Cost	Replacement Cost (Net Realizable Value) at Year-End	Quantity on Hand
Alfred Sung Shi	$22	$20	80
Animale	15	16	75
Azzaro	10	10	50
Mambo	16	17	30
OP Juice	8	7	400

You realize that you'll need to multiply the quantity of each item by the lower of cost and net realizable value per unit. You emailed your friend Owen for Excel help.

So you don't have any idea how to pick the lower of cost and net realizable value? You can do this several different ways, but the easiest is to use the MIN command. Set up your spreadsheet similar to the table you sent me, and then add two new columns. In the first new column, enter the command "= MIN(cost cell, net realizable value cell)" where cost cell is the cell containing the cost per unit and net realizable value cell is the cell containing the net realizable value per unit. Next, in the second new column, multiply the quantity by the lower of cost or net realizable value per unit, and then SUM the column.

Required:

1. Prepare a spreadsheet that calculates total lower of cost and net realizable value for inventory, applied on an item—by—item basis.
2. Prepare a journal entry to record the inventory lower of cost and net realizable value write—down.

CONTINUING CASE

LO7-3, 7-5 **CC7-1 Accounting for Changing Inventory Costs**

In October 2017, Nicole of Nicole's Getaway Spa (NGS) eliminated all existing inventory of cosmetic items. The trouble of ordering and tracking each product line had exceeded the profits earned. In December, a supplier asked her to sell a prepackaged spa kit. Feeling she could manage a single product line, Nicole agreed. NGS would make monthly purchases from the supplier at a cost that included production costs and a transportation charge. The spa would use a perpetual inventory system to keep track of its new inventory.

On December 30, 2017, NGS purchased ten units at a total cost of $6 per unit. NGS purchased thirty more units at $8 in February 2018, but returned five defective units to the supplier. In March, NGS purchased fifteen units at $10 per unit. In May, fifty units were purchased at $10 per unit; however, NGS took advantage of a 2/10, n/30 discount from the supplier. In June, NGS sold fifty units at a selling price of $12 per unit and thirty—five units at $10 per unit.

Required:

1. Explain whether the transportation cost included in each purchase should be recorded as a cost of the inventory or immediately expensed.
2. Compute the Cost of Goods Available for Sale, Cost of Goods Sold, and Cost of Ending Inventory using the first—in, first—out (FIFO) method.
3. Calculate the inventory turnover ratio (to one decimal place), using the inventory on hand at December 31, 2017, as the beginning inventory. The supplier reported that the typical inventory turnover ratio was 7.9. How does NGS's ratio compare?

LO7-3, 7-4 **CC7-2 Wiki Art Gallery (WAG)**

LEVEL UP

Refer to the Wiki Art Gallery (WAG) instructional case in Appendix D and read the case in sufficient depth to answer the following questions.

1. What inventory costing method(s) does Wiki Art Gallery (WAG) use for determining the cost of artwork purchased as individual pieces?
   a. WAG uses FIFO.
   b. WAG uses Specific Identification.
   c. WAG uses a combination of FIFO and Specific Identification.
   d. WAG uses a combination of Average Cost and Specific Identification.

2. What assumption is WAG making when accounting for the cost of artwork purchased in lots?
   a. WAG is assuming the first artwork purchased is the first artwork sold.
   b. WAG is assuming the last artwork purchased is the first artwork sold.

   c. WAG is assuming the pieces of artwork are interchangeable and do not vary in value.

   d. WAG is assuming the pieces of artwork are uniquely identifiable.

3. For the twenty original oil paintings that were purchased on August 20, determine the amounts that WAG included in the cost of artwork sold and cost of artwork remaining in ending inventory after the sale of two pieces to TEAC.

   a. Cost of artwork sold includes $20,000 and ending inventory includes $20,000.

   b. Cost of artwork sold includes $10,000 and ending inventory includes $10,000.

   c. Cost of artwork sold includes $18,000 and ending inventory includes $2,000.

   d. Cost of artwork sold includes $2,000 and ending inventory includes $18,000.

4. Assume that the two paintings sold to TEAC represented 40 percent of the total value of the twenty original oil paintings purchased on August 20. Determine the amounts WAG would include in the cost of artwork sold and cost of artwork remaining in ending inventory after the sale of two pieces to TEAC.

   a. Cost of artwork sold would include $8,000 and ending inventory would include $12,000.

   b. Cost of artwork sold would include $12,000 and ending inventory would include $8,000.

   c. Cost of artwork sold would include $8,000 and ending inventory would include $20,000.

   d. Cost of artwork sold would include $20,000 and ending inventory would include $8,000.

5. WAG's notes to the financial statements indicate the company reports its inventory at the lower of cost or market. What facts suggest a write–down may be required but has not been recorded by WAG?

   a. The market value of inventory is estimated by WAG's management, and Rob may be biased in thinking that WAG's inventory can be sold to TEAC.

   b. WAG's inventory contains aging, less–attractive items.

   c. The 2011 income statement does not include an inventory write–down expense.

   d. All of the above.

Endnotes

1. By showing all purchases taking place before any Sales and Cost of Goods Sold are computed, we are demonstrating a periodic inventory system. You might think it's odd that we use a periodic system when we said in Chapter 6 that most modern companies use perpetual inventory systems. We actually have several good reasons for doing this, which we explain in Supplement 7A in this chapter, where we also explain how cost flow assumptions are applied in more complex situations involving perpetual inventory systems. For purposes of examples shown in the chapter and for problem materials at the end of this chapter, we assume no shrinkage (a topic discussed in Chapter 6).

2. We apply lower of cost or net realizable value on an item basis. It also may be applied on a product line basis.

3. Samsung Electronics Co., Notes to the 2016 Consolidated Financial Statements, page 76.

4. If inventory is sold immediately after the $100 purchase, the weighted average cost will need to be calculated again ($138.75 ÷ 15 = $9.25 per unit). Notice the change in weighted average cost from $7.75 to $9.25 per unit. Because the weighted average unit cost changes, weighted average perpetual is also called the *moving average method*.

THAT WAS
THEN

In previous chapters, we quietly assumed that all sales on account ultimately are collected as cash.

THIS IS
NOW

In this chapter, you'll learn how companies handle the situation where customers don't pay all that they owe.

CHAPTER 8

Receivables, Bad Debt Expense, and Interest Revenue

©Danita Delimont/Alamy

FOCUS COMPANY:
VF Corporation (VFC)
www.vfc.com

One of the most challenging parts of your academic and professional career will be managing events that you can't completely control. Think, for example, about a group project that you must complete this term. You may believe that, in theory, the work should take only six days from start to finish. You know from experience, however, that someone in your group is likely to be late with the assigned work or may fail to complete it at all.

The problem is that you don't know who it will be or how long the delay will be—these matters are largely beyond your control. To allow for the possibility that someone might be late, you could set a shorter time period (say, four days) to complete the work. Establishing a two-day allowance will give you a realistic basis for planning and successfully completing the project.

This situation is similar to a problem faced by many companies, including VF Corporation, or simply VFC. VFC is the company responsible for making North Face jackets, JanSport backpacks, Wrangler jeans, and Vans shoes. VFC sells its products on account to major customers including Walmart, Macy's, and Target, as well as to many smaller retailers that you likely haven't heard of including Adventure 16, Paragon Sports, and Tactics.

After making a sale to its customers, VFC faces the challenge of trying to collect the amount owed. Inevitably, some of VFC's customers will not pay the full amount owed, either because they dispute the price or quality of VFC's products, or because the customers have run into financial difficulties. This risk of failing to collect the full amount of its Accounts Receivable is a major concern

Logo courtesy of VFC.

ORGANIZATION OF THE CHAPTER

Understand the business	Study the accounting methods	Evaluate the results	Review the chapter
• Advantages and disadvantages of extending credit	• Accounts receivable and bad debts • Methods for estimating bad debts • Notes receivable and interest revenue • Recording notes receivable and interest revenue	• Receivables turnover analysis	• Demonstration Cases • Chapter Summary • Solutions to Self-Study Practice • Key Terms • Homework Helper • Practice Material

for VFC's managers and investors, and it presents interesting challenges for the company's accountants.

The challenge is that, at the time sales are made, VFC can't identify which particular customers will be "bad" customers. In this chapter, you'll learn about a method of accounting for such uncertainties—one that is similar to the allowance approach you took with your group project. This method allows VFC's managers to report in a timely manner how much money the company is likely to collect from customers. Also in this chapter, you will learn about notes receivable, which arise from selling or lending to others under contract.

Understand the Business

ADVANTAGES AND DISADVANTAGES OF EXTENDING CREDIT

What factors do managers consider when extending credit on account (accounts receivable) or lending to others under contract (notes receivable)? VFC allows business customers like Walmart and Target to open accounts and buy items on credit, yet its stores do not extend this option to you—the individual consumer. The reason VFC is willing to create an account receivable for business customers but not individual consumers is that doing so involves different advantages and disadvantages. The advantage of extending credit is that it helps customers buy products and services, thereby increasing the seller's revenues. The disadvantages of extending credit are that the following additional costs are introduced:

LEARNING OBJECTIVE 8-1

Describe the trade-offs of extending credit.

1. **Increased wage costs.** If credit is extended, VFC will have to hire people to (*a*) evaluate whether each customer is creditworthy, (*b*) track how much each customer owes, and (*c*) follow up to collect the receivable from each customer.

2. **Bad debt costs.** Inevitably, some customers dispute what they owe or they run into financial difficulties and pay only a fraction, or none,

of their account balances. These bad debts, as they are called, can be a significant additional cost of extending credit. At January 2, 2016, VFC estimated that over 1.8 percent of its receivables would not be collected.

3. **Delayed receipt of cash.** Even if VFC were to collect in full from customers, it would likely have to wait thirty to sixty days before receiving the cash. During this period, VFC may have to take out a short—term bank loan to pay for other business activities. The interest on such a loan would be another cost of extending credit to customers.

Most managers find that the additional revenue (or, more accurately, the gross profit) to be gained from selling on account to business customers is greater than the additional costs mentioned above. Similar advantages and disadvantages are considered when deciding whether to create notes receivable. A **note receivable** is created when a formal written contract (note) is estab—lished outlining the terms by which a company will receive amounts it is owed.

Note receivable: A promise that requires another party to pay the business accord-ing to a written agreement.

Notes receivable differ from accounts receivable in that notes generally charge interest from the day they are signed to the day they are collected. Notes receivable are viewed as a stronger legal claim than accounts receivable, but a new note needs to be created for every transaction, so they are used less fre—quently—typically when a company sells large—dollar—value items (e.g., cars), offers extended payment periods, or lends money to individuals or businesses.

SPOTLIGHT ON Business Decisions

Deciding Whether to Grant Credit

Many companies, including VFC, do not grant credit to individual consumers because the expected costs outweigh the benefits. However, some companies, such as Target Corporation, have been able to profit by extending credit to individuals. Through its Target credit card program, Target has allowed consumers to purchase merchandise on credit. For Target, extending credit allowed the company to generate additional net profit,* even in 2008-2010, when the economy struggled and Target's bad debts soared:

Credit program results (in millions):	2007	2008	2009	2010	2011	2012
Gross profit	$ 1,896	$ 2,064	$ 1,922	$ 1,604	$1,399	$1,341
Wages and administration expense	485	491	439	452	567	575
Bad debt expense	**481**	**1,251**	**1,185**	**528**	**154**	**196**
Interest expense	133	167	97	83	72	13
Additional net profit	$ 797	$ 155	$ 201	$ 541	$ 606	$ 557

*Target Corporation Form 10-K, Item 7, Management's Discussion and Analysis.

Study the Accounting Methods

Estimate and report the effects of uncollectable accounts.

Accounts receivable:
Amounts owed to a business by its customers. Also called *trade receivables* or *receivables*.

ACCOUNTS RECEIVABLE AND BAD DEBTS

You already know from earlier chapters that **accounts receivable** arise from the sale of goods or services on credit. What you may not know is that some accounts receivable are never collected. Like that "friend" of yours who *says* he'll pay you later, but for one reason or another never gets around to it, some customers just do not pay their bills.

Two objectives when accounting for accounts receivable and bad debts are to (1) report Accounts Receivable at the amount the company expects to collect (net realizable value) and (2) match the cost of bad debts to the accounting period in which the related credit sales are made. These two objectives point to the same solution: reduce both Accounts Receivable and Net Income by the amount of credit sales that are unlikely to be collected as cash.

The only problem with this solution is that time will pass before VFC discovers which particular credit sales and customer balances aren't going to be collected. These bad debts will likely be discovered in an accounting period following the sale, rather than in the same period as the sale. As Exhibit 8.1 shows, if you record sales in one period, when they occur, and bad debts in a different period, when they are discovered, you will violate the expense recognition (matching) principle. This failure to match Bad Debt Expense with Sales Revenue in the same period will lead to distorted views of Net Income in the period of the sale as well as in the period the bad debt is discovered.

EXHIBIT 8.1	**Distortion Occurs if Bad Debts Are Not Matched to Sales**

| PERIOD 1 | | PERIOD 2 | |
(Credit Sale Occurs)		(Bad Debt Discovered)	
Sales Revenues	$10,000	Sales Revenues	$ 0
Cost of Goods Sold	8,000	Cost of Goods Sold	0
Bad Debt Expense	0	Bad Debt Expense	1,000
Net Income	$ 2,000	Net Income (Loss)	$ (1,000)

Clearly, we need to record bad debts in the same period as the sale. The only way to do this is to record an estimate of the amount of bad debts that are likely to arise. Later, the accounting records can be adjusted when uncollectable amounts become known with certainty. This approach is called the **allowance method** and it follows a two-step process:

1. Make an end-of-period adjustment to record the estimated bad debts in the period credit sales occur.

2. Remove (write off) specific customer balances when they are known to be uncollectable.

Allowance method: An accounting method that reduces accounts receivable (as well as net income) for an estimate of uncollectable accounts (bad debts).

1. Adjust for Estimated Bad Debts

Credit sales, when first recorded, affect both the balance sheet (an increase in Accounts Receivable) and the income statement (an increase in Sales Revenue). Thus, to account for any bad credit sales that have been recorded in Sales Revenue and Accounts Receivable, we record offsetting amounts on both the balance sheet and income statement. This adjustment is made at the end of each accounting period to reduce Accounts Receivable (using a contra-asset account called *Allowance for Doubtful Accounts*) and reduce Net Income (using an expense account called **Bad Debt Expense**).

Bad debt expense: Reports the estimated amount of this period's credit sales that customers will fail to pay.

If VFC were to estimate $900 of bad debts this period, the effects on the accounting equation and adjusting journal entry to record them would be as follows:

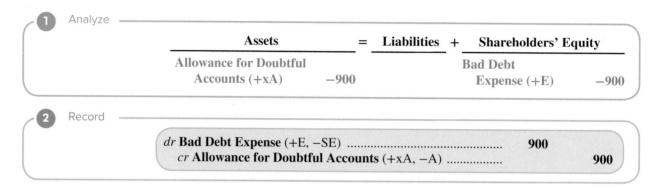

1 Analyze

Assets		=	Liabilities	+	Shareholders' Equity	
Allowance for Doubtful Accounts (+xA)	−900				Bad Debt Expense (+E)	−900

2 Record

dr **Bad Debt Expense** (+E, −SE) 900
    cr **Allowance for Doubtful Accounts** (+xA, −A) 900

Exhibit 8.2 uses blue and red text to show how the accounts in the end—of—period adjusting entry partially offset the original sales on account. The exhibit also shows where the accounts appear in the balance sheet and income statement.

EXHIBIT 8.2   Recording and Reporting Estimated Bad Debts

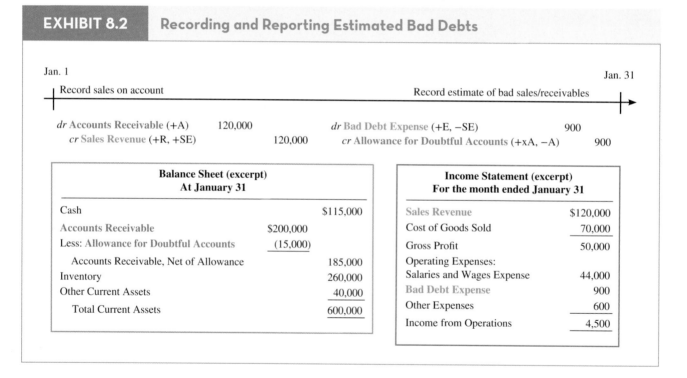

Jan. 1   Jan. 31

Record sales on account   Record estimate of bad sales/receivables

dr Accounts Receivable (+A)   120,000   dr Bad Debt Expense (+E, −SE)   900
     cr Sales Revenue (+R, +SE)   120,000   cr Allowance for Doubtful Accounts (+xA, −A)   900

Balance Sheet (excerpt) At January 31		
Cash		$115,000
Accounts Receivable	$200,000	
Less: Allowance for Doubtful Accounts	(15,000)	
Accounts Receivable, Net of Allowance		185,000
Inventory		260,000
Other Current Assets		40,000
Total Current Assets		600,000

Income Statement (excerpt) For the month ended January 31	
Sales Revenue	$120,000
Cost of Goods Sold	70,000
Gross Profit	50,000
Operating Expenses:	
Salaries and Wages Expense	44,000
Bad Debt Expense	900
Other Expenses	600
Income from Operations	4,500

🏈 COACH'S TIP

Accounts Receivable, Net of Allowance (shown in Exhibit 8.2) is not a separate account. It is a subtotal that is computed by subtracting the contra-asset account *Allowance for Doubtful Accounts* from the asset account *Accounts Receivable*. This subtotal can also be referred to as the *Net Realizable Value*.

Like all contra—asset accounts, such as Accumulated Depreciation, the Allowance for Doubtful Accounts is a permanent account, so its balance carries forward from one accounting period to the next. Bad Debt Expense, which is a temporary account, will have its balance closed (zeroed out) at the end of each accounting period. Consequently, the balance in the Allowance for Doubtful Accounts will differ from the balance in Bad Debt Expense, except during the first year that the Allowance for Doubtful Accounts is used. This explains why the Allowance for Doubtful Accounts in the balance sheet in Exhibit 8.2 does not equal the Bad Debt Expense in the January income statement.

For billing and collection purposes, VFC internally keeps a sepa—rate accounts receivable account (called a subsidiary account) for each customer. The total of these accounts is reported as Accounts Receivable on the balance sheet. Given this, you might wonder why the estimated uncollectable accounts aren't taken directly out of these individual accounts. It's because, at the time the Allowance for Doubtful Accounts is estimated, no one knows which particular customers' accounts receivable are uncollectable. If VFC were to remove the specific customer accounts believed to be uncollectable, it would lose track of which customers still owed money. If this were to happen, VFC would no longer know which customers it should continue pursuing for payment.

2. Remove (Write Off) Specific Customer Balances

Throughout the year, when it becomes clear that a particular customer will never pay, VFC removes the customer's account from the accounts receivable records. By removing the receivable, VFC no longer needs to make an allowance for it, so the company removes the corresponding amount from the Allowance for Doubtful Accounts. Removing the uncollectable account and a corresponding amount from the allowance is called a **write-off**. The purpose of writing off some or all of a customer's account balance is to remove amounts that are known with near certainty to have no chance of collection.

Write-off: An uncollectable account and its corresponding allowance that has been removed from the accounting records.

To illustrate, assume VFC decides to write off an $800 receivable from Fast Fashions. VFC would record an $800 decrease in Accounts Receivable, which would be offset by an $800 decrease in the contra-account Allowance for Doubtful Accounts. These accounting equation effects and the journal entry to record them follow.

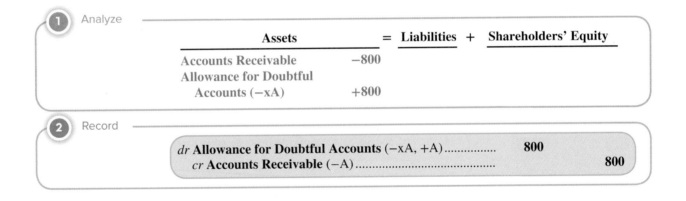

① Analyze

Assets		= Liabilities +	Shareholders' Equity
Accounts Receivable	−800		
Allowance for Doubtful Accounts (−xA)	+800		

② Record

dr Allowance for Doubtful Accounts (−xA, +A)	800	
cr Accounts Receivable (−A)		800

Notice that a write-off does not affect income statement accounts. The estimated Bad Debt Expense relating to these uncollectable accounts was already recorded with an adjusting entry in the period the sale was recorded. Therefore, no additional expense is incurred when the account is finally written off.

The effects of these two steps on VFC's accounting records can be summarized in terms of the following changes in the related T-accounts:

Accounts Receivable (A)			Allow. for Doubtful Accts. (xA)			Bad Debt Expense (E, SE)		
1/1 Bal.	200,000				14,100 1/1 Bal.	1/1 Bal.	0	
					900 (1) Estimate	(1) Estimate	900	
1/31 Bal.	200,000				15,000 1/31 Bal.	1/31 Bal.	900	
		800 (2) Write-off	(2) Write-off	800				
End. Bal.	199,200				14,200 End. Bal.			

Notice that the write−off decreased both the total Accounts Receiv−able and Allowance for Doubtful Accounts by the same amount ($800). Consequently, the *net* receivable balance after the write−off ($185,000 = $199,200 = $14,200) is unchanged from the net receivable balance before the write−off ($185,000 = $200,000 = $15,000). Write−offs merely remove receivable balances that were previously accounted for as uncollectible.

Summary of the Allowance Method

Here is a summary of the two main steps in the allowance method:

Step, Timing, and Journal Entry	FINANCIAL STATEMENT EFFECTS	

1. Adjust for estimated bad debts at the end of each period
 	
dr Bad Debt Expense (+E, −SE)
   cr Allowance for Doubtful
     Accounts (+xA, −A)
	Balance Sheet
	Accounts Receivable *no effect*
	  Less: Allowance increase
	Accounts Receivable, Net decrease
		Income Statement
		Revenues *no effect*
		Expenses
		  Bad Debt Expense increase
		Net Income decrease

2. Write off specific customer balances when known to be uncollectable
 	
dr Allowance for Doubtful
   Accounts (−xA, +A)
   cr Accounts Receivable (−A)
	Balance Sheet
	Accounts Receivable decrease
	  Less: Allowance decrease
	Accounts Receivable,
	  Net *no effect*
		Income Statement
		Revenues *no effect*
		Expenses
		  Bad Debt Expense *no effect*
		Net Income *no effect*

HOW'S IT GOING?

Self-Study Practice 8.1

Indicate the effect (+/−/No Effect) of each of the following hypothetical situations on net income and total assets.

	Net Income	Total Assets
1. Polaris Industries recorded an increase in estimated bad debts on December 31.		
2. Kellogg's wrote off twelve customer account balances during the year.		

After you have finished, check your answers with the solution, which follows the chapter summary.

METHODS FOR ESTIMATING BAD DEBTS

In the examples given so far, we simply stated the estimated amount of uncollectables to record. In the workplace, these bad debts must be estimated. Such estimates may be based on either (1) a percentage of credit sales for the period or (2) an aging of accounts receivable. Both methods are acceptable under ASPE and IFRS. The percentage of credit sales method is simpler to apply, but the aging method is generally more accurate. Some companies use the simpler method on a weekly or monthly basis and the more accurate method on a quarterly or annual basis.

Percentage of Credit Sales Method

The **percentage of credit sales method** estimates bad debt expense by multiplying the historical percentage of bad debt losses by the current period's credit sales. Assume, for example, that VFC has experienced bad debt losses of ¾ of 1 percent of credit sales in prior periods. If credit sales in January total $120,000, VFC could estimate the month's bad debt expense as follows:

Percentage of credit sales method: Estimates bad debts based on the historical percentage of sales that lead to bad debt losses. Also called the *income statement approach*.

Credit sales this month	$120,000
× Bad debt loss rate (0.75%)	× 0.0075
Bad debt expense this month	$ 900

This estimate would be recorded using the journal entry previously shown.

Aging of Accounts Receivable Method

While the percentage of credit sales method focuses on estimating Bad Debt Expense for the period, the **aging of accounts receivable method** focuses on estimating the ending balance in the Allowance for Doubtful Accounts. The aging method gets its name because it is based on the "age" of each amount in Accounts Receivable. The older and more overdue an account receivable becomes, the less likely it is to be collectable. Based on this idea, credit managers and accountants use their experience to estimate what portion of receivables of a specific age will not be paid.

Aging of accounts receivable method: Estimates uncollectable accounts based on the age of each account receivable. Also called the *balance sheet approach*.

To illustrate the aging of accounts receivable method, we assume VFC applies this method to its accounts receivable balances on February 28, after taking into account February sales and cash collections. The aging method includes three steps, as shown in Exhibit 8.3:

1. Prepare an aged listing of accounts receivable with totals for each age category. Most accounting software will produce this report automatically by counting back the number of days to when each receivable was first recorded.

2. Estimate bad debt loss percentages for each category. The percentage each company uses varies according to its circumstances

---

EXHIBIT 8.3   Estimating Uncollectable Amounts with an Aging of Accounts Receivable

Customer	Total	Number of Days Unpaid			
		0–30	31–60	61–90	Over 90
Adam's Sports	$ 700	$ 400	$ 200	$ 100	
Momentum Clothes	2,300				$2,300
Others (not shown to save space)	189,000	97,600	49,800	37,900	3,700
Zoom Athletics	6,000	4,000	2,000		
Total Accounts Receivable	**$198,000**	**$102,000**	**$52,000**	**$38,000**	**$6,000**
Estimated Uncollectable (%)		× 2%	× 10%	× 20%	× 40%
Estimated Uncollectable ($)	**$ 17,240**	**$ 2,040**	**$ 5,200**	**$ 7,600**	**$2,400**

←Step ❶ –Age

←Step ❷ –Estimate

←Step ❸ –Compute

and past experience. Generally, higher percentages are applied to increasingly older receivables.

 Compute the total estimate by multiplying the totals in step 1 by the percentages in step 2 and then summing across all categories. The total across all aging categories ($2,040 + $5,200 + $7,600 + $2,400 = $17,240) equals the balance to which the Allowance for Doubtful Accounts will need to be adjusted at the end of the period.

The amount computed in step 3 is the desired balance in the Allowance for Doubtful Accounts, not the amount of the adjust— ment. To compute the amount of the adjustment, you must determine how much to increase (credit) or decrease (debit) the Allowance for Doubtful Accounts to reach the desired adjusted balance computed in step 3. Assume, for example, that VFC had an unadjusted credit bal— ance in the Allowance for Doubtful Accounts of $15,000 on March 31 and computed a desired credit balance of $17,240 as shown in Exhibit 8.3. An adjustment of $2,240 ($17,240 − $15,000) needs to be recorded as a credit to the account. A corresponding amount is debited to Bad Debt Expense, as follows:

Allowance for		
dr − Doubtful Accounts cr +		
	15,000	Unadj. bal.
	?	AJE
	17,240	Desired bal.

1 Analyze

	Assets	= Liabilities +	Shareholders' Equity
	Allowance for Doubtful Accounts (+xA)	−2,240	Bad Debt Expense (+E) −2,240

2 Record

dr Bad Debt Expense (+E, −SE)	2,240	
cr Allowance for Doubtful Accounts (+xA, −A)		2,240

3 Summarize

dr − Allow. for Doubtful Accts. (xA) cr +			dr + Bad Debt Expense (E, SE) cr −		
	15,000	Unadj. bal.	Beg. bal.	900	
	2,240	AJE	AJE	2,240	
	17,240	Adj. bal.	End. bal.	3,140	

Although the Allowance for Doubtful Accounts normally has a credit balance, it may in some situations have a debit balance before it is adjusted. This happens when a company has recorded write—offs that exceed previous estimates of uncollectable accounts. If this hap— pens, you can still calculate the amount of the adjustment needed to reach the desired balance under the aging of accounts receivable method. The only difference is that to reach the desired balance, you need to record an amount equal to the desired balance *plus* the existing debit balance.

After the adjustment is recorded, the Allowance for Doubtful Accounts will once again return to a credit balance. Assume, for example, that VFC had an unadjusted debit balance in the Allowance for Doubtful Accounts of $7,000 on February 28 and computed a desired credit balance of $17,240 as

Allowance for		
dr − Doubtful Accounts cr +		
7,000		Unadj. bal.
	?	AJE
	17,240	Desired bal.

shown in Exhibit 8.3. An adjustment of $24,240 ($17,240 + $7,000) needs to be recorded as a credit to the account. A corresponding amount is debited to Bad Debt Expense:

1 Analyze

Assets		= Liabilities +	Shareholders' Equity
Allowance for Doubtful Accounts (+xA)	−24,240		Bad Debt Expense (+E) −24,240

2 Record

dr **Bad Debt Expense (+E, −SE)** 24,240
  cr **Allowance for Doubtful Accounts (+xA, −A)** 24,240

3 Summarize

dr − Allow. for Doubtful Accts. (xA) *cr* +		*dr* + Bad Debt Expense (E, SE) *cr* −	
Unadj. bal. 7,0000		Beg. bal. 900	
	24,240 AJE	AJE 24,240	
	17,240 Adj. bal.	End. bal. 25,140	

SPOTLIGHT ON Business Decisions

Focus Collection Efforts with the Aged Listing of Accounts Receivable

The aged listing of accounts receivable, as shown in Exhibit 8.3, is useful when estimating uncollectable accounts. It also is useful when credit managers identify customers at risk of failing to pay their accounts. Some sources report that this risk doubles every month that an account ages beyond ninety days. Knowing this, employees in VFC's credit department would be especially concerned with the $2,300 shown in Exhibit 8.3 as receivable from Momentum Clothes. If a follow-up phone call does not prompt the customer to pay, VFC could turn the account over to a collection agency.

HOW'S IT GOING?

Self-Study Practice 8.2

For the years ended March 31, 2017, and 2016, Maddie Enterprises reported credit balances in the Allowance for Doubtful Accounts of $4,514 and $3,583, respectively. It also reported that write-offs during the year ended March 31, 2017, amounted to $7,273 (all numbers in thousands of dollars). Assuming no other changes in the account, what amount did Maddie Enterprises record as Bad Debt Expense for the period? Use the following T-accounts to solve for the missing value.

dr − Allow. for Doubtful Accts. (xA) *cr* +		*dr* + Bad Debt Expense (E, SE) *cr* −	
	3,583 March 31, 2016	Beg. bal. 0	
☐	☐ Estimate	Estimate ☐	
	March 31, 2017	March 31, 2017	

After you have finished, check your answers with the solution, which follows the chapter summary.

Other Issues

Revising Estimates Bad debt estimates always differ somewhat from the amounts that are later written off. To ensure that bad debts and the allowance for doubtful accounts do not become materially misstated over time, companies revise overestimates of prior periods by lowering estimates in the current period, or they raise estimates in the current period to correct underestimates of prior periods.

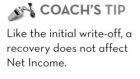
Account Recoveries In the same way that someone you've written off as a friend might do something to win you back, a customer might pay an account balance that was previously written off. Collection of a previously written—off account is called a recovery and it is accounted for in two parts. First, put the receivable back on the books by recording the opposite of the write—off. Second, record the collection of the account. To illustrate, let's assume that VFC collects the $800 from Fast Fashions that was previously written off. This recovery would be recorded with the following journal entries:

Reverse the write-off

(1)	*dr* **Accounts Receivable** (+A)	800	
	cr **Allowance for Doubtful Accounts** (+xA, −A)		800

Record the collection

(2)	*dr* **Cash** (+A)	800	
	cr **Accounts Receivable** (−A)		800

Look closely at the journal entries for recording a recovery and you'll see that Accounts Receivable is debited and then credited for $800. It's tempting to cancel these two out, but don't do it, because it would create an inaccurate credit history for the customer. After all is said and done, the customer's balance was removed because it was actually collected, not written off, so the accounting records should reflect that.

Alternative Methods You should be aware that some small companies don't use the allowance method. Instead, they use an alternative approach called the direct write—off method, which we demonstrate in Supplement 8A near the end of this chapter. This alternative method records Bad Debt Expense only when a company writes off specific accounts. Although this alternative method is easier to use, it overstates the value of Accounts Receivable and it violates the expense recognition principle, as explained in Supplement 8A. Thus, it is not considered a generally accepted accounting method.

NOTES RECEIVABLE AND INTEREST REVENUE

A company reports Notes Receivable if it uses a promissory note to document its right to collect money from another party. This usually happens in the following three situations: (1) the company loans money to employees or businesses, (2) the company sells expensive items for which customers require an extended payment period, or (3) the company converts an existing account receivable to a note receivable to allow an extended payment period.

The accounting issues for notes receivable are similar to those for accounts receivable, with one exception. Unlike accounts receivable, which are interest free until they become overdue, notes receivable charge interest from the day they are created to the day they are due (their maturity date). Although interest on a note receivable is earned each day, interest payments typically are received only once or twice a year. This means that a company with a note receivable needs to accrue Interest Revenue and Interest Receivable. Let's look at how to calculate interest.

Calculating Interest

To calculate interest, you need to consider three variables: (1) the principal, which is the amount of the note receivable, (2) the annual interest rate charged on the note, and (3) the time period covered in the interest calculation. Because interest rates are always stated as an annual percentage even if the note is for less than a year, the time period is the portion of a year for which interest is calculated. Ask yourself how many months out of twelve or how many days out of 365 the interest period covers. Then use the following **interest formula** to calculate the interest:

$$\text{Interest (I)} = \text{Principal (P)} \times \text{Interest Rate (R)} \times \text{Time (T)}$$

Many financial institutions use the number of days out of 365 to compute interest. In doing homework assignments, assume that the time is measured in terms of number of months out of twelve. See Exhibit 8.4 for the computation of interest for three notes with different terms and different lengths of interest periods. Notice how the time variable depends on the interest period, not the due date for the note.

COACH'S TIP

The "time" variable refers to the portion of a year for which interest is calculated, not the portion of the note's entire life. A two-month interest calculation on a three-year note has a time variable of 2/12 not 2/36.

Interest formula: $I = P \times R \times T$, where I = interest calculated, P = principal, R = annual interest rate, and T = time period covered in the interest calculation (number of months out of 12).

EXHIBIT 8.4	Sample Interest Computations

GIVEN INFORMATION		INTEREST CALCULATION				
Terms of Note	Interest Period	Principal	Rate	Time	Interest
$200,000, 6%, due in 2 years	November 1–October 31	$200,000 ×	6% ×	12/12 =	$12,000
$200,000, 6%, due in 1 year	January 1–October 31	200,000 ×	6 ×	10/12 =	10,000
$200,000, 6%, due in 100 days	November 1–December 31	200,000 ×	6 ×	2/12 =	2,000

RECORDING NOTES RECEIVABLE AND INTEREST REVENUE

The four key events that occur with any note receivable are (1) establishing the note, (2) accruing interest earned but not received, (3) recording interest payments received, and (4) recording principal payments received. Assume that on November 1, 2016, VFC lent $100,000 to a company by creating a note that required the company to pay VFC 6 percent interest and the $100,000 principal on October 31, 2017. VFC prepared year–end financial statements as of December 31, 2016, but made no other adjustments for interest during the year.

Establishing a Note Receivable

The $100,000 loan that created the note receivable has the following accounting equation effects, which VFC would record using the following journal entry:

1 Analyze

Assets		= Liabilities	+	Shareholders' Equity
Note Receivable	+100,000			
Cash	−100,000			

2 Record

dr **Note Receivable** (+A)	100,000	
cr **Cash** (−A)		100,000

Notice that no interest is recorded on the day the note is established. Interest is earned over time.

Accruing Interest Earned

Under accrual basis accounting, interest revenue is recorded when it is earned. Rather than record the interest earned as each day passes, VFC waits until it either receives an interest payment or reaches the end of its accounting period.

The timeline in Exhibit 8.5 shows how VFC should account for the interest revenue earned from the note over its one–year term. Between the date of the note's creation (November 1, 2016) and the year–end (December 31, 2016), VFC earned two months of interest revenue (the red portion of the timeline) because the note was outstanding for all of November and December 2016. As you learned in Chapter 4, when a company has earned interest in the current period but has not yet recorded the interest, the company must make an adjusting entry at the end of the current period to accrue the interest earned. The amount of interest for two months is computed as:

$$\text{Interest (I)} = \text{Principal (P)} \times \text{Interest Rate (R)} \times \text{Time (T)}$$
$$\$1,000 \ = \ \$100,000 \ \times \ 6\% \ \times \ 2/12$$

EXHIBIT 8.5 Use of a Timeline to Keep Track of Interest Periods

388 CHAPTER 8 Receivables, Bad Debt Expense, and Interest Revenue

The effect of this adjustment, along with the adjusting journal entry to record the $1,000 of interest revenue that is receivable on December 31, 2016, is as follows:

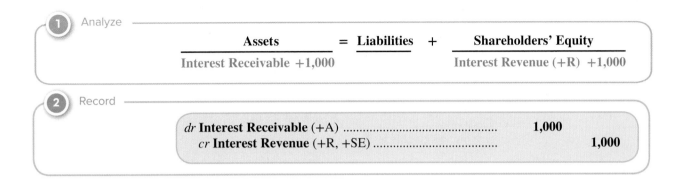

1 Analyze

Assets	=	Liabilities	+	Shareholders' Equity
Interest Receivable +1,000				Interest Revenue (+R) +1,000

2 Record

dr Interest Receivable (+A) 1,000
    cr Interest Revenue (+R, +SE) 1,000

Recording Interest Received

On October 31, 2017, VFC receives a cash interest payment of $6,000 (= $100,000 × 6% × 12/12). As shown on the following timeline, this $6,000 of interest includes the $1,000 that was accrued as Interest Receivable at December 31, 2016, plus $5,000 earned during the ten−month period from January 1 to October 31, 2017, which had yet to be recorded.

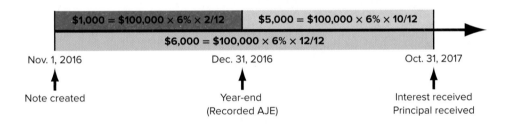

$1,000 = $100,000 × 6% × 2/12 $5,000 = $100,000 × 6% × 10/12

$6,000 = $100,000 × 6% × 12/12

Nov. 1, 2016	Dec. 31, 2016	Oct. 31, 2017
Note created	Year-end (Recorded AJE)	Interest received Principal received

When VFC receives the interest payment, it will record the $6,000 increase in cash, and it will reduce the $1,000 Interest Receivable that was previ−ously recorded and record the remaining $5,000 as interest revenue in 2017. These effects and the journal entry to record them follow:

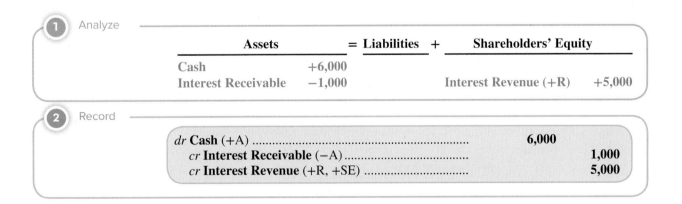

1 Analyze

Assets		= Liabilities	+	Shareholders' Equity	
Cash	+6,000				
Interest Receivable	−1,000			Interest Revenue (+R)	+5,000

2 Record

dr Cash (+A) 6,000
    cr Interest Receivable (−A) 1,000
    cr Interest Revenue (+R, +SE) 5,000

Recording Principal Received

The collection of a note receivable is accounted for just like the collection of an account receivable. Assuming that VFC receives the $100,000 principal that is due, the accounting equation effects and journal entry for this transaction would be as follows:

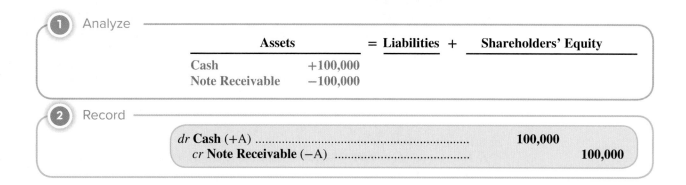

1 Analyze

Assets		= Liabilities +	Shareholders' Equity
Cash	+100,000		
Note Receivable	−100,000		

2 Record

dr **Cash (+A)** 100,000
     cr **Note Receivable (−A)** 100,000

Accounting for Uncollectable Notes

Just as companies may not collect their accounts receivable in full, they also might not collect the full principal (and interest) that they are owed on a note receivable. When the collection of notes receivable is in doubt, a company

HOW'S IT GOING?

Self-Study Practice 8.3

Assume that Maddie Enterprises loaned $12,000 to an employee on October 1, 2016, by creating a note that required the employee to pay the principal plus interest of 8 percent on September 30, 2017. Assume that the company makes adjusting entries only at year-end on December 31.

1. Record the creation of the note.
2. Record any necessary end-of-period adjusting entry to be made at the end of 2016.
3. Record the receipt of interest and principal on September 30, 2017.

After you have finished, check your answers with the solution, which follows the chapter summary.

SPOTLIGHT ON Ethics

Resetting the Clock

Earlier in this chapter, you saw that as customer balances get older, the Allowance for Doubtful Accounts should be increased. Because increases in the Allowance for Doubtful Accounts require increases in Bad Debt Expense, the result of older customer accounts should be a decrease in Net Income.

A credit manager at MCI, a U.S. telecommunications company, knew about these accounting effects. To avoid reducing net income, he "reset the clock" on amounts owed by customers. He did so by making loans to customers, who then used the money to pay off their account balances. By replacing old accounts receivable with new notes receivable, he avoided recording approximately $70 million in bad debts.

His scheme didn't last long, though. After the fraud was revealed, the credit manager spent several years in prison and he has been working to pay off over $10 million in fines. To learn more about this fraud, see Skills Development Case S8-4 at the end of this chapter.

should record an Allowance for Doubtful Accounts against the Notes Receivable, just as it records an Allowance for Doubtful Accounts against Accounts Receivable.

Evaluate the Results

RECEIVABLES TURNOVER ANALYSIS

Managers, directors, investors, and creditors can evaluate the effectiveness of a company's credit-granting and collection activities by conducting a receivables turnover analysis. The idea behind a receivables turnover analysis is shown in Exhibit 8.6. When a company sells goods or services on credit, its receivables balance goes up, and when it collects from customers, the receivables balance goes down. This process of selling and collecting is called **receivables turnover** and it is repeated over and over for each customer during each accounting period.

EXHIBIT 8.6	Receivables Turnover Analysis

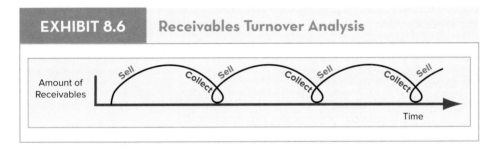

The receivables turnover ratio indicates how many times, on average, this process of selling and collecting is repeated during the period. The higher the ratio, the faster the collection of receivables. And the faster the collection of receivables, the shorter your company's operating cycle, which means more cash available for running the business. A low turnover ratio can be a warning sign, suggesting that the company is allowing too much time for customers to pay.

As you learned earlier from the Aging of Accounts Receivable Method, the longer an account goes without being collected, the bigger the risk that it will never be collected. Analysts watch for changes in the receivables turnover ratio because a sudden decline may mean that a company is recording sales of merchandise that customers are likely to return later. It also may mean that the company is selling to less financially secure customers or is allowing customers more time to pay their accounts to entice them to buy as much as possible—a practice known as channel stuffing.

Rather than evaluate the number of times accounts receivable turn over during a year, some people find it easier to think in terms of the length of time (in days) it takes to collect accounts receivable (called **days to collect**). Converting the year's receivables turnover ratio into the average days to collect is easy: simply divide 365 by the year's receivables turnover ratio. This alternative measure provides the same basic information about the company's ability to collect receivables, but it's a little easier to interpret. In terms of Exhibit 8.6, the *receivables turnover ratio* counts the number of loops in a given period of time, whereas *days to collect* tells you the average number of days between loops.

Comparison to Benchmarks

Credit Terms By calculating days to collect, you can compare a company's collection performance to its stated collections policy. You might remember from Chapter 6 that when companies sell on account, they specify the length of credit period (as well as any discounts for prompt payment). By comparing the number of days to collect to the length of credit period, you can gain a sense of whether customers are complying with the stated policy. Managers inside a company watch this closely, and so do investors and creditors on the outside. Why? If customers appear to be disregarding the stated credit period, this may be a sign they are dissatisfied with the product or service they bought.

SPOTLIGHT ON Financial Reporting

Days to Collect Hurt by a Weak Economy

Kellogg Company (also known as Kellogg's, and Kellogg)—the cereal maker—provides information about its normal credit policies in its annual report. Kellogg's stated policy is to require payment from customers within sixteen days of making a sale (1/15, n/16). During the financial crisis of 2008 and 2009, the company experienced an increase in its days to collect from about nineteen to twenty-seven days, suggesting that customers were finding it difficult to meet the stated credit terms. Other companies also experienced a jump in days to collect between 2007 and 2009, including Caterpillar (68 to 85 days), Hewlett-Packard (43 to 53 days), and K.Swiss (35 to 47 days). Even now, more than eight years later, Kellogg and these other companies are still working to reduce their days to collect.

Other Companies Receivables turnover ratios and the number of days to collect often vary across industries. To illustrate, we have calculated these measures in Exhibit 8.7 for VFC, Kellogg, and Skechers (a footwear company). As Exhibit 8.7 shows, VFC turned over its receivables 9.4 times, which is once every 38.8 days. Kellogg had a turnover ratio of 10.3 times, which means a collection period of about 35.4 days. Skechers shuffled close behind, with a receivables turnover ratio of 10.2 times, which is about 35.8 days to collect.

Because these measures typically vary between industries, you should focus on comparing a company's turnover only with other companies in the same industry or with its own figures from prior periods. If you detect a significant decline in receivables turnover and lengthening in days to collect, you should question whether the company has estimated a sufficient amount for uncollectable accounts. For practice at computing and comparing to prior periods, try the Self—Study Practice that follows Exhibit 8.7.

EXHIBIT 8.7   Summary of Receivables Turnover Ratio Analyses

Company	Relevant Information (in millions)			Fiscal 2015 Receivables Turnover Calculation	Fiscal 2015 Days to Collect Calculation
		2015	2014		
VFC	Net Sales	$12,251	$12,155	$\dfrac{\$12,251}{(\$1,320 + \$1,276)/2} = 9.4\,\text{times}$	$\dfrac{365 \text{ days}}{9.4 \text{ times}} = 38.8 \text{ days}$
	Net Accounts Receivable	1,320	1,276		
		2015	2014		
Kellogg	Net Sales	$13,525	$14,580	$\dfrac{\$13,525}{(\$1,344 + \$1,276)/2} = 10.3\,\text{times}$	$\dfrac{365 \text{ days}}{10.3 \text{ times}} = 35.4 \text{ days}$
	Net Accounts Receivable	1,344	1,276		
		2015	2014		
Skechers	Net Sales	$3,147	$2,378	$\dfrac{\$3,147}{(\$344 + \$272)/2} = 10.2\,\text{times}$	$\dfrac{365 \text{ days}}{10.2 \text{ times}} = 35.8 \text{ days}$
	Net Accounts Receivable	344	272		

HOW'S IT GOING?

Self-Study Practice 8.4

VFC reported net accounts receivable of $1,360 (millions) at the end of fiscal 2013.

a. Use this information, along with that in Exhibit 8.7, to calculate VFC's receivables turnover and days to collect in 2014.

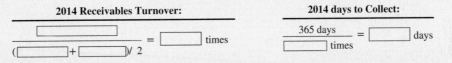

2014 Receivables Turnover:

$\dfrac{\boxed{}}{(\boxed{} + \boxed{})/\ 2} = \boxed{}$ times

2014 days to Collect:

$\dfrac{365 \text{ days}}{\boxed{} \text{ times}} = \boxed{}$ days

b. Did VFC's receivables turnover improve or decline from 2014 [calculated in (a)] to 2015 as shown in Exhibit 8.7?

After you have finished, check your answers with the solution, which follows the chapter summary.

Speeding Up Collections

Factoring Receivables   To generate the cash needed to pay for a company's business activities, managers must ensure that receivables are collected on a timely basis. One way to speed up collections of sluggish receivables is to start hounding customers for payment. But this forceful approach is time consuming and costly, and can annoy customers and cause them to take their business elsewhere.

An alternative approach is to sell outstanding accounts receivable to another company (called a factor). In **factoring**, your company receives cash for the receivables it sells to the factor (minus a factoring fee) and the factor then has the right to collect the outstanding amounts owed by your customers. Factoring is a fast and easy way for your company to get cash for its receivables, but it has costs.

Factoring: An arrangement where receivables are sold to another company (called a *factor*) for immediate cash (minus a factoring fee).

First, factoring could send a potentially negative message to the users of the financial statements because it might be seen as a last resort for collecting accounts. Second, the factoring fee can be as much as 3 percent of the receivables sold. In a recent annual report, VFC reported that it sold $240 million of receivables to a factor and was charged a fee of $400,000, which VFC reported as a Miscellaneous Expense. Other companies that regularly sell their receivables may report the cost of factoring on the income statement as a selling expense.

Credit Card Sales Another way to avoid lengthy collection periods is to allow customers to pay for goods using national credit cards like Visa, MasterCard, and American Express. Unlike private credit card programs, where the seller pursues collection from customers, national credit card com—panies and PayPal pay the seller within one to three days of the sale. Most banks accept credit card receipts as overnight deposits into the company's bank account as if they were cash. This not only speeds up the seller's cash collection, but also reduces losses from customers writing bad cheques.

But, just like factoring, these benefits come at a cost. PayPal and credit card companies charge a fee for their services, often around 3 percent of the total sales price. If credit card sales amounted to $100,000, a credit card fee of $3,000 would be deducted, leaving the equivalent of $97,000 cash. These transaction fees are included with selling expenses on the income statement.

SPOTLIGHT ON Controls

Segregating Collections and Write-Offs

One way to control accounts receivable is to ensure that the same person does not both receive collections from customers and write off account balances. This segregation of duties helps to prevent errors and fraud. Without adequate segregation between these duties, a single dishonest employee could divert customer payments to his or her own bank account and then cover up the theft by writing off the customer's balance.

SPOTLIGHT ON IFRS and ASPE

Topic	ASPE	IFRS
Methods for Estimating Bad Debts	• Both the percentage of credit sales method and the aging of accounts receivable method are acceptable under ASPE.	• Both the percentage of credit sales method and the aging of accounts receivable method are acceptable under IFRS.
Direct Write-off Method	• The direct write-off method is not acceptable under ASPE.	• The direct write-off method is not acceptable under IFRS.
Expense Recognition Principle	• The expense recognition principle, which was introduced in Chapter 3, is the process of recording expenses (such as bad debt expense) on the basis that there is a direct associa-tion between the costs incurred and the earning of income.	• Expenses are recognized in the income statement on the basis that there is a direct association between the costs incurred and the earning of income, even though the term *matching principle* has been removed from the conceptual framework for IFRS. This is referred to as the *expense recognition principle*.

DIRECT WRITE-OFF METHOD

As described earlier in this chapter, an alternative method exists to account for uncollectable accounts. This alternative approach, called the **direct write–off method**, does not estimate bad debts and does not use an Allowance for Doubtful Accounts. Instead, it reports Sales when they occur and Bad Debt Expense when it is discovered. This method is not acceptable under ASPE or IFRS. Consequently, it isn't used very often for external financial reporting.

The reason the direct write–off method isn't considered a GAAP method is that it reports Accounts Receivable at the total amount owed by customers (an overly optimistic point of view) rather than what is estimated to be collectable (a more realistic viewpoint). The direct write–off method also breaks the expense recognition (matching) principle by recording Bad Debt Expense in the period that customer accounts are determined to be bad rather than matching the expense to the revenues reported in the period when the credit sales are actu-ally made. As illustrated in Exhibit 8.1, the failure to match Bad Debt Expense to Sales has a distorting effect on Net Income in the period of the sale as well as in later periods when bad debts are discovered. The only advantage of this method is that it doesn't require estimation of uncollectable amounts.

Under the direct write–off method, no journal entries are made until a bad debt is discovered. Below is the journal entry used by the direct write–off method to record $1,000 of Bad Debt Expense when a customer account is determined to be uncollectable:

dr **Bad Debt Expense** (+E, −SE)	1,000	
cr **Accounts Receivable** (−A)		1,000

LEARNING OBJECTIVE 8-S1

Record bad debts using the direct write-off method.

Direct write-off method:
A non-GAAP alternative to the allowance method of accounting for uncollectable accounts.

Review the Chapter

This section provides a chance to solidify your understanding of key points. It's worth your time to work through the following demonstration cases, scan the chapter summary, test your understanding of key terms, and then practise, practise, practise.

DEMONSTRATION CASE A: BAD DEBTS

Shooby Dooby Shoe (SDS) reported credit sales of $95,000 during January 2017. Later in 2017, SDS determined that it would not be able to collect a $500 account balance that was owed by a deceased customer (Captain Cutler). SDS uses the percentage of credit sales method for estimating monthly Bad Debt Expense, and the aging of accounts receivable method at its December 31 year–end.

Required:

1. If SDS estimates that 1 percent of credit sales will result in bad debts, what will be the effect on the accounting equation of recording the January 2017 estimate? Prepare the journal entry to record this estimate.
2. Show how the write–off of the account receivable from Captain Cutler would affect the accounting equation, and prepare the journal entry to record the write–off.

3. Assume that SDS estimates that $11,000 of its year–end Accounts Receivable is uncollect–able as shown below. As of December 31, 2017, the Allowance for Doubtful Accounts had an unadjusted credit balance of $3,000. Show the accounting equation effects of recording the bad debt estimate, and prepare a journal entry to record this estimate.

		Number of Days Unpaid			
	Total	0–30	31–60	61–90	Over 90
Total Accounts Receivable	$171,000	$50,000	$80,000	$40,000	$1,000
Estimated Uncollectable (%)		× 1%	× 5%	× 15%	× 50%
Estimated Uncollectable ($)	$ 11,000	$ 500	$ 4,000	$ 6,000	$ 500

4. Assume the same facts as in requirement 3, except that as of December 31, 2017, the Allowance for Doubtful Accounts had an unadjusted *debit* balance of $3,000. Show the accounting equation effects of recording the bad debt estimate, and prepare a journal entry to record this estimate.

5. Assume that SDS reported total sales of $950,000 in 2017, with Net Accounts Receivable of $160,000 at December 31, 2017 and $167,586 at December 31, 2016. Calculate the receiv–ables turnover ratio for 2017.

6. If the receivables turnover ratio was 6.4 in 2016, what was the number of days to collect in 2017? Given your calculations in requirement 4, conclude whether SDS collections were faster or slower in 2017 than in 2016.

Suggested Solution

1. The percentage of credit sales method multiplies historical bad debt losses (1 percent) by this period's credit sales ($95,000) to directly estimate the amount of Bad Debt Expense to record ($950 = 1% × $95,000).

Assets	=	Liabilities	+	Shareholders' Equity	
Allowance for Doubtful				**Bad Debt Expense (+E)**	**−950**
Accounts (+xA) **−950**					

dr Bad Debt Expense (+E, −SE)(0.01 × $95,000)............................. 950
  cr Allowance for Doubtful Accounts (+xA, −A)................................. 950

2.

Assets	=	Liabilities	+	Shareholders' Equity
Accounts Receivable **−500**				
Allowance for Doubtful Accounts (−xA) **+500**				

dr Allowance for Doubtful Accounts (−xA, +A)............................. 500
  cr Accounts Receivable (−A)... 500

3. Under the aging of accounts receivable method, we determine the estimated balance for the Allowance for Doubtful Accounts ($11,000) and then subtract its unadjusted balance ($3,000) to determine the amount of the adjustment ($8,000 = $11,000 − $3,000).

Assets	=	Liabilities	+	Shareholders' Equity	
Allowance for Doubtful				**Bad Debt Expense (+E)**	**−8,000**
Accounts (+xA) **−8,000**					

dr Bad Debt Expense (+E, −SE)... 8,000
  cr Allowance for Doubtful Accounts (+xA, −A)............................ 8,000

4. Under the aging of accounts receivable method, we determine the estimated balance for the Allowance for Doubtful Accounts ($11,000) and then add its unadjusted debit balance ($3,000) to determine the amount of the adjustment ($14,000 = $11,000 + $3,000).

Assets	=	Liabilities	+	Shareholders' Equity
Allowance for Doubtful				Bad Debt Expense (+E) −14,000
Accounts (+xA) −14,000				

dr Bad Debt Expense (+E, ×SE)... 14,000
    cr Allowance for Doubtful Accounts (+xA, −A)................................   14,000

5. Receivables turnover ratio is calculated as Net Sales divided by Average Accounts Receivable. The average accounts receivable in 2017 was $163,793 [= ($160,000 + $167,586)/2], so the receivables turnover ratio for 2017 was 5.8 (= $950,000 ÷ $163,793).

6. Days to collect is calculated as 365 divided by receivables turnover ratio. The 6.4 turnover in 2016 equates to fifty−seven days (and the 5.8 turnover in 2017 equates to sixty−three days). Collections are slower in 2017 than in 2016.

DEMONSTRATION CASE B: NOTES RECEIVABLE

Let's assume that, as of February 28, 2017, Rocky Mountain Chocolate Factory, Inc. (RMCF) reported it had approximately $240,000 of Notes Receivable, with an annual interest rate of 8 percent. As a public company, RMCF prepares financial statements for external reporting every quarter, ending on May 31, August 31, November 30, and February 28. Assume that the notes were created on March 1, 2016, when money was loaned to another company, and that RMCF receives interest payments semi−annually, on July 31 and January 31.

Required:

1. Using the interest formula, calculate the amount of interest that RMCF earns each month on the notes.
2. Using the interest formula, calculate the amount of interest payment that RMCF received on July 31, 2016, and on January 31, 2017.
3. Prepare a timeline showing the amount of interest earned each quarter and received on each payment date.
4. Prepare journal entries to record the note's issuance, interest earned, and interest payments received for each quarter and on each payment date.

Suggested Solutions

1. Interest earned = Principal × Interes Rate × Time
                = $240,000 × 8% × 1/12
                = $1,600 per month

2. The period from March 1 to July 31 is five months, whereas the period from August 1 to January 31 is six months.

    Interest Payment = Principal × Interest Rate × Time
                  = $240,000 × 8% × 5/12
                  = $8,000 on July 31

    Interest Payment = Principal × Interest Rate × Time
                  = $240,000 × 8% × 6/12
                  = $9,600 on January 31

3. Timeline

March 1	May 31	July 31	Aug. 31	Nov. 30	Jan. 31	Feb. 28
$4,800	$3,200	$1,600	$4,800	$3,200	$1,600	
$8,000			$9,600			

4. Journal Entries

March 1, 2016 (Notes Issued)

dr Notes Receivable (+A)..	240,000	
cr Cash (−A)...		240,000

May 31, 2016 (Interest Accrued)

dr Interest Receivable (+A)	4,800	
cr Interest Revenue (+R, +SE).........................		4,800

July 31, 2016 (Interest Payment Received)

dr Cash (+A)..	8,000	
cr Interest Receivable (−A).........................		4,800
cr Interest Revenue (+R, +SE).......................		3,200

August 31, 2016 (Interest Accrued)

dr Interest Receivable (+A).........................	1,600	
cr Interest Revenue (+R, +SE).......................		1,600

November 30, 2016 (Interest Accrued)

dr Interest Receivable (+A).........................	4,800	
cr Interest Revenue (+R, +SE).......................		4,800

January 31, 2017 (Interest Payment Received)

dr Cash (+A)	9,600	
cr Interest Receivable (−A).........................		6,400
cr Interest Revenue (+R, +SE).......................		3,200

February 28, 2017 (Interest Accrued)

dr Interest Receivable (+A).........................	1,600	
cr Interest Revenue (+R, +SE).......................		1,600

CHAPTER SUMMARY

LO8-1 **Describe the trade-offs of extending credit.**

- By extending credit to customers, a company is likely to attract a greater number of customers willing to buy from it.
- The additional costs of extending credit include increased wage costs, bad debt costs, and delayed receipt of cash.

LO8-2 **Estimate and report the effects of uncollectable accounts.**

- Under generally accepted accounting principles, companies must use the allowance method to account for uncollectables. This method involves the following steps:
    1. Estimate and record uncollectables with an end–of–period adjusting journal entry that increases Bad Debt Expense (debit) and increases the Allowance for Doubtful Accounts (credit).
    2. Identify and write off specific customer balances in the period that they are deter– mined to be uncollectable.
- The adjusting entry (in step 1) reduces Net Income as well as Net Accounts Receivable. The write–off (in step 2) has offsetting effects on Accounts Receivable and the Allowance for Doubtful Accounts, ultimately yielding no net effect on Net Accounts Receivable or on Net Income.

LO8-3 **Compute and report interest on notes receivable.**

- Interest is calculated by multiplying the principal, interest rate, and time period (number of months out of twelve). As time passes and interest is earned on the note, accountants must record an adjusting journal entry that accrues the interest revenue that is receivable on the note.

Compute and interpret the receivables turnover ratio.

- The receivables turnover ratio measures the effectiveness of credit–granting and collection activities. It reflects how many times average trade receivables were recorded and collected during the period.
- Analysts and creditors watch this ratio because a sudden decline may mean that a company is extending payment deadlines in an attempt to prop up lagging sales. Or it may mean that a company is recording sales of merchandise that customers are likely to return later.

ACCOUNTING DECISION TOOLS

Name of Measure	Formula	What It Tells You
Receivables turnover ratio	$\dfrac{\text{Net Sales Revenue}}{\text{Average Net Receivables}}$	• The number of times receivables turn over during the period • A higher ratio means faster (better) turnover
Days to collect	$\dfrac{365}{\text{Receivables Turnover Ratio}}$	• Average number of days from sale on account to collection • A higher number means a longer (worse) time to collect

SOLUTIONS TO SELF-STUDY PRACTICE

Solution to SP8.1

	Net Income	Total Assets
1.	—	—
2.	NE	NE*

*The decrease in Accounts Receivable is offset by the decrease in Allowance for Doubtful Accounts.

Solution to SP8.2

$dr -$	Allow. for Doubtful Accts.	$cr +$
	3,583	March 31, 2016
Write–offs 7,273	8,204	Estimate
	4,514	March 31, 2017

$dr +$	Bad Debt Expense	$cr -$
Beg. bal.	0	
Estimate	8,204	
March 31, 2017	8,204	

Beginning + Bad debt estimate − Write−offs = Ending
3,583 + X − 7,273 = 4,514
X = 8,204

The bad debt estimate is $8,204.

Solution to SP8.3

1. dr Note Receivable (+A)... 12,000
   cr Cash (−A).. 12,000

2. dr Interest Receivable (+A) ($12,000 × 8% × 3/12)............ 240
   cr Interest Revenue (+R, + SE)... 240

3. dr Cash (+A) ($12,000 × 8% × 12/12)................................. 960
   cr Interest Receivable (−A) ($12,000 × 8% × 3/12)........... 240
   cr Interest Revenue (+R, + SE) ($12,000 × 8% ×9/12)...... 720

   dr Cash (+A)... 12,000
   cr Note Receivable (−A)... 12,000

Solution to SP8.4

a. $\dfrac{\$12,155}{(\$1,276 + \$1,360)/2} = 9.2$ times

$365 \div 9.2 = 39.6$ days

b. VFC's receivables turnover was just slightly better in 2014 (0.1 days faster).

KEY TERMS

Accounts Receivable	Days to Collect	Note Receivable
Aging of Accounts Receivable Method	Direct Write–Off Method	Percentage of Credit Sales Method
Allowance Method	Factoring	Receivables Turnover
Bad Debt Expense	Interest Formula	Write–Off

Complete definitions can also be found in the glossary in the end of this text.

HOMEWORK HELPER

Alternative terms

- Days to Collect is also called *days' sales outstanding*.

Helpful reminders

- The percentage of credit sales method calculates the amount to record as Bad Debt Expense. The aging of accounts receivable method calculates the desired balance in the Allowance for Doubtful Accounts. This desired balance is compared to the existing balance to determine the amount to record as Bad Debt Expense.

- Interest rates are always for a full year. To calculate interest for a shorter period, multiply the interest rate by the fraction of the year for which you are calculating interest.

Frequent mistakes

- Some students mistakenly think a write–off is an expense. It isn't. It is merely a way to clean up the accounts receivable records. Under the allowance method, no Bad Debt Expense is recorded when removing (writing off) specific customer accounts.

PRACTICE MATERIAL

QUESTIONS (💲 Symbol indicates questions that require analysis from more than one perspective.)

1. What are the advantages and disadvantages of extending credit to customers?

2. In April 2006, Kohl's Corporation decided to discontinue its Kohl's credit card operations. What factors would this department store company have considered prior to making this decision? 💲

3. Which basic accounting principles does the allowance method of accounting for bad debts satisfy?

4. Using the allowance method, is Bad Debt Expense recognized in the period in which (a) sales related to the uncollectable account were made or (b) the seller learns that the customer is unable to pay?

5. What is the effect of the write–off of uncollectable accounts (using the allowance method) on (a) net income and (b) net accounts receivable?

6. How does the use of calculated estimates differ between the aging of accounts receivable method and the percentage of credit sales method?

7. A local phone company had a customer who rang up $300 in charges during September 2016, but did not pay. Despite reminding the customer of this balance, the company was unable to collect in October, November, or December. In March 2017, the company finally gave up and wrote off the account balance. What amount of Sales, Bad Debt Expense, and Net Income would the phone company report from these events in 2016 and 2017 if it used the allowance method of accounting for uncollectable accounts? Assume that the company estimates 5 percent of credit sales will go bad.

8. What is the primary difference between accounts receivable and notes receivable?

9. What are the three components of the interest formula? Explain how this formula adjusts for interest periods that are less than a full year.

10. Assume that, as of February 1, 2017, Tim Hortons had $100,000 of Notes Receivable due before January 31, 2018, $1,268,000 of Accounts Receivable, and $249,000 in its Allowance for Doubtful Accounts (all related to accounts receivable). How should these accounts be reported on a balance sheet prepared following ASPE?

11. Does an increase in the receivables turnover ratio generally indicate faster or slower collection of receivables? Explain.

12. What two approaches can managers take to speed up sluggish collections of receivables? List one advantage and disadvantage for each approach.

13. When customers experience economic difficulties, companies consider extending longer credit periods. What are the possible consequences of longer credit periods on Sales, Accounts Receivable, Allowance for Doubtful Accounts, Net Income, and the receivables turnover ratio? 🔄

14. (Supplement 8A) Describe how (and when) the direct write–off method accounts for uncollectable accounts. What are the disadvantages of this method?

15. (Supplement 8A) Refer to question 7. What amounts would be reported if the direct write–off method was used? Which method (allowance or direct write–off) more accurately reports the financial results?

MINI-EXERCISES

M8-1 Evaluating the Decision to Extend Credit

LO8-1

a. Nutware Productions Inc. generated sales of $30,000 and gross profit of $10,000 last year. The company estimates that it would have generated sales of $60,000 if it had extended credit, but this would involve additional costs for associated wages and bad debts totalling $25,000. Should the company extend credit?

b. Assume Reitmans (Canada) Limited currently allows customers to purchase merchandise using national credit cards like Visa and MasterCard, yet discontinued its own private credit card program. What pros and cons would lead Reitmans to continue with national credit cards but not its own private credit card program? Assume in its annual report for the year ended January 31, 2017, Reitmans removed $56 million of credit card transactions awaiting settlement from Accounts Receivable and instead reported them as Cash and Cash Equivalents. What characteristic of national credit cards makes this reclassification appropriate?

M8-2 Evaluating the Decision to Extend Credit

LO8-1

Last year, Pastis Productions reported $100,000 in sales and $40,000 in cost of goods sold. The company estimates it would have doubled its sales had it allowed customers to buy on credit, but it also would have incurred $50,000 in additional expenses relating to wages, bad debts, and interest. Should Pastis Productions extend credit?

M8-3 Reporting Accounts Receivable and Recording Write-Offs Using the Allowance Method

LO8-2

At the end of 2016, Donnelly Fitness Centre has adjusted balances of $800,000 in Accounts Receivable and $55,000 in Allowance for Doubtful Accounts. On January 2, 2017, the company learns that certain customer accounts are not collectable, so management authorizes a write–off of these accounts totalling $5,000.

a. Show how the company would have reported its receivable accounts on December 31, 2016. As of that date, what amount did Donnelly expect to collect?

b. Prepare the journal entry to write off the accounts on January 2, 2017.

c. Assuming no other transactions occurred between December 31, 2016, and January 3, 2017, show how Donnelly would have reported its receivable accounts on January 3, 2017. As of that date, what amount did Donnelly expect to collect? Has this changed from December 31, 2016? Explain why or why not.

M8-4 Recording Recoveries Using the Allowance Method

Let's go a bit further with the example in M8–3. Assume that on February 2, 2017, Donnelly received a payment of $500 from one of the customers whose balance had been written off. Prepare the journal entries to record this transaction.

M8-5 Recording Write-Offs and Bad Debt Expense Using the Allowance Method

Prepare journal entries for each transaction listed.

a. During the period, customer balances are written off in the amount of $17,000.
b. At the end of the period, bad debt expense is estimated to be $14,000.

M8-6 Determining Financial Statement Effects of Write-Offs and Bad Debt Expense Using the Allowance Method

Using the following categories, indicate the effects of the following transactions. Use + for increase and − for decrease, and indicate the accounts affected and the amounts.

Assets	=	Liabilities	+	Shareholders' Equity

a. During the period, customer balances are written off in the amount of $10,000.
b. At the end of the period, the bad debt expense is estimated to be $8,000.

M8-7 Estimating Bad Debts Using the Percentage of Credit Sales Method

Assume Simple Co. had credit sales of $250,000 and cost of goods sold of $150,000 for the period. Simple uses the percentage of credit sales method and estimates that ½ percent of credit sales would result in uncollectable accounts. Before the end–of–period adjustment is made, the Allowance for Doubtful Accounts has a credit balance of $250.

a. What amount of Bad Debt Expense would the company record as an end–of–period adjustment?
b. Prepare the journal entry to record the end–of–period adjustment for bad debts.

M8-8 Estimating Bad Debts Using the Aging Method

Assume that Simple Co. had credit sales of $250,000 and cost of goods sold of $150,000 for the period. Simple uses the aging method and estimates that the appropriate ending balance in the Allowance for Doubtful Accounts is $1,600. Before the end–of–period adjustment is made, the Allowance for Doubtful Accounts has a credit balance of $250.

a. What amount of Bad Debt Expense would the company record as an end–of–period adjustment?
b. Prepare the journal entry to record the end–of–period adjustment for bad debts.

M8-9 Using the Interest Formula to Compute Interest

Complete the following table by computing the missing amounts (?) for the following inde–pendent cases.

Principal Amount on Note Receivable	Annual Interest Rate	Time Period	Interest Earned
a. $100,000	10%	6 months	?
b. ?	10%	12 months	$4,000
c. $50,000	?	9 months	$3,000

M8-10 Recording Note Receivable Transactions

Nova Corporation hired a new product manager and agreed to provide her a $20,000 relocation loan on a six–month, 7 percent note. Prepare journal entries to record the following transactions for Nova Corporation. Rather than use letters to reference each transaction, use the date of the transaction.

a. The company loans the money on January 1, 2016.
b. The new employee pays Nova the full principal and interest on its maturity date.

M8-11 Recording Note Receivable Transactions

LO8-3

RecRoom Equipment Company received an $8,000, six—month, 6 percent note to settle an $8,000 unpaid balance owed by a customer. Prepare journal entries to record the following transactions for RecRoom. Rather than use letters to reference each transaction, use the date of the transaction.

a. The note is accepted by RecRoom on November 1, 2017, causing the company to increase its Notes Receivable and decrease its Accounts Receivable.
b. RecRoom adjusts its records for interest earned to December 31, 2017.
c. RecRoom receives the principal and interest on the note's maturity date.

M8-12 Reporting Accounts and Notes Receivable in a Classified Balance Sheet

LO8-2

Assume that Caterpillar, Inc. reported the following accounts and amounts (in millions) in its December 31, 2017, year—end financial statements. Prepare the current assets section of a classified balance sheet. Assume that the Allowance for Doubtful Accounts relates to Accounts Receivable rather than Notes Receivable.

Accounts Payable	$ 4,827	Long-Term Debt	$22,834
Accounts Receivable	9,788	Long-Term Notes Receivable	15,743
Accumulated Depreciation	10,963	Notes Receivable—Current	8,731
Allowance for Doubtful Accounts	391	Other Current Assets	1,988
Cash and Cash Equivalents	2,736	Other Current Liabilities	14,033
Inventories	8,781	Other Non-current Assets	9,105
Loans Payable—Current	7,209	Property, Plant, and Equipment	23,487

M8-13 Determining the Effects of Credit Policy Changes on Receivables Turnover Ratio and Days to Collect

LO8-4

Indicate the most likely effect of the following changes in credit policy on the receivables turnover ratio and days to collect (+ for increase, − for decrease, and NE for no effect).
  a. Granted credit to less creditworthy customers
  b. Granted credit with shorter payment deadlines
  c. Increased effectiveness of collection methods

M8-14 Evaluating the Effect of Factoring on the Receivables Turnover Ratio and Computing the Cost of Factoring

LO8-4

After noting that its receivables turnover ratio had declined, Imperative Company decided for the first time in the company's history to sell $500,000 of receivables to a factoring company. The factor charges a factoring fee of 3 percent of the receivables sold. How much cash does Imperative receive on the sale? Calculate the factoring fee and describe how it is reported by Imperative Company. All else equal, how will this affect Imperative's receivables turnover ratio in the future?

M8-15 (Supplement 8A) Recording Write-Offs and Reporting Accounts Receivable Using the Direct Write-Off Method

Complete all the requirements of M8–3, except assume that Extreme Fitness uses the direct write—off method. Note that this means Extreme does not have an Allowance for Doubtful Accounts balance.

EXERCISES

E8-1 Recording Bad Debt Expense Estimates and Write-Offs Using the Aging of Receivables Method

LO8-2

At the end of 2017, Blackberry Hill Productions, Inc. used the aging of accounts receivable method to estimate that its Allowance for Doubtful Accounts should be $19,750. The account had an unadjusted credit balance of $10,000 at December 31, 2017.

Required:

Prepare journal entries for each transaction.

1. The appropriate bad debt adjustment was recorded for the year 2017.
2. On January 31, 2018, an account receivable for $1,000 from March 2017 was determined to be uncollectable and was written off.

LO8-2 **E8-2 Determining Financial Statement Effects of Bad Debt Expense Estimates and Write-Offs**

For each transaction listed in E8−1, indicate the amount and direction (+ or −) of effects on the financial statement accounts and on the overall accounting equation.

Assets	=	Liabilities	+	Shareholders' Equity

LO8-2 **E8-3 Recording, Reporting, and Evaluating a Bad Debt Estimate Using the Percentage of Credit Sales Method**

During the year ended December 31, 2017, Kelly's Camera Equipment had sales revenue of $170,000, of which $85,000 was on credit. At the start of 2017, Accounts Receivable showed a $10,000 debit balance, and the Allowance for Doubtful Accounts showed an $800 credit balance. Collections of accounts receivable during 2017 amounted to $68,000.

Use the following data for 2017 to answer the questions:

a. On December 10, 2017, a customer balance of $1,500 from a prior year was determined to be uncollectable, so it was written off.
b. On December 31, 2017, a decision was made to continue the accounting policy of basing estimated bad debt losses on 2 percent of credit sales for the year.

Required:

1. Give the required journal entries for the two events in December 2017.
2. Show how the amounts related to Accounts Receivable and Bad Debt Expense would be reported on the balance sheet and income statement for 2017.
3. On the basis of the data available, does the 2 percent rate appear to be reasonable? Explain.

LO8-2 **E8-4 Recording Write-Offs and Recoveries**

Prior to recording the following, E. Perry Electronics, Incorporated, had a credit balance of $2,000 in its Allowance for Doubtful Accounts.

Required:

Prepare journal entries for each transaction.

1. On August 31, 2017, a customer balance for $300 from a prior year was determined to be uncollectable and was written off.
2. On December 15, 2017, the customer balance for $300 written off on August 31, 2017, was collected in full.

LO8-2 **E8-5 Determining Financial Statement Effects of Write-Offs and Recoveries**

For each transaction listed in E8−4, indicate the amount and direction (+ or −) of effects on the financial statement accounts and on the overall accounting equation.

Assets	=	Liabilities	+	Shareholders' Equity

LO8-2 **E8-6 Computing Bad Debt Expense Using Aging of Accounts Receivable Method**

Young and Old Corporation (YOC) uses two aging categories to estimate uncollectable accounts. Accounts less than sixty days are considered young and have a 5 percent uncollectable rate. Accounts more than sixty days are considered old and have a 35 percent uncollectable rate.

Required:

1. If YOC has $100,000 of young accounts and $400,000 of old accounts, how much should be reported in the Allowance for Doubtful Accounts?
2. If YOC's Allowance for Doubtful Accounts currently has an unadjusted credit balance of $40,000, how much should be credited to the account?
3. If YOC's Allowance for Doubtful Accounts has an unadjusted debit balance of $5,000, how much should be credited to the account?
4. Explain how YOC's Allowance for Doubtful Accounts could have a debit balance.

Check Figure
[Req. 3]:
Credit to
Allowance for
Doubtful Accounts
= $150,000

E8-7 Computing Bad Debt Expense Using Aging of Accounts Receivable Method

LO8-2

Brown Cow Dairy uses the aging approach to estimate Bad Debt Expense. The balance of each account receivable is aged on the basis of three time periods as follows: (1) 1 to 30 days old, $12,000; (2) 31 to 90 days old, $5,000; and (3) more than 90 days old, $3,000. Experience has shown that for each age group, the average loss rate on the amount of the receivable due to uncollectibility is (1) 3 percent, (2) 15 percent, and (3) 30 percent, respectively. At December 31, 2017 (end of the current year), the Allowance for Doubtful Accounts balance was $800 (credit) before the end–of–period adjusting entry is made.

Required:

1. Prepare a schedule to estimate an appropriate year–end balance for the Allowance for Doubtful Accounts.
2. What amount should be recorded as Bad Debt Expense for the current year?
3. If the unadjusted balance in the Allowance for Doubtful Accounts was a $600 debit balance, what would be the amount of Bad Debt Expense in 2017?

E8-8 Recording and Reporting Allowance for Doubtful Accounts Using the Percentage of Credit Sales and Aging of Accounts Receivable Methods

LO8-2

Innovations Corp (IC) uses the percentage of credit sales method to estimate bad debts each month and then uses the aging method at year–end. During November 2017, IC sold services on account for $100,000 and estimated that ½ of one percent of those sales would be uncollectible. At its December 31 year–end, total Accounts Receivable is $89,000, aged as follows: (1) 1 to 30 days old, $75,000; (2) 31 to 90 days old, $10,000; and (3) more than 90 days old, $4,000. Experience has shown that for each age group, the average rate of uncollectibility is (1) 1 percent, (2) 15 percent, and (3) 40 percent, respectively. Before the end–of–year adjusting entry is made, the Allowance for Doubtful Accounts has a $1,600 credit balance at December 31, 2017.

Required:

1. Prepare the November 2017 adjusting entry for bad debts.
2. Prepare a schedule to estimate an appropriate year–end balance for the Allowance for Doubtful Accounts.
3. Prepare the December 31, 2017, adjusting entry.
4. Show how the various accounts related to accounts receivable should be shown on the December 31, 2017, balance sheet.

Check Figure
[Req. 3]:
Bad Debt Expense
= $2,250

E8-9 Recording and Determining the Effects of Write-Offs, Recoveries, and Bad Debt Expense Estimates on the Balance Sheet and Income Statement

LO8-2

Academic Dishonesty Investigations Ltd. operates a plagiarism detection service for universities and colleges.

Required:

1. Prepare journal entries for each transaction below.
   a. On March 31, ten customers were billed for detection services totalling $25,000.
   b. On October 31, a customer balance of $1,500 from a prior year was determined to be uncollectable and was written off.
   c. On December 15, a customer paid an old balance of $900, which had been written off in a prior year.
   d. On December 31, $500 of bad debts were estimated and recorded for the year.

2. Complete the following table, indicating the amount and effect (+ for increase, − for decrease, and NE for no effect) of each transaction. Ignore income taxes.

Transaction	Net Receivables	Net Sales	Income from Operations
(a)			
(b)			
(c)			
(d)			

LO8-3 **E8-10 Recording Note Receivable Transactions, Including Accrual Adjustment for Interest**

The following transactions took place for Christoff Solutions Ltd.

2016

July 1 Loaned $70,000 to an employee of the company and received back a one−year, 10 percent note.
Dec. 31 Accrued interest on the note.

2017

July 1 Received interest and principal on the note. (No interest has been recorded since December 31.)

Required:

Prepare the journal entries that Christoff Solutions Ltd. would record for the above transactions.

LO8-3 **E8-11 Recording Note Receivable Transactions, Including Accrual Adjustment for Interest**

The following transactions took place for Parkell's Grocery.

Jan. 1 Loaned $50,000 to a company cashier and received back a one−year, 7 percent note
June 30 Accrued interest on the note
Dec. 31 Received interest and principal on the note.(No interest has been recorded since June 30.)

Required:

Prepare the journal entries that Parkell's Grocery would record for the above transactions.

LO8-3 **E8-12 Recording Note Receivable Transactions, Including Accrual Adjustment for Interest**

To attract retailers to its shopping centre, the Makepiece Mall is going to lend money to tenants under formal contracts, provided that they use it to renovate their store space. On November 1, 2017, the company loaned $100,000 to a new tenant on a one−year note with a stated annual interest rate of 6 percent. Interest is to be received by Makepiece Mall on April 30, 2018, and at maturity on October 31, 2018.

Required:

Prepare journal entries that Makepiece Mall would record related to this note on the following dates: (*a*) November 1, 2017; (*b*) December 31, 2017 (Makepiece Mall's fiscal year−end); (*c*) April 30, 2018; and (*d*) October 31, 2018.

LO8-2, 8-4 **E8-13 Using Financial Statement Disclosures to Infer Write-Offs and Bad Debt Expense and to Calculate the Receivables Turnover Ratio**

Microsoft Corporation develops, produces, and markets a wide range of computer software, including the Windows operating system. Assume Microsoft reported the following information about Net Sales Revenue and Accounts Receivable (in millions).

	June 30, 2017	June 30, 2016
Accounts Receivable, Net of Allowances of $153 and $117	$13,589	$11,338
Net Revenues	60,420	51,122

Assume that, according to its annual report, Microsoft recorded Bad Debt Expense of $88 million and did not recover any previously written off accounts during the year ended June 30, 2017.

Required:

1. What amount of accounts receivable was written off during the year ended June 30, 2017?
2. What was Microsoft's receivables turnover ratio (to one decimal place) in the current year?
3. Does your answer in requirement 2 suggest the collectibility of Accounts Receivable improved (or deteriorated) in 2017, relative to 2016 when the turnover was 4.6?

E8-14 Using Financial Statement Disclosures to Infer Bad Debt Expense

LO8-2

Assume the 2017 annual report for Sears Holding Corporation contained the following information (in millions):

	2017	2016
Accounts Receivable	$881	$781
Allowance for Doubtful Accounts	42	37
Accounts Receivable, Net	$839	$744

A footnote to the financial statements disclosed that accounts receivable write–offs amounted to $13 million during 2017 and $3 million during 2016. Assume that Sears did not record any recoveries.

Required:

Determine the Bad Debt Expense for 2017 based on the above facts.

E8-15 Determining the Effects of Uncollectable Accounts on the Receivables Turnover Ratio

LO8-2, 8-4

Refer to the information about Sears given in E8–14.

Required:

Complete the following table indicating the direction of the effect (+ for increase, − for decrease, and NE for no effect) of each transaction during 2017:

Transaction	Net Credit Sales	Average Net Accounts Receivable	Receivables Turnover Ratio
a. Writing off $13,000,000 in uncollectable accounts.			
b. Recording bad debt expense.			

LO8-4   **E8-16 Analyzing and Interpreting Receivables Turnover Ratio and Days to Collect**

Assume that a recent annual report for FedEx Corporation contained the following data (in millions):

	May 31	
	2017	**2016**
Accounts Receivable	$ 4,517	$ 4,078
Less: Allowance for Doubtful Accounts	158	136
Accounts Receivable, Net of Allowance	$ 4,359	$ 3,942
Net Sales (assume all on credit)	$37,953	$35,214

**Check Figure
[Req. 1]:**
Receivables
Turnover Ratio = 9.1
times

Required:

1. Determine the receivables turnover ratio and days to collect for 2017. Round your answers to one decimal place.
2. Explain the meaning of each number.

LO8-2, 8-4   **E8-17 Determining the Effects of Bad Debt Write-Offs on the Receivables Turnover Ratio**

During 2017, Jesse Jericho Enterprises Corporation recorded credit sales of $650,000. At the beginning of the year, Accounts Receivable, Net of Allowance was $50,000. At the end of the year, *after* the Bad Debt Expense adjustment was recorded but *before* any bad debts had been written off, Accounts Receivable, Net of Allowance was $49,000.

Required:

1. Assume that on December 31, 2017, accounts receivable totalling $6,000 for the year were determined to be uncollectable and written off. What was the receivables turnover ratio for 2017? Round to one decimal place.
2. Assume instead that on December 31, 2017, $7,000 of accounts receivable was determined to be uncollectable and written off. What was the receivables turnover ratio for 2017? Round to one decimal place.
3. Explain why the answers to requirements 1 and 2 differ or do not differ.

LO8-S1   **E8-18 (Supplement 8A) Recording Write-Offs and Reporting Accounts Receivable Using the Direct Write-Off Method**

Trevorson Electronics is a small company privately owned by Jon Trevorson, an electrician who installs wiring in new homes. Because the company's financial statements are prepared for internal purposes only, Jon uses the direct write–off method. During 2016, its first year of operations, Trevorson Electronics sold $30,000 of services on account. The company collected $26,000 of these receivables during the year, and Jon believed that the remaining $4,000 was fully collectable. In 2017, Jon discovered that none of the $4,000 would be collected, so he wrote off the entire amount. To make matters worse, Jon sold only $5,000 of services during the year.

Required:

**Check Figure
[Req. 2]:**
2017 Net Income =
$1,000

1. Prepare journal entries to record the transactions in 2016 and 2017.
2. Using only the information provided (ignore other operating expenses), prepare comparative income statements for 2016 and 2017. Was 2016 really as profitable as indicated by its income statement? Was 2017 quite as bad as indicated by its income statement? What should Jon do if he wants better information for assessing his company's ability to generate profit?

COACHED PROBLEMS

CP8-1 Recording Accounts Receivable Transactions Using the Percentage of Credit Sales and Aging of Accounts Receivable Methods

The A.T. Cross Company is well known for its Cross pens. The company recently reported the following amounts in its unadjusted trial balance as of December 31.

	Debits	Credits
Accounts Receivable	$30,691,000	
Allowance for Doubtful Accounts		$ 952,000
Sales Revenue		158,312,000

Required:

1. Assume Cross uses ¼ of 1 percent of sales to estimate its bad debt expense for the year. Prepare the adjusting journal entry required at December 31, for recording Bad Debt Expense.

   TIP: The percentage of credit sales method directly calculates Bad Debt Expense.

2. Assume that Cross uses the aging of accounts receivable method and estimates that $1,007,000 of Accounts Receivable will be uncollectible. Prepare the adjusting journal entry required at December 31 for recording bad debt expense.

   TIP: The aging of accounts receivable method focuses on calculating what the adjusted Allowance for Doubtful Accounts balance should be. You need to consider the existing balance when determining the adjustment. 1007 000 - 952 000

3. Repeat requirement 2, except this time assume the unadjusted balance in Cross's Allowance for Doubtful Accounts at December 31, was a debit balance of $10,050.

4. If one of Cross's main customers declared bankruptcy, what journal entry would be used to write off its $10,000 balance?

CP8-2 Interpreting Disclosure of Allowance for Doubtful Accounts

McDonald's Corporation is the world's largest chain of hamburger fast–food restaurants. It has an Allowance for Doubtful Accounts that relates to its accounts and notes receivable. Assume that in its 2017 financial statements, McDonald's reported the following changes in the Allowance for Doubtful Accounts (in thousands):

Balance at Beginning of Period	Charged to Bad Debt Expense	Amounts Written Off	Balance at End of Period
$711	$341	$335	$717

Required:

1. Create a T–account for the Allowance for Doubtful Accounts and enter into it the amounts from the above schedule. Then write the T–account in equation format to prove that the above items account for the changes in the account.

   TIP: The allowance increases when estimates are charged to Bad Debt Expense and when recoveries are reported. The allowance decreases when accounts are written off.

Receivables, Bad Debt Expense, and Interest Revenue   CHAPTER 8   409

2. Record summary journal entries related to (*a*) estimating bad debt expense, and (*b*) write–offs of specific balances during the year.

> TIP: Use the generic account name Receivables to refer to the combined accounts receivable and notes receivable.

3. If McDonald's had written off an additional $20,000 of accounts receivable during the period and the ending allowance balance was estimated to be $717, how would Net Receivables have been affected? How would Net Income have been affected? Explain why.

LO8-3   **CP8-3 Recording Notes Receivable Transactions**

Jung & Newbicalm Advertising (JNA) recently hired a new creative director, Howard Rachell, for its Bay Street office in Toronto. To persuade Howard to move from Vancouver, JNA agreed to advance him $100,000 on April 30, 2017, on a one–year, 10 percent note, with interest payments required on October 31, 2017, and April 30, 2018. JNA issues quarterly financial statements on March 31, June 30, September 30, and December 31.

Required:

1. Prepare the journal entry that JNA will make to record the promissory note created on April 30, 2017.

> TIP: See Demonstration Case B for a similar problem.

2. Prepare the journal entries that JNA will make to record the interest accruals at each quarter end and interest payments at each payment date.

> TIP: Interest receivable will be accrued at the end of each quarter, and then will be reduced when the interest payment is received.

3. Prepare the journal entry that JNA will make to record the principal payment at the maturity date.

LO8-2, 8-3   **CP8-4 Accounting for Accounts and Notes Receivable Transactions**

P & K Consultants has provided business consulting services for several years. The company uses the percentage of credit sales method to estimate bad debts for internal monthly report–ing purposes. At the end of each quarter, the company adjusts its records using the aging of accounts receivable method. The company entered into the following selected transactions during the first quarter of 2017.

a. During January, the company provided services for $200,000 on credit.
b. On January 31, the company estimated bad debts using 1 percent of credit sales.
c. On February 4, the company collected $100,000 of accounts receivable.
d. On February 15, the company wrote off a $500 account receivable.
e. During February, the company provided services for $150,000 on credit.
f. On February 28, the company estimated bad debts using 1 percent of credit sales.
g. On March 1, the company loaned $12,000 to an employee who signed a 10 percent note, due in three months.
h. On March 15, the company collected $500 on the account written off one month earlier.
i. On March 31, the company accrued interest earned on the note.
j. On March 31, the company adjusted for uncollectable accounts, based on the following aging analysis, which includes the preceding transactions (as well as others not listed). Prior to the adjustment, Allowance for Doubtful Accounts has an unadjusted credit balance of $6,000.

| Customer | Total | Number of Days Unpaid | | | |
		0–30	31–60	61–90	Over 90
Arrow Ergonomics	$ 1,000	$ 500	$ 400	$ 100	
Asymmetry Architecture	2,000				$2,000
Others (not shown to save space)	85,000	34,000	42,000	5,000	4,000
Weight Whittlers	2,000	2,000			
Total Accounts Receivable	**$90,000**	**$36,500**	**$ 42,400**	**$5,100**	**$6,000**
Estimated Uncollectable (%)		**2%**	**10%**	**20%**	**40%**

Required:

1. For items (*a*) through (*j*), analyze the amount and direction (+ or −) of effects on specific financial statement accounts and the overall accounting equation, and prepare journal entries.
2. Show how the receivables related to these transactions would be reported in the current assets section of a classified balance sheet.
3. Name the accounts related to Accounts Receivable and Note Receivable that would be reported on the income statement and indicate whether they would appear before, or after, Income from Operations.

CP8-5 Analyzing Allowance for Doubtful Accounts, Receivables Turnover Ratio, and Days to Collect   LO8-4

Mattel and Hasbro are two of the largest and most successful toymakers in the world, in terms of the products they sell and their receivables management practices. To evaluate their ability to collect on credit sales, consider the following information assuming it was reported in their annual reports (amounts in millions).

	Mattel			Hasbro		
Fiscal Year Ended:	**2017**	**2016**	**2015**	**2017**	**2016**	**2015**
Net Sales	$5,856	$5,431	$5,918	$4,002	$4,068	$4,022
Accounts Receivable	1,168	774	900	992	1,072	644
Allowance for Doubtful Accounts	22	25	26	31	33	32
Accounts Receivable, Net of Allowance	1,146	749	874	961	1,039	612

Required:

1. Calculate the receivables turnover ratios and days to collect for Mattel and Hasbro for 2017 and 2016. (Round your final answers to one decimal place.)
   TIP: In your calculations, use *average* Accounts Receivable, Net of Allowance.
2. Which of the companies was quicker to convert its receivables into cash in 2017? in 2016?

GROUP A PROBLEMS

PA8-1 Recording Accounts Receivable Transactions Using the Aging Method   LO8-2

Kraft Foods Inc. is the second−largest food company in the world. Assume the company recently reported the following amounts in its unadjusted trial balance (in millions) as of December 31, 2017:

	Debits	Credits
Accounts Receivable	$4,833	
Allowance for Doubtful Accounts		$ 129
Sales (assume all on credit)		42,201

Required:

1. Assume Kraft uses ½ of 1 percent of sales to estimate its Bad Debt Expense for the year. Prepare the adjusting journal entry required for the year, assuming no Bad Debt Expense has been recorded yet.
2. Assume instead that Kraft uses the aging of accounts receivable method and estimates that $233 million of its Accounts Receivable will be uncollectable. Prepare the adjusting journal entry required at December 31, 2017, for recording Bad Debt Expense.
3. Repeat requirement 3, this time assuming the unadjusted balance in Kraft's Allowance for Doubtful Accounts at December 31, 2017, was a debit balance of $20 million.
4. If one of Kraft's main customers declared bankruptcy in 2018, what journal entry would be used to write off its $15 million balance?

Check Figure
[Req. 1]:
Bad Debt Expense
= $211

PA8-2 Interpreting Disclosure of Allowance for Doubtful Accounts

Wheelys, Inc. designs and sells footwear with a wheel in the heel, worn by sometimes—annoying kids at shopping malls. It recently disclosed the following information concerning the Allowance for Doubtful Accounts in its annual report.

SCHEDULE II Valuation and Qualifying Accounts (dollars in thousands)				
Allowance for Doubtful Accounts	Balance at Beginning of Year	Additions Charged to Bad Debt Expense	Write-Offs	Balance at End of Year
2017	$ 189	$ 0	$ 69	$ 120
2016	410	333	554	189
2015	130	435	?	410

Required:

1. Create a T—account for the Allowance for Doubtful Accounts and enter into it the 2017 amounts from the above schedule. Then write the T—account in equation format to prove that the above items account for the changes in the account.
2. Wheelys reported sales of $70 million in 2017. Why might its Bad Debt Expense equal zero that year?
3. Record summary journal entries for 2016 related to (a) estimating Bad Debt Expense and (b) writing off specific balances.
4. Supply the missing dollar amount noted by ? for 2015.
5. If Wheelys had written off an additional $20 of Accounts Receivable during 2017 and the ending allowance balance was estimated to be $120 (dollars in thousands), how would Net Receivables have been affected? How would Net Income have been affected? Explain why.

PA8-3 Recording Notes Receivable Transactions

C&Q Marketing (CQM) recently hired a new marketing director, Jeff Otos, for its main office. As part of the arrangement, CQM agreed on February 28, 2017, to advance Jeff $50,000 on a one—year, 8 percent note, with interest to be paid at maturity on February 28, 2018. CQM prepares financial statements on June 30 and December 31.

Required:

1. Prepare the journal entry that CSM will make when the note is established.
2. Prepare the journal entries that CSM will make to accrue interest on June 30 and December 31.
3. Prepare the journal entry that CSM will make to record the interest and principal pay—ments on February 28, 2018.

PA8-4 Accounting for Accounts and Notes Receivable Transactions

LEVEL
UP

Web Wizard, Inc., has provided information technology services for several years. The com—pany uses the percentage of credit sales method to estimate bad debts for internal monthly reporting purposes. At the end of each quarter, the company adjusts its records using the aging of accounts receivable method. The company entered into the following selected trans—actions during the first quarter of 2017:

a. During January, the company provided services for $40,000 on credit.
b. On January 31, the company estimated bad debts using 1 percent of credit sales.
c. On February 4, the company collected $20,000 of accounts receivable.
d. On February 15, the company wrote off a $100 account receivable.
e. During February, the company provided services for $30,000 on credit.

f. On February 28, the company estimated bad debts using 1 percent of credit sales.

g. On March 1, the company loaned $2,400 to an employee who signed a 6 percent note, due in six months.

h. On March 15, the company collected $100 on the account written off one month earlier.

i. On March 31, the company adjusted for uncollectable accounts, based on the following aging analysis, which includes the preceding transactions (as well as others not listed). Prior to the adjustment, Allowance for Doubtful Accounts had an unadjusted credit balance of $1,200.

j. On March 31, the company accrued interest earned on the note.

Customer	Total	Number of Days Unpaid			
		0–30	31–60	61–90	Over 90
Altavista Tourism	$ 200	$ 100	$ 80	$ 20	
Bayling Bungalows	400				$ 400
Others (not shown to save space)	17,000	6,800	8,400	1,000	800
Xciting Xcursions		400			
Total Accounts Receivable	**$18,000**	**$7,300**	**$8,480**	**$1,020**	**$1,200**
Estimated Uncollectable (%)		**2%**	**10%**	**20%**	**40%**

Required:

1. For items (a) through (j), analyze the amount and direction (+ or −) of effects on specific financial statement accounts and the overall accounting equation and prepare journal entries.

2. Show how the receivables related to these transactions would be reported in the current assets section of a classified balance sheet.

3. Name the accounts related to Accounts Receivable and Note Receivable that would be reported on the income statement and indicate whether they would appear before or after Income from Operations.

PA8-5 Analyzing Allowance for Doubtful Accounts, Receivables Turnover Ratio, and Days to Collect   LO8-4

eXcel

Coca–Cola and PepsiCo are two of the largest and most successful beverage companies in the world in terms of the products that they sell and their receivables management practices. To evaluate their ability to collect on credit sales, consider the following information assumed to have been reported in their 2017, 2016, and 2015 annual reports (amounts in millions).

Fiscal Year Ended:	Coca-Cola			PepsiCo		
	2017	2016	2015	2017	2016	2015
Net Sales	$31,944	$28,857	$24,088	$43,251	$39,474	$35,137
Accounts Receivable	3,141	3,373	2,650	3,784	3,670	3,147
Allowance for Doubtful Accounts	51	56	63	70	69	64
Accounts Receivable, Net of Allowance	3,090	3,317	2,587	3,714	3,601	3,083

Required:

1. Calculate the receivables turnover ratios and days to collect for Coca–Cola and PepsiCo for 2017 and 2016. (Round to one decimal place.)

2. Which of the companies is quicker to convert its receivables into cash?

Check Figure:
Coca-Cola's 2016 Days to Collect = 37.2 days

GROUP B PROBLEMS

LO8-2   **PB8-1 Recording Accounts Receivable Transactions Using the Allowance Method**

Intel Corporation is a well–known supplier of computer chips, boards, systems, and software building blocks. Assume the company recently reported the following amounts (in millions) in its unadjusted trial balance at its year–end of December 27, 2017:

	Debits	Credits
Accounts Receivable	$1,729	
Allowance for Doubtful Accounts		$ 17
Sales (assume all on credit)		37,586

Required:

1. Assume Intel uses ¼ of 1 percent of sales to estimate its Bad Debt Expense for the year. Prepare the adjusting journal entry required for the year, assuming no Bad Debt Expense has been recorded yet.
2. Now assume that Intel uses the aging of accounts receivable method and estimates that $40 million of its Accounts Receivable will be uncollectable. Prepare the adjusting journal entry required at December 27, 2017, for recording Bad Debt Expense.
3. Repeat requirement 2, except this time assume the unadjusted balance in Intel's Allowance for Doubtful Accounts at December 27, 2017, was a debit balance of $20 million.
4. If one of Intel's main customers declared bankruptcy in 2018, what journal entry would be used to write off its $15 million balance?

LO8-2   **PB8-2 Interpreting Disclosure of Allowance for Doubtful Accounts**

Xerox Corporation is the company that made the photocopier popular, although it now describes itself as a technology and services enterprise that helps businesses deploy document management strategies and improve productivity. Assume it recently disclosed the following information concerning the allowance for doubtful accounts in its annual report.

		SCHEDULE II		
		Valuation and Qualifying Accounts		
		(in millions)		
Allowance for Doubtful Accounts	**Balance at Beginning of Year**	**Additions Charged to Bad Debt Expense**	**Write-Offs**	**Balance at End of Year**
2017	$ 128	$ 72	$ 69	$ 131
2016	116	?	42	128
2015	136	27	?	116

Required:

1. Create a T–account for the Allowance for Doubtful Accounts and enter into it the 2017 amounts from the above schedule. Then write the T–account in equation format to prove that the above items account for the changes in the account.
2. Record summary journal entries for 2017 related to (a) estimating bad debt expense and (b) writing off specific balances.
3. Supply the missing dollar amounts noted by ? for 2016 and 2015.
4. If Xerox had written off an additional $20 million of accounts receivable during 2017 and the ending allowance balance was estimated to be $131 million, how would that have affected Net Accounts Receivable? How would the write–off have affected Net Income? Explain.

Check Figure [Req. 3]:
2016 Additions Charged to Bad Debt Expense = $54 million

PB8-3 Recording Notes Receivable Transactions

Stintson Company recently agreed to loan an employee $100,000 for the purchase of a new house. The loan was executed on May 31, 2017, and is a one–year, 6 percent note, with interest payments required on November 30, 2017, and May 31, 2018. Stinson issues quarterly financial statements on March 31, June 30, September 30, and December 31.

Required:

1. Prepare the journal entry that Stinson will make when the note is established.
2. Prepare the journal entries that Stinson will make to record the interest accruals at each quarter end and interest payments at each payment date.
3. Prepare the journal entry that Stinson will make to record the principal payment at the maturity date.

PB8-4 Accounting for Accounts and Notes Receivable Transactions

Fleet Events Corporation has provided event–planning services for several years. The company uses the percentage of credit sales method to estimate bad debts for internal monthly reporting purposes. At the end of each quarter, the company adjusts its records using the aging of accounts receivable method. The company entered into the following selected transactions during the first quarter of 2017:

a. During January, the company provided services for $300,000 on credit.
b. On January 31, the company estimated bad debts using 1 percent of credit sales.
c. On February 4, the company collected $250,000 of accounts receivable.
d. On February 15, the company wrote off a $3,000 account receivable.
e. During February, the company provided services for $250,000 on credit.
f. On February 28, the company estimated bad debts using 1 percent of credit sales.
g. On March 1, the company loaned $15,000 to an employee who signed a 4 percent note, due in nine months.
h. On March 15, the company collected $3,000 on the account written off one month earlier.
i. On March 31, the company accrued interest earned on the note.
j. On March 31, the company adjusted for uncollectable accounts, based on the following aging analysis, which includes the preceding transactions (as well as others not listed). Prior to the adjustment, Allowance for Doubtful Accounts had an unadjusted credit balance of $9,000.

Customer	Total	Number of Days Unpaid			
		0–30	31–60	61–90	Over 90
Aerosmit	$ 2,000	$ 1,000	$ 1,000		
Biggie Small	2,000			$ 1,000	$ 1,000
Others (not shown to save space)	99,000	39,000	42,000	9,000	9,000
ZZ Tip	7,000	7,000			
Total Accounts Receivable	**$110,000**	**$47,000**	**$43,000**	**$10,000**	**$10,000**
Estimated Uncollectable (%)		**2%**	**10%**	**20%**	**40%**

Required:

1. For items (a) through (j), analyze the amount and direction (+ or −) of effects on specific financial statement accounts and the overall accounting equation, and prepare journal entries.
2. Show how the receivables related to these transactions would be reported in the current assets section of a classified balance sheet.
3. Name the accounts related to Accounts Receivable and Note Receivable that would be reported on the income statement and indicate whether they would appear before or after Income from Operations.

PB8-5 Analyzing Allowance for Doubtful Accounts, Receivables Turnover Ratio, and Days to Collect

Walmart and Target are two of the largest and most successful retail chains in the world. To evaluate their ability to collect on credit sales, consider the following fictional information reported in their annual reports (amounts in millions).

	Walmart			Target		
Fiscal Year Ended January 31:	**2017**	**2016**	**2015**	**2017**	**2016**	**2015**
Net Sales	$401,244	$374,307	$344,992	$62,894	$61,471	$57,878
Accounts Receivable, Net of Allowance	3,905	3,642	2,840	8,084	8,054	6,194

Check Figure:
Walmart's 2017
Receivables
Turnover Ratio =
106.3

Required:

1. Calculate the receivables turnover ratios and days to collect for Walmart and Target for the years ended January 31, 2017, and 2016. (Round to one decimal place.)
2. Which of the companies is quicker to convert its receivables into cash?
3. How did the economic difficulties in 2016 to 2017 affect the accounts receivable collections?

COMPREHENSIVE PROBLEMS

C8-1 Recording and Reporting Credit Sales and Bad Debts Using the Aging of Accounts Receivable Method (Chapters 6 and 8)

Okay Optical, Inc. (OOI) began operations in January 2017, selling inexpensive sunglasses to large retailers like Walmart and other smaller stores. Assume the following transactions occurred during its first six months of operations:

January 1	Sold merchandise to Walmart for $20,000; the cost of these goods to OOI was $12,000
February 12	Received payment in full from Walmart
March 1	1Sold merchandise to Tony's Pharmacy on account for $3,000; the cost of these goods to OOI was $1,400
April 1	Sold merchandise to Travis Pharmaco on account for $8,000; the cost to OOI was $4,400
May 1	Sold merchandise to Anjuli Stores on account for $2,000; the cost to OOI was $1,200
June 17	Received $6,500 on account from Travis Pharmaco

Required:

1. Complete the following aged listing of customer accounts at June 30.

		Unpaid Since			
Customer	Total Balance	June (one month)	May (two months)	April (three months)	March (over three months)
Anjuli Stores	$ 2,000		$ 2,000		
Tony's Pharmacy	3,000				$3,000
Travis Pharmaco					
Walmart					

2. Estimate the Allowance for Doubtful Accounts required at June 30, 2017, assuming the following uncollectable rates: one month, 1 percent; two months, 5 percent; three months, 20 percent; more than three months, 40 percent.

3. Show how OOI would report its accounts receivable on its June 30 balance sheet. What amounts would be reported on an income statement prepared for the six–month period ended June 30, 2017?

4. Bonus Question: In July 2017, OOI collected the balance due from Tony's Pharmacy but discovered that the balance due from Travis Pharmaco needed to be written off. Using this information, determine how accurate OOI was in estimating the Allowance for Doubtful Accounts needed for each of these two customers and in total.

C8-2 Evaluating Accounts Receivable Management (Chapters 6 and 8)

LO6-4, 8-4

WorldBiz operates divisions around the world. Its European division—EuroBiz (EB)—has recently reported the following information to you at WorldBiz's head office. You are trying to decide whether to direct your internal audit staff to investigate more closely.

From the Financial Statement Notes	2017	2016	2015
Accounts Receivable, Gross	$100,000	$ 60,000	$ 40,000
Allowance for Doubtful Accounts	(5,000)	(6,000)	(4,000)
Accounts Receivable, Net	95,000	54,000	36,000
Other Information Gathered			
Net Sales Revenue	$590,000	$540,000	$490,000
Accounts Receivable, Write-offs	6,900	6,100	6,100
Bad Debt Expense	5,900	8,100	7,350
Sales Discounts (2/10, n/30)	3,000	9,000	5,000

Required:

1. For each of the years, calculate the proportion of gross accounts receivable estimated to be uncollectible as allowed for in the Allowance for Doubtful Accounts. Round to one decimal place. Which year does not align with the other two?

2. For each of the years, calculate the proportion of Net Sales Revenue that Bad Debt Expense represents. Round to one decimal place. Which year does not align with the other two?

3. Did customers take greater (or lesser) advantage of sales discounts in 2017 than in 2016 and 2015? Does this indicate customers were more (or less) likely to promptly pay their balances in 2017 as compared to prior years?

4. Calculate the average days to collect in 2017 and 2016. Does this measure indicate custom–ers paid their balances faster (or slower) in 2017 as compared to 2016?

5. Given your answers to requirements 1 through 4, indicate (Yes or No) whether you should direct your internal audit staff to investigate EB's receivables management practices more closely.

SKILLS DEVELOPMENT CASES

S8-1 Finding Financial Information

LO8-2, 8-4

Refer to the summarized financial statements of The Home Depot in Appendix A at the back of this book.

1. Does the company report Accounts Receivable or an Allowance for Doubtful Accounts in its financial statements? Explain why it does or does not.

2. Compute the company's receivables turnover ratio and days to collect for the year ended January 29, 2017.

S8-2 Comparing Financial Information

Refer to the financial statements of Lowe's Companies, Inc. in Appendix B at the back of this book.

1. Does the company report Accounts Receivable or an Allowance for Doubtful Accounts in its financial statements? Explain why it does or does not.
2. Based on your observations for requirement 1, describe the usefulness of the receiv— ables turnover ratio and days to collect analyses for companies that are involved in home improvement retail sales.

S8-3 Internet-Based Team Research: Examining an Annual Report

As a team, select an industry to analyze. Using the Internet, each team member should access the annual report for one publicly traded company in the industry, with each member select— ing a different company. (See S1–3 in Chapter 1 for a description of possible resources for these tasks.)

Required:

1. On an individual basis, each team member should write a short report that incorporates the following:
   a. Calculate the receivables turnover ratio for the current and prior years. (To obtain the beginning accounts receivable number for the prior year, you will need the prior year's annual report.)
   b. Explain any change between the two years.
2. Then, as a team, write a short report comparing and contrasting your companies using these attributes. Discuss any patterns across the companies that you as a team observe. Provide potential explanations for any differences discovered.

S8-4 Ethical Decision Making: A Real-Life Example

You work for a company named MCI and you have been assigned the job of adjusting the company's Allowance for Doubtful Accounts balance. You obtained the following fictional aged listing of customer account balances for December.

		Accounts Receivable Aged Listing—December 31				
Customer	Total	0–30 days	31–60 days	61–90 days	91–120 days	Over 120 days
AfriTel	$ 40,000	$ 20,000	$ 10,000	$ 5,000	$ 5,000	$ 0
CT&T	0	0	0	0	0	0
GlobeCom	28,000	0	18,000	8,000	1,000	1,000
Hi-Rim	35,000	0	0	0	0	35,000
Level 8	162,000	63,000	44,000	29,000	13,000	13,000
NewTel	0	0	0	0	0	0
Telemedia	0	0	0	0	0	0
Others	485,000	257,000	188,000	28,000	11,000	1,000
TOTAL	**$750,000**	**$340,000**	**$260,000**	**$70,000**	**$30,000**	**$50,000**

Historically, bad debt loss rates for each aging category have been 1 percent (0 to 30 days), 5 percent (31 to 60 days), 8 percent (61 to 90 days), 10 percent (91 to 120 days), and 50 percent (over 120 days). Using these rates, you calculate a desired balance for the allowance. No entries have been made to the account since the end of November when the account had a credit balance of $46,820.

To check the reasonableness of the calculated balance, you obtain the aged listings for prior months (on the next page). As you scan the listings, you notice an interesting pattern. Several account balances, which had grown quite large by the end of November, disappeared in the final month of the year. You ask the accounts receivable manager, Walter Pavlo, what happened. He said the customers "obtained some financing...I guess out of nowhere," and they must have used it to pay off their account balances.

| | Total Accounts Receivable as of . . . | | | | | |
Customer	Q1 (March 31)	Q2 (June 30)	Q3 (September 30)	Q4 (October 31)	Q4 (November 30)	Q4 (December 31)
AfriTel	$ 19,000	$ 19,000	$ 21,000	$ 16,000	$ 20,000	$ 40,000
CT&T	0	30,000	100,000	100,000	100,000	0
GlobeCom	29,000	28,000	31,000	27,000	28,000	28,000
Hi-Rim	0	0	25,000	35,000	35,000	35,000
Level 8	229,000	229,000	198,000	174,000	190,000	162,000
NewTel	0	0	25,000	25,000	25,000	0
Telemedia	0	0	2,000	2,000	2,000	0
Others	524,000	489,000	375,000	503,000	463,000	485,000
TOTAL	**$ 801,000**	**$795,000**	**$ 777,000**	**$882,000**	**$863,000**	**$750,000**

Required:

1. Calculate the balance that should be reported in Allowance for Doubtful Accounts as of December 31.
2. Prepare the adjusting journal entry that is required on December 31.
3. Show how Accounts Receivable would be reported on the balance sheet at December 31.
4. If the balances for CT&T, NewTel, and Telemedia at the end of November continued to exist at the end of December (in the over 120 days category), what balance would you have estimated for the Allowance for Doubtful Accounts on December 31? Would this have changed MCI's net income in the current year? Explain.
5. A few days later, you overhear Pavlo talking about the account receivable from Hi–Rim. Apparently, MCI will soon loan Hi–Rim some money, creating a note receivable. Hi–Rim will use the money to pay off the Accounts Receivable balance it owes to MCI. You are aware that Pavlo receives a bonus based on MCI's net income. Should you investigate this matter further? Explain why or why not.

Epilogue: The events described above are based on an article in the June 10, 2002, issue of Forbes magazine that describes how, in the mid–1990s, Walter Pavlo was pressured to commit accounting fraud at MCI. Ironically, MCI was later taken over by WorldCom—the company that went on to commit the world's largest accounting fraud at the time.

S8-5 Ethical Decision Making: A Mini-Case

LO8-2

Having just graduated with a business degree, you're excited to begin working as a junior accountant at Sunny Optics, Inc. The company supplies lenses, frames, and sunglasses to opticians and retailers throughout the country. Sunny Optics is currently in the process of finalizing its third quarter (Q3) operating results. All Q3 adjusting entries have been made, except for bad debt expense. The preliminary income statement for Q3 is shown below, along with reported results for Q2 and Q1.

SUNNY OPTICS, INC.
Quarterly Income Statements
(in thousands)

	Q3 (preliminary)	Q2 (as reported)	Q1 (as reported)
Net Sales	$135,800	$135,460	$130,100
Cost of Goods Sold	58,400	58,250	55,990
Gross Profit	77,400	77,210	74,110
Selling, General, and Administrative Expenses	56,560	53,975	53,690
Bad Debt Expense	—	6,050	4,200
Income before Income Tax Expense	20,840	17,185	16,220
Income Tax Expense	5,620	5,155	5,020
Net Income	$ 15,220	$ 12,030	$ 11,200

The corporate controller has asked you to examine the Allowance for Doubtful Accounts and use the aged listing of accounts receivable to determine the adjustment needed to record estimated bad debts for the quarter. The controller states that, "Although our customers are somewhat slower in paying this quarter, we can't afford to increase the Allowance for Doubtful Accounts. If anything, we need to decrease it—an adjusted balance of about $8,000 is what I'd like to see. Play around with our estimated bad debt loss rates until you get it to work."

You were somewhat confused by what the controller told you, but you chalked it up to your lack of experience and decided to analyze the Allowance for Doubtful Accounts. You summarized the transactions recorded in the Allowance for Doubtful Accounts using the T–account below:

Allowance for Doubtful Accounts (xA)			
		7,900	January 1 bal. fwd.
Q1 Write–offs	4,110	4,200	Q1 Bad debts estimate
		7,990	March 31 adjusted
Q2 Write–offs	4,120	6,050	Q2 Bad debts estimate
		9,920	June 30 adjusted
Q3 Write–offs	4,030	—	
		5,890	September 30 unadjusted

Required:

1. What bad debts estimate for Q3 will produce the $8,000 balance that the controller would like to see?
2. Prepare the adjusting journal entry that would be required to record this estimate.
3. If the entry in requirement 2 is made, what does it do to the Q3 income and the trend in earnings? (Assume that Income Tax Expense does not change.)
4. Reconsider the statement the controller made to you. Is his suggestion a logical way to use the aging method to estimate bad debts?
5. What would be the Q3 net income if the Bad Debt Expense estimate was 4.5 percent of sales, as in Q2? What would this do to the trend in net income across the three quarters? (Assume that Income Tax Expense does not change.)
6. Is there any evidence of unethical behaviour in this case? Explain your answer.

S8-6 Critical Thinking: Analyzing

Problem Solved Company has been operating for five years as a software consulting firm. During this period, it has experienced rapid growth in Sales Revenue and in Accounts Receivable. To solve its growing receivables problem, the company hired you as its first corporate controller. You have put into place more stringent credit—granting and collection procedures that you expect will reduce receivables by approximately one—third by year—end. You have gathered the following data (in thousands of dollars) related to the changes:

	Beginning of Year	End of Year (projected)
Accounts Receivable	$1,000,608	$660,495
Less: Allowance for Doubtful Accounts	36,800	10,225
Accounts Receivable Net	$963,808	$650,270
	Prior Year	Current Year (projected)
Net Sales (assume all on credit)	$7,515,444	$7,015,069

Required:

1. Compute, to one decimal place, the accounts receivable turnover ratio based on three different assumptions:

    a. The stringent credit policies reduce Accounts Receivable, Net and decrease Net Sales as projected in the table.
    b. The stringent credit policies reduce Accounts Receivable, Net as projected in the table but do not decrease Net Sales from the prior year.
    c. The stringent credit policies are not implemented, resulting in no change from the beginning of the year Accounts Receivable balance and no change in Net Sales from the prior year.

2. On the basis of your findings in requirement 1, write a brief memo to the chief financial officer explaining the potential benefits and drawbacks of more stringent credit policies and how they are likely to affect the accounts receivable turnover ratio.

S8-7 Using an Aging Schedule to Estimate Bad Debts and Improve Collections from Customers

LO8-2

eXcel

Assume you were recently hired by Caffe D'Amore, the company that formulated the world's first flavoured instant cappuccino and now manufactures several lines of coffee—flavoured cappuccino mixes. Given the company's tremendous sales growth, Caffe D'Amore's receivables also have grown. Your job is to evaluate and improve collections of the company's receivables.

By analyzing collections of accounts receivable over the past five years, you were able to estimate bad debt loss rates for balances of varying ages. To estimate this year's uncollectable accounts, you jotted down the historical loss rates on the last page of a recent aged listing of outstanding customer balances (see below).

		Number of Days Unpaid				
Customer	Total	1–30	31–60	61–90	91–120	Over 120
Subtotal from previous page	$280,000	$150,000	$60,000	$40,000	$20,000	$10,000
Jumpy Jim's Coffee	1,000					1,000
Pasadena Coffee Company	24,500	14,500	8,000	2,000		
Phillips Blender House	17,000	12,000	4,000		1,000	
Pugsly's Trading Post	26,600	19,600	7,000			
Q-Coffee	12,400	8,400	3,000	1,000		
Special Sips	10,000	6,000	4,000			
Uneasy Isaac's	3,500	500				3,000
Total accounts receivable	**$375,000**	**$211,000**	**$86,000**	**$43,000**	**$21,000**	**$14,000**
Bad debt loss rates		1%	5%	10%	15%	30%

Required:

1. Enter the above totals in a spreadsheet and then insert formulas to calculate the total estimated uncollectable balance.

2. Prepare the year—end adjusting journal entry to adjust the Allowance for Doubtful Accounts to the balance you calculated above. Assume the allowance account has an unad—justed credit balance of $8,000.

3. Of the customer account balances shown above on the last page of the aged listing, which should be your highest priority for contacting and pursuing collection?

4. Assume Jumpy Jim's Coffee account is determined to be uncollectable. Prepare the journal entry to write off the entire account balance.

CONTINUING CASES

LO8-2, 8-4 **CC8-1 Accounting for Receivables and Uncollectable Accounts**

The following transactions occurred over the months of September to December 2017 at Nicole's Getaway Spa (NGS).

September	Sold spa merchandise to Ashley Welch Beauty for $1,800 on account; the cost of these goods to NGS was $900.
October	Sold merchandise to Kelly Fast Nail Gallery for $450 on account; the cost of these goods to NGS was $200.
November	Sold merchandise to Raea Gooding Wellness for $300 on account; the cost of these goods to NGS was $190.
December	Received $1,200 from Ashley Welch Beauty for payment on its account.

Required:

1. Prepare journal entries for each of the transactions. Assume a perpetual inventory system.

2. Estimate the Allowance for Doubtful Accounts required at December 31, 2017, assuming NGS uses the aging of accounts receivable method with the following uncollectable rates: one month, 2 percent; two months, 6 percent; three months, 20 percent; more than three months, 35 percent.

3. The Allowance for Doubtful Accounts balance was $50 (credit) before the end—of—period adjusting entry was made. Prepare the journal entry to account for the Bad Debt Expense.

4. Assume the end of the previous year showed net accounts receivable of $800, and net sales for the current year is $9,000. Calculate the accounts receivable turnover ratio (round to one decimal place).

5. Audrey's Mineral Spa has an accounts receivable turnover ratio of 9.0 times. How does NGS compare to this competitor?

LO8-3, 8-4 **CC8-2 Wiki Art Gallery (WAG)**

Refer to the Wiki Art Gallery (WAG) instructional case in Appendix D and read the case in sufficient depth to answer the following questions.

1. What method for recording bad debts does Wiki Art Gallery (WAG) use and does this method conform to generally acceptable accounting principles?

   a. WAG uses the direct write—off method, which is not in accordance with GAAP.

   b. WAG uses the allowance method with estimates based on aging of receivables, which is in accordance with GAAP.

   c. WAG uses the allowance method with estimates based on percentage of sales, which is in accordance with GAAP.

   d. WAG uses the allowance method with estimates based on percentage of sales, which is not in accordance with GAAP.

2. Which of the following suggests WAG has not adequately allowed for bad debts in 2011?

   a. WAG changed its bad debt estimation percentage between 2010 and 2011.

   b. WAG changed its bad debt estimation method between 2010 and 2011.

   c. WAG calculated bad debts on artwork sales but not artist fees.

   d. WAG calculated bad debts on artist fees but not artwork sales.

3. WAG wrote off uncollectible customer accounts in 2011. Using information in Note 2 of the financial statements, determine the total amount of the 2011 write–off, and indicate whether this amount was greater than, equal to, or less than the amount of estimated bad debts recorded in 2011.

   a. WAG wrote off $300 in 2011, which is equal to the amount of bad debts estimated in 2011.
   b. WAG wrote off $250 in 2011, which is less than the amount of bad debts estimated in 2011.
   c. WAG wrote off $50 in 2011, which is less than the amount of bad debts estimated in 2011.
   d. WAG wrote off $347 in 2011, which is greater than the amount of bad debts estimated in 2011.

4. Calculate the number of days to collect in 2011, and explain what it suggests about the collectibility of the amount reported as net accounts receivable.

   a. The number of days to collect was 3.7, which suggests WAG is unlikely to collect the amount reported as net accounts receivable.
   b. The number of days to collect was 98.1, which suggests WAG is unlikely to collect the amount reported as net accounts receivable.
   c. The number of days to collect was 3.7, which suggests WAG is likely to collect the amount reported as net accounts receivable.
   d. The number of days to collect was 98.1, which suggests WAG is likely to collect the amount reported as net accounts receivable.

5. What would be the financial impact if WAG were to increase its estimate of bad debts in 2011?

   a. WAG's bad debt expense would increase.
   b. WAG's net income would decrease.
   c. WAG's net assets would decrease.
   d. All of the above.

THAT WAS
THEN

In the past few chapters, you learned about the sale of goods and services to customers.

THIS IS
NOW

This chapter focuses on the assets that enable companies to produce and sell goods and services.

YOUR LEARNING OBJECTIVES

Understand the business

LO9-1 Define, classify, and explain the nature of long-lived assets.

Study the accounting methods

LO9-2 Apply the cost principle to the acquisition of long-lived assets.

LO9-3 Apply various depreciation methods as economic benefits are used up over time.

LO9-4 Explain the effect of asset impairment on the financial statements.

LO9-5 Analyze the disposal of long-lived tangible assets.

LO9-6 Analyze the acquisition, use, and disposal of long-lived intangible assets.

Evaluate the results

LO9-7 Interpret the fixed asset turnover ratio.

LO9-8 Describe factors to consider when comparing companies' long-lived assets.

Review the chapter

Chapter Summary

Supplemental material

LO9-S1 Analyze and report depletion of natural resources..

CHAPTER 9

Long-Lived Tangible and Intangible Assets

Shenval/Alamy Images

FOCUS COMPANY:
Cedar Fair
www.cedarfair.com

Most people agonize over how much money to spend on a house or which car to buy. After all, they will own these expensive items for many years to come. The same concerns exist when companies acquire long-lived assets. One of the major challenges that business managers face is determining the right amount to invest in long-lived assets.

The task is especially challenging for companies such as Disney, Six Flags, and Cedar Fair, which operate amusement parks. Unlike merchandising companies, an amusement park cannot build up an inventory of unused roller-coaster seats to be sold sometime in the future. If managers build more rides than needed to satisfy guests, some rides will run with empty seats. Although the company will still incur all the costs of running the rides, it will generate only a fraction of the potential revenue. On the other hand, amusement parks can also run into trouble if they have too few rides to satisfy patrons. Fortunately for managers, accounting reports provide information to evaluate a company's investment in long-lived assets.

In this chapter, you will study specific long-lived asset decisions made by Cedar Fair, which owns and operates eleven amusement parks, four water parks, and five hotels throughout North America. You will see the significant effect that long-lived assets can have on a company's financial statements. Although manufacturing companies, retailers, and even airlines must deal with the same issues as Cedar Fair, the impact on this amusement park company is particularly significant because it relies almost exclusively on long-lived assets. As of December 31, 2015, in fact, Cedar Fair's rides, hotels, and other long-lived assets accounted for more than 90 percent of its total assets.

Logo courtesy of Cedar Fair.

ORGANIZATION OF THE CHAPTER

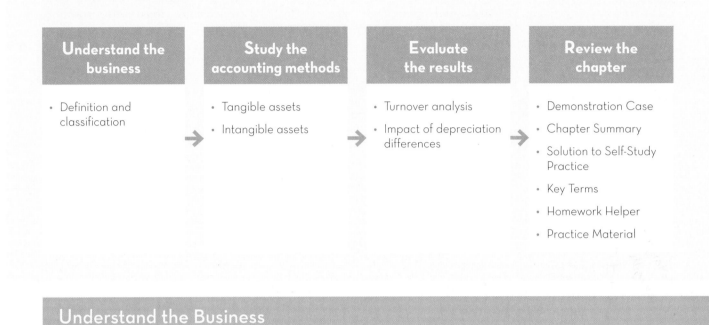

Understand the business	Study the accounting methods	Evaluate the results	Review the chapter
• Definition and classification	• Tangible assets • Intangible assets	• Turnover analysis • Impact of depreciation differences	• Demonstration Case • Chapter Summary • Solution to Self-Study Practice • Key Terms • Homework Helper • Practice Material

Understand the Business

DEFINITION AND CLASSIFICATION

Long–lived assets are business assets acquired for use over one or more years. These assets are not intended for resale. Instead, they are considered "productive" assets in the sense that they enable the business to produce the goods or services that the business then sells to customers. Examples include the ovens in which Pizza Palace bakes pizza, the stores where Walmart sells merchandise, and the legal rights that restrict use of the Under Armour logo. So when you hear the term *long–lived assets*, think more broadly than just rusty old equipment.

This class of assets includes two major types: tangible and intangible.

1. **Tangible assets.** These are long–lived assets that have physical substance, which simply means that you can see, touch, or kick them. The most prominent examples of tangible assets are land, buildings, machinery, vehicles, office equipment, and furniture and fixtures. These assets are typically grouped into a single line item on the balance sheet called *Property, Plant, and Equipment*. Because many long–lived tangible assets are fixed in place, they are also known as fixed assets. Cedar Fair's tangible assets include roller coasters, hotels, and land in Canada and the United States.

2. **Intangible assets.** These long–lived assets have special rights but no physical substance. The existence of most intangible assets is indicated only by legal documents that describe their rights. Compared to the tangible assets that you see in daily life, such as store buildings and cash registers, intangible assets are probably less familiar to you. For this reason, we'll describe the various types of intangibles in detail later in this chapter. For now you can think of this category as including brand names, trademarks, and licensing rights, such as the ones that allow Cedar Fair to use PEANUTS® characters throughout its amusement parks.

A third category of long–lived assets that are depleted over time, like oil wells or gold mines, is common in natural resource industries. This chapter's Supplement 9A describes how to account for these natural resource assets.

LEARNING OBJECTIVE 9-1

Define, classify, and explain the nature of long-lived assets.

Long-lived assets: Resources owned by a business that enable it to produce the goods or services that are sold to customers.

Exhibit 9.1 shows how Cedar Fair reported long–lived assets on its 2015 balance sheet. From this exhibit, you can see how important tangible and intangible assets are to Cedar Fair. Of the nearly $2 billion in total assets at December 31, 2015, Cedar Fair owned long–lived assets totalling $1.7 billion ($1,515 + $211 = $1,726, in millions).

EXHIBIT 9.1	Cedar Fair's Assets

	AT DECEMBER 31	
(in millions)	2015	2014
Assets		
Current Assets	$ 196	$ 204
(details omitted to save space)		
Property and Equipment		
Land	268	276
Land Improvements	381	367
Buildings	648	600
Rides and Equipment	1,561	1,536
Construction in Progress	51	70
Property and Equipment, at cost	2,909	2,849
Less: Accumulated Depreciation	(1,394)	(1,323)
Property and Equipment, Net	1,515	1,526
Goodwill and Other Intangible Assets	211	228
Other Assets	73	80
Total Assets	$1,995	$2,038

Study the Accounting Methods

TANGIBLE ASSETS

In this section, you will study the accounting decisions that relate to long–lived assets. We'll start with tangible long–lived assets and consider key accounting decisions related to their (1) acquisition, (2) use, and (3) disposal. Accounting for intangible assets will be the focus of the last part of this section.

Most companies own a variety of tangible assets. Earlier chapters introduced you to the most common examples: land, buildings, equipment, and vehicles. Other, less common examples include land improvements and construction in progress—both of which Cedar Fair reported on its balance sheet in Exhibit 9.1. Land improvements include the sidewalks, pave–ment, landscaping, fencing, lighting, and sprinkler systems that are added to improve the usefulness of land. Land improvements differ from land in that they deteriorate over time, whereas land is assumed to last forever. Construction in progress includes the costs of constructing new buildings and equipment. When construction is finished, these costs are moved from this account into the building or equipment account to which they relate.

Acquisition of Tangible Assets

The general rule for tangible assets under the cost principle is that all rea–sonable and necessary costs to acquire and prepare an asset for use should be recorded as a cost of the asset. Accountants say costs have been **capitalized** when they are recorded as assets (rather than as expenses).

Deciding whether a cost is a reasonable and necessary cost to acquire or prepare tangible assets for use can involve a great deal of judgment. Because capitalizing costs has a significant impact on both the balance sheet (it increases assets) and the income statement (it decreases expenses), some dishonest accountants and managers have exploited the judgment involved in this decision by capitalizing costs that should have been expensed. A well–known example of this tactic is described in the following Spotlight on Ethics. As you read the feature and the next couple of pages, focus on distinguishing between what types of costs should be capitalized and what types should be expensed.

The illustration that follows shows the types of costs that should be capitalized when a tangible asset is acquired. All are necessary for acquiring and preparing tangible assets for use. Notice that they are not limited to the amounts paid to purchase or construct the assets. For example, the Land account at Cedar Fair would include legal fees for title searches, fees for land surveys, and commissions paid to brokers. Take a moment right now to read the lists of costs that should be capitalized when buildings (middle) and equipment (right) are acquired.

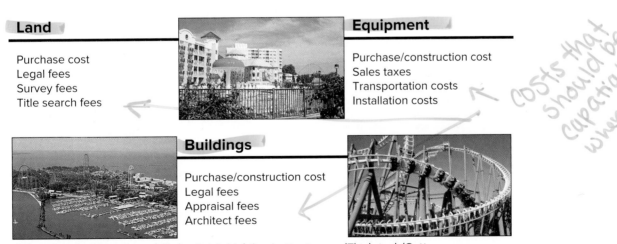

Land

Purchase cost
Legal fees
Survey fees
Title search fees

Equipment

Purchase/construction cost
Sales taxes
Transportation costs
Installation costs

Buildings

Purchase/construction cost
Legal fees
Appraisal fees
Architect fees

Costs that should be capitalized when TASSET is acquired

(left and centre): Courtesy of Cedar Point; (right): ©Jupiter images/Thinkstock/Getty

If a company buys land, a building, or a piece of used equipment and incurs demolition, renovation, or repair costs before it can be used, these additional costs would be capitalized as a cost of the land, building, or equipment. These costs are capitalized because they are needed to prepare the asset for use.

In some cases, land, buildings, and equipment are purchased together, such as when Cedar Fair bought five amusement parks, including Canada's Wonderland, from Paramount Parks for $1.2 billion. When this type of "basket purchase" occurs, the total cost is split among the assets in proportion to the market value of the assets as a whole. For example, if Cedar Fair was to pay $10 million for a hotel and the land surrounding it, based on an appraisal that estimates that the land contributes 40 percent of the property's value and the building contributes 60 percent, Cedar Fair would record 40 percent of the total cost as land ($4 million) and the other 60 percent as buildings ($6 million). Splitting the total purchase price among individual assets is necessary because they may be used over different periods. For example, the hotel may be used over fifty years. However, land is never used up, so any costs assigned to Land will remain in that account until Cedar Fair sells the land.

Total Cost
$10 million

40% | Percent of total value | 60%

$4 million
Land

$6 million
Buildings

To illustrate how the costs of tangible assets are recorded, let's consider the Top Thrill Dragster that Cedar Fair purchased from Intamin, a Swiss roller coaster manufacturer. When it was purchased, the Top Thrill Dragster was the biggest, fastest roller coaster in the world. Some of its specs are shown in the following graphic.

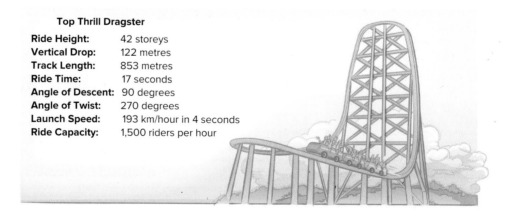

Top Thrill Dragster

Ride Height:	42 storeys
Vertical Drop:	122 metres
Track Length:	853 metres
Ride Time:	17 seconds
Angle of Descent:	90 degrees
Angle of Twist:	270 degrees
Launch Speed:	193 km/hour in 4 seconds
Ride Capacity:	1,500 riders per hour

Assume the list price for the roller coaster (including sales tax) was $26 million but that Cedar Fair received a $1 million discount. In other words, the roller coaster's net purchase price to Cedar Fair was $25 million. Assume, too, that Cedar Fair paid $125,000 to have the roller coaster delivered and another $625,000 to have it assembled and prepared for use. Since these expenditures are necessary to acquire and prepare the asset for use, Cedar Fair would capitalize the expenditures as part of the cost of the asset as follows:

List price	$26,000,000
Less: Discount	1,000,000
Net invoice price	25,000,000
Add: Transportation costs paid by Cedar Fair	125,000
Installation costs paid by Cedar Fair	625,000
Total cost of the roller coaster	$25,750,000

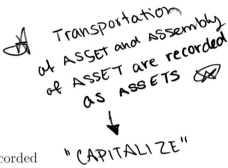

Transportation of ASSET and assembly of ASSET are recorded as ASSETS

"CAPITALIZE"

The total $25,750,000 cost would be the amount Cedar Fair recorded in the Rides and Equipment account regardless of how the company paid for or financed the roller coaster. If we assume Cedar Fair signed a note for the new roller coaster and paid cash for the transportation and installation costs, the accounting equation effects and journal entry would be:

1 Analyze

Assets		=	Liabilities		+	Shareholders' Equity
Cash	−750,000		Note Payable	+25,000,000		
Rides and Equipment	+25,750,000					

2 Record

dr **Rides and Equipment** (+A)	25,750,000	
cr **Cash** (−A)		750,000
cr **Note Payable** (+L)		25,000,000

🔦 HOW'S IT GOING?

Self-Study Practice 9.1

In a recent year, the Newton Bakery Company opened a new baking plant that can make 200,000 buns per hour. The equipment cost $21 million. Assume that Newton Bakery financed the equipment purchase using a promissory note and paid in cash $900,000 of sales tax, $60,000 of transportation costs, and $40,000 of installation costs before the equipment could be used. Indicate the effects of the purchase on the accounting equation and give the journal entry to record the purchase.

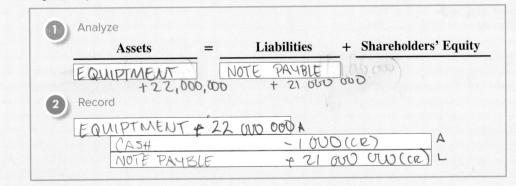

1 Analyze

Assets	=	Liabilities	+	Shareholders' Equity
EQUIPTMENT +22,000,000		NOTE PAYBLE + 21 000 000		

2 Record

EQUIPTMENT $ 22 000 000		A
CASH	− 1 000 (CR)	A
NOTE PAYBLE	+ 21 000 000 (CR)	L

After you have finished, check your answers with the solution, which follows the chapter summary.

IngramPublishing

Before we leave this section, we should mention that not all fixed asset costs are capitalized. The cost of some fixed assets, like staplers or scissors, is such a small dollar amount that it's not worth the trouble of recording them as fixed assets. Ford Motor Company, with over $23 billion in property and equipment, reports in its financial statement notes that it expenses all expenditures less than $2,500. Such policies are acceptable because immaterial amounts (small in relation to the company) will not affect users' analysis of financial statements. Also, when purchases are made in Canada, the applicable Goods and Services Tax (GST) and Provincial Sales Tax (PST), or a Harmonized Sales Tax (HST), increase the purchase price. These taxes are dealt with in more detail in Chapter 10. Other costs that are expensed when incurred include insurance for fixed assets, interest on loans to purchase fixed assets, and ordinary repairs and maintenance, as discussed in the next section.

Use of Tangible Assets

Maintenance Costs Incurred During Use   Most tangible assets require substantial expenditures over the course of their lives to maintain or enhance their operation. Maintenance is a big deal in the roller coaster industry, where safety is vital. Companies in this industry spend a lot of money on two types of maintenance: (1) ordinary repairs and maintenance and (2) extraordinary repairs and maintenance.

Ordinary repairs and maintenance: Expenditures for routine operating upkeep of long-lived assets that are recorded as expenses.

✱minor maintence upkeep.

(Greasing tracks)

1. Ordinary repairs and maintenance. **Ordinary repairs and main-tenance** are expenditures for the routine maintenance and upkeep of long–lived assets. Just like an oil change for your car, these are recurring, relatively small expenditures that do not directly increase an asset's usefulness. Because these costs occur frequently to maintain the asset's productive capacity for a short time, they are recorded as expenses in the current period. Because these expenses are matched to revenues, ordinary repairs and maintenance are sometimes called revenue expenditures.

    In the case of Cedar Fair, ordinary repairs and maintenance would include greasing the tracks on the Behemoth roller coaster at Canada's Wonderland outside of Toronto. It would also include replacing the lights on the century–old Antique Carousel and tight-ening the seams on the Barracuda Blaster water slide.

Extraordinary repairs: Expenditures that increase a tangible asset's economic usefulness in the future and are recorded as increases in asset accounts, not as expenses.

✱ Bigger | less Frequent expenses

2. Extraordinary repairs, overhauls, replacements, and additions. In con-trast to ordinary repairs and maintenance, **extraordinary repairs** occur infrequently, involve large expenditures, and increase an asset's economic usefulness by enhancing its efficiency, capacity, or life span. Examples include additions, major overhauls, complete reconditioning, and major replacements and improvements, such as the complete replacement of the passenger train on a roller coaster. Because these costs increase the usefulness of tangible assets beyond their original condition, they are added to the appropriate long–lived asset accounts. And because doing so means capitalizing costs, these extraordinary repairs, replacements, and additions are called capital expenditures.

Depreciation Expense   In addition to repairs and maintenance expense, a company reports depreciation every period that buildings and equipment are used to generate revenue. Depreciation doesn't involve

Self-Study Practice 9.2

As you know from living in a house, apartment, or dorm, buildings often require maintenance and repair. For each of the following expenditures, indicate whether it should be expensed in the current period or capitalized.

Expense or Capitalize?

1 Replacing electrical wiring throughout the building. C — *extends life*
2 Repairing the hinge on the front door of the building. E — *does not increase usefulness*
3 Yearly cleaning of the building's air-conditioning filters. E — *does not increase usefulness*
4 Making major structural improvements to a clubhouse. C — *extends life*

★ *Capitalize when it benefits/ adds to ASSET. Expens when it does not* ★

After you have finished, check your answers with the solution, which follows the chapter summary.

new payments for using the asset. Rather, **depreciation** (or *amortization*) is the allocation of existing costs that were already recorded as a long–lived asset. Think of the cost of a long–lived asset as a big prepayment for future benefits. As that asset is used, those prepaid benefits are used up, so the asset needs to be decreased each period. This decrease in the asset creates an expense, which is reported on the income statement and matched against the revenue generated by the asset, as required by accrual accounting. Amortization is the same process of allocating the cost of an asset over its limited useful life. The term *amortization* is used for intangible assets, whereas the term *depreciation* is used for tangible assets. Intangible assets are covered later in this chapter.

As you learned in Chapter 4, depreciation affects one income statement account and one balance sheet account. The income statement account, Depreciation Expense, reports the depreciation of the current period. The balance sheet account, Accumulated Depreciation, contains the current period's depreciation as well as that of prior periods. It is an *accumulation* over several periods. The effects of $130 of depreciation on the accounting equation and the journal entry to record them are as follows:

Depreciation: (1) The process of allocating the cost of buildings, vehicles, and equipment to the accounting periods in which they are used; also referred to as *amortization.* (2) The allocation of the cost of long-lived tangible assets over their productive lives using a systematic and rational method. Also called *amortization.*

1 Analyze

	Assets	= Liabilities +	Shareholders' Equity	
Accumulated Depreciation (+xA)	−130		Depreciation Expense (+E)	−130

2 Record

dr **Depreciation Expense (+E, −SE)** 130
  cr **Accumulated Depreciation (+xA, −A)** 130

Exhibit 9.2 shows how Cedar Fair reported its depreciation in 2015. The income statement on the right shows the $126 million of Depreciation Expense in 2015. The balance sheet on the left shows that this $126 million, when combined with depreciation of prior years, brought the total Accumulated Depreciation to $1,394 million at December 31, 2015. The $1,515 difference between the Property and Equipment's $2,909 cost and $1,394 of Accumulated Depreciation is called the **book value** (or *carrying value*). Most companies report a breakdown of these totals by class of asset (e.g., buildings, equipment) in their financial statement notes.

EXHIBIT 9.2   Reporting Depreciation on the Balance Sheet and Income Statement

Balance Sheet (in millions)	Dec. 31, 2015
Assets	
Property and Equipment, at cost	$ 2,909
Less: Accumulated Depreciation	(1,394)
Property and Equipment, net	1,515

Income Statement (in millions)	2015
Net Revenues	$1,236
Operating Expenses:	
Food and Operating Expenses	623
Depreciation Expense	126
Selling, General, and Other	171
Loss on Disposals and Impairments	21
Total Operating Expenses	941
Income from Operations	295

Book value (carrying value): The amount an asset or liability is reported at ("carried at") in the financial statements. For assets, it's the acquisition cost less accumulated depreciation. It is also known as *net book value* or *book value*.

One way to interpret the information in Exhibit 9.2 is that the Property and Equipment's $2,909 million cost represents the assets' total economic benefits. Thus, $126 million of Depreciation Expense means Cedar Fair used up almost 5 percent ($126/$2,909 = 0.043) of the assets' benefits in 2015. As of December 31, 2015, almost 48 percent ($1,394/$2,909 = 0.479) of their total benefits had been used up.

To fully understand the depreciation numbers in Exhibit 9.2, you need to know how they are calculated. Depreciation calculations are based on the following three items:

1. **Asset cost.** This includes all of the asset's capitalized costs, including the purchase cost, sales tax, legal fees, and other costs needed to acquire and prepare the asset for use.

Residual value: The estimated amount to be recovered at the end of the company's estimated useful life of an asset. Also called *salvage value.*

2. **Residual value.** **Residual value** (or *salvage value*) is an estimate of the amount the company will receive when it disposes of the asset. Cedar Fair will recover some of the initial cost of its roller coasters when it disposes of them by either selling them "as is" to local amusement companies or by dismantling them and selling their parts to other roller-coaster or scrap metal companies.

Useful life: The expected service life of an asset under the present owner.

3. **Useful life.** **Useful life** is an estimate of the asset's useful economic life to the company (not its economic life to all potential users). It may be expressed in terms of years or units of capacity, such as the number of units it can produce or the number of kilometres it will travel. Land is the only tangible asset that's assumed to have an unlimited (indefinite) useful life. Because of this, land is not depreciated.

The basic idea of depreciation is to match the economic benefit that will be used up (asset cost minus residual value) to the periods in which the asset will be used to generate revenue (useful life). Residual value is considered when calculating depreciation because we want to leave a little of the asset's cost in the accounts after we have finished depreciating it. We do this because, when we dispose of the asset, we're likely to get back some of the money we initially paid for it. So the amount to be depreciated over the asset's life is the difference between its cost and residual value, an amount called the **depreciable cost**. A company should record depreciation each year of an asset's useful life until its total accumulated depreciation equals its depreciable cost. After that, the company should report no additional depreciation, even if the company continues to use the asset.

If every company used the same techniques for calculating depreciation, we'd stop right here. But they don't. Companies own different assets and use them differently, so they are allowed to choose from several depreciation methods. These alternative depreciation methods produce different patterns of depreciation as represented by the depreciation amounts recorded each year.

Depreciation Methods   The depreciation method chosen for each type of property, plant, and equipment should reflect the pattern in which those assets' economic benefits are used up. We discuss the three most common depreciation methods:

1. **Straight-line**—when usage is the same each period
2. **Units-of-production**—when usage varies each period
3. **Declining-balance**—when the asset is more efficient (generates more revenues) in early years but less so over time

To show how each method works, let's assume that Cedar Fair acquired a new go-kart ride on January 1. The relevant information is shown in Exhibit 9.3.

Depreciable cost The portion of the asset's cost that will be used in generating revenue; calculated as asset cost minus residual value.

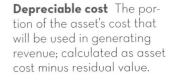

LEARNING OBJECTIVE **9-3**

Apply various depreciation methods as economic benefits are used up over time.

EXHIBIT 9.3	Information for Depreciation Computations

CEDAR FAIR—Acquisition of a New Go-Kart Ride	
Cost, purchased on January 1	$62,500
Estimated residual value	$ 2,500
Estimated useful life	3 years; 100,000 km

Straight-Line Method   Managers choose the **straight-line depreciation method** when an asset is expected to be used up in equal amounts each period of the asset's estimated useful life. Here is the straight-line formula for estimating annual depreciation expense:

Straight-line depreciation method: For tangible and intangible assets, the systematic and rational allocation of the cost of the asset in equal periodic amounts over its useful life.

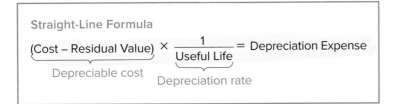

Straight-Line Formula

$$\underbrace{(\text{Cost} - \text{Residual Value})}_{\text{Depreciable cost}} \times \underbrace{\frac{1}{\text{Useful Life}}}_{\text{Depreciation rate}} = \text{Depreciation Expense}$$

In the straight-line formula, (Cost − Residual Value) is the total amount to be depreciated (the depreciable cost). The depreciation rate is 1/ Useful Life. Using the information in Exhibit 9.3, the depreciation expense for Cedar Fair's new ride is $20,000 per year, calculated in the following depreciation schedule:

Straight–line (Cost − Residual Value) × (1/Useful Life)		INCOME STATEMENT	BALANCE SHEET		
Year	Yearly Computation	Depreciation Expense	Cost	Accumulated Depreciation	Book Value
At acquisition			$62,500	$ 0	$62,500
Year 1	($62,500 − $2,500) × (1/3)	$20,000	62,500	20,000	42,500
Year 2	($62,500 − $2,500) × (1/3)	20,000	62,500	40,000	22,500
Year 3	($62,500 − $2,500) × (1/3)	20,000	62,500	60,000	2,500
	Total	$60,000			

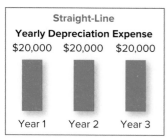

Straight-Line
Yearly Depreciation Expense
$20,000 $20,000 $20,000
Year 1   Year 2   Year 3

Take a moment to study the straight–line depreciation schedule. Notice that as the name *straight–line* suggests,

1. Depreciation Expense is a constant amount each year;
2. Accumulated Depreciation increases by an equal amount each year; and
3. Book Value decreases by the same equal amount each year.

Notice, too, that at the end of the asset's life, accumulated depreciation ($60,000) equals the asset's depreciable cost ($62,500 − $2,500), and book value ($2,500) equals residual value.

As you will see with other depreciation methods, the amount of depreciation depends on estimates of an asset's useful life and residual value at the end of that life. A question people often ask is: How do accountants estimate useful lives and residual values? While some of this information can be obtained from the asset's supplier or from other sources, such as reseller databases or insurance companies, the simple answer is that professional judgment is required. Because useful lives and residual values are difficult to estimate with precision, accountants are encouraged to update their calculations regularly (see Changes in Depreciation Estimates later in the chapter).

Units-of-production depreciation method: Allocates the cost of an asset over its useful life based on the relationship of its periodic output to its total estimated output.

Units-of-Production Method   Choose the **units–of–production depreciation method** if the amount of asset production varies significantly from period to period. An asset's production can be defined in terms of kilometres, products, or machine hours. This is the units–of–production formula for estimating depreciation expense:

Units-of-Production Formula

$$(\text{Cost} - \text{Residual Value}) \times \frac{\text{Actual Production This Period}}{\text{Estimated Total Production}} = \text{Depreciation Expense}$$

Depreciable cost

Depreciation rate

If the go–kart ride in Exhibit 9.3 was driven 30,000 kilometres in Year 1, 50,000 kilometres in Year 2, and 20,000 kilometres in Year 3, the units—of—production method would calculate depreciation in each year of the asset's life as follows:

Units—of—production (Cost − Residual Value) × (Actual/Estimated Total Production)		INCOME STATEMENT	BALANCE SHEET		
Year	Yearly Computation	Depreciation Expense	Cost	Accumulated Depreciation	Book Value
At acquisition			$62,500	$ 0	$62,500
Year 1	($62,500 − $2,500) × (30,000 km/ 100,000 km) = Dep Expense	$18,000	62,500	18,000 +36 000 ~ 30,000	44,500
Year 2	($62,500 − $2,500) × (50,000 km/ 100,000 km)	30,000	62,500	48,000 +12 000	= 14,500 −12 000
Year 3	($62,500 − $2,500) × (20,000 km/ 100,000 km)	12,000	62,500	60,000	2,500
	Total	$60,000			

Under the units—of—production method, the depreciation expense, accumulated depreciation, and book value vary from period to period, depending on the number of units produced.

Declining-Balance Method

The **declining—balance depreciation method** is more often used to report depreciation expense in the early years of an asset's life when the asset is more efficient, and less in later years as the asset become less efficient. Because this method speeds up depreciation reporting, it is sometimes called an *accelerated deprecia— tion method*. Accelerated methods are used more frequently for financial reporting purposes in countries such as Canada and Japan, as well as for tax reporting (a point we discuss in greater detail later).

The declining—balance method applies a depreciation rate to the book value of the asset at the beginning of each accounting period. Notice that the formula below uses the asset's book value (which is Cost − Accumu— lated Depreciation) rather than depreciable cost (Cost − Residual Value). This slight difference in the formula produces declining amounts of depre— ciation as the asset ages. In the first year of an asset's life, the beginning balance in Accumulated Depreciation is zero. However, with each passing year, as additional depreciation is recorded, the Accumulated Depreciation balance increases, causing the amount of double—declining depreciation expense to decline each year.

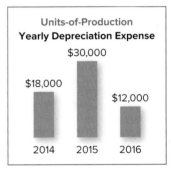
Units-of-Production Yearly Depreciation Expense
$30,000
$18,000
$12,000
2014   2015   2016

Declining-balance depreciation method: Assigns more depreciation to early years of an asset's life and less depreciation to later years.

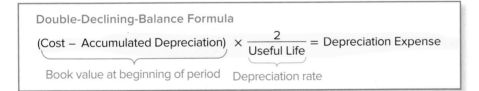
Double-Declining-Balance Formula
(Cost − Accumulated Depreciation) × 2/Useful Life = Depreciation Expense
Book value at beginning of period   Depreciation rate

The depreciation rate for the declining balance method also differs from that used in the straight—line method. In the formula above, we show a rate of 2/Useful Life, which is the most common declining depreciation rate. Because the (2/Useful Life) rate used in the formula is double the straight—line rate, this particular version of the declining—balance method is called the double—declining—balance depreciation method.

Because residual value is not included in the formula for the declining—balance method of computing depreciation expense, you must take extra care to ensure that an asset's book value is not depreciated beyond its residual value. If the calculated amount of depreciation for the year would reduce the book value below the asset's residual value, you must record a lower amount of depreciation so that the book value will equal the residual value. If this happens in a year prior to the last year of the asset's useful life, no additional depreciation is calculated, to keep book value equal to residual value. The following depreciation schedule illustrates this point.

Double–declining–balance (Cost – Accumulated Depreciation) × (2/Useful Life)		INCOME STATEMENT	BALANCE SHEET		
Year	Yearly Computation	Depreciation Expense	Cost	Accumulated Depreciation	Book Value
At acquisition			$62,500	$ 0	$62,500
Year 1	($62,500 – $0) × (2/3)	$41,667	62,500	41,667	20,833
Year 2	($62,500 – $41,667) × (2/3)	13,889	62,500	55,556	6,944
Year 3	($62,500 – $55,556) × (2/3)	4,629	62,500	60,185	2,315
		4,444	62,500	60,000	2,500
	Total	$60,000			

Double-Declining
Yearly Depreciation Expense

$41,667
$13,889
$4,444
Year 1   Year 2   Year 3

Notice that the calculated depreciation expense for Year 3 ($4,629) would not be recorded because it would cause the asset's book value to fall below its residual value. Instead, in the final year of the asset's life, just enough depreciation ($4,444) is recorded to make the book value of the asset equal its residual value of $2,500.

Summary of Depreciation Methods   See Exhibit 9.4 for a summary of the depreciation expense that would be reported in each year of our example under the three alternative depreciation methods. Notice that the amount of depreciation expense recorded in each year of an asset's life depends on the method that is used. That means that the amount of net income that is reported can vary, depending on the depreciation method used. At the end of an asset's life, after it has been fully depreciated, the total amount of depreciation will equal the asset's depreciable cost, regardless of the depreciation method used.

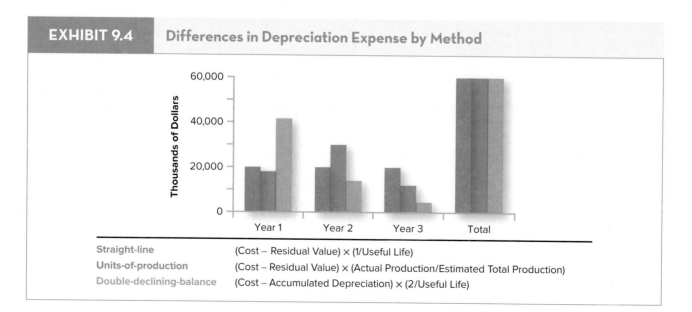

EXHIBIT 9.4   Differences in Depreciation Expense by Method

Thousands of Dollars

Straight-line   (Cost – Residual Value) × (1/Useful Life)
Units-of-production   (Cost – Residual Value) × (Actual Production/Estimated Total Production)
Double-declining-balance (Cost – Accumulated Depreciation) × (2/Useful Life)

Different depreciation methods can be used for different classes of assets provided they are used consistently over time so that financial statement users can compare results across periods. The straight–line method is the preferred choice because it is the easiest to use and understand, and it does a good job of matching depreciation expense to revenues when assets are used evenly over their useful lives. The units–of–production method is the typical choice when asset use fluctuates significantly from period to period. Declining–balance methods apply best to assets that are most productive when they are new but quickly lose their usefulness as they get older.

 HOW'S IT GOING?

Self-Study Practice 9.3

Assume that Cedar Fair has acquired new equipment at a cost of $24,000. The equipment has an estimated life of six years, an estimated operating life of 5,000 hours, and an estimated residual value of $3,000. Determine depreciation expense for the **second year** under each of the following methods:

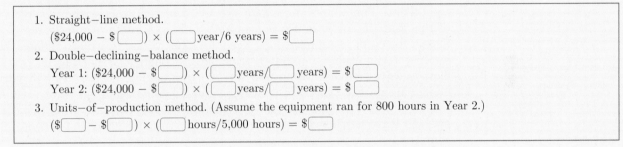

1. Straight–line method.
   ($24,000 − $☐) × (☐year/6 years) = $☐
2. Double–declining–balance method.
   Year 1: ($24,000 − $☐) × (☐years/☐years) = $☐
   Year 2: ($24,000 − $☐) × (☐years/☐years) = $☐
3. Units–of–production method. (Assume the equipment ran for 800 hours in Year 2.)
   ($☐ − $☐) × (☐hours/5,000 hours) = $☐

After you have finished, check your answers with the solution, which follows the chapter summary.

Partial-Year Depreciation Calculations   Purchases of long–lived assets seldom occur on the first day of the accounting period. Consequently, the need arises to calculate depreciation for periods shorter than a year. Under the straight–line and declining–balance methods, the annual depreciation is multiplied by the fraction of the year for which depreciation is being calculated.

For purposes of these calculations, accountants typically assume that assets were purchased at the beginning of the month nearest to the actual purchase date. For example, if Cedar Fair purchased the go–kart ride on October 7, it would have owned the asset for about three months during the year ended December 31. Thus, straight–line depreciation for the ride that year would be calculated by multiplying the annual straight–line depre– ciation of $20,000 by 3 ÷ 12, representing the three months of twelve that Cedar Fair owned it. Similarly, if an asset is disposed of during the year, the annual depreciation is multiplied by the fraction of the year during which the asset was owned. These partial–year modifications are not required in the units–of–production method because that method is based on actual production for the period. If the accounting period is shorter than a year, the level of actual production already reflects that shorter period.

Tax Depreciation   Before we leave the topic of depreciation methods, we should note that most companies use one method of depreciation for reporting to shareholders and a different method for determining income taxes. Keeping two sets of accounting records like this is both ethical and legal because the primary objective of financial reporting differs from that of income tax reporting.

Financial Reporting	Income Tax Reporting
Objective: Provide economic information about a business that is useful in projecting its future cash flows.	*Objective*: Raise sufficient tax revenues to pay for the expenditures of the federal government and to encourage certain social and economic behaviours.

Capital cost allowance (CCA): The depreciation process required by the Canada Revenue Agency for calculating taxable income and income taxes.

One of the behaviours the government wants to encourage is economic renewal and growth. For this reason, Canada Revenue Agency allows companies to deduct larger amounts of tax depreciation in the early years of an asset's life than those allowed by ASPE and IFRS. The Canada Revenue Agency requires corporations to use the **capital cost allowance (CCA)** method when calculating taxable income and taxes owed to the government.

The CCA calculation method is similar, but not identical, to the declining–balance method that was illustrated earlier in this chapter. For example, in order to encourage spending on technology, the government might set the CCA rate at 100 percent for a certain piece of medical equipment. This allows a company to write off or expense the whole cost of this asset in the year it was acquired. This is great for saving taxes, but if that piece of equipment was used for five years, it would violate the expense recognition (matching) principle for financial reporting purposes. This is why companies keep two sets of records. The CCA rates will vary depending on the type of asset. For example, some buildings have a CCA rate of 4 percent, while computer hardware has a CCA rate of 55 percent. We will leave further discussion of this topic to more advanced accounting courses.

Changes in Depreciation The amount of depreciation and amortization depends on three items: an asset's recorded cost, its estimated useful life, and its estimated residual value. When any one of these items changes, the amount of depreciation needs to change. For example, Cedar Fair changed its amortization calculations when it shortened the estimated useful life of certain intangible assets after deciding to discontinue its licensing agreement with Nickelodeon. In other instances, when the company made extraordinary repairs that increased a roller coaster's recorded cost, it needed to revise depreciation for the remaining years of that asset's estimated life.

To compute the new depreciation expense due to the changes described above, substitute the book value for the original acquisition cost, the new residual value for the original residual value, and the estimated remaining life for the original useful life. As an illustration, note the formula using the straight–line method:

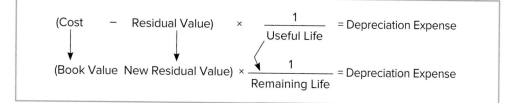

Assume Cedar Fair purchased the largest and fastest roller coaster in the world for $60,000,000, with an estimated useful life of twenty years and estimated residual value of $3,000,000. Shortly after the start of year five, Cedar Fair changed the initial estimated life to twenty–five years and lowered the estimated residual value to $2,400,000. At the end of year five, the computation of the new amount for depreciation expense is as follows:

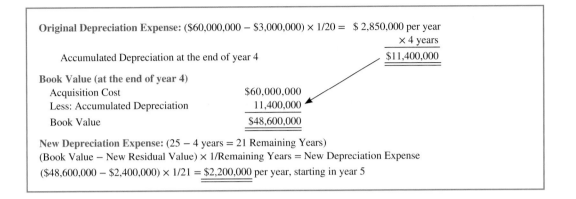

Original Depreciation Expense: ($60,000,000 − $3,000,000) × 1/20 = $ 2,850,000 per year
                                                                                × 4 years
        Accumulated Depreciation at the end of year 4 $11,400,000

Book Value (at the end of year 4)
    Acquisition Cost $60,000,000
    Less: Accumulated Depreciation   11,400,000
    Book Value $48,600,000

New Depreciation Expense: (25 − 4 years = 21 Remaining Years)
(Book Value − New Residual Value) × 1/Remaining Years = New Depreciation Expense
($48,600,000 − $2,400,000) × 1/21 = $2,200,000 per year, starting in year 5

Companies may also change depreciation methods (e.g., from declining–balance to straight–line), although such a change requires significantly more disclosure, as described in intermediate account–ing textbooks. Under ASPE and IFRS, changes in accounting estimates and depreciation methods should be made only when a new estimate or accounting method better measures the periodic income of the business.

SPOTLIGHT ON Canada

Differences in the Capitalization and Depreciation of Capital Assets

The Government of Canada is accountable to the public for the funds that it administers to First Nations communities. This is why Indigenous and Northern Affairs Canada (INAC) requires First Nations to provide annual audited consolidated financial statements. As was mentioned in Chapter 1, First Nations communities are expected to follow Generally Accepted Accounting Principles (GAAP) for public sector entities, such as government organizations, when preparing these financial statements.

The government reporting model does not provide direction on accounting for capital assets, other than to indicate that the financial statements should provide information about physical assets. Many First Nations financial statements that have been submitted to the government provide a bal-ance for capital assets at amortized cost on the Statement of Financial Position.

Such statements tend to record the depreciation of the capital assets as a decrease in the capital asset equity account. As will be discussed further in Chapter 13, differences in financial reporting prac-tices can influence ratios, and the analysis performed on those ratios will differ between organizations. Therefore, users of financial information need to be vigilant and cautious of these differences and what they reveal financially about an organization.

It is this discrepancy in reporting versus expectations that has prompted the current Federal gov-ernment to seek input on how to best address the mutual transparency and accountability between First Nations and the Government of Canada, as well as other unique communities, so that reports adequately reflect and satisfy both sides.

Source: Financial Reporting by First Nations by The Canadian Institute of Chartered Accountants, URL: http://www.frascanada.ca /standards-for-public-sector-entities/resources/reference-materials/item14957.pdf

Asset Impairment Losses

LEARNING OBJECTIVE **9-4**

Explain the effect of asset impairment on the financial statements.

Impairment: Occurs when the cash to be generated by an asset is estimated to be less than the carrying value of that asset.

As a result of recording depreciation, an asset's book value declines as it ages. However, because depreciation is not intended to report an asset at its current value, an asset's book value could exceed its current value, particularly if the asset becomes impaired. **Impairment** occurs when events or changed circumstances interfere with a company's ability to recover the value of the asset through future operations. If this occurs, the book value should be written down to what the asset is worth (called *fair value*), with the amount of the write–down reported as an impairment loss. Impairment losses are classified as an operating expense on the income statement and reported above the Income from Operations subtotal, as shown in Exhibit 9.2.

Cedar Fair recorded a $3 million write–down about fifteen years ago after a rare engineering phenomenon called *vortex shedding* caused a steel support tower in one of its VertiGo slingshot rides to snap during the off–season. More recently, in 2012, the company recorded a $25 million write–down of its Wildwater Kingdom water park rides. To see how this event would be accounted for, assume that the book value of the rides at this theme park was $30 million. If the fair value of the rides was estimated to be $5 million—an amount that represents what other amusement park companies and scrap dealers might be expected to pay for the rides—then the impairment loss would be calculated as $30 million minus $5 million. The effects of this $25 million impairment and the journal entry to record it would be as follows:

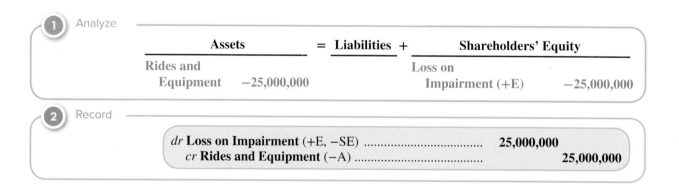

1 Analyze

Assets	= Liabilities +	Shareholders' Equity
Rides and Equipment −25,000,000		Loss on Impairment (+E) −25,000,000

2 Record

dr **Loss on Impairment (+E, −SE)** 25,000,000
  cr **Rides and Equipment (−A)** 25,000,000

Disposal of Tangible Assets

LEARNING OBJECTIVE **9-5**

Analyze the disposal of long-lived tangible assets.

A business may voluntarily decide not to hold a long–term asset for its entire life. For example, your local gym might decide to replace its treadmills with elliptical trainers. Or, if a company discontinues a product, it may sell the equipment that was used to make the product. To get rid of used assets, companies do just what you do. They trade them in on a new asset, sell them on eBay, or "retire" them to a junkyard.

The disposal of a depreciable asset usually requires two accounting adjustments:

1. **Update the Depreciation Expense and Accumulated Depreciation accounts.** If a long–lived asset is disposed of during the year, it should be depreciated to the date of disposal using the partial–year calculations explained earlier.

2. **Record the disposal.** All disposals of long–lived assets require that you account for (1) the book value of the items given up,

(2) the value of the items received on disposal, and (3) any difference between the two amounts, which reflects a gain or loss on the disposal to be reported on the income statement.

Earlier in this chapter, you saw how to compute and record depreciation expense on a long–lived asset (step 1 above), so let's look instead at an example where we have to record only the disposal (step 2). Assume that, at the end of year 6, Cedar Fair sold one of its junior roller coasters for $50,000 cash. The original $100,000 cost of this equipment was depreciated using the straight–line method over ten years with no residual value ($10,000 depreciation expense per year), resulting in $60,000 of accumulated depreciation at the time of disposal. A gain (or loss) on disposal represents the difference between the proceeds from selling the asset and the asset's book value (BV), computed as follows:

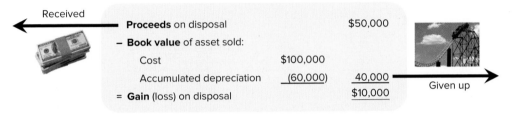

Received

Proceeds on disposal	$50,000
− **Book value** of asset sold:	
Cost	$100,000
Accumulated depreciation	(60,000) 40,000
= **Gain** (loss) on disposal	$10,000

Given up

Money: ©Comstock/PunchStock RF; Roller Coaster: ©Image State Royalty Free/Alamy Images

The effects of the gain and roller coaster disposal on Cedar Fair follow, along with the journal entry to record them.

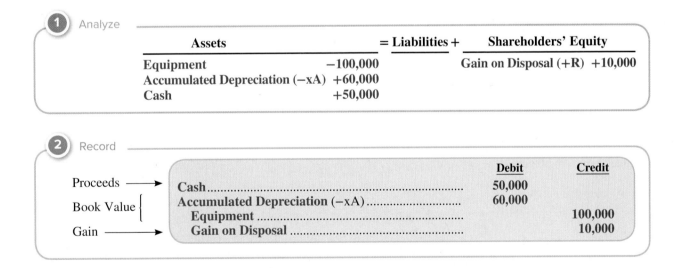

1 Analyze

Assets		= Liabilities +	Shareholders' Equity
Equipment	−100,000		Gain on Disposal (+R) +10,000
Accumulated Depreciation (−xA)	+60,000		
Cash	+50,000		

2 Record

	Debit	Credit
Proceeds ⟶ Cash	50,000	
Book Value { Accumulated Depreciation (−xA)	60,000	
Equipment		100,000
Gain ⟶ Gain on Disposal		10,000

Gains (and losses) on disposal are included in the income statement. In the previous example, had the book value exceeded the selling price, Cedar Fair would have reported a loss on disposal. A loss on disposal is recorded just like any expense (with a debit), as shown in Exhibit 9.2, for Cedar Fair and in the following Self–Study Practice.

HOW'S IT GOING?

Self-Study Practice 9.4

Assume that Cedar Fair sold the roller coaster described above at the end of year six for $25,000 cash. Also assume that depreciation had been updated to that point in time, resulting in Accumulated Depreciation of $60,000 on the asset that originally cost $100,000. Complete the accounting equation effects and the journal entry for this disposal below.

1 Analyze

Assets		= Liabilities + Shareholders' Equity
Equipment	−100,000	
Accumulated Depreciation (−xA)		
Cash	+25,000	

2 Record

	Debit	Credit

After you have finished, check your answers with the solution, which follows the chapter summary.

INTANGIBLE ASSETS

LEARNING OBJECTIVE 9-6

Analyze the acquisition, use, and disposal of long-lived intangible assets.

Trademark: A special name, image, or slogan identified with a product or company.

Copyright: A form of protection provided to the original authors of literary, musical, artistic, dramatic, and other works of authorship.

Patent: A right to exclude others from making, using, selling, or importing an invention.

Intangible assets are long−lived assets that lack physical substance. Their existence is indicated by legal documents of the types described below.

- **Trademark.** A **trademark** is a special name, image, or slogan identified with a product or company, like the name Kleenex or the image of the McDonald's golden arches. The symbol ® signifies a trade−mark registered with the Canadian Intellectual Property Office and ™ indicates an unregistered trademark. Both types of trademark are considered intangible assets.

- **Copyright.** A **copyright** gives the owner the exclusive right to pub−lish, use, and sell a literary, musical, artistic, or dramatic work for a period not exceeding fifty years after the author's death. Some countries' copyright laws extend this period to seventy years. The book you are reading is copyrighted. It is illegal, therefore, for an instructor to copy several chapters from this book and hand them out in class without first obtaining permission from the copyright owner.

- **Patent.** A **patent** is an exclusive right granted by the federal gov−ernment for a period of twenty years, typically to whoever invents a new product or discovers a new process. The patent declares the owner to be the only one who can use, manufacture, or sell the patented item. This protection is intended to encourage people to be inventive because it prevents others from simply copying innovations until after the inventor has had time to profit from the new product or process. One of the first roller−coaster patents was granted in 1884 for what was then called a "gravity pleasure road."

- **Technology.** **Technology assets** include software and Web development work. Amazon.com reported $1.5 billion of these assets at the end of 2015. Most companies use up intangible technology assets over a relatively short time (three to seven years).

- **Licensing rights.** **Licensing rights** are limited permissions to use something according to specific terms and conditions. Your university or college likely has obtained the licensing right to make computer programs available for use on your campus network. A licensing right also allows Cedar Fair to showcase SNOOPY ® at its parks.

- **Franchise.** A **franchise** is a contractual right to sell certain products or services, use certain trademarks, or perform activities in a geographical region. For example, a business can buy franchise rights that allow it to use the Tim Hortons name, store format, recipes, and ingredients by paying a franchise fee averaging $50,000 per store.[1]

- **Goodwill.** **Goodwill** tops the charts as the most frequently reported intangible asset. It encompasses lots of good stuff like a favourable location, an established customer base, a great reputation, and successful business operations. Although many companies have probably built up their own goodwill, it is not permitted under GAAP to report it as an intangible asset on the balance sheet unless it has been purchased from another company. To understand the reasons behind this, keep reading. We explain them in the next section.

Acquisition, Use, and Disposal

Acquisition   Generally, the costs of an intangible asset are capitalized as an asset, if the asset clearly produces future economic benefits that flow to the company and the costs can be reliably measured. Most companies acquire intangible assets only when these conditions exist, so the costs of purchased intangible assets are usually capitalize when incurred.

A more challenging situation arises when a company self-generates its own intangible asset through internal research and development projects. In these circumstances, research costs are reported as **research and development expenses** as they are incurred. The primary reason that the cost of self-developed intangibles is reported as an expense rather than an asset is that it's easy for people to claim that they've developed a valuable (but invisible) intangible asset. In special circumstances, when a company has reached the stage at which its research and development efforts have yielded an identifiable intangible asset that will clearly produce future benefits that flow to the company, any further development costs—if they can be reliably measured—are capitalized as an intangible asset. As with all limited-life assets, the costs of intangible assets are amortized over their expected periods of benefit.

Goodwill is a peculiar intangible asset because it represents the value paid for the unidentifiable assets of another business. You might wonder how to put a value on something you can't identify, but it is possible. When one company buys another business, the purchase price often is greater than the appraised value of all of the **net assets** of the business. Why would a company pay more for a business as a whole than it would pay if it bought the assets individually? In order to obtain its goodwill, which encompasses intangible benefits such as its good location or strong management team.

Technology assets: Acquired computer software and development costs.

Licensing rights: The limited permission to use property according to specific terms and conditions set out in a contract.

Franchise: A contractual right to sell certain products or services, use certain trademarks, or perform activities in a certain geographical region.

Goodwill: The premium a company pays to obtain the favourable reputation associated with another company.

Research and development expenses: Expenditures that may someday lead to patents, copyrights, or other intangible assets; the uncertainty about their future benefits requires that they be expensed.

Net assets: The shorthand term used to refer to assets minus liabilities.

Reporting Goodwill After a Business Acquisition

When Cedar Fair bought five theme parks from Paramount Parks it paid $1.2 billion, which exceeded the then fair value of Paramount's net assets ($890 million). As shown below, Cedar Fair paid this extra $310 million to acquire the goodwill associated with the theme parks' businesses.

Cedar Fair Purchase of Five Paramount Parks Theme Parks (in millions)		
Purchase price		$1,200
Assets purchased and liabilities assumed		
Current assets	$ 70	
Property and equipment	1,000	
Intangible assets	80	
Debt and other liabilities	(260)	
Net assets, at fair value Goodwill		890
Goodwill		$ 310

For most companies, goodwill is not amortized but, instead, is tested annually for impairment and written down if its value is found to be impaired.

Use The accounting rules that apply to the use of intangible assets after they have been purchased depend on whether the intangible asset has a limited or unlimited life.

Amortization: The process of allocating the cost of intangible assets over their limited useful lives. Similar to depreciation.

- **Limited life.** The cost of intangible assets with a limited life (copyrights, patents, licensing rights, and franchises) is spread on a straight-line basis over each period of useful life in a process called **amortization**, which is similar to depreciation. Most companies do not estimate a residual value for their intangible assets because, unlike tangible assets that can be sold as scrap, intangibles usually have no value at the end of their useful lives. Amortization is reported as an expense each period on the income statement and accumulated on the balance sheet in the contra-asset account Accumulated Amortization.

To illustrate, assume Cedar Fair purchased a patent for an uphill water coaster for $800,000 and intends to use it for twenty years. Each year, the company would record $40,000 in Amortization Expense ($800,000 ÷ 20 years). The effect of this amortization and the journal entry to record it are as follows:

1 Analyze

Assets	= Liabilities +	Shareholders' Equity
Accumulated Amortization (+xA) −40,000		Amortization Expense (+E) −40,000

2 Record

	Debit	Credit
Amortization Expense	40,000	
Accumulated Amortization (+xA)		40,000

- **Unlimited life.** Intangibles with unlimited or indefinite lives (trademarks and goodwill) are not amortized.

All intangible assets are tested at least annually for possible impairment, just like long-lived tangible assets. If an intangible asset is impaired, its book value is written down (reduced) to its fair value and the amount of the reduction is reported as an expense. For example, in 2010, Cedar Fair determined that declining economic conditions had impaired its Goodwill and Other Intangible Assets by approximately $2 million. These assets were written down on the balance sheet to their remaining fair value with the $2 million reduction reported as an operating expense on the income statement.

Disposal   Just like long-lived tangible assets, disposal of intangible assets results in gains (or losses) if the amounts received on disposal are greater than (less than) their book values.

The accounting rules for long-lived tangible and intangible assets are summarized and compared in the Homework Helper at the end of the chapter.

SPOTLIGHT ON The World

Differences between ASPE and IFRS

IFRS differs from ASPE in many ways, particularly when accounting for tangible and intangible assets. The following are two of the most significant differences:

1. ASPE requires tangible and intangible assets to be recorded at cost and not revalued for later increases in asset values. In contrast, IFRS allows companies the option of reporting these assets at fair values (e.g., appraisals), provided they use the fair value method consistently each year.

2. IFRS requires companies to capitalize costs of developing intangible assets, such as prototypes or models for making new products or tools. ASPE generally expenses such development costs because of the uncertainty of their ultimate value.

As countries continue to adopt IFRS, you should carefully read the financial statement notes of companies that you analyze. Cedar Fair chose to use historical costs, but it could have chosen to use fair value, instead. This and other differences are summarized in the Spotlight on IFRS and ASPE.

Evaluate the Results

TURNOVER ANALYSIS

A primary goal of financial analysts is to evaluate how well management uses long-lived tangible assets to generate revenues. The fixed asset turnover ratio provides a good measure of this aspect of managerial performance. It is calculated as shown in the table below. The denominator uses the value of *average* net fixed assets (property and equipment) over the same period as the revenues in the numerator. You can calculate the average net fixed assets by summing the beginning and ending balances in fixed assets (net of accumulated depreciation) and dividing by 2.

LEARNING OBJECTIVE 9-7

Interpret the fixed asset turnover ratio.

ACCOUNTING DECISION TOOLS

Name of Measure	Formula	What It Tells You
Fixed asset turnover ratio	$\dfrac{\text{Net Sales Revenue}}{\text{Average Net Fixed Assets}}$	• Indicates dollars of sales generated for each dollar invested in fixedassets (long-lived tangible assets) • A higher ratio implies greater efficiency

The fixed asset turnover ratio measures the sales dollars generated by each dollar invested in (tangible) fixed assets. Just as the number of litres per kilometre provides a measure of a car's fuel efficiency, the fixed asset turnover ratio provides a measure of fixed asset operating efficiency. Generally speaking, a high or increasing turnover ratio relative to others in the industry suggests better—than—average use of fixed assets in the sense that each dollar of fixed assets is generating higher than average revenue.

Be aware that fixed asset turnover ratios can vary across industries because capital intensity—the need for tangible assets—varies widely. Compared to Cedar Fair and Six Flags, a company such as Yahoo! needs fewer fixed assets to generate revenue, so it has a higher turnover ratio. Exhibit 9.5 shows the fixed asset turnover ratios for three companies in 2015. Cedar Fair generated approximately 81 cents of revenue for every dollar invested in net fixed assets, whereas Six Flags generated about $1.05 of revenue in comparison to every dollar invested in net fixed assets. Look closely at the ratios and you can see the reason for the difference. Cedar Fair has invested more in long—lived tangible assets than Six Flags. When asked about this during an analyst conference call, Cedar Fair's CEO explained, "...we made a strategic decision to spend a few extra million dollars...to make rides longer (with) smoother transitions. I am convinced that consumers will reward you for these differences."

EXHIBIT 9.5   Summary of Fixed Asset Turnover Ratio Analyses

Company		Relevant Information (in millions)		2015 Fixed Asset Turnover Calculation
		2015	2014	
Cedar Fair. L.P.	Net sales	$1,236	$1,160	$\dfrac{\$1{,}236}{(\$1{,}515 + \$1{,}527)/2} = 0.81$
	Net fixed assets	1,515	1,527	
Six Flags	Net sales	$1,264	$1,176	$\dfrac{\$1{,}264}{(\$1{,}198 + \$1{,}218)/2} = 1.05$
	Net fixed assets	1,198	1,218	
YAHOO!	Net sales	$4,968	$4,618	$\dfrac{\$4{,}968}{(\$1{,}547 + \$1{,}488)/2} = 3.27$
	Net fixed assets	1,547	1,488	

Check that you can compute the fixed asset turnover ratio by trying the Self–Study Practice that follows.

Self-Study Practice 9.5

Cedar Fair reported net fixed assets of $1,506 (million) at December 31, 2013.

1. Use this information, with that in Exhibit 9.5, to calculate Cedar Fair's fixed asset turnover ratio in 2014.

$$\frac{1160}{(1527 + 1506)/2} = \boxed{0.77}$$

2. Did Cedar Fair's fixed asset turnover improve or decline from 2014 (calculated in question 1) to 2015 (shown in Exhibit 9.5)?

After you have finished, check your answers with the solution, which follows the chapter summary.

SPOTLIGHT ON Financial Reporting

Fixed Asset Turnover Before and After the Financial Crisis

Revenue at amusement parks declined in 2009 as people became increasingly concerned about their jobs and the economy. They didn't go to the parks as often, and when they did go, they spent less on food, merchandise, and games. This decline in revenue led to a significant drop in the fixed asset turnover ratios of the three amusement parks shown in the accompanying graph. Fortunately, this decline was short-lived. When the economy began to recover in 2010, the companies reported significant increases in their fixed asset turnover ratios, driven by increases in admissions and concessions revenue.

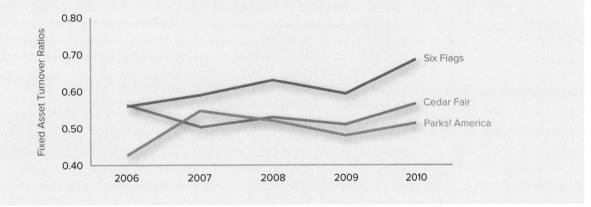

IMPACT OF DEPRECIATION DIFFERENCES

Just as differences in the nature of business operations affect financial analyses and the conclusions you draw from them, so, too, do differences in depreciation. Depreciation varies from one company to the next as a result of differences in depreciation methods, estimated useful lives, and

LEARNING OBJECTIVE 9-8

Describe factors to consider when comparing companies' long-lived assets.

COACH'S TIP

For tips and practice involving the calculations in Exhibit 9.6, try Skills Development Case S9-7 at the end of this chapter.

estimated residual values. In this section, we present a simple example to show how different depreciation methods can affect financial analysis throughout the life of a long—lived asset. Do not be fooled by the simplicity of the example. Differences in depreciation can have a significant impact in the real world.

Assume that Cedar Fair and Six Flags each acquired a new roller coaster at the beginning of the year for $15.5 million. The two companies estimate that the roller coasters will have residual values of $1.5 million at the end of their seven—year useful lives. Assume, too, that everything about the roller coasters is identical. However, Cedar Fair uses the straight—line depreciation method and Six Flags uses the double—declining—balance method. Exhibit 9.6 shows the yearly depreciation reported by the two companies (rounded to the nearest thousand dollars).

EXHIBIT 9.6 Straight-Line versus Double-Declining-Balance Depreciation Schedules

CEDAR FAIR (STRAIGHT—LINE)				SIX FLAGS (DOUBLE—DECLINING—BALANCE)		
Depreciation Expense	Accumulated Depreciation	Book Value	Year	Depreciation Expense	Accumulated Depreciation	Book Value
$2,000,000	$ 2,000,000	$13,500,000	1	$4,429,000	$ 4,429,000	$11,071,000
2,000,000	4,000,000	11,500,000	2	3,163,000	7,592,000	7,908,000
2,000,000	6,000,000	9,500,000	3	2,259,000	9,851,000	5,649,000
2,000,000	8,000,000	7,500,000	4	1,614,000	11,465,000	4,035,000
2,000,000	10,000,000	5,500,000	5	1,153,000	12,618,000	2,882,000
2,000,000	12,000,000	3,500,000	6	823,000	13,441,000	2,059,000
2,000,000	14,000,000	1,500,000	7	559,000	14,000,000	1,500,000

Notice that early in the asset's life, before year 4, the straight—line depreciation expense reported by Cedar Fair is less than the declining—balance depreciation expense reported by Six Flags. Thus, even if the two companies attract exactly the same number of customers and earn exactly the same total revenues, their reported net incomes will differ each year simply because they use two different (but equally acceptable) methods of depreciation. This example shows why a user of financial statements needs to understand the accounting methods companies use.

These differences in depreciation affect more than just depreciation expense, however. Taking this example one step further, assume that the two companies sell the roller coasters at the end of year 4 for $6,000,000. Because the disposal occurs on the last day of the year, the companies will record a full year of depreciation prior to the disposal. Thus, at the time of disposal, Cedar Fair's roller coaster has a book value of $7,500,000, but Six Flags' roller coaster has a book value of $4,035,000 (the highlighted line in Exhibit 9.6). To account for the disposal at the end of year 4, the companies record what they received, remove what they gave up (the book value of the asset), and recognize a gain or loss for the difference between the two. Exhibit 9.7 shows the calculations for the two companies.

EXHIBIT 9.7 — Calculation of Gain/Loss on Disposal

	Cedar Fair	Six Flags
Selling price	$ 6,000,000	$6,000,000
Book value (see Exhibit 9.6)	(7,500,000)	(4,035,000)
Gain (loss) on disposal	$(1,500,000)	$1,965,000

Based on the information in Exhibit 9.7, which company appears to be better managed? Someone who does not understand accounting is likely to say that Six Flags is better managed because it reported a gain on disposal, whereas Cedar Fair reported a loss. But you know that cannot be right, because both companies experienced exactly the same events. They bought the same asset at the same cost ($15.5 million) and sold it for the same amount of money ($6 million). The only difference between them is that Cedar Fair reported less depreciation over the years leading up to the disposal, so its roller coaster had a larger book value at the time of disposal. Six Flags reported more depreciation, so its roller coaster had a smaller book value at the time of disposal. As a financial statement user, you should realize that *any gain or loss on disposal that is reported on the income statement tells you as much about the method used to depreciate the asset as about management's apparent ability to successfully negotiate the sale of long–lived assets.*

Although the previous example concerned different depreciation methods, the same effects can occur for two companies that use the same depreciation method but different estimated useful lives or residual values. Useful lives can vary for several reasons, including differences in (1) the type of equipment each company uses, (2) the frequency of repairs and maintenance, (3) the frequency and duration of use, and (4) the degree of conservatism in management's estimates. How large can these differences be? Even within the same industry, sizable differences can occur. The notes to the financial statements of various companies in the airline industry, for example, reveal the following differences in the estimated useful lives of airplanes and other flight equipment:

Company	Estimated Life (in years)
US Airways	Up to 30
Air Canada	Up to 25
Alaska Airlines	Up to 20
Singapore Airlines	Up to 15

Some analysts try to sidestep such differences in depreciation calculations by focusing on financial measures that exclude the effects of depreciation. One popular measure is called **EBITDA** (pronounced some–thing like *e bit duh*), which stands for Earnings Before Interest, Taxes, Depreciation, and Amortization." Analysts calculate EBITDA by start–ing with net income and then adding back depreciation and amortization expense (as well as non–operating expenses such as interest and taxes). The idea is that this measure allows analysts to conduct financial analyses with–out having to deal with possible differences in depreciation and amortization.

EBITDA: Abbreviation for "earnings before interest, taxes, depreciation, and amortization," which is a measure of operating perfor-mance that some managers and analysts use in place of net income.

Topic	ASPE	IFRS
Component Allocation	• Significant separable costs of component parts are allocated to those parts when practicable	• Requires that property, plant, and equipment parts with significant costs be depreciated separately. There is no mention of practicability, which results in more recognition of components than under ASPE.
Cost versus Fair Value	• Must record at cost • Adjust for depreciation and impairment • Do not record increases in value	• Choose between either cost or fair value. • Adjust for depreciation and impairment. • If using fair value, record increases in value.
Research and Development	• Expense all costs of researching and developing intangible assets	• Expense research costs, but capitalize measurable costs of developing intangible assets.
Goodwill Disclosure		• Under IFRS, an intangible asset is defined as an identifiable non-monetary asset without physical substance. Goodwill is not considered to be an identifiable asset and therefore does not meet the definition of an intangible asset. Because of this, goodwill needs to be disclosed separately.

Supplement 9A

NATURAL RESOURCES

LEARNING OBJECTIVE 9-S1

Analyze and report depletion of natural resources.

Depletion: The process of allocating a natural resource's cost over the period of its extraction or harvesting.

Industries such as oil and gas, mining, and timber harvesting rely signifi-cantly on a third category of long–lived assets called *natural resources*. These natural resources, whether in the form of oil wells, mineral deposits, or timber tracts, provide the raw materials for products that are sold by companies like ExxonMobil and International Paper. When a company first acquires or develops a natural resource, the cost of the natural resource is recorded in conformity with the cost principle. As the natural resource is used up, its acquisition cost must be split among the periods in which revenues are earned in conformity with the expense recognition ("matching") principle. The term **depletion** describes the process of allocating a nat–ural resource's cost over the period of its extraction or harvesting. The units–of–production method is often used to compute depletion.

Depletion is similar to the concepts of depreciation and amortization discussed earlier in the chapter for tangible and intangible assets, with one important exception. When a natural resource such as timberland is depleted, the company obtains inventory (logs). Because depletion of the natural resource is necessary to obtain the inventory, the depletion computed during a period is added to the cost of the inventory, not expensed in the period. For example, if a timber tract costing $530,000 is depleted over its estimated cutting period based on a cutting rate of approximately 20 percent per year, it would be depleted by $106,000 each year. Recording this depletion would have the following effects on the company's account—ing equation, which would be recorded with the journal entry shown below:

1 Analyze

Assets		= Liabilities +	Shareholders' Equity
Timber Inventory	+106,000		
Accumulated			
Depletion (+xA)	−106,000		

2 Record

	Debit	Credit
Timber Inventory	106,000	
Accumulated Depletion (+xA)............................		106,000

Just as Accumulated Depreciation is subtracted from Equipment, Accumulated Depletion is subtracted from the long—lived asset Timber Tract on the balance sheet. Timber Inventory remains as an asset on the balance sheet until it is sold, at which time its cost is removed from the balance sheet and reported on the income statement as an expense called *Cost of Goods Sold*.

Review the Chapter

This section provides a chance to solidify your understanding of key points. It's worth your time to work through the following demonstration case, scan the chapter summary, test your understanding of key terms, and then practise, practise, practise.

DEMONSTRATION CASE

Diversified Industries (DI) started as a house construction company. In recent years, it has expanded into heavy construction, ready—mix concrete, sand and gravel, construction supplies, and earth—moving services. The company completed the following transactions during 2017. Amounts have been simplified.

Jan. 1   Management decided to buy a ten—year—old building for $175,000 and the land on which it was situated for $130,000. DI paid $100,000 in cash and signed a note payable for the rest.

Jan. 3   DI paid $38,000 in cash for renovations to the building prior to its use.

July 10   DI paid $1,200 cash for ordinary repairs on the building.

Dec. 31   DI determined year—end adjustments.

On December 31, DI considered the following information to determine year–end adjustments:

a. The building will be depreciated on a straight–line basis over an estimated useful life of thirty years. The estimated residual value is $33,000.

b. DI purchased another company two years ago at $100,000 more than the fair values of the net assets acquired. The goodwill has an unlimited life.

c. At the beginning of the year, DI owned equipment with a cost of $650,000 and accu–mulated depreciation of $150,000. The equipment is being depreciated using the double–declining–balance method, with a useful life of twenty years and no residual value.

d. At year–end, DI tested its long–lived assets for possible impairment of their value. Included was a piece of old excavation equipment with a cost of $156,000 and book value of $120,000, after making the adjustment for (*c*). Due to its smaller size and lack of safety features, the old equipment has limited use. The future cash flows and fair value are expected to be $35,000. Goodwill was found to be not impaired.

December 31, 2017, is the end of the annual accounting period.

Required

1. Indicate the accounts affected and the amount and direction (+ for increase and − for decrease) of the effect of each of the preceding events and required adjustments on the financial statement categories at the end of the year. Use the following headings:

Date	Assets	=	Liabilities	+	Shareholders' Equity

2. Prepare the journal entries to record each event that occurred during the year and the adjusting journal entries required at December 31.
3. Which accounts would be reported on the income statement? Where?
4. Show how the December 31, 2017, balance sheet would report these long–lived tangible and intangible assets.
5. Assuming that the company had Net Sales of $1,000,000 for the year and a book value of $500,000 for fixed assets at the beginning of the year, compute the fixed asset turnover ratio. Explain its meaning and evaluate it relative to the prior year's ratio of 1.5.

Suggested Solution

1. Effects of events (with computations in notes below the table)

Date	Assets		=	Liabilities		+	Shareholder's Equity	
Jan. 1	Cash	−100,000		Note Payable	+205,000			
	Land	+130,000						
	Building	+175,000						
Jan. 3 (Note 1)	Cash	−38,000						
	Building	+38,000						
July 10 (Note 2)	Cash	−1,200					Repairs and Maintenance Expense (+E)	−1,200
Dec. 31 (a) (Note 3)	Accumulated Depreciation (+xA)	−6,000					Depreciation Expense (+E)	−6,000
Dec. 31 (b) (Note 4)	No entry							
Dec. 31 (c) (Note 5)	Accumulated Depreciation (+xA)	−50,000					Depreciation Expense (+E)	−50,000
Dec. 31 (d) (Note 6)	Equipment	−85,000					Impairment Loss (+E)	−85,000

Notes

(1) Capitalize the $38,000 expenditure because it is necessary to prepare the asset for use.

(2) This is an ordinary repair and should be expensed.

(3)

Cost of building		Straight—line depreciation (building)
Initial payment	$175,000	($213,000 cost − $33,000 residual value) ×
Renovations prior to use	38,000	1/30 years = $6,000 annual depreciation
Acquisition cost	$213,000	

(4) Goodwill has an indefinite life and is therefore not amortized. Goodwill is tested for impairment but, as described later in the case, was found to be not impaired.

(5) Double—declining—balance depreciation (equipment)
($650,000 cost − $150,000 accumulated depreciation) × 2/20 years = $50,000 depreciation for the year.

(6) Asset impairment test
The book value of the old equipment ($120,000) exceeds expected future cash flows ($35,000). The asset has become impaired, so it needs to be written down to its fair value:

Impairment loss:	
Book Value	$120,000
Fair Value	(35,000)
Impairment Loss	$ 85,000

2. Journal entries for events during the year

Jan. 1, 2017	dr Land (+A).....................................	130,000	
	dr Building (+A).................................	175,000	
	cr Cash (−A)		100,000
	cr Note Payable (+L)		205,000
Jan. 3, 2017	dr Building (+A)	38,000	
	cr Cash (−A)		38,000
July 10, 2017	dr Repairs and Maintenance Expense (+E, –SE)	1,200	
	cr Cash (−A)		1,200

Adjusting journal entries at December 31, 2017

a. dr Depreciation Expense (+E, −SE) 6,000
   cr Accumulated Depreciation—Building (+xA, −A).......... 6,000

b. No adjusting journal entry required because goodwill is assumed to have an unlimited (or indefinite) life.

c. dr Depreciation Expense (+E, −SE) ....`..... 50,000
   cr Accumulated Depreciation—Equipment (+xA, −A) 50,000

d. dr Impairment Loss (+E, −SE).. 85,000
   cr Equipment (−A)... 85,000

3. The income statement would report Depreciation Expense, Repairs and Maintenance Expense, and Impairment Loss as operating expenses included in the computation of Income from Operations.

4. Partial balance sheet, December 31, 2017

Assets	
Property, Plant, and Equipment	
Land	$130,000
Building	213,000
Equipment	565,000*
Property, Plant, and Equipment, at cost	908,000
Less: Accumulated Depreciation	(206,000)†
Property, Plant, and Equipment, net	702,000
Goodwill	100,000

* $565,000 = $650,000 - $85,000
† $206,000 = $6,000 + $150,000 + $50,000

5. Fixed asset turnover ratio

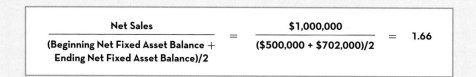

$$\frac{\text{Net Sales}}{(\text{Beginning Net Fixed Asset Balance} + \text{Ending Net Fixed Asset Balance})/2} = \frac{\$1,000,000}{(\$500,000 + \$702,000)/2} = 1.66$$

The fixed asset turnover ratio measures the company's efficiency at using its investment in property, plant, and equipment to generate sales. Approximately $1.66 of sales were generated for each dollar of fixed assets, which is an improvement over the previous year's turnover ratio of 1.5.

CHAPTER SUMMARY

LO9-1 **Define, classify, and explain the nature of long-lived assets.**

- Long−lived assets are those that a business retains for long periods of time for use in the course of normal operations rather than for sale. They may be divided into tangible assets (land, buildings, equipment) and intangible assets (including goodwill, patents, and franchises).

LO9-2 **Apply the cost principle to the acquisition of long-lived assets.**

- The acquisition cost of property, plant, and equipment is the cash−equivalent purchase price plus all reasonable and necessary expenditures made to acquire and prepare the asset for its intended use. Expenditures made after the asset is in use are either expensed or capitalized as a cost of the asset:

  a. Expenditures are expensed if they recur frequently, involve relatively small amounts, and do not directly lengthen the asset's useful life. These are considered ordinary repairs and maintenance expense.

  b. Expenditures are capitalized as a cost of the asset if they provide benefits for one or more accounting periods beyond the current period. This category includes extraordinary repairs, replacements, and additions.

LO9-3 **Apply various depreciation methods as economic benefits are used up over time.**

- In conformity with the expense recognition ("matching") principle, the cost of long−lived tangible assets (less any estimated residual value) is allocated to depreciation expense over each period benefited by the assets.

- Because of depreciation, the book value of an asset declines over time and net income is reduced by the amount of the expense.

- Common depreciation methods include straight−line (a constant amount over time), units−of−production (a variable amount over time), and double−declining−balance (a decreasing amount over time).

Explain the effect of asset impairment on the financial statements.   LO9-4

- When events or changes in circumstances reduce the estimated future cash flows of a long–lived asset below its book value, the book value of the asset should be written down, with the amount of the write–down reported as an impairment loss.

Analyze the disposal of long-lived tangible assets.   LO9-5

When assets are disposed of through sale or abandonment
- record additional depreciation arising since the last adjustment was made;
- remove the cost of the old asset and its related accumulated depreciation;
- recognize the cash proceeds (if any); and
- recognize any gains or losses when the asset's book value is not equal to the cash received.

Analyze the acquisition, use, and disposal of long-lived intangible assets.   LO9-6

- Intangible assets are recorded at cost, but only when purchased. The costs of most inter–nally developed intangible assets are expensed as research and development when incurred.
- Intangibles are reported at book value on the balance sheet.
- Amortization is calculated for intangibles with limited useful lives, using the straight–line method.
- Intangibles with unlimited useful lives, including goodwill, are not amortized, but are reviewed for impairment.

Interpret the fixed asset turnover ratio.   LO9-7

- The fixed asset turnover ratio measures the company's efficiency at using its investment in property, plant, and equipment to generate sales. Higher turnover ratios imply greater efficiency.

Describe factors to consider when comparing companies' long-lived assets.   LO9-8

- Companies in different industries require different levels of investment in long–lived assets. Beyond that, you should consider whether differences exist in depreciation methods, estimated useful lives, and estimated residual values, which can affect the book value of long–lived assets as well as ratios calculated using these book values and any gains or losses reported at the time of asset disposal.

ACCOUNTING DECISION TOOLS

Name of Measure	Formula	What It Tells You
Fixed asset turnover ratio	$$\frac{\text{Net Sales Revenue}}{\text{Average Net Fixed Assets}}$$	• Dollars of sales generated for each dollar invested in (tangible) fixed assets • A higher ratio implies greater efficiency

SOLUTIONS TO SELF-STUDY PRACTICE

Solution to SP9.1

1.

Assets	=	Liabilities	+	Shareholders' Equity
Equipment +22,000,000		Note Payable +21,000,000		
Cash −1,000,000				

dr Equipment (+A)	22,000,000	
cr Cash (−A)		1,000,000
cr Note Payable (+L)		21,000,000

Solution to SP9.2

1. Capitalize—Extends life
2. Expense—Does not increase usefulness
3. Expense—Does not increase usefulness
4. Capitalize—Extends life

Solution to SP9.3

1. ($24,000 − $3,000) × 1 year/6 years = $3,500
2. Year 1: ($24,000 − $0) × 2 years/6 years = $8,000
   Year 2: ($24,000 − $8,000) × 2 years/6 years = $5,333
3. ($24,000 − $3,000) × (800 hours/5,000 hours) = $3,360

Solution to SP9.4

1.

Assets		=	Liabilities	+	Shareholders' Equity	
Equipment	−100,000				Loss on Disposal (+E)	−15,000
Acc. Deprec.	+60,000					
Cash	+25,000					

2.

dr Cash (+A)	25,000	
dr Accumulated Depreciation (−xA, +A)	60,000	
dr Loss on Disposal (+E)	15.000	
cr Equipment (−A)		100,000

Solution to SP9.5

1. $\dfrac{\$1,160}{(\$1,527+\$1,506)/2} = 0.77$

2. Cedar Fair's fixed asset turnover increased in 2015 in comparison to 2014.

KEY TERMS

Amortization
Book Value (Carrying Value)
Capital Cost Allowance (CCA)
Capitalized
Copyright
Declining–Balance Depreciation
Method
Depletion
Depreciable Cost
Depreciation

EBITDA
Extraordinary Repairs
Franchise
Goodwill
Impairment
Licensing Rights
Long–Lived Assets
Net Assets
Ordinary Repairs and
Maintenance

Patent
Research and Development
Expenses
Residual Value
Straight–Line Depreciation Method
Technology Assets
Trademark
Units–of–Production Depreciation
Method
Useful Life

Complete definitions can also be found in the glossary at the end of this text.

Stage	Subject	Tangible Assets	Intangible Assets
Acquire	**Purchased asset**	Capitalize all related costs	Capitalize all related costs
Use	***Repairs and maintenance***		
	Ordinary	Expense related costs	Not applicable
	Extraordinary	Capitalize related costs	Not applicable
	Depreciation/amortization		
	Limited life	One of several methods: • Straight-line • Units-of-production • Declining-balance	Straight-line method
	Unlimited life	Do not depreciate (e.g., land)	Do not amortize (e.g., goodwill)
	Impairment test	Write down if necessary	Write down if necessary
Dispose	***Report gain (loss) when . . .***	Receive more (less) on disposal than book value	Receive more (less) on disposal than book value

Alternative terms

- Declining–balance depreciation methods are also called *accelerated methods*.
- Tangible assets are also called *fixed assets* or *plant assets*.
- Residual value is also called *salvage value*.

Helpful reminders

- See Exhibit 9.2 for an income statement showing where to report Depreciation Expense, Impairment Losses, and Losses (Gains) on Disposal of Assets.
- Declining–balance depreciation methods subtract Accumulated Depreciation, not residual value, from the asset's cost. For this reason, it is important to stop depreciating the asset when its book value equals its residual value.
- The following T–accounts illustrate changes in long–lived asset accounts:

Equipment (A)		Accumulated Depreciation (xA)	
Beg. bal.			Beg. bal.
Purchases (at cost)	**Disposals** (at cost)		
	Impairment (loss in value)	**Disposals** (amount accumulated)	**Depreciation** (this year)
End. bal.			End. bal.

Frequent mistakes

- Depreciation does not represent a decline in the current value of an asset; declines in asset values are recorded as impairment losses, not depreciation. The purpose of depreciation is to allocate the cost of a long–lived asset to each period in which the asset is used to generate revenue.
- When recording an asset disposal, remove its cost and accumulated depreciation separately, rather than removing just its book value from the asset's account.

PRACTICE MATERIAL

QUESTIONS (Ⓢ Symbol indicates questions that require analysis from more than one perspective.)

1. Define *long–lived assets*. What are the two common categories of long–lived assets? Describe each.

2. Under the cost principle, what amounts should be recorded as a cost of a long–lived asset?

3. What is the term for recording costs as assets rather than as expenses? Describe how the decision to record costs as assets rather than expenses affects the balance sheet and income statement in the period the costs are incurred and in future periods.

4. Waste Management, Inc. regularly incurs costs (e.g., salaries, legal fees, travel) to find new locations for landfill sites. What reasons support capitalizing these costs? What reasons support expensing these costs? ⑤

5. Distinguish between ordinary repairs and extraordinary repairs. How is each accounted for?

6. Describe the relationship between the expense recognition principle and accounting for long–lived assets.

7. Why are different depreciation methods allowed?

8. In computing depreciation, three values must be known or estimated. Identify and describe each.

9. What type of depreciation expense pattern is used under each of the following methods and when is its use appropriate?

    a. The straight–line method

    b. The units–of–production method

    c. The double–declining–balance method

10. After merging with Northwest Airlines, Delta Airlines increased the estimated useful life and increased the estimated residual value of its flight equipment. All else equal, how would each of these changes affect Delta's Depreciation Expense and Net Income? ⑤

11. A local politician claimed, "to reduce the government's deficit, it's time we require companies to start paying their deferred income tax liabilities." Explain to the politician what deferred income taxes represent and why they should not be viewed as accounts payable to the government. ⑤

12. What is an *asset impairment?* How is it accounted for?

13. What is *book value?* When equipment is sold for more than book value, how is the transaction recorded? How is it recorded when the selling price is less than book value?

14. Distinguish between depreciation and amortization.

15. Define *goodwill.* When is it appropriate to record goodwill as an intangible asset? When is its value decreased?

16. Blue Sky Flights reports the cost of its aircraft in a single category called *Flight Equipment*. What impact will IFRS have on this aspect of Blue Sky's accounting? ⑤

17. How is the fixed asset turnover ratio computed? Explain its meaning.

18. Johnson & Johnson, the maker of Tylenol, uses U.S. GAAP. Bayer, the maker of Aspirin, uses IFRS. Explain what complications might arise when comparing the Property, Plant, and Equipment category of these two companies. ⑤

19. Over what period should an addition to an existing long–lived asset be depreciated? Explain.

20. (Supplement 9A) How does depletion affect the balance sheet and income statement? Why is depletion accounted for in a manner that differs from depreciation?

MINI-EXERCISES

LO9-1, 9-3, 9-6   **M9-1 Classifying Long-Lived Assets and Related Cost Allocation Concepts**

For each of the following long–lived assets, indicate its nature and related cost allocation concept. Use the abbreviations shown on the right:

Asset	Nature	Cost Allocation		Nature
1. Property	_____	_____	B	Building
2. Delivery vans	_____	_____	E	Equipment
3. Warehouse	_____	_____	I	Intangible
4. Trademark	_____	_____	L	Land
5. New engine	_____	_____		
6. Franchise	_____	_____		**Cost Allocation**
7. Software license	_____	_____	A	Amortization
8. Computers	_____	_____	D	Depreciation
9. Production plant	_____	_____	NO	No cost allocation

M9-2 Deciding Whether to Capitalize or Expense

Canadian Golf Corporation operates over 110 golf courses throughout the country. For each of the following transactions, enter the correct letter to show whether the cost should be capitalized (C) or expensed (E).

Transactions

_____ 1. Purchased a golf course in Kelowna, British Columbia.

_____ 2. Paid a landscaping company to clear 100 acres of land on which to build a new course.

_____ 3. Paid a landscaping company to apply fertilizer to the fairways on its Coyote Hills Golf Course.

_____ 4. Hired a building maintenance company to build a 2,000 square metre addition to a clubhouse.

_____ 5. Hired a building maintenance company to replace the locks on a clubhouse and equipment shed.

_____ 6. Paid an advertising company to create a campaign to build goodwill.

M9-3 Deciding Whether to Capitalize an Expense

LO9-2, 9-6

For each of the following items, enter the correct letter to show whether the expenditure should be capitalized (C) or expensed (E).

Transactions

_____ 1. Purchased a machine, $70,000; gave long-term note

_____ 2. Paid $600 for ordinary repairs

_____ 3. Purchased a patent, $45,300 cash

_____ 4. Paid cash, $200,000, for addition to old building

_____ 5. Paid $20,000 for monthly salaries

_____ 6. Paid $250 for routine maintenance

_____ 7. Paid $16,000 for extraordinary repairs

M9-4 Computing Book Value (Straight-Line Depreciation)

LO9-3

Calculate the book value of a two-year-old machine that cost $200,000, has an estimated residual value of $40,000, and has an estimated useful life of four years. The company uses straight-line depreciation.

M9-5 Computing Book Value (Units-of-Production Depreciation)

Calculate the book value of a two–year–old machine that cost $200,000, has an estimated residual value of $40,000, and has an estimated useful life of 20,000 machine hours. The company uses units–of–production depreciation and ran the machine 3,000 hours in year 1 and 8,000 hours in year 2.

M9-6 Computing Book Value (Double-Declining-Balance Depreciation)

Calculate the book value of a two–year–old machine that cost $200,000, has an estimated residual value of $40,000, and has an estimated useful life of four years. The company uses double–declining–balance depreciation. Round to the nearest dollar.

M9-7 Calculating Partial-Year Depreciation

Calculate the amount of depreciation to report during the year ended December 31, 2017, for equipment that was purchased at a cost of $33,000 on September 1, 2017. The equipment has an estimated residual value of $3,000 and an estimated useful life of five years or 20,000 hours. Assume the equipment was used for 1,000 hours from September 1 to December 31. Calculate the amount of depreciation if the company uses (*a*) straight–line, (*b*) double–declining–balance, and (*c*) units–of–production depreciation.

M9-8 Understanding the Significance of Asset Impairment Losses and Gains on Disposal

Liz Claiborne Inc. reported $145 million of Income from Operations for its year ended December 31, 2011. This income included a gain on sale of the Liz Claiborne family of brand names to J. C. Penney for total proceeds of $268 million. At the time of disposal, the brand names had a book value of zero because they had been developed internally by Liz Claiborne Inc. Soon after the disposal, in January 2012, the company changed its name to Fifth & Pacific Companies to reflect the sale of its Liz Claiborne brand names. For its year ended December 28, 2013, Fifth & Pacific reported Income from Operations of $73.9 million after deducting the following asset impairment losses:

Juicy Couture brand impairment loss	$ 1.7 million
TRIFARI brand impairment loss	3.3 million
Mexx impairment loss	6.1 million
Total impairment losses	$11.1 million

a. Determine the gain on sale that Liz Claiborne reported in 2011 when it disposed of its brand names.

b. What would have been the company's Income (Loss) from Operations for this year had it not sold its Liz Claiborne brand names?

c. Determine the Income from Operations that Fifth & Pacific would have reported in 2013 had its impairment losses been zero.

d. What percentage of operating income (before impairment) did the 2013 impairment losses represent?

M9-9 Recording the Disposal of a Long-Lived Asset

Prepare journal entries to record the transactions that follow.

a. Mortell Limited disposed of two computers at the end of their useful lives. The computers had cost $4,800 and their Accumulated Depreciation was $4,800. No proceeds were received.

b. Assume the same information as in (*a*), except that Accumulated Depreciation, updated to the date of disposal, was $3,600.

M9-10 Reporting and Recording the Disposal of a Long-Lived Asset (Straight-Line Depreciation)

LO9-5

As part of a major renovation at the beginning of the year, Hunter Pharmaceuticals, Inc. sold shelving units (store fixtures) that were ten years old for $1,000 cash. The shelves originally cost $6,400 and had been depreciated on a straight–line basis over an estimated useful life of ten years with an estimated residual value of $400. Assuming that depreciation has been recorded to the date of sale, show the effect of the disposal on the accounting equation. Prepare the journal entry to record the sale of the shelving units.

M9-11 Capitalizing versus Expensing Intangible Asset Costs

LO9-6

Most highly visible companies spend significant amounts of money to protect their intel–lectual property, ensuring that no one uses this property without direct permission. For example, to include logos throughout this book, we had to obtain written permission from each company—a process that stretched over nearly a year and often resulted in requests being denied. Discuss whether companies should capitalize or expense the money paid to employees who evaluate requests for use of their logos and who search for instances where the companies' intellectual property has been used without permission. Draw an analogy to similar costs incurred for employees responsible for the use and upkeep of tangible assets.

M9-12 Computing Goodwill and Patents

LO9-6

Taste–T Company has been in business for thirty years and has developed a large group of loyal restaurant customers. Downter's Foods made an offer to buy Taste–T Company for $6,000,000. The market value of Taste–T's recorded assets, net of liabilities, on the date of the offer is $5,600,000. Taste–T also holds a patent for a fluting machine that the com–pany invented (the patent with a market value of $200,000 was never recorded by Taste–T because it was developed internally). How much has Downter's Foods included for intangibles in its offer of $6,000,000? Assuming Taste–T accepts this offer, which company will report Goodwill on its balance sheet?

M9-13 Computing and Evaluating the Fixed Asset Turnover Ratio

LO9-7

The following information was reported by Amuse Yourself Parks (AYP) for 2012:

Net fixed assets (beginning of year)	$8,450,000
Net fixed assets (end of year)	8,250,000
Net sales for the year	4,175,000
Net income for the year	1,700,000

Compute the company's fixed asset turnover ratio for the year. What can you say about AYP's fixed asset turnover ratio when compared to Cedar Fair's 2012 ratio as seen in Exhibit 9.5?

M9-14 Computing Revised Depreciation After Change in Cost and Estimated Life

LO9-3

Plummer Industries purchased a machine for $43,800 and is depreciating it with the straight–line method over a life of eight years, using a residual value of $3,000. At the beginning of the sixth year, an extraordinary repair was made costing $7,500, the estimated useful life was extended to thirteen years, and no change was made to the estimated residual value. Calculate depreciation expense for year 6, rounded to the nearest dollar.

M9-15 (Supplement 9A) Recording Depletion for a Natural Resource

LO9-S1

Saskatchewan Forestry Company purchased a timber tract for $600,000 and estimates that it will be depleted evenly over its ten–year useful life with no residual value. Show the journal entry that would be recorded if 10 percent of the total timber is cut and placed into inventory during the current year.

EXERCISES

LO9-1, 9-7 **E9-1 Preparing a Classified Balance Sheet**

Assume the following is a list of account titles and amounts (in millions) reported at December 31, 2017, by Hasbro, Inc., a leading manufacturer of games, toys, and interactive entertainment software for children and families:

Buildings and Improvements	$195	Goodwill	$475
Prepaids and Other Current Assets	171	Machinery and Equipment	413
Allowance for Doubtful Accounts	32	Accumulated Depreciation	403
Other Non-current Assets	200	Inventories	301
Cash and Cash Equivalents	630	Other Intangibles	568
Accounts Receivable	644	Land and Improvements	7

Required:

1. Prepare the asset section of a classified balance sheet for Hasbro, Inc., assuming Hasbro follows ASPE.
2. Assuming that Hasbro's 2017 Net Sales Revenue was $4,022 (million) and its Net Fixed Assets was $188 (million) at December 30, 2016, calculate the fixed asset turnover ratio for 2017. Has the company generated more or less revenue from each dollar of fixed assets than in 2016, when the ratio was 20.75?

LO9-2, 9-3 **E9-2 Computing and Recording a Basket Purchase and Straight-Line Depreciation**

Bridgadoon Consulting bought a building and the land on which it is located for $182,000 cash. The land is estimated to represent 70 percent of the purchase price. The company paid $22,000 for building renovations before it was ready for use.

Required:

Check Figure:
[Req. 4]:
Book value of
land and building
at end of year
2 = $192,000

1. Explain how the renovation costs should be accounted for.
2. Give the journal entry to record all expenditures. Assume that all transactions were for cash and they occurred at the start of the year.
3. Compute straight–line depreciation on the building at the end of one year, assuming an estimated twelve–year useful life and a $4,600 estimated residual value.
4. What should be the book value of the land and building at the end of year 2?

LO9-2, 9-3 **E9-3 Determining Financial Statement Effects of an Asset Acquisition and Straight-Line Depreciation**

Conover Corp. ordered a machine on January 1, 2017, at a purchase price of $30,000. On delivery, January 2, 2017, the company paid $8,000 on the machine and signed a note payable for the balance. On January 3, 2017, it paid $250 for freight on the machine. On January 5, Conover paid installation costs relating to the machine amounting to $1,500. On December 31, 2017 (the end of the accounting period), Conover recorded depreciation on the machine using the straight–line method with an estimated useful life of ten years and an estimated residual value of $2,750.

Required:

1. Indicate the effects (accounts, amounts, and + or −) of each transaction (on January 1, 2, 3, and 5) on the accounting equation. Use the following schedule:
2. Compute the acquisition cost of the machine.

Date	Assets	=	Liabilities	+	Shareholders' Equity

3. Compute the depreciation expense to be reported for 2017.
4. What should be the book value of the machine at the end of 2018?

LO9-2, 9-3

E9-4 Recording Straight-Line Depreciation and Repairs

Wiater Company operates a small manufacturing facility. On January 1, 2017, an asset account for the company showed the following balances:

Manufacturing equipment	$160,000
Accumulated depreciation through 2016	110,000

During the first week of January 2017, the following expenditures were incurred for repairs and maintenance:

Routine maintenance and repairs on the equipment	$ 1,850
Major overhaul of the equipment that improved efficiency	21,000

The equipment is being depreciated on a straight–line basis over an estimated life of fifteen years with a $10,000 estimated residual value. The annual accounting period ends on December 31.

Required:

Indicate the effects (accounts, amounts, and + or −) of the following two items on the accounting equation, using the headings shown below.

1. The adjustment for depreciation made at the end of 2016.
2. The two expenditures for repairs and maintenance during January 2017.

Item	Assets	=	Liabilities	+	Shareholders' Equity

LO9-2, 9-3

E9-5 Determining Financial Statement Effects of Straight-Line Depreciation and Repairs

Refer to the information in E9–4.

Check Figure:
[Req. 2]:
Remaining estimated
life beginning of
2017 = 4 years

Required:

1. Give the adjusting journal entry that would have been made at the end of 2016 for depreciation on the manufacturing equipment.
2. Starting at the beginning of 2017, what is the remaining estimated life of the equipment?
3. Give the journal entries to record the two expenditures for repairs and maintenance during 2017.

LO9-3

E9-6 Computing Depreciation Under Alternative Methods

PlasticWorks Corporation bought a machine at the beginning of the year at a cost of $12,000. The estimated useful life was five years, and the residual value was $2,000. Assume that the estimated productive life of the machine is 10,000 units. Expected annual production was: year 1, 3,000 units; year 2, 3,000 units; year 3, 2,000 units; year 4, 1,000 units; and year 5, 1,000 units.

Required:

1. Complete a depreciation schedule for each of the alternative methods:
   a. Straight–line
   b. Units–of–production
   c. Double–declining–balance

		Income Statement	Balance Sheet		
Year	Computation	Depreciation Expense	Cost	Accumulated Depreciation	Book Value
At acquisition					
1					

2. Which method will result in the highest net income in year 2? Does this higher net income mean the machine was used more efficiently under this depreciation method?

LO9-3 **E9-7 Computing Depreciation Under Alternative Methods**

Sonin Company purchased and installed electronic payment equipment at its drive−in restaurant at the beginning of the year at a cost of $27,000. The equipment has an estimated residual value of $1,500. The equipment is expected to process 255,000 payments over its three−year useful life. Per year, expected payment transactions are 61,200 in year 1, 140,250 in year 2, and 53,550 in year 3.

Required:

Complete an depreciation schedule for each of the alternative methods:
1. Straight−line
2. Units−of−production
3. Double−declining−balance

| | | Income Statement | | Balance Sheet | | |
Year	Computation	Depreciation Expense	Cost	Accumulated Depreciation	Book Value
At acquisition					
1					

LO9-3 **E9-8 Inferring Asset Age from Straight-Line Depreciation**

On January 1, 2017, the records of Great Grass Corp. (GGC) showed the following regarding production equipment:

Equipment (estimated residual value, $4,000)	$14,000
Accumulated Depreciation (straight-line, one year)	2,000

Required:

Based on the data given, compute the estimated useful life of the equipment.

LO9-4 **E9-9 Exploring Financial Statement Effects of Asset Impairment**

Refer to E9−8.

Required:

If GGC's management estimated that the equipment had future cash flows and a fair value of only $6,800 at December 31, 2017, how would this affect GGC's balance sheet and income statement? Explain.

LO9-5 **E9-10 Demonstrating the Effect of Book Value on Reporting an Asset Disposal**

FedEx Corporation is the world's leading express−distribution company. In addition to the world's largest fleet of all−cargo aircraft, the company uses more than 53,700 ground vehicles to pick up and deliver packages. Assume that FedEx sold a delivery truck for $16,000 that it originally purchased for $28,000. The company had recorded depreciation for three years.

Required:

Check Figure:
[Req. 1(b)]:
Loss on disposal = $2,000

1. Calculate the amount of gain or loss on disposal, assuming that Accumulated Depreciation was: (*a*) $12,000, (*b*) $10,000, and (*c*) $15,000.
2. Using the following structure, indicate the effects (accounts, amounts, and + or −) for the disposal of the truck in each of the three preceding situations:

Date	Assets	=	Liabilities	+	Shareholders' Equity

3. Based on the three preceding situations, explain how the amount of depreciation recorded up to the time of disposal affects the amount of gain or loss on disposal.

4. Prepare the journal entry to record the disposal of the truck for each situation in requirement 1.

E9-11 Computing and Reporting the Acquisition and Amortization of Three Different Intangible Assets

LO9-6

Kreiser Company had three intangible assets at the end of 2017 (end of the accounting year):

  a. A patent was purchased from J. Miller on January 1, 2017, for a cash cost of $5,640. When purchased, the patent had an estimated life of fifteen years.

  b. A trademark was registered with the federal government for $10,000. Management estimated that the trademark could be worth as much as $200,000 because it has an indefinite life.

  c. On January 1, 2017, computer licensing rights were purchased for $60,000. The rights are expected to have a four-year useful life to the company.

Required:

1. Compute the acquisition cost of each intangible asset.

2. Compute the amortization of each intangible for the year ended December 31, 2017.

3. Show how these assets and any related expenses should be reported on the balance sheet and income statement for 2017.

E9-12 Recording the Purchase, Amortization, and Impairment of a Patent

LO9-4, 9-6

Conrad Inc. purchased a patent for $1,000,000 for "a specialty line of patented switch plate covers and outlet plate covers specifically designed to light up automatically when the power fails." Assume the switch plate patent was purchased January 1, 2017, and it is being depreciated over a period of ten years. Assume that Conrad Inc. does not use an accumulated amortization account but instead charges amortization directly against the intangible asset account.

Required:

1. Describe the effects of the purchase and amortization of the switch plate patent on the 2017 balance sheet and income statement.

2. Give the journal entries to record the purchase and amortization of the switch plate patent in 2017.

3. After a year of unsuccessful attempts to manufacture the switch plate covers, Conrad Inc. determined the patent was significantly impaired and its book value on January 1, 2017, was written off. Describe the financial statement effects of accounting for the asset impairment and give the journal entry to record the impairment.

E9-13 Computing and Interpreting the Fixed Asset Turnover Ratio from a Financial Analyst's Perspective

LO9-7

Assume the following data were included in a recent Apple Inc. annual report (in millions):

	2014	2015	2016	2017
Net sales	$13,931	$19,315	$24,006	$32,479
Net property, plant, and equipment	817	1,281	1,832	2,455

Required:

1. Compute Apple's fixed asset turnover ratio for 2015, 2016, and 2017. Round your answer to one decimal place.

2. Was Apple able to maintain its strong financial performance in recent years when the economy was beginning to falter?

Check Figure:
[Req. 1]:
2017 Fixed Asset
Turnover = 15.2

E9-14 Computing Depreciation and Book Value for Two Years Using Alternative Depreciation Methods and Interpreting the Impact on the Fixed Asset Turnover Ratio

Torge Company bought a machine for $65,000 cash. The estimated useful life was five years, and the estimated residual value was $5,000. Assume that the estimated useful life in productive units is 150,000. Units actually produced were 40,000 in year 1 and 45,000 in year 2.

Required:

1. Determine the appropriate amounts to complete the following schedule. Show computations.

	Depreciation Expense for		Book Value at the End of	
Method of Depreciation	Year 1	Year 2	Year 1	Year 2
Straight-line				
Units-of-production				
Double-declining-balance				

2. Which method would result in the lowest net income for year 1? For year 2?
3. Which method would result in the lowest fixed asset turnover ratio for year 1? Why?

E9-15 Determining Financial Statement Effects of a Change in Estimate

Refer to E9–4.

Required:

1. Indicate the effects (accounts, amounts, and + or −) of the 2017 adjustment for depreciation of the manufacturing equipment, assuming no change in the estimated life or residual value. Show computations.

Date	Assets	=	Liabilities	+	Shareholders' Equity

2. Give the adjusting entry that should be made at the end of 2017 for depreciation.

E9-16 (Supplement 9A) Calculating and Reporting Depletion

Lucky Lake Oil Company (LLOC) paid $3,000,000 for an oil reserve estimated to hold 50,000 barrels of oil. Oil production is expected to be 10,000 barrels in year 1, 30,000 barrels in year 2, and 10,000 barrels in year 3. LLOC expects to begin selling barrels from its oil inventory in year 2.

Required:

Assuming these estimates are accurate, describe the amounts, financial statements, and classifications that would be used for the oil reserves and oil inventory at the end of year 1.

COACHED PROBLEMS

CP9-1 Computing Acquisition Cost and Recording Depreciation Under Three Alternative Methods

At the beginning of the year, McCoy Company bought three used machines from Colt, Inc. The machines immediately were overhauled, installed, and started operating. Because the machines were different, each was recorded separately in the accounts.

	Machine A	Machine B	Machine C
Amount paid for asset	$6,600	$25,600	$6,400
Installation costs	300	600	200
Renovation costs prior to use	1,500	400	1,000
Repairs after production began	400	350	325

By the end of the first year, each machine had been operating 8,000 hours.

Required:

1. Compute the cost of each machine. Explain the rationale for capitalizing or expensing the various costs.

   TIP: Total cost for all three machines is $42,600.

2. Give the journal entry to record depreciation expense at the end of year 1, assuming the following:

| Machine | Estimates | | Depreciation Method |
	Life	Residual Value	
A	5 years	$ 500	Straight-line
B	40,000 hours	1,000	Units-of-production
C	5 years	2,000	Double-declining-balance

> TIP: Remember that the formula for double-declining-balance uses cost minus accumulated depreciation (not residual value).

LO9-5

CP9-2 Recording and Interpreting the Disposal of Long-Lived Assets

During 2017, Bhumika Company disposed of two different assets. On January 1, 2017, prior to the assets' disposal, the accounts reflected the following:

Asset	Original Cost	Residual Value	Estimated Life	Accumulated Depreciation (straight-line)
Machine A	$76,200	$4,200	15 years	$57,600 (12 years)
Machine B	20,000	3,000	8 years	12,750 (6 years)

The machines were disposed of in the following ways:

a. Machine A: This machine was sold on January 2, 2017, for $8,200 cash.
b. Machine B: On January 2, 2017, this machine suffered irreparable damage from an accident and was removed immediately by a salvage company at no cost.

Required:

1. Give the journal entries related to the disposal of each machine at the beginning of 2017.

> TIP: When no cash is received on disposal, the loss on disposal will equal the book value of the asset at the time of disposal.

> TIP: Loss on disposal for Machine A equals $10,400.

> TIP: Loss on disposal for Machine B equals $7,250.

2. Explain the accounting rationale for the way that you recorded each disposal.

LO9-2, 9-3, 9-6

CP9-3 Analyzing and Recording Long-Lived Asset Transactions with Partial-Year Depreciation

Palmer Cook Productions manages and operates two rock bands. The company entered into the following transactions during a recent year.

January 2	Purchased a tour bus for $80,000 by paying $20,000 cash and signing a $60,000 note
January 8	Bus painted with the logos of the two bands at a cost of $350, on account
January 30	Wrote a cheque for the amount owed on account for the work completed on January 8
February 1	Purchased new speakers and amplifiers and wrote a cheque for the full $12,000 cost
February 8	Paid $250 cash to tune up the tour bus
March 1	Paid $20,000 cash and signed a $190,000 note to purchase a small office building and land; appraisal indicated that the building and land contributed equally to the total price
March 31	Paid $90,000 cash to acquire the goodwill and certain tangible assets of KrisMyt, Inc.; fair values of the tangible assets acquired were $20,000 for band equipment and $60,000 for recording equipment

Required:

1. Analyze the accounting equation effects and record journal entries for each of the transactions.

   TIP: Goodwill is recorded as the excess of the purchase price over the fair value of individual assets.

2. For the tangible and intangible assets acquired in the preceding transactions, determine the amount of depreciation and amortization that Palmer Cook Productions should report for the quarter ended March 31. For convenience, the equipment and vehicle are depreciated the same way, using the straight−line method with a useful life of five years and no resid−ual value. The building is depreciated using the double−declining−balance method, with a ten−year useful life and residual value of $20,000.

   TIP: Calculate depreciation and amortization from the acquisition date to the end of the quarter.

3. Prepare a journal entry to record the depreciation and amortization calculated in requirement 2.

4. What advice would you offer the company in anticipation of switching to IFRS in the future?

   TIP: Consider whether the vehicle and different types of equipment should be grouped together.

GROUP A PROBLEMS

LO9-1, 9-7   **PA9-1 Preparing a Classified Balance Sheet**

The following is a list of account titles and amounts (in thousands) reported at June 30, 2017, by Darian's Dirt Bikes, Inc., a retail distributor of motorcycles:

Buildings and Improvements	$292	Goodwill	$ 79
Prepaids and Other Current Assets	120	Machinery and Equipment	646
Allowance for Doubtful Accounts	15	Accumulated Depreciation	421
Other Non-current Assets	30	Inventories	740
Cash and Cash Equivalents	59	Other Intangibles	100
Accounts Receivable	330	Land and Improvements	23

Required:

1. Prepare the asset section of a classified balance sheet for Darian's Dirt Bikes, Inc. using ASPE.

2. Using Darian's Dirt Bikes, Inc.'s 2017 Net Sales Revenue of $2,520 (thousand) and its Net Fixed Assets of $471 (thousand) at June 30, 2016, calculate the fixed asset turnover ratio for 2017. Has the company generated more or less revenue from each dollar of fixed assets than in 2016, when the ratio was 5.00?

LO9-2, 9-3   **PA9-2 Computing Acquisition Cost and Recording Depreciation Under Three Alternative Methods**

e**X**cel

At the beginning of the year, CCZ Corporation bought three used machines from Pequita Compression Incorporated. The machines immediately were overhauled, installed, and started operating. Because the machines were different from each other, each was recorded separately in the accounts.

	Machine A	Machine B	Machine C
Cost of the asset	$10,000	$31,500	$22,000
Installation costs	1,600	2,100	800
Renovation costs prior to use	600	1,400	1,600
Repairs after production began	500	400	700

By the end of the first year, each machine had been operating 7,000 hours.

Check Figure:
[Req. 1]:
Machine C total
cost = $24,400

Required:

1. Compute the cost of each machine. Explain the rationale for capitalizing or expensing the various costs.

2. Give the journal entry to record depreciation expense at the end of year 1, assuming the following:

| Machine | Estimates | | Depreciation Method |
	Life	Residual Value	
A	4 years	$1,000	Straight-line
B	33,000 hours	2,000	Units-of-production
C	5 years	1,400	Double-declining-balance

PA9-3 Recording and Interpreting the Disposal of Long-Lived Assets

LO9-5

During 2017, Ly Company disposed of two different assets. On January 1, 2017, prior to disposal of the assets, the accounts reflected the following:

Asset	Original Cost	Residual Value	Estimated Life	Accumulated Depreciation (straight-line)
Machine A	$24,000	$2,000	5 years	$17,600 (4 years)
Machine B	59,200	3,200	14 years	48,000 (12 years)

The machines were disposed of in the following ways:

a. Machine A: This machine was sold on January 1, 2017, for $5,750 cash.
b. Machine B: On January 1, 2017, this machine suffered irreparable damage from an accident and was removed immediately by a salvage company at no cost.

Required:

1. Give the journal entries related to the disposal of each machine at the beginning of 2017. Transaction "a" relates to the recording of the 2017 depreciation and transaction "b" relates to the recording of the disposal of the machine.
2. Explain the accounting rationale for the way that you recorded each disposal.

PA9-4 Analyzing and Recording Long-Lived Asset Transactions with Partial-Year Depreciation

LO9-2, 9-3, 9-6

Casting Crown Construction entered into the following transactions during a recent year:

January 2	Purchased a bulldozer for $200,000 by paying $20,000 cash and signing a $180,000 note
January 3	Replaced the steel tracks on the bulldozer at a cost of $20,000, purchased on account
January 30	Wrote a cheque for the amount owed on account for the work completed on January 3
February 1	Replaced the seat on the bulldozer and wrote a cheque for the full $600 cost
March 1	Paid $2,400 cash for the rights to use computer software for a two-year period

Required:

1. Analyze the accounting equation effects and record journal entries for each of the transactions.
2. For the tangible and intangible assets acquired in the preceding transactions, determine the amount of depreciation and amortization that Casting Crown Construction should report for the quarter that ended March 31. The equipment is depreciated using the double-declining-balance method with a useful life of five years and $40,000 residual value.
3. Prepare a journal entry to record the depreciation and amortization calculated in requirement 2.
4. What advice would you offer the company in anticipation of switching to IFRS in the future?

Check Figure:
[Req. 3]:
Total depreciation and amortization expense = $22,100

PA9-5 Recording Transactions and Adjustments for Tangible and Intangible Assets

LO9-1, 9-2, 9-3, 9-4, 9-5, 9-6

The following transactions and adjusting entries were completed by Gravure Graphics International, a paper-packaging company. The company uses straight-line depreciation for trucks and other vehicles, double–declining–balance depreciation for buildings, and straight–line amortization for patents.

January 2, 2016	Paid $95,000 cash to purchase storage shed components
January 3, 2016	Paid $5,000 cash to have the storage shed erected; storage shed has an estimated life of ten years and a residual value of $10,000
April 1, 2016	Paid $38,000 cash to purchase a pickup truck for use in the business; truck has an estimated useful life of five years and a residual value of $8,000
May 13, 2016	Paid $250 cash for repairs to the pickup truck
July 1, 2016	Paid $20,000 cash to purchase patent rights on a new paper bag manufacturing process; patent is estimated to have a remaining useful life of five years
December 31, 2016	Recorded depreciation and amortization on the pickup truck, storage shed, and patent
June 30, 2017	Sold the pickup truck for $33,000 cash (Record the depreciation on the truck prior to recording its disposal.)
December 31, 2017	Recorded depreciation on the storage shed; determined that the patent was impaired and wrote off its remaining book value (i.e., wrote down the book value to zero)

Required:

Give the journal entries required on each of the above dates.

GROUP B PROBLEMS

LO9-1, 9-7 **PB9-1 Preparing a Classified Balance Sheet**

The following is a list of account titles and amounts (in thousands) reported at December 31, 2017, by Megan's Veterinary Clinic:

Buildings and Improvements	$95	Goodwill	$45
Prepaids and Other Current Assets	71	Machinery and Equipment	43
Allowance for Doubtful Accounts	3	Accumulated Depreciation	43
Other Non-current Assets	20	Inventories	31
Cash and Cash Equivalents	63	Other Intangibles	58
Accounts Receivable	64	Land and Improvements	7

Check Figure:
[Req. 2]:
2017 Fixed Asset
Turnover = 3.65

Required:

1. Prepare the asset section of a classified balance sheet for Megan's Veterinary Clinic, using ASPE.
2. Using Megan's Veterinary Clinic's 2017 Net Sales Revenue of $402 (thousand) and its Net Fixed Assets of $118 (thousand) at December 31, 2016, calculate the fixed asset turnover ratio for 2017. Has the company generated more or less revenue from each dollar of fixed assets than in 2016, when the ratio was 2.75?

LO9-2, 9-3 **PB9-2 Computing Acquisition Cost and Recording Depreciation under Three Alternative Methods**

At the beginning of the year, Oakmountain Company bought three used machines from Canadian Manufacturing, Inc. The machines immediately were overhauled, installed, and started operating. Because the machines were different from each other, each was recorded separately in the accounts.

	Machine A	Machine B	Machine C
Amount paid for asset	$19,600	$10,100	$9,800
Installation costs	300	500	200
Renovation costs prior to use	100	300	600
Repairs after production began	220	900	480

By the end of the first year, each machine had been operating 4,000 hours.

Required:

1. Compute the cost of each machine. Explain the rationale for capitalizing or expensing the various costs.
2. Give the journal entry to record depreciation expense at the end of year 1, assuming the following:

	Estimates		
Machine	Life	Residual Value	Depreciation Method
A	7 years	$1,100	Straight-line
B	40,000 hours	900	Units-of-production
C	4 years	2,000	Double-declining-balance

PB9-3 Recording and Interpreting the Disposal of Long-Lived Assets

LO9-5

During 2017, Rayon Corporation disposed of two different assets. On January 1, 2017, prior to disposal of the assets, the accounts reflected the following:

Asset	Original Cost	Residual Value	Estimated Life	Accumulated Depreciation (straight-line)
Machine A	$60,000	$11,000	7 years	$28,000 (4 years)
Machine B	14,200	1,925	5 years	7,365 (3 years)

The machines were disposed of in the following ways:

a. Machine A: This machine was sold on January 2, 2017, for $33,500 cash.
b. Machine B: On January 2, 2017 this machine suffered irreparable damage from an accident and was removed immediately by a salvage company at no cost.

Required:

1. Give the journal entries related to the disposal of each machine at the beginning of 2017.
2. Explain the accounting rationale for the way in which you recorded each disposal.

Check Figure:
[Req. 1]:
Gain on Disposal for
Machine A = $1,500

PB9-4 Analyzing and Recording Long-Lived Asset Transactions with Partial-Year Depreciation

LO9-2, 9-3, 9-6

Grondy's Restaurant Company (GRC) entered into the following transactions during a recent year.

April 1	Purchased a new food locker for $5,000 by paying $1,000 cash and signing a $4,000 note
April 2	Installed an air–conditioning system in the food locker at a cost of $3,000, purchased on account
April 30	Wrote a cheque for the amount owed on account for the work completed on April 2
May 1	A local carpentry company repaired the restaurant's front door; GRC wrote a cheque for the full $120 cost
June 1	Paid $9,120 cash for the rights to use the name and store concept created by a different restaurant that has been successful in the region; for the next four years, GRC will operate under the Mullet Restaurant name

Required:

1. Analyze the accounting equation effects and record journal entries for each of the transactions.
2. For the tangible and intangible assets acquired in the preceding transactions, determine the amount of depreciation and amortization that Grondy's Restaurant Company should report for the quarter ended June 30. For convenience, the food locker and air–conditioning system are depreciated as a group using the straight–line method, with a useful life of five years and no residual value.

3. Prepare a journal entry to record the depreciation and amortization calculated in requirement 2.

4. What advice would you offer the company in anticipation of switching to IFRS in the future?

LO9-1, 9-2, 9-3, 9-4, 9-5, 9-6

PB9-5 Recording Transactions and Adjustments for Tangible and Intangible Assets

The following transactions and adjusting entries were completed by Super Swift, a local delivery company. The company uses straight–line depreciation for delivery vehicles, double–declining–balance depreciation for buildings, and straight–line amortization for franchise rights.

January 2, 2016	Paid $75,000 cash to purchase a small warehouse building near the airport; building has an estimated life of 20 years and a residual value of $15,000
July 1, 2016	Paid $40,000 cash to purchase a delivery van; van has an estimated useful life of five years, and a residual value of $8,000
October 2, 2016	Paid $400 cash to paint a small office in the warehouse building
October 13, 2016	Paid $150 cash to get the oil changed in the delivery van
December 1, 2016	Paid $60,000 cash to Clairmont Parcel Service (CPS) to begin operating a Super Swift business as a franchise using the name The CPS Store; this franchise right expires in five years
December 31, 2016	Recorded depreciation and amortization on the delivery van, warehouse building, and franchise right
June 30, 2017	Sold the warehouse building for $64,000 cash (Record the depreciation on the building prior to recording its disposal.)
December 31, 2017	Recorded depreciation on the delivery van and amortization on the franchise right; determined that the franchise right was not impaired in value

Required:

Give the journal entries required on each of the above dates.

COMPREHENSIVE PROBLEM

LO3-3, 4-2, 8-2, 9-2, 9-3

C9-1 Accounting for Operating Activities (Including Depreciation) and Preparing Financial Statements

Consider the following, thinking about what you learned in Chapters 3, 4, 8, and 9.

Grid Iron Prep Inc. (GIPI) is a service business incorporated in January 2017 to provide personal training for athletes aspiring to play college or university football. The following transactions occurred during the year ended December 31, 2017.

a. GIPI issued shares in exchange for $90,000 cash.

b. GIPI purchased a gymnasium building and gym equipment at the beginning of the year for $50,000, 80 percent of which related to the gymnasium and 20 percent to the equipment.

c. GIPI paid $250 cash to have the gym equipment refurbished before it could be used.

d. GIPI collected $36,000 cash in training fees during the year, of which $2,000 were customer deposits to be earned in 2018.

e. GIPI paid $23,000 of wages and $7,000 in utilities.

f. GIPI provided $3,000 in training during the final month of the year and expected collection in 2018.

g. GIPI will depreciate the gymnasium building using the double–declining–balance method over twenty years. Gym equipment will be depreciated using the straight–line method, with an estimated residual value of $2,250 at the end of its four–year useful life.

h. GIPI received a bill for $350 of advertising done during December. The bill has not been paid or recorded.

i. GIPI will record an estimated 5 percent of its Accounts Receivable as not collectable.

j. GIPI's income tax rate is 30 percent. Assume depreciation for tax is the same amount as depreciation for financial reporting purposes.

Required:

1. Prepare journal entries to record the transactions and adjustments listed in transactions (*a*) through (*j*).
2. Prepare GIPI's annual income statement, statement of retained earnings, and classified balance sheet using ASPE.

SKILLS DEVELOPMENT CASES

S9-1 Finding Financial Information

LO9-2, 9-3, 9-7

Refer to the summarized financial statements of The Home Depot in Appendix A.

Required:

1. The total amount of Accumulated Depreciation (and accumulated depreciation on leasehold improvements) at January 29, 2017, is $18,512 million. What percentage is this of the total cost of property and equipment?
2. In the year ended January 29, 2017, The Home Depot reported Depreciation and Amortization Expense of $1,754 million. What percentage of net sales is it?
3. What is the fixed asset turnover ratio for the current year?
4. For each of the preceding questions, where could you locate the information?

S9-2 Comparing Financial Information

LO9-2, 9-3, 9-7, 9-8

Refer to the summarized financial statements of The Home Depot in Appendix A and Lowe's Companies, Inc. in Appendix B.

Required:

1. What method of depreciation does Lowe's Companies, Inc. use?
2. What amount of Accumulated Depreciation did Lowe's Companies, Inc. report at February 3, 2017? What percentage is this of the total cost of property and equipment? Is this a larger (or smaller) percentage of the total cost of property and equipment than for The Home Depot (in S9–1)? What does it suggest to you about the length of time the assets have been depreciated?
3. Lowe's Companies, Inc.'s estimated useful life of buildings is between five and forty years. In some cases, this could be shorter or longer than that estimated by The Home Depot. How will this affect the fixed asset turnover ratios of the two companies?
4. What amount of Depreciation Expense was reported on Lowe's Companies, Inc.'s income statement for the year ended February 3, 2017? What percentage of net sales is it? Compare this percentage to that of The Home Depot and describe what this implies about the two companies' operations.
5. What is Lowe's Companies, Inc.'s fixed asset turnover ratio for the current year? Compare this ratio to that of The Home Depot and describe what it implies about the operations of the two companies.

S9-3 Internet-Based Team Research: Examining an Annual Report

LO9-1, 9-3, 9-6, 9-7

As a team, select an industry to analyze. Using the Internet, each team member should access the annual report for one publicly traded company in the industry, with each member selecting a different company. (See S1–3 in Chapter 1 for a description of possible resources for these tasks.)

Required:

1. On an individual basis, each team member should write a short report that incorporates
   a. a description of the depreciation methods used;
   b. a computation of the percentage of fixed asset cost that has been depreciated and a description of what it implies about the length of time the assets have been depreciated;
   c. a computation of the fixed asset turnover ratios for the current and prior years, and a description of what this tells you about the efficiency of the company's asset use; and
   d. a description of the kinds of intangible assets, if any, that the company reports on the balance sheet.

2. Then, as a team, write a short report comparing and contrasting your companies using these attributes. Discuss any patterns across the companies that you, as a team, observe. Provide potential explanations for any differences discovered.

LO9-2, 9-7 **S9-4 Ethical Decision Making: A Real-Life Example**

Assume you work as a staff member in a large accounting department for a multinational public company. Your job requires you to review documents relating to the company's equipment purchases. Once you've verified that purchases were properly approved, you prepare journal entries to record the equipment purchases in the accounting system. Typically, you handle equipment purchases of $100,000 or less.

This morning, you were contacted by the executive assistant to the chief financial officer. She says that the CFO has asked to see you immediately in his office. Although your boss's boss has attended a few meetings where the CFO was present, you have never met the CFO during your three years with the company. Needless to say, you are anxious about the meeting.

When you enter the CFO's office, you are warmly greeted with a smile and friendly handshake. The CFO compliments you on the great work that you've been doing for the company. You soon feel a little more comfortable, particularly when the CFO mentions that he has a special project for you.

He states that he and the chief executive officer have negotiated significant new arrangements with the company's equipment suppliers, which require the company to make advance payments for equipment to be purchased in the future. The CFO says that, for various reasons he doesn't want to discuss, he will be processing the payments through the operating division of the company rather than through the equipment accounting group.

Given that the payments will be made through the operating division, they will initially be classified as operating expenses of the company. He indicates that clearly these advance payments for property and equipment should be recorded as assets, so he will be contacting you at the end of every quarter to make an adjusting journal entry to capitalize the amounts inappropriately classified as operating expenses. He advises you that a new account, called Prepaid Equipment, has been established for this purpose.

He quickly wraps up the meeting by telling you that it is important that you not talk about the special project with anyone. You assume he doesn't want others to become jealous of your important new responsibility.

A few weeks later, at the end of the first quarter, you receive a voice mail from the CFO stating, "The adjustment that we discussed is $771,000,000 for this quarter." Before deleting the message, you replay it to make sure you heard it right. Your company generates over $8 billion in revenues and incurs $6 billion in operating expenses every quarter, but you've never made a journal entry for that much money. So, just to be sure there's no mistake, you send an email to the CFO confirming the amount. He phones you back immediately to abruptly inform you, "There's no mistake. That's the number." Feeling embarrassed that you may have annoyed the CFO, you quietly make the adjusting journal entry.

For each of the remaining three quarters in that year and for the first quarter in the following year, you continue to make these end-of-quarter adjustments. The "magic number," as the CFO likes to call it, was $560,000,000 for Q2, $742,745,000 for Q3, $941,000,000 for Q4, and $818,204,000 for Q1 of the following year. During this time, you've had several meetings and lunches with the CFO where he provides you with the magic number, sometimes supported with nothing more than a Post-it note with the number written on it. He frequently compliments you on your good work and promises that you'll soon be in line for a big promotion.

Despite the CFO's compliments and promises, you are growing increasingly uncomfortable with the journal entries that you've been making. Typically, whenever an ordinary equipment purchase involves an advance payment, the purchase is completed a few weeks later. At that time, the amount of the advance is removed from an Equipment Deposit account and transferred to the appropriate equipment account. This hasn't been the case with the CFO's special project. Instead, the Prepaid Equipment account has continued to grow, now standing at over $3.8 billion. There's been no discussion about how or when this balance will be reduced, and no depreciation has been recorded for it.

Just as you begin to reflect on the effect the adjustments have had on your company's fixed assets, operating expenses, and operating income, you receive a call from the vice–president for internal audit. She needs to talk with you this afternoon about "a peculiar trend in the company's fixed asset turnover ratio and some suspicious journal entries that you've been making."

Required:

1. Complete the following table to determine what the company's accounting records would have looked like had you not made the journal entries as part of the CFO's special project. Comment on how the decision to capitalize amounts, which were initially recorded as operating expenses, has affected the level of income from operations in each quarter.

(millions of dollars)	Q1 Year 1 (March 31)		Q2 Year 1 (June 30)		Q3 Year 1 (September 30)		Q4 Year 1 (December 31)		Q1 Year 2 (March 31)	
	With the Entries	Without the Entries	With the Entries	Without the Entries	With the Entries	Without the Entries	With the Entries	Without the Entries	With the Entries	Without the Entries
Property and Equipment, Net	$38,614	$	$35,982	$	$38,151	$	$38,809	$	$39,155	$
Sales Revenues	8,825	8,825	8,910	8,910	8,966	8,966	8,478	8,478	8,120	8,120
Operating Expenses	7,628		8,526		7,786		7,725		7,277	
Income from Operations	1,197		384		1,180		753		843	

2. Using the publicly reported numbers (which include the special journal entries that you recorded), compute the fixed asset turnover ratio (rounded to two decimal places) for the periods ended Q2 to Q4 of year 1 and Q1 of year 2. What does the trend in this ratio suggest to you? Is this consistent with the changes in operating income reported by the company?

3. Before your meeting with the vice–president for internal audit, you think about the above computations and the variety of peculiar circumstances surrounding the "special project" for the CFO. What in particular might have raised your suspicion about the real nature of your work?

4. Your meeting with internal audit was short and unpleasant. The vice–president indicated that she had discussed her findings with the CFO before meeting with you. The CFO claimed that he, too, had noticed the peculiar trend in the fixed assets turnover ratio, but that he hadn't had a chance to investigate it further. He urged internal audit to get to the bottom of things, suggesting that perhaps someone might be making unapproved journal entries. Internal audit had identified you as the source of the journal entries and had been unable to find any documents that approved or substantiated the entries. She ended the meeting by advising you to find a good lawyer. Given your current circumstances, describe how you would have acted earlier had you been able to foresee where it might lead you.

5. In the real case on which this one is based, the internal auditors agonized over the question of whether they had actually uncovered a fraud or whether they were jumping to the wrong conclusion. The *Wall Street Journal* mentioned this on October 30, 2002, by stating, "it was clear...that their findings would be devastating for the company. They worried about whether their revelations would result in layoffs. Plus, they feared that they would somehow end up being blamed for the mess." Beyond the personal consequences mentioned in this quote, describe other potential ways in which the findings of the internal auditors would likely be devastating for the publicly traded company and those associated with it.

Epilogue: This case is based on a fraud committed at WorldCom (now owned by Verizon). The case draws its numbers, the nature of the unsupported journal entries, and the CFO's role in carrying out the fraud from a report issued by WorldCom's bankruptcy examiner. Year 1 in this case was actually 2001 and year 2 was 2002. This case excludes other fraudulent activities that contributed to WorldCom's $11 billion fraud. The 63–year–old CEO was sentenced to twenty–five years in prison for planning and executing the biggest fraud in the history of

American business. The CFO, who cooperated in the investigation of the CEO, was sentenced to five years in prison.

LO9-3 ### S9-5 Ethical Decision Making: A Mini-Case

Assume you are one of three members of the accounting staff working for a small private company. At the beginning of this year, the company expanded into a new industry by acquiring equipment that will be used to make several new lines of products.

The owner and general manager of the company has indicated that, as one of the conditions for providing financing for the new equipment, the company's bank will receive a copy of the company's annual financial statements. Another condition of the loan is that the company's total assets cannot fall below $250,000. Violation of this condition gives the bank the option to demand immediate repayment of the loan.

Before making the adjustment for this year's depreciation, the company's total assets are reported at $255,000. The owner has asked you to take a look at the facts regarding the new equipment and "work with the numbers to make sure everything stays onside with the bank."

A depreciation method has not yet been adopted for the new equipment. Equipment used in other parts of the company is depreciated using the double—declining—balance method. The cost of the new equipment was $35,000 and the manager estimates it will be worth "at least $7,000" at the end of its four—year useful life. Because the products made with the new equipment are only beginning to catch on with consumers, the company used the equipment to produce just 4,000 units this year. It is expected that, over all four years of its useful life, the new equipment will make a total of 28,000 units.

Required:

1. Calculate the depreciation that would be reported this year under each of the three meth—ods shown in this chapter. Which of the methods would meet the owner's objective?
2. Evaluate whether it is ethical to recommend that the company use the method identified in requirement 1. What two parties are most directly affected by this recommendation? How would each party benefit from or be harmed by the recommendation? Does the recom—mendation violate any laws or applicable rules? Are there any other factors that you would consider before making a recommendation?

LO9-3, 9-5, 9-8 ### S9-6 Critical Thinking: Analyzing the Effects of Depreciation Policies on Income

As an aspiring financial analyst, you have applied to a major Bay Street firm for a summer job. As part of the screening process, the firm provides you with a short case study and asks you to evaluate the financial success of two hypothetical companies that started operations on January 1, 2016. Both companies operate in the same industry, use very similar assets, and have very similar customer bases. Among the additional information provided about the companies are the following comparative income statements.

	Fast Corporation		Slow Corporation	
	2017	2016	2017	2016
Net Sales	$ 60,000	$ 60,000	$60,000	$60,000
Cost of Goods Sold	20,000	20,000	20,000	20,000
Gross Profit	40,000	40,000	40,000	40,000
Selling, General, and Administrative Expenses	19,000	19,000	19,000	19,000
Depreciation Expense	3,555	10,667	5,000	5,000
Gains (Losses) on Disposal	2,222	—	(2,000)	—
Income from Operations	$ 19,667	$ 10,333	$14,000	$16,000

Required:

Prepare an analysis of the two companies to determine which company is better managed. If you could request two additional pieces of information from these companies' financial statements, describe specifically what they would be and explain how they would help you to make a decision.

To make some extra money, you've started preparing templates of business forms and schedules for others to download from the Internet (for a small fee). After relevant information is entered into each template, it automatically performs calculations using formulas you have entered into the template. For the depreciation template, you decide to produce two worksheets—one that calculates depreciation and book value under the straight–line method and another that calculates these amounts using the double–declining–balance method.

The templates perform straightforward calculations of depreciation and book value when given the cost of an asset, its estimated useful life, and its estimated residual value. These particular templates won't handle disposals or changes in estimates—you plan to create a deluxe version for those functions. To illustrate that your templates actually work, you enter the information used to produce the depreciation schedules shown in Exhibit 9.6, with Cedar Fair and Six Flags as examples.

Although you're confident you can use appropriate formulas in the spreadsheet to create a template for the straight–line method, you're a little uncertain about how to make the double–declining–balance method work. As usual, you email your friend Owen for advice. Here's what he said:

From: Owentheaccountant@yahoo.com
To: Helpme@hotmail.com
Cc:
Subject: Excel Help

I wish I'd thought of charging money for showing people how to do ordinary accounting activities. You'd have made me rich by now. Here's how to set up your worksheets. Begin by creating an "input values" section. This section will allow someone to enter the asset cost, residual value, and estimated life in an area removed from the actual depreciation schedule. You don't want someone accidentally entering amounts over formulas that you've entered into the schedule.

The cells from the input values section will be referenced by other cells in the depreciation schedule. You will want to enter formulas into the cells for the first year row, and then copy and paste them into rows for the other years. When doing this, you will need to use what is called an "absolute reference," which means that the cell reference does not change when one row is copied and pasted into a different row. Unlike an ordinary cell reference that has a format of A1, an absolute reference has the format of A1, which prevents the spreadsheet from changing either the column (A) or row (1) when copying the cell to other cells. You may find this useful when preparing both the straight-line and double-declining-balance schedules.

To create the depreciation schedules, use five columns labelled (1) year, (2) beginning of year accumulated depreciation, (3) depreciation, (4) end of year accumulated depreciation, and (5) end of year book value.

The double-declining-balance template will be the trickiest to create because you need to be concerned that the book value is not depreciated below the residual value in the last year of the asset's life. To force the template to automatically watch for this, you will need to use the IF function. I have included a screenshot of a template I created, using the IF function to properly calculate depreciation for all years of the asset's life. Notice the formula shown in the formula bar at the top.

Required:

Create the spreadsheet templates to calculate depreciation and book value using the straight—line and double—declining—balance methods. Demonstrate that the template works by reproducing the schedules in Exhibit 9.6.

> **TIP:** To switch between displaying cell formulas and their values, press CTRL and ~ (tilde) at the same time. Also, use Excel's help feature to obtain further information about the IF function.

CONTINUING CASES

LO9-3, 9-5 **CC9-1 Accounting for the Use and Disposal of Long-Lived Assets**

Nicole's Getaway Spa (NGS) purchased a hydrotherapy tub system to add to the wellness programs at NGS. The machine was purchased at the beginning of the year at a cost of $5,000. The estimated useful life was five years, and the residual value was $500. Assume that the estimated productive life of the machine is 15,000 hours. Expected annual production is: year 1, 4,100 hours; year 2, 2,500 hours; year 3, 3,400 hours; year 4, 1,800 hours; and year 5, 3,200 hours.

Required:

1. Complete a depreciation schedule for each of the alternative methods.
   a. Straight—line
   b. Units—of—production
   c. Double—declining—balance
2. Assume NGS sold the hydrotherapy tub system for $2,100 at the end of year 3. Prepare the journal entry to account for the disposal of this asset under the three different methods.
3. The following amounts were forecast for year 3: Sales Revenues, $42,000; Cost of Goods Sold, $33,000; Other Operating Expenses, $4,000; and Interest Expense, $800. Create an income statement for year 3 for each of the different depreciation methods, ending at Income Before Income Tax Expense. (Don't forget to include a loss or gain on disposal for each method.)

LO9-3, 9-4 **CC9-2 Wiki Art Gallery (WAG)**

Refer to the Wiki Art Gallery (WAG) instructional case in Appendix D and read the case in sufficient depth to answer the following questions.

1. What method for depreciation does Wiki Art Gallery use and is this method generally accepted?
   a. WAG uses the capitalization method, which is in accordance with GAAP.
   b. WAG uses the straight—line method, which is in accordance with GAAP.
   c. WAG uses the declining—balance method, which is in accordance with GAAP.
   d. WAG uses the units—of—production method, which is in accordance with GAAP.

2. Calculate the amount of 2011 depreciation expense that WAG recorded on the old computer equipment and on the new computer equipment.
   a. WAG recorded $206 on the old equipment and $180 on the new equipment.
   b. WAG recorded $825 on the old equipment and $180 on the new equipment.
   c. WAG recorded $825 on the old equipment and $386 on the new equipment.
   d. Cannot be determined with the information provided.

3. Which aspect(s) of WAG's accounting for website development costs in 2011 may be inappropriate?
   a. WAG capitalized $9,000 despite $7,000 being a regularly recurring cost.
   b. WAG began amortizing only after the website development costs were paid.
   c. The six—year useful life overstates the likely period of benefit.
   d. All of the above.

4. By what amount would WAG's net income change if WAG were to adopt a two–year usef3ul life for the new computer equipment, appropriately capitalize the Web development cost, and amortize the capitalized Web costs over a three–year life?

   a. WAG's net income would decrease by $928.

   b. WAG's net income would decrease by $1,233.

   c. WAG's net income would decrease by $1,867.

   d. WAG's net income would decrease by $7,928.

Endnote

1. Tim Hortons, Franchising Program: http://www.timhortons.com/ca/en/corporate/franchise–ca–faq.php

CHAPTER 10

Liabilities

THAT WAS

THEN

Previous chapters focused on items related to the assets section of the balance sheet.

THIS IS

NOW

This chapter focuses on items related to the liabilities section of the balance sheet.

YOUR LEARNING OBJECTIVES

Understand the business

LO10-1 Explain the role of liabilities in financing a business.

Study the accounting methods

LO10-2 Explain how to account for common types of current liabilities.

LO10-3 Analyze and record bond liability transactions.

LO10-4 Describe how to account for contingent liabilities.

Evaluate the results

LO10-5 Calculate and interpret the debt-to-assets ratio and the times interest earned ratio.

Review the chapter

Chapter Summary

Supplemental material

LO10-S1 Use straight-line bond amortization.

LO10-S2 Use effective-interest bond amortization.

LO10-S3 Use simplified effective-interest bond amortization.

LunaseeStudios/Shutterstock.com

FOCUS COMPANY:

General Mills

www.generalmills.com

GENERAL MILLS

They've turned in the reports, and they're just waiting to hear their letter grade. They're expecting an A and will be devastated if it's a B. Sounds like some high-achieving students, right? It could be. But it's actually the Jolly Green Giant, Lucky the Leprechaun, the Pillsbury Doughboy, and their corporate bosses at General Mills. That's right. This magically delicious company and all its characters receive a letter grade, just like you and your friends.

Their grading process differs a bit from yours, because their grade is assigned by credit-rating agencies like Standard & Poor's, Fitch, and Moody's, indicating the company's ability to pay its liabilities on a timely basis. Another difference is that their grades can range from AAA to D. The AAA rating is given to companies in rock-solid financial condition, and the D goes to those likely to pay less than half of what they owe. In general, anything above BB is considered a good to high-quality credit rating, which is what General Mills typically earns. Anything below BB is called "junk."

In this chapter, you will learn about the accounting procedures and financial ratios used to report and interpret liabilities, and how they influence credit ratings. Although we focus on corporate reporting and analyses, this chapter can also help you to understand the kind of information others use to evaluate your own personal credit rating.

Logo courtesy of General Mills.

ORGANIZATION OF THE CHAPTER

Understand the Business

THE ROLE OF LIABILITIES

The balance sheet excerpt in Exhibit 10.1 shows that, at the end of its 2015 fiscal year, General Mills had financed its $22.0 billion of total assets using a combination of liabilities ($15.8 billion) and equity ($6.2 billion). For General Mills and many other companies, liabilities play a significant role in financing most business activities. Liabilities are created when a company buys goods and services on credit, obtains short–term loans to cover gaps in cash flows, and issues long–term debt to obtain money for expanding into new regions and markets.

The importance of liabilities was highlighted during the recent global financial crisis. Soon after banks restricted their lending activities and suppliers tightened their credit terms, companies began to fail. Circuit City, for example, filed for bankruptcy protection just one week after its suppliers required the company to pay cash on delivery (COD).

General Mills survived the financial crisis because it was able to pay suppliers on time and its BBB+ credit rating helped it obtain short–term

LEARNING OBJECTIVE 10-1

Explain the role of liabilities in financing a business.

EXHIBIT 10.1	Excerpt from General Mills' Balance Sheet	GENERAL MILLS

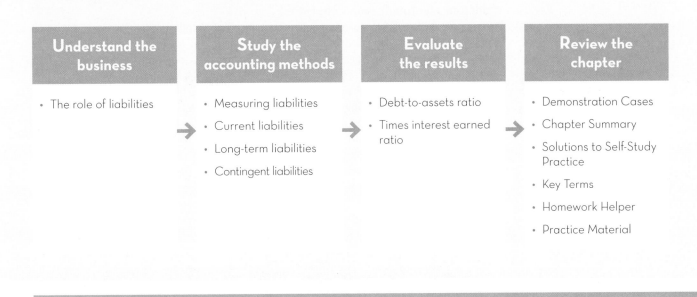

Balance Sheet Excerpt (in millions)			
Assets		**Liabilities and Shareholders' Equity**	
Current Assets		Current Liabilities	
Cash and Cash Equivalents	$ 334	Accounts Payable	$ 1,684
Accounts Receivable (net)	1,387	Accrued Liabilities (see Exhibit 10.2)	1,590
Inventory	1,541	Notes Payable	616
Prepaid Rent and Other	524	Current Portion of Long–Term Debt	1,000
Total Current Assets	3,786	Total Current Liabilities	4,890
Land, Building, and Equipment	3,783	Long–Term Debt	7,608
Goodwill	8,875	Other Liabilities	3,295
Other Intangible Assets	4,677	Total Liabilities	15,793
Other Assets	844	Shareholders' Equity (summarized)	6,172
Total Assets	$21,965	Total Liabilities and Equity	$21,965

financing as needed. To provide long–term financial stability, the company also arranged debt financing that will not come due until the year 2040. With these critical sources of financing in place, the company was able to ride out the rough economic times.

To help financial statement users know when liabilities must be repaid, companies prepare a classified balance sheet, as shown in Exhibit 10.1. In Chapter 2, you learned that a classified balance sheet reports current liabilities separate from other liabilities. Technically, current liabilities are defined as short–term obligations that will be paid with current assets within the company's current operating cycle or within one year of the balance sheet date, whichever is longer.

Practically, this definition can be simplified as *liabilities that are due within one year* (because most companies have operating cycles that are shorter than a year). This means that, as shown in Exhibit 10.1, General Mills will have to pay nearly $4.9 billion in the upcoming year. An additional $7.6 billion in long–term debt and $3.3 billion in other liabilities will need to be paid in the longer term. Although these long–term obligations rarely get a separate subheading of their own, people often refer to them as *non–current* or *long–term liabilities*.

Current liabilities: (1) Debts and obligations that are expected to be paid, settled, or fulfilled within twelve months of the balance sheet date. (2) Short-term obligations that will be paid with current assets within the current operating cycle or one year, whichever is longer.

Explain how to account for common types of current liabilities.

How much to begin

How much is added

How much is paid off

Study the Accounting Methods

MEASURING LIABILITIES

As Exhibit 10.1 illustrates, General Mills owed various types of liabilities at the end of its 2015 fiscal year. In this section, we will describe each of these liabilities and the methods used to account for them. In general, the amount reported for each liability is the result of three factors:

1. **The initial amount of the liability.** Initially, the company records each liability at the amount of cash a creditor would accept to settle the liability immediately after a transaction or event creates the liability.

2. **Additional amounts owed to the creditor.** The company increases liabilities, whenever additional obligations arise, by purchasing goods and services, receiving customer deposits, or incurring interest charges over time.

3. **Payments or services provided to the creditor.** The company decreases liabilities whenever the company makes a payment or provides services to the creditor.

Notice that a liability is first recorded at the amount initially owed, which excludes interest charges. Interest arises only when time passes, so no interest is recorded on the day the company purchases an item on account or the day the company receives a loan.

CURRENT LIABILITIES

Let's look more closely at each current liability listed in Exhibit 10.1.

Accounts Payable

You've used this account in previous chapters, so we'll keep this discussion short. Accounts Payable is increased (credited) when a company receives goods or services on credit, and it is decreased (debited) when the company pays on its account. Accounts Payable is interest free unless it becomes overdue.

Accrued Liabilities

Chapter 4 showed how to use an adjusting journal entry at the end of the accounting period to record increases in both Wages Expense (debit) and Wages Payable (credit) when a company had incurred but not yet paid that period's wages. Similar adjustments were made for interest incurred but not paid and income taxes incurred but not paid. Because these adjustments are called *accruals*, the liabilities (Wages Payable, Interest Payable, etc.) are generally referred to as *accrued liabilities*. **Accrued liabilities** relate to various unpaid expenses, including advertising, electricity, corporate income tax, interest, payroll tax, and warranties. General Mills itemizes its $1.6 billion of Accrued Liabilities in a note to its financial statements, similar to Exhibit 10.2.

> **Accrued liabilities:** Liabilities for expenses that have been incurred but not yet billed or paid at the end of the accounting period. Also called *accrued expenses*.

Have been incurred not yet paid.

EXHIBIT 10.2	Examples of Accrued Liabilities

(in millions)	2015
Accrued Advertising	$ 565
Accrued Payroll	362
Accrued Taxes	21
Accrued Interest	92
Other	550
Total Accrued Liabilities	$1,590

Accrued Payroll In addition to Wages Payable, companies record liabilities for other aspects of payroll. Two significant payroll liabilities relate to payroll deductions and employer payroll taxes.

Payroll Deductions Payroll deductions are amounts subtracted from employees' gross earnings to determine their net pay. Gross earnings are computed by multiplying the time worked by the pay rate promised by the employer (40 hours × $15 per hour = $600 gross earnings). From these gross earnings, certain payroll deductions are subtracted for items such as federal, provincial, and territorial income taxes; Canada Pension Plan (CPP); and Employment Insurance (EI). The tear–away portion of the paycheque shown in Exhibit 10.3 illustrates payroll deductions totalling $149.30. Net pay equals gross earnings less payroll deductions ($450.70 = $600.00 − $149.30).

You might think your employer keeps the deductions from your gross earnings, but that's not true. Your employer is obligated to remit those deductions to another organization or government agency on your behalf. As Exhibit 10.3 shows, payroll deductions create current liabilities for your employer.

Payroll deductions are either required by law or voluntarily requested by employees. The law requires that employers deduct federal and provincial

EXHIBIT 10.3	Accounting for Gross Earnings, Payroll Deductions, and Net Pay

GENERAL MILLS CANADA CORP.
5825 Explorer Drive
Mississauga, ON L4W 5P6

Cheque No. 222

Date: January 10, 2017

PAY FOUR HUNDRED FIFTY AND 70/100 **DOLLARS**

To the Order of
ANDREA PALMER
223 Pickard Bay
Edmonton, AB T5A 2S5

$450.70

For illustration only.

DETACH AND RETAIN THIS PORTION FOR YOUR RECORDS

GROSS EARNINGS			PAYROLL DEDUCTIONS					NET PAY
HOURS	HOURLY RATE	GROSS	INCOME TAXES	CPP	EI	OTHER	TOTAL	$450.70
40.00	$15.00	$600.00	$100.55	$28.50	$10.25	$10.00	$149.30	

Wages Expense   Current Liabilities   Cash Payment

or territorial income taxes from each employee's gross earnings. The law also requires that each employee support the Canada Pension Plan and the Employment Insurance Act through employee payroll deductions. Employers use these same methods to account for any other payroll deduc— tions (including voluntary deductions for charitable donations, union dues, retirement savings, parking, etc.). The employer classifies payroll deductions as *current* liabilities because they must be paid within the current year.

To illustrate how to record these items, let's assume (for simplicity) that General Mills has 1,000 workers just like the employee in Exhibit 10.3. The accounting equation effects and journal entry would be as follows:

① Analyze

Assets	=	Liabilities		+	Shareholders' Equity	
Cash −450,700		Withheld Income Tax Payable	+100,550		Wages Expense (+E)	−600,000
		CPP Contributions Payable	+28,500			
		EI Contributions Payable	+10,250			
		United Way Contributions Payable	+10,000			

② Record

dr Wages Expense (+E, −SE)	600,000	
cr Withheld Income Tax Payable (+L)		100,550
cr CPP Contributions Payable (+L)		28,500
cr EI Contributions Payable (+L)		10,250
cr United Way Contributions Payable (+L)		10,000
cr Cash (−A)		450,700

Employer Payroll Taxes Beyond paying employees and remitting payroll deductions, employers have other responsibilities that lead to substantial addi— tional labour costs. In the remainder of this section, we consider two employer payroll taxes: Canada Pension Plan and Employment Insurance contributions.

All employers are required to match the amount paid by employees to the Canada Pension Plan. In addition, employers are required by the Employment Insurance Act to pay 1.4 times the total employee contribution. So what does this all mean? It means that employers pay slightly more to the Employment Insurance program than employees do, whereas for the Canada Pension Plan, the costs are the same for the employer as they are for the employee.

To illustrate how these payroll expenses affect the accounting records, let's assume General Mills was required to contribute $28,500 for CPP (100 percent of total employee contributions = $28,500) and $14,350 for Employment Insurance (1.4 times the total employee contributions = 1.4 × $10,250). These payroll taxes are extra costs the employer incurs beyond the costs of salaries and wages, so they are reported as an additional operating expense on the income statement. Until they have been paid, the liabilities for these taxes are recorded in current liability accounts, as follows:

① Analyze

Assets	=	Liabilities		+	Shareholders' Equity	
		CPP Contributions Payable	+28,500		Payroll Tax	
		EI Contributions Payable	+14,350		Expense (+E)	−42,850

② Record

dr Payroll Tax Expense (+E, −SE).......................................	42,850	
cr CPP Contributions Payable (+L)		28,500
cr EI Contributions Payable (+L)		14,350

When the employer pays these taxes (and the payroll deductions shown earlier), it decreases the liability accounts (with debits) and decreases its Cash account (with a credit).

Accrued Income Taxes Corporations pay taxes not only on payroll but also on income they earn, just as you do. A corporation's tax return, which the CRA calls a T2, is similar to a company's income statement, except that it calculates *taxable* income by subtracting tax–allowed expenses from revenues. This taxable income is then multiplied by a tax rate, which ranges for corporations from about 15 to 38 percent. Corporate income taxes are due three months after year–end, although most corporations are required to pay advance instalments during the year.

COACH'S TIP

The adjusting journal entry to accrue income taxes was presented in Chapter 4, Income Taxes Incurred but Not Yet Recorded.

Notes Payable

The next liability reported by General Mills in Exhibit 10.1 is Notes Payable. This liability represents the amount the company owes to others as a result of issuing promissory notes. It is the flip side of the notes receivable transactions that were explained in Chapter 8.

Four key events occur with any note payable: (1) establishing the note, (2) accruing interest incurred but not paid, (3) recording interest paid, and (4) recording principal paid. Financial effects are recorded for each of these four events. As an example, assume that on November 1, 2017, General Mills borrowed $100,000 cash on a one–year note that required General Mills to pay 6 percent interest and $100,000 principal, both on October 31, 2018.

1. **Establish the note payable.** The $100,000 loan that created the note payable has the following accounting equation effects, which General Mills would record using the following journal entry:

① Analyze

	Assets		=	Liabilities		+	Shareholders' Equity
Cash	+100,000			Note Payable	+100,000		

② Record

dr **Cash (+A)**	100,000	
cr **Note Payable (+L)**		100,000

2. **Accrue interest incurred but not paid.** Interest occurs as time passes. It is not owed the day the note is established, but rather it accumulates as each day passes. Under accrual accounting, interest must be recorded as it is incurred over time. The timeline in Exhibit 10.4 shows how General Mills should account for the interest incurred on the note over its one–year term. In reality, General Mills would record an adjustment each month or quarter for interest incurred in that period, but for simplicity, we have assumed it occurs only once, at the end of the year. From the date the note was established (November 1, 2017) to the end of the year (December 31, 2017), General Mills incurred two months of interest expense.

COACH'S TIP

This example shows how to account for the note from the borrower's perspective. The same example is presented from the lender's perspective in Chapter 8, Notes Receivable and Interest Revenue.

EXHIBIT 10.4 | **Timeline for Notes Payable**

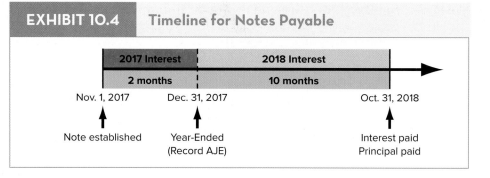

The amount of interest to record for *two* months is computed using the interest formula, as follows:

> Interest (I) = Principal (P) × Interest Rate (R) × Time (T)
> $1,000   = $100,000   ×   6%   ×   2/12

The effect of this adjustment, along with the adjusting journal entry to record the $1,000 of interest expense payable on December 31, 2017, is as follows:

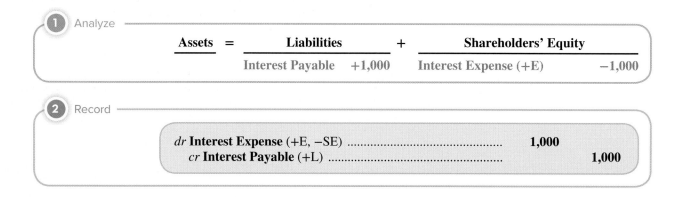

1 Analyze

Assets	=	Liabilities	+	Shareholders' Equity
		Interest Payable +1,000		Interest Expense (+E) −1,000

2 Record

dr **Interest Expense (+E, −SE)** 1,000
    cr **Interest Payable (+L)** 1,000

3. **Record interest paid.** The timeline in Exhibit 10.4 indicates that on October 31, 2018, General Mills pays both the principal and the interest. Although the company is likely to pay both amounts with a single cheque, it is instructive to consider these payments separately. In this step, we analyze and record the interest payment. The interest payment is $6,000 (which is equal to $100,000 × 6% × 12/12). As shown in the following timeline, this $6,000 interest pay—ment includes the $1,000 that was accrued as Interest Payable at December 31, 2017, plus $5,000 interest expense incurred during the ten months between January 1 and October 31, 2018.

The $6,000 interest payment is analyzed and recorded as follows:

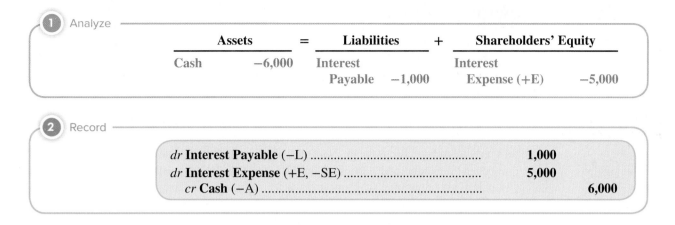

Analyze

	Assets		=	Liabilities	+	Shareholders' Equity	
Cash		−6,000		Interest Payable	−1,000	Interest Expense (+E)	−5,000

Record

dr Interest Payable (−L) 1,000
dr Interest Expense (+E, −SE) 5,000
  cr Cash (−A)   6,000

4. **Record principal paid.** The accounting equation effects and journal entry to record the $100,000 principal payment on October 31, 2018, are as follows:

Analyze

	Assets		=	Liabilities		+	Shareholders' Equity
Cash		−100,000		Note Payable	−100,000		

Record

dr Note Payable (−L) 100,000
  cr Cash (−A)...   100,000

HOW'S IT GOING?

Self-Study Practice 10.1

Assume Starbucks issues a 5 percent, $12,000 note on December 1. How would this transaction and the month-end interest adjustment affect the accounting equation?

Analyze

	Assets	=	Liabilities	+	Shareholders' Equity
December 1					
December 31					

After you have finished, check your answers with the solution, which follows the chapter summary.

Current Portion of Long-Term Debt

Remember when you were in Grade 9 and it seemed as if it would be forever before you'd graduate from high school? At that time, graduation was something that would happen in the long term. Later, when you were in Grade 12, graduation became a current event—one that was less than a year away. A similar progression occurs with long–term debt.

If a company borrows money with the promise to repay it in two years, the loan is classified as a long–term debt. The company reports only the accrued interest on the loan as a current liability in that year's balance sheet. After a year has passed, however, the loan becomes a current liability (just as your graduation became a current event when you reached your fourth year). When that happens, the borrower must report the loan in the Current Liabilities section of the balance sheet. Rather than create a different account for this, accountants simply remove the amount of principal to be repaid in the upcoming year from the total long-term debt and report it as a current liability, Current Portion of Long-Term Debt.

The final line item in the Current Liabilities section of the General Mills balance sheet provides an example (see Exhibit 10.1). Notice that in 2015, General Mills reported a current liability for the $1,000 million of long-term debt that was expected to be paid in 2016. This reclassification of long-term debt into current liabilities is needed so that the balance sheet accurately reports the dollar amount of existing liabilities that will be paid in the upcoming year.

HOW'S IT GOING?

Self-Study Practice 10.2

Assume that on December 31, 2016, Netflix borrowed $10,000, a portion of which is to be repaid each year on November 30. Specifically, Netflix will make the following principal payments: $1,000 in 2017, $2,000 in 2018, $3,000 in 2019, and $4,000 in 2020. Show how this loan will be reported on the balance sheets on December 31, 2017, and 2016, assuming that principal payments will be made when required.

	At December 31	
	2017	2016
Current Liabilities:		
Current Portion of Long-Term Debt	$	$
Long-Term Debt		
Total Liabilities	$9,000	$10,000

After you have finished, check your answers with the solution, which follows the chapter summary.

Additional Current Liabilities

Because of the nature of General Mills' business, the company does not have some current liabilities that are common to other companies. This section covers two such liabilities.

Sales Tax Payable Retail companies are required to charge a provincial sales tax (PST) in all provinces and territories but Alberta. In addition to PST, the federal government charges a goods and services tax (GST) of 5 percent. In the provinces of Nova Scotia, New Brunswick, Newfoundland and Labrador, Prince Edward Island, and Ontario, the provincial sales tax is combined with the GST to form a single harmonized sales tax (HST).

The provincial sales tax rates vary from province to province, as do the goods and services to which the tax is applied and the way the tax is applied. Retailers collect sales tax from consumers at the time of sale and forward it to the provincial and federal governments. Just like payroll taxes, the tax collected by the company is reported as a current liability until it is forwarded to the government. Sales tax is not an expense to the retailer because it is simply collected and passed on to the government. So if Best Buy sold a television in Saskatchewan (where the PST rate is 6 percent) for $1,000 cash plus taxes, Best Buy would collect $1,110 cash, earn $1,000 in sales revenue, recognize a $60 liability (= 6% × $1,000) for the provincial sales tax collected, and also recognize a $50 liability (= 5% × $1,000) for the GST collected. The financial effects of this sale are analyzed below and would be recorded with the journal entry that follows.

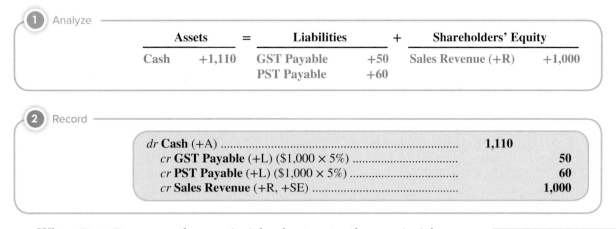

1 Analyze

Assets		=	Liabilities		+	Shareholders' Equity	
Cash	+1,110		GST Payable	+50		Sales Revenue (+R)	+1,000
			PST Payable	+60			

2 Record

dr **Cash** (+A)	1,110	
cr **GST Payable** (+L) ($1,000 × 5%)		50
cr **PST Payable** (+L) ($1,000 × 5%)		60
cr **Sales Revenue** (+R, +SE)		1,000

When Best Buy pays the provincial sales tax to the provincial government and pays the GST to the federal government, its accountants will reduce both PST Payable and GST Payable (with a debit) and reduce Cash (with a credit). If Best Buy sold this same television in Ontario, where the HST is 13 percent, the accountants would recognize a $130 liability (= 13% × $1,000) in the HST Payable account (with a credit). This would then be reduced (with a debit) when Best Buy paid off this current liability. Best Buy would collect $1,130 cash, and still earn $1,000 in sales revenue. Although the sales tax rate was different in these two examples, Best Buy earns only the sales price of the television and remits the sales tax collected to the federal and provincial governments.

COACH'S TIP

The sale shown above would be accompanied (in a perpetual inventory system) by an increase in Cost of Goods Sold (recorded with a debit) and a decrease in Inventory (recorded with a credit).

Deferred Revenue In Chapter 4, you learned that some companies receive cash before they provide goods or services to customers. Airlines are paid in advance of providing flights, retailers receive cash for gift cards that can be used for future purchases of goods and services, and other companies receive money for subscriptions before the subscriptions begin. Live Nation Entertainment (LYV), the owner of Ticketmaster, provides a great example of this type of liability. Consider what happened when LYV received $6 million cash on December 9, 2016, when tickets went on sale for Garth Brooks and Trisha Yearwood concerts to take place on February 17 and 18, 2017, at Rogers Place. Because LYV received cash before providing concert services, accountants initially record a liability in the account Deferred Revenue. As the concert services were provided, LYV reduced this liability and reported the earned concert fees as revenue.

That is, LYV recorded the following financial effects and related journal entries on December 9, 2016, when it received $6 million for advance ticket sales for the February 2017 concerts:

1. Receive cash and create a liability (on December 9):

1 Analyze

Assets		=	Liabilities		+	Shareholders' Equity
Cash	+6		Deferred Revenue	+6		

2 Record

dr **Cash** (+A)	6	
cr **Deferred Revenue** (+L)		6

2. Fulfill part of the liability and earn revenue (February 17):

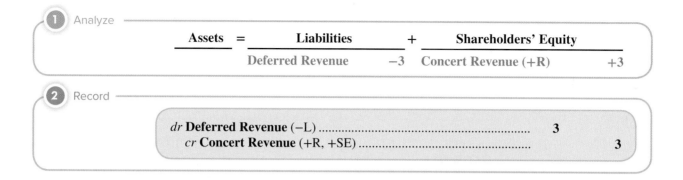

1 Analyze

Assets	=	Liabilities		+	Shareholders' Equity	
		Deferred Revenue	−3		Concert Revenue (+R)	+3

2 Record

    dr Deferred Revenue (−L) 3
    cr Concert Revenue (+R, +SE) 3

When the February 18 concert was held, LYV made another adjust—ment, just like the one in step 2, to show that it fulfilled its remaining obligation and earned $3 million more in concert revenue.

SPOTLIGHT ON Business Decisions

Jumpstarting a Business with Crowdfunding

Crowdfunding has become a popular way for small business ventures to raise funds from large numbers of individuals over the Internet. People have made movies, developed mobile apps, and published books using crowdfunding. These arrangements can take different forms, including presales, loans, and equity investments.

Presales

Made popular by Kickstarter, most presale arrangements use an all-or-nothing funding model where you ask people to pledge money to your venture and later you collect that money from them if your project reaches its funding goals. In exchange for their payments, you give these backers an "award" such as an exclusive deal from your business.

How do you account for this arrangement? The same way Ticketmaster accounts for its presales of concert tickets, shown in the previous section. At first, record nothing because your proposal and the backers' pledges represent only an exchange of promises. But when you reach your funding goal and receive the money, record increases in both Cash and Deferred Revenue for the promise made to backers. Later, when you fulfill that performance obligation, reduce Deferred Revenue and report the funding as revenue, and also expense the cost of awards given out.

Loans

A different crowdfunding arrangement known as peer-to-peer lending, or P2P for short, makes it possible for people with money to lend to others without involving banks. The process at Prosper begins with borrowers requesting a loan amount and providing a reason for the loan. Lenders evaluate all the loan requests and then bid on the loans they want to fund. This form of crowdfunding is accounted for as a note payable with interest accrued and paid monthly.

©Medioimages/Photodisc/Getty Images RF

LONG-TERM LIABILITIES

Like most companies, General Mills reports several long–term liabilities on its balance sheet (see Exhibit 10.1). Common long–term liabilities include long–term notes payable, deferred income taxes, and bonds payable. Long–term notes payable are accounted for in the same way as the short–term notes payable discussed in the previous section (except, of course, long–term notes are on the books for more than one year). This section focuses on accounting for bonds that a company issues to obtain a significant amount of financing. After you become more familiar with this form of long–term debt financing, we will compare it to alternative forms of long–term (equity) financing in Chapter 11.

Bonds

Occasionally, governments and very large companies such as General Mills need to borrow more money than any single lender can provide. In January 2013, for example, General Mills needed to borrow $1 billion. Because issu–ing a promissory note for such a large amount of money was impractical, the company instead issued bonds. A sample bond certificate is shown here.

Bonds are financial instruments that outline the future payments a company promises to make in exchange for receiving a sum of money now. From the company's perspective, the bond is a long–term liability. From the bondholder's perspective, the bond is an investment. For an investor, bonds can be attractive because they return higher interest rates than bank savings accounts, and after a company issues the bonds, they can be traded on established exchanges such as the Toronto Stock Exchange.

As you can see from the sample bond certificate, three key elements of a bond are (1) the **maturity date**, (2) the amount payable on the maturity date (often called the **face value**), and (3) the **stated interest rate**. In most cases, the face value of each bond is $1,000. The stated interest rate is always expressed as an annual rate although many bonds require interest payments every six months (i.e., semi–annually). Each interest payment is computed by multiplying the face value times the stated interest rate (times the frac–tion of the year if payments are made semi–annually). As you will see later, for good economic reasons, bonds may be priced at amounts above or below their face value. A bond's price does not affect the amount of each interest payment, however. For example, a 6 percent bond with a face value of $1,000 will always pay interest of $60 cash each year (= $1,000 × 6% × 12/12).

Bond Pricing

Neither the company nor its financial advisers determine the price at which bonds are issued. Instead, investors in the market establish the issue price. The bond **issue price** represents the amount

Maturity date: The date on which a bond is due to be paid in full.

Face value: The amount payable on a bond's maturity date.

Stated interest rate: The rate stated on the face of the bond, which is used to compute interest payments.

Issue price: The amount of money that a lender pays (and the company receives) when a bond is issued.

Can be more or less than face

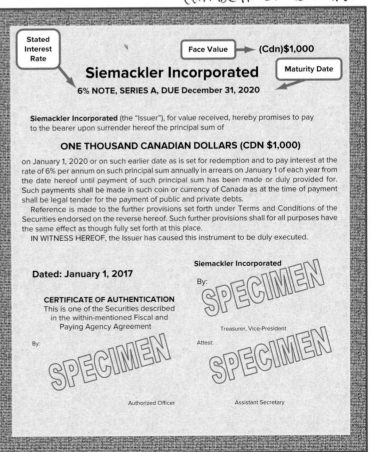

Present value: (1) A mathematical calculation that determines the amount that one or more payments made in the future are worth today. (2) The current value of an amount to be received in the future; it is calculated by discounting a future amount for compound interest.

that investors are willing to pay on the issue date in exchange for the cash payments that the company promises to make over the life of the bond. Theoretically, this amount is based on a mathematical calculation called a **present value**, which is described in Appendix C at the back of this book. (Case C of the appendix shows the calculations for a $1,000, 6 percent General Mills bond.)

SPOTLIGHT ON Financial Reporting

Bond Prices in the Financial Press

The financial press (and Yahoo! Finance Bonds Center) report bond prices each day based on transactions that occurred on the bond exchange. The following is typical of the information you will find:

| Company Name | Maturity | INTEREST RATE | | Bond Price |
		Stated	Market	
Apple Inc.	2043	3.85	4.40	87.49
General Mills, Inc.	2018	6.00	4.00	107.26
McDonald's Corporation	2017	5.80	5.00	116.83

This listing reports that the General Mills bond will mature in the year 2018. It has a stated interest rate of 6.00 percent. At the present time, 4.00 is the typical interest rate earned by investors in the market when buying similar bonds. Because the 6.00 percent stated interest rate is better than the 4.00 percent market interest rate, investors are attracted to the General Mills bond. Consequently, they are willing to pay a higher bond price. The bond price is quoted as a percentage of face value. In this case, investors were willing to pay 107.26 percent of face value, or $1,072.60 for each $1,000 bond (107.26% · $1,000).

When companies issue bonds, they try to offer competitive interest rates. However, changing economic events can cause the bond's stated interest rate to differ from the market's desired rate, which affects the bond's attractiveness and its price. After a bond has issued, the market's desired rate fluctuates frequently, which affects the bond price in the market. Daily fluctuations in the market do not directly involve the company, so they are not considered to be transactions of the company. Except in rare situations, the company continues to account for its bonds using the bond price and interest rates that existed when the bonds were first issued to the market.

Accounting for a Bond Issue

Although it is useful to know how to determine bond prices, it is not a necessary step in accounting for a bond issue. Instead, what we need to know is the amount of cash the company receives from investors when the bonds are first issued. This amount may be equal to the face value, above the face value, or below the face value. A bond issued for more than its face value is said to have been issued at a **premium**, which is the excess of the bond's issue price over its face value. A bond issued for less than its face value is said to have been issued at a **discount**, which is the amount

Premium: The amount by which a bond's issue price exceeds its face value.

Discount: The amount by which a bond's issue price is less than its face value.

by which the issue price falls short of the bond's face value. The following sections show how to account for bonds issued at face value, at a premium, and at a discount.

Bonds Issued at Face Value   If General Mills receives $100,000 cash in exchange for issuing 100 bonds at their $1,000 face value, the transaction will be analyzed and recorded as follows:

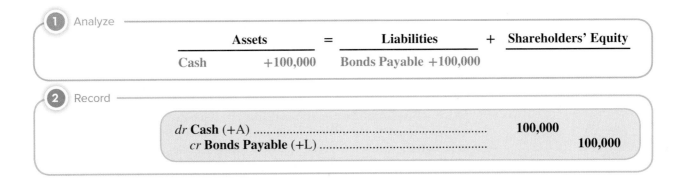

	Assets	=	Liabilities	+	Shareholders' Equity
Cash	+100,000		Bonds Payable +100,000		

2 Record

dr **Cash (+A)** 100,000
    cr **Bonds Payable (+L)** 100,000

Bonds Issued at a Premium   If General Mills issues 100 of its $1,000 bonds at a price of $107.26, the company will receive $107,260 (= 100 × $1,000 × 1.0726). Thus, the cash–equivalent amount is $107,260, which represents the total liability on that date. The company's accountants will distinguish the $100,000 total face value from the $7,260 premium by recording them in separate liability accounts as follows:

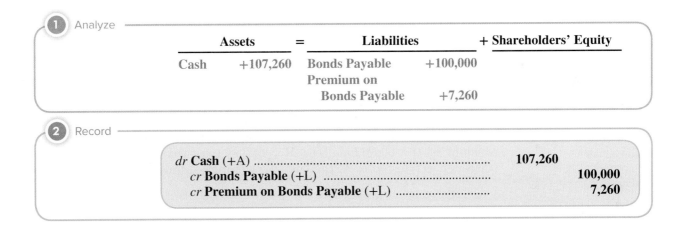

1 Analyze

	Assets	=	Liabilities		+ Shareholders' Equity
Cash	+107,260	Bonds Payable	+100,000	
		Premium on		
		Bonds Payable	+7,260	

2 Record

dr **Cash (+A)** 107,260
    cr **Bonds Payable (+L)** 100,000
    cr **Premium on Bonds Payable (+L)** 7,260

Why would bondholders be willing to pay a premium? For the same reason that you might pay a premium to acquire tickets to a great concert or a big game. If a bond offers something attractive, such as a high interest rate, bondholders may be willing to pay a premium to acquire it.

Bonds Issued at a Discount   If General Mills receives $93,376 for bonds with a total face value of $100,000, the cash–equivalent amount is $93,376, which represents the liability on that date. As shown in the Analyze step below, the discount of $6,624 (which equals $100,000 − $93,376) offsets the face value, so accountants will record it in a contra–liability account, which we identify using "xL." A contra–liability account is recorded as a debit as in the journal entry that follows:

COACH'S TIP

Although Discount on Bonds Payable is recorded with a debit, it is not an asset—it is a contra-liability.

	Assets	=	Liabilities		+ Shareholders' Equity
Cash	+93,376		Bonds Payable	+100,000	
			Discount on Bonds		
			Payable (+xL)	−6,624	

② Record

dr **Cash** (+A) 93,376

dr **Discount on Bonds Payable** (+xL, −L) 6,624

    cr **Bonds Payable** (+L) 100,000

Why would companies be willing to discount a bond? The answer is that they must if they want to issue it. If a bond promises to pay inter−est at a stated rate of 6 percent when other financial instruments offer 8 percent, no one will be willing to buy the bond unless the company dis−counts it. The discount reduces the initial bond price for investors without changing the stated interest payments and the face value paid to them. In effect, a discount increases the return that bondholders earn on their initial investment.

To illustrate, suppose you could buy a $1,000 bond that pays a stated interest rate of 6 percent and matures in one year. After one year, you would receive the stated interest of $60 ($1,000 × 6% × 12/12) plus the face value of $1,000. If you had paid $1,000 for the bond, you would receive 1.06 times as much as your initial investment [($60 + $1,000) ÷ $1,000]—a return of 6 percent. If, instead, the bond price was discounted $19, so that you paid only $981 for it, you would receive 1.08 times as much as your initial investment [($60 + $1,000) ÷ $981 = 1.08]—a return of 8 percent. This percentage represents both the bondholder's rate of return and the company's cost of borrowing. It is commonly referred to as the **market interest rate**.

Market interest rate: The rate of interest that investors demand from a bond.

Reporting Bond Liabilities The total face value of a bond plus any related premium or minus any related discount is reported in the liabilities section of the balance sheet as in Exhibit 10.5 for our three examples. The amount of the bond liability, after taking into account any premium or discount, is referred to as the bond's carrying value.

EXHIBIT 10.5	**Balance Sheet Reporting of Bond Liabilities**

Bonds issued at a premium		Bonds issued at face value		Bonds issued at a discount	
Bonds Payable	$100,000	Bonds Payable	$100,000	Bonds Payable	$100,000
Premium on Bonds Payable	7,260			Discount on Bonds Payable	(6,624)
Carrying Value	107,260			Carrying Value	93,376

To determine whether a bond will be issued at a premium, at face value, or at a discount, you need consider only the relationship between the stated interest rate on the bond (what the bond pays in cash) and the market interest rate (the return that bondholders require). Exhibit 10.6 illustrates this relationship.

EXHIBIT 10.6   Relationships Between Interest Rates and Bond Pricing

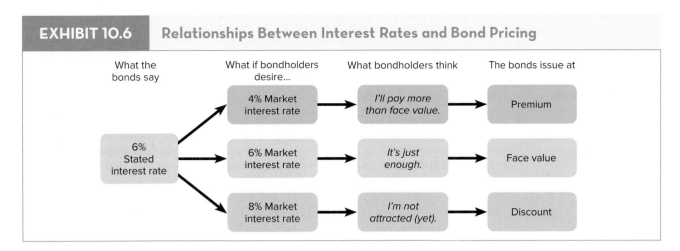

Before you continue, try the following Self—Study Practice.

HOW'S IT GOING?

Self-Study Practice 10.3

For each of the following independent situations, indicate whether the bonds were issued at a premium, at a discount, or at face value.

1. Stated interest rate = 7% and market interest rate = 7%.
2. Stated interest rate = 5% and market interest rate = 6%.
3. Bond issue price = $10,100 and bond face value = $10,000.

After you have finished, check your answers with the solutions, which follow the chapter

Interest Expense

As time passes, a bond liability creates interest expense, which is matched to each period in which the liability is owed. Because interest expense arises from a financing decision (not an operating decision), it is reported below the Income from Operations line on the company's income statement.

Interest on Bonds Issued at Face Value   For bonds issued at face value, the process of calculating and recording interest on bonds is similar to that for Notes Payable. Assume, for example, that General Mills issues bonds on January 1, 2017, at their total face value of $100,000. If the bonds carry an annual stated interest rate of 6 percent payable in cash on December 31 of each year, General Mills will need to accrue an expense and liability for interest at the end of each accounting period. For the first month, which ended January 31, 2017, assuming no previous accrual of interest, General Mills would record interest of $500 (= $100,000 × 6% × 1/12) as follows:

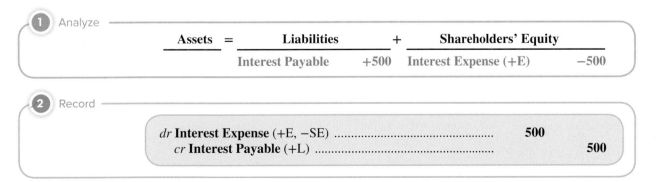

① Analyze

Assets	=	Liabilities	+	Shareholders' Equity	
		Interest Payable	+500	Interest Expense (+E)	−500

② Record

dr Interest Expense (+E, −SE)	500	
cr Interest Payable (+L)		500

General Mills would continue to calculate and record interest this way each month until the interest is paid. When interest is paid, Interest Payable will be decreased (with a debit) and Cash will be decreased (with a credit) for the amount paid.

Interest on Bonds Issued at a Premium   When bonds are issued at a premium, the bond issuer receives more cash on the issue date than it repays on the maturity date. For example, in our earlier illustration of bonds issued at a premium, General Mills received $107,260 but repays only $100,000 at maturity. The $7,260 difference isn't exactly "free money" for General Mills but rather is a reduction in the company's cost of borrowing. For accounting purposes, we match the reduced borrowing cost to the periods in which interest expense is recorded. This process, called **bond amortization**, makes the Interest Expense smaller than the actual interest payment and, at the same time, causes the balance in Premium on Bonds Payable to decline each period, as shown in Exhibit 10.7.

bond amortization: The bond discount or premium amount is amortized over the life of the bond until the bond's maturity date, and this amortization becomes part of its interest expense over the life of the bond.

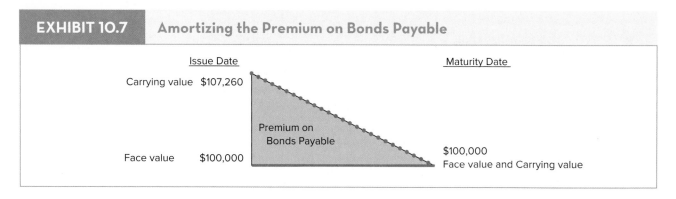

EXHIBIT 10.7   Amortizing the Premium on Bonds Payable

Issue Date — Carrying value $107,260
Face value $100,000
Premium on Bonds Payable
Maturity Date — $100,000 Face value and Carrying value

Procedures for amortizing bond premiums are explained in chapter Supplements 10A, 10B, and 10C. If you have been assigned any of these supplements, don't jump to them yet. We'll tell you later when it's best to read them.

Interest on Bonds Issued at a Discount   When bonds are issued at a discount, the bond issuer receives less cash on the issue date than it repays on the maturity date. For example, in our earlier illustration of bonds issued at a discount, General Mills receives $93,376 on the issue date but repays $100,000 at maturity. For General Mills, the $6,624 discount represents an extra cost of borrowing, over and above each interest payment.

For accounting purposes, we match the extra borrowing cost to the periods in which interest is recorded. This amortization causes the Interest Expense to be more than the interest payment and at the same time, causes Discount on Bonds Payable to decrease each period. As the Discount on Bonds Payable decreases, the carrying value of the liability increases until it reaches $100,000 on the maturity date, as illustrated in Exhibit 10.8.

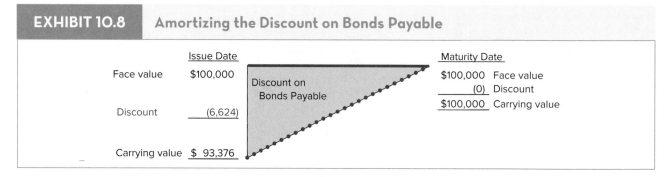

EXHIBIT 10.8   Amortizing the Discount on Bonds Payable

Issue Date
Face value $100,000
Discount (6,624)
Carrying value $ 93,376
Discount on Bonds Payable
Maturity Date
$100,000 Face value
(0) Discount
$100,000 Carrying value

At this point, you should read any of the assigned chapter supplements, then come back here and continue with the remainder of this section.

Bond Retirements

Retirement at Maturity   Most bonds are retired (paid off) at maturity. If interest has been fully paid at the time of maturity, the only remaining account to settle will be Bonds Payable. Assuming the General Mills bonds in our example were retired with a payment equal to their $100,000 face value, the transaction would be analyzed and recorded as follows:

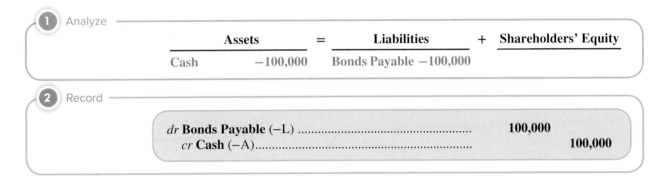

Early Retirement   Rather than wait until the maturity date to retire bonds, a company may retire them early. Companies with a lot of cash often retire their bonds early to avoid the related interest expense. Even companies that do not have extra cash may decide to retire their bonds early if interest rates have fallen since issuing the original bonds. In this case, the companies would issue new bonds at the lower interest rate and use the money they receive from the new bonds to retire the old ones before maturity. Again, this decision reduces future interest expense, which increases future earnings.

The early retirement of bonds has three financial effects. The company (1) pays cash, (2) eliminates the bond liability, and (3) reports either a gain or a loss. A gain arises if the cash paid to retire the bonds is less than the carrying value of the bond liability. A loss is incurred if the company pays more than the carrying value at the time of retirement.

To illustrate these effects, assume that ten years ago, General Mills issued $100,000 of bonds at face value. If the company retired the bonds now at a bond price of $103, General Mills made a payment of $103,000 (= $100,000 × 1.03) to retire the bonds. This transaction would be analyzed and recorded as follows:

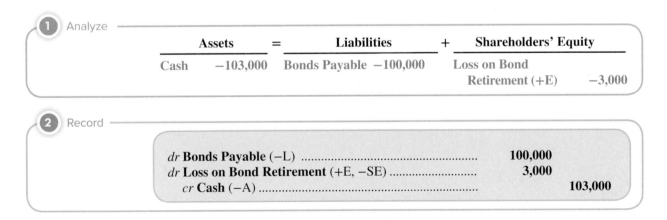

Notice two features of this example. First, because the bond retirement is a financing decision, the loss would be reported after the Income from

Operations line on the income statement. Second, this retirement example does not involve the removal of a bond discount or bond premium account because the bonds were issued at face value. If the bonds had been issued below or above face value, any premium or discount balance that existed at the time of retirement would need to be removed, as well.

Types of Bonds

When you first start learning about bonds, the number of new terms that describe the bonds might seem to be limitless. These terms can generally be grouped into two categories: (1) those that describe the type of organization that issued the bonds, and (2) those that describe specific features of the bond. In the first category are bonds issued by the Government of Canada, municipal organizations such as cities and towns, and corporations. In the second category are bonds that are backed by collateral (*secured*) or not (*debentures*) that the issuing corporation can call in and exchange for cash (*callable*) or convert into corporate shares (*convertible*), and that mature in a series of instalments (*serial bonds*) or include no periodic interest payments (*zero–coupon bonds* and *strips*). The basic procedures shown in the previous sections for recording bond liabilities and interest expense apply equally to these various types of bonds.

CONTINGENT LIABILITIES

LEARNING OBJECTIVE 10-4

Describe how to account for contingent liabilities.

Contingent liabilities:
Potential liabilities that have arisen as a result of a past transaction or event; their ultimate outcome will not be known until a future event occurs or fails to occur.

Contingent liabilities are potential liabilities that arise as a result of past transactions or events, but their ultimate resolution depends (is contin–gent) on a future event. Contingent liabilities differ from other liabilities discussed in this chapter because their dependence on a future event intro–duces a great deal of uncertainty.

For example, consider the product warranties on watches and com–puters. These warranties obligate the company to repair defective products for a limited time, but the ultimate cost of those repairs depends on future events including the number of warranty claims, labour rates, and supply costs. Imagine trying to estimate the cost of the eight–year, 100,000–mile warranty on Tesla's unproven car battery.

Even more uncertainty is introduced when accounting for lawsuits against a company. Some suits may be defended successfully but others may result in huge penalties, such as the $2.75 billion Starbucks was ordered to pay three years after backing out of an agreement with Kraft to distribute packaged coffee to grocery stores.

Given the uncertainties of contingent events, accounting rules require the company to evaluate whether it is likely to be found liable and, if so, whether the amount of the liability is estimable. If the liability is prob–able, an expense and liability are accrued as shown in Exhibit 10.9. If a contingent liability is reasonably possible but not probable, or its amount cannot be reasonably estimated, a liability is not recorded in the accounting records. Instead, any potential liability and related loss is described in a note to the financial statements, as shown below in a General Mills excerpt.

SPOTLIGHT ON The World

Just How Certain Are You?

Under ASPE, contingent liabilities (and corresponding losses) are recorded if the estimated loss is prob-able. Under IFRS, contingent liabilities (and corresponding losses) are recorded if the estimated loss is "more likely than not" to occur. The threshold under IFRS is lower than that under ASPE, which should cause more contingent liabilities to be reported on the balance sheet under IFRS than under ASPE. This and other differences between IFRS and ASPE are summarized in the Spotlight on IFRS and ASPE feature.

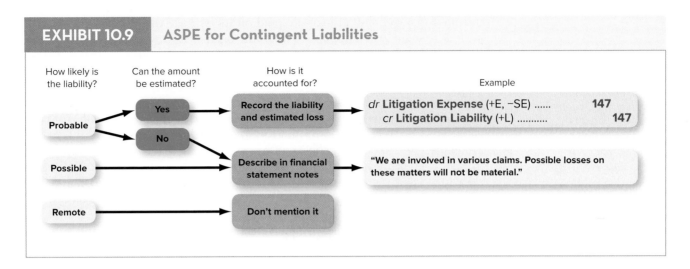

EXHIBIT 10.9 ASPE for Contingent Liabilities

How likely is the liability?	Can the amount be estimated?	How is it accounted for?	Example
Probable	Yes	Record the liability and estimated loss	*dr* **Litigation Expense** (+E, −SE) ...... 147 *cr* **Litigation Liability** (+L) 147
Possible	No	Describe in financial statement notes	"We are involved in various claims. Possible losses on these matters will not be material."
Remote		Don't mention it	

Now that you have seen how liabilities are accounted for inside a company, let's consider them again from the outside. How do users evaluate liabilities?

Evaluate the Results

It's tempting to think of liabilities as bad, but debt can be good if it is managed well. What does it mean to manage it well? First, don't take on too much debt. Second, pay what is owed when it is owed. Two ratios commonly used in business to evaluate these two aspects of debt management are (1) the debt−to−assets ratio and (2) the times interest earned ratio.

LEARNING OBJECTIVE 10-5

Calculate and interpret the debt-to-assets ratio and the times interest earned ratio.

ACCOUNTING DECISION TOOLS

Name of Measure	Formula	What It Tells You
1. Debt-to-assets ratio	$\dfrac{\text{Total Liabilities}}{\text{Total Assets}}$	• The percentage of assets financed by creditors • A higher ratio means greater financing risk
2. Times interest earned ratio	$\dfrac{(\text{Net Income} + \text{Interest Expense} + \text{Income Tax Expense})}{\text{Interest Expense}}$	• Whether sufficient resources are generated from operations to cover interest costs • The higher the number the better the coverage

DEBT-TO-ASSETS RATIO

The **debt−to−assets ratio** compares total liabilities to total assets. It is usually calculated to three decimal places and can be expressed as a percentage by multiplying by 100. This ratio indicates the proportion of total assets that are financed by liabilities. It's important to know the proportion of assets financed by liabilities because liabilities have to be repaid whether or not a company is doing well financially. If assets are financed mainly by debt, rather than equity, then this ratio will be high, which would suggest the company has adopted a risky financing strategy.

What makes this a risky financing strategy is the possibility that the company will not be able to generate enough profit from its debt−financed

Debt-to-assets ratio: Indicates financing risk by computing the proportion of total assets financed by debt.

[handwritten note:] IF D2AR is higher in Yr2 than Yr1, creditors were providing a greater portion of Assets. IF TIER is higher Yr2 than Yr1 company is more successfull at covering interest costs.

business to cover the interest charged on its debt. If this occurs over several periods, causing the company to default on its payments, the company can be forced into bankruptcy.

The balance sheet of General Mills, in Exhibit 10.1, reports total liabilities of $15,793 and total assets of $21,965. Thus, the debt–to–assets ratio is $15,793 ÷ $21,965 = 0.719 or 71.9 percent. This ratio implies that creditors have provided financing for nearly three–quarters of the assets of General Mills. Is this ratio too high? Not according to industry data, which indicates General Mills relies less on debt financing than its competitors in the food processing industry. For example, in early 2016, Kellogg had a ratio of 86.0 percent, and Campbell Soup had a ratio of 80.4 percent. These comparisons suggest that General Mills has not adopted as risky a financing strategy as its industry competitors. However, to be sure, analysts will more closely examine the relationship between the company's interest expense and its earnings, as discussed below.

TIMES INTEREST EARNED RATIO

One way to judge whether a company is generating enough income from operations to cover its interest expense is to compute the **times interest earned ratio** (also called a *fixed charge coverage ratio*).

The accounting decision tools box above shows the formula for the times interest earned ratio. Notice that in this ratio, interest and income tax expenses are added back into net income. The reason for this is simple: analysts want to know whether a company generates enough income to cover its interest expense before the costs of financing and taxes. In general, a high times interest earned ratio is viewed more favourably than a low one. A high ratio indicates an extra margin of protection if the company's profitability declines in the future.

Using information from the fiscal year–end 2015 income statement reported by General Mills, we can compute the times interest earned ratio as follows:

$$\frac{\text{Net Income} + \text{Interest Expense} + \text{Income Tax Expense}}{\text{Interest Expense}} = \frac{\$1{,}259 + \$315 + \$587}{\$315} = 6.86$$

This ratio means that General Mills generates $6.86 of income (before the costs of financing and taxes) for each dollar of interest expense. Reaching this level of interest coverage was important to General Mills because its long–term debt note reported that loan covenants required a minimum ratio of 2.5.

You may see a times interest earned ratio that is less than 1.0 or even negative. When the times interest earned ratio is less than 1.0, a company is not generating enough operating income to cover its interest expense. Companies with recurring negative times interest earned ratios run the risk of defaulting on their interest payments, and in severe cases, face bankruptcy.

SPOTLIGHT ON The World

Violated Loan Covenants

Most lending agreements allow the lender to revise loan terms (e.g., interest rates, due dates) if a borrower's financial condition deteriorates significantly. These escape hatches, called **loan covenants**, are often based on financial statement ratios such as debt-to-assets and times interest earned. Under ASPE, if a company violates loan covenants on long-term debt but renegotiates the loan prior to releasing its financial statements, the debt remains classified as long-term. Under IFRS, the company must reclassify that long-term debt as a current liability even if renegotiated.

Topic	ASPE	IFRS
Presentation of callable long-term debt (due to a violations of a debt covenant)	The debt can remain as long-term debt if the company renegotiates the loan prior to releasing its financial statements.	The debt must be reported as a current liability.
Recognition of contingent liabilities	Recognize the liability if the occurrence of the future event is "likely," meaning that it is highly probable and also measurable.	Recognize the liability if the occurrence of the future event is "probable," meaning more likely than not and also measurable. This is a lower standard than under ASPE.
Measurement of liabilities	Generally measured at amortized cost using the effective-interest method or the straight-line method.	Generally measured at amortized cost using only the effective-interest method.

Supplement 10A

STRAIGHT-LINE METHOD OF AMORTIZATION

Exhibits 10.7 and 10.8 illustrate how a bond premium or discount decreases each year until it is completely eliminated on the bond's maturity date. This process is called *amortizing the bond premium or discount*.

The **straight—line amortization method** reduces the premium or discount by an equal amount each period. Because this method results in an equal amount each period, it is easy to apply. However, it distorts the financial results somewhat because it produces an equal Interest Expense each period, even though the bond's carrying value changes each period. For this reason, ASPE allows the straight—line method to be used only when it does not materially differ from the effective—interest method of amortization (presented in Supplement 10B). This is different, however, under IFRS, where the effective—interest method of amortization is required.

LEARNING OBJECTIVE **10-S1**

Use straight-line bond amortization.

Straight-line amortization method: For bonds payable, evenly allocates the amount of bond premium or discount over each period of a bond's life to adjust interest expense for differences between its stated interest rate and market interest rate.

Bond Premiums

In our earlier example of bonds issued at a premium, General Mills received $107,260 on the issue date (January 1, 2017) but repays only $100,000 at maturity (December 31, 2020). The $7,260 difference is considered a reduction in the company's borrowing cost over the four—year period the bond is owed. Under the straight—line method, this $7,260 is spread evenly as a reduction in interest expense over the four years ($7,260 ÷ 4 = $1,815 per year). So when General Mills makes its yearly $6,000 cash payment for interest, it will report Interest Expense of only $4,185 ($6,000 − $1,815). The remainder of the $6,000 cash payment is reported as a reduction in the bond liability, as follows:

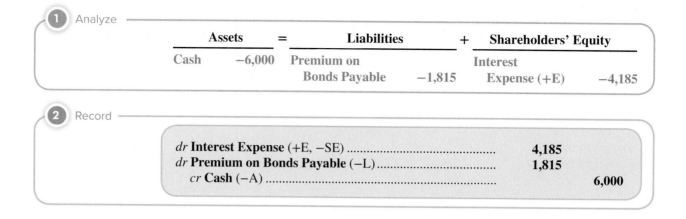

Analyze

	Assets	=	Liabilities	+	Shareholders' Equity
Cash	−6,000		Premium on Bonds Payable −1,815		Interest Expense (+E) −4,185

Record

dr Interest Expense (+E, −SE) 4,185
dr Premium on Bonds Payable (−L) 1,815
 cr Cash (−A) 6,000

In effect, the $6,000 payment includes both an interest component ($4,185) and a repayment of the bond liability ($1,815). The account-ing equation effects and journal entry shown above will be recorded each year on December 31 until the bonds mature. The following bond amortization schedule summarizes the journal entry effects each period (on the left) and the updated balance sheet account balances (on the right):

	Bond Premium Amortization Schedule: Straight–Line Method					
	Journal Entry Components			Balance Sheet Accounts		
	(A)	(B)	(C) (= A − B)	(D)	(E)	(F) (= D + E)
Period Ended	Cash Paid	Amortized Premium	Interest Expense	Bonds Payable	Premium on Bonds Payable	Carrying Value
01/01/2017				$100,000	$7,260	$107,260
12/31/2017	$6,000	$1,815	$4,185	100,000	5,445	105,445
12/31/2018	6,000	1,815	4,185	100,000	3,630	103,630
12/31/2019	6,000	1,815	4,185	100,000	1,815	101,815
12/31/2020	6,000	1,815	4,185	100,000	0	100,000

Bond Discounts

A discount arises when the bond issuer receives less cash than the issuer repays at maturity. In effect, a discount increases the company's cost of borrowing, so amortization of the discount causes interest expense to be higher than the interest payment each period. To report this effect, accoun-tants record a decrease in Discount on Bonds Payable and an increase in Interest Expense.

In our earlier example, General Mills received $93,376 for four–year bonds with a total face value of $100,000, implying a discount of $6,624. Using the straight–line method, amortization of the discount in each of the four years that the bonds remain unpaid would be $1,656 (= $6,624 ÷ 4). This amount would be added to the interest to be paid ($6,000) to calculate the amount of Interest Expense ($7,656). The effects would be recorded as follows:

	Assets	=	Liabilities	+	Shareholders' Equity	
Cash	−6,000		Discount on Bonds Payable (−xL) +1,656		Interest Expense (+E)	−7,656

② Record

dr Interest Expense (+E, −SE) 7,656
   cr Discount on Bonds Payable (−xL, +L)......................... 1,656
   cr Cash (−A) 6,000

The accounting equation effects and journal entry shown above would be recorded each year on December 31 until the bonds mature. The following bond amortization schedule summarizes the effects that must be recorded each period (on the left), producing the end–of–year balance sheet account balances (on the right):

Bond Premium Amortization Schedule: Straight–Line Method

| | Journal Entry Components | | | | Balance Sheet Accounts | | |
	(A)	(B)	(C) (= A + B)		(D)	(E)	(F) (= D − E)
Period Ended	Cash Paid	Amortized Premium	Interest Expense		Bonds Payable	Discount on Bonds Payable	Carrying Value
01/01/2017					$100,000	$6,624	$93,376
12/31/2017	$6,000	$1,656	$7,656		100,000	4,968	95,032
12/31/2018	6,000	1,656	7,656		100,000	3,312	96,688
12/31/2019	6,000	1,656	7,656		100,000	1,656	98,344
12/31/2020	6,000	1,656	7,656		100,000	0	100,000

Supplement 10B

EFFECTIVE-INTEREST METHOD OF AMORTIZATION

The **effective–interest method of amortization** is considered a conceptually superior method of accounting for bonds because it correctly calculates interest expense by multiplying the true cost of borrowing times the amount of money actually owed to investors. The true cost of borrowing is the market interest rate that investors used to determine the bond issue price. The actual amount owed to investors is the carrying value of the bond, which equals the cash received when the bond was issued plus any interest that has been incurred but not yet paid. It can then be understood why this is the required method under IFRS, where financial statements on a global basis are to be comparative.

To clearly understand the effective–interest method, it helps to see how a bond's issue price depends on the market interest rate. As we mentioned in the chapter, investors in the market decide how much to pay for a bond by using a mathematical calculation called a present value. You can read instructions about how to calculate present values in Appendix C, but for now, just focus on understanding what a present value is.

LEARNING OBJECTIVE 10-S2

Use effective-interest bond amortization.

Effective-interest method of amortization: Allocates the amount of bond premium or discount over each period of a bond's life in amounts corresponding to the bond's carrying value.

Present value is the idea that something is worth more if you get it today than if you get it sometime in the future. For example, if someone offered to pay you $100,000 today or $100,000 five years from now, you'd be better off taking it today. You could invest the money and earn interest for five years, making it worth more than $100,000. The same idea explains why you could be equally happy with receiving $100,000 in five years or some smaller amount today. To figure out how much this smaller amount is, you just calculate the present value of $100,000. The only pieces of information you need for this calculation are (1) the amounts to be received in the future, (2) the number of months between now and then, and (3) the interest rate you expect to earn during that time.

In the bond context, investors calculate the present value of the amounts received periodically (at the stated interest rate) and at maturity (the face value), using the interest rate that they want to earn. We have summarized this calculation in Exhibit 10B.1 for General Mills' 6 percent, four–year bond.

EXHIBIT 10.B1   Computing the Present Value of Bond Payments

	MARKET INTEREST RATES		
	4%	6%	8%
Present value of $100,000 face value (principal) paid four years from now	$ 85,480	$ 79,210	$73,503
Present value of $6,000 (6% stated interest rate) paid once a year for four years	21,780	20,790	19,873
Bond price	**$107,260**	**$100,000**	**$93,376**

Exhibit 10B.1 shows three different scenarios, each one involving a different market interest rate but the same 6 percent stated interest rate. The first column calculates the amount of money that investors would be willing to give up if they needed to earn interest of 4 percent on the amount they pay for the bond. The second column calculates the amount investors would pay if they wanted to earn an interest rate of 6 percent. The third column calculates the amount that investors would be willing to pay if they wanted to earn 8 percent on the amount they pay for the bond. (For detailed calculations underlying the amounts in Exhibit 10B.1, see Appendix C.)

Notice that when the bond pays interest at a rate that exactly matches the rate required by investors in the market (6 percent), they are willing to pay face value ($100,000) for it. If the 6 percent interest rate stated on the bond is more than investors require (4 percent), they will pay a premium for the bond (as shown in the first column). If the 6 percent interest promised is less than the market interest rate (8 percent), investors will pay less than face value for the bond, resulting in a discounted bond price as indicated in the third column. Let's now look at what happens to a bond premium and discount under the effective–interest amortization method.

Bond Premiums

In our earlier example of a bond premium, General Mills promised to make cash interest payments each year at a rate of 6 percent. Investors found this stated interest rate attractive, so the bond issued at a $7,260 premium. When General Mills adds this $7,260 premium to the $100,000 face value, it reports a carrying value of $107,260 (= $100,000 + $7,260) on January 1, 2017.

Exhibit 10B.1 indicates that the $107,260 total implies the market interest rate was 4 percent. General Mills uses this market interest rate to calculate its Interest Expense on the bond, using a variation of the interest formula. For example, General Mills calculates Interest Expense in the first year, which ended on December 31, 2017, as follows:

2017	Interest (I)	=	Principal (P)	×	Interest Rate (R)	×	Time (T)
	Interest Expense	=	Carrying Value	×	Market Interest Rate	×	n/12
	$4,290	=	$107,260	×	4%	×	12/12

Use the information *stated* on the *face* of the bond to calculate the *cash* interest payment:

	Interest (I)	=	Principal (P)	×	Interest Rate (R)	×	Time (T)
	Cash Payment	=	Face Value	×	Stated Interest Rate	×	n/12
	$6,000	=	$100,000	×	6%	×	12/12

Because the $6,000 cash interest payment exceeds the $4,290 Interest Expense by $1,710 ($6,000 − $4,290 = $1,710), General Mills records a $1,710 reduction in its bond liability. In effect, the $6,000 cash payment includes both an interest component ($4,290) and a partial repayment of the bond liability ($1,710), as analyzed and recorded below:

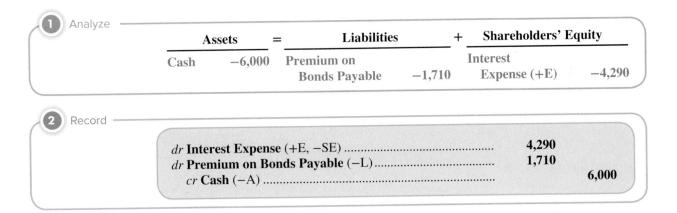

1 Analyze

Assets		=	Liabilities		+	Shareholders' Equity	
Cash	−6,000	=	Premium on Bonds Payable	−1,710	+	Interest Expense (+E)	−4,290

2 Record

dr Interest Expense (+E, −SE)	4,290	
dr Premium on Bonds Payable (−L)	1,710	
cr Cash (−A)		6,000

Similar calculations and accounting effects occur each period until the bonds mature. The only thing to watch out for is that the carrying value of the bond liability decreases each year because the cash payment includes a partial repayment of the bond liability. For example, after the above entry is recorded on December 31, 2017, the Premium on Bonds Payable decreases by $1,710, from $7,260 to $5,550. Thus, the Interest Expense for the second year of the bond (for the year ended December 31, 2018) is as shown.

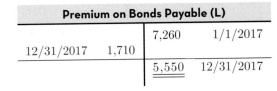

Premium on Bonds Payable (L)			
		7,260	1/1/2017
12/31/2017	1,710		
		5,550	12/31/2017

2018	Interest (I)	=	Principal (P)	×	Interest Rate (R)	×	Time (T)
	Interest Expense	=	Carrying Value	×	Market Interest Rate	×	n/12
	$4,222	=	$105,550	×	4%	×	12/12

The following bond amortization schedule summarizes the effects that must be recorded each period (on the left), producing the end−of−year balance sheet account balances (on the right):

Bond Premium Amortization Schedule: Effective−Interest Method

	Journal Entry Components			Balance Sheet Accounts		
	(A)	(B)	(C) (= A − B)	(D)	(E)	(F) (= D + E)
Period Ended	Cash Paid	Interest Expense	Amortized Premium	Bonds Payable	Premium on Bonds Payable	Carrying Value
01/01/2017				$100,000	$7,260	$107,260
12/31/2017	$6,000	$4,290	$1,710	100,000	5,550	105,550
12/31/2018	6,000	4,222	1,778	100,000	3,772	103,772
12/31/2019	6,000	4,151	1,849	100,000	1,923	101,923
12/31/2020	6,000	4,077	1,923	100,000	0	100,000

Bond Discounts

In our earlier example of a bond discount, General Mills promised to make cash interest payments each year at a rate of 6 percent. Investors did not find this stated interest rate attractive, so the bond issued at a $6,624 dis−count. When General Mills subtracts this $6,624 discount from the $100,000 face value, it reports a carrying value of $93,376 (= $100,000 − $6,624) on January 1, 2017. Exhibit 10B.1 indicates that the $93,376 implies the market interest rate was 8 percent. General Mills uses this market interest rate to calculate its Interest Expense on the bond, as we did in the case of a bond premium. The Interest Expense for the first year, ended December 31, 2017, is calculated as shown.

2017	Interest (I)	=	Principal (P)	×	Interest Rate (R)	×	Time (T)
	Interest Expense	=	Carrying Value	×	Market Interest Rate	×	n/12
	$7,470	=	$93,376	×	8%	×	12/12

Use the information *stated* on the *face* of the bond to calculate the cash interest payment.

	Interest (I)	=	Principal (P)	×	Interest Rate (R)	×	Time (T)
	Cash Payment	=	Face Value	×	Stated Interest Rate	×	n/12
	$6,000	=	$100,000	×	6%	×	12/12

Because the $7,470 Interest Expense is more than the $6,000 cash paid, General Mills records the $1,470 difference ($7,470 − $6,000 = $1,470) as an increase in its bond liability. As illustrated in Exhibit 10.8, the increase in the bond liability is achieved by decreasing the contra–liability Discount on Bonds Payable. These effects are analyzed and recorded as follows:

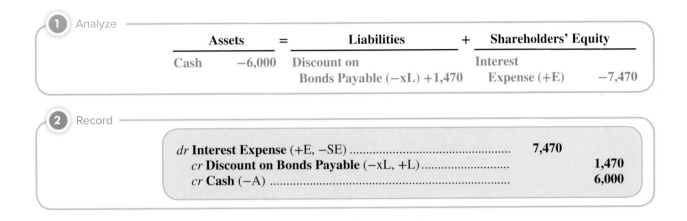

The T–account shows how the above journal entry reduces Discount on Bonds Payable. A reduction of this contra–liability account increases the carrying value of the long–term liability, as you can see by moving from left to right in Exhibit 10B.2.

Discount on Bonds Payable (xL)			
1/1/2017	6,624		
		1,470	12/31/2017
12/31/2017	5,154		

EXHIBIT 10.B2	Sample Balance Sheet Reporting of Bond Discount

GENERAL MILLS
Balance Sheet (excerpt)

	January 1, 2017	December 31, 2017
Long–Term Liabilities		
Bonds Payable	$100,000	$100,000
Discount on Bonds Payable	(6,624)	(5,154)
Carrying Value	93,376	94,846

Let's now consider the interest expense for 2018. As in 2017, the 2018 interest expense is calculated using the market interest rate. However, the carrying value of bonds owed at the end of 2017 increased, as shown in Exhibit 10B.2. Thus, interest expense also will increase in 2018, calculated as follows:

COACH'S TIP

The interest expense for 2018 is greater than that for 2017 because the carrying value was greater in 2018 than in 2017.

2018	Interest (I)	=	Principal (P)	×	Interest Rate (R)	×	Time (T)
	Interest Expense	=	Carrying Value	×	Market Interest Rate	×	n/12
	$7,588	=	$94,846	×	8%	×	12/12

Because the Interest Expense ($7,588) is greater than the cash payment ($6,000), the bond liability is increased (by reducing the contra–liability).

This is reflected in the accounting equation and recorded with the journal entry on December 31, 2018:

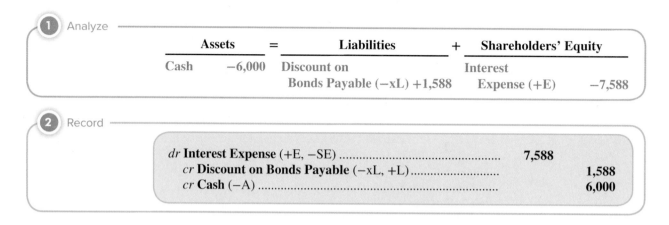

1 Analyze

Assets	=	Liabilities	+	Shareholders' Equity
Cash	−6,000	Discount on Bonds Payable (−xL) +1,588		Interest Expense (+E) −7,588

2 Record

dr Interest Expense (+E, −SE) 7,588
   cr Discount on Bonds Payable (−xL, +L)......................... 1,588
   cr Cash (−A) 6,000

The following bond amortization schedule summarizes the effects that must be recorded each period (on the left), producing the end−of−year balance sheet account balances (on the right):

Bond Premium Amortization Schedule: Effective−Interest Method

	Journal Entry Components			Balance Sheet Accounts		
	(A)	(B)	(C) (= B − A)	(D)	(E)	(F) (= D − E)
Period Ended	Cash Paid	Interest Expense	Amortized Premium	Bonds Payable	Discount on Bonds Payable	Carrying Value
01/01/2017				$100,000	$6,624	$ 93,376
12/31/2017	$6,000	$7,470	$1,470	100,000	5,154	94,846
12/31/2018	6,000	7,588	1,588	100,000	3,566	96,434
12/31/2019	6,000	7,715	1,715	100,000	1,851	98,149
12/31/2020	6,000	7,851	1,851	100,000	0	100,000

Supplement 10C

SIMPLIFIED EFFECTIVE-INTEREST AMORTIZATION

LEARNING OBJECTIVE 10-S3

Use simplified effective-interest bond amortization.

The approach shown in this supplement presents a simplified explanation of how to account for bond liabilities and interest expense. Remember that the effective−interest method is required by IFRS and can be used for ASPE. You should be aware that this approach involves taking a shortcut. While the shortcut will help you to focus on the line items that ultimately are reported on the financial statements, it requires that we ignore a few accounts that are typically used behind the scenes in real−world account− ing systems. Be sure to check your course syllabus to see whether you are expected to read this supplement.

If you're like most people, you probably have to concentrate really hard when you are told the carrying value of a bond is increased by decreasing a contra−liability account. You may even whisper this thought quietly to yourself a few times before it starts making sense. In this section, we present a shortcut when accounting for bonds that will allow you to avoid thinking in "double negatives" like this. Hopefully, it will also help you to stop whispering to yourself when you read.

Accounting for the Bond Issue

The shortcut involves simplifying only one aspect of what you studied earlier in this chapter. Rather than record a discount or premium in a separate account, we combine the discount or premium with the bond's face value in a single account that we will call *Bonds Payable, Net*. This name is used to remind you that we are focusing on what is ultimately reported in the financial statements rather than what is actually used behind the scenes. The following journal entries demonstrate how the shortcut is applied to three earlier bond examples (issued at a premium, at face value, and at a discount).

	Premium	Face Value	Discount
dr **Cash** (+A)	107,260	100,000	93,376
cr **Bonds Payable, Net** (+L)	107,260	100,000	93,376

Interest Expense

As time passes, the company incurs Interest Expense on its bond liability. Because the bond liability was recorded in a single account, the interest calculation is the same whether the bond has been issued at a premium or discount. The following version of the interest formula is used to compute Interest Expense.

Interest (I)	=	Principal (P)	×	Interest Rate (R)	×	Time (T)
Interest Expense	=	Bonds Payable, Net	×	Market Interest Rate	×	n/12

The market interest rate is determined by using present value techniques (discussed in Appendix E) that relate the bond's issue price to the payments promised over the life of the bond. The market interest rate also can be determined using the XIRR and RATE functions in Excel, or the online bond calculator app at fncalculator.com.

Bond Premiums

Our bond premium example indicated that General Mills received $107,260 on the issue date, which we would record in Bonds Payable, Net, using the journal entry shown above. The $107,260 issue price implies a 4 percent market interest rate. The bonds promise to pay the 6 percent stated interest rate on their total face value of $100,000. This information is used to compute Interest Expense and the annual cash payment as follows:

2017	Interest (I)	=	Principal (P)	×	Interest Rate (R)	×	Time (T)
	Interest Expense	=	Bonds Payable, Net	×	Market Interest Rate	×	n/12
	$4,290	=	$107,260	×	4%	×	12/12

	Interest (I)	=	Principal (P)	×	Interest Rate (R)	×	Time (T)
	Cash Payment	=	Face Value	×	Stated Interest Rate	×	n/12
	$6,000	=	$100,000	×	6%	×	12/12

Because the $6,000 cash interest payment exceeds the $4,290 Interest Expense by $1,710 ($6,000 − $4,290 = $1,710), General Mills records a $1,710 reduction in Bonds Payable, Net. In effect, the $6,000 cash payment includes both an interest component ($4,290) and a partial repayment of the bond liability ($1,710), as analyzed and recorded below:

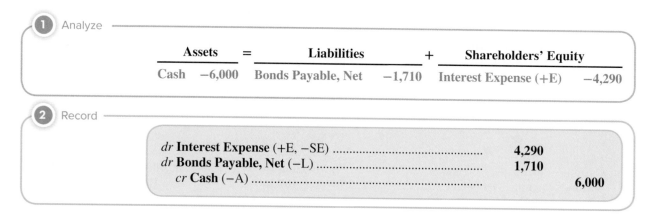

Analyze						
Assets	**=**	**Liabilities**		**+**	**Shareholders' Equity**	
Cash −6,000		Bonds Payable, Net −1,710			Interest Expense (+E) −4,290	

Record

dr Interest Expense (+E, −SE) 4,290
dr Bonds Payable, Net (−L) 1,710
    cr Cash (−A) 6,000

Bonds Payable, Net (L)		
	107,260	1/1/2017
12/31/2017 1,710		
	105,550	12/31/2017

Similar calculations and accounting effects occur each period until the bonds mature. The only thing to watch out for is that Bonds Payable, Net decreases each year because the cash payment includes a partial repayment of the bond liability. For example, after the above entry is recorded on December 31, 2017, Bonds Payable, Net decreases by $1,710, from $107,260 to $105,550. This new balance is used to compute Interest Expense for the second year of the bond (for the year ended December 31, 2018):

2018	Interest (I)	=	Principal (P)	×	Interest Rate (R)	×	Time (T)
	Interest Expense	=	Bonds Payable, Net	×	Market Interest Rate	×	n/12
	$4,222	=	$105,550	×	4%	×	12/12

Because the $6,000 annual cash payment exceeds the $4,222 Interest Expense by $1,778 ($6,000 − $4,222 = $1,778), General Mills records a $1,778 reduction in Bonds Payable, Net in 2018. In effect, the $6,000 cash payment includes both an interest component ($4,222) and a partial repayment of the bond liability ($1,778). As the following amortization schedule shows, the bond liability continues to decrease until, at maturity, it reaches the bonds' face value ($100,000).

	Bond Premium Amortization Schedule: Simplified Method				
	Beginning of Year	Changes During the Year			End of Year
	(A)	(B)	(C)	(D) = (C − B)	(E) = (A − D)
Period	Bonds Payable, Net	Interest Expense	Cash Paid	Reduction in Bonds Payable, Net	Bonds Payable, Net
1/1/17–12/31/17	$107,260	$4,290	$6,000	$1,710	$105,550
1/1/18–12/31/18	105,550	4,222	6,000	1,778	103,772
1/1/19–12/31/19	103,772	4,151	6,000	1,849	101,923
1/1/20–12/31/20	101,923	4,077	6,000	1,923	100,000

Bond Discounts

Our bond discount example indicated that General Mills received $93,376 on the issue date, which we would record in Bonds Payable, Net, using the journal entry shown on the facing page. This issue price implies an 8 percent market interest rate. The bonds promise to pay the 6 percent stated interest rate on their total face value of $100,000. This information is used to compute Interest Expense and the annual cash payment as follows:

2017	Interest (I)	=	Principal (P)	×	Interest Rate (R)	×	Time (T)
	Interest Expense	=	Bonds Payable, Net	×	Market Interest Rate	×	n/12
	$7,470	=	$93,376	×	8%	×	12/12

	Interest (I)	=	Principal (P)	×	Interest Rate (R)	×	Time (T)
	Cash Payment	=	Face Value	×	Stated Interest Rate	×	n/12
	$6,000	=	$100,000	×	6%	×	12/12

Because the $7,470 Interest Expense is more than the $6,000 cash paid, General Mills records the $1,470 difference ($7,470 − $6,000 = $1,470) as an increase in its liability Bonds Payable, Net as follows:

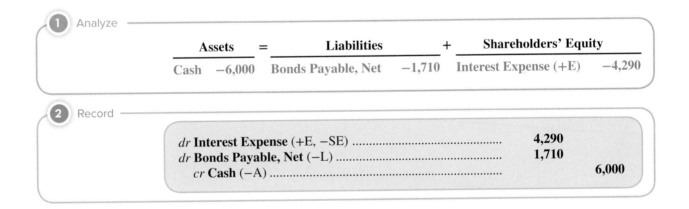

1 Analyze

Assets	=	Liabilities	+	Shareholders' Equity
Cash −6,000		Bonds Payable, Net −1,710		Interest Expense (+E) −4,290

2 Record

```
dr Interest Expense (+E, −SE) .............................................    4,290
dr Bonds Payable, Net (−L) ...............................................    1,710
      cr Cash (−A) ...............................................................             6,000
```

Recording the $1,470 as the liability Bonds Payable, Net is appropriate because General Mills will pay this amount at maturity, as part of the face value of the bond.

Similar calculations and accounting effects occur each period until the bonds mature. The only thing to watch out for is that Bonds Payable, Net increases each year because the cash pay‑ ment is less than the interest expense. For example, after the above entry is recorded on December 31, 2017, Bonds Payable, Net increases by $1,470, from $93,376 to $94,846. This new balance is used to compute Interest Expense for the second year of the bond (for the year ended December 31, 2018):

Bonds Payable, Net (L)	
93,376	1/1/2017
1,470	12/31/2017
94,846	12/31/2017

2018	Interest (I)	=	Principal (P)	×	Interest Rate (R)	×	Time (T)
	Interest Expense	=	Bonds Payable, Net	×	Market Interest Rate	×	n/12
	$7,588	=	$94,846	×	8%	×	12/12

Because the $7,588 Interest Expense exceeds the $6,000 annual cash payment by $1,588 ($7,588 − $6,000 = $1,588), General Mills records a $1,588 increase in Bonds Payable, Net in 2018. In effect, the $1,588 in unpaid interest will be paid at maturity. As the following amortization schedule shows, the bond liability continues to increase until, at maturity, it reaches the bonds' face value ($100,000).

Bond Premium Amortization Schedule: Simplified Method

	Beginning of Year	Changes During the Year			End of Year
	(A)	(B)	(C)	(D) = (B − C)	(E) = (A + D)
Period	Bonds Payable, Net	Interest Expense	Cash Paid	Reduction in Bonds Payable, Net	Bonds Payable, Net
1/1/17–12/31/17	$93,376	$7,470	$6,000	$1,470	$ 94,846
1/1/18–12/31/18	94,846	7,588	6,000	1,588	96,434
1/1/19–12/31/19	96,434	7,715	6,000	1,715	98,149
1/1/20–12/31/20	98,149	7,851	6,000	1,851	100,000

Review the Chapter

This section provides a chance to solidify your understanding of key points. It's worth your time to work through the following demonstration cases, scan the chapter summary, test your understanding of key terms, and then practise, practise, practise.

DEMONSTRATION CASE A: ACCRUED LIABILITIES AND DEFERRED REVENUE

Online Games, Inc. reported the following information in its accounting records on December 31, 2017:

Annual subscription payments received in December 2017 for 2018 services	$12,000
Gross salaries earned by employees (December 26–31, 2017)	3,600
Income taxes withheld from employees (December 26–31, 2017)	610
CPP withheld from employees (December 26–31, 2017)	170
EI withheld from employees (December 26–31, 2017)	60
Net payment to employees (made on December 31, 2017)	2,760

The 2018 subscription payments will be earned equally during each month of 2018. The employees were paid $2,760 on December 31, 2017, but the withholdings have not yet been remitted, nor have the employer CPP and EI contributions.

Required:

1. Describe how the 2018 subscription payments should be reported in the balance sheet and income statement on (*a*) December 31, 2017, and (*b*) January 31, 2018.
2. Show the accounting equation effects and give the journal entries for (*a*) the receipt of annual subscription payments in December 2017, and (*b*) any required adjustments for the subscription payments on January 31, 2018.
3. Compute the total payroll costs relating to the period from December 26–31, 2017.
4. Show the accounting equation effects and give the journal entries on December 31, 2017, to adjust for payroll costs relating to December 26–31, 2017.

Suggested Solution

1. a. On December 31, 2017, the $12,000 of advance subscription payments would be reported on the balance sheet as a current liability called *Deferred Revenue*. No amounts relating to 2018 subscription services would be reported in the 2017 income statement.

   b. On January 31, 2018, one month of subscription services would be earned, so Deferred Revenue on the balance sheet would be reduced by $1,000 (= $12,000 × 1/12) and Subscription Revenue on the income statement would be increased by $1,000.

2. a. December 2017 (receipt of 2018 subscription payments)

Assets	=	Liabilities	+	Shareholders' Equity
Cash +12,000		Deferred Revenue +12,000		

   dr Cash (+A) 12,000
       cr Deferred Revenue (+L)   12,000

   b. January 31, 2018 (earned one month of 2018 subscriptions)

Assets	=	Liabilities	+	Shareholders' Equity
		Deferred Revenue −1,000		Subscription Revenue (+R) +1,000

   dr Deferred Revenue (−L) 1,000
       cr Subscription Revenue (+R, +SE)   1,000

3. Computation of total payroll costs

Salaries and wages:	Net pay to employees	$2,760
	Income taxes withheld from employees	610
	CPP withheld from employees	170
	EI withheld from employees	60
	Total cost of salaries and wages	3,600
Employer payroll taxes:	CPP (employer matching contribution)	170
	EI (employer contribution 1.4 times the amount withheld from the employee)	84
Total payroll costs		$3,854

4. Salaries and wage costs

Assets	=	Liabilities	+	Shareholders' Equity
		Withheld Income		
Cash −2,760		Taxes Payable +610		Salaries and Wages Expense (+E) −3,600
		CPP Payable +170		
		EI Payable +60		

dr Salaries and Wages Expense (+E, −SE)	3,600	
cr Withheld Income Taxes Payable (+L)		610
cr CPP Payable (+L)		170
cr EI Payable (+L)		60
cr Cash (−A)		2,760

5. Employer–related payroll costs

Assets	=	Liabilities	+	Shareholders' Equity
		CPP Payable (+L) +170		Payroll Tax Expense (+E) −254
		EI Payable (+L) +84		

dr Payroll Tax Expense (+E, −SE)...................................	254	
cr CPP Payable (+L)...		170
cr EI Payable (+L)..		84

DEMONSTRATION CASE B: NOTES PAYABLE AND ACCRUED INTEREST

On December 31, 2017, assume that Caterpillar Inc. had $20.9 billion in Cash, Short–Term Investments, and Accounts Receivable, Net, and $26.1 billion in current liabilities. On December 3, 2017, assume that Caterpillar received $350 million when it issued promissory notes that will mature in 2022. The notes pay interest at the annual rate of 7.00 percent, which was comparable to other interest rates available in the market. Caterpillar's fiscal year ends on December 31.

Required:

1. Describe which sections of Caterpillar's classified balance sheet are affected by its issuance of promissory notes.
2. Give the journal entry on December 3, 2017, to record the issuance of the notes.
3. Give the journal entry on December 31, 2017, to record one month of interest expense, assuming none had been accrued prior to that date.

Suggested Solutions

1. The issuance of notes increases Caterpillar's Cash (a current asset) and its Notes Payable (a long–term liability) by $350 million.
2. December 3, 2017 (issuance date)

dr Cash (+A)..	350,000,000	
cr Notes Payable (+L).......................................		350,000,000

3. December 31, 2017 (accrual of interest expense for one month)

dr Interest Expense (+E, −SE)	2,041,667	
($350,000,000 × 7.00% × 1/12)...............		
cr Interest Payable (+L).................................		2,041,667

DEMONSTRATION CASE C: BONDS PAYABLE

To raise funds to build a new plant, Reed Company issued bonds with the following terms:

> Face value of the bonds: $100,000.
> Dates: Issued January 1, 2017; due in 5 years on January 1, 2022.
> Interest rate: 6 percent per year, payable on December 31 each year.

The bonds were issued on January 1, 2017, at 104.3, implying a 5 percent market rate of interest. The annual accounting period for Reed Company ends on December 31.

Required:

1. How much cash did Reed Company receive from the issuance of the bonds? Show computations.
2. What was the amount of premium on the bonds payable? Over how many months should the premium be amortized?
3. Show the accounting equation effects and give the journal entry on January 1, 2017, for recording the issuance of the bonds.
4. (Supplement 10A) Show the accounting equation effects and give the journal entry required on December 31, 2017, relating to interest on the bond. Use the straight−line amortization method.
5. (Supplement 10B) Show the accounting equation effects and give the journal entry required on December 31, 2017, relating to interest on the bond. Use the effective−interest amortization method.
6. (Supplement 10C) Show the accounting equation effects and give the journal entries required on January 1, 2017, relating to the bond issuance, and on December 31, 2017, relating to interest on the bond. Use the simplified effective−interest amortization method.

Suggested Solution

1. Issue price of the bonds: $100,000 × 104.3\% = \$104,300$.
2. Premium on the bonds payable: $\$104,300 − \$100,000 = \$4,300$.

   Months amortized: From January 1, 2017 (date of issue), to January 1, 2022 (maturity date)
   $$= 5 \text{ years} × 12 \text{ months per year} = 60 \text{ months}$$

3. January 1, 2017 (issuance date)

Assets	=	Liabilities	+	Shareholders' Equity
Cash +104,300		Bonds Payable +100,000		
		Premium on		
		Bonds Payable +4,300		

dr Cash (+A) 104,300
   cr Premium on Bonds Payable (+L)   4,300
   cr Bonds Payable (+L)   100,000

4. December 31, 2017

Assets	=	Liabilities	+	Shareholders' Equity
Cash −6,000		Premium on		Interest Expense (+E) −5,140
		Bonds Payable −860		

dr Premium on Bonds Payable (−L)   860
($4,300 × 12/60 months) ....
dr Interest Expense (+E, −SE) ($6,000 − $860) 5,140
   cr Cash (−A) ($100,000 × 6\% × 12/12)   6,000

5. December 31, 2017

Assets	=	Liabilities	+	Shareholders' Equity
Cash −6,000		Premium on		Interest Expense (+E) −5,215
		Bonds Payable −785		

dr Interest Expense (+E, −SE) ($104,300 × 5\% × 12/12) 5,215
dr Premium on Bonds Payable (−L) ($6,000 − $5,215) 785
   cr Cash (−A) ($100,000 × 6\% × 12/12)   6,000

6. January 1, 2017 (issuance date)

Assets	=	Liabilities	+	Shareholders' Equity
Cash +104,300		Bonds Payable, Net +104,300		

dr Cash (+A) 104,300

   cr Bonds Payable, Net (+L)   104,300

December 31, 2017 (interest accrual)

Assets	=	Liabilities	+	Shareholders' Equity
Cash −6,000		Bonds Payable, Net −785		Interest Expense (+E) −5,215

dr Interest Expense (+E, −SE) ($104,300 × 5% × 12/12) 5,215

dr Bonds Payable, Net (−L) ($6,000 − $5,215) 785

   cr Cash (−A) ($100,000 × 6% × 12/12)   6,000

CHAPTER SUMMARY

LO10-1 **Explain the role of liabilities in financing a business.**

- Liabilities play a vital role in allowing a business to buy goods and services on credit, cover gaps in cash flows, and expand into new regions and markets.

- Liabilities are classified as *current* if due to be paid with current assets within the current operating cycle of the business or within one year of the balance sheet date (whichever is longer). All other liabilities are considered long term.

LO10-2 **Explain how to account for common types of current liabilities.**

- Liabilities are initially reported at their cash−equivalent value, which is the amount of cash that a creditor would accept to settle the liability immediately after the transaction or event occurred.

- Liabilities are increased whenever additional obligations arise (including interest) and are reduced whenever the company makes payments or provides services to the creditor.

LO10-3 **Analyze and record bond liability transactions.**

- For most public issuances of debt (bonds), the amount borrowed by the company does not equal the amount repaid at maturity. The effect of a bond discount is to provide the borrower less money than the value stated on the face of the bond, which increases the cost of borrowing above the interest rate stated on the bond. The effect of a bond premium is to provide the borrower with more money than the face value repaid at maturity, which decreases the cost of borrowing below the stated interest rate.

- Interest Expense reports the cost of borrowing, which equals the periodic interest payments plus (or minus) the amount of the bond discount (or premium) amortized in that interest period.

LO10-4 **Describe how to account for contingent liabilities.**

- A contingent liability is a potential liability (and loss) that has arisen as a result of a past transaction or event. Its ultimate outcome will not be known until a future event occurs or fails to occur. Under ASPE, it is recorded when likely and estimable.

LO10-5 **Calculate and interpret the debt-to-assets ratio and the times interest earned ratio.**

- The debt−to−assets ratio is calculated by dividing total liabilities by total assets. It indicates the percentage of assets financed by creditors, with a higher ratio indicating a riskier financing strategy.

- The times interest earned ratio measures a company's ability to meet its interest obliga-tions with resources generated from its profit−making activities.

ACCOUNTING DECISION TOOLS

Name of Measure	Formula	What It Tells You
1. Debt-to-Assets ratio	$\dfrac{\text{Total Liabilities}}{\text{Total Assets}}$	• The percentage of assets financed by creditors • A higher ratio means greater financing risk
2. Times interest earned ratio	$\dfrac{(\text{Net Income} + \text{Interest Expense} + \text{Income Tax Expense})}{\text{Interest Expense}}$	• Whether sufficient resources are generated to cover interest costs • The higher the number the better the coverage

SOLUTION TO SELF-STUDY PRACTICE

Solution to SP10.1

	Assets	=	Liabilities	+	Shareholders' Equity	
Dec. 1	Cash +12,000		Note Payable +12,000		Interest Expense (+E)	−50
Dec. 31			Interest Payable +50		($50 = $12,000 × 5% × 1/12)	

Solution to SP10.2

	At December 31	
	2017	2016
Current Liabilities		
Current Portion of Long−Term Debt	$2,000	$ 1,000
Long−Term Debt	7,000	9,000
Total Liabilities	$9,000	$10,000

Solution to SP10.3

1. Face value
2. Discount—investors not attracted to lower stated rate
3. Premium—investors pay more than face value

KEY TERMS

Accrued Liabilities

Bond Amortization

Contingent Liabilities

Current Liabilities

Debt−to−Assets Ratio

Discount

Effective−Interest Method of Amortization

Face Value

Issue Price

Market Interest Rate

Maturity Date

Premium

Present Value

Stated Interest Rate

Straight−Line Amortization Method

Times Interest Earned Ratio

Complete definitions can also be found in the glossary at the end of this text.

HOMEWORK HELPER

Alternative terms

- The stated interest rate on a bond is also called the *coupon rate* or *contract rate*. The market interest rate is also called the *effective–interest rate* or *yield rate*.
- The word *amortize* comes from the Latin root word *mort*, which means to kill or elimi–nate; as bond discounts and premiums are amortized, they are gradually eliminated.

Helpful reminders

- From the employer's perspective, payroll deductions create liabilities, not expenses. They are not expenses because they do not increase the employer's wages and salaries cost; they simply redirect part of the wages and salaries payments to a government agency or other organization rather than to employees.
- Bonds are issued above face value (at a premium) if their stated interest rate is attractive (more than the market interest rate). If bonds have issued at a premium, their periodic cash payments will be greater than the interest expense, causing a reduction in the bond liability's carrying value.
- Bonds are issued below face value (at a discount) if their stated interest is unattractive (less than the market interest rate). If bonds have issued at a discount, their periodic cash payments will be less than the interest expense, causing an increase in the bond liability's carrying value.

Frequent mistakes

- Use the stated interest rate, not the market interest rate, to calculate the cash paid periodically on a bond. (The market interest rate is used to calculate Interest Expense when using the effective–interest method.)

PRACTICE MATERIAL

QUESTIONS (Ⓢ Symbol indicates questions that require analysis from more than one perspective.)

1. Describe three ways in which liabilities are used to finance business activities.
2. Define *liability*. What is the difference between a current liability and a long–term liability?
3. What three factors influence the dollar amount reported for liabilities?
4. Define *accrued liability*. Give an example of a typical accrued liability.
5. Why is Deferred Revenue considered a liability?
6. Why are payroll taxes and sales taxes considered liabilities?
7. Your company plans to hire an employee at a yearly salary of $70,000. Someone in your company says the actual cost will be lower because of payroll deductions. Someone else says it will be higher. Who is right? What is likely to be the total cost to the company? Explain. Ⓢ
8. If a company has a long–term loan that has only two years remaining until it matures, how is it reported on the balance sheet (*a*) this year and (*b*) next year?
9. What are the reasons that some bonds are issued at a discount and others are issued at a premium?
10. What is the difference between the stated interest rate and the market interest rate on a bond?
11. Will the stated interest rate be higher than the market interest rate or will the market interest rate be higher than the stated interest rate when a bond is issued at (*a*) face value, (*b*) a discount, and (*c*) a premium?
12. What is the carrying value of a bond payable?
13. How do you calculate the debt–to–assets ratio? What does this ratio tell you?

14. What is the difference between a secured bond and a debenture? Which carries more risk for the lender?

15. What is a contingent liability? How is a contingent liability reported under ASPE? How does this differ under IFRS?

16. (Supplement 10A) How is interest expense calculated using the straight–line method of amortization for a bond issued at (*a*) a discount and (*b*) a premium?

17. (Supplement 10B) How is interest expense calculated using the effective–interest method of amortization for a bond issued at (*a*) a discount and (*b*) a premium?

18. (Supplement 10C) How is interest expense calculated using the simplified approach to the effective–interest method for a bond issued at (*a*) a discount and (*b*) a premium?

MINI-EXERCISES

M10-1 Recording Deferred Revenues
LO10-2

A local theatre company sells 1,500 season ticket packages at a price of $250 per package. The first show in the five–show season starts this week. Show the accounting equation effects and prepare the journal entries related to (*a*) the sale of the season tickets before the first show, and (*b*) the revenue earned after putting on the first show.

M10-2 Recording Sales and Provincial Tax
LO10-2

Ahlers Clocks is a retailer of wall, mantel, and grandfather clocks, and is located in the Empire Mall in Red Deer, Alberta. Assume that a grandfather clock was sold for $10,000 cash plus 4 percent sales tax. The clock had originally cost Ahlers $6,000. Show the accounting equation effects and prepare the journal entries related to this transaction. Assume Ahlers uses a per-petual inventory system, as explained in Chapter 6.

M10-3 Calculating Payroll Tax Liabilities
LO10-2

Lightning Electronics is a mid–size manufacturer of lithium batteries. The company's pay-roll records for the November 1–14 pay period show that employees earned wages totalling $100,000 but that employee income taxes totalling $14,000, Canada Pension Plan (CPP) totalling $2,250, and Employment Insurance (EI) totalling $3,000 were withheld from this amount. The net pay was directly deposited into the employees' bank accounts.

a. What was the amount of net pay?

b. Prepare the journal entry or entries that Lightning would use to record the payroll. Include both employee and employer taxes.
   Tip: Employer CPP equals employee CPP. Employer EI equals 1.4 times employee EI.

M10-4 Reporting Current and Non-current Portions of Long-Term Debt
LO10-2

Assume that on December 1, 2017, your company borrowed $14,000, a portion of which is to be repaid each year on November 30. Specifically, your company will make the following prin-cipal payments: 2018, $2,000; 2019, $3,000; 2020, $4,000; and 2021, $5,000. Show how this loan will be reported in the December 31, 2017 and 2018 balance sheets, assuming that principal payments will be made when required.

M10-5 Recording a Note Payable
LO10-2

Greener Pastures Corporation borrowed $1,000,000 on November 1, 2017. The note carried a 6 percent interest rate with the principal and interest payable on June 1, 2018. Show the accounting equation effects and prepare the journal entries for (*a*) the note issued on November 1, and (*b*) the interest accrual on December 31.

M10-6 Reporting Interest and Long-Term Debt, Including Current Portion
LO10-2

Barton Chocolates used a promissory note to borrow $1,000,000 on July 1, 2017, at an annual interest rate of 6 percent. The note is to be repaid in yearly instalments of $200,000, plus accrued interest, on June 30 of every year until the note is paid in full (on June 30, 2022). Show how the results of this transaction would be reported in a classified balance sheet pre-pared as of December 31, 2017.

M10-7 Determining Bond Discount or Premium from Quoted Price

On February 10, 2014, finance.yahoo.com/bonds quoted a bond price of 140.2 for Ford Motor Company's 9.3 percent bonds maturing on March 1, 2030. Were the bonds selling at a discount or premium? Does this mean the market interest rate for comparable bonds was higher or lower than 9.3 percent?

LO10-3 **M10-8 Computing and Reporting a Bond Liability**

E−Tech Initiatives Limited plans to issue $500,000 of ten−year, 4 percent bonds. Interest is payable annually on December 31. All of the bonds will be issued on January 1, 2018.

a. Show how the bonds would be reported on the balance sheet at January 2, 2018, if they were issued at 98.

b. Show how the bonds would be reported on the balance sheet at January 2, 2018, if they were issued at 103.

LO10-3 **M10-9 Recording Bonds Issued at Face Value**

Waterbahn Waterslide Company issued 25,000 ten−year, 6 percent, $100 bonds on January 1, 2017, at face value. Interest is payable each December 31. Show the accounting equation effects and prepare journal entries for (a) the issuance of these bonds on January 1, 2017, and (b) the interest payment on December 31, 2017.

LO10-4 **M10-10 Reporting a Contingent Liability**

Buck's Coffee Shop is famous for its large servings of hot coffee. After a famous case involving McDonald's, the lawyer for Buck's warned management (during 2009) that it could be sued if someone were to spill hot coffee and be burned. "With the temperature of your coffee, I can guarantee that it's just a matter of time before you're sued for $1,000,000." Buck's owner felt that the likelihood was remote.

Unfortunately, in 2012, the lawyer's prediction came true when a customer filed suit. After consulting with his attorney, the owner of Buck's felt that a loss was possible but not likely or probable. The case went to trial in 2013 and the jury awarded the customer $400,000 in damages, which the company immediately appealed. Although accepting that a loss was probable, Buck's owner believed that a lower amount could be negotiated. During 2014, the customer and the company settled their dispute for $150,000. What is the proper reporting of this liability each year under ASPE? Would the reporting differ under IFRS?

LO10-5 **M10-11 Computing the Debt-to-Assets Ratio and the Times Interest Earned Ratio**

The balance sheet for Shaver Corporation reported the following: cash, $5,000; short−term investments, $10,000; net accounts receivable, $35,000; inventory, $40,000; prepaids, $10,000; equipment, $100,000; current liabilities, $40,000; notes payable (long−term), $70,000; total shareholders' equity, $90,000; net income, $3,320; interest expense, $4,400; income before income taxes, $5,280. Compute Shaver's debt−to−assets ratio and times interest earned ratio. Based on these ratios, does it appear Shaver relies mainly on debt or equity to finance its assets? Is it probable that Shaver will be able to meet its future interest obligations?

LO10-5 **M10-12 Analyzing the Impact of Transactions on the Debt-to-Assets Ratio**

BSO, Inc. has assets of $600,000 and liabilities of $450,000, resulting in a debt−to−assets ratio of 0.75. For each of the following transactions, determine whether the debt−to−assets ratio will increase, decrease, or remain the same. Each item is independent.

a. Purchased $20,000 of new inventory on credit

b. Paid accounts payable in the amount of $50,000

c. Recorded accrued salaries in the amount of $100,000

d. Borrowed $250,000 from a local bank, to be repaid in ninety days

LO10-S1 **M10-13 (Supplement 10A) Recording Bond Issuance and Interest Payment (Straight-Line Amortization)**

Simko Company issued $600,000 of ten−year, 5 percent bonds on January 1, 2017. The bonds were issued for $580,000. Interest is payable annually on December 31. Using straight−line amortization, prepare journal entries to record (*a*) the bond issuance on January 1, 2017 and (*b*) the payment of interest on December 31, 2017.

M10-14 (Supplement 10B) Recording Bond Issuance and Interest Payment (Effective-Interest Amortization)

LO10-S2

Clem Company issued $800,000 of ten–year, 5 percent bonds on January 1, 2017. The bonds sold for $741,000. Interest is payable annually on December 31. Using effective–interest amortization, prepare journal entries to record (*a*) the bond issuance on January 1, 2017, and (*b*) the payment of interest on December 31, 2017. The market interest rate on the bonds is 6 percent.

M10-15 (Supplement 10C) Recording Interest Accrual and Interest Payment (Simplified Approach to Effective-Interest Amortization)

LO10-S3

On January 1, 2014, Buchheit Enterprises reported $95,000 in a liability called *Bonds Payable, Net*. This liability related to a $100,000 bond with a stated interest rate of 5 percent that was issued when the market interest rate was 6 percent. Assuming that interest is paid December 31 each year, prepare the journal entry to record interest paid on December 31, 2017, using the simplified effective–interest method shown in Supplement 10C.

EXERCISES

E10-1 Determining Financial Statement Effects of Transactions Involving Notes Payable

LO10-2

Many businesses borrow money during periods of increased business activity to finance inventory and accounts receivable. Hudson's Bay Company (HBC) is Canada's largest department store. Each Christmas, HBC builds up its inventory to meet the needs of Christmas shoppers. A large portion of Christmas sales are on credit. As a result, HBC often collects cash from the sales several months after Christmas. Assume that on November 1, 2017, HBC borrowed $6 million cash from Downtown Bank and signed a promissory note that matures in six months. The interest rate was 7.5 percent payable at maturity. The accounting period ends December 31.

Required:

1. Indicate the accounts, amounts, and effects (+ for increase, − for decrease, and NE for no effect) of the (*a*) issuance of the note on November 1, (*b*) impact of the adjusting entry on December 31, 2017, and (*c*) the payment of the note and interest on April 30, 2018, on the accounting equation. Use the following structure for your answer:

Date	Assets	=	Liabilities	+	Shareholders' Equity

2. If HBC needs extra cash every Christmas season, should management borrow money on a long–term basis to avoid negotiating a new short–term loan each year? Explain your answer.

E10-2 Recording a Note Payable Through Its Time to Maturity

LO10-2

Use the information in E10–1 to complete the following requirements.

Required:

1. Give the journal entry to record the note on November 1, 2017.
2. Give any adjusting entry required on December 31, 2017.
3. Give the journal entry to record payment of the note and interest on the maturity date, April 30, 2018, assuming that interest has not been recorded since December 31, 2017.

E10-3 Recording Payroll Costs

LO10-2

Macier Company completed the salary and wage payroll for March 2017. The payroll provided the following details:

Salaries and wages earned	$230,000
Employee income taxes withheld	50,200
Canada Pension Plan	2,500
Employment Insurance	750

Required:

1. Considering both employee and employer payroll taxes, use the preceding information to calculate the total labour cost for the company.

   TIP: Employer CPP equals employee CPP. Employer EI equals 1.4 times employee EI.

2. Prepare the journal entry to record the payroll for March, including employee deductions but excluding employer payroll taxes.

3. Prepare the journal entry to record the employer's CPP and EI contributions.

LO10-2

E10-4 Recording Payroll Costs With and Without Withholdings

Assume that an employee of Rocco Rock Company earns $1,000 of gross wages during the current pay period and is required to remit to the government $100 for income tax and $50 for CPP and EI together. Consider the following two procedures for paying the employee:

Procedure 1 (Withholdings)	Procedure 2 (No Withholdings)
Rocco Rock Company pays the employee net wages of $850 and will remit income taxes and CPP/EI on behalf of the employee.	Rocco Rock Company pays the employee gross wages of $1,000 and the employee is responsible for remitting income taxes and CPP/EI.

Required:

1. Ignoring employer payroll taxes, under each procedure calculate (*a*) the total labour cost for the company and (*b*) the amount of cash the employee will have after satisfying all responsibilities to the government.

2. Explain why procedure 1 (withholdings) is the approach required by the government.

3. Considering that employers are responsible for matching employees' CPP/EI contributions, explain why employers might also prefer procedure 1 over procedure 2.

4. Prepare the journal entries required by the employer under procedure 1, assuming that the employee is paid in cash, but the withholdings and matching employer CPP/EI contribution have not yet been paid. (Assume employer EI equals employee EI.)

LO10-2, 10-5

E10-5 Determining the Impact of Current Liability Transactions, Including Analysis of the Debt-to-Assets Ratio

Bryanger Company sells a wide range of inventories that are initially purchased on account. Occasionally, a short−term note payable is used to obtain cash for current use. The following transactions were selected from those occurring during the year:

a. On January 10, purchased merchandise on credit for $18,000; company uses a perpetual inventory system

b. On March 1, borrowed $40,000 cash from City Bank and signed a promissory note with a face amount of $40,000, due at the end of six months, accruing interest at an annual rate of 8 percent, payable at maturity

Required:

1. For each of the transactions, indicate the accounts, amounts, and effects (+ for increase, − for decrease, and NE for no effect) on the accounting equation. Use the following structure:

Date	Assets	=	Liabilities	+	Shareholders' Equity

2. What amount of cash is paid on the maturity date of the note?

3. Indicate the impact of each transaction (+ for increase, − for decrease, and NE for no effect) on the debt−to−assets ratio. Assume Bryant Company had $300,000 in total liabilities and $500,000 in total assets, yielding a debt−to−assets ratio of 0.60, prior to each transaction.

E10-6 Determining and Recording the Financial Statement Effects of Deferred Subscription Revenue

LO10-2

Reader's Digest Association is a publisher of magazines, books, and music collections. The following note is from a recent annual report:

> **Revenues**
>
> Sales of our magazine subscriptions are deferred (as unearned revenue) and recognized as revenues proportionately over the subscription period.

Assume that Reader's Digest (a) collected $394 million in 2016 for magazines that will be delivered later in 2016 and 2017, and (b) delivered $190 million worth of magazines on these subscriptions in 2016.

Required:

1. Using the information given, indicate the accounts, amounts, and accounting equation effects (+ for increase, − for decrease, and NE for no effect) of the transactions involving $394 million and $190 million.
2. Using the information given, prepare the journal entries that would be recorded in 2016 and 2017.

E10-7 Preparing Journal Entries to Record Issuance of Bonds and Payment of Interest

LO10-3

On January 1, Applied Tech Corporation (ATC) issued $600,000 in bonds that mature in ten years. The bonds have a stated interest rate of 10 percent. When the bonds were issued, the market interest rate was 10 percent. The bonds pay interest once per year on December 31.

Required:

1. Determine the price at which the bonds were issued and the amount that ATC received at issuance.
2. Prepare the journal entry to record the bond issuance.
3. Prepare the journal entry to record the interest payment on December 31. Assume no interest was accrued earlier in the year.

E10-8 Preparing Journal Entries to Record Issuance of Bonds at Face Value, Payment of Interest, and Early Retirement

LO10-3

On January 1, InnoSolutions, Inc. issued $200,000 in bonds at face value. The bonds have a stated interest rate of 6 percent. The bonds mature in ten years and pay interest once per year on December 31.

Required:

1. Prepare the journal entry to record the bond issuance.
2. Prepare the journal entry to record the interest payment on December 31. Assume no interest was accrued earlier in the year.
3. Assume the bonds were retired immediately after the first interest payment at a quoted price of 102. Prepare the journal entry to record the early retirement of the bonds.

Check Figure
[Req. 3]:
Loss on bond
retirement =
$4,000

E10-9 Describing the Effects of a Premium Bond Issue and Interest Payment on the Financial Statement

LO10-3

Grocery Corporation received $300,328 for 11 percent bonds issued on January 1, 2018, at a market interest rate of 8 percent. The bonds had a total face value of $250,000, stated that interest would be paid each December 31, and stated that they mature in ten years

Required:

Complete the following table for each account by indicating (a) whether it is reported on the Balance Sheet (B/S) or Income Statement (I/S); (b) the dollar amount by which the account increases (+), decreases (−), or does not change (0) when Grocery Corporation issues the bonds; and (c) the direction of change in the account [increase (+), decrease (−), or no change (0)] when Grocery Corporation records the interest payment on December 31.

Account	(a) Financial Statement	(b) Issuance	(c) Interest Paid
Bonds Payable			
Discount on Bonds Payable			
Interest Expense			
Premium on Bonds Payable			

E10-10 Calculating and Interpreting the Debt-to-Assets Ratio and Times Interest Earned Ratio

According to one report, Kraft Foods Inc. sells enough Kool–Aid® mix to make 4,500 litres of the drink every minute during the summer and over 2.5 billion litres each year. Assume at December 31, 2017, the company reported no short–term investments but did report the following amounts (in millions) in its financial statements:

	2017	2016
Total Assets	$ 12,940	$ 12,000
Total Liabilities	10,060	9,060
Interest Expense	260	260
Income Tax Expense	240	245
Net Income	1,040	960

Required:

1. Compute the debt–to–assets ratio and times interest earned ratio (to two decimal places) for 2017 and 2016.
2. Use your answers to requirement 1 to determine whether, in 2017, (a) creditors were pro– viding a greater (or lesser) proportion of financing for Kraft's assets and (b) Kraft was more (or less) successful at covering its interest costs, as compared to 2016.

E10-11 (Supplement 10A) Recording the Effects of a Premium Bond Issue and First Interest Period (Straight-Line Amortization)

Refer to the information in E10−9 and assume that Grocery Company uses the straight–line method to amortize the bond premium.

Required:

1. Prepare the journal entry to record the bond issuance.
2. Prepare the journal entry to record the interest payment on December 31, 2018.

E10-12 (Supplement 10B) Recording the Effects of a Premium Bond Issue and First Interest Period (Effective-Interest Amortization)

Refer to the information in E10−9 and assume Grocery Company uses the effective–interest method to amortize the bond premium.

Check Figure [Req. 2]:
Debit "Premium on Bonds Payable" for $3,474

Required:

1. Prepare the journal entry to record the bond issuance.
2. Prepare the journal entry to record the interest payment on December 31, 2018.

E10-13 (Supplement 10C) Recording the Effects of a Premium Bond Issue and First Interest Period (Simplified Effective-Interest Amortization)

LO10-S3

Refer to the information in E10—9 and assume Grocery Company accounts for the bond using the shortcut approach shown in chapter Supplement 10C.

Required:

1. Prepare the journal entry to record the bond issuance.
2. Prepare the journal entry to record the interest payment on December 31, 2018.

E10-14 (Supplement 10A) Recording the Effects of a Discount Bond Issue and First Interest Payment, and Preparing a Discount Amortization Schedule (Straight-Line Amortization)

LO10-S1

On January 1, 2017, when the market interest rate was 9 percent, Selton Corporation completed a $200,000, 8 percent bond issue for $187,163. The bonds were dated January 1, 2017, pay interest each December 31, and mature in ten years on December 31, 2026. Seton amortizes the bond discount using the straight—line method.

Required:

1. Prepare the journal entry to record the bond issuance.
2. Prepare the journal entry to record the interest payment on December 31, 2017.
3. Prepare a bond discount amortization schedule for these bonds. Round calculations to the nearest dollar.

E10-15 (Supplement 10B) Recording the Effects of a Discount Bond Issue and First Interest Payment and Preparing a Discount Amortization Schedule (Effective-Interest Amortization)

LO10-S2

Refer to the information in E10—14 and assume Selton Corporation uses the effective—interest method to amortize the bond discount.

Required:

1. Prepare the journal entry to record the bond issuance.
2. Prepare the journal entry to record the interest payment on December 31, 2017.
3. Prepare a bond discount amortization schedule for these bonds. Round calculations to the nearest dollar.

E10-16 (Supplement 10C) Recording the Effects of a Discount Bond Issue and First Interest Payment and Preparing a Discount Amortization Schedule (Simplified Effective-Interest Amortization)

LO10-S3

Refer to the information in E10—14 and assume Selton Corporation accounts for the bond using the simplified effective—interest method shown in Supplement 10C.

Required:

1. Prepare the journal entry to record the bond issuance.
2. Prepare the journal entry to record the interest payment on December 31, 2017.
3. Prepare a bond discount amortization schedule for these bonds. Round calculations to the nearest dollar.

**Check Figure
[Req. 2]:**
Interest Expense =
$16,845

COACHED PROBLEMS

CP10-1 Determining Financial Effects of Transactions Affecting Current Liabilities with Evaluation of Effects on the Debt-to-Assets Ratio

LO10-2, 10-5

Assume that EZ Curb completed the following transactions during 2017. December 31, 2017 is the end of the annual accounting period.

Jan. 8	Purchased merchandise on account at a cost of $14,000 (Assume a perpetual inventory system.)
Jan. 17	Paid for the January 8 purchase
Apr. 1	Received $40,000 from National Bank after signing a twelve–month, 6 percent, promissory note
June 3	Purchased merchandise on account at a cost of $18,000
July 5	Paid for the June 3 purchase
Aug. 1	Rented out a small office in a building owned by EZ Curb and collected six months' rent in advance, amounting to $6,000 (Use an account called *Deferred Rent Revenue*.)
Dec. 20	Received a $100 deposit from a customer as a guarantee to return a large trailer "borrowed" for thirty days
	TIP: Consider whether EZ Curb has an obligation to return the money when the trailer is returned.
Dec. 31	Determined that wages of $6,500 were earned but not yet paid on December 31 (ignore payroll taxes)
Dec. 31	Adjusted the accounts at year–end, relating to interest
Dec. 31	Adjusted the accounts at year–end, relating to rent

Required:

1. For each listed transaction and related adjusting entry, indicate the accounts, amounts, and effects (+ for increase, – for decrease, and NE for no effect) on the accounting equation, using the following format:

$$\underline{\text{Date}} \qquad \underline{\text{Assets}} \quad = \quad \underline{\text{Liabilities}} \quad + \quad \underline{\text{Shareholders' Equity}}$$

2. For each transaction and related adjusting entry, state whether the debt–to–assets ratio is increased or decreased or there is no change. (Assume EZ Curb's debt–to–assets ratio has always been less than 1.0.)

LO10-2   **CP10-2 Recording and Reporting Current Liabilities**

eXcel   Using data from CP10–1, complete the following requirements.

Required:

1. Prepare journal entries for each of the transactions.
2. Prepare any adjusting entries required on December 31, 2017.
3. Show how all of the liabilities arising from these items are reported on the balance sheet at December 31, 2017.
4. Complete requirement 2 of CP10–1, if you have not already done so.

LO10-4   **CP10-3 Determining Financial Statement Reporting of Contingent Liabilities**

Brunswick Corporation is a multinational company that manufactures and sells marine and recreational products. A prior annual report contained the following information:

Litigation

A jury awarded $44.4 million in damages in a suit brought by Independent Boat Builders, Inc., a buying group of boat manufacturers and its 22 members. Under the antitrust laws, the damage award has been tripled, and the plaintiffs will be entitled to their attorney's fees and interest. The Company has filed an appeal contending the verdict was erroneous as a matter of law, both as to liability and damages.

---

contingent liability

Required:

What are the alternative ways in which Brunswick could account for this litigation?

  TIP: Consider the different possible outcomes that could arise from the appeal.

CP10-4 (Supplement 10A) Recording Bond Issuance and Interest Payments (Straight-Line Amortization)

LO10-S1

SWest Corporation issued bonds with the following details:

> Face value: $600,000
> Interest: 9 percent per year payable each December 31
> Terms: Bonds dated January 1, 2014, due five years from that date

The annual accounting period ends December 31. The bonds were issued at 104 on January 1, 2017, when the market interest rate was 8 percent. Assume the company uses straight—line amortization and adjusts for any rounding errors when recording interest expense in the final year.

Required:

1. Compute the issue price of the bonds in dollars (show computations).

    TIP: The issue price typically is quoted at a percentage of face value.

2. Give the journal entry to record the issuance of the bonds.

3. Give the journal entries to record the payment of interest on December 31, 2017, and 2018.

4. How much interest expense would be reported on the income statements for 2017 and 2018? Show how the liability related to the bonds should be reported on the balance sheets at December 31, 2017, and 2018.

CP10-5 (Supplement 10B) Recording Bond Issuance and Interest Payments (Effective-Interest Amortization)

LO10-S2

Complete the requirements of CP10—5, assuming SWest Corporation uses effective—interest amortization.

CP10-6 (Supplement 10C) Recording Bond Issuance and Interest Payments (Simplified Approach to Effective-Interest Amortization)

LO10-S3

Complete the requirements of CP10—5, assuming SWest Corporation uses simplified effective interest amortization shown in Supplement 10C.

CP10-7 (Supplement 10A) Completing an Amortization Schedule (Straight-Line Amortization)

LO10-S1

The Peg Corporation (TPC) issued bonds and received cash in full for the issue price. The bonds were dated and issued on January 1, 2017. The stated interest rate was payable at the end of each year. The bonds mature at the end of four years. The following schedule has been prepared (amounts in thousands):

Date	Cash	Interest	Amortization	Balance
January 1, 2017				$6,101
End of year 2017	$450	$425	$25	?
End of year 2018	450	?	25	6,051
End of year 2019	450	?	25	6,026
End of year 2020	450	424	26	6,000

Required:

1. Complete the amortization schedule.

    TIP: The switch in amortization from $25 to $26 in 2020 is caused by rounding.

2. What was the maturity amount (face value) of the bonds?

3. How much cash was received at date of issuance of the bonds?

4. Was there a premium or a discount? If so, which, and how much was it?

5. How much cash is paid for interest each period and will be paid in total for the full life of the bond issue?
6. What is the stated interest rate?
7. What is the market interest rate?
8. What amount of interest expense should be reported on the income statement each year?
9. Show how the bonds should be reported on the balance sheet at the end of 2018 and 2019.

LO10-S2, 10-S3 **CP10-8 (Supplements 10B and 10C) Completing an Amortization Schedule (Effective-Interest Amortization or Simplified Effective-Interest)**

Hondor Corporation issued bonds and received cash in full for the issue price. The bonds were dated and issued on January 1, 2017. The stated interest rate was payable at the end of each year. The bonds mature at the end of four years. The schedule on the next page has been completed (amounts in thousands):

Date	Cash	Interest	Amortization	Balance
January 1, 2017				$6,101
End of year 2017	$450	$427	$23	6,078
End of year 2018	450	426	24	6,054
End of year 2019	450	?	?	?
End of year 2020	450	?	28	6,000

Required:

1. Complete the amortization schedule.
2. What was the maturity amount (face value) of the bonds?
3. How much cash was received at date of issuance (sale) of the bonds?
4. Was there a premium or a discount? If so, which and how much was it?
5. How much cash is paid for interest each period and will be paid in total for the full life of the bond issue?
6. What is the stated interest rate?
   TIP: The stated interest rate can be calculated by comparing the cash payment to the face value of the bond.
7. What is the market interest rate?
8. What amount of interest expense should be reported on the income statement each year?
9. Show how the bonds should be reported on the balance sheet at the end of 2017 and 2018.

GROUP A PROBLEMS

LO10-2, 10-5 **PA10-1 Determining Financial Effects of Transactions Affecting Current Liabilities with Evaluation of Effects on the Debt-to-Assets Ratio**

Jack Hammer Company completed the following transactions. The annual accounting period ends December 31.

Apr. 30 Received $600,000 from Commerce Bank after signing a twelve–month, 6 percent, promissory note

June 6 Purchased merchandise on account at a cost of $75,000 (Assume a perpetual inventory system.)

July 15 Paid for the June 6 purchase

Aug. 31 Signed a contract to provide security services to a small apartment complex and collected six months' fees in advance, amounting to $24,000 (Use an account called *Deferred Revenue.*)

Dec. 31 Determined salary and wages of $40,000 were earned but not yet paid as of December 31 (ignore payroll taxes)

Dec. 31 Adjusted the accounts at year–end, relating to interest

Dec. 31 Adjusted the accounts at year–end, relating to security services

Required:

1. For each listed transaction and related adjusting entry, indicate the accounts, amounts, and effects (+ for increase, − for decrease, and NE for no effect) on the accounting equation, using the following format:

$$\underline{\text{Date}} \qquad \underline{\text{Assets}} \quad = \quad \underline{\text{Liabilities}} \quad + \quad \underline{\text{Shareholders' Equity}}$$

2. For each item, state whether the debt—to—assets ratio is increased or decreased or there is no change. (Assume Jack Hammer's debt—to—assets ratio is less than 1.0.)

Check Figure [Req. 2]: Aug. 31 transaction increases the debt-to-assets ratio

PA10-2 Recording and Reporting Current Liabilities with Evaluation of Effects on the Debt-to-Assets Ratio

LO10-2, 10-5

Using data from PA10−1, complete the following requirements.

Required:

1. Prepare journal entries for each of the transactions.
2. Prepare all adjusting entries required on December 31.
3. Show how all of the liabilities arising from these items are reported on the balance sheet at December 31.
4. Complete requirement 2 of PA10−1, if you have not already done so.

PA10-3 Recording and Reporting Current Liabilities

LO10-2

Lakeview Company completed the following two transactions. The annual accounting period ends December 31.

a. On December 31, calculated the payroll, which indicates gross earnings for wages ($80,000), payroll deductions for income tax ($8,000), payroll deductions for CPP ($5,000) and EI ($1,000), payroll deductions for Canadian Cancer Society ($3,000), and employer contributions for CPP (matching) and EI ($1,400). Employees were paid in cash, but payments for the corresponding payroll deductions have not yet been made and employer taxes have not yet been recorded.

b. Collected rent revenue of $6,000 on December 10 for office space that Lakeview rented to another business. The rent collected was for thirty days from December 11 to January 10 and was credited in full to Deferred Revenue.

Required:

1. Give the journal entries to record payroll on December 31.
2. Give (a) the journal entry for the collection of rent on December 10 and (b) the adjusting journal entry on December 31.
3. Show how any liabilities related to these items should be reported on the company's balance sheet at December 31.

PA10-4 Comparing Bonds Issued at Par, Discount, and Premium

LO10-3

Net Work Corporation, whose annual accounting period ends on December 31, issued the following bonds:

> Date of bonds: January 1, 2017
> Maturity amount and date: $200,000 due in 10 years (December 31, 2026)
> Interest: 10 percent per year payable each December 31
> Date issued: January 1, 2017

Check Figure [Req. 1]: Case B has an unamortized discount of $6,000

Required:

1. Provide the following amounts to be reported on the January 1, 2017, financial statements immediately after the bonds were issued:

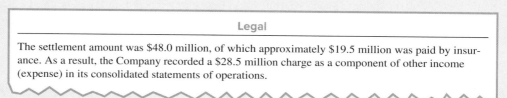

	Case A (issued at 100)	Case B (issued at 97)	Case C (issued at 101)
a. Bonds Payable	$	$	$
b. Unamortized premium (or discount)			
c. Carrying Value			

2. Assume that you are an investment adviser and a friend has written to you asking, "Why should I buy a bond at a premium when I can find one at a discount? Isn't that stupid? It's like paying list price for a car instead of negotiating a discount." Write a brief message in response to the question.

LO10-3 **PA10-5 Determining Financial Statement Reporting of Contingent Liabilities**

Macromedia, Inc. is the original maker of Shockwave and Flash technologies. One of its annual reports indicated that a lawsuit had been filed against the company and five of its former officers for securities fraud in connection with allegedly making false or misleading statements about its financial results. The lawsuit was settled out of court, as described in the following note:

Legal

The settlement amount was $48.0 million, of which approximately $19.5 million was paid by insurance. As a result, the Company recorded a $28.5 million charge as a component of other income (expense) in its consolidated statements of operations.

Required:

Explain why Macromedia didn't record a contingent liability under GAAP when the lawsuit was first filed.

LO10-S1 **PA10-6 (Supplement 10A) Recording Bond Issue, Interest Payments (Straight-Line Amortization), and Early Bond Retirement**

On January 1, 2017, Loop de Loop Raceway issued 600 bonds, each with a face value of $1,000, a stated interest rate of 5 percent paid annually on December 31, and a maturity date of December 31, 2019. On the issue date, the market interest rate was 6 percent, so the total proceeds from the bond issue were $583,950. Loop de Loop uses the straight–line bond amortization method.

Required:

1. Prepare a bond amortization schedule.
2. Give the journal entry to record the bond issue.
3. Give the journal entries to record the interest payments on December 31, 2017, and 2018.
4. Give the journal entry to record the interest and face value payment on December 31, 2019.
5. Assume the bonds are retired on January 1, 2019, at a price of 98. Give the journal entries to record the bond retirement.

LO10-S2 **PA10-7 (Supplement 10B) Recording Bond Issue, Interest Payments (Effective-Interest Amortization), and Early Bond Retirement**

On January 1, 2017, Surreal Manufacturing issued 600 bonds, each with a face value of $1,000, a stated interest rate of 3 percent paid annually on December 31, and a maturity date of December 31, 2019. On the issue date, the market interest rate was 4 percent, so the total proceeds from the bond issue were $583,352. Surreal uses the effective–interest bond amorti–zation method.

Required:

1. Prepare a bond amortization schedule.
2. Give the journal entry to record the bond issue.

3. Give the journal entries to record the interest payments on December 31, 2017, and 2018.

4. Give the journal entry to record the interest and face value payment on December 31, 2019.

5. Assume the bonds are retired on January 1, 2019, at a price of 101. Give the journal entry to record the bond retirement.

PA10-8 (Supplement 10C) Recording Bond Issue, Interest Payments (Simplified Effective-Interest Amortization), and Early Bond Retirement

LO10-3

Assume the same facts as PA10–7, except that Surreal uses the simplified effective–interest bond amortization method, as shown in Supplement 10C.

Required:

1. Prepare a bond amortization schedule.

2. Give the journal entry to record the bond issue.

3. Give the journal entries to record the interest payments on December 31, 2017, and 2018.

4. Give the journal entry to record the interest and face value payment on December 31, 2019.

5. Assume the bonds are retired on January 1, 2019, at a price of 101. Give the journal entry to record the bond retirement.

GROUP B PROBLEMS

PB10-1 Determining Financial Effects of Transactions Affecting Current Liabilities with Evaluation of Effects on the Debt-to-Assets Ratio

LO10-2, 10-5

TigerCom completed the following transactions. The annual accounting period ends December 31.

Jan. 3	Purchased merchandise on account at a cost of $24,000 (Assume a perpetual inventory system.)
Jan. 27	Paid for the January 3 purchase
Apr. 1	Received $80,000 from Atlantic Bank after signing a twelve–month, 5 percent, promissory note
June 13	Purchased merchandise on account at a cost of $8,000
July 25	Paid for the June 13 purchase
Aug. 1	Rented out a small office in a building owned by TigerCom and collected eight months' rent in advance, amounting to $8,000 (Use an account called Deferred Rent Revenue.)
Dec. 31	Determined wages of $12,000 were earned but not yet paid on December 31 (Ignore payroll taxes.)
Dec. 31	Adjusted the accounts at year–end, relating to interest
Dec. 31	Adjusted the accounts at year–end, relating to rent

Required:

1. For each listed transaction and related adjusting entry, indicate the accounts, amounts, and effects (+ for increase, − for decrease, and NE for no effect) on the accounting equation, using the following format:

Date	Assets	=	Liabilities	+	Shareholders' Equity

2. For each item, state whether the debt–to–assets ratio is increased or decreased or there is no change. (Assume Tiger Company's debt–to–assets ratio is less than 1.0.)

PB10-2 Recording and Reporting Current Liabilities with Evaluation of Effects on the Debt-to-Assets Ratio

LO10-2, 10-5

Using data from PB10–1, complete the following requirements.

Required:

1. Prepare journal entries for each of the transactions through August 1.
2. Prepare any adjusting entries required on December 31.
3. Show how all of the liabilities arising from these items are reported on the balance sheet at December 31.
4. Complete requirement 2 of PB10–1, if you have not already done so.

LO10-2 **PA10-3 Recording and Reporting Current Liabilities**

Sandler Company completed the following two transactions. December 31 is the end of the annual accounting period.

a. On December 31, calculated the payroll, which indicates gross earnings for wages ($260,000), payroll deductions for income tax ($28,000), payroll deductions for CPP ($15,000) and EI ($5,000), payroll deductions for United Way ($4,000), employer contri- butions for CPP (matching), and EI ($7,000). Employees were paid in cash, but payments for the corresponding payroll deductions have not yet been made and employer taxes have not yet been recorded.

b. Collected rent revenue of $1,500 on December 10 for office space that Sandler rented to another business. The rent collected was for 30 days from December 11 to January 10 and was credited in full to Deferred Revenue.

Required:

1. Give the journal entries to record payroll on December 31.
2. Give (a) the journal entry for the collection of rent on December 10 and (b) the adjusting journal entry on December 31.
3. Show how any liabilities related to these items should be reported on the company's balance sheet at December 31.

LO10-3 **PB10-4 Comparing Bonds Issued at Par, Discount, and Premium**

Marshalls Corporation completed a $500,000, 7 percent bond issue on January 1, 2017. The bonds pay interest each December 31 and mature ten years from January 1, 2017.

Required:

1. Provide the following amounts to be reported on the January 1, 2017, financial statements immediately after the bonds were issued:

	Case A (issued at 100)	Case B (issued at 98)	Case C (issued at 102)
a. Bonds Payable	$	$	$
b. Unamortized premium (or discount)			
c. Carrying Value			

2. Assume that you are an investment adviser and a retired person has written to you asking, "Why should I buy a bond at a premium when I can find one at a discount? Isn't that stupid? It's like paying list price for a car instead of negotiating a discount." Write a brief message in response to the question.

LO10-3 **PB10-5 Recording and Explaining the Early Retirement of Debt**

ABC Entertainment, Inc. owns and operates 361 movie theatres worldwide, with 5,203 screens in Canada. Assume the company issued 11 percent bonds in the amount of $53,000,000 and then used all of these cash proceeds to retire bonds with a coupon rate of 13.6 percent. At that time, the 13.6 percent bonds had a carrying value of $50,000,000.

Required:

1. Prepare the journal entries to record the issuance of the 11 percent bonds and the early retirement of the 13.6 percent bonds. Assume both sets of bonds were issued at face value.

2. How should ABC report any gain or loss on this transaction?

3. What dollar amount of interest expense is ABC saving each year by replacing the 13.6 percent bonds with the 11 percent bonds?

PB10-6 (Supplement 10A) Recording Bond Issue, Interest Payments (Straight-Line Amortization), and Early Bond Retirement

LO10-S1

On January 1, 2017, Methodical Manufacturing issued 100 bonds, each with a face value of $1,000, a stated interest rate of 5 percent, paid annually on December 31, and a maturity date of December 31, 2019. On the issue date, the market interest rate was 4.25 percent, so the total proceeds from the bond issue were $102,070. Methodical uses the straight–line bond amortization method.

Required:

1. Prepare a bond amortization schedule.
2. Give the journal entry to record the bond issue.
3. Give the journal entries to record the interest payments on December 31, 2017 and 2018.
4. Give the journal entry to record the interest and face value payment on December 31, 2019.
5. Assume the bonds are retired on January 1, 2019, at a price of 102. Give the journal entries to record the bond retirement.

PB10-7 (Supplement 10B) Recording Bond Issue, Interest Payments (Effective-Interest Amortization), and Early Bond Retirement

LO10-S2

Refer to PB10–5. Assume Methodical uses the effective–interest bond amortization method.

Required:

1. Prepare a bond amortization schedule.
2. Give the journal entry to record the bond issue.
3. Give the journal entries to record the interest payments on December 31, 2017, and 2018.
4. Give the journal entry to record the interest and face value payment on December 31, 2019.
5. Assume the bonds are retired on January 1, 2019, at a price of 101. Give the journal entry to record the bond retirement.

Check Figure [Req. 3]:
Interest expense Dec. 31/18 = $4,310

PB10-8 (Supplement 10C) Recording Bond Issue, Interest Payments (Simplified Effective-Interest Amortization), and Early Bond Retirement

LO10-S3

Assume the same facts as PB10–5, but now assume that Methodical uses the simplified effective–interest bond amortization method, as shown in Supplement 10C.

Required:

1. Prepare a bond amortization schedule.
2. Give the journal entry to record the bond issue.
3. Give the journal entries to record the interest payments on December 31, 2017, and 2018.
4. Give the journal entry to record the interest and face value payment on December 31, 2019.
5. Assume the bonds are retired on January 1, 2019, at a price of 101. Give the journal entry to record the bond retirement.

COMPREHENSIVE PROBLEM

C10-1 Calculating Interest and Depreciation Expenses and Effects on Loan Covenant Ratios

LO9-3, 9-7, 10-2, 10-5

Use what you learned in Chapters 9 and 10 when considering the following.

Zoom Car Corporation (ZCC) plans to purchase approximately 100 vehicles on December 31, 2017, spending $2 million plus 11 percent total sales tax. ZCC expects to use the vehicles for five years and then sell them for approximately $420,000. ZCC anticipates the following average vehicle use over each year ended December 31:

	2018	2019	2020	2021	2022
Kilometres per year	15,000	20,000	10,000	10,000	5,000

To finance the purchase, ZCC signed a five–year promissory note on December 31, 2017, for $1.8 million, with interest paid annually at the market interest rate of 6 percent. The note carries loan covenants that require ZCC to maintain a minimum times interest earned ratio of 3.0 and a minimum fixed asset turnover ratio of 1.0. ZCC forecasts that the company will generate the following sales and preliminary earnings (prior to recording depreciation on the vehicles and interest on the note). For purposes of this question, ignore income tax.

(in thousands)	2018	2019	2020	2021	2022
Sales Revenue	$2,000	$2,500	$2,800	$2,900	$3,000
Income before depreciation and interest expense	1,000	1,200	1,400	1,500	1,600

Required:

1. Calculate the amount of interest expense that would be recorded each year.
2. Calculate the depreciation expense that would be recorded each year, using the (a) straight–line, (b) double–declining–balance, and (c) units–of–production depreciation method.
3. Using your answers to requirements 1 and 2, determine net income and the two loan covenant ratios in each year, assuming the company chooses the (a) straight–line, (b) double–declining–balance, and (c) units–of–production depreciation method.
4. Using your answers to requirement 3, indicate whether the loan covenants would be violated under the (a) straight–line, (b) double–declining–balance, and (c) units–of–production depreciation method.

SKILLS DEVELOPMENT CASES

LO10-5 **S10-1 Finding Financial Information**

Refer to the summarized financial statements of The Home Depot in Appendix A.

Required:

1. Calculate the company's debt–to–assets ratio for the year ended January 29, 2017.
2. Calculate, to two decimal places, the company's times interest earned ratio for the year ended January 29, 2017. Does this ratio cause you any concern about the company's ability to meet future interest obligations as they become due?

LO10-5 **S10-2 Comparing Financial Information**

Refer to the summarized financial statements of The Home Depot in Appendix A and Lowe's Companies, Inc.'s in Appendix B at the back of this book.

Required:

1. Calculate and express as a percentage, the companies' debt–to–assets ratios using amounts reported in the financial statements for the year ending in early 2017. What do the differences in this ratio suggest about the companies' reliance on creditors? Does it appear that The Home Depot or Lowe's Companies, Inc. has a riskier financing strategy?
2. Calculate, to two decimal places, the companies' times interest earned ratios for the 2016 fiscal year end. Does it appear that The Home Depot or Lowe's Companies, Inc. will be better able to meet future interest obligations as they become payable?

LO10-1, 10-2, 10-3, 10-4, 10-5

As a team, select an industry to analyze. Using the Internet, each team member should access the annual report for one publicly traded company in the industry, with each member selecting a different company. (See S1–3 in Chapter 1 for a description of possible resources for these tasks.)

Required:

1. On an individual basis, each team member should write a short report that incorporates the following:

   a. What are the most significant types of current liabilities owed by the company?

   b. Read the company's financial statement note regarding long–term debt and commitments and contingencies. Does the company have any significant amounts coming due in the next five years?

   c. Compute and analyze the debt–to–assets ratio and times interest earned ratio.

2. Then, as a team, write a short report comparing and contrasting your companies using these attributes. Discuss any patterns across the companies that the team observes. Provide potential explanations for any differences discovered.

S10-4 Ethical Decision Making: A Real-Life Example

LO10-3

Many retired people invest a significant portion of their money in bonds issued by corporations because of their relatively low risk. During the 1980s, significant inflation caused some interest rates to rise to as high as 15 percent. Retired people who bought bonds that paid only 6 percent continued to earn at the lower rate. During the 1990s, inflation subsided and interest rates declined. Many corporations took advantage of the callability feature of these bonds and retired the bonds early. Many of these retired high–interest–rate bonds were replaced with low interest rate bonds.

Required:

In your judgment, is it ethical for corporations to continue paying low interest rates when rates increase but to call bonds when rates decrease? Why or why not?

S10-5 Ethical Decision Making: A Mini-Case

LO10-3

Assume that you are a portfolio manager for a large insurance company. The majority of the money you manage is from retired schoolteachers who depend on the income you earn on their investments.

You have invested a significant amount of money in the bonds of a large corporation and have just received news released by the company's president explaining that it is unable to meet its current interest obligations because of deteriorating business operations related to increased international competition. The president has a recovery plan that will take at least two years. During that time, the company will not be able to pay interest on the bonds, and she admits that if the plan does not work, bondholders will probably lose more than half of their money.

As a creditor, you can force the company into immediate bankruptcy and probably get back at least 90 percent of the bondholders' money. You also know that your decision will cause at least 10,000 people to lose their jobs if the company ceases operations.

Required:

Given only these two options, what should you do? Consider who would be helped or harmed by the two options.

S10-6 Critical Thinking: Evaluating Effects on the Debt-to-Assets Ratio

LO10-5

Assume you work as an assistant to the chief financial officer of Fashions First, Inc. The CFO reminds you that the fiscal year–end is only two weeks away and that he is looking to you to ensure the company stays in compliance with its loan covenant to maintain a a debt–to–assets ratio of no more than 75 percent. A review of the general ledger indicates that cash and other liquid assets total $690,000 and current liabilities are $570,000. Your company has an excess of Cash ($300,000) and an equally large balance in Accounts Payable ($270,000), although none of its Accounts Payable are due until next month.

Required:

1. Determine whether the company is currently in compliance with its loan covenant.

2. Assuming the level of assets and liabilities remains unchanged until the last day of the fiscal year, evaluate whether Fashions First should pay down $90,000 of its Accounts Payable on the last day of the year, before the Accounts Payable become due.

LO10-S1

S10-7 (Supplement 10A) Preparing a Bond Amortization Schedule (Straight-Line Amortization)

Assume the authors of a popular introductory accounting text have hired you to create spreadsheets that will calculate bond discount amortization schedules like those shown in this chapter. As usual, you email your friend Owen for some guidance. Much to your disappointment, you receive an auto—reply message from Owen indicating that he's gone skiing in New Zealand.

After a bit of panicking, you realize you can refer to Owen's previous email messages for spreadsheet advice that will help you complete this task. From his advice for Chapter 9, you decide to create a data input section for the stated interest rate, market interest rate, face value, issue price, and years to maturity.

The spreadsheet file also will have a separate amortization schedule worksheet that contains only formulas, references to the cells in the data input section, and references to other cells in the amortization schedule. All amounts will be rounded to the nearest dollar (using the Round function in Excel), which means the discount amortization in the final year might be off a few dollars (unless you use the IF function in Excel to eliminate any remaining discount in the final year of the bond's life, in the same way that Owen showed in Chapter 9 for declining—balance depreciation).

Required:

Prepare a worksheet that uses formulas to reproduce the straight—line bond discount amortization schedule shown in Supplement 10A. Display both the completed spreadsheet and a "formulas revealed" (Ctrl ~) version of it.

LO10-S2

S10-8 (Supplement 10B) Preparing a Bond Amortization Schedule (Effective-Interest Amortization)

Refer to the information in S10—7 and prepare a worksheet that uses formulas to reproduce the effective—interest bond discount amortization schedule shown in Supplement 10B. Display both the completed spreadsheet and a "formulas revealed" (Ctrl ~) version of it.

LO10-S3

S10-9 (Supplement 10C) Preparing a Bond Amortization Schedule (Simplified Effective-Interest Amortization)

Refer to the information in S10—7 and prepare a worksheet that uses formulas to reproduce the bond discount amortization schedule shown for simplified effective—interest amortization in Supplement 10C. Display both the completed spreadsheet and a "formulas revealed" (Ctrl ~) version of it.

CONTINUING CASE

LO10-2

CC10-1 Accounting for Debt Financing

Nicole thinks that her business, Nicole's Getaway Spa (NGS), is doing really well and she is planning a large expansion. With such a large expansion, Nicole will need to finance some of it using debt. She signed a one—year note for $50,000, payable to the bank with a 6 percent interest rate. The note was issued October 1, 2017, interest is payable semi—annually, and the end of Nicole's accounting period is December 31.

Required:

1. Prepare the journal entries required from the issuance of the note until its maturity on September 30, 2018, assuming that no entries are made other than at the end of the accounting period, when interest is payable and when the note reaches its maturity.

2. Is there any similarity between the way Notes Payable and Notes Receivable are accounted for? Explain.

Refer to the Wiki Art Gallery (WAG) instructional case in Appendix D and read the case in sufficient depth to answer the following questions.

1. Note 4 to WAG's financial statements indicates that the note payable increased from $20,000 to $25,000. Assume this change in loan balance occurred when the terms of the loan were adjusted on May 31, 2011. Use the interest formula to calculate the amount of interest expense for the periods from October 1, 2010, to May 31, 2011, and from May 31, 2011, to September 30, 2011. What do your calculations suggest about the interest reported by WAG during the 2011 fiscal year?

   a. Interest from October 1, 2010, to May 31, 2011, should be $1,000, and interest from May 31, 2011, to September 30, 2011, should be $1,500. These calculations suggest WAG understated its 2011 interest expense by $1,780.

   b. Interest from October 1, 2010, to May 31, 2011, should be $667, and interest from May 31, 2011, to September 30, 2011, should be $500. These calculations suggest WAG understated its 2011 interest expense by $447.

   c. Interest from October 1, 2010, to May 31, 2011, should be $1,000, and interest from May 31, 2011, to September 30, 2011, should be $500. These calculations suggest WAG understated its 2011 interest expense by $780.

   d. Interest from October 1, 2010, to May 31, 2011, should be $800, and interest from May 31, 2011, to September 30, 2011, should be $400. These calculations suggest WAG understated its 2011 interest expense by $480.

2. What was the effect of Rob cutting his salary by $2,000?

   a. It decreased WAG's selling price by $2,000.

   b. It increased WAG's selling price by $2,000.

   c. It increased WAG's selling price by $10,000.

   d. This was a kind gesture that better aligned Rob's take—home pay with Stephen's cut in dividends. It had no effect on WAG's selling price.

THIS IS
NOW

This chapter focuses on equity financing, as reported in the shareholders' equity section of the balance sheet.

YOUR LEARNING OBJECTIVES

Understand the business

LO11-1 Explain the role of shares (also called *stocks*) in financing a corporation.

Study the accounting methods

LO11-2 Explain and analyze common share transactions.

LO11-3 Explain and analyze cash dividends, stock dividends, and stock split transactions.

LO11-4 Describe the characteristics of preferred shares and analyze transactions affecting preferred shares.

Evaluate the results

LO11-5 Analyze the earnings per share (EPS), return on equity (ROE), and price/earnings (P/E) ratios.

Review the chapter

Chapter Summary

Supplemental material

LO11-S1 Account for owners' equity in other forms of business.

CHAPTER 11

Shareholders' Equity

Keith Homan/ Shutterstock.com

FOCUS COMPANY:

Molson Coors
Brewing Company
www.molsoncoors.com

News about company shares, or stocks, is everywhere. You've probably read it in the *Globe and Mail*, listened to it on CBC Radio, or searched for it at Yahoo! Finance. Behind this fascination with shares is a dream that many people have: taking a small amount of money and turning it into a fortune. That's what Molson Coors Brewing Company has managed to do.

John Molson opened the Molson Brewery in Montreal in 1786. This brewery is the oldest in North America and continues to produce beer on the site of the original brewery. The company went public in 1945, and has expanded into a successful brewing company well-known in households across Canada. This success has arisen through partnerships with other major brewers (such as merging with Adolph Coors in 2005), and the development of new brands of beer. Molson Coors Brewing Company offers a diverse portfolio of beer brands, including Molson Canadian (lager), Molson Canadian Light, Molson Canadian 67, Coors Light, Molson Dry, Rickard's, Old Style Pilsner, and Carling, just to name a few!

To obtain financing for growing these brands, Molson Coors Brewing Company issued its shares to investors through the New York Stock Exchange, under the stock ticker symbol TAP. Investors who purchased one share of the company in January of 2007 paid $38.98 per share. Ten years later, those shares were trading for $97.62 per share, which is an increase in share value of 2.5 times.

In this chapter, you will see how companies like Molson Coors Brewing Company account for a variety of share transactions, including issuances, splits, and dividends. By the end of the chapter, you should understand many of the terms used in the news about company shares.

Logo courtesy of Molson Coors Brewing Company.

ORGANIZATION OF THE CHAPTER

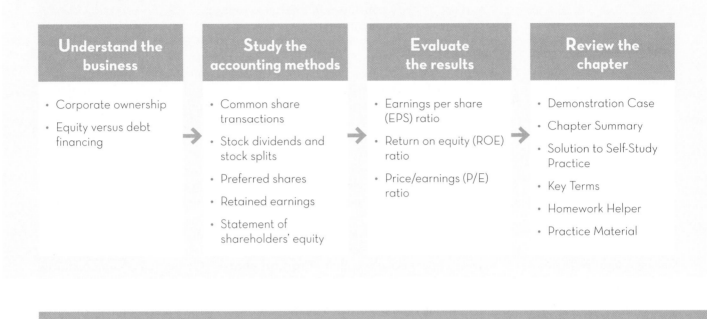

Understand the business	Study the accounting methods	Evaluate the results	Review the chapter
• Corporate ownership • Equity versus debt financing	• Common share transactions • Stock dividends and stock splits • Preferred shares • Retained earnings • Statement of shareholders' equity	• Earnings per share (EPS) ratio • Return on equity (ROE) ratio • Price/earnings (P/E) ratio	• Demonstration Case • Chapter Summary • Solution to Self-Study Practice • Key Terms • Homework Helper • Practice Material

Understand the Business

CORPORATE OWNERSHIP

If you were to write down the names of fifty familiar businesses, probably all of them would be corporations. This is understandable because corporations account for a large percentage of the total sales reported by Canadian businesses.[1] Many Canadians own shares in corporations, either directly or indirectly through a mutual fund or pension program.

You probably recall from Chapter 1 that the act of creating a corporation is costly, so why is the corporate form so popular? One reason is that it limits the legal liability of its owners. Another is that corporations can raise large amounts of money because investors can easily participate in a corporation's ownership. This ease of participation is related to several factors.

- **Shares can be purchased in small amounts.** You could have become one of Molson Coors' owners in 2017 by buying a share of the company for just over $97.
- **Ownership interests are transferable.** The shares of public companies are regularly bought and sold on established markets such as the Toronto Stock Exchange (TSX) or the New York Stock Exchange (NYSE). Molson Coors shares are traded on the NYSE and TSX under the ticker symbol TAP and TPX.B–T respectively.
- **Shareholders (or stockholders) are not liable for the corporation's debts.** Creditors have no legal claim on the personal assets of shareholders, as they do on the personal assets belonging to owners of sole proprietorships and partnerships. So if you owned shares in the old Eaton's department store, which went bankrupt and was liquidated in 1999, you would have lost what you paid to buy the shares, but unless you personally guaranteed the company's debt, you wouldn't have had to chip in to help pay the hundreds of millions of dollars that the company owed.

The law recognizes a corporation as a separate legal entity. It may own assets, incur liabilities, expand and contract in size, sue others, be sued,

LEARNING OBJECTIVE 11-1

Explain the role of shares (also called *stocks*) in financing a corporation.

and enter into contracts independently of its owners. A corporation exists separate and apart from its owners, which means it doesn't die when its owners die. Thomas Edison died in 1931, but the company he founded (General Electric) continues in existence today.

To protect everyone's rights, the creation and oversight of cor‐porations are tightly regulated by law. Corporations are created by submitting an application to the government (provincial, territorial, or federal). Because laws vary across Canada, you might decide to create a corporation in a province or territory other than the one in which it operates. If the application to create a corporation is approved, the province or territory issues a charter, also called the *articles of incor‐poration*, which spells out information about the corporation such as its name, address, nature of business, and ownership structure. Federally incorporated companies are regulated by the Canada Business Corpo‐rations Act (CBCA), while provincially and territorially incorporated companies are regulated by the legislation of the corresponding province or territory.

The ownership structure of a corporation can vary from one company to the next. In the most basic form, a corporation must have one type of shares, appropriately called **common shares**. Owners of common shares usually enjoy a number of benefits:

> **Common shares:** The basic voting shares issued by a corporation to shareholders.

1. **Voting rights.** For each share you own, you get a set number of votes on major issues. Some classes of common shares can carry more votes than others, so watch for this if you care about voting on which accounting firm will be appointed as external auditors and who will serve on the board of directors. The board of directors is the group that appoints the corporation's officers and governs top manage‐ment, as shown in Exhibit 11.1.

2. **Dividends.** Shareholders receive a share of the corporation's profits when distributed as dividends.

EXHIBIT 11.1	Typical Organizational Structure of a Corporation

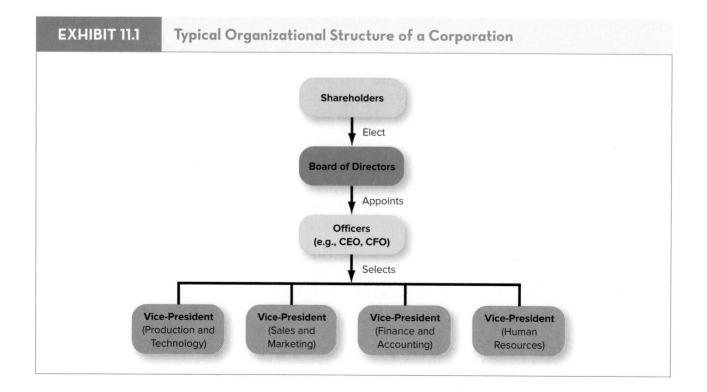

3. **Residual claim.** If the company ceases operations, shareholders share in any assets remaining after creditors have been paid.

4. **Pre-emptive rights.** To retain their ownership percentages, exist—ing shareholders may be given the first chance to buy newly issued shares before they are offered to others.

EQUITY VERSUS DEBT FINANCING

Whenever a company needs a large amount of long—term financing, its executives have to decide whether to obtain it by issuing new shares to investors (called equity financing) or by borrowing money from lenders (debt financing). Each form of financing has certain advantages over the other, as listed in Exhibit 11.2. These factors play a big role in determining whether equity or debt financing is most appropriate for each particular corporation.

One company, for example, might be primarily concerned about the impact of financing on income taxes and decide to rely on debt financ—ing because its interest payments are tax deductible. Another company might be so concerned about being able to pay its existing liabilities that it can't afford to take on additional debt. By using equity financ—ing, which doesn't have to be repaid, the company could obtain the financing it needs. Ultimately, the decision to pursue additional equity or debt financing depends on the circumstances.

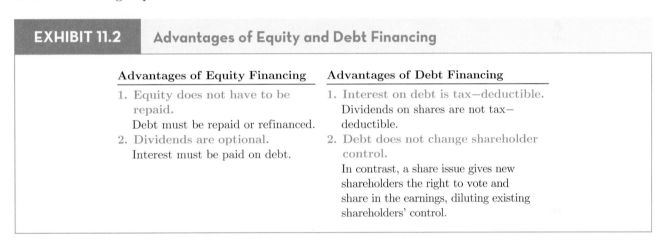

EXHIBIT 11.2	Advantages of Equity and Debt Financing

Advantages of Equity Financing	Advantages of Debt Financing
1. Equity does not have to be repaid. Debt must be repaid or refinanced.	1. Interest on debt is tax—deductible. Dividends on shares are not tax—deductible.
2. Dividends are optional. Interest must be paid on debt.	2. Debt does not change shareholder control. In contrast, a share issue gives new shareholders the right to vote and share in the earnings, diluting existing shareholders' control.

SPOTLIGHT ON The World

JOBS Act Enables Crowdfunding Equity

Until recently, equity financing for start-up companies was typically limited to the personal savings of company founders, or their friends and relatives. But now, in some countries, that's changing. In the United States, for example, the Jumpstart Our Business Startups (JOBS) Act aims to help start-up companies raise money from a large number of small investors over the Internet.

Prompted by the JOBS Act, the U.S. Securities and Exchange Commission (SEC) plans to allow companies to raise up to $1 million annually via crowdfunding portals. Companies will have to fulfill certain requirements, such as filing financial statements with the SEC each year, and investors will be limited to investing less than 10 percent of their annual income. Only time will tell whether equity crowdfunding replaces your rich, surly uncle as a source of equity.

The first point to note is that all transactions between a company and its shareholders affect the company's balance sheet accounts only. They do not affect the company's income statement.

COMMON SHARE TRANSACTIONS

Exhibit 11.3 shows the balance sheet accounts that Molson Coors Brewing Company reported in the shareholders' equity section of its balance sheet at the end of its 2015 fiscal year. It includes four main elements:

1. **Contributed Capital.** This reports the amount of capital the company received from investors' contributions in exchange for the company's common shares. For this reason, contributed capital represents paid—in capital. As Exhibit 11.3 suggests, contributed capital can include several components, which we'll explain later in this section.

2. **Retained Earnings.** This reports the cumulative amount of net income earned by the company less the cumulative amount of dividends declared since the corporation was first organized. Retained Earnings represents earned capital.

3. **Treasury Shares.** This reports shares that were previously issued to and owned by shareholders but have been reacquired and are now held by the corporation. To fully understand treasury shares, it's helpful to follow share transactions through from authorization to issuance and repurchase, as we do in the following section.

4. **Accumulated Other Comprehensive Income (Loss).** This reports unre—alized gains and losses, which are temporary changes in the value of certain assets and liabilities the company holds. They can relate to pensions, financial investments, and foreign currency translation differ—ences, such as for Molson Coors Brewing Company's foreign operations.

EXHIBIT 11.3	Explanation of Molson Coors Brewing Company Shareholders' Equity

MOLSON COORS BREWING COMPANY
Partial Balance Sheets
As of December 31

(in millions, except share amounts)	2015	2014	Explanation
SHAREHOLDERS' EQUITY			
Contributed Capital			
Common Shares, no par value	$ 713	$ 772	Basic voting shares
Authorized: 500,000,000 shares			Maximum number of shares
Issued: 191,400,000 shares			Number of shares distributed
Paid—in Capital	4,000	3,871	Amount in excess of par value
Total Contributed Capital	4,713	4,643	Total equity paid in by investors
Retained Earnings	4,496	4,440	Total equity earned by the company
Treasury Shares (9.5 million shares)	(471)	(321)	Shares reacquired by the company
Accumulated Other Comprehensive Income (Loss)	(1,695)	(898)	Unrealized gains and losses, net
Total Shareholders' Equity	$ 7,043	$ 7,864	

A corporation's charter indicates the maximum number of common shares that the corporation is allowed to issue. Look closely at the Contributed Capital section of Exhibit 11.3 and you will see that Molson Coors has **authorized shares** of 500 million. The next line in Exhibit 11.3 tells us how many shares have actually been issued. At the end of 2015, 191.4 million common shares had been issued. **Issued shares** will be owned forever by one shareholder or another, unless the company repurchases them.

The CBCA requires that, for the most part, repurchased shares be cancelled (retired). Only in certain jurisdictions in Canada and in limited circumstances can repurchased shares be held by a company, at which point they become known as **treasury shares**. Treasury shares are used more often in the United States or by Canadian companies that are listed on U.S. stock exchanges. During the time that treasury shares are held by a corporation, the shares do not carry voting, dividend, or other shareholder rights. Shares that are owned by shareholders (not the corporation itself) are called **outstanding shares**.

Because of the limited application of treasury shares in Canada, we felt it would be more beneficial to leave the detailed discussion of, and accounting application for, treasury shares out of the text material.

The relationships among authorized, issued, outstanding, and treasury shares are shown in Exhibit 11.4. Be aware that the number of outstanding shares (181.9 million) is not reported on the face of the balance sheet but, instead, has to be computed as the difference between issued shares (191.4 million) and treasury shares (9.5 million). Knowing this will help you compute earnings per share, which is a key financial ratio discussed later in this chapter and expressed in terms of the number of outstanding shares.

Authorized shares: The maximum number of shares of a corporation that can be issued, as specified in the charter.

Issued shares: Shares that have been distributed by the corporation.

Treasury shares: Issued shares that have been reacquired by the company.

Outstanding shares: Shares that are currently held by shareholders (not the corporation itself).

EXHIBIT 11.4	Authorized, Issued, Outstanding, and Treasury Shares

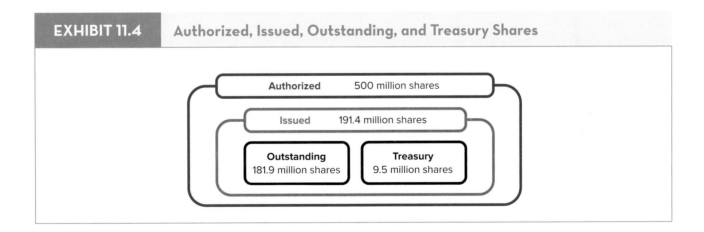

Authorized	500 million shares
Issued	191.4 million shares
Outstanding 181.9 million shares	**Treasury** 9.5 million shares

Share Authorization   Before a share can be issued, its specific rights and characteristics must be authorized and defined in the corporate charter. This authorization does not affect the accounting records, but it does establish certain characteristics that, later, will affect how shares are accounted for. One characteristic of importance is the share's par value.

A **par value share** is a share with an insignificant value as specified by the corporate charter. *Par value* has little meaning today. It is a concept from long ago, originally introduced to prevent shareholders from removing contributed capital of businesses that were about to go bankrupt. Stronger laws and regulations exist today to prevent this from happening, so par value no longer has this use.

In fact, the CBCA prohibits the use of par values, but they are still seen in some areas in Canada and are very common in the United States. So the CBCA allows the issuance of **no–par value shares**, which are similar to shares with par value except that they do not have a specified legal value per share. In any event, par value is a legal concept and is not related in any way to the market value of the company's shares.

COACH'S TIP

Don't confuse par value as it relates to shares with par value as it relates to bonds. They differ in meaning and in the methods used to account for them.

Share Issuance   A share issuance occurs when a corporation distributes its shares to existing or new shareholders, usually in exchange for cash. The very first issuance of a company's shares to the public is called an initial public offering, or IPO. This is what most people are referring to when they say a private company is *going public*. If a company has issued shares previously, additional issuances of new shares by the company are called seasoned new issues. Whether shares are issued as part of an IPO or as a seasoned new issue, a company accounts for them in the same way.

Most share issuances are cash transactions. To illustrate the accounting for a share issuance, assume that during the next fiscal year, Molson Coors issues 100,000 no–par value shares at the $10 per share market price existing at the time of issuance. Here are the accounting equation effects of this share issuance and the journal entry to record them:

1 Analyze

	Assets	= Liabilities +	Shareholders' Equity	
Cash	+1,000,000		Common Shares	+1,000,000

2 Record

dr **Cash** (+A) (100,000 × $10) 1,000,000
   cr **Common Shares** (+SE) 1,000,000

Notice that the increase in common shares is the number of shares sold times the issue price per share. This is because the corporate charter did not specify a par value for the shares (no–par value shares), so the total proceeds from the share issuance will be entered into the Common Shares account, as you learned in Chapter 2.

COACH'S TIP

Remember the separate entity assumption in Chapter 1, which states that owners' transactions are recorded only if they directly involve the corporation.

Shares Exchanged Between Investors   When a company issues shares to the public, the transaction is between the issuing corporation and an investor. After this initial share issuance, an investor can exchange shares for cash provided by other investors without directly affecting the corporation. For example, if investor Marita Gorski disposed of 1,000 shares of Molson Coors to Jacques Grenier, the company would not record a journal entry on its books. Gorski received cash for the shares, and Grenier received shares for the cash he paid. Molson Coors did not receive or pay anything. These transactions involve only the owners of the company and not the corporation itself. It's like an auto dealer who records the initial sale of a car to a customer but doesn't later record another sale when the customer sells the car to someone else.

Shares Used to Compensate Employees To encourage employees to work hard for a corporation, employee pay packages often include a combination of base pay, cash bonuses, and stock options. Stock options give employees the option to acquire the company's shares at a predetermined price, often equal to the then–current market price. If employees work hard and meet the corporation's goals, the company's share price will increase. Employees can exercise their option to acquire the company's shares at the lower predetermined price and sell it at the higher price for a profit.

If the share price declines, employees haven't lost anything. Accounting rules require that, at the time the company grants stock options, an expense must be reported for the estimated cost associated with stock options, even if the option price equals the current share price. The specific accounting procedures for this will be discussed in an intermediate accounting course.

SPOTLIGHT ON Ethics

At Whose Expense?

Some critics claim that stock options, which are intended to give the senior executives of a company the same goals as shareholders, often come at the expense of existing shareholders. When senior executives exercise their stock options to acquire new shares, existing shareholders lose voting power because their percentage of ownership in the company is diluted. Furthermore, critics contend that stock options create an incentive for senior executives to overstate financial results in an attempt to falsely increase the company's share price so they can exercise their options for huge personal gains.

Repurchase of Shares A corporation may want to repurchase its shares from existing shareholders to (1) distribute excess cash to shareholders, (2) send a signal to investors that the company believes its own shares are worth acquiring, (3) obtain shares so that new shares can be issued as payment for purchases of other companies, (4) obtain shares so that new shares can be issued to employees as part of employee stock option plans, and (5) reduce the number of outstanding shares to increase per–share measures of earnings and share value. (See the Spotlight on Business Decisions box below).

If a company repurchases its shares for reasons (2), (3), or (4), it will hold them in the company treasury for a period of time until they are reissued. Remember that in most situations and in most jurisdictions in Canada, the CBCA requires that repurchased shares to be cancelled. Therefore we will look only at cancelling the shares; what happens as the result of companies holding them in treasury is covered in most intermediate accounting classes.

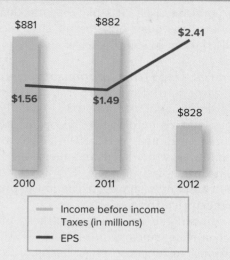
Assume that during the next fiscal year, Molson Coors repurchased 50,000 shares for $5 per share (50,000 shares × $5 = $250,000). Molson Coors would first have to calculate the carrying (book) value of the outstanding shares at the time of this repurchase. Exhibit 11.3 shows that at its fiscal year—end on December 31, 2015, Molson Coors had a total of 191.4 million common shares issued for a total consideration of $713 million, or an average issue price of $3.73 per share. Molson Coors therefore paid $5 per share to repurchase shares that had (on average) originally been issued for $3.73.

One could say that Molson Coors lost money on this repurchase of shares. However, our accounting rules prohibit gains and losses on share transactions from going through the income statement, primarily to restrict companies from trading their own shares to manipulate earnings. Instead, these "losses" are debited directly to **Retained Earnings**, as shown below. Molson Coors would have accounted for this transaction as follows:

Retained earnings:
Cumulative earnings of a company that are not distributed to the owners; profits from the current year and all prior years that are reinvested ("retained") in the business.

① Analyze

Assets		= Liabilities	+	Shareholders' Equity	
Cash	−250,000	=		Common Shares (−SE)	−186,500
				Retained Earnings (−SE)	−63,500

② Record

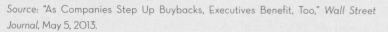

dr **Common Shares** (−SE) (50,000 × $3.73) 186,500
dr **Retained Earnings** (−SE) [50,000 × ($5 − $3.73)] 63,500
　cr **Cash** (−A) (50,000 × $5) 250,000

Contributed surplus:
The accumulation of differences when a company issues and sells shares at a price greater than their original issue price.

If Molson Coors had repurchased the shares for $1 instead of for $5, creating a "gain" instead of a "loss," the credit needed to balance the journal entry would have been made to a Contributed Capital account called **Contributed Surplus**, as follows:

	Assets	= Liabilities +	Shareholders' Equity	
Cash	−50,000		Common Shares (−SE)	−186,500
			Contributed Surplus (+SE)	+136,500

② Record

dr **Common Shares** (−SE) (50,000 × $3.73) 186,500
   cr **Cash** (−A) (50,000 × $1) 50,000
   cr **Contributed Surplus** (+SE) [50,000 × ($3.73 − $1.00)] 136,500

HOW'S IT GOING?

Self-Study Practice 11.1

1. Assume that Oakley, Inc. issued 1,000 of its common shares, no-par value, for $20 per share. Show the accounting equation effects and journal entry for this transaction.

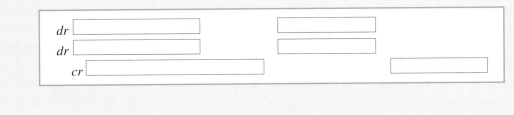

① Analyze

	Assets	= Liabilities +	Shareholders' Equity
Cash	[ ]		[ ] +20,000

② Record

dr [ ]   [ ]
  cr [ ]   [ ]

2. Assume that Oakley repurchased and cancelled 500 of its common shares in the stock market when they were selling for $25 per share. Show the journal entry to record this transaction.

dr [ ]   [ ]
dr [ ]   [ ]
  cr [ ]   [ ]

After you have finished, check your answers with the solution, which follows the chapter summary.

Cash Dividends on Common Shares

Investors acquire common shares because they expect a return on their investment. This return can come in two forms: dividends and increases in share price. Some investors prefer to buy shares that pay little or no div—idend (called a growth investment), because companies that reinvest the majority of their earnings tend to increase their future earnings potential along with their share price. Google, for example, has never paid a dividend,

LEARNING OBJECTIVE 11-3

Explain and analyze cash dividends, stock dividends, and stock split transactions.

yet if your parents had paid $1,000 to buy 100 Google shares when they were first issued on August 19, 2004, the investment would be worth about $84,000 at the time this chapter was being written. Rather than wait for growth in share value, other investors, such as retired people who need a steady income, prefer to receive their return in the form of dividends. These people often seek shares that consistently pay dividends (called an income investment), such as Coca–Cola shares, which have paid cash dividends each year since 1920.

SPOTLIGHT ON Business Decisions

Dividend Cuts in Difficult Times

Under pressure to save cash during a global economic crisis, such as in 2009, many big-name companies reversed or cut their policy to pay cash dividends. Although dividends are discretionary, companies are reluctant to cut them because doing so suggests the company is facing significant financial challenges. Several companies and the percentage of dividend cuts in 2009 (as compared to prior years) are shown in the table.

General Electric	67%	CBS Corp.	81%
Motorola, Inc.	75%	Black & Decker	71%

A corporation does not have a legal obligation to pay dividends. It is a decision made by the board of directors, and it is made each time a dividend is to be paid. Some boards of directors may decide to use the company's cash flows to pay off interest–bearing debt, instead. So cut–ting dividends doesn't always indicate that a company is having financial difficulties. A company's board of directors also need to consider two key financial requirements when declaring a cash dividend:

1. **Sufficient retained earnings.** The corporation must have accu–mulated a sufficient amount of Retained Earnings to cover the amount of the dividend. Incorporation laws often restrict cash dividends to the balance in Retained Earnings. A company may be further restricted by clauses in its loan agreements that require an even larger minimum balance in Retained Earnings. If the company were to violate such a loan covenant, a lender could require renegotiation of the loan and possibly demand its imme–diate repayment. Because restrictions on Retained Earnings can severely limit the ability to pay dividends, accounting rules require that companies disclose any restrictions in their financial statement notes.

2. **Sufficient cash.** The corporation must have sufficient cash to pay the dividend. Cash can be used in many ways, so the mere fact that Retained Earnings has a large credit balance does not mean that the company has sufficient cash to pay a dividend. Remember, retained earnings are not cash.

However, once the board of directors formally declares a dividend, a liability is created. The company would send out a press release containing very important information, such as the amount of the cash dividend per share and when the cash dividend is to be paid.

A cash dividend involves four important dates, only three of which require accounting entries. To illustrate, consider the huge cash dividend that Molson Coors declared and paid during its 2015 fiscal year.

1. **Declaration Date.** On the **declaration date** the board of directors formally approves the dividend, thereby creating a legal liability for the corporation. The dividend is accounted for by increasing Dividends Payable and increasing a temporary account called Dividends Declared. Because dividends are a distribution of the company's prior earnings, this Dividends Declared account is deducted from Retained Earnings when it is closed at year–end. Until then, the temporary account is accounted for as a decrease in Shareholders' Equity, as shown below. Although they reduce Retained Earnings, dividends are not an expense. Rather, they are a distribution of prior profits. The accounting equation effects and journal entry to record the cash dividend declared would be as follows:

Declaration date: The date on which the board of directors officially approves a dividend, thereby creating a liability.

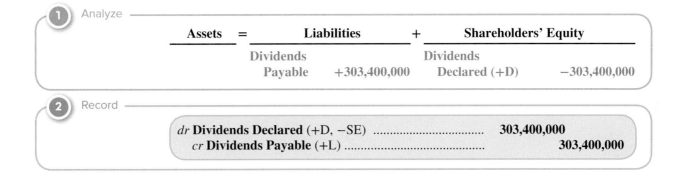

2. **Date of Record.** The shares of public companies are bought and sold constantly; it takes time to determine who should receive the dividend payment after the dividend has been declared. The **record date** is the cut–off date for determining the specific shareholders to be paid the dividend. The dividend is payable only to those names listed on the date of record. No journal entry is recorded on this date.

3. **Date of Payment.** The **payment date** is the date on which the cash is disbursed to pay the dividend liability owed to each shareholder. The distribution of cash and reduction in liability are recorded on this date as follows:

Record date: The date on which the corporation prepares the list of current shareholders as shown on its records; dividends can be paid only to the shareholders who own shares on that date.

Payment date: The date on which a cash dividend is paid to the shareholders of record.

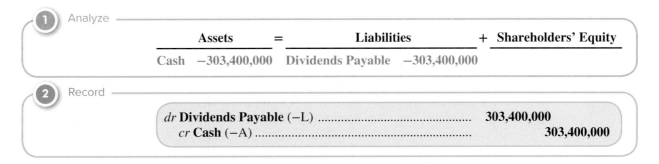

4. Year-End. All temporary accounts, including Dividends Declared, are closed into Retained Earnings at each accounting year—end. This closing journal entry zeroes out the temporary account Dividends Declared by transferring its (debit) balance to its permanent home in Retained Earnings. The closing entry has no effect on total share—holders' equity.

1 Analyze

Assets	=	Liabilities	+	Shareholders' Equity	
				Dividends Declared	+303,400,000
				Retained Earnings	−303,400,000

2 Record

	Debit	Credit
Retained Earnings	303,400,000	
Dividends Declared		303,400,000

HOW'S IT GOING?

Self-Study Practice 11.2

Answer the following questions concerning dividends:

1. On which dividend date is a liability created?
2. A cash outflow occurs on which dividend date?
3. What are the two fundamental requirements for the payment of a dividend?

After you have finished, check your answers with the solution, which follows the chapter summary.

STOCK DIVIDENDS AND STOCK SPLITS

Stock Dividends

Stock dividends: Additional shares of a corporation distributed to shareholders in the form of dividends.

The term *dividend*, when used alone with no adjectives, implies a cash dividend. However, some dividends are not paid in cash but in additional shares. These dividends, called **stock dividends**, are distributed to a corporation's shareholders on a pro rata basis at no cost to the shareholder. The term *pro rata basis* means that each shareholder receives additional shares equal to the percentage of shares held. A shareholder who owns 10 percent of the outstanding shares would receive 10 percent of any additional shares issued as a stock dividend.

How are stock dividends accounted for? Stock dividends are recorded by transferring an amount from Retained Earnings to contributed capital accounts. The CBCA requires that stock dividends be valued at the current market price of the shares. Regardless of value, a stock dividend affects only the balances within shareholders' equity; it does not change a company's total shareholders' equity.

Why would a company issue a stock dividend? On the surface, a stock dividend may seem pointless: it does not affect ownership percentages and it does not change total shareholders' equity. Three possible explanations for stock dividends are as follows:

1. **To lower the market price per share.** If you increase the number of shares without changing the company in any other way, the price per share will fall proportionately: twenty shares at $100 per share become forty shares at $50 per share after a 100 percent stock dividend. A company may declare stock dividends to make the company's shares more affordable to small investors.

2. **To demonstrate commitment to shareholders while conserving cash during difficult times.** This reason was given by the Marriott hotel company during the financial crisis of 2009, when it replaced its regular cash dividend with a stock dividend. Unlike a cash dividend, a stock dividend does not involve cash payments or any distribution of assets. But the stock dividend did allow Marriott to continue boasting that it had declared a dividend "in every year since going public in 1953."

3. **To signal an expectation of significant future earnings.** Companies can declare future cash dividends only when they maintain an adequate balance in Retained Earnings through profitable operations. Because stock dividends cause a reduction in Retained Earnings, companies will declare stock dividends only if they expect sufficient future earnings to replenish the balance in Retained Earnings after a stock dividend. Nike used this reasoning to explain its 100 percent stock dividend in 2012; the company's CEO said it was a sign of "the ongoing confidence we have in our strategy to generate long-term profitable growth."

Let's assume a company issued a 2 percent stock dividend when the share price was $4 per share, and there were 10.8 million common shares outstanding prior to the stock dividend. The company would account for this stock dividend by moving $864,000 (= 10.8 million × 2% × $4 share value) from Retained Earnings to Common Shares as follows:

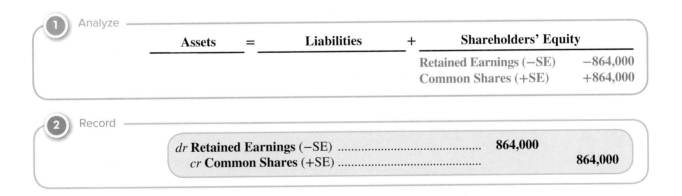

	Assets	=	Liabilities	+	Shareholders' Equity	
					Retained Earnings (−SE)	−864,000
					Common Shares (+SE)	+864,000

2 Record

dr **Retained Earnings (−SE)**	864,000	
cr **Common Shares (+SE)**		864,000

Before we leave this section, we must caution you about a potential point of confusion. Some companies refer to 100 percent stock dividends as a "stock split effected as a stock dividend." Although they *say* stock split, they actually mean a stock dividend as described above. A true stock split is different, both in terms of how it is done and how it is accounted for, as we discuss in the following section.

Stock Splits

Stock split: An increase in the total number of authorized shares by a specified ratio; does not affect retained earnings.

Stock splits are not dividends. While they are similar to a stock dividend, they are quite different in terms of how they occur and how they affect the shareholders' equity accounts. In a **stock split**, the total number of authorized shares is increased by a specified amount, such as 2 for 1. In this instance, each issued share is called in and two new shares are issued in its place. Cash is not affected when the company splits its shares, so the total resources of the company do not change. It's just like taking a four–slice pizza and cutting each slice into two smaller slices.

Typically, a stock split involves reducing the carrying value of all issued shares, so that the total carrying value of the shares is unchanged. For instance, if a company with one million shares outstanding executes a 2–for–1 stock split, with a total issue price of $4,000,000, it reduces the per–share carrying value of its shares and doubles the number of outstanding shares. The decrease in carrying value per share offsets the increase in the number of shares, so the financial position of the company is not affected and no journal entry is needed. By reading the following illustration from left to right, you can see these offsetting effects on the number of shares and book value per share.

Shareholders' Equity	Before a 2–for–1 Stock Split	After a 2–for–1 Stock Split
Number of shares outstanding	1,000,000	2,000,000
Carrying value per share	$ 4	$ 2
Total carrying value outstanding	$ 4,000,000	$ 4,000,000
Retained earnings	6,500,000	6,500,000
Total shareholders' equity	$10,500,000	$10,500,000

Exhibit 11.5 shows the typical components of the shareholders' equity section of the balance sheet and highlights amounts (in blue) that are changed by a 2–for–1 stock split, a 100 percent stock dividend, and an equivalent ($10,000) cash dividend. Notice that the cash dividend is the only distribution that affects total shareholders' equity because it is the only one that distributes the company's resources to shareholders.

EXHIBIT 11.5	**Comparison of Distribution to Shareholders**			

| | | | AFTER | |
Shareholders' Equity	BEFORE	2–for–1 Stock Split	100% Stock Dividend	$10,000 Cash Dividend
Contributed Capital				
Number of common shares outstanding	1,000,000	2,000,000	2,000,000	1,000,000
Carrying value per common share	$ 0.01	$ 0.005	$ 0.01	$ 0.01
Common shares	$ 10,000	$ 10,000	$ 20,000	$ 10,000
Retained Earnings	650,000	650,000	640,000	640,000
Total shareholders' equity	$ 660,000	$ 660,000	$ 660,000	$ 650,000

Choosing Between Stock Dividends and Stock Splits

Both stock dividends and stock splits increase the number of shares outstanding and decrease the market price per share. A key difference between them is that a stock dividend causes a reduction in Retained Earnings, whereas a "true" stock split doesn't (see Exhibit 11.5).

By itself, this accounting difference might not mean much. Remember, though, that to declare a cash dividend, a company must maintain an adequate balance in Retained Earnings. If you're managing a company that you expect will struggle financially in the future, you'll prefer a stock split because it doesn't reduce Retained Earnings, so it doesn't reduce your ability to declare cash dividends in the future.

On the other hand, if you expect your company will be financially successful in the near future, you won't care that a stock dividend reduces Retained Earnings because future earnings will replenish that account to allow cash dividends to be declared. In fact, you'll probably *want* to declare a stock dividend to show how confident you are of your company's financial outlook. This reasoning suggests that **a company's board of directors may declare a stock dividend rather than a stock split to signal to financial statement users that the company expects significant future earnings** (which will replenish the reduction in Retained Earnings caused by the stock dividend).

HOW'S IT GOING?

Self-Study Practice 11.3

Vandalay Industries wanted to reduce the market price of its shares, so it issued 10,000 new common shares in a 10 percent stock dividend when there were 100,000 shares outstanding and the market value was $30 per share.

1. Prepare the journal entry that Vandalay would use to record this transaction.
2. What journal entry would be required if the transaction instead involved a 2-for-1 stock split? Theoretically, what would be the new share price after the split?

After you have finished, check your answers with the solution, which follows the chapter summary.

PREFERRED SHARES

In addition to common shares, some corporations issue **preferred shares** to a select group of investors. This special form of shares differ from common shares, typically in the following ways:

> **LEARNING OBJECTIVE 11-4**
>
> Describe the characteristics of preferred shares and analyze transactions affecting preferred shares.

1. **Preferred shares allow different voting rights.** Preferred shares can carry anywhere from no voting rights to "super" voting rights. This flexibility allows a corporation to separate share ownership from voting control. No voting rights are useful if you want to raise financing from a key shareholder who already owns a lot of common shares but you don't want the shareholder to take control. Super voting rights are useful if you want to issue shares to the public but not give up voting control. Recently, Facebook and Google have adopted such a dual–share structure.

> **Preferred shares:** Shares that have specific rights than are different from those of common shares.

2. **Dividends on preferred shares, if any, may be paid at a fixed rate.** The rate is specified as a dollar amount per share. For example, a "$0.60 preferred share" pays dividends each year of $0.60 per share. A fixed dividend can be attractive to certain investors, such as company founders or retirees, who seek a stable income from their investments.

3. **Preferred shares carry priority over common shares.** Preferred shareholders have higher priority than common shareholders if a corporation distributes assets to its owners through dividends or at liquidation. That is, any dividends the corporation declares must be paid to preferred shareholders before they can be paid to common shareholders. Also, if the corporation goes out of business, its assets will be sold and used to pay creditors and then preferred shareholders. Holders of common shares are paid last from whatever assets remain after paying the holders of preferred shares.

SPOTLIGHT ON The World

Preferred Shares

Under IFRS, preferred shares are typically classified as shareholders' equity. However, if the issuing company is contractually obligated to pay dividends or redeem the shares at a future date, then preferred shares are classified as a liability. This classification can dramatically affect financial ratios that use total shareholders' equity (e.g., return on equity, discussed later in this chapter) or total liabilities (e.g., debt-to-assets ratio, discussed in Chapter 10).

Preferred Share Issuance

Just like a common share issuance, a preferred share issuance increases a company's cash and its shareholders' equity. To illustrate, assume that a company issued 10,000 preferred shares for $5 per share ($5 × 10,000 shares = $50,000 cash received). As shown below, the Preferred Shares account increases by the share price for each share issued ($5 × 10,000 = $50,000) and so does the amount of cash received.

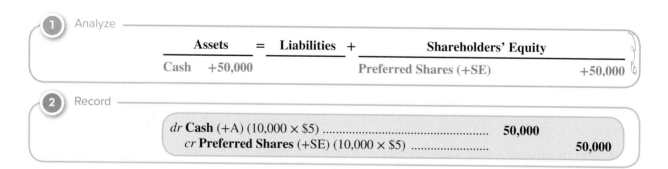

Preferred Share Dividends

Because investors who acquire preferred shares are not entitled to voting rights that are available to investors in common shares, preferred shares offer dividend preferences. The two most common dividend preferences are called *current* and *cumulative*.

Current Dividend Preference A current dividend preference requires that dividends on preferred shares be paid before any dividends are paid to holders of common shares. This preference is a feature of all pre—ferred shares. After the current dividend preference has been met, and if no other preference exists, dividends may be paid to the common shareholders. To illustrate, consider the following example:

Flavoria Company
Preferred shares outstanding: 6 percent; book value $40,000; 2,000 shares
Common shares outstanding: book value $50,000; 5,000 shares

Assume that the preferred shares carry only a current dividend preference and that the company declared dividends totalling $8,000 in 2016 and $10,000 in 2017. In each year, a fixed amount of the total dividends would first go to the preferred shareholders, and only the excess would go to the common shareholders.

Year	Total Dividends Declared	Dividends on 6% Preferred Shares[*]	Dividends on Common Shares[†]
2016	$ 8,000	$2,400	$5,600
2017	10,000	2,400	7,600

[*] Dividends on preferred shares = Total book value of shares ($40,000) × 6% dividend = $2,400
[†] Dividends on common shares = Total dividends declared − Dividends on preferred shares

Had Flavoria Company not declared dividends in 2016, preferred share—holders would have had preference with regard to $2,400 of dividends only in 2017. The current dividend preference does not carry over to later years unless the preferred shares are designated as cumulative, as discussed next.

Cumulative Dividend Preference A cumulative dividend prefer—ence states that if all or a part of the current dividend is not paid in full, the cumulative unpaid amount, known as **dividends in arrears**, must be paid before any future common dividends can be paid. Of course, if the preferred shares are non—cumulative, dividends can never be in arrears; any preferred dividends that are not declared are permanently lost. Because preferred shareholders are unwilling to accept this unfavourable feature, preferred shares are usually cumulative.

To illustrate the cumulative preference, assume that Flavoria Com—pany has the same amount of shares outstanding as in the last example. In this case, however, assume that dividends were in arrears for 2014 and 2015. The following table shows that, in 2016, dividends in arrears are satisfied first, followed by the current dividend preference, and the excess goes to common shareholders. In 2017, preferred dividends include only the current preference of that year because dividends in arrears were fulfilled in 2016.

Current dividend preference: The feature of preferred shares that grants priority on preferred dividends over common dividends.

Cumulative dividend preference: Preferred share feature that requires current dividends not paid in full to accumulate for every year in which they are not paid. These cumulative unpaid amounts (called *dividends in arrears*) must be paid before any common dividends can be paid.

Dividends in arrears: Cumulative unpaid amount as a result of cumulative dividend preference that must be paid before any common dividends can be paid.

		DIVIDENDS ON 6% PREFERRED SHARES		
Year	Total Dividends Declared	In Arrears*	Current†	Dividends on Common Shares‡
2016	$ 8,000	$4,800	$2,400	$5,600
2017	10,000	—	2,400	7,600

* Dividends in arrears preference = Book value of total shares ($40,000) × 6% dividend × 2 years = $4,800

† Current dividend preference = Book value of total shares ($40,000) × 6% dividend = $2,400

‡ Dividends on common shares = Total dividends declared − Total dividends on preferred shares

Because dividends are not an actual liability until the board of directors declares them, dividends in arrears are not reported on the balance sheet. Instead, they are disclosed in the notes to the financial statements.

RETAINED EARNINGS

As its name suggests, the Retained Earnings account represents the company's total earnings that have been retained in the business (rather than being distributed to shareholders). The balance in this account increases when the company reports net income, and it decreases when the company reports a net loss (expenses greater than revenues) or declares cash or stock dividends to shareholders. Think of retained earnings as the amount of equity that the company itself has generated for shareholders (through profitable operations) but not yet distributed to them.

Should a company ever accumulate more net losses than net income over its life, it will report a negative (debit) balance in the Retained Earnings account. This amount is (1) shown in parentheses in the shareholders' equity section of the balance sheet, (2) deducted when computing total shareholders' equity, and (3) typically called an Accumulated Deficit rather than Retained Earnings.

STATEMENT OF SHAREHOLDERS' EQUITY

Previous chapters indicated that companies report a statement of retained earnings to show how net income increased and dividends decreased the retained earnings balance during the period. While this information is useful, it doesn't tell the full story because Retained Earnings is only one of the shareholders' equity accounts. To show the causes of changes in all shareholders' equity accounts, public companies report a more comprehensive version of the statement of retained earnings called the statement of shareholders' equity. The statement of shareholders' equity has a column for each shareholders' equity account and shows the factors that increased and decreased these account balances during the period.

Exhibit 11.6 shows a modified version of Molson Coors' statement for its fiscal year ended December 31, 2015. Notice how the beginning and ending balances for each account correspond to the comparative balance sheet (in Exhibit 11.3). From Exhibit 11.6, we can quickly see the most significant share transactions for Molson–Coors during its 2015 fiscal year: the issuance and repurchase of common shares, net income, and its dividend on common shares.

EXHIBIT 11.6   Statement of Shareholders' Equity

MOLSON COORS BREWING COMPANY
Statement of Shareholders' Equity

(in millions)	Common Shares	Paid–In Capital	Retained Earnings	Treasury Shares	Accumulated Other Comprehensive Income (Loss)
December 31, 2014	772	3,871	4,440	(321)	(898)
Share Issuances/ (Repurchases)	(59)	129		(150)	
Net Income			359		
Dividends			(303)		
Foreign translation adjustments					(797)
December 31, 2015	713	4,000	4,496	(471)	(1,695)

Evaluate the Results

Now that you know how dividends and other shareholders' equity transactions are accounted for inside a company, it's time to evaluate things from the outside. In this section, you will learn to use three ratios to evaluate how well a company appears to be using its capital to generate returns for the company and, ultimately, for its shareholders.

LEARNING OBJECTIVE 11-5

Analyze the earnings per share (EPS), return on equity (ROE), and price/earnings (P/E) ratios.

EARNINGS PER SHARE (EPS)

The most famous of all ratios, earnings per share (EPS), reports how much profit is earned for each common share outstanding. The calculation of EPS can involve many details and intricacies, but in its basic form, it is computed by dividing net income by the average number of common shares outstanding. Because preferred shares have priority over common shares, any dividends on preferred shares are subtracted from net income when computing EPS. Most companies report EPS on the income statement immediately below Net Income or in the notes to the financial statements.[2]

You might be wondering why *earnings* per share is so popular when dividends and share prices ultimately determine the return to shareholders. The reason is that current earnings can predict future dividends and share prices. If a company generates increased earnings in the current year, it will be able to pay higher dividends in future years. In other words, current EPS influences expectations about future dividends, which investors factor into the current share price.

Another reason that EPS is so popular is that it allows you to easily compare results over time. For example, assume a company earned net income of $3.6 million in the third quarter of 2017, compared to $3.3 million for the same quarter in the previous year. It's hard to know whether the increase is good for shareholders because it's possible that the increase in net income was accompanied by an increase in the number of shares outstanding. By considering earnings on a per–share basis, we adjust for the effect of additional shares issued, resulting in a clearer picture of what increases mean for each investor.

COACH'S TIP

Outstanding shares are issued shares minus treasury shares.

Name of Measure	Formula	What It Tells You
1. Earnings per share (EPS) ratio	$\dfrac{\text{Net Income}}{\text{Average Number of Common Shares Outstanding}}$	• The amount of income generated for each common share owned by shareholders • A higher ratio means greater profitability
2. Return on equity (ROE) ratio	$\dfrac{\text{Net Income}}{\text{Average Shareholders' Equity}}$	• The amount of income earned for each dollar of shareholders' equity • A higher ratio means shareholders are likely to enjoy greater returns
3. Price/earnings (P/E) Ratio	$\dfrac{\text{Current Share Price (per share)}}{\text{Earnings per Share (annual)}}$	• How many times more than the current year's earnings investors are willing to pay for a company's common share • A higher number means investors anticipate an improvement in the company's future results

Exhibit 11.7 shows how to calculate EPS for Molson Coors Brewing Company and one of its competitors Anheuser–Busch Inbev, the brewers of Budweiser among other brands.

We should caution you against comparing EPS across companies. The number of shares outstanding for one company can differ dramatically from the number outstanding for a different company, simply because one chooses to issue more shares than the other. Also, as you saw in earlier chapters, net income can be affected by differences in how two companies cost inventory (Chapter 7), estimate bad debts (Chapter 8), depreciate long–lived tangible assets (Chapter 9), and estimate losses from contingent liabilities (Chapter 10). So, while EPS is an effective and widely used measure for comparing a company with itself over time, it is not appropriate for comparing across companies.

RETURN ON EQUITY (ROE)

Like EPS, return on equity (ROE) reports a company's return to investors. However, rather than relating net income to the average *number* of shares outstanding, the return on equity (ROE) ratio relates net income to the average *dollars* of shareholder investment and earn– ings reinvested in the company.[3] Because ROE uses dollars contributed to and reinvested in the company, this ratio can be appropriately com– pared across companies.

According to Yahoo! Finance, the average return on equity for the alcoholic beverage industry in 2015 was 11.5 percent. As Exhibit 11.7 reports, Molson Coors' 2015 ROE was 4.8 percent, down from 6.2 percent in the prior year. Look closely at the ROE calculation and you will find the main factor responsible for the decrease. Molson Coors' net income was down from $514.0 million to $359.5 million.

According to the management discussion and analysis in Molson Coors' annual report, the company experienced lower levels of net income due to competitive challenges and weak consumer demand continued across some of their largest markets. Anheuser–Busch, on the other hand, is well above the industry average with a ROE of 17.9 percent for 2015. In Anheuser–Busch's case, the company was able to report a higher return by using a strategy called financial leverage. Rather than relying on equity financing, Anheuser–Busch relies heavily on debt. Anheuser–Busch has been able to generate more profit from using these

COACH'S TIP

The denominator in the return on equity formula contains average shareholders' equity. Remember that this represents both contributed capital and retained earnings.

EXHIBIT 11.7   Summary of EPS, ROE, and P/E Ratio Analyses

MOLSON COORS BREWING COMPANY

(millions, except share price)	2015	2014	2013
Net income	$ 359.5	$ 514.0	$ 567.3
Average # shares outstanding	185.3	184.9	183.0
Shareholders' equity	$7,043	$7,863	$8,605
Price per share	$ 93.92	$ 74.52	$ 56.15

	2015	2014
$EPS = \dfrac{Net\ income}{Avg.\ \#\ shares}$	$\dfrac{\$359.5}{185.3}$ $= \$1.94$	$\dfrac{\$514.0}{184.9}$ $= \$2.78$
$ROE = \dfrac{Net\ income}{Average\ SE}$	$\dfrac{\$359.5}{(\$7,043 + \$7,86)/2}$ $= 0.048$ or 4.8%	$\dfrac{\$514.0}{(\$7,863 + \$8,605)/2}$ $= 0.062$ or 6.2%
$P/E = \dfrac{Share\ price}{EPS}$	$\dfrac{\$93.92}{\$1.94}$ $= 48.4$	$\dfrac{\$74.52}{\$2.78}$ $= 26.81$

ANHEUSER-BUSCH INBEV

(millions, except share price)	2015	2014	2013
Net income	$ 8,273	$ 9,216	$14,394
Average # shares outstanding	1,638	1,634	1,617
Shareholders' equity	$42,137	$49,972	$50,365
Price per share	$ 125.00	$ 112.32	$ 106.46

	2015	2014
$EPS = \dfrac{Net\ income}{Avg.\ \#\ shares}$	$\dfrac{\$8,273}{1,638}$ $= \$5.05$	$\dfrac{\$9,216}{1,634}$ $= \$5.64$
$ROE = \dfrac{Net\ income}{Average\ SE}$	$\dfrac{\$8,273}{(\$42,137 + \$49,972)/2}$ $= 0.179$ or 17.9%	$\dfrac{\$9,216}{(\$49,972 + \$50,365)/2}$ $= 0.184$ or 18.4%
$P/E = \dfrac{Share\ price}{EPS}$	$\dfrac{\$125.0}{\$5.05}$ $= 24.8$	$\dfrac{\$112.32}{\$5.64}$ $= 19.9$

borrowed funds than it incurred for interest on that debt. As a result, Anheuser–Busch was able to generate a superior return on equity for shareholders. Financial leverage isn't always the best strategy, though, as the Dr Pepper Snapple Group discovered during the global financial crisis when its 2008 Interest Expense on debt financing was greater than its Income from Operations.

PRICE/EARNINGS (P/E) RATIO

While EPS and ROE are useful for evaluating a company's return to shareholders, they don't help you determine what a reasonable price would be for the company's shares. Sophisticated techniques to value a company are taught in advanced courses in finance, but for this course, let's focus on a simple tool. The price/earnings ratio is the most basic way to determine the value that investors place on a company's common shares. The P/E ratio, as most people call it, measures how many times more than current year's earnings investors are willing to pay for a company's shares. It is calculated as shown in Exhibit 11.7 by dividing a company's EPS for the year into the share price at the time its EPS is reported.

Generally, a relatively high P/E ratio means investors expect the company to improve in the future and increase its profits, so they have factored in the future earnings when determining the current share price. A relatively low P/E ratio typically means that they don't expect strong future performance. P/E ratios can vary significantly across industries, so you'll find them most meaningful when comparing a company with itself or with competitors in the same industry over time. Molson Coors showed a P/E ratio in 2015 of 48.4, which exceeded the industry average of 32.5. This suggests that investors were anticipating good things to come from Molson Coors.

Self-Study Practice 11.4

Molson Coors reported shareholders' equity of $7,967 (millions) at its 2012 fiscal year-end.

Use this information, along with that in Exhibit 11.7, to calculate Molson Coors' earnings per share (EPS), return on equity (ROE), and price/earnings (P/E) ratios for 2013.

2013 EPS:	2013 ROE:	2013 P/E:
☐ = ☐	$\dfrac{\boxed{}}{(\boxed{} + \boxed{})/2}$ = ☐	$\dfrac{\boxed{}}{\boxed{}}$ = ☐

After you have finished, check your answers with the solution, which follows the chapter summary.

SPOTLIGHT ON IFRS and ASPE

Topic	ASPE	IFRS
Presentation of changes in Shareholders' Equity accounts	• Changes in retained earnings are presented in the Statement of Retained Earnings. • Changes in capital accounts are disclosed in the notes to the financial statements.	• Changes in *all* equity accounts are presented in a separate statement called Statement of Changes in Equity.
Disclosure of Earnings per Share	• The disclosure of Earnings per Share is not required.	• The disclosure of Earnings per Share is required.

LEARNING OBJECTIVE 11-S1

Account for owners' equity in other forms of business.

Supplement 11A

OWNER'S EQUITY FOR OTHER FORMS OF BUSINESS

Owner's Equity for a Sole Proprietorship

A sole proprietorship is an unincorporated business owned by one person. For a sole proprietorship owned by H. Simpson, only two owner's equity accounts are needed: (1) a capital account for the proprietor (H. Simpson, Capital) and (2) a drawings (or withdrawal) account for the proprietor (H. Simpson, Drawings).

The capital account of a sole proprietorship serves two purposes: (1) to record investments by the owner and (2) to accumulate periodic income or loss. The drawings account is used to record the owner's withdrawals of cash or other assets from the business, similar to recording dividends declared by corporations. The drawings account is closed to the capital account at the end of each accounting period. Thus, after the drawings account is closed, the capital account reflects the cumulative total of all capital contributions by the owner and all earnings of the business less all withdrawals from the entity by the owner.

In most respects, the accounting for a sole proprietorship is the same as for a corporation. Exhibit 11A.1 presents the recording of selected transactions of Homer's Dough Store and a statement of owner's equity, which replaces the statement of retained earnings or statement of shareholders' equity.

January 1

H. Simpson started a sole proprietorship by placing $150,000 cash in a bank account opened for the business. The accounting equation effects and journal entry follow:

Assets		=	Liabilities	+	Owner's Equity	
Cash	+150,000				H. Simpson, Capital	+150,000

dr Cash (+A)..	150,000
cr H. Simpson, Capital (+OE).............................	150,000

During the year

Each month during the year, Simpson withdrew $1,000 cash from the business for personal living costs. Accordingly, each month the financial effects and required journal entry are:

Assets		=	Liabilities	+	Owner's Equity	
Cash	−1,000				H. Simpson, Drawing (+D)	−1,000

dr H. Simpson, Drawings (+D, −OE)	1,000
cr Cash (−A)...	1,000

Note: At December 31, after the last withdrawal, the drawings account reflected a debit balance of $12,000.

December 31

The usual journal entries for the year, including adjusting and closing entries for the revenue and expense accounts, resulted in revenue of $48,000 and expenses of $30,000. The net income of $18,000 was closed to the capital account as follows:

Assets	=	Liabilities	+	Owner's Equity	
				Revenues (−R)	−48,000
				Expenses (−E)	+30,000
				H. Simpson, Capital	+18,000

dr Individual Revenue Accounts (−R, −OE)	48,000
cr Individual Expense Accounts (−E, +OE).........	30,000
cr H. Simpson, Capital (+OE).............................	18,000

December 31

The drawings account was closed as follows:

Assets	=	Liabilities	+	Owner's Equity	
				H. Simpson, Capital	−12,000
				H. Simpson, Drawings (−D)	+30,000

dr H. Simpson, Capital (−OE)..................................	12,000
cr H. Simpson, Drawings (−D, +OE)....................	12,000

HOMER'S DOUGH STORE
Statement of Owner's Equity
For the Year Ended December 31

H. Simpson, Capital, January 1	$ 0
Add: Capital contribution	150,000
Add: Net income	18,000
Total	168,000
Less: Withdrawals	(12,000)
H. Simpson, Capital, December 31	$156,000

Because a sole proprietorship does not pay income taxes, its financial statements do not report Income Tax Expense or Income Tax Payable. Instead, the net income of a sole proprietorship is taxed when it is included on the owner's personal income tax return. Likewise, the owner's salary is not recognized as an expense in a sole proprietorship because an employer/employee contractual relationship cannot exist with only one party involved. The owner's salary is therefore accounted for as a distribution of profits—a withdrawal—instead of salary expense, as it would be in a corporation.

Owner's Equity for a Partnership

A partnership is defined as "an association of two or more persons to carry on as co—owners of a business for profit." Small businesses and professionals such as accountants, doctors, and lawyers often use the partnership form of business.

A partnership is formed by two or more persons reaching mutual agreement about the terms of the relationship. The law does not require an application for a charter, as in the case of a corporation. Instead, the agreement between the partners constitutes a partnership contract. This agreement should specify matters such as division of income, management responsibilities, transfer or sale of partnership interests, disposition of assets upon liquidation, and procedures to be followed in case of the death of a partner. If the partnership agreement does not specify these matters, the applicable provincial or territorial laws are binding.

In comparison to a corporation, the primary advantages of a partner—ship are (1) ease of formation, (2) complete control by the partners, and (3) lack of income taxes on the business itself. The primary disadvantage is the unlimited liability of each partner for the partnership's debts. If the partnership does not have sufficient assets to satisfy outstanding debt, creditors of the partnership can seize each partner's personal assets. In some cases, this can even result in one partner being held responsible for another partner's share of the partnership's debt.

As with a sole proprietorship, accounting for a partnership follows the same underlying principles as any other form of business organization, except for those entries that directly affect owners' equity. Accounting for partners' equity follows the same pattern as for a sole proprietorship, except that separate capital and drawings accounts must be established for each partner. Investments by each partner are credited to that partner's Capital account and withdrawals are debited to the respective Drawings account. The net income of a partnership is divided among the partners in accordance with the partnership agreement and credited to each account. The respective Drawings accounts are closed to the partner Capital accounts. After the closing process, each partner's Capital account reflects the cumulative total of all that partner's investments plus that partner's share of the partnership earnings less all of that partner's withdrawals.

Exhibit 11A.2 presents selected journal entries and partial financial statements for AB Partnership to illustrate the accounting for the distri—bution of income and partners' equity.

A separate statement of partners' capital, similar to a corporation's statement of shareholders' equity, is customarily prepared to supplement the balance sheet, as shown next.

Another Business Form

In addition to sole proprietorships, partnerships, and corporations, another form of business exists in Canada. This form blends features of the "pure" organizational forms described earlier in this chapter to create a hybrid business form called a limited liability partnership (LLP). The LLP is an increasingly common form of business that combines legal characteristics of

EXHIBIT 11.A2 | **Accounting for Partners' Equity**

January 1

A. Able and B. Baker organized AB Partnership on this date. Able contributed $60,000 cash and Baker contributed $40,000 cash to the partnership, and they agreed to divide net income (and net loss) 60 percent and 40 percent, respectively. The financial effects of this investment on the business and the journal entry to record them are as follows:

Assets	= Liabilities	+	Partner's Equity	
Cash +100,000			A. Able, Capital	+60,000
			B. Baker, Capital	+40,000

dr Cash (+ A)..	100,000	
cr A. Able, Capital (+OE)....................................		60,000
cr B. Baker, Capital (+OE)...................................		40,000

During the year

The partners agreed that Able would withdraw $1,000 and Baker $650 per month in cash. Accordingly, each month the following financial effects were recorded with the journal entry that appears below:

Assets	= Liabilities	+	Partner's Equity	
Cash −1,650			A. Able, Drawing (+D)	−1,000
			B. Baker, Drawings (+D)	−650

dr A. Able, Drawings (+D, −OE)...............................	1,000	
dr B. Baker, Drawings (+D, −OE)............................	650	
cr Cash (+A)		1,650

Note: At December 31, after the last withdrawals, the Drawings account for Able had a debit balance of $12,000 and the Drawings account for Baker had a debit balance of $7,800.

December 31

Assume that the normal closing entries for the revenue and expense accounts resulted in revenue of $78,000, expenses of $48,000, and net income of $30,000. The partnership agreement specified Able would receive 60 percent of net income ($18,000 = 60% × $30,000) and Baker would get 40 percent ($12,000 = 40% × $30,000). The financial effects and related closing entry follow:

Assets	= Liabilities	+	Partner's Equity	
			Revenues (−R)	−78,000
			Expenses (−E)	+48,000
			A. Able, Capital	+18,000
			B. Baker, Capital	+12,000

dr Individual Revenue Accounts (−R, −OE)	78,000	
cr Individual Expense Accounts (−E, +OE)..........		48,000
cr A. Able, Capital (+OE) (60% × $30,000)..........		18,000
cr B. Baker, Capital (+OE) (40% × $30,000)		12,000

December 31

The financial effects of closing the drawings accounts and the related closing journal entry are as follows:

Assets	= Liabilities	+	Partner's Equity	
			A. Able, Capital	−12,000
			B. Baker, Capital	−7,800
			A. Able, Drawings (−D)	+12,000
			B. Baker, Drawings (−D)	+7,800

dr A. Able, Capital (−OE)...	12,000	
dr B. Baker, Capital (−OE)..	7,800	
cr A. Able, Drawings (−D, +OE)............................		12,000
cr B. Baker, Drawings (−D, +OE)...........................		7,800

AB PARTNERSHIP
Statement of Partners' Equity
For the Year Ended December 31

	A. Able	B. Baker	Total
Partners' equity, January 1	$ 0	$ 0	$ 0
Add: Additional contributions during the year	60,000	40,000	100,000
Add: Net income for the year	18,000	12,000	30,000
Totals	78,000	52,000	130,000
Less: Drawings during the year	(12,000)	(7,800)	(19,800)
Partners' equity, December 31	$66,000	$44,200	$110,200

corporations (such as a separate legal identity and limited liability) with the tax treatment of partnerships (where tax is paid by the individual owners rather than by the business entity itself). Accounting for a limited liability partnership generally follows the methods shown earlier in this chapter.

The financial statements of an LLP follow the same format as those for a partnership, which differs from a corporation in the following ways: (1) the financial statements include an additional section entitled Distribution of Net Income; (2) the owners' equity section of the balance sheet is detailed for each owner; (3) the income statement does not report income tax expense because this form of business does not pay income tax (owners must report their share of the entity's profits on their individual tax returns); and (4) unless other contractual arrangements exist, amounts paid to the owners are not recorded as expenses but instead are accounted for as withdrawals of capital.

Review the Chapter

This section provides a chance to solidify your understanding of key points. It's worth your time to work through the following demonstration cases, scan the chapter summary, test your understanding of key terms, and then practise, practise, practise.

DEMONSTRATION CASE A: SHARE ISSUANCE AND REPURCHASES

This case focuses on selected transactions from the first year of operations of Zoogle Corporation, which became a public company on January 1, 2014, for the purpose of operating a lost–pet search business. The charter authorized the following shares:

Common: 20,000 shares
Preferred: $5; non-cumulative; 5,000 shares

The following summarized transactions were completed on the dates indicated:

Jan. 1	Zoogle issued a total of 8,000 common shares for cash at $50 per share.
Feb. 1	Zoogle sold 2,000 preferred shares at $102 per share; cash was collected in full.
July 1	Zoogle purchased 400 common shares that had been issued earlier. Zoogle Corporation paid the shareholder $54 per share and cancelled the shares.
Dec. 1	The board declared a cash dividend on the preferred shares, payable on December 22 to shareholders of record as of December 15.
Dec. 22	The cash dividends declared on December 1 were paid.

Required:

1. Give the appropriate journal entries, and show calculations for each transaction.
2. Prepare the shareholders' equity section of the balance sheet for Zoogle Corporation at December 31. Assume that the balance in Retained Earnings after closing entries is $31,000.

Suggested Solution

1. Journal entries

Jan. 1	*dr* Cash (+A) ($50 × 8,000 shares)	400,000	
	cr Common Shares (+SE)		400,000
Feb. 1	*dr* Cash (+A) ($102 × 2,000 shares)	204,000	
	cr Preferred Shares (+SE)		204,000
July 1	*dr* Common Shares (−SE) ($50 × 400)	20,000	
	dr Retained Earnings (−SE) [$400 × ($54 − $50)] ...	1,600	
	cr Cash (−A) ($54 × 400 shares)		21,600
Dec. 1	*dr* Dividends Declared (+D, −SE)		
	[2,000 preferred shares × $5]	10,000	
	cr Dividends Payable (+ L)		10,000
Dec. 22	*dr* Dividends Payable (−L).................................	10,000	
	cr Cash (− A)		10,000

2. Shareholders' equity section of the balance sheet

ZOOGLE CORPORATION
Partial Balance Sheet
At December 31

Shareholders' Equity

Contributed Capital

Preferred shares: $5; 5,000 authorized; 2,000 issued and outstanding shares	$204,000	
Common shares: 20,000 authorized; 7,600 issued and outstanding shares	380,000	
Total Contributed Capital		$584,000
Retained Earnings		31,000
Total Shareholders' Equity		615,000

DEMONSTRATION CASE B: CASH AND STOCK DIVIDENDS

This case extends Demonstration Case A by focusing on dividend transactions occurring during Zoogle Corporation's second year. The following summarized transactions were completed on the dates indicated:

Nov. 1	To make the company's shares more affordable, the board declared a 100 percent stock dividend on the outstanding common shares. The share price at that time on the open market was $49.80.
Nov. 30	The stock dividend from Nov. 1 was issued on the common shares.
Dec. 1	The board declared a cash dividend on the preferred shares, payable on December 26, to shareholders of record as of December 15.
Dec. 26	The cash dividends declared on December 1 were paid.

Required:

Give the appropriate journal entries, and show calculations for each transaction.

Suggested Solution

Nov. 1	*dr* Retained Earnings (−SE)	378,480	
	cr Common Shares Distributable (+SE)		378,480
	[(7,600 common shares issued and outstanding) × $49.80]		

Note: Because the stock dividend was only *declared* on November 1, the company would credit a Common Shares Distributable account, as the common shares have yet to be distributed. Then, when the stock dividend is actually *issued*, the company would debit this same Common Shares Distributable account and credit the Common Shares account. This journal entry is shown below.

Nov. 30	*dr* Common Shares Distributable (−SE)	378,480	
	cr Common Shares (+SE)		378,480
Dec. 1	*dr* Dividends Declared (+D, −SE)	10,000	
	cr Dividends Payable (+L)		10,000
	(2,000 preferred shares × $5 dividend rate)		
Dec. 26	*dr* Dividends Payable (−L)	10,000	
	cr Cash (−A)		10,000

CHAPTER SUMMARY

LO11-1   Explain the role of shares (also called stocks) in financing a corporation.

- The law recognizes corporations as separate legal entities. Owners invest in a corporation and receive shares that can be bought from and sold to other investors. Shares provide a number of rights, including the right to vote, to receive dividends, and to share in residual assets at liquidation.

LO11-2   Explain and analyze common share transactions.

- A number of key transactions involve common shares: (1) initial issuance of shares, (2) repurchase and cancellation of shares, (3) repurchase of shares into treasury, and (4) reissuance of treasury shares. The first two transactions were illustrated in this chapter. Note that these transactions have only balance sheet effects; corporations do not report income arising from gains or losses on transactions involving their own shares.

LO11-3   Explain and analyze cash dividends, stock dividends, and stock split transactions.

- Cash dividends reduce shareholders' equity (Retained Earnings) and create a liability (Dividends Payable) when they are declared by the board of directors (on the date of declaration). The liability is reduced when the dividends are paid (on the date of payment).

- Stock dividends are pro rata distributions of a company's shares to existing owners. The transaction typically is accounted for by transferring an amount out of Retained Earnings and into contributed capital accounts.

- A stock split also involves the distribution of additional shares to owners but no additional amount is transferred into the contributed capital accounts. Instead, the book value of the shares is reduced.

LO11-4   Describe the characteristics of preferred shares and analyze transactions affecting preferred shares.

- Preferred shares provide investors with certain advantages, including current dividend preferences and an advantage with regard to asset distribution in the event that the corporation is liquidated.

- If preferred shares carry cumulative dividend rights, any part of current dividends that are not paid (called *dividends in arrears*) must be paid in full before any additional dividends can be paid.

Analyze the earnings per share (EPS), return on equity (ROE), and price/earnings (P/E) ratios.

- The earnings per share (EPS) ratio is calculated by dividing net income by the average number of common shares outstanding during the year. This ratio makes it easy to com—pare a company's earnings over time but it does not allow reliable comparisons across companies because it does not adjust for likely differences in the number of shares that each company has outstanding.
- The return on equity (ROE) ratio relates earnings to each dollar contributed to and retained by the company. Because it is calculated using dollar amounts contributed to and retained by a company, it allows comparisons to be made across companies.
- The price/earnings (P/E) ratio relates the company's current share price to its most recent annual earnings per share, indicating the value that investors place on the company's shares.

ACCOUNTING DECISION TOOLS

Name of Measure	Formula	What It Tells You
1. Earnings per share (EPS) ratio	$\dfrac{\text{Net Income}}{\text{Average Number of Common Shares Outstanding}}$	• The amount of income generated for each common share owned by shareholders • A higher ratio means greater profitability
2. Return on equity (ROE) ratio	$\dfrac{\text{Net Income}}{\text{Average Shareholders' Equity}}$	• The amount of income earned for each dollar of shareholders' equity • A higher ratio means shareholders are likely to enjoy greater returns
3. Price/earnings (P/E) Ratio	$\dfrac{\text{Current Share Price}}{\text{Earnings per Share (annual)}}$	• How many times more than the current year's earnings investors are willing to pay for a company's common share • A higher number means investors anticipate an improvement in the company's future results

SOLUTIONS TO SELF-STUDY PRACTICE

Solution to SP11.1

1. *dr* Cash (+A) 20,000
      cr Common Shares (+SE) (1,000 × $20)) 20,000

2. *dr* Common Shares (−SE) (500 × $20) 10,000
      dr Retained Earnings (−SE) 2,500
      cr Cash (−A) (500 × $25) 12,500

Solution to SP11.2

1. Declaration date
2. Date of payment
3. Dividends can be paid only if sufficient retained earnings and sufficient cash are both available.

Solution to SP11.3

1. *dr* Retained Earnings (−SE) 300,000
      cr Common Shares (+SE) 300,000

2. No journal entry is required in the case of a stock split. Theoretically, the new price would be one−half of what it was before the 2−for−1 split ($30 × 1/2 = $15).

Solution to SP11.4

EPS: $567.3 ÷ 183.0 = $3.10
ROE: $567.3 ÷ [($8,605 + $7,967)/2] = 0.068 or 6.8%
P/E: $56.15 ÷ $3.10 = 18.1

KEY TERMS

Authorized Shares

Common Shares

Contributed Surplus

Cumulative Dividend Preference

Current Dividend Preference

Declaration Date

Dividends in Arrears

Issued Shares

No–Par Value Shares

Outstanding Shares

Par Value Share

Payment Date

Preferred Shares

Record Date

Retained Earnings

Stock Dividends

Stock Split

Treasury Shares

Complete definitions are also included in the glossary at the end of this text.

HOMEWORK HELPER

Alternative terms

- Shareholders are also called *stockholders*.

Helpful reminders

- Stock dividends are recorded at the current market price of the share.

Frequent mistakes

- Do not record a liability for dividends in arrears at the end of each year. They are recorded as a liability only when dividends are declared on the cumulative preferred shares.

PRACTICE MATERIAL

QUESTIONS (§ Symbol indicates questions that require analysis from more than one perspective.)

1. Identify the primary advantages of the corporate form of business.

2. What are the relative advantages of equity financing? What are the relative advantages of debt financing?

3. Just prior to filing for bankruptcy protection in 2009, General Motors (GM) asked its bondholders to exchange their investment in GM's bonds for GM shares. The bondholders rejected this proposal. Why might GM have proposed this exchange? Why might the bondholders have rejected it? §

4. Explain each of the following terms: (*a*) authorized common shares, (*b*) issued common shares, and (*c*) outstanding common shares.

5. What are the differences between common shares and preferred shares?

6. What is the distinction between par value and no–par value shares?

7. What are the usual characteristics of preferred shares?

8. What are the two basic sources of shareholders' equity? Explain each.

9. What are treasury shares? Why do corporations acquire treasury shares?

10. What are the two financial requirements to support the declaration of a cash dividend? What are the effects of a cash dividend on assets and shareholders' equity?

11. What is the difference between cumulative and non–cumulative preferred shares?

12. What is a stock dividend? How does a stock dividend differ from a cash dividend?

13. What are the primary reasons for issuing a stock dividend?

14. Your company has been very profitable and expects continued financial success. Its share price has reached a point where the company needs to make the cost of shares more affordable. Would you recommend a stock dividend or a stock split? Why? §

15. Identify and explain the three important dates related to dividends.

16. Why is the EPS number so popular? What are its limitations?

17. How do share repurchases affect the EPS and ROE ratios?

18. What is one interpretation of a high P/E ratio?

19. You work for a public company that has relied heavily on debt financing in the past and is now considering a preferred share issuance to reduce its debt–to–assets ratio. Debt–to–assets is one of the key ratios in your company's loan covenants. Should the preferred shares have a fixed annual dividend rate or a dividend that is determined yearly? In what way might this decision be affected by IFRS? 🜚

MINI-EXERCISES

M11-1 Equity versus Debt Financing

LO11-1

Indicate whether each of the following relates to equity (E) or debt (D) financing, and whether it makes that form of financing more, or less, favourable.

1. Interest is tax deductible.
2. Dividends are optional.
3. It must be repaid.
4. Additional stock issuances dilute existing shareholders' control.

M11-2 Analyzing and Recording the Issuance of Common Shares

LO11-2

To expand operations, Artagon Consulting issued 100,000 shares of previously unissued common shares for $75 per share. Analyze the accounting equation effects and record the journal entry for the share issuance.

M11-3 Analyzing and Recording the Issuance of No-Par Value Common Shares

LO11-2

Refer to M11–2. Assume the issued shares have no par value. Analyze the accounting equation effects and record the journal entry for the issuance of the no–par value shares at $75. Do the effects on total assets, total liabilities, and total shareholders' equity differ from those in M11–2?

M11-4 Comparing Common Shares and Preferred Shares

LO11-4

Your parents have just retired and have asked you for some financial advice. They have decided to invest $100,000 in a company very similar to Molson Coors Brewing Company. The company has issued both common and preferred shares. Which type of shares would you recommend? What factors are relevant to this recommendation?

M11-5 Determining the Effects of Share Issuance and Share Repurchase and Cancellation Transactions

LO11-2

TransUnited Limited issued 5,000 shares for $50 per share in one year, and it issued 10,000 shares for $37 per share in the following year. The year after that, the company reacquired and cancelled 20,000 shares of its own shares for $45 per share. Determine the dollar amount impact (increase, decrease, or no change) of each of these transactions on the following classifications:

1. Total assets
2. Total liabilities
3. Total shareholders' equity
4. Net income

M11-6 Determining the Amount of a Dividend

LO11-3

Netpass Company has 300,000 shares of common shares authorized, 270,000 shares issued, and 100,000 shares of treasury stock. The company's board of directors declares a dividend of $1 per common share. What is the total amount of the dividend that will be paid?

M11-7 Recording Dividends

LO11-3

On April 15, the board of directors for AuctionPro declared a cash dividend of 40 cents per share payable to shareholders of record on May 20. The dividends will be paid on June 14. The company has 500,000 shares outstanding. Prepare any necessary journal entries for each date.

LO11-3 **M11-8** **Determining the Impact of a Stock Dividend**

Stone Tools, Inc. announced a 100 percent stock dividend. Determine the impact (+ for increase, − for decrease, or NE for no effect) of this dividend on the following:

1. Total assets NE
2. Total liabilities NE
3. Common shares INCREASE
4. Total shareholders' equity NE
5. Market value per share of common shares DECREASE

LO11-3 **M11-9** **Determining the Impact of a Stock Split**

Complete the requirements of M11−8 assuming that the company announced a 2−for−1 stock split.

LO11-4 **M11-10** **Determining the Amount of a Preferred Dividend**

Colliers Inc. has 100,000 shares of cumulative preferred shares outstanding. The preferred shares pay dividends in the amount of $2 per share, but because of cash flow problems, the company did not pay any dividends last year. The board of directors plans to pay dividends in the amount of $1 million this year. What amount will go to preferred shareholders? How much will be available for dividends to common shareholders?

LO11-5 **M11-11** **Calculating and Interpreting Earnings per Share (EPS) and Return on Equity (ROE)**

Academy Driving School reported the following in its financial statements:

	Year 2	Year 1
Number of common shares	11,500	11,500
Net income	$ 23,000	$ 18,000
Cash dividends paid on common shares	$ 3,000	$ 3,000
Total shareholders' equity	$240,000	$220,000

Calculate the EPS and ROE for Year 2. Another driving school in the same city reported a higher net income ($45,000) in the same year, yet its EPS and ROE ratios were lower than those for the Academy Driving School. Explain how this apparent inconsistency could occur.

LO11-2, 11-3 **M11-12** **Determining the Impact of Transactions on Components of Earnings per Share (EPS) and Return on Equity (ROE)**

Indicate the direction of effect (+ for increase, − for decrease, or NE for no effect) of each of the following transactions on the accounting equation in the table below. The first transaction is shown as an example.

	Assets	=	Liabilities	+	Shareholders' Equity
a. Purchased and cancelled 50 shares for $5,000; the original price paid for these shares was also $5,000 in total	Cash −5,000				Common shares (+xSE) −5,000
b. Declared and paid a cash dividend of $600					
c. Declared and issued a stock dividend valued at $10,000 on no−par common shares					
d. Sold inventory for $80 cash, when it had cost $55					
e. Issued common shares at par for $60,000 cash					

M11-13 Inferring Financial Information Using the P/E Ratio

LO11-5

In 2016, Rec Room Sports reported earnings per share of $8.50 when its share price was $212.50. In 2017, its earnings increased by 20 percent. If the P/E ratio remains constant, what is the price of the shares? Explain.

M11-14 (Supplement 11 A) Comparing Owner's Equity to Shareholders' Equity

LO11-S1

On January 2, Daniel Harrison contributed $20,000 to start his business. At the end of the year, the business had generated $30,000 in sales revenues, incurred $18,000 in operating expenses, and distributed $5,000 in the form of dividends for Daniel to use to pay some personal expenses. Prepare (a) a statement of owner's equity, assuming this is a sole proprietorship, (b) the owner's equity section of the balance sheet, assuming this is a sole proprietorship, and (c) the shareholder's equity section of the balance sheet, assuming this is a corporation with no—par value shares.

EXERCISES

E11-1 Reporting Shareholders' Equity and Determining Dividend Policy

LO11-2, 11-3

Beamsley Corporation was organized in 2017 to operate a financial consulting business. The charter authorized 12,000 common shares, no par value. During the first year, the following selected transactions were completed:

a. Issued 6,000 shares of common shares for cash at $20 per share.
b. Issued 2,000 shares of common shares for cash at $23 per share.

Required:

1. Show the effects of each transaction on the accounting equation.
2. Give the journal entry required for each of these transactions.
3. Prepare the shareholders' equity section as it should be reported on the 2017 year—end balance sheet. At year—end, the accounts reflected a profit of $100.
4. Beamsley Corporation has $30,000 in the company's bank account. Should the company declare cash dividends at this time? Explain.

Check Figure
[Req. 3]:
Total shareholders'
equity = $166,100

E11-2 Preparing the Shareholders' Equity Section of the Balance Sheet

LO11-2, 11-4

Norwest Aviation received its charter during January 2017. The charter authorized the fol—lowing shares:

Preferred shares: 8 percent; no-par value; authorized 20,000 shares
Common shares: no-par value; authorized 50,000 shares

During 2017, the following transactions occurred in the order given:

a. Issued a total of 40,000 common shares to the company's founders for $11 per share
b. Issued 5,000 preferred shares at $18 per share
c. Issued 3,000 common shares at $14 per share and 1,000 preferred shares at $28
d. Net income for the first year was $48,000

Required:

Prepare the shareholders' equity section of the balance sheet at December 31, 2017.

E11-3 Reporting the Shareholders' Equity Section of the Balance Sheet

LO11-2, 11-3, 11-4

Shelby Corporation was organized in January 2017 by ten shareholders to operate an air—conditioning sales and service business. The charter issued by the province authorized the following shares:

Common shares: no-par value; 200,000 shares
Preferred shares: no-par value; 6 percent; 50,000 shares

During January and February 2017, the following share transactions were completed:

a. Collected $40,000 cash from each of the ten organizers and issued 2,000 common shares to each of them

b. Issued 15,000 preferred shares at $25 per share; collected in cash
Net income for 2017 was $40,000; cash dividends declared and paid at year–end were $10,000.

Required:

Prepare the shareholders' equity section of the balance sheet at December 31, 2017.

LO11-2, 11-4 **E11-4 Determining the Effects of the Issuance of Common and Preferred Shares**

RiteSide Limited was issued a charter on January 15, 2017, that authorized the following shares:

> Common shares: no-par value; 100,000 shares; one vote per share
> Preferred shares: 7 percent; no-par value $10 per share; 5,000 shares; non-voting

During 2017, the following selected transactions were completed in the order given:

a. Issued 20,000 common shares at $18 cash per share
b. Issued 3,000 preferred shares at $22 cash per share
At the end of 2017, the accounts showed net income of $38,000.

Required:

1. Prepare the shareholders' equity section of the balance sheet at December 31, 2017.
2. Assume that you are a common shareholder. If RiteSide Limited needed additional capital, would you prefer to have it issue additional common shares or additional preferred shares? Explain.

LO11-2, 11-4 **E11-5 Recording and Reporting Shareholders' Equity Transactions**

Ava School of Learning obtained a charter at the start of 2017 that authorized 50,000 shares of no–par value common shares and 20,000 no–par value preferred shares. During 2017, the following selected transactions occurred:

a. Collected $40 cash per share from four individuals and issued 5,000 common shares to each
b. Issued 6,000 shares of common shares to an outside investor at $40 cash per share
Issued 8,000 shares of preferred shares at $20 cash per share

Check Figure [Req. 2]:
Total shareholders' equity = $1,236,000

Required:

1. Give the journal entries indicated for each of these transactions.
2. Prepare the shareholders' equity section of the balance sheet at December 31, 2017. At the end of 2017, the accounts reflected net income of $36,000. No dividends were declared.

LO11-2, 11-3 **E11-6 Recording Shareholders' Equity Transactions**

The annual report for Malibu Beachwear reported the following transactions affecting share–holders' equity:

a. Repurchased and cancelled $3.5 million common shares
b. Declared and paid cash dividends in the amount of $254.2 million
c. Issued 100 percent common stock dividend involving 222.5 million additional shares with a total par value of $556.3 million

Required:

1. Indicate the effect (increase, decrease, or no effect) of each of these transactions on total assets, liabilities, and shareholders' equity.
2. Prepare journal entries to record each of these transactions.

E11-7 Computing Dividends on Preferred Shares and Analyzing Differences

LO11-3, 11-4

At December 31, 2016, the records of Hoffman Company reflected the following balances in the shareholders' equity accounts:

> Common shares: par $12 per share; 40,000 shares outstanding
> Preferred shares: 8 percent; par $10 per share; 6,000 shares outstanding
> Retained earnings: $220,000

On January 1, 2017, the board of directors was considering the distribution of a $62,000 cash dividend. No dividends were paid during 2015 and 2016.

Required:

1. Determine the total and per–share amounts that would be paid to the common sharehold–ers and to the preferred shareholders under two independent assumptions:

   a. The preferred shares are non–cumulative.
   b. The preferred shares are cumulative.

2. Briefly explain why the dividends per common share were less for the second assumption.
3. What factors would cause a more favourable dividend for the common shareholders?

Check Figure [Req. 1(a)]: Dividends paid to common shareholders = $57,200

E11-8 Recording the Payment of Dividends and Preparing a Statement of Retained Earnings

LO11-2, 11-3

The 2017 annual report for Sneer Corporation disclosed that the company declared and paid preferred dividends in the amount of $119.9 million in 2017. It also declared and paid dividends on common shares in the amount of $2 per share. During 2017, Sneer had 1,000,000,000 common shares authorized; 387,570,300 shares had been issued. The balance in Retained Earnings was $1,554 million on December 31, 2016, and 2017 Net Income was $858 million.

Required:

1. Prepare journal entries to record the declaration, and payment, of dividends on (a) pre–ferred and (b) common shares.
2. Using the information given above, prepare a statement of retained earnings for the year ended December 31, 2017.

E11-9 Analyzing Stock Dividends

LO11-3

LEVEL UP

On December 31, 2016, the shareholders' equity section of the balance sheet of R & L Corporation reflected the following:

Common shares (no-par value; authorized 60,000 shares; outstanding 25,000 shares)	$250,000
Contributed surplus	12,000
Retained earnings	75,000

On February 1, 2017, the board of directors declared a 12 percent stock dividend to be issued April 30, 2017. The market value of the shares on February 1, 2017, was $18 per share.

Required:

1. For comparative purposes, prepare the shareholders' equity section of the balance sheet (a) immediately before the stock dividend and (b) immediately after the stock dividend.

   TIP: Use two columns for the amounts in this requirement.

2. Explain the effects of this stock dividend on the assets, the liabilities, and the components of shareholders' equity.

LO11-3 **E11-10 Accounting for Dividends During the Credit Crisis**

A press release contained the following announcement:

> Castleton, Sask., April 30, 2017: Ridgeton Corporation announced today that its Board of Directors declared a quarterly cash dividend of $0.12 per share of the Corporation's outstanding common shares, payable June 26, 2017, to shareholders of record at the close of business on June 12, 2017. This represents a reduction from the $0.42 quarterly dividend paid by the Corporation since 2015. Frederick Furter, chairman and chief executive officer, said, "In today's uncertain and challenging economic environment, we believe it is important to preserve liquidity. By lowering the dividend to $0.12 per quarter, we will reduce cash outflows by $54 million in 2017. This action will strengthen our balance sheet, improve our credit metrics, and provide greater financial flexibility."

At the time of the press release, Ridgeton had 150,000,000 shares authorized and 60 million outstanding. The par value for the company's shares is $0.50 per share.

Required:

1. Prepare journal entries as appropriate for each of the three dates mentioned above.
2. Explain how a dividend cut from $0.42 to $0.12 will strengthen the company's balance sheet.

LO11-3 **E11-11 Comparing Stock Dividends and Splits**

On July 1, 2017, Jones Limited had the following share structure:

Common shares (par $1; 200,000 authorized shares; 150,000 issued and outstanding)	$150,000
Contributed surplus	88,000
Retained earnings	172,000

Required:

Complete the following table based on three independent cases involving share transactions:

Check Figure [Case 2]:
Retained Earnings = $22,000

Case 1: The board of directors declared and issued a 10 percent stock dividend when the share price was $8 per share.
Case 2: The board of directors declared and issued a 100 percent stock dividend when the share price was $8 per share.
Case 3: The board of directors voted a 2—for—1 stock split. The share price prior to the split was $8 per share.

		Case 1	Case 2	Case 3
Items	**Before Share Transactions**	**After 10% Stock Dividend**	**After 100% Stock Dividend**	**After Stock Split**
Number of shares outstanding				
Par per share	$ 1	$	$	$
Common shares account	$	$	$	$
Contributed surplus	88,000			
Retained earnings	172,000			
Total shareholders' equity	$	$	$	$

LO11-4 **E11-12 Analyzing Dividends in Arrears**

Like many start—up companies, DomainCo struggled with cash flows as it developed new business opportunities. A student found a financial statement for DomainCo stating that the increase in dividends in arrears on preferred shares this year was $264,000.

The student who read the note suggested that the DomainCo preferred share would be a good investment because of the large amount of dividend income that would be earned when the company started paying dividends again: "As the owner of the shares, I'll get dividends for the period I hold the shares plus some previous periods when I didn't even own the shares." Do you agree? Explain.

E11-13 Determining the Impact of Cash and Stock Dividends

LO11-3, 11-4

Superior Corporation has the following shares outstanding:

> Preferred shares: 6 percent; par $15; 8,000 outstanding shares
> Common shares: par $8; 30,000 outstanding shares

On October 1, 2017, the board of directors declared dividends as follows:

> Preferred shares: Full cash preference amount, payable December 20, 2017
> Common shares: 10 percent common stock dividend (i.e., one additional share for each 10 held), to be issued on December 20, 2017

On December 20, 2017, the market prices were preferred shares, $40, and common shares, $32.

Required:

Indicate the direction and amount of change in total assets, liabilities, and shareholders' equity as a result of: (*a*) declaration of the cash dividend on October 1, (*b*) payment of the cash dividend on December 20, and (*c*) a 10 percent common stock dividend on December 20.

E11-14 Determining the Financial Statement Effects of Cash and Stock Dividends

LO11-3, 11-4

Lynn Company has outstanding 60,000 common shares of $10 par value and 25,000 preferred shares of $20 par value (8 percent). On December 1, 2017, the board of directors voted an 8 percent cash dividend on the preferred shares and a 10 percent stock dividend on the common shares. At the date of declaration, the common share price was $35 and the preferred share price was $20 per share. The dividends are to be paid, or issued, on February 15, 2018. The annual accounting period ends December 31.

Required:

Explain the comparative effects of the two dividends on the assets, liabilities, and shareholders' equity (*a*) through December 31, 2017, (*b*) on February 15, 2018, and (*c*) in regard to the overall effects from December 1, 2017, through February 15, 2018. Use the following structure:

Item	Comparative Effects Explained	
	Cash Dividend on Preferred	Stock Dividend on Common
(a) Through December 31, 2017:		
Effect on Assets		
Effect on Liabilities		
Effect on Shareholders' Equity		

E11-15 Preparing a Statement of Retained Earnings and Partial Balance Sheet and Evaluating Dividend Policy

LO11-3, 11-5

At December 31, 2017, the following account balances were selected from the records of beverage maker Blake Corporation after all adjusting entries were completed:

Common shares (no-par value; authorized 100,000 shares; issued 35,000 shares)	$525,000
Contributed surplus	180,000
Dividends declared and paid in 2017	28,000
Retained earnings, January 1, 2017	76,000

Net income for the year was $48,000.

Required:

1. Prepare the statement of retained earnings for the year ended December 31, 2017, and the shareholders' equity section of the balance sheet at December 31, 2017.
2. Compute the ROE ratio for 2017, assuming total shareholders' equity on December 31, 2016 was $629,000. How does it compare to the ratios shown in Exhibit 11.7?

LO11-2, 11-5 **E11-16 Determining the Effect of a Share Repurchase on EPS and ROE**

J. Bartley Pools Inc. reported the following in its financial statements for the quarter ended March 31, 2017.

	December 31, 2016	March 31, 2017
Common shares (no par value; 50,000 shares outstanding)	$ 50,000	$ 50,000
Contributed surplus	30,000	30,000
Retained earnings	20,000	20,000
Total shareholders' equity	$ 100,000	$100,000

During the quarter ended March 31, 2017, Bartley reported Net Income of $5,000 and declared and paid cash dividends totalling $5,000.

Required:

1. Calculate earnings per share (EPS) and return on equity (ROE) for the quarter ended March 31, 2017.
2. Assume that Bartley repurchases 10,000 of its common shares at a price of $2 per share on April 1, 2017. Also assume that during the quarter ended June 30, 2017, Bartley reported Net Income of $5,000, and declared and paid cash dividends totalling $5,000. Calculate earnings per share (EPS) and return on equity (ROE) for the quarter ended June 30, 2017.
3. Based on your calculations in requirements 1 and 2, what can you conclude about the impact of a share repurchase on EPS and ROE?

LO11-S1 **E11-17 (Supplement 11 A) Comparing Shareholders' Equity Sections for Alternative Forms of Organization**

Assume for each of the following independent cases that the annual accounting period ends on December 31, 2017, and that the total of all revenue accounts was $150,000 and the total of all expense accounts was $130,000.

Case A: Assume that the company is a *sole proprietorship* owned by Proprietor A. Prior to the closing entries, the Capital account reflected a credit balance of $50,000 and the Drawings account showed a balance of $8,000.

Check Figure [Case B, Req. 2]: Total Partners' Equity = $84,000

Case B: Assume that the company is a *partnership* owned by Partner A and Partner B. Prior to the closing entries, the owners' equity accounts reflected the following balances: A, Capital, $40,000; B, Capital, $38,000; A, Drawings, $5,000; and B, Drawings, $9,000. Profits and losses are divided equally.

Case C: Assume that the company is a *corporation*. Prior to the closing entries, the shareholders' equity accounts showed the following:

Capital shares: par $10; authorized 30,00 shares; outstanding 15,000 shares	
Contributed surplus: $5,000	
Retained earnings: $65,000	

Required:

1. Give all the closing entries required at December 31, 2017, for each of the separate cases.
2. Show how the equity section of the balance sheet would appear at December 31, 2017, for each case. Show computations.

COACHED PROBLEMS

CP11-1 Analyzing Accounting Equation Effects, Recording Journal Entries, and Preparing a Partial Balance Sheet Involving Share Issuance and Repurchase Transactions

LO11-2

Worldwide Company obtained a charter from the province in January that authorized 200,000 no-par value common shares. During the first year, the company earned $38,200 and the following selected transactions occurred in the order given:

a. Issued 60,000 shares of the common shares at $12 cash per share
b. Reacquired and cancelled 2,000 shares at $15 cash per share from shareholders
c. Issued 1,000 common shares at $18 cash per share

Required:

1. Indicate the effects of each transaction on the accounting equation.
2. Prepare journal entries to record each transaction.
3. Prepare the shareholders' equity section of the balance sheet at December 31.

   TIP: Because this is the first year of operations, Retained Earnings has a zero balance at the beginning of the year.

   TIP: Total Retained Earnings at December 31 equals $770,200.

CP11-2 Recording Stock Dividends

LO11-3

Activision Blizzard, Inc. reported the following in the notes to its financial statements.

> *Stock Split*—In July, the Board of Directors approved a two-for-one split of our outstanding common shares effected in the form of a stock dividend ("the split"). The split was paid September 5 to shareholders of record as of August 25. The par value of our common stock was maintained at the pre-split amount of $.000001 per share.

Required:

1. Describe the effects that this transaction would have had on the company's financial statements. Assume that 600 million shares were outstanding at the time of the transaction, trading at a stock price of $33.

   TIP: Although the financial statements refer to a stock split, the transaction actually involved a 100 percent stock dividend.
2. Why might the board of directors have decided to declare a stock dividend rather than a stock split?

CP11-3 Finding Missing Amounts

LO11-2, 11-3, 11-5

At December 31, the records of Nortech Corporation provided the following selected and incomplete data:

> Common shares: no changes during the current year
>
> Shares authorized: 5,000,000
>
> Shares issued, _____ ; issue price $2 per share
>
> Net income for the current year: $147,750
>
> Common Shares account: $200,000
>
> Dividends declared and paid during the year: $25,000
>
> Retained Earnings balance, beginning of the year: $155,000

Required:

1. Complete the following:

   Shares issued _____

   Shares outstanding _____

   > TIP: To determine the number of shares issued, divide the balance in the Common Share account by the issue price per share.

2. Earnings per share is $_____ (Round your answer to two decimal places.)
3. Dividends paid per common share is $_____

LO11-2, 11-3, 11-4

CP11-4 Comparing Stock and Cash Dividends

Water Tower Company had the following shares outstanding and Retained Earnings at December 31, 2017:

Common shares (outstanding 30,000 shares)	$240,000
Preferred shares (7%; outstanding, 6,000 shares)	60,000
Retained earnings	280,000

On December 31, 2017, the board of directors considered the distribution of a cash dividend to the common and preferred shareholders. No dividends were declared during 2015 or 2016. Three independent cases are assumed:

Case A: The preferred shares are non–cumulative; the total amount of 2017 dividends would be $30,000.
Case B: The preferred shares are cumulative; the total amount of 2017 dividends would be $12,600. Dividends were not in arrears prior to 2015.
Case C: Same as Case B, except the amount is $66,000.

Required:

Compute the amount of 2017 dividends, in total and per share, that would be payable to each class of shareholders for each case. Show computations.

> TIP: Preferred shareholders with cumulative dividends are paid dividends for any prior years (in arrears) *and* for the current year before common shareholders are paid.

LO11-5

CP11-5 Computing and Interpreting Return on Equity (ROE) and Price/Earnings (P/E) Ratios

Avery's Rentals, Inc. and Rent–A–Matic, Inc. are two publicly traded rental companies. They reported the following in their 2017 financial statements (in millions of dollars, except per–share amounts and share prices):

	Avery's Rentals, Inc.		Rent-A-Matic, Inc.	
	2017	2016	2017	2016
Net income	$ 90.2	$ 80.3	$ 139.6	$ 76.3
Total shareholders' equity	761.5	673.4	1,079.2	947.1
Earnings per share	1.69	1.48	2.10	1.11
Share price when annual results reported	26.67	21.54	19.37	18.35

Required:

1. Compute the 2017 ROE for each company. Express ROE as a percentage rounded to one decimal place. Which company appears to generate greater returns on shareholders' equity in 2017?

   > TIP: Remember that the bottom of the ROE ratio uses the *average* shareholders' equity.

2. Compute the 2017 P/E ratio for each company (rounded to one decimal place). Do investors appear to value one company more than the other? Explain.

GROUP A PROBLEMS

PA11-1 Analyzing Accounting Equation Effects, Recording Journal Entries, and Preparing a Partial Balance Sheet Involving Shares Issuance and Purchase Transactions

LO11-2

Doulane Marine obtained a charter from the province in January 2017 that authorized 1,000,000 common shares. During the first year, the company earned $429,000 and the following selected transactions occurred in the order given:

a. Issued 700,000 common shares at $54 cash per share
b. Reacquired and cancelled 25,000 shares at $50 cash per share

Required:

1. Indicate the effects of each transaction on the accounting equation.
2. Prepare journal entries to record each transaction.
3. Prepare the shareholders' equity section of the balance sheet at December 31, 2017.

PA11-2 Recording Cash Dividends

LO11-3

Metro Chocolate Corp. produces chocolate bars and snacks under the brand names Blast and Soothe. A press release contained the following information:

> March 5, 20XX—Metro Chocolate Corp. today announced that its Board of Directors has declared a special "one-time" cash dividend of $1.00 per share on its one million outstanding common shares. The dividend will be paid on April 30 to shareholders of record at the close of business on March 26.

Required:

1. Prepare any journal entries that Metro Chocolate Corp. should make as a result of information in the press release. Assume that the company has 1.0 million shares outstanding on March 5, the par value is $0.01 per share, and the share price is $10 per share.
2. What two requirements would the board of directors have considered before making the dividend decisions?

PA11-3 Finding Missing Amounts

LO11-2, 11-3, 11-5

At December 31, 2017, the records of Kozmetsky Corporation provided the following selected and incomplete data:

> Common shares: no changes during 2017
> Shares authorized: 5,000,000.
> Shares issued,_____; issue price $1 per share.
> Net income for 2017: $4,800,000
> Common Shares account: $1,500,000
> Dividends declared and paid during 2017: $2 per share
> Retained Earnings balance, January 1, 2017: $82,900,000

Required:

1. Complete the following:
   Shares issued _____
   Shares outstanding _____
2. Earnings per share is $_____ (Round your answer to two decimal places.)
3. Total dividends paid on common shares during 2017 is $_____

PA11-4 Comparing Stock and Cash Dividends

Ritz Company had the following shares outstanding and Retained Earnings at December 31, 2017:

Common shares (500,000 outstanding shares)	$500,000
Preferred shares (8 percent; 21,000 outstanding shares)	210,000
Retained earnings	900,000

On December 31, 2017, the board of directors is considering the distribution of a cash dividend to the common and preferred shareholders. No dividends were declared during 2015 or 2016. Three independent cases are assumed:

Case A: The preferred shares are non–cumulative; the total amount of 2017 dividends would be $30,000.

Case B: The preferred shares are cumulative; the total amount of 2017 dividends would be $30,000. Dividends were not in arrears prior to 2015.

Case C: Same as Case B, except the amount is $75,000.

Required:

Compute the amount of dividends, in total and per share, payable to each class of shareholders for each case. Show computations. Round per share amounts to two decimal places.

LO11-5 **PA11-5 Computing and Interpreting Return on Equity (ROE) and Price/Earnings (P/E) Ratios**

Two magazine companies reported the following in their 2017 financial statements (in thousands of dollars, except earnings per share amounts and share prices):

	Business Now		Fun and Games	
	2017	**2016**	**2017**	**2016**
Net income	$ 55,000	$ 54,302	$ 91,420	$ 172,173
Total shareholders' equity	587,186	512,814	894,302	934,098
Earnings per share	3.20	3.19	2.10	3.98
Share price when annual results reported	54.40	51.04	32.55	59.70

Required:

1. Compute the 2017 ROE for each company (express ROE as a percentage rounded to one decimal place). Which company appears to generate greater returns on shareholders' equity in 2017?
2. Compute the 2017 P/E ratio for each company. Do investors appear to value one company more than the other? Explain.
3. Fun and Games reacquired 32,804 (thousand) common shares in 2017 at $4 per share. Recalculate the company's ROE for 2017, assuming that this share repurchase did not occur. Does this new ROE change your interpretation of the ROE ratios calculated in requirement 1?

GROUP B PROBLEMS

LO11-2 **PB11-1 Analyzing Accounting Equation Effects, Recording Journal Entries, and Preparing a Partial Balance Sheet Involving Shares Issuance and Purchase Transactions**

Whyville Corporation obtained its charter from the province in January 2017, which authorized 500,000 common shares. During the first year, the company earned $58,000 and the following selected transactions occurred in the order given:

a. Issued 200,000 shares of the common shares at $23 cash per share
b. Reacquired and cancelled 5,000 shares at $24 cash per share

Required:

1. Indicate the effects of each transaction on the accounting equation.
2. Prepare journal entries to record each transaction.
3. Prepare the shareholders' equity section of the balance sheet at December 31, 2017.

PB11-2 Recording Cash and Stock Dividends

LO11-3

Yougi Corp., an animation studio, issued a press release that contained the following information:

> April 1, 20XX—Yougi Corp. today announced that its Board of Directors has declared a cash dividend of $0.50 per share on 605,000 outstanding preferred shares. The dividend will be paid on or before May 31, 20XX, to preferred shareholders of record at the close of business on May 26, 20XX. The Board of Directors also announced a 100 percent common stock dividend will occur on May 31, 20XX, on its 1,900,000 outstanding $0.01 par common shares for shareholders of record on May 26, 20XX.

Required:

1. Prepare any journal entries that Yougi Corp. should make as the result of information in the preceding report.
2. What two requirements would the board of directors have considered before making the dividend decision?

PB11-3 Finding Missing Amounts

LO11-2, 11-3, 11-5

At December 31, 2017, the records of Seacrest Enterprises provided the following selected and incomplete data:

> Common shares: no changes during 2017
>
> Shares authorized: 5,000,000.
>
> Shares issued,_____; issue price $1 per share.
>
> Net income for 2017: $4,800,000
>
> Common Shares account: $1,500,000
>
> Dividends declared and paid during 2017: $2 per share
>
> Retained Earnings balance, January 1, 2017: $82,900,000

Required:

1. Complete the following:
   Shares issued _____
   Shares outstanding _____
2. Earnings per share is $_____ (Round your answer to two decimal places.)
3. Total dividends paid on common shares during 2017 is $_____

PB11-4 Comparing Stock and Cash Dividends

LO11-2, 11-3, 11-4

At December 31, 2017, Carlos Company had the following Retained Earnings and shares outstanding:

Common shares (490,000 outstanding shares)	$490,000
Preferred shares (8%; 19,000 outstanding shares)	190,000
Retained earnings	966,000

On December 31, 2017, the board of directors considered the distribution of a cash dividend to the common and preferred shareholders. No dividends were declared during 2015 or 2016. Three independent cases are assumed:

Case A: The preferred shares are non–cumulative; the total amount of 2017 dividends would be $24,000.

Case B: The preferred shares are cumulative; the total amount of 2017 dividends would be $24,000. Dividends were not in arrears prior to 2015.

Case C: Same as Case B, except the amount is $67,000.

Check Figure
[Case C]:
Dividend paid to common shareholders = $21,400

Required:

Compute the amount of 2017 dividends, in total and per share, payable to each class of share—holders for each case. Show computations. Round per—share amounts to two decimal places.

LO11-5 **PB11-5 Computing and Interpreting Return on Equity (ROE) and Price/Earnings (P/E) Ratio**

Two music companies reported the following in their 2017 financial statements (in thousands of dollars, except earnings per share amounts and share prices):

	Urban Youth		Sound Jonx	
	2017	2016	2017	2016
Net income	$ 27,500	$ 24,302	$ 41,500	$ 36,739
Total shareholders' equity	387,101	300,399	516,302	521,198
Earnings per share	1.10	1.00	0.95	0.85
Share price when annual results reported	20.35	18.50	16.15	14.45

Required:

Check Figure [Req. 1]: 2017 ROE for Urban Youth = 8.0%

1. Compute the 2017 ROE for each company (express ROE as a percentage rounded to one decimal place). Which company appears to generate greater returns on shareholders' equity in 2017?
2. Compute the 2017 P/E ratio for each company. Do investors appear to value one company more than the other? Explain.
3. Sound Jonx reacquired 5,000 (thousand) common shares in 2017 at $13 per share. Recalculate the company's ROE for 2017 assuming that this share repurchase did not occur. Does this new ROE change your interpretation of the ROE ratios calculated in requirement 1?

COMPREHENSIVE PROBLEM

LO8-2, 9-3, 10-3, 11-2, 11-3 **C11-1 Financial Reporting of Write-off, Bond Issuance, and the Issuance, Purchase, Reissuance, and Cash Dividends that Relate to Common Shares.**

Consider the following, using what you learned in Chapters 8, 10, and 11.
American Laser, Inc. reported the following account balances on January 1.

Accounts Receivable	$ 5,000
Accumulated Depreciation	30,000
Allowance for Doubtful Accounts	2,000
Bonds Payable	0
Buildings	247,000
Cash	10,000
Common Shares, 10,000 shares of $1 issue price	10,000
Notes Payable (long-term)	10,000
Retained Earnings	120,000

The company entered into the following transactions during the year.

Jan. 15	Issued 5,000 common shares for $50,000 cash
Feb. 15	Reacquired and cancelled 3,000 common shares for $33,000 cash
Mar. 15	Issued 2,000 common shares for $24,000 cash
Aug. 15	Issued 600 common shares for $4,600 cash
Sept. 15	Declared (but did not yet pay) a $1 cash dividend on each outstanding com—mon shares
Oct. 1	Issued 100 10—year, $1,000 bonds, at a quoted bond price of 101
Oct. 3	Wrote off a $500 balance due from a customer who went bankrupt

Required:

1. Analyze the effects of each transaction on total assets, liabilities, and shareholders' equity.

2. Prepare journal entries to record each transaction.

3. Enter the January 1 balances into T−accounts, post the journal entries from requirement 2, and determine ending balances.

4. Prepare the non−current liabilities and stockholders' equity sections of the balance sheet at December 31. At the end of the year, the adjusted net income was $20,000.

5. Prepare the closing entry for Dividends.

SKILLS DEVELOPMENT CASES

S11-1 Finding Financial Information

LO11-2, 11-3, 11-5

Refer to the summarized financial statements of The Home Depot in Appendix A at the back of this book.

Required:

1. According to the income statement, how have The Home Depot's net earnings changed over the past year? Has the company's basic earnings per share changed over the past year? Are these patterns consistent?

S11-2 Comparing Financial Information

LO11-2, 11-3, 11-5

Refer to the summarized financial statements of The Home Depot in Appendix A and Lowe's Companies Inc. in Appendix B at the back of this book.

Required:

1. The Home Depot had 1.776 billion common shares issued at January 29, 2017. Did Lowe's Companies Inc. have more or fewer common shares issued than The Home Depot at the fiscal year−end 2016?

2. From the Retained Earnings column in the Statement of Shareholders' Equity, what total amount of cash dividends did Lowe's Companies Inc. declare during the year ended February 3, 2017?

3. How have Lowe's Companies Inc.'s net earnings changed over the past three years? How has the company's basic earnings per share changed over the past three years?

S11-3 Internet-Based Team Research: Examining an Annual Report

LO11-3, 11-5

As a team, select an industry to analyze. Using the Internet, each team member should access the annual report for one publicly traded company in the industry, with each member select− ing a different company. (See S1−3 in Chapter 1 for a description of possible resources for these tasks.)

Required:

1. On an individual basis, each team member should write a short report that incorporates the following:
   a. What is the ownership structure for this company and how does this structure impact the reporting in the financial statements?
   b. Has the company declared cash or stock dividends during the past three years?
   c. What is the trend in the company's EPS over the past three years?
   d. Compute and analyze the return on equity ratio over the past two years.

2. Then, as a team, write a short report comparing and contrasting your companies using these attributes. Discuss any patterns across the companies that you as a team observe. Provide potential explanations for any differences discovered.

S11-4 Ethical Decision Making: A Real-Life Example

LO11-1, 11-2

Activision became a public company with an initial public offering of shares on June 9, 1983, at $12 per share. In June 2002, Activision issued 7.5 million additional shares to the public at approximately $33 per share in a seasoned new issue. In October 2002, when its shares were trading at about $22 per share, Activision executives announced that the company would spend up to $150 million to reacquire shares from investors. On January 8, 2003, the *Wall Street Journal* reported that several analysts were criticizing Activision's executives because the company had issued the shares to the public at a high price ($33) and then were offering to reacquire them at the going share market price, which was considerably lower than the issue price in 2002.

Required:

1. Do you think it was inappropriate for Activision to offer to reacquire the shares at a lower share price in October 2002?

2. Would your answer to question 1 be different if Activision had not issued additional shares in June 2002?

3. The *Wall Street Journal* article referred to above also reported that, in December 2002, Activision executives had purchased, for their own personal investment portfolios, 530,000 shares in the company at the then–current price of $13.32 per share. If you were an investor, how would you feel about executives buying shares in their own company?

4. Would your answer to question 3 be different if you also learned that the executives had disposed of nearly 2.5 million shares of Activision earlier in the year, when the price was at least $26.08 per share?

LO11-3   S11-5 **Ethical Decision Making: A Mini-Case**

You are the president of a very successful Internet company that has had a remarkably profitable year. You have determined that the company has more than $10 million in cash generated by operating activities and that it is not needed in the business. You are thinking about paying it out to shareholders as a special dividend. You discuss the idea with your vice–president, who reacts angrily to your suggestion:

> "Our share price has gone up by 200 percent in the last year alone. What more do we have to do for the owners? The people who really earned that money are the employees who have been working 12 hours a day, six or seven days a week to make the company successful. Most of them didn't even take vacations last year. I say we have to pay out bonuses and nothing extra for the shareholders."

As president, you know that you are hired by the board of directors, which is elected by the shareholders.

Required:

What is your responsibility to both groups? To which group would you give the $10 million? Why?

LO11-3   S11-6 **Critical Thinking: Making a Decision as an Investor**

You have retired after a long and successful career as a business executive and now spend a good portion of your time managing your retirement portfolio. You are considering three basic investment alternatives. You can invest in (*a*) corporate bonds paying 7 percent interest, (*b*) conservative shares that pay substantial dividends (typically 5 percent of the share price every year), and (*c*) growth–oriented technology shares that pay no dividends.

Required:

Analyze each of these alternatives and select one. Justify your selection.

LO11-1, 11-3   S11-7 **Charting Share Price Movement Around Important Announcement Dates**

Using the Internet, find either an earnings or dividend announcement for two different companies. Using a source such as bigcharts.com, determine the closing share price for each company for each day during the five business days before and after the announcement. Using a separate worksheet for each company, prepare a line chart of its share price movement.

Required:

Examine the charts for each company. Does the share price appear to change as a consequence of the announcements? Explain why or why not.

CONTINUING CASES

CC11-1 Accounting for Equity Financing

LO11-1, 11-2
11-3, 11-4, 11-2

Nicole has been financing Nicole's Getaway Spa (NGS) using equity financing. Currently, NGS has authorized 100,000 $0.30 preferred shares and 200,000 common shares. Outstanding shares include 50,000 preferred shares and 40,000 common shares.

Recently the following transactions have taken place.

a. NGS repurchased and cancelled 1,000 common shares for $10 a share.
b. NGS issued 1,000 preferred shares for $12 a share.
c. On November 12, the board of directors declared a cash dividend on each outstanding pre-ferred share.
d. The dividend was paid December 20.

Required:

1. Prepare the journal entries needed for each of the transactions.
2. If you were a common shareholder concerned about your voting rights, would you prefer Nicole to issue additional common shares or additional preferred shares? Why?
3. Describe the overall effect of each transaction on the assets, liabilities, and shareholders' equity of the company. (Use + for increase, − for decrease, and NE for no effect.)
4. How would each transaction affect the ROE ratio?

CC11-2 Wiki Art Gallery (WAG)

LO11-3, 11-5

Refer to the Wiki Art Gallery (WAG) instructional case in Appendix D and read the case in sufficient depth to answer the following questions.

1. Is there any evidence that Rob failed to follow generally accepted accounting principles when preparing WAG's 2011 and 2010 financial statements?
   a. Yes, dividends should have increased rather than decreased from 2010 to 2011.
   b. Yes, as a public company, WAG is required to report its price/earnings ratio.
   c. Yes, dividends should not be reported on the income statement.
   d. No, there were no violations of generally accepted accounting principles.
2. Stephen and Rob agreed to base their agreement on an "earnings multiplier." Which of the following is an alternative name for this concept?
   a. Earnings per share (EPS) ratio
   b. Return on equity (ROE) ratio
   c. Price/earnings (P/E) ratio
   d. None of the above

Endnotes

1. Supplement 11A near the end of this chapter discusses accounting for owners' equity in proprietorships, partnerships, and other business forms.
2. Although companies report their annual EPS numbers only at the end of their fiscal years, most analysts find it useful to update annual EPS as each quarter's results are reported. To do this, analysts will compute their own "trailing twelve months" (TTM) EPS measure by summing the most recent four quarters of EPS. This way, they can get a timely measure of year-long EPS without having to wait until the end of the fiscal year.
3. If a company has preferred shares outstanding, the ROE ratio can be adjusted to focus on the common shareholders' perspective. Simply deduct any preferred dividends from net income and exclude any preferred share accounts from the calculation of average shareholders' equity. This adjustment is not required in the case of Molson Coors Brewing Company because all its issued shares are common shares.

CHAPTER 12

THAT WAS

THEN

In the previous chapters, you learned about the income statement, statement of retained earnings, and balance sheet.

THIS IS

NOW

This chapter focuses on the fourth main financial statement—the statement of cash flows.

Statement of Cash Flows

ThamKC/Shutterstock.com

FOCUS COMPANY:

Under Armour, Inc.

www.underarmour.com

Have you ever studied your bank statements to see how much money you bring in and pay out during a typical month? You don't have to be a financial genius to know that if you spend more than you earn, your savings will quickly disappear, and you will need to get a loan or some other source of financing to see you through.

Most businesses face the same issues you do. In 2015, for example, Under Armour, Inc.—famous for its frictionless sportswear—paid more cash for its day-to-day operating activities than it brought in from selling its brand of clothing. To ensure the company's long-term survival, managers had to stay on top of this change in the cash situation. Fortunately, the company had saved a great deal of cash in prior years. Managers were also able to negotiate some new loans to keep the business from running out of cash. The company was also able to generate financing by issuing shares for cash.

Just like Under Armour's managers, investors and creditors also monitor a company's cash inflows and outflows. Investors want to know whether Under Armour is likely to pay dividends, and creditors want to know whether Under Armour is likely to pay them the amounts they are owed. The statement of cash flows provides them with the information necessary to make such predictions. Similar to your personal bank statement, the statement of cash flows reports changes in a company's cash situation.

Logo courtesy of Under Armour.

ORGANIZATION OF THE CHAPTER

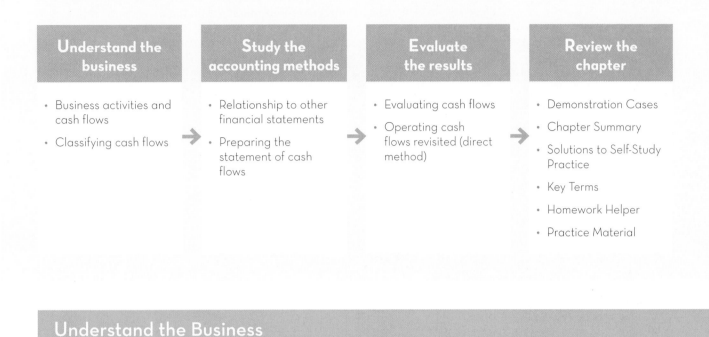

Understand the business	Study the accounting methods	Evaluate the results	Review the chapter
• Business activities and cash flows • Classifying cash flows	• Relationship to other financial statements • Preparing the statement of cash flows	• Evaluating cash flows • Operating cash flows revisited (direct method)	• Demonstration Cases • Chapter Summary • Solutions to Self-Study Practice • Key Terms • Homework Helper • Practice Material

Understand the Business

BUSINESS ACTIVITIES AND CASH FLOWS

So far in the course, we've analyzed business activities to identify their financial effects on assets, liabilities, shareholders' equity, revenues, and expenses. We've emphasized that business activities have financial effects even when they don't involve cash. That's why accrual accounting exists. When accurately reported, accrual—based net income is the best measure of a company's profitability during the period.

Despite its importance, net income is not what companies use when they pay wages, dividends, or loans. These activities require cash, so financial statement users need information about the company's cash and changes in its cash. Neither the balance sheet nor the income statement provides this information. The balance sheet shows a company's cash balance at a point in time, but it doesn't explain the activities that caused changes in its cash. Cash may have been generated by the company's day—to—day operations, by the sale of the company's buildings, or by the negotiation of new loans. The income statement doesn't explain changes in cash because it focuses just on the operating results of the business, excluding cash that is received or paid when taking out or paying down loans, issuing or buying the com—pany's own shares, and selling or investing in long—lived assets.

Also, the timing of cash receipts and payments may differ from the accrual—based income statement, which reports revenues when they are earned and expenses when they are incurred. Under Armour, for example, reported a hefty amount of net income in each quarter of 2015, yet its related cash flows were negative in all four of those quarters. Such differences between net income and cash flows are the reason that the Accounting Stan—dards for Private Enterprises (ASPE) and International Financial Reporting Standards (IFRS) require every company to report a statement of cash flows.

The statement of cash flows shows each major type of busi—ness activity that caused a company's cash to increase or decrease during the accounting period. For purposes of this statement, *cash* is defined to include cash and cash equivalents. As explained in Chapter 5,

LEARNING OBJECTIVE 12-1

Identify cash flows arising from operating, investing, and financing activities.

cash equivalents are short term, highly liquid investments purchased within three months of maturity. They are considered equivalent to cash because they are both (1) readily convertible to known amounts of cash and (2) so close to maturity that their value is unlikely to change.

SPOTLIGHT ON Ethics

Cash Isn't Estimated

Critics of accrual-based net income claim it can be manipulated because it relies on many estimates (of bad debts, inventory market values, assets' useful lives), but cash flows do not involve estimates so they are not easily manipulated. A cash balance changes only when cash has been received or paid.

One particularly dramatic illustration of the subjectivity of net income, but not cash, involved the bankruptcy of a department store chain operated by the W. T. Grant Company. Through biased estimates, the company reported net income for nine consecutive years then shocked everyone when it declared bankruptcy and shut down the following year. At the time, a statement of cash flows wasn't required. Had it been required, the company would have reported negative operating cash flows in seven of the previous ten years.

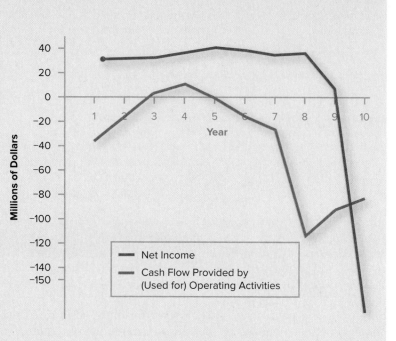

Source: James A. Largay, III, and Clyde P. Stickney, "Cash Flows, Ratio Analysis and the W. T. Grant Company Bankruptcy," *Financial Analysts Journal* 36:4, July/August 1980, pp. 51–54.

CLASSIFYING CASH FLOWS

The statement of cash flows requires that all cash inflows and outflows be classified according to how they relate to the company's operating, investing, or financing activities. This classification of cash flows is useful because most companies experience different cash flow patterns as they develop and mature.

Think back to Chapter 2 when Pizza Palace had just started. The first thing the owner needed to get his idea off the ground was financing, which he could then use to invest in assets that later would be needed to operate his business. At this early stage, financing and investing cash flows were crucial for Pizza Palace. For an established business, like Walmart in Chapter 6, operating activities often are the focus.

Financial statement users are interested in a company's ability to generate operating cash flows that will allow it to continue investing in additional assets and repay the financing it originally obtained. Creditors and investors will tolerate poor operating cash flows for only so long before they stop lending to or investing in the company. For any company to survive in the long run, the amount of cash generated through daily operating activities has to exceed the amount spent on them.

A condensed version of Under Armour's statement of cash flows is pre-sented in Exhibit 12.1. Don't worry about the details in the three cash flow categories yet. For now, focus on the categories' totals. Notice that each category can result in net cash inflows (represented by a positive number) or net cash outflows (in brackets to represent by a negative number). The sum of these three categories [$(100) + $(847) + $484 = $(463)] represents the overall change in cash on the balance sheet between the beginning and end of the period ($593 + $(463) = $130).

EXHIBIT 12.1	Under Armour's Condensed Statement of Cash Flows

UNDER ARMOUR, INC. Statement of Cash Flows For the Year Ended December 31, 2015		Explanations
(in millions)		
Cash Flows from Operating Activities		Cash flows related to day–to–day activities
Net income	$233	Assume net income (NI) generates cash inflow
Depreciation	23	Depreciation decreased NI but didn't decrease cash
Changes in current assets and current liabilities	(356)	Differences in the timing of net income and cash flows
Net cash used in operating activities	(100)	Indicates overall cash impact of operating activities
Cash Flows Used in Investing Activities		Cash flows related to long–term assets
Purchase of equipment	(256)	Cash was used to purchase equipment
Purchase of intangible and other assets	(591)	Cash was used to purchase intangibles
Net cash used in investing activities	(847)	Indicates overall cash impact of investing activities
Cash Flows from Financing Activities		Cash flows from transactions with lenders, investors
Additional borrowings of long–term debt	665	Cash received from borrowing
Payments on long–term debt	(266)	Cash used to repay amounts previously borrowed
Proceeds from share issuance	85	Cash received from issuing shares
Net cash provided by financing activities	484	Indicates overall cash impact of financing activities
Net Change in Cash and Cash Equivalents	(463)	$(100) + $(847) + 484 = (463)
Cash and cash equivalents, beginning of year	593	Cash balance at beginning of the period
Cash and cash equivalents, end of year	$130	Cash balance at end of the period (on balance sheet)

Under Armour's cash flows in Exhibit 12.1 show that the company's day–to–day operational cash outflows were greater than the company's day–to–day operational cash inflows by $100 million. Under Armour invested $847 million in additional long–term assets, financed by prior year cash balances and the $484 million of net cash inflow from financing activities. To learn the specific causes of these cash flows, you would consider the details of each category, as we will do now.

Operating Activities

Cash flows from operating activities (or cash flows from operations) are the cash inflows and outflows related directly to the revenues and expenses reported on the income statement. Operating activities involve day–to–day business activities with customers, suppliers, employees, landlords, and others. Typical cash flows from operating activities include the following:

Cash flows from operating activities (cash flows from operations): Cash inflows and outflows related to components of net income. Also called *cash flows from operations*.

Inflows	Outflows
Cash provided by	Cash used for
Collecting from customers	Purchasing services (electricity, etc.) and goods for resale
Receiving dividends	Paying salaries and wages
Receiving interest	Paying income taxes
	Paying interest

The difference between these cash inflows and outflows is reported on the statement of cash flows as a subtotal, Net Cash Provided by (Used for) Operating Activities.

Investing Activities

Cash flows from investing activities: Cash inflows and outflows related to the sale or purchase of investments and long-lived assets.

Cash flows from investing activities are the cash inflows and outflows related to the purchase and disposal of investments, such as securities, and long–lived assets. Typical cash flows from investing activities include:

Inflows	Outflows
Cash provided by	*Cash used for*
Sale or disposal of property, plant, and equipment	Purchase of property, plant, and equipment
Sale or maturity of investments in securities	Purchase of investments in securities

The difference between these cash inflows and outflows is reported on the statement of cash flows as a subtotal, Net Cash Provided by (Used in) Investing Activities.

Financing Activities

Cash flows from financing activities: Cash inflows and outflows related to financing sources external to the company (owners and lenders).

Cash flows from financing activities include exchanges of cash with shareholders and cash exchanges with lenders (for principal on loans). Common cash flows from financing activities include:

Inflows	Outflows
Cash provided by	*Cash used for*
Borrowing from lenders through formal debt contracts	Repaying principal to lenders
Issuing shares to owners	Repurchasing shares from owners
	Paying cash dividends to owners

The difference between these cash inflows and outflows is reported on the statement of cash flows as a subtotal, Net Cash Provided by (Used in) Financing Activities.

One way to classify cash flows into operating, investing, and financing categories is to think about the balance sheet accounts to which the cash flows relate. Although exceptions exist, a general rule is that operating cash flows cause changes in current assets and current liabilities, investing cash flows affect non–current assets, and financing cash flows affect non–current liabilities or shareholders' equity accounts.[1] Exhibit 12.2 shows how this general rule relates the

EXHIBIT 12.2 Relationships Between Classified Balance Sheet and Statement of Cash Flows (SCF) Categories

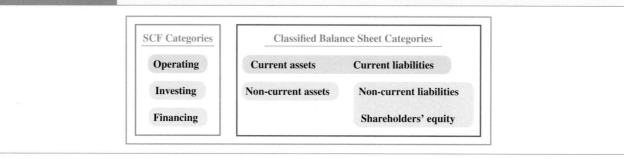

Self-Study Practice 12.1

Brunswick Corporation produces the Life Fitness line of gym equipment. A listing of some of its cash flows follows. Indicate whether each item is disclosed in the operating activities (O), investing activities (I), or financing activities (F) section of the statement of cash flows.

☐ 1. Shares issued to shareholders

☐ 2. Collections from customers

☐ 3. Interest paid on debt

☐ 4. Purchase of plant and equipment

☐ 5. Purchase of investment securities

☐ 6. Cash dividends paid

After you have finished, check your answers with the solution, which follows the chapter summary.

SPOTLIGHT ON The World

Classification Choices Under IFRS

To create consistency across companies, ASPE restricts interest and dividend classifications to a single category. IFRS, on the other hand, allows managers to choose between categories, as follows:

	Company Pays		Company Receives	
	Dividends	Interest	Dividends	Interest
ASPE	F	O	O	O
IFRS	O, F	O, F	O, I	O, I

ASPE classifies dividends paid as *financing* because they are transactions with shareholders. IFRS allows dividends paid to be classified as *operating* to assist users in determining the company's ability to pay dividends out of operating cash flows. ASPE requires the other three items to be classified as *operating* because they enter into the determination of net income. IFRS allows interest paid to be classified as *financing* because it is a cost of obtaining financial resources. IFRS allows interest and dividends received to be classified as *investing* because they are returns on investments.

three sections of the statement of cash flows (SCF) to each of the main sections of a classified balance sheet.

Study the Accounting Methods

RELATIONSHIP TO OTHER FINANCIAL STATEMENTS

The statement of cash flows is intended to provide a cash–based view of a company's business activities during the accounting period. It uses the same transactions that have been reported in the income statement and balance sheet but converts them from the accrual basis to a cash basis. This conversion involves analyzing the income statement and the changes in balance sheet accounts, and relating these changes to the three cash flow categories. To prepare a statement of cash flows, you need the following:

1. **Comparative balance sheets,** showing beginning and ending balances, used in calculating the cash flows from all activities (operating, investing, and financing).

2. **A complete income statement,** used primarily in calculating cash flows from operating activities.

3. **Additional data** concerning selected accounts that increase and decrease as a result of investing and/or financing activities.

The approach to preparing the cash flow statement focuses on changes in the balance sheet accounts. It relies on a simple rearrangement of the balance sheet equation.

Assets = Liabilities + Shareholders' Equity

First, assets can be split into cash and all other assets, which we'll call **non–cash assets:**

Cash + Non-cash Assets = Liabilities + Shareholders' Equity

If we move the non–cash assets to the right side of the equation, we get the following:

Cash = Liabilities + Shareholders' Equity = Non-cash Assets

Given this relationship, the changes in cash between the beginning and end of the period must equal the changes in the amounts on the right side of the equation between the beginning and end of the period:

Change in Cash = Change in (Liabilities + Shareholders' Equity − Non-cash Assets)

This equation says that changes in cash must be accompanied by and can be accounted for by the changes in liabilities, shareholders' equity, and non–cash assets.

PREPARING THE STATEMENT OF CASH FLOWS

Based on the idea that the change in cash equals the sum of the changes in all other balance sheet accounts, we use the following steps to prepare the statement of cash flows:

 Determine the change in each balance sheet account. From this year's ending balance, subtract this year's beginning balance (i.e., last year's ending balance).

Identify the cash flow category or categories to which each account relates. Use Exhibit 12.2 as a guide, but be aware that some accounts may include two categories of cash flows. Retained Earnings, for example, can include both financing cash flows (paying dividends) and operating cash flows (generating net income). Similarly, Accumulated Depreciation can be affected by operating activities (depreciation for using equipment in daily operations) as well as investing activities (disposing of equipment).

③ Create schedules that summarize operating, investing, and financing cash flows. Let's start with operating cash flows.

Direct and Indirect Reporting of Operating Cash Flows

Two alternative methods may be used when presenting the operating activities section of the statement of cash flows.

1. The **direct method** reports the total cash inflow or outflow from each main type of transaction (i.e., transactions with customers, suppliers, employees, etc.). The difference between these cash inflows and outflows equals the Net Cash Provided by (Used in) Operating Activities.

2. The **indirect method** starts with net income from the income statement and adjusts it by eliminating the effects of items that do not involve cash (e.g., depreciation) and including items that do have cash effects. Adjusting net income for these items yields the amount of Net Cash Provided by (Used in) Operating Activities.

Direct method: Reports the components of cash flows from operating activities as gross receipts and gross payments.

Indirect method: Presents the operating activities section of the cash flow statement by adjusting net income to compute cash flows from operating activities.

Direct Method		Indirect Method	
Cash collected from customers	$3,809		
Cash paid to suppliers of inventory	(2,312)		
Cash paid to employees and suppliers of services	(1,421)	Net income	$233
Cash paid for interest	(22)	Depreciation	23
Cash paid for income tax	(154)	Changes in current assets and current liabilities	(356)
Net cash provided by (used in) operating activities	$ (100)	Net cash provided by (used in) operating activities	$(100)

The point to remember about the direct and indirect methods is that they are simply different ways to arrive at the same number. Net cash flows provided by (used in) operating activities are always the same under the direct and indirect methods. Also, the choice between the two methods affects only the operating activities section of the statement of cash flows, not the investing and financing sections.

EXHIBIT 12.3 Information for Preparing a Statement of Cash Flows

Current assets you have less cash

UNDER ARMOUR, INC.
Balance Sheet*

(in millions)	Dec. 31, 2015	Dec. 31, 2014		Change	Related Cash Flow Section
			Step ①		Step ②
Assets					
Current Assets:					
Cash and Cash Equivalents	$ 130	$593		−463	Cash
Accounts Receivable	434	280		+154	O
Inventories	783	537		+246	O
Prepaid Expenses	152	139		+13	O
Total Current Assets	1,499	1,549			
Equipment	626	370		+256	I
Less: Accumulated Depreciation	(87)	(64)		−23	O (Note 2 below implies not I.)
Intangible and Other Assets	831	240		+591	I
Total Assets	$2,869	$2,095			
Liabilities and Shareholders' Equity					
Current Liabilities:					
Accounts Payable	$ 201	$210		−9	O
Accrued Liabilities	278	212		+66	O
Total Current Liabilities	479	422			
Long−Term Debt	722	323		+399	F
Total Liabilities	1,201	745			
Shareholders' Equity:					
Contributed Capital	579	494		+85	F
Retained Earnings	1,089	856		+233	O (Note 1 below implies not F.)
Total Shareholders' Equity	1,668	1,350			
Total Liabilities and Shareholders' Equity	$2,869	$2,095			

Current liabilities you have less cash

UNDER ARMOUR, INC.
Income Statement*
For the Year Ended December 31, 2015

(in millions)	
Net Sales	$3,963
Cost of Goods Sold	2,057
Gross Profit	1,906
Operating Expenses:	
Selling, General, and Administrative Expenses	1,474
Depreciation Expense	23
Total Operating Expenses	1,497
Income from Operations	409
Interest Expense	22
Net Income before Income Tax Expense	387
Income Tax Expense	154
Net Income	$ 233

Additional data

1. No dividends were declared or paid.
2. No disposals or impairments of equip−ment or intangibles occurred.
3. Equipment costing $256 million and intangibles and Other Asset costing $591 million were purchased with cash.
4. Long−term debt of $266 million was repaid and $665 million in new loans was issued.
5. Shares were issued for $85 million.

*Certain balances have been adjusted to simplify the presentation.

Direct versus Indirect Method Presentation

ASPE and IFRS currently allow companies to use either the direct or indirect method. The Financial Accounting Standards Board (FASB) and the International Accounting Standards Board (IASB) have spoken in the past about removing this choice and allowing only the direct method, because the direct method is more detailed and shows the operating cash receipts and cash payments. This is consistent with the objective of a cash flow statement. However, the indirect method shows the reconciliation of accrual income to cash flows from operations, which is an advantage over the direct method. If this proposal were to be adopted, it would significantly change the way companies report their statement of cash flows. Currently, about 99 percent of large Canadian companies, including Bombardier, use the indirect method.

We focus on the indirect method in the following section because it is currently the most commonly used method in Canada. The direct method is presented in the last section of this chapter.

Determining Operating Cash Flows Using the Indirect Method

When using the indirect method, the schedule of operating activities has the following format. We explain each of these items below and then, in Under Armour's Operating Cash Flows—Indirect Method, we demonstrate how to use Under Armour's information in Exhibit 12.3 to create such a schedule.

Net income
Items included in net income that do not involve cash
   +Depreciation
   + Losses on disposal of long–term assets or retirement of long–term debt
   −Gains on disposal of long–term assets or retirement of long–term debt
Changes in current assets and current liabilities
   +Decreases in current assets
   −Increases in current assets
   −Decreases in current liabilities
   +Increases in current liabilities

Net cash flow provided by (used in) operating activities

Net income. When preparing a schedule to determine operating cash flows using the indirect method, start with net income as reported on the last line of the company's income statement. By starting with net income, it's as if we are assuming all revenues resulted in cash inflows and all expenses resulted in cash outflows. But we know this is not true, so we adjust net income to eliminate items that are included in net income but do not involve cash and to include items that were excluded from net income but do involve cash.

+ Depreciation. When initially recording depreciation in the accounting system, we increase Depreciation Expense (with a debit) and increase Accumulated Depreciation (with a credit). Notice that depreciation does not involve cash. To eliminate the effect of having deducted Depreciation Expense in the income statement, we add it back in the statement of cash flows.

+Losses on disposal of long—term assets and retirement of long—term debt. — Gains on disposal of long—term assets and retirement of long—term debt. When long—term assets are disposed of and when long—term debt has been retired early, a corresponding loss or gain can result from these transactions. The amount of the loss is reported on the income statement and reduces the amount of net income the company would have otherwise reported. The amount of the gain is also reported on the income statement and increases the amount of net income the company would have otherwise reported. However, this loss or gain amount is not usually the same as the cash flow that resulted from the transaction.

The actual cash flow is the cash proceeds received on the disposal of the long—term asset or the cash payment paid to retire the long—term debt. Therefore we need to eliminate the effect of having incurred the loss or gain by adding back the loss or subtracting the gain in the statement of cash flows. Then we can properly deal with the cash proceeds received on the disposal of the long—term asset in the investing section of the cash flow statement, and the cash payment to retire the long—term debt is dealt with in the financing section of the cash flow statement. Supplement 12A later in this chapter explains in more detail how these transactions affect the statement of cash flows.

+Decreases in current assets. Adding decreases in current assets serves two purposes. First, it eliminates the effects of some transactions that decreased net income but did not affect cash in the current period. For example, when Supplies are used, net income decreases but cash is not affected. To eliminate these non—cash effects from our cash flow computations, we must add back decreases in Supplies and other current assets. Second, adding decreases in current assets allows us to include the cash effects of other transactions that did not affect net income in the current period but did increase cash. For example, Cash increases when Accounts Receivable are collected. These cash inflows are captured by adding the amount by which this current asset had decreased.

— Increases in current assets. Subtracting increases in current assets similarly serves two purposes. First, it eliminates the effects of transactions that increased net income but did not affect cash in the current period. For example, net income increases when a company provides services on account, but cash is not affected. We eliminate these non—cash effects by subtracting increases in current assets. Second, subtracting increases in current assets allows us to include the cash effects of other transactions that did not affect net income in the current period but did decrease cash. For example, Cash decreases when a company prepays its insurance or rent, but net income isn't affected until these assets are used up. The cash outflows can be captured by subtracting the increase in these current assets.

— Decreases in current liabilities. Subtracting decreases in current liabilities serves two purposes. First, it eliminates the effects of transactions that increased net income but did not affect cash. For example, a company decreases Deferred Revenue and increases net income in the current period when it fulfills its prior obligations to provide services, but cash is not affected. To eliminate these non—cash effects, we subtract decreases in current liabilities. Second, subtracting decreases in current liabilities allows us to include the cash effects of other transactions that did not affect net income in the current period but did decrease cash. For example, Cash decreases when a company pays wages that were incurred and expensed in a previous period. These cash outflows are captured by subtracting decreases in current liabilities.

+ Increases in current liabilities. Adding increases in current liabilities serves two purposes. First, it eliminates the effects of transactions that decreased net income but did not affect cash. For example, when interest is accrued, a company decreases net income but its cash is not affected. To eliminate these non–cash effects, we add back increases in current liabilities. Second, adding increases in current liabilities allows us to include the cash effects of other transactions that did not affect net income in the current period but did increase cash. For example, Cash and Deferred Revenue increase when the company receives cash in advance of providing services. Adding the increase in current liabilities captures these cash inflows.

Under Armour's Operating Cash Flows—Indirect Method

The preceding approach to preparing an operating cash flow schedule can be applied to Under Armour's information in Exhibit 12.3. We start by calculating the changes in all balance sheet accounts (in Step ❶) and classifying whether the changes involve operating (O), investing (I), and/ or financing (F) activities (in Step ❷). Cash is not classified as O, I, or F because the change in Cash is reported at the bottom of the statement of cash flows rather than within its three sections. Next, we use the amount of the change in each account marked by an O in Exhibit 12.3 to complete Step ❸, which involves preparing an operating cash flow schedule for Under Armour (in Exhibit 12.4).

Understanding the causes of increases or decreases in each current asset and current liability is the key to understanding the logic behind the items in the schedule. Look at Exhibit 12.4 right now, and then take your time reading the following explanations and make sure you understand the reasons for each item.

| EXHIBIT 12.4 | Under Armour's Schedule of Operating Cash Flows ❸ |

Item	Amount (in millions)	Explanation
Net income	$ 233	Starting point, from the income statement
Items included in net income that do not involve cash		
+ Depreciation	23	Depreciation is a non–cash expense
Changes in current assets and current liabilities		
–Increase in Accounts Receivable	(154)	Cash collections less than sales on account
–Increase in Inventories	(246)	Purchases are more than cost of goods
–Increase in Prepaid Expenses	(13)	Prepayments greater than related expenses
–Decrease in Accounts Payable	(9)	Payments to suppliers less than purchases
+Increase in Accrued Liabilities	66	Cash payments less than accrued expenses
Net cash flow provided by (used in) operating activities	$(100)	Overall increase in cash from operations

Net Income + Depreciation. Net income and depreciation are always the first two lines to appear in a statement of cash flows prepared using the indirect method. They begin the process of converting net income to operating cash flows. They also begin the process of explaining the change in Cash by accounting for changes in the other balance sheet accounts. In the case of Under Armour, the $233 million of net income fully accounts for the change in Retained Earnings (the company had no dividends). Similarly, the $23 million of depreciation accounts for the change in Accumulated Depreciation (the company had no disposals).[2]

COACH'S TIP

The depreciation add-back is not intended to suggest that depreciation creates an increase in cash. Rather, it just shows that depreciation does not cause a decrease in cash. This is a subtle, but very important, difference in interpretation.

Increase in Accounts Receivable.   Accounts Receivable increases when sales are made on account and it decreases when cash is collected from customers. An overall increase in this account, then, implies that cash collections were less than sales on account. To convert from the higher sales number that is included in net income to the lower cash collected from customers, we subtract the difference ($154 million).

Another way to remember whether to add or subtract the difference is to think about whether the overall change in the account balance is explained by a debit or credit. If the change in the account is explained by a credit, the adjustment in the cash flow schedule is reported like a cor—responding debit to cash (added). In Under Armour's case, the increase in Accounts Receivable is explained by a debit, so the adjustment in the cash flow schedule is reported like a credit to cash (a decrease), as follows:

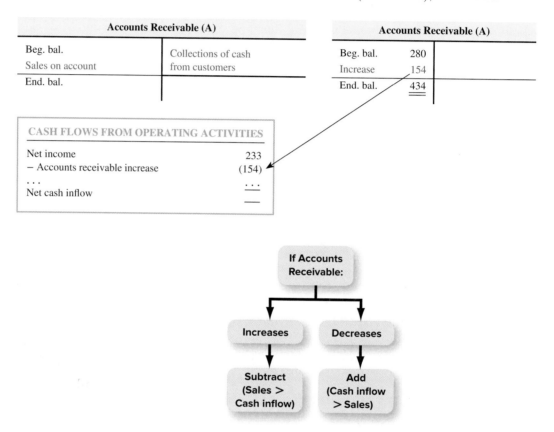

Increase in Inventory.   The income statement reports the cost of goods sold during the period, but cash flow from operating activities must report cash purchases of inventory. As shown in the T—account below, purchases of goods increase the balance in inventory, and recording cost of goods sold (COGS) decreases the balance in inventory.

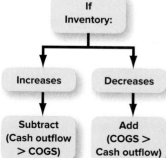

Inventories (A)	
Beg. bal.	
Purchases	Cost of goods sold
End. bal.	

Inventories (A)	
Beg. bal.	537
Increase	246
End. bal.	783

Under Armour's $246 million inventory increase means that the amount of cash outflow for inventory purchases is more than the cost of goods sold. The increase due to purchases must be subtracted from net income to convert to cash flow from operating activities in Exhibit 12.4. (A decrease would be added.)

Increase in Prepaid Expenses.   The income statement reports expenses of the period, but cash flow from operating activities must reflect the cash payments. Cash prepayments increase the balance in prepaid expenses, and recording of expenses decreases the balance in prepaid expenses.

Prepaid Expenses (A)	
Beg. bal.	
Cash prepayments	Used–up (expensed)
End. bal.	

Prepaid Expenses (A)		
Beg. bal.	139	
Increase	13	
End. bal.	152	

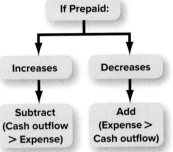

If Prepaid:
Increases → Subtract (Cash outflow > Expense)
Decreases → Add (Expense > Cash outflow)

Under Armour's $13 million increase in Prepaid Expenses means that cash prepayments this period were more than expenses. These extra cash prepayments must be subtracted in Exhibit 12.4. (A decrease would be added.)

Decrease in Accounts Payable.   Cash flow from operations must reflect cash purchases, but not all purchases are for cash. Purchases on account increase Accounts Payable, and cash paid to suppliers decreases Accounts Payable.

Accounts Payable (L)	
	Beg. bal.
Cash payments	Purchases on account
	End. bal.

Accounts Payable (L)		
	Beg. bal.	210
Decrease	9	
	End. bal.	201

If Accounts Payable:
Decreases → Subtract (Cash outflow > Purchases)
Increases → Add (Purchases > Cash outflow)

Accounts Payable decreased by $9 million, which means that cash payments to suppliers were greater than purchases on account. Thus, to show the higher cash outflow, the decrease in Accounts Payable must be subtracted in Exhibit 12.4. (An increase would be added.)

Increase in Accrued Liabilities.   The income statement reports all accrued expenses, but the cash flow statement must reflect only the actual payments for expenses. Recording accrued expenses increases the balance in Accrued Liabilities, and cash payments for the expenses decreases Accrued Liabilities.

Accrued Liabilities (L)	
	Beg. bal.
Cash payments	Accrued expenses
	End. bal.

Accrued Liabilities (L)		
	Beg. bal.	212
	Increase	66
	End. bal.	278

If Accrued Liabilities:
Decreases → Subtract (Cash outflow > Accruals)
Increases → Add (Accruals > Cash outflow)

Under Armour's Accrued Liabilities increased by $66 million, which indicates that more expenses were accrued than paid. Consequently, this difference (representing less cash paid) must be added back in Exhibit 12.4. (A decrease would be subtracted.)

By scanning Exhibit 12.3, you can see that you have now considered the changes in all balance sheet accounts that relate to operating activities (marked by the letter O). The last step in determining the net cash flow provided by (used in) operating activities is to calculate a total. As shown in Exhibit 12.4, the combined effects of all operating cash flows are a net outflow of $100 million.

Now that you have seen how to compute operating cash flows using the indirect method, take a moment to complete the following Self–Study Practice.

HOW'S IT GOING?

Self-Study Practice 12.2

Indicate whether the following items taken from Brunswick Corporation's cash flow statement would be added (+), subtracted (−), or not included (NA) in the reconciliation of net income to cash flow from operations using the direct method.

☐ 1. Decrease in inventories

☐ 2. Increase in accounts payable

☐ 3. Depreciation expense

☐ 4. Increase in accounts receivable

☐ 5. Increase in accrued liabilities

☐ 6. Increase in prepaid expenses

After you have finished, check your answers with the solution, which follows the chapter summary.

Under Armour's Investing Cash Flow Calculations

LEARNING OBJECTIVE 12-3

Report cash flows from investing activities.

To prepare the investing section of the statement of cash flows, you must analyze accounts related to long–lived tangible and intangible assets.[3] Unlike the analysis of operating activities, where you were concerned only with the *net* change in selected balance sheet accounts, an analysis of investing (and financing) activities requires that you identify and separately report the causes of *both* increases and decreases in account balances. The following examples are the ones that you will encounter most frequently:

Related Balance Sheet Accounts	Investing Activity	Cash Flow Effect
Property, Plant, and Equipment	Purchase of property, plant, and equipment for cash	Outflow
	Sale of property, plant, and equipment for cash	Inflow
Intangible Assets	Purchase of intangible assets	Outflow
	Sale of intangible assets	Inflow

Under Armour's balance sheet (Exhibit 12.3) shows two investing assets (noted with an I) that changed during the year: Equipment, and Intangible and Other Assets.

Equipment. To determine the cause of the change in the Equipment account, accountants would examine the detailed accounting records for equipment. Purchases of equipment increase the account, and disposals of equipment decrease it. The additional data in Exhibit 12.3 indicates that Under Armour purchased equipment for $256 million cash. This purchase is a cash outflow, which we subtract in the schedule of investing activities in Exhibit 12.5. In our example, this purchase fully accounts for the change in the Equipment balance, as shown in the Equipment T–account. Thus, we

EXHIBIT 12.5 — Under Armour's Schedule of Investing Cash Flows ③

Item	Amount (in millions)	Explanation
Purchase of equipment	$ (256)	Payment of cash for equipment
Purchase of intangible and other assets	(591)	Payment of cash for intangibles
Net cash provided by (used in) investing activities	(847)	Subtotal for the statement of cash flows

can assume that Under Armour did not dispose of any equipment during the year. Supplement 12A explains how disposals of property, plant, and equipment affect the statement of cash flows.

Equipment (A)			
Beg. bal.	370		
Purchases	256	Disposals	0
End. bal.	626		

Intangible and Other Assets.   A similar approach is used to determine cash flows associated with intangible assets. Analysis of Under Armour's detailed records indicates that the company did not have any reductions in its intangible assets as a result of disposals, impairments, or amortization during the year. However, Under Armour did purchase intangible assets for $591 million cash, as noted in the additional data in Exhibit 12.3. This cash outflow is subtracted in the schedule of investing activities in Exhibit 12.5.

Under Armour's Financing Cash Flow Calculations

This section of the cash flow statement includes changes in liabilities owed to owners (Dividends Payable) and financial institutions (Notes Payable and other types of debt), as well as changes in shareholders' equity accounts. Interest is considered an operating activity, so it is excluded from financing cash flows. The following examples are the ones that you will encounter most often:

LEARNING OBJECTIVE 12-4

Report cash flows from financing activities.

Related Balance Sheet Accounts	Financing Activity	Cash Flow Effect
Notes Payable	Borrowing cash from banks or other financial institutions	Inflow
	Repayment of loan principal	Outflow
Bonds Payable	Issuance of bonds for cash	Inflow
	Repayment of bond face value	Outflow
Contributed Capital	Issuance of shares for cash	Inflow
	Repurchase of shares with cash	Outflow
Retained Earnings	Payment of cash dividends	Outflow

To compute cash flows from financing activities, you should review changes in all debt and shareholders' equity accounts. Increases and decreases must be identified and reported separately. Under Armour's balance sheet in Exhibit 12.3 indicates that Long-Term Debt and Contributed Capital changed during the period as a result of financing cash flows (noted with an F).

COACH'S TIP

Dividends paid are financing cash flows. Dividends received, however, are operating cash flows.

Long-Term Debt. The additional data in Exhibit 12.3 indicates that Long–Term Debt was affected by both cash inflows and outflows, as shown in the T–account below. These cash flows are reported separately in the schedule of financing activities shown in Exhibit 12.6.

Long–term Debt (L)			
		Beg. bal.	323
Repayments	266	Borrowings	665
		End. bal.	722

Contributed Capital. Under Armour did not repurchase shares during the year, but it did issue shares for $85 million cash. This share issuance fully accounts for the change in Contributed Capital, as shown in the following T–account. This cash inflow is listed in the schedule of financing activities in Exhibit 12.6.

Contributed Capital (SE)	
Beg. bal.	494
Shares issued	85
End. bal.	579

COACH'S TIP

If you have difficulty remembering the order in which to report operating (O), investing (I), and financing (F) cash flows, say to yourself, "O, IF only I could remember!"

Retained Earnings. Net income increases Retained Earnings and any div–idends declared decrease Retained Earnings. Net income has already been accounted for as an operating cash flow. In Under Armour's case, no dividends were declared or paid in 2015 (see the additional notes in Exhibit 12.3). As shown in the following T–account, dividends would have decreased Retained Earnings if they had been declared; their payment would have been reported as a cash outflow in the financing section of the statement of cash flows.

Retained Earnings (SE)			
		Beg. bal.	856
Dividends	0	Net income	233
		End. bal.	1,089

EXHIBIT 12.6	Under Armour's Schedule of Financing Cash Flows ③

Item	Amount (in millions)	Explanation
Additional borrowings of long–term debt	$665	Cash received when new loan obtained
Payments on long–term debt	(266)	Cash paid on loan principal
Proceeds from share issuance	85	Cash received from shareholders for new shares
Net cash provided by financing activities	484	Subtotal for the statement of cash flows

Under Armour's Statement of Cash Flows

Now that you have determined the cash flows for the three main types of business activities in Exhibits 12.4, 12.5, and 12.6, you can prepare the statement of cash flows in a proper format. Exhibit 12.7 shows the state–ment of cash flows for Under Armour using the indirect method. Notice that the $463 million subtotal for Net increase (decrease) in cash and cash equivalents combines cash flows from operating, investing, and financing activities to produce an overall net change in cash. This net change is added to the beginning cash balance to arrive at the ending cash balance, which is the same cash balance as reported on the balance sheet.

EXHIBIT 12.7	Under Armour's Statement of Cash Flows (Indirect Method)

UNDER ARMOUR, INC.
Statement of Cash Flows*
For the Year Ended December 31, 2015

(in millions)	
Cash Flows from Operating Activities	
Net income	$233
Adjustments to reconcile net income to net cash provided by operating activities:	
Depreciation	23
Changes in current assets and current liabilities	
Accounts Receivable	(154)
Inventories	(246)
Prepaid Expenses	(13)
Accounts Payable	(9)
Accrued Liabilities	66
Net cash provided by (used in) operating activities	(100)
Cash Flows from Investing Activities	
Purchase of equipment	(256)
Purchase of intangible and other assets	(591)
Net cash provided by (used in) investing activities	(847)
Cash Flows from Financing Activities	
Additional borrowings of long–term debt	665
Payments on long–term debt	(266)
Proceeds from share issuance	85
Net cash provided by (used in) financing activities	484
Net increase (decrease) in cash and cash equivalents	(463)
Cash and cash equivalents at beginning of period	593
Cash and cash equivalents at end of period	$130
Supplemental Disclosures	
Cash paid for interest	$ 22
Cash paid for income tax	154

*Certain amounts have been adjusted to simplify the presentation.

COACH'S TIP

When doing homework problems, assume that all changes in non-current account balances are caused by cash transactions (unless the problem also describes changes caused by non-cash investing and financing activities).

Supplemental Disclosures. In addition to their cash flows, all companies are required to report material investing and financing transactions that did not have cash flow effects (called non–cash investing and financing activities). For example, the purchase of a

$10,000 piece of equipment with a $10,000 note payable to the supplier does not cause either an inflow or an outflow of cash. As a result, these activities are not listed in the three main sections of the statement of cash flows. This important information is normally presented for users in a supplementary schedule to the statement of cash flows or in the financial statement notes. Supplementary information must also disclose (for companies using the indirect method) the amount of cash paid for interest and for income taxes. An example of this disclosure is shown at the bottom of Exhibit 12.7.

Evaluate the Results

Unlike the income statement, which summarizes its detailed information in one number (net income), the statement of cash flows does not provide a summary measure of cash flow performance. Instead, it must be evaluated in terms of the cash flow pattern suggested by the subtotals of each of the three main sections. As we discussed at the beginning of this chapter, expect different patterns of cash flows from operating, investing, and financing activities, depending on how well established a company is. An established, healthy company will show positive cash flows from operations, which are sufficiently large to pay for replacing existing property, plant, and equipment, and to pay dividends to shareholders. Any additional cash (called free cash flow) can be used in the future to (1) expand the business through additional investing activities, (2) repay existing financing, or (3) simply build up the company's cash balance. After considering where the company stands in relation to this big picture, you should then look at the details within each of the three sections.

EVALUATING CASH FLOWS

Cash Flows from Operating Activities

The operating activities section indicates how well a company is able to generate cash internally through its operations and management of current assets and current liabilities. Most analysts believe this is the most important section of the statement because, in the long run, operations are the only continuing source of cash. Investors will not invest in a company if they do not believe that cash generated from operations will be available to pay dividends or expand the company. Similarly, creditors will not lend money or extend credit if they believe that cash generated from operations will be insufficient to repay them.

When evaluating the operating activities section of the statement of cash flows, consider the absolute amount of cash flow (is it positive or negative?), keeping in mind that operating cash flows have to be positive over the long run for a company to be successful. Also, look at the relationship between operating cash flows and net income.

All other things equal, when net income and operating cash flows are similar, there is a likelihood that revenues are realized in cash and that expenses are associated with cash outflows. Any major deviations should be investigated. In some cases, a deviation may be nothing to worry about, but in others, it could be the first sign of big problems to come. Four potential causes of deviations to consider include the following:

1. **Seasonality.** As in Under Armour's case, seasonal variations in sales and inventory levels can cause the relationship between net income

and cash flow from operations to fluctuate from one quarter to the next. Usually this isn't a cause for alarm.

2. **The corporate life cycle (growth in sales).** New companies often experience rapid sales growth. When sales are increasing, accounts receivable and inventory normally increase faster than the cash flows being collected from sales. This often causes oper-ating cash flows to be lower than the related net income. This isn't a big deal, provided that the company can obtain cash from financing activities until operating activities begin to generate more positive cash flows.

3. **Changes in revenue and expense recognition.** Most cases of fraudulent financial reporting involve aggressive revenue recogni-tion (recording revenues before they are earned) or delayed expense recognition (failing to report expenses when they are incurred). Both of these tactics cause net income to increase in the current period, making it seem as though the company has improved its performance. Neither of these tactics, though, affects cash flows from operating activities. As a result, if revenue and expense rec-ognition policies are changed to boost net income, cash flow from operations will be significantly lower than net income, providing one of the first clues that the financial statements might contain errors or fraud.

4. **Changes in working capital management.** Working capital is a measure of the amount by which current assets exceed current liabilities. If a company's current assets (such as accounts receivable and inventories) are allowed to grow out of control, its operating cash flows will decrease. More efficient management will have the opposite effect. To investigate this potential cause more closely, use the inventory and accounts receivable turnover ratios covered in Chapters 7 and 8.

SPOTLIGHT ON Business Decisions

Lehman Brothers' Operating Cash Flows and the Financial Crisis

Lehman Brothers Holdings, Inc. was one of the largest and most profitable financial services com-panies in the world. But cash flow and working capital management problems led to the company's bankruptcy only a month before the stock market crash of 2008. The following comparison of Lehman's net income and net operating cash flows reveals the company's problems:

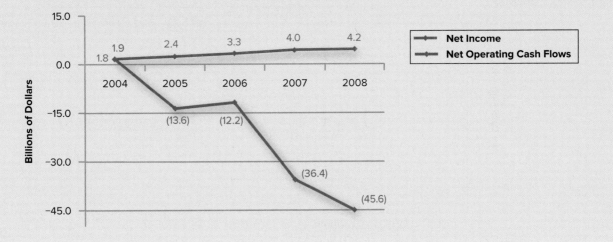

Cash Flows from Investing Activities

Although it might seem counterintuitive at first, healthy companies tend to show negative cash flows in the investing section of the statement of cash flows. A negative total for this section means the company is spending more to acquire new long–term assets than it is taking in from selling its existing long–term assets. That's normal for any healthy, growing company. In fact, if you see a positive total cash flow in the investing activities section, you should be concerned because it could mean the company is selling off its long–term assets just to generate cash inflows. If a company sells off too many long–term assets, it may not have a sufficient base to continue running its business effectively, which would likely lead to further decline in the future.

Cash Flows from Financing Activities

Unlike the operating and investing activities sections, where a healthy company typically shows positive and negative cash flows, respectively, the financing activities section does not have an obvious expected direction for cash flows. For example, a healthy company that is growing rapidly could need financing cash inflows to fund its expansion. In this case, the company could take out new loans or issue new shares, both of which would result in positive net cash flows from financing activities. Alternatively, a healthy company could use its cash resources to repay existing loans, pay dividends, or repurchase shares, all of which would result in negative net cash flows from financing activities.

Thus, it's not possible to evaluate the company's financing cash flows by simply determining whether they are positive or negative on an overall basis. Rather, you will need to consider detailed line items within this section to assess the company's overall financing strategy. (Is the company moving toward greater reliance on risky debt financing?)

Overall Patterns of Cash Flows

Just as most products go through a series of developmental phases, most companies have life cycles. The corporate life cycle includes an introductory phase when the company is being established, a growth phase when the company's presence expands, a maturity phase when the company stabilizes, and finally a decline phase when the company loses its way. During each of these phases, a company is likely to show different patterns of net cash flows from operating, investing, and financing activities. Exhibit 12.8

EXHIBIT 12.8   Phases of Corporate Life Cycle

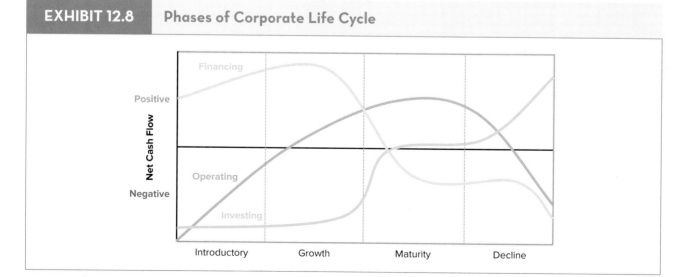

illustrates the cash flow patterns that suggest the life cycle phase being experienced by a company. Although exceptions to these patterns can exist, they can help you to better understand and evaluate a company's cash flows.

As Exhibit 12.8 suggests, most companies in the introductory (start–up) phase experience negative net operating cash flows. Negative cash flows arise during this phase because companies pay cash out to employees and suppliers but haven't established a large enough customer base to generate sizable cash inflows from customers. Also during the introductory phase, these companies are spending significant amounts of cash on long–term assets (e.g., equipment and buildings), resulting in negative investing cash flows.

To fund these negative investing and operating cash flows, companies in the introductory phase rely heavily on cash obtained through financing activities (e.g., borrowing from lenders and obtaining contributions from shareholders). If a company survives the introductory phase, it will enter a growth phase, which is similar to the introductory phase except that oper–ating cash flows turn positive because the company has improved its cash inflows from customers.

In the maturity phase, the company continues to enjoy positive operat–ing cash flows, but no longer has opportunities for expanding the business, so it stops spending cash on investing activities and instead uses its cash for financing activities such as repaying lenders and returning excess cash to shareholders. Finally, during the decline phase, a company's operating cash flows again become negative, prompting lenders to demand repayment of loans (i.e., negative financing cash flows). To fund these repayments, the company sells off its long–term assets, resulting in significantly positive investing cash flows.

OPERATING CASH FLOWS REVISITED (DIRECT METHOD)

In this section, we demonstrate how to determine operating cash flows using the direct method of presentation. You might ask whether it's worth learning how to use this approach when fewer than one percent of public companies report with it. That's a fair question. But you also should ask why *aren't* more companies using it when the IASB favours it over the indirect method? Some argue that companies do not use the direct method of presentation because it reveals too much about their operations. As we show below, useful insights can be gained about a company by analyzing its operating cash flows using the direct method of presentation.

Exhibit 12.9 presents Under Armour's statement of cash flows using the direct method. Because this method lists each operating cash flow component, it allows more detailed analyses of operating cash flows. For example, the direct method would allow Under Armour's managers to determine that a 10 percent increase in product costs in 2015 would have required an additional cash outflow to inventory suppliers of $230.3 million (=10% × $2,303 million). To cover these additional cash outflows, Under Armour could raise prices by 6.1 percent, which would gener–ate a $232 million (= 6.1% × $3,809 million) cash inflow from customer collections.

The direct method also provides financial statement users with more information to identify potential relationships between cash inflows and outflows. An increase in some activities, such as sales, generally leads to an increase in cash inflows from customers and cash outflows to inventory suppliers. However, an increase in sales activity only loosely affects other

LEARNING OBJECTIVE **12-6**

Report and interpret cash flows from operating activities using the direct method.

EXHIBIT 12.9   Under Armour's Statement of Cash Flows (Direct Method)

UNDER ARMOUR, INC. Statement of Cash Flows For the Year Ended December 31, 2015		Explanation
(in millions)		
Cash Flows from Operating Activities		Cash flows related to day–to–day activities
Cash collected from customers	$3,809	Cash collected on account and from any cash sales
Cash paid to suppliers of inventory	(2,312)	Cash paid in the current period to acquire inventory
Cash paid to employees and suppliers of services	(1,421)	Cash paid for salaries, wages, utilities, rent, etc.
Cash paid for interest	(22)	Separate reporting of these items fulfills the role of
Cash paid for income tax	(154)	the supplemental disclosures in Exhibit 12.7
Net cash provided by (used in) operating activities	(100)	Indicates overall cash impact of operating activities
Cash Flows from Investing Activities		Cash flows related to long–term assets
Purchase of equipment	(256)	Cash was used to purchase equipment
Purchase of intangible and other assets	(591)	Cash was used to purchase intangibles
Net cash provided by (used in) investing activities	(847)	Indicates overall cash impact of investing activities
Cash Flows from Financing Activities		Cash flows from transactions with lenders, investors
Proceeds from long–term debt	665	Cash received from borrowing
Payments on long–term debt	(266)	Cash used to repay amounts previously borrowed
Proceeds from share issuances	85	Cash received from issuing shares
Net cash provided by (used in) financing activities	484	Indicates overall cash impact of financing activities
Net Change in Cash and Cash Equivalents	(463)	$(100) + $(847) + $484 = $(463)
Cash and cash equivalents, beginning of year	593	Cash balance at beginning of the period
Cash and cash equivalents, end of year	$ 130	Cash balance at end of the period (on balance sheet)

cash outflows, such as interest paid on loans. Knowing the detailed com-ponents of operating cash flows allows analysts to more reliably predict a company's future cash flows.[4]

In the remainder of this section, we describe how to prepare the state-ment of cash flows using the direct method. We focus on preparing just the operating activities section. For instructions on preparing the investing and financing activities sections, which are identical under both the direct and indirect methods, see Under Armour's Investing Cash Flow Calculations and Under Armour's Financing Cash Flow Calculations.

Reporting Operating Cash Flows with the Direct Method

The direct method presents a summary of all operating transactions that result in either a debit or a credit to cash. It is prepared by adjusting each revenue and expense on the income statement from the accrual basis to the cash basis. We will complete this process for all of the revenues and expenses reported in the Under Armour income statement in Exhibit 12.3 to show the calculations underlying the operating cash flows in Exhibit 12.9. Notice that with the direct method, we work directly with each rev-enue and expense listed on the income statement and ignore any totals or subtotals (such as net income).

Converting Sales Revenues to Cash Inflows.   When sales are recorded, Accounts Receivable increases, and when cash is collected, Accounts Receivable decreases. This means that if Accounts Receivable increases by $154 million, then cash collections were $154 million less than sales on account. To convert sales revenue to the cash collected, we need to subtract $154 million from Sales Revenue. The following flow chart shows this visually:

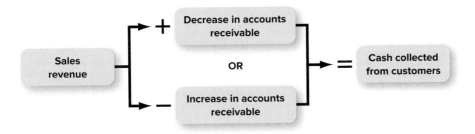

Using information from Under Armour's income statement and balance sheet presented in Exhibit 12.3, we compute cash collected from customers as follows:

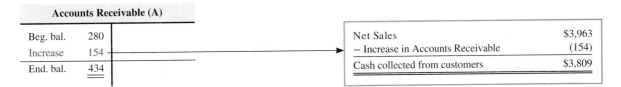

Accounts Receivable (A)		
Beg. bal.	280	
Increase	154	
End. bal.	434	

Net Sales	$3,963
− Increase in Accounts Receivable	(154)
Cash collected from customers	$3,809

Converting Cost of Goods Sold to Cash Paid to Suppliers.

Cost of Goods Sold represents the cost of merchandise sold during the accounting period, which may be more or less than the amount of cash paid to suppliers during the period. In Under Armour's case, Inventory increased during the year, implying the company purchased more merchandise than it sold. If the company paid cash to suppliers of inventory, it would have paid more cash to suppliers than the amount of Cost of Goods Sold. So, the increase in Inventory must be added to Cost of Goods Sold to compute cash paid to suppliers.

Typically, companies buy inventory on account from suppliers (as indicated by an Accounts Payable balance on the balance sheet). Consequently, we need to consider more than just the change in Inventory to convert Cost of Goods Sold to cash paid to suppliers. The credit purchases and payments that are recorded in Accounts Payable must also be considered. Credit purchases increase Accounts Payable, and cash payments decrease it. The overall decrease in Accounts Payable reported by Under Armour in Exhibit 12.3 indicates that cash payments were more than credit purchases, so the difference must be added in the computation of total cash payments to suppliers.

In summary, to fully convert Cost of Goods Sold to a cash basis, you must consider changes in both Inventory and Accounts Payable as follows:

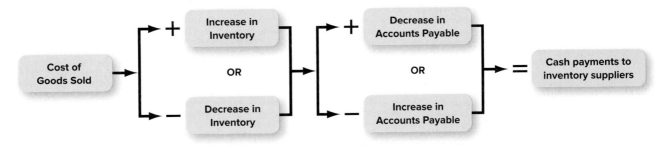

Using information from Exhibit 12.3, we compute cash paid to suppliers as follows:

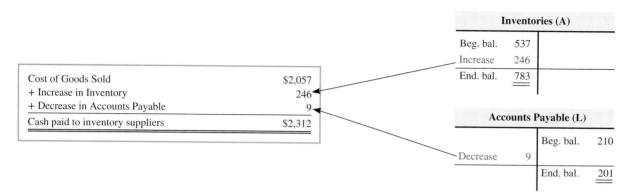

Inventories (A)		
Beg. bal.	537	
Increase	246	
End. bal.	783	

Cost of Goods Sold	$2,057
+ Increase in Inventory	246
+ Decrease in Accounts Payable	9
Cash paid to inventory suppliers	$2,312

Accounts Payable (L)		
	Beg. bal.	210
Decrease	9	
	End. bal.	201

Converting Operating Expenses to a Cash Outflow.

The total amount of an expense on the income statement may differ from the cash outflow associated with that activity. Some amounts, like prepaid rent, are paid before they are recognized as expenses. When prepayments are made, the balance in the asset Prepaid Expenses increases. When expenses are recorded, Prepaid Expenses decreases. When we see Under Armour's prepaid expenses increase by $13 million during the year, it means the company paid more cash than it recorded as operating expenses. This amount must be added in computing cash paid to service suppliers for operating expenses.

Some other expenses, like wages, are paid for after they are incurred. In this case, when expenses are recorded, the balance in Accrued Liabilities increases. When payments are made, Accrued Liabilities decreases. When Under Armour's Accrued Liabilities increased by $66 million, it means the company paid that much less cash than it recorded as operating expenses. This amount must be subtracted when computing cash paid to employees and service suppliers for operating expenses.

Generally, operating expenses such as Selling, General, and Administrative Expenses can be converted from the accrual basis to the cash basis in the following manner:

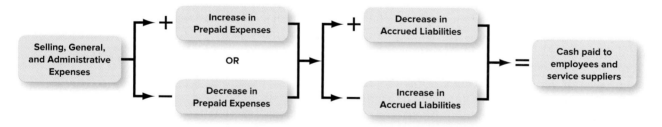

Using information from Exhibit 12.3, we can compute the total cash paid as follows:

Prepaid Expenses (A)		
Beg. bal.	139	
Increase	13	
End. bal.	152	

Selling, General, and Administrative Expenses	$1,474
+ Increase in Prepaid Expenses	13
− Increase in Accrued Liabilities	(66)
Cash paid to employees and suppliers of services	$1,421

Accrued Liabilities (L)		
	Beg. bal.	212
	Increase	66
	End. bal.	278

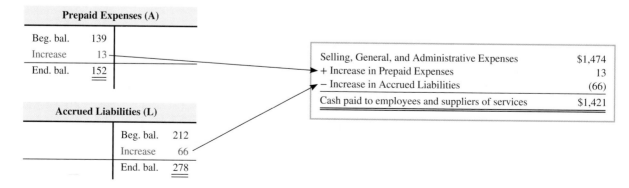

You don't have to convert Depreciation Expense on the income statement to the cash basis for the statement of cash flows because depreciation doesn't involve cash. It merely reports previously incurred costs as an expense in the current period. Non–cash expenses like depreciation (or, similarly, revenues that don't affect cash) are omit–ted when the statement of cash flows is prepared using the direct method. Because of this, be sure to exclude any Depreciation Expense that might have been included in Selling, General, and Administrative Expenses.

The next account listed on the income statement in Exhibit 12.3 is Interest Expense of $22 million. Because the balance sheet does not report Interest Payable, we will assume all of the interest was paid in cash. Thus, interest expense equals interest paid.

Interest Expense	$22
No change in Interest Payable	0
Cash paid for interest	$22

The same logic can be applied to income taxes. Under Armour pres–ents Income Tax Expense of $154 million. Exhibit 12.3 does not report an Income Tax Payable balance, so we assume income tax paid is equal to income tax expense.

Income Tax Expense	$154
No change in Income Tax Payable	0
Cash paid for income tax	$154

You have now seen in this section how to determine each amount reported in the operating activities section of a statement of cash flows prepared using the direct method. For a quick check on your understanding of this material, complete the Self–Study Practice that follows.

HOW'S IT GOING?

Self-Study Practice 12.3

Indicate whether the following items taken from a cash flow statement would be added (+), subtracted (−), or not included (NA) when calculating cash flow from operations using the direct method under ASPE.

  1. Cash paid to suppliers

  2. Payment of dividends to shareholders

  3. Cash collections from customers

  4. Purchase of plant and equipment for cash

  5. Payments of interest to lenders

  6. Payment of taxes to the government

After you have finished, check your answers with the solution, which follows the chapter summary.

Topic	ASPE	IFRS
Classification of interest and dividends		
• Dividends paid	• Dividends paid that are charged directly to retained earnings are presented as a financing cash flow.	• Dividends paid can be presented as either an operating or a financing cash flow.
• Interest paid	• Interest paid that is recognized in net income is presented as an operating cash flow.	• Interest paid can be presented as either an operating or a financing cash flow.
• Dividends received	• Dividends received are classified as an operating cash flow.	• Dividends received can be presented as either an operating or an investing cash flow.
• Interest received	• Interest received is classified as an operating cash flow.	• Interest received can be presented as either an operating or an investing cash flow.
Disclosures		
• Income taxes	• Income taxes paid are not required to be disclosed on the statement of cash flows.	• Income taxes paid are required to be disclosed on the statement of cash flows.
• Restrictions on cash and cash equivalents	• The amounts of cash and cash equivalents that are restricted for a particular use are required to be disclosed on the statement of cash flows.	• The amounts of cash and cash equivalents that are restricted for a particular use are required to be disclosed on the statement of cash flows, along with an explanation of the restrictions.

Supplement 12A

REPORTING DISPOSALS OF PROPERTY, PLANT, AND EQUIPMENT (INDIRECT METHOD)

LEARNING OBJECTIVE 12-S1

Report cash flows from property, plant, and equipment (PPE) disposals using the indirect method.

COACH'S TIP

If you're a little rusty on the journal entry to record this disposal, it would be worth your time to review Disposal of Tangible Assets in Chapter 9.

Whenever a company sells property, plant, and equipment (PPE), it records three things: (1) decreases in the PPE accounts for the assets sold, (2) an increase in the Cash account for the cash received on disposal, and (3) a gain if the cash received is more than the book value of the assets sold (or a loss if the cash received is less than the book value of the assets sold). The only part of this transaction that qualifies for the statement of cash flows is the cash received on disposal. This cash inflow is classified as an investing activity, just like the original equipment purchase.

Okay, that seems straightforward. So, why do we have a separate chapter supplement for this kind of transaction? Well, there is one complicating factor. Gains and losses on disposal are included in the computation of net income, which is the starting point for the operating activities section when prepared using the indirect method. Just as we had to add back the depreciation subtracted on the income statement, we also have to add back losses reported on disposals of PPE. As the following example shows, the flip side is true for gains on disposal (they are subtracted).

To illustrate, assume that Under Armour sold a piece of its manufacturing equipment for $7 million. The equipment originally cost $15 million and had $10 million of accumulated depreciation at the time of disposal. The disposal would have been analyzed and recorded as follows (in millions):

(1) Analyze

Assets		= Liabilities	+	Shareholders' Equity	
Cash	+7			Gain on Disposal (+R)	+2
Accumulated Depreciation (−xA)	+10				
Equipment	−15				

(2) Record

dr **Cash** (+A)	7	
dr **Accumulated Depreciation** (−xA, +A)	10	
cr **Equipment** (−A)		15
cr **Gain on Disposal** (+R, +SE)		2

The $7 million inflow of cash would be reported as an investing activity. The $10 million and $15 million are taken into account when considering changes in the Accumulated Depreciation and Equipment account balances. Lastly, the $2 million Gain on Disposal was included in net income, so we must remove (subtract) it in the operating activities section of the statement. Thus, the disposal would affect two parts of the statement of cash flows:

Cash flows provided by (used in) operating activities	
Net income	$233
Adjustments to reconcile net income to net cash from operations:	
. . .	. . .
Gain on disposal of property, plant, and equipment	(2)
. . .	. . .
Net cash provided by (used in) operating activities	. . .
Cash provided by (used in) investing activities	
Additions to property, plant, and equipment	. . .
Cash received from disposal of property, plant, and equipment	7
. . .	. . .
Net cash provided by (used in) investing activities	. . .

Supplement 12B

T-ACCOUNT APPROACH (INDIRECT METHOD)

When we began our discussion of preparing the statement of cash flows, we noted that changes in cash must equal the sum of the changes in all other balance sheet accounts. Based on this idea, we used the following three steps to prepare the statement of cash flows:

LEARNING OBJECTIVE **12-S2**

Use the T-account approach for preparing an indirect method statement of cash flows.

1. Determine the change in each balance sheet account. From this year's ending balance, subtract this year's beginning balance (i.e., last year's ending balance).

2. Identify the cash flow category or categories to which each account relates. Use Exhibit 12.2 as a guide, but be aware that some accounts may include two categories of cash flows. Retained Earnings, for example, can include both financing cash flows (paying dividends) and operating cash flows (generating net income). Similarly, Accumulated Depreciation can be affected by operating activities (depreciation for using equipment in daily operations) as well as investing activities (disposing of equipment).

3. Create schedules that summarize operating, investing, and financing cash flows.

Instead of creating separate schedules for each section of the state—ment, many accountants prefer to prepare a single large T—account to represent the changes that have taken place in cash subdivided into the three sections of the cash flow statement. Such an account is pre—sented in Panel A of Exhibit 12B.1. The cash account in Panel A shows

---

EXHIBIT 12B.1 **T-Account Approach to Preparing the Statement of Cash Flows (Indirect Method)**

Panel A: Changes in Cash Account

Cash (A)

Operating				
(1) Net Income	233		154	(3) Accounts Receivable
(2) Depreciation Expense	23		246	(4) Inventory
(7) Accrued Liabilities	66		13	(5) Prepaid Expenses
			9	(6) Accounts Payable
			100	Net Cash Used in Operating Activities
Investing				
			256	(8) Purchased Equipment
			591	(9) Purchased Intangibles
			847	Net Cash Used in Investing Activities
Financing				
(10) Additional Long-Term Debt	665		266	(11) Payment of Long-Term Debt
(12) Proceeds from Share Issuance	85			
Net Cash Provided by Financing Activities	484			
			463	Net Decrease in Cash
Beg. Bal.	593			
End. Bal.	130			

Panel B: Changes in Non-cash Accounts

Accounts Receivable (A)

Beg. Bal.	280	
(3) Increase	154	
End. Bal.	434	

Inventory (A)

Beg. Bal.	537	
(4) Increase	246	
End. Bal.	783	

Prepaid Expenses (A)

Beg. Bal.	139	
(5) Increase	13	
End. Bal.	152	

Equipment (A)

Beg. Bal.	370		
(8) Purchases	256	Disposals	0
End. Bal.	626		

Accumulated Depreciation-Equipment (xA)

		Beg. Bal.	64
Disposals	0	(2) Decrease	23
		End. Bal.	87

Intangibles and Other Assets (A)

Beg. Bal.	240		
(9) Purchases	591	Disposals	0
End. Bal.	831		

Accounts Payable (L)

		Beg. Bal.	210
(6) Decrease	9		
		End. Bal.	201

Accrued Liabilities (L)

		Beg. Bal.	212
		(7) Increase	66
		End. Bal.	278

Long-Term Debt (L)

		Beg. Bal.	323
(11) Payments	266	(10) Borrowings	665
		End. Bal.	722

Contributed Capital (SE)

		Beg. Bal.	494
Shares Repurchased	0	(12) Shares Issued	85
		End. Bal.	579

Retained Earnings (SE)

		Beg. Bal.	856
Dividends	0	(1) Net Income	233
		End. Bal.	1,089

increases in cash as debits and decreases in cash as credits. Note how each section matches the three schedules that we prepared for Under Armour's cash flows presented in Exhibits 12.4, 12.5, and 12.6. Panel B includes the same T–accounts for the non–cash balance sheet accounts we used in our discussion of each cash flow statement section in the body of the chapter. Note how each change in the non–cash balance sheet accounts has a number referencing the change in the cash account that it accompanies. Use the information in the cash flow T–account in Exhibit 12B.1 to prepare the statement of cash flows in proper format, as shown in Exhibit 12.7.

Review the Chapter

This section provides a chance to solidify your understanding of key points. It's worth your time to work through the following demonstration cases, scan the chapter summary, test your understanding of key terms, and then practise, practise, practise.

DEMONSTRATION CASE A: INDIRECT METHOD

During a recent year (ended April 30), Best Beverage Corp. reported net income of $25,000. The company also reported the following activities:

a. Purchased equipment for $6,000 in cash

b. Issued shares for $1,000 in cash

c. Depreciation of equipment was $9,000 for the year

Its comparative balance sheet is presented below.

BEST BEVERAGE CORP Balance Sheet Year Ended April 30		
	Current Year	Prior Year
Assets		
Current assets:		
Cash and cash equivalents	$ 84,000	$ 48,7000
Accounts receivable	53,600	50,000
Inventory	39,600	39,000
Prepaid expenses	5,500	15,000
Equipment	206,000	200,000
Accumulated depreciation	(126,700)	(117,700)
Total assets	$ 262,000	$ 235,000
Liabilities and shareholders' equity		
Current liabilities:		
Accounts payable	$ 48,000	$ 49,000
Accrued liabilities	44,000	42,000
Total current liabilities	92,000	91,000
Shareholders' equity:		
Contributed capital	10,000	9,000
Retained earnings	160,000	135,000
Total shareholders' equity	170,000	144,000
Total liabilities and shareholders' equity	$ 262,000	$ 235,000

Required:

Based on this information, prepare the cash flow statement using the indirect method. Evaluate the cash flows reported in the statement.

Suggested Solution

BEST BEVERAGE CORP. Balance Sheet At April 30			STEP 1	STEP 2	BEST BEVERAGE CORP. Statement of Cash Flows For the Year Ended April 30	
	Current Year	**Prior Year**	**CHANGE**	**SCF SECTION**		
Assets					**Cash Flows from Operating Activities**	
Cash and Cash Equivalents	$ 84,000	$ 48,700	+35,300	Cash	Net income	$25,000
Accounts Receivable	53,600	50,000	+3,600	O	Adjustments to reconcile net income to net cash provided by operating activities:	
Inventory	39,600	39,000	+600	O	Depreciation	9,000
Prepaid Expenses	5,500	15,000	−9,500	O	Changes in current assets and current liabilities:	
Equipment	206,000	200,000	+6,000	I	Accounts Receivable	(3,600)
Accum. Depreciation	(126,700)	(117,700)	−9,000	O	Inventory	(600)
Total Assets	$ 262,000	$ 235,000			Prepaid Expenses	9,500
Liabilities and Shareholders' Equity					Accounts Payable	(1,000)
					Accrued Liabilities	2,000
Accounts Payable	$ 48,000	$ 49,000	−1,000	O	Net cash provided by operating activities	40,300
Accrued Liabilities	44,000	42,000	+2,000	O	**Cash Flows from Investing Activities**	
Common Shares	10,000	9,000	+1,000	F	Purchase of equipment	(6,000)
Retained Earnings	160,000	135,000	+25,000	O	Net cash used in investing activities	(6,000)
Total Liabilities and Shareholders' Equity					**Cash Flows from Financing Activities**	
	$ 262,000	$ 235,000			Proceeds from issuance of common shares	1,000
					Net cash provided by financing activities	1,000
					Net Increase in Cash and Cash Equivalents	35,300
					Cash and Cash Equivalents at beginning of year	48,700
					Cash and Cash Equivalents at end of year	$84,000

Best Beverage reported positive profits and even higher cash flows from operations for the year. This difference between the two is caused primarily by depreciation and decreases in prepaid expenses. This also suggests that Best Beverage is carefully managing its current assets and current liabilities so that it has more than sufficient cash on hand to cover the costs of purchases of additional equipment without the need to borrow additional funds. This increase in cash can be used for future expansion or to pay future dividends to shareholders.

DEMONSTRATION CASE B: DIRECT METHOD

The managers at Best Beverage Corp. would like to know the impact on cash flows of a 10 percent increase in product costs.

Required:

Based on the information given in Demonstration Case A and the income statement shown below, prepare a statement of cash flows using the direct method. By what amount would cash outflows have increased if product costs were 10 percent higher? By what percentage would Best Beverage have to increase its prices to cover a 10 percent increase in cash outflows for product costs? (Assume a price increase will not adversely affect sales volume.)

BEST BEVERAGE CORP.
Income Statement
For the Year Ended April 30

Sales Revenue	$636,000
Cost of Goods Sold	240,000
Gross Profit	396,000
Office Expenses	242,000
Depreciation Expense	9,000
Income from Operations	145,000
Interest Expense	0
Income before Income Taxes	145,000
Income Tax Expense	120,000
Net Income	$ 25,000

Suggested Solution

BEST BEVERAGE CORP.
Statement of Cash Flows
For the Year Ended April 30

Cash Flows from Operating Activities	
Cash collected from customers	$632,400
Cash paid to suppliers of inventory	(241,600)
Cash paid to employees and suppliers of services	(230,500)
Cash paid for income taxes	(120,000)
Net cash provided by operating activities	40,300
Cash Flows from Investing Activities	
Purchase of equipment	(6,000)
Net cash used in investing activities	(6,000)
Cash Flows from Financing Activities	
Proceeds from issuance of common stock	1,000
Net cash provided by financing activities	1,000
Net Increase in Cash and Cash Equivalents	35,300
Cash and Cash Equivalents at beginning of year	48,700
Cash and Cash Equivalents at end of year	$ 84,000

Cash collected from customers = Sales Revenue − Increase in Accounts Receivable = $636,000 − 3,600
= $632,400

Cash paid for inventory = Cost of Goods Sold + Increase in Inventories + Decrease in Accounts Payable
= $240,000 + 600 + 1,000 = $241,600

Cash paid to employees, etc. = Office Expenses − Decrease in Prepaids − Increase in Accrued Liabilities
= $242,000 − 9,500 − 2,000 = $230,500

If product costs were 10 percent higher, total cash paid to inventory suppliers would have increased by $24,160 ($241,600 × 10%). To cover these additional cash outflows, Best Beverage could increase prices by $24,160, which compared to current collections from customers is 3.8 percent ($24,160 ÷ $632,400).

CHAPTER SUMMARY

LO12-1   **Identify cash flows arising from operating, investing, and financing activities.**

- The statement has three main sections:
  1. Cash flows from operating activities, which are related to earning income from normal operations
  2. Cash flows from investing activities, which are related to the acquisition and sale of productive assets
  3. Cash flows from financing activities, which are related to external financing of the enterprise

- The net cash inflow or outflow for the period is the same amount as the increase or decrease in cash and cash equivalents for the period on the balance sheet. Cash equivalents are highly liquid investments purchased within three months of maturity.

LO12-2   **Report cash flows from operating activities using the indirect method.**

- The indirect method for reporting cash flows from operating activities reports a conversion of net income to net cash flow from operating activities.
- The conversion involves additions and subtractions for (1) non−cash expenses (such as depreciation expense) and revenues that do not affect current assets or current liabilities, and (2) changes in each of the individual current assets (other than cash) and current liabilities (other than debt to financial institutions, which relates to financing).

LO12-3   **Report cash flows from investing activities.**

- Investing activities reported on the cash flow statement include cash payments to acquire fixed assets and investments, and cash proceeds from the sale of fixed assets and investments.

LO12-4   **Report cash flows from financing activities.**

- Cash inflows from financing activities include cash proceeds from issuance of debt and common shares. Cash outflows include cash principal payments on debt, cash paid for the repurchase of the company's shares, and cash dividend payments. Cash payments associated with interest are a cash flow from operating activities.

LO12-5   **Interpret cash flows from operating, investing, and financing activities.**

- A healthy company will generate positive cash flows from operations, some of which will be used to pay for purchases of property, plant, and equipment. Any additional cash (called *free cash flow*) can be used to further expand the business, pay down some of the company's debt, or simply build up the cash balance. A company is in trouble if it is unable to generate positive cash flows from operations in the long run, because eventually creditors will stop lending to the company and shareholders will stop investing in it.

LO12-6   **Report and interpret cash flows from operating activities using the direct method.**

- The direct method for reporting cash flows from operating activities accumulates all of the operating transactions that result in either a debit or a credit to cash into categories. The most common inflows are cash received from customers and dividends, and interest on investments. The most common outflows are cash paid for purchase of services and goods for resale, salaries and wages, income taxes, and interest on liabil−ities. It is prepared by adjusting each item on the income statement from an accrual basis to a cash basis.

SOLUTIONS TO SELF-STUDY PRACTICE

Solution to SP12.1

1. F, 2. O, 3. O, 4. I, 5. I, 6. F

Solution to SP12.2

1. +, 2. +, 3. +, 4. −, 5. +, 6. −

Solution to SP12.3

1. −, 2. NA, 3. +, 4. NA, 5. −, 6. −

KEY TERMS

Cash Flows from Financing Activities
Cash Flows from Investing Activities
Cash Flows from Operating Activities (Cash Flows from Operations)
Direct Method
Indirect Method

Complete definitions are also included in the glossary at the end of this text.

HOMEWORK HELPER

Helpful reminders

- Although some exceptions exist, operating activities typically affect current assets and current liabilities, investing activities typically affect non−current assets, and financing activities typically affect non−current liabilities and shareholders' equity accounts.
- The typical additions and subtractions that are required when using the indirect method to reconcile net income with cash flow from operating activities are as follows:

Item	Additions and Subtractions to Reconcile Net Income to Cash Flow From Operating Activities*	
	When Item Increases	When Item Decreases
Depreciation	+	n/a
Accounts Receivable	−	+
Inventory	−	+
Prepaid Expenses	−	+
Accounts Payable	+	−
Accrued Liabilities	+	−

*This summary excludes additions and subtractions for losses and gains arising on disposal of certain assets, which are discussed in Supplement 12A.

> **COACH'S TIP**
>
> Notice in this table that, to reconcile net income to cash flows from operations, you
> - add the change when the current asset decreases or current liability increases, and
> - subtract the change when the current asset increases or current liability decreases.

- The following adjustments are commonly made to convert income statement items to the related operating cash flow amounts for the direct method:

Income Statement Account	+/− Change in Balance Sheet Account(s)	= Operating Cash Flow
Sales Revenue	+ Decrease in Accounts Receivable (A) − Increase in Accounts Receivable (A)	= Cash collected from customers
Cost of Goods Sold	+ Increase in Inventory (A) − Decrease in Inventory (A) − Increase in Accounts Payable (L) + Decrease in Accounts Payable (L)	= Cash paid to suppliers of inventory
Other Expenses	+ Increase in Prepaid Expenses (A) − Decrease in Prepaid Expenses (A) − Increase in Accrued Expenses (L) + Decrease in Accrued Expenses (L)	= Cash paid to employees and suppliers of services (e.g., wages, rent, utilities)
Interest Expense	− Increase in Interest Payable (L) + Decrease in Interest Payable (L)	= Cash paid for interest
Income Tax Expense	− Increase in Income Taxes Payable (Deferred Taxes) (L) + Decrease in Income Taxes Payable (Deferred Taxes) (L)	= Cash paid for income tax

• Do not merely report the net change in all balance sheet accounts. Some accounts (typically those affected by investing and financing activities) include both inflows and outflows of cash, which must be reported separately.

PRACTICE MATERIAL

QUESTIONS (⊖ Symbol indicates questions that require analysis from more than one perspective.)

1. Compare the purposes of the income statement, the balance sheet, and the statement of cash flows.

2. What information does the statement of cash flows report that is not reported on the other required financial statements?

3. What are cash equivalents? How are they reported on the statement of cash flows?

4. What are the major categories of business activities reported on the statement of cash flows? Define each of these activities.

5. What are the typical cash inflows from operating activities? What are the typical cash outflows from operating activities?

6. Describe the types of items used to compute cash flows from operating activities under the two alternative methods of reporting.

7. Under the indirect method, depreciation expense is added to net income to report cash flows from operating activities. Does depreciation cause an inflow of cash?

8. Explain why cash outflows during the period for purchases and salaries are not specifi-cally reported on a statement of cash flows prepared using the indirect method.

9. Explain why a $50,000 increase in inventory during the year must be included in com-puting cash flows from operating activities under both the direct and indirect methods.

10. Loan covenants require that E–Gadget Corporation (EGC) generate $200,000 cash from operating activities each year. Without intervention during the last month of the current year, EGC will generate only $180,000 cash from operations. What are the pros and cons of each of the following possible interventions: (*a*) pressuring customers to pay over-due accounts, (*b*) delaying payment of amounts owing to suppliers, and (*c*) purchasing additional equipment to increase depreciation? ⊖

11. As a junior analyst, you are evaluating the financial performance of Digil Corporation. Impressed by this year's growth in sales (20 percent increase), receivables (40 percent increase), and inventories (50 percent increase), you plan to report a favourable eval-uation of the company. Your supervisor cautions you that those increases may signal difficulties rather than successes. When you ask what she means, she just says you should look at the company's statement of cash flows. What do you think you will find there? What are the cash flow effects when a company's receivables and inventories increase faster than its sales? ⊖

12. What are the typical cash inflows from investing activities? What are the typical cash outflows from investing activities?

13. What are the typical cash inflows from financing activities? What are the typical cash outflows from financing activities?

14. What are non–cash investing and financing activities? Give one example. How are non–cash investing and financing activities reported on the statement of cash flows?

15. (Supplement 12A) How is the sale of equipment reported on the statement of cash flows using the indirect method?

MINI-EXERCISES

LO12-1, 12-5 **M12-1 Identifying Companies from Cash Flow Patterns**

Based on the cash flows shown, classify each of the following cases as a growing start–up company (S), a healthy, established company (E), or an established company facing financial difficulties (F), and explain why you chose this classification.

	Case 1	Case 2	Case 3
Cash provided by (used for) operating activities	$ 3,000	$(120,000)	$ 80,000
Cash provided by (used for) investing activities	(70,000)	10,000	(40,000)
Cash provided by (used for) financing activities	75,000	75,000	(30,000)
Net change in cash	8,000	(35,000)	10,000
Cash position at beginning of year	2,000	40,000	30,000
Cash position at end of year	$ 10,000	$ 5,000	$ 40,000

M12-2 Matching Items Reported to Cash Flow Statement Categories (Indirect Method)

LO12-1, 12-2

The Buckle, Inc. included the following in its statement of cash flows presented using the indirect method. Indicate whether each item is disclosed in the operating activities (O), investing activities (I), or financing activities (F) section of the statement, or use (NA) if the item does not appear on the statement.

_____ 1. Purchase of investments   _____ 4. Depreciation

_____ 2. Proceeds from issuance of shares   _____ 5. Accounts payable (decrease)

_____ 3. Purchase of property and equipment   _____ 6. Inventories (increase)

M12-3 Determining the Effects of Account Changes on Cash Flows from Operating Activities (Indirect Method)

LO12-2

Indicate whether each item would be added (+) or subtracted (−) in the computation of cash flow from operating activities using the indirect method.

_____ 1. Depreciation   _____ 4. Accounts receivable increase

_____ 2. Inventories decrease   _____ 5. Accrued liabilities increase

_____ 3. Accounts payable decrease

M12-4 Computing Cash Flows from Operating Activities (Indirect Method)

LO12-2

For each of the following independent cases, compute cash flows from operating activities. Assume the list below includes all balance sheet accounts related to operating activities. (Amounts in parentheses represent decreases.)

	Case A	Case B	Case C
Net Income	$200,000	$ 20,000	$360,000
Depreciation Expense	40,000	150,000	80,000
Accounts Receivable	100,000	(200,000)	(20,000)
Inventory increase	(50,000)	(100,000)	50,000
Accounts Payable	(110,000)	120,000	70,000
Accrued Liabilities	60,000	(220,000)	(80,000)

M12-5 Computing Cash Flows from Operating Activities (Indirect Method)

LO12-2

For the following two independent cases, show the cash flows from the operating activities section of the statement of cash flows for Year 2 using the indirect method.

	Case A		Case B	
	Year 2	Year 1	Year 2	Year 1
Sales Revenue	$10,000	$9,000	$21,000	$18,000
Cost of Goods Sold	6,000	5,500	12,000	11,000
Gross Profit	4,000	3,500	9,000	7,000
Depreciation Expense	1,000	1,000	2,000	1,500
Salaries Expense	2,500	2,000	5,000	5,000
Net Income	500	500	2,000	500
Accounts Receivable	300	400	750	600
Inventories	600	500	790	800
Accounts Payable	800	700	800	850
Salaries Payable	1,000	1,200	200	250

M12-6 Computing Cash Flows from Investing Activities

Based on the following information, compute cash flows from investing activities under ASPE.

Cash collections from customers	$800	Sale of investments	$300
Purchase of used equipment	350	Dividends received	100
Depreciation expense	200	Interest received	200

M12-7 Computing Cash Flows from Financing Activities

Based on the following information, compute cash flows from financing activities under ASPE.

Purchase of investments	$ 250
Dividends paid	800
Interest paid	400
Additional borrowing from bank	2,000

M12-8 Computing Cash Flows Under IFRS

Using the data from M12–6, calculate the maximum investing cash inflows that could be reported under IFRS. Using data from M12–7 calculate the maximum financing cash flows that could be reported under IFRS.

M12-9 Reporting Non-cash Investing and Financing Activities

Which of the following transactions would be considered non–cash investing and financing activities?

____ 1. Additional borrowing from bank

____ 2. Purchase of equipment with investments

____ 3. Dividends paid in cash

____ 4. Purchase of a building with a promissory note

M12-10 Interpreting Cash Flows from Operating, Investing, and Financing Activities

Quantum Dot Corporation is a nanotechnology company that manufactures "quantum dots," which are tiny pieces of silicon consisting of 100 or more molecules. Quantum dots can be used to illuminate very small objects, enabling scientists to see the blood vessels beneath a mouse's skin ripple with each heartbeat, at the rate of 100 times per second. Evaluate this research–intensive company's cash flows, assuming the following was reported in its statement of cash flows.

	Current Year	Previous Year
Cash Flows from Operating Activities		
Net cash provided by (used for) operating activities	$ (50,790)	$ (46,730)
Cash Flows from Investing Activities		
Purchases of research equipment	(250,770)	(480,145)
Proceeds from selling all short-term investments	35,000	0
Net cash provided by (used for) investing activities	(215,770)	(480,145)
Cash Flows from Financing Activities		
Additional long-term debt borrowed	100,000	200,000
Proceeds from shares issuance	140,000	200,000
Cash dividends paid	0	(10,000)
Net cash provided by (used for) financing activities	240,000	390,000
Net increase (decrease) in cash	(26,560)	(136,875)
Cash at beginning of period	29,025	165,900
Cash at end of period	$ 2,465	$ 29,025

M12-11 Computing Cash Flows from Operating Activities (Direct Method)

For each of the following independent cases, compute cash flows from operating activities using the direct method. Assume the list below includes all items relevant to operating activities.

	Case A	Case B	Case C
Sales revenue	$70,000	$55,000	$95,000
Cost of goods sold	35,000	32,000	65,000
Depreciation expense	10,000	2,000	10,000
Other operating expenses	5,000	13,000	8,000
Net income	20,000	8,000	12,000
Accounts receivable increase (decrease)	(1,000)	4,000	3,000
Inventory increase (decrease)	2,000	0	(4,000)
Accounts payable increase (decrease)	0	3,000	(2,000)
Accrued liabilities increase (decrease)	1,000	(2,000)	1,000

M12-12 Computing Cash Flows from Operating Activities (Direct Method)　　　　LO12-6

Refer to the two cases presented in M12–5, and show the cash flow from the operating activities section of the Year 2 statement of cash flows, using the direct method.

EXERCISES

E12-1 Matching Items Reported to Cash Flow Statement Categories (Indirect Method)　　　　LO12-1, 12-2

Nike, Inc. is the best–known sports shoe, apparel, and equipment company in the world because of its association with sports stars such as LeBron James and Serena Williams. Some of the items included in its recent statement of cash flows prepared using the indirect method are listed here. Indicate whether each item is disclosed in the operating activities (O), investing activities (I), or financing activities (F) section of the statement, or use (NA) if the item does not appear on the statement.

_____ 1. Additions to long–term debt

_____ 2. Depreciation

_____ 3. Additions to property, plant, and equipment

_____ 4. Increase (decrease) in notes payable (The amount is owed to financial institutions.)

_____ 5. (Increase) decrease in other current assets

_____ 6. Cash received from disposal of property, plant, and equipment

_____ 7. Reductions in long–term debt

_____ 8. Issuance of shares

_____ 9. (Increase) decrease in inventory

_____ 10. Net income

E12-2 Understanding the Computation of Cash Flows from Operating Activities (Indirect Method)　　　　LO12-2

Suppose your company sells services of $150 in exchange for $100 cash and $50 on account. Depreciation of $40 also is recorded.

Required:

1. Show the journal entries to record these transactions.
2. Calculate the amount that should be reported as net cash flow from operating activities.
3. Calculate the amount that should be reported as net income.
4. Show how the indirect method would convert net income (requirement 3) to net cash flow from operating activities (requirement 2).
5. What general rule about converting net income to operating cash flows is revealed by your answer to requirement 4?

E12-3 Understanding the Computation of Cash Flows from Operating Activities (Indirect Method)

Suppose your company sells goods for $300, of which $200 is received in cash and $100 is on account. The goods cost your company $125 in a previous period. Your company also recorded wages of $70, of which only $30 has been paid in cash.

Required:

1. Show the journal entries to record these transactions.
2. Calculate the amount that should be reported as net cash flow from operating activities.
3. Calculate the amount that should be reported as net income.
4. Show how the indirect method would convert net income (requirement 3) to net cash flow from operating activities (requirement 2).
5. What general rule about converting net income to operating cash flows is revealed by your answer to requirement 4?

E12-4 Understanding the Computation of Cash Flows from Operating Activities (Indirect Method)

Suppose your company sells services of $150 in exchange for $120 cash and $30 on account. Depreciation of $50 also is recorded.

Required:

1. Show the journal entries to record these transactions.
2. Calculate the amount that should be reported as net cash flow from operating activities.
3. Calculate the amount that should be reported as net income.
4. Show how the indirect method would convert net income (requirement 3) to net cash flow from operating activities (requirement 2).
5. What general rule about converting net income to operating cash flows is revealed by your answer to requirement 4?

E12-5 Preparing and Evaluating a Simple Statement of Cash Flows (Indirect Method)

Suppose your company's income statement reports $105 of net income, and its comparative balance sheet indicates the following.

	Beginning	Ending
Cash	$ 35	$205
Accounts Receivable	75	175
Inventory	260	135
Total	$370	$515
Wages Payable	$ 10	$ 50
Retained Earnings	360	465
Total	$370	$515

Required:

1. Prepare the operating activities section of the statement of cash flows, using the indirect method.
2. Identify the most significant cause of the difference between the company's net income and net cash flow from operating activities.

E12-6 Preparing and Evaluating a Simple Statement of Cash Flows (Indirect Method)

Suppose the income statement for Goggle Company reports $70 of net income, after deducting depreciation of $35. The company bought equipment costing $60 and obtained a long-term bank loan for $60. The company's comparative balance sheet, at December 31, indicates the following:

	Previous Year	Current Year	Change
Cash	$ 35	$205	
Accounts Receivable	75	175	
Inventory	260	135	
Equipment	500	560	
Accumulated Depreciation	(45)	(80)	
Total	$825	$995	
Wages Payable	$ 10	$ 50	
Long-Term Debt	445	505	
Contributed Capital	10	10	
Retained Earnings	360	430	
Total	$825	$995	

Required:

1. Calculate the change in each balance sheet account, and indicate whether each account relates to operating, investing, and/or financing activities.
2. Prepare a statement of cash flows using the indirect method.
3. In one sentence, explain why an increase in accounts receivable is subtracted.
4. In one sentence, explain why a decrease in inventory is added.
5. In one sentence, explain why an increase in wages payable is added.
6. Are the cash flows typical of a start—up, a healthy, or a troubled company? Explain.

Check Figure [Req. 2]: Net change in cash = $170

E12-7 Reporting Cash Flows from Operating Activities (Indirect Method)

LO12-2

The following information pertains to Guy's Gear Company:

Sales		$ 80,000
Expenses:		
Cost of Goods Sold	$50,000	
Depreciation Expense	6,000	
Salaries Expense	12,000	68,000
Net Income		$ 12,000
Accounts Receivable decrease	$ 5,000	
Merchandise Inventory increase	8,000	
Salaries Payable increase	500	

Required:

Present the operating activities section of the statement of cash flows for Guy's Gear Company using the indirect method.

E12-8 Reporting and Interpreting Cash Flows from Operating Activities from an Analyst's Perspective (Indirect Method)

LO12-2, 12-5

New Vision Company completed its income statement and balance sheet for 2017 and pro—vided the following information:

Service Revenue		$66,000
Expenses:		
Salaries	$42,000	
Depreciation	7,300	
Utilities	7,000	
Other	1,700	58,000
Net Income		$ 8,000
Decrease in Accounts Receivable	$12,000	
Bought a small service machine	5,000	
Increase in Salaries Payable	9,000	
Decrease in Other Accrued Liabilities	4,000	

Required:

1. Present the operating activities section of the statement of cash flows for New Vision Company using the indirect method.
2. Of the potential causes of differences between cash flow from operations and net income, which are the most important to financial analysts?

LO12-2, 12-5 **E12-9 Reporting and Interpreting Cash Flows from Operating Activities from an Analyst's Perspective (Indirect Method)**

Pizza International Inc. operates 700 family restaurants around the world. The company's annual report contained the following information (in thousands):

Operating Activities			
Net loss	$ (9,482)	Decrease in accounts payable	$ 2,282
Depreciation	33,305	Decrease in accrued liabilities	719
Increase in accounts receivables	170	Increase in income taxes payable	1,861
Decrease in inventories	643	Reduction of long-term debt	12,691
Increase in prepaid expenses	664	Additions to equipment	29,073

Required:

1. Based on this information, compute cash flow from operating activities using the indirect method.
2. What were the major reasons that Pizza International was able to report positive cash flow from operations despite having a net loss?
3. Of the potential causes of differences between cash flow from operations and net income, which are the most important to financial analysts?

LO12-2 **E12-10 Inferring Balance Sheet Changes from the Cash Flow Statement (Indirect Method)**

Colgate–Palmolive was founded in 1806. Assume its statement of cash flows reported the following information (in millions) for the year ended December 31, 2017:

Operating Activities	
Net Income	$2,313
Depreciation	376
Cash effect of changes in	
Accounts Receivable	40
Inventories	(10)
Accounts Payable	(65)
Other	557
Net Cash Provided by Operations	$3,211

Required:

Based on the information reported in the operating activities section of the statement of cash flows for Colgate–Palmolive, determine whether the following accounts increased or decreased during the period: Accounts Receivable, Inventories, and Accounts Payable.

LO12-2 **E12-11 Inferring Balance Sheet Changes from the Cash Flow Statement (Indirect Method)**

The statement of cash flows for Apple Inc. contained the following information (in millions) for the year ended September 25, 2010:

Operating Activities	
Net Income	$14,013
Depreciation	1,027
Changes in current assets and current liabilities:	
Accounts Receivable	(2,142)
Inventories	(596)
Accounts Payable	6,307
Deferred Revenue	1,217
Other adjustments	(1,231)
Net Cash Provided by Operations	$18,595

Required:

For each of the four current asset and liability accounts listed in the operating activities section of the statement of cash flows, determine whether the account balances increased or decreased during the period.

E12-12 Preparing and Evaluating a Statement of Cash Flows (Indirect Method) from Comparative Balance Sheets and Income Statements

LO12-1, 12-2, 12-3, 12-4, 12-5

Consultex Company was founded in 2014 as a small financial consulting business. The company had done reasonably well in 2014–2016, but noticed that its cash was beginning to dwindle early in 2017. In January 2017, Consultex had paid $16,000 to purchase land and repaid $2,000 principal on an existing promissory note. In March 2017, the company paid $2,000 cash in dividends and $1,000 to repurchase Consultex shares that had previously been issued for $1,000. To improve its cash position, Consultex borrowed $5,000 by signing a new promissory note in May 2017 and also issued shares to a new private investor for $12,000 cash. Comparative balance sheets and income statements for the most recent fiscal year are presented below.

CONSULTEX COMPANY
Balance Sheet
October 31

	2017	2016
Assets		
Cash	$11,000	$14,000
Accounts Receivable	14,000	12,000
Prepaid Rent	2,000	3,000
Land	26,000	10,000
Total Assets	$53,000	$39,000
Liabilities and Shareholders' Equity		
Wages Payable	$ 2,000	$ 3,000
Income Taxes Payable	1,000	1,000
Notes Payable (long–term)	15,000	12,000
Contributed Capital	20,000	9,000
Retained Earnings	15,000	14,000
Total Liabilities and Shareholders' Equity	$53,000	$39,000

CONSULTEX COMPANY
Income Statement
For the Year Ended October 31

	2017	2016
Sales Revenue	$158,000	$161,000
Wages Expense	98,000	97,000
Rent Expense	36,000	30,000
Other Operating Expenses	19,700	20,000
Income before Income Tax Expense	4,300	14,000
Income Tax Expense	1,300	4,200
Net Income	$ 3,000	$ 9,800

Required:

1. Prepare a properly formatted statement of cash flows for Consultex for the year ended October 31, 2017 (using the indirect method).
2. What one thing can Consultex reasonably change in 2018 to avoid depleting its cash?

LO12-2   **E12-13 Calculating and Understanding Operating Cash Flows Relating to Inventory Purchases (Indirect Method)**

The following information was reported by three companies. When completing the require-ments, assume that any and all purchases on account are for inventory.

	Azure Corporation	Best Bikes	Charlotte's Cycles
Cost of goods sold	$175	$175	$350
Inventory purchases from suppliers made using cash	200	0	200
Inventory purchases from suppliers made on account	0	200	200
Cash payments to suppliers on account	0	160	160
Beginning inventory	100	100	200
Ending inventory	125	125	250
Beginning accounts payable	0	80	80
Ending accounts payable	0	120	120

Required:

1. What amount did each company deduct on the income statement related to inventory?
2. What total amount did each company pay out in cash during the period related to inven-tory purchased with cash and on account?
3. By what amount do your answers in 1 and 2 differ for each company?
4. By what amount did each company's inventory increase (decrease)? By what amount did each company's accounts payable increase (decrease)?
5. Using the indirect method of presentation, what amount(s) must each company add (deduct) from net income to convert from accrual to cash basis?
6. Describe any similarities between your answers to requirements 3 and 5. Are these answers the same? Why or why not?

LO12-3, 12-4   **E12-14 Reporting Cash Flows from Investing and Financing Activities**

LEVEL UP

Rowen Furniture Corporation reported the following activities in a recent quarter:

Net income	$ 4,135	Payments to reduce long-term debt	$ 46
Purchase of property, plant, and equipment	871	Sale of investments	134
Borrowings under line of credit (bank)	1,417	Cash proceeds from sale of property and equipment	6,594
Proceeds from issuance of shares	11	Cash dividends paid	277
Cash received from customers	29,164	Interest paid	90

Required:

Based on this information, present the cash flows from investing and financing activities sections of the cash flow statement, using ASPE.

LO12-3, 12-4, 12-5   **E12-15 Reporting and Interpreting Cash Flows from Investing and Financing Activities with Discussion of Management Strategy**

Payton Place Industries, Inc. is a manufacturer of steel products for customers such as House Depot and Private Motors. In the year ended December 31, 2017, it reported the following activities:

O Net income	$ 24,068	⟂ Proceeds from sale of property, plant, and equipment	$28,669
⟂ Purchase of property, plant, and equipment	21,595	O Decrease in accounts receivable	12,273
F Payments on notes payable (bank)	184,937	~~~~ Proceeds from notes payable (bank) F	53,439
F Net proceeds from share issuance	250	Payment of dividends F	5,985
O Depreciation	33,907	Other financing cash outflows F	1,694

Required:

1. Based on this information, present the cash flows from the investing and financing activities sections of the cash flow statement.

2. Referring to your response to requirement 1, comment on whether you think Payton's cash flows are typical of a healthy or a struggling company.

E12-16 (Supplement 12A) Determining Cash Flows from the Sale of Property

LO12-S1

During fiscal 2017, M&Q Entertainment sold its Ferentio assets for $20,360,000 cash and recorded a gain on disposal of $18,360,000, which was included in the company's net income of $43,445,000.

Required:

1. Show how the disposal would be reported on the statement of cash flows, using the following format (which assumes the indirect method):

(in thousands)	
Cash flows from operating activities	
Net income	$43,445
Gain on sale of property	
Cash flows from investing activities	
Proceeds from disposition of property	

2. Compute the book value of the Ferentio assets that were sold.

E12-17 (Supplement 12A) Determining Cash Flows from the Sale of Equipment

LO12-S1

During the period, Teen's Trends sold some excess equipment at a loss. The following information was collected from the company's accounting records:

From the Income Statement	
Depreciation expense	$ 500
Loss on sale of equipment	4,000
From the Balance Sheet	
Beginning equipment	12,500
Ending equipment	6,500
Beginning accumulated depreciation	2,000
Ending accumulated depreciation	2,200

No new equipment was bought during the period.

Required:

For the equipment that was sold, determine its original cost, its accumulated depreciation, and the cash received from the sale.

E12-18 (Supplement 12B) Preparing a Statement of Cash Flows, Indirect Method: T-Account Approach

LO12-S2

Golf Universe is a regional and online golf equipment retailer. The company reported the following for the current year:

- Purchased a long-term investment for cash, $15,000
- Paid cash dividend, $12,000
- Sold equipment for $6,000 cash (cost, $21,000; accumulated depreciation, $15,000)
- Issued no-par common shares, 500 shares at $12 cash per share
- Net income was $20,200
- Depreciation expense was $3,000

Its comparative balance sheet is presented below.

	Beginning Balances	Ending Balances
Balance Sheet Items		
Cash	$ 20,500	$ 19,200
Accounts Receivable	22,000	22,000
Merchandise Inventory	68,000	75,000
Investments	0	15,000
Equipment	114,500	113,500
Accumulated Depreciation	32,000	20,000
Total	$193,000	$204,700
Accounts Payable	17,000	14,000
Wages Payable	2,500	1,500
Income Taxes Payable	3,000	4,500
Notes Payable	54,000	74,000
Contributed Capital	100,000	106,000
Retained Earnings	16,500	24,700
Total	$193,000	$204,700

Required:

1. Using what you learned in Supplement 12B, complete a T−account worksheet to be used to prepare the statement of cash flows for the current year.
2. Based on the T−account worksheet, prepare the statement of cash flows for the current year in proper format.

COACHED PROBLEMS

LO12-1   CP12-1 **Determining Cash Flow Statement Effects of Transactions**

For each of the following transactions, indicate whether operating (O), investing (I), or financing activities (F) are affected and whether the effect is a cash inflow (+) or outflow (−), or write (NE) if the transaction has no effect on cash.

   TIP: Think about the journal entry recorded for the transaction. The transaction affects net cash flows if and only if the account Cash is affected.

____ 1. Purchased new equipment by signing a promissory note
____ 2. Recorded and paid income taxes to the federal government
____ 3. Issued shares for cash
____ 4. Prepaid rent for the following period
____ 5. Recorded an adjusting entry for expiration of a prepaid expense
____ 6. Paid cash to purchase new equipment
____ 7. Issued long−term debt for cash
____ 8. Collected payments on account from customers
____ 9. Recorded and paid salaries to employees

LO12-2   CP12-2 **Computing Cash Flows from Operating Activities (Indirect Method)**

The income statement and selected balance sheet information for Hamburger Heaven for the year ended December 31, 2017, are presented below.

Income Statement

Sales Revenue	$2,060
Expenses:	
Cost of Goods Sold	900
Depreciation Expense	200
Salaries Expense	500
Rent Expense	250
Insurance Expense	80
Interest Expense	60
Utilities Expense	50
Net Income	$ 20

Selected Balance Sheet Accounts

	2017	2016
Merchandise Inventory	$ 82	$ 60
Accounts Receivable	380	450
Accounts Payable	200	210
Salaries Payable	29	20
Utilities Payable	20	60
Prepaid Rent	2	10
Prepaid Insurance	14	5

TIP: Prepaid Rent decreased in 2017 because the amount taken out of Prepaid Rent (and sub—tracted from net income as Rent Expense) was more than the amount paid for rent in cash during 2017.

Required:

Prepare the cash flows from operating activities section of the 2017 statement of cash flows using the indirect method.

CP12-3 Preparing a Statement of Cash Flows (Indirect Method)

LO12-2, 12-3, 12-4, 12-5

eXcel

Hunter Company is developing its annual financial statements at December 31, 2017. The statements are complete except for the statement of cash flows. The completed comparative balance sheets and income statement are summarized below:

	2017	2016
Balance Sheet at December 31		
Cash	$ 44,000	$ 18,000
Accounts Receivable	27,000	29,000
Merchandise Inventory	30,000	36,000
Property and Equipment	111,000	102,000
Less: Accumulated Depreciation	(36,000)	(30,000)
	$176,000	$155,000
Accounts Payable	$ 25,000	$ 22,000
Wages Payable	800	1,000
Note Payable, Long-Term	38,000	48,000
Contributed Capital	80,000	60,000
Retained Earnings	32,200	24,000
	$176,000	$155,000
Income Statement for 2017		
Sales	$100,000	
Cost of Goods Sold	61,000	
Other Expenses	27,000	
Net Income	$ 12,000	

→ purchase

Additional notes:

a. Bought equipment for cash, $9,000

b. Paid $10,000 on the long–term note payable

c. Issued new shares for $20,000 cash

d. Declared and paid a $3,800 cash dividend

e. Other expenses included depreciation, $6,000; wages, $10,000; taxes, $3,000; other, $8,000

f. Accounts Payable includes only inventory purchases made on credit. Because there are no liability accounts relating to taxes or other expenses, assume that these expenses were fully paid in cash.

Required:

1. Prepare the statement of cash flows for the year ended December 31, 2017, using the indirect method.

> TIP: Net cash flows provided by operating activities equal $28,800.
>
> TIP: Net cash used in investing activities equals $9,000.
>
> TIP: Net cash provided by financing activities equals $6,200.

2. Use the statement of cash flows to evaluate Hunter's cash flows.

> TIP: Demonstration case A provides a good example of information to consider when evaluating cash flows.

LO12-2, 12-3, 12-4, 12-5

CP12-4 Preparing and Interpreting a Statement of Cash Flows (Indirect Method)

Soft Touch Company was started several years ago by two golf instructors. The company's comparative balance sheets and income statement appear below, along with additional information.

	2017	2016
Balance Sheet at December 31		
Cash	$12,000	$ 8,000
Accounts Receivable	2,000	3,500
Equipment	11,000	10,000
Less: Accumulated Depreciation	(3,000)	(2,500)
	$22,000	$19,000
Accounts Payable	$ 1,000	$ 2,000
Wages Payable	1,000	1,500
Long-Term Bank Loan Payable	3,000	1,000
Contributed Capital	10,000	10,000
Retained Earnings	7,000	4,500
	$22,000	$19,000
Income Statement for 2017		
Lessons Revenue	$75,000	
Wages Expense	70,000	
Depreciation Expense	500	
Income Tax Expense	2,000	
Net Income	$ 2,500	

Additional Data:

a. Bought new golf clubs using cash, $1,000

b. Borrowed $2,000 cash from the bank during the year

c. Accounts Payable includes only purchases of services made on credit for operating purposes. Because there are no liability accounts relating to income tax, assume that this expense was fully paid in cash.

Required:

1. Prepare the statement of cash flows for the year ended December 31, 2017, using the indirect method.

> TIP: Net cash flows provided by operating activities equal $3,000.

TIP: Net cash used in investing activities equals $1,000.

TIP: Net cash provided by financing activities equals $2,000.

2. Use the statement of cash flows to evaluate the company's cash flows.

TIP: Demonstration Case A provides a good example of information to consider when evaluating cash flows.

CP12-5 Computing Cash Flows from Operating Activities (Direct Method)

Refer to the information in CP12—2.

Required:

Prepare the cash flows from operating activities section of the 2017 statement of cash flows using the direct method.

TIP: Convert the cost of goods sold to cash paid to suppliers by adding the increase in inventory and subtracting the increase in accounts payable.

CP12-6 Preparing and Interpreting a Statement of Cash Flows (Direct Method)

Refer to CP12—4.

Required:

Complete requirements 1 and 2 using the direct method.

TIP: Remember to exclude depreciation expense when converting to the cash basis.

CP12-7 (Supplement 12A) Preparing and Interpreting a Statement of Cash Flows with Loss on Disposal (Indirect Method)

Assume the same facts as CP12—4, except for additional data item (*a*) and the income statement. Instead of using the data from item (*a*), assume that the company bought new golf clubs for $3,000 cash and sold existing clubs for $1,000 cash. The clubs that were sold cost $2,000 and had Accumulated Depreciation of $500 at the time of sale. The income statement follows.

Income Statement for 2017	
Lessons Revenue	$75,000
Wages Expense	68,000
Depreciation Expense	1,000
Loss on Disposal of Equipment	500
Income Tax Expense	1,000
Net Income	$ 2,500

Required:

1. Prepare the statement of cash flows for the year ended December 31, 2017, using the indirect method.
2. Use the statement of cash flows to evaluate the company's cash flows.

GROUP A PROBLEMS

PA12-1 Determining Cash Flow Statement Effects of Transactions

Motif Furniture designs and sells modern furniture. For each of the following first–quarter transactions, indicate whether operating (O), investing (I), or financing activities (F) are affected and whether the effect is a cash inflow (+) or outflow (−), or write (NE) if the transaction has no effect on cash.

_____ 1. Bought used equipment for cash

_____ 2. Paid cash to purchase new equipment

_____ 3. Declared and paid cash dividends to shareholders

_____ 4. Collected payments on account from customers

_____ 5. Recorded an adjusting entry to record accrued salaries expense

LO12-3, 12-4, 12-5, 12-6

LO12-3, 12-4, 12-5, 12-6

LO12-S1

LO12-1

_____ 6. Recorded and paid interest on debt to creditors
_____ 7. Repaid principal on loan from bank
_____ 8. Prepaid rent for the following period
_____ 9. Made payment to suppliers on account

LO12-2 **PA12-2 Computing Cash Flows from Operating Activities (Indirect Method)**

The income statement and selected balance sheet information for Direct Products Company for the year ended December 31, 2017 are as follows:

Income Statement	
Sales Revenue	$48,600
Expenses:	
Cost of Goods Sold	21,000
Depreciation Expense	2,000
Salaries Expense	9,000
Rent Expense	4,500
Insurance Expense	1,900
Interest Expense	1,800
Utilities Expense	1,400
Net Income	$ 7,000

Selected Balance Sheet Accounts	2017	2016
Accounts Receivable	$560	$580
Merchandise Inventory	990	770
Accounts Payable	440	460
Prepaid Rent	25	20
Prepaid Insurance	25	28
Salaries Payable	100	70
Utilities Payable	20	15

Check Figure:

Net cash flow from operating activities = $8,813

Required:

Prepare the cash flows from operating activities section of the 2017 statement of cash flows using the indirect method.

LO12-2, 12-3, 12-4, 12-5

PA12-3 Preparing a Statement of Cash Flows (Indirect Method)

XS Supply Company is developing its annual financial statements at December 31, 2017. The statements are complete except for the statement of cash flows. The completed comparative balance sheets and income statement are summarized:

	2017	2016
Balance Sheet at December 31		
Cash	$ 34,000	$ 29,000
Accounts Receivable	35,000	28,000
Merchandise Inventory	41,000	38,000
Property and Equipment	121,000	100,000
Less: Accumulated Depreciation	(30,000)	(25,000)
	$201,000	$170,000
Accounts Payable	$ 36,000	$ 27,000
Wages Payable	1,200	1,400
Note Payable, Long-Term	38,000	44,000
Contributed Capital	88,600	72,600
Retained Earnings	37,200	25,000
	$201,000	$170,000
Income Statement for 2017		
Sales	$120,000	
Cost of Goods Sold	70,000	
Other Expenses	37,800	
Net Income	$ 12,200	

Additional Data:

a. Bought equipment for cash, $21,000

b. Paid $6,000 on the long—term note payable

c. Issued new shares for $16,000 cash

d. No dividends were declared or paid

e. Other expenses included depreciation, $5,000; wages, $20,000; taxes, $6,000; other, $6,800

f. Accounts Payable includes only inventory purchases made on credit. Because there are no liability accounts relating to taxes or other expenses, assume that these expenses were fully paid in cash.

Required:

1. Prepare the statement of cash flows for the year ended December 31, 2017, using the indirect method.
2. Evaluate the statement of cash flows.

PA12-4 Preparing and Interpreting a Statement of Cash Flows (Indirect Method)

LO12-2, 12-3, 12-4, 12-5

Heads Up Company was started several years ago by two hockey instructors. The company's comparative balance sheets and income statement appear on the next page, along with additional information.

	2017	2016
Balance Sheet at December 31		
Cash	$ 6,000	$4,000
Accounts Receivable	1,000	1,750
Equipment	5,500	5,000
Less: Accumulated Depreciation	(1,500)	(1,250)
	$11,000	$9,500
Accounts Payable	$ 500	$1,000
Wages Payable	500	750
Long-Term Bank Loan Payable	1,500	500
Contributed Capital	5,000	5,000
Retained Earnings	3,500	2,250
	$11,000	$9,500
Income Statement for 2017		
Lessons Revenue	$ 37,500	
Wages Expense	35,000	
Depreciation Expense	250	
Income Tax Expense	1,000	
Net Income	$ 1,250	

Additional notes:

a. Bought new hockey equipment for cash, $500

b. Borrowed $1,000 cash from the bank during the year

c. Accounts Payable includes only purchases of services made on credit for operating purposes. Because there are no liability accounts relating to income tax, assume that this expense was fully paid in cash.

Required:

1. Prepare the statement of cash flows for the year ended December 31, 2017, using the indirect method.
2. Use the statement of cash flows to evaluate the company's cash flows.

PA12-5 Computing Cash Flows from Operating Activities (Direct Method)

LO12-6

Refer to the information in PA12–2.

Required:

Prepare the cash flows from operating activities section of the 2017 statement of cash flows using the direct method.

Check Figure:
Cash payments to suppliers = $(21,240)

PA12-6 Preparing and Interpreting a Statement of Cash Flows (Direct Method)

LO12-3, 12-4, 12-5, 12-6

Refer to PA12–4.

Required:

Complete requirements 1 and 2 using the direct method.

LO12-S1 **PA12-7 (Supplement 12A) Preparing and Interpreting a Statement of Cash Flows with Loss on Disposal (Indirect Method)**

Assume the same facts as PA12—4, except for the income statement and additional item (*a*). The new income statement is shown below. Instead of item (*a*) from PA12—4, assume that the company bought new equipment for $1,800 cash and sold existing equipment for $500 cash. The equipment that was sold was purchased for $1,300 and had Accumulated Depreciation of $250 at the time of sale.

Income Statement for 2017	
Lessons Revenue	$37,500
Wages Expense	35,000
Depreciation Expense	500
Loss on Disposal of Equipment	550
Income Tax Expense	200
Net Income	$ 1,250

Required:

1. Prepare the statement of cash flows for the year ended December 31, 2017, using the indirect method.
2. Use the statement of cash flows to evaluate the company's cash flows.

GROUP B PROBLEMS

LO12-1 **PB12-1 Determining Cash Flow Statement Effects of Transactions**

For each of the following transactions, indicate whether operating (O), investing (I), or financing activities (F) are affected and whether the effect is a cash inflow (+) or outflow (−), or write (NE) if the transaction has no effect on cash.

_____ 1. Received deposits from customers for products to be delivered the following period
_____ 2. Principal repayments on loan
_____ 3. Paid cash to purchase new equipment
_____ 4. Received proceeds from loan
_____ 5. Collected payments on account from customers
_____ 6. Recorded and paid salaries to employees
_____ 7. Paid cash for building construction
_____ 8. Recorded and paid interest to debt holders

LO12-2 **PB12-2 Computing Cash Flows from Operating Activities (Indirect Method)**

The income statement and selected balance sheet information for Calendars Incorporated for the year ended December 31, 2017, is presented below.

Income Statement	
Sales Revenue	$78,000
Expenses:	
Cost of Goods Sold	36,000
Depreciation Expense	16,000
Salaries Expense	10,000
Rent Expense	2,500
Insurance Expense	1,300
Interest Expense	1,200
Utilities Expense	1,000
Net Income	$10,000

Selected Balance Sheet Accounts		
	2017	2016
Merchandise Inventory	$ 430	$ 490
Accounts Receivable	1,800	1,500
Accounts Payable	1,200	1,300
Salaries Payable	450	300
Utilities Payable	100	0
Prepaid Rent	50	100
Prepaid Insurance	70	90

Required:

Prepare the cash flows from operating activities section of the 2017 statement of cash flows using the indirect method.

PB12-3 Preparing a Statement of Cash Flows (Indirect Method)

LO12-2, 12-3, 12-4, 12-5

Audio City Inc. is developing its annual financial statements at December 31, 2017. The statements are complete except for the statement of cash flows. The completed comparative balance sheets and income statement are summarized as follows:

	2017	2016
Balance Sheet at December 31		
Cash	$ 63,000	$ 65,000
Accounts Receivable	15,000	20,000
Merchandise Inventory	22,000	20,000
Property and Equipment	210,000	150,000
Less: Accumulated Depreciation	(60,000)	(45,000)
	$250,000	$210,000
Accounts Payable	$ 8,000	$ 19,000
Wages Payable	2,000	1,000
Note Payable, Long-Term	60,000	75,000
Contributed Capital	100,000	70,000
Retained Earnings	80,000	45,000
	$250,000	$210,000
Income Statement for 2017		
Sales	$190,000	
Cost of Goods Sold	90,000	
Other Expenses	60,000	
Net Income	$ 40,000	

Additional notes:

a. Bought equipment for cash, $60,000

b. Paid $15,000 on the long–term note payable

c. Issued new shares for $30,000 cash

d. Dividends of $5,000 were paid in cash

e. Other expenses included depreciation, $15,000; wages, $20,000; taxes, $25,000

f. Accounts Payable includes only inventory purchases made on credit. Because a liability relating to taxes does not exist, assume that the taxes were fully paid in cash.

Required:

1. Prepare the statement of cash flows for the year ended December 31, 2017, using the indi– rect method.
2. Evaluate the statement of cash flows.

Check Figure [Req. 1]:
Net decrease in cash during the year = $(2,000)

PB12-4 Preparing and Interpreting a Statement of Cash Flows (Indirect Method)

LO12-2, 12-3, 12-4, 12-5

Buddies' Dive In Company was started several years ago by two diving instructors. The company's comparative balance sheets and income statement are presented below, followed by additional information.

	2017	2016
Balance Sheet at December 31		
Cash	$ 3,200	$4,000
Accounts Receivable	1,000	500
Prepaid Expenses	100	50
	$ 4,300	$4,550
Wages Payable	$ 350	$1,100
Contributed Capital	1,200	1,000
Retained Earnings	2,750	2,450
	$ 4,300	$4,550
Income Statement for 2017		
Lessons Revenue	$33,950	
Wages Expense	30,000	
Other Operating Expenses	3,650	
Net Income	$ 300	

Additional notes:

a. Prepaid Expenses relate to rent paid in advance.

b. Other Operating Expenses were paid in cash.

c. An owner contributed capital by paying $200 cash in exchange for company shares.

Required:

1. Prepare the statement of cash flows for the year ended December 31, 2017, using the indirect method.
2. Use the statement of cash flows to evaluate the company's cash flows.

LO12-6   **PB12-5 Computing Cash Flows from Operating Activities (Direct Method)**

Refer to the information in PB12–2.

Required:

Prepare the cash flows from the operating activities section of the 2017 statement of cash flows using the direct method.

LO12-3, 12-4,   **PB12-6 Preparing and Interpreting a Statement of Cash Flows (Direct Method)**
12-5, 12-6
Refer to PB12–4.

Check Figure   **Required:**
[Req. 1]:
Net decrease in   Complete requirements 1 and 2 using the direct method.
cash during the
year = $(800)
SKILLS DEVELOPMENT CASES

LO12-1, 12-5   **S12-1 Finding Financial Information**

Refer to the summarized financial statements of The Home Depot Inc. in Appendix A at the back of this book.

Required:

1. Which of the two basic reporting approaches for the cash flows from operating activities did The Home Depot use if their cash flow statement starts with Net Income?
2. In the 2016 fiscal year, The Home Depot generated $9,783 million from operating activities. Give some examples as to where The Home Depot might spend this money?

LO12-1, 12-5   **S12-2 Comparing Financial Information**

Refer to the summarized financial statements of The Home Depot in Appendix A and Lowe's Companies Inc. in Appendix B at the end of this book.

Required:

1. Which of the two basic reporting approaches for the cash flows from operating activities did Lowe's Companies Inc. use? Is this the same as what The Home Depot used?

2. What amount of cash did Lowe's Companies Inc. receive from disposing of property and equipment during the year ended February 3, 2017?

3. In the 2016 fiscal year, Lowe's Companies Inc. generated $5,617 million from operating activities. Where did Lowe's Companies Inc. spend this money? List the two largest cash outflows reported in the investing or financing activities sections.

S12-3 Internet-Based Team Research: Examining an Annual Report

LO12-5

As a team, select an industry to analyze. Using the Internet, each team member should access the annual report for one publicly traded company in the industry, with each member selecting a different company. (See S1–3 in Chapter 1 for a description of possible resources for these tasks.)

Required:

1. On an individual basis, each team member should write a short report that incorporates the following:

   a. Has the company generated positive or negative operating cash flows during the past three years?

   b. Has the company been expanding over that period? If so, what appears to have been the source of financing for this expansion (operating cash flow, additional borrowing, issuance of shares)?

   c. Compare and analyze the difference between net income and operating cash flows over the past three years.

2. Then, as a team, write a short report comparing and contrasting your companies using these attributes. Discuss any patterns across the companies that you as a team observe. Provide potential explanations for any differences discovered.

S12-4 Ethical Decision Making: A Real-Life Example

LO12-1, 12-5

In a press release on February 19, 2004, the U.S. Securities and Exchange Commission described a number of fraudulent transactions that Enron executives concocted in an effort to meet the company's financial targets. One particularly well–known scheme is called the "Nigerian barge" transaction. According to court documents, Enron arranged to sell three electricity–generating power barges moored off the coast of Nigeria. The "buyer" was the investment banking firm of Merrill Lynch. Although Enron reported this transaction as a sale in its income statement, it turns out that this was no ordinary sale. Merrill Lynch didn't really want the barges and had agreed to buy them only because Enron guaranteed, in a secret side deal, that it would arrange for the barges to be bought back from Merrill Lynch within six months of the initial transaction. In addition, Enron promised to pay Merrill Lynch a hefty fee for doing the deal. In an interview on National Public Radio on August 17, 2002, Michigan Senator Carl Levin declared, the "case of the Nigerian barge transaction was, by any defini–tion, a loan."

Required:

1. Discuss whether the Nigerian barge transaction should have been considered a loan rather than a sale. As part of your discussion, consider the following questions. Doesn't the Merrill Lynch payment to Enron at the time of the initial transaction automatically make it a sale, not a loan? What aspects of the transaction are similar to a loan? Which aspects suggest revenue has not been earned by Enron?

2. The income statement effect of recording the transaction as a sale rather than as a loan is fairly clear: Enron was able to boost its revenues and net income. What is somewhat less obvious, but nearly as important, are the effects on the statement of cash flows. Describe how including the transaction with sales of other Enron products, rather than as a loan, would change the statement of cash flows.

3. How would the difference in the statement of cash flows (described in your response to requirement 2) affect financial statement users?

S12-5 Ethical Decision Making: A Mini-Case

Assume that you serve on the board of a local golf and country club. In preparation for renegotiating the club's bank loans, the president indicates that the club needs to increase its operating cash flows before the end of the current year.

The club's treasurer reassures the president and other board members that he knows a couple of ways to boost the club's operating cash flows. First, he says, the club can sell some of its accounts receivable to a collections company that is willing to pay the club $97,000 up front for the right to collect $100,000 of the overdue accounts. That will immediately boost operating cash flows. Second, he indicates that the club paid about $200,000 the previous month to relocate the 18th fairway and green closer to the clubhouse.

The treasurer indicates that although these costs have been reported as expenses in the club's own monthly financial statements, he feels an argument can be made for reporting them as part of land and land improvements (a long–lived asset) in the year–end financial statements that would be provided to the bank. He explains that, by recording these payments as an addition to a long–lived asset, they will not be shown as a reduction in operating cash flows.

Required:

1. Does the sale of accounts receivable to generate immediate cash harm or mislead anyone? Would you consider it an ethical business activity?
2. What category in the statement of cash flows is used when reporting cash spent on long–lived assets, such as land improvements? What category is used when cash is spent on expenses, such as costs for regular upkeep of the grounds?
3. What facts are relevant to deciding whether the costs of the 18th hole relocation should be reported as an asset or as an expense? Is it appropriate to make this decision based on the impact it could have on operating cash flows?
4. As a member of the board, how would you ensure that an ethical decision is made?

S12-6 Critical Thinking: Interpreting Adjustments Reported on the Statement of Cash Flows from a Management Perspective (Indirect Method)

QuickServe, a chain of convenience stores, was experiencing some serious cash flow difficulties because of rapid growth. The company did not generate sufficient cash from operating activities to finance its new stores, and creditors were not willing to lend money because the company had not produced any income for the previous three years.

The new controller for QuickServe proposed a reduction in the estimated life of store equipment to increase depreciation expense, thus, "we can improve cash flows from operating activities because depreciation expense is added back on the statement of cash flows." Other executives were not sure that this was a good idea because the increase in depreciation would make it more difficult to report positive earnings: "Without income, the bank will never lend us money."

Required:

What action would you recommend for QuickServe? Why?

S12-7 Using a Spreadsheet that Calculates Cash Flows from Operating Activities (Indirect Method)

*e**X**cel*

You've recently been hired by B2B Consultants to provide financial advisory services to small–business managers. B2B's clients often need advice on how to improve their operating cash flows, and given your accounting background, you're frequently called on to show them how operating cash flows would change if they were to speed up their sales of inventory and their collections of accounts receivable or delay their payment of accounts payable.

Each time you're asked to show the effects of these business decisions on the cash flows from operating activities, you get the uneasy feeling that you might inadvertently miscalculate their effects. To deal with this once and for all, you email your friend Owen and ask him to prepare a template that automatically calculates the net operating cash flows from a simple comparative balance sheet. You received his reply today.

Hey pal. I like your idea of working smarter, not harder. Too bad it involved me doing the thinking. Anyhow, I've created a spreadsheet file that contains four worksheets. The first two tabs (labelled BS and IS) are the input sheets where you would enter the numbers from each client's comparative balance sheets and income statement. Your clients are small, so this template allows for only the usual accounts. Also, I've assumed that depreciation is the only reason for a change in accumulated depreciation. If your clients' business activities differ from these, you'll need to contact me for more complex templates. The third worksheet calculates the operating cash flows using the indirect method and the fourth does this calculation using the direct method. I'll attach the screenshots of each of the worksheets so you can create your own. To answer "what if" questions, all you'll need to do is change selected amounts in the balance sheet and income statement.

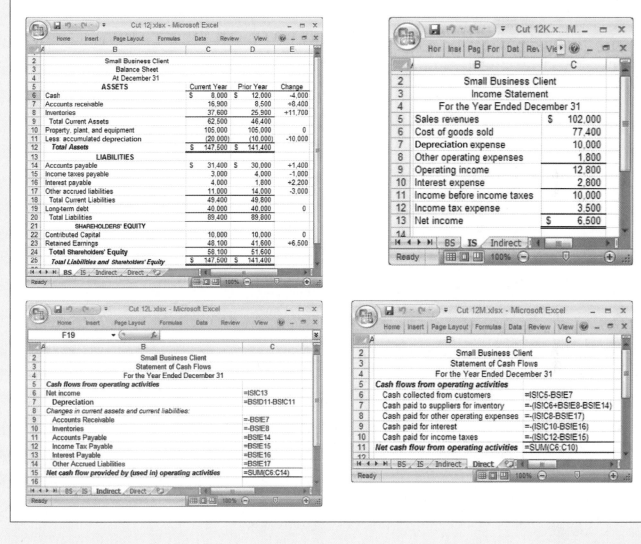

Required:

Copy the account balances from the worksheets for the balance sheet and income statement into a spreadsheet file. Enter formulas into the balance sheet worksheet to compute the change in each account balance, and then enter the formulas for the statement of cash flows (indirect method only) into a third worksheet. From this third worksheet, report the net cash flow provided by (used in) operating activities.

S12-8 Using a Spreadsheet That Calculates Cash Flows from Operating Activities (Direct Method)

Refer to the information presented in S12–7.

Required:

Complete the same requirements using the direct method only.

S12-9 Using a Spreadsheet to Answer "What If" Management Questions (Indirect or Direct Method)

Change the amounts for selected balance sheet accounts in the spreadsheets created for either S12–7 or S12–8 to calculate the net cash flows from operating activities if, just before the current year–end, the company's management took the actions listed in the following requirements. Consider each question independently, unless indicated otherwise.

Required:

1. What if the company collected $10,000 of the accounts receivable?
2. What if the company had paid down its interest payable by an extra $2,000?
3. What if the company waited an additional month before paying $6,000 of its accounts payable?
4. What if the company had reported $5,000 more depreciation expense?
5. What if all four of the above events had taken place at the same time?

CONTINUING CASES

CC12-1 Accounting for Cash Flows

During a recent year (ended December 31, 2017), Nicole's Getaway Spa (NGS) reported net income of $2,300. The company reported the following activities:

a. Increase in inventories of $400

b. Depreciation of $3,000

c. Increase of $2,170 in prepaid expenses

d. Payments of $4,600 on long–term debt

e. Purchased new spa equipment for $7,582

f. Payments on accounts payable exceeded purchases by $320

g. Collections on accounts receivable exceeded credit sales by $859

h. Issued $10,000 of common shares

Required:

Based on this information, prepare a statement of cash flows for the year ended December 31, 2017, using the indirect method. Assume the cash balance at December 31, 2016, was $7,000.

CC12-2 Wiki Art Gallery (WAG)

Refer to the Wiki Art Gallery (WAG) instructional case in Appendix D and read the case in sufficient depth to answer the following questions.

WAG reported $140,000 in total revenues in 2011. What amount of cash did WAG collect in 2011 from its customers (artwork buyers and artists)?

a. $140,000

b. $78,400

c. $71,550

d. $61,650

Endnotes

1. Intermediate accounting courses discuss in detail exceptions to this general rule. Exceptions include investing activities that affect current assets (e.g., short−term investments) and financing activities that affect current liabilities (for example, dividends payable and short−term notes payable).

2. Amortization and impairment losses (discussed in Chapter 9) are handled in exactly the same way as depreciation. Gains and losses on fixed asset disposals also are dealt with in a similar manner and are discussed in this chapter's Supplement 12A.

3. Investing activities also affect other assets described in Appendix E (investments in other companies). Although not shown here, the cash flows for investments are similar to those shown in this section for equipment and intangible assets.

4. Steven F. Orpurt and Yoonseok Zang, "Do Direct Cash Flow Disclosures Help Predict Future Operating Cash Flows and Earnings?" *The Accounting Review 84*:3, May 2009, pp. 893–936.

THAT WAS
THEN

In the previous chapters, you learned how to report and interpret the financial effects of various business activities.

THIS IS
NOW

This chapter synthesizes previous chapters by evaluating the financial statements and accounting decisions of a publicly traded company.

YOUR LEARNING OBJECTIVES

Understand the business

LO13-1 Describe the purposes and uses of horizontal, vertical, and ratio analyses.

Study the accounting methods

LO13-2 Use horizontal (trend) analyses to recognize financial changes that unfold over time.

LO13-3 Use vertical (common-size) analyses to understand important relationships within financial statements.

LO13-4 Calculate financial ratios to assess profitability, liquidity, and solvency.

Evaluate the results

LO13-5 Interpret the results of financial analyses.

LO13-6 Describe how analyses depend on key accounting decisions and concepts.

Review the chapter

Chapter Summary

Supplemental material

LO13-S1 Describe how non-recurring and other comprehensive income items are reported.

LO13-S2 Describe significant differences between ASPE and IFRS.

CHAPTER 13

Measuring and Evaluating Financial Performance

Niloo/Shutterstock.com

FOCUS COMPANY:
The Home Depot, Inc.
www.homedepot.ca

Measuring and evaluating financial performance is like judging gymnastics or figure skating at the Olympics. You have to know three things: (1) the general categories to evaluate for each event, (2) the particular elements to consider within each category, and (3) how to measure performance for each element. On the financial side, managers and analysts follow the same process. They evaluate general categories such as profitability, liquidity, and solvency, which are separated into particular elements such as gross profit margin and net profit margin. For each of these elements, analysts measure performance by computing various percentages and ratios, which themselves are based on information reported in the financial statements.

In this chapter, we focus on The Home Depot, the largest home improvement specialty retailer in the world. The Home Depot currently operates in ten Canadian provinces, fifty American states, the District of Columbia, Puerto Rico, the U.S. Virgin Islands, and Mexico. The company has 182 stores in Canada and employs over 27,000 people in Canada alone. Yet the company's continued success still requires innovations to increase sales in existing markets and to successfully enter new markets. At the same time, The Home Depot must control costs while maintaining a high level of customer service in its stores. Finally, The Home Depot's management must anticipate the actions of its rival, Lowe's, and address changes in overall demand for building products over which it has little control.

How do managers, analysts, investors, and creditors assess The Home Depot's success in meeting these challenges? This is the purpose of financial statement analysis. Our discussion begins with an explanation of how to analyze financial statements to understand the financial results of a company's business activities. We conclude the chapter with a review of the key accounting decisions that analysts consider when evaluating financial statements.

ORGANIZATION OF THE CHAPTER

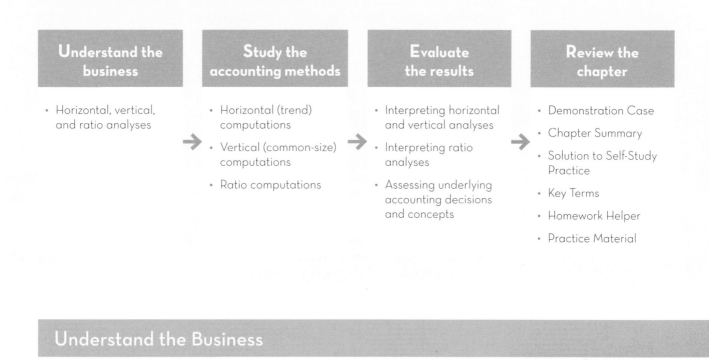

Understand the business	Study the accounting methods	Evaluate the results	Review the chapter
• Horizontal, vertical, and ratio analyses	• Horizontal (trend) computations • Vertical (common-size) computations • Ratio computations	• Interpreting horizontal and vertical analyses • Interpreting ratio analyses • Assessing underlying accounting decisions and concepts	• Demonstration Case • Chapter Summary • Solution to Self-Study Practice • Key Terms • Homework Helper • Practice Material

Understand the Business

As you first learned in Chapter 1, the goal of accounting is to provide information that allows decision makers to understand and evaluate the results of business activities. Throughout the course, you have learned how financial statements are used in a variety of decisions. Managers analyze financial statements to evaluate past financial performance and make future decisions. Creditors use financial statements to assess compliance with loan covenants. And, of course, analysts use financial statements to generate advice for investors and others.

You have learned that no single number fully captures the results of all business activities, nor does it predict a company's success or failure. Instead, to understand and evaluate the results of business activities, you need to look at a business from many different angles. An understanding of whether a business is successful will emerge only after you have learned to combine all of your evaluations into a complete picture or story that depicts the company's performance. Our goal for this chapter is to demonstrate how you can do this, relying on horizontal, vertical, and ratio analyses to develop the "story" of how well a company has performed.

LEARNING OBJECTIVE 13-1

Describe the purposes and uses of horizontal, vertical, and ratio analyses.

HORIZONTAL, VERTICAL, AND RATIO ANALYSES

Most good stories have a plot, which the reader comes to understand as it unfolds over time or as one event relates to another. Financial analyses work the same way.

Horizontal (trend) analyses are conducted to help financial statement users recognize important financial changes that unfold over time. Horizontal analyses compare individual financial statement line items horizontally (from one period to the next), with the general goal of identifying significant, sustained changes (trends). These changes are typically described in terms of dollar amounts and year–over–year percentages. For example, trend analyses could be used to determine the dollar amount and percentage by which Cost of Goods Sold increased this year, relative to prior years.

Vertical analyses focus on important relationships between items on the same financial statement. These items are compared vertically (one account balance versus another) and are typically expressed as percentages to reveal the relative contributions made by each financial statement item. For example, vertical analyses could show that operating expenses consume one-quarter of a company's net sales revenue.

Ratio analyses are conducted to understand relationships among various items reported in one or more of the financial statements. Ratio analyses allow you to evaluate how well a company has performed, given the level of other company resources. For example, while vertical analyses can show that Cost of Goods Sold consumes 65 percent of Net Sales and horizontal analyses can show that this percentage has increased over time, ratio analyses can relate these amounts to inventory levels to evaluate inventory management decisions.

Before we show you how to calculate horizontal, vertical, and ratio analyses (in the next section), we must emphasize that no analysis is complete unless it leads to an interpretation that helps financial statement users understand and evaluate a company's financial results. Without interpretation, these computations can appear as nothing more than a list of disconnected numbers.

Study the Accounting Methods

HORIZONTAL (TREND) COMPUTATIONS

LEARNING OBJECTIVE **13-2**

Use horizontal (trend) analyses to recognize financial changes that unfold over time.

Horizontal (trend) analyses: Compare results across time, often expressing changes in account balances as a percentage of prior year balances. Also called *horizontal analysis* or *time - series analysis.*

Horizontal (trend) analyses help financial statement users to recognize financial changes that unfold over time. This approach compares individual financial statement items from year to year with the general goal of identifying significant sustained changes or trends. For example, trend analysis can be used to determine the dollar and percentage changes in the cost of goods sold this year relative to prior years. Because this type of analysis compares the results on each line of the financial statements across several years, trend analysis is also known as horizontal analysis. Because it compares results over a series of periods, it is sometimes called time–series analysis.

Regardless of the name, trend analyses are usually calculated in terms of year–to–year dollar and percentage changes. A year–to–year percentage change expresses the current year's dollar change as a percentage of the prior year's total using the following calculation:

$$\text{Year-to-Year Change (\%)} = \frac{\text{Change This Year}}{\text{Prior Year's Total}} \times 100 = \frac{(\text{Current Year's Total} - \text{Prior Year's Total})}{\text{Prior Year's Total}} \times 100$$

To demonstrate how to calculate a trend, we analyze The Home Depot's financial statements. Summaries of The Home Depot's balance sheets and income statements from five recent years appear in Exhibits 13.1 and 13.2. Dollar and percentage changes from fiscal year 2015 compared to 2014[1] are shown to the right of the account balances in the balance sheet and income statement for fiscal 2015. The dollar changes were calculated by subtracting fiscal 2014 balances from fiscal 2015 balances. The percentage changes were calculated by dividing those differences by the fiscal 2014 balances. For example, in Exhibit 13.1, we see that Cash and Cash Equivalents increased by $493 (= $2,216 − $1,723) in fiscal 2015 relative to fiscal 2014 (all numbers in millions). That dollar amount represented an increase of 28.6 percent (= ($493 ÷ $1,723) × 100). Dollar and percentage changes are provided for the comparison of the remaining fiscal years. These were calculated using the same formula for any two comparative years.

THE HOME DEPOT
Balance Sheets
(in millions)

Year Ended:	January 31, 2016 (Fiscal 2015)	Increase (Decrease) Amount	Percentage*	February 1, 2015 (Fiscal 2014)	Increase (Decrease) Amount	Percentage*
Assets						
Current Assets						
Cash and Cash Equivalents	$ 2,216	$ 493	28.6%	$ 1,723	$ 206	(10.7)%
Accounts Receivable, Net	1,890	406	27.4	1,484	86	6.2
Inventories	11,809	730	6.6	11,079	22	0.2
Other Current Assets	1,078	62	6.1	1,016	121	13.5
Total Current Assets	16, 993	1,691	11.1	15,302	23	0.2
Property and Equipment, Net	22,191	(529)	(2.3)	22,720	(628)	(2.7)
Goodwill	2,102	749	55.4	1,353	(64)	(5.0)
Other Assets	1,263	692	121.2	571	(31)	(5.1)
Total Assets	$42,549	$ 2,603	6.5	$39,946	$ (572)	(1.4)
Liabilities and Shareholders' Equity						
Current Liabilities	$12,526	$ 1,257	11.2	$11,269	$520	4.8
Long–Term Liabilities	23,707	(4,352)	22.5	19,355	2,108	12.2
Total Liabilities	36,233	5,609	18.3	30,624	2,628	9.4
Shareholders' Equity	6,316	(3,006)	(32.2)	9,322	(3,200)	(25.6)
Total Liabilities and Shareholders' Equity	$42,549	$ 2,603	6.5	$39,946	$ (572)	(1.4)

Year Ended:	February 2, 2014 (Fiscal 2013)	Increase (Decrease) Amount	Percentage*	February 3, 2013 (Fiscal 2012)	Increase (Decrease) Amount	Percentage*	January 29, 2012 (Fiscal 2011)
Assets							
Current Assets							
Cash and Cash Equivalents	$ 1,929	$ (565)	(22.7)%	$ 2,494	$ 507	25.5%	$ 1,987
Accounts Receivable, Net	1,398	3	0.2	1,395	150	12.0	1,245
Inventories	11,057	347	3.2	10,710	385	3.7	10,325
Other Current Assets	895	122	15.8	773	(190)	(19.7)	963
Total Current Assets	15,279	(93)	(0.6)	15,372	852	5.9	14,520
Property and Equipment, Net	23,348	(721)	(3.0)	24,069	(379)	(1.6)	24,448
Notes Receivable	—	(140)	(100.0)	140	5	3.7	135
Goodwill	1,289	119	10.2	1,170	50	4.5	1,120
Other Assets	602	269	80.8	333	38	12.9	295
Total Assets	$40,518	$ (566)	(1.4)	$ 41,084	$ 566	1.4	$40,518
Liabilities and Shareholders' Equity							
Current Liabilities	$10,749	$ (713)	(6.2)	$ 11,462	$2,086	22.2	$ 9,376
Long–Term Liabilities	17,247	5,402	45.6	11,845	(1,399)	(10.6)	13,244
Total Liabilities	27,996	4,689	20.1	23,307	687	3.0	22,620
Shareholders' Equity	12,522	(5,255)	(29.6)	17,777	(121)	(0.7)	17,898
Total Liabilities and Shareholders' Equity	$40,518	$ (566)	(1.4)	$ 41,084	$ 566	1.4	$40,518

*Amount of Increase (Decrease) ÷ Prior Fiscal Year × 100

THE HOME DEPOT
Income Statements
(in millions)

		Increase (Decrease)			Increase (Decrease)	
Year Ended:	**January 31, 2016 (Fiscal 2015)**	**Amount**	**Percentage***	**February 1, 2015 (Fiscal 2014)**	**Amount**	**Percentage***
Net Sales Revenue	$88,519	$5,343	6.4%	$83,176	$4,364	5.5%
Cost of Sales	58,254	3,467	6.3	54,787	2,890	5.6
Gross Profit	30,265	1,876	6.6	28,389	1,474	5.5
Operating and Other Expenses	18,491	571	3.2	17,920	171	1.0
Interest and Other Expense	753	260	52.7	493	(206)	(29.5)
Income Tax Expense	4,012	381	10.5	3,631	549	17.8
Net Income	$ 7,009	$ 664	10.5	$ 6,345	$ 960	17.8
Basic Earnings per Share	$ 5.49	$ 0.75	15.8	$ 4.74	$ 0.96	25.4

		Increase (Decrease)			Increase (Decrease)		
Year Ended:	**February 2, 2014 (Fiscal 2013)**	**Amount**	**Percentage***	**February 3, 2013 (Fiscal 2012)**	**Amount**	**Percentage***	**January 29, 2012 (Fiscal 2011)**
Net Sales Revenue	$78,812	$4,058	5.4%	$74,754	$4,359	6.2%	$70,395
Cost of Sales	51,897	2,985	6.1	48,912	2,779	6.0	46,133
Gross Profit	26,915	1,073	4.2	25,842	(1,580)	6.5	24,262
Operating and Other Expenses	17,749	(327)	(1.8)	18,076	475	2.7	17,601
Interest and Other Expense	699	154	28.3	545	(48)	(8.1)	593
Income Tax Expense	3,082	396	14.7	2,686	501	22.9	2,185
Net Income	$ 5,385	$ 850	18.7	$ 4,535	$ 652	16.8	$ 3,883
Basic Earnings per Share	$ 3.78	$ 0.75	24.8	$ 3.03	$ 0.54	21.7	$ 2.49

* Amount of Increase (Decrease) ÷ Prior Fiscal Year × 100

In a later section, we will explain and evaluate the underlying causes of significant changes in account balances. But before we leave this topic, we must note that not all large percentage changes will be significant. For example, the 27.4 percent increase in Accounts Receivable is a significant change on the balance sheet (Exhibit 13.1). However, the $406 increase is relatively small when compared to other changes, such as the $4,352 decrease in Long–Term Liabilities. To avoid focusing on unimportant changes, use the percentage changes to identify potentially significant changes, but then check the dollar change to make sure that it, too, is significant.

Vertical (common-size) analyses: Express each financial statement amount as a percentage of another amount on the same financial statement.

VERTICAL (COMMON-SIZE) COMPUTATIONS

A second type of analysis, **vertical (common–size) analysis**, focuses on important relationships within a financial statement. When a company is growing or shrinking overall, it is difficult to tell from the dollar amounts whether the proportions within each statement category are changing. Common–size financial statements provide this information by expressing each financial statement amount as a percentage of another amount on that statement. The usefulness of common–size statements is illustrated in Exhibits 13.3 and 13.4 by showing The Home Depot's balance sheet and income statements presented in the common–size format.

In a common–size balance sheet, each asset appears as a percentage of total assets, and each liability or shareholders' equity item appears as a percentage of total liabilities and shareholders' equity. Exhibit 13.3, for

Use vertical (common-size) analyses to understand important relationships within financial statements.

EXHIBIT 13.3 Vertical (Common-Size) Analysis of The Home Depot's Summarized Balance Sheets

THE HOME DEPOT
Balance Sheets
(in millions)

	January 31, 2016 (Fiscal 2015)	Percentage*	February 1, 2015 (Fiscal 2014)	Percentage*	February 2, 2014 (Fiscal 2013)	Percentage*	February 3, 2013 (Fiscal 2012)	Percentage*	January 29, 2012 (Fiscal 2011)	Percentage*
Assets										
Current Assets										
Cash and Cash Equivalents	$ 2,216	5.21%	$ 1,723	4.3%	$ 1,929	4.8%	$ 2,494	6.1%	$ 1,987	4.9%
Accounts Receivable, Net	1,890	4.4	1,484	3.7	1,398	3.5	1,395	3.4	1,245	3.1
Inventories	11,809	27.8	11,079	27.7	11,057	27.3	10,710	26.1	10,325	25.5
Other Current Assets	1,078	2.5	1,016	2.5	895	2.2	773	1.9	963	2.4
Property and Equipment, Net	22,191	52.2	22,720	56.9	23,348	57.6	24,069	58.6	24,448	60.3
Notes Receivable	––	0.0	––	0.0	––	0.0	140	0.3	135	0.3
Goodwill	2,102	4.9	1,353	3.4	1,289	3.2	1,170	2.8	1,120	2.8
Other Assets	1,263	3.0	571	1.4	602	1.5	333	0.8	295	0.7
Total Assets	$42,549	100%	$39,946	100%	$40,518	100%	$41,084	100%	$40,518	100%
Liabilities and Shareholders' Equity										
Current Liabilities	$12,526	29.4%	$11,269	28.2%	$10,749	26.5%	$11,462	27.9%	$ 9,376	23.1%
Long–Term Liabilities	23,707	55.7	19,355	48.5	17,247	42.6	11,845	28.8	13,244	32.7
Shareholders' Equity	6,316	14.8	9,322	23.3	12,522	30.9	17,777	43.3	17,898	44.2
Total Liabilities and Shareholders' Equity	$42,549	100%	$39,946	100%	$40,518	100%	$41,084	100%	$40,518	100%

*Numbers might not add due to rounding.

EXHIBIT 13.4 **Vertical (Common-Size) Analysis of The Home Depot's Summarized Income Statements**

THE HOME DEPOT
Income Statements
(in millions)

Year Ended:	January 31, 2016 (Fiscal 2015)	Percentage*	February 1, 2015 (Fiscal 2014)	Percentage*	February 2, 2014 (Fiscal 2013)	Percentage*	February 3, 2013 (Fiscal 2012)	Percentage*	January 29, 2012 (Fiscal 2011)	Percentage*
Net Sales Revenue	$88,519	100%	$83,176	100%	$78,812	100%	$74,754	100%	$70,395	100%
Cost of Sales	58,254	65.8	54,787	65.9	51,897	65.8	48,912	65.4	46,133	65.5
Gross Profit	30,265	34.2	28,389	34.1	26,915	34.2	25,842	34.6	24,262	34.5
Operating and Other Expenses	18,491	20.9	17,920	21.5	17,749	22.5	18,076	24.2	17,601	25.0
Interest and Other Expense	753	0.9	493	0.6	699	0.9	545	0.7	593	0.8
Income Tax Expense	4,012	4.5	3,631	4.4	3,082	3.9	2,686	3.6	2,185	3.1
Net Income	$ 7,009	7.9	$ 6,345	7.6	$ 5,385	6.8	$ 4,535	6.1	$ 3,883	5.5

*Numbers might not add due to rounding.

example, which presents The Home Depot's common–size balance sheets, shows Cash and Cash Equivalents was 5.2 percent of total assets [= ($2,216 ÷ $42,549) × 100] at the end of fiscal 2015.

The common–size income statement reports each income statement item as a percentage of sales. For example, in Exhibit 13.4, which presents common–size income statements for The Home Depot for fiscal 2011 to 2015, cost of sales equalled 65.8 percent of net sales revenue in 2015 [= ($58,254 ÷ $88,519) × 100]. These common–size financial statements can be very useful to management and analysts in comparing results over a series of years and enable them to highlight key areas of concern. For example, gross profit has remained steady over the five years shown in Exhibit 13.4, at around 34 percent. If gross profit all of a sudden took a big decline to 25 percent, this would be shown in these common–size financial statements and would prompt management to look into the cause of such a decline.

RATIO COMPUTATIONS

LEARNING OBJECTIVE 13-4

Calculate financial ratios to assess profitability, liquidity, and solvency.

Ratio analyses help financial statement users to understand relationships among various items reported in the financial statements. These analyses compare the amounts for one or more line items to the amounts for other line items in the same year. Ratio analyses are useful because they con–sider differences in the sizes of the amounts being compared, similar to common–size statements. In fact, some of the most popular ratios, such as net profit margin and the debt–to–assets ratio, are taken directly from the common–size statements. Ratios allow users to evaluate how well a com–pany has performed given the level of its other resources.

Most analysts classify ratios into three categories:

1. **Profitability** ratios, which relate to the company's performance in the current period—in particular, the company's ability to generate income

2. **Liquidity** ratios, which relate to the company's short–term sur–vival—in particular, the company's ability to use current assets to repay liabilities as they become due

3. **Solvency** ratios, which relate to the company's long–run sur–vival—in particular, the company's ability to repay lenders when debt matures and to make the required interest payments prior to the date of maturity

Profitability: The extent to which a company generates income.

Liquidity: The extent to which a company is able to pay its currently maturing obligations.

Solvency: The ability to survive long enough to repay lenders when debt matures.

Exhibit 13.5 organizes the ratios introduced in previous chapters according to these three categories, and demonstrates Home Depot's calculations for fiscal 2015 using data from Exhibits 13.1 and 13.2.

EXHIBIT 13.5 Common Ratios Used in Financial Statement Analysis (See also the Accounting Decision Tools feature of each chapter.)

Profitability Ratios

THE HOME DEPOT
Fiscal 2015

(1) $\text{Net Profit Margin} = \dfrac{\text{Net Income}}{\text{Net Sales Revenue}} \times 100$ Ch. 3

$\dfrac{\$7,009}{\$88,519} \times 100 = 7.9\%$

(2) $\text{Gross Profit Percentage} = \dfrac{\text{Net Sales Revenue} - \text{Cost of Goods Sold}}{\text{Net Sales Revenue}} \times 100$ Ch. 6

$\dfrac{\$88,519 - \$58,254}{\$88,519} \times 100 = 34.2\%$

(3) $\text{Fixed Asset Turnover} = \dfrac{\text{Net Sales Revenue}}{\text{Average Net Fixed Assets}}$ Ch. 9

$\dfrac{\$88,519}{(\$22,191 + \$22,720)/2} = 3.94$

(4) $\text{Return on Equity (ROE)} = \dfrac{\text{Net Income}}{\text{Average Shareholders''s Equity}} \times 100$ Ch. 11

$\dfrac{\$7,009}{(\$6,316 + \$9,322)/2} \times 100 = 89.6\%$

(5) $\text{Earnings per Share (EPS)} = \dfrac{\text{Net Income*}}{\text{Average Number of Common Shares Outstanding}}$ Ch. 11

$\dfrac{\$7,009}{1,277} = \$5.49$

(6) $\text{Price/Earnings Ratio} = \dfrac{\text{Share Price**}}{\text{EPS}}$ Ch. 11

$\dfrac{\$132.25}{\$5.49} = 24.1$

Liquidity Ratios

(7) $\text{Receivable Turnover} = \dfrac{\text{Net Sales Revenue}}{\text{Average Net Receivables}}$ Ch. 8

$\dfrac{\$88,519}{(\$1,890 + \$1,484)/2} = 52.5$

$\text{Days to Collect} = \dfrac{365}{\text{Receivables Turnover Ratio}}$ Ch. 8

$\dfrac{365}{52.5} = 7.0$

(8) $\text{Inventory Turnover} = \dfrac{\text{Cost of Goods Sold}}{\text{Average Inventory}}$ Ch. 7

$\dfrac{\$58,254}{(\$11,809 + \$11,079)} = 5.1$

$\text{Days to Sell} = \dfrac{365}{\text{Inventory Turnover Ratio}}$ Ch. 7

$\dfrac{365}{5.1} = 71.6$

(9) $\text{Current Ratio} = \dfrac{\text{Current Assets}}{\text{Current Liabilities}}$ Ch. 2

$\dfrac{\$16,993}{\$12,526} = 1.36$

Solvency Ratios

(10) $\text{Debt–to–Assets} = \dfrac{\text{Total Liabilities}}{\text{Total Assets}}$ Ch. 10

$\dfrac{\$36,233}{\$42,549} = 0.85$

(11) $\text{Times Interest Earned} = \dfrac{\text{Net Income} + \text{Interest Expense} + \text{Income Tax Expense}}{\text{Interest Expense}}$ Ch. 10

$\dfrac{\$7,009 + \$753 + \$4,012}{\$753} = 15.64$

*If a company has preferred shares outstanding, preferred dividends are subtracted from net income in the numerator to assess the earnings for each common share. The dividends and average number of shares shown above were reported in The Home Depot's annual report.

**Share price is the closing price reported for the day on which the company first reports its annual earnings in a press release.

Self-Study Practice 13.1

For the year ended January 29, 2016, Lowe's reported net income of $2.5 billion on sales of $59.1 billion. If the company's cost of sales that year was $38.5 billion, what was the company's gross profit percentage and net profit margin? If sales were $56.2 billion in the prior year, what was the year-over-year percentage decrease in the most recent year?

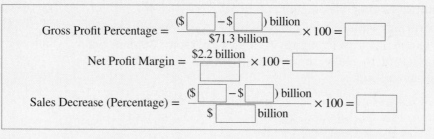

$$\text{Gross Profit Percentage} = \frac{(\$\boxed{} - \$\boxed{}) \text{ billion}}{\$71.3 \text{ billion}} \times 100 = \boxed{}$$

$$\text{Net Profit Margin} = \frac{\$2.2 \text{ billion}}{\boxed{}} \times 100 = \boxed{}$$

$$\text{Sales Decrease (Percentage)} = \frac{(\$\boxed{} - \$\boxed{}) \text{ billion}}{\$\boxed{} \text{ billion}} \times 100 = \boxed{}$$

After you have finished, check your answers with the solution, which follows the chapter summary.

Evaluate the Results

INTERPRETING HORIZONTAL AND VERTICAL ANALYSES

As noted earlier, financial statement analyses are not complete unless they lead to interpretations that help users understand and evaluate a company's financial results. When interpreting analyses, your goals should be to understand what each analysis is telling you and then to combine your findings into a coherent "story" that explains the results of the company's business activities. We demonstrate how to do this, beginning with interpretations of each set of analyses shown in Exhibits 13.1 to 13.5 and later concluding with an overall summary of The Home Depot's results.

Trends Revealed in Horizontal Analyses

LEARNING OBJECTIVE 13-5

Interpret the results of financial analyses.

Horizontal (trend) analysis of The Home Depot's balance sheet in Exhibit 13.1 shows that the company grew in fiscal 2015. Overall, total assets increased 6.5 percent with the majority of this being in Goodwill and Other Assets. This was due to the $1.7 billion acquisition of Interline Brands, Inc., which is a leading national distributor and direct marketer of broad–line MRO (maintenance, repair and operation) products, that The Home Depot intends to leverage.

The other significant change indicated by the balance sheet is that the company relied more on debt and less on equity financing. The Home Depot explains the activities of the company in the Management's Discussion and Analysis (MD&A) section of its 2015 annual report. Additional long–term debt of $4.0 billion was issued in fiscal 2015 and was used in conjunction with operating cash flows to fund $7.0 billion of share repurchases, pay $3.0 billion of dividends, purchase Interline (as mentioned above), and fund $1.5 billion in capital expenditures.

Horizontal analysis of The Home Depot's income statement in Exhibit 13.2 shows a 6.4 percent increase in Net Sales Revenue and a 6.3 percent increase in Cost of Sales, as a result of more customer transactions. There were over 59 million more sales transactions than in 2014. As well, on average, most sales transactions were 1.6 percent higher in sales price over the prior year.

Because the increase in Net Sales Revenue (6.4 percent) was slightly larger than the increase in Cost of Goods Sold (6.3 percent), The Home Depot saw an increase in 2015 Gross Profit. However, its operating expenses also increased 3.2 percent in 2015, in part because of extra expenses related to the data breach that was discovered in the third quarter of fiscal 2014. According to the MD&A, The Home Depot completed a major payment security project that provides enhanced encryption of payment card data at the point of sale in all U.S. and Canadian stores.

The Home Depot also rolled out EMV chip card technology in the U.S. stores, which adds extra layers of payment card protection for customers who use EMV-enabled chip cards. The Canadian stores were already enabled with EMV chip card technology. The final changes in The Home Depot's expenses relate to interest and income tax expenses, which increased as a direct result of carrying more debt and earning more income.

Relationships Noted in Vertical Analyses

Vertical (common-size) analysis of The Home Depot's balance sheet in Exhibit 13.3 highlights key elements of the company. Its most significant assets have always been Inventories and Property and Equipment, with these assets representing 27.8 and 52.2 percent respectively of The Home Depot's total assets. As noted in the horizontal analysis, the company's financing strategy shifted in 2015. As a result of the additional debt issued and share repurchases, debt became a significantly greater source of financing (85.1 percent) than equity (14.9 percent) at the end of fiscal 2015.

Vertical analysis of The Home Depot's income statement in Exhibit 13.4 indicates that Cost of Sales and Operating Expenses are the most important determinants of the company's profitability. Cost of Sales consumed 65.8 percent of Sales in 2015, and Operating Expenses consumed an additional 20.9 percent. Much of the increase in the company's Net Income (from 7.6 percent of Sales in 2014 to 7.9 percent in 2015) is explained by greater control of these two categories of expenses, as suggested by the horizontal analyses.

These findings from the vertical analyses serve to underscore findings from the horizontal analyses. The emerging story is that The Home Depot's success depends on its ability to use significant investments in Inventory as well as Property and Equipment to generate sales. By focusing on customer service, more efficient operating practices, and expense control, The Home Depot was able to improve its net income in a recovering but still challenging economy.

INTERPRETING RATIO ANALYSES

As shown throughout other chapters in this book, benchmarks help when interpreting a company's ratios. These benchmarks can include the company's prior year results as well as the results of close competitors or the average for the industry. In a competitive economy, companies strive to outperform one another, so comparisons against other companies can provide clues about who is likely to survive and thrive in the long run.

In the following analyses, we compare The Home Depot's financial ratios for fiscal years 2011 to 2015, and in some cases to those for Lowe's and the home improvement industry as a whole. (Summarized financial statements for The Home Depot for fiscal 2015 are provided in Appendix A and the Annual Report for Lowe's fiscal 2015 year-end is provided in Appendix B.)

Profitability Ratios

The analyses in this section focus on the level of profits The Home Depot generated during the period. We will analyze ratios (1) through (6) from

Exhibit 13.5. The first two profitability ratios come right from the common–size income statement in Exhibit 13.4.

1. Net Profit Margin. Net profit margin represents the percentage of revenue that ultimately makes it into net income after deducting expenses. Using equation (1) in Exhibit 13.5, the calculation of The Home Depot's net profit margin for each of the five years yields the following:

Fiscal Year	2015	2014	2013	2012	2011
Net Profit Margin $= \dfrac{\text{Net Income}}{\text{Net Sales Revenue}} \times 100 =$	7.9%	7.6%	6.8%	6.1%	5.5%

As discussed in the previous sections, the slowly improving economy, additional sales transactions, and controlling costs helped boost The Home Depot's profits in 2015. The company's net profit margin continues to increase over the five year period. Lowe's net profit margin saw a similar increase over this period, rising from 3.7 percent to 4.3 percent.

2. Gross Profit Percentage. The horizontal analysis indicated that The Home Depot's gross profit increased from 2014 to 2015 in terms of total dollars, but it did not indicate whether that increase was caused by greater total sales or also by more profit per sale. The gross profit percentage addresses these possibilities by indicating how much profit was made, on average, on each dollar of sales after deducting the cost of goods sold. The Home Depot's gross profit percentage for the five–year period was as follows:

Fiscal Year	2015	2014	2013	2012	2011
Gross Profit Percentage $= \dfrac{\text{Net Sales Revenue} - \text{Cost of Goods Sold}}{\text{Net Sales Revenue}} \times 100$	34.2%	34.1%	34.2%	34.6%	34.5%

This analysis shows that in 2015, after deducting the cost of merchandise sold, 34.2 cents of each sales dollar was left to cover other costs, such as employee wages, advertising, and utilities, and to provide profits to the shareholders. The slight increase in the gross profit percentage from 2014 to 2015 (34.1 percent to 34.2 percent) means that The Home Depot made 0.1 cents more gross profit on each dollar of sales in 2015 than in 2014.

There are two potential explanations for this slight increase. The first is that The Home Depot charged higher selling prices without experiencing a corresponding increase in the cost of merchandise and the second is that The Home Depot obtained merchandise at a lower unit cost. The MD&A section of The Home Depot's annual report explained that the increase in gross profit percentage came from both higher selling prices and a decrease in product costs.

3. Fixed Asset Turnover. The fixed asset turnover ratio indicates how much revenue the company generates in sales for each dollar invested in fixed assets, such as store buildings and the property they sit on. Following are The Home Depot's fixed asset turnover ratios for the same five years:

Fiscal Year	2015	2014	2013	2012	2011
Fixed Asset Turnover $= \dfrac{\text{Net Sales Revenue}}{\text{Average Net Fixed Assets}} =$	3.94	3.61	3.32	3.08	2.84

This analysis shows that The Home Depot had $3.94 of sales in 2015 for each dollar invested in fixed assets. By looking at the components of this ratio, we can see that an increase in 2015 sales and a decrease in net fixed assets both contributed to the ratio's increase for 2015. Increased sales resulted from the improvement in the economy and additional sale transactions in 2015 compared to fiscal 2014. Net fixed assets decreased due to a disciplined approach to capital allocation and controlling these costs. The Home Depot's fixed asset turnover ratio has been continuously increasing, and it continues to be higher than one of its main competitors, Lowe's, whose fixed asset turnover ratio was 2.98 in 2015. In terms of using fixed assets to generate sales revenue, The Home Depot had a competitive advantage over Lowe's in 2015. In other words, The Home Depot was operating more efficiently than its major competitor.

4. Return on Equity (ROE). The return on equity ratio compares the amount of net income earned for common shareholders to the average amount of common shareholders' equity. Like the interest rate on your bank account, ROE reports the net amount earned during the period as a percentage of each dollar contributed by shareholders and retained in the business. The Home Depot's ROE ratios for the same five–year period were:

Fiscal Year		2015	2014	2013	2012	2011
Return on Equity (ROE) = $\dfrac{\text{Net Income}}{\text{Average Shareholders' Equity}} \times 100 =$		89.6%	58.1%	35.5%	25.4%	21.1%

The Home Depot's ROE increase from 58.1 to 89.6 percent was inevitable, given our previous analyses. Specifically, horizontal analysis indicated that the company had decreased its shareholders' equity through a share repurchase, and it had increased its net income in 2015 through more profitable operations. Taken together, these results imply that net income as a percentage of average shareholders' equity was sure to rise in 2015. Seeing that The Home Depot experienced increases in net income for all five years and it also reported lower shareholders' equity for all five years due to share repurchases, it is consistent that the ROE for this five–year period has continued to increase year after year.

5. Earnings per Share (EPS). Earnings per Share indicates the amount of earnings generated for each common share outstanding. Consistent with the increase in ROE, the EPS ratio increased from $4.74 in 2014 to $5.49 in 2015, as shown below. This represents an increase of $0.75 per share ($5.49 − $4.74). The following are the remaining EPS ratios, which show the same consistent upward trend that we have seen already in prior ratios:

Fiscal Year		2015	2014	2013	2012	2011
Earnings per Share (EPS) = $\dfrac{\text{Net Income*}}{\text{Average Number of Common Shares Outstanding}} =$		$5.49	$4.74	$3.78	$3.03	$2.49

6. Price/Earnings (P/E) Ratio. The P/E ratio relates the company's share price to its EPS, as follows:

Fiscal Year		2015	2014	2013	2012	2011
Price/Earnings Ratio = $\dfrac{\text{Share Price**}}{\text{EPS}} =$		24.1	22.0	19.9	21.9	18.0

Using the going price for The Home Depot's shares when its 2015 and 2014 earnings were announced during the last week of January 2016 and the first week of February 2015, the P/E ratios were 24.1 and 22.0, respectively. This means investors were willing to pay 24.1 times earnings to buy a share of The Home Depot's shares in early 2016 (versus 22.0 times earnings a year earlier). The increase from the prior year suggests that investors were more optimistic about the company's future prospects than they had been a year earlier. Improvement in the general economy combined with The Home Depot's strategies for better organizational efficiency contributed to this optimism. We can see from the five–year trend that The Home Depot's P/E ratio increased each year with the exception of fiscal 2013. There were lingering concerns about economies throughout the world that had dampened enthusiasm for The Home Depot's shares, as it had for many other companies.

Let's pause to summarize what we've learned so far. The Home Depot enjoyed improvement in 2015. Additional customer traffic resulted in increased sales, which contributed to increases in gross profit percentage and net profit margin. Greater sales revenue in 2015 combined with a disciplined approach to capital allocation and controlling costs boosted the fixed asset turnover in 2015. These improved results were magnified in the ROE and EPS ratios because The Home Depot reduced its shareholders' equity and the number of outstanding common shares in 2015 through share repurchases. Investors were impressed by these improvements in 2015 along with The Home Depot outperforming the competition, as shown by the higher P/E ratio after the fiscal 2015 results were reported.

Liquidity Ratios

The analyses in this section focus on a company's ability to survive in the short term by converting assets to cash that can be used to pay current liabilities as they come due. We interpret ratios (7) through (9) from Exhibit 13.5.

7. Receivables Turnover. Most home improvement retailers have low levels of accounts receivable relative to sales revenue because they collect the majority of their sales immediately in cash. Although the formula calls for net credit sales in the top of the ratio, companies rarely report their credit sales and cash sales separately. Consequently, financial statement users typically use total net sales revenue in the formula, which results in a receivables turnover ratio that is not terribly meaningful for businesses that make few sales on account. The formula is presented in Exhibit 13.5 simply to remind you of how it's calculated.

8. Inventory Turnover. The inventory turnover ratio indicates how frequently inventory is bought and sold during the year. The measure "days to sell" converts the inventory turnover ratio into the average number of days needed to sell each purchase of inventory.

Fiscal Year	2015	2014	2013	2012	2011
Inventory Turnover $= \dfrac{\text{Cost of Goods Sold}}{\text{Average Inventory}} =$	5.1	5.0	4.8	4.7	4.4
Days to Sell $= \dfrac{365}{\text{Inventory Turnover Ratio}} =$	71.6	73.0	76.0	77.7	83.0

The Home Depot's inventory turned over slightly more in 2015 compared to 2014. These results were encouraging to The Home Depot because the company continued to introduce a wide range of innovative new products for their do–it–yourself, do–it–for–me, and professional customers. The goal in carrying more inventory was to better meet customer needs, but this strategy increased the risk that the new products would not sell as quickly. On average, its inventory took 71.6 days to sell.

These results are encouraging because almost every retailer's success depends on its ability to offer customers the right product when they need it at a price that beats the competition. The number of days to sell has continued to decrease since 2011, due to the mechanization of The Home Depot's rapid deployment centre network and a continuous focus on operating and optimizing the supply chain network. The Home Depot enjoys a faster inventory turnover than other competitors such as Lowe's (where inventory takes an average of 87.1 days to sell) because it carries fewer big–ticket items.

Turnover ratios vary significantly from one industry to the next. Companies in the food industry (restaurants and grocery stores) have high inventory turnover ratios because their inventory is subject to spoilage. Companies that sell expensive merchandise (automobiles and high–fashion clothes) have much slower turnover because sales of those items are infrequent, but these companies must carry lots of inventory so that customers have a wide selection to choose from when they do buy.

9. Current Ratio. The current ratio compares current assets to current liabilities, as follows:

Fiscal Year	2015	2014	2013	2012	2011
Current Ratio = $\dfrac{\text{Current Assets}}{\text{Current Liabilities}}$ =	1.36	1.36	1.42	1.34	1.55

The current ratio measures the company's ability to pay its current liabilities. The Home Depot's ratio in 2015 remained consistent with that of 2014, ending the year with a ratio of 1.36. This ratio has fluctuated over the five–year period and was at its highest in 2011 at 1.55. This is in comparison with Lowe's, whose current ratio dropped from 1.05 in 2014 to 1.01 in 2015. In some instances, a decrease in current ratio is a cause for concern. But in this industry, a current ratio greater than 1.0 is deemed acceptable. Lowe's had a very good reason for its lower current ratio in comparison to 2014, as explained in the following Spotlight.

SPOTLIGHT ON Business Decisions

Lowe's **Helps Suppliers Collect on Account**

The decrease in Lowe's current ratio in 2015 was caused in part by an increase in its Accounts Payable. That increase in Accounts Payable resulted from suppliers giving Lowe's more favourable payment terms, including a longer period to settle its Accounts Payable.

Why would suppliers be willing to allow this? Lowe's participates in supply chain financing or "reverse factoring." Here's how it works. Lowe's tells a finance company what it owes to particular suppliers. The finance company then contacts the suppliers and offers to take over the collection of the Lowe's account balance. Just like a normal factoring arrangement (discussed in Chapter 8), the finance company pays the supplier right away.

The finance company charges the supplier a smaller-than-normal factoring fee because it knows Lowe's balance will be easily collected—Lowe's has openly told the finance company how much it owes. The supplier appreciates collecting right away and being charged a smaller factoring fee, so it gives Lowe's more favourable payment terms. Lowe's has reported in prior-year annual reports that it has made this supply chain financing possible for 15 percent of its suppliers.

Solvency Ratios

The analyses in this section focus on The Home Depot's ability to survive over the long term—that is, its ability to repay debt when it matures, pay interest until that time, and finance the replacement and/or expansion of long-term assets. We interpret ratios (10) and (11) from Exhibit 13.5.

10. Debt—to—Assets. The debt—to—assets ratio indicates the proportion of total assets that creditors finance. Remember that creditors must be paid regardless of how difficult a year the company may have had. The higher this ratio, the riskier the company's financing strategy. The Home Depot's ratio for the five—year period was:

Fiscal Year		2015	2014	2013	2012	2011
Debt-to-Assets $= \dfrac{\text{Total Liabilities}}{\text{Total Assets}} =$		0.85	0.77	0.69	0.57	0.56

The Home Depot's ratio of 0.85 in 2015 indicates that creditors con-tributed 85 percent of the company's financing, implying that it was the main source of financing. The debt—to—assets ratio increased from 2014 to 2015 as a result of issuing new notes and repurchasing common shares, which we learned earlier in the analysis. Lowe's, which had a debt—to—as-sets ratio of 0.76 in 2015, relies less on debt financing and more on equity financing.

11. Times Interest Earned. The times interest earned ratio indicates how many times the company's interest expense was covered by its operating results. This ratio is calculated using accrual—based interest expense and net income before interest and income taxes, as follows:

Fiscal Year		2015	2014	2013	2012	2011
Times Interest Earned $= \dfrac{\text{Net Income + Interest Expense + Income Tax Expense}}{\text{Interest Expense}} =$		15.6	21.2	13.1	14.3	11.2

A times interest earned ratio above 1.0 indicates that net income (before the costs of financing and taxes) is sufficient to cover the company's inter—est expense. The Home Depot's ratio of 15.6 in 2015 indicates the company was generating more than enough profit to cover its interest expense. This ratio has fluctuated throughout the last five years but was always greater than 1.0, which means the company was always in a good position to cover its interest expense.

HOW'S IT GOING?

Self-Study Practice 13.2

Show the computations for the following two ratios for The Home Depot for fiscal 2014. Use the information in Exhibits 13.1 and 13.2.
   1. Times interest earned ratio
   2. Current ratio

After you have finished, check your answers with the solution, which follows the chapter summary.

Different Reporting Standards Can Make Ratio Analysis Complex

As discussed in Chapter 1, there are various sets of financial reporting standards in Canada. Specific groups, like the First Nations communities, are expected to follow Generally Accepted Accounting Principles (GAAP) for public sector entities.

Under this government model, the presentation of financial assets should be separately identified. For many of the financial statements submitted to the government by First Nations communities, financial assets were not specifically identified. Instead, these assets and liabilities were differentiated in two ways: as either current or long-term. As you learned in Chapter 2, a classified balance sheet is required to report assets and liabilities as current or long-term under ASPE. So, it appears that some First Nations communities were using a combination of accounting standards for their financial reporting, given that there is currently not a set of accounting standards geared specifically to Aboriginal organizations.

As discussed in Chapter 1, the objective of external financial reporting is to provide useful financial information to external users for decision-making purposes. Financial information is much more useful if it is comparable. Users of financial information may be making decisions as to whether or not to grant a loan to that organization. When different organizations follow different financial reporting standards in Canada, it can result in different outcomes when analyzing these ratios, and users need to be aware of the differences when making those decisions.

Source: "Financial Reporting by First Nations," The Canadian Institute of Chartered Accountants: http://www.frascanada.ca /standards-for-public-sector-entities/resources/reference-materials/item14957.pdf

ASSESSING UNDERLYING ACCOUNTING DECISIONS AND CONCEPTS

Accounting Decisions

In the analyses just presented, we compared The Home Depot's results with those of Lowe's. When appropriate, we discussed how differences in the two companies' strategies (e.g., relying on debt versus equity financing) and business operations (e.g., carrying big–ticket versus less–expensive items) affected their financial ratios. We should also consider whether differences between the two companies' financial ratios might be caused by differences in their accounting decisions.

Please note is that both companies' financial statements have been audited by an independent public accounting firm. Appendix B presents the auditors' report for Lowe's, which indicates an *unqualified opin-ion* that the companies' financial statements can be relied upon because they are fairly presented. (*Unqualified* in this context means that the auditors are offering those opinions with no restrictions or "quali-fications.") With this overall assurance, we then consider the specific accounting decisions that are summarized in the first note to the financial statements. Exhibit 13.6 shows the policies that three home improvement retailers follow in accounting for inventory and depreciation—two line items that can have a noticeable impact on a retailer's results. Take a moment to study the exhibit.

As you can see, the three companies follow similar but not identical policies. The Home Depot and Lowe's use the FIFO method of accounting

LEARNING OBJECTIVE 13-6

Describe how analyses depend on key accounting decisions and concepts.

EXHIBIT 13.6	Comparison of Accounting Methods		
	The Home Depot	**Lowe's**	**Builders FirstSource**
Inventory	FIFO	FIFO	Weighted Average Cost
Depreciation	Straight line Buildings: 5–45 yrs Equipment: 2–20 yrs	Straight line Buildings: 5–40 yrs Equipment: 3–15 yrs	Straight line Buildings: 20–40 yrs Equipment: 3–10 yrs

for inventory and cost of goods sold; Builder's FirstSource uses the weighted average method. Although these two methods result in different numbers, the overall impact on the companies' financial ratios should be minor because inventory costs did not rise rapidly in 2015.

All three companies calculate depreciation using the straight–line method, with a similar range of estimated useful lives for buildings and equipment. Because buildings and equipment make up such a large portion of each company's assets, these similarities go a long way toward making their financial results comparable. In conclusion, although the companies' accounting policies have some differences, these policies are unlikely to have a major impact on our comparisons.

 SPOTLIGHT ON The World

Caution Required When Comparing Financial Statements

Lowe's dominates the Canadian home improvement industry, as does The Home Depot in the United States. Kingfisher plc is Europe's largest home improvement retailer, with market-leading positions in the United Kingdom, France, Poland, Turkey, and China. Direct comparisons of financial statements, however, should be made with caution, as companies may be using different standards for financial reporting purposes. In this case, for example, Kingfisher follows IFRS, while The Home Depot and Lowe's use U.S. GAAP. We have seen in prior chapters that using different methods (such as FIFO versus weighted average) can result in different outcomes in financial reporting. Therefore, it is important to be aware of these differences between companies.

Accounting Concepts

Before wrapping up this chapter, it's worth revisiting the accounting concepts that were introduced in previous chapters. At this stage of the course, you should have developed a fairly good understanding of the rules of accounting and be better able to appreciate why accounting relies on these particular concepts. Exhibit 13.7 presents the conceptual framework for financial accounting and reporting that was first introduced in Chapter 1. The concepts that you have already learned about in prior chapters are highlighted in red in Exhibit 13.7.

As shown in Exhibit 13.7, the primary objective of financial accounting and reporting is to provide useful financial information that people external to a company can use in making decisions about the company. To be useful, this information must be relevant and faithfully represent the underlying business.

EXHIBIT 13.7   Conceptual Framework for Financial Accounting and Reporting

Objective of External Financial Reporting

To provide useful financial information to external users for decision making (Ch. 1)

- It must be relevant and a faithful representation of the business.
- It is more useful if it is comparable, verifiable, timely, and understandable.

Elements to Be Measured and Reported

- Assets, Liabilities, Shareholders' Equity, Revenues, Expenses, Dividends (Ch. 1)

Concepts for Measuring and Reporting Information

- **Assumptions:**   Unit of Measure (Ch. 1), Separate Entity (Ch. 1), Going Concern, Time Period (Ch. 3)
- **Principles:**   Cost (Ch. 2), Revenue and Expense Recognition (Ch. 3), Full Disclosure

Exhibit 13.7 includes two accounting concepts that have not been introduced in previous chapters, so we will explain them here. The **going-concern assumption** quietly underlies accounting rules. It is the belief that any business will be capable of continuing its operations long enough to realize the economic benefits of its assets and meet its obligations in the normal course of business. If a company judges that it will be unable to meet its obligations for at least one year after the financial statements are issued, it must disclose this in the financial statement notes. In severe cases, it may need to adjust the amount and classification of items in its financial statements. Some of the factors that commonly contribute to going-concern problems are listed in Exhibit 13.8. Notice that some of the analyses presented earlier in this chapter are key considerations.

The other principle of accounting that was not previously explained is full disclosure. Simply put, according to the **full disclosure principle**, financial reports should present all information that is needed to properly interpret the results of the company's business activities. This doesn't mean that every single transaction needs to be explained in detail, but rather that adequate information needs to be presented to allow financial statement users to fairly interpret reports about the company's income, financial position, and cash flows.

Before closing the book on this topic (and possibly this course), take a moment to complete the following Self-Study Practice. It'll give you a

Going-concern assumption: A business is assumed to be capable of continuing its operations long enough to meet its obligations. Also called the *continuity assumption.*

Full disclosure principle: Financial statements should present information needed to understand the financial results of the company's business activities.

EXHIBIT 13.8   Factors Contributing to Going-Concern Problems

Revealed by Financial Analyses	Revealed by Other Analyses
• Declining sales	• Loss of a key supplier or customer
• Declining gross profit	• Insufficient product innovation/quality
• Significant one-time expenses	• Significant barriers to expansion
• Fluctuating net income	• Loss of key personnel without replacement
• Insufficient current assets	• Unfavourable long-term commitments
• Excessive reliance on debt financing	• Inadequate maintenance of long-lived assets
• Negative operating cash flows	• Loss of a key franchise, license, or patent

Self-Study Practice 13.3

Match each statement below with the concept to which it most closely relates.

1. Everything comes down to dollars and cents.
2. That's not our issue. It's for somebody else to report.
3. If it relates to this period, you'd better report it.
4. I've told you everything you could possibly want to know.
5. At that rate, you may not survive past the end of the year.
6. I know it's a long time, but let's break it down into stages.

(a) Separate entity
(b) Revenue and expense recognition
(c) Going concern
(d) Unit of measure
(e) Time period
(f) Full disclosure

After you have finished, check your answers with the solution, which follows the chapter summary.

good idea of whether you need a detailed review of the concepts introduced in earlier chapters or whether you're ready to move on to review and practise key aspects of this chapter.

You have now seen enough to interpret most basic financial statements. When analyzing real–world financial statements, you will probably encounter non–recurring or other special items reported in the income statement. These items are discussed in Supplement 13A, which follows.

Supplement 13A

NON-RECURRING AND OTHER SPECIAL ITEMS

Non-recurring Items

Until 2005, three different types of non–recurring items were reported in income statements: discontinued operations, extraordinary items, and the cumulative effects of changes in accounting methods. Recently, however, new accounting standards have nearly eliminated income statement reporting of extraordinary items and the cumulative effects of changes in accounting methods. In fact, the definition of extraordinary has become so restricted that few events—not even BP's $20 billion of losses that arose from the April 2010 oil spill in the Gulf of Mexico— qualify as extraordinary. The cumulative effects of changes in accounting methods are reported as adjustments to Retained Earnings rather than as part of the income statement in the period when the change is made. (The technical procedures used to make these adjustments are discussed in intermediate accounting courses.) That leaves only one non–recurring item—discontinued operations.

Discontinued operations:
Result from the disposal of a major component of the business and are reported net of income tax effects.

Discontinued operations result from a strategic shift, such as abandoning or selling a major business component. Because an abandoned or sold business unit will not affect financial results in future years, its results for the current year are reported on a separate line of the income statement following Income Tax Expense. This discontinued operations line includes any gain or loss on disposal of the discontinued operation as well as any operating income generated before its disposal. Because this appears below the Income Tax Expense line, any related tax effects are netted against (included with) the gains or losses on discontinued operations. Exhibit 13A.1 shows how The Home Depot reported discontinued operations back in 2010.

THE HOME DEPOT, INC.	(in millions)
Net Sales	$66,176
Cost of Sales	43,764
Gross Profit	22,412
Selling, General, and Administrative Expenses	15,902
Depreciation Expense	1,707
Income from Operations	4,803
Interest and Other Expenses, Net	821
Income from Continuing Operations Before Income Tax Expense	3,982
Income Tax Expense	1,362
Net Income from Continuing Operations	2,620
Income from Discontinued Operations, Net of Tax	41
Net Income	$ 2,661

Other Special Items: ASPE versus IFRS

In some cases, you may see that companies include additional items on their income statements after the net income line. These items may be added to or subtracted from net income to arrive at the amount of comprehensive income. These companies would be using IFRS because ASPE does not use comprehensive income.

As you can learn in detail in intermediate financial accounting courses, these items represent gains or losses relating to changes in the value of certain balance sheet accounts. While most gains and losses are included in the computation of net income, some (relating to changes in foreign currency exchange rates and the value of certain investments, for example) are excluded from net income and included only in comprehensive income. The main reason for excluding these gains and losses from net income is that the changes in value that created them may well disappear before they are ever realized (when the company sells the related assets or discharges the related liabilities). For this reason, most analysts will take a moment to consider the size of these special items in relation to net income. If the amount is not large, they will exclude the items in calculating profitability ratios.

Supplement 13B

REVIEWING AND CONTRASTING ASPE AND IFRS

In this supplement, we review and contrast ASPE and IFRS as they relate to topics raised in earlier chapters of this text. We begin with a theoretical discussion of similarities and differences between ASPE and IFRS that potentially affect the accounting rules for specific topics. We then follow with a summary of specific topic discussions.

LEARNING OBJECTIVE 13-S2

Describe significant differences between ASPE and IFRS.

Overview

Generally speaking, ASPE and IFRS are similar in that both aim to guide businesses in reporting financial information that is relevant and that faithfully represents the underlying activities of businesses. At a basic level, these accounting rules describe (1) when an item should be recognized in the account—ing system, (2) how that item should be classified (e.g., asset or expense, rev—enue or liability), and (3) the amount at which each item should be measured.

Although some exceptions exist, both ASPE and IFRS require that items be recorded only after an exchange between the company and another party. Initially, these items are recorded at the value they enter the company (called the *entry price* or *historical cost*). Later, this value may be revised (upward or downward) as a result of events or changes in circumstances. The new value may be (1) the entry price adjusted for items such as interest or depreciation, (2) a current market price, or (3) another computed amount (such as the *fair value* or *exit price* that the company would pay or receive in the future for that item).

Many differences between ASPE and IFRS that we have noted in this book relate to cases where IFRS requires or allows companies to report items using values that differ from those required or allowed by ASPE. For example, in Chapter 7, we noted that IFRS allows (and ASPE prohibits) the reversal of write—downs in inventory value. Similarly, in Chapter 9, we noted that IFRS allows companies to report fixed assets at fair values. Intermediate accounting courses will expand on these situations and add others. For now, though, just focus on gaining a general awareness of the ways in which accounting rules may differ. Refer to the following Spotlight on IFRS and ASPE, which gives a quick review of the specific cases introduced in previous chapters.

SPOTLIGHT ON IFRS and ASPE

Specific Topics Introduced in Earlier Chapters

Chapter 1
- Discusses financial reporting standards in Canada and the basic differences between ASPE and IFRS.

Chapter 2
- Discusses differences in the level of detail in ASPE versus IFRS materials, and the increased role for transaction analysis skills and judgment in accounting.

Chapter 4
- Discusses how IFRS uses a five-step model for determining when to recognize revenue.

Chapter 7
- Explains that IFRS prohibits LIFO.
- Discusses how IFRS allows (and ASPE prohibits) reversals of write-downs when inventory recovers in value.

Chapter 9
- Discusses IFRS's accounting for component costs.
- Discusses IFRS's accounting for R & D and revaluation at fair value.

Chapter 10
- Discusses IFRS's current classification of long-term debt involving violated loan covenants.
- Discusses IFRS's threshold for accruing contingent liabilities.

Chapter 11
- Discusses classification of some preferred shares as a liability.

Chapter 12
- Illustrates differences in classification of dividends and interest received and paid, under IFRS and ASPE.

Chapter 13
- Discusses the potential impact of accounting differences on ratio analyses.

Review the Chapter

This section provides a chance to solidify your understanding of key points. It's worth your time to work through the following demonstration case, scan the chapter summary, test your understanding of key terms, and then practise, practise, practise.

DEMONSTRATION CASE

The information below was taken from Avericana Company's annual report.

eXcel

(in millions)	Year Ended January 26, 2017 (Fiscal 2016)
Net Sales Revenue	$90,837
Cost of Goods Sold	61,054
Net Income	5,761

	January 26, 2017 (Fiscal 2016)	January 27, 2016 (Fiscal 2015)
Inventory	$12,822	$11,401
Current Assets	18,000	15,269
Property and Equipment, Net	26,605	24,901
Total Assets	52,263	44,405
Current Liabilities	12,931	12,706
Total Liabilities	27,233	17,496

Required:

1. Compute the following ratios for Avericana for the year ended January 26, 2017.
   - Fixed Asset Turnover
   - Return on Equity
   - Days to Sell
   - Current Ratio
   - Debt–to–Assets
2. Interpret the meaning of the ratios you calculated in requirement 1.

Suggested Solution

1. Calculating ratios:

Fixed Asset Turnover	= Net Sales Revenue/Average Net Fixed Assets
	= $90,837 \div [(\$26,605 + \$24,901) \div 2]$
	= 3.53
Return on Equity	= Net Income/Average Shareholders' Equity
	= $5,761 \div [(\$25,030 + \$26,909) \div 2]$
	= 0.2218, or 22.2%
Days to Sell	= $365 \div$ Inventory Turnover Ratio
	= $365 \div$ (Cost of Goods Sold/Average Inventory)
	= $365 \div [\$61,054 \div [(\$12,822 + \$11,401) \div 2]]$
	= 72
Current Ratio	= Current Assets/Current Liabilities
	= $18,000 \div \$12,931$
	= 1.39

$$\begin{aligned}
\text{Debt--to--Assets} \quad &= \text{Total Liabilities/Total Assets} \\
&= \$27{,}233 \div \$52{,}263 \\
&= 0.52
\end{aligned}$$

2. Interpreting ratios:

- The fixed asset turnover ratio of 3.53 means that, on average, Americana generated $3.53 of sales for each dollar of fixed assets.

- The return on equity of 22.2 percent means that Americana's net income for the year was 22.2 percent of the amount investors contributed to and left in the company.

- The days to sell ratio of 72 means that, on average, 72 days elapsed between the time Americana acquired the inventory and the time the company sold it.

- The current ratio of 1.39 means that at year--end Americana had $1.39 of current assets for each dollar of current liabilities.

- The debt--to--assets ratio of 0.52 means that Americana relied on short--term and long--term debt to finance 52 percent of its assets, implying that shareholders' equity financed 48 percent ($= 100 - 52$) of its total assets.

CHAPTER SUMMARY

LO13-1 **Describe the purposes and uses of horizontal, vertical, and ratio analyses.**

- Horizontal analyses (also called *trend analyses*) compare financial statement items to comparable amounts in prior periods with the goal of identifying sustained changes or trends.

- Vertical analyses create common--size financial statements that express each line of the income statement (or balance sheet) as a percentage of total sales (or total assets).

- Ratio analyses compare one or more financial statement items to an amount for other items for the same year. Ratios take into account differences in the size of amounts to allow for evaluations of performance given existing levels of other company resources.

LO13-2 **Use horizontal (trend) analyses to recognize financial changes that unfold over time.**

- Trend analyses involve computing the dollar amount by which each account changes from one period to the next and expressing that change as a percentage of the balance for the prior period.

LO13-3 **Use vertical (common-size) analyses to understand important relationships within financial statements.**

- Vertical (common--size) analyses indicate the proportions within each financial statement category.

LO13-4 **Calculate financial ratios to assess profitability, liquidity, and solvency.**

- Financial ratios are commonly classified with relation to profitability, liquidity, or solvency. Exhibit 13.5 lists common ratios in these three categories and shows how to compute them.

- Profitability ratios focus on measuring the adequacy of a company's income by comparing it to other items reported on the financial statements.

- Liquidity ratios measure a company's ability to meet its current debt obligations.

- Solvency ratios measure a company's ability to meet its long--term debt obligations.

LO13-5 **Interpret the results of financial analyses.**

- Financial analyses are not complete unless they lead to an interpretation that helps financial statement users understand and evaluate a company's financial results.

- In order to understand whether a business is successful, analysts must know how to combine analyses into a complete picture or story that depicts the company's performance.

- To assist in developing this picture or story, most analysts use benchmarks for comparison, such as the company's performance in prior years or competitors' performance in the current year.

- Before comparing across companies or time periods, users should determine the extent to which differences in accounting decisions (e.g., methods used to account for inventory, depreciation, contingent liabilities, etc.) might reduce comparability or consistency of the financial information being compared.
- Many accounting concepts were presented throughout earlier chapters, all of which aim to make accounting information more useful for creditors and investors. Two new concepts were explained in this chapter:
  1. Going–concern (continuity) assumption—a business is assumed able to continue to operate into the foreseeable future.
  2. Full disclosure principle—a company's financial statements should provide all informa–tion that is important to users' decisions.

ACCOUNTING DECISION TOOLS

See Exhibit 13.5 for a summary.

SOLUTIONS TO SELF-STUDY PRACTICE

Solution to SP13.1

Gross Profit Percentage $= (\$59.1 - \$38.5)/\$59.1 \times 100$
$$= 34.9\%$$

Net Profit Margin $= \$2.5/\$59.1 \times 100$
$$= 4.2\%$$

Sales Decrease (Percentage) $= (\$59.1 - \$56.2)/\$56.2 \times 100$
$$= -5.2\%$$

Solution to SP13.2

1. $(\$6,345 + \$493 + \$3,631)/\$493 = 21.2$
2. $\$15,302 \div \$11,269 = 1.36$

Solution to SP13.3

1. (d) 2. (a) 3. (b) 4. (f) 5. (c) 6. (e)

KEY TERMS

Comprehensive Income	Going–Concern Assumption	Profitability
Discontinued Operations	Horizontal (Trend) Analyses	Solvency
Full Disclosure Principle	Liquidity	Vertical (Common–Size) Analyses

Complete definitions are also included in the glossary in the end of this text.

HOMEWORK HELPER

Helpful reminders

- Ratios that include both income statement and balance sheet accounts require you to calculate an average for the balance sheet accounts rather than just using the end–of–pe–riod balance. An average ensures that the balance sheet data cover the same period as the income statement data.
- To calculate averages for the current and prior years, you will need three years of balance sheet data. (The statement of shareholders' equity reports three years of shareholders'

equity data. To calculate averages for other balance sheet accounts, you will need comparative balance sheets from at least two annual reports.)

• The pronoun for referring to a specific company is "its," not "their."

Frequent mistakes

• In calculating year–over–year percentages, divide the change in the account balance by its balance from the prior year, not the current year.

PRACTICE MATERIAL

QUESTIONS (⑤ Symbol indicates questions that require analysis from more than one perspective.)

1. What is the general goal of trend analysis?

2. How is a year–over–year percentage calculated?

3. What is ratio analysis? Why is it useful?

4. What benchmarks are commonly used for interpreting ratios?

5. In what three categories of performance are most financial ratios reported? To what, in particular, do each of these categories relate?

6. Why are some analyses called *horizontal* and others called *vertical*?

7. Slow Cellar's current ratio increased from 1.2 to 1.5. What is one favourable interpretation of this change? What is one unfavourable interpretation of this change? ⑤

8. From last year to this year, Colossal Company's current ratio increased and its inventory turnover decreased. Does this imply a higher, or lower, risk of obsolete inventory? ⑤

9. From last year to this year, Mechanic International reported that its Net Sales increased from $300,000 to $400,000, and its Gross Profit increased from $90,000 to $130,000. Was the Gross Profit increase caused by (*a*) an increase in sales volume only, (*b*) an increase in gross profit per sale only, or (*c*) a combination of both? Explain your answer. ⑤

10. Explain whether the following situations, taken independently, would be favourable or unfavourable: (*a*) increase in gross profit percentage, (*b*) decrease in inventory turnover ratio, (*c*) increase in earnings per share, (*d*) decrease in days to collect, and (*e*) increase in net profit margin.

11. What are the two essential characteristics of useful financial information? What other characteristics enhance the usefulness of financial information?

12. What is the primary objective of financial reporting?

13. What is the full disclosure principle?

14. What is the going–concern assumption? What is a going–concern problem? What factors can contribute to such a problem?

15. (Supplement 13A) Name the most commonly reported non–recurring item, and explain where and how it is reported on the income statement.

16. (Supplement 13B) How are the Accounting Standards for Private Enterprises similar to International Financial Reporting Standards and how are they different?

17. (Supplement 13B) TechCo is a U.S. company that uses the LIFO inventory method. You plan to compare its ratios to Euroten, but you are concerned because Euroten uses IFRS. What accounting policy difference is certain to exist between the two companies? Of the ratios in Exhibit 13.5, name five that will be affected by this difference. ⑤

MINI-EXERCISES

LO13-2 **M13-1 Calculations for Horizontal Analyses**

Using the following income statements, perform the calculations needed for horizontal analyses. Round percentages to one decimal place.

LOCKEY FENCING CORPORATION
Income Statements
For the Years Ended December 31

	2017	2016
Net Sales	$100,000	$75,000
Cost of Goods Sold	58,000	45,000
Gross Profit	42,000	30,000
Selling, General, and Administrative Expenses	9,000	4,500
Income from Operations	33,000	25,500
Interest Expense	3,000	3,750
Income Before Income Tax	30,000	21,750
Income Tax Expense	9,000	6,525
Net Income	$ 21,000	$15,225

M13-2 Calculations for Vertical Analyses
LO13-3

Refer to M13−1. Perform the calculations needed for vertical analyses. Round percentages to one decimal place.

M13-3 Interpreting Horizontal Analyses
LO13-5

Refer to the calculations from M13−1. What are the two most significant year−over−year changes in terms of dollars and in terms of percentages? Give one potential cause of each of these changes.

M13-4 Interpreting Vertical Analyses
LO13-5

Refer to the calculations from M13−2. Which of the ratios from Exhibit 13.5 have been included in these calculations? Have these two ratios improved or deteriorated in 2017 com−pared to 2016?

M13-5 Inferring Financial Information Using Gross Profit Percentage
LO13-4

Your campus computer store reported Sales Revenue of $168,000. The company's gross profit percentage was 60.0 percent. What amount of Cost of Goods Sold did the company report?

M13-6 Inferring Financial Information Using Gross Profit Percentage and Year-over-Year Comparisons
LO13-2, 13-3, 13-4

A consumer products company reported a 25 percent increase in sales from 2016 to 2017. Sales in 2016 were $200,000. In 2017, the company reported Cost of Goods Sold in the amount of $150,000. What was the gross profit percentage in 2017? Round to one decimal place.

M13-7 Computing the Return on Equity Ratio
LO13-4

Given the following data, compute the 2017 return on equity ratio (expressed as a percentage with one decimal place).

	2017	2016
Net Income	$ 1,850,000	$ 1,600,000
Shareholders' Equity	10,000,000	13,125,000
Total Assets	24,000,000	26,000,000
Interest Expense	400,000	300,000

M13-8 Analyzing the Inventory Turnover Ratio
LO13-4, 13-5

A manufacturer reported an inventory turnover ratio of 8.6 during 2016. During 2017, man−agement introduced a new inventory control system that was expected to reduce average inventory levels by 25 percent without affecting sales volume. Given these circumstances, would you expect the inventory turnover ratio to increase or decrease during 2017? Explain.

LO13-4   **M13-9**   **Inferring Financial Information Using the Current Ratio**

Mystic Laboratories reported total assets of $11,200,000 and noncurrent assets of $1,480,000. The company also reported a current ratio of 1.5. What amount of current liabilities did the company report?

LO13-4   **M13-10**   **Inferring Financial Information Using the P/E Ratio**

In 2016, Big W Company reported earnings per share of $2.50 when its shares were selling for $50.00. If its 2017 earnings increase by 10 percent and the P/E ratio remains constant, what will be the price of its shares?

LO13-4, 13-5   **M13-11**   **Identifying Relevant Ratios**

Identify the ratio that is relevant to answering each of the following questions.

1. How much net income does the company earn from each dollar of sales?
2. Is the company financed primarily by debt or equity?
3. How many dollars of sales were generated for each dollar invested in fixed assets?
4. How many days, on average, does it take the company to collect on credit sales made to customers?
5. How much net income does the company earn for each dollar that owners have invested in it?
6. Does the company's net income convert into more or less cash flow from operating activities?
7. Does the company have sufficient assets to convert into cash for paying liabilities as they come due in the upcoming year?

LO13-4, 13-5   **M13-12**   **Interpreting Ratios**

Generally speaking, do the following indicate good news or bad news?

1. Increase in times interest earned ratio
2. Decrease in days to sell
3. Increase in gross profit percentage
4. Decrease in EPS
5. Increase in asset turnover ratio

LO13-6   **M13-13**   **Analyzing the Impact of Accounting Alternatives**

Nevis Corporation operates in an industry where costs are falling. The company is considering changing its inventory method from FIFO to Weighted Average and wants to determine the impact that the change would have on selected accounting ratios in future years. In general, what impact would you expect on the following ratios: net profit margin, fixed asset turnover, and current ratio?

LO13-6   **M13-14**   **Describing the Effect of Accounting Decisions on Ratios**

For each of the following three accounting choices, indicate the decision that will yield (*a*) a higher net profit margin and (*b*) a lower current ratio. If the decision does not affect the ratio, indicate No Effect.

1. Straight–line versus accelerated depreciation (in the first year of the asset's life).
2. FIFO versus weighted average (in periods of constantly rising costs and rising inventory levels).
3. Straight–line depreciation with a four–year useful life versus a seven–year useful life (no residual value).

EXERCISES

LO13-2, 13-3, 13-5   **E13-1**   **Preparing and Interpreting a Schedule for Horizontal and Vertical Analyses**

Assume the average price of a litre of gas in 2017 jumped $0.17 (16 percent) from $1.04 in 2016 to $1.21 in 2017. Let's see whether this change is reflected in the income statement of Suncor Energy Inc. for the year ended December 31, 2017 (amounts in billions).

	2017	2016
Total Revenues	$273	$221
Costs of Crude Oil and Products	171	133
Other Operating Costs	59	56
Income Before Income Tax Expense	43	32
Income Tax Expense	19	13
Net Income	$ 24	$ 19

Required:

1. Conduct a horizontal analysis by calculating the year–over–year changes in each line item, expressed in dollars and in percentages (rounded to one decimal place). How did the change in gas prices compare to the changes in Suncor's total revenues and costs of crude oil and products?

2. Conduct a vertical analysis by expressing each line as a percentage of total revenues (round to one decimal place). Excluding income tax and other operating costs, did Suncor earn more profit per dollar of revenue in 2017 compared to 2016?

LO13-4, 13-5

E13-2 Computing and Interpreting Profitability Ratios

Use the information for Suncor Energy Inc. in E13–1 to complete the following requirements.

Required:

1. Compute the gross profit percentage for each year (one decimal place). Assuming that the change for 2016 to 2017 is the beginning of a sustained trend, is Suncor likely to earn more or less gross profit from each dollar of sales in 2018?

2. Compute the net profit margin for each year (expressed as a percentage with one decimal place). Given your calculations here and in requirement 1, explain whether Suncor did a better or worse job of controlling expenses other than the costs of crude oil and products in 2017 relative to 2016.

3. Assume Suncor reported average net fixed assets of $85 billion in 2017 and $74 billion in 2016. Compute the fixed asset turnover ratios for both years (rounded to two decimal places). Did the company better utilize its investment in fixed assets to generate revenues in 2017 or 2016?

4. Assume Suncor reported average shareholders' equity of $82 billion in 2017 and $73 billion in 2016. Compute the return on equity ratios for both years (expressed as a percentage with one decimal place). Did the company generate greater returns for shareholders in 2017 or 2016?

**Check Figure
[Req. 3]:**
2017 Fixed Asset
Turnover = 3.21

LO13-2, 13-3, 13-3

E13-3 Preparing and Interpreting a Schedule for Horizontal and Vertical Analyses

Assume the average cost of computer equipment fell 20.9 percent between 2016 and 2017. Let's see whether these changes are reflected in the income statement of Computer Tycoon Inc. for the year ended December 31, 2017.

	2017	2016
Sales Revenues	$98,913	$121,761
Cost of Goods Sold	59,249	71,583
Gross Profit	39,664	50,178
Selling, General, and Administrative Expenses	36,943	36,934
Interest Expense	565	474
Income Before Income Tax Expense	2,156	12,770
Income Tax Expense	1,024	5,540
Net Income	$ 1,132	$ 7,230

Required:

1. Conduct a horizontal analysis by calculating the year–over–year changes in each line item, expressed in dollars and in percentages (rounded to one decimal place). How did the change in computer prices compare to the changes in Computer Tycoon's sales revenues?

2. Conduct a vertical analysis by expressing each line as a percentage of total revenues (rounded to one decimal place). Excluding income tax, interest, and selling, general, and administrative expenses, did Computer Tycoon earn more profit per dollar of sales in 2017 compared to 2016?

LO13-4, 13-5 **E13-4 Computing Profitability Ratios**

Use the information in E13–3 to complete the following requirements.

Required:

**Check Figure
[Req. 4]:**
2017 Return on
Equity = 2.1%

1. Compute the gross profit percentage for each year (rounded to one decimal place). Assuming that the change for 2016 to 2017 is the beginning of a sustained trend, is Computer Tycoon likely to earn more or less gross profit from each dollar of sales in 2018?

2. Compute the net profit margin for each year (expressed as a percentage with one decimal place). Given your calculations here and in requirement 1, explain whether Computer Tycoon did a better or worse job of controlling operating expenses in 2017 relative to 2016.

3. Computer Tycoon reported average net fixed assets of $54,200 in 2017 and $45,100 in 2016. Compute the fixed asset turnover ratios for both years (rounded to two decimal places). Did the company better utilize its investment in fixed assets to generate revenues in 2017 or 2016.

4. Computer Tycoon reported average shareholders' equity of $54,000 in 2017 and $40,800 in 2016. Compute the return on equity ratios for both years (expressed as a percentage with one decimal place). Did the company generate greater returns for shareholders in 2017 than in 2016?

LO13-4, 13-5 **E13-5 Computing a Commonly Used Solvency Ratio**

Use the information in E13–3 to complete the following requirement.

Required:

Compute the times interest earned ratios for 2017 and 2016. In your opinion, does Computer Tycoon generate sufficient net income (before taxes and interest) to cover the cost of debt financing?

LO13-4 **E13-6 Matching Each Ratio with Its Computational Formula**

Match each ratio or percentage with its formula by entering the appropriate letter for each numbered item.

Ratios or Percentages	Formula
____ 1. Current ratio	A. Net income ÷ Net sales revenue
____ 2. Net profit margin	B. (Net sales revenue − Cost of goods sold) ÷ Netsales revenue
____ 3. Inventory turnover ratio	
____ 4. Gross profit percentage	C. Current assets ÷ Current liabilities
____ 5. Fixed asset turnover	D. Cost of goods sold ÷ Average inventory
____ 6. Return on equity	E. Net credit sales revenue ÷ Average netreceivables
____ 7. Times interest earned	F. Net income ÷ Average number of common shares outstanding
____ 8. Debt–to–assets ratio	
____ 9. Price/earnings ratio	G. Total liabilities ÷ Total assets
____ 10. Receivables turnover ratio	H. (Net income + Interest expense + Income taxexpense) ÷ Interest expense
____ 11. Earnings per share	
	I. Current market price per share ÷ Earningsper share
	J. Net income ÷ Average total shareholders' equity
	K. Net sales revenue ÷ Average net fixed assets

E13-7 Computing and Interpreting Selected Liquidity Ratios

LO13-4, 13-5

Double West Suppliers (DWS) reported sales for the year of $300,000, all on credit. The average gross profit percentage was 40 percent on sales. Account balances are as follows:

	Beginning	Ending
Accounts receivable (net)	$45,000	$55,000
Inventory	60,000	40,000

Required:

1. Compute the turnover ratios for accounts receivable and inventory (rounded to one decimal place).
2. By dividing 365 by your ratios from requirement 1, calculate the average days to collect receivables and the average days to sell inventory (rounded to one decimal place).
3. Explain what each of these ratios and measures mean for DWS.

**Check Figure
[Req. 2]:**
Average days to
sell = 101.4 days

E13-8 Computing and Interpreting Liquidity Ratios

LO13-4, 13-5

Assume that for the 2017 fiscal year, AstroCo reported sales revenue of $2.8 billion and cost of goods sold of $1.6 billion.

Fiscal Year	2017	2016
Balance Sheet	(in millions)	
Cash	$ 70	$ 35
Accounts Receivable, less allowance of $15 and $15	430	410
Inventories	240	230
Prepaid Expenses	10	15
Other Current Assets	410	345
Accounts Payable	95	65
Wages Payable	50	60
Income Tax Payable	10	70
Other Current Liabilities	210	205

Required:

Assuming that all sales are on credit, compute the current ratio (rounded to two decimal places), inventory turnover ratio (rounded to one decimal place), and accounts receivable turnover ratio (rounded to one decimal place) for 2017. Explain what each ratio means for AstroCo.

E13-9 Computing the Accounts Receivable and Inventory Turnover Ratios

LO13-4, 13-5

Procter & Gamble is a multinational corporation that manufactures and markets many prod—ucts that you use every day. In 2017, assume that sales for the company were $83,503 (all amounts in millions) and that all sales were on credit. The average gross profit percentage was 51.3 percent. Account balances are as follows:

	Beginning	Ending
Accounts receivable (net)	$6,761	$6,629
Inventory	8,416	6,819

Required:

1. Compute the turnover ratios for accounts receivable and inventory (rounded to one decimal place).
2. By dividing 365 by your ratios from requirement 1, calculate the average days to collect receivables and the average days to sell inventory.
3. Interpret what these ratios and measures mean for P&G.

E13-10 Inferring Financial Information from Profitability and Liquidity Ratios

Loonie Corporation stores feature quality merchandise at low prices to meet the needs of mid−dle−, low−, and fixed−income families. For the year ended January 30, 2017, the company reported average inventories of $1,352 (in millions) and an inventory turnover of 5.47. Average total fixed assets were $1,272 (in millions), and the fixed asset turnover ratio was 8.22.

Required:

Check Figure [Req. 1]:
Net sales = $10,456 (in millions)

1. Calculate Loonie's gross profit percentage (expressed as a percentage with one decimal place). What does this imply about the amount of gross profit made from each dollar of sales?

   TIP: Work backward from the fixed asset turnover and inventory turnover ratios to compute the amounts needed for the gross profit percentage.

2. Is this an improvement from the gross profit percentage of 28.2 percent earned during the previous year?

E13-11 Analyzing the Impact of Selected Transactions on the Current Ratio

In its most recent annual report, Laurentian Beverages reported current assets of $54,000 and a current ratio of 1.80. Assume that the following transactions were completed:

a. Purchased merchandise for $6,000 on account
b. Purchased a delivery truck for $10,000, paying $1,000 cash and signing a two−year prom−issory note for the balance

Required:

Compute the updated current ratio, rounded to two decimal places, after each transaction.

E13-12 Analyzing the Impact of Selected Transactions on the Current Ratio

In its most recent annual report, Sunrise Corp. reported current assets of $1,090,000 and cur−rent liabilities of $602,000. Assume that the following transactions were completed:

a. Sold long−term assets for cash
b. Accrued severance pay for terminated employees
c. Wrote down the carrying value of certain inventory items that were deemed to be obsolete
d. Acquired new inventory by signing an eighteen−month promissory note (The supplier was not willing to provide normal credit terms.)

Required:

Determine for each transaction, whether the Sunrise's current ratio, and each of its two com−ponents, will increase, decrease, or have no change.

E13-13 Analyzing the Impact of Selected Transactions on the Current Ratio

SportChek is Canada's largest retailer of sporting goods and sports apparel and footwear, with over 130 stores across the couontry. Assume one of the SportChek stores reported current assets of $88,000 and its current ratio was 1.75. Assume that the following transactions were completed:

a. Paid $6,000 on accounts payable
b. Purchased a delivery truck for $10,000 cash
c. Wrote off a bad account receivable for $2,000
d. Paid previously declared dividends in the amount of $25,000

Required:

Compute the updated current ratio, rounded to two decimal places, after each transaction.

E13-14 Analyzing the Impact of Selected Transactions on the Current Ratio

A company has current assets that total $500,000 and a current ratio of 2.00, and uses the perpetual inventory method. Assume that the following transactions are completed:

a. Sold $12,000 in merchandise on short−term credit for $15,000
b. Declared but did not pay dividends of $50,000
c. Paid prepaid rent in the amount of $12,000

d. Paid previously declared dividends in the amount of $50,000

e. Collected an account receivable in the amount of $12,000

f. Reclassified $40,000 of long–term debt as a current liability

Required:

Compute the updated current ratio, rounded to two decimal places, after each transaction.

E13-15 Analyzing the Impact of Alternative Inventory Methods on Selected Ratios

LO13-6

Company A uses the FIFO method to cost inventory, and Company B uses the LIFO method. The two companies are exactly alike except for the difference in inventory costing methods. Costs of inventory items for both companies have been falling steadily in recent years, and each company has increased its inventory each year. Ignore income tax effects.

Required:

Identify which company will report the higher amount for each of the following ratios. If it is not possible to identify which will report the higher amount, explain why.

1. Current ratio
2. Debt–to–assets ratio
3. Earnings per share

COACHED PROBLEMS

CP13-1 Analyzing Comparative Financial Statements Using Horizontal Analyses

LO13-2, 13-5

eXcel

The comparative financial statements for Golden Corporation, prepared at December 31, 2017, showed the following summarized data:

	2017	2016	Increase (Decrease) 2014 over 2013 Amount	Percentage
Income Statement				
Sales revenue	$ 180,000	$ 165,000		
Cost of goods sold	110,000	100,000		
Gross profit	70,000	65,000		
Operating expenses	53,300	50,400		
Interest expense	2,700	2,600		
Income before income taxes	14,000	12,000		
Income tax expense	4,000	3,000		
Net income	$ 10,000	$ 9,000		
Balance Sheet				
Cash	$ 4,000	$ 8,000		
Accounts receivable (net)	19,000	23,000		
Inventory	40,000	35,000		
Property and equipment (net)	45,000	38,000		
	$ 108,000	$ 104,000		
Current liabilities (no interest)	16,000	19,000		
Long-term liabilities (6% interest)	45,000	45,000		
Common shares (par $5)	30,000	30,000		
Additional paid-in capital	5,000	5,000		
Retained earnings	12,000	5,000		
	$ 108,000	$ 104,000		

Handwritten annotations: 5× 30,000 = 150,000; 30,000/5 = 6,000; 47,00; 40,000; SE (next to Common shares, Additional paid-in capital, Retained earnings)

Required:

1. Complete the two final columns shown beside each item in Golden Corporation's compara-tive financial statements. Round the percentages to one decimal place.

   TIP: Calculate the increase (decrease) by subtracting 2016 from 2017. Calculate the percentage by dividing the amount of increase (decrease) by the 2016 balance.

2. Is there anything significant that jumps out at you from the horizontal (trend) analyses? Explain.

LO13-4, 13-5 **CP13-2 Analyzing Comparative Financial Statements Using Selected Ratios**

Use the data given in CP13–1 for Golden Corporation.

Required:

1. Compute the gross profit percentage for 2017 and 2016. Round the percentages to one decimal place. Is the trend going in the right direction?

2. Compute the net profit margin for 2017 and 2016. Round the percentages to one decimal place. Is the trend going in the right direction?

3. Compute the earnings per share for 2017 and 2016. Does the trend look good or bad? Explain.

   TIP: To calculate EPS, use the balance in Common Shares to determine the number of shares outstanding. Common Shares equals the par value per share times the number of shares.

4. Shareholders' equity totalled $30,000 at the end of 2015. Compute the return on equity (ROE) ratios for 2016 and 2017. Express the ROE as percentages rounded to one decimal place. Is the trend going in the right direction?

5. Net property and equipment totalled $35,000 at the end of 2015. Compute the fixed asset turnover ratios for 2017 and 2016. Round the ratios to two decimal places. Is the trend going in the right direction?

6. Compute the debt–to–assets ratios for 2017 and 2016. Round the ratios to two decimal places. Is debt providing financing for a larger or smaller proportion of the company's asset growth? Explain.

7. Compute the times interest earned ratios for 2017 and 2016. Round the ratios to one deci-mal place. Do they look good or bad? Explain.

8. After Golden released its 2017 financial statements, the company's shares were trading at $30. After the release of its 2016 financial statements, the company's share price was $21 per share. Compute the P/E ratios for both years, rounded to one decimal place. Does it appear that investors have become more (or less) optimistic about Golden's future success?

LO13-3, 13-5 **CP13-3 Vertical Analysis of a Balance Sheet**

Electric Arts is a video game company. A condensed balance sheet for Electric Arts and a partially completed vertical analysis are presented below.

ELECTRIC ARTS, INC. Balance Sheet (summarized) March 31, 2017 (in millions)					
Cash and Short–Term Investments	$ 1,273	27%	Accounts Payable	$ 91	2%
Accounts Receivable	206	4	Accrued Liabilities	717	(d)
Inventories	100	2	Long–Term Debt	1,109	24
Other Current Assets	1,006	(a)	Total Liabilities	1,917	(e)
Intangibles	1,297	(b)	Contributed Capital	2,378	51
Property and Equipment	537	(c)	Retained Earnings	351	8
Other Assets	227	5	Total Shareholders' Equity	2,729	59
Total Assets	$ 4,646	100%	Total Liabilities & Shareholders' Equity	$4,646	100%

Required:

1. Complete the vertical analysis by computing each line item from (a) through (e) as a per—centage of total assets. Round to the nearest whole percentage.

    TIP: Inventories were 2 percent of total assets, computed as ($100/$4,646) × 100.

2. What percentages of Electric Arts' assets relate to intangibles versus property and equip—ment? What business reasons would explain this relative emphasis?

CP13-4 Vertical Analysis of an Income Statement

A condensed income statement for Electric Arts and a partially completed vertical analysis follow.

ELECTRIC ARTS, INC. Income Statement (summarized) For the Year Ended March 31 (in millions)				
	2017		**2016**	
Net Revenues	$ 3,654	100%	$ 4,212	100%
Cost of Goods Sold	1,866	(a)	2,127	50
Research and Development Expense	1,229	(b)	1,359	32
Sales and Marketing Expense	730	(c)	691	16
General and Administrative Expense	515	14	862	21
Income (Loss) from Operations	(686)	(19)	(827)	(19)
Other Revenue (Expenses)	(20)	(1)	(28)	(1)
Income (Loss) before Income Tax	(706)	(20)	(855)	(20)
Income Tax Recovery (Expense)	29	1	(233)	(6)
Net Income (Loss)	$ (677)	(d)%	$(1,088)	(26)%

Required:

1. Complete the vertical analysis by computing each line item from (a) through (d) as a per—centage of Net Revenues. Round to the nearest whole percentage.

    TIP: Research and Development was 32 percent of Net Revenues in 2016, which was computed as ($1,359/$4,212) × 100.

2. Does Electric Arts' 2017 Cost of Goods Sold, as a percentage of Net Revenues, represent better or worse performance as compared to 2016?

CP13-5 Interpreting Profitability, Liquidity, Solvency, and P/E Ratios

Kohl's Corporation is a national retail department store in the United States. Assume the company's total revenues for the year ended January 29, 2017, were $18 billion. J.C. Penney is a similar—sized department store company with $18 billion of revenues. The following ratios for the two companies were obtained for that fiscal year from reuters.com/finance:

Ratio	Kohl's	J.C. Penney
Gross profit percentage	38.2%	39.2%
Net profit margin	6.0%	2.1%
Return on equity	14.0%	7.38%
EPS	$3.75	$1.57
Inventory turnover ratio	3.81	3.46
Current ratio	2.08	2.41
Debt-to-assets ratio	0.96	0.98
P/E ratio	14.2	23.3

Required:

1. Which company appears more profitable? Describe the ratio(s) that you used to reach this decision.

2. Which company appears more liquid? Describe the ratio(s) that you used to reach this decision.

3. Which company appears more solvent? Describe the ratio(s) that you used to reach this decision.

4. Are the conclusions from your analyses in requirements 1 to 3 consistent with the value of the two companies, as suggested by their P/E ratios? If not, offer one explanation for any apparent inconsistency.

   TIP: Remember that the share price in the top of the P/E ratio represents investors' expecta— tions about future financial performance, whereas the bottom number reports past financial performance.

LO13-4, 13-5, 13-6   **CP13-6 Using Ratios to Compare Alternative Investment Opportunities**

The 2017 financial statements for the Armstrong and Blair companies are summarized here:

	Armstrong Company	Blair Company
Balance Sheet		
Cash	$ 35,000	$ 22,000
Accounts Receivable, Net	40,000	30,000
Inventory	100,000	40,000
Property and Equipment, Net	180,000	300,000
Other Assets	45,000	408,000
Total Assets	$ 400,000	$ 800,000
Current Liabilities	$ 100,000	$ 50,000
Long-Term Debt	60,000	370,000
Total Liabilities	160,000	420,000
Common Share (par $10)	150,000	200,000
Additional Paid-In Capital	30,000	110,000
Retained Earnings	60,000	70,000
Total Liabilities and Shareholders' Equity	$ 400,000	$ 800,000
Income Statement		
Sales Revenue (1/3 on credit)	$ 450,000	$810,000
Cost of Goods Sold	(245,000)	(405,000)
Expenses (including interest and income tax)	(160,000)	(315,000)
Net Income	$ 45,000	$ 90,000
Selected Data from 2016 Statements		
Accounts Receivable, Net	$ 20,000	$ 38,000
Inventory	92,000	45,000
Property and Equipment, Net	180,000	300,000
Long-Term Debt	60,000	70,000
Total Shareholders' Equity	231,000	440,000
Other Data		
Estimated value of each share at end of 2017	$ 18	$ 27

The companies are in the same line of business and are direct competitors in a large met—ropolitan area. Both have been in business approximately ten years, and each has had steady growth. One—third of both companies' sales are on credit.

Despite these similarities, the management of each has a different viewpoint in many respects. Blair is more conservative, and as its president said, "We avoid what we consider to be undue risk." Both companies use straight—line depreciation, but Blair estimates slightly shorter useful lives than Armstrong does. No shares were issued in 2017, and neither company is publicly held. Blair Company has an annual audit by a CA but Armstrong Company does not.

Required:

1. Calculate the ratios in Exhibit 13.5 for which sufficient information is available. Round all calculations to two decimal places.

    TIP: To calculate EPS, use the balance in Common Shares to determine the number of shares outstanding. Common Shares equals the par value per share times the number of shares.

2. A client of yours has decided to buy shares in one of the two companies. Based on the data given, prepare a comparative written evaluation of the ratio analyses (and any other available information) and conclude with your recommended choice.

    TIP: Comment on how accounting differences affect your evaluations, if at all.

CP13-7 Analyzing an Investment by Comparing Selected Ratios

LO13-5

You have the opportunity to invest $10,000 in one of two companies from a single industry. The only information you have is in the table below. The word *high* refers to the top third of the industry; *average* is the middle third; *low* is the bottom third.

Ratio	Company A	Company B
Current	High	Average
Inventory turnover	Low	Average
Debt-to-assets	High	Average
Times interest earned	Low	Average
Price/earnings	Low	Average

Required:

Which company would you select? Write a brief explanation for your recommendation.

    TIP: When interpreting ratios, think about how they are related to one another. For example, the current ratio and the inventory turnover ratio both include the Inventory balance. This means that the low inventory turnover ratio can help you to interpret the high current ratio.

GROUP A PROBLEMS

PA13-1 Analyzing Financial Statements Using Horizontal and Ratio Analyses

LO13-2, 13-5

The comparative financial statements prepared at December 31, 2017, for Pinnacle Plus showed the following summarized data:

			Increase (Decrease) 2017 over 2016	
	2017	2016	Amount	Percentage
Income Statement				
Sales Revenue*	$ 110,000	$ 99,000		
Cost of Goods Sold	52,000	48,000		
Gross Profit	58,000	51,000		
Operating Expenses	36,000	33,000		
Interest Expense	4,000	4,000		
Income before Income Tax Expense	18,000	14,000		
Income Tax Expense (30%)	5,400	4,200		
Net Income	$ 12,600	$ 9,800		
Balance Sheet				
Cash	$ 49,500	$ 18,000		
Accounts Receivable, Net	37,000	32,000		
Inventory	25,000	38,000		
Property and Equipment, Net	95,000	105,000		
Total Assets	$ 206,500	$193,000		
Accounts Payable	$ 42,000	$ 35,000		
Income Tax Payable	1,000	500		
Note Payable, Long-Term	40,000	40,000		
Total Liabilities	83,000	75,500		
Contributed Capital (9,000 shares)	90,000	90,000		
Retained Earnings†	33,500	27,500		
Total Liabilities and Shareholders' Equity	$ 206,500	$193,000		

*One-half of all sales are on credit.
†During 2017, cash dividends amounting to $6,600 were declared and paid.

Required:

1. Complete the two final columns shown beside each item in Pinnacle's comparative financial statements. Round the percentages to one decimal place.
2. Is there anything significant that jumps out at you from the horizontal analyses? Explain.

LO13-4, 13-5 **PA13-2 Analyzing Comparative Financial Statements Using Selected Ratios**

Use the data given in PA13–1 for Pinnacle Plus.

Required:

Check Figure [Req. 3]:
2017 Earnings per Share = $1.40

1. Compute the gross profit percentage in 2017 and 2016. Round the percentages to one decimal place. Is the trend going in the right direction?
2. Compute the net profit margin for 2017 and 2016. Round the percentages to one decimal place. Is the trend going in the right direction?
3. Compute the earnings per share for 2017 and 2016. Does the trend look good or bad? Explain.
4. Shareholders' equity totaled $100,000 at the end of 2015. Compute the return on equity (ROE) ratios for 2017 and 2016. Express the ROE as percentages rounded to one decimal place. Is the trend going in the right direction?
5. Net property and equipment totaled $110,000 at the end of 2015. Compute the fixed asset turnover ratios for 2017 and 2016. Round the ratios to two decimal places. Is the trend going in the right direction?

6. Compute the debt–to–assets ratios for 2017 and 2016. Round the ratios to two decimal places. Is debt providing financing for a larger or smaller proportion of the company's asset growth? Explain.

7. Compute the times interest earned ratios for 2017 and 2016. Round the ratios to one decimal place. Do they look good or bad? Explain.

8. After Pinnacle Plus released its 2017 financial statements, the company's shares were trading at $18. After the release of its 2016 financial statements, the company's share price was $15 per share. Compute the P/E ratios for both years, rounded to one decimal place. Does it appear that investors have become more (or less) optimistic about Pinnacle's future success?

PA13-3 Vertical Analysis of a Balance Sheet

LO13-3, 13-5

A condensed balance sheet for Simultech Corporation and a partially completed vertical analysis are presented below.

SIMULTECH CORPORATION
Balance Sheet (summarized)
January 31, 2017
(in millions)

Cash and Short–Term Investments	$ 433	29%	Current Liabilities	$ 409	27%
Accounts Receivable	294	19	Long–Term Liabilities	495	33
Inventories	206	14	Total Liabilities	904	(b)
Other Current Assets	109	(a)	Contributed Capital	118	(c)
Property and Equipment	27	2	Retained Earnings	492	30
Other Assets	445	29	Total Shareholders' Equity	610	(d)
Total Assets	$1,514	100%	Total Liabilities & Shareholders' Equity	$1,514	100%

Required:

1. Complete the vertical analysis by computing each line item from (a) through (d) as a percentage of total assets. Round to the nearest whole percentage.

2. What percentages of Simultech's assets relate to inventories versus property and equipment? What does this tell you about the relative significance of these two assets to Simultech's business?

3. What percentage of Simultech's assets is financed by total shareholder's equity? By total liabilities?

PA13-4 Vertical Analysis of an Income Statement

LO13-3, 13-5

A condensed income statement for Simultech Corporation and a partially completed vertical analysis are presented below.

SIMULTECH CORPORATION
Income Statement (summarized)
(in millions)

	For the Years Ended			
	January 31, 2017		January 31, 2016	
Sales Revenues	$2,062	100%	$2,200	100%
Cost of Goods Sold	1,637	79	1,721	(d)
Selling, General, and Administrative Expenses	333	(a)	346	16
Other Operating Expenses	53	3	12	1
Interest Expense	22	(b)	26	1
Income before Income Tax Expense	17	1	95	(e)
Income Tax Expense	6	0	33	1
Net Income	$ 11	(c)%	$ 62	(f)%

Required:

1. Complete the vertical analysis by computing each line item from (a) through (f) as a percentage of sales revenues. Round to the nearest whole percentage.
2. Does Simultech's Cost of Goods Sold for the year ended January 31, 2017, as a percentage of revenues, represent better or worse performance as compared to that for the year ended January 31, 2016?
3. Do the percentages for items (c) and (f) that you calculated in requirement 1 indicate whether Simultech's net profit margin has changed over the two years?

LO13-4, 13-5   **PA13-5 Interpreting Profitability, Liquidity, Solvency, and P/E Ratios**

Coke and Pepsi are well–known international brands. Coca–Cola sells more than $35 billion worth of beverages each year while annual sales of Pepsi products exceed $43 billion. Compare the two companies as a potential investment based on the following ratios:

Ratio	Coca-Cola	PepsiCo
Gross profit percentage	63.9%	54.1%
Net profit margin	33.6%	10.9%
Return on equity	37.7%	29.4%
EPS	$ 5.06	$ 3.91
Receivables turnover ratio	8.6	10.6
Inventory turnover ratio	5.1	8.9
Current ratio	1.17	1.11
Debt-to-assets	0.57	0.68
P/E ratio	12.6	16.2

Required:

1. Which company appears more profitable? Describe the ratio(s) that you used to reach this decision.
2. Which company appears more liquid? Describe the ratio(s) that you used to reach this decision.
3. Which company appears more solvent? Describe the ratio(s) that you used to reach this decision.
4. Are the conclusions from your analyses in requirements 1 to 3 consistent with the value of the two companies, as suggested by their P/E ratios? If not, offer one explanation for any apparent inconsistency.

LO13-4, 13-5, 13-6   **PA13-6 Using Ratios to Compare Loan Requests from Two Companies**

The 2017 financial statements for Royale and Cavalier companies are summarized below.

	Royale Company	Cavalier Company
Balance Sheet		
Cash	$ 25,000	$ 45,000
Accounts Receivable, Net	55,000	5,000
Inventory	110,000	25,000
Property and Equipment, Net	550,000	160,000
Other Assets	140,000	57,000
Total Assets	$ 880,000	$ 292,000

Current Liabilities	$ 120,000	$ 15,000
Long-Term Debt	190,000	55,000
Contributed Capital (24,000 shares; 10,500 shares)	480,000	210,000
Contributed Surplus	50,000	4,000
Retained Earnings	40,000	8,000
Total Liabilities and Shareholders' Equity	$ 880,000	$ 292,000
Income Statement		
Sales Revenue	$ 800,000	$ 280,000
Cost of Goods Sold	(480,000)	(150,000)
Expenses (including interest and income tax)	(240,000)	(95,000)
Net Income	$ 80,000	$ 35,000
Selected Data from 2016 Statements		
Accounts Receivable, Net	$ 47,000	$ 11,000
Long-Term Debt	190,000	55,000
Property and Equipment, Net	550,000	160,000
Inventory	95,000	38,000
Total Shareholders' Equity	570,000	202,000
Other Data		
Per share price at end of 2017	$ 14.00	$ 11.00

These two companies are in the same business and the same province but in different cities. One–half of Royale's sales and one–quarter of Cavalier's sales are on credit. Each company has been in operation for about ten years. Both companies received an unqualified audit opinion on the financial statements. Royale Company wants to borrow $75,000 cash, and Cavalier Company is asking for $30,000. The loans will be for a two–year period. Both companies estimate bad debts based on an aging analysis, but Cavalier has estimated slightly higher uncollectable rates than Royale. Neither company issued shares in 2017.

Required:

1. Calculate the ratios in Exhibit 13.5 for which sufficient information is available. Round all calculations to two decimal places.

2. Assume that you work in the loan department of a local bank. You have been asked to analyze the situation and recommend which loan is preferable. Based on the data given, your analysis prepared in requirement 1, and any other information (e.g., accounting policies and decisions), give your choice and the supporting explanation.

PA13-7 Analyzing an Investment by Comparing Selected Ratios   LO13-5

You have the opportunity to invest $10,000 in one of two companies from a single industry. The only information you have is shown here. The word *high* refers to the top third of the industry; *average* is the middle third; *low* is the bottom third.

Ratio	Company A	Company B
Current	Low	High
Inventory turnover	High	Low
Debt-to-assets	Low	Average
Times interest earned	High	Average
Price/earnings	High	Average

Required:

Which company would you select? Write a brief explanation for your recommendation.

LO13-2, 13-5   **PB13-1** **Analyzing Financial Statements Using Horizontal and Ratio Analyses**

The comparative financial statements prepared at December 31, 2017, for Tiger Audio showed the following summarized data:

	2017	2016	Increase (Decrease) 2017 over 2016 Amount	Percentage
Income Statement				
Sales Revenue	$222,000	$185,000		
Cost of Goods Sold	127,650	111,000		
Gross Profit	94,350	74,000		
Operating Expenses	39,600	33,730		
Interest Expense	4,000	3,270		
Income before Income Tax Expense	50,750	37,000		
Income Tax Expense (30%)	15,225	11,100		
Net Income	$ 35,525	$ 25,900		
Balance Sheet				
Cash	$ 40,000	$ 38,000		
Accounts Receivable, Net	18,500	16,000		
Inventory	25,000	22,000		
Property and Equipment, Net	127,000	119,000		
Total Assets	$210,500	$195,000		
Accounts Payable	$ 27,000	$ 25,000		
Income Tax Payable	3,000	2,800		
Note Payable, Long-Term	75,500	92,200		
Total Liabilities	105,500	120,000		
Contributed Capital (25,000 shares outstanding)	25,000	25,000		
Retained Earnings	80,000	50,000		
Total Liabilities and Shareholders' Equity	$210,500	$195,000		

Required:

1. Complete the two final columns shown beside each item in Tiger Audio's comparative financial statements. Round the percentages to one decimal place.
2. Does anything significant jump out at you from the year−over−year analyses?

LO13-4, 13-5   **PB13-2** **Analyzing Comparative Financial Statements Using Selected Ratios**

Use the data given in PB13−1 for Tiger Audio.

Required:

Check Figures: [Req. 4]: 2017 Return on Equity = 39.5%

1. Compute the gross profit percentage in 2017 and 2016. Is the trend going in the right direction?
2. Compute the net profit margin for 2017 and 2016. Is the trend going in the right direction?
3. Compute the earnings per share for 2017 and 2016. Does the trend look good or bad? Explain.
4. Shareholders' equity totalled $65,000 at the end of 2015. Compute the return on equity ratios for 2017 and 2016. Is the trend going in the right direction?

5. Net property and equipment totalled $115,000 at the end of 2015. Compute the fixed asset turnover ratios for 2017 and 2016. Is the trend going in the right direction?

6. Compute the debt−to−assets ratios for 2017 and 2016. Is debt providing financing for a larger or smaller proportion of the company's asset growth? Explain.

7. Compute the times interest earned ratios for 2017 and 2016. Do they look good or bad? Explain.

8. After Tiger released its 2017 financial statements, the company's shares were trading at $17. After the release of its 2016 financial statements, the company's share price was $12 per share. Compute the P/E ratios for both years. Does it appear that investors have become more or less optimistic about Tiger's future success?

PB13-3 Vertical Analysis of a Balance Sheet

LO13-3, 13-5

A condensed balance sheet for Northwest Airlines and a partially completed vertical analysis are presented below.

NORTHWEST AIRLINES
Balance Sheet (summarized)
December 31, 2017 (in millions)

Cash	$ 1,261	8%	Current Liabilities	$ 3,305	(b)%
Accounts Receivable	195	1	Long−Term Liabilities	5,921	38
Inventory of Parts and Supplies	243	2	Total Liabilities	9,226	60
Other Current Assets	2,580	17	Contributed Capital	1,100	7
Property and Equipment, Net	10,578	(a)	Retained Earnings	5,137	33
Other Assets	606	4	Total Shareholders' Equity	6,237	(c)
Total Assets	$15,463	100%	Total Liabilities & Shareholders' Equity	$ 15,463	100%

Required:

1. Complete the vertical analysis by computing each line item from (a) through (c) as a per−centage of total assets. Round to the nearest whole percentage.

2. What percentages of Northwest's assets relate to inventory of parts and supplies versus property and equipment? What does this tell you about the relative significance of these two assets to Northwest's business?

3. What percentage of Northwest's assets is financed by total shareholders' equity? By total liabilities?

PB13-4 Vertical Analysis of an Income Statement

LO13-3, 13-5

A condensed income statement for Northwest Airlines and a partially completed vertical analysis are presented below.

NORTHWEST AIRLINES
Income Statement (summarized)
For the Year Ended December 31
(in millions)

	2017		2016	
Sales Revenues	$12,104	100%	$10,350	100%
Salaries, Wages, and Benefits	3,704	31	3,468	(d)
Fuel, Oil, Repairs, and Maintenance	3,620	(a)	3,044	29
Other Operating Expenses	3,792	(b)	3,576	35
Other Expenses (Revenues)	243	2	98	1
Income before Income Tax Expense	745	6	164	(e)
Income Tax Expense	286	2	65	1
Net Income	$ 459	(c)%	$ 99	(f)%

Required:

1. Complete the vertical analysis by computing each line item from (a) through (f) as a percentage of sales revenues. Round to the nearest whole percentage.
2. Does the percentage that you calculated in requirement 1(a) suggest that Northwest tried to increase its profit by cutting repairs and maintenance costs in 2017 compared to 2016?
3. Refer to the percentages that you calculated in requirements 1(c) and 1(f). Is Northwest's net profit margin improving or declining?

LO13-4, 13-5   **PB13-5 Interpreting Profitability, Liquidity, Solvency, and P/E Ratios**

Mattel and Hasbro are the two largest manufacturers of games and toys in the world. Mattel sells some $9 billion of products each year, while annual sales of Hasbro products exceed $4 billion. Compare the two companies as a potential investment based on the following assumed ratios:

Ratio	Mattel	Hasbro
Gross profit percentage	45.5%	57.7%
Net profit margin	6.5%	7.3%
Return on equity	17.1%	21.8%
EPS	$ 1.05	$ 2.18
Receivables turnover ratio	8.9	10.5
Inventory turnover ratio	6.2	5.7
Current ratio	2.38	2.54
Debt-to-assets ratio	0.31	0.35
P/E ratio	15.9	13.8

Required:

1. Which company appears more profitable? Describe the ratio(s) that you used to reach this decision.
2. Which company appears more liquid? Describe the ratio(s) that you used to reach this decision.
3. Which company appears more solvent? Describe the ratio(s) that you used to reach this decision.
4. Are the conclusions from your analyses in requirements 1 to 3 consistent with the value of the two companies, as suggested by their P/E ratios? If not, offer one explanation for any apparent inconsistency.

LO13-4, 13-5, 13-6   **PB13-6 Using Ratios to Compare Loan Requests from Two Companies**

The 2017 financial statements for the Thor and Gunnar companies are summarized below.

	Thor Company	Gunnar Company
Balance Sheet		
Cash	$ 35,000	$ 54,000
Accounts Receivable, Net	77,000	6,000
Inventory	154,000	30,000
Property and Equipment, Net	770,000	192,000
Other Assets	196,000	68,400
Total Assets	$ 1,232,000	$ 350,400
Current Liabilities	$ 168,000	$ 18,000
Long-Term Debt (12% interest rate)	266,000	66,000

Contributed Capital (33,600 shares; 12,600 shares)	672,000	252,000
Contributed Surplus	70,000	4,800
Retained Earnings	56,000	9,600
Total Liabilities and Shareholders' Equity	$ 1,232,000	$ 350,400
Income Statement		
Sales Revenue	$ 1,120,000	$ 336,000
Cost of Goods Sold	(672,000)	(180,000)
Expenses (including interest and income tax)	(336,000)	(114,000)
Net Income	$ 112,000	$ 42,000
Selected Data from 2016 Statements		
Accounts Receivable, Net	$ 65,800	$ 13,200
Inventory	133,000	45,600
Property and Equipment, Net	770,000	192,000
Long-Term Debt (12% interest rate)	266,000	66,000
Total Shareholders' Equity	798,000	266,400
Other Data		
Per share price at end of 2017	$ 13.20	$ 19.60

These two companies are in the same business and in the same province but in different cities. One–half of Thor's sales and one–quarter of Gunnar's sales are on credit. Each company has been in operation for about ten years. Both companies received an unqualified audit opinion on the financial statements. Thor Company wants to borrow $105,000, and Gunnar Company is asking for $36,000. The loans will be for a two–year period. Neither company issued shares in 2017.

Required:

1. Calculate the ratios in Exhibit 13.5 for which sufficient information is available. Round all calculations to two decimal places.
2. Assume that you work in the loan department of a local bank. You have been asked to analyze the situation and recommend which loan is preferable. Based on the data given, your analysis prepared in requirement 1 and any other information, give your choice and the supporting explanation.

PB13-7 Analyzing an Investment by Comparing Selected Ratios   LO13-5

You have the opportunity to invest $10,000 in one of two companies from a single industry. The only information you have is shown here. The word *high* refers to the top third of the industry; *average* is the middle third; *low* is the bottom third.

Ratio	Company A	Company B
EPS	High	High
Return on equity	High	Average
Debt-to-assets	High	Low
Current	Low	Average
Price/earnings	Low	High

Required:

Which company would you select? Write a brief explanation for your choice.

SKILLS DEVELOPMENT CASES

LO13-4, 13-5 **S13-1 Computing Ratios**

To benchmark Lowe's financial results, we reported the following ratios for The Home Depot fiscal year ended January 27, 2017: fixed asset turnover (3.32), days to sell (71.6), and debt—to—assets (0.90). Show that you can compute these ratios using the financial statements of Lowe's Companies, Inc. in Appendix B.

S13-2 Evaluating Financial Information

The Lumber Yard Ltd. competes with Hardesty Inc. in product lines such as hardwood flooring, noise—reducing underlay, and mouldings. Assume the two companies reported the following financial results in fiscal 2017:

	The Lumber Yard Ltd.	Hardesty Inc.
Gross profit percentage	35.0%	34.2%
Net profit margin	4.7%	4.6%
Return on equity	21.1%	12.9%
Earnings per share	$ 0.83	$ 1.51

Required:

1. Explain how The Lumber Yard Ltd. could have a substantially higher gross profit per—centage than Hardesty Inc. but a nearly identical net profit margin. What does this suggest about the relative ability of the two companies to control operating expenses?
2. Explain how The Lumber Yard Ltd. could have a higher return on equity but lower earn—ings per share. What does this suggest about the companies' relative number of outstanding shares? What other explanations could account for this seemingly contradictory pattern?

LO13-1, 13-2, 13-3, 13-4, 13-5, 13-6 **S13-3 Internet-Based Team Research: Examining an Annual Report**

As a team, select an industry to analyze. Using the Internet, each team member should access the annual report for one publicly traded company in the industry, with each member select—ing a different company. (See S1—3 in Chapter 1 for a description of possible resources for these tasks.)

Required:

1. On an individual basis, each team member should write a short report that incorporates horizontal and vertical analyses, and as many of the ratios from the chapter as are applica—ble given the nature of the selected company.
2. Then, as a team, write a short report comparing and contrasting your companies using these attributes. Discuss any patterns across the companies that you as a team observe. Provide potential explanations for any differences discovered. Consider the impact of dif—ferences in accounting policies.

LO13-6 **S13-4 Ethical Decision Making: A Real-Life Example**

One study done by Weiss Ratings focused on auditors' ability to predict bankruptcy. The study criticized auditors for failing to identify and report going—concern problems for audit clients that later went bankrupt. Based on a sample of forty—five bankrupt companies, the Weiss study concluded that if auditors had noted unusual levels for just two of seven typical financial ratios, they would have identified 89 percent of the sample companies that later went bankrupt.

A follow—up to the Weiss study found that if the criteria in the Weiss study had been applied to a larger sample of non—bankrupt companies, 46.9 percent of non—bankrupt com—panies would have been predicted to go bankrupt.[2] In other words, the Weiss criteria would have incorrectly predicted bankruptcy for nearly half of the companies in the follow—up study and would have led the auditors to report that these clients had substantial going—concern problems when, in fact, they did not.

Discuss the negative consequences that arise when auditors fail to identify and report going–concern problems. Who is harmed by these failures? Discuss the negative consequences that arise when auditors incorrectly report going–concern problems when they do not exist. Who is harmed by these errors? In your opinion, which of the potential consequences is worse?

S13-5 Ethical Decision Making: A Mini-Case

LO13-4, 13-5

Capital Investments Corporation (CIC) requested a sizable loan from First Canadian Bank to acquire a large piece of land for future expansion. CIC reported current assets of $1,900,000 (including $430,000 in cash) and current liabilities of $1,075,000. First Canadian denied the loan request for a number of reasons, including the fact that the current ratio was below 2:1.

When CIC was informed of the loan denial, the controller of the company immediately paid $420,000 that was owed to several trade creditors. The controller then asked First Canadian to reconsider the loan application. Based on these abbreviated facts, would you recommend that First Canadian approve the loan request? Why? Are the controller's actions ethical?

S13 6 Critical Thinking: Analyzing the Impact of Alternative Depreciation Methods on Ratio Analysis

LO13-4, 13-5, 13-6

Speedy Company uses the double–declining–balance method to depreciate its property, plant, and equipment, and Turtle Company uses the straight–line method. The two companies are exactly alike except for the difference in depreciation methods.

Required:

1. Identify the financial ratios discussed in this chapter that are likely to be affected by the difference in depreciation methods.
2. Which company will report the higher amount for each ratio that you have identified in response to requirement 1? If you cannot be certain, explain why.

S13-7 Using a Spreadsheet to Calculate Financial Statement Ratios

LO13-2, 13-3

Enter the account names and dollar amounts from the comparative balance sheets in Exhibit 13.1 into a worksheet in a spreadsheet file. Create a second copy of the worksheet in the same spreadsheet file.

Required:

1. To the right of the comparative numbers in the first worksheet, enter the necessary formulas to compute the amount and percent change as shown in Exhibit 13.1.
2. To the right of each column in the second worksheet, enter the necessary formulas to create common–size statements similar to those shown in Exhibit 13.3.

CONTINUING CASE

CC13-1 Evaluating Profitability, Liquidity, and Solvency

LO13-4, 13-5

Looking back over the past few years, it is clear that Nicole Mackisey has accomplished a lot running her business, Nicole's Getaway Spa (NGS). Nicole is curious about her company's performance as she compares its financial statements.

	2017	2016	2015
Balance Sheet			
Cash	$ 6,700	$ 4,200	$ 3,800
Accounts Receivable, Net	2,000	2,500	1,800
Inventory	1,200	3,000	1,600
Prepaid Expenses	750	1,050	200
Other Current Assets	300	350	200
Total Current Assets	10,950	11,100	7,600

Property and Equipment	64,000	79,000	27,000
Total Assets	$ 74,950	$ 90,100	$ 34,600
Current Liabilities	$ 8,000	$ 8,000	$ 9,000
Long-Term Liabilities	35,000	50,000	14,000
Total Liabilities	43,000	58,000	23,000
Contributed Capital	25,000	30,000	10,900
Retained Earnings	6,950	2,100	700
Total Shareholders' Equity	31,950	32,100	11,600
Total Liabilities and Shareholders' Equity	$ 74,950	$ 90,100	$ 34,600
Income Statement			
Sales Revenue	$ 80,000	56,000	$ 44,000
Cost of Goods Sold	65,000	48,000	35,000
Gross Profit	15,000	8,000	9,000
Operating Expenses	4,000	2,000	7,000
Income from Operations	11,000	6,000	2,000
Interest Expense	1,000	3,100	800
Income Before Income Tax Expense	10,000	2,900	1,200
Income Tax Expense	3,050	800	500
Net Income	$ 6,950	2,100	700

Required:

1. Was NGS more profitable in 2016 or 2017? Use the gross profit percentage, return on equity, and asset turnover ratio to help in making a decision. Round each ratio to two decimal places.
2. Was NGS more liquid in 2016 or 2017? Use the current ratio to help in making a decision. Round the ratio to two decimal places.
3. Was NGS more solvent in 2016 or 2017? Use the debt–to–assets ratio and times interest earned ratio to help in making a decision. Round each ratio to two decimal places.

Endnotes

1. Like many retail companies, The Home Depot's fiscal year–end is at the end of January.
2. Michael D. Akers, Meredith A. Maher, and Don E. Giacomino, "Going–Concern Opinions: Broadening the Expectations Gap," *CPA Journal*, October 2003. Retrieved June 12, 2009, from www.nysscpa.org/cpajournal/2003/1003/features/f103803.htm.

APPENDIX A

Summarized Financial Statements of The Home Depot

Note: The materials in this appendix have been summarized from multiple full annual reports of The Home Depot, Inc. for fiscal years 2012 through 2016. The complete annual reports can be found online.

The Home Depot Summarized Consolidated Balance Sheets

The materials in this appendix have been summarized from multiple full annual reports of The Home Depot, Inc. for fiscal years 2012 through 2016. This information has been provided to allow you to complete financial statement analysis with real life data. Questions involving this data are found in the Skills Development Cases at the end of every chapter.

EXHIBIT A.1 The Home Depot's Summarized Balance Sheets

THE HOME DEPOT
Balance Sheets
(in millions)

Year Ended:	January 29, 2017 (Fiscal 2016)	January 31, 2016 (Fiscal 2015)	February 1, 2015 (Fiscal 2014)	February 2, 2014 (Fiscal 2013)	February 3, 2013 (Fiscal 2012)
Assets					
Current Assets					
Cash and Cash Equivalents	$ 2,538	$ 2,216	$ 1,723	$ 1,929	$ 2,494
Accounts Receivable, Net	2,029	1,890	1,484	1,398	1,395
Inventories	12,549	11,809	11,079	11,057	10,710
Other Current Assets	608	1,078	1,016	895	773
Total Current Assets	17,724	16,993	15,302	15,279	15,372
Property and Equipment, Net	21,914	22,191	22,720	23,348	24,069
Notes Receivable			—	—	140
Goodwill	2,093	2,102	1,353	1,289	1,170
Other Assets	1,235	1,263	571	602	333
Total Assets	$ 42,966	$ 42,549	$ 39,946	$ 40,518	$ 41,084
Liabilities and Shareholders' Equity					
Current Liabilities	$ 14,133	$ 12,526	$ 11,269	$ 10,749	$ 11,462
Long–Term Liabilities	24,500	23,707	19,355	17,247	11,845
Total Liabilities	38,633	36,233	30,624	27,996	23,307
Shareholders' Equity	4,333	6,316	9,322	12,522	17,777
Total Liabilities and Shareholders' Equity	$ 42,966	$ 42,549	$ 39,946	$ 40,518	$ 41,084

The Home Depot Summarized Consolidated Statements of Earnings

The materials in this appendix have been summarized from multiple full annual reports of The Home Depot, Inc. for fiscal years 2012 through 2016. This information has been provided to allow you to complete financial statement analysis with real life data. Questions involving this data are found in the Skills Development Cases at the end of every chapter.

EXHIBIT A.2 The Home Depot's Summarized Statements of Earnings

THE HOME DEPOT
Statements of Earnings
(in millions)

Year Ended:	January 29, 2017 (Fiscal 2016)	January 31, 2016 (Fiscal 2015)	February 1, 2015 (Fiscal 2014)	February 2, 2014 (Fiscal 2013)	February 3, 2013 (Fiscal 2012)
Net Sales Revenue	$94,595	$ 88,519	$83,176	$ 78,812	$ 74,754
Cost of Sales	62,282	58,254	54,787	51,897	48,912
Gross Profit	32,313	30,265	28,389	26,915	25,842
Operating and Other Expenses	18,886	18,491	17,920	17,749	18,076
Interest and Other Expense	936	753	493	699	545
Income Tax Expense	4,534	4,012	3,631	3,082	2,686
Net Income	$ 7,957	$ 7,009	$ 6,345	$ 5,385	$ 4,535

Excerpts from the Fiscal 2016 Annual Report of Lowe's Companies, Inc.

Notes: The materials that follow in the appendix have been selected from the full annual report of Lowe's Companies, Inc. for fiscal year 2016, which ended February 3, 2017. The complete annual report is available from the Lowe's website at www.lowes.ca.

MANAGEMENT'S REPORT ON INTERNAL CONTROL OVER FINANCIAL REPORTING

Management of Lowe's Companies, Inc. and its subsidiaries is responsible for establishing and maintaining adequate internal control over financial reporting (Internal Control) as defined in Rule 13a–15(f) under the Securities Exchange Act of 1934, as amended. Our Internal Control was designed to provide reasonable assurance to our management and the Board of Directors regarding the reliability of financial reporting and the preparation and fair presentation of published financial statements.

All internal control systems, no matter how well designed, have inherent limitations, including the possibility of human error and the circumvention or overriding of controls. Therefore, even those systems determined to be effective can provide only reasonable assurance with respect to the reliability of financial reporting and financial statement preparation and presentation. Further, because of changes in conditions, the effectiveness may vary over time.

Our management, with the participation of the Chief Executive Officer and Chief Financial Officer, evaluated the effectiveness of our Internal Control as of February 3, 2017. In evaluating our Internal Control, we used the criteria set forth by the Committee of Sponsoring Organizations of the Treadway Commission (COSO) in Internal Control—Integrated Framework (2013). Based on our management's assessment, we have concluded that, as of February 3, 2017, our Internal Control is effective.

Under guidelines established by the SEC, companies are permitted to exclude acquisitions from their first assessment of internal control over financial reporting following the date of acquisition. Management's assessment of the effectiveness of the Company's internal control over financial reporting excluded RONA Inc. (RONA), a wholly owned subsidiary of Lowe's Companies, Inc., that consisted of the net assets purchased from RONA in May 2016. RONA represented 8.9% and 3.4% of the Company's consolidated total assets and consolidated net sales, respectively, as of and for the year ended February 3, 2017. This acquisition is more fully discussed in Note 2 to our Consolidated Financial Statements for fiscal year 2016.

Deloitte & Touche LLP, the independent registered public accounting firm that audited the financial statements contained in this Annual Report, was engaged to audit our Internal Control. Their report appears on page 34.

Report of Independent Registered Public Accounting Firm

To the Board of Directors and Shareholders of Lowe's Companies, Inc.
Mooresville, North Carolina

We have audited the accompanying consolidated balance sheets of Lowe's Companies, Inc. and subsidiaries (the "Company") as of February 3, 2017, and January 29, 2016, and the related consolidated statements of earnings, comprehensive income, shareholders' equity, and cash flows for each of the three fiscal years in the period ended February 3, 2017. Our audits also included the financial statement schedule listed in the Index at Item 15. These financial statements and financial statement schedule are the responsibility of the Company's management. Our responsibility is to express an opinion on the financial statements and financial statement schedule based on our audits.

We conducted our audits in accordance with the standards of the Public Company Accounting Oversight Board (United States). Those standards require that we plan and perform the audit to obtain reasonable assurance about whether the financial statements are free of material misstatement. An audit includes examining, on a test basis, evidence supporting the amounts and disclosures in the financial statements. An audit also includes assessing the accounting principles used and significant estimates made by management, as well as evaluating the overall financial statement presentation. We believe that our audits provide a reasonable basis for our opinion.

In our opinion, such consolidated financial statements present fairly, in all material respects, the financial position of the Company at February 3, 2017, and January 29, 2016, and the results of its operations and its cash flows for each of the three fiscal years in the period ended February 3, 2017, in conformity with accounting principles generally accepted in the United States of America. Also, in our opinion, such financial statement schedule, when considered in relation to the basic consolidated financial statements taken as a whole, presents fairly, in all material respects, the information set forth therein.

We have also audited, in accordance with the standards of the Public Company Accounting Oversight Board (United States), the Company's internal control over financial reporting as of February 3, 2017, based on the criteria established in Internal Control—Integrated Framework (2013) issued by the Committee of Sponsoring Organizations of the Treadway Commission and our report dated April 3, 2017, expressed an unqualified opinion on the Company's internal control over financial reporting.

/s/ DELOITTE & TOUCHE LLP

Charlotte, North Carolina

April 3, 2017

LOWE'S COMPANIES, INC.
CONSOLIDATED STATEMENTS OF EARNINGS
(in millions, except per share and percentage data)

Fiscal years ended on	February 3, 2017	% Sales	January 29, 2016	% Sales	January 30, 2015	% Sales
Net sales	$ 65,017	100.00%	$ 59,074	100.00%	$ 56,223	100.00%
Cost of sales	42,553	65.45	38,504	65.18	36,665	65.21
Gross margin	22,464	34.55	20,570	34.82	19,558	34.79
Expenses:						
Selling, general and administrative	15,129	23.27	14,105	23.88	13,272	23.60
Depreciation and amortization	1,489	2.29	1,494	2.53	1,494	2.66
Operating income	5,846	8.99	4,971	8.41	4,792	8.53
Interest, net	645	0.99	552	0.93	516	0.92
Pre—tax earnings	5,201	8.00	4,419	7.48	4,276	7.61
Income tax provision	2,108	3.24	1,873	3.17	1,578	2.81
Net earnings	$ 3,093	4.76%	$ 2,546	4.31%	$ 2,698	4.80%
Basic earnings per common share	$ 3.48		$ 2.73		$ 2.71	
Diluted earnings per common share	$ 3.47		$ 2.73		$ 2.71	
Cash dividends per share	$ 1.33		$ 1.07		$ 0.87	

LOWE'S COMPANIES, INC.
CONSOLIDATED BALANCE SHEETS
(in millions, except par value and percentage data)

	February 3, 2017	% Total	January 29, 2016	% Total
Assets				
Current assets:				
Cash and cash equivalents	$ 558	1.6 %	$ 405	1.3%
Short−term investments	100	0.3	307	1.0
Merchandise inventory, net	10,458	30.4	9,458	30.3
Other current assets	884	2.6	391	1.3
Total current assets	12,000	34.9	10,561	33.9
Property, less accumulated depreciation	19,949	58.0	19,577	62.6
Long−term investments	366	1.1	222	0.7
Deferred income taxes, net	222	0.6	241	0.8
Goodwill	1,082	3.1	154	0.5
Other assets	789	2.3	511	1.5
Total assets	$ 34,408	100.0 %	$ 31,266	100.0%
Liabilities and shareholders' equity				
Current liabilities:				
Short−term borrowings	$ 510	1.5 %	$ 43	0.1%
Current maturities of long−term debt	795	2.3	1,061	3.4
Accounts payable	6,651	19.3	5,633	18.0
Accrued compensation and employee benefits	790	2.3	820	2.6
Deferred revenue	1,253	3.6	1,078	3.4
Other current liabilities	1,975	5.7	1,857	6.1
Total current liabilities	11,974	34.7	10,492	33.6
Long−term debt, excluding current maturities	14,394	41.8	11,545	36.9
Deferred revenue − extended protection plans	763	2.2	729	2.3
Other liabilities	843	2.6	846	2.7
Total liabilities	27,974	81.3	23,612	75.5
Commitments and contingencies				
Shareholders' equity:				
Preferred stock − $5 par value, none issued	—	—	—	—
Common stock − $.50 par value				
Shares issued and outstanding:				
February 3, 2017 866				
January 29, 2016 910	433	1.3	455	1.5
Capital in excess of par value	—	—	—	—
Retained earnings	6,241	18.1	7,593	24.3
Accumulated other comprehensive loss	(240)	(0.7)	(394)	(1.3)
Total shareholders' equity	6,434	18.7	7,654	24.5
Total liabilities and shareholders' equity	$ 34,408	100.0%	$ 31,266	100.0%

See accompanying notes to consolidated financial statements.

	Common Stock		Capital in Excess of Par Value	Retained Earnings	Accumulated Other Comprehensive Income/(Loss)	Total Lowe's Companies, Inc. Shareholders' Equity	Non controlling Interest	Total Equity
	Shares	Amount						
Balance January 31, 2014	1,030	$ 515	$ —	$ 11,355	$ (17)	$ 11,853	$ —	$11,853
Net earnings				2,698		2,698		2,698
Other comprehensive loss					(86)	(86)		(86)
Tax effect of non–qualified stock options exercised and restricted stock vested			41			41		41
Cash dividends declared, $0.87 per share				(858)		(858)		(858)
Share–based payment expense			111			111		111
Repurchase of common stock	(75)	(37)	(286)	(3,604)		(3,927)		(3,927)
Issuance of common stock under share–based payment plans	5	2	134			136		136
Balance January 30, 2015	960	$ 480	$ —	$ 9,591	$ (103)	$ 9,968	$ —	$ 9,968
Net earnings				2,546		2,546		2,546
Other comprehensive loss					(291)	(291)		(291)
Tax effect of non–qualified stock options exercised and restricted stock vested			61			61		61
Cash dividends declared, $1.07 per share				(991)		(991)		(991)
Share–based payment expense			112			112		112
Repurchase of common stock	(54)	(27)	(298)	(3,553)		(3,878)		(3,878)
Issuance of common stock under share–based payment plans	4	2	125			127		127
Balance January 29, 2016	910	$ 455	$ —	$ 7,593	$ (394)	$ 7,654	$ —	7,654
Net earnings				3,091		3,091	2	3,093
Other comprehensive income					154	154		154
Tax effect of non–qualified stock options exercised and restricted stock vested			57			57		57
Cash dividends declared, $1.33 per share				(1,169)		(1,169)		(1,169)
Share–based payment expense			104			104		104
Repurchase of common stock	(48)	(24)	(279)	(3,274)		(3,577)		(3,577)
Issuance of common stock under share–based payment plans	4	2	136			138		138
Non–controlling interest resulting from acquisition						—	109	109
Dividends paid to non–controlling interest holders						—	(2)	(2)
Purchase of non–controlling interest		(18)				(18)	(109)	(127)
Balance February 3, 2017	866	$ 433	$ —	$ 6,241	$ (240)	$ 6,434	$ —	$ 6,434

See accompanying notes to consolidated financial statements.

LOWE'S COMPANIES, INC.
CONSOLIDATED STATEMENTS OF CASH FLOWS
(in millions)

Fiscal years ended on	February 3, 2017	January 29, 2016	January 30, 2015
Cash flows from operating activities:			
Net earnings	$ 3,093	$ 2,546	$ 2,698
Adjustments to reconcile net earnings to netcash provided by operating activities:			
Depreciation and amortization	1,590	1,587	1,586
Deferred income taxes	28	(68)	(124)
Loss on property and other assets, net	143	30	25
Loss on cost method and equity method investments	302	594	57
Share—based payment expense	90	117	119
Changes in operating assets and liabilities:			
Merchandise inventory, net	(178)	(582)	170
Other operating assets	(183)	(34)	83
Accounts payable	653	524	127
Other operating liabilities	79	70	188
Net cash provided by operating activities	**5,617**	**4,784**	**4,929**
Cash flows from investing activities:			
Purchases of investments	(1,192)	(934)	(820)
Proceeds from sale/maturity of investments	1,254	884	805
Capital expenditures	(1,167)	(1,197)	(880)
Contributions to equity method investments, net	—	(125)	(241)
Proceeds from sale of property and other long—term assets	37	57	52
Purchases of derivative instruments	(103)	—	—
Proceeds from settlement of derivative instruments	179	—	—
Acquisition of business, net	(2,356)	—	—
Other, net	(13)	(28)	(4)
Net cash used in investing activities	**(3,361)**	**(1,343)**	**(1,088)**
Cash flows from financing activities:			
Net change in short—term borrowings	466	43	(386)
Net proceeds from issuance of long—term debt	3,267	1,718	1,239
Repayment of long—term debt	(1,173)	(552)	(48)
Proceeds from issuance of common stock under share—based payment plans	139	125	137
Cash dividend payments	(1,121)	(957)	(822)
Repurchase of common stock	(3,595)	(3,925)	(3,905)
Other, net	(75)	55	24
Net cash used in financing activities	**(2,092)**	**(3,493)**	**(3,761)**
Effect of exchange rate changes on cash	**(11)**	**(9)**	**(5)**
Net increase/(decrease) in cash and cash equivalents	153	(61)	75
Cash and cash equivalents, beginning of year	405	466	391
Cash and cash equivalents, end of year	**$ 558**	**$ 405**	**$ 466**

See accompanying notes to consolidated financial statements.

YEARS ENDED FEBRUARY 3, 2017, JANUARY 29, 2016, AND JANUARY 30, 2015

NOTE 1. SUMMARY OF SIGNIFICANT ACCOUNTING POLICIES

Lowe's Companies, Inc. and subsidiaries (the Company) is the world's second–largest home improvement retailer and operated 2,129 stores in the United States, Canada, and Mexico at February 3, 2017. Below are those accounting policies considered by the Company to be significant.

Fiscal Year

Fiscal Year—The Company's fiscal year ends on the Friday nearest the end of January. Fiscal 2016 contained 53 weeks, and fiscal years 2015 and 2014 each contained 52 weeks. All references herein for the years 2016, 2015, and 2014 represent the fiscal years ended February 3, 2017, January 29, 2016, and January 30, 2015, respectively.

Principles of Consolidation

The consolidated financial statements include the accounts of the Company and its wholly owned or controlled operating subsidiaries. All intercompany accounts and transactions have been eliminated.

Foreign Currency

The functional currencies of the Company's international subsidiaries are generally the local currencies of the countries in which the subsidiaries are located. Foreign currency denominated assets and liabilities are translated into U.S. dollars using the exchange rates in effect at the consolidated balance sheet date. Results of operations and cash flows are translated using the average exchange rates throughout the period. The effect of exchange rate fluctuations on translation of assets and liabilities is included as a component of shareholders' equity in accumulated other comprehensive loss. Gains and losses from foreign currency transactions are included in selling, general and administrative (SG&A) expense.

Use of Estimates

The preparation of the Company's financial statements in accordance with accounting principles generally accepted in the United States of America requires management to make estimates that affect the reported amounts of assets, liabilities, sales and expenses, and related disclosures of contingent assets and liabilities. The Company bases these estimates on historical results and various other assumptions believed to be reasonable, all of which form the basis for making estimates concerning the carrying values of assets and liabilities that are not readily available from other sources. Actual results may differ from these estimates.

Cash and Cash Equivalents

Cash and cash equivalents include cash on hand, demand deposits, and short–term investments with original maturities of three months or less when purchased. Cash and cash equivalents are carried at amortized cost on the consolidated balance sheets. The majority of payments due from financial institutions for the settlement of credit card and debit card transactions process within two business days and are, therefore, classified as cash and cash equivalents.

Investments

As of February 3, 2017, investments consisted primarily of money market funds, municipal obligations, certificates of deposit, and municipal floating rate obligations, all of which are classified as available–for–sale. Available–for–sale securities are recorded at fair value, and unrealized gains and losses are recorded, net of tax, as a component of accumulated other comprehensive income. Gross unrealized gains and losses were insignificant at February 3, 2017, and January 29, 2016.

The proceeds from sales of available—for—sale securities were $505 million, $394 million, and $283 million for 2016, 2015, and 2014, respectively. Gross realized gains and losses on the sale of available—for—sale securities were not significant for any of the periods presented.

Investments with a stated maturity date of one year or less from the balance sheet date or that are expected to be used in current operations are classified as short—term investments. All other investments are classified as long—term. Invest—ments classified as long—term at February 3, 2017, will mature in one to 38 years, based on stated maturity dates.

The Company classifies as investments restricted balances primarily pledged as collateral for the Company's extended protection plan program. Restricted balances included in short—term investments were $81 million at February 3, 2017, and $234 million at January 29, 2016. Restricted balances included in long—term investments were $354 million at February 3, 2017, and $202 million at January 29, 2016.

Merchandise Inventory

The majority of the Company's inventory is stated at the lower of cost or market using the first—in, first—out method of inventory accounting. Inventory for certain subsidiaries representing approximately 8% of the consolidated inventory balance as of February 3, 2017, is stated at lower of cost or market using other inventory meth—ods, including the weighted average cost method and the retail inventory method. The cost of inventory includes certain costs associated with the preparation of inventory for resale, including distribution center costs, and is net of vendor funds.

The Company records an inventory reserve for the anticipated loss associated with selling inventories below cost. This reserve is based on management's current knowledge with respect to inventory levels, sales trends, and historical experience. Management does not believe the Company's merchandise inventories are subject to significant risk of obsolescence in the near term, and management has the ability to adjust purchasing practices based on anticipated sales trends and general economic conditions. However, changes in consumer purchasing patterns could result in the need for additional reserves. The Company also records an inventory reserve for the estimated shrinkage between physical inventories. This reserve is based primarily on actual shrink results from previous physical inventories. Changes in the estimated shrink reserve are made based on the timing and results of physical inventories.

The Company receives funds from vendors in the normal course of business, principally as a result of purchase volumes, sales, early payments, or promotions of vendors' products. Generally, these vendor funds do not represent the reimbursement of specific, incremental, and identifiable costs incurred by the Company to sell the vendor's product. Therefore, the Company treats these funds as a reduction in the cost of inventory as the amounts are accrued, and are recognized as a reduction of cost of sales when the inventory is sold. Funds that are determined to be reim—bursements of specific, incremental, and identifiable costs incurred to sell vendors' products are recorded as an offset to the related expense. The Company develops accrual rates for vendor funds based on the provisions of the agreements in place. Due to the complexity and diversity of the individual vendor agreements, the Company performs analyses and reviews historical trends throughout the year and confirms actual amounts with select vendors to ensure the amounts earned are appropriately recorded. Amounts accrued throughout the year could be impacted if actual purchase volumes differ from projected annual purchase volumes, especially in the case of pro—grams that provide for increased funding when graduated purchase volumes are met.

Credit Programs

The Company has an agreement with Synchrony Bank (Synchrony), formerly GE Capital Retail, under which Synchrony purchases at face value commercial business accounts receivable originated by the Company and services these accounts. This agreement expires in December 2023, unless terminated sooner by the parties. The Company primarily accounts for these transfers as sales of the accounts receivable. When the Company transfers its commercial business accounts receivable, it retains certain interests in those receivables, including the funding of a loss reserve and its obligation related to Synchrony's ongoing servicing of the receivables sold. Any gain or loss on the sale is determined based on the previous carrying amounts of the transferred assets allocated at fair value between the receivables sold and the interests retained. Fair value is based on the present value of expected future cash flows, taking into account the key assumptions of anticipated credit losses, payment rates, late fee rates, Synchrony's servicing costs, and the discount rate commensurate with the uncertainty involved. Due to the short-term nature of the receivables sold, changes to the key assumptions would not materially impact the recorded gain or loss on the sales of receivables or the fair value of the retained interests in the receivables.

Total commercial business accounts receivable sold to Synchrony were $2.8 billion in 2016, $2.6 billion in 2015, and $2.4 billion in 2014. The Company recognized losses of $32 million in 2016, $36 million in 2015, and $38 million in 2014 on these receivable sales as SG&A expense, which primarily relates to the fair value of obligations related to servicing costs that are remitted to Synchrony monthly. At February 3, 2017, and January 29, 2016, the fair value of the retained interests was determined based on the present value of expected future cash flows and was insignificant.

Sales generated through the Company's proprietary credit cards are not reflected in receivables. Under an agreement with Synchrony, credit is extended directly to customers by Synchrony. All credit program-related services are performed and controlled directly by Synchrony. The Company has the option, but no obligation, to purchase the receivables at the end of the agreement in December 2023. Tender costs, including amounts associated with accepting the Company's proprietary credit cards, are included in SG&A expense in the consolidated statements of earnings.

The total portfolio of receivables held by Synchrony, including both receivables originated by Synchrony from the Company's proprietary credit cards and commercial business accounts receivable originated by the Company and sold to Synchrony, approximated $9.6 billion at February 3, 2017, and $8.8 billion at January 29, 2016.

Property and Depreciation

Property is recorded at cost. Costs associated with major additions are capitalized and depreciated. Capital assets are expected to yield future benefits and have original useful lives which exceed one year. The total cost of a capital asset generally includes all applicable sales taxes, delivery costs, installation costs, and other appropriate costs incurred by the Company, including interest in the case of self-constructed assets. Upon disposal, the cost of properties and related accumulated depreciation is removed from the accounts, with gains and losses reflected in SG&A expense in the consolidated statements of earnings.

Property consists of land, buildings and building improvements, equipment, and construction in progress. Buildings and building improvements includes owned buildings, as well as buildings under capital lease and leasehold improvements.

Equipment primarily includes store racking and displays, computer hardware and software, forklifts, vehicles, and other store equipment.

Depreciation is provided over the estimated useful lives of the depreciable assets. Assets are depreciated using the straight-line method. Leasehold improvements and assets under capital lease are depreciated over the shorter of their estimated useful lives or the term of the related lease, which may include one or more option renewal periods where failure to exercise such options would result in an economic penalty in such amount that renewal appears, at the inception of the lease, to be reasonably assured. During the term of a lease, if leasehold improvements are placed in service significantly after the inception of the lease, the Company depreciates these leasehold improvements over the shorter of the useful life of the leasehold assets or a term that includes lease renewal periods deemed to be reasonably assured at the time the leasehold improvements are placed into service. The amortization of these assets is included in depreciation expense in the consolidated financial statements.

Long-Lived Asset Impairment/Exit Activities

The carrying amounts of long-lived assets are reviewed whenever certain events or changes in circumstances indicate that the carrying amounts may not be recoverable. A potential impairment has occurred for long-lived assets held-for-use if projected future undiscounted cash flows expected to result from the use and eventual disposition of the assets are less than the carrying amounts of the assets. An impairment loss is recorded for longlived assets held—for—use when the carrying amount of the asset is not recoverable and exceeds its fair value.

Excess properties that are expected to be sold within the next 12 months and meet the other relevant held—for—sale criteria are classified as long—lived assets held—for—sale. Excess properties consist primarily of retail outparcels and property associated with relocated or closed locations. An impairment loss is recorded for long—lived assets held—for—sale when the carrying amount of the asset exceeds its fair value less cost to sell. A long—lived asset is not depreciated while it is classified as held—for—sale.

For long—lived assets to be abandoned, the Company considers the asset to be disposed of when it ceases to be used. Until it ceases to be used, the Company continues to classify the asset as held—for—use and tests for potential impairment accordingly. If the Company commits to a plan to abandon a long—lived asset before the end of its previously estimated useful life, its depreciable life is re—evaluated.

The Company recorded long—lived asset impairment losses of $43 million during 2016, including $34 million for operating locations and $9 million for excess properties classified as held—for—use. The Company recorded impairment losses of $10 million during 2015, including $8 million for operating locations and $2 million for excess properties classified as held—for—use. The Company recorded long—lived asset impairment of $28 million during 2014, including $26 million for operating locations and $2 million for excess properties classified as held—for—use. Impairment losses are included in SG&A expense in the consolidated statements of earnings. Fair value measurements associated with long—lived asset impairments are further described in Note 4 to the consolidated financial statements.

The net carrying amount of excess properties that do not meet the held—for—sale criteria is included in other assets (noncurrent) on the consolidated balance sheets and totaled $174 million and $131 million at February 3, 2017, and January 29, 2016, respectively.

When locations under operating leases are closed, a liability is recognized for the fair value of future contractual obligations, including future minimum lease payments, property taxes, utilities, common area maintenance, and other ongoing expenses, net of estimated sublease income and other recoverable items. When the Company commits to an exit plan and communicates that plan to affected employees, a liability is recognized in connection with one—time employee termination benefits. Subsequent changes to the liabilities, including a change resulting from a revision to either the timing or the amount of estimated cash flows, are recognized in the period of change. Expenses associated with exit activities are included in SG&A expense in the consolidated statement of earnings.

Goodwill

Goodwill is the excess of the purchase price over the fair value of identifiable net assets acquired, less liabilities assumed, in a business combination. The Company reviews goodwill for impairment at the reporting unit level, which is one level below the operating segment level. Goodwill is not amortized but is evaluated for impairment at least annually on the first day of the fourth quarter or whenever events or changes in circumstances indicate that it is more likely than not that the carrying amount may not be recoverable.

The first step of the goodwill impairment test used to identify potential impairment compares the fair value of a reporting unit with its carrying amount, including goodwill. Fair value represents the price a market participant would be willing to pay in a potential sale of the reporting unit and is based on discounted future cash flows. If the fair value exceeds carrying value, then no goodwill impairment has occurred. If the carrying value of the reporting unit exceeds its fair value, a second step is required to measure possible goodwill impairment loss. The second step includes hypothetically valuing the tangible and intangible assets and liabilities of the reporting unit as if the reporting unit had been acquired in a business combination. Then, the implied fair value of the reporting unit's goodwill is compared to the carrying value of that goodwill. If the carrying value of the reporting unit's goodwill exceeds the implied fair value of the goodwill, an impairment loss is recognized in an amount equal to the excess, not to exceed the carrying value.

A reporting unit is an operating segment or a business unit one level below that operating segment, for which discrete financial information is prepared and regularly reviewed by segment management. During fiscal year 2016, goodwill was allocated to the following reporting units: U.S. Home Improvement, Orchard Supply Hardware (Orchard), Canada – Retail, and Canada – Distribution.

During the third quarter of fiscal year 2016, due to a strategic reassessment of the Orchard operations, the Company determined potential indicators of impairment within the reporting unit existed, and quantitatively evaluated the Orchard reporting unit for impairment. The Company classified this fair value measurement as Level 3. See Note 4 for additional information on the Company's fair value measurements. The Company performed a discounted cash flow analysis for the Orchard reporting unit. The discounted cash flow model included management assumptions for expected sales growth, expansion plans, capital expenditures, and overall operational forecasts. The analysis led to the conclusion that the goodwill allocated to the Orchard reporting unit had no implied value. Accordingly, the full carrying value of $46 million relating to Orchard goodwill was impaired during the third quarter.

The changes in the carrying amount of goodwill for 2016, 2015, and 2014 were as follows:

(in millions)

	2016	2015	2014
Goodwill, balance at beginning of year	$ 154	$ 154	$ 155
Acquisitions	1,015		
Impairment	(46)	–	(1)
Foreign currency translation adjustments	(41)	–	–
Goodwill, balance at end of year	$ 1,082	$ 154	$ 154

In May 2016, the Company completed its acquisition of RONA, Inc. (RONA). As a result of the acquisition, goodwill increased $976 million which was allocated to the Canada – Retail and Canada – Distribution reporting units. See Note 2 for additional information on the RONA acquisition.

Gross carrying amounts and cumulative goodwill impairment losses are as follows:

(in millions)

	February 3, 2017		January 29, 2016	
	Gross Carrying Amount	Cumulative Impairment	Gross Carrying Amount	Cumulative Impairment
Goodwill	$ 1,129	$ (47)	$ 155	$ (1)

Equity Method Investments

The Company's investments in certain unconsolidated entities are accounted for under the equity method. The balance of these investments is included in other assets (noncurrent) in the accompanying consolidated balance sheets. The balance is increased to reflect the Company's capital contributions and equity in earnings of the investees. The balance is decreased for its equity in losses of the investees, for distributions received that are not in excess of the carrying amount of the investments, and for any other than temporary impairment losses recognized. The Company's equity in earnings and losses of the investees and other than temporary impairment losses are included in SG&A expense.

Equity method investments are evaluated for impairment whenever events or changes in circumstances indicate that a decline in value has occurred that is other than temporary. Evidence considered in this evaluation includes, but would not necessarily be limited to, the financial condition and near–term prospects of the investee, recent operating trends and forecasted performance of the investee, market conditions in the geographic area or industry in which the investee operates and the Company's strategic plans for holding the investment in relation to the period of time expected for an anticipated recovery of its carrying value. Investments that are determined to have a decline in value deemed to be other than temporary are written down to estimated fair value. See Note 3 for additional information on the investment in the Australian joint venture.

Leases

For lease agreements that provide for escalating rent payments or free-rent occupancy periods, the Company recognizes rent expense on a straight-line basis over the non-cancellable lease term and option renewal periods where failure to exercise such options would result in an economic penalty in such amount that renewal appears, at the inception of the lease, to be reasonably assured. The lease term commences on the date that the Company takes possession of or controls the physical use of the property. Deferred rent is included in other liabilities (noncurrent) on the consolidated balance sheets.

When the Company renegotiates and amends a lease to extend the non-cancellable lease term prior to the date at which it would have been required to exercise or decline a term extension option, the amendment is treated as a new lease. The new lease begins on the date the lease amendment is entered into and ends on the last date of the non-cancellable lease term, as adjusted to include any option renewal periods where failure to exercise such options would result in an economic penalty in such amount that renewal appears, at the inception of the lease amendment, to be reasonably assured. The new lease is classified as operating or capital under the authoritative guidance through use of assumptions regarding residual value, economic life, incremental borrowing rate, and fair value of the leased asset(s) as of the date of the amendment.

Accounts Payable

The Company has an agreement with a third party to provide an accounts payable tracking system which facilitates participating suppliers' ability to finance payment obligations from the Company with designated third-party financial institutions. Participating suppliers may, at their sole discretion, make offers to finance one or more payment obligations of the Company prior to their scheduled due dates at a discounted price to participating financial institutions. The Company's goal in entering into this arrangement is to capture overall supply chain savings, in the form of pricing, payment terms, or vendor funding, created by facilitating suppliers' ability to finance payment obligations at more favorable discount rates, while providing them with greater working capital flexibility.

The Company's obligations to its suppliers, including amounts due and scheduled payment dates, are not impacted by suppliers' decisions to finance amounts under this arrangement. However, the Company's right to offset balances due from suppliers against payment obligations is restricted by this arrangement for those payment obligations that have been financed by suppliers. As of February 3, 2017, and January 29, 2016, $1.6 billion and $1.3 billion, respectively, of the Company's outstanding payment obligations had been placed on the accounts payable tracking system, and participating suppliers had financed $1.0 billion and $921 million, respectively, of those payment obligations to participating financial institutions.

Other Current Liabilities—Other current liabilities on the consolidated balance sheets consist of:

(in millions)	February 3, 2017	January 29, 2016
Self-insurance liabilities	$ 327	$ 343
Accrued dividends	304	255
Sales tax liabilities	210	140
Accrued interest	194	179
Accrued property taxes	108	111
Other	832	829
Total	$ 1,975	$ 1,857

Self-Insurance

The Company is self—insured for certain losses relating to workers' compensation, automobile, property, and general and product liability claims. The Company has insurance coverage to limit the exposure arising from these claims. The Company is also self—insured for certain losses relating to extended protection plan and medical and dental claims. Self—insurance claims filed and claims incurred but not reported are accrued based upon management's estimates of the discounted ultimate cost for self—insured claims incurred using actuarial assumptions followed in the insurance industry and historical experience. Although management believes it has the ability to reasonably estimate losses related to claims, it is possible that actual results could differ from recorded self—insurance liabilities. The total self—insurance liability, including the current and non—current portions, was $831 million and $883 million at February 3, 2017, and January 29, 2016, respectively.

The Company provides surety bonds issued by insurance companies to secure payment of workers' compensation liabilities as required in certain states where the Company is self—insured. Outstanding surety bonds relating to self—insurance were $243 million and $240 million at February 3, 2017, and January 29, 2016, respectively.

Income Taxes

The Company establishes deferred income tax assets and liabilities for temporary differences between the tax and financial accounting bases of assets and liabilities. The tax effects of such differences are reflected in the consolidated balance sheets at the enacted tax rates expected to be in effect when the differences reverse. A valuation allowance is recorded to reduce the carrying amount of deferred tax assets if it is more likely than not that all or a portion of the asset will not be realized. The tax balances and income tax expense recognized by the Company are based on management's interpretation of the tax statutes of multiple jurisdictions.

The Company establishes a liability for tax positions for which there is uncer—tainty as to whether or not the position will be ultimately sustained. The Company includes interest related to tax issues as part of net interest on the consolidated financial statements. The Company records any applicable penalties related to tax issues within the income tax provision.

Shareholders' Equity

The Company has a share repurchase program that is executed through purchases made from time to time either in the open market or through private market trans—actions. Shares purchased under the repurchase program are retired and returned to authorized and unissued status. Any excess of cost over par value is charged to additional paid—in capital to the extent that a balance is present. Once additional paid—in capital is fully depleted, remaining excess of cost over par value is charged to retained earnings.

Revenue Recognition

The Company recognizes revenues, net of sales tax, when sales transactions occur and customers take possession of the merchandise. A provision for antic—ipated merchandise returns is provided through a reduction of sales and cost of sales in the period that the related sales are recorded. Revenues from product installation services are recognized when the installation is completed. Deferred revenues associated with amounts received for which customers have not yet taken possession of merchandise or for which installation has not yet been com—pleted were $755 million and $619 million at February 3, 2017, and January 29, 2016, respectively.

Revenues from stored—value cards, which include gift cards and returned merchandise credits, are deferred and recognized when the cards are redeemed. The liability associated with outstanding stored—value cards was $498 million and $459 million at February 3, 2017, and January 29, 2016, respectively, and these amounts are included in deferred revenue on the consolidated balance sheets. The Company recognizes income from unredeemed stored—value cards at the point at which redemption becomes remote. The Company's stored—value cards have no expiration date or dormancy fees. Therefore, to determine when redemption is remote, the Company analyzes an aging of the unredeemed cards based on the date of last stored—value card use. The amount of revenue recognized from unredeemed stored—value cards for which redemption was deemed remote was not significant for 2016, 2015, and 2014.

Cost of Sales and Selling, General and Administrative Expenses

The following lists the primary costs classified in each major expense category:

Cost of Sales

- Total cost of products sold, including:
  - Purchase costs, net of vendor funds;
  - Freight expenses associated with moving merchandise inventories from vendors to retail stores;
  - Costs associated with operating the Company's distribution network, including payroll and benefit costs and occupancy costs;
- Costs of installation services provided;
- Costs associated with delivery of products directly from vendors to customers by third parties;
- Costs associated with inventory shrinkage and obsolescence;
- Costs of services performed under the extended protection plan.

Selling, General and Administrative

- Payroll and benefit costs for retail and corporate employees;
- Occupancy costs of retail and corporate facilities;
- Advertising;
- Costs associated with delivery of products from stores and distribution centers to customers;
- Third—party, in—store service costs;
- Tender costs, including bank charges, costs associated with credit card interchange fees and amounts associated with accepting the Company's proprietary credit cards;
- Costs associated with self—insured plans, and premium costs for stop—loss coverage and fully insured plans;
- Long—lived asset impairment losses and gains/losses on disposal of assets;
- Other administrative costs, such as supplies, and travel and entertainment.

Advertising

Costs associated with advertising are charged to expense as incurred. Advertising expenses were $893 million, $769 million, and $819 million in 2016, 2015, and 2014, respectively.

Shipping and Handling Costs

The Company includes shipping and handling costs relating to the delivery of products directly from vendors to customers by third parties in cost of sales. Shipping and handling costs, which include third—party delivery costs, salaries, and vehicle operations expenses relating to the delivery of products from stores and distribution centers to customers, are classified as SG&A expense. Shipping and handling costs included in SG&A expense were $700 million, $607 million and $548 million in 2016, 2015, and 2014, respectively.

Store Opening Costs

Costs of opening new or relocated retail stores, which include payroll and supply costs incurred prior to store opening and grand opening advertising costs, are charged to expense as incurred.

Comprehensive Income

The Company reports comprehensive income in its consolidated statements of comprehensive income and consolidated statements of shareholders' equity. Comprehensive income represents changes in shareholders' equity from non-owner sources and is comprised of net earnings adjusted primarily for foreign currency translation adjustments. Net foreign currency translation losses, net of tax, classified in accumulated other comprehensive loss were $240 million, $394 million, and $103 million at February 3, 2017, January 29, 2016, and January 30, 2015, respectively.

Segment Information

The Company's home improvement retail operations represent a single reportable segment. Key operating decisions are made at the Company level in order to maintain a consistent retail store presentation. The Company's home improvement retail stores sell similar products and services, use similar processes to sell those products and services, and sell their products and services to similar classes of customers. In addition, the Company's operations exhibit similar long-term economic characteristics. The amounts of long-lived assets and net sales outside of the U.S. were approximately 8.7% and 5.7%, respectively, at February 3, 2017, and were not significant at January 29, 2016, and January 30, 2015.

Reclassifications

Certain prior period amounts have been reclassified to conform to current classifications.

NOTE 5. PROPERTY AND ACCUMULATED DEPRECIATION

Property is summarized by major class in the following table:

	Estimated Depreciable Lives, In Years	February 3, 2017	January 29, 2016
(in millions)			
Cost			
Land	N/A	$ 7,329	$ 7,086
Buildings and building improvements	5–40	18,147	17,451
Equipment	2–15	10,978	10,863
Construction in progress	N/A	464	513
Total Cost		**36,918**	**35,913**
Accumulated depreciation		(16,969)	(16,336)
Property, less accumulated depreciation		**$ 19,949**	**$ 19,577**

NOTE 9. SHAREHOLDERS' EQUITY

Authorized shares of preferred stock were 5.0 million ($5 par value) at February 3, 2017, and January 29, 2016, none of which have been issued. The Board of Directors may issue the preferred stock (without action by shareholders) in one or more series, having such voting rights, dividend and liquidation preferences, and such conversion and other rights as may be designated by the Board of Directors at the time of issuance.

Authorized shares of common stock were 5.6 billion ($.50 par value) at February 3, 2017, and January 29, 2016.

The Company has a share repurchase program that is executed through purchases made from time to time either in the open market or through private off-market transactions. Shares purchased under the repurchase program are retired and returned to authorized and unissued status. On March 20, 2015, the Company's Board of Directors authorized a $5.0 billion share repurchase under the program with no expiration, which was announced on the same day. On January 27, 2017, the Company's Board of Directors authorized an additional $5.0 billion share repurchase under the program with no expiration, which was announced on the same day. As of February 3, 2017, the Company had $5.1 billion remaining under the program.

During the year ended February 3, 2017, the Company entered into Accelerated Share Repurchase (ASR) agreements with third-party financial institutions to repurchase a total of 19.1 million shares of the Company's common stock for $1.4 billion. At inception, the Company paid the financial institutions using cash on hand and took initial delivery of shares. Under the terms of the ASR agreements, upon settlement, the Company would either receive additional shares from the financial institution or be required to deliver additional shares or cash to the financial institution. The Company controlled its election to either deliver additional shares or cash to the financial institution and was subject to provisions which limited the number of shares the Company would be required to deliver.

The final number of shares received upon settlement of each ASR agreement was determined with reference to the volumeweighted average price of the Company's common stock over the term of the ASR agreement. The initial repurchase of shares under these agreements resulted in an immediate reduction of the outstanding shares used to calculate the weighted-average common shares outstanding for basic and diluted earnings per share.

These ASR agreements were accounted for as treasury stock transactions and forward stock purchase contracts. The par value of the shares received was recorded as a reduction to common stock with the remainder recorded as a reduction to capital in excess of par value and retained earnings. The forward stock purchase contracts were considered indexed to the Company's own stock and were classified as equity instruments. During the year ended February 3, 2017, the Company also repurchased shares of its common stock through the open market totaling 27.6 million shares for a cost of $2.1 billion.

The Company also withholds shares from employees to satisfy either the exercise price of stock options exercised or the statutory withholding tax liability resulting from the vesting of restricted stock awards and performance share units.

Shares repurchased for 2016 and 2015 were as follows:

(in millions)	2016		2015	
	Shares	Cost	Shares	Cost
Share repurchase program	46.7	$ 3,500	53.6	$ 3,811
Shares withheld from employees	1.0	77	0.9	67
Total share repurchases	47.7	$ 3,577	54.5	$ 3,878

Reductions of $3.3 billion and $3.6 billion were recorded to retained earnings, after capital in excess of par value was depleted, for 2016 and 2015, respectively.

APPENDIX C

Present and Future Value Concepts

Time value of money: The idea that money received today is worth more than the same amount received in the future because money received today can be invested to earn interest over time.

The concepts of present value (PV) and future value (FV) are based on the time value of money. The **time value of money** is the idea that, quite simply, money received today is worth more than money received one year from today (or at any other future date), because it can be used to earn interest. If you invest $1,000 today at 10 percent, you will have $1,100 in one year. So $1,000 in one year is worth less than $1,000 today because you lose the opportunity to earn interest on that $1,000.

In some business situations, you will know the dollar amount of a cash flow that will occur in the future and will need to determine its value now. This situation is known as a present value problem. The opposite situation occurs when you know the dollar amount of a cash flow that occurs today and need to determine its value at some point in the future. These situations are called **future value** problems. As mentioned previously, the value of money changes over time because money can earn interest. The following table illustrates the basic difference between present value and future value problems:

	Now	Future
Present value	?	$1,000
Future value	$1,000	?

Present and future value problems may involve two types of cash flow: a single payment or an annuity (which is the fancy word for a series of equal cash payments). Combining two types of time value of money problems with two types of cash flows yields four different situations:

1. Future value of a single payment

2. Present value of a single payment

3. Future value of an annuity

4. Present value of an annuity

Most inexpensive hand–held calculators and any spreadsheet program can perform the detailed mathematical computations required to solve future value and present value problems. In later courses and in all business situations, you will probably use a calculator or computer to solve these problems. At this stage, we encourage you to solve problems using Tables C.1 through C.4 near the end of this appendix. We believe that using the tables will give you a better understanding of how and why present and future value concepts apply to business problems. The tables give the value of a $1 cash flow (single payment or annuity) for different periods (n) and at different interest rates (i). If a problem involves payments other than $1, multiply the value from the table by the amount of the payment.[1] Just before the tables near the end of this appendix, we explain how to use Excel to compute present values.

FUTURE VALUE OF A SINGLE AMOUNT

In problems involving the future value of a single amount, you will be asked to calculate how much money you will have in the future as the result of investing a certain amount in the present. If you were to receive a gift of $10,000, for instance, you might decide to put it into a savings account and use the money as a down payment on a home after you graduate. The future value computation would tell you how much money will be available when you graduate.

To solve a future value problem, you need to know three things:

1. Amount to be invested

2. Interest rate (i) the amount will earn

3. Number of periods (n) in which the amount will earn interest

The future value concept is based on compound interest, which simply means that interest is calculated on top of interest. Thus, the amount of interest for each period is calculated using the principal plus any interest not paid out in prior periods. Graphically, the calculation of the future value of $1 for three periods at an interest rate of 10 percent can be represented as follows:

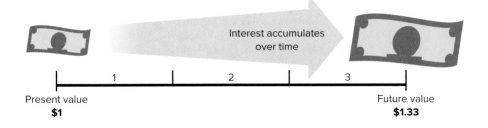

Present value
$1

Interest accumulates over time

Future value
$1.33

Assume that on January 1, 2017, you deposit $1,000 in a savings account at 10 percent annual interest, compounded annually. At the end of three years, the $1,000 will have increased to $1,331 as follows:

Year	Amount at Start of Year	+	Interest During the Year	=	Amount at End of Year
1	$1,000	+	$1,000 × 10% = $100	=	$1,100
2	1,100	+	1,100 × 10% = 110	=	1,210
3	1,210	+	1,210 × 10% = 121	=	1,331

We can avoid the detailed arithmetic by referring to Table C.1, Future Value of $1 (on page C–13). For $i = 10\%$, $n = 3$, we find the value 1.3310. We then compute the balance at the end of year 3 as follows:

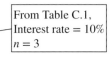

From Table C.1,
Interest rate = 10%
$n = 3$

$$\$1,000 \times 1.3310 = \$1,331$$

Note that the increase of $331 is due to the time value of money. It is interest revenue to the owner of the savings account and interest expense to the bank.

PRESENT VALUE OF A SINGLE AMOUNT

The present value of a single amount is the worth to you today of receiving that amount sometime in the future. For instance, you might be offered an opportunity to invest in a financial instrument that would pay you $1,000 in three years. Before you decided whether to invest, you would want to determine the present value of the instrument.

To compute the present value of an amount to be received in the future, we must discount (a procedure that is the opposite of compounding) at i interest rate for n periods. In discounting, the interest is subtracted rather than added, as it is in compounding. Graphically, the present value of $1 due at the end of the third period with an interest rate of 10 percent can be represented as follows:

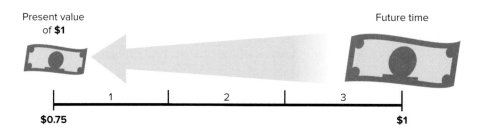

Present value of **$1**

Future time

| 1 | 2 | 3 |

$0.75

$1

Assume that today is January 1, 2017, and you have the opportunity to receive $1,000 cash on December 31, 2019. At an interest rate of 10 percent per year, how much is the $1,000 payment worth to you on January 1, 2017? You could discount the amount year by year,[2] but it is easier to use Table C.2, Present Value of $1 (on page C−13). For $i = 10\%$, $n = 3$, we find that the present value of $1 is 0.7513. The present value of $1,000 to be received at the end of three years can be computed as follows:

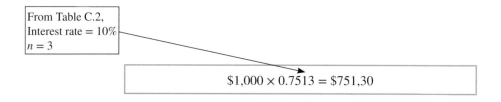

From Table C.2,
Interest rate = 10%
$n = 3$

$1,000 × 0.7513 = $751,30

It's important to learn not only how to compute a present value but also to understand what it means. The $751.30 is the amount you would pay now to have the right to receive $1,000 at the end of three years, assuming an interest rate of 10 percent. Conceptually, you should be indifferent between having $751.30 today and receiving $1,000 in three years. If you had $751.30 today but wanted $1,000 in three years, you would deposit the money in a savings account that pays 10 percent interest and it would grow to $1,000 in three years. Alternatively, if you had a contract that promised you $1,000 in three years, you could sell it to an investor for $751.30 in cash today because it would permit the investor to earn the difference in interest.

What if you could earn only 6 percent during the three−year period from Jan− uary 1, 2017, to December 31, 2019? What would be the present value on January 1, 2017, of receiving $1,000 on December 31, 2019? To answer this we would take the same approach, using Table C.2, except that the interest rate would change to $i = 6\%$. Referring to Table C.2, we see the present value factor for $i = 6\%$, $n = 3$, is 0.8396. Thus, the present value of $1,000 to be received at the end of three years, assuming a 6 percent interest rate, would be computed as $1,000 × 0.8396 = $839.60. Notice that when we assume a 6 percent interest rate the present value is greater than when we assumed a 10 percent interest rate. The reason for this difference is that, to reach $1,000 three years from now, you'd need to deposit more money in a savings account now if it earns 6 percent interest than if it earns 10 percent interest.

🌀 HOW'S IT GOING?

Self-Study Practice C.1

1. If the interest rate in a present value problem increases from 8 percent to 10 percent, will the present value increase or decrease?
2. What is the present value of $10,000 to be received 10 years from now if the interest rate is 5 percent, compounded annually?
3. If $10,000 is deposited now in a savings account that earns 5 percent interest compounded annually, how much will it be worth 10 years from now?

After you have finished, check your answers in the Solution to Self-Study Practice section later in this appendix.

The Power of Compounding

Compound interest is a remarkably powerful economic force. In fact, the ability to earn interest on interest is the key to building economic wealth. If you save $1,000 per year for the first ten years of your career, you will have more money when you retire than you would if you had saved $15,000 per year for the last ten years of your career. This surprising outcome occurs because the money you save early in your career will earn more interest than the money you save at the end of your career. If you start saving money now, the majority of your wealth will not be the money you saved but the interest your money was able to earn.

The table below shows how a single investment of $1,000 today grows over time at the investment community's historic average growth rate of 10 percent. Two important lessons are revealed in the table: (1) you can earn a lot of interest through the effects of compounding (in just ten years, you will earn $1,600 interest on a $1,000 investment), and (2) start early (notice that the balance more than doubles every ten years, so letting your investment sit an extra decade could make you twice as rich).

Period	Value
Now	$ 1,000
10 years	$ 2,600
20 years	$ 6,700
30 years	$ 17,400
40 years	$ 45,300
50 years	$ 17,400
60 years	$304,500
70 years	$789,700

Computing Future and Present Values of an Annuity

Instead of a single payment, many business problems involve multiple cash payments over a number of periods. An **annuity** is a series of consecutive payments character-ized by the following:

Annuity: A series of periodic cash receipts or payments that are equal in amount each interest period.

1. An equal dollar amount each interest period
2. Interest periods of equal length (year, half a year, quarter, or month)
3. An equal interest rate each interest period

Examples of annuities include monthly payments on a car or house, yearly contri-butions to a savings account, and monthly pension benefits.

FUTURE VALUE OF AN ANNUITY

If you are saving money for some purpose, such as a new car or a trip to Europe, you might decide to deposit a fixed amount of money in a savings account each month. The future value of an annuity computation will tell you how much money will be in your savings account at some point in the future.

The future value of an annuity includes compound interest on each payment from the date of payment to the end of the term of the annuity. Each new payment accumulates less interest than prior payments, only because the number of periods remaining in which to accumulate interest decreases. The future value of an annuity of $1 for three periods at 10 percent may be represented graphically as

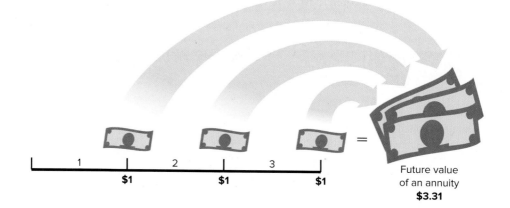

Future value
of an annuity
$3.31

Assume that each year for three years, you deposit $1,000 cash in a savings account at 10 percent interest per year. You make the first $1,000 deposit on December 31, 2017, the second one on December 31, 2018, and the third and last one on December 31, 2019. The first $1,000 deposit earns compound interest for two years (for total principal and interest of $1,210); the second deposit earns interest for one year (for total principal and interest of $1,100). The third deposit earns no interest because it was made on the day that the balance is computed. So the total amount in the savings account at the end of three years is $3,310 (= $1,210 + $1,100 + $1,000).

To calculate the future value of this annuity, we could compute the interest on each deposit, similar to what's described above. However, a faster way is to refer to Table C.3, Future Value of Annuity of $1 (on page C–14). For $i = 10\%$, $n = 3$, we find the value 3.3100. The future value of your three deposits of $1,000 each can be computed as follows:

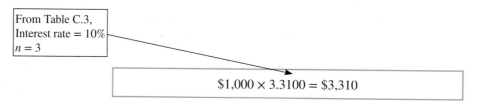

From Table C.3,
Interest rate = 10%
$n = 3$

$1,000 × 3.3100 = $3,310

PRESENT VALUE OF AN ANNUITY

The present value of an annuity is the value now of a series of equal amounts to be received (or paid out) for some specified number of periods in the future. It is computed by discounting each of the equal periodic amounts. A good example of this type of problem is a retirement program that offers employees a monthly income after retirement. The present value of an annuity of $1 for three periods at 10 percent can be represented graphically:

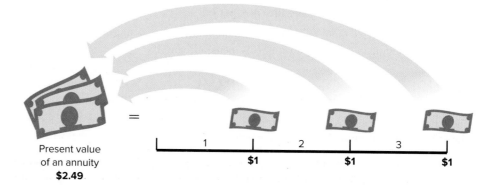

Present value
of an annuity
$2.49

Assume you are to receive $1,000 cash on each December 31, 2017, 2018, and 2019. How much would the sum of these three $1,000 future amounts be worth on January 1, 2017, assuming an interest rate of 10 percent per year? One way to determine this is to use Table C.2 to calculate the present value of each single amount as follows:

		FACTOR FROM TABLE C.2		
Year	Amount	$i = 10\%$		Present Value
1	$1,000	$\times$	0.9091 ($n = 1$)	$=$	$ 909.10
2	$1,000	$\times$	0.8264 ($n = 2$)	$=$	826.40
3	$1,000	$\times$	0.7513 ($n = 3$)	$=$	751.30
		Total present value	$=$	$2,486.80

Alternatively, we can compute the present value of this annuity more easily by using Table C.4, Present Value of Annuity of $1, as follows:

$1,000 \times 2.4869 = $2,487$ (rounded)

From Table C.4,
Interest rate = 10%
$n = 3$

INTEREST RATES AND INTEREST PERIODS

The preceding illustrations assumed annual periods for compounding and discount—ing. Although interest rates are almost always quoted on an annual basis, many compounding periods encountered in business are less than one year. When interest periods are less than a year, the values of n and i must be restated to be consistent with the length of the interest compounding period.

To illustrate, 12 percent interest compounded annually for five years requires the use of $n = 5$ and $i = 12\%$. If compounding is quarterly, however, there will be four interest periods per year (20 interest periods in five years), and the quarterly interest rate is one quarter of the annual rate (3 percent per quarter). Therefore, 12 percent interest compounded quarterly for five years requires use of $n = 20$ and $i = 3\%$.

Accounting Applications of Present Values

Many business transactions require the use of future and present value concepts. In finance classes, you will see how to apply future value concepts. In this section, we apply present value concepts to three common accounting cases.

Case A: Present Value of a Single Amount

On January 1, 2017, assume that General Mills bought some new delivery trucks. The company signed a note and agreed to pay $200,000 on December 31, 2018, an amount representing the cash equivalent price of the trucks plus interest for two years. The market interest rate for this note was 12 percent.

1. How should the accountant record the purchase?

Answer   This case requires the computation of the present value of a single amount. In conformity with the cost principle, the cost of the trucks is their current

cash equivalent price, which is the present value of the future payment. The problem can be shown graphically as follows:

January 1, 2017   December 31, 2017   December 31, 2018

? $200,000

The present value of the $200,000 is computed as follows:

From Table C.2,
Interest rate = 12%
n = 2

$$\$200,000 \times 0.7972 = \$159,440$$

This transaction has the following financial effects, and would be recorded with
the journal entry shown below.

Assets		=	Liabilities		+	Shareholders' Equity
Delivery Trucks	+159,440		Note Payable	+159,440		

dr **Delivery Trucks** (+A) 159,440
    cr **Note Payable** (+L) 159,440

COACH'S TIP

The interest is recorded in the
Note Payable account because
it would be paid as part of the
note at maturity. Alternatively,
the interest could be recorded
in an Interest Payable account
separate from the Note Payable.

2. How should the effects of interest be reported at the end of 2017 and 2018?

Answer   Interest expense would be calculated, reported, and recorded as follows:

December 31, 2017

Interest = Principal × Rate × Time

= $159,440 × 12% × 12/12

= $19,132 (rounded)

Assets	=	Liabilities		+	Shareholders' Equity	
		Note Payable	+19,132		Interest Expense (+E)	−19,132

dr **Interest Expense** (+E, −SE) 19,132
    cr **Note Payable** (+L) 19,132

December 31, 2018

> Interest = Principal × Rate × Time
> = ($159,440 + $19,132) × 12% × 12/12
> = $21,428 (rounded)

Assets	=	Liabilities		+	Shareholders' Equity	
		Note Payable	+21,428		Interest Expense (+E)	−21,428

> *dr* **Interest Expense** (+E, −SE) 21,428
>   *cr* **Note Payable** (+L)   21,428

3. What is the effect of the $200,000 debt payment made on December 31, 2018?

Answer At this date, the amount to be paid is the balance in Note Payable, after it has been updated for interest pertaining to 2018, as shown in the T−account. Notice that, just prior to its repayment, the balance for the note on December 31, 2018, is the same as the maturity amount on the due date.

The debt payment has the following financial effects, and would be recorded with the journal entry shown below.

Note Payable (L)	
159,440	Jan. 1, 2017
19,132	Interest 2017
21,428	Interest 2018
200,000	Dec. 31, 2018

Assets	=	Liabilities		+	Shareholders' Equity
Cash	−200,000	Note Payable	−200,000		

> *dr* **Note Payable** (−L) 200,000
>   *cr* **Cash** (−A)   200,000

Case B: Present Value of an Annuity

On January 1, 2017, assume that General Mills bought new milling equipment. The company elected to finance the purchase with a note payable to be paid off in three years in annual instalments of $163,686. Each instalment includes principal plus interest on the unpaid balance at 11 percent per year. The annual instalments are due on December 31, 2017, 2018, and 2019. This can be shown graphically as follows:

1. What is the amount of the note?

Answer The note is the present value of each instalment payment, $i = 11\%$ and $n = 3$. This is an annuity because the note repayment is made in three equal instalments. The amount of the note is computed as follows:

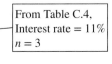

From Table C.4,
Interest rate = 11%
$n = 3$

> $163,686 × 2.4437 = $400,000

The acquisition on January 1, 2017, would be accounted for as follows:

Assets		=	Liabilities		+	Shareholders' Equity
Milling Equipment	+400,000		Note Payable	+400,000		

dr **Milling Equipment** (+A)	400,000	
cr **Note Payable** (+L)		400,000

2. How should the payments made at the end of each year be accounted for?

Answer

<u>December 31, 2017</u>

Each payment includes both interest and principal. The interest part of the first payment is calculated as

$$\text{Interest} = \text{Principal} \times \text{Rate} \times \text{Time}$$
$$= \$400,000 \times 11\% \times 12/12$$
$$= \$44,000$$

Now that we know the interest component, the principal portion of the first payment of $163,686 can be calculated ($163,686 − $44,000 = $119,686). Thus, the first payment on December 31, 2017, would be accounted for as

Assets		=	Liabilities		+	Shareholders' Equity	
Cash	−163,686		Note Payable	−119,686		Interest Expense (+E)	−44,000

dr **Interest Expense** (+E, −SE)	44,000	
dr **Note Payable** (−L) ($163,686 − $44,000)	119,686	
cr **Cash** (−A)		163,686

<u>December 31, 2018</u>

The interest portion of the second and third payments would be calculated in the same way, although notice that the principal balance in the Note Payable account changes after each payment.

$$\text{Interest} = \text{Principal} \times \text{Rate} \times \text{Time}$$
$$= [(\$400,000 - \$119,686) \times 11\% \times 12/12]$$
$$= \$30,835$$
$$\text{Principal} = \text{Payment} - \text{Interest}$$
$$= \$163,686 - \$30,835$$
$$= \$132,851$$

Assets	=	Liabilities	+	Shareholders' Equity	
Cash −163,686		Note Payable −132,851		Interest Expense (+E)	−30,835

dr **Interest Expense** (+E, −SE) 30,835
dr **Note Payable** (−L) 132,851
   cr **Cash** (−A) 163,686

December 31, 2019

Interest = Principal × Rate × Time

      = [($400,000 − $119,686 − $132,851) × 11% × 12/12]

      = $16,223 (adjusted to accommodate rounding)

Principal = Payment − Interest

      = $163,686 − $16,223

      = $147,463

Assets	=	Liabilities	+	Shareholders' Equity	
Cash −163,686		Note Payable −147,463		Interest Expense (+E)	−16,223

dr **Interest Expense** (+E, −SE) 16,223
dr **Note Payable** (−L) 147,463
   cr **Cash** (−A) 163,686

Case C: Present Value of a Single Amount and an Annuity

On January 1, 2017, assume that General Mills issued 100 four–year $1,000 bonds. The bonds pay interest annually at a rate of 6 percent of face value. What total amount would investors be willing to pay for the bonds if they require an annual return of (a) 4 percent, (b) 6 percent, or (c) 8 percent?

Answer This case requires the computation of the present value of a single amount (the $100,000 face value paid at maturity) plus the present value of an annuity (the annual interest payments of $6,000). The problem can be shown graphically as follows:

Note Payable (L)	
	400,000 Jan. 1, 2017
Dec. 31, 2017 119,686	
Dec. 31, 2018 132,851	
Dec. 31, 2019 147,463	
	0 Dec. 31, 2019

January 1, 2017	December 31, 2017	December 31, 2018	December 31, 2019	December 31, 2020	
Bond issued	Pay interest $6,000	Pay interest $6,000	Pay interest $6,000	Pay interest $6,000	← **INTEREST**
?				$100,000 Repaid	← **FACE VALUE**

COACH'S TIP

Each interest payment of $6,000 is calculated as $100,000 × 6% × 12/12.

(a) 4 Percent Market Interest Rate

The present value of the $100,000 face value is computed as follows:

From Table C.2,
Interest rate = 4%
$n = 4$

$$\$100,000 \times 0.8548 = \$85,480$$

The present value of the $6,000 annuity is computed as follows:

From Table C.4,
Interest rate = 4%
$n = 4$

$$\$6,000 \times 3.6299 = \$21,780*$$

*Adjusted to accommodate rounding in the present value factor.

The present value of the total bond payments, computed using the discount rate of 4 percent, is $107,260 (= $85,480 + $21,780).

(b) 6 Percent Market Interest Rate

The present value of the $100,000 face value is computed as follows:

From Table C.2,
Interest rate = 6%
$n = 4$

$$\$100,000 \times 0.7921 = \$79,210$$

The present value of the $6,000 annuity is computed as follows:

From Table C.4,
Interest rate = 6%
$n = 4$

$$\$6,000 \times 3.4651 = \$20,790*$$

*Adjusted to accommodate rounding in the present value factor.

The present value of the total bond payments, computed using the discount rate of 6 percent, is $100,000 (= $79,210 + $20,790).

(c) 8 Percent Market Interest Rate

The present value of the $100,000 face value is computed as follows:

From Table C.2,
Interest rate = 8%
$n = 4$

$$\$100,000 \times 0.7350 = \$73,503*$$

*Adjusted to accommodate rounding in the present value factor.

The present value of the $6,000 annuity is computed as follows:

From Table C.4,
Interest rate = 8%
$n = 4$

$$\$6,000 \times 3.3121 = \$19,873$$

The present value of the total bond payments, computed using the discount rate of 8 percent, is $93,376 (= $73,503 + $19,873).
The following table summarizes these calculations:

COACH'S TIP

The present values in (a), (b), and (c) demonstrate the calculation of the bond issue prices used in Chapter 10.

	MARKET INTEREST RATES		
	4%	6%	8%
Present value of $100,000 face value (principal) paid four years from now	$ 85,480	$ 79,210	$ 73,503
Present value of $6,000 (interest) paid once a year for four years	21,780	20,790	19,873
Bond price	**$107,260**	**$100,000**	**$93,376**

Of course, these calculations are just the starting point for understanding how bond liabilities are determined and reported. If necessary, review Chapter 10 for information about how bond liabilities are accounted for.

PRESENT VALUE COMPUTATIONS USING EXCEL

While the present value tables are useful for educational purposes, most present value problems in business are solved with calculators or Excel spreadsheets. Because of the widespread availability of Excel, we will show you how to solve present value problems using Excel. Slightly different versions of Excel are available. The illustrations in this text are based on Microsoft Office 2007 and later.

Present Value of a Single Payment

The calculation of a present value amount is based on a fairly simple mathematical formula:

$$PV = Payment/(1 + i)^n$$

In this formula, *payment* is the cash payment made at some point in the future, i is the interest rate each period, and n is the number of periods in the problem. We could use this formula to solve all problems involving the present value of a single payment. It is, of course, easier to use a present value table (like the one in this appendix) which is derived by solving the present value formula for various interest rates and numbers of periods. Unfortunately, a table that included all interest rates and numbers of periods actually encountered in business would be too large to work with. As a result, most accountants and analysts use Excel to compute a present value.

To compute the present value of a single payment in Excel, you enter the present value formula in a cell, using the format required by Excel. You should select a cell and enter the following formula:

$$= Payment/(1 + i)\hat{}n$$

To illustrate, if you want to solve for the present value of a $100,000 payment to be made in five years with an interest rate of 10 percent, you would enter the following in the function field:

$$= 100{,}000/(1.10)^5$$

Based on this entry, Excel would compute a present value of $62,092.13. This answer is slightly different from the answer you would have if you used the present value tables at the end of this appendix. The tables are rounded based on four digits. Excel does not round and, therefore, provides a more accurate computation.

Present Value of an Annuity

The formula for computing the present value of an annuity is a little more complicated than that for computing the present value of a single payment. As a result, Excel has been programmed to include the formula so that you do not have to enter it yourself.

To compute the present value of an annuity in Excel, select a cell, click on the Formulas tab, and then click on the Financial icon and the following dropdown box will appear:

Scroll down and click on PV. A new dropdown box will appear:

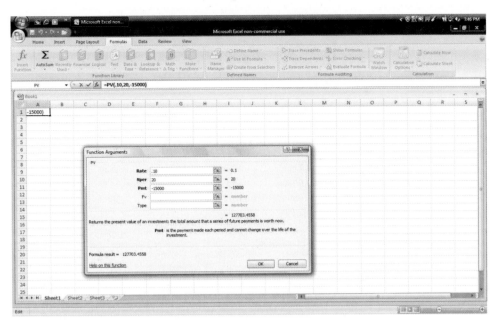

In this box, enter the interest rate, 10 percent in this example, beside Rate. Notice that the rate must be entered as a decimal (i.e., .10). Enter the number of periods (20) beside Nper. Excel has an unusual convention associated with the payment. It must be entered as a negative amount (−15000) beside Pmt. Do not include a comma or brack−ets with the amount you enter. When you click OK, Excel will enter the present value in the cell you selected. In this example, the value determined by Excel is $127,703.46.

Present Value Tables

| TABLE C.1 | Future Value of $1 |

Periods	2%	3%	3.75%	4%	4.25%	5%	6%	7%	8%
0	1.0000	1.0000	1.0000	1.0000	1.0000	1.0000	1.0000	1.0000	1.0000
1	1.02	1.03	1.0375	1.04	1.0425	1.05	1.06	1.07	1.08
2	1.0404	1.0609	1.0764	1.0816	1.0868	1.1025	1.1236	1.1449	1.1664
3	1.0612	1.0927	1.1168	1.1249	1.1330	1.1576	1.1910	1.2250	1.2597
4	1.0824	1.1255	1.1587	1.1699	1.1811	1.2155	1.2625	1.3108	1.3605
5	1.1041	1.1593	1.2021	1.2167	1.2313	1.2763	1.3382	1.4026	1.4693
6	1.1262	1.1941	1.2472	1.2653	1.2837	1.3401	1.4185	1.5007	1.5869
7	1.1487	1.2299	1.2939	1.3159	1.3382	1.4071	1.5036	1.6058	1.7138
8	1.1717	1.2668	1.3425	1.3686	1.3951	1.4775	1.5938	1.7182	1.8509
9	1.1951	1.3048	1.3928	1.4233	1.4544	1.5513	1.6895	1.8385	1.9990
10	1.2190	1.3439	1.4450	1.4802	1.5162	1.6289	1.7908	1.9672	2.1589
20	1.4859	1.8061	2.0882	2.1911	2.2989	2.6533	3.2071	3.8697	4.6610
Periods	9%	10%	11%	12%	13%	14%	15%	20%	25%
0	1.0000	1.0000	1.0000	1.0000	1.0000	1.0000	1.0000	1.0000	1.0000
1	1.09	1.10	1.11	1.12	1.13	1.14	1.15	1.20	1.25
2	1.1881	1.2100	1.2321	1.2544	1.2769	1.2996	1.3225	1.4400	1.5625
3	1.2950	1.3310	1.3676	1.4049	1.4429	1.4815	1.5209	1.7280	1.9531
4	1.4116	1.4641	1.5181	1.5735	1.6305	1.6890	1.7490	2.0736	2.4414
5	1.5386	1.6105	1.6851	1.7623	1.8424	1.9254	2.0114	2.4883	3.0518
6	1.6771	1.7716	1.8704	1.9738	2.0820	2.1950	2.3131	2.9860	3.8147
7	1.8280	1.9487	2.0762	2.2107	2.3526	2.5023	2.6600	3.5832	4.7684
8	1.9926	2.1436	2.3045	2.4760	2.6584	2.8526	3.0590	4.2998	5.9605
9	2.1719	2.3579	2.5580	2.7731	3.0040	3.2519	3.5179	5.1598	7.4506
10	2.3674	2.5937	2.8394	3.1058	3.3946	3.7072	4.0456	6.1917	9.3132
20	5.6044	6.7275	8.0623	9.6463	11.5231	13.7435	16.3665	38.3376	86.7362

TABLE C.2 — Present Value of $1

Periods	2%	3%	3.75%	4%	4.25%	5%	6%	7%	8%
1	0.9804	0.9709	0.9639	0.9615	0.9592	0.9524	0.9434	0.9346	0.9259
2	0.9612	0.9426	0.9290	0.9246	0.9201	0.9070	0.8900	0.8734	0.8573
3	0.9423	0.9151	0.8954	0.8890	0.8826	0.8638	0.8396	0.8163	0.7938
4	0.9238	0.8885	0.8631	0.8548	0.8466	0.8227	0.7921	0.7629	0.7350
5	0.9057	0.8626	0.8319	0.8219	0.8121	0.7835	0.7473	0.7130	0.6806
6	0.8880	0.8375	0.8018	0.7903	0.7790	0.7462	0.7050	0.6663	0.6302
7	0.8706	0.8131	0.7728	0.7599	0.7473	0.7107	0.6651	0.6227	0.5835
8	0.8535	0.7894	0.7449	0.7307	0.7168	0.6768	0.6274	0.5820	0.5403
9	0.8368	0.7664	0.7180	0.7026	0.6876	0.6446	0.5919	0.5439	0.5002
10	0.8203	0.7441	0.6920	0.6756	0.6595	0.6139	0.5584	0.5083	0.4632
20	0.6730	0.5537	0.4789	0.4564	0.4350	0.3769	0.3118	0.2584	0.2145

Periods	9%	10%	11%	12%	13%	14%	15%	20%	25%
1	0.9174	0.9091	0.9009	0.8929	0.8850	0.8772	0.8696	0.8333	0.8000
2	0.8417	0.8264	0.8116	0.7972	0.7831	0.7695	0.7561	0.6944	0.6400
3	0.7722	0.7513	0.7312	0.7118	0.6931	0.6750	0.6575	0.5787	0.5120
4	0.7084	0.6830	0.6587	0.6355	0.6133	0.5921	0.5718	0.4823	0.4096
5	0.6499	0.6209	0.5935	0.5674	0.5428	0.5194	0.4972	0.4019	0.3277
6	0.5963	0.5645	0.5346	0.5066	0.4803	0.4556	0.4323	0.3349	0.2621
7	0.5470	0.5132	0.4817	0.4523	0.4251	0.3996	0.3759	0.2791	0.2097
8	0.5019	0.4665	0.4339	0.4039	0.3762	0.3506	0.3269	0.2326	0.1678
9	0.4604	0.4241	0.3909	0.3606	0.3329	0.3075	0.2843	0.1938	0.1342
10	0.4224	0.3855	0.3522	0.3220	0.2946	0.2697	0.2472	0.1615	0.1074
20	0.1784	0.1486	0.1240	0.1037	0.0868	0.0728	0.0611	0.0261	0.0115

TABLE C.3 — Future Value of Annuity of $1

Periods*	2%	3%	3.75%	4%	4.25%	5%	6%	7%	8%
1	1.0000	1.0000	1.0000	1.0000	1.0000	1.0000	1.0000	1.0000	1.0000
2	2.02	2.03	2.0375	2.04	2.0425	2.05	2.06	2.07	2.08
3	3.0604	3.0909	3.1139	3.1216	3.1293	3.1525	3.1836	3.2149	3.2464
4	4.1216	4.1836	4.2307	4.2465	4.2623	4.3101	4.3746	4.4399	4.5061
5	5.2040	5.3091	5.3893	5.4163	5.4434	5.5256	5.6371	5.7507	5.8666
6	6.3081	6.4684	6.5914	6.6330	6.6748	6.8019	6.9753	7.1533	7.3359
7	7.4343	7.6625	7.8386	7.8983	7.9585	8.1420	8.3938	8.6540	8.9228
8	8.5830	8.8923	9.1326	9.2142	9.2967	9.5491	9.8975	10.2598	10.6366
9	9.7546	10.1591	10.4750	10.5828	10.6918	11.0266	11.4913	11.9780	12.4876
10	10.9497	11.4639	11.8678	12.0061	12.1462	12.5779	13.1808	13.8164	14.4866
20	24.2974	26.8704	29.0174	29.7781	30.5625	33.0660	36.7856	40.9955	45.7620

Periods*	9%	10%	11%	12%	13%	14%	15%	20%	25%
1	1.0000	1.0000	1.0000	1.0000	1.0000	1.0000	1.0000	1.0000	1.0000
2	2.09	2.10	2.11	2.12	2.13	2.14	2.15	2.20	2.25
3	3.2781	3.3100	3.3421	3.3744	3.4069	3.4396	3.4725	3.6400	3.8125
4	4.5731	4.6410	4.7097	4.7793	4.8498	4.9211	4.9934	5.3680	5.7656
5	5.9847	6.1051	6.2278	6.3528	6.4803	6.6101	6.7424	7.4416	8.2070
6	7.5233	7.7156	7.9129	8.1152	8.3227	8.5355	8.7537	9.9299	11.2588
7	9.2004	9.4872	9.7833	10.0890	10.4047	10.7305	11.0668	12.9159	15.0735
8	11.0285	11.4359	11.8594	12.2997	12.7573	13.2328	13.7268	16.4991	19.8419
9	13.0210	13.5975	14.1640	14.7757	15.4157	16.0853	16.7858	20.7989	25.8023
10	15.1929	15.9374	16.7220	17.5487	18.4197	19.3373	20.3037	25.9587	33.2529
20	51.1601	57.2750	64.2028	72.0524	80.9468	91.0249	102.4436	186.6880	342.9447

*There is one payment each period

TABLE C.4 — Present Value of Annuity of $1

Periods*	2%	3%	3.75%	4%	4.25%	5%	6%	7%	8%
1	0.9804	0.9709	0.9639	0.9615	0.9592	0.9524	0.9434	0.9346	0.9259
2	1.9416	1.9135	1.8929	1.8861	1.8794	1.8594	1.8334	1.8080	1.7833
3	2.8839	2.8286	2.7883	2.7751	2.7620	2.7232	2.6730	2.6243	2.5771
4	3.8077	3.7171	3.6514	3.6299	3.6086	3.5460	3.4651	3.3872	3.3121
5	4.7135	4.5797	4.4833	4.4518	4.4207	4.3295	4.2124	4.1002	3.9927
6	5.6014	5.4172	5.2851	5.2421	5.1997	5.0757	4.9173	4.7665	4.6229
7	6.4720	6.2303	6.0579	6.0021	5.9470	5.7864	5.5824	5.3893	5.2064
8	7.3255	7.0197	6.8028	6.7327	6.6638	6.4632	6.2098	5.9713	5.7466
9	8.1622	7.7861	7.5208	7.4353	7.3513	7.1078	6.8017	6.5152	6.2469
10	8.9826	8.5302	8.2128	8.1109	8.0109	7.7217	7.3601	7.0236	6.7101
20	16.3514	14.8775	13.8962	13.5903	13.2944	12.4622	11.4699	10.5940	9.8181

Periods*	9%	10%	11%	12%	13%	14%	15%	20%	25%
1	0.9174	0.9091	0.9009	0.8929	0.8550	0.8772	0.8696	0.8333	0.8000
2	1.7591	1.7355	1.7125	1.6901	1.6681	1.6467	1.6257	1.5278	1.4400
3	2.5313	2.4869	2.4437	2.4018	2.3612	2.3216	2.2832	2.1065	1.9520
4	3.2397	3.1699	3.1024	3.0373	2.9745	2.9137	2.8550	2.5887	2.3616
5	3.8897	3.7908	3.6959	3.6048	3.5172	3.4331	3.3522	2.9906	2.6893
6	4.4859	4.3553	4.2305	4.1114	3.9975	3.8887	3.7845	3.3255	2.9514
7	5.0330	4.8684	4.7122	4.5638	4.4226	4.2883	4.1604	3.6046	3.1611
8	5.5348	5.3349	5.1461	4.9676	4.7988	4.6389	4.4873	3.8372	3.3289
9	5.9952	5.7590	5.5370	5.3282	5.1317	4.9464	4.7716	4.0310	3.4631
10	6.4177	6.1446	5.8892	5.6502	5.4262	5.2161	5.0188	4.1925	3.5705
20	9.1285	8.5136	7.9633	7.4694	7.0248	6.6231	6.2593	4.8696	3.9539

*There is one payment each period.

SOLUTION TO SELF-STUDY PRACTICE

Solution to SPC.1

1. The present value will decrease.   2. $10,000 × 0.6139 = $6,139   3. $10,000 × 1.6289 = $16,289

KEY TERMS

Annuity   Future Value   Time Value of Money

Complete definitions are also included in the glossary at the end of this text.

PRACTICE MATERIAL

QUESTIONS

	TABLE VALUES		
	i = 5%	i = 10 %	i = 14%
	n = 4	n = 7	n = 10
FV of $1			
PV of $1			
FV of annuity of $1			
PV of annuity of $1			

1. Explain the concept of the time value of money.

2. Explain the basic difference between future value and present value.

3. If you deposited $10,000 in a savings account that earns 2 percent, how much would you have at the end of ten years? Use a convenient format to display your computations.

4. If you hold a valid contract that will pay you $8,000 cash ten years from now and the going rate of interest is 10 percent, what is its present value? Use a convenient format to display your computations.

5. What is an annuity?

6. Use the Present Value Tables in this appendix to complete the following schedule:

7. If you deposit $1,000 at the end of each period for ten interest periods and you earn 8 percent interest, how much would you have at the end of period ten?

MINI-EXERCISES

MC-1 Computing the Present Value of a Single Payment

What is the present value of $500,000 to be paid in ten years, with an interest rate of 8 percent?

MC-2 Computing the Present Value of an Annuity

What is the present value of ten equal payments of $15,000, with an interest rate of 10 percent?

MC-3 Computing the Present Value of a Complex Contract

As a result of a slowdown in operations, Mercantile Stores is offering employees who have been terminated a severance package of $100,000 cash, another $100,000 to be paid in one year, and an annuity of $30,000 to be paid each year for twenty years. What is the present value of the package, assuming an interest rate of 8 percent?

MC-4 Computing the Future Value of an Annuity

You plan to retire in twenty years. Calculate whether it is better for you to save $25,000 a year for the last ten years before retirement or $15,000 for each of the twenty years. Assume you are able to earn 10 percent interest on your investments.

EXERCISES

EC-1 Computing Growth in a Savings Account: A Single Amount

On January 1, 2017, you deposited $6,000 in a savings account. The account will earn 10 percent annual compound interest, which will be added to the fund balance at the end of each year.

Required:

(Round your answers to the nearest dollar.)
1. What will be the balance in the savings account at the end of ten years?
2. What will the interest be for the ten years?
3. How much interest revenue did the fund earn in 2017? How much will it earn in 2018?

EC-2 Computing Deposit Required and Accounting for a Single-Sum Savings Account

On January 1, 2017, Alan King decided to transfer an amount from his chequing account into a savings account that later will provide $80,000 to send his son to university (four years from now). The savings account will earn 8 percent, which will be added to the fund each year—end.

Required:

(Show computations and round your answers to the nearest dollar.)
1. How much must Alan deposit on January 1, 2017?
2. Give the January 1, 2017 journal entry that Alan should make to record the transfer.
3. What will the interest be for the four years?
4. Give the journal entry that Alan should make on (a) December 31, 2017, and (b) December 31, 2018.

EC-3 Recording Growth in a Savings Account with Equal Periodic Payments

On each December 31, you plan to transfer $2,000 from your chequing account into a savings account. The savings account will earn 9 percent annual interest, which will be added to the savings account balance at each year—end. The first deposit will be made December 31, 2017 (at the end of the period).

Required:

(Show computations and round your answers to the nearest dollar.)
1. Give the required journal entry on December 31, 2017.
2. What will be the balance in the savings account at the end of the tenth year (i.e., ten deposits)?

3. What will be the total amount of interest earned on the ten deposits?
4. How much interest revenue will the fund earn in 2018? In 2019?
5. Give all journal entries that will be required at the end of 2018 and 2019.

EC-4 Computing Growth for a Savings Fund with Periodic Deposits

On January 1, 2017, you start making plans to take a trip around the world when you graduate in four years. Your grandmother wants to deposit sufficient funds for this trip into a savings account for you. On the basis of a budget, you estimate that the trip currently would cost $15,000. Being the generous and sweet lady she is, your grandmother decided to deposit $3,500 into the fund at the end of each of the next four years, starting on December 31, 2017. The savings account will earn 6 percent annual interest, which will be added to the savings account at each year-end.

Required:

(Show computations and round your answers to the nearest dollar.)
1. How much money will you have for the trip at the end of year four (i.e., after four deposits)?
2. What will be the total amount of interest earned over the four years?
3. How much interest revenue will the fund earn in 2017, 2018, 2019, and 2020?

EC-5 Computing Value of an Asset Based on Present Value

You have the chance to purchase an oil well. Your best estimate is that the oil well's net royalty income will average $25,000 per year for five years. There will be no residual value at that time. Assume that the cash inflow occurs at each year-end and that, considering the uncertainty in your estimates, you expect to earn 15 percent per year on the investment. What should you be willing to pay for this investment right now?

COACHED PROBLEM

CPC-1 Comparing Options Using Present Value Concepts

After hearing a knock at your front door, you are surprised to see the Prize Patrol from a large, well-known magazine subscription company. It has arrived with the good news that you are the winner of $20 million. You discover that you have three options: (1) you can receive $1 million per year for the next twenty years, (2) you can have $8 million today, or (3) you can have $2 million today and receive $700,000 for each of the next twenty years. Your financial adviser tells you that it is reasonable to expect to earn 10 percent on investments. Which option do you prefer? What factors influence your decision?

> TIP: All three scenarios require you to determine today's value of the various payment options. These are present value problems.

GROUP A PROBLEM

PAC-1 Comparing Options Using Present Value Concepts

You are the successful senior vice-president of a large bank, and you are preparing for retirement. After visiting the Human Resources office, you found that you have several retirement options: (1) you can receive an immediate cash payment of $1 million, (2) you can receive $60,000 per year for life (your remaining life expectancy is 20 years), or (3) you can receive $50,000 per year for ten years and then $70,000 per year for life (this option is intended to give you some protection against inflation). You have determined that you can earn 8 percent on your investments. Which option do you prefer and why?

GROUP B PROBLEM

PBC-1 Comparing Options Using Present Value Concepts

After incurring a serious injury caused by a manufacturing defect, your friend has sued the manufacturer for damages. Your friend received three offers from the manufacturer to settle the lawsuit: (1) receive an immediate cash payment of $100,000, (2) receive $6,000 per year for life (your friend's remaining life expectancy is twenty years), or (3) receive $5,000 per year for ten years and then $7,000 per year for life (this option is intended to compensate your friend for increased aggravation of the injury over time). Your friend can earn 8 percent interest and has asked you for advice. Which option would you recommend and why?

Endnotes

1. Present value and future value problems involve cash flows. The basic concepts are the same for cash inflows (receipts) and cash outflows (payments). No fundamental differences exist between present value and future value calculations for cash payments versus cash receipts.

2. The detailed discounting is as follows:

Periods	Interest for the Year	Present Value*
1	$1,000 − ($1,000 × 1/1.10) = $90.91	$1,000 − $90.91 = $909.09
2	$909.09 − ($909.09 × 1/1.10) = $82.65	$909.09 − $82.65 = $826.44
3	$826.44 − ($826.44 × 1/1.10) = $75.14†	$826.44 − $75.14 = $751.30

*Verifiable in Table C.2.
†Adjusted for rounding

APPENDIX D

Wiki Art Gallery Inc.

The Setting

Wiki Art Gallery (WAG) is a privately owned business started in 2006 by two students. Rob Wilco combined his entrepreneurial business interests with Stephen Conley's knowledge of artwork to create an online art gallery that they named WAG.

WAG's start—up years were challenging. The owners contributed their savings to the company but initially earned little return on their significant investments of money and time. Propelled by a belief that their work would pay off, they persevered. Now it appears their luck is changing. WAG became profitable in late 2009 and has reported a sizeable net income for the year ended September 30, 2011.

Both owners are excited by this turn of events. In the summer of 2010, Stephen indicated he would like to buy out Rob, which coincided with Rob's desire to leave WAG and embark on a new career. Acknowledging his limited accounting knowl—edge, Stephen has approached you for advice.

As a private company, WAG's shares do not have a readily determinable price. Consequently, Stephen and Rob have agreed to calculate the buyout price using an *earnings multiplier* equal to five times WAG's net income for the year ended September 30, 2011. Although Rob has been a reliable friend and business partner in the past, Stephen is concerned that WAG's fiscal 2011 results could be misstated or biased because WAG does not obtain an annual audit. Stephen would like you to advise him whether WAG's fiscal 2011 net income fairly reports the company's financial success, given that the purchase price he will pay Rob is to be based on WAG's 2011 net income.

Background Information

Stephen explained that WAG obtains revenues from two sources. First, WAG purchases art from promising artists and sells it to individuals and traditional art galleries. Second, WAG charges annual fees to artists in exchange for displaying their work in its online galleries. WAG's expenses relate to salaries, the cost WAG incurs for the artwork it sells, depreciation on WAG's computer equipment, web—site maintenance, and other administrative costs (e.g., bad debts, interest, income taxes).

WAG has many transactions with artists and customers throughout the year. Stephen described some of the particularly significant events that hap—pened during the year ended September 30, 2011, which you summarized in Exhibit 1. He also provided you comparative income statements for the years ended September 30, 2011 and 2010 (see Exhibit 2) and excerpts from WAG's notes to the financial statements (see Exhibit 3).

Stephen has asked you, an experienced financial accountant and business adviser, to prepare a report that identifies and evaluates financial reporting choices that Rob has made that may have resulted in a biased measure of WAG's 2011 financial success. Specifically, for each accounting judgment or method that Rob has applied that might not fairly measure WAG's 2011 net income, you should (1) describe the choice, (2) evaluate whether it is allowed under Canadian GAAP, (3) use WAG's specific information to explain how it leads to an unfair measure of WAG's 2010 net income, and (4) propose an alternative choice that is in accordance with Canadian GAAP and would yield a fairer measure of WAG's 2011 net income.

Stephen would like you to focus on accounting choices, rather than business decisions, given his primary focus on the fairness of WAG's 2011 net income. He indicated that he would consult with you about business decisions after his purchase of WAG, but for now, he wants you to focus on providing the accounting advice he currently needs.

WAG: SIGNIFICANT 2010–2011 EVENTS

- Rob has been WAG's primary decision maker with respect to business operations. Rob manages the company's relationship with the bank, he prepares WAG's annual financial statements and tax returns, and he is WAG's representative at art auctions, buying artwork for WAG by the piece or in lots. In exchange for this work, Rob is paid an annual salary of $30,000 by WAG.

  Stephen's involvement to date has drawn on his art knowledge by helping artists determine appropriate prices at which to offer their artwork on WAG's website and advising Rob on art auction purchases. Because he has less involvement in WAG's day–to–day business, Stephen is paid a smaller salary. Like Rob, however, he receives 50 percent of WAG's dividends.

  Until 2011, WAG had paid total monthly dividends of $400. But at the end of May 2011, WAG's bank required the company to suspend its dividends and accept a higher interest rate on its loans because WAG had violated its debt–to–assets loan covenant. Rob told Stephen that it seemed unfair for Rob to continue to receive the same salary when Stephen's dividends had dried up, so Rob voluntarily cut his total salary in fiscal 2011 by $2,000.

- WAG replaced its computer server with a new Dell server on January 3, 2011. The previous server cost $1,650, had been depreciated straight–line over a two–year period with zero residual value, and was disposed of on eBay at a price equal to its book value ($619). The new server cost $2,400.

- Soon after the new server became operational, Rob asked WAG's website consultant to redesign its site. The new site, which went live on March 31, 2011, features a more user–friendly environment, offers e–commerce capabilities for online sales of artwork, and is linked to social networking sites. Rob anticipates that more users will visit the site, which could potentially increase revenue from artwork sales. The bill for WAG's website work in fiscal 2011 totalled $9,000, of which $2,000 was for the new site development and $7,000 was for regular maintenance for the year. Rob thought this cost was fair and the work seems to promise many benefits so he capitalized the full amount when he paid the bill on August 31, 2011.

- As a result of the new website features, WAG increased the fee it charges artists for displaying and assisting in the sale of their artwork. Through March 31, 2011, the monthly fee was $20 per artist. Beginning April 1, 2011, the fee increased to $40 per artist. Although the artists were excited by broader exposure and increased traffic to WAG's site, they weren't thrilled with the increase in annual fees. Many of WAG's 165 artist members indicated that they were already struggling to make ends meet during these difficult economic times.

- For most of 2011, WAG's monthly sales were comparable to 2010. However, WAG entered into a series of lucrative transactions late in the year. On August 30, Rob had managed to buy twenty original oil paintings as a single lot costing $20,000—an average cost of $1,000 per piece. Then, in early September, he sold the two best pieces in an online art auction, for $25,000 each. Rob was thrilled, not only at the gross profit, but also at the opportunities to expand WAG's reach through future online auctions.

The buyer of the two pieces, known only by his login ID, TEAC (The Eccentric Art Collector), emailed Rob in early October 2011 to express interest in buying other art on WAG's website. Rob said he would be happy to discuss it further, but first wanted TEAC to take delivery of and begin paying for the two pieces that WAG sold him in September. Rob sees TEAC's enquiry as a sign that WAG will find buyers for other less attractive items remaining in the twenty-piece lot and in the rest of WAG's extensive, but aging, inventory.

EXHIBIT D.1 WAG's Comparative Income Statements

Wiki Art Gallery, Inc.
Income Statements
For the Years Ended September 30

	2011	2010
Revenue from Sales and Service		
Artwork Sales	$ 80,600	$30,400
Artist Fees	59,400	39,600
	140,000	70,000
Expenses		
Amortization Expenses	125	0
Bad Debt Expenses	297	198
Cost of Artwork Sold	22,375	20,000
Depreciation Expenses	386	825
Divident Expenses	3,200	4,800
Income Tax Expenses	18,836	560
Interest Expenses	720	1,200
Salaries Expenses	29,500	31,500
Web Maintenance and Other	1,500	8,500
Net Income	$ 63,061	$ 2,417

Note 1: Significant Accounting Policies

Basis of Accounting.   The Company prepares its financial statements in accordance with Canadian accounting standards for private enterprises.

Revenue Recognition.   The Company records revenue from artwork sales when the Company and customer agree upon a selling price. The Company records revenue from artist fees as it is earned each month. Bad debts on artist fees are estimated by the percentage of credit sales method, using an average estimated rate of 0.5 percent. Write–offs are determined and recorded at each year–end.

Inventory.   The Company records its inventory of artwork at the lower of cost or net realizable value. Cost is determined using the specific identification method for individual pieces and using average cost for art purchased in lots. Cost of artwork sold is recorded in the period of sale. Net realizable value is estimated by the Company's management, taking into account the aesthetic of each piece.

Equipment.   The Company records equipment at cost (see Note 3). Depreciation is recorded on a straight–line basis over the equipment's estimated useful life, which is currently estimated to be ten years.

Intangible Assets.   The Company capitalizes intangible assets at the costs incurred to create those assets (see Note 3). Amortization is recorded on a straight–line basis over the useful life of the intangible assets, which is currently estimated to be six years.

Note 2: Accounts Receivable

	2011	2010
Receivables from Artwork Buyers	$53,700	$ 3,200
Receivables from Artists	15,000	3,900
Less: Allowance for Doubtful Accounts	(250)	(300)
Accounts Receivable, Net	$68,450	$ 6,800

Note 3: Capital Assets

	2011	2010
Computer Equipment	$ 2,400	$ 1,650
Less: Accumulated Depreciation	(180)	(825)
Equipment, Net	2,220	825
Intangible Web Development, Net	8,875	–0–
Capital Assets, Net	$11,095	$ 825

Note 4: Long-term Debt

	2011	2010
Note Payable, due May 31, 2017	$25,000	$20,000

Effective May 31, 2011, interest on the note was adjusted from 5 to 6 percent per annum.

©American Accounting Association

The original article published in the U.S. Phillips, *Fundamentals of Financial Accounting*, 4th edition, referred to U.S. GAAP. The text here has been changed to Canadian GAAP.

APPENDIX E

Investments in Other Corporations

Introduction

Along with financial hardship, the 2008 stock market crash generated a great deal of criticism of the accounting rules applied to investments in other corporations. As you will read in Appendix E, these rules use fair values when accounting for certain types of investments. Critics complained that use of fair values ("mark–to–market accounting") had forced companies to report losses simply because the economic crisis had caused reductions in their investment values. Critics argued that these losses did not accurately reflect reality and that each reported loss caused further reductions in investment value, like the downward spiral of a toilet flush. Supporters of the account– ing rules countered that the rules themselves did not cause the economic crisis; rather that they merely exposed the underlying economic problems that were pre–existing.

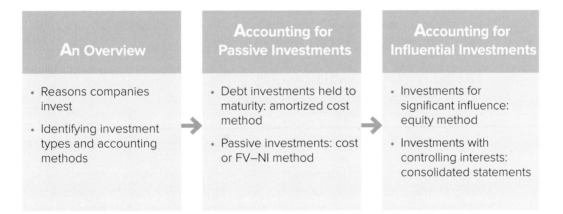

An Overview	**Accounting for Passive Investments**	**Accounting for Influential Investments**
• Reasons companies invest • Identifying investment types and accounting methods	• Debt investments held to maturity: amortized cost method • Passive investments: cost or FV–NI method	• Investments for significant influence: equity method • Investments with controlling interests: consolidated statements

Have you ever wondered how big companies become big? The answer, for many companies, is *by investing in other companies*. One such business is Rogers Communications, which is best known for being Canada's largest wireless phone carrier. However, Rogers Communications does much more than that. It owns tele– vision stations, magazine and trade publications, sports television networks, radio stations, and the Toronto Blue Jays Major League Baseball team.

The company has achieved its diversity in part by investing in the shares of other companies and has spent considerable amounts of money purchasing other compa– nies. For example, in 2013, it acquired Score Media Inc., Mountain Cablevision Ltd., Blackiron Data ULC, and Pivot Data Centres. According to its 2013 annual report, Rogers purchased Score Media Inc. for a cash consideration of $167 million and later rebranded it as Sportsnet 360. In addition, the company's investment portfolio con– sisted of more than $1,487 million worth of shares of other companies.

In this appendix, you will see how to account for three different types of investments using ASPE. To understand these investments and the reasons why they are accounted for in certain ways, you first need to answer the question: Why do companies invest in other companies?

REASONS COMPANIES INVEST

Many factors motivate managers to invest in securities. Some do so because the very nature of their business requires it. For example, pension funds, insurance companies, and mutual funds receive large sums of cash from their clients. To generate earnings—an important source of revenue in these companies—they invest the cash in the securities of other companies. Investments are significant assets to these companies.

Other managers invest in securities to even out seasonal fluctuations in cash. A manager whose company has extra cash at the end of a busy season may want to earn a return on the idle funds until they are needed for other purposes, such as repaying loans, purchasing property and equipment, or paying dividends. Excess cash can be invested in the shares and bonds of other companies, either long or short term. Managers may also invest excess cash to provide a cushion against future downturns in the economy or unanticipated emergencies. Such investments in securities are referred to as passive investments because the investors are not interested in influencing or controlling the companies that issued the securities.

Sometimes managers want to expand their company's presence in a related industry or market. They do so by investing in another company with the purpose of influencing, but not controlling, the company's policies and activities.

Finally, managers may want to control another company, either by pur-chasing it directly or by becoming the majority shareholder. In this case, the two companies combine their financial reports into consolidated financial statements, as Rogers Communications has done. In the notes to its 2016 annual report, Rogers reported just over $1 billion invested in publicly traded companies, $169 million invested in private companies and $958 million in investments that were accounted for using the equity method. As we discuss below, this means that Rogers had significant influence over these companies.

IDENTIFYING INVESTMENT TYPES AND ACCOUNTING METHODS

The accounting methods used to record investments are directly related to the purpose of the investment.

Passive Investments in Debt and Equity Securities

Passive investments: Are purchased with excess funds with the intent of earning a return.

Investors make **passive investments** to earn a high rate of return on funds that may be needed in the future for either short– or long–term purposes. This category includes investments in both debt securities (bonds and notes) and equity securities (shares):

- Investments in equity securities are presumed to be passive if the invest-ing company owns less than 20 percent of the other company's outstanding voting shares or any amount of non–voting shares. The cost method or *fair value through net income* (FV–NI) method can be used to measure and report these investments.

- Investments in debt securities are always considered to be passive. If they are meant to be sold before maturity, they are treated as equity securities and reported using the market value method (also called *fair market value method*). If the company intends and has the ability to hold them until the maturity date, however, the company measures and reports them at amortized cost.

Investments in Shares for Significant Influence

Active investments are those in which a company owns enough shares in another business to influence or control that business. An investor or company that owns enough voting shares of another company to have an important impact on its operating and financing policies is said to have significant influence. Significant influence is presumed to exist if the investing company owns from 20 to 50 percent of the outstanding voting shares. However, other factors may also indicate significant influence, including membership on the board of directors of the other company, participation in its policy–making processes, evidence of material transactions between the two companies, an interchange of managerial personnel, and technological dependency. The equity method is used to measure and report this type of investment.

Investments in Shares for Control

Control is the ability to determine the operating and financial policies of another company through ownership of its voting shares. For all practical purposes, control is presumed when the investing company owns more than 50 percent of the outstanding voting shares. These investments are accounted for by combining the two companies' financial records, using the consolidated statement method.

The three investment types and the appropriate measuring and reporting methods for each can be summarized as shown in Exhibit E.1.

EXHIBIT E.1	Accounting for Investments in Other Corporations' Shares			
Level of Involvement in Decision Making (Percentage of Ownership)	Reason for the Investment		Method of Accounting	How It Works
Control (more than 50%)	Take over the company	→	Consolidation	Combine the financial statements of parent and subsidiaries
Significant Influence (20–50%)	Influence the company	→	Equity Method	Record investment at cost, add percentage share of net income, deduct percentage share of dividends
Passive (less than 20%)	Invest excess cash to earn greater return	→	Cost or FV–NI Method	Record investment at cost but adjust this cost basis to market value at period–end if these investments are traded in an active market; report dividends and gains/losses as investment income on the income statement

Let's look more closely at the accounting and reporting rules for each of these investment types.

Accounting for Passive Investments

DEBT INVESTMENTS HELD TO MATURITY: AMORTIZED COST METHOD

When management plans to hold a bond investment until the maturity date (when the principal is due), it is reported in the financial account appropriately named Investments Held to Maturity. Bonds should be classified as investments held to maturity if management has both the intent and the ability to hold them until the maturity date. These bonds are reported at amortized cost—that is, at cost adjusted for the amortization of any bond discount or premium. We illustrate how to account for these investments from their purchase date through the maturity date.

Bond Purchases

On the date of purchase, a bond may be acquired at face value, for less than face value (at a discount), or for more than face value (at a premium). Following the cost principle, the bond's total cost is debited to the Investments Held to Maturity account.

To illustrate, assume that on October 1, 2017, Horizon Telemedia Inc. paid the face value of $100 million for 8 percent bonds due to mature on October 1, 2022. The 8 percent interest is paid each September 30. Management plans and has the ability to hold the bonds for five years until their maturity date. The purchase of the bonds on October 1, 2017, would be accounted for as follows (amounts in millions):

1 Analyze

Assets		=	Liabilities	+	Shareholders' Equity
Investments Held to Maturity	+100				
Cash	−100				

2 Record

dr **Investments Held to Maturity (+A)** 100
    cr **Cash (−A)** 100

Interest Earned

In this illustration, the company purchased the bonds at face value. Because there is no premium or discount to amortize, the book value remains constant over the life of the investment. In such situations, the revenue earned on the investment each period is measured as the amount of interest collected in cash or accrued at year−end. The fol−lowing accrual of $2 million in interest would be required on December 31 [$100 million face value × 0.08 (or 8%) × 3/12 of a year (since the October 1 purchase)]:

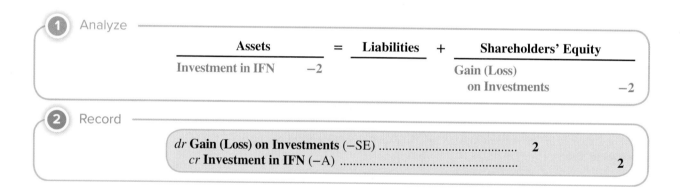

1 Analyze

Assets		=	Liabilities	+	Shareholders' Equity	
Investment in IFN	−2				Gain (Loss) on Investments	−2

2 Record

dr **Gain (Loss) on Investments (−SE)** 2
    cr **Investment in IFN (−A)** 2

On September 30, 2018, when the investor receives a full year of interest ($2 million each quarter × 4 quarters = $8 million), the following effects are recorded:

1 Analyze

Assets		=	Liabilities	+	Shareholders' Equity	
Cash	+8				Interest Revenue (+R)	+6
Interest Receivable	−2					

2 Record

dr **Cash (+A)** 8
    cr **Interest Receivable (−A)** 2
    cr **Interest Revenue (+R, +SE)** 6

Succeeding interest payments would be accounted for in the same way. On the income statement, Interest Revenue is reported in the Other Items section.

Principal at Maturity

When the bonds mature on October 1, 2022, the journal entry to record receipt of the $100 million face value payment will be

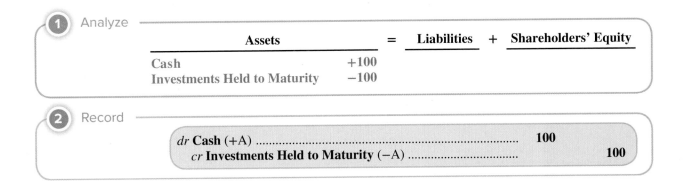

① Analyze

Assets		=	Liabilities	+	Shareholders' Equity
Cash	+100				
Investments Held to Maturity	−100				

② Record

dr **Cash (+A)** 100
    cr **Investments Held to Maturity (−A)** 100

Note the following:

- If the bond investment is sold before maturity, any difference between the market value (the proceeds from the sale) and the net book value (the unamortized cost) is reported in the income statement as a gain or loss on the sale.
- If management intends to sell the bonds before (or is unable to hold them until) the maturity date, they should be treated in the same way as passive investments, which we discuss in the next section.

PASSIVE INVESTMENTS: COST OR FV–NI METHOD

When the investing company owns less than 20 percent of the outstanding voting shares in another company or any level of non–voting shares, its investment in equity securities is considered passive. Among the assets and liabilities shown on the balance sheet, only passive investments in marketable securities (i.e., shares and debt that are not held to maturity) are reported using either the cost method or the fair value through net income (FV–NI) method.

Classifying Passive Investments

Passive investments can be traded actively with the objective of generating short–term profits on changes in the price of securities. This approach is sim–ilar to the one taken by many mutual funds whose portfolio managers actively buy and sell securities. On the balance sheet, these investments are classified as current assets.

Most companies do not actively trade the securities of other companies. Instead they invest in them to earn a return on funds they may need in the near future for operating purposes. These investments are classified as either current or non–cur–rent assets, depending on whether management intends to sell them within the next year.

We will focus on analyzing passive investing activities for a fictional company in the next section.

Recording and Reporting Passive Investments

Exhibit E.2 shows the fictional balance sheet for Horizon Telemedia Inc. (HTI), where its Investments in Marketable Securities account is reported at $357 million for the year 2017.

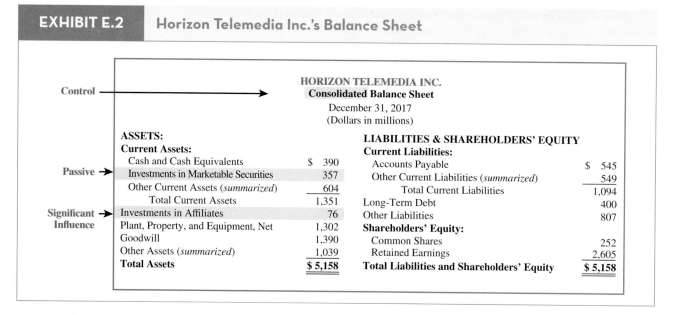

Here is how the cost method is applied:

- Assume that Horizon Telemedia Inc. invests in equity securities, acquiring a passive interest in the shares of other companies. These assets are reported on the balance sheet (Exhibit E.2) as Investments in Marketable Securities on HTI's balance sheet.

- At the end of each reporting period, the company is required to assess whether there are any indications that the value of the investment in the other company's shares may be impaired. When there is an indication of impairment, the carrying amount of the investment should be reduced. Accountants use a special account, a valuation allowance, to show the change in the value below acquisition cost. If the value of the investment has decreased, the valuation allowance is subtracted from the cost of the investment. If the value of the investment increases, then the valuation allowance is reversed only by the original amount set up in the allowance account for that investment. Hence, the carrying amount of the investment can never be greater than the original cost of the investment.

- Because a journal entry must affect at least two accounts, the other half of the adjusting entry is made to another account called *Impairment Loss*, which is reported on the income statement and affects the calculation of net income.

This process may sound complicated, so let's simplify it a little. Let's assume that HTI had no passive investments at the end of 2016. In the following example, we apply the cost method to a sample securities purchase.

Purchase of Shares   Assume that on January 2, 2017, HTI purchased 1,000,000 common shares of Internet Financial News (IFN) for $60 per share, paying

$60,000,000. On that date, 10,000,000 shares were outstanding, so HTI owned 10 percent of IFN (1,000,000 ÷ 10,000,000). This investment would be treated as a passive investment that is recorded initially (on January 2, 2017) at cost:

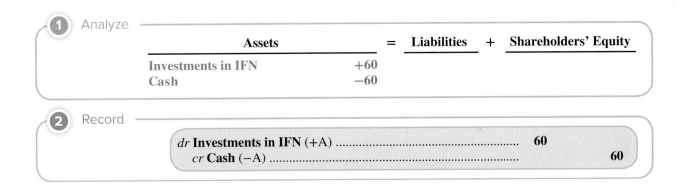

Dividends Earned   Investments in equity securities earn a return from two sources: (1) price increases and (2) dividend income. Price increases (or decreases) are analyzed both at year–end and when a security is sold. On the income state–ment, dividends earned are reported as Investment Income (or Dividend Revenue) and included in the computation of net income for the period. Let's assume that on December 15, 2017, HTI received a $1 per share cash dividend from IFN totalling $1,000,000 ($1 × 1,000,000 shares). The dividend received (in millions of dollars) is accounted for as follows:

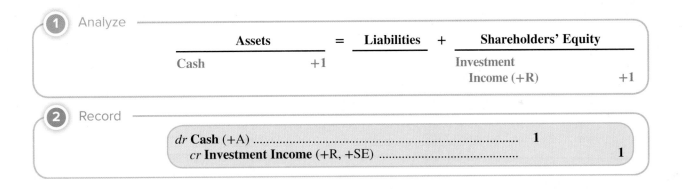

Year-End Valuation   At the end of the accounting period, HTI needs to assess the value of the investment. Some investments may not be traded in an active market, in which case, the company must keep the investment recorded at cost and take into account any adverse changes that have occurred that will impact the future cash flows of the investment. This impairment requires adjusting the account to the impaired value at the end of each period, using the valuation account Impairment Allowance. The offset to the Impairment Allowance is the Impairment Loss on Investments account. If the Impairment Allowance account has a debit balance, it is added to the Investment account. If it has a credit balance, it is subtracted from the Investment account The Impairment Loss on Investment account is then reported in the income statement. This impacts net income, which eventually will be closed to Retained Earnings. Thus, the accounting equation remains in balance.

Investments that are traded in an active market must be "marked to market" or in other words, be recorded at the market value. For example, let's assume that IFN had a $58 per share market value at the end of the year. That is, the invest– ment lost value ($60 − $58 = $2 per share).

The following chart shows the computation of any gain or loss in the passive investments portfolio. The amounts are given in millions of dollars:

Year: 2017	(in millions)	
Market value	$ 58	($58 per share × 1 million shares)
−Cost	− 60	($60 per share × 1 million shares)
Amount for adjusting entry to mark this investment to market	($ 2)	

Investment in IFN			
02/01/17	60		
		2	AJE
12/31/17	58		

On December 31, 2017, HTI would mark its investment to market as follows:

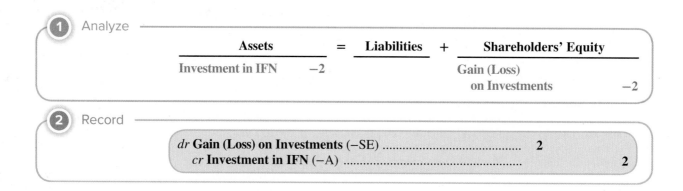

1 Analyze

	Assets		=	Liabilities	+	Shareholders' Equity	
Investment in IFN		−2				Gain (Loss) on Investments	−2

2 Record

dr **Gain (Loss) on Investments (−SE)** 2
  cr **Investment in IFN (−A)** 2

On the 2017 balance sheet under Investments in Marketable Securities, HTI would report its investment in IFN at a fair value of $58 million. The company also would report on the income statement an impairment loss of $2 million. One other item that would be reported on the income statement for 2017 would be investment income of $1 million (from dividends received), classified under Other Items.

Now let's assume that HTI held the IFN securities through the year 2018. At the end of 2018, the shares had a market value of $61 per share. The adjustment for 2018 is computed as follows:

Year: 2018	in millions	
Market value	$ 61	($61 per share × 1 million shares)
−Current recorded book value	− 58	($58 per share × 1 million shares)
	$ 3	

Investment in IFN	
12/31/17	58
AJE	3
12/31/18	61

On December 31, 2018, the investment is marked to market as follows:

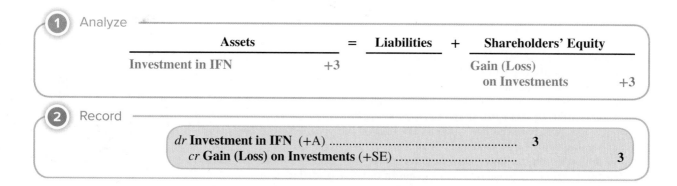

1 Analyze

	Assets		=	Liabilities	+	Shareholders' Equity	
Investment in IFN		+3				Gain (Loss) on Investments	+3

2 Record

dr **Investment in IFN (+A)** 3
  cr **Gain (Loss) on Investments (+SE)** 3

On the 2018 balance sheet under Investments in Marketable Securities, HTI would report its Investment in IFN at a fair value of $61 million. The company would also report on the income statement for 2018 a gain of $3 million. The balance sheet account would be reported as shown below at December 31, 2018.

On the Balance Sheet:	(in millions)
Assets	
Investments in Marketable Securities	$61

Sale of Shares   Let's assume that on March 17, 2019, Horizon Telemedia Inc. sold all of its investment in IFN for $64 per share. The company received $64 million in cash ($64 × 1,000,000 shares) for shares purchased at $60 million in 2017 ($60 × 1,000,000 shares). On that date, accountants record a $3 million realized gain on the sale and then eliminate the Investment in IFN account.

You may be wondering why the gain is for only $3 million and not $4 million, which is the difference between the amount of cash received from the sale of the investment and the cost of the investment ($64 million − $60 million). The difference is due to the fact that this investment had a readily available market price and was therefore marked to market every period. When this investment was adjusted to market value over the previous two years, the journal entries recorded a net gain of $1 million (a $2 million loss in 2017 and a $3 million gain in 2018). Therefore, $1 million of the total $4 million gain has already been recognized, and the gain to record at the time of sale is for $3 million, as shown below.

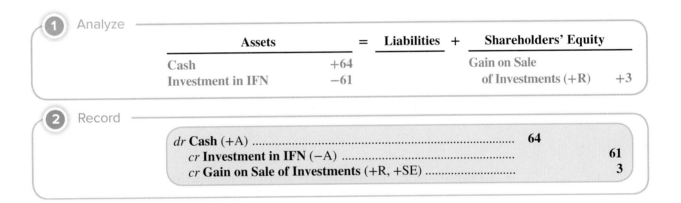

1 Analyze				
Assets		**= Liabilities +**	**Shareholders' Equity**	
Cash	+64		Gain on Sale	
Investment in IFN	−61		of Investments (+R)	+3

2 Record

dr **Cash (+A)** 64
    cr **Investment in IFN (−A)** 61
    cr **Gain on Sale of Investments (+R, +SE)** 3

SPOTLIGHT ON Financial Reporting

Passive Investments and the Fair Value Requirement

International Financial Reporting Standards (IFRS) require companies to account for passive investments at **fair value**. Fair value is the price the seller would receive if the assets were sold.

Accounting for Influential Investments

INVESTMENTS FOR SIGNIFICANT INFLUENCE: EQUITY METHOD

For a variety of reasons, an investor may want to exert significant influence (by owning 20 to 50 percent of a company's outstanding voting shares) without becoming the controlling shareholder (by acquiring over 50 percent of the voting shares):

- A retailer might want to influence a manufacturer to ensure certain prod—ucts are designed to the retailer's specifications.
- A manufacturer might want to influence a computer consulting firm to incor—porate the firm's cutting—edge technology into its manufacturing processes.
- A manufacturer might recognize that a parts supplier lacks experienced management and could prosper with additional managerial support.

When an investor can exert significant influence over an investee (the company it partially owns), accountants must use the equity method to value the investment. As you have seen, when Horizon Telemedia Inc. invests in securities as a passive investor, the company reports those investments on the balance sheet as Investments in Marketable Securities. However, when HTI owns 20 to 50 percent of the outstanding voting shares, the company is presumed to be taking a more active role as an investor. On the balance sheet, Horizon Telemedia reports these long—term investments for significant influence as Investments in Affiliates (see Exhibit E.2).

Recording Investments Under the Equity Method

With a passive investment (less than 20 percent share ownership), an investor usu—ally cannot influence the investee's operating and financing activities—for example, by compelling the investee to pay dividends. So the investor reports any dividends received from the investee as dividend revenue.

Under the equity method, however, the investor's 20 to 50 percent ownership in a company presumes significant influence over the investee's operating and financ—ing policies. Often the investee's board of directors may include a representative of the investor who influences the investee's board to declare dividends among other decisions. Because of this influence, the investment is accounted for as if the two companies were one. That is, the net income the investee earned increases the investee's net assets (assets minus liabilities). Likewise, the investor should report a portion of the investee's net income as its income and an increase in the invest—ment account. Dividends paid by the investee decrease the investee's net assets. Similarly, the receipt of dividends by the investor is treated as a reduction of the investment account, not revenue. A summary follows:

Net Income of Investee. When the investee reports net income for the year, the investor records investment income equal to its **percentage share of the investee's net income** and increases the asset account Investments in Affiliates. (If the investee reports a net loss, the investor records the opposite effect.)

Dividends Paid by Investee. If the investee declares and pays dividends to the investor during the year (a financing decision), the investor reduces the investment account and increases cash.

+	Investments in Affiliates (A)	−
Beginning balance		
Purchases of shares in affiliated companies	Sales of shares in affiliated companies	
Investor's percentage share of investee's net income (also credit Equity in Investee Earnings)	Investor's percentage share of investee's net loss (also debit Equity in Investee Losses)	
	Investor's percentage share of investee's dividends declared for the period (also debit Cash)	
Ending balance		

Purchase of Shares For simplicity, let's assume that at the end of 2016, Horizon Telemedia had no long–term investments in companies over which it exerted significant influence. Horizon Telemedia purchased 4 million shares of the outstanding voting shares of IFN on January 2, 2017, for $240 million cash. Because IFN had 10 million shares of common shares outstanding, HTI acquired a 40 percent interest (4 million ÷ 10 million shares) and was presumed to have significant influence over the investee. Therefore, HTI must use the equity method to account for the investment. The purchase of the asset would be recorded at cost in Investments in Affiliates on January 2, 2017.

1 Analyze

Assets		=	Liabilities	+	Shareholders' Equity
Investments in Affiliates	+240				
Cash	−240				

2 Record

dr **Investments in Affiliates** (+A) 240
    cr **Cash** (−A) 240

Investee Earnings Because the investor can influence the investee's income–earning process, the investor bases its investment income on the investee's earnings rather than on the dividends paid. In 2017, IFN reported net income of $50 million. Horizon Telemedia's percentage share of that income, $20 million (40% × $50 million), would be recorded on December 31, 2017, as follows:

1 Analyze

Assets	= Liabilities	+	Shareholders' Equity
Investments in Affiliates +20			Equity in Investee Earnings (+R) +20

2 Record

dr **Investments in Affiliates** (+A) 20
    cr **Equity in Investee Earnings** (+R, +SE) 20

If reporting a net loss, the investor records its share of the loss by decreasing the investment account and recording the loss under Equity in Investee Losses. Equity in Investee Earnings (or Losses) is reported in the Other Items section of the income statement, along with interest revenue and interest expense.

Dividends Received Because Horizon Telemedia can influence the dividend policies of its investees, the company should *not* record any dividends it receives as investment income. Instead, dividends reduce its investment account. On December 1, 2017, IFN declared and paid a cash dividend of $2 per share to shareholders. HTI received $8 million in cash ($2 per share × 4 million shares) from IFN, and recorded this on December 1, 2017, as follows:

1 Analyze

Assets		=	Liabilities	+	Shareholders' Equity
Investments in Affiliates	−8				
Cash	+8				

2 Record

dr **Cash** (+A) 8
    cr **Investments in Affiliates** (−A) 8

The cumulative effects of the IFN purchase, earnings, and dividends for 2017 are reflected in the following T–accounts (in millions of dollars):

Investments in Affiliates (A)				
1/1/17	0			
Purchases	240			
Share of investee net earnings	20	8	Share of investee dividends	
12/31/17	252			

	Equity in Investee Earnings (R)	
	0	1/1/17
	20	Share of investee net earnings
	20	12/31/17

COACH'S TIP

Because Horizon Telemedia owned 40 percent of IFN prior to the sale (4 million of the 10 million shares outstanding), it will then own 30 percent (3 million of 10 million shares) after the sale. Thus, it must still apply the equity method.

Sale of Shares Companies record any sale of shares in affiliated companies in the same way as sales of other assets. Investment in Affiliates is reduced by the percentage of shares sold, Cash is debited, and the difference is recorded as either a Gain (or Loss) on Sale of Investments.

Let's assume that on January 2, 2018, Horizon Telemedia decided to sell 1,000,000 of the 4,000,000 shares it owned in IFN for $70 million. That rep–resents 25 percent of Horizon Telemedia's Investment in Affiliates. One–fourth of the balance in the account is equal to $63 million ($252 million × 0.25), so the accounting effects on January 2, 2018, are the following:

1 Analyze

Assets		=	Liabilities	+	Shareholders' Equity	
Cash	+70				Gain on Sale of	
Investments in Affiliates	−63				Investments (+R)	+7

2 Record

> dr **Cash** (+A) 70
>   cr **Investments in Affiliates** (−A) 63
>   cr **Gain on Sale of Investments** (+R, +SE) 7

Reporting Investments Under the Equity Method

On the balance sheet, Investments in Affiliates is reported as a long–term asset. However, as the year–end entries show, the investment account does not reflect either cost or market value. Instead, the following occurs:

- The investment account increases with the cost of the purchased shares and the proportional share of the investee's income.

- The investment account decreases with the dividends received from the investee, the proportional share of any investee losses, and any sale of shares in the investee.

At the end of the accounting period, accountants do not adjust the invest–ment account to reflect changes in the market value of securities accounted for under the equity method. When the securities are sold, accountants record the difference between the cash received and the book value of the investment as a Gain (Loss) on Sale of Investments and report the amount on the income statement in the Other Items section.

Improper Influence

A key assumption in accounting is that all transactions occur at "arm's length." That is, each party to the transaction is acting separately in his or her own self-interest. But when one company exerts significant influence over another (i.e., when it owns 20 to 50 percent of the voting common shares), it is unreasonable to assume that transactions between the two companies are carried out at arm's length.

Consider what might happen if an investor company could affect the investee's dividend policy. If the investor reported dividends paid by the investee as dividend income, the investor could manipulate its own income by influencing the other company's dividend policy. In a bad year, the investor might request large dividend payments to bolster its income. In a good year, it might try to cut dividend payments to build up the investee's retained earnings, which would support large dividends in the future.

The equity method prevents this type of manipulation. Instead of recognizing dividends as income, this method bases income from the investment on a percentage of the affiliated company's reported net income.

INVESTMENTS WITH CONTROLLING INTERESTS: CONSOLIDATED STATEMENTS

Why Control Other Companies?

Before we discuss financial reporting of investments that involve ownership of more than 50 percent of another company's outstanding voting shares, we should consider the reasons for acquiring this level of ownership. Following are some of these reasons:

1. **Vertical integration.** In this type of acquisition, one company acquires another company that operates on a different level in the distribution channel.

2. **Horizontal growth.** Horizontal acquisitions involve companies that operate on the same level of the distribution channel.

3. **Synergy.** Two companies operating together may be more profitable than two companies operating separately. Rogers Communications has created or purchased a number of broadcast and Internet services. Merging these companies and sharing news content may create more profits than operating separate entities could.

Understanding why one company has acquired control over other companies is a key factor in understanding that company's business strategy.

What Are Consolidated Statements?

Any corporate acquisition involves two companies. A merger occurs when one company purchases all assets and liabilities of another company and the acquired company's corporate status is terminated and its business operations are merged with the acquiring corporation. When the acquired company retains its corporate status, the company that gains control is the **parent company** and the acquired corporation is the **subsidiary company.**[1] Following is a list of three corporations and some of the well-known companies they own:

Parent company: The entity that gains a controlling influence over another company (a subsidiary).

Subsidiary company: A business that is controlled by another company (the parent).

Gap Inc.	YUM! Brands, Inc.	The Walt Disney Company
Gap	Pizza Hut	ABC Television Network
Old Navy	KFC	ESPN
Banana Republic	Taco Bell	Disneyland
Piperlime	WingStreet	Walt Disney World
Athleta		Marvel Entertainment
INTERMIX		Lucasfilm Ltd.

Consolidated financial statements: The financial statements of parent and subsidiary companies combined into a single set of financial statements.

COACH'S TIP

Because a single set of financial statements covers both the parent company and its subsidiaries, external users such as shareholders and banks (and you) will not be able to obtain financial statements for individual subsidiaries.

When one company acquires another, the results of their operations must be reported together in consolidated statements. **Consolidated financial statements** combine the operations of two or more companies into a single set of statements, usually identified by the word *consolidated* in the statement titles. For example, the title of the statement in Exhibit E.2 is *Consolidated* Balance Sheet. Consolidated statements can be thought of as adding together the financial statements for two or more companies so that they appear to be a single company. Thus, the cash accounts for the companies are summed, along with the inventory accounts, the land accounts, and all other accounts. Combining all financial information into one set of consolidated statements gives users better information on the size and scope of operations in companies controlled by the parent corporation.

When consolidated statements are prepared, intercompany items, such as loans from the parent company to the subsidiaries, must be eliminated. Remember that consolidated statements imply that a single company exists when, in fact, there are two or more separate legal entities. Intercompany items do not exist in a single corporation. For example, a debt that the parent owes to its subsidiary is not reported on a consolidated statement because a company cannot owe money to itself. Accounting for business acquisitions and preparing consolidated financial statements are discussed in detail in advanced accounting courses.

DEMONSTRATION CASE A: PASSIVE INVESTMENTS

Cascon Equipment Corporation sells and services a major line of farm equipment. Both sales and service operations have been profitable. The following transactions affected the company during 2017:

a. Jan. 1   Purchased 2,000 common shares in Dear Company at $40 per share. Purchase represented 1 percent of the shares outstanding. Management intends to trade these shares actively.

b. Dec. 28   Received $4,000 cash dividend on Dear Company shares.

c. Dec. 31   Determined that the current market price of Dear shares was $39.

Required:

1. Prepare the journal entry for each of these transactions.
2. What accounts and amounts will be reported on the balance sheet at the end of 2017 and on the income statement for 2017?

Suggested Solution

1. *a.* *dr* Investment in Dear Company (+A) 80,000

   cr Cash (−A) (2,000 shares × $40) 80,000

   b. *dr* Cash (+A) 4,000

   cr Investment Income (+R, +SE) 4,000

   c. *dr* Loss on Investments (+E, −SE) 2,000

   cr Investment in Dear Company (−A) 2,000

Year: 2017		
Market value	$78,000	$39 per share × 2,000 shares)
− Cost	−80,000	($40 per share × 2,000 shares)
Adjustment needed to record investment at market value	$ (2,000)	A realized loss to income

2. On the balance sheet   On the income statement

Current Assets		Other Items	
Investment in Dear Company	$ 78,000	Investment Income	$4,000
		Loss on investment	(2,000)

E-14   APPENDIX E   Investments in Other Corporations

DEMONSTRATION CASE B: EQUITY METHOD

On January 1, 2017, Connaught Company purchased 40 percent of the outstanding voting shares of London Company on the open market for $85,000 cash. London declared $10,000 in cash dividends on December 1, 2017, and reported net income of $60,000 for the year on December 31, 2017.

Required:

1. Prepare the journal entries for 2017.
2. What accounts and amounts were reported on Connaught's balance sheet at the end of 2017 and on Connaught's income statement for 2017?

Suggested Solution

1.

Jan. 1	*dr* Investments in Affiliates (+A)............................	85,000
	cr Cash (−A)		85,000
Dec. 1	*dr* Cash (+A) (40% × $10,000)	4,000
	cr Investments in Affiliates (−A)		4,000
Dec. 31	*dr* Investments in Affiliates (+A)	24,000
	(40% × $60,000)	
	cr Equity in Investee Earnings (+R, +SE)		24,000

2. On the balance sheet   On the income statement

Non-current Assets		Other Items	
Investments in Affiliates	$ 105,000	Equity in Investee Earnings	$24,000
$ 85,000 cost			
− 4,000 dividends			
+ 24,000 percentage of investee's net income			
$ 105,000 balance in Investments account			

KEY TERMS

Consolidated Financial Statements   Passive Investments

Parent Company   Subsidiary Company

Complete definitions are also included in the glossary in the end of this text.

PRACTICE MATERIAL

QUESTIONS

1. When is it appropriate to use consolidation, equity, and market value methods for an investment in another corporation?

2. What are the differences between the accounting methods used for passive investments and those used for investments involving a significant influence?

3. What are the differences between the accounting methods used for investments involving a significant influence and those used for investments involving control?

4. What are consolidated financial statements and what do they attempt to accomplish?

5. Under the equity method, dividends received from the investee company are not recorded as revenue. Recording dividends as revenue would involve double counting. Explain.

6. What are the two sources of return for passive investments?

MINI-EXERCISES

MC-1 Recording Equity Method Securities Transactions

On January 2, 2017, Ubuy.com paid $100,000 to acquire 25 percent (10,000 shares) of the common shares of E−Net Enterprises. The accounting period for both companies ends December 31. Give the journal entries for the purchase on January 2 and for each of the following transactions that occurred during 2017:

July 2   E–Net declared and paid a cash dividend of $3 per share.
Dec. 31   E–Net reported net income of $200,000.

MC-2 Determining Financial Statement Effects of Equity Method Securities

Using the following categories, indicate the effects (direction and amount) of the transactions listed in ME–1. Use + for increase and – for decrease.

	Balance Sheet				Income Statement		
Transaction	Assets	Liabilities	Shareholders' Equity		Revenues	Expenses	Net Income

MC-3 Recording Passive Investment Transactions

During 2017, Princeton Company acquired some of the 50,000 outstanding common shares of Cox Corporation as trading securities. The accounting period for both companies ends December 31. Give the journal entries for each of the following transactions that occurred during 2014:

July 2   Purchased 8,000 shares of Cox common shares at $28 per share.
Dec. 15   Cox Corporation declared and paid a cash dividend of $2 per share.
    31   Determined the current market price of Cox shares to be $29 per share.

MC-4 Determining Financial Statement Effects of Passive Investment Transactions

Using the following categories, indicate the effects (direction and amount) of the transactions listed in ME–3. Use + for increase and – for decrease.

	Balance Sheet				Income Statement		
Transaction	Assets	Liabilities	Shareholders' Equity		Revenues	Expenses	Net Income

MC-5 Recording the Purchase and Sale of a Passive Investment

Rocktown Corporation bought 600 shares of General Esterdies on March 20, 2017, for its trading securities portfolio at $29 per share. Rocktown sold the shares at $33 per share on June 23, 2017. Prepare the journal entries to record the transactions on each of these dates, assuming that the investment had not yet been adjusted to market value (i.e., the investment was still recorded at cost at the time of sale).

EXERCISES

EE-1 Recording and Reporting an Equity Method Security

Felicia Company acquired 21,000 of the 60,000 outstanding common shares of Nurces Corporation during 2017 as a long–term investment. The annual accounting period for both companies ends December 31. The following transactions occurred during 2017:

Jan. 10   Purchased 21,000 common shares of Nurces at $12 per share.
Dec. 31   Nurces Corporation reported net income of $90,000.
Dec. 31   Nurces Corporation declared and paid a cash dividend of $0.60 per share.
Dec. 31   Determined the market price of Nurces shares to be $11 per share.

Required:

1. What accounting method should the company use? Why?

2. Give the journal entries for each of these transactions. If no entry is required, explain why.

3. Show how the long–term investment and the related revenue should be reported on the 2017 financial statements of Felicia Company.

EE-2 Recording Gains for Passive Investments

On June 30, 2016, MetroMedia Unlimited purchased 10,000 shares of Mitekii for $20 per share. The following information pertains to the price per share of Mitekii shares:

	Price
12/31/2016	$24
12/31/2017	31

Required:

1. Assume that the shares are traded on an open market. Prepare the journal entries required on each date given.
2. Show how the investment and gains would be reported at the end of 2017 and 2016 on the classified balance sheet and income statement.

EE-3 Recording Losses for Passive Investments

On March 10, 2016, Gesalt Solutions Inc. purchased 5,000 shares of Sperior Technologies for $50 per share. The following information pertains to the price per share of Sperior Technologies shares:

	Price
12/31/2016	$45
12/31/2017	42

Required:

1. Assume that the shares are traded on an open market. Prepare the journal entries required on each date given.
2. Show how the investment and losses would be reported at each year—end on the classified balance sheet and income statement.

COACHED PROBLEMS

CPE-1 Recording Passive Investments and Investments for Significant Influence

On August 4, 2015, Cappio Corporation purchased 1,000 shares of Maxweller Company for $45,000. The following information applies to the shares price of Maxweller Company:

	Price
12/31/2016	$52
12/31/2017	$47
12/31/2017	38

Maxweller Company declares and pays cash dividends of $2 per share on June 1 of each year.

Required:

1. Prepare journal entries to record the facts in the case, assuming that Maxweller shares are traded on an open market.
2. Prepare journal entries to record the facts in the case, assuming that Cappio uses the equity method to account for the investment. Cappio owns 30 percent of Maxweller, and Maxweller reported $50,000 of net income each year.

CPE-2 Comparing Methods to Account for Various Levels of Ownership of Voting Shares

Bart Company had 30,000 outstanding common shares for $10 per share. On January 1, 2017, Homer Company purchased some of these shares at $25 per share, with the intent of holding them for a long time. At the end of 2017, Bart Company reported the following: net income, $50,000, and cash dividends declared and paid during the year, $25,500. The market value of Bart Company shares at the end of 2017 was $22 per share.

Required:

1. This problem involves two separate cases. For each case (shown in the table below), iden—tify the method of accounting that Homer Company should use. Explain why.

    TIP: Divide the number of shares purchased by the number outstanding to determine the per—centage of ownership.

2. Give the journal entries for Homer Company at the dates indicated for each of the two independent cases. If no entry is required, explain why. Use the following format:

	Case A: 3,600 Shares Purchased	Case B: 10,500 Shares Purchased
Journal entries made by Homer Company:		
a. To record the acquisition of Bart Company at January 1, 2017.		
b. To recognize the income reported by Bart Company for 2017.		
c. To recognize the dividends declared and paid by Bart Company.		
d. Entry to recognize the market value effect at end of 2017.		

3. Complete the following schedule to show the separate amounts that should be reported on the 2017 financial statements of Homer Company:

	Dollar Amounts	
	Case A	Case B
Balance sheet		
Investments		
Income Statement		
Investment Income		
Gain on Investments		
Equity in Investee Earnings		

4. Explain why assets and investment income for the two cases are different.

GROUP A PROBLEMS

PAE-1 Recording Passive Investments and Investments for Significant Influence

On July 12, 2015, Rossow Corporation purchased 1,000 shares of Reimer Company for $30,000. The following information applies to the share price of Reimer Company:

	Price
12/31/2015	$33
12/31/2016	$28
12/31/2017	20

Reimer Company declares and pays cash dividends of $2 per share on May 1 of each year.

Required:

1. Prepare journal entries to record the facts of the case, assuming that Reimer shares are traded on an open market.
2. Prepare journal entries to record the facts of the case, assuming that Rossow uses the equity method to account for the investment. Rossow owns 30 percent of Reimer, and Reimer reported $50,000 of net income each year.

PAE-2 Comparing the Market Value and Equity Methods

Lisa Company had 100,000 outstanding common shares. On January 10, 2017, Marg Company purchased a block of these shares in the open market at $20 per share, with the intent of holding the shares for a long time. At the end of 2017, Lisa reported net income of $300,000 and cash dividends of $0.60 per share. At December 31, 2017, Lisa Company shares were selling at $18 per share.

Required:

1. This problem involves two separate cases. For each case (shown in the table below), iden—tify the method of accounting that Marg Company should use. Explain why.

2. Give the journal entries for Marg Company at the dates indicated for each of the two independent cases. If no entry is required, explain why. Use the following format:

	Case A: 10,000 Shares Purchased	Case B: 40,000 Shares Purchased
Journal entries made by Marg Company:		
a. To record the acquisition of Lisa Company on January 10, 2017		
b. To recognize the income reported by Lisa Company for 2017		
c. To recognize the dividends declared and paid by Lisa Company		
d. Entry to recognize the market value effect at end of 2017		

3. Complete the following schedule to show the separate amounts that should be reported on the 2017 financial statements of Marg Company:

	Dollar Amounts	
	Case A	Case B
Balance sheet		
Investments		
Income Statement		
Investment Income		
Loss on Investments		
Equity in Investee Earnings		

4. Explain why assets and investment income for the two cases are different.

Endnote

1. The discussion assumes acquisition of 100 percent of another company. Any acquisition of 51 to 99 percent of another company creates a minority interest that is discussed in advanced accounting courses.

A

Accounting Standards for Private Enterprises (ASPE) Rules of accounting that address issues that are more relevant in a private enterprise environment and therefore can be used by private enterprises only.

Accounting A system of analyzing, recording, and summarizing the results of a business's activities and then reporting the results to decision makers.

Accounts Receivable Amounts owed to a business by its customers. Also called *trade receivables* or *receivables*.

Accounts Accumulate and report the effects of each different business activity.

Accrual Basis Accounting Reports revenues when they are earned and expenses when they are incurred, regardless of the timing of cash receipts or payments; required under GAAP.

Accrued Liabilities Liabilities for expenses that have been incurred but not yet billed or paid at the end of the accounting period. Also called *accrued expenses*.

Adjusted Trial Balance A list of all accounts and their adjusted balances to check on the equality of recorded debits and credits.

Adjusting Journal Entries (AJEs) Record the effects of each period's adjustments in a debits−equal−credits format.

Adjustments Entries made at the end of every accounting period to report revenues and expenses in the proper period and assets and liabilities at appropriate amounts.

Aging of Accounts Receivable Method Estimates uncollectable accounts based on the age of each account receivable. Also called the *balance sheet approach*.

Allowance Method An account−ing method that reduces accounts receivable (as well as net income) for an estimate of uncollectable accounts (bad debts).

Amortization The process of allocating the cost of intangible assets over their limited useful lives. Similar to depreciation.

Annuity A series of periodic cash receipts or payments that are equal in amount each interest period.

Assets Resources presently owned by a business that generate future economic benefits.

Authorized Shares The maximum number of shares of a corporation that can be issued, as specified in the charter.

B

Bad Debt Expense Reports the estimated amount of this period's credit sales that customers will fail to pay.

Balance Sheet Reports the amount of assets, liabilities, and shareholders' equity of a business at a point in time.

Bank Reconciliation Process of using both the bank statement and the case accounts of a business to determine the appropriate amount of cash in a bank account, after taking into consideration delays or errors in processing cash transactions.

Basic Accounting Equation $A + L = SE$, where A = assets, L = liabilities, and SE = shareholders' equity.

Bond Amortization The bond discount or premium amount is amortized over the life of the bond until the bond's maturity date, and this amortization becomes part of its interest expense over the life of the bond.

Book Value (Carrying Value) The amount an asset or liability is reported at ("carried at") in the financial statements. For assets, it's the acquisition cost less accumulated depreciation. It is also known as *net book value* or *book value*.

C

Canadian Auditing Standards (CAS) Provide auditors with up−to−date tools and required procedures in order to carry out high−quality financial statement audits in today's complex business environment.

Canadian Auditing Standards (CAS) Provide auditors with up−to−date tools and required procedures in order to carry out high−quality financial statement audits in today's complex business environment.

Capital Cost Allowance (CCA) The depreciation process required by the Canada Revenue Agency for calculating taxable income and income taxes.

Capitalized To have recorded a cost as a long−lived asset, rather than an expense.

Carrying Value (Net Book Value, Book Value) The amount an asset or liability is reported at ("carried at") in the financial statements. For assets, it's the acquisition cost less accumulated depreciation. It is also known as *net book value* or *book value*.

Cash Basis Accounting Reports revenues when cash is received and expenses when cash is paid; this is not allowed under GAAP.

Cash Equivalents Short−term, highly liquid investments purchased within three months of maturity.

Cash Flows from Financing Activities Cash inflows and outflows related to financing sources external to the company (owners and lenders).

Cash Flows from Investing Activities Cash inflows and outflows related to the sale or purchase of investments and long−lived assets.

Cash Flows from Operating Activities (Cash Flows from Operations) Cash inflows and outflows related to components of net income. Also called *cash flows from operations*.

Cash Money or any instrument that banks will accept for deposit and immediate credit to a company's account, such as a cheque, money order, or a bank draft.

Chart of Accounts A summary of all account names (and corresponding account numbers) used to record financial results in the accounting system.

Classified Balance Sheet A balance sheet that classifies current assets and current liabilities separately from long–term assets and long–term liabilities.

Common Shares The basic voting shares issued by a corporation to shareholders.

Consolidated Financial Statements The financial statements of parent and subsidiary companies combined into a single set of financial statements.

Contingent Liabilities Potential liabilities that have arisen as a result of a past transaction or event; their ultimate outcome will not be known until a future event occurs or fails to occur.

Contra–Account An account that is an offset to, or reduction of, another account.

Contributed Surplus The accumulation of differences when a company issues and sells shares at a price greater than their original issue price.

Copyright A form of protection provided to the original authors of literary, musical, artistic, dramatic, and other works of authorship.

Cost of Goods Sold (CGS) Equation Expresses the relationship between inventory on hand, purchased, and sold; BI + P − EI = CGS or BI + P − CGS = EI.

Cost Principle Assets and liabilities should initially be recorded at their original cost to the company.

Credit The right side of an account, or the act of entering an amount into the right side of an account.

Cumulative Dividend Preference Preferred share feature that requires current dividends not paid in full to accumulate for every year in which

they are not paid. These cumulative unpaid amounts (called *dividends in arrears*) must be paid before any common dividends can be paid.

Current Assets Expected to be used up or converted into cash within 12 months of the balance sheet date.

Current Dividend Preference The feature of preferred shares that grants priority on preferred dividends over common dividends. (526)

Current Liabilities (1) Debts and obligations that are expected to be paid, settled, or fulfilled within twelve months of the balance sheet date. (2) Short–term obligations that will be paid with current assets within the current operating cycle or one year, whichever is longer.

D

Days to Collect A measure of the average number of days from the time a sale is made on account to the time it is collected.

Days to Sell A measure of the average number of days from the time inventory is bought to the time it is sold.

Debit The left side of an account, or the act of entering an amount into the left side of an account.

Debt–to–Assets Ratio Indicates financing risk by computing the proportion of total assets financed by debt.

Declaration Date The date on which the board of directors officially approves a dividend, thereby creating a liability.

Declining–Balance Depreciation Method Assigns more depreciation to early years of an asset's life and less depreciation to later years.

Deferred Revenue A liability representing a company's obligation to provide goods or services to customers in the future.

Depletion The process of allocating a natural resource's cost over the period of its extraction or harvesting.

Depreciable Cost The portion of the asset's cost that will be used in generating revenue; calculated as asset cost minus residual value.

Depreciation (1) The process of allocating the cost of buildings, vehicles, and equipment to the accounting periods in which they are used; also referred to as *amortization*. (2) The allocation of the cost of long–lived tangible assets over their productive lives using a systematic and rational method. Also called *amortization*.

Direct Method Reports the components of cash flows from operating activities as gross receipts and gross payments.

Direct Write–Off Method A non–GAAP alternative to the allowance method of accounting for uncollectable accounts.

Discontinued Operations Result from the disposal of a major component of the business and are reported net of income tax effects.

Discount The amount by which a bond's issue price is less than its face value.

Dividends in Arrears Cumulative unpaid amount as a result of cumulative dividend preference that must be paid before any common dividends can be paid.

E

EBITDA Abbreviation for "earnings before interest, taxes, depreciation, and amortization," which is a measure of operating performance that some managers and analysts use in place of net income.

Effective–Interest Method of Amortization Allocates the amount of bond premium or discount over each period of a bond's life in amounts corresponding to the bond's carrying value.

Expense Recognition Principle (Matching) The requirement under accrual basis accounting to record expenses in the same period as the revenues they generate, not necessarily the period in which cash is paid for them.

Expenses Costs of business necessary to earn revenues.

Extraordinary Repairs Expenditures that increase a tangible asset's economic usefulness in the future and are recorded as increases in asset accounts, not as expenses.

F

Face Value The amount payable on a bond's maturity date.

Factoring An arrangement where receivables are sold to another company (called a *factor*) for immediate cash (minus a factoring fee).

Financial Statements Accounting reports that summarize the financial results of business and financing activities.

First–In, First–Out (FIFO) Assumes that the costs of the first goods purchased (first in) are the costs of the first goods sold (first out).

FOB (Free on Board) Destination A term of sale indicating that goods are owned by the seller until they are delivered to the customer.

FOB (Free on Board) Shipping Point A term of sale indicating that goods are owned by the customer the moment they leave the seller's premises.

Franchise A contractual right to sell certain products or services, use certain trademarks, or perform activities in a certain geographical region.

Fraud A fraud is an attempt to deceive others for personal gain.

Full Disclosure Principle Financial statements should present information needed to understand the financial results of the company's business activities.

Future Value The sum to which an amount will increase as the result of compound interest.

G

Generally Accepted Accounting Principles (GAAP) Rules of accounting approved by the Canadian Institute of Chartered Accountants for use in Canada.

Generally Accepted Accounting Principles (GAAP) Rules of accounting approved by the Canadian Institute of Chartered Accountants for use in Canada.

Going–Concern Assumption A business is assumed to be capable of continuing its operations long enough to meet its obligations. Also called the *continuity assumption.*

Goods Available for Sale The sum of beginning inventory and purchases for the period.

Goodwill The premium a company pays to obtain the favourable reputation associated with another company.

Gross Profit (or Gross Margin) Net sales minus cost of goods sold. It is a subtotal, not an account.

Gross Profit Percentage A ratio indicating the percentage of profit earned on each dollar of sales, after considering the cost of products sold.

H

Horizontal (Trend) Analyses Compare results across time, often expressing changes in account balances as a percentage of prior year balances. Also called *horizontal analysis* or *time–series analysis.*

I

Impairment Occurs when the cash to be generated by an asset is estimated to be less than the carrying value of that asset.

Imprest System A process that controls the amount paid to others by limiting the total amount of money available for making payments to others.

Income Statement Reports the amount of revenues less expenses for a period of time. Also called the *statement of operations.*

Indirect Method Presents the operating activities section of the cash flow statement by adjusting net income to compute cash flows from operating activities.

Interest Formula $I = P \times R \times T$, where I = interest calculated, P = principal, R = annual interest rate, and T = time period covered in the interest calculation (number of months out of 12).

Internal Control Processes by which a company provides

reasonable assurance regarding the reliability of the company's financial reporting, the effectiveness and efficiency of its operations, and its compliance with applicable laws and regulations.

International Financial Reporting Standards (IFRS) Rules of accounting created by the International Accounting Standards Board (IASB) for international use.

Inventory Turnover The process of buying and selling inventory.

Inventory Assets acquired for resale to customers.

Issue Price The amount of money that a lender pays (and the company receives) when a bond is issued.

Issued Shares Shares that have been distributed by the corporation.

J

Journal Entries Indicate the effects of each day's transactions in a debits–equal–credits format.

Journals Used to record the effects of each day's transactions, organized by date.

L

Last–In, First–Out (LIFO) Assumes that the most recently purchased units (last in) are sold first (first out).

Ledger Used to summarize the effects of journal entries on each account; organized by account.

Liabilities Amounts presently owed by a business.

Licensing Rights The limited permission to use property according to specific terms and conditions set out in a contract.

Liquidity The extent to which a company is able to pay its currently maturing obligations.

Loan Covenants Terms of a loan agreement that, if broken, entitle the lender to renegotiate loan terms or to force repayment.

Long–Lived Assets Resources owned by a business that enable it to produce the goods or services that are sold to customers.

Lower of Cost and Net Realizable Value (LC&NRV) A valuation rule that requires Inventory to be written down when its net realizable value or current replacement cost falls below its original historical cost. Can also be referred to as *lower of cost and market value*.

M

Manufacturing Companies Sell goods that they have made themselves.

Market Interest Rate The rate of interest that investors demand from a bond.

Maturity Date The date on which a bond is due to be paid in full.

Merchandising Companies Sell goods that have been obtained from a supplier.

Multi—step Income Statement Presents important subtotals, such as gross profit, to help distinguish core operating results from other, less significant items that affect net income.

N

Net Assets The shorthand term used to refer to assets minus liabilities.

Net Income The excess of revenues over expenses.

Net Profit Margin Indicates how much profit is earned from each dollar of revenue.

Non—current Assets and liabilities that do not meet the definition of current. Also described as long—term.

No—Par Value Shares Shares that have no specified legal value per share in the corporate charter.

Note Receivable A promise that requires another party to pay the business according to a written agreement.

NSF (Not Sufficient Funds) Cheques Cheques written for an amount greater than the funds available to cover them.

O

Ordinary Repairs and Maintenance Expenditures for routine operating upkeep of long—lived assets that are recorded as expenses.

Outstanding Shares Shares that are currently held by shareholders (not the corporation itself).

P

Par Value Share A share with an insignificant value as specified in the corporate charter. The specified value has no relationship to the market value of the share.

Parent Company The entity that gains a controlling influence over another company (a subsidiary).

Passive investments Are purchased with excess funds with the intent of earning a return.

Patent A right to exclude others from making, using, selling, or importing an invention.

Payment Date The date on which a cash dividend is paid to the shareholders of record.

Percentage of Credit Sales Method Estimates bad debts based on the historical percentage of sales that lead to bad debt losses. Also called the *income statement approach*.

Periodic Inventory System A system in which ending inventory and cost of goods sold are determined only at the end of the accounting period based on a physical inventory count.

Permanent Account An account that tracks financial results from year to year by carrying its ending balances into the next year.

Perpetual Inventory System A system in which a detailed inventory record is maintained by recording each purchase and sale of inventory during the accounting period.

Post—Closing Trial Balance An internal report prepared as the last step in the accounting cycle to check that debits equal credits and all temporary accounts have been closed.

Posting The process of transferring details of journal entries into the corresponding ledger accounts.

Preferred Shares Shares that have specific rights than are different from those of common shares.

Premium The amount by which a bond's issue price exceeds its face value.

Present Value (1) A mathematical calculation that determines the amount that one or more payments made in the future are worth today. (2) The current value of an amount to be received in the future; it is calculated by discounting a future amount for compound interest.

Private Enterprise Does not have publicly traded shares in an open market, nor does it hold assets in a fiduciary capacity for someone else. Has the option to use IFRS or ASPE.

Profitability The extent to which a company generates income.

Publicly Accountable Profit—Oriented Enterprise Has shares or debt trading in a public market or holds assets in a fiduciary capacity for someone else and is required to use IFRS.

Purchase Discount A cash discount received for prompt payment of a purchase on account.

Purchase Returns and Allowances A reduction in the cost of inventory purchases associated with unsatisfactory goods.

R

Receivables Turnover The process of selling and collecting on account. The receivables turnover ratio determines the average number of times this process occurs during the period.

Record Date The date on which the corporation prepares the list of current shareholders as shown on its records; dividends can be paid only to the shareholders who own shares on that date.

Research and Development Expenses Expenditures that may someday lead to patents, copyrights, or other intangible assets; the uncertainty about their future bene—fits requires that they be expensed.

Residual Value The estimated amount to be recovered at the end of the company's estimated useful life of an asset. Also called *salvage value*.

Restricted Cash Not available for general use but rather restricted for a specific purpose.

Retained Earnings Cumulative earnings of a company that are not distributed to the owners; profits from the current year and all prior years that are reinvested ("retained") in the business.

Revenue Recognition Principle The requirement under accrual basis accounting to record revenues when they are earned, not necessarily when cash is received for them.

Revenues Amounts earned by selling goods or services to customers.

S

Sales Discount A sales price reduction given to customers for prompt payment of their account balance.

Sales Returns and Allowances Refunds and price reductions given to customers after goods have been sold and found unsatisfactory.

Sarbanes—Oxley Act (SOX) Cre—ated by the U.S. Congress after the fall of Enron due to accounting fraud. Includes regulations on many topics, including internal control systems and certification of executives.

Segregation of Duties An internal control that involves separating employees' duties so that the work of one person can be used to check the work of another person.

Separate Entity Assumption The financial reports of a business are assumed to include the results of only that business's activities.

Service Companies Sell services rather than physical goods.

Shareholders' Equity The amount invested and reinvested in a com—pany by its shareholders. Also called *owners' equity or stockholders' equity*.

Shrinkage The cost of inventory lost to theft, fraud, and error.

Single—Step Income Statement Reports net income by subtracting a single group of expenses from a single group of revenues.

Solvency The ability to survive long enough to repay lenders when debt matures.

Specific Identification The inven—tory costing method that identifies the cost of the specific item that was sold.

Stated Interest Rate The rate stated on the face of the bond, which is used to compute interest payments.

Statement of Cash Flows Reports the operating, investing, and financ—ing activities that caused increases and decreases in cash during the period.

Statement of Cash Flows Reports the operating, investing, and financ—ing activities that caused increases and decreases in cash during the period.

Statement of Retained Earnings Reports the way that net income and the distribution of dividends affected the financial position of the company during the period.

Stock Dividends Additional shares of a corporation distributed to share—holders in the form of dividends.

Stock Split An increase in the total number of authorized shares by a specified ratio; does not affect retained earnings.

Straight—Line Amortization Method For bonds payable, evenly allocates the amount of bond pre—mium or discount over each period of a bond's life to adjust interest expense for differences between its stated interest rate and market interest rate.

Straight—Line Depreciation Method For tangible and intangible assets, the systematic and rational allocation of the cost of the asset in equal periodic amounts over its useful life.

Subsidiary Company A business that is controlled by another company (the parent).

T

T—Account A simplified version of a ledger account used for summariz—ing the effects of journal entries.

Technology Assets Acquired com—puter software and development costs.

Temporary Accounts Accounts that track financial results for a limited period of time by having their balances zeroed out at the end of each accounting year.

Time Period Assumption The long life of a company is divided into shorter periods, such as months, quarters, and years.

Time Value of Money The idea that money received today is worth more than the same amount received in the future because money received today can be invested to earn interest over time.

Times Interest Earned Ratio Divides net income before inter—est and taxes by interest expense to determine the extent to which earnings before taxes and financing costs are sufficient to cover interest incurred on debt. Also called a *fixed charge coverage ratio*.

Trademark A special name, image, or slogan identified with a product or company.

Transactions An exchange or event that has a direct economic effect on the assets, liabilities, or shareholders' equity of a business.

Treasury Shares Issued shares that have been reacquired by the company.

Trial Balance An internal report that lists all accounts and their bal—ances to check on the equality of total recorded debits and total recorded credits.

U

Unit of Measure Assumption Results of business activities should be reported in an appropriate mon—etary unit, which in Canada is the Canadian dollar.

Units—of—Production Depreciation Method Allocates the cost of an asset over its useful life based on the relationship of its periodic output to its total estimated output.

Useful Life The expected service life of an asset under the present owner.

V

Vertical (Common—Size) Analyses Express each financial statement amount as a percentage of another amount on the same financial statement.

Voucher System A process for approving and documenting all purchases and payments on account.

W

Weighted Average Cost An inventory costing assumption that uses the weighted average unit cost of the goods available for sale for both cost of goods sold and ending inventory.

Write—Off An uncollectable account and its corresponding allowance that has been removed from the account—ing records.

acquisition, 426–430
  capitalized, 426
  defined, 425
  demonstration case, 451–454
  depreciation, 430–437
  disposal of, 440–441
  extraordinary repairs, 430
  fixed asset turnover ratio, 445–447
  gain/loss on disposal, 449
  IFRS vs. ASPE, 445
  impairment losses, 440
  maintenance costs, 430
  ordinary repairs and maintenance, 430
  use of, 430–439
tax
  accrued income taxes, 485
  capital cost allowance (CCA), 438
  cash flow effects, 337–338
  depreciation, 437–438
  payroll tax, 484–485
  sales tax payable, 486–489
taxes payable, 8
technology assets, 443
temporary accounts, 185–186
time lag, 250
time period assumption, 111, 112
time-series analysis, 646
times interest earned ratio, 499, 500, 517, 651, 658
trademark, 442
transaction analysis
  basic accounting equation, 54
  chart of accounts, 54, 55
  debit/credit framework, 62, 118
  demonstration case, 132
  duality of effects, 54
  examples, 54–58
  expanded accounting equation, 118-123
  IFRS vs. ASPE, 74
transactions. *See also* operating activities; recording
    transactions
  defined, 53
  external exchanges, 53
  internal exchanges, 53
  recording and summarizing, 59–61, 118–123
transaction analysis. *See* transaction analysis
transportation costs, 288–289
treasury shares, 542, 543
trend analysis. *See* horizontal (trend) analysis
trial balance
  adjusted, 181–183
  balance sheet and, 68–70
  defined, 124

demonstration case, 76–78, 131–134
unadjusted trial balance, 124–126, 171, 181

U

unadjusted trial balance
  adjustments, 171
  deferral adjustments, 172
  demonstration case, 134, 190
  sample, 126
  trial balance, 124–126
unearned revenue. *See* deferred revenue
unit of measure assumption, 11
units-of-production depreciation method, 433, 434–435, 436–437
unqualified audit opinion, 659
unqualified opinion, 659
useful life, 432, 434

V

vertical (common-size) analysis
  computations, 648–650
  defined, 648
  described, 646
  relationships noted in, 653
vortex shedding, 440
voucher system, 245

W

weighted average cost
  cost flow assumptions, 334
  cost flow calculation, 336
  defined, 334
  financial statement effects, 335, 337, 348
  periodic inventory system, 347–348
  perpetual inventory system, 347–348
Whistleblower Program, 237
wholesalers, 283
work in process inventory, 331
write-off, 381–382, 386

Y

year-to-year percentage change, 646

Z

zero-coupon bonds, 498

Chapter Title	Chapter Focus Company	Company Logo	Type of Company	Key Ratios
1 Business Decisions and Financial Accounting	**Pizza Palace, Inc.**	PIZZA PALACE	Restaurant	
2 The Balance Sheet	**Pizza Palace, Inc.**	PIZZA PALACE	Restaurant	Current Ratio
3 The Income Statement	**Pizza Palace, Inc.**	PIZZA PALACE	Restaurant	Net Profit Margin
4 Adjustments, Financial Statements, and Financial Results	**Pizza Palace, Inc.**	PIZZA PALACE	Restaurant	Coach, Inc. Deere & Company Regis Corporation
5 Fraud, Internal Control, and Cash	**Koss Corporation**	KOSS	Headphones Designer & Manufacturer	Debt-to-Assets Ratio
6 Merchandising Operations and the Multi-step Income Statement	**Walmart**	Walmart	Superstore chain	Gross Profit Percentage Ratio
7 Inventory and Cost of Goods Sold	**Hudson's Bay Company**	HBC HUDSON'S BAY COMPANY	Department store	Inventory Turnover Ratio

Chapter Title	Chapter Focus Company	Company Logo	Type of Company	Key Ratios
8 Receivables, Bad Debt Expense, and Interest Revenue	**VF Corporation (VCF)**		Apparel and footwear company	Receivables Turnover Ratio
9 Long-Lived Tangible and Intangible Assets	**Cedar Fair**		Entertainment company	Fixed Asset Turnover Ratio
10 Liabilities	**General Mills**		Food company	Times Interest Earned Ratio
11 Shareholders' Equity	**Molson Coors Brewing Company**		Food and beverage manufacturer	Earnings per Share (EPS), Return on Equity (ROE), Price/Earnings (P/E) Ratios
12 Statement of Cash Flows	**Under Armour**		Athletic clothing and accessories company	Brunswick Corporation
13 Measuring and Evaluating Financial Performance	**The Home Depot, Inc.**		Retailer of home improvement, construction products and services	Comprehensive Summary (Exhibit 13.5)